WHERE t

AND Snowboard 2001

The Reuters Guide
to the World's Best Winter Sports Resorts

Edited by
Chris Gill
and
Dave Watts

NortonWood

REUTERS

Published in Great Britain by
NortonWood Publishing
The Old Forge
Norton St Philip
Bath BA3 6LW
United Kingdom

tel 01373 834227
fax 01373 834106
e-mail mailbox@snow-zone.co.uk

This edition published 2000

10 9 8 7 6 5 4 3 2 1

ISBN 0 9536371 1 5

A CIP catalogue entry for this book is available from the British Library.

Editors Chris Gill and Dave Watts
Assistant editors Martin Hall, Mandy Crook, Minnie Burlton, Catherine Weakley, Emma Morris
Australia/NZ editor Bronwen Gora
Contributors Chris Allan, Alan Coulson, Nicky Holford, James Hooke, Tim Perry, Adam Ruck, Helena Wiesner, Ian Porter
Nightlife consultant Bert Walsh
Advertising manager Sam Palmer

Design by Fox Design Consultants
Production by Guide Editors
Production manager Ian Stratford
Production assistant Ross Bruniges
Proof-reader Sally Vince
Printed and bound in Italy
by Conti Tipocolor

Book trade sales are handled by
Portfolio Books Ltd
Unit 5 Perivale Industrial Park
Horsenden Lane South
Greenford UB6 7RL
tel 020 8997 9000
fax 020 8997 9097
e-mail sales@portfoliobooks.com

Individual copies of the book can be bought by credit card from www.amazon.co.uk or through our own web site at:
www.snow-zone.co.uk
or by phoning:
01373 834227

Resort reports

We are always grateful for readers' feedback on the resorts they visit. The 100 most useful reports earn a free copy of the new edition.

Send resort reports via our web site at:
www.snow-zone.co.uk
or send an e-mail message to:
reports@snow-zone.co.uk
or write to:
Where to Ski and Snowboard
FREEPOST
The Old Forge
Norton St Philip
Bath
BA3 6UB

Contents

About this book

it's simply the best

We believe that *Where to Ski and Snowboard* is the best guide to ski and snowboard resorts that you can buy.

We're ahead of our rivals in five key ways:

• Despite the fact that we use colour printing fully, by making the most of technology we are able to go to press later than competing guides and bring the book **up to date for the season ahead** – the 2000/01 season. To see what we mean, check out our What's new chapter, crammed with new resort developments.

• To help you compile a shortlist of resorts, we work hard to make our information **reader-friendly**, with cost ratings, star-ratings for the main aspects of each resort, and crystal-clear lists of resort plus-points and minus-points at the start of each chapter.

• We don't hesitate to express **critical views**. We learned our craft at Consumers' Association, where one of us became editor of *Holiday Which?* magazine and the other editor of *Which?* itself, and so a consumerist attitude comes naturally to us.

• Our resort chapters give an **unrivalled level of detail** – including scale plans showing the extent and layout of each major resort, as well as all the facts you need to have at your fingertips.

• We include scores of **colour photographs**, carefully chosen so that you can see for yourself what different resorts are like.

The merits of *Where to Ski and Snowboard* are now widely recognised – not least in the national press, as the glowing quotes on the front and back covers show. But we're not resting on our laurels. This edition has more photos and more piste maps than ever, for example.

We're delighted that *Where to Ski and Snowboard* will now have the support of Reuters. Their sponsorship will mean that we can continue to expand our coverage and improve our presentation each year, opening up an ever-larger lead over rival guides.

Enjoy your skiing and riding this season.

Chris Gill and Dave Watts
Norton St Philip, 14 July 2000

Get this edition FREE!

We reckon *Where to Ski and Snowboard* is a bargain at only £15.99. But if you plan to take a winter sports holiday this winter or the next, you can buy the book safe in the knowledge that you can get the cost of it refunded. See page 8.

Using the book

FINDING A RESORT

The bulk of the book consists of chapters devoted to individual major resorts, some also covering minor resorts that share the same lift system. These chapters are ordered alphabetically and grouped by country – first, the four major Alpine countries in alphabetical order; then the US and Canada (where resorts are grouped by states or regions); then minor European countries; then Australasia.

Premier league

The rest

Short cuts to the resorts that might suit you are provided by a table of comparative **ratings** on page 74 and a series of shortlists of resorts with particular merits on page 80.

At the back of the book is an **index** to the resort chapters, combined with a **directory** giving basic information on other minor resorts. The UK tour operators offering **package holidays** in each resort are listed in the index, too.

READING A CHAPTER

The **cost** of visiting each resort is rated on a scale of one to six – (1) to (6) – reflecting the typical cost of a one-week trip based on a half-board package from the UK, plus a lift pass and an allowance for lunch in mountain restaurants. We assume two people sharing a room – even in the US, where package prices are often based on four people sharing.

Star-ratings summarise our view of the resort in 11 respects, including how well it suits different standards of skier/boarder. The more stars, the better.

We give international phone and fax numbers of the **tourist office** (the lift company in North America). Normally, substitute a zero for the +code if calling from within the country concerned. Note that the Italian system is different, and that you must leave in the zero (as we have) when dialling internationally.

Our **mountain maps** show the resorts' own gradings of runs – so those for the US and Canada show green, blue and black runs, and no red ones (unlike Europe). On some maps we also follow the North American convention of using black diamonds to indicate expert terrain.

We use the following symbols to identify **fast or high-capacity lifts**:

- fast chair-lift
- gondola
- cable-car
- funicular railway

There's further guidance on using our information in Choosing your resort on page 66 – designed to be helpful particularly to people with narrow experience of different resorts, who may not appreciate how big the differences can be.

Who do one billion people look to
for their daily news?

Issues of the season

the editors have their say

HAVE A NICE JOUR?

Since the first edition of this book in 1994 we have been extolling the virtues of North American skiing, partly because of the the excellent and cheerful service you get in the States and Canada. And we have urged European resorts to emulate American standards. We're happy to say that we detect signs of Alpine improvement.

Courchevel has unashamedly copied American ideas. It now has grooming maps available at all main lift stations showing which trails were groomed the previous night – a great idea, common in American resorts, which enabled us to spot that the black run Jockeys had been groomed and to have a wonderful fast cruise down a deserted slope that is normally a top-to-bottom mogul field. On the back of the map is the weather forecast for the next few days in diagram form to avoid language difficulties. Courchevel has also introduced singles queues at lots of lifts – though the difficulty of getting different nationalities to understand what is going on is leading to some some pretty bad accidents, with too many people trying to get on at the same time. St Anton also has a few singles queues, and has cracked the language problem by playing recorded tapes in different languages telling people what to do to make the lift queue as short as possible. Back in France, readers' reports on Val-d'Isère are now full of comments on friendly staff – and (incredibly) reservations about 'over-enthusiastic' grooming of the slopes.

But, ironically, last season we picked up the first signs of slipping standards in American service. In Breckenridge we heard complaints from British guests staying at a hotel where the rooms were dirty and the breakfast staff surly and slow. We stayed at a condo where the front desk was open only half the advertised hours because of 'staff shortage'. In Vail we came across weekend queues that weren't being properly organised and in danger of becoming a European-style scrum. We walked into a hotel restaurant at 9.15pm to be told it was closed; when we pointed out that it was advertised as serving until 9.30pm we got grudging service (and lousy steaks). In more than one ski rental shop, we rejected 'performance' skis because they were in poor condition, and got blank stares in reply.

When we pointed these failings out to the resort bosses they agreed it was a problem – and said the underlying reason was full employment in the US, meaning that resorts in Colorado have thousands of unfilled vacancies.

PLUS ÇA CHANGE ...

Of course, the change is a partial one. The Ecole du Ski Français is a continuing source of horror stories, particularly about its inability to deal responsibly with children. This year one reporter tells of two ESF instructors shouting at her 4-year-olds in French in front of 40 screaming children. And, not for the first time, we have reports of ESF instructors – in Val-d'Isère and Val-Thorens, this time – losing or even abandoning kids on the slopes. There are many exceptions, of course, but all too often the attitude of the ESF is one of arrogance.

What do the world's top 350,000 traders have in common?

www.reuters.com

THE SMELL OF THE GREASEPAINT ...

Another of the fundamental problems faced by Alpine resorts is less easy to tackle: piste crowding. For years now we have been preaching the message that most US resorts offer a more satisfying holiday for the simple reason that the slopes are generally free of crowds. In Europe, that's a rare state of affairs, and getting rarer. What's more, this is no longer just something that affects our enjoyment – it's now common for pistes to become dangerously crowded.

One weekend in St Anton last season we saw several bad collisions in the so-called Happy Valley, into which skiers and riders are funnelled from all the runs above. On one stretch, each skier was within a ski's length of the people ahead, behind and on both sides. In these circumstances, if one falls, you all fall.

In contrast, our March visit to Colorado saw us skiing on many occasions with no one else in sight. Even in Vail, of all places, we had acres to ourselves on a snowy day in Blue Sky Basin. In Aspen-Snowmass, where the ski company prides itself on the lack of crowds, we repeatedly skied long trails without seeing another person.

The importance of these differences can hardly be overstated. It remains true that the dramatic mountains and huge lift networks of the Alps are unmatched in America. But the fact is that in the Alps the activities that our winter holidays revolve around are becoming less enjoyable every year. It's partly the result of ever more efficient lifts, but it is also the result of the relentless increase in visitor beds. Something to do with geese and golden eggs comes to mind.

AHEAD OF THE GAME

When celebrities – or British teenagers – die as a result of skiing into trees, the stories hit the headlines and we all start worrying: should we be wearing helmets? And as the crowding on Alpine pistes gets worse, that will lead to more head injuries, too. The evidence is that helmets do reduce injuries. But there are drawbacks.

One of your editors used a helmet for most of last season to find out what it's like. Result: overheating was a problem later in the season – and when the helmet was abandoned for a day or two the renewed sense of freedom was mightily enjoyable. If you think you might share these reactions, you can't simply adopt helmet-wearing on the common-sense grounds that it must be a worthwhile precaution. You have to weigh the benefits against the drawbacks.

The debate over the value of helmets was given a relatively firm footing for the first time in January 1999, when the US Consumer Product Safety Commission (CPSC) produced a report. On the basis of a study of injuries during the previous season, it concluded that the use of helmets could prevent or reduce the severity of almost half the head injuries to adults, and over half of those to children, and could prevent about a dozen deaths a year in the US. These findings are consistent with a much earlier study in Sweden.

In the US, head injuries accounted for 12 per cent of serious injuries in 1993, 15 per cent in 1997. This represents 12,700 injuries, resulting from an estimated 55 million skier-days or part-days spent on the slopes, or one injury per 4300 skier-days. Ski for 15 days a year for 40 years, and you have a one in seven chance of a head injury. According to the CPSC, you can virtually halve this chance by wearing a helmet. Of course the CPSC stuff all relates to skiing in America, where trees are part of the deal practically everywhere, and where skiing among those trees is much more common than in

Europe. And the CPSC's review of deaths from head injuries did find that collisions with trees were much the most common cause.

But the picture is different with non-fatal head injuries. Most resulted from contact with the mountain or with skis following a fall. Impacts on other objects or other people were much less common.

Editorial conclusions? One of us plans to wear a helmet in future, and especially when skiing in trees, but to look for one with better ventilation. The other isn't (yet) sufficiently convinced to sacrifice the wind in his hair. If you're convinced, take a look at the special SkiSafe offer advertised below – an insurance industry initiative to encourage helmet wearing by offering helmets at cut prices.

ANOTHER INTERESTING ITEM™

We're often amused by the American tendency to claim all kinds of names as trade marks. The home of excessive trade marking is, of course, Vail, where the names of practically all the lifts on Vail Mountain™, the Back Bowls™ and Blue Sky Basin™ are claimed to be trade marks, along with lift stations such as Mid-Vail™ and restaurants such as Two Elk Lodge™. Not forgetting of course the Activities Desk™ and Mountain Welcome Tour™.

The cookie is taken, though, by Winter Park (Colorado's Favorite®). The top of the mountain here is known as Parsenn Bowl™. The Parsenn, above Davos, is a rather special mountain for various reasons. The idea that the words Parsenn Bowl can be recognised as representing Winter Park strikes us as faintly ludicrous.

A PISTE IS A PISTE – OR IS IT?

We've gone on in these pages before about the need for resorts to be absolutely clear about what their various run designations mean, so that visitors can take appropriate precautions. You need to know whether that run shown in yellow on the map and labelled ski-route is marked out on the mountain, whether it is protected against avalanches and whether it is patrolled.

But our concern about these distinctions is nothing compared with the fit we suffered while standing in front of a piste map at Kleine Scheidegg, the meeting point of the slopes above Wengen and Grindelwald. The big display map had a discreet little notice stating calmly that various pistes – blue, red and black – did not benefit from an end of day piste patrol. We read this little notice several times. It couldn't really be saying that, could it? Yes, it could. The English was excellent, as you'd expect in that part of the world, and unequivocal.

We know the value of end-of-day piste patrols. Many years ago, at the end of his first day on skis, Chris found himself alone on a tricky red run above Davos as darkness fell on a freezing January night. The

story involves an irresponsible friend, a frozen wrist watch and two failed attempts to ride a steep T-bar alone – and it has a happy ending only because the end-of-day patrol got Chris down to Davos just as a full-scale search of the Jakobshorn was about to start.

We expressed our concerns about this lunatic policy to the Jungfrau railway company that runs the mountain, and asked for an explanation and a change. We got the second – all its runs will in future be properly patrolled – but not the first. So we still don't know what particular form of madness was to blame.

THE GOOD SKIING AND SNOWBOARDING GUIDE: A CLARIFICATION

The Good Skiing and Snowboarding Guide is a guide to winter sports resorts, in most respects similar to this one, but in one respect quite different. It is published by *Which?*, the famously impartial consumer organisation, and so does not carry advertising. *Which?* reckons this is an advantage to be pressed, and described the 1999 Guide as 'untainted by advertising'.

Provoked by the implication that advertising affects adversely the quality of this book, in our 2000 edition we went on to the front foot. We explained that it is only because of advertising revenue that *Where to Ski and Snowboard* has been able to adopt ever-higher standards of research and presentation.

We went on to note that *Which?* is rather selective about which aspects of the Guide operation it publicises. The publishers of the Guide objected to our remarks, and as a result we have agreed to publish the following clarification:

In Where to Ski and Snowboard 2000 we said that the editors of and contributors to The Good Skiing and Snowboarding Guide accepted free facilities from resorts, airlines and tour operators. The publishers of The Good Skiing and Snowboarding Guide, Which? Ltd, have asked us to make clear that the Guide's editors and contributors are freelance writers who work for a variety of publications, and that when they accept free facilities of this kind they do so only as freelance individuals or as representatives of other publications, and never in the name of The Good Skiing and Snowboarding Guide, Which? Ltd or Consumers' Association. It is a fundamental principle of CA that it accepts no free samples, free holidays, free meals or any other handouts from those whose products and services are under review, or from suppliers or anyone else who might threaten CA's integrity.

We are happy to oblige.

DAVOS-RELATED ITEMS R US™

The main way up into the main Davos ski area is the ancient Parsennbahn funicular, to which with regret we award the title of 'worst lift in the world' – it can generate enormous queues of one and a half hours or more to get up the mountain and the same to get down again when the snow is too bad to ski down (which is often). There were plans to replace it with a high-capacity gondola, but these have now been scrapped. So it looks like Clinton, Blair and their high-powered friends who attend the World Economic Summit every winter in Davos will continue to spend half their day waiting in queues if they want to go skiing. Canny Prince Charles, however, takes his sons William and Harry down the valley to Klosters each year and gets into the ski area by the back door (using the cable-car named after him) to reach the same ski area an hour or more before Clinton and Blair would arrive.

What's new?

lifts and snow for 2001

The main news from the resorts of Europe and North America.

Austria

Alpbach The 2000 T-bar to the resort high point has been replaced by a four-seater chair-lift.

Ellmau A second six-pack to the Hartkaiser-Brandstadl area is planned for next season.

Hintertux The world's highest jumbo-gondola (each cabin holds 24 people), from Tuxerfernhaus at 2660m to 3250m, opened in April 2000. For 2000/01 an eight-person gondola will replace the existing double chair-lift from the base area.

Ischgl For 2000/01, a quad is being upgraded to an eight-seater and another quad and six-pack will replace existing T-bars on the Ischgl side. Over in Samnaun, yet another six-pack is replacing a T-bar.

Kitzbühel A fast quad has replaced the Talsen T-bar, at Jochberg. The Pengelstein lift is to be upgraded to a fast quad for 2000/01.

Mayrhofen The gondola from Hippach to Penken is being upgraded.

Obertauern Three new chairs, including a six-pack, were installed last season. For 2000/01 a fast quad replaces the Kurvenlift T-bar.

Saalbach-Hinterglemm For 2000/01 two lifts on the south-facing slopes above Hinterglemm will be replaced by high-speed chairs.

St Anton Big improvements have been made in preparation for the Alpine Skiing World Championships to be held here from 28 Jan to 10 Feb 2001. A new 8-person gondola from Nasserein up to Gampen opens for 2000/01. The railway line and station are being moved to the outskirts of town, making it possible to ski right into the centre.

Schladming The old gondola from Haus is being replaced by an eight-seater gondola. And the slow double chair-lift from Rohrmoos on Hochwurzen is being replaced by a six-pack.

Sölden For 1999/2000 a fast quad from Giggijoch speeded up the link to Sölden's glaciers. 2000/01 sees a new gondola on the Tiefenbach glacier and a six-pack from Langegg to Giggijoch.

Söll For 2000/01 the old single-seat chair to the Hohe Salve will be replaced by an eight-seater gondola. In Hopfgarten, a queue-prone T-bar (a key link on the Ski Welt circuit) is being replaced by a six-pack.

France

As we went to press, construction work on the Mont Blanc Tunnel was supposed to start during the summer of 2000. But the likely opening date is still unclear.

Alpe-d'Huez Improvements for 2000/01 include a second stage to the Marmottes gondola (replacing the old Clocher chair) and a two-seater chair to replace the Chatelard drag-lift. Snowmaking has been greatly extended and for 2000/01 a further huge investment is planned, adding almost 50 per cent to the installation.

Avoriaz/Morzine For 2000/01 the gondola from Ardent to above Les Lindarets is being replaced by a higher-capacity one.

Châtel For 2000/01 the chair from Les Combes to Cornebois is to be replaced by a fast quad.

Les Contamines A new gondola on the back side of the mountain, from Belleville to La Ruelle, replaces the old chair-lift for 2000/01.

Courchevel For 2000/01 the slow chair from Les Creux to La Vizelle will be replaced by a six-pack. In 1650 the old access gondola is being replaced. Extra cabins are being added to the La Tania gondola, and new snowmaking is being installed on the run back to the resort.

Flaine Three new chair-lifts in the Vernant bowl below Les Grands Vans have improved connections between Flaine and the outlying villages. 2000/01 sees the old chair-lift from Flaine Forêt to Les Grands Vans replaced by France's first fast eight-person chair. More cabins are being added to the Grandes Platières gondola.

La Plagne/Les Arcs For 2000/01 the queue-prone Grande Rochette gondola from Plagne Centre is being replaced. There are plans to link the Les Arcs and La Plagne slopes by cable-car in the next couple of years, forming the world's third biggest linked ski area.

Puy-St-Vincent 10km of new pistes have taken the total up to 60km. The old gondola to mid-mountain is being replaced by a fast quad.

Serre-Chevalier Serre-Chevalier is getting a new six-pack from the base of Chantemerle towards the Prorel sector.

Val-d'Isère 2000/01 will see the defunct Cascade chair-lift, on the Pissaillas glacier, replaced by two quad chair-lifts.

Valmorel A new quad chair-lift from the bottom of the Madeleine chair up to the top of the Beaudin sector will be ready for 2000/01.

Vars/Risoul A fast quad from Clos Chardon on the Risoul side to the Pic de Chabrières in Vars will improve cross-border links for 2000/01.

ITALY

Turin has been chosen to host the 2006 Olympic Winter Games; most of the Alpine events will be held at Sansicario and Sestriere, with the freestyle competitions at Sauze d'Oulx.

COURMAYEUR There's a new blue run down to Dolonne, with buses back to town – so you no longer have to download on the cable-car.

LIVIGNO The antique chair-lift from Monte Sponda to the top of Monte della Neve is being replaced by a six-pack for 2000/01.

MADONNA DI CAMPIGLIO There was a new fast quad at the Pinzola slopes. For 2000/01 another new fast quad will go from the valley floor to the Pradalago area.

MONTEROSA SKI There are plans to replace the old cable-car from Alagna and install a new chair-lift.

SELVA/SELLA RONDA For 1999/2000 gondolas replaced the cable-cars from Ortisei to Seceda and Alpe di Siusi. Two new quad chairs are due to replace old ones towards Corvara from Arabba, speeding up the anticlockwise Sella Ronda circuit. A gondola will replace an old single-person chair in Colfosco. In Canazei, two chairs on Belvedere are being upgraded to a six-pack and a quad.

SESTRIERE New chairs are to replace the Combetta and Garnel drags.

SWITZERLAND

ADELBODEN The T-bar from Aebi to Sillerenbühl was replaced by a new six-pack for 1999/2000.

AROSA For 2000/01 a quad chair-lift will replace two existing slow chairs from mid-mountain to near the top of the Weisshorn.

ENGELBERG There's a new six-pack on Titlis. The drag-lift across the

200 KM OF SLOPES
NOW IT'S TIME TO HAVE FUN !
FORFAIT ARAVIS
6 JOURS
WWW.ARAVIS.COM
MASSIF DES
ARAVIS
FRANCE
LA CLUSAZ
TEL. 33 4 50 32 65 00
LE GRAND-BORNAND
TEL. 33 4 50 02 78 00
SAINT-JEAN-DE-SIXT
TEL. 33 4 50 02 70 14

frozen lake at Trübsee is to be replaced by a chair.

Saas-Fee The two-person Plattjen gondola has been replaced by a fast, six-person one.

Villars A six-seat chair to Grand Chamossaire was built last year. For 2000/01 there will be a new chair on the far side of Meilleret.

Wengen The avalanche-damaged Männlichen cable-car station has been rebuilt close to the main street.

United States

California

Heavenly A new gondola from downtown South Lake Tahoe opens for 2000/01. Work on a pedestrian village at the base is under way.

Lake Tahoe Squaw has two new six-packs and there's another for 2000/01. Work on a new alpine village is under way. In Kirkwood accommodation is up by 70 per cent and three new lifts will open up 125 acres of expert terrain for 2000/01. A new chair-lift opens 200 acres of expert terrain in Northstar next year.

Mammoth Mountain Further developments at the slope-side mini-village at Juniper Springs are under way: the two lifts out are being replaced by the Eagle chair – Mammoth's first fast six-seater.

Colorado

Aspen More terrain is being opened in Highland Bowl (the G Zones) at Highlands and phase two of the new base area is nearly complete.

Breckenridge The Quicksilver fast quad has been replaced by the first double-loading fast six-person chair in the US.

Copper Mountain The new car-free resort centre is almost complete.

Crested Butte An extra 274 acres are to be added to the Extreme Limits by reopening Teocalli Bowl.

Keystone 2000/01 will see a new six-pack on the back side of Keystone Mountain – speeding up the return from North Peak.

Steamboat The American Skiing Company's signature Grand Summit hotel will be open at the base of the slopes for 2000/01.

Vail-Beaver Creek 520 acres of largely ungroomed terrain, served by two fast quads, has been opened in the new Blue Sky Basin area – a season ahead of schedule. Another fast quad and a further 125 acres of terrain will be ready for 2000/01. There are 100 acres of new gladed terrain at Beaver Creek.

Winter Park The first phase of Winter Park's slope-side village is open. New shops and restaurants are planned for next season.

Utah

Park City's three unlinked ski resorts, Park City Mountain Resort, Deer Valley and the Canyons, are getting a new joint lift pass.

The Canyons The first stage of the resort village is complete. Peak 5, with 300 acres of new terrain, opened last year. An eighth mountain and 300 more acres of new terrain opens for 2000/01.

Deer Valley There's a new family ski area, served by a triple chair-lift, on Empire Canyon – a new day lodge will be ready for 2001/02. A fast quad has replaced the old triple chair-lift from the base lodge to Silver Lake Lodge and the chair back to Bald Eagle is now a quad.

Park City In preparation for the 2002 Olympics, a new base lodge – Legacy Lodge – opened in May 2000.

Snowbasin Snowmaking was installed in 1999. With over 520 guns covering 580 acres, it is one of America's biggest installations. By

Get your money back

Where to Ski and Snowboard can be yours free

You can reclaim the price of Where to Ski and Snowboard when you book a winter sports holiday for the 2000/01 or 2001/02 seasons. All you have to do is book the holiday through the specialist ski travel agency Ski Solutions. On your final invoice the price of the book will be knocked off the cost of your holiday.

Ski Solutions is Britain's original and leading ski travel agency. You can buy whatever kind of holiday you want through them, so you're not losing out on choice.

Ski Solutions sells the complete range of package holidays offered by all the bonded tour operators in Britain. And if that choice isn't enough, they can tailor-make a holiday just for you, based on any form of travel and any kind of accommodation. No one is better placed to find you what you want than Ski Solutions.

Phone Ski Solutions on

020 7471 7700

Claiming a refund

Claiming your refund is easy. At the back of the book are two vouchers. When you make your definite booking, tell Ski Solutions that you want to claim a refund. Cut out the vouchers and send one to Ski Solutions and the other to Where to Ski and Snowboard (the addresses are on the vouchers). That's it.

free!

Get next year's edition FREE

There are too many resorts for us to visit them all every year, and too many hotels, bars and mountain restaurants for us to see. So we are very keen to encourage more readers to send in reports on their holiday experiences. As usual, we'll be giving 100 copies of the next edition to the writers of the best reports.

There are five main kinds of feedback we need:
- what you particularly **liked and disliked** about the resort
- what aspects of the resort came as a **surprise** to you
- your other suggestions for **changes to our evaluation** of the resort – changes we should make to the ratings, verdicts, descriptions etc
- your experience of **queues** and other weaknesses in the lift system, and of the **ski school** and associated childcare arrangements
- your feedback on **individual facilities** in the resort – the hotels, bars, restaurants (including mountain restaurants), nightspots, equipment shops, sports facilities etc.

You can send your reports to us in three ways. In order of preference, they are:
- by e-mail to: reports@snow-zone.co.uk (don't forget to give us your mailing address)
- printed on paper, word-processed
- handwritten on a form that we can provide.

Where to Ski and Snowboard, FREEPOST, The Old Forge, Norton St Philip, Bath BA3 6UB

January 2001 the new base lodge will be complete.

Snowbird 500 acres of terrain and a new fast quad in Mineral Basin, on the back of the mountain, were opened last season.

The Rest of the West

Big Sky A new lift opened up 200 acres of new terrain last season.

Jackson Hole 2500 acres of backcountry terrain in the Teton National Park and Bridger Teton National Forest were opened last season. A chair-lift replaces the drag at the base of the Hobacks for 2000/01.

New England

Killington Work on a resort village at Snowshed is due to start in summer 2001. Yet more snowmaking is being installed.

Smugglers' Notch A new lift accessed a new beginner area with five trails and a new lodge in Morse Bowl for 1999/2000. A new water reservoir will increase snowmaking by 66 per cent for 2000/01.

Canada

Western Canada

Banff-Lake Louise Lake Louise is adding another fast quad chair from the base for 2000/01.

Fernie The Bear T-bar is being replaced by a fast quad, improving access to both Lizard and Cedar Bowls.

Panorama 1000 acres of new terrain, adding 50 per cent to the existing area, should be open for 2000/01. A new gondola connects the lower and upper villages and there's new expert terrain in Canadian Bowl.

Whistler Two fast quad chairs on Whistler mountain, in parallel with the gondola, were installed for last season. A new base lodge at Whistler Creek will be ready for 2000/01.

Eastern Canada

Tremblant 20 per cent has been added to the slopes by the opening of the new Versant Soleil area, served by a fast quad. A new beginner run from top to bottom of the north side is planned for 2000/01.

Andorra

The new link between Pas de la Casa and Soldeu, via Pla de les Pedres (Pas de la Casa) and Solana (Soldeu), was open last season. But as we went to press the resorts had still not agreed on a joint lift pass.

Pal/Arinsal A new fast quad accesses three new runs at Seturia, in Pal. A gondola linking Pal and Arinsal will be ready for 2000/01.

Pas de la Casa There's a new beginners' area at the Funicamp mid-station. And new drag-lifts here and at Cubil. The beginners' area in Pas de la Casa has also been expanded and the snowmaking capacity increased. For 2000/01 a high-speed six-pack and a quad chair will replace five existing drag-lifts.

Soldeu There's a new six-pack from Pla Riba Escorxada to Tossa dels Espiolets. An eight-seater gondola now links Canillo and El Forn. Planned for 2000/01 is a gondola, two quad chairs and a restaurant at Canillo with new access to the slopes.

Spain

Baqueira-Beret There's a new six-pack and new snowmaking on Beret. Another chair, new pistes and more snowmaking are proposed for next year.

by Chris Gill

Avalanche danger

be prudent, be prepared

Happily, the winter of 1999/2000 produced nothing like the tragedies of the previous season, when freak snowfalls resulted in twice the normal number of avalanche deaths in Austria (because of the single tragic incident at Galtür) and deaths in France and Switzerland that were 50 per cent up on the norm. Nevertheless, when the final figures for the season are published they will doubtless show once again that over 100 people lost their lives in slides in the Alps. Here's some guidance on how to avoid joining the statistics.

First, let's get the risks in perspective. The risk of avalanche involved in staying in Alpine villages and skiing or riding on open, controlled pistes is very low. If you want to worry about death and injury, worry about the risk of collisions (on the pistes or, more particularly, on the roads leading to your resort) rather than the risk of avalanche.

But the risk is not zero: 1999 was exceptional, but it was not unique. Avalanches do occasionally hit villages. Readers with long memories may recall, for example, that in 1988 exceptional depths of snow above St Anton led to a massive and fatal avalanche through the eastern part of the village. In that season, avalanche deaths in Austria recorded in the 'other' category – which excludes skiers and boarders, and includes people in buildings – totalled 10 (out of a total of 40). The devastating avalanches in early 1999 produced an 'other' deaths figure for Austria reaching an unprecedented 40; it is more usually in the range zero to five.

SNOWPIX.COM / CHRIS GILL

The avalanche is real (above Grindelwald in Switzerland) and gives some idea of the devastating scale of these things; the rescue operation is a training exercise ↓

Avalanches also occasionally hit pistes. French avalanche statistics reveal that in November 1992 an avalanche hit a group of 10 skiers on an open piste in Savoie and killed seven of them. But, again, such incidents are exceptional. There have been only two other deaths on French pistes in the last decade, and three in Austria.

So who are these 100-plus people who are killed by Alpine avalanches during a typical winter? In short, they are off-piste skiers and boarders. The Austrian and French statistics distinguish between people going off-piste and people touring – presumably on the

The portable Recco Rescue System detector (bottom) is used by trained rescue staff to find people buried by avalanches who have Recco reflectors fitted to their ski boots (below) or built into their clothing ↓

basis of whether they have used lifts to get up the mountain. In Austria, deaths among those touring (ie those making their way through the mountains unaided) outnumber those using lifts to go off-piste by five to two. In France, the numbers of mortalities in these two groups are much more balanced, and in some years it's those going off-piste who dominate the statistics. Whatever: people skiing and boarding outside the controlled pistes account for the great bulk of the avalanche accidents and deaths.

What's more, the great bulk of the avalanches that cause the accidents do not occur spontaneously. In the last decade, over 80 per cent of the avalanches in France resulting in death or injury were triggered, usually by those involved in the accident. This statistic is clearly connected to another, which is that 80 per cent of the avalanches were of the slab variety, starting from a fracture across the slope rather than a point. It's the weight of the skier or rider on the slope that causes the fracture and starts the avalanche. In some years, the proportion of injurious avalanches reckoned to be slab slides triggered by skiers and riders approaches 100 per cent of the total.

It's interesting to compare European statistics with the picture in America. Avalanche deaths in the US average a fairly modest 19 per year – fourth in the international league, fractionally above Italy and below France, Austria and Switzerland. But the biggest single group of fatalities in the States is people riding snowmobiles – a group that scarcely exists in Europe; take them out of the US figures and you're left with less than 15 deaths a year, exactly half the French figure.

There are good reasons for this. The precipitous, rocky mountains of the Alps are inherently more dangerous places than the more rounded, wooded mountains on which people go skiing and boarding in the States. But, at the same time, the record of the American resorts in dealing with avalanche risk is impressive.

American resorts take responsibility for a lot more steep, avalanche-prone terrain than European resorts do – if it's inside the resort boundary, it's the resort's responsibility. Yet in the last 15 years there have been only three deaths from avalanches in American ski areas – two in 1985/86 and one in early 1999, when a slide at Jackson Hole swept a snowboarder over a cliff to his death. It's clear that for the adventurous skier or rider who doesn't want the expense or fuss of the precautions necessary for going off-piste safely in the Alps, the in-bounds steeps of places such as Aspen-Snowmass and Snowbird are a safe bet.

US statistics also hold some valuable lessons in general. They show that most avalanche deaths occur in the group that is at high risk of accidental death in general: 70 per cent of fatalities are males in their late teens to late 20s. This same group has 74 per cent of all fatal road accidents. If you're in that group, perhaps you should acknowledge that you're prone to excessive risk-taking, and start taking special care instead.

The appeal of skiing and riding in deep, virgin snow away from the crowds on the pistes is clear to anyone who has tried it. The keys to surviving the experience are prudence and preparation.

If you're going to act prudently, you need reliable information about the terrain and the snow you're venturing on to. For most people, most of the time, this means going with a reliable and qualified local ski instructor or mountain guide, who knows the terrain and can assess the conditions and your ability, and make sure that you are not exposed to unacceptable risk. But it's important to develop your own awareness of avalanche hazards, too. Following a scary incident in the Trois Vallées a couple of seasons ago, I will no longer go seriously off-piste without personally checking the current avalanche hazard rating. (My instructor told me the rating that day was 2 – moderate; I later learned that it was 4 – high.)

You need to be prepared to survive an avalanche. Some of those who are hit by avalanches are killed by the force of the slide, or are quickly suffocated. Many survive the immediate impact, but are buried in the debris. In these circumstances, minutes count: most people who survive are found and pulled out within 15 minutes of the avalanche. The chances of survival decline rapidly thereafter.

In practice, what this means is that you need to be equipped to maximise the chance of being found quickly if you're buried.

If you are making major off-piste expeditions – 'backcountry' ski touring, or doing long runs away from the nearest lift system – everyone in the party should be fully prepared for avalanche rescue and survival. This means having both the right equipment – crucially, radio transceivers so that those not buried can locate those who are – and appropriate training in its use. Make sure you get some practice as well as the theory – it isn't easy.

If you are going off-piste within or close to a lift network, it's likely that any avalanche will trigger the resort rescue services, and in these circumstances you can hope that a more rapid and precise system for locating buried people will swing into action: Recco.

Most major resorts covered in this book are now equipped with Recco detectors, and many have several portable detectors distributed around the slopes for speedy rescue. Some helicopter rescue services, which cover many resorts, also carry Recco detectors. Under each resort covered in this book, in the Mountain facts section, we tell you if Recco says its detectors are in use.

To take advantage of the system, you need to be equipped with Recco reflectors. The detectors emit a directional radio signal on a frequency of 917 MHz. When the signal hits a Recco reflector, even under 10m of snow, the frequency is doubled and sent back to the receiver in the detector. The trained operator can then instantly pinpoint the buried victim. Detectors can easily be used from helicopters searching for victims.

Recco reflectors are small, inconspicuous and cheap – and require no batteries or other maintenance. Reflectors are sewn into some brands of clothing, normally on the arms. Failing that, you can buy self-adhesive ones to stick on your boots for only £12.95 a pair – a price not worth bothering about for something that may save your life. They are offered at half price when you buy a new pair of ski (or snowboard) boots from Snow + Rock.

The Swiss Alpine Club, Swiss Air Rescue and the Federal Institute for the Study of Snow and Avalanches in Davos have recommended that all skiers and snowboarders wear Recco reflectors. We agree.

by **Dave Watts and Chris Gill**

Ski clinics

improving your skiing

If you would like to improve your skiing, we recommend trying one of the increasing number of specialist ski improvement clinics that are run by qualified British instructors. No longer are you stuck with the group or private lessons that the local ski schools have to offer.

For years, we have been getting reports of how good special week-long clinics taught by British ski instructors are. But it wasn't until 1999 that we tried one ourselves. Then Chris went on an Ali Ross ski clinic in Tignes. It was one of Ali's 'standard' courses, aimed at people stuck on the famous intermediate plateau. By the middle of the week, Ali had the whole group skiing powder. Ali Ross Ski Clinics is represented by Ski Solutions, which will fix whatever accommodation you want in Tignes – see page 69.

We wish we'd discovered ski clinics like this before. They eliminate language problems, ensure a week of intensive instruction with fellow pupils of roughly the same ability and ambitions, and mean that the psychological aspects of this tricky activity do not get pushed aside. Most offer instruction half of each day.

Optimum's charming Chalet Tarentaise was renovated by the owners Martin and Deirdre Rowe; it has a cosy rustic living room and bar and fairly basic bedrooms (all with shower, though). It is in the tiny hamlet of Le Pré, with a chair-lift into the Les Arcs skiing. Group are a maximum of eight and most courses are designed to help skiers get off a learning plateau, with video analysis twice a week. They can arrange heli-skiing and run occasional weeks where you ski different resorts daily. We can vouch personally for the chalet and the food – and we have had glowing reports of the courses.

Triple 8 Ski Systems courses are run in Tignes by BASI-qualified instructors led by Hugh Pelling. They offer five-day Performance Skiing courses with no more than six in a class, a session spent on snow blades and video analysis twice a week. They also have a five-day Family Package with parents and children developing their skills together and offer a Skier Alignment service to ensure your body and equipment are working as efficiently together as possible. They can arrange catered chalet accommodation in one of the few real chalets in Tignes and self-catered apartments.

Warren Smith is a dynamic British ski instructor who runs a Ski Academy in Verbier. He runs courses for private groups and special week-long mogul, carving, new school and powder/free-ride camps. He also runs summer courses on the Tignes glacier (call 01442 266449 or visit www.warrensmith-skisynergy.com).

Tour operator Le Ski has its own ski school and lots of chalets in Courchevel 1650. As well as normal group and private lessons, it runs three-day free-ride courses designed to improve bumps and powder technique for good skiers, red/blue check-up clinics, ladies-only sessions and race training sessions – phone for details.

Other highly regarded courses are taught in various resorts by The Ski Company, run by Sally Chapman and Phil Smith, both BASI trainers. The five-day courses are mostly for all-round performance, but they also have special weeks such as off-piste, slalom or carving.

McGarry The Ski System has chalets in Châtel and runs week-long improvement courses that we've had good reports of.

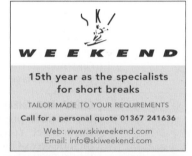

by **Dave Watts**

Renting a place

for economy or luxury

Sponsored by

Erna Low

Renting an apartment in a ski resort is a great way to have a holiday. It gives you privacy to enjoy time with your friends or family without having others around (as you'd get in a hotel or a chalet), and it gives you the freedom to eat as you wish, without being tied to half-board.

You can make an apartment or rented chalet holiday into whatever you want: rent a big place with lots of family or friends or a small place for an intimate time alone with your partner; go for economy by renting a cheap place and packing people in or for luxury by renting a place with lots of space and facilities such as a swimming pool, sauna, cable TV and phone.

Until recently most apartment holidays have been sold as a way of holidaying on the cheap. And apartment holidays have the image of being basic, with cramped accommodation and a small kitchenette on which to rustle up meals on the cheap. They can be like that, but they don't have to be.

CHEAP AND CHEERFUL

If your main priority is to keep costs down, an apartment holiday is the best bet. You can get amazing-value self-drive packages that include cross-Channel fares and a week's apartment rental for well under £100 a head in low season. Most of these are to big-name French resorts with great skiing and riding. Driving is very easy these days, with motorways virtually all the way from Calais to most major resorts (except the last hour or so) – see pages 48 and 53 for chapters on Driving to the Alps and Driving to France.

Normally, to get the cheapest price you really have to pack people in to a small space – say four people sleeping in a one-room 'studio' that doubles up as living room and bedroom, with cooking facilities in a corner. And you have to go in a low-season week.

MGM RESIDENCES

MGM is setting new standards in French self-catering properties →

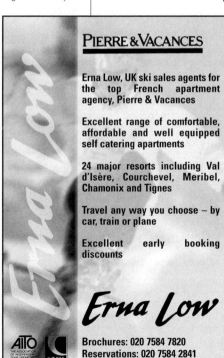

Prices in France, in particular, are very dependent on the week you go because all the French tend to go on holiday at the same times. And the French school holidays are spread throughout February and early March – different regions of France have their own 'half-term' weeks – making the whole of February busy and expensive. So a four-person studio in La Plagne booked through Erna Low is priced at £356 (£89 a head,) including the cross-Channel fare, for the week beginning 6 January, but it more than doubles in price to £820 (£205 a head) for the high-season week beginning 17 February.

If you don't fancy the idea of four adults living and sleeping in one room for a week, you can pay extra for more space and rooms. For an extra bedroom in the La Plagne apartment building, the price goes up to £478 (£119.50 each) for the January week and £1131 (£282.75) in February – so more space need not cost a fortune.

Most cheap-and-cheerful apartments are in blocks owned by big apartment company specialists such as Pierre & Vacances and Maeva. They are generally well positioned for the pistes, but don't expect too much in the way of luxury furniture or fittings.

THE LUXURY OPTION

Although apartment holidays can be the economy option they don't have to be. For the last few years, for example, my main skiing holidays with my wife and a couple of friends have been based in apartments, and we certainly haven't found ourselves slumming it. We like to have a long lunch on the mountain and often aren't very hungry at night, so we go down the local deli and buy luxury snacks such as smoked salmon and oysters, to go with fresh bread, paté, local cheeses and a few good bottles of wine – cooking isn't really our

PIERRE & VACANCES

It's cool to have your own funicular up to an apartment with great views in Méribel-Mottaret, right in the centre of the huge Three Valleys ↘

idea of self-catering! A couple of nights we might go out to a local restaurant – but we love the freedom to choose for ourselves rather than being forced into a half-board regime.

And we go for spacious apartments – a big living room with a good view and two bedrooms. In Zermatt, we've had a top-floor apartment in a four-star hotel with a view of the Matterhorn and the use of a swimming pool, sauna and bar – for only £250 a head. Last winter we rented a luxurious, beautifully furnished apartment with a separate kitchen kitted out with a big cooker, a fridge-freezer, a washing machine and a dishwasher, right on the Bellecôte piste down to the main lifts in Courchevel 1850 (more expensive at £400 a head, but it was early March and in Europe's most expensive resort).

We've tended to book our apartments independently and do a lot of research to make sure they suit our needs. But now more spacious and luxurious apartments are being offered by UK tour operators. Erna Low, for example, now arranges more self-drive ski and snowboard holidays to France than any other UK tour operator and has just introduced a series of luxury apartments that have been developed by a company called MGM in 10 French resorts.

All of these are 'beautifully furnished, most with swimming pool and sauna and all in perfect locations at the foot of the slopes,' says the brochure. Both editors of this guide stayed in one that had just opened in Les Arcs 1800 last season; it had a superb leisure centre with a lovely pool, sauna, steam room and fully equipped gym together with a personal trainer in attendance.

For a four-room apartment for eight people in this development in Les Arcs the cost will be £812 for the 6 January week or £1672 for 17 February including cross-Channel fares. That works out at £101 each in January or £209 in February – or if you just put six people in it £135 and £279 respectively.

MGM has similar developments in Méribel Village, Les Menuires, Val-d'Isère (where they also have 10-person chalets), La Plagne (at Aime 2000), Pralognan-la-Vanoise, Chamonix, Les Houches, Argentière and Les Saisies.

WHAT TO LOOK FOR

If you are thinking of renting an apartment, we recommend you do some homework so you know what you are getting. In particular:

- ask for the total floor space (for our 'luxury' option I look for at least $50m^2$ for four people; studios for four people usually vary between $20m^2$ and $28m^2$, for two people between $13m^2$ and $20m^2$)
- even better, ask for a floor plan with the dimensions of each room
- if you want spacious comfort, fill a place with half the number of people it is advertised as being able to hold
- check out its location on a map of the resort
- if it is in a new area away from the main resort, check what shops there are and how frequently and how late the buses run
- check it has the facilities you want (eg dishwasher, phone, Sky TV)
- ask what is and is not included (in some cases you may have to pay extra for bed linen and towels and perhaps for cleaning the apartment on your departure)
- ask how much deposit you have to pay and when you get it back
- bear in mind that top-floor apartments are likely to have better views and be quieter than lower ones
- if you are renting through a UK tour operator, check what type of cross-Channel transport is included in the price, if any.

by **Chris Gill**

Luxury chalets

the ultimate holiday

So you're planning a week in the Trois Vallées, and you're going to push the boat out and treat yourself to a rather special holiday. Will it be the pampering of a swanky hotel, with flunkies on the door and a Michelin-starred restaurant? Or the privacy of a private rented chalet, and dinner in a different restaurant every night? Or a UK tour operator's catered chalet, with cooking done by a young Brit who lives in?

Put like that, the catered chalet sounds like it comes a poor third. Obviously, some catered chalets would do exactly that. But the best are something else: for my money, the best catered chalets offer the definitive indulgent skiing holiday. They offer an unbeatable combination of comfort, privacy and good food – and service of a kind that is geared to your needs, not to some theoretical concept of your needs.

THE CHALET HOLIDAY

The catered chalet holiday is a uniquely British idea. Tour operators install their own cooks and housekeepers in private chalets which they take over for the season. In the early days this meant roughing it in creaky old buildings, cramped bedrooms with spartan furniture and paper-thin walls, with six or more people sharing a bathroom and a loo. And the chalet girl – always a girl, in those days – was often straight out of college or finishing school and more intent on having a fun season on the slopes than preparing gourmet meals and pandering to your every whim. The main attractions were convivial company, a cosy living room (with a roaring log fire if you were lucky), unlimited free wine with the evening meal and a good price. But for a truly comfortable holiday you went to a hotel.

But now times have changed. You can still get economy chalets, and some companies still employ staff who are there mainly to have a good time for a year. But the general standard of catered chalets has risen, and a new breed of genuinely luxurious chalets has found its way on to the market. These generally have huge, airy living rooms with great views and most or all bedrooms with en suite bathrooms, and are staffed by professional chefs or mature couples who regard catering or hotel-keeping as their chosen profession.

THE LUXURY CHALET HOLIDAY

In a word association game, 'luxury chalet' might trigger various reactions; my own might be 'champagne and canapés'. I reckon the hour before dinner, when you and your friends gradually assemble in front of the log fire to chew over the events of the day, is the time when the chalet's blend of pampering and privacy reaches its peak.

For others, the essence of the luxury chalet holiday might come at the start of the day, with the earlier but equally gradual assembly for breakfast, triggered by the scent of fresh coffee and warming croissants wafting up to the bedrooms. Enthusiasts will already be kitted up for the slopes; but those who are in a more relaxed frame of mind may be padding about in their fluffy bath robes and slippers – perhaps taking their orange juice out on to the sunny balcony to make the most of the crisp morning air and the views before knuckling down to breakfast itself. Others might relish the moment when they slide into the ski boots that have been dried out and warmed overnight. You might look forward to relaxing in the bath to enjoy the giant cocktail you have mixed with your 'duty-free' booze. Or the ultimate post-skiing treat of a Swedish massage.

For many, the highlight will be dinner; it will not offer the choice of a restaurant, but in my experience it will be of a quality that few could hope to better – and will be served in more relaxed and comfortable surroundings (and of course complete privacy). This is one area where luxury operators have made great leaps forward. Most now employ professional cooks rather than the traditional chalet girl, and the result no longer resembles an amateur dinner party. And there is generally wine of a quality that matches the food – indeed, there will often be a choice of wines.

I should emphasise that not all 'luxury' chalets have boot warmers and sunny balconies, not all have a tame masseur on hand, and not all provide provide champagne and canapés as part of the basic deal. But you get the general picture. And there may, on the other hand, be other luxuries – tea in bed, satellite TV, use of a sauna or hot-tub.

What most luxury chalets do have in common is a huge, deeply comfortable living room. This is often what makes the place so irresistible. Ideally, it has oceans of space, picture windows looking out on to fabulous sweeping views, deep sofas in front of that open log fire and a rustic antique cabinet filled with alcoholic delights. If, like me, you're the kind of chalet-goer who is disinclined to stir from the fireside after dinner, it's a real treat to pour a cognac and put your feet up in a chalet that has a real sense of style.

But it's arguable that the biggest single advance that these upmarket chalets represent is in the more functional matter of bathrooms. For years, people who would never dream of booking a hotel room without en suite bathroom went without that simple convenience in the Alps, simply because most chalets didn't have them. Now, lots of chalets do – though it's still necessary to point out that not all the bedrooms in all the chalets offered by the smarter operators are en suite.

Many of these upmarket chalets have been designed for occupation by the family that owns them or at least built them. The result is that the bedrooms vary much more than in purpose-built hotel or apartment accommodation. If you're the lucky ones who get the best room, you may find yourself in a simply stunning 'master' bedroom with acres of space, an immaculate white carpet and a wall of windows looking out on a deserted valley – and an equally impressive bathroom with spa bath. But it has to be said that some otherwise excellent chalets are slightly let down – in comparison with the 4-star and even 5-star hotels they compete with on price – by the other bedrooms. Space in some rooms may be at a premium, even if the furnishings are impressively luxurious. Make sure you know what you're getting, and who is going to sleep where.

The ideal chalet is located right on the piste, but conveniently close to the village centre – yet tucked away from the main streets, so that there are no problems with noise in the early hours. Some luxury chalets come close to this ideal, but you can't assume that high quality and a prime position go together automatically. Many of the best chalets are recently built ones which by definition are most likely to be located on the fringes of the resort. Happily, the operators of these chalets mostly run good minibus services.

LOTUS SUPERTRAVEL

Chalet Founets is my current favourite in Courchevel – but will The Ski Company's new Colombe displace it? →

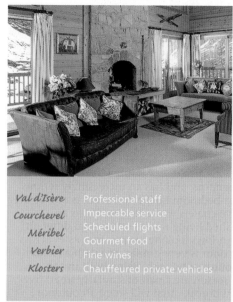

CREME DE LA CREME

You can find isolated luxury chalets in all sorts of places, from Austria to Aspen, but the breed in general is still not widespread: most are concentrated in the more upmarket French mega-resorts of Méribel, Courchevel and Val-d'Isère.

The greatest concentration is found in Méribel, particularly in the hands of long-time local specialist Meriski. One of our favourites is the four-bedroom Iberis. The splendidly spacious and tastefully furnished pine-panelled sitting room has huge floor-to-ceiling windows. There's an extravagantly luxurious master bedroom, complete with walk-in wardrobe and jacuzzi bath. Mira Bellum is another captivating place, with an interesting split-level living space. Meriski has around a dozen chalets altogether, none falling far short of the luxury category, including three new ones for the coming season: Liandon, only 200m from the piste, and two newly built ones in the Mussillon area, designed to give splendid views from their top-floor sitting rooms – Marielene and Mariefleur.

The Ski Company Ltd is perhaps the most upmarket of all the established luxury chalet operators, and has an increasingly serious presence in Méribel. Its eight-bedroom Lodge de Burgin is one of the most spectacularly impressive chalets we have seen. It has an enormous, beautifully furnished living room with several different sitting areas and a wall of windows looking over to the pistes across the valley. The Génépi next door is very similar, but with a jacuzzi bath in every room and an outdoor hot-tub. Being built in the Brames area for the coming season are a pair of similarly smart five-bedroom chalets, Aurore and Boreale, that will share an outdoor heated swimming pool.

The pick of Scott Dunn Ski's four properties in Méribel is the Grand Ours, with its six bedrooms spread over three floors and the sunny living room/balcony on the middle one. Simply Ski's best Méribel properties are the stylish chalet hotel Rousillon, where the compact bedrooms have balconies and great views, and the seven-bedroom chalet Névé, right on the slopes, with outdoor hot tub.

Courchevel is well established as the smartest resort in France, and clearly doesn't lack smart chalets – but relatively few of them find their way on to the UK package market. My current favourite is Lotus Supertravel's five-bedroom Founets, which has a lovely high-ceilinged sitting/dining room and a great position only yards from both the Bellecôte piste and the Bergerie bar-restaurant. Supertravel's Eboulis and Maisonnée chalets are worth looking at, too. The big news this winter is that The Ski Company Ltd has found a suitable property here – the four-bedroom Colombe. This is being built over the summer to an unusual design on four floors, with the top-floor sitting/dining room giving great views in two opposing directions (and a lift to get you up there from your bedroom).

FlexiSki's chalet Anemone is beautifully rustic, and one of Courchevel's originals. Scott Dunn Ski has several properties. In a league of its own (and about 50 per cent more expensive than anything else in Scott Dunn's programme) is the five-bedroom Alaska, complete with indoor swimming pool. That apart, the most impressive is a very grand apartment with wonderful views, the Cristal de Roche penthouse, just a few yards from the heart of Courchevel 1850. Two other fine luxury chalet-apartments are the brand-new Pralong units, right opposite the button lift of the same name. Coblette has a steam room and is right on the Chenus piste.

In Val-d'Isère The Ski Company Ltd has an impressive enclave of four modern luxury chalets right out at the southern extremity of the resort, with massive, well-furnished living rooms, huge windows and splendid views. YSE's Mountain Lodges offer no picture windows but have splendidly atmospheric and comfortable living rooms, with stone walls and ample leather sofas. Scott Dunn Ski has several properties in Val, the most impressive being the Abri du Houard, right by the piste and with fantastic views; eight people can wallow luxuriously in 360 square metres of living space plus sauna, hot-tub and table-tennis room. Opale next door is smaller but still luxurious. New for this season is Sanville, with a glorious galleried living room.

Verbier is with some justification thought of as the chalet capital of the Alps but, here again, there are relatively few luxury properties on the UK market. The Ski Company Ltd's chalet Goodwood is much the best we've seen – a fabulously comfortable and stylish place in a great position, tucked away down a side street a few yards from the main square, a bearable walk from the Medran lift station. Flexiski's Bouvreuil is not so grand, but tastefully rustic, and close to Medran.

In Austria, St Anton is probably the main chalet resort. FlexiSki, Simply Ski and Mark Warner all have upmarket chalet hotels here, but personally I'm itching to see Haus Fauner, the four-bedroom 'superchalet' that Lotus Supertravel is having built this summer, in an excellent position close to both the skiing and the town.

Not surprisingly, the standard of luxury chalets we've inspected in North America is even higher than in Europe. Specialist operators Ski Independence and Ski the American Dream have excellent chalet-style properties in resorts such as Vail and Whistler, and in the latter Simply Ski has an impressive handful, including the genuinely luxurious chalets Eagle and Muirfield, the latter new this season.

Selected luxury chalets

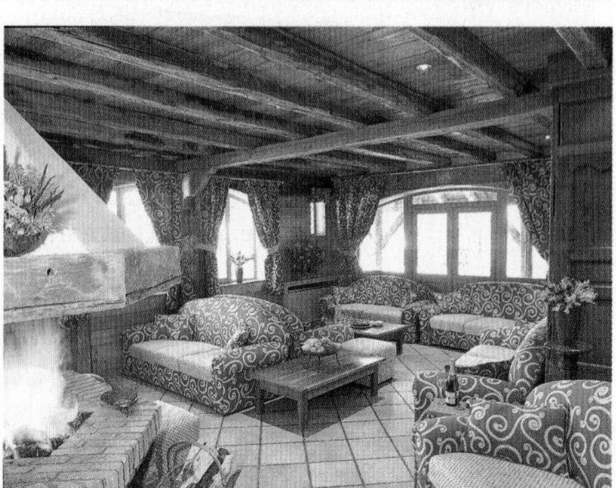

by **Dave Watts**

Good gear guide

new kit means more fun

Ski and snowboard equipment has made huge leaps forward in recent years. Gone are the days of skinny skis and a long learning curve to get good at skiing, and gone are the days when you had to spend ages fiddling with awkward straps at the top of every lift when you tried snowboarding. Gone too are uncomfortable and ill-fitting boots. Equipment has improved beyond recognition and the result is that sliding down mountains has never been so easy and so much fun, whether you are a complete beginner, an intermediate or an expert.

Prices in the UK are now as competitive as in Europe. Readers used to get annoyed when they bought gear in the UK and then found it on sale significantly cheaper in ski resorts. That has changed as a result of manufacturers starting to price in euros and UK retailers being determined to match European prices. And if you buy in America, remember that you'll have to pay duty and VAT when you bring your gear back to the UK.

UK prices for ski and snowboard equipment have generally remained the same or fallen compared with last season. And some retailers have price-match guarantees. Snow + Rock, for example, offers a price pledge to give customers the confidence to purchase in the UK and know that they are getting a fair deal compared with purchasing abroad (call 0845 100 1000 for full details).

SHORTER, FATTER, WIDER

That's the way skis are going, driven by the free-ride revolution which started three years ago. Salomon, for example, have a ski range that is now oriented mainly towards free-riding. Free-ride skis are wider and more shaped than conventional skis, so that they float in powder, cut through the crud off-piste and carve like a dream on piste. Just as rear-entry boots became extinct a few years ago, traditional skinny skis are dead and all they do now is collect dust.

ROSSIGNOL

Rossignol's new T-Power skis are 20 per cent shorter than conventional skis →

Rossignol's new T-Power range has skis that are generally 20 per cent shorter and 20 per cent lighter than conventional skis. For example, an expert skier who might otherwise ski a 190cm long ski

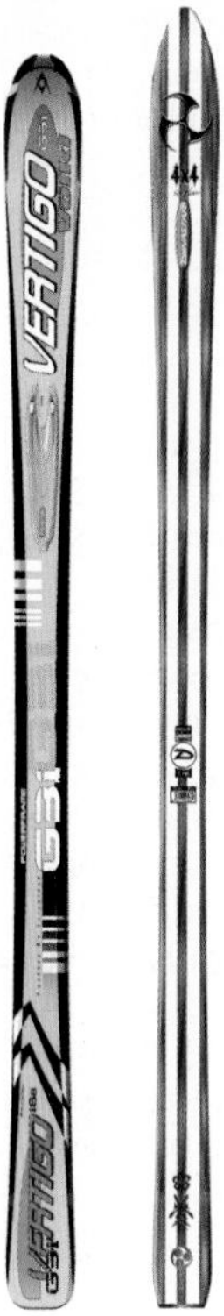

↑ The Volkl Vertigo G31 (left) and Dynastar 4x4 Vertical Maui (right) are two of the season's coolest new freeride skis

VOLKL / DYNASTAR

would be recommended a 167cm length T-Power ski.

And new free-ride skis abound. One of the coolest looking new lines is Dynastar's Maui range of 4x4 skis with retro-style wood graphics. And one of the best that I tried in both the Snow + Rock and *Daily Mail Ski & Snowboard* magazine's ski tests was the Volkl Vertigo G31 – this performed perfectly on- and off-piste and I even preferred it to my previous favourite, the Salomon XScream.

Pretty much every manufacturer now has an expert extreme, pro-model, backcountry ski, perfect for heli-skiing in Alaska and being seen carrying to and from Val-d'Isère bars. Salomon's AK (Alaska – geddit?) Rocket has been joined by K2's AK Launcher, Head's Monster Cross, Dynastar's 4x4 Big and Fischer's Alltrax Big Stix. These babies come in huge dimensions – typically 116mm at the front, 84mm at the waist and 110mm at the tail, compared with a slalom race ski's typical dimensions of 102mm, 63mm and 90mm respectively. Perfect weapons for floating in neck-deep powder, less ideal for cruising the blues!

Salomon's huge AK Rocket is perfect for heli-skiing and floating in neck-deep powder ↑

SALOMON

TWIN TIPS AND SKIBOARDS FOR ALL

Last season's *Daily Mail Ski & Snowboard* magazine's Ski of the Year, Salomon's Teneighty, took the market by storm. Not just great in the half-pipe and fun-park throwing flips and 360s, it also performs on-piste and floats like a dream in powder and crud off the groomed terrain. Next season it will have strong competition from pretty much every major manufacturer, which all have their own all-terrain twin tips – Rossignol Pow'Air, Fischer Unlimited, Volkl V, Dynastar Agyl, Head Air Head and K2 Enemy. Salomon is keeping the 1080 and adding a cheaper 720 aimed at younger, less affluent kids.

The Dynastar Agyl is one of the new breed of twin-tip skis →

DYNASTAR

Look in the half-pipes and terrain-parks around the world now and you'll see as many skiers as snowboarders strutting their stuff. Skiing has become trendy again and many hip snowboarders are finding their boards way too restrictive and are changing back to two planks instead of one.

All the major manufacturers now have at least one pair of skiboards in their range – defined as less than a metre long and with fixed rather than releasing safety bindings. They take very little time to get to grips with and provide a totally different on-snow thrill. Skiboarding gives snowbound youngsters (and the occasional adolescent wrinkly) street cred. While all manufacturers have cruisey carving skiboards that will take the first-time snow visitor around the

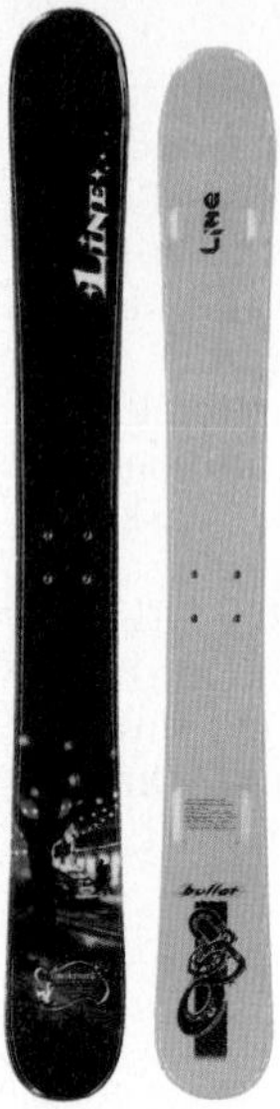

↑ Line is a small manufacturer leading the way in skiboard development

LINE

mountain by the second day, there is a revolution happening. Aggressive street skaters, snowboarders and fun-loving skiers are taking up the challenge of the terrain-parks. These short skiboards enable this new breed of snow dweller to deliver tricks (hucks) that snowboarders and skiers would never have thought imaginable. If you feel that your long boards are cramping your style, check these out. New small manufacturers such as Line are leading the way.

STAYING FLEXIBLE

Carving means allowing the shape/geometry of the ski to take you into the turn rather than physically driving the ski around, or having to use years of acquired technique which many skiers do not possess. To maximise edge grip you need to be able to push the ski into reverse camber and feel the whole ski flex beneath your feet. Conventional bindings prevent perfect flexing of the ski because they are mounted straight on the ski and then your boot is clamped in giving a 'flat spot' under your foot. This coming season sees lots of innovations to eliminate the flat spot. Leading the marketing hype will be Salomon's new Pilot system, where the binding is attached to the sides rather than the top of the skis through specially drilled holes, allowing the ski to flex naturally and giving even quicker edge grip and transmission of power from boot to ski. Atomic is introducing a boot with a Tritech system where the sole of the boot flexes to allow full flexing of the ski. Fischer has an Accelerator plate and Dynastar an autodrive floating plate on to which the bindings are mounted to allow free flexing of the ski.

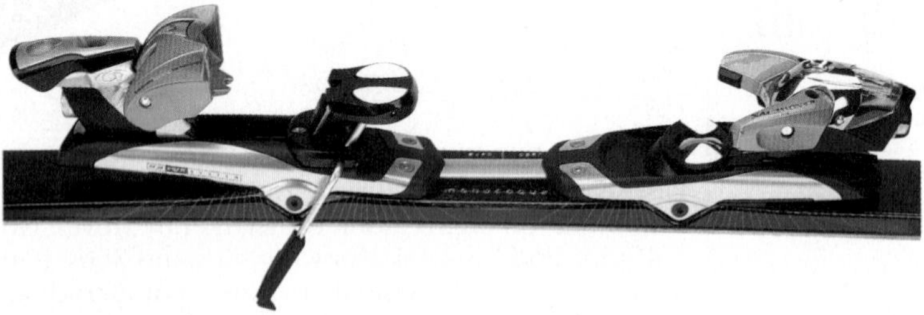

Salomon's new Pilot bindings and skis are designed to allow the ski to flex naturally →

SALOMON

COMFORT ZONE

The big news on the boot front is that custom-fit inner boots are becoming the norm. Nearly all manufacturers now have – in at least some of their boots – inner boots that can be heated up (usually by a sophisticated hair dryer type of device). They then automatically mould to the shape of your foot when you put the boot on. Indeed, Rossignol now has Thermo Fit inner boots throughout its entire boot range. You can also buy separate inner boots called Zip-Fit, which are made of cork and oil. These mould to the shape of your foot, last for ages and can be swapped from boot to boot if you change your boots or demo a new pair. I have heard only good reports of them, but I have not tried them myself yet.

Lange has a new boot that is designed to reduce the danger of anterior cruciate ligament injuries in backward falls and near falls. It has a hinge on the back allowing the rear of the boot to move backwards under extreme pressure, so reducing the stretching of the ligament on the front of the knee. The boot will be on sale in the US in 2000/01 and in Europe the following season.

A few unique new products are available this season, including

SNOW + ROCK
Hi Energy Sports
www.snowandrock.com
8 SHOPS* - 4 SEASONS - 1 ADVENTURE
SNOW+ROCK DIRECT:
0845 100 1000 - WWW.SNOWANDROCK.COM
*NEW STORE NOW OPEN IN COVENT GARDEN

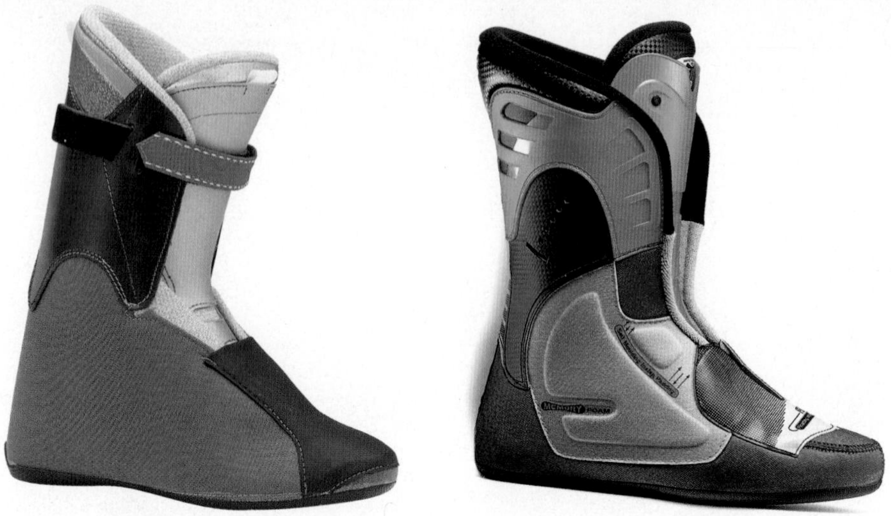

↑ Inner boots which mould to your foot such as Tecnica's (right) are good, and Zip-Fit (left) has one which fits different makes of boots

ZIP-FIT / TECNICA

K2's Aggressor Clicker boot, which will work in its skiboards, snowboards and in touring bindings – a true cross-category boot, it says. Rossignol has a Free Trek Venture ski with a binding that can be used with ski, snowboard and hiking boots and in telemark, touring and fixed heel positions. It is designed to allow you access to every part of the mountain, whatever method of descent you choose.

GET ON BOARD

Both the editors of this guidebook now board – one of them regularly. And increasing numbers of readers are now getting on board, judging by the resort reports we receive. If you still haven't tried it, why not give it a go? Once you have got over the first few days of falling around as you did when learning to ski it is great fun, and the thrill of making your first linked turns makes you feel like a kid again.

There is a basic choice between hard and soft boots. Hard boots look pretty similar to ski boots at first sight. But they are much more popular on the Continent than with British or US snowboarders and we would recommend going for soft boots – which are a complete contrast to ski boots and give you a great sense of freedom. And this coming season sees great strides forward with drastically improved fit, comfort and performance from all the major manufacturers, such as North Wave, Ride, K2, Nitro and Burton. This follows the entry into the market of Salomon with market-leading fit and performance, which the other players have to emulate. The added bonus of all this competition is that the prices have come down. For example, one of last season's highest performance boots, the Salomon Malamute Custom-fit, then retailed for £199 and will sell for £179 this coming season.

With soft boots, the traditional way to attach your feet to the board is with straps that are part of the binding – again, these have been changed over the years to make them much easier to use, with further changes this coming season improving response, power, comfort and support. Personally, as relative beginners, we prefer step-in bindings, where your boot clicks in to the binding rather in the same way that a ski boot does. Again, this season sees further

Salomon's Malamute is one of the highest-performance snowboard boots and is £20 cheaper than last season →

SALOMON

improvements in the comfort, performance and convenience of step-in boots.

With boards, my recommendation for relative beginner boarders is an easy to ride 'Free-ride' board – these are designed for all-mountain use. Other options for more advanced riders are 'Freestyle' boards (for doing tricks and riding half-pipes), Alpine 'Freecarve' boards for use with hard boots and 'Race' boards. For advanced free-riders, one of the most innovative things on the board front this season is the new M2 3D core from Ride Snowboards, giving the boards fantastic performance enhancement without losing any of their ease of riding characteristics. The Ride Fuel and Timeless feature this new construction.

BODY FACTOR

Before last season I had a bad back and could hardly walk at times. I visited a local physio but without much effect. So I took myself off to Snow + Rock's Body Factor unit at its M25 branch. An osteopath there sorted me out in just three sessions (giving me exercises to do as well). My back got better and saw me through the season without problems – fantastic! Body Factor also does fitness assessments, treats all kinds of sports injury, makes custom-moulded orthotics (footbeds) and has a ski alignment programme. There's now another branch at the new Covent Garden store, which includes a full rehabilitation and work-out gym. For details or an appointment call 01932 564364.

RIDE

Ride's Fuel board has a new M2 3D core for added performance ↓

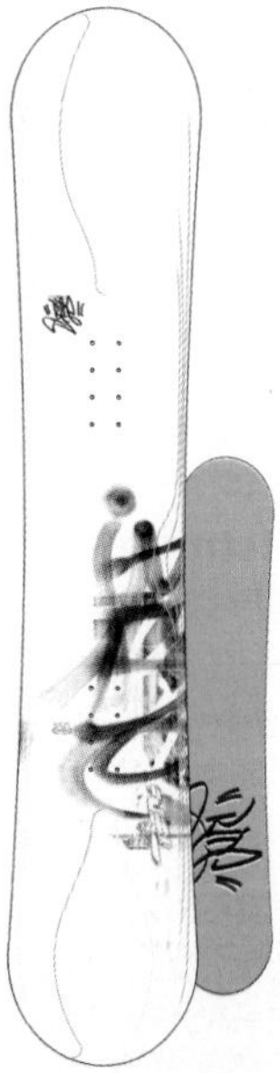

SNOW + ROCK

WHY BUY BRITISH?

Snow + Rock has a six-point charter for why it makes sense to buy your ski and snowboard gear in Britain rather than in your resort:

- British ski shops are reputed to be among the most technical and highly trained in the world.
- Britain has a greater international choice of product, not governed by a regional or national bias. Do not expect to get the same choice of product or the same range of sizes in a resort shop.
- After-sales service is important. You can return to the shop for further boot fitting and adjustment and for ski services. Warranty problems can easily be dealt with. Snow + Rock offers a comfort guarantee for boots and a suitability guarantee for skis.
- You can buy from knowledgeable staff who speak English. Most technicians will have tried and tested the product and are not trying to sell you an end of line product or an item that is totally inappropriate for your skiing ability.
- You can make the most of your precious week or two on the slopes without wasting time looking for equipment in the resort.
- Snow + Rock offers a price pledge (see first page of this chapter).

by **Dave Watts**

Weekends on the slopes

the quick fix break

We love weekend skiing. Just one day off work can give you three great days on the slopes, leaving you with the feeling of having been away for ages and returning to work feeling really refreshed. And it does not need to cost you an arm and a leg.

Last season I had a couple of great weekends away. The first was in Austria when we flew to Zürich from Heathrow on the 8.30pm Swissair flight after a full day in the office. We picked up a rental car and arrived in Lech shortly after midnight. The day dawned sunny and we had a marvellous day cruising the pistes and sampling the deserted off-piste slopes of Austria's chicest resort. Après-ski was a couple of drinks at the Tanbergerhof with its pavement umbrella bar followed by a flute of champagne at the bar of the amazing Strolz emporium. This is one of the flashiest ski shops in the world – catering for the beautiful people shopping for £1000 ski suits, fur coats and hand-made, made-to-measure ski boots. Next day we drove to St Anton and skied the steep, ungroomed slopes of the Valluga before moving on to Ischgl (only an hour away) for the night. This was a complete contrast to Lech. The bars and clubs heaved with crowds and blasted out music. Tea-time après-ski was enlivened by the scantily clad dancing girls on the bar of the 4-star Hotel Elisabeth at the foot of the slopes. On Sunday we were able to cruise the high, snowsure intermediate slopes that this underrated resort shares with duty-free Samnaun in Switzerland for a full day before the three-hour drive back to Zürich for the 8.30pm flight to London. We arrived back feeling as if we had had a full week's skiing – and for just one day off work. This trip was arranged by Momentum Ski, a tailor-made ski holiday specialist that I have always found very helpful and reliable.

Late in the season I took a £70 return Buzz flight from Stansted to Lyon to join some friends already out in Optimum's Chalet Tarentaise (see page 26), arriving late on a Friday night after a two-and-a-half hour drive from the airport. The local Les Arcs ski area was already closed (it was late April/early May) but the vast expanse of the Espace Killy (Tignes-Val-d'Isère) was still open and only a 20-minute drive away. We spent Saturday and Sunday up on the area's high glacier slopes which were still in tremendous shape. On Monday I went out with the Alpine Experience off-piste guiding service based in Val-d'Isère and had a couple of great spring-snow descents to round off my season. It was possible to ski right until the lifts closed before changing and leaving to catch Buzz's 9.30pm return flight from Lyon to Stansted, ready for work on Tuesday morning. Again, one day off work meant being able to ski for three full days – this time a great way to round off the season.

Over the years I've had great weekends in lots of resorts, including Chamonix (the classic weekend destination because of its proximity to Geneva airport), Flaine, the Portes du Soleil, Courchevel, Val-d'Isère, Schladming, Zell am See, Flims, Saas-Fee and Verbier, for example.

↑ Chamonix is one of the most popular weekend resorts

SNOWPIX.COM / CHRIS GILL

ARRANGING THE WEEKEND

The key to making the most of your time is to catch late flights each way – and it obviously helps if you live near a suitable airport. Swissair has well-timed flights for both Geneva and Zürich from Heathrow. EasyJet had suitable flights from both Luton and Liverpool to Geneva and Zürich. Buzz's late flight back from Lyon to Stansted was particularly useful for a relaxing last day on the slopes. Alitalia has lots of flights to Milan and Venice.

We don't recommend flying to Munich if you are travelling out on a Friday or back on a Sunday – the queues on the motorway can be horrendous as the whole of Munich seems to go weekend skiing and the airport is on the far side of the city from the Alps. We nearly missed our Sunday evening flight back one weekend despite leaving Schladming a good hour before the locals' recommended departure time. Similarly, it makes sense to allow plenty of time if you are driving back to Lyon airport on a Sunday evening – again we encountered very heavy traffic after leaving Courchevel in what we thought had been good time.

Booking a rental car or taxi in advance is usually cheaper than arranging one after you arrive. Several tour operators can arrange that as part of a complete weekend package. Taxis can be ridiculously expensive compared with the cost of renting a car. For example, expect to pay around £200 or more each way between Geneva airport and Courchevel by taxi – a small car for the weekend would be much less than the one-way taxi price. In our experience train and public bus times between airports and resorts are more suitable for week-long visitors than for weekenders looking for maximum time on the slopes.

Using a weekend specialist, such as one of those advertising in this chapter, makes sense if you don't want the hassle of making your own arrangements or renting a car. They know the best resorts to go to, can arrange transfers by their own staff or through local companies, and have special deals with hotels that do them good room rates or that might not otherwise take weekend bookings. Some of them have weekend chalet accommodation too. Some also arrange special weekend courses (eg with off-piste guides or even heli-skiing weekends). And local tour operator representatives and contacts can save valuable time arranging lift passes (beware of big weekend queues on Saturday and Sunday mornings) and equipment hire and advise on local restaurants and other facilities.

Several operators do a lot of 'corporate' business: fixing weekend breaks for companies that want a conference away from the office, or want to reward successful employees or loyal customers.

CHOOSING A RESORT

As for choosing a resort, there are various considerations. Many people think they should go for a resort within a short drive of your arrival airport. But by definition, resorts close to major airports are close to large numbers of people poised to hit the slopes on fine weekends, which can mean queues for the lifts, crowds on the slopes and competition for hotel beds. But these days most resorts are within striking distance of a major airport and an hour's extra transfer time is not really that much if it gets you to quieter slopes.

Resorts close to Geneva include Chamonix, St Gervais, Megève and Les Contamines (all in the Mont Blanc area and sharing an area lift pass), Flaine and La Clusaz in France, and Villars and Les Diablerets in Switzerland. All these are within an hour or so of Geneva by car. Verbier and Crans-Montana in Switzerland are a bit further, as are the Three Valleys and other Tarentaise resorts – even Val-d'Isère can be reached in under three hours now – and Morzine and the Portes du Soleil resorts in France.

Flying to Zürich opens up lots of other possibilities. Flims-Laax and Davos and Klosters are probably the closest big resorts, and less-well known Engelberg and Andermatt are within easy reach. St Anton and Lech in Austria are within striking distance, as are the resorts of the Montafon valley.

In Italy, Courmayeur is a popular and attractive weekend destination. It used to be easily accessible from Geneva via the Mont Blanc tunnel – but while the tunnel is shut Turin is the nearest international airport. Resorts such as Sauze d'Oulx and Sestriere are also easily accessible from Turin.

Unless you are booking at short notice when you know the snow is good, we'd be tempted to avoid low resorts such as Megève and Villars – unless you

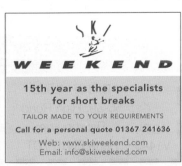

Weekends of excitment?
Start here!
SkiMcNeill.com
Flexible, tailormade ski holidays in Europe's top resorts
Snow reports
Resort Info
Late Offers
ATOL 4138
ABTA 43398
IATA

have transport to get you to more snowsure slopes. And because you don't want your whole weekend ruined by a white-out if it snows all the time, we'd also be tempted to avoid very high resorts where the skiing is entirely above the tree-line – which would rule out places such as Tignes and Val-Thorens in France, Obergurgl in Austria and Cervinia in Italy.

WHAT ABOUT PRICE?

The cost can vary enormously. The flight and transfer or car hire are the expensive fixed costs and obviously make a weekend proportionately more expensive than a full week. But as we said before, you do get three days' skiing (half a full week) for only one day off work, and the three days makes a substantial break. A four-night break is, of course even better – it only costs two days off work and means you can travel out and back on Thursday and Monday evenings (quieter than Fridays and Sundays).

In general you can expect to pay £400 or more a head for flights, car hire and a double room in a 3-star hotel for three nights, assuming two people sharing. With lift passes and meals you could be looking at £500 or £600 or more. But you can do it more cheaply. Last season, for example, there were weekends on offer by some weekend specialist tour operators at under £300 for scheduled flights, three nights' bed and breakfast and car hire. And if you are prepared to rough it and travel overnight by coach both ways, companies such as Harris Holidays (under its brand name Freedom 2 Travel) have weekends on offer starting at just £99 (1999/2000 prices).

by **Chris Allan**

Drive to the Alps

and ski where you please

The days when driving from Britain to the Alps was the preserve of the most intrepid of motorists have long gone. The advent of the Channel Tunnel and the tremendous improvements made to the motorway networks in northern France and the Alps have made life much, much easier for the growing number of Brits who decide to drive down. You can now get to most resorts easily in a day. The advantages? It's less hassle, it gives you tremendous freedom once you're in the Alps – the kind of freedom you're probably used to on summer holidays – and it can save money.

If you've never tried driving to the Alps, you don't know what you're missing. For a start, it simplifies the whole business of getting all your kit from here to there: you just load up at one end and unload at the other, without tangling with airport trolleys. If you're taking your family or going self-catering, just think of all the extra things you can cram in that you'd otherwise have to leave behind.

But for us, the freedom factor is the key. If the snow's bad in your resort, if the lift queues are horrendous or if the resort you've plumped for is a let-down, car drivers can try somewhere else.

Another plus-point is that you can extend the standard six-day holiday by two days while taking only one extra day off work. We do it by crossing the Channel early on a Friday morning and returning nine days later on the Sunday evening. Of course, you need accommodation for the Friday night on the way out, and for the Saturday night on the way back. On the trip out, we often take advantage of this to spend a day in a different resort before moving on to our final destination late on the Saturday. You could stop off in Valmorel before going on to the Three Valleys, for example.

After a full day on the slopes on the final Saturday, driving towards the Channel for a few hours before stopping for the night means you won't find Sunday's journey too demanding.

AS YOU LIKE IT

If you fancy visiting several resorts, you can use one as a base and make day-trips to nearby places when it suits you. This way, you can still take advantage of tour operator prices and get a discount for driving. The discount varies from operator to operator and also depends on whether you go in high or low season – but you can expect to get from around £70 to £120.

The key to turning this kind of holiday into a success is to go for a base that offers easy road access to other resorts. Our suggestions for France are in the special chapter following this one.

A good choice in Austria is the Tirol. The resorts to the east of Innsbruck offer many options for day-trippers. Söll is a convenient base for exploring the other resorts nearby, including Alpbach and Kitzbühel. Further east, in Salzburg province, you can use Zell am See as a base for excursions to Bad Gastein and Saalbach, while Flachau is a convenient base for visiting the resorts covered by the Top Tauern lift pass, such as Schladming and Obertauern. Western Austria is not

WINTER TYRES

For several seasons now we have used Snowtrac tyres made by a specialist Dutch company, Vredestein, and been very happy with them, both on-snow and off. They are made in common car sizes from 175/70 R13 up to 195/65 R15, and are usually available from stock. The UK warehouse is in Wellingborough. **t** 01933 677770.

ideal for this sort of holiday, but from St Anton you could make day-trips to Lech, Zürs, Ischgl and Serfaus.

You could consider resorts on the Swiss side of the Portes du Soleil, such as Morgins and Champéry, as a base for trips to resorts such as Verbier, Crans-Montana and Chamonix, as well as visiting the Portes du Soleil resorts. Although eastern Switzerland provides more of a challenge to day-trippers, you might find that it's well worth the effort. Lenzerheide is about the best choice of base camp. Flims, Arosa, Davos and St Moritz are all within striking distance. From St Moritz you could even go over to Livigno in Italy.

Because many resorts are so remote, Italy isn't easily recommendable for day trippers.

AROUND THE ALPS IN SEVEN DAYS

If you want to ski as much of the Alps as possible, consider making a Grand Tour by car, moving every day or two to a different resort and enjoying the complete freedom of going where you want, when you want. Except in high season, there's no need to book any accommodation before you go. So you can decide at the last minute which part of the Alps to visit – where the snow is best, perhaps.

A touring holiday doesn't mean you'll be spending more time on the road than on the piste – provided you plan your route carefully. An hour's drive after the lifts have shut is all it need take. Our special chapter on driving to the French Alps covers the possibilities there.

Many of the areas that are great for day-trippers are also worth considering if you're going on tour. These include western Austria and the Tirol. Take western Austria, for example; you could start with Lech, Zürs and St Anton, move on to Serfaus and Ischgl, then go down to Obergurgl, perhaps stopping at Sölden on the way.

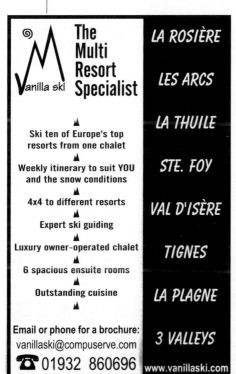

Italy is far more suitable for tourers than day trippers provided you're prepared to put up with some slow drives on winding passes. You could start in Livigno, drive to Bormio and then to the Dolomites, visiting Madonna di Campiglio and Selva, and finish your Italian expedition in Cortina.

Eastern Switzerland also offers a very attractive touring holiday. You could start in Davos/Klosters, take in Lenzerheide and Arosa and end up in Flims. You could even include St Moritz if you're prepared to put up with a little extra driving. Again in Switzerland, you could easily combine several resorts in the Bernese Oberland – Gstaad, Adelboden, Grindelwald and Lauterbrunnen, where trains go up to Wengen and Mürren.

There's no need to confine yourself to one country. You

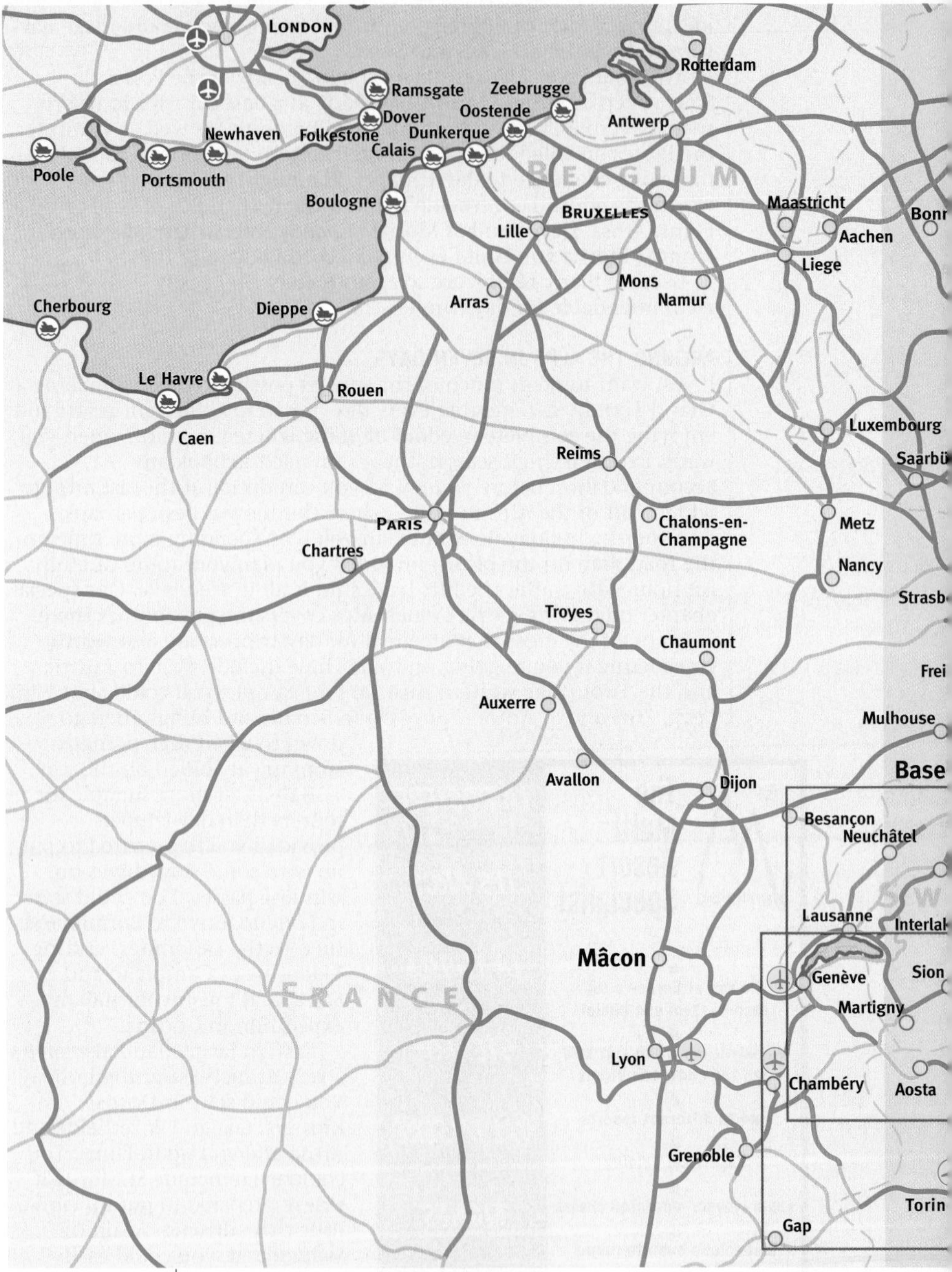

This map should help you plan your route to the Alps. All the main routes from the Channel and all the routes up into the mountains funnel through three 'gateways', picked out on the map in larger type – Mâcon, Basel and Ulm. Decide which gateway suits your destination, and pick a route to it. Occasionally, different Channel ports will lead you to use different gateways.

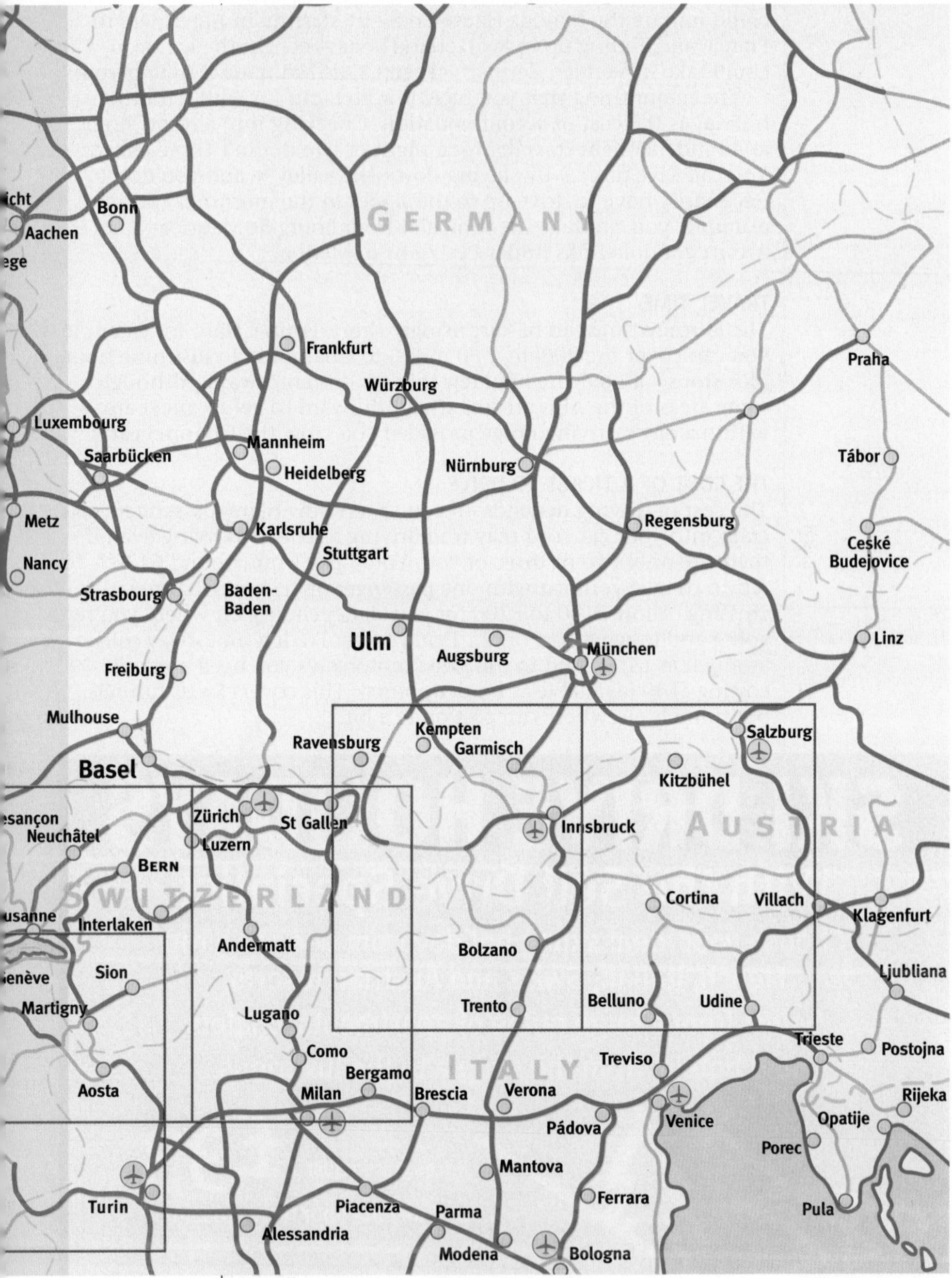

The boxes on the map correspond to the areas covered by the more detailed maps at the start of the main country sections of the book:
Austria page 84
France page 182
Italy page 324
Switzerland page 374.

could imitate the famous Haute-Route by starting in Argentière in France and ending up in Switzerland's Saas-Fee. On the way you could take in Verbier, Zermatt – even Crans-Montana if time permits.

The major thing that you have to watch out for with a touring holiday is the cost of accommodation. Checking into a resort hotel as an independent traveller for a night or two doesn't come cheap. You can save money by staying down the valley – and you don't necessarily have to drive up to the slopes in the morning. For example, you can take the funicular from Bourg-St-Maurice to Les Arcs; a gondola links Brides-Les-Bains to Méribel.

TRAVEL TIME

The journey time can be surprisingly short. From Calais, for example, you can cover the 900km (560 miles) to Chamonix in just nine hours plus stops – all but the final few miles is on motorways. Although some areas of the Alps are less straightforward to get to, most are within a day's driving range provided you cross the Channel early.

THE COST OF A TICKET TO DRIVE

The cost of driving depends, of course, on how many passengers you cram into your car. You may find driving as cheap as flying even if there are only two or three of you. You'll pay from around £130 return to take your car with one passenger on a short Channel crossing. Allow £100 to £200 for petrol, depending on where you're going and in what sort of car. Don't forget French motorway tolls – as much as £100. And to use Swiss motorways you need a permit costing SF40 (available at border points). This covers Swiss tunnels, but tunnels elsewhere can cost quite a bit.

by **Chris Gill**

Drive to the French Alps

to make the most of them

If you've read the preceding chapter, you'll have gathered that we are keen on driving to the Alps. But we're particularly keen on driving to the French Alps. The drive is a relatively short one, whereas many of the transfers from Geneva airport are relatively long. And the route from the Channel is through France rather than Germany, which for Francophiles like us means it's a pleasant prospect rather than a grim one.

TRAVEL TIME

The French Alps are the number-one destination for British car-borne skiers. The journey time is surprisingly short. From Calais, for example, you can comfortably cover the 900km (560 miles) to Chamonix in about nine hours plus stops – with the exception of the final few miles, the whole journey is on motorways. And except on peak weekends the traffic is relatively light.

With some southern exceptions, all the resorts of the French Alps are within a day's driving range, provided you cross the Channel early in the day (or overnight). And the weekend traffic jams that used to make such a nightmare (for drivers and coach passengers alike) of the journey from Albertville to the Tarentaise resorts are pretty much a thing of the past, thanks to road improvements.

DAY-TRIP BASES

Most people driving to the French Alps do it simply because they find it a more relaxing way to get themselves, their kit and perhaps their kids to their chosen resort. But, as we have explained in the previous chapter, having a car opens up different kinds of holiday for the more adventurous. Day tripping, for example.

In the southern French Alps, Serre-Chevalier and Montgenèvre are ideal bases for day tripping. They are within easy reach of one another, and Montgenèvre is at one end of the Milky Way lift network, which includes Sauze d'Oulx and Sestriere in Italy. Puy-St-Vincent is an underrated resort that is well worth a visit – as is Risoul. The major resorts of Alpe-d'Huez and Les Deux-Alpes are also within range, as is the cult off-piste resort of La Grave.

The Chamonix valley is an ideal destination for day trippers. The Mont-Blanc pass covers the lifts of Chamonix, Les Contamines, Megève and others. Flaine and its satellites are also fairly accessible – so is Verbier in Switzerland if the intervening passes are open.

MOVING ON

A look at the map on the next page shows that a different approach will pay dividends in the Tarentaise region of France. Practically all the resorts here, from Valmorel to Val-d'Isère, are found at the end of long winding roads up from the main valley. You could visit them all from a base such as Aime, but it would be hard work. If instead you stayed in a different resort each night, moving on from one to the next in the early evening, you could have the trip of a lifetime. Imagine a week in which you could explore the Three Valleys, La Plagne, Les Arcs, and Val-d'Isère/Tignes.

GETTING THERE

The map in our Driving to the Alps chapter shows the main routes across France to the Alps. Whatever route you prefer across the Channel, the gateway to the French Alps is Mâcon and the initial target is Beaune. If you're taking the short crossing to Calais, Boulogne or Dunkirk, the route is via Reims, Troyes and Dijon. From Le Havre or Caen your route sounds even simpler: the A13 to Paris then the A6 south. But you have to get through or around Paris. The most direct way around the city is the notorious périphérique – a hectic, multi-lane urban motorway close to the centre, with exits every few hundred yards. But this is not the quickest route if it is jammed with traffic. The more reliable alternative is to take a series

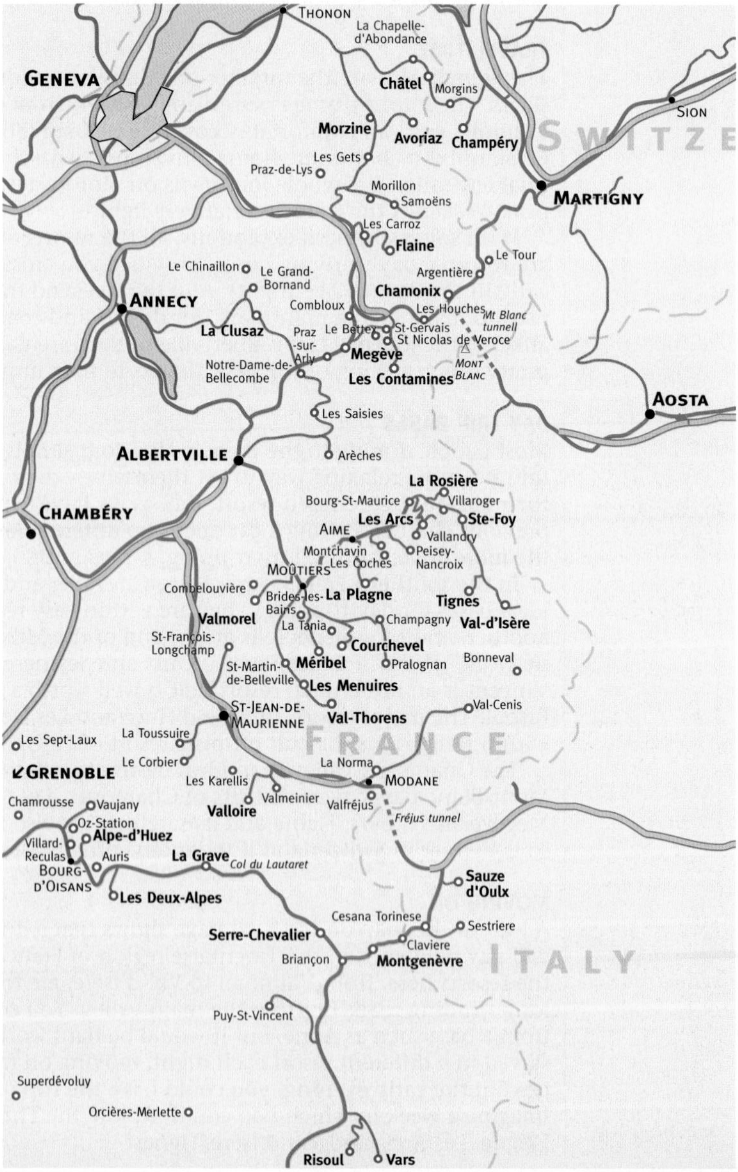

0 30
Scale in km

of motorways and dual carriageways through the south-west fringes of Greater Paris. The route (or one of the routes – there are a couple of variants) is signed, but not easy to follow without a detailed map and a good navigator to shout instructions.

MAKING THE MOST OF THE TRIP

The journey across France can be a holiday in itself. Here are some suggestions for stopovers en route.

Arras

One plan we sometimes employ is to cross the Channel quite late in the day and to stop for the night an hour or so into France. Our favourite spot, without doubt, is Arras – an astonishing little town with two central squares surrounded by ornate arcades.

Paris

What better way to celebrate the start or end of your French holiday than with a slap-up meal in a Parisian restaurant? Don't be afraid to tangle with the Paris traffic – just be ready to use your horn. For comfortable modern rooms with the great convenience of a secure garage, we use the Mercure Tour Eiffel hotel.

Disneyland

If you have kids of the right age, you will already know about this. If the budget will stand it, we'd recommend blowing some of it on staying at the theme park in the Newport Bay Club hotel.

Burgundy and points south

On the way back, we like to spend a last day on the slopes and then drive for two or three hours. Mâcon has a reasonable choice of hotels and restaurants, including the Michelin-starred Pierre. Tournus has several stars. Chalon-sur-Saône has plenty of choice.

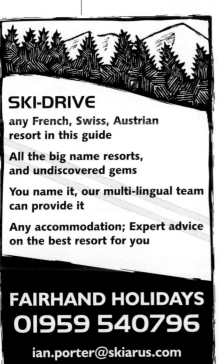

by **Dave Watts**

Taking to the air

cheap flights galore

EasyJet started the first cheap scheduled flights to the Alps by flying to Geneva in the 1997/98 season. They still have the biggest range of flights on offer but have now been joined by three other cut-price airlines. And this competition has made the bigger, established airlines smarten up their acts and offer some competitive deals. This is great news for independent skiers or riders, who can now get flights for under £100, rent a car for a week for under £200 (£50 each between four) and have affordable holidays they arrange themselves.

Last season I used three of the cheap airlines – EasyJet, Buzz and Go – during our various trips to the Alps. (I did not have the opportunity to try out the fourth, Ryanair.) All three were pretty much on time, and their no-frills service and pay-as-you-eat food is all you need on a short flight of 90 minutes or less. They are particularly convenient for me because I live only 20 minutes from Stansted and 40 from Luton, the airports they operate from. From Heathrow I used Swissair, which has well-timed flights for weekend or short-break trips and offers competitive fares through agents if you book a package. It may also be cheaper than the 'cheap' airlines when flights start to get full and 'cheap' prices rise.

By the time we went to press, most of the airlines had not firmed up their programmes for the the 2000/01 season. What we talk about here is what applied last season.

All the cheap airlines are ticketless, and none of them works through travel agents. You book direct with the airline over the telephone or on the Internet (there's usually a discount of a few pounds for booking on the Web because it is cheaper for the airline). You pay by credit card and either print out your own confirmation (if you book on the Web) or receive it in the post or by fax. Prices vary according to demand, and in general the cheapest flights (which they quote in their adverts) are for midweek flights early or late in the day, booked months in advance. As a flight fills up, the prices charged go up. But you may also get a bargain by booking at the last minute if the flight is not full. In general, prices start at about £40 one-way or £70 return.

Policies about flexibility vary. EasyJet's prices are made up of a price for the outward journey and another for the return leg – you can book either journey separately or book both and add the two fares together. If you book and then want to change the date or time of your flight (or even the name of the passenger), you pay an administration fee and any difference between the fares. Such changes can be made up to an hour before the original scheduled flight departure time. Buzz, on the other hand, offers a 'Done Deal' fare, where you cannot make any changes after you've booked, or a (very much more expensive) flexible fare which allows you to change your flight without charge. And when I tried to book a one-way flight they quoted the full return flexible fare – just like a standard scheduled airline might do.

AIRLINE CONTACT DETAILS

Phone numbers for the major airlines are listed on page 609.

With Buzz I also had a problem with the baggage limit. Four of us were travelling together, and we had three ski bags (including a double ski bag containing skis and a board), a couple of big cases and some smaller ones. In total we were within the weight limit, but on the way out to the Alps the check-in staff insisted that we checked in separately and had our luggage weighed individually. This meant scrabbling about in the check-in area, repacking to even out weights as far as possible. And we still ended up having to pay a bit in excess baggage. Ridiculous (and a rip-off). On the way back, the check-in staff at Lyon just gave a Gallic shrug and waved us through.

Last season EasyJet had several flights a day from Luton to both Geneva and Zürich. It also flew from Liverpool, Gatwick and Stansted to Geneva. And it had flights from Luton and Liverpool to Nice (great for a weekend in Isola 2000) and Barcelona (handy for Andorra).

Go (a subsidiary of British Airways) flew from Stansted to Zürich, Lyon (good for most French resorts), Munich (handy for Austria), Venice (for the Dolomites), Milan (for western Italian resorts) and Barcelona (for Andorra). Buzz (a subsidiary of KLM) flew from Stansted to Lyon and Milan. Ryanair went from Stansted to Turin (nearer than Milan for western Italian resorts), Venice, Carcassonne (for Andorra and the French Pyrenees) and St-Etienne (40 minutes south-west of Lyon and within striking distance of the French Alps).

Swissair operated several direct flights a day from Heathrow and Manchester to Zürich and from Heathrow to Geneva, and are likely to continue to do so. Late flights (8pm or later) to and from Heathrow to both Geneva and Zürich make short breaks particularly easy if you live in the south-east – you can work all day Thursday, catch a late flight out, have three days on the slopes and still be back at work on Monday morning. Crossair (a Swissair subsidiary) have useful flights on Saturdays to Sion, less than half an hour's transfer to, for example, Nendaz (for Verbier's slopes) and Crans-Montana, and a bit further to Saas-Fee, Zermatt and Verbier.

Alitalia flies direct from Heathrow to Milan, which gives access to many of the Italian resorts. Direct flights from Gatwick to Venice are handy for the Dolomite resorts.

EASYJET

EasyJet started the cheap flight boom to the Alps three seasons ago →

by **Martin Hall**

Travel by train

it can be less of a strain

Taking the train to the Alps can be a great way to get more time on the slopes without taking more time off work. You can leave on Friday night, arriving in your resort on Saturday morning, and return on the following Saturday night, arriving back home on the Sunday – eight days' skiing for five days out of the office. Even if you opt for a different service that doesn't deliver the eight-day week, travelling by train is one of the most restful ways to get to the Alps – provided your journeys to and from the railway stations at either end are not too stressful.

The most popular train destination, with several different direct and indirect services, is the Tarentaise valley in France. You can step off the train in Bourg-St-Maurice and on to a funicular straight up to Arc 1600, and there are quick bus transfers to the other famous mega-resorts of this region – Val-d'Isère, Tignes, La Plagne, Courchevel and Méribel, with slightly longer transfers to Les Menuires and Val-Thorens.

But you can travel by train, one way or another, to many other resorts. And many traditional resorts, especially in Switzerland, are on the rail network and therefore reachable without resorting to buses. How many times you'll have to change trains is another matter.

DIRECT TRAIN SERVICES TO THE FRENCH ALPS

Since 1997, Eurostar has offered a truly direct service to the Alps – you board the train at London Waterloo and disembark at Moûtiers or Bourg-St-Maurice in the Tarentaise valley, without changing trains en route. The special winter services run from New Year through to the end of April. Standard return tickets start at around £160 but seats can also be booked as part of a package holiday. You can travel by day or overnight. The overnight service affords you two extra days skiing or boarding – it leaves on Friday night, arriving early on Saturday morning, and returns late Saturday evening, arriving back in London on Sunday morning. The service uses standard Eurostar carriages with no special sleeping arrangements – you just doze (or not) in your seat. The daytime service gives you no more than the standard six days on the slopes: both outward and return services leave on Saturday morning, arriving late afternoon. The outbound service also stops at Ashford, in Kent, and Aime (between Moûtiers and Bourg-St-Maurice). The return service doesn't stop at Aime.

All the other train services to the Alps involve a change somewhere along the line, but they can still be fairly convenient and also allow for extra time on the slopes. Unlike Eurostar, many of the other services are equipped with sleeping compartments.

The Snowtrain is another weekly overnight service to the Tarentaise giving an eight-day week on the slopes, but it starts from Calais. It runs throughout the winter season, leaving Calais on Friday night and arriving in the Alps the following morning – first stop is Chambéry, then Moûtiers, Aime, and finally Bourg-St-Maurice. For the return journey you leave the Alps on Saturday evening, arriving in Calais early on Sunday morning. You cross the Channel by ferry from Dover (you can pay a supplement for a coach transfer from London or make your own arrangements and travel as a foot passenger). The train works on a charter basis and can be booked only through UK tour operators – they have allocated spaces on each service. Overnight amenities include on-board couchettes (six drop-down berths to a compartment) and a disco/bar. Beware, it can get very noisy and crowded. It is possible to book a compartment for the exclusive use of four or five people on both legs of the journey.

There is a similar Friday night sleeper service to the Tarentaise starting from Paris. You take the Eurostar to Paris from London Waterloo and change platforms at Paris Gare du Nord for an overnight train (again with couchettes) to the Alps. The return journey leaves the Alps on Saturday evening, arriving in Paris early on Sunday morning. The service starts at about £200 return and, again, it is possible to pay a supplement for a private compartment for four or five. A number of tour operators offer this service as part of an overall package.

There are a number of indirect services available on the French railway throughout the week but most mean crossing Paris from the Gare du Nord to the Gare de Lyon – the change of stations is not difficult, with a direct metro, regular buses and plenty of taxis at your disposal. Indirect services to many Alpine destinations via Brussels or Lille also run every day of the week and involve only a change of platform. This can be easier than going via Paris, and the timing of the slower overnight services via Brussels may be more suitable for some holidaymakers; the services tend to be less frequent and are often more expensive, but are worth considering at peak dates.

Motorail is another option, getting your car to the Alps without having to drive it. The services are not cheap, but the train takes a lot of the strain out of long journeys and saves on hotel and petrol costs, as well as substantial extra mileage on your car. Most services run overnight, with a choice of couchette or sleeper accommodation. Vehicles are usually loaded one hour before departure and available for pick up half an hour after arrival. You should book your trip well in advance – at least 80 days in advance is recommended on most services.

The main motorail options of interest to British skiers are the French railway services from Paris to Briançon, Lyon, Moûtiers and St-Gervais. The Belgian railway runs services from Brussels to Milan and Venice.

by Chris Gill

Family holidays

there's nothing like them

Tempted to get back on the slopes now that you've started a family? If you are, you're probably a bit concerned about all sorts of angles. There's the cost, of course; but at least that's a simple matter, without emotional baggage; either you can meet it or you can't. Other issues involve much more complicated considerations. If they're too young to ski, there's the question of how they'll be looked after while you spend your days pretending you are childless again. If they're old enough, there's the even more tricky question of how they should be taught. Do you hand them over to some arrogant bonehead in the Ecole du Ski Français? Seek out the world's most sensitive private instructor? Devote your holiday to passing on your own highly developed flaws in technique? These are questions I'll try to shed some light on, from my own experience.

But let's get one thing clear at the start: skiing holidays with your kids can be one of the highlights of the year, for you and possibly for them. (Kids brought up on annual skiing holidays don't seem to regard them as anything special, I'm sorry to say.) Whereas it's all too easy for summer holidays to descend into wrangles over how you should spend your time, skiing/boarding holidays present a great opportunity for you and the kids to spend your days happily engaged in the same activity. They soon get to the point where they can keep up with you; the problem is that they go past that point, and before long you can't keep up with them.

WHERE SHOULD YOU GO?

It's easy to give too much weight to the matter of choosing your resort. In principle, a traffic-free resort has considerable attractions – either a purpose-built one such as Flaine or Valmorel or an accidental one like Wengen or Saas-Fee. Of course, the terrain needs to be suitable – and if you're reading this I presume it's because your children haven't yet been skiing. So ideally look for resorts to which we give a high rating for beginners, which means resorts that have not only good nursery slopes but also good easy runs to progress to. But we have had very successful holidays in places that are far from ideal, and which you might be tempted to dismiss.

One is Chamonix; the fragmented nature of the slopes and the isolated valley-bottom location of the main nursery slopes here are real drawbacks, but in the end the success of the week depends much more on what the kids spend their time doing, and with whom. Another non-ideal place is Verbier, where the main difficulty we found was in finding easy ways back to the resort from areas with good long easy runs – something that is explained in more detail in the Verbier chapter. My point here is that despite these difficulties we had a great time, and wouldn't hesitate to go back.

BABIES AND TODDLERS: WHO SHOULD LOOK AFTER THEM?

There are day nurseries in most resorts (except in Italy, where Mamma is expected to shoulder her responsibilities without interruption), with or without ski tuition as part of the deal, open to anyone. But bear in mind that there are also individual hotels with their own in-house nurseries, usually (but not always) without ski tuition available.

The big question about such resort-based facilities is language. Not only the language skills of those running the nurseries, about which enquiries can be made, but the language of the other children, about which you've got to make assumptions. This is only one respect in which resorts in the US and Canada have an edge over the Alps; the others are that you can count on a fun attitude, and a high staff to child ratio. But the result of the last is high charges – much higher than we're used to in Europe.

We made repeated use of UK tour operators' childcare facilities when our two children were at this stage, and would recommend anyone to do the same. There's more about this below.

INFANTS AND JUNIORS: WHO SHOULD TEACH THEM?

In our household there is nothing so likely to produce outpourings of undying affection for Mum and Dad as a mention of the possibility of attending ski school. 'Oh no! We want to spend our holiday with you two, not in some boring old school,' is the general tenor of the response.

Mind you, Alex (now 12) has good grounds for objecting, since his first experience of ski school was disastrous. When he was four we went to Val-d'Isère at a time when the little 'alternative' school we intended to use was out of action, and had no alternative but to use the ESF. It was understaffed and oversubscribed, and run with the arrogance and indifference to children's happiness that still seems to characterise French institutions of this kind (see Val-d'Isère and Val-

Thorens chapters). After the first morning, we and other parents in our large chalet-hotel organised our own DIY classes instead.

After that we gave Alex a year off to recover. The next year, we went to Courchevel and adopted a formula that we have used with some success on several occasions since: we spent half the day with the kids, on the snow, and then they spent half a day in the 'snow-club' run by our tour operator, in this case Ski Esprit. In our half-day sessions with Alex, he learned to ski well enough to descend some of Courchevel's long greens. Laura, then three, did a bit of sledging. In the afternoons they did a lot of snowballing and video-watching.

The next year, we went to New England. We somehow succeeded in establishing that Alex was going to go to kids' ski school and that Laura was going into the resort crèche, doing some sledging and messing about in the snow but not attempting to ski. When we got to Killington, we discovered that this was not an option: the crèche was an entirely indoor affair. Laura wasn't going to put up with that, so she opted to join ski school.

Our first experience of American kids' ski schools was very successful. Those guys really know how to motivate their pupils. On his first day Alex was taken to the top of the mountain, from which point his group skied all the way down to the bottom. On day two, they skied a run designated black – not a severe one, but a black all the same. Laura meanwhile had learnt the basics of doing 'pizza pies' (snowploughs) by the time we moved on to Smugglers' Notch three days later. There, Alex went all over the mountain with his class, and delighted in showing me his favourite runs at the end of the day. Laura made steady progress and completed the end-of-week slalom test successfully – not bad for someone who hadn't planned to start skiing at all. Oh, and she fell in love with her hunky instructor.

The next year we went to Chamonix, and plugged into morning classes organised by Ski Esprit but taught by the ESF. In the afternoons, we skied with one or both children – calling on Ski Esprit's crèche to look after one of them as necessary. Alex made good progress, but Laura was rather put off by the combination of drag-lifts (not nearly so easy as the slow chairs used on the kids' slopes in Killington and Smugglers' Notch) and a rather severe-looking woman instructor.

That was a couple of years ago. Since then, we've made less use of ski schools. Both kids have grown enormously in confidence and competence, Alex especially, and we seem to be able to make the days work out by spending them partly together and partly in parent–child pairs. Of course, both of them would benefit from more lessons, and when I'm feeling responsible I'm inclined to decree that they should have them at the first available opportunity. When it comes to the crunch, I often seem to soften.

MAKING THE MOST OF YOUR TOUR OPERATOR

For an ever-increasing number of British skiers, travelling with a tour operator that provides childcare is the key to an enjoyable family holiday. If your tour operator undertakes to relieve you of some or all of the chores of childcare during your holiday, you get some or all of the pleasures of a skiing holiday as it was in the old days, pre-kids.

The possibilities range from the provision of a nanny to look after your particular small group to organised 'clubs' designed to provide entertaining group activities, especially for older children.

We've had highly successful holidays with Ski Esprit and with

TEEN ski
PGL Teenski uniquely offers a fully inclusive Ski & Snowboard package for teenagers aged 12-17 years.
For a full colour brochure
Freecall
0500 749147
www.pgl.co.uk
PGL has 44 years' experience in organising holidays for children and teenagers. Teenski combines an action-packed all inclusive week, along with the opportunity to take part in a ski and snowboard holiday in the company of other like minded fun loving teenagers, whilst accompanied by our experienced and enthusiastic PGL Staff.
PGL

SKIING AND SNOWBOARDING FOR THE DISCERNING TRAVELLER
• Child care in renowned family friendly resorts for children aged 6 months to 10 years
• Crèches and Clubs in Courchevel and La Plagne
• Private Nanny Service in Verbier, Courchevel and La Plagne
• Highly trained, friendly and professional child care staff
SIMPLY Ski
24 hour brochure hotline:
020 8541 2222
For further information call:
020 8541 2209
www.simplyski.co.uk
ABTA V1337 ATOL 1922

Ski Esprit
The Family Ski Specialist
offers children the chance to:
• Ski
• Snowboard
• Snowblade
With activity clubs and in-chalet nurseries
Ring now for your brochure
01252 618300
www.ski-esprit.co.uk
ABTA V3614
AITO

2000/01
..... One Parent Savers and family moneysavers,
Whizz Kids Clubs for 4-10 yrs,
Pepi Penguin Club for 6 months - 4 years,
Resort Crèches with qualified nannies ....
For a brochure see your travel agent or phone 01235 824324 quoting ref: 9709
Crystal HOLIDAYS
IATA
FTO
www.crystalski.co.uk

Mark Warner, both pioneers of chalet holidays with childcare that go to some highly satisfactory big-league resorts. In recent years Esprit has successfully developed its own dedicated kids' ski classes. The key factor, in our experience, is to go to a chalet (or at least a resort) where the operator will have enough clients to guarantee the availability of playmates for the kids.

But there are lots of alternatives. During the 1990s, the travel trade woke up to the fact that there is a booming market for childcare. Holidays in Club Med's 'villages' (ie mega-hotels) in a wide range of resorts, mainly in France and Switzerland, include everything but equipment, and this usually includes childcare. Of the big mainstream UK operators, Crystal probably has the most wide-ranging childcare, with crèches or nanny service in over two dozen resorts. Simply Ski is a chalet specialist that concentrates its childcare in two resorts: Montchavin and Courchevel 1300. Upmarket chalet company Scott Dunn Ski runs a crèche in Courchevel and has nannies in its other three big-name resorts.

Snowbizz is a one-resort operation that has a virtual monopoly on an excellent and underrated small resort in the southern French Alps, Puy-St-Vincent. Its comprehensive childcare arrangements include ski-guiding for children, and evening amusements at a modest charge. Accommodation is in apartments. Ski Famille is another small operator concentrating on a single French resort – Les Gets, linked to Morzine, in the northern Alps. The company has several catered chalets, generally with special bedrooms for the children. There is comprehensive free day care for the kids.

Another possibility is that of packing your teenage kids off on an all-inclusive week with the activity-holiday outfit PGL.

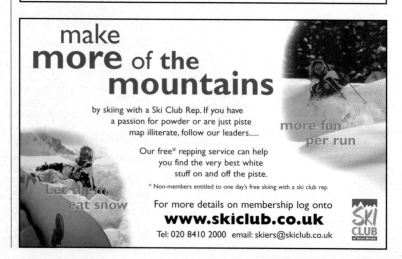

Val Thorens
2300
Mottaret
1700
Les Menuires
1815
Courchevel
Altiport
1700
Méribel
1400
La Tania

Choosing your resort

get it right first time

Most people get to go skiing or boarding only once or twice a year – and then only for a week at a time. So choosing the right resort is crucially important. This book is designed to help you get it right first time. Here is some advice on how to use our information to best effect – particularly for the benefit of readers with relatively narrow experience of different resorts. Chamonix, Châtel and Courchevel are all French resorts, but they are as similar as chalk and Camembert.

Lots of factors need to be taken into account. The weight you attach to each of them depends on your own personal preferences, and on the make-up of the group you are going on holiday with. On page 80 you'll find 20 shortlists of resorts which are outstanding in various key respects.

Each resort chapter is organised in the same way, to help you choose the right resort. This short introduction takes you through the structure and what to find under each heading we use.

WHICH RESORT?

We start each chapter with a one-line verdict, in which we aim to sum up the resort in a few words. If you like the sound of it, you might want to go next to our What it Costs rating, in the margin. These ratings, ranging from ① to ⑥, reflect the total cost of a week's holiday from Britain, including a typical package of flights plus half-board accommodation, a lift pass and meals and drinks on the spot. As you might expect with a six-point scale, 3 means on the low side of average, 4 means on the high side. Further on in the margin copy we give the cost of lift passes in local currency; these are for the 2000/01 season if the resort had decided prices by the time we went to press, otherwise we use the 1999/2000 prices. Below the What it Costs rating, in the How it Rates section, we rate each resort from 11 points of view – the more stars the better. (All these star ratings are brought together in one chart, starting on page 74, after this chapter.) Still looking at the information in the margin, in most chapters we have a What's New section; this is likely to be of most use and interest in resorts you already know – perhaps resorts you've resolved to stay away from until they fix some fundamental problem with the lift network or install more snowmaking.

For major resorts, the next things to look at are our lists of the main good and bad points about the resort and its slopes, picked out with ⊕ and ⊖. These lists are followed by a summary in **bold type**, in which we've aimed to weigh up the pros and cons, coming off the fence and giving our view of who might like it. These sections should give you a good idea of whether the resort is likely to suit *you,* and whether you should read our detailed analysis of it. Then, we have a special summary of the resort from the particular point of view of snowboarders – whether the slopes present special attractions or problems, how much you can expect to have to use drag-lifts, whether you'll find specialist schools and shops and lively snowboard bars in the resort.

You'll know by now whether this is, for example, a high, hideous, purpose-built resort with superb, snowsure skiing for all standards of skier but absolutely no nightlife, or whether it's a pretty, traditional village with gentle wooded skiing, ideal for beginners if only there was some snow. We then look at each aspect in more detail.

THE RESORT

Resorts vary enormously in character and charm. At the extremes of the range are the handful of really hideous modern apartment-block resorts thrown up in France in the 1960s – step forward, Les Menuires and Flaine – and the captivating old traffic-free mountain villages of which Switzerland has an unfair number. But it isn't simply a question of old versus new. Some purpose-built places (such as Valmorel) can have a much friendlier feel than some traditional resorts with big blocky buildings (eg Davos). And some places can be remarkably strung out (eg Vail) whereas others are surprisingly compact (eg Wengen).

The landscape can have an important impact – whether the resort is at the bottom of a narrow, shady valley (eg Ischgl) or on a sunny shelf with panoramic views (eg Crans-Montana). Some places are working towns as well as ski resorts (eg Bormio). Some are full of bars, discos and shops (eg St Anton). Others are peaceful backwaters (eg Arabba). Traffic may choke the streets (eg Sölden). Or the village may be traffic-free (eg Mürren).

In this first section of each chapter, we try to sort out the character of the place for you. Later, in the Staying There section, we tell you more about the hotels, restaurants, bars and so on.

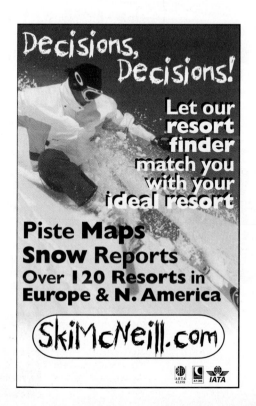

Britain's original and largest specialist ski travel agency – the first and only place you need to call to book your ski holiday
We are a ski travel agency as opposed to a ski tour operator. When you call us you immediately place at your disposal a choice of thousands of holidays offered by a wide variety of different reputable, fully bonded tour operators, both large and small.
You don't have to ski alone ... to be an individual
SKI SOLUTIONS
We sell you the holiday you want, not the holiday we need to sell
Reclaim the cost of
Where to Ski and Snowboard 2001
Book through Ski Solutions and we'll refund the cost of this book – see page 8.

THE MOUNTAINS

The slopes Some mountains and lift networks are vast and complex, while others are much smaller and lacking variation. The description here tells you how the area divides up into different sectors and how the links between them work.

Snow reliability This is a crucial factor for many people, and one which varies enormously. In some resorts you don't have to worry at all about a lack of snow, while others (including some very big names) are notorious for treating their paying guests to ice, mud and slush. Whether a resort is likely to have decent snow on its slopes normally depends on the height, the direction most of the slopes face (north good, south bad), its snow record and how much artificial snow it has. But bear in mind that in the Alps high resorts tend to have rocky terrain where the runs will need more snow than those on the pasture land of lower resorts. Many resorts have increased their snowmaking capacity in recent years and we list the latest amount they claim to have in Mountain Facts and comment on it in the Snow reliability text. Bear in mind that snowmaking can operate only if temperatures are low enough (typically –2°C or less). So it's much more useful in midwinter than in spring.

For experts, intermediates, beginners Most (though not all) resorts have something to offer beginners, but relatively few will keep an expert happy for a week's holiday. As for intermediates, whether a resort will suit you really depends on your standard and inclinations. Places such as Cervinia and Obergurgl are ideal for those who want easy cruising runs, but have little to offer intermediates looking for more challenge. Others, such as Sölden and Val-d'Isère, may intimidate the less confident intermediate who doesn't know the area well. Some, such as the Trois Vallées and Portes du Soleil, have vast amounts of terrain so that you can cover different ground each day. But some other well known names, such as Obergurgl, Courmayeur, Livigno, and many American resorts, have surprisingly small areas of pistes.

For cross-country We don't pretend that this is a guide for avid cross-country skiers. But if you or one of your group wants to try it, our summary here will help you gauge whether the resort is worth considering or a washout. It looks not just at the amount of cross-country available but also at its scenic beauty and whether or not the tracks are likely to have decent snow (many are at low altitude).

Queues Another key factor. Most resorts have improved their lift systems enormously in the last 10 years, and monster queues are largely a thing of the past. Crowding on the pistes is more of a worry in many resorts, and we mention problems of this kind here.

Mountain restaurants Here's a subject that divides people clearly into two opposing camps. To some, having a decent lunch in civilised surroundings – either in the sun, contemplating amazing scenery, or in a cosy hut, sheltered from the elements – makes or breaks their holiday. Others regard a prolonged midday stop as a waste of valuable time, as well as valuable spending money. We are firmly in the former camp. We get very disheartened by places with miserable restaurants and miserable food (eg some resorts in America); and there are some resorts that we go to regularly partly because of the cosy huts and excellent cuisine (eg Zermatt).

Schools and guides This is an area where we rely heavily on readers' reports of their own or their friends' experiences. The only way to judge a ski school is by trying it. Reports on schools are always extremely valuable and frequently record disappointment.

Facilities for children If you need crèche facilities, don't go to Italy. In other countries, facilities for looking after and teaching children can vary enormously between resorts. We say what is available in each resort, including what's on offer from UK tour operators – often the most attractive option for Brits. But, again, to be of real help we need reports from people who've used the facilities.

STAYING THERE

In some resorts, such as St Anton and Zermatt, choosing where in the resort to stay is very important – otherwise you might end up with long treks to and from the lifts or being woken at 2am by noisy revellers. We tell you what to take into account. Our village plans are drawn to scale, and give a good idea of the size of each place.

How to go The basic choice is between catered chalets, hotels and self-catering accommodation. The catered chalet holiday remains a peculiarly British phenomenon. A tour operator takes over a chalet (or a hotel in some cases), staffs it with young Brits (or Antipodeans), fills it with British guests, provides half-board and free wine, and lets you drink your duty-free booze without hassle. You can take over a complete chalet, or share one with other groups. It is a relatively economical way of visiting the expensive top resorts.

Hotels, of course, can vary a lot but, especially in France and Switzerland, can work out very expensive. In North America, watch out for supplements: rooms are often capable of sleeping four, and UK tour operators are inclined to base their standard brochure prices on the assumption that you fill all available bed spaces.

Apartments can be very economical but French ones, in particular, tend to be very small – it's not unusual for brochure prices to be

Get next year's edition free

There are too many hotels, nightspots and mountain restaurants for us to see them all every year – so we need reports on your holiday experiences. As usual, the 100 best reports will earn copies of next year's edition.

We want to know:

- what you particularly **liked and disliked** about the resort
- what aspects of the resort came as a **surprise** to you
- your suggestions for **changes to our evaluation** of the resort
- your experience of lift **queues** and of the **ski school** and associated childcare
- your feedback on other **individual facilities** – hotels, bars, restaurants etc

e-mail: reports@snow-zone.co.uk
mail: our address is at the front of the book; we'll send a form if you like.

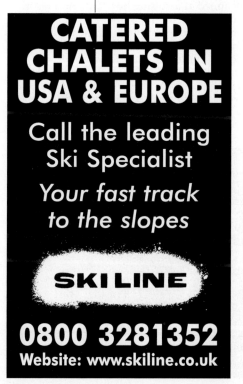

based on four people sleeping in a one-room studio, for example. To be comfortable, pay extra for under-occupancy.

We also look at what's available for independent travellers who want to fix their own hotels or self-catering accommodation. With hotels we've given each a price rating from ① to ⑤ – the more coins, the pricier the hotel.

Staying up the mountain / down the valley If there are interesting options for staying on the slopes above the resort village or in valley towns below it, we've picked them out. The former is often good for avoiding early-morning scrums for the lifts, the latter for cutting costs considerably.

Eating out The range of restaurants varies widely. Even some big resorts, such as Les Arcs, may have little choice because most of the clientele stay in their apartments or chalets. Others, such as Val-d'Isère, have a huge range available, including national and regional cuisine, pizzas, fondues and international fare. American resorts generally have an excellent range of restaurants – everyone eats out. This is an area where we rely a lot on reporters recommending restaurants that were good last season – and we are often able to recommend some out-of-the-way restaurants that you might not otherwise find (eg in the Les Arcs and Saas-Fee chapters).

Après-ski Tastes and styles vary enormously. Most resorts have pleasant places in which to have an immediate post-skiing beer or hot chocolate. Some then go dead. Others have noisy bars and discos until the early hours. And, especially in Austrian resorts, there may be a lot of events such as tobogganing and bowling that are organised by British tour operator reps. We are largely dependent for this section on hearing from reporters who are keen après-skiers.

Off the slopes This is largely aimed at assessing how suitable a resort is for someone who doesn't intend to use the slopes – a non-skiing spouse or elderly relative or friend, for example. In some resorts, such as most French purpose-built places, there is really nothing to amuse them. In others, such as Seefeld in Austria, there are more people walking, skating, curling and swimming than there are people skiing or boarding. Excursion possibilities vary widely. And there are great variations in the practicality of meeting skiers and boarders for lunch up the mountain.

SKIWORLD
19th Season
The largest independent ski tour operator
• Choose from catered chalets, self-catering and hotels in 24 snow sure resorts in Europe & North America.
• 22 regional flight options.
• 4 Train services for shorter transfers and more time to ski.
• Quality schedule flights including non-stop services to Denver & Vancouver.
• New for 2000/2001 weekend breaks and tailor made holidays.
call us now on:
Europe 020 7602 4826
USA 020 7602 7444
Email: sales@skiworld.ltd.uk
ABTA V2151
ATOL 2036

USA & CANADA
Ski from your own front door and return*
VIP Local Departure Service™ from your front door to the airport and return*
Top quality hotels, resorts and chalets
Great money saving two centre holidays
Scheduled flights with the world's leading airlines
Super savings for children and teens
Excellent value city stay options
Call for brochure on 01293 450892
www.canadaski.net
*Available for parties of four or more departing from one address
Connections
WORLDWIDE
ABTA V4585
10 York Way, Lancaster Road, High Wycombe. HP12 3PY
ATOL 2850

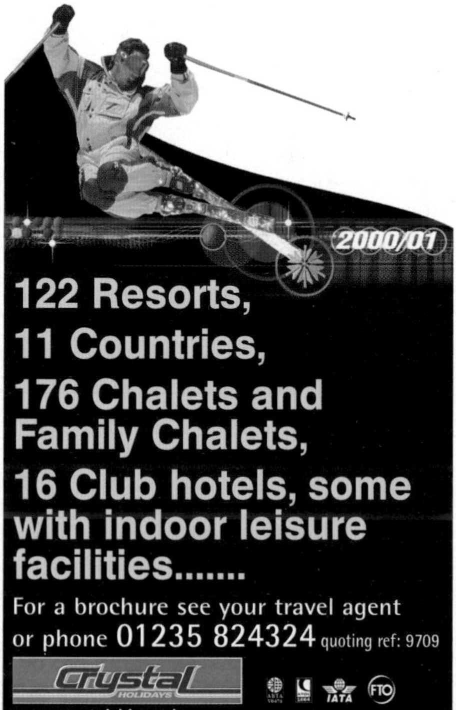
2000/01
122 Resorts,
11 Countries,
176 Chalets and Family Chalets,
16 Club hotels, some with indoor leisure facilities.......
For a brochure see your travel agent or phone 01235 824324 quoting ref: 9709
Crystal HOLIDAYS
IATA
FTO
www.crystalski.co.uk

Resort ratings at a glance

The following six pages bring together the ratings we give each resort for 11 key characteristics. You'll find these ratings at the start of each resort chapter too. Use the tables here to compare resorts directly for the aspects that are most important to you. You'll be able to see at a glance which resorts come out top and bottom of the pile.

AUSTRIA

	Alpbach	Bad Gastein	Ellmau	Hintertux	Ischgl	Kitzbühel	Lech
Page	87	88	95	100	106	111	117
Snow	**	***	**	*****	****	**	****
Extent	*	****	****	**	***	****	****
Experts	*	***	*	***	***	***	****
Intermediates	**	****	****	***	****	****	****
Beginners	****	**	****	*	**	**	****
Convenience	**	**	***	**	***	**	***
Queues	***	***	****	***	***	**	***
Restaurants	***	****	**	**	**	****	**
Scenery	***	***	***	***	***	***	***
Resort charm	*****	***	***	***	****	****	****
Off-slope	***	****	***	*	***	*****	***

	Mayrhofen	Neustift	Obergurgl	Obertauern	Saalbach-Hinterglemm	St Anton	St Johann in Tirol
Page	125	132	133	138	139	146	154
Snow	***	*****	*****	****	***	****	**
Extent	**	**	**	**	****	****	**
Experts	*	**	**	***	**	*****	*
Intermediates	***	***	***	****	****	***	***
Beginners	**	**	****	*****	***	*	****
Convenience	*	*	****	****	****	***	***
Queues	*	***	*****	****	***	**	***
Restaurants	****	**	**	***	****	***	****
Scenery	***	***	***	***	***	***	***
Resort charm	***	****	****	**	****	****	***
Off-slope	****	***	**	**	**	***	***

	Schladming	Seefeld	Sölden	Söll	Westendorf	Wildschönau	Zell am See
Page	158	162	163	164	169	170	173
Snow	***	**	****	**	**	**	**
Extent	***	*	***	****	*	*	**
Experts	**	*	**	*	*	*	**
Intermediates	****	**	****	****	**	**	***
Beginners	****	*****	**	***	****	****	***
Convenience	***	*	***	**	***	***	**
Queues	****	***	**	***	****	****	**
Restaurants	****	***	***	**	***	**	***
Scenery	***	***	***	***	***	***	***
Resort charm	****	****	**	***	****	***	***
Off-slope	****	*****	**	**	**	**	****

FRANCE

	Alpe-d'Huez	Les Arcs	Avoriaz	Chamonix	Châtel	La Clusaz	Les Contamines	Courchevel
Page	185	193	199	203	211	216	222	223
Snow	****	****	***	****	**	**	****	****
Extent	****	***	*****	***	*****	***	**	*****
Experts	****	****	***	*****	***	***	**	****
Intermediates	****	****	****	**	****	****	***	*****
Beginners	*****	****	****	*	**	****	***	*****
Convenience	****	****	****	*	**	***	**	****
Queues	****	***	**	**	***	***	***	****
Restaurants	****	**	****	***	***	****	****	****
Scenery	****	***	***	*****	***	****	***	***
Resort charm	*	*	**	****	***	****	****	**
Off-slope	***	*	*	*****	**	***	**	***

	Les Deux-Alpes	Flaine	La Grave	Isola 2000	Megève	Les Menuires	Méribel	Montgenèvre
Page	233	238	244	245	248	254	257	265
Snow	****	****	***	***	**	****	****	****
Extent	***	****	**	**	*****	*****	*****	****
Experts	****	****	*****	**	**	****	****	**
Intermediates	**	*****	*	***	****	*****	*****	****
Beginners	***	*****	*	*****	***	***	***	*****
Convenience	***	*****	***	*****	**	*****	***	****
Queues	**	****	****	***	****	****	****	****
Restaurants	**	**	**	**	*****	***	****	**
Scenery	****	****	****	***	***	***	***	***
Resort charm	**	*	***	*	****	*	***	***
Off-slope	**	*	*	*	****	*	***	*

	Morzine	La Plagne	Puy-St-Vincent	Risoul	La Rosière	St-Martin-de-Belleville	Ste-Foy	Serre-Chevalier
Page	269	275	284	285	286	288	290	291
Snow	**	****	***	***	***	***	***	****
Extent	*****	****	**	***	***	*****	*	****
Experts	***	***	***	**	**	****	****	***
Intermediates	****	*****	***	****	***	*****	***	****
Beginners	***	*****	***	****	*****	***	**	****
Convenience	**	*****	*****	****	***	***	***	***
Queues	***	**	****	****	***	****	*****	***
Restaurants	***	**	***	***	*	****	*	***
Scenery	***	****	***	***	***	***	***	****
Resort charm	***	*	**	**	***	****	***	***
Off-slope	***	*	*	*	*	*	*	**

FRANCE (continued) – ITALY

	Tignes	Val-d'Isère	Valmorel	Val-Thorens	Vars
Page	296	303	312	317	321
Snow	*****	*****	***	*****	***
Extent	*****	*****	***	*****	***
Experts	*****	*****	**	****	**
Intermediates	*****	*****	****	*****	****
Beginners	**	***	*****	****	***
Convenience	****	***	*****	*****	****
Queues	****	****	****	***	****
Restaurants	**	**	**	****	**
Scenery	***	***	***	***	***
Resort charm	**	***	****	**	**
Off-slope	*	**	**	**	**

ITALY

	Bardonecchia	Bormio	Cervinia	Cortina d'Ampezzo	Courmayeur	Livigno	Madesimo
Page	326	327	330	335	340	345	349
Snow	**	***	*****	***	****	****	***
Extent	***	**	***	***	**	**	*
Experts	*	*	*	**	***	**	***
Intermediates	***	***	****	***	****	***	**
Beginners	**	**	*****	*****	**	****	***
Convenience	**	***	***	*	*	**	***
Queues	***	***	***	***	****	****	***
Restaurants	***	****	***	****	****	***	**
Scenery	***	***	****	*****	****	***	***
Resort charm	*	****	**	****	****	***	**
Off-slope	**	****	*	*****	***	**	*

	Madonna di Campiglio	Monterosa Ski	Pila	Sauze d'Oulx	Selva/Sella Ronda	Sestriere	La Thuile
Page	350	351	352	353	358	366	368
Snow	***	***	***	**	****	***	****
Extent	***	***	**	*****	*****	****	***
Experts	**	**	**	**	***	***	**
Intermediates	****	****	****	****	*****	****	****
Beginners	****	**	***	**	****	***	****
Convenience	**	****	***	**	***	****	***
Queues	***	****	****	***	***	***	****
Restaurants	****	**	***	***	****	**	*
Scenery	****	****	***	***	*****	***	***
Resort charm	***	***	***	**	***	*	***
Off-slope	***	*	**	*	***	*	**

SWITZERLAND

	Adelboden	Andermatt	Arosa	Champéry	Crans-Montana	Davos
Page	376	377	378	379	384	389
Snow	**	****	***	**	**	****
Extent	***	*	**	*****	***	*****
Experts	**	****	*	***	**	****
Intermediates	***	**	***	****	****	*****
Beginners	****	*	****	**	***	**
Convenience	***	***	***	*	**	**
Queues	***	**	****	****	***	**
Restaurants	**	*	****	***	***	***
Scenery	***	***	***	****	****	****
Resort charm	****	****	**	****	**	**
Off-slope	****	**	****	***	****	*****

	Engelberg	Flims	Grindelwald	Gstaad	Mürren	Saas-Fee
Page	395	396	401	405	406	410
Snow	***	***	**	*	***	*****
Extent	**	****	***	****	*	**
Experts	***	***	**	**	***	***
Intermediates	***	*****	*****	***	***	****
Beginners	**	****	***	***	**	*****
Convenience	*	***	**	*	***	***
Queues	***	***	**	***	***	***
Restaurants	***	***	***	***	**	***
Scenery	***	***	*****	***	*****	****
Resort charm	***	***	****	****	*****	*****
Off-slope	***	***	****	****	***	****

	St Moritz	Verbier	Villars	Wengen	Zermatt
Page	415	421	430	431	436
Snow	****	***	**	**	****
Extent	*****	*****	**	***	****
Experts	****	*****	**	**	*****
Intermediates	****	***	***	****	****
Beginners	**	**	****	***	*
Convenience	**	**	***	***	*
Queues	**	***	***	***	***
Restaurants	****	***	***	****	*****
Scenery	****	****	***	*****	*****
Resort charm	*	***	****	*****	*****
Off-slope	*****	***	****	****	****

UNITED STATES

	CALIFORNIA Heavenly	Mammoth	COLORADO Aspen	Breckenridge	Copper Mountain	Crested Butte	Keystone	Steamboat
Page	450	457	462	469	474	475	479	484
Snow	****	****	*****	*****	*****	****	*****	****
Extent	***	***	****	**	**	**	**	***
Experts	***	****	*****	****	****	****	***	***
Intermediates	****	****	*****	****	****	***	****	****
Beginners	****	****	*****	****	****	****	****	*****
Convenience	*	**	**	***	****	***	**	***
Queues	****	****	****	****	****	*****	****	****
Restaurants	*	*	****	**	*	*	***	***
Scenery	****	***	***	***	***	***	***	***
Resort charm	*	**	****	***	**	****	**	**
Off-slope	**	*	****	***	*	**	**	**

	Telluride	Vail-Beaver Creek	Winter Park	UTAH Alta	The Canyons	Deer Valley	Park City	Snowbasin
Page	490	491	498	505	506	507	508	513
Snow	****	*****	*****	*****	****	****	****	*****
Extent	**	****	***	*	***	**	***	***
Experts	****	****	****	*****	***	***	****	****
Intermediates	***	*****	****	***	***	****	****	****
Beginners	*****	*****	*****	***	***	****	****	**
Convenience	****	***	***	****	****	****	***	*
Queues	*****	***	****	***	****	****	****	*****
Restaurants	*	**	***	**	***	****	**	*
Scenery	****	***	***	****	***	***	***	****
Resort charm	****	****	**	**	**	***	***	**
Off-slope	**	***	*	*	**	**	***	*

	Snowbird	REST OF THE WEST Big Sky	Jackson	Sun Valley	Taos	NEW ENGLAND Killington	Smugglers'	Stowe
Page	515	519	520	526	527	533	537	540
Snow	*****	****	****	***	****	***	***	***
Extent	*	***	***	***	**	**	*	*
Experts	*****	*****	*****	***	*****	***	***	***
Intermediates	***	****	**	****	***	***	***	****
Beginners	**	****	***	***	**	****	****	****
Convenience	*****	****	***	**	***	*	*****	*
Queues	**	*****	***	****	****	****	****	****
Restaurants	*	*	*	****	*	*	*	**
Scenery	***	***	***	***	***	***	***	***
Resort charm	*	**	****	***	***	**	**	****
Off-slope	*	**	***	***	**	*	*	*

UNITED STATES – CANADA – AND THE REST

		WESTERN CANADA				EASTERN CANADA
	Sunday River	Banff	Fernie	Panorama	Whistler	Tremblant
Page	541	547	556	559	560	569
Snow	***	****	****	***	****	****
Extent	**	****	***	**	****	**
Experts	**	****	*****	****	*****	***
Intermediates	****	****	**	***	*****	***
Beginners	****	***	****	****	****	****
Convenience	***	*	****	***	****	****
Queues	****	****	****	****	***	***
Restaurants	***	**	*	*	**	**
Scenery	***	****	****	***	***	***
Resort charm	**	***	**	**	***	****
Off-slope	*	****	**	*	**	***

	ANDORRA			SPAIN
	Arinsal	Pas de la Casa	Soldeu	Baqueira-Beret
Page	571	574	575	578
Snow	***	***	***	***
Extent	*	***	**	***
Experts	*	*	*	***
Intermediates	**	***	***	****
Beginners	***	****	****	**
Convenience	***	****	***	***
Queues	***	***	***	***
Restaurants	*	***	*	**
Scenery	***	**	***	***
Resort charm	*	*	*	**
Off-slope	*	*	*	*

	NORWAY	SWEDEN	NEW ZEALAND
	Hemsedal	Åre	Queenstown
Page	586	588	597
Snow	****	***	**
Extent	*	**	*
Experts	**	**	***
Intermediates	****	****	***
Beginners	***	****	***
Convenience	*	***	*
Queues	****	****	***
Restaurants	*	***	*
Scenery	**	***	****
Resort charm	**	***	**
Off-slope	*	***	*****

Resort shortlists

to simplify the decision

To choose the ideal resort for your own holiday, you first need to identify the key things which are most important to you. Then the ratings, the general summary and the lists of pros and cons at the start of each resort chapter will help you spot resorts to suit you. But for a real short cut, here are lists of the best ten or so resorts for 20 different categories. Most lists embrace European and North American resorts, but some we've confined to the Alps, because America has too many qualifying resorts (eg for beginners) or because America does things differently, making comparisons invalid (eg for off-piste).

SOMETHING FOR EVERYONE
Resorts with everything from reassuring nursery slopes to real challenges for experts
Alpe-d'Huez, France p185
Les Arcs, France p193
Aspen-Snowmass , Colorado p462
Courchevel, France p223
Flaine, France p238
Lech/Zürs, Austria p117
Mammoth, California p457
Vail, Colorado p491
Val-d'Isère, France p303
Whistler, Canada p560

INTERNATIONAL OVERSIGHTS
Resorts that deserve as much attention as the ones we go back to every year, but don't seem to get it
Alta, Utah p505
Andermatt, Switzerland p377
Bad Gastein, Austria p88
Big Sky, Montana p519
Flims-Laax, Switzerland p396
Ischgl, Austria p106
Monterosa Ski, Italy p351
Sun Valley, Idaho p526
Telluride, Colorado p490
Western Canada p544

RELIABLE SNOW IN THE ALPS
Alpine resorts with good snow records or lots of snowmaking, and high or north-facing slopes
Argentière, France p203
Cervinia, Italy p330
Courchevel, France p223
Hintertux, Austria p100
Lech/Zürs, Austria p117
Obergurgl, Austria p133
Saas-Fee, Switzerland p410
Val-d'Isère/Tignes, France pp303/296
Val-Thorens, France p317
Zermatt, Switzerland p436

OFF-PISTE WONDERS
Alpine resorts where, with the right guidance and equipment, you can have the time of your life
Alpe-d'Huez, France p185
Andermatt, Switzerland p377
Argentière/Chamonix, France p203
Davos/Klosters, Switzerland p389
La Grave, France p244
Lech/Zürs, Austria p117
Monterosa Ski, Italy p351
St Anton, Austria p146
Val-d'Isère/Tignes, France pp303/296
Verbier, Switzerland p421

BLACK RUNS
Resorts with steep, mogully, lift-served slopes within the safety of the piste network
Alta/Snowbird, Utah pp505/515
Andermatt, Switzerland p377
Argentière/Chamonix, France p203
Aspen-Snowmass , Colorado p462
Courchevel, France p223
Jackson Hole, Wyoming p520
Taos, New Mexico p527
Whistler, Canada p560
Winter Park, Colorado p498
Zermatt, Switzerland p436

CHOPAHOLICS
Resorts where you can quit the conventional lift network and have a day riding helicopters or cats
Aspen-Snowmass , Colorado p462
Crested Butte, Colorado p475
Fernie, Canada p556
Grand Targhee, Wyoming p520
Lech/Zürs, Austria p117
Monterosa Ski, Italy p351
Panorama, Canada p559
Verbier, Switzerland p421
Whistler, Canada p560
Zermatt, Switzerland p436

HIGH-MILEAGE PISTE-BASHING
Extensive intermediate slopes with big lift networks
Alpe-d'Huez, France p185
Davos/Klosters, Switzerland p389
Flims/Laax, Switzerland p396
Milky Way: Sauze d'Oulx (Italy), Montgenèvre (France) pp353/265
La Plagne, France p275
Portes du Soleil, France/Switz p283
Selva/Sella Ronda, Italy p358
Trois Vallées, France p302
Val-d'Isère/Tignes, France pp303/296
Whistler, Canada p560

MOTORWAY CRUISING
Long, gentle, super-smooth pistes to bolster the frail confidence of those not long off the nursery slope
Les Arcs, France p193
Aspen-Snowmass, Colorado p462
Breckenridge, Colorado p469
Cervinia, Italy p330
Cortina, Italy p335
Courchevel, France p223
Megève, France p248
La Plagne, France p275
La Thuile, Italy p368
Vail, Colorado p491

RESORTS FOR BEGINNERS
Alpine resorts with gentle, snowsure nursery slopes and easy longer runs to progress to
Alpe-d'Huez, France p185
Les Arcs, France p193
Cervinia, Italy p330
Courchevel, France p223
Isola 2000, France p245
Montgenèvre, France p265
Pamporovo, Bulgaria p579
La Plagne, France p275
Saas-Fee, Switzerland p410
Soldeu, Andorra p575

MODERN CONVENIENCE
Resorts where there's plenty of slope-side accommodation to make life easy in those heavy ski boots
Les Arcs, France p193
Avoriaz, France p199
Courchevel, France p223
Flaine, France p238
Isola 2000, France p245
Les Menuires, France p254
Obertauern, Austria p138
La Plagne, France p275
Valmorel, France p312
Val-Thorens, France p317

WEATHERPROOF SLOPES
Alpine resorts with snowsure slopes if the sun shines, and trees in case it doesn't
Les Arcs, France p193
Courchevel, France p223
Courmayeur, Italy p340
Flims, Switzerland p396
Montchavin/Les Coches, France p275
Schladming, Austria p158
Selva, Italy p358
Serre-Chevalier, France p291
Sestriere, Italy p366
La Thuile, Italy p368

BACK-DOOR RESORTS
Cute little villages linked to big, bold ski areas, giving you the best of two different worlds
Les Brévières (Tignes), France p296
Les Carroz (Flaine), France p238
Champagny (La Plagne), France p275
Falera (Flims), Switzerland p396
Leogang (Saalbach), Austria p139
Montchavin (La Plagne), France p275
Le Pré (Les Arcs), France p193
St-Martin (Three Valleys), France p288
Stuben (St Anton), Austria p146
Vaujany (Alpe-d'Huez), France p185

SNOWSURE BUT SIMPATICO

Alpine resorts with high-rise slopes, but low-rise, traditional-style buildings

Andermatt, Switzerland p377
Arabba, Italy p358
Argentière, France p203
Les Contamines, France p222
Ischgl, Austria p106
Lech/Zürs, Austria p117
Obergurgl, Austria p133
Obertauern, Austria p138
Saas-Fee, Switzerland p410
Zermatt, Switzerland p436

SPECIALLY FOR FAMILIES

Resorts where you can easily find accommodation surrounded by snow, not by traffic and fumes

Les Arcs, France p193
Avoriaz, France p199
Flaine, France p238
Isola 2000, France p245
Montchavin (La Plagne), France p275
Mürren, Switzerland p406
Risoul, France p285
Saas-Fee, Switzerland p410
Valmorel, France p312
Wengen, Switzerland p431

BUDGET BALANCING

Resorts where cheap packages, cheap lifts, cheap drinks and meals will mean a cheap holiday

Arinsal, Andorra p571
Bardonecchia, Italy p326
Borovets, Bulgaria p580
Kranjska Gora, Slovenia p582
Livigno, Italy p345
Monterosa Ski, Italy p351
Poiana Brasov, Romania p581
Sauze d'Oulx, Italy p353
Sierra Nevada, Spain p577
Soldeu, Andorra p575

SPECIAL MOUNTAIN RESTAURANTS

Alpine resorts where the mountain restaurants can really add an extra dimension to your holiday

Alpe-d'Huez, France p185
La Clusaz, France p216
Courmayeur, Italy p340
Kitzbühel, Austria p111
Megève, France p248
St Johann in Tirol, Austria p154
St Moritz, Switzerland p415
Selva, Italy p358
Söll, Austria p164
Zermatt, Switzerland p436

DRAMATIC SCENERY

Resorts where the mountains are not just high and snowy, but precipitous too

Banff, Canada p547
Chamonix, France p203
Cortina, Italy p335
Courmayeur, Italy p340
Heavenly, California p450
Jungfrau resorts (Grindelwald, Mürren, Wengen), Switzerland pp401/406/431
Saas-Fee, Switzerland p410
St Moritz, Switzerland p415
Selva, Italy p358
Zermatt, Switzerland p436

VILLAGE CHARM

Resorts with traditional character that enriches your holiday – from mountain villages to mining towns

Alpbach, Austria p87
Champéry, Switzerland p379
Courmayeur, Italy p340
Crested Butte, Colorado p475
Lech, Austria p117
Mürren, Switzerland p406
Saas-Fee, Switzerland p410
Telluride, Colorado p490
Wengen, Switzerland p431
Zermatt, Switzerland p436

LIVELY NIGHTLIFE

Alpine resorts where you'll have no difficulty finding somewhere to boogy, and someone to do it with

Chamonix, France p203
Ischgl, Austria p106
Kitzbühel, Austria p111
Saalbach, Austria p139
St Anton, Austria p146
Sauze d'Oulx, Italy p353
Sölden, Austria p163
Soldeu, Andorra p575
Val-d'Isère, France p303
Verbier, Switzerland p421

OTHER AMUSEMENTS

Resorts where those not interested in skiing or boarding can still find plenty to do

Bad Gastein, Austria p88
Chamonix, France p203
Cortina, Italy p335
Davos, Switzerland p389
Kitzbühel, Austria p111
Megève, France p248
St Moritz, Switzerland p415
Seefeld, Austria p162
Wengen, Switzerland p431
Zell am See, Austria p173

Austria

Austria had been losing ground steadily as far as attracting British skiers was concerned. In the 1970s and early 1980s it was the most popular country for the British. But it lost out to the growth of the French mega-resorts. And then it was hit by Italian resorts, which gained ground as the lira fell against the pound – Italy became much cheaper than Austria. But last season it made a big rebound and overtook Italy again in popularity on the British market.

We have made some extensive tours of Austrian resorts in the last couple of seasons and are struck by just how different it is to the other Alpine nations. It deserves more attention than it gets from today's skiers and boarders who have only ever experienced France. Austria is the land of cute little villages clustered around onion-domed churches; of friendly wooded mountains, reassuring to beginners and timid intermediates in a way that bleak snowfields and craggy peaks will never be; of friendly, welcoming people who don't find it demeaning to speak their guests' language; and of jolly beer-fuelled après-ski action, starting in many resorts in mid-afternoon with dancing in on-mountain restaurants and going on as long as you have the legs for it. And it does no harm to the Austrian campaign that the resorts have made great strides in their attempt to catch up on the snowmaking front – most have radically increased their snowmaking capacity in recent years. In midwinter, especially, lack of snow generally goes hand in hand with low night-time temperatures, even at low altitudes, and snowmaking comes into its own.

It's the après-ski that strikes most first-time visitors as being Austria's unique selling point. The few French resorts that have lively après-ski are dominated by British or Scandinavian holidaymakers (and resort workers and ski-bums). The French are noticeable by their absence and you could be in London or Stockholm rather than France. But Austrian après-ski remains very Austrian. Huge quantities of beer and schnapps are drunk, German is the predominant language and German drinking songs are common. So is incredibly loud Europop music. People pack into mountain restaurants at the end of the day and dance in their ski boots on the dance floor, on the tables, on the bar, on the roof beams, wherever there's room. There are open-air ice bars on the mountain, umbrella bars and countless transparent 'igloos' in which to shelter from bad weather. In many resorts the bands don't stop playing or the DJs working until darkness falls, when the happy punters slide off down the mountain in the dark to find another watering hole in town. After dinner the drinking and dancing starts again – for those who take time out for dinner, that is.

Of course, not all Austrian resorts conform to this image. But lots of big name ones with the best and most extensive slopes do. St Anton, Saalbach-Hinterglemm, Ischgl and Zell am See for example, fit this bill. And they have other things in common with most Austrian resorts, of which there are a huge number, large and small.

One thing they all have in common is reliably comfortable accommodation – whether it's in four-star hotels with pools, saunas and spas, or in great-value family-run guest houses, of which Austria

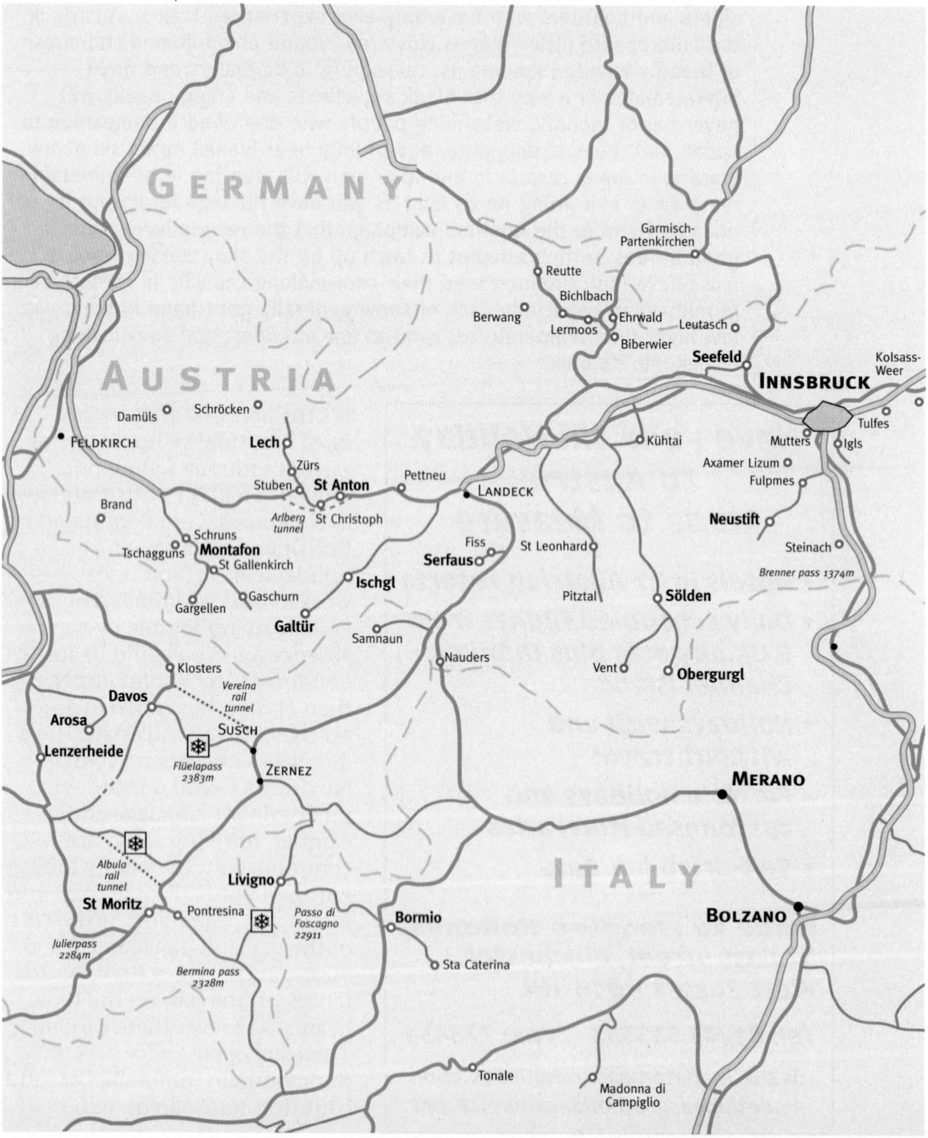

has thousands. The accommodation scene is very much dominated by hotels and guest houses; catered chalets and self-catering packages are in general much less widely available (though there are one or two resorts, such as St Anton and Kitzbühel, where chalets are more easily come by).

Most Austrian resorts are real, friendly villages on valley floors, with skiing and boarding on the wooded slopes above them. They have expanded enormously since the war, but practically all the development has been in traditional chalet style, and the villages generally look good even without the snow that is the saving grace of many French and even some Swiss resorts. Unlike Courchevel and Verbier, many Tirolean resorts are as busy in August as in February.

Outside the big-name resorts the skiing is often quite limited.

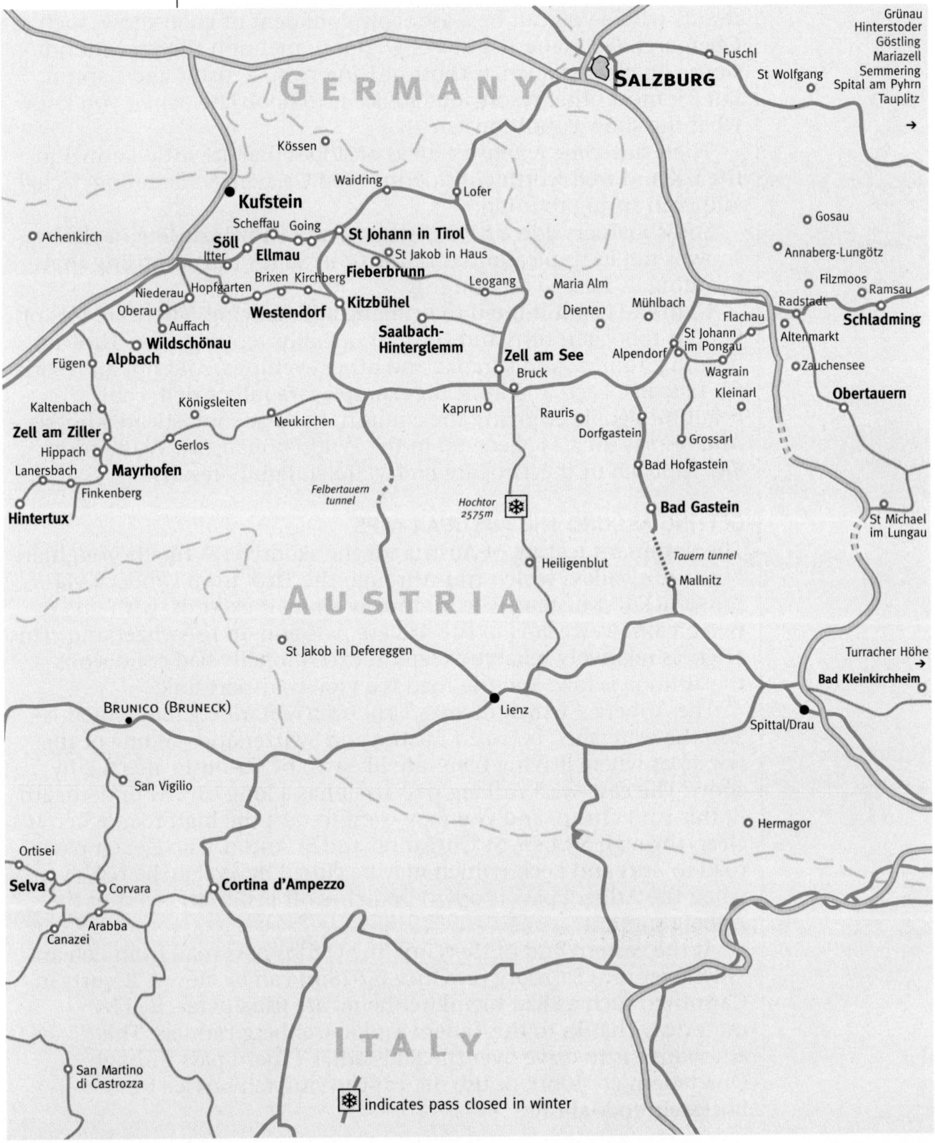

There are many Austrian resorts that a keen skier could explore fully in half a day. Those who start their skiing careers in such resorts may not be worried by this; those who have tried the bigger areas of France and developed a taste for them may find the list of acceptable Austrian resorts quite a short one.

Unfortunately, several of the resorts on that shortlist bring you up against another problem – low altitude, and therefore poor snow conditions. Kitzbühel is at 760m, Söll at 700m, Zell am See at 775m. The top heights of Austrian resorts are relatively low, too – typically 1800m to 2000m; as we have noted above, snowmaking is becoming more widespread, but it works only when the conditions are right.

The resorts of the Arlberg area, at the western end of the Tirol – St Anton, Lech and Zürs – stand apart from these concerns, with excellent snow records and extensive skiing. And there are other resorts where you can be reasonably confident of good snow, such as Obergurgl, Obertauern and Ischgl, not to mention the year-round slopes on glaciers such as those at Hintertux, Neustift and Kaprun. But for most other resorts our advice is to book late, when you know what the snow conditions are like.

There are some extensive areas of slopes that are little-known in the UK and well worth considering. Bad Gastein, Schladming, Ischgl and Lech spring to mind.

Snowboarders don't need big areas; and snowboarding in slushy snow is not as unpleasant as skiing in it. So it's not surprising that boarding in Austria is booming.

Nightlife is not limited to drinking and dancing. There are lots of floodlit toboggan runs and UK tour operator reps organise Tirolean, bowling, fondue and karaoke and other evenings. And not all resorts are raucous. Lech and Zürs, for example, are full of rich, cool, beautiful people enjoying the comfort of 4-star sophisticated hotels. And resorts such as Niederau in the Wildschönau and Westendorf and Alpbach in the Tirol are pretty, quiet, family resorts.

GETTING AROUND THE AUSTRIAN ALPS

The dominant feature of Austria for the ski driver is the thoroughfare of the Inn valley, which runs through the Tirol from Landeck via Innsbruck to Kufstein. The motorway along it extends, with one or two breaks, westwards to the Arlberg pass and on to Switzerland. This artery is relatively reliable except in exceptionally bad conditions – the altitude is low, and the road is a vital transport link.

The Arlberg – which divides Tirol from Vorarlberg, but which is also the watershed between Austria and Switzerland – is one of the few areas where driving plans are likely to be seriously affected by snow. The east–west Arlberg pass itself has a long tunnel underneath it; this isn't cheap, and you may want to take the high road when it's clear, through Stuben, St Christoph and St Anton. The Flexen pass road to Zürs and Lech (which may be closed by avalanche risk even when the Arlberg pass is open) branches off just to the west of the Arlberg summit.

At the eastern end of the Tirol, the Gerlos pass road from Zell am Ziller over into Salzburg province (1628m) can be closed. Resorts in Carinthia, such as Bad Kleinkirchheim, are usually reached by motorway thanks to the Tauern and Katschberg tunnels. The alternative is to drive over the Radstädter Tauern pass through Obertauern (1740m), or use the car-carrying rail service from Böckstein to Mallnitz.

Alpbach 1000m

Traditional charm with slopes perfect for practising technique

WHAT IT COSTS

3

HOW IT RATES

The slopes

Snow	**
Extent	*
Experts	*
Intermediates	**
Beginners	****
Convenience	**
Queues	***
Restaurants	***

The rest

Scenery	***
Resort charm	*****
Off-slope	***

What's new

The 2000 T-bar, up to the resort high point at 2025m was replaced by a four-seater chair-lift last season. Snowmaking has been installed from the gondola mid-station to the base and more is planned.

A new eight-person gondola to replace the one-seater chair to the top of Reith should be ready for 2001.

Plans to link the area to Wildschönau are still being discussed – this would be a great step forward for both areas.

MOUNTAIN FACTS

Altitude	670m-2025m
Lifts	19
Pistes	45km
Blue	15%
Red	70%
Black	15%
Artificial snow	23km

TOURIST OFFICE

Postcode A-6236
t +43 (5336) 600-0
f 600-200
info@alpbach-tirol.at
www.alpbach.at

Alpbach is an old British favourite – there is even a British club, the Alpbach Visitors. We go there partly out of habit, but also because it is exceptionally pretty and friendly – 'it has great character and atmosphere,' says one visitor – and because its small mountain is not without interest, even for experts.

THE RESORT

Alpbach is captivating both in summer and winter. It's near the head of a valley, looking south towards the Wiedersbergerhorn, where most of the slopes are. Traditional chalets crowd around the little church, and open snowfields (including the nursery slopes) are yards away. The Inn valley is a few miles north, and trips east to Kitzbühel or west to Innsbruck are possible. The Hintertux and Stubai glaciers are within reach.

THE MOUNTAIN

Alpbach's **slopes**, on two flanks of the Wiedersbergerhorn, are small and simple. The main gondola goes from isolated Achenwirt (830m), a mile away but served by a free shuttle-bus and taxis. Slower lifts go from Inneralpbach (1050m) to the east, and meet above Hornboden (1850m), then a new quad chair takes you up to 2025m. The small area at Reith is on the lift pass. There's some good free-riding terrain and two half-pipes for **snowboarders**.

Alpbach cannot claim great **snow reliability**; but at least most slopes face north. The village nursery slope and, increasingly, other runs have artificial snow. A recent reporter found the bottom section of the home run icy and tricky despite excellent snowfalls.

Alpbach isn't ideal for **experts**, but the reds and the three blacks are not without challenge, and runs of 1000m vertical are not to be sniffed at. There are a number of off-piste routes to the valley, short tours are offered, and the schools take the top classes off-piste.

There is great **intermediate** terrain; the problem is that it's limited. This resort is for practising technique on familiar slopes, not high mileage.

Beginners love the sunny, handy nursery slopes. Higher slopes can be used, but not for confidence-building: most longer runs are red.

Pretty **cross-country** trails rise up beyond Inneralpbach; the most testing is about 8km long and climbs 300m.

Serious **queues** are rare, thanks to the efficient gondola. But the resort does attract some weekend trade.

The area has squeezed in many **mountain restaurants**. Recommended are the Hornboden at the top of the mountain, the cosy Böglalm at Inneralpbach, the Kolberhof, Achenwirt and the Asthütte for the sun.

Alpbach and Alpbach Aktiv are the **ski schools**. We have had excellent reports on both in the past; however, one recent reporter tells of a high dropout rate from the Aktiv school and poor English spoken by the instructor in her multi-national class. Both take **children**. Babysitters can be arranged by the tourist office.

STAYING THERE

Alpbach is small, so there's no need to worry about where you stay. The very centre is most convenient, both for the bus and for après-ski. The backwater of Inneralpbach is convenient for the slopes, and suits families.

Hotels and pensions dominate in UK packages. Of the smart 4-star places, the Alpbacherhof and historical Böglerhof get most votes. But simpler Haus Thomas, Haus Theresia, Haus Angelika and Haus Leirerhäusl are recommended by visitors. The Alphof is 'excellent', as long as your room is not above the disco. Some self-catering is available via the tourist office and the Alpbach Visitors Club.

For **eating out**, hotels Reblaus, Jakober, Berghof and Post are popular, as is the Wiedersbergerhorn in Inneralpbach – worth a taxi-ride.

Après-ski is typically Tirolean at peak times, with lots of noisy tea-time beer-swilling in the bars of central hotels such as the Jakober and the Post. In the evening the Waschkuchl is good for a drink. The Birdy Pub and Weinstahdl have late-night dancing. However, it's pretty quiet during the rest of the season.

Off-slope activities include pretty walks, and trips to Innsbruck.

Bad Gastein 1000m

Traditional spa resort with huge ski area and few Brits

WHAT IT COSTS

3

HOW IT RATES

The slopes	
Snow	***
Extent	****
Experts	***
Intermediates	****
Beginners	**
Convenience	**
Queues	***
Restaurants	****
The rest	
Scenery	***
Resort charm	***
Off-slope	****

- ➕ Four separate, varied areas with a huge number of slopes both above and below the tree-line
- ➕ Great for confident intermediates, with lots of long, challenging reds – and great cruising and carving in the Schlossalm sector
- ➕ More snowsure than most low-altitude Austrian resorts, with the high Sportgastein area as back-up
- ➕ Lots of good, atmospheric, traditional mountain restaurants
- ➕ Plenty of off-slope facilities, many related to its origins as a spa resort

- ➖ Unless you have a car, you need to choose your location with care or budget for a lot of pricey taxi rides – the lift bases are widely spread and the bus service is a disgrace
- ➖ Spa-town atmosphere is not to everyone's taste, and Bad Gastein itself can suffer from local traffic on the narrow streets; Bad Hofgastein is a better base for many people
- ➖ Near-beginners and timid intermediates must be wary of leaving the Schlossalm sector

The Gastein valley isn't widely known in Britain. It deserves better: its slopes are impressively extensive, and mainly quite challenging – great for intermediates who are happy on real red runs. But the place doesn't cater properly for air-package holidaymakers without a car. With five mountains, of which only two are linked, the valley really needs an efficient bus service instead of the current token offering.

With its grand hotels, trinket shops and cramped gorge-like setting, central Bad Gastein itself is a far cry from your standard chalet-style Austrian village. But staying above the centre near the lifts offers a more normal winter sports experience, and both Bad Hofgastein and Dorfgastein, respectively a few km and a few more km down the valley, are equally well worth considering as a base.

BAD GASTEIN TO

The Gastein valley has five separate, mountains, only two of them linked and all well worth exploring ↓

What's new

Last season a new eight-person gondola opened from Angertal to Schlossalm. And a FunCenter for kids and teenagers opened at the top of Stubnerkogel, with a climbing area, kids' movies, Sony Playstations and free Internet access.

For 2000/01 an old chair-lift on Graukogel will be replaced by a new two-seater. And they are hoping to replace old T-bars on Schlossalm by chair-lifts, though plans weren't definite when we went to press. The snowmaking capacity will be increased.

MOUNTAIN FACTS

Altitude	840m-2685m
Lifts	51
Pistes	200km
Blue	24%
Red	66%
Black	10%
Artificial snow	60km
Recco detectors used	

boarding *The Gastein valley is starting to embrace boarding, at least on the slopes. There is a snowboard park with a half-pipe in the Dorfgastein area and further snowboard facilities in other sectors. The valley plays host to lots of events. But apart from the main access lifts, most of the lifts are drags, particularly above Bad Hofgastein. And there are few easy slopes, so it's not ideal for beginners. There's a fair bit to do in the evenings, but it's not as lively and as boarder-friendly as lots of other Austrian resorts.*

The resort

Bad Gastein sits at the head of eastern Austria's Gastein valley. It is an old spa that had its heyday many years ago; it has now spread widely, but still has a compact core where the buildings are a bizarre combination (smart, modern, hotel-shopping-casino complex, baroque town hall and concrete multi-storey car park) laid out in a cramped horseshoe set in what is virtually a gorge, complete with waterfall crashing beneath the main street. It mainly attracts a quite formal German/Austrian clientele.

The thick surrounding woods lend some charm, and the main road and railway bypass the centre – though it can still get choked with traffic.

The slopes are spread around, up and down the valley, with a big sector directly accessible from the fringes of Bad Gastein and Bad Hofgastein (also a spa, but a more open, modern and less stuffy-feeling village).

Dorfgastein is a more relaxed and rustic village a little further down the valley, with its own extensive slopes linked with those of Grossarl, in the next valley to the east

The mountains

On the whole, this is an area that suits confident intermediates best; most of the slopes are graded red, and rightly so. Where there is a blue option, it is not always a very attractive one – and not always as easy as a timid intermediate might hope.

Buses and trains covered by the lift pass run between the spread-out slopes. But they are not very frequent and can be a bit of a scrum. Every reporter we hear from complains about the bus service; a car is most definitely an asset if you want to get around the different sectors. Rail excursions are easy to Zell am See and St Johann im Pongau. Drivers can visit snowsure Obertauern and Kaprun.

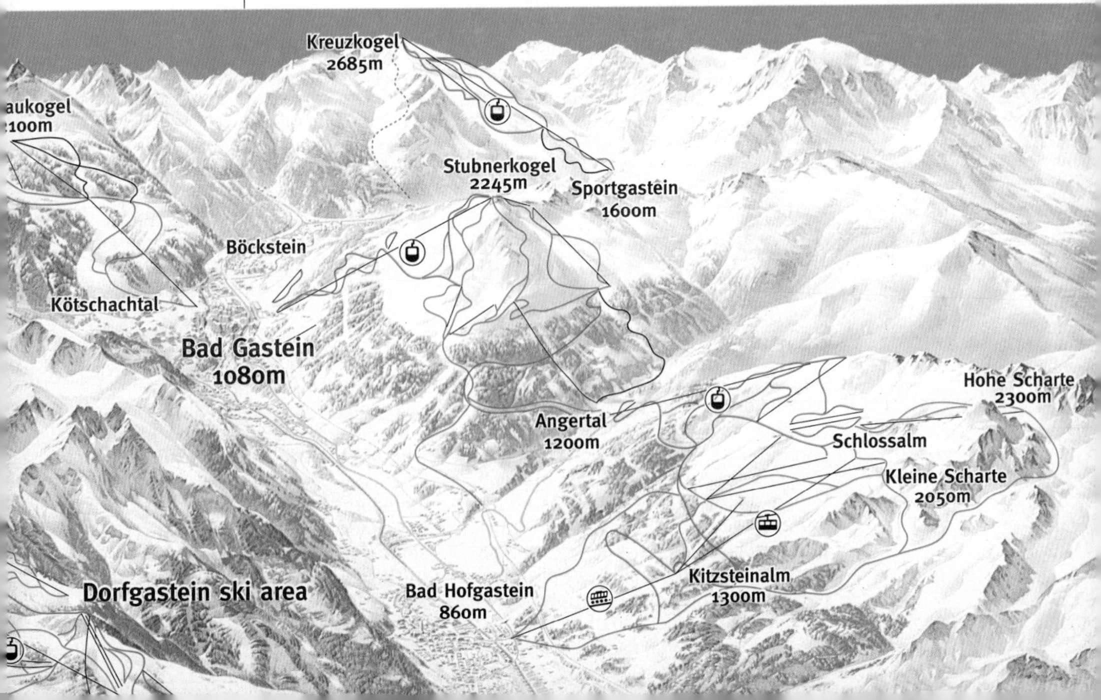

LIFT PASSES

2000/01 prices in schillings

Gastein Super Ski Pass
Covers all lifts in Gastein valley and Grossarl, and buses, trains and road tolls between the resorts (while lifts are open).
Beginners Day- and points-tickets for baby lifts.
Main pass
1-day pass 430
6-day pass 2,050 (low season 1900)
Senior citizens
Over 65 male, 60 female: 6-day pass 1900
Children
Under 15: 6-day pass 1230
Under 6: free pass
Alternative periods
5 skiing days in 7, and 12 skiing days in 14 passes available.
Alternative passes
Gastein Super Ski Pass only available for 1½ days or more. Passes for shorter periods cover only Bad Gastein/Bad Hofgastein. Single ascent passes available for lifts in Dorfgastein and Sportgastein.

THE SLOPES
Extensive but fragmented

The extensive main slopes are made up of two distinct sectors, with a link via the side valley of Angertal.

From the upper part of Bad Gastein a gondola goes up to **Stubnerkogel**, from where you can head back to the resort or down to Angertal. From Angertal a new gondola goes to the **Schlossalm** sector above Bad Hofgastein, from where a variety of pistes lead off in different directions. The runs back to Angertal are south-facing and low, but well covered by artificial snowmakers.

The much smaller **Graukogel** area lies at the other side of Bad Gastein, reached by an inadequate bus service. It is a steep, straightforward mountain. With pistes running through the forest, the area is a great asset in bad weather and quiet at other times.

Reached by bus or train, the higher, more exposed **Sportgastein**, 9km south of Bad Gastein, has the best snow in the area and is served by an eight-person gondola; but there are few pistes – basically, variants on the long run back down to the main lift.

In the opposite direction, **Dorfgastein** offers another extensive area of intermediate runs – mainly red.

SNOW RELIABILITY
Good for a low-altitude resort

Although the area is of typically Austrian low altitude, this part of the Alps has a relatively good snow record and there is a battery of snowmakers in crucial sections. There are a lot of lifts and runs above mid-station height, and the higher sector of Sportgastein is an important fallback.

FOR EXPERTS
More fast cruises than challenge

There are few black runs but there are long, testing reds with steepish terrain for fast cruising or mogul-bashing, depending on the conditions.

Graukogel has the World Cup slopes, and provides some challenge on its upper slopes. The other main sectors have plenty of opportunities to go off-piste, with or without hiking.

Sportgastein is worth the trip – there are off-piste possibilities on the front of the mountain, and a long off-piste trail off the back drops almost 1500m from Kreuzkogel to Heilstollen in the valley (on the bus route). Remember to check the bus times carefully or a long wait (or walk) could await you at the bottom. Dorfgastein has the least demanding slopes in the area, but there is a fine black run from mid-mountain to the village.

FOR INTERMEDIATES
Not for leisurely cruisers

Good intermediates will love all the areas on the lift pass – more than enough to keep you happy for a week. A particular delight is the beautiful 8km red run, well away from the lifts, from Höhe Scharte down to Bad Hofgastein. The open north-facing slopes of Stubnerkogel down into Angertal are good, for both interest and snow-cover – try the red down to Hartlgut at the end of the day and a train ride home after a few beers. The same is true of the Graukogel runs.

For early intermediates, the area as a whole is uncomfortably challenging. But Grossarl (linked to Dorfgastein) and Schlossalm are less demanding than other sectors, and the open bowl around the main cluster of restaurants at Schlossalm is splendid cruising (and carving) territory.

FOR BEGINNERS
Unsuitable slopes

Nursery slopes are dotted around the valley, but none combines convenience with reassuringly gentle gradients. The transition to longer runs is not an easy one, either.

FOR CROSS-COUNTRY
Extensive, if low and fragmented

There is an impressive 90km of trails, but all are along the valley floor, making only the small loop at Sportgastein reasonably reliable for snow. Another drawback is the scattered nature of the loops. Bad Hofgastein is by far the best base for cross-country skiing, with long trails stretching almost to Bad Gastein.

QUEUES
Buses are the problem

There are few problems outside the peak season in late February. The powerful gondola at Sportgastein put paid to the queues there when conditions were poor elsewhere. Morning queues to get out of the valley and for the Bad Hofgastein mid-station cable-car are the worst.

Queues for the infrequent buses linking the various villages and lift stations are more of a problem.

SCHOOLS/GUIDES

99/00 prices in schillings

Bad Gastein
Manager Werner Pflaum
Classes 6 days
5hr: 10am-3pm, 1hr lunch; 3hr: 1pm-4pm
6 full days: 1590
Children's classes
Ages: up to 14
6 full days including lunch: 2750
Private lessons
55 min
490 for 55 min; each additional person 250

Luigi
Manager Luigi Kravanja
Classes 6 days
5hr: 10am-3pm with 1hr lunch
6 full days: 1550
Children's classes
Ages: 4 to 14
6 full days including lunch: 2650
Private lessons
1hr or full-day
450 for 1hr; each additional person 250

CHILDCARE

Both ski schools run ski kindergartens.

There is a kindergarten at the Grüner Baum hotel, taking children aged 3 to 8, from 9.30 to 4pm. Skiing is available, with a special lift.

ACTIVITIES

Indoor Fitness centre (swimming, sauna, gym), thermal baths, squash, tennis, bowling, indoor golf, darts, casino, museum, theatre, concerts
Outdoor Natural ice rinks (skating and curling), sleigh rides, horse-riding, ice climbing, toboggan runs, ski-bob, 35km cleared paths

MOUNTAIN RESTAURANTS
One of the pleasures of this area

Numerous atmospheric, traditional huts are dotted around. Good value and good food are the norm. Bad Gastein's places are more expensive than those in the rest of the valley, but still cheap compared to most of the Alps.

Bad Hofgastein's smart Schlossalm has a large terrace, plus yodelling! Jolly places include Aeroplanstadl on the 8km Höhe Scharte run, Hamburger Skiheim at Schlossalm (with 'barbecue in the snow') and the Panoramastube in Dorfgastein. The Wengeralm, also above Dorf, is a cosy, upmarket refuge with a good terrace. We've had good reports of the restaurants at Sportgastein.

SCHOOLS AND GUIDES
English widely spoken

The two schools do have good reputations (for their English as well as the tuition). But a reporter complained this year that neither ski school offered good, demanding off-piste guiding that he was used to getting in places like St Anton.

FACILITIES FOR CHILDREN
Reasonable

With its fragmented areas and rather serious slopes, Bad Gastein hardly seems an ideal resort for small children, but there are facilities for all-day care, of which the ski kindergarten at the Grüner Baum sounds the most inviting.

Staying there

Getting around Bad Gastein is not easy, so it is worth picking your location with care. For getting to the slopes (and for something like a ski-resort ambience), the best place to stay is in the upper part of town, close to the Stubnerkogel gondola station. But consider flat Bad Hofgastein – a less tiring alternative to hilly Bad Gastein.

HOW TO GO
Packages mainly to hotels

Although apartments make up nearly 15 per cent of the total beds available, British tour operators sell mainly hotel-based packages. The nearest thing to a catered chalet is Ski Miquel's Tannenburg, a traditional-style old hotel run as a chalet-hotel. It is a short walk from the gondola and we've had good reports of its 'good atmosphere, very pleasant communal rooms and bar, large en-suite bedrooms – would definitely return' and 'couldn't praise the food highly enough'.

Hotels This is an upmarket spa resort, and it has lots of smart hotels with excellent spa facilities – there are almost as many 4-star places as 3-star ones.

(5) **Elisabethpark** Luxury hotel popular with Brits looking for excellent facilities, style, comfort and formality. Poorly placed for the slopes, but does run a courtesy bus.

(4) **Salzburger Hof** 4-star with excellent spa facilities, a longish walk from the village gondola.

(4) **Wildbad** Luxurious 4-star within reasonable walking distance of the main lift.

(4) **Schillerhof** Reliable 3-star in good position, opposite Graukogel lift.

(4) **Grüner Baum** Splendidly secluded Relais & Châteaux place, tucked away in the Kötschachtal.

(3) **Mozart** Well placed for buses. Good, simple and filling food.

(3) **Alpenblick** Good value, informal 3-star; well placed for the slopes.

Self-catering Plenty of apartments are available for rent but you have to book them directly.

EATING OUT
Something for most tastes

There is a fair range of restaurants, including surprisingly fine Chinese and seafood places. The Bellevue Alm is one of the liveliest places to eat at, while the à la carte menus at the 3-star hotels Nussdorferhof and Mozart are good value. The Junger Stube was recommended by a reporter for 'atmosphere and traditional food'.

APRES-SKI
Varied, but no oom-pah-pah

Soaking in one of the spas is a popular activity – see below.

There are elegant tea rooms, sophisticated dances, numerous bars, discos and casinos, but the general ambience is rather subdued.

This part of Austria has not imported the informal Tirolean-style 'oom-pah-pah' jollity. There is tea-dancing at the Bellevue Alm though. The best tea rooms are the Causerie, in the Elisabethpark and the Wiener Café/Pilsstube in the Salzburger Hof. Weismayr's, Eden's and Manfreda's

↑ High open bowls turn into tree-lined trails lower down

BAD GASTEIN TO

GETTING THERE

Air Salzburg, transfer 2hr. Linz or Munich, transfer 3½hr.

Rail Mainline station in resort.

bars are pleasant for a quiet drink. The Hexen Haüsl is a more informal little wooden schnapps bar.

Haggenblooms has live music, gets full of young Swedes and is 'brilliant' says a reporter. The Bunny Bar is more sophisticated than its name suggests. The various functions in the Grüner Baum are the most informal hotel entertainment, but the elegant Ritz and Felsen bars in the Salzburger Hof and the Elisabethpark respectively are more typical of the scene later on.

The Gatz and High Life are the main clubs. The casino gives you a generous amount of free chips, so those with will power and/or luck can have a surprisingly inexpensive couple of hours there. Bowling and a casino trip are likely to be organised by tour operator reps.

OFF THE SLOPES

Great variety of things to do

Provided you don't mind the style of the place, Bad Gastein has a lot to offer off the slopes, whether you're active or not. The spas are supposed to have a regenerative effect thanks to the high radon content. The Gastein

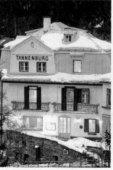

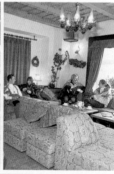

TOURIST OFFICE

Postcode A-5640
t +43 (6434) 25310
f 253137
info@gastein.com
www.gastein.com

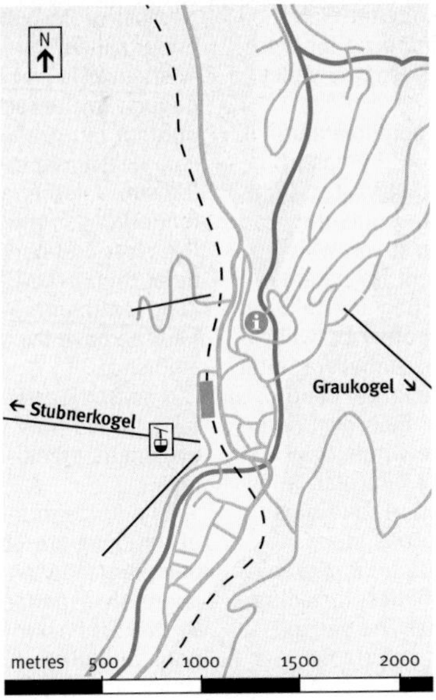

Healing Gallery is a highlight – a train takes you down into an old gold-digging tunnel where you can lie on benches inhaling radon in steam-room-like heat and humidity for a couple of hours. We find all this a bit strange: radon is a radioactive, carcinogenic gas, and we spend a fortune keeping it out of our homes in the UK. The Rock Pool is a large indoor pool hewn out of the rock, heated naturally by hot springs.

Meeting up the mountain is no problem for pedestrians, though getting to the best mountain restaurants isn't easy.

There are organised coach trips to Kitzbühel, Salzburg and Goldegg Castle, and trains run to the resorts of Zell am See and St Johann im Pongau.

Bad Hofgastein 860m

Bad Hofgastein is a sizeable, quiet, old spa village set out spaciously in a broad section of the valley. It has an impressive old Gothic church, traditional-style buildings, elegant quiet hotels, narrow alleys and a babbling brook. Everything is kept in pristine order.

Although rather sprawling, the village has a pleasant pedestrianised area which acts as a central focus. Because of the spa 'cures' there's a relatively high number of people just pottering about during the day, notably at the curling rinks in Kurpark. The place looks very pretty in the evenings, under the soft glow of night lamps. The large public spa building, the Kurzentrum, is the only relative blot on the landscape, though it's not exactly an eyesore.

The best location to stay is in the pedestrian zone, which is relatively handy for most things including the slopes. A high proportion of hotels are a long walk from the lift station – but there is a shuttle-bus.

Bad Hofgastein's lift is a short funicular that takes you up to a mid-station (1302m), above which most of the slopes are found. Here, you have a choice between a cable-car and two-stage chair. Both the funicular and the much lower capacity cable-car can generate big queues (30 minutes in rush hour during peak season is not unusual). At such times, the chair is an obvious alternative to the cable-car and there's closed-circuit TV at the funicular base station which shows you the situation up at the cable-car.

Beginners staying in Bad Hofgastein have to catch a bus to the limited

BAD GASTEIN TO

Come on in, the water's radioactive →

nursery area over at Angertal. Bad Hofgastein makes a fine base for cross-country skiers when its lengthy valley-floor trails have snow.

We have received complimentary reports of the schools in the past, but haven't heard from recent visitors. One is based at Angertal, and runs the village ski kindergarten there, which can be very inconvenient for parents. Lack of many English-speaking children to play with may be another drawback.

Bad Hofgastein is essentially a hotel resort. They tend to be large, good quality and many have their own fine spa facilities. Some are within easy walking distance of the funicular, a few provide courtesy transport, and most of the rest are close to bus stops.

The Palace Gastein is a big 4-star with superb leisure facilities, including pool and thermal baths. The elegant Germania is similarly comfortable.

The high-quality Norica is atypically modern in design, but is well positioned in the pedestrian zone. The Alpina is another well located 4-star, five minutes from the slopes. The Astoria is well appointed but quite poorly positioned and doesn't supply courtesy transport.

The Kurpark has been recommended for its good food, service and location in the pedestrian zone. Gasthof Reiter is poorly positioned but provides a useful inexpensive, informal B&B.

There is a good range of restaurants, and many hotels offer good formal dining. The Moserkeller is an intimate restaurant, and Pension Maier one of the better informal places. The Pyrkerhöhe, on the slopes just above town, is worth an evening excursion. The Tele Pizza Bar cooks outside on an open fire at lunchtimes in fine weather. It's also good inside in the evenings, as are the Tschickeria and Da Dimo pizza and pasta places.

Après-ski is very quiet by Austrian standards. Some reporters have been disappointed; others have loved the peacefulness.

There are, however, a few animated places around. Last time we were there, the Picolo ice bar in the centre of town was lively immediately after the lifts close. Frankie's bar was quite lively and popular with locals. Evergreen had a friendly atmosphere. Visions was a spacious modern disco, while Match Box and C'est la Vie had loud music and were full of teenagers when we looked in.

Most of Bad Hofgastein's clientele prefer something more sedate. Café Weitmoser is an historic little castle popular for its cakes at tea-time. The outdoor bar of the Osterreichischer Hof is a pleasant spot to catch the last of the sun. Another atmospheric tea-time rendezvous is the Tennishalle. Later, the West End bar is a cosy place for a quiet drink. The Glocknerkeller in Hotel Zum Toni and the Rondo bar in Hotel Käruten have live music in a low-key ambience.

The Bad Gastein casino provides taxis to and from town. A bowling evening is organised by tour operator reps.

The Kurzentrum is the centrepiece of the things to do off the slopes, being arguably an even more impressive spa facility than that of Bad Gastein. It has an impressive thermal pool, and offers a range of therapies. Other off-slope amenities include artificial and natural ice skating, indoor tennis, squash, sleigh rides. Lovely walks and riding.

Dorfgastein 830m

Those who wish to try the Gastein valley slopes but prefer not to stay in large, commercialised villages should consider Dorfgastein. Prices are lower, and the atmosphere is friendlier and more informal – a contrast to its rather cold setting, sheltered from the sun.

The extensive slopes are more suitable for early intermediates than the steeps above Bad Gastein. Runs are long and varied, amid lovely scenery. Unfortunately the low-altitude nursery slopes can be cold and icy. Bad Hofgastein's funicular is 15 minutes away by bus (infrequent and sometimes crowded).

Those not interested in venturing that far can buy a local pass at 75 per cent of the Gastein Valley pass price.

There are a few shops and après-ski places, a short walk or bus-ride from the slopes. Café St Ruperb is a nice village pizzeria. The Kirchenwirt and Römerhof are comfortable hotels, while Pension Skihausl is cheaper, does good food, and is next to the slopes.

There is an outdoor heated pool with sauna-solarium, a bowling alley and a ski kindergarten.

Ellmau 800m

A quiet base from which to access the extensive Ski Welt area

WHAT IT COSTS

3

HOW IT RATES

The slopes

Snow	**
Extent	****
Experts	*
Intermediates	****
Beginners	****
Convenience	***
Queues	****
Restaurants	**

The rest

Scenery	***
Resort charm	***
Off-slope	***

What's new

The snowmaking capacity in the Ski Welt has been hugely increased in recent years. It now covers 125km of pistes (half the pistes in the Ski Welt) and is the largest snowmaking facility anywhere in Austria.

For 2000/01 a high-speed six-seater chair-lift will replace a T-bar up to the Hartkaiser-Brandstadl area. This joins another six-pack that was installed for last season.

Amazingly, they are also building a new T-bar (we thought T-bars were dead!) to improve the link between Ellmau and Scheffau.

MOUNTAIN FACTS

Altitude	620m-1830m
Lifts	92
Pistes	250km
Blue	43%
Red	48%
Black	9%
Artificial snow	125km

- ⊕ Part of Ski Welt, Austria's largest linked ski and snowboard area
- ⊕ Pretty, easy slopes
- ⊕ Excellent nursery slopes (but snow reliability can be a problem)
- ⊕ Massive recent investment in snowmaking has paid off
- ⊕ Cheap by Austrian standards
- ⊕ Quiet, charming family resort – more appealing than neighbouring Söll

- ⊖ Poor natural snow record but increased snowmaking does compensate
- ⊖ Village a bus-ride from slopes
- ⊖ Short runs make getting about the Hartkaiser area very slow. New chairs will help. A poor piste map doesn't
- ⊖ Lack of nightlife other than rep-organised events
- ⊖ Little for experts or good intermediates

Like nearby Söll, Ellmau gives access to the large, unthreatening Ski Welt circuit, with good slopes for early intermediates. The resort is a pleasant, quiet alternative to Söll, and offers more holiday amenities than other neighbours such as Scheffau.

Although Ellmau's natural snow record is bad, continuing investment in snowmakers has made a big difference. The snow may not always be in tip-top condition, but at least there'll be some. A reader has commented, 'Massive investment in artificial snow and new lifts have improved the situation considerably, though cruising through green fields of grazing sheep seems a bit odd!' The new chairs which replace drags at Hartkaiser make it possible to move around the mountain a bit quicker now, though of course the runs will still be short. Now if they could sort out the inefficient bus service ...

boarding *Ellmau is a good place to try boarding. Local slopes are easy and you can stick to the funicular and chair-lifts when you get off the nursery slopes. And if the snow deteriorates to slush, it makes the boarding easier. For decent boarders it's more limited – the slopes of the Ski Welt are tame and fresh powder is not the norm. But there is a fun-park and quarter-pipe near Söll. Nightlife is in short supply – good for a family with some members learning to board but a disaster area if you're looking for a rave.*

The resort

Ellmau sits at the north-eastern corner of the Ski Welt, between St Johann and Wörgl. Although a sizeable resort, and becoming more commercialised each year, it remains quiet and pretty, with traditional chalet-style buildings, welcoming bars and shops, and a picturesque old church. Its Alpine charm is spoilt a little by the main road along its edge, and by a frequent lack of snow on rooftops and streets. Buses around the resort, necessary if you stay in the village, attract complaint: 'Infrequent, to almost non-existent during the day. We waited over an hour for the bus back to Ellmau in –10°C temperatures.'

By Austrian standards the nightlife is rather tame, and although off-slope diversions have improved, the village doesn't really amount to more than a pleasant dormitory for slope users.

Make sure you get an Ellmau guest card entitling you to various discounts, including to the Kaiserbad leisure centre.

The mountains

The Ski Welt is the largest mountain circuit in Austria. It links Going, Scheffau (covered in this chapter), Söll, Itter, Hopfgarten and Brixen. But it hardly compares in size, and certainly not in quality, to St Anton, Ischgl, Saalbach or the Gastein valley. Most runs are not difficult. We receive

LIFT PASSES

2000/01 prices in schillings

Ski Welt Wilder Kaiser-Brixental
Covers all lifts in the Wilder Kaiser-Brixental area from Going to Westendorf, and the ski-bus.

Beginners Points tickets (25 points 75). Small drags are 5 points.

Main pass
1-day pass 380
6-day pass 1890

Children
Under 16: 6-day pass 1070
Under 6: free pass

Short-term passes
Single ascent on some lifts, passes from 11am, noon, 1pm and 'taster' pass.

Alternative periods
5 in 7 days, 7 in 10 days and 10 in 14 days.

Notes Discounts for physically disabled visitors and seniors.

Alternative passes
Kitzbüheler Alpenskipass covers lots of resorts in the East Tirol (adult 6-day 2200, children 1100; plus 50 for electronic Keycard), including access to swimming pools.

complaints that it is slow to get about, thanks both to the number of short connecting runs, and the piste map: 'A complete work of fiction, I'd have been better equipped with the London A-Z.' New chair-lifts on Hartkaiser should speed things up a bit.

Westendorf is covered by the Ski Welt pass, though separate. Kitzbühel, Waidring, Fieberbrunn and St Johann are in easy reach for day trips and covered by the Kitzbüheler Alpenskipass.

THE SLOPES

Improving links around the area

Ellmau is close to the best slopes in the area, above Scheffau. The funicular railway on the edge of the village takes you up to Hartkaiser, from where a fine long red (a favourite with reporters) leads down to Blaiken (Scheffau's lift station). A choice of gondola or two-stage chair goes back to Brandstadl, the start of three varied, long alternatives back to Blaiken.

Immediately beyond Brandstadl, the slopes become rather bitty; an array of short runs and lifts link Brandstadl to Zinsberg. From Zinsberg, excellent, long, south-facing pistes lead down to Brixen. Then it's a short bus-ride to Westendorf's pleasant separate area. Part-way down to Brixen you can head towards Söll – either by the steep Hohe Salve or avoiding the latter using a series of easy runs. Hohe Salve also provides access to a long, west-facing run to Hopfgarten.

Returning all the way to Ellmau has always been time consuming but should be speeded up by the new lifts.

Ellmau and Going share a pleasant little area of slopes on Astberg, slightly apart from the rest of the area, and well suited to the unadventurous and to families. One piste leads to the funicular for access to the rest of Ski Welt. The main Astberg chair is rather inconveniently positioned, midway between Ellmau and Going.

SNOW RELIABILITY

Now with more artificial help

With a very low average height, and important links that get a lot of sun, the snowmaking that the Ski Welt has installed in recent seasons is essential. At 125km and covering half the area's pistes, it is one of Austria's biggest artificial snow installations. We were there in January 1999, before any major snowfalls, and snowmaking was keeping the links open well. It did not, however, prevent slush and icy patches forming – usually slush on south-facing slopes, ice on north-facing ones. A reporter noted that the snow-guns 'operated 24 hours a day' and that though grooming was generally good, 'some runs down to the valley floor were closed'.

The north-facing Eiberg area above Scheffau holds its snow well. Or go to the high Steinplatte area – covered by the Kitzbüheler Alpenskipass.

FOR EXPERTS

Not suitable

There's a steep plunge off the Hohe Salve summit, and a little mogul field between Brandstadl and Neualm, but the area isn't really suitable except for

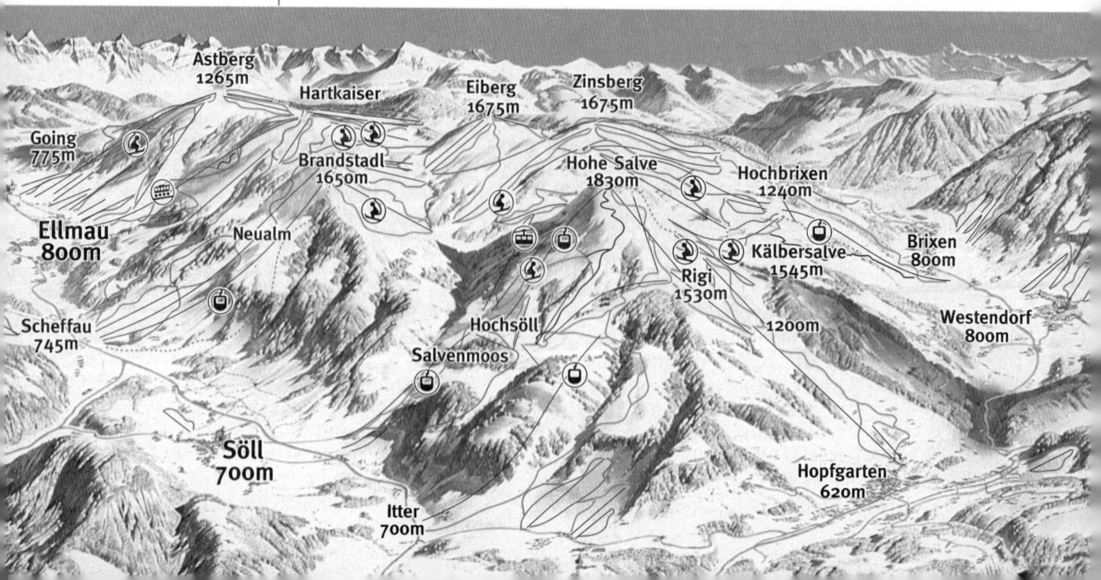

↑ You don't ski on the Wilder Kaiser mountains, but they do make a picturesque backdrop to the village

ELLMAU TO

GETTING THERE

Air Salzburg, transfer 2hr.

Rail Wörgl (18km), St Johann in Tirol (10km), Kufstein (20km), bus to resort.

those prepared to seek out worthwhile off-piste opportunities. The ski route from Brandstadl down to Scheffau is a highlight and you can go off-piste with a guide from Brandstadl to Söll.

FOR INTERMEDIATES

Great for cruisers and families

With good snow, the Ski Welt is a paradise for early intermediates and those who love easy cruising. There are lots of blue runs and many of the reds in truth deserve a blue grading. It is a big area and you really get a feeling of travelling around – we skied it for two days and felt we only scratched the surface. The main challenge you may find is when the snow isn't perfect – ice and slush can make even gentle slopes seem tricky. In general the most difficult slopes are those from the mid-stations to the valleys: the most direct of the runs between Brandstadl and Blaiken, the pistes down to Brixen and the run from Hochsöll back to Söll, for example. Higher up the red from Hohe Salve to Rigi is a good cruise on relatively good snow. For timid intermediates the quiet, easy slopes of Astberg are on hand to Ellmau guests.

FOR BEGINNERS

One of the best Ski Welt villages

Ellmau has an array of good nursery slopes – snow permitting. The main ones are at the Going end, but there are some by the road to the funicular, smaller but still very satisfactory. The Astberg chair opens up a more snowsure plateau at altitude. The Brandstadl-Hartkaiser area has a section of short, easy runs, and near-beginners looking for a rest from drags have a nice long piste running the length of the funicular.

FOR CROSS-COUNTRY

Plenty of valley trails

When there is snow, there are long, quite challenging trails along the valley to St Johann and Kirchdorf, and an easier one to Scheffau and via Söll to Itter. But trails at altitude are lacking.

QUEUES

Few local problems

Continued introduction of new lifts has greatly improved this once queue-prone area. The Blaiken gondola has queues at weekends and when snow is poor elsewhere, when the higher lifts on and around Eiberg get busy too.

SCHOOLS/GUIDES

1999/2000 prices in schillings

1st Ellmau
Classes 6 days
4hr: 10am-noon and 2pm-4pm
6 full days: 1350
Children's classes
Ages: 3 to 14
6 full days: 1290
Private lessons
Hourly or full day (4hr) 470 for 1hr; additional person 200

Ellmau-Hartkaiser
Classes 6 days
4hr: 10am-noon and 2pm-4pm
6 full days: 1300
Children's classes
Ages: 3 to 14
6 full days: 1250
Private lessons
Hourly or full day
450 for 1hr; each additional person 200

Top
Classes 6 days
4hr: 10am-noon and 2pm-4pm
6 full days: 1690
Children's classes
Ages: 4 to 14
6 full days: 1300

CHILDCARE

Ist school has a playroom open from 9am. Hartkaiser school opened a ski nursery last season. Top school welcomes children and provides lunchtime care on request. There is also a village non-skiing kindergarten.

The poor valley bus service and the roundabout links between Hartkaiser and the rest of the Ski Welt have generated more complaints about how long it takes to get around the area than about lift queues.

MOUNTAIN RESTAURANTS
Stick to the little huts

'Little huts good, big huts bad' is a simple but fairly accurate description. The smaller places are fairly consistent in providing wholesome, good-value food in pleasant surroundings. The Rübezahl above Ellmau is our favourite. It is very rustic – with wooden carvings, low doors, several rooms and excellent food. The hut at Neualm has also been recommended. The larger self-service restaurants are rather functional (the Jochstube at Eiberg is an exception) and suffer queues. Going is a good spot for a quiet lunch.

SCHOOLS AND GUIDES
Good on the whole

The three schools have good reputations – except that classes tend to be very large. As well as the main schools there are mountaineering schools that organise tours in the Wilder Kaiser and the Kitzbühel mountains.

FACILITIES FOR CHILDREN
Fine in theory

Ellmau is an attractive resort for families. Kindergarten facilities seem to be perfectly satisfactory and include fun ideas such as a mini train to the lifts. We have had no recent reports, however.

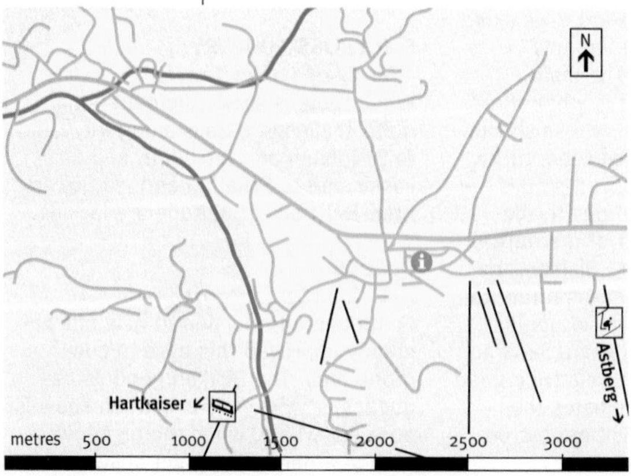

Staying there

Ellmau has a compact centre, but its accommodation is scattered, and the bus service unreliable.

Hotel position is quite important: those keen to hit the slopes as early as possible will want to be close to the funicular. Après-skiers will want to be more central, close to the village facilities – but up to 20 minutes' walk or a bus-ride from the funicular. Near-beginners might want to be near the Astberg chair, halfway between Ellmau and Going.

HOW TO GO
Lots of chalet-style hotels

Ellmau is essentially a hotel and pension resort, though there are apartments that can be booked locally.
Hotels Ellmau is typical of Austrian resorts that have expanded since World War II, with many comfortable, modern, chalet-style hotels.
(((((5) **Bär** Elegant but relaxed Relais & Châteaux chalet that seems almost out of place in Ellmau – twice the price of any other hotel.
(((3) **Hochfilzer** Central, well equipped (it has an outdoor hot-tub) and popular with reporters: 'What a gem. I have stayed in no better hotel for a ski holiday in my life.'
(((3) **Christoph** Large, comfortable, multi-facility place in secluded position on the outskirts – handy for funicular.
(((3) **Sporthotel** Similar in style to the Christoph, but opposite the school and main nursery slopes.
(((3) **Alte Post** Pleasant and central, though not self-evidently 'alte'.
(1) **Gasthof Au** Cheapest in town, five minutes from the funicular and ten from the centre.
Self-catering There is a wide variety. Basically you get what you pay for. The Bauer Annemarie is under the same management as the hotel Christoph and equally well placed for lifts.

WHERE TO EAT
Hotel-dominated

Most people are on half-board so there are not many restaurants. The hotel Hochfilzer has a reputation for good food. There are a couple of pizzerias. Café Bettina, midway between the funicular and town, is good for afternoon coffee and cakes.

ACTIVITIES

Indoor Swimming pool, sauna, solarium, tennis, squash, bowling, billiards, ski museum, theatre
Outdoor Winter hiking, natural ice rink, curling, toboggan run, sleigh rides, cleared walking paths, paragliding, hang-gliding, mountaineering school

TOURIST OFFICE

Postcode A-6352
t +43 (5358) 2301
f 3443
ellmau@netway.at
www.ellmau.com

APRES-SKI
Limited but varied programme

The rep-organised events include bowling, sleigh rides, Tirolean folklore and inner-tubing, but there is little else. Reporters have enjoyed their immediate après-ski at local mountain huts. Later on they favoured the Memory bar and the Dorfstüberl, though both were very quiet: 'The bars never really got busy. The only noise in the resort was the Austrian band that played on your return from the slopes.'

OFF THE SLOPES
Excellent sports centre

The Kaiserbad leisure centre is good. There are many excursions available, including Innsbruck, Salzburg, Rattenburg and Vitipeno. St Johann in Tirol is a nice little town only a few miles away by bus. Other facilities are very limited. Valley walks are spoilt by the busy main road.

Scheffau 745m

Scheffau is one of the most attractive of the Ski Welt villages: a rustic little place complete with pretty white church, it is spacious yet not sprawling, and has a definite centre. It is tucked away a kilometre off the busy main Wörgl road, which increases the charm factor at the cost of slope convenience (the Ski Welt lifts are at Blaiken, on the opposite side of the main road). The nursery slopes are in the village, however, and this makes Scheffau a poor choice for mixed-ability parties – though one regular visitor finds even real beginners can make it up to Brandstadl by the end of the week. If convenience is all important to you, you have the option of staying in Blaiken, where there are several more hotels.

A gondola and parallel two-stage chair give rapid and generally queue-free access directly to the Ski Welt's best (and most central and snowsure) section of pistes.

The pistes above Blaiken are some of the longest and steepest in the Ski Welt. Nearby Eiberg is the place to go when snow is poor, and the slopes are more extensive since drags were replaced by four-seater chairs.

The village nursery slope is adequate when snow-cover is good enough. Higher slopes suitable for novices are an inconvenient and expensive distance away up the main mountain, though there are plenty of options for improving beginners.

There can be weekend queues for the gondola. At such times the two-stage valley chair can be a useful alternative – though the VIP pass for Scheffau guests means you can slide past day trippers in the queue.

The school is well regarded, but groups can be large and bilingual.

The 4-star Alpin is one of the best hotels and has the only pool in town. The Wilder Kaiser is the best hotel at Blaiken. Nearby are the good value gasthofs Waldhof, Aloisia and Blaiken.

There aren't many village restaurants, and those staying in B&B places are advised to book tables.

Regulars find Scheffau friendly and restful. Après-ski is unlikely to draw Blaiken residents up the hill. The usual rep-organised events such as bowling and tobogganing are available.

Walking apart, there is little to do off the slopes. Tour operators organise trips to Innsbruck and Salzburg.

Scheffau is a good family choice: both the ski kindergarten and non-ski nursery have good reputations.

Going 775m

Going is a tiny, attractively rustic village, well placed for the limited but quiet slopes of the Astberg and for the vast area of nursery slopes between here and Ellmau. Prices are low, but it's not an ideal place for covering the whole of the Ski Welt on the cheap.

Going is ideal for families looking for a quiet time, particularly if they have a car for transport to Scheffau or St Johann when the Astberg's low runs have poor snow.

Hintertux 1500m

Powerful new lifts and excellent snow in a bleak setting

WHAT IT COSTS

3

HOW IT RATES

The slopes

Snow	*****
Extent	**
Experts	***
Intermediates	***
Beginners	*
Convenience	**
Queues	***
Restaurants	**

The rest

Scenery	***
Resort charm	***
Off-slope	*

TOURISMUSVERBAND TUX

Hintertux's year-round glacier slopes are popular with boarders – the British Snowboard Championships were held there last season ↓

Hintertux has one of the best glaciers in the world and its slopes are open 365 days a year. It's popular with national ski teams for summer training. In winter, it provides guaranteed good snow even when lower resorts are suffering badly. The village itself is small, with few diversions. The traditional old villages of Madseit and Juns are pleasant but Lanersbach is a more attractive option.

THE RESORT

Tiny Hintertux is bleakly set at the dead end of the Tux valley. Ringed by steep mountains except to the north, the village is often in shade. It is little more than a small collection of hotels and guest houses; there is another, smaller group of hotels near the lifts, which lie a 15-minute walk away from the village, across a car park which fills with day-visitors' cars and coaches, especially when snow is poor in lower resorts. Lanersbach, the largest of the villages in the valley, is 5km down the road, has its own ski area and a regular free shuttle-bus to Hintertux.

THE MOUNTAINS

Hintertux's **slopes** are fairly extensive and, for a glacier, surprisingly challenging. A series of speedy new gondolas now takes you in three stages from the base at 1500m to the top of the glacier at 3250m in under 20 minutes. Two gondolas (including a new one for 2000/01) go from the base to Sommerbergalm. From here two more gondolas including a 24-person jumbo go on up to Tuxer Ferner Haus, beside the glacier. Then a further new 24-person gondola whisks you up to Gefrorene Wand ('frozen face') at 3250m. At Tuxer Ferner Haus, a fast quad chair serves the slopes below Tuxer Joch; from the top of this sector, an excellent secluded off-piste run goes down to the base station. Between the top of the glacier and Tuxer Ferner Haus there are further chairs and drag-lifts to play on and links across to another 1000m-vertical chain of lifts below Grosser Kaserer on the west. Behind Gefrorene Wand is the area's one sunny piste served by a triple chair. Descent to the valley involves a short ascent to

Tux
im Zillertal
1300 m - 3250 m
... das grüne Gletschertal
Mountains of snow
• Ski and snowboard paradise: 122 km excellent runs for every standard, breathtaking mountain scenery, 32 modern lifts, longest run 12 km, skiing down to the valley
• Sunny, familiar, challenging - and no waiting periods on the Eggalm and Rastkogel skiareas
• The Hintertux glacier is the favourite training ground of the World Cup skiing stars
• Top restaurants on the mountains and in the valley, tyrolean hospitality and après-ski; adventure program with snowboard-contests, snow festivals and floodlit hiking trails and toboggan runs
Year round skiing on the Hintertux glacier - Europe´s most exciting skiing, at the heart of Austria´s Tyrol
Package Holidays:
7 nights accomodation, tux sports bus until 2 a.m. and 6 days superski pass per person:
***-category Bed and breakfast from ATS 4.470,– (£ 235)
***-category halfboard from ATS 5.555,– (£ 292)
****-category halfboard from ATS 6.709,– (£ 353)
MonoGraficDesign
Rooms/Brochures/Information
Tourismusverband Tux • A-6293 Tux •
Lanersbach 472 • Tel. 0043/5287/8506
Fax 0043/5287/8508 • http://www.tux.at,
with live-weather panorama • e-mail: info@tux.at
Tux
... das grüne Gletschertal
ENGLISH SPOKEN
Hintertuxer Gletscher

What's new

Hintertux has invested millions in its lift system in recent years and for the 2000/01 season you will be able to ride state-of-the-art high-speed gondolas from the base at 1500m to the top of the glacier at 3250m in under 20 minutes.

The latest addition, which opened in April 2000, was the world's highest jumbo-gondola, with each cabin holding 24 people, going from Tuxerfernhaus at 2660m to 3250m.

For 2000/01 a new eight-person gondola will replace the existing double chair-lift from the base area. This will supplement the existing gondola and should eliminate queues there even on the busiest days.

MOUNTAIN FACTS

Altitude	1300m-3250m
Lifts	33
Pistes	122km
Blue	35%
Red	52%
Black	13%
Artificial snow	10km

TOURIST OFFICE

Postcode A-6293
t +43 (5287) 8506
f 8508
info@tux.at
www.tux.at

Sommerbergalm on the way, now achieved by a fast six-seater chair-lift.

Snowboarders will find two year-round half-pipes on the glacier, and a fun-park at Hinteranger. There are also some great off-piste opportunities.

Even off the glacier, the other slopes are high and face north, making for very reliable **snow-cover**.

There is more to amuse **experts** here than on any other glacier, with a couple of serious black runs at glacier level and steep slopes and off-piste ski routes beneath.

The area particularly suits good or aggressive **intermediates**. The long runs down from Gefrorene Wand and Kaserer are fun. And there is a pleasant, tree-lined ski route to the valley from Sommerbergalm and another from Tuxer Joch. Moderate intermediates will love the glacier,

This is not a resort for **beginners**. But there are nursery slopes down the valley at Madseit and Juns.

There are 18km of **cross-country** trails, alongside the Tux creek, between Madseit and Lanersbach.

There used to be huge **queues** at Hintertux when snow was poor elsewhere. But the splendid new lifts have largely solved this problem.

Queues for the inadequate **mountain restaurants** are worse. Gletscherhütte, at the top, has great views.

The **ski school** has a good reputation. There's a **children's** section, and Lanersbach has a nursery.

The Ziller Super Ski pass covers all the lifts and buses in the Ziller valley.

STAYING THERE

Most **hotels** are large and comfortable and have spa facilities, but there are also more modest pensions. Close to lifts are the 4-star Neuhintertux and Vierjahreszeiten. Pensions Kössler and Willeiter are in the heart of the village. There are plenty of **apartments**.

Restaurants are mainly hotel-based. The Vierjahreszeiten café is pleasant and informal.

There is very little **nightlife**. The Rindererhof has a lively tea dance.

The spa facilities are excellent but, in general, for **off-slope** activities you're much better off in Mayrhofen.

Being based in Lanersbach has its pluses, especially for drivers, who can get to the glacier in 10 minutes, or head down the Ziller valley – but there are regular free buses too and a new night bus which runs until 2am.

Lanersbach 1300m

Lanersbach is an attractive, spacious, traditional village spoilt only a little by the busy road up to Hintertux, which passes the main lift. Happily, the area around the pretty church is hidden away off the road, yet within walking distance of the lift. The village is small and uncommercialised, but it has all you need in a resort. And prices are relatively low.

The slopes of Eggalm, accessed by a cable-car, have a high point of 2300m at Beil, and a small network of pleasantly varied, mostly wooded pistes leading back to the village and across towards the Rastkogel sector, above nearby Vorderlanersbach. This sector (accessed by its own modern gondola) goes higher (top station 2500m); it is not so pretty or interesting, but you can ski from it to the Eggalm sector. The two sectors total 33km of piste. Snow conditions are usually good, at least in early season; by Austrian standards, these are high slopes and there is some snowmaking, but the Vorderlanersbach sector, in particular, gets a lot of sun.

There are no pistes to challenge experts, but there is a fine off-piste route starting a short walk from the Lanersbach top station and finishing at the village. Intermediates will enjoy the wonderfully uncrowded, well-groomed runs. Lanersbach's nursery slope is rather small.

This is the best base in the area for cross-country.

Lanersbach is essentially a hotel resort. The Lanersbachherof is a good 4-star with pool, sauna, steam and Jacuzzi close to the lifts but is also on the main road. The cheaper 3-star Pinzger and Alpengruss are similarly situated. Restaurants are mainly hotel-based and nightlife is quiet by Austrian standards.

Off-slope facilities are fairly good considering the size of the resort. Some hotels have pools, hot-tubs and fitness rooms open to non-residents. Outside the village is a tennis centre with squash and ten-pin bowling. Mayrhofen is a worthwhile excursion and Salzburg is just within range.

The non-ski nursery takes children from age two, the school from four. Lanersbach is generally child-friendly, though a lack of other English-speaking children to play with could be a problem.

Innsbruck 575m

A cultured city base for a range of little ski resorts

WHAT IT COSTS

3

MOUNTAIN FACTS

Altitude	575m-3210m
Lifts	63
Pistes	130km
Blue	35%
Red	42%
Black	23%
Artificial snow	24km

Innsbruck is not a ski resort in the usual sense. It is a historic university city of 130,000 inhabitants, with a vibrant cultural life, set at a major Alpine crossroads, and a major tourist destination in summer. Its local slopes are of mainly local interest. But the city has twice hosted the Olympic Winter Games, and it lies at the heart of a little group of resorts that share a lift pass and are accessible by efficient bus services. Among them, as it happens, is one of the three or four best glacier areas in the Alps – the Stubaier Gletscher, covered in the separate chapter on Neustift, on page 132.

The Inn valley is a broad, flat-bottomed trench hereabouts, but Innsbruck manages to fill it from side to side. It is a sizeable city, and as you would expect from its Olympic background it has an excellent range of winter sports facilities, as well as a captivating car-free medieval core. It has smart modern shopping areas, trendy bars and restaurants, museums (including, of course, one devoted to the Olympics), concert halls, theatres, a zoo and other attractions that you might seek out on a summer holiday, but normally wouldn't expect to find when going skiing.

Winter diversions off the slopes include 300km of cross-country trails, some at valley level but others appreciably above it; curling and skating at the Olympic centre, including public ice-hockey sessions; several toboggan runs totalling 50km, the longest (above Birgitz) an impressive 10km and 960m vertical; and rides on a four-man bob at Igls.

Not the least of the attractions of staying in such a place is that you don't pay ski resort prices for anything.

There are hotels, inns and guest-houses of every standard and style, with 3-star and 4-star hotels forming the nucleus. Among the more distinctive hotels are the grand 5-star Europa Tyrol, the ancient 4-star Goldener Adler and the 3-star Weisses Kreuz, in the central pedestrian zone, and the 4-star art nouveau Best Western Neue Post.

As well as the traditional Austrian restaurants there's a wide choice of Italian ones, plus a smattering of more exotic alternatives from Mexican to Japanese.

There is an impressive 1400m vertical of slopes on the south-facing slopes of **Seegrube-Nordkette**. The focus of the slopes at Seegrube (1905m) is reached by cable-car rising 1050m from Hungerburg on the

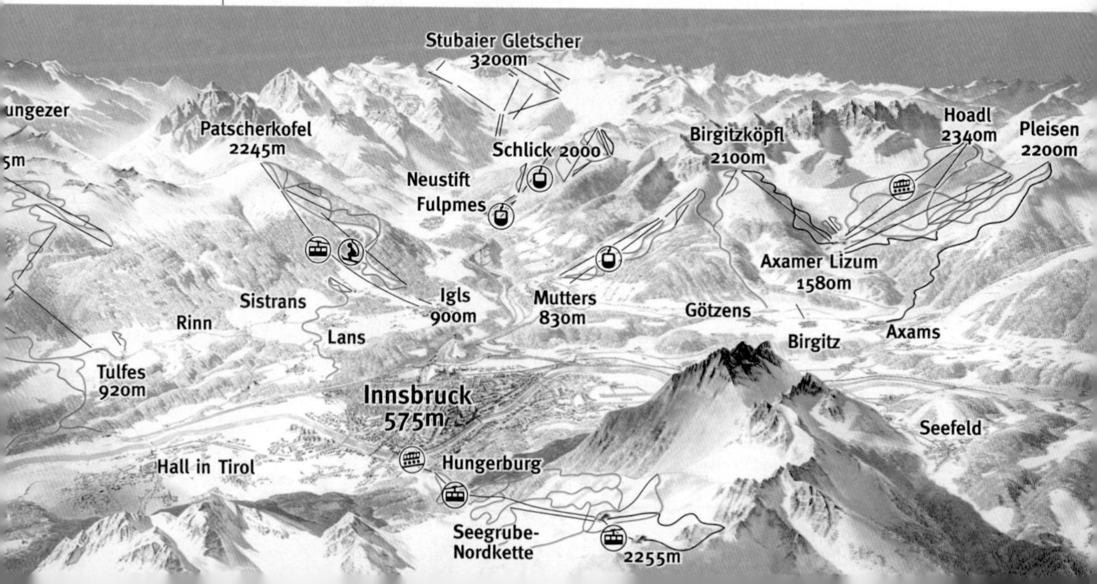

← Igls sits on a shelf about 350m vertical above Innsbruck, with the wooded slopes of Patscherkofel rising immediately above it

INNSBRUCK TOURISMUS / MICHAEL GILHAUS

outskirts of the city (with buses and a funicular up to the cable-car departure station). Although there are red runs to the valley, the snow is not reliable. You go up here expecting to ski the red runs of 370m vertical below Seegrube, served by a chair-lift. A further stage of the cable-car rises 350m vertical to access the Karinne ski route, which is said to be fearsomely steep (up to 70 per cent gradient). You can ski it with a guide and collect not only a T-shirt but a certificate to prove you did it.

But for visitors, if not for residents, skiing usually means heading for the opposite side of the Inn trench, to east or west of the side valley that runs southwards towards the Brenner pass and Italy. The Brenner road is a major pipeline for goods and tourists travelling between Germany and Italy, and opens up the possibility of excursions to the resorts of the Dolomites, such as Selva.

The standard Innsbruck lift pass covers the lifts in all the resorts dealt with here, and Schlick 2000 and the Stubai glacier (see Neustift chapter). The extraordinary Super-Skipass includes days in Kitzbühel to the east and St Anton to the west. Free ski-bus services run to and from all these areas, but only at the beginning and end of the day. A car makes life in general more convenient, especially if you are staying in one of the outlying villages rather than in downtown Innsbruck.

There are snowboard parks in the Seegrube and Axamer Lizum sectors, and at Schlick 200 and the Stubai glacier.

IGLS 900m

Igls seems almost a suburb of Innsbruck – the city trams run out to the village – but really it is a resort in its own right. Its famous downhill race course is an excellent piste.

The village of Igls is small and quiet, with not much in the way of diversions apart from the beautiful walks, the Olympic bob run and the tea shops. But you can stay there, and a couple of UK operators sell packages to its comfortable hotels. Most are small – one exception being the family-run 5-star Sporthotel, which occupies the prime site, centrally placed between the tram station and the cable-car station. These are mostly concentrated in the centre of the village, a bit of a walk from the cable-car station.

The skiing on Patscherkofel revolves around the excellent, varied, long red run that formed the men's downhill course in 1976, when Franz Klammer took ski racing (and the Olympic gold medal) by storm. There is a blue-run variation on this run, and off-piste possibilities. A cable-car rises 1050m from the village. At the top, a chair rises a further 275m to the summit of Patscherkofel at 2245m, and a new fast quad and a couple of drags serve slopes below the cable-car station. There is a short beginner lift at village level, and another a short bus-ride up the hill.

AXAMER LIZUM 1580m

The mountain outpost of the Inn-side village of Axams is a simple ski station and nothing more, but it does have the best slopes around Innsbruck – and the most reliable snow conditions.

Axamer Lizum could scarcely offer a

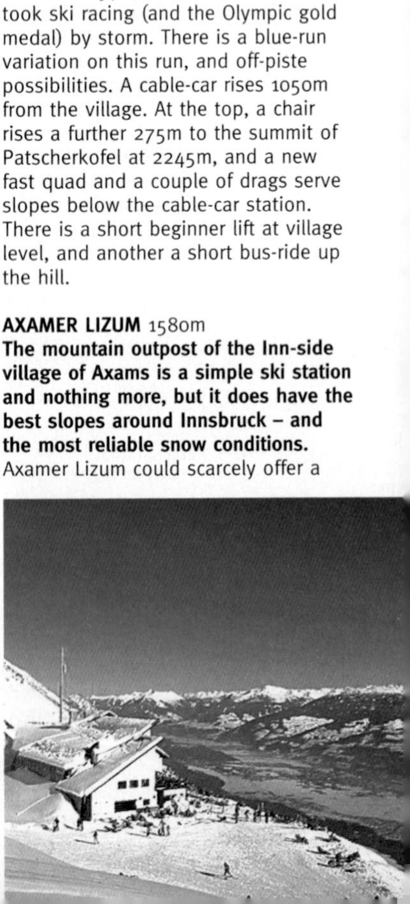

INNSBRUCK TOURISMUS / MICHAEL GILHAUS

From the sunny top cable-car station at Seegrube there are grand views southwards across the Inn valley →

↑ If the bob-run is too scary and ice skating too tricky, there are always the countless toboggan runs

INNSBRUCK TOURISMUS / MICHAEL GILHAUS

sharper contrast to Igls. If offers much more varied slopes and a network of lifts, with the base station at a much higher altitude. The slopes here hosted all the Olympic Alpine events in 1976 except the men's downhill (which was at Igls), and this is the standard local venue for weekend sport – hence the huge car park which is the most prominent feature of the 'resort'.

You can stay up here (there is a 4-star hotel at the lift base, the Lizumerhof), but it's difficult to see why you would want to. (If you want a holiday in a skiing service station with nothing to amuse you in the evenings, you might as well go somewhere that has rather more extensive slopes than these.)

The main slopes on Hoadl (2340m) and Pleisen (2200m) are blues and reds, almost entirely above the trees but otherwise nicely varied. The vertical of the main east-facing slopes above the main lift station is 'only' 700m, but for good skiers at least there is the possibility of a 1300m descent at the end of the day to the outskirts of Axams – an easy 6.5km black run.

On the opposite side of the base station, a chair-lift serves a fairly easy black slope. Beyond it are links to the slopes above Mutters, but the lifts on those slopes are closed for the time being (see below).

There is accommodation not far away at lower altitude in Axams – including four 3-star hotels – and in other nearby villages such as Götzens (one 4-star hotel, two 3-star gasthofs) and Birgitz (two 3-star hotels).

TOURIST OFFICE

Postcode A-6021
t +43 (512) 59850
f 59850-7
info@innsbruck.tvb.co.at
www.tiscover.com/innsbruck

MUTTERS 830m

Almost as close to Innsbruck as Igls, Mutters is a charming rustic village at the foot of long slopes of 900m vertical – the lifts are closed for the moment, awaiting the construction of a new gondola (projected for 2001/02).

Of course, you can still base yourself here and use the other surrounding resorts – and in principle ski back to the village off-piste from Axamer Lizum (a short drive away). The half-dozen hotels in the village divide equally into 3-star and 4-star categories.

TULFES 920m

Tulfes gets rather overshadowed by the Olympic resorts of Igls and Axamer Lizum, but it has some worthwhile runs.

The runs are on the north-facing slopes of Glungezer. A chair-lift from a car park above the village serves red and blue runs of 600m vertical. This leads to a drag up to the tree line serving a red run of 500m vertical. And this in turn leads to two drags serving open red runs from the top height of 2305m – almost 1400m above the village.

Like Igls, the village sits on the shelf on the south side of the Inn valley. There are a dozen hotels and gasthofs, of which the pick is probably the 3-star Neuwirt.

INNSBRUCK TOURISMUS / MICHAEL GILHAUS

Götzens is one of several rustic villages around Innsbruck with comfortable accommodation →

Ischgl

1400m

Pretty, wild party town with snowsure slopes

WHAT IT COSTS

5

HOW IT RATES

The slopes

Snow	****
Extent	***
Experts	***
Intermediates	****
Beginners	**
Convenience	***
Queues	***
Restaurants	**

The rest

Scenery	***
Resort charm	****
Off-slope	***

What's new

The lift system is being continuously improved. In addition to the existing eight high-speed chairs and three gondolas, for 2000/01 they are upgrading a quad to be an eight-seater and installing another quad and another six-pack to replace existing T-bars on the Ischgl side. Over in Samnaun, yet another six-pack is replacing a T-bar.

They are also installing more snowmaking and rebuilding and expanding two mountain restaurants.

In 1999/2000 the resort introduced a refund service if the road to and from the resort is shut because of avalanche danger. They will pay for you to stay in accommodation equivalent to that which you have booked in the resort for as long as the road is closed.

- ➕ Charming old Tirolean village, expanded in sympathetic fashion
- ➕ High slopes with reliable snow
- ➕ Lots of good intermediate runs, extending over the Swiss border to duty-free Samnaun
- ➕ Impressive lift system
- ➕ Very lively après-ski

- ➖ Not ideal for beginners, for various reasons
- ➖ Few tough runs for experts
- ➖ A few T-bars still to be eradicated
- ➖ Few British tour operators go there
- ➖ Wild après-ski may not be to everyone's taste

Ischgl is changing fast. It is a strange mixture of pretty, traditional Tirolean village, pricey, upmarket hotels and drunken, bawdy après-ski, dominated by German and Scandinavian males. On our last visit there were dancing girls, scantily clad in national costume, cavorting on the bar of a plush 4-star hotel at the foot of the slopes from 4pm to 6.30, and drunks weaving their way through the treacherous streets all evening. But the resort remains quite trendy and attracts top-draw entertainers for open-air concerts – Elton John, Diana Ross, Madonna, Bon Jovi, Tina Turner, Bob Dylan and Rod Stewart to name a few.

The slopes are extensive, high, snowsure and ideal for intermediate cruising – some of the best intermediate terrain in Austria. And the efficient lift system now boasts eight high-speed chair-lifts (including six-seaters) and three gondolas – with more to come (including an eight-seater) for next season.

boarding *Ischgl has long been popular with boarders. Between Idalp, the main station above the town, and Idjoch, a chair-ride further up, is a big half-pipe and excellent fun-park. The lifts are generally boarder-friendly; where there is a drag, there's often a chair option. The area is well suited to beginners and intermediates; experts will love Ischgl after fresh snow, but nearby St Anton is even better. The town rocks at night, with some very lively bars.*

The resort

The village is in the long, narrow Paznaun valley and the lower, steep, north-facing slopes and the village get almost no sun in early season.

The main street is virtually traffic-free, with architecture which is a mixture of old original buildings, traditional Tirolean-style hotels and shops, and modern recent additions. The village is long and narrow, but you can walk from one end to the other in 10 minutes or so. But it's far from flat, – and the ups and downs can be quite treacherous when there's snow or ice on the ground. There's now a rather sordid underground walkway from the centre of town to the Fimba gondola which cuts out some nasty hills.

There's a selection of lively bars, an excellent sports centre and a fair number of shops to stroll round. But early evening drunks can be intrusive.

The mountains

Ischgl is a fair-sized, relatively high, snowsure area ideal for intermediates. Most pistes are red, with very few black or easy blue runs. Being able to pop over to duty-free Samnaun in Switzerland adds spice to the area. The local lift pass covers Samnaun and the more expensive Silvretta pass covers this area plus Galtür, and smaller Kappl and See – all linked by an infrequent bus service. Visiting St Anton is easy with a car.

THE SLOPES

Cross-border cruising

The main slopes start at the top of three gondolas. From both ends of the village you can get up to the sunny **Idalp** plateau at 2310m, where the schools and guides meet. At the east end of town the third gondola goes about 300m higher to Pardatschgrat,

MOUNTAIN FACTS

Altitude	1400m-2870m
Lifts	42
Pistes	200km
Blue	25%
Red	60%
Black	15%
Artificial snow	48km
Recco detectors used	

from where it's an easy run down to Idalp – with the alternative of testing red and black runs towards Ischgl. Lifts radiate from Idalp, leading to a wide variety of mainly north-west- and west-facing intermediate runs. Idalp is the hub of the slopes and can get very crowded, especially at ski school meeting time and the end of the day.

A short piste brings you to the lifts serving the **Höllenkar** bowl, leading up to the area's south-western extremity at Palinkopf. There are further lifts beyond Höllenkar, on the Fimbatal.

The mountain ridge above Idalp forms the border with Switzerland. On the Swiss side the hub of activity is **Alp Trida** at 2265m, surrounded by south- and east-facing runs with great views. From here an enjoyable, scenic red run goes down to the hamlet of Compatsch, from where there is a bus to Ravaisch – for the cable-car back – and Samnaun.

From the Palinkopf area there is a very beautiful run to Samnaun itself, down an unspoilt valley. It is not difficult, but doesn't always have ideal snow conditions and is prone to closure by avalanche risk.

SNOW RELIABILITY
Very good

All the slopes, except the runs back to the resort, are above 2000m and much of those on the Ischgl side are north-west- or north-facing. So snow conditions are often good here even when they're poor elsewhere (which can lead to crowds when bus-loads of visitors arrive from lower resorts). There is snowmaking on some runs all the way down from Idjoch to Ischgl.

FOR EXPERTS
Not much on-piste challenge

Ischgl can't compare with nearby St Anton for exciting slopes, and some of the runs marked black on the piste map barely deserve their rating. But there is plenty of beautiful off-piste to be found with a guide – and because there are few experts around, it doesn't get tracked out quickly. The wooded lower slopes of the Fimbatal are delightful in a snowstorm.

The best steep piste is the Fimba Nord run from Pardatschgrat towards Ischgl. If snow is poor near the bottom, you can do the top half of this repeatedly by catching the gondola at the mid-station. A variant will take you down a black to Velilltal, with return by chair-lift or, conditions permitting, an unpisted ski-route back to Ischgl.

FOR INTERMEDIATES
Something for everyone

Most of the slopes are wide, forgiving and ideal for intermediates. No matter what your standard, you should be able to find runs to suit you (though the high slopes can be bleak and windswept in bad weather).

At the tough end of the spectrum our favourite runs are those from

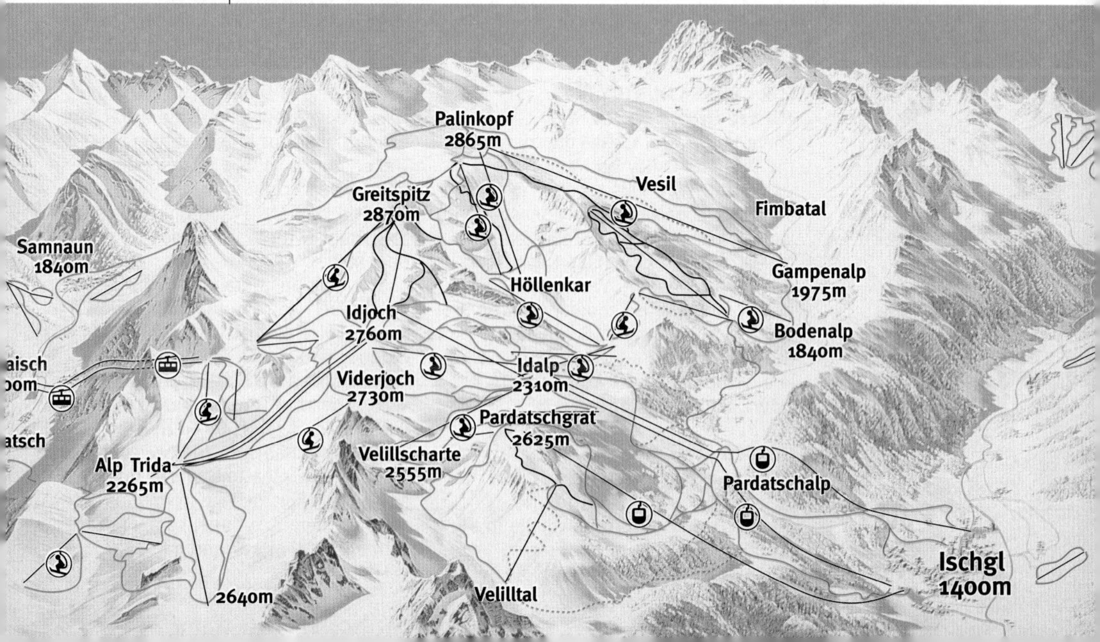

Après-ski starts early in Ischgl – beers on the mountain, followed by dancing girls in town ➔

ISCHGL TO

Palinkopf down to Gampenalp and on along the valley to the secluded restaurant at Bodenalp. You can do the top of these runs repeatedly, taking the chair-lift back up from Gampenalp.

There are also interesting and challenging black runs down the Hollspitz chair, and from both the top and bottom of the drag-lift from Idjoch up to Greitspitz. The reds from Pardatschgrat and Velillscharte down the beautiful valley to Velilltal and the red from Greitspitz into Switzerland are great for quiet, high-speed cruising.

For easier motorway cruising, there is lots of choice, including the Swiss side, where the runs from the border down to Alp Trida should prove ideal. So should the runs that take you back to Idalp on the return journey. But there are frequent moans from intermediates about the red runs down to Ischgl itself; neither is easy, conditions can be tricky, and it can be worryingly crowded at the end of the day with too many people skiing beyond their ability (perhaps helped by a schnapps or two too many).

FOR BEGINNERS
Not ideal

Beginners go up the mountain to Idalp, where there are good, sunny, snowsure nursery slopes and a short beginners' drag-lift. The blue runs on the east side of the bowl offer pleasant progression for fast learners. But away from this area there are few runs ideal for the near-beginner. You'd do better to learn elsewhere and come to Ischgl as an intermediate.

FOR CROSS-COUNTRY
Plenty in the valley

There is 48km of cross-country track in the Paznaun valley between Ischgl, Galtür and Wirl. This tends to be pretty sunless, especially in early season, and is away from the main slopes, which makes meeting downhillers for lunch rather inconvenient. We've also seen people doing cross-country high up in the Fimbatal, towards Gampenalp, though this isn't an official trail. Galtür is a better choice for cross-country skiers, with 60km of loops.

QUEUES
An amazing transformation

Ischgl used to be renowned for its queues to get out of the village in the morning. But now three village gondolas transport 6700 people an hour between them. Once on the mountain high-speed chairs whizz you around and the double-decker cable-car from Samnaun has cut the queues there – you are more likely to have to wait for the next scheduled departure than to queue. One remaining bottleneck to get back to Idalp in late afternoon from the Höllenkar valley should disappear with a new eight-seater chair replacing a quad for 2000/01.

MOUNTAIN RESTAURANTS
Mostly large and crowded

In general, Ischgl isn't the place to go for either culinary delights or charming, small mountain restaurants – most tend to be self-service. The Paznauner Taya, above Bodenalp, is an attractive, rustic chalet, but it gets very crowded. There is table-service upstairs and often a band playing on the terrace. Down in Fimbatal is the quieter rustic restaurant (with-table service) at Bodenalp.

The main restaurant at Idalp has a big self-service cafeteria, and a good table-service alternative (with a sunny outdoor terrace with splendid views). There's also a smaller, crowded self-service nearby. The restaurant at Pardatschgrat tends to be quieter.

The restaurants on the Swiss side at Alp Trida are pleasant, and Marmotte has pricey table service as well as self-service. There is a huge, sunny terrace with an outdoor bar and barbecue.

LIFT PASSES

2000/01 prices in schillings

VIP Skipass
Covers all lifts in Ischgl, Samnaun and Mathon and local buses.

Main pass
1-day pass 415
6-day pass 2060
(low season 1880)

Senior citizens
Over 60: 6-day pass 1620

Children
Under 16: 6-day pass 1270
Under 7: free pass

Short-term passes
Single and multi-ascent passes for main lifts; half-day pass from 11.30 (365); trial pass from 2pm (225).

Alternative periods
5 skiing days in 7 (2015), 10 days in 14 (3215).

Notes VIP Skipass is only available to those staying in Ischgl, Samnaun or Mathon on presentation of guest card. Discounts for physically disabled and groups.

Alternative passes
Silvretta ski pass covers Ischgl, Samnaun, Galtür, Kappl and See (adult 6-day 2560), 66 lifts and use of ski-bus; See is 15km away.

Credit cards No

SCHOOLS/GUIDES

2000/01 prices in schillings

Ischgl-Silvretta
Classes 6 days
4hr: 10.30-12.30 and 1.30-3.30
6 full days: 1650
Children's classes
Ages: from 6
6 full days including lunch: 2130
Private lessons
Half- (2hr) or full-day (4hr)
1300 for half-day; each additional person 200

CHILDCARE

The childcare facilities are all up the mountain at Idalp. There's a ski kindergarten for children aged 3 to 5; from age 5 they go into a slightly more demanding regime in an 'adventure garden'; lunch is included in both arrangements, which are open 6 days a week. Toilet-trained children can be left at a non-ski nursery; lunch is available.

GETTING THERE

Air Innsbruck, transfer 2hr. Zürich, transfer 5hr.

Rail Landeck (30km); frequent buses from station.

SCHOOLS AND GUIDES
Good despite language problems

The school meets up at Idalp and starts very late (10.30 to 12.30 and 1.30 to 3.30) – perhaps to allow people to get over their hangovers from the nightlife! This year we've had a rave report of both adult and children's classes. 'Mixed language but the best instruction I've ever had,' said an adult intermediate. 'Mixed language but excellent – very patient and small group. Can stay with class through lunch,' said a satisfied parent.

As well as normal lessons the school organises off-piste tours – this area is one of the best in the Alps for touring.

FACILITIES FOR CHILDREN
High-altitude options

The childcare facilities are all up at Idalp, but we have no first-hand reports of the service they provide. We have, however, heard from reporters who both stayed at hotel Sonne with six-month-old babies and were delighted with the private baby minder the hotel arranged.

Staying there

On or near the main street or near the bottom of the Pardatsch and Fimba gondolas are the best places to stay. The main lift stations are an easy walk, après-ski is on your doorstep and the new village tunnel makes getting around quick and safe. Beware of accommodation across the bypass road at the far side of the valley floor from the village – though this does have the advantage of getting more sun.

HOW TO GO
Few packages

Very few British tour operators now feature Ischgl – mainly because they find it difficult to get firm allocations of affordable accommodation.

Hotels There is a good selection from luxurious and expensive to basic B&Bs.

(5) **Trofana Royal** One of Austria's most luxurious hotels, with prices to match. Huge, sumptuous spa facilities.

(5) **Madlein** Convenient, modern family-run chalet in traditional style. Reportedly comfortable rooms. Swimming pool, sauna, steam room and solarium. Nightclub and disco.

(5) **Elisabeth** Owned by same family as the Madlein. Right by the Pardatsch gondola with lively après-ski (dancing girls), pool, sauna and steam room.

(5) **Solaria** Near the Madlein and just as luxurious, but with a 'friendly family atmosphere'. Nice wood-panelled wine bar. Swimming pool, fitness room.

(5) **Piz Tasna** Up hill behind church: 'quiet location, friendly, lovely views over village, excellent food'.

(4) **Goldener Adler** Traditional 250-year-old hotel in the middle of village. Wood-panelled and painted restaurant. Sauna, steam room, hot-tub, solarium.

(4) **Sonne** Highly rated by reporters. In the centre of the village. Lively stube, with traditional squeeze-box music. Sauna, steam room, hot-tub, solarium.

(3) **Astoria** Comfortable B&B hotel that faces the main Silvrettabahn gondola.

(3) **Christine** Probably the best B&B in town. Near the centre of town and the Silvretta gondola.

(3) **Erna** Small, central B&B. Firmly recommended by a reporter who has holidayed in Ischgl 20 times.

(2) **Alpenrose** Popular, good-value pension close to Pardatschgratbahn.

(2) **Dorfschmeide** Small, good-value, central B&B recommended by reporter.

Self-catering Some attractive apartments are available.

EATING OUT
Plenty of choice

Our favourite places for dinner are the traditional Austrian restaurants and stubes, of which there's a wide choice. The Goldener Adler probably serves the best food around and has a splendid traditional dining room. The Wippas stube in the Sonne is lively and serves good food. For pizza there's the very popular and 'excellent' Nona and the Trofana-Alm, which is as much a bar as a restaurant, and for fondue there's the Kitzloch with its galleried tables overlooking the dance floor. La Bamba is a restaurant-bar serving Mexican specialities. The Grillalm, Salner and Tirol are also popular eateries.

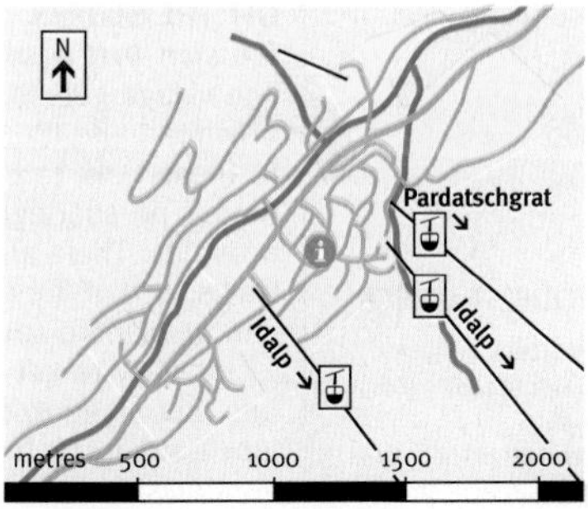

The runs back to Ischgl are steep, shady and wooded, in contrast to the gentle, sunny, open bowls above →

ISCHGL TO

ACTIVITIES

Indoor Silvretta Centre (bowling, billiards, swimming pool, sauna, steam baths, solarium), museum, library, cinema, gallery, tennis courts

Outdoor Curling, skating, sleigh rides, hiking tours, 7km floodlit toboggan run

TOURIST OFFICE

Postcode A-6561
t +43 (5444) 5266
f 5636
tvb.ischgl@netway.at
www.ischgl.com

APRES-SKI
Very lively

Ischgl is one of the liveliest resorts in the Alps, from early afternoon on. Lots of revellers are still in their ski boots late in the evening. On our latest visit there did seem to be many more men than women – lots of them young and fairly drunk by mid-evening.

The Kitzloch, at the bottom of the run down from Pardatschgrat, is one of the liveliest places at the end of the day – dancing on tables and communal congas are common. Niki's Stadl across the road is worth a visit too, with comedy spots as well as music. The Elisabeth hotel by the Pardatschgratbahn has popular indoor and outdoor bars with scantily-clad dancing girls. The Post hotel also has a busy outdoor bar beneath a giant umbrella. The Sunn-Alm at the hotel Sonne gets crowded and has live music. The Kuhstahl under the Sporthotel Silvretta and Fire & Ice over the road are both lively all evening. Guxa and Allegra liven up after dinner and the Golden Eagle is 'good for live bands'. The dancing girls from the Elisabeth move to the Wunderbar at the hotel Madlein in the evenings and wear even less. Our favourite club was the place underneath the hotel Post which has ancient Roman theme decor.

OFF THE SLOPES
No sun but a nice pool

The village gets little sun in the middle of winter, and the resort is best suited to those keen to hit the slopes. But there's no shortage of off-slope activities. There are 24km of marked walks, a 7km floodlit toboggan run and a splendid sports centre.

It's easy to get around the valley by bus. But meeting on the slopes for lunch, except at the tops of the gondolas, is a problem for pedestrians.

STAYING DOWN THE VALLEY
Too far without a car

Ischgl is fairly isolated. Landeck is the nearest big town. It has good shopping and is well positioned for trips to the surrounding resorts, including Serfaus, Nauders, Sölden and St Anton.

Galtür 1585m

You could consider staying up the valley instead, in Galtür. It has hit the headlines for the last couple of years because of avalanche disasters – last season's really nowhere near the village, the centre of which has been rebuilt and fortified against further avalanches since the 1999 disaster.

It is a charming, peaceful, traditional village clustered around a pretty little church, amid impressive mountain scenery. Quieter, sunnier and cheaper than Ischgl, it is a good base for a quiet family holiday. There are good 3-star and 4-star hotels – the Almhof, Ballunspitz and Flüchthorn have been recommended. The nightlife is quiet, but there are a couple of jolly bars.

Galtür's own slopes are not particularly challenging, but its black runs are ideal for intermediates, and there are fine nursery slopes, plus plenty of 'graduation' pistes for improvers. The school has a high reputation – and we've had a good report about its teaching of children.

If you intend to visit Ischgl a lot, bear in mind that the bus service isn't very frequent and finishes early.

Off-slope facilities are limited, but there's a natural ice rink and a sports centre with pool, tennis and squash.

Samnaun 1840m

Samnaun is a small, quiet village, and its duty-free status makes it a useful stopover for restocking on booze and tobacco. A reporter warns that most duty-free outlets are closed on Sunday.

Kitzbühel 760m

Wonderful town and extensive slopes, but unreliable snow

WHAT IT COSTS

3

HOW IT RATES

The slopes

Snow	**
Extent	****
Experts	***
Intermediates	****
Beginners	**
Convenience	**
Queues	**
Restaurants	****

The rest

Scenery	***
Resort charm	****
Off-slope	*****

What's new

A high-speed quad replaced the Talsen T-bar, at Jochberg, for 1999/2000. Extensive snowmaking was also installed in the area. There was also a new snowboard park on the Kitzbüheler Horn.

2000/01 sees the Pengelstein lift upgraded to a covered fast quad. And snowmaking is being further extended around the slopes.

- ⊕ Large, attractive, varied slopes offering a sensation of travel both on- and off-piste
- ⊕ Beautiful medieval town centre (but see minus points)
- ⊕ Vibrant nightlife
- ⊕ Plenty of off-slope amenities, both for the sporty and the not-so-sporty
- ⊕ A surprisingly large amount of cheap and cheerful accommodation
- ⊕ Jolly mountain restaurants

- ⊖ Unreliable snow (though increasing amount of snowmaking)
- ⊖ Surprisingly little expert terrain
- ⊖ Disjointed slopes, with quite a lot of bussing to get around them
- ⊖ Town's charm spoilt by heavy traffic
- ⊖ Disappointing nursery area
- ⊖ Crowded pistes

Kitzbühel is an impressive name to drop in the pub. Every *Ski Sunday* viewer knows that the Hahnenkamm race-course is the most challenging on the World Cup circuit, helping the resort to cultivate a reputation as a rather special place. But the race course is untypical of Kitzbühel's slopes – and there is nothing very special about coping with icy, slushy or bare slopes. We have visited Kitz countless times, and rarely found decent snow on the lower slopes. It does of course get good snow at times and has invested serious money in snowmaking. But Kitzbühel's low altitude means that its problems won't go away.

The resort is very far from exclusive. It has its expensive, elegant hotels, but it also has a huge amount of hotel and guest-house accommodation that is quite inexpensive – and not surprisingly attracts quite a few low-budget visitors, many of whom are young and intent on a good time.

We have received fewer reports on Kitzbühel lately, but enthusiasts enjoy its unique combination of historic town and extensive slopes.

KITZBÜHEL TO

The Trattalm bowl on the Kitzbüheler Horn is gloriously sunny, and almost 1000m above the town →

LIFT PASSES

2000/01 prices in schillings

Kitzbühel
Covers all lifts in Kitzbühel, Kirchberg, Jochberg, Pass Thurn, Bichlalm and Aschau, linking buses, and swimming pool.

Main pass
1-day pass 430
6-day pass 2080 £119
(low season 1915)

Senior citizens
Over 60: 6-day pass 1665

Children
Under 19: 6-day pass 1665
Under 15: 6-day pass 1040
Under 6: free pass

Short-term passes
Single ascent tickets for the major lifts; hourly refunds on day tickets; day tickets can be bought in half-hourly steps from 11am.

Notes 5% reduction for groups of over 15 people. The season pass is valid in Gstaad and Davos/Klosters.

Alternative passes
Kitzbüheler Alpenskipass covers 5 large ski areas – Schneewinkl (St Johann), Ski Region Kitzbühel, Ski Welt Wilder Kaiser, Bergbahnen Wildschönau and Alpbachtal (adult 6-day 2200).

MOUNTAIN FACTS

Altitude	800m-2000m
Lifts	60
Pistes	158km
Blue	50%
Red	42%
Black	8%
Artificial snow	57km
Recco detectors used	

boarding *Kitzbühel was slow off the mark with boarding, keeping to its image of World Cup Downhill venue/skier party town. However, things have changed, and now there is a half-pipe, fun-park and boarder-cross course on the Kitzbüheler Horn, an area with few drag-lifts. Half of all lifts in the area are drags, but all main lifts are gondolas and chair-lifts – the area suits beginners and intermediates well. The town is lively at night, with plenty of bars and clubs; the Londoner Pub is the main place with boarder appeal.*

The resort

Set at a junction of broad, pretty valleys, Kitzbühel is a large, animated town, with separate areas of local slopes on each side. The beautiful walled medieval centre – complete with quaint church, cobbled streets and attractively painted buildings – is traffic-free during the day and a compelling place to stay.

But the much-publicised old town is only a small part of Kitzbühel; the resort spreads widely, and busy roads surround the old town reducing the charm factor markedly.

Visitors used to peaceful little Austrian villages are likely to be disappointed by its urban nature. But for those who like it, the sophisticated, glitzy, towny ambience is what 'makes' Kitzbühel. There are swanky shop windows to gaze in and cafés to while away the time in. It is also handily placed for visiting Salzburg and Innsbruck, as well as lots of nearby resorts covered by the Kitzbüheler Alpenskipass.

The mountains

Snow and lift queues permitting, the mountain suits intermediates well. Although experts can find things to do, there are many better places for them. Kitz's total area is large, and includes access to sizeable Kirchberg. Lots of resorts in the Tirol can be reached by car or train – and if you buy the wide-ranging Kitzbüheler Alpenskipass you are covered to visit many of them.

THE SLOPES
Big but bitty

Kitzbühel's slopes are divided into four areas – three sizeable and one much smaller. Two of the major areas are just connected by piste in one direction. All are served by a reasonably effective bus service.

The **Hahnenkamm** is by far the largest, and accessible from the town. It is reached via a gondola or two chair-lifts, from the top of which a choice of steep and gentle runs lead down into Ehrenbachgraben; from there several chair-lifts fan out. One takes you to the gentle peak of Steinbergkogel, the high point of the sector at 1975m. Beyond is the slightly lower peak of Pengelstein. On the far side of Pengelstein several long runs lead down to the west of the resort; shuttle-buses link their end-points at Aschau and Skirast with Obwiesen, Kirchberg and Kitz. Another lift from Ehrenbachgraben goes up to Ehrenbachhöhe, the focal point of the sector, linked by lifts and runs to Kirchberg and Klausen, on the road between Kitzbühel and Kirchberg.

Pengelstein is the start of the 'ski safari' route to the higher area of **Jochberg-Pass Thurn**. The piste from Pengelstein finishes at Trampelpfad, a short walk or taxi-ride from the Jochberg lifts. A parallel piste from Steinbergkogel ends at Hechenmoos – more than a walk from Jochberg, but you can get the shuttle-bus from here. Jochberg-Pass Thurn is well worth the excursion, with better snow and fewer crowds than the local slopes – but runs are short and there are lots of T-bars. Pass Thurn is the terminus of the shuttle-bus, where it is worth ending the day to ensure a bus seat.

The very small **Bichlalm** area is of little interest except for getting away from the crowds and working on your suntan. When conditions are good, the top station (Stuckkogel) accesses an off-piste route to Fieberbrunn. A train returns you to Kitz.

The **Kitzbüheler Horn** is equally sunny, with repercussions on snow-cover, but many slopes are above the 1270m-high mid-station, accessed by a modern gondola starting close to the railway station, but some way from the centre. The second stage leads to the sunny Trattalm bowl at around 1660m, but the alternative cable-car takes you up to the summit of the Horn, from where a fine, solitary east-facing piste leads down into the Raintal on the far side, with a chair-lift returning to the ridge. There are widely spread blue, red and black runs back towards town.

The piste map has recently been greatly improved by the addition of altitudes and mountain restaurants. And a reporter praises 'the Bergbahn Info people in bright jackets at the main lift stations who are there to offer advice on closures, directions etc'.

SNOW RELIABILITY
More snowmaking now

In a normal year, snow on the lower slopes can be thin or non-existent at times. The problem is that Kitzbühel's slopes have one of the lowest average heights in the Alps. The expansion of snowmaking in recent years has improved matters when it's cold enough to make snow – major runs right down to Kitzbühel, Kirchberg, Klausen and Jochberg are now covered and more is planned for 2000/01. But many slopes still remain unprotected. The best plan is to book late when snow-cover is known to be good. Otherwise, take a car for snow-searching excursions.

FOR EXPERTS
Plan to go off-piste

Steep pistes are concentrated in the ring of runs down into the bowl of Ehrenbachgraben, the most direct of which are challenging mogul fields. Nearby is the Streif red, the basis for the famous Hahnenkamm Downhill race – see the feature panel over the page. When conditions allow there is plenty of off-piste potential, some of it safely close to pistes, some requiring a guide.

FOR INTERMEDIATES
Lots of alternatives

The Hahnenkamm area is prime intermediate terrain. Good intermediates will want to do the World Cup downhill run, of course. And the long 1000m-vertical blue to Klausen from Ehrenbachhöhe is also satisfying. The long runs down to the Kirchberg–Aschau road make a fine end to the day; earlier, they are rather spoilt by the lack of return lifts.

The east-facing Raintal run on the Horn is an excellent slope for good intermediates to hone their skills on. The long runs back to town from the ridge don't offer much challenge.

The runs above Jochberg are particularly good for mixed abilities. Less adventurous types have some fine runs either side of Pengelstein, including the safari route, and the Hieslegg piste above Aschau. The short high runs at the top of the Pass Thurn area are ideal if you're more timid. There are also easy reds down to both Pass Thurn and Jochberg. Much of the Horn and Bichlalm is also cruising territory, including very long glides to town when snow conditions allow.

FOR BEGINNERS
Not ideal

The Hahnenkamm nursery slopes are no more than adequate, and prone to poor snow conditions. The Horn has a high, sunny nursery-like section, and precocious learners will soon be cruising home from there on the long Hagstein piste. There are plenty of other easy runs to progress to.

SCHOOLS/GUIDES

2000/01 prices in schillings

Hahnenkamm
Classes 6 days
4hr: 2hr am and pm
6 full days 1600
Children's classes
Ages: up to 14
6 full days 1850
Private lessons
On request.

Kitzbüheler Horn
Classes 6 days
4hr: 2hr am and pm
6 full days 1650
Children's classes
6 full days 1800
Private lessons
On request.

Red Devils
Classes 6 days
4hr: 2hr am and pm
6 full days 1600
Children's classes
Ages: 4 to 11
6 full days 1850
Private lessons
On request.

Total
Classes 6 days
4hr: 9.30-11.30 and 1pm-3pm
6 full days 1600
Children's classes
Ages: 4 to 11
6 full days 1750
Private lessons
On request.

CHILDCARE

All four schools cater for small children, offering lunchtime supervision as well as tuition on baby slopes – generally from age 3. There is no non-ski nursery, but babysitters and nannies can be hired.

THE HAHNENKAMM DOWNHILL

Kitzbühel's Hahnenkamm downhill race, held in mid-January each year, is the toughest as well as one of the most famous on the World Cup circuit. On the race weekend the town is packed and there is a real carnival atmosphere, with bands, people in traditional costumes and huge (and loud) cowbells everywhere.

The race itself starts with a steep icy section before you hit the famous Mausfalle and Steilhang, where even Franz Klammer used to get worried. The course (now thankfully served by snow-guns) starts near the top of the new gondola and drops 860m to finish amid the noise and celebrations right on the edge of town. Ordinary mortals can try all but the steepest parts of the course after the race weekend, whenever the snow is good enough – it's an easy red run mostly. But the course is normally closed from the start of the season until after the race.

FOR CROSS-COUNTRY
Plentiful but low

There are nearly 35km of trails dotted about, but all are at valley level and prone to lack of snow. When the snow is good, try the quiet Reith area.

QUEUES
Still a drawback

Replacing the old Hahnenkamm cable-car with a speedy six-person gondola has vastly reduced morning queues. However, elsewhere on the mountain bad snow conditions can lead to queues. In good snow, however, reporters say they've had queue-free slopes even in high season. But both the Horn and the Hahnenkamm can have overcrowded pistes. Reporters have also complained about warning signs for avalanche danger and closed or icy pistes being in German only.

MOUNTAIN RESTAURANTS
A highlight

'One of the reasons we keep going back,' says one of our Kitz regulars. There are many restaurants, now thankfully marked on the piste map. Avoid the large self-service places and stick to the smaller huts. On the Horn the Hornköpfl-Hütte has good food, reasonable prices, sunny terraces and few queues. Alpenhaus is good for a lively lunch, the Gipfelhaus (recently renovated) is quieter with 'good views and food'. The 'busy' Alderhütte has also been recommended. The Bichlalm in the next-door sector is also good if you want some peace. At Pass Thurn–Jochberg the Jägerwurzhütte and Trattenbachalm are recommended, and Panoramaalm has great views. The Ochsalm, Seidalm and Brandseit in the Hahnenkamm sector are good – and there are many others. The new (rather pricey) Hochkitzbühel table-service restaurant at the top of the gondola has good food, but the service is 'not brilliant'.

SCHOOLS AND GUIDES
Off-piste guiding a bargain

There are now half-a-dozen competing schools. The original school, Rudi Sailer's famous Red Devils, runs regular off-piste guiding groups. In contrast to the 200-strong Red Devils, the other schools emphasise their small scale and personal nature. Ernst Hinterseer's Total school is the best established of these and includes video analysis. A reporter says: 'Never seen so many British instructors. Good reports all round.'

FACILITIES FOR CHILDREN
Not an ideal choice

Provided your children are able and willing to take classes, you can deposit them at any of the schools. The Total school has supervision until 5pm.

Staying there

The size of Kitz makes choice of location important. The old town is charming, and gives you most options. It's reasonably equidistant from the two main lift stations either side of town, both being within walking distance. However, the Hahnenkamm is very much the larger (and more snowsure) of the two areas, and many visitors prefer to be as close as possible to its gondola. But the Hahnenkamm nursery slopes are often lacking in snow, and then novices are taken up the Horn.

The bus service around town is good, and 'extra buses are put on when needed,' says a reporter. Having

GETTING THERE

Air Salzburg, transfer $1\frac{1}{2}$hr. Munich, transfer 2hr. Innsbruck, transfer $1\frac{1}{2}$hr.

Rail Mainline station in resort. Postbus every 15 min from station.

ACTIVITIES

Indoor Aquarena Centre (2 pools, sauna, solarium, mud baths, aerated baths, underwater massage – free entry with lift pass), indoor tennis hall, 2 squash courts, fitness centre, beauty centre, bridge, indoor riding school, local theatre, library, museum, chess club, casino

Outdoor Ice rink (curling and skating), horse-riding, sleigh rides, toboggan run, ballooning, ski-bobs, flying school, wildlife park, hang-gliding, paragliding, 40km of cleared walking paths (free guided tours), copper mine tours

a car is very useful for quick access to the Pass Thurn–Jochberg area, the Klausen gondola and for making the most of the Kitzbüheler Alpenskipass.

HOW TO GO
Mainly hotels and pensions

Kitz is essentially a hotel resort, and UK package offerings reflect this.

Chalets A few tour operators run chalet-hotels here.

Hotels There is an enormous choice, especially of 4-star and 3-star hotels.

((((5 **Tennerhof** Much-extended, luxuriously converted farmhouse in big garden with renowned restaurant. Beautiful panelled rooms.

((((5 **Schloss Lebenberg** Modernised 'castle' with smart pool, and free shuttle-bus to make up for secluded but inconvenient location. Free nursery for kids aged 3-plus.

(((4 **Weisses Rössl** Smartly traditional, with welcoming bar–sitting room (open fire); recently awarded its fifth star.

(((4 **Goldener Grief** Historic inn, elegantly renovated; vaulted lobby-sitting area, panelled bar, casino.

(((4 **Jägerwirt** Modern 'chalet' that gets a rave report for helpful staff and 'wonderful food'. Not ideally placed.

((3 **Schweizerhof** Comfortable chalet in unbeatable position right by Hahnenkamm gondola.

((3 **Maria Theresia** Big, comfortable modern chalet.

((3 **Hahnenhof** Small converted farmhouse retaining rustic charm.

((3 **Strasshofer** An old favourite – 'central, family-run, friendly, good food, quiet rooms at back'.

(1 **Mühlbergerhof** Small, friendly pension in good position.

Self-catering Although there are plenty of apartments in Kitz, very few are available through tour operators. Many of the best (and best-positioned) places are attached to hotels. The 4-star Garni Ludwig and 3-star Garni Christophorus, Haselsberger and Pension Hillebrand all have good apartments close to the gondola.

EATING OUT
Something for everyone

There is a wide range of restaurants to suit all pockets, including pizzerias and fast food outlets (even McDonald's). Some 4-star hotels have excellent restaurants; the Maria Theresia is recommended. But the Unterberger Stuben ('excellent but expensive' says a reporter) vies with Schwedenkapelle for the 'best in town' award. Good, cheaper places include the Huberbräu-Stüberl, Sportstüberl and Zinnkrug. Goldene Gams has changed from serving traditional Austrian to 'modern French cuisine', says a reporter. On Fridays and Saturdays you can dine at the top of the Hahnenkamm gondola.

APRES-SKI
A main attraction

Nightlife is a great selling point of Kitz. There's something for all tastes, from throbbing bars full of teenagers to quiet little places popular with local workers, nice cafés full of calories and self-consciously smart spots for fur-coat flaunting.

Much of the action starts quite late; immediately after the slopes close the town is jolly without being much livelier than many other Tirolean resorts – try the Mockingstube, near

KITZBÜHEL TO

The medieval town – largely traffic-free during the day – really is something special ➔

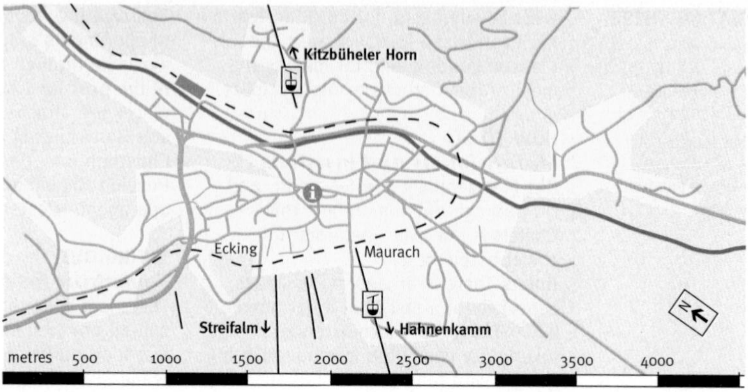

the gondola, which often has live music. Cafés Praxmair, Kortschak and Langer are among the most atmospheric tea-time places for cakes and pastries. Stamperl is a very lively bar. Later the lively Big Ben British pub, American-style Highways bar and Das Lichtl get packed. Seppi's Pub is recommended for sport on TV, pizzas and the eccentric owner with his 'huge moustache'. Royal, Olympia and Take 5 are the main discos. The Londoner Pub is the loudest, most crowded place in town, with sing-along and dance-along music: 'Crowded, smoky, ridiculously expensive but great,' says one of our regular reporters.

Tour reps organise plenty of the usual events, and there's also a casino for more formal entertainment. A reporter says there's 'table dancing at the Go Go Bar Café Romantica 2km out of town – we weren't tempted.'

OFF THE SLOPES
Plenty to do

The Aquarena leisure centre is covered by the lift pass and very impressive, with two pools, sauna, solarium and various health activities. One of the many other diversions is a surprisingly worthwhile museum. The railway also affords plenty of scope for excursions (eg to Salzburg and Innsbruck) and reps organise coach trips.

TOURIST OFFICE

Postcode A-6370
t +43 (5356) 621550
f 62307
info@kitzbuehel.com
www.kitzbuehel.com

Kirchberg 850m

Anyone going to Kirchberg expecting a quiet, rustic little haven from which to access Kitzbühel's slopes will be sadly disappointed. Kirchberg has a lot in common with its neighbour: it is a large, spread out, crowded, lively, commercialised village very popular with young Brits, Scandinavians and Germans. It suffers similar traffic congestion and inconvenient layout to its famous neighbour, without the compensating medieval town centre. Nor are prices much lower here.

There is a choice of schools: here as in Kitz there is a Total school. Meeting points are spread about. Beginners, for example, start over on the Gaisberg mountain, on the opposite side of town from the main area. There are non-ski and ski kindergartens at Obwiesen, 2.5km out of town, near the Elisabeth–Zeinlach hotel complex. And the village Krabbelstube crèche will accept babies.

Like Kitz, Kirchberg is essentially a hotel-pension resort, with a wide choice of modern chalet-style places available. Choice of location is important. Beginners have slopes within walking distance of the village, but the more experienced wishing to avoid crowded bus journeys should look for a hotel a couple of kilometres out of town near the Maierl chair.

The 3-star Elisabeth and Zeinlach twin-hotel complex, even further out at Obwiesen, provides the best slope-side accommodation. These hotels are particularly good for families, with shared games and playroom amenities, and kindergartens on hand (see above). Those preferring a central village location will appreciate the 4-star Tiroler Adler, which has a fine leisure complex. The 3-star Sporthotel Landhaus Brauns is also comfortable and has a good position by the nursery slopes.

Nightlife is very lively both in bars and in discos, to the point of rowdiness at times. Good bars include the traditionally Austrian Kupferstubn, the Boomerang, the Londoner (with frequent live music), Gismo and Fuchslokal.

Lech 1450m

Charming luxury for the beautiful people

WHAT IT COSTS

6

HOW IT RATES

The slopes

Snow	****
Extent	****
Experts	****
Intermediates	****
Beginners	****
Convenience	***
Queues	***
Restaurants	**

The rest

Scenery	***
Resort charm	****
Off-slope	***

What's new

For 1999/2000 there was a new hands-free electronic lift pass system. A magic carpet lift was installed to cut out the climb from the ski bridge to the Zürsersee fast quad. Pavements were widened and roads narrowed in the centre of the village.

From 2000/01 the Kriegerhorn-Zuger Hochlicht cable-car will not work (the area is served by an alternative chair). The old Rüfikopf cable-car will get new panoramic cabins and the restaurant at the top will be refurbished. The Hasensprung chair will be speeded up by adding a moving carpet to speed loading.

LECH TO

The American we visited Lech with in January said it was his idea of 'everything a cute Alpine village should be – simply awesome!' ➔

- ➕ Picturesque Alpine village
- ➕ Fair-sized, largely intermediate piste network plus good off-piste terrain
- ➕ Easy access to the tougher slopes of St Anton and other Arlberg resorts
- ➕ Sunny slopes with excellent snow record and extensive snowmaking
- ➕ Lively après-ski scene
- ➕ Very chic resort, with some very comfortable hotels

- ➖ Very expensive, and credit cards not always accepted by hotels, shops, restaurants or lift pass office
- ➖ Surprising dearth of atmospheric mountain restaurants other than in the mini-resort of Oberlech
- ➖ Very few tough pistes
- ➖ Blue runs back to the village are rather steep for nervous novices
- ➖ Still a few antiquated lifts

Lech and its higher neighbour Zürs are the most glamorous and expensive resorts in Austria. Their shared slopes could fairly easily be linked with those of St Anton – but then their rich and royal visitors would be forced to mingle with hoi polloi from their equally famous but less exclusive neighbour.

Lech is for those who don't mind fur coats, do like well groomed, snowsure, cruising pistes, and are content to enjoy a winter holiday in pampered comfort and style in a traditional Alpine village. There are challenging slopes available (mainly off-piste) and the tougher slopes of St Anton are only a short bus- or car-ride away. But it is the part-timer, who enjoys the après and the strolling as much as the winter sports, who will get the most out of the resort. It helps to have a deep pocket.

boarding *Lech's upper-crust image has not stood in the way of its snowboarding development, and it continues to improve its facilities. Chairs and cable-cars, with hardly any drags, and perfectly manicured pistes make the area ideal for beginner and intermediate boarders – lessons are with the local ski school. There's also a good fun-park above the town at the Schlegelkopf, with jumps, a boarder-cross and a half-pipe, and more confident boarders should hire a guide and track some powder. The town slips back to being an up-market ski destination in the evenings – bars tend to be in 4-star hotels populated by 'beautiful people'.*

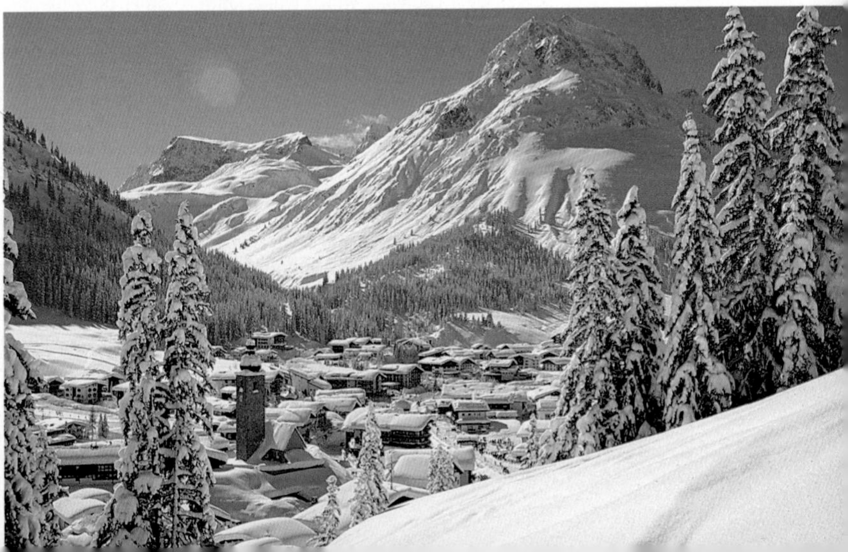

MOUNTAIN FACTS

Altitude 1450m-2450m

Arlberg region

Lifts	84
Pistes	260km
Blue	25%
Red	50%
Black	25%
Artificial snow	37km

Recco detectors used

LIFT PASSES

2000/01 prices in schillings

Arlberg Ski pass
Covers all St Anton, St Christoph, Lech, Zürs and Stuben lifts, and linking bus between Rauz and Zürs.
Beginners Limited day passes covering a few lifts; adventurous second-week skiers need an area pass.
Main pass
1-day pass 485
6-day pass 2230
(low season 2010)
Senior citizens
Over 65 male, 60 female: 6-day pass 1950
Children
Under 15: 6-day pass 1450
Under 6: 'Snowman' ticket
Short-term passes
Single ascent tickets on some lifts throughout Arlberg. Half-day tickets (adults 360) from noon, afternoon 'taster' tickets (205) from 3pm. Day tickets have by-the-hour reimbursement.
Notes 6-day pass prices are for Arlberg 'Special' pass, available to adults and children staying in the Arlberg area (normal adult 6-day pass, 2410). Main pass also covers Klösterle (10 lifts), 7km west of Stuben. Discounts during wedel, firn and snow crystal weeks.

The resort

Like other glitz-and-glamour resorts, such as Courchevel and Zermatt, Lech and Zürs attract some visitors who simply want to be seen, but also have great attractions for the rest of us.

The clientele is largely German and Austrian, with very few Brits. The fur coat count is one of the highest in the Alps. And it helps to be able to afford a helicopter transfer out: Lech lies in a small, high valley reachable in winter only by driving over the Flexen Pass from Stuben (Zürs is just below the top of the pass). This road can be closed for days on end after an exceptional snowfall.

The village offers cosy old-world Austrian charm with modern convenience. While some of the best hotels are right in the centre, they are not obtrusive. The village remains picturesque despite its growth and popularity – there is a domed church and covered wooden bridge over the gurgling river that runs down one side of the main street; on the other side are enticing and pricey shops. In good weather the centre is a picture of open-air cafés, dancing in the street and a fashion show of fur coats and horse-drawn carriages, with good views of the mountains on all sides.

The top hotels are owned by a few families and have large numbers of regular guests who come back year after year.

Oberlech is a small, traffic-free collection of 4-star hotels and chalets set on the piste above Lech and served by a cable-car which works until 1am, allowing access to Lech's much livelier nightlife and shopping. If you stay there, luggage is delivered efficiently from Lech to your hotel via underground tunnels, leaving you unburdened for the short, snowy walk from the cable-car.

Zug is a hamlet, 3km from Lech, which connects with the Lech–Oberlech area. The small amount of accommodation is mostly bed and breakfast with one 4-star hotel, the Rote Wand, which serves the best Kaiserschmarren (a delicious pancake and fruit dessert) in the Arlberg. From Lech, Zug makes a good night out: you can take a horse-drawn sleigh for a fondue at the Rote Wand, Klösterle or Auerhahn, followed by a visit to the Rote Wand disco.

The mountains

Lech and Zürs are working hard on improving their links. There are still some old two-seaters, but new fast chairs have improved the network considerably in recent years. The runs, with a lot of gentle wide blues and reds, flatter leisurely cruisers and suit most of the clientele. As well as Lech and Zürs, the Arlberg lift pass covers St Anton, St Christoph and Stuben, all reachable by car or bus.

THE SLOPES

One-way traffic

The main slopes centre on **Oberlech**, 300m above Lech, and are reached from the village by chair-lifts as well as the cable-car. The wide, open pistes are perfect for intermediates and there is also lots of off-piste potential for experts. **Zuger Hochlicht** is the highest point of this sector, at 2380m, and views from here, and Kriegerhorn below, are stunning. As at St Anton, the toughest runs here are now classed as 'ski routes' or 'high-touring routes' rather than pistes, with all the resulting confusion (see the St Anton chapter). Most of the official pistes back to the main slopes from Zuger Hochlicht are gentle blues, but the only way down to Zug is one of the ski routes.

The linked Lech–Zürs–Lech circuit can be done only in a clockwise direction. To get to Zürs you take the **Rüfikopf** cable-car from the centre of Lech. From the top there are long cruisey pistes, via a couple of lifts, down to Zürs. In school holidays and other busy periods the linking lifts and runs on the circuit can get crowded.

All the slopes at Zürs are above the tree-line, with two areas on either side of the village. The more difficult runs are off the top of **Trittkopf** – on the same side as the runs down from Lech. On the other side of the valley, chairs go up to **Seekopf** and Zürsersee with intermediate runs down. There's a chair up to **Muggengrat** (at 2450m the highest point of the Zürs area) from below Zürsersee. This has a blue back under it and a lovely long red away from all the lifts back down to Zürs. But most people head for the Madloch chair. This accesses the long itinerary run all the way back to Lech. You can peel off part-way down and head for Zug and the chair-lift up to the Kriegerhorn above Oberlech.

A LITTLE HISTORY

The first settlers in Lech came from the Valais region of Switzerland in the 11th century. Skiing started in the early 1900s. The Lech ski school was founded in 1925 and the first T-bar was built in 1939. Patrick Ortlieb, Olympic Downhill champion at Albertville in 1992, was born and learned his skiing in Oberlech.

SNOW RELIABILITY

One of Austria's best

Lech and Zürs both get a lot of snow, but Austrian weather station records show a big difference between them despite their proximity. Lech gets an average of almost 8m of snow between December and March, almost twice as much as St Anton and three times as much as Kitzbühel, but Zürs gets half as much again as Lech. The altitude is high by Austrian resort standards and there is excellent snowmaking on Lech's sunny lower slopes.

This combination, together with excellent grooming, means that the Lech–Zürs area normally has good coverage from December until April. And the snow is frequently better here than on St Anton's predominantly south-facing slopes.

FOR EXPERTS

Off-piste is main attraction

There are only two black pistes on the map, although there are the two types of off-piste route referred to above. The official recommendation is to visit these with a guide, though many ignore the advice. The truth is that experts will get a lot more out of the area if they do have a guide, as there is plenty of excellent off-piste other than the marked routes, much of it accessed by long traverses. Especially in fresh snow, it can be wonderful.

Many of the best runs start from Zuger Hochlicht or the Steinmähder chair, which finishes just below it. Some routes involve a short climb to access bowls of untracked powder. From the Kriegerhorn there are shorter off-piste runs down towards Lech and a very scenic long run down to Zug. One of the problems with all these, however, is that most are south or west-facing and can suffer from getting a lot of sun.

At the end of the season, when the snow is deep and settled, the off-piste off the shoulder of the Wöstertäli from the top of the Rüfikopf cable-car down to Lech can be superb. There are also good runs from the top of the Trittkopf cable-car in the Zürs sector, including a tricky one above the Flexen Pass down to Stuben.

Experts will also enjoy cruising some of the steeper red runs and will want to visit St Anton during the week, where there are more challenging pistes as well as more off-piste.

Heli-lifts are available to a couple of remote spots.

Zürs 172

Lech 1450

Stuben 140

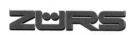

FOR INTERMEDIATES
Flattering variety for all

The pistes in the Oberlech area are nearly all immaculately groomed blue runs, the upper ones above the trees, the lower ones in wide swathes cut through them. It is ideal territory for leisurely cruisers not wanting surprises. And even early intermediates will be able to take on the circuit to Zürs and back, the only significant red involved being the beautiful long (and not at all difficult) 'ski route' back to Lech from the top of the Madloch chair in Zürs.

More adventurous intermediates should take the fast Steinmähder chair to just below Zuger Hochlicht, or the cable-car all the way up, and from there take the scenic red run all the way to Zug (the latter part on a 'ski route' rather than a piste). And if you feel ready to have a stab at some off-piste, Lech is a good place to try it.

Zürs has many more interesting red runs, on both sides of the valley. We particularly like the west-facing reds down from the Trittkopf cable-car and the usually quiet red run back to Zürs from the Muggengrat chair, which starts in a steep bowl.

FOR BEGINNERS
Easy slopes in all areas

The main nursery slopes are in Oberlech, but there is also a nice isolated area in the village dedicated purely to beginners. There are good, easy runs to progress to, both above and below Oberlech.

FOR CROSS-COUNTRY
Picturesque valley trail

There are two cross-country trails in Lech. The longer one is 15km; it begins in the centre of town and leads through the beautiful Zug valley, following the Lech river and ending up outside Zug. The other begins behind the church and goes to Stubenbach (another hamlet in the Lech area). In Zürs there is a 3km track starting at Zürs and going to the Flexen Pass. This starts at 1600m and climbs to 1800m.

QUEUES
Some bottlenecks at peak times

The region proudly boasts that it limits numbers on the slopes to 14,000 a day for a more enjoyable experience, and there have been significant lift improvements in recent years. On our visit last season we thought traffic on the circuit through Zürs, particularly, has improved thanks to the fast Zürsersee quad chair-lift which has relieved pressure on the Seekopf chair. But there are one or two remaining problems – notably the Schlegelkopf fast quad out of Lech. The crucial Madloch chair at the top of the Zürs area must still generate queues of people on the one-way circuit going to Lech, but recent reporters have not complained. Other bottlenecks can include the Zuger Hochlicht lift and any of the cable-cars. The Oberlech region rarely causes any problems.

MOUNTAIN RESTAURANTS
Few atmospheric places

There are surprisingly few cosy Alpine restaurants in the area. A jolly area for lunch is at Oberlech, where there are several big sunny terraces set prettily around the piste; our favourite is the Goldener Berg. Quite often you'll find a live band playing outside one of the restaurants.

One of the best mountain restaurants is Seekopf (reached by the Seekopf chair-lift) which has a lovely sun terrace. The traditional Schröfli Alm, not marked on the piste map but just above the bottom of the Seekopf lift, is a pleasant traditional chalet. Also popular is the self-service Palmenalpe above Zug, but it does get very crowded. The Mohnenfluh, at the top of the Lech nursery lift, does 'excellent' food.

Many people go back to the villages for lunch. For a gourmet blow-out in Zürs, Chesa Verde in the hotel Edelweiss and the hotel Hirlanda's restaurant both feature in the Gault-Millau gourmet's guide (as does the Arlberg in Lech), and the Lorünser does a 'magnificent' buffet. The hotel Rote Wand in Zug serves more casual fare. Café Schneider in Lech serves good local dishes. Hus Nr 8, at the end of the route back from Zürs, is 300 years old and has good traditional food.

SCHOOLS AND GUIDES
Excellent in parts

The ski schools of Lech, Oberlech and Zürs all have good reputations and the instructors speak good English. Group lessons are divided into no fewer than 10 ability levels. One past visitor enjoyed 'the best tuition I have ever had'. In peak periods it might be as well to book in advance as many of the instructors are hired regularly every year by an exclusive clientele.

FACILITIES FOR CHILDREN
Oberlech's fine, but expensive

Oberlech does make an excellent choice for families who can afford it, particularly as it's so convenient for the slopes. The Sonnenburg and the Goldener Berg have in-house kindergartens. Reporters tell us the Oberlech school is great for children, with small classes, good English spoken and lunch offered.

Staying there

Lech is big enough for some of the cheaper accommodation to be quite a walk from the lifts. Unless you're heavily into nightlife, staying up in Oberlech is very attractive. Reporters have recommended both the Goldener Berg and the Burg for food, service, comfort, facilities (pool and sauna) and views from your own balcony.

HOW TO GO
Surprising variety

There is quite a variety of accommodation from luxury hotels through to simple but spotless B&Bs.
Hotels There are three 5-star hotels, over 30 4-star and countless more modest places.

(((((5) **Arlberg** Patronised by royalty and a number of celebrities. Elegantly rustic chalet, centrally placed. Pool.
(((((5) **Post** Lovely old Relais & Chateaux place on main street with pool and sauna.
((((4) **Krone** One of the oldest buildings in the village, in prime spot by river.
((((4) **Tannbergerhof** Splendidly atmospheric inn on main street, with outdoor bar and hugely popular disco (tea-time as well as later). Pool.
((((4) **Haldenhof** Friendly and well-run, with antique furnishings and a fine collection of prints and paintings.
((((4) **Sonnenburg** (Oberlech) Luxury on-piste chalet (popular for lunch). Good children's facilities. Pool.
((((4) **Monzabon** Excellent restaurant and wine cellar. Pool.
((2) **Haus Angerhof** Beautiful ancient pension, with wood panels and quaint little windows.
((2) **Haus Fernsicht** Pension with spa facilities.
((2) **Haus Rudboden** Right by the nursery slopes.

Self-catering There is lots available to independent bookers.
Chalets There are a couple of catered chalets run by British tour operators.

EATING OUT
Not necessarily expensive

There are over 50 restaurants in Lech, nearly all of them in hotels. For reasonably priced meals try the Montana, which serves French cuisine and has an excellent wine cellar, the Krone, Ambrosius (above a shopping arcade), or the Post, which serves Austrian nouvelle-type food. The Madlochblick has a typically Austrian restaurant, very cosy with good solid food. Hus Nr 8 is one of the best non-hotel restaurants (see mountain restaurants) and does good fondue. For pasta and other Italian fare there is Pizzeria Charly. In Oberlech there is a good fondue at the Alte Goldener Berg, a tavern built in 1432. In Zug the Rote Wand is excellent for fondues and a good night out. Also try the Alphorn, the Klösterle and the Olympia.

One reporter recommends Gasthaus Älpele near Zug, 3km from the road – up the valley on the cross-country route, for its atmosphere and good food. Transport is arranged by the restaurant in the form of covered wagons attached to a snowcat.

SCHOOLS/GUIDES

2000/01 prices in schillings

Lech and Oberlech
Classes 6 days
4hr: 10am-noon and 1pm-3pm
6 full days 2010 (low season 1830)
Children's classes
Ages: 3½ to 13
6 full days 1840 (low season: 1680)
Private lessons
Full day only
2410 for 1 day; each additional person 200

CHILDCARE

There are ski kindergartens in Lech and Oberlech taking children from age 3, from 9am to 4.30.

GETTING THERE

Air Zürich, transfer 3hr. Innsbruck, transfer 2hr.

Rail Langen (15km); 12 buses daily from station, buses connect with international trains.

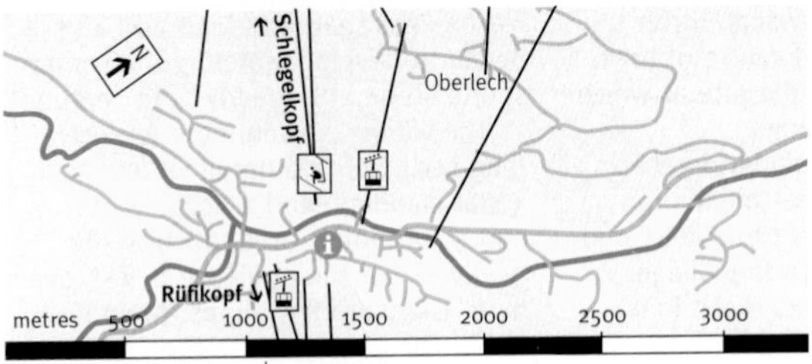

APRES-SKI

Good but pricey

The smart, modern-style Fux bar and restaurant has live music and is one of the latest trendy places.

The umbrella bar of the Burg hotel at Oberlech is popular immediately after the slopes close, as is the champagne bar in Oberlech's Hotel Montana. Then the 'beautiful people' head for the Hotel Krone's ice bar which has a lovely setting by the river, or to the outdoor bar of the Tannbergerhof. Inside the Tannbergerhof, there's a tea dance disco. The bar in the Strolz store is good for people-watching in bad weather. Later on, the Arlberg Hotel's Scotch Club disco (owned and run by former Olympic champion, Egon Zimmermann), and those in the hotels Almhof-Schneider and Krone liven up. The latter's Side Step specialises in 60s and 70s music. S'Pfefferkörndl is a good place for a drink, and you can get a steak or pizza there until late. For a change of scene the Rote Wand in Zug has a disco.

Taxi James is a shared mini-bus taxi which charges a flat fare for any journey in Lech/Zürs – you phone and it picks you up within half an hour.

OFF THE SLOPES

Poseurs' paradise

Many visitors to Lech don't indulge in sports. If you're armed with limitless funds the shopping possibilities are enticing, and the main street is often

LECH TO

Lech is doing all it can to keep traffic out of its pretty village centre ↓

ACTIVITIES

Indoor Tennis, hotel swimming pools and saunas, squash, cinema, museum, art gallery, hotel spas
Outdoor 25km of cleared walking paths, toboggan run (from Oberlech), artificial ice rink (skating, curling), sleigh rides, billiards, helicopter rides

TOURIST OFFICE

Postcode A-6764
t +43 (5583) 21610
f 3155
lech-info@lech.at
www.lech.at

ZÜRS TO

Zürs gets exceptional amounts of snow ↓

filled with fur-clad browsers. Strolz's plush emporium in the centre of town is a good place to up the rate at which you're spending schillings.

It's easy for pedestrians to get to Oberlech or Zug to meet friends for lunch on the slopes – or for skiers and boarders to get back to the village. The village outdoor bars make ideal posing positions – but make sure you are immaculately groomed or you'll feel out of place. An excursion to St Anton, to see how the other half live, is possible, though Lech clientele may feel more at home getting off the bus at chic St Christoph. For the more active there are 25km of walking paths and a variety of sporting activities – the walk along the river to Zug is especially beautiful.

Zürs 1720m

Ten minutes' drive towards St Anton from Lech, Zürs is almost on the Flexen Pass, with good snow virtually guaranteed. Zürs was a tiny hamlet used only for farming during the summer until (in the late 1890s) the Flexen Pass road was built and Zürs began to develop, entering the winter sports scene in the early 20th century.

The village is even more exclusive than Lech, with no hotels of less than 3-star standing, and a dozen 4-star and 5-star hotels around which life revolves. But the opulence is less overt here. There are few shops. Nightlife is quiet. There's a disco in the Edelweiss hotel and a piano bar in the Alpenhof. Mathie's-Stüble and Kaminstüble are worth trying, as is Vernissage, at the Skiclub Alpenrose, which is reported to be the best night spot in town. Serious dining means the Zürserhof and the Lorünser; make sure your wallet will stand a visit before you go – credit cards are not accepted. For something cheaper try spaghetti in the basement of the Edelweiss. Princess Caroline (who stays at the Lorünser) once managed this here at 5am.

Zürs has its own school, but many of the instructors are booked for the entire season by regular clients, and more than 80 per cent of them are hired privately. The resort also has its own kindergarten.

Stuben 1405m

Stuben is linked by lifts and pistes to St Anton, but is on the Vorarlberg side of the Arlberg pass (St Anton is over in the Tirol). There are infrequent but timetabled buses between the village and Lech and Zürs.

Dating back to the 13th century, Stuben is a small unspoilt village where personal service and quiet friendliness are the order of the day. Modern developments are kept to a minimum. The only concessions to the new era are a few unobtrusive hotels, a school, two or three bars, a couple of banks and a few little shops. The old church and traditional buildings, usually snow-covered, make Stuben a really charming Alpine village.

The north-facing local slopes retain snow well, though the queue-free but slow village chair can be a cold ride. A quicker and warmer way to get to St Anton in the morning, if you have a car, is to drive down the road to Rauz.

Stuben has sunny nursery slopes separate from the main slopes, but lack of progression runs make it unsuitable for beginners. Evenings are quiet, but several places have a pleasant atmosphere. The charming old Post is a very comfortable 4-star renowned for its fine restaurant.

Mayrhofen 630m

For keen skiers, the last resort – but a British favourite

WHAT IT COSTS

3

HOW IT RATES

The slopes

Snow	***
Extent	**
Experts	*
Intermediates	***
Beginners	**
Convenience	*
Queues	*
Restaurants	****

The rest

Scenery	***
Resort charm	***
Off-slope	****

- ⊕ Excellent children's amenities
- ⊕ Lively après-ski – though it's easily avoided if you prefer peace
- ⊕ Wide range of off-slope facilities
- ⊕ Snowsure by Tirol standard, plus the Hintertux glacier nearby
- ⊕ Various nearby areas on the same lift pass, and reached by free bus

- ⊖ Slopes are on two widely separated mountains and there are no runs back to the village itself
- ⊖ Ahorn sector is still served by a slow cable-car and is a bus ride from town, the Penken gondola is more convenient but neither is queue-free
- ⊖ Confined local slopes, with mainly short runs
- ⊖ Little to challenge experts
- ⊖ Sprawling, commercialised village

Mayrhofen is a British favourite that wears two distinctly different hats. Many young or youngish visitors like it for its lively nightlife. But it's also an excellent family resort, with highly regarded kindergartens and a fun pool with special children's area. Fortunately, the liveliest of the nightlife is confined to a few very popular places, easily avoided by families in such a large village.

We've at last been able to include a piste map (over the page). The slopes may look extensive, but do a few calculations with the altitudes and you'll see that most of the runs are very short – typically 300m to 400m vertical.

Despite lift improvements, this is still an inconvenient resort. On the plus side, it's fairly easy to explore other resorts in the valley, including the excellent glacier up at Hintertux. But if you plan to spend a lot of time at the glacier, consider staying in Lanersbach, described in the Hintertux chapter.

J P FANKHAUSER / MAYRHOFEN TO

Broad views are not the least of the attractions ↓

What's new

Direct access to the Penken has improved in the last five years thanks to the Penken gondola and the Penken Express chair.

The Horbergbahn gondola from Hippach to Penken is being upgraded – with increased capacity – for 2000/01. Snowmaking is being extended as well.

There are plans for a new six-pack and a fast quad up to Schafskopf for 2001.

LIFT PASSES

2000/01 prices in schillings

Mayrhofen/Zillertal
Coverage depends on period – see notes.

Main pass
1-day pass 370
6-day pass (including glacier) 2130

Children
Under 14: 6-day pass (including glacier) 1300
Under 6: free pass

Short-term passes
Passes available from 11am, noon and 2pm.

Alternative periods
Zillertaler ski pass available for 4 days' skiing in 6, 5 days in 7, 6 days in 7 and 10 days in 14.

Notes Up to 3-day passes covers Penken, Horberg-Gerent and Ahorn areas only; 4-day and over includes all 147 Ziller valley lifts (including Hintertux glacier), 475km of piste, ski-bus and railway. Reduced pass price for 14- to 18-year-olds (6-day including glacier 1720)

Alternative passes
Zillertaler ski pass also available without Hintertux glacier (6 days 1780 for adults, 1420 for 14- to 18-year olds, 1070 for children).

boarding *Mayrhofen is not ideal for learning to snowboard – the nursery slopes are inconvenient and the lifts are mainly drags. For intermediates though, the slopes are good and the gondolas and chair-lifts mean that few drags have to be negotiated. There is a fun-park and a half-pipe on the Gerent slopes at the top of the Penken area. More advanced riders will enjoy the Hintertux glacier, further up the valley – it's a boarder-friendly place (except for the drag-lifts), with two permanent half-pipes and some good off-piste possibilities. Budget prices and lively nightlife make Mayrhofen a popular boarder destination – it played host (along with Hintertux) to the 2000 British Snowboard Championships last season.*

The resort

Mayrhofen is a large resort sitting in the flat-bottomed Zillertal – big enough to be called a town, but not towny in character. It's essentially a traditional little village of a few bars, restaurants, hotels and sports shops – multiplied twenty-fold. As the village has grown, architecture has been kept traditional, but the place is so sprawling and commercialised it isn't really charming.

The main street is surrounded by almost every kind of tourist amenity – except convenient lifts. The Penken lift station is on the edge of the village centre, while the Ahorn cable-car is out in the suburbs, about 1km from the centre. The free bus service is frequent and efficient, though it finishes early (5pm).

Despite its 'lively' image, Mayrhofen is not dominated by lager louts. They exist, but tend to gather in a few easily avoided bars. The central hotels are mainly slightly upmarket, and overall the resort feels pleasantly civilised.

The mountains

Of Mayrhofen's two mountains Penken is mainly suitable for intermediates, and Ahorn only for beginners. Neither has much for experts. A frequent free bus serves other resorts covered by the pass, notably Hintertux, Lanersbach and Gerlos – but we hear you need to be up early to beat the queues. If you buy a lift pass in advance through a tour operator, make sure it covers the Hintertux glacier.

THE SLOPES
Highly inconvenient

Lifts to the two main sectors are a bus-ride apart, and you often have to take them down as well as up. And if the lifts are closed by wind during the day, there's nothing for it but a long and tricky walk down a piste or a ski-route – as one reporter found out in 1999.

The only trail from mountains to Mayrhofen (or, at least, to the outskirts of the town) is a winding run down from **Ahorn** (black on the map), and moving between mountains or lunching in the village means a serious waste of slope time. **Penken** is also accessible via the Hippach and Finkenberg gondolas, a couple of kilometres either side of the resort. You can get back to either of these on snow if cover is good, and then take a bus to town – the Finkenberg piste is only a path, graded red. Signposting and marking of runs is good.

SNOW RELIABILITY
Good by Austrian standards

Although the highest lift goes no higher than 2250m, the area is reasonably good for snow-cover because (apart from the unreliable valley runs) all of Mayrhofen's slopes are above 1580m. There is also one of the best glaciers in the Alps within day-trip range, at Hintertux. Snowmaking is being extended for 2000/01.

FOR EXPERTS
Not ideal

Mayrhofen itself doesn't have much for experts. But there are worthwhile challenges to be found, including off-piste areas, you can go touring, and reporters staying here and visiting the other resorts on the valley lift pass have been more than happy. The long unpisted trail to Hippach is the only testing local slope, and is rarely in good order – as a recent report from a repeat visitor testifies: 'Snow conditions were the best I've known, yet some parts were extremely tricky due to poor snow cover.'

FOR INTERMEDIATES
Problematic

Mayrhofen's slopes are small enough to disappoint avid piste-bashers, yet just difficult enough to be unappetising

MOUNTAIN FACTS

Altitude	630m-2250m
Lifts	29
Pistes	102km
Blue	26%
Red	53%
Black	21%
Artificial snow	4½km

for nervous intermediates. If you fall between the two, the short, mainly open runs spread across the Penken and next-door Gerent may suit you.

If you're willing to travel, each of the main mountains covered by the Ziller valley pass is large and varied enough for an interesting day out.

FOR BEGINNERS
Overrated: big drawbacks

Despite its reputation for teaching, Mayrhofen is not ideal for beginners. The Ahorn nursery slopes are excellent – high, extensive and sunny – but it's a tiresome journey to reach them (and to get home in the afternoon). The overcrowded slopes and restaurants add to the hassle. The Penken nursery area is less satisfactory. And there are few long blues to progress to from the nursery slopes.

FOR CROSS-COUNTRY
Go to Lanersbach

In theory there is a fine 20km trail along the valley to Zell am Ziller, plus small loops conveniently in, or close to, the village. But snow at 600m is not reliable. Vorderlanersbach has a much higher, more snowsure trail running to Madseit.

QUEUES
A problem at peak times

The Penken gondola opened in 1995, theoretically ending morning and evening queues among the worst in the Alps. It has three times the old lift's capacity; but that doesn't mean it is queue-free – one peak-period visitor tells of a 'disorganised scrum' for boarding. And nothing has been done to address the lengthy queues for the Ahorn cable-car.

Once away from the busy area near the Penken lift, slopes are surprisingly queue-free, though there are still quite a few slow old lifts. Buses to and from the more out-of-town gondolas are often crowded, especially the Finkenberg one, which also serves Hintertux.

MOUNTAIN RESTAURANTS
Penken good, Ahorn bad

Most of Penken's many mountain restaurants are attractive, sunny and serve good-value food – Vroni's is highly recommended but can get very crowded. The Schneekar restaurant at the top of the Gerent section is also recommended. Penkenjoch, at the top of the Finkenberg gondola, is remote from the Mayrhofen crowds. The Ahorn's restaurants are inadequate for the hordes using them.

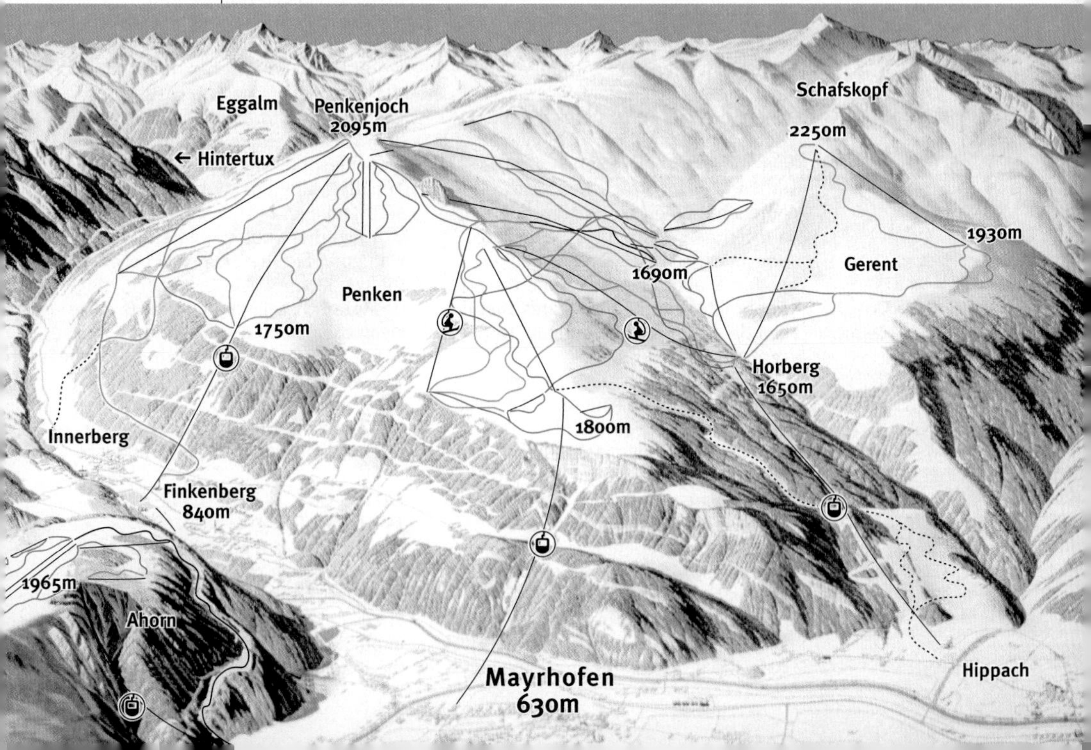

SCHOOLS/GUIDES

1999/2000 prices in schillings

Mayrhofen
Classes 5 days
2½hr: 10am-12.30 or 1pm-3.30
5 half days 1190
Children's classes
Ages: 4 to 14
6 full days including lunch 2320
Private lessons
Hourly and daily
500 for 1hr; each additional person 200

SMT Mayrhofen Total
Classes 6 days
4hr: 10am-noon and 1pm-3pm
6 full days 1540
Children's classes
Ages: 4 to 14
6 full days including lunch 2320
Private lessons
Hourly and daily
500 for 1hr; each additional person 200

Mount Everest
Classes 6 days
4hr: 10am-noon and 1pm-3pm
6 full days 1490
Children's classes
Ages: 5 to 14
6 full days including lunch 2270
Private lessons
Hourly
500 for 1hr; each additional person 200

CHILDCARE

All three ski schools at Penken run children's classes, and ski kindergartens where lunch is provided. All take children aged 4 or 5 to 12 or 14, and appear to operate only until the end of ski teaching at 3.30.

Wuppy's Kinderland non-skiing nursery at the fun pool complex takes children aged 3 months to 7 years, 9am to 5pm, Monday to Friday.

SCHOOLS AND GUIDES

You name it, they do it – well

Mayrhofen's popularity is founded on its three ski schools, which between them provide a wide range of services, including snowboarding. We have received many positive reports on many of them in the past and one recent reporter was delighted with her two-day private lesson with the SMT school. There's also guiding around the Zillertal, and tours with the Mount Everest School to the Hoher Riffler and Rastkogel summits.

FACILITIES FOR CHILDREN

Excellent but inconvenient

Mayrhofen has put childcare at the centre of its pitch, and all the facilities are excellent. But you may prefer to take your offspring to resorts where they don't have to be bussed around and ferried up and down the mountain.

Staying there

In such a large, sprawling village, with two widely separated lifts, location is important. The original centre, around the market, church and bus/railway stations, is now on the edge of things. The most convenient area is on the main street, as close as possible to the Penken gondola station.

HOW TO GO

Plenty of mainstream packages

There is a wide choice of hotel holidays available from UK tour operators, but few catered chalets.

Hotels There are dozens of cheap pensions, but most British visitors stay in the larger, better hotels. Most of the hotels packaged by UK tour operators are centrally located close to village amenities, a walk from the Penken gondola, and a bus-ride from the Ahorn lift. One reporter warns that it can be a bit noisy if you stay 'too centrally'.

((((5 **Elisabeth** The resort's only 5-star hotel, an opulent chalet in a fair position near the post office.

(((4 **Manni's** Well-placed, smartly done out; pool.

(((4 **Kramerwirt** Lovely Tirolean hotel simply oozing character. A recent visitor reports 'friendly and helpful staff, comfortable rooms, varied and interesting half-board menu'.

((3 **Strass** Best placed of the 4-stars, very close to the Penken gondola. Lively bars, disco, fitness centre, solarium, pool and children's playroom, but rooms lack style.

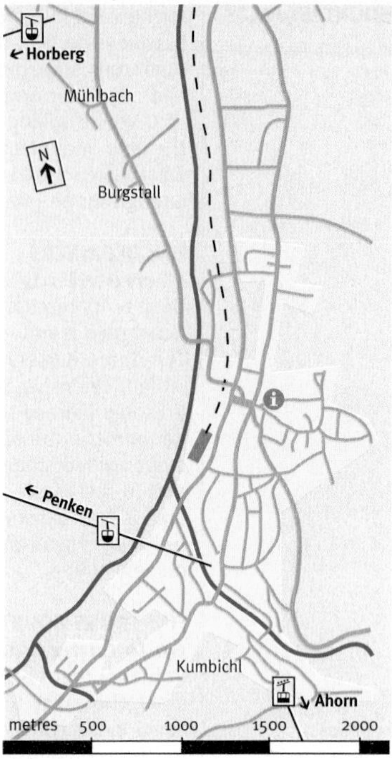

((3 **Rose** Well placed, 'a few minutes' walk from the centre, yet far enough to be able to sleep'. Good food.

((3 **Neue Post** Conveniently situated family-run 4-star on the main street – 'good food and nice big rooms'.

((3 **Waldheim** Smallish, cosy 3-star gasthof, close to the Penken lift.

((3 **St Georg** Poorly positioned for amenities, but ideal for those wanting a multi-facility quality hotel in peaceful surroundings.

((3 **Jägerhof** Another peaceful hotel with good facilities, mid-way between the two lifts.

(1 **Mozart** 'Excellent value' B&B. 'Nice clean rooms and a very good breakfast buffet'. 15-minute walk from the centre.

(1 **Claudia**, **Monika** Cheap little twin guest houses in a good position.

(1 **Kumbichl**, **Kumbichlhof** Adjoining pensions, next to the Ahorn cable-car.

EATING OUT

Wide choice

Most visitors are on half-board, but there is a large choice of restaurants catering for most tastes and budgets. The Hotel Rose has a particularly good, informal restaurant. The restaurants in the Kramerwirt, Neuhaus ('excellent

GETTING THERE

Air Salzburg, transfer 3hr. Munich, transfer 2½hr. Innsbruck, transfer 1hr.

Rail Local line through to resort; regular buses from station.

ACTIVITIES

Indoor Bowling, adventure pool, 2 hotel pools open to the public, massage, sauna, squash, fitness centre, indoor tennis centre at Hotel Berghof (3 courts, coaching available), indoor riding-school, pool and billiards, stamp-swapping, cinema

Outdoor Skating-rink, curling, horse-riding, horse sleigh rides and racing, 45km cleared paths, hang-gliding, paragliding, tobogganing (2 runs of 2.5km), snowrafting, ski-bobs

TOURIST OFFICE

Postcode A-6290
t +43 (5285) 6760
f 6760 33
mayrhofen@zillertal.tirol.at
www.mayrhofen.com

standards of food and service'), and Gasthaus Ländenhof are also recommended. Manni's is good for pizzas ('a genuine pleasure to eat there') and Kaiser Brundl, opposite the Neuhaus, has been recommended for its extensive menu (traditional and international dishes) and good food, though one recent reporter complained of appalling service on one occasion. Wirthaus zum Griena is a 'wonderful old wooden building offering traditional farmhouse cuisine'.

APRES-SKI
Lively but not rowdy

Nightlife is a great selling point. Mayrhofen has all the standard Tirolean-style entertainments, such as folk dancing, bier kellers and tea dances, along with bowling, sleigh rides, tobogganing, but also some seriously lively bars and discos.

At close of play, the Happy End umbrella bar, at the top of the Penken gondola, is lively and the Ice bar, in the hotel Strass (near the Penken gondola base station), gets packed out. Micky's is another recommended après-ski bar.

Some of the other bars in the Strass are rocking places later on – the Lobby bar has live music and the Sport's Arena club has a good atmosphere and has been described as the 'trendiest in the Tirol'. Mo's American theme bar and Scotland Yard are also popular with reporters. The Schlussel disco can be 'wild'. Try Rundum or Am Kamin (in the hotel Elisabeth) if you're after more Manhattan than Mayrhofen. The Neue Post bar and the Passage are recommended for a quiet drink.

OFF THE SLOPES
Good for all

The village travel agency arranges trips to Italy, and Innsbruck is easily reached by train. There are also good walks and sports amenities, including the swimming pool complex – with saunas, solariums and lots of other fun features. Pedestrians have no trouble getting up the mountain to meet friends for lunch.

Finkenberg 840m

Finkenberg is a welcome alternative to Mayrhofen, being a much smaller, quieter village with good access to and from the Penken. It is no more than a collection of traditional-style hotels, bars, cafés and private homes awkwardly dispersed along a steep section of the busy main road between Mayrhofen and Lanersbach. There are two distinct halves – the original village around the church, and a cluster of buildings conveniently close to the gondola station, just over five minutes' walk away.

The gondola gives queue-free access to the Penken (those based in Mayrhofen tend to use the Hippach gondola rather than this one as an alternative to the Penken) and a speedy ride home for beginners (and everyone else when the Katzenmoos path is not open).

Finkenberg has a nursery slope in the village which, given good snow, means that beginners do not need to buy the full lift pass. But it's a sunless spot, and good conditions are far from certain at this altitude.

Cross-country skiers have to get a bus up to Lanersbach.

There are two schools. The Finkenberg School has a particularly good reputation.

Like Mayrhofen, Finkenberg prides itself on giving children a good time. There's a non-ski crèche and the ski nursery takes children from age four.

All hotels are within walking distance of the gondola, and many of the more distant ones run minibuses to the lift station. Restaurants are mostly hotel-based.

Finkenberg is quiet in the evenings. The main après-ski spots are the Laterndl Pub and Finkennest, and there are rep-organised events such as tobogganing and bowling. Mayrhofen is a short taxi-ride away and offers a far wider choice of evening action.

Swimming, curling and ice-skating are available, and the local walks have been recommended, but those not using the slopes find themselves spending a lot of time in Mayrhofen.

Montafon

650m-1430m

Extensive slopes, well off the beaten package path

WHAT IT COSTS

3

The 40km-long Montafon valley contains no less than eleven resorts and five main lift systems. Packages from the UK are few (accommodation on a serious scale is not easy to find), but for the independent traveller the valley is well worth a look – especially the Silvretta Nova area (linking Gaschurn and St Gallenkirch) and high, tiny, isolated Gargellen.

MOUNTAIN FACTS

Altitude	700m-2395m
Lifts	66
Pistes	197km
Blue	56%
Red	37%
Black	7%
Artificial snow	62km

TOURIST OFFICE

Postcode A-6780
t +43 (5556) 722530
f 74856
tourismus.information@montafon.at
www.montafon.at

ALPENSZENE MONTAFON

Extensive slopes, above and below the tree line ↓

The Montafon is neglected by the UK travel trade, partly because of its location in Vorarlberg, west of the Arlberg pass – easy enough to reach from Zürich (and from the German motorways), but not so easy from the standard Austrian charter airport of Salzburg. More importantly, the valley lacks the large hotels that mainstream UK tour operators apparently need.

The valley runs parallel with the nearby Swiss border from the medieval city of Bludenz. The first sizeable community you come to is Vandans, linked to its own ski area by gondola. Next are Schruns, at the foot of one of the major lift networks, and Tschagguns, across the valley. Further up are St Gallenkirch and Gaschurn, at opposite ends of the other major area. Up a side valley from St Gallenkirch is Gargellen, close to the Swiss border – a tiny village, but quite widely known in Britain.

The valley road goes on up to Partenen, where it climbs steeply to Bielerhöhe and the Silvrettasee dam at about 2000m, at the foot of glaciers and Piz Buin (of suncream fame). In summer you can drive over the pass to Galtür and Ischgl. In winter Bielerhöhe is a great launch pad for ski-tours, and there are cross-country trails totalling 14km on and around the frozen lake. You get there by taking a cable-car from Partenen, and then mini-buses.

There are more ordinary cross-country trails along the valley, and an 11km woodland trail at Kristberg (1440m), above the Silbertal. Trails total 100km.

The shared valley lift pass covers the respectable post-bus service and the trains that run as far as Schruns, as well as the 66 lifts – so exploration of the valley does not require a car.

The top heights hereabouts – going from 2000m to 2400m – are no match for the nearby Arlberg resorts; but there is plenty of skiing above the mid-mountain lift stations at around 1500m, and most of the slopes are not excessively sunny, so snow reliability (aided by snowmaking on quite a big scale) is reasonable. Practically all of the pistes are accurately graded blue or red, but there are plentiful off-piste opportunities (including some 'ski routes'). There are snowboard fun-parks in most sectors. Tobogganing is popular, and there is a floodlit 6km run down to the Gortipohl lift base.

What's new

There's a new eight-person gondola from Gargellen up to the main Schafberg slopes, speeding up access to the main slopes.

Snowmaking on Silvretta Nova has been extended down to the valley lift stations – almost one-third of the mountain is now covered by snowmaking. The Spatla drag-lift, near the top of Versettla, has been replaced by a four-seater chair-lift.

There's a new skier services building by the Kapell restaurant, on Hochjoch. And there's a huge new children's area here as well.

Snowmaking in Grabs and Golm has also been extended.

'Hands-free' electronic lift passes are now available.

ALPENSZENE MONTAFON

On-mountain dining and revelry is a major feature of this area – especially on Silvretta Nova ↓

GARGELLEN 1425m

Gargellen is a real backwater – a tiny village tucked up a side valley, with a small but varied piste network on Schafberg that is blissfully quiet.

The new eight-person gondola out of the village must seem rather out of place in this tiny collection of hotels and guest houses, huddled in the bottom of a steep-sided, narrow valley. The runs it takes you to are gentle, with not much to choose between the blues and reds; but there is lots of off-piste terrain, and a couple of excellent away-from-the-lifts runs at the extremities of the area. There are three pleasant mountain restaurants, including two rustic huts at the tree line; a party is held weekly at Obwaldhütte after the lifts close, followed by a torchlit descent. (Slide shows and bridge are more typical evening entertainments.) There are several pistes to the valley, and with care you can ski to the door of the hotel Madrisa (and others). Behind the hotel is a rather steep nursery slope.

A special feature is the day-tour around the Madrisa – a small-scale off-piste adventure taking you over to Klosters in Switzerland. It involves a 300m climb, but is otherwise easy.

SCHRUNS 700m

Schruns is the most rounded resort in the valley – a towny little place, with the shops in its car-free centre catering for locals and for summer tourists.

A cable-car and gondola go up from points outside the village into the Hochjoch slopes, now accessible also from the Silbertal, around the side of the mountain. Above the trees is a fair-sized area of easy blue runs, with the occasional red alternative. There are restaurants at strategic points – the Wormser Hütte is a climbing refuge with 'stunning' views. The blue run from Kreuzjochsattel back to Schruns is 12km long and over 1600m vertical.

Easily accessible across the valley are the limited slopes of Grabs, above the rather formless village of Tschagguns, and the more extensive area of Golm, where a gondola goes from Vandans up to a handful of chairs and drags serving easy slopes above the trees. A single red run returns to the valley station.

As you are reminded at every opportunity, Ernest Hemingway ensconced himself in Schruns in 1925/26, and his favourite drinking table in the hotel Taube is still there to be admired. The Löwen and the Alpenhof Messmer are elegant, well-equipped 4-stars with big pools, the former a hub of the après-ski scene.

GASCHURN / ST GALLENKIRCH 900m

Silvretta Nova is the biggest lift and piste network in the valley. As a results, Germans' cars fill to overflowing the huge car parks at the valley lift stations. Gaschurn is an attractive place to stay.

The two main resorts here are quite different. Whereas St Gallenkirch is strung along the main road and spoilt by traffic, Gaschurn is a pleasant village, bypassed by the valley traffic, with the wood-shingled Posthotel Rössle in the centre.

The lift network covers two parallel ridges running north–south, with most of the runs on their east- and west-facing flanks. This is the most challenging area in the valley, with as many red as blue runs, and an occasional nominal black. Most of the slopes are above the tree line, typically offering 300m or 400m vertical.

There is lots of off-piste potential, including some seriously challenging (and quite dangerous) slopes down into the central valley.

There are lots of mountain restaurants, many impressive in different ways. At the top of one ridge is the state-of-the-art Nova Stoba, with seats for over 1500 people in 17 different rooms catering for different markets, including splendid panelled rooms with table-service. The big terrace bar gets seriously boisterous. At the top of the other ridge is the splendidly woody Valisera Hüsli.

Neustift 990m

Access to one of the best glaciers in the world

WHAT IT COSTS

(3)

HOW IT RATES

The slopes

Snow	*****
Extent	**
Experts	**
Intermediates	***
Beginners	**
Convenience	*
Queues	***
Restaurants	**

The rest

Scenery	***
Resort charm	****
Off-slope	***

What's new

The glacier lifts have been further upgraded in recent years, with most recently a six-pack replacing the Eisjoch T-bars.

A new Fernau chair will speed the journey to the to station of Gaiskar for 2000/01. And a new 100m half-pipe will be built on the glacier.

MOUNTAIN FACTS

Altitude	1000m-3210m
Lifts	19
Pistes	55km
Blue	52%
Red	24%
Black	24%
Artificial snow	7km

These statistics relate to the Stubai glacier alone. The Stubai-Superski lift pass covers 45 lifts and 90km of pistes.

TOURIST OFFICE

Postcode A-6167
t +43 (5226) 2228
f 2529
tv.neustift@neustift.at
www.stubaital.at

Neustift has its own little area of slopes where unadventurous intermediates can potter happily, but it's the Stubai Gletscher – 20km away and one of the best glaciers in Austria (or the world) – that earns Neustift its place in this book.

THE RESORT

Neustift is a very attractive, traditional Tirolean village halfway along the Stubai valley. It is the closest large community to the Stubai glacier, but there are other resorts down the valley. Fulpmes (with its satellite village of Telfes) has more extensive local slopes (Schlick 2000). Milders has some slopes too (Serleslifte). The Stubai-Superski lift pass covers all these resorts, the glacier and the shuttle-bus. The half-hourly service to the glacier is inadequate.

THE MOUNTAINS

Neustift's limited local **slopes** consist of a narrow chain of runs and lifts from Elferhütte at 2080m down to the village. Apart from one short blue run at altitude, the pistes are all red. This area is on the south-east side of the valley; there is a nursery area at village level, on the other side.

The Stubai glacier is a much more extensive area of runs between 3200m and 2300m reached via a choice of two-stage gondolas. The glacier is broken up by rocky peaks, giving more sense of variety than is normal on a glacier. There is also a lovely 10km route (Wilde Grub'n) from the glacier down via a deserted bowl to the valley at 1750m. Start at the top of the glacier and you have a descent of about 1450m and 14km.

On the glacier, **snow reliability** is rarely a problem. Our regular reporter goes each year in May to round off the season, and most of the area is open in summer. The lower local slopes face roughly north, but are of typically modest Austrian altitude. The sunny village nursery slopes are unreliable.

The village slopes do not have much for **experts**, and the glacier does not have the challenge of Hintertux's. But there are some good long runs, including a 4km itinerary route down the east side of the glacier. Two new black runs have improved the variety – one is a pretty steep mogul field.

For **intermediates**, the local slopes are neither easy nor extensive – so the main appeal is to the confident intermediate who wants to practise technique rather than get around. The glacier is splendid territory.

This is not a resort for **beginners**; the village nursery slopes are attractive, but too sunny – though they do have snowmakers.

The glacier attracts **snowboarders** in large numbers. The fun-park will have a new 100m half-pipe for nest season.

There are 100km of **cross-country** trails in the Stubaital, including some reached by the lifts serving Fulpmes and Milders, and some on the glacier.

Regular improvements, including a new gondola and fast chairs, over the last few years have virtually eliminated what **queues** there were in the past.

The **mountain restaurants** are a mixture of primitive mountaineering huts and impersonal cafeterias. There are great views from the cute little cabin at Jochdohle (at 3150m, Austria's highest restaurant), and the Dresdner Hütte at 2300m is recommended as charming and uncrowded.

There are **ski schools** both in Neustift itself and at the glacier. Guides are available. **Children** can be looked after all day.

STAYING THERE

If you fly into Innsbruck, you can be in the resort an hour later. There are lots of 4-star and 3-star **hotels**. The 3-star Tirolerhof is excellent – comfortable and relaxed, good food. It has its own ski school and hire shop. The central 4-star Sonnhof is also recommended. For families, a visitor suggests the 4-star Gasteigerhof in Gasteig, with pool.

Most **restaurants** are hotel-based. Visitors recommend Bellefonte's pizzas, and the atmospheric Hoferwirt. **Après-ski** is focused on the Dorf, Bierfassl, Hully Gully and the Romansstuben.

Neustift has quite a lot to offer **off the slopes**: a good leisure centre and numerous activities. All the villages have impressive toboggan runs. Innsbruck is 45 minutes away by bus.

Obergurgl 1930m

High, snowsure slopes with loyal clientele

WHAT IT COSTS

(4)

HOW IT RATES

The slopes

Snow	*****
Extent	**
Experts	**
Intermediates	***
Beginners	****
Convenience	****
Queues	*****
Restaurants	**

The rest

Scenery	***
Resort charm	****
Off-slope	**

- ⊕ Glaciers apart, one of the Alps' most reliable resorts for snow – especially good for a late-season holiday
- ⊕ Excellent area for beginners, timid intermediates and families
- ⊕ Normally queue- and crowd-free
- ⊕ Retains village charm despite modern development
- ⊕ Jolly tea-time après-ski
- ⊕ Obergurgl and Hochgurgl slopes are now linked by gondola

- ⊖ Small area with no tough pistes
- ⊖ Very bleak setting, with no sheltered slopes for bad weather
- ⊖ Few off-slope amenities except in hotels
- ⊖ Quiet nightlife by Austrian standards
- ⊖ For a small Austrian resort, rather expensive

A dedicated group of visitors go back every year to Obergurgl or Hochgurgl, some of our reporters among them. Whichever of the two resorts they are loyal to, they love its high, snowsure, easy intermediate slopes, its end-of-the-valley seclusion and civilised atmosphere, its jolly tea-time après-ski and its comfortable, expensive hotels. There aren't many beds, so you need to book early to avoid disappointment.

But some first-timers are disappointed. Even accepting the exposed setting, some yearn for a more substantial village, some for more variety of terrain, some simply for more runs. They have a point. If we're going to a bleak, high, snowsure resort where there is nothing to do but ski or board, we'd rather go somewhere with rather more skiing or boarding to do (like Tignes, for example).

boarding *Obergurgl is a traditional ski destination, attracting an affluent and (dare we say it?) 'older' clientele. But the resort has made an attempt at accommodating snowboarding and there's a fun-park and quarter pipe on the Festkogl in Obergurgl. The resort has a low proportion of drag-lifts, which makes it good for beginners too, and there's also some off-piste potential. Evenings tend to be a bit tame for hardcore boarders – fever-pitch is usually a 'conga' round the bar. Sölden, 20 minutes by road, has stacks of lively bars and clubs though.*

What's new

The neighbouring sectors of Obergurgl and Hochgurgl have been linked by lift for the last couple of seasons – the eight-person Top Express gondola means that you no longer need to come down off the mountain and take a bus from one to the other.

For the 1999/2000 season snowmaking was extended to almost every run and now covers 90% of all the pistes.

For 2000/01 all ski passes will be electronic hands-free cards you keep in your pocket. And guests will be able to buy their passes at the hotel reception desk. Ticket offices will at long last accept credit card payments.

The resort

Obergurgl is based on a traditional old village, set in a remote, bleak spot, the dead end of a long road up past Sölden. It is the highest parish in Austria and is usually under a blanket of snow from November until May. The surrounding mountains are bleak, with an array of avalanche barriers giving them a forbidding appearance. Obergurgl has no through-traffic and few day visitors. The village centre is mainly traffic-free and entirely so at night.

Despite its small size, this is a village of parts. At the entrance to the resort is a cluster of hotels near the main gondola, which takes you to all the local slopes. The road then passes another group of hotels around the ice rink, up the hillside to the left, before coming to the village proper. This starts with an attractive little square with church, fountain, and the original village hotel (the Edelweiss und Gurgl). Just above there's a chair-lift to the local slopes.

Village atmosphere is jolly during the day and immediately after the slopes close, but can be subdued later at night; there are some nightspots, but most people stay in their hotels. The resort is popular with British families and well-heeled groups looking for a relaxing winter break.

Hochgurgl, a bus-ride away, is little more than a handful of hotels at the foot of its own slopes – now linked to Obergurgl's by gondola.

MOUNTAIN FACTS

Altitude	1800m-3080m
Lifts	23
Pistes	110km
Blue	32%
Red	50%
Black	18%
Artificial snow	25km

The mountains

Now that the slopes of Obergurgl and Hochgurgl are linked by lift, a day here can be more varied than in the past. But for a well-known and popular resort, the slopes are still surprisingly limited, and lacking interest or challenge for adventurous intermediates or better. You also don't get a sense of travel, as you do in bigger Alpine resorts: you just go up and down north-west facing slopes, not from area to area or down into a valley and up the other side. There are, however, some good off-piste runs to explore with a guide. The lift pass is quite expensive for the extent of slopes and number of lifts (though prices have been frozen this season).

For a day out, it's a short bus or car trip to Sölden (good, quite steep and extensive intermediate slopes), and a long car trip to Kühtai (a worthwhile high area near Innsbruck). Much closer is the tiny touring launch-pad of Vent.

THE SLOPES
Fragmented cruising

Obergurgl is the smaller of the two linked areas. It is in two sections, well linked by piste in one direction, more loosely in the other.

The Festkogl gondola, from near the village entrance, and the Rosskar fast quad chair-lift, from the centre of the village – next to the Gaisberg lift – go to the highest area. This is served by two drags and two chairs, one of which reaches 3035m. From these runs you can head back to the gondola base or over to Gaisberg, with its high point of 2670m at Hohe Mut, reached by a long, slow chair. There are four other short lifts here, and also one that comes up from Obergurgl's village square. Follow this access lift back to town and you can take the new Rosskar lift up, or pole or walk to the Festkogl gondola and start the circuit again.

The new Top Express gondola is the obvious way to travel between the two sectors during lift opening hours. But there is still the alternative of a regular and reliable free shuttle-bus to Untergurgl. From there, a chair-lift goes up to **Hochgurgl** (also reachable by car, or by bus that leaves a few times a day). Another chair-lift takes you from Hochgurgl to the heart of its mountain, served by drag- and chair-lifts. From the high point on Wurmkogl (3080m) there are spectacular views of the Dolomites.

A single tree-lined run leads down from Hochgurgl to the bottom of the Untergurgl chair and the bus home.

The 8km run from the Festkogl station back to the village is floodlit on Tuesday and Saturday nights.

SNOW RELIABILITY
Excellent

Obergurgl has high slopes and is arguably the most snowsure of Europe's non-glacier resorts – even without its extensive snowmaking. It has a justifiably popular mid-December white week, and regular late-season visitors who book well in advance. But there are virtually no tree-lined runs, wind and white-outs can shut the lifts and, especially in early season, severe cold can curtail enthusiasm.

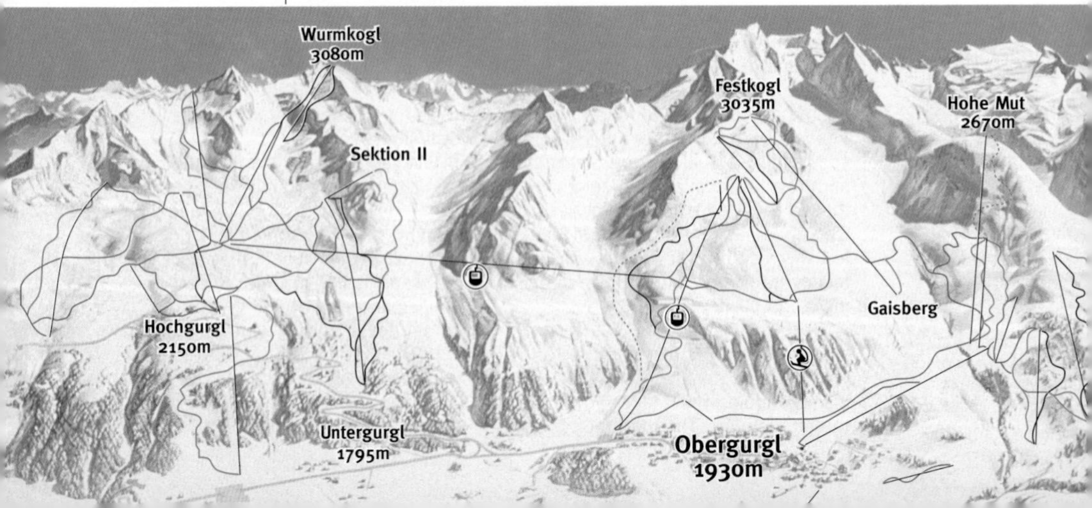

High, snowy bowls: that's what Obergurgl is all about ➔

OBERGURGL TO

LIFT PASSES

2000/01 prices in schillings.

Obergurgl ski pass
Covers all lifts in Obergurgl and Hochgurgl, and local ski-bus.

Beginners Lift pass or points card.

Main pass
1-day pass 460
6-day pass 2230
(low season 1960)

Senior citizens
Over 60: 6-day pass 1360

Children
Under 16: 6-day pass 1360
Under 8: free pass

Short-term passes
Half-day (from 11am, noon, 1pm or 2pm).

Alternative periods
5 days' skiing in 7 and 11 days' skiing in 14 passes available.

FOR EXPERTS
Not generally recommendable

There is a fair amount of enjoyable off-piste to be found with a guide – especially from Obergurgl – and the top school groups often go off-piste at times when there is little avalanche danger. This is a well-known area for ski touring, and we have reports of very challenging expeditions on the glaciers at the head of the valley.

The most challenging official piste is the Hohe Mut mogul field beneath the slow, old chair-lift at Gaisberg. But this is often irritatingly awkward rather than pleasurable, being icy, worn and difficult to follow in places. Other blacks are rather overgraded – they could easily be red – and there are few challenges. Experts will soon tire of cruising the mainly short runs, no matter how powdery the snow.

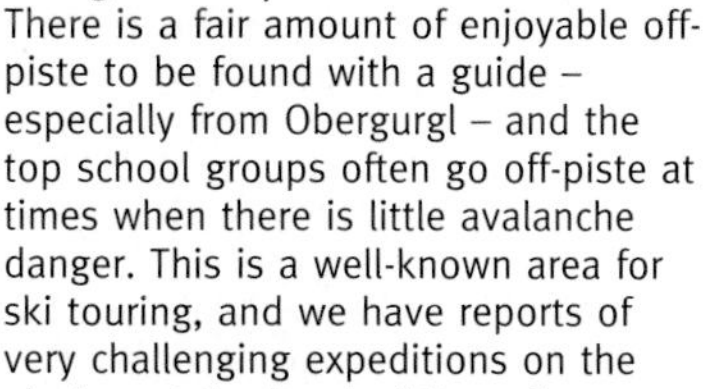

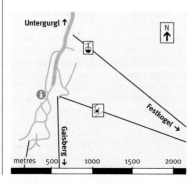

FOR INTERMEDIATES
Good but limited

There is some perfect intermediate terrain here, made even better by the normally flattering snow conditions. The problem is, there's not much of it. Keen piste-bashers will quickly tire of travelling the same runs and be itching to catch the bus to Sölden, down the valley – unfortunately, there is no pass-sharing arrangement.

Hochgurgl has the bigger area of easy runs, and these make good cruising. For more challenging intermediate runs, head to the Vorderer Wurmkogellift, on the right as you look at the mountain.

The run down from Hochgurgl to the bus stop at Untergurgl is about the only tree-lined piste in the area, and about the only long run served by artificial snow. Less confident intermediates can find this tricky and may be best advised to take the gondola back to Obergurgl.

The Obergurgl area has more red than blue runs but most offer no great challenge to a confident intermediate. The area served by chair-lifts at the top of the Festkogl gondola is easy cruising. And there is a long enjoyable run down the length of the gondola (floodlit twice a week), with a scenic off-piste route in the adjoining valley.

In the Gaisberg area, there are very easy runs in front of the Nederhütte and back towards town. The bottom

SCHOOLS/GUIDES

2000/01 prices in schillings

Obergurgl
Classes 6 days
4hr: 10am-noon and 2pm-4pm
6 full days 1880
Children's classes
Ages: from 5
6 full days including lunch: 2960
Private lessons
Half and full day
1520 for half-day; each additional person 150

Hochgurgl
Classes 6 days
4hr: 10am-noon and 2pm-4pm
6 full days 1880
Children's classes
Ages: from 5
6 full days 1880
Private lessons
Hourly, half and full day
750 for 1hr, for 1 to 2 people; each additional person 200.
1500 for half day, for 1 to 2 people; each additional person 200

CHILDCARE

The ski schools at Obergurgl and Hochgurgl take children over the age of 5. The Obergurgl school runs a non-skiing kindergarten for children from the age of 3.

The village kindergarten in Obergurgl also takes children from the age of 3.

The Alpina, Austria and Hochfirst hotels (among others) have in-house kindergartens.

drag-lifts here serve very short but sometimes surprisingly tricky and bumpy runs.

FOR BEGINNERS
Fine for first-timers or improvers

There is an adequate nursery slope above Obergurgl, and the Gaisberg run under the chair out of the village can be completed as soon as a modicum of control is achieved.

Near beginners can travel from the top of the four-person Wurmkogl chair to Hochgurgl village (600m vertical) without any problems. However, a recent reporter complained that the Hochgurgl nursery slopes are inconveniently placed for complete beginners to have to walk to.

The quality of the snow makes the area a good (but relatively expensive) choice for beginners compared with most lower Austrian resorts.

CROSS-COUNTRY
Limited but snowsure

Three small loops, one each at Obergurgl, Untergurgl and Hochgurgl, give just 12km of trail. All are relatively snowsure and pleasantly situated. Tuition is available.

QUEUES
No problems

Lift queues are rare – even at Christmas and New Year. The resort is too remote to attract day trippers, and its authorities do not encourage 'bussing-in' when lower villages are struggling for snow.

MOUNTAIN RESTAURANTS
Little choice

Compared with most Austrian resorts, mountain huts are not very numerous and not very special. At Gaisberg the Nederhütte is jolly, and often with live music and dancing on the tables; David's Skihütte is friendly, cheerful, good value and recently refurbished. The Schönwieshütte, a 10-minute walk from the piste, has excellent views, as does the small hut at the top of the Hohe Mut chair. At Hochgurgl, the tiny hut at Wurmkogl has stunning views into Italy and basic food. Many people return to Obergurgl and Hochgurgl for lunch. Hotels Edelweiss and Jenewein in Obergurgl are convenient, if expensive. Café Josl is cheaper. In Hochgurgl, hotel Riml has excellent reasonably priced food.

SCHOOLS AND GUIDES
Mainly good news

We've had nothing but good reports of the Obergurgl school in the last couple of years, with good English spoken and excellent tuition and organisation: 'highly efficient, very thorough testing of pupils before being put into a class', 'big effort to make school fun'. But we've also heard that class sizes have climbed to as many as 15.

FACILITIES FOR CHILDREN
Check out your hotel

For a village with obvious appeal to families, Obergurgl doesn't seem to put itself out to cater for children. There is no ski kindergarten for tots who want to start early, but there is now lunchtime supervision for ski school and non-skiing kindergarten children. Many hotels offer childcare of one sort or another, and the Alpina has been particularly recommended.

Staying there

The Rosskar chair-lift and the gondola link to Hochgurgl have meant that position is no longer much of an issue in Obergurgl; most places are now close enough to a convenient lift. The Festkogl gondola area at the village entrance is good for getting to the slopes and for ease of access by car. However, it's a long walk or a shuttle-bus from the village centre and the nursery slopes.

Accommodation around the ice rink is perched above the village, with very steep, sometimes treacherous walks to and from other amenities. It's a very short slide to the chair-lifts and a pole, walk or slide to the Festkogl gondola.

Many of Obergurgl's middle-aged clientele much prefer the convenience of staying in the village centre, close to the Gaisberg and Rosskar lifts. Drivers have underground parking bang in the centre of town.

The usual advantages of staying in a mountainside mini-resort like Hochgurgl are convenience for the slopes, good snow and no queues. Obergurgl itself scores well in these respects, but Hochgurgl, despite its location on the slopes at 2150m, is not conveniently arranged. From practically all the half-dozen hotels you have to negotiate roads and/or staircases to get to or from the snow. Hochgurgl is quieter than Obergurgl at night.

GETTING THERE

Air Innsbruck, transfer 2hr. Salzburg, transfer 3hr. Munich, transfer 4hr.

Rail Train to Ötz; regular buses from station, transfer 1½hr.

ACTIVITIES

Indoor Swimming pool (at Hotel Muhle, open to the public), saunas, whirlpools, steam baths, massage, bowling, pool and billiards, squash, table tennis, shooting range
Outdoor Natural skating rink (open in the evenings), curling, sleigh rides, snow-shoe outings

TOURIST OFFICE

Postcode A-6456
t +43 (5256) 6466
f 6353
info@obergurgl.com
www.obergurgl.com

HOW TO GO
Plenty of good hotels

Most package accommodation is in hotels and pensions, but there are a number of comfortable apartments. Demand for rooms in Obergurgl exceeds supply, and for once it is true that you should book early to avoid disappointment.

Hotels Obergurgl's accommodation is of high quality: most hotels are 4-stars, and none is less than a 3-star. Hochgurgl's hotels include the most luxurious one in the area (the hotel Hochgurgl).

Within each rating, hotels are uniformly comfortable. In our fat file of reports we have hardly any complaints. The main ones come from couples staying in the Deutschmann who had to share tables.

A cheaper option for the independent traveller is to stay down the valley in Untergurgl, where the 4-star Jadghof is recommended.

(((④ **Edelweiss und Gurgl** The focal hotel – biggest, oldest, among the most appealing; on the central square. Pool.
(((④ **Alpina de Luxe** Big, smart chalet with excellent children's facilities – kindergarten and playroom. Pool.
(((④ **Hochfirst** Recommended by recent reporter. Good spa facilities, comfortable, 4 or 5 minutes from gondola.
(((④ **Jenewein** Recently refurbished, friendly staff, excellent food; good central position next to main lift.
(((④ **Berggasthof Gamper** Best rooms very comfortable, good food; at far end of village, past the square.
(((④ **Crystal** If you don't mind the ocean-liner appearance, one of the best hotels in the Festkogl lift area.
((③ **Fender** Good all-rounder with friendly staff; central.
((③ **Wiesental** Comfortable, well positioned, good value.
((③ **Granat-Schlössl** Amusing pseudo-castle, surprisingly affordable.
(② **Alpenblume** Good B&B hotel well-placed for Festkogl lift.
(② **Haus Gurgl** B&B near Festkogl lift; friendly, pizzeria, same owners as Edelweiss und Gurgl.
Hochgurgl has equally good hotels.
((((⑤ **Hochgurgl** The most luxurious in the area – the only 5-star. Pool.
((③ **Sporthotel Ideal** Well situated for access to the slopes. Pool.
((③ **Laurin** Well equipped, traditional rooms, excellent food.

Self-catering The Lohmann is a high-standard large modern apartment block, well placed for the slopes, less so for the village centre below. The 3-star Pirchhütt has apartments close to the Festkogl gondola, and the Wiesental hotel has more central ones.

EATING OUT
Wide choice, limited range

Hotel dining rooms and à la carte restaurants dominate. The commendable Pic Nic and Krumpn's Stadl are the only independent restaurants, and hotel Madeleine has a good separate pizzeria. Hotel Alpina has a particularly good reputation for its food, while the restaurant at the Berggasthof Gamper is pleasantly cosy. The two restaurants in the Edelweiss und Gurgl are reportedly 'superb'. Nederhütte and David's Skihütte are both open in the evenings if you fancy venturing up the mountain for a change.

APRES-SKI
Lively early, quiet later

Obergurgl is more animated in the evening than you might expect. The Nederhütte mountain restaurant has a lively tea dance three times a week, and the Umbrella Bar outside the Edelweiss hotel is popular at close of play when the weather is good.

Later on, the crowded Krumpn's Stadl barn is the liveliest place in town with live music on alternate nights – it's also recommended for its fondues. The Josl, Jenewein and Edelweiss, and Gurgl hotels have atmospheric bars. The Bajazzo is a more sophisticated late-night haunt. (Our specialist reporter particularly recommends the 5-litre cylinders of draught beer, delivered to your table.) The Edelweissbar and Austriakeller are discos. Hochgurgl is very quiet at night except for Toni's Almhütte bar in the Olymp Sporthotel – one of three places with live music. There's also the African Bar disco.

OFF THE SLOPES
Very limited

There isn't much to do during the day. Innsbruck is over two hours away by post-bus. Sölden (20 minutes away) has a leisure centre and shopping facilities. Pedestrians can walk to restaurants in the Gaisberg area to meet friends for lunch. The Hochfirst hotel has a good health centre.

Obertauern 1740m

Small but varied area, with great snow record

WHAT IT COSTS

5

HOW IT RATES

The slopes

Snow	****
Extent	**
Experts	***
Intermediates	****
Beginners	*****
Convenience	****
Queues	****
Restaurants	***

The rest

Scenery	***
Resort charm	**
Off-slope	**

What's new

Three new chairs were installed last season, including a high-speed, six-seater chair-lift. For 2000/01 a new high-speed quad will replace the Kurvenlift T-bar.

MOUNTAIN FACTS

Altitude	1740m-2335m
Lifts	26
Pistes	120km
Blue	50%
Red	35%
Black	15%
Artificial snow	50km

TOURIST OFFICE

Postcode A-5562
t +43 (6456) 7252
f 7515
info@ski-obertauern.com
www.ski-obertauern.com

Obertauern's excellent snow record takes precedence, for some, over its lack of village charm and limited slopes. It has a small intermediate circuit, good beginners' slopes, some challenges and a typically jolly Austrian atmosphere.

THE RESORT

In the land of postcard resorts grown out of rustic villages, Obertauern is something of an oddity – a mainly modern development at the top of the Tauern pass road. Built in (high-rise) chalet style, it's not unattractive – but there is no real central focus of shops and bars, and a lack of local transport.

THE MOUNTAINS

The Tauern pass road divides the **slopes** into two unequal parts, well linked to make a user-friendly circuit that can be travelled clockwise or anticlockwise. However, reporters complain about the piste map and poor piste marking that makes getting lost in bad weather easy. Most pistes are on the sunny slopes to the north: a wide, many-faceted basin of mostly gentle runs, with a few steepish mogulled pitches punctuated by long schusses. Vertical range is limited, and runs are short. Visitors used to big areas will soon see it all. There is a **snowboard** fun-park at Hochalm.

Zehnerkar and Gamsleiten to the south-west have some of Obertauern's most difficult runs. You can travel the circuit in a couple of hours.

The resort's key attraction is the exceptional **snow reliability** of its high bowl. But it is often windy, which can mean lifts close and snow blows away.

Experts naturally incline towards the south-west slopes. There are some genuinely steep pisted and off-piste runs from the Gamsleiten chair, but it is prone to closure. For more challenge, join off-piste guided groups.

For **intermediates** the biggest draw is Obertauern's circuit. Stay low for easier pistes, or try the tougher runs higher up. The central point of the north area is Hochalm, from where the Seekareck and Panorama chairs take you to challenging, often mogully runs. The chair to Hundskogel leads to a red and a black. And over at the Plattenkar quad there are two splendid reds.

Obertauern has very good nursery slopes for **beginners**, close to the village. After the first couple of lessons you can go up the mountain, because the Schaidberg chair leads to a drag-lift serving a high-altitude beginners' slope and it is an easy run back home.

There are 17km of **cross-country** trails in the heart of the resort.

When neighbouring resorts don't share Obertauern's good snow, non-residents arrive by the bus-load. The lift system is very impressive and is continually being upgraded – seven new lifts in the last few years are eliminating the **queues** of the past. Recent reporters have experienced no queues but lifts closed by bad weather can be more of a problem.

The **mountain restaurants** are plentiful and good, but crowded. The Kringsalm is the largest, but small huts are more atmospheric ('Often full of groups of Austrians and Germans singing,' says a reporter). The old Lürzeralm at village level was praised.

Of the several **schools and guides**, most tour operators use the Krallinger – and its kindergarten. We have good reports of both, despite large classes.

STAYING THERE

Practically all **accommodation** is in hotels (mostly 3-star and 4-star) and guest houses. Location is not a major worry. The Petershubel, Steiner, Passe Schutz, Edelweiss, Gamsleiten, Enzian and Alpina have been recommended.

Eating out is mostly in hotels (the Enzian is recommended) and the busy après-ski bars at the foot of the north-side lifts. The Hochalm restaurant at the top of the quad chair sometimes serves early-evening meals.

Après-ski is lively and varied. The Latschnstub'n has a terrace, music and dancing and is good at tea-time. Later, try the Lürzeralm, which has farmyard-style decor and a disco. The Taverne has various bars, a pizzeria and disco.

Off the slopes there's an excellent sports centre (no pool, but with tennis) but little else to do in bad weather. Salzburg is an easy trip. For lunch, the Kringsalm can be reached on foot.

Saalbach-Hinterglemm 1000m

Attractive villages, lively nightlife and good intermediate runs

WHAT IT COSTS

4

HOW IT RATES

The slopes

Snow	***
Extent	****
Experts	**
Intermediates	****
Beginners	***
Convenience	****
Queues	***
Restaurants	****

The rest

Scenery	***
Resort charm	****
Off-slope	**

What's new

For 2000/01 two lifts on the south-facing slopes above Hinterglemm will be replaced by high-speed chairs with bubbles for protection in cold weather. A six-seater will replace a slow old double chair to Spieleckkogel and a four-seater will replace a T-bar to Reiterkogel.

Last season a new hands-free electronic lift pass system was installed so you can now keep your pass in a pocket. More snowmaking was also installed.

- + Large, well-linked, intermediate circuit with open and tree-lined runs
- + Saalbach is a big but pleasant, affluent village, lively at night
- + Both village main streets traffic-free
- + Atmospheric mountain restaurants all over the mountain
- + Sunny slopes
- + Large snowmaking installation and excellent piste maintenance

- − Large number of low, south-facing slopes that suffer from the sun
- − Not much for experts
- − Nursery slopes in Saalbach are not ideal – sunny, and busy in parts
- − Saalbach spreads along the valley and some rooms are far from central
- − Hinterglemm is just a long road with no real centre
- − Can get rowdy at night

Like many Austrian resorts Saalbach-Hinterglemm has a pretty, traditional-style village and very lively nightlife, but unlike many it combines this with a very extensive circuit of slopes on both sides of a valley, and runs are linked by an efficient modern lift system. Its slopes resemble a French resort more than a traditional Austrian one – with the added advantage of excellent traditional mountain restaurants dotted around.

The main downside is the snow. Although it has impressive snowmaking, one side of the valley faces south and these slopes, especially the lower ones, deteriorate quickly in good weather.

Saalbach's après-ski is very lively – and can get rowdy – and is dominated by Scandinavian and German visitors. It rocks from 3pm until the early hours non-stop. There are also large parties of British schoolchildren around at times.

boarding *Saalbach is great for boarding. Slopes are extensive, lifts are mainly chairs and gondolas (though there are some connecting drags), and there are pistes to appeal to beginners, intermediates and experts alike. For experienced boarders there's good off-piste terrain, a large half-pipe on the Bernkogel above Saalbach, another below Hochalm and a fun-park on the north-facing slopes just above Hinterglemm. There are also dedicated 'carving' zones for boarders and skiers. And the nightlife is some of the liveliest in Europe.*

SAALBACH-HINTERGLEMM TO

Wherever you are on Saalbach's extensive circuit, you are never far from an attractive mountain hut →

The resort

Saalbach and Hinterglemm, their centres 4km apart, expanded along a narrow dead-end valley floor until, a few years ago, they adopted a single identity. Their slopes are spread across north- and south-facing mountainsides, with lifts and runs connecting the villages via both sides.

Saalbach is one of the most attractive winter villages in Austria. Wedged into the narrow valley, with pisted slopes coming right down to the traffic-free village centre, its traditional-style buildings are huddled together around a classic onion-domed church. Most buildings are modern reproductions – the main exceptions are the Post Inn and the church – and the result is pretty close to Austrian charm with French convenience.

Saalbach is a strange mixture. The attractive, largely traffic-free, main street is lined with expensive, upmarket hotels, restaurants and shops, festooned with fairy lights, but further out there are more cheap and cheerful pensions. The clientele are similarly mixed, with rich BMW and Mercedes drivers rubbing shoulders in the bars and clubs with teenagers (including British school kids) looking for a good time.

Hinterglemm is a more scattered, less appealing collection of hotels and holiday homes, with a small, traffic-free zone in the centre. It offers a cheaper, though not inexpensive, alternative to Saalbach, with far better access to the north-facing slopes.

Leogang is a quiet village in the next valley to the north, its long, north-facing slopes forming a spur from the main area.

MOUNTAIN FACTS

Altitude	930m-2095m
Lifts	52
Pistes	200km
Blue	50%
Red	33%
Black	17%
Artificial snow	30km
Recco detectors used	

The mountains

The slopes form a 'circus' almost exclusively suitable for intermediates, much of it on lightly wooded slopes. Few runs are likely either to bore the aggressive intermediate or worry the timid one. There are sufficient open sections and changes of pitch and direction to give pistes variety, but not many genuinely black pistes.

Several resorts in Salzburg province are reachable by road – including Bad Hofgastein, Kaprun and Zell am See, the last a short bus-ride away.

THE SLOPES
User-friendly circuit

The complete circuit of the valley can only be travelled anticlockwise – going clockwise, at Vorderglemm there is no way up the slope on the opposite side of the valley. You can do a truncated clockwise circuit, crossing to the south side of the valley at Saalbach itself. The valley floor is very narrow, so there is very little walking necessary when changing sides. Where you end up at the end of the day is not important because of the excellent bus service which runs every 20 minutes.

A good deal of the south-facing slopes is above 1400m, albeit with rather short runs. Five sectors can be identified – from west to east, **Hochalm**, **Reiterkogel**, **Bernkogel**, **Kohlmaiskopf** and **Wildenkarkogel**. The last connects via Schönleitenhütte to Leogang – a small, high, open area, leading to a long, narrow, north-facing slope down to Leogang village, broadening towards the bottom. An eight-person gondola brings you most of the way back.

The connections across Saalbach-Hinterglemm's south-facing slopes work well: when traversing the whole hillside you need to descend to the valley floor only once, in whichever direction you go. At Saalbach a very short walk across the main street gets you from the Bernkogel piste to the Kohlmaiskopf lift and vice versa. Both these runs are well endowed with snowmakers to ensure the link normally remains open, and there is a choice of lifts going up, including a multi-cabin cable-way to Kohlmaiskopf.

The north-facing slopes are different in character – two distinct mountains, with long runs from both to the valley. Access from Saalbach is by a solitary, queue-prone cable-car to **Schattberg**. The high, open, sunny slopes behind the peak are now served by a fast quad chair.

From Schattberg, long runs go down to Saalbach village, Vorderglemm and Hinterglemm. From the latter, lifts go not only to Schattberg but also to the other north-facing mountain, **Zwölferkogel**, served by a two-stage eight-person gondola. Drags serve open slopes on the sunny side of the peak, and a high-capacity gondola provides a link from the south-facing Hochalm area.

LIFT PASSES

2000/01 prices in schillings

Saalbach-Hinterglemm-Leogang
Covers all the lifts in Saalbach, Hinterglemm and Leogang, and the ski-bus.

Main pass
1-day pass 430
6-day pass 2070 £118
(low season 1845)

Senior citizens
Over 65 male, 60 female 6-day pass 1240

Children
Under 19: 6-day pass 1865 (10% off)
Under 15: 6-day pass 1240
Under 7: free pass

Short-term passes
Day pass price reduced hourly from 11am; single and return tickets on main lifts.

Notes Can pay extra 120 for free use of indoor pool in Hinterglemm. £6 Sun ticket for pedestrians: 7-day pass 660. Points cards for beginners.

SNOW RELIABILITY
Better than most of the Tirol

Saalbach's array of snowmakers cover several main runs on the lower half of the mountain, on both sides of the valley. The resort also claims to be in a 'snow pocket'. Good piste maintenance helps to keep the slopes in the best possible condition, but an altitude range of 930m to 2100m is only a slight advance on Kitzbühel. As 60 per cent of runs face south, Saalbach suffers when the sun comes out. Both north and south sides can develop icy patches, as we found on a January 1999 visit.

FOR EXPERTS
Little steep stuff

There are few testing slopes. Off-piste guides are available, but snow conditions and forest tend to limit the potential. The north-facing slopes are steeper than those on the south-facing side of the valley. The long (4km) run beneath the length of the Schattberg cable-car is the only truly black run – a fine fast bash first thing in the morning if it has been groomed. The other long black from Zwölferkogel is really a red with just a couple of short, steeper pitches. The World Cup downhill run from Zwölferkogel is interesting, as is the 5km Schattberg West-Hinterglemm red (and its scenic 'ski route' variant).

FOR INTERMEDIATES
Paradise

This area is ideal for both the great British piste-basher, eager to clock up the miles, and the more leisurely cruiser. The south-facing pistes have mainly been cut through the pine forest at an angle, allowing movement across the area on easy runs.

For those looking for more of a challenge, the most direct routes down from Hochalm, Reiterkogel, Kohlmaiskopf and Hochwartalm are good fun. All the south-facing slopes are uniformly pleasant and, as a result, everyone tends to be fairly evenly distributed over them. Only the delightful blue from Bernkogel to Saalbach gets really crowded at times. The alternative long ski route is very pleasant, taking you through forest and meadows.

The north-facing area has some more challenging runs, and a section of relatively high, open slopes around Zwölferkogel, which often have good snow. None of the black runs is beyond an adventurous intermediate, while the long pretty cruise from Limbergalm to Vorderglemm gets you away from lifts for most of the time and is particularly quiet and pleasant first thing in the morning.

Our favourite intermediate run was the long cruise down on excellent north-facing snow to Leogang – over 1000m of vertical.

FOR BEGINNERS
Best for improvers

Saalbach's two nursery slopes are very well positioned for convenience, right next to the village centre. But they are both south-facing, and the upper one gets a lot of intermediate traffic taking a short cut between the Kohlmaiskopf and Bernkogel areas. The lower one is very small, but the lift is free.

Alternatives are trips to the short, easy runs at Bernkogel and Schattberg. There is also a little slope at the foot of the Schattberg but the school seems loath to use it – so it's great for pottering about on your own at lunchtime. It's rather sunless and a little steeper than the other nursery areas, but perfectly usable.

Hinterglemm's spacious nursery area is separate from the main slopes. Being north-facing, it is much more reliable for snow later on in the season, but it consequently misses out on the sun in mid-winter.

There are lots of easy blue runs to move on to, especially on the south-facing side of the valley.

FOR CROSS-COUNTRY
Go to Zell am See

Trails run beside the road along the valley floor from Saalbach to Vorderglemm and between Hinterglemm and the valley end at Lindlingalm. In mid-winter these trails get very little sun, and are not very exciting. The countryside beyond nearby Zell am See offers more scope.

QUEUES
Busy, but only one long delay

The Schattberg cable-car is an obvious problem, with waiting routine in the morning peak period. Otherwise, much depends on snow conditions. When all runs are in good shape there are few problems, other than small morning peak queues to leave Saalbach. If the snow is poor, the Bernkogel chair and the following drag get very busy, as do any lifts servicing the better snow.

SAALBACH-HINTERGLEMM TO

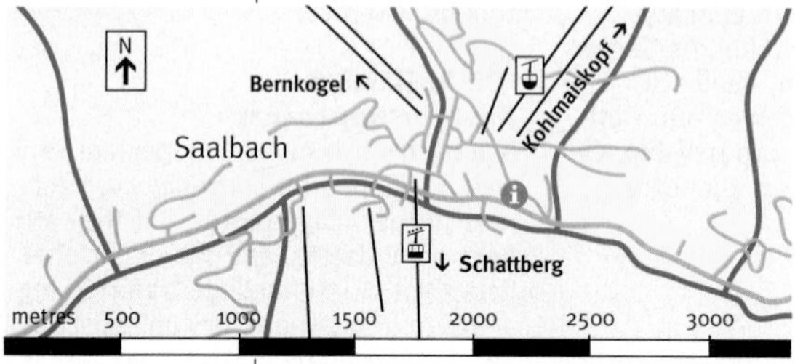

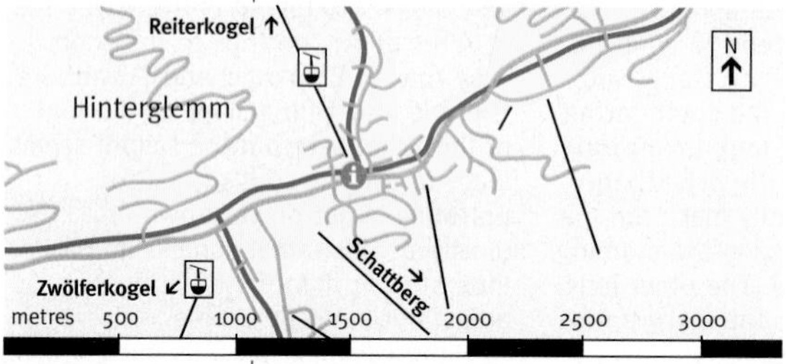

Saalbach-Hinterglemm does not get as overrun at weekends as other Tirolean resorts – it's less accessible for the Munich hordes than the Ski Welt area and its neighbours.

MOUNTAIN RESTAURANTS

Excellent quality and quantity

The whole area is liberally scattered with attractive little huts that serve good food. And they do not simply rely on good weather; many have pleasant rustic interiors and a lively ambience.

On the south-facing slopes, the Panorama on the Kohlmaiskopf slope, Waleggeralm on Hochalm and Turneralm close to Bründelkopf serve particularly good food. The little Bernkogelalm hut, overlooking Saalbach, has a great atmosphere. A reporter recommends the Bärnalm near the top of the Bernkogel chair ('good food, good value') and the Burgeralm ('3km up the toboggan track, marvellous atmosphere and reindeer steaks before a 1am descent'). The Wildenkarkogel Hütte has a big terrace and possibly the loudest mountain-top music we've heard, with resident DJ from mid-morning.

On the north-facing slopes, the

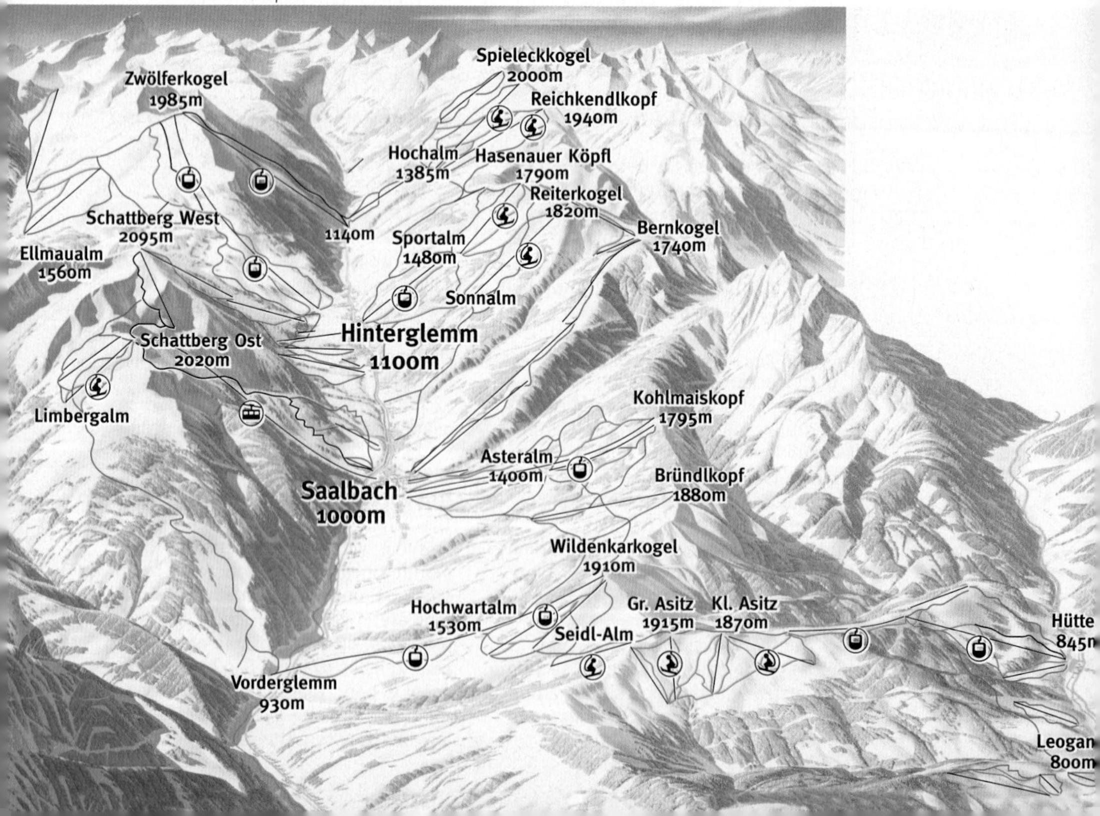

SCHOOLS/GUIDES

1999/2000 prices in schillings

Hannes Füstauer
Classes 6 days
4hr: 10am-noon and 1pm-3pm
1 full day 540
6 full days 1640
Children's classes
Ages: from 5
1 full day 540
6 full days 1640
Private lessons
Half- and full-day
1150 for 2hr, for 1 to 2 people; each additional person 100.
2300 for 4hr, for 1 to 2 people; each additional person 200

Wolfgang Zink
Classes 6 days
4hr: 10am-noon and 1pm-3pm
1 full day 540
6 full days 1640
Children's classes
Ages: from 6
1 full day 540
6 full days 1640
Private lessons
Hourly and daily
600 for 1hr, for 1 to 2 people; each additional person 100.
1200 for 2hr, for 1 to 2 people; additional person 200.
2400 for 4hr, for 1 to 2 people; each additional person 200

CHILDCARE

Some of the ski schools take children from age 4 or 5 and can provide lunchtime care – there are special areas in both villages.

Several hotels have nurseries, and some in Hinterglemm are open to non-residents.

Bergstadl halfway down the red run from Schattberg West has stunning views and good food. Ellmaualm, at the bottom of the Zwölferkogel's upper slopes, is a quiet, sunny retreat with good food and 'palatial loos'. The 12er Treff umbrella bar at the top of the Zwölferkogel gondola is good for lounging in the sun.

SCHOOLS AND GUIDES
An excess of choice

We're all in favour of competition between schools but visitors to Saalbach-Hinterglemm may feel that they are faced with rather too much of this good thing. Two or three schools offers a choice; nine or ten begins to look like a recipe for confusion. We have had good reports of the Wolf and Zink schools and the 'excellent' Snowboard Academy.

FACILITIES FOR CHILDREN
Hinterglemm tries harder

Saalbach doesn't go out of its way to sell itself to families, although it does have a ski kindergarten. Hinterglemm, perhaps seeing itself as more of a family resort, has some good hotel-based nursery facilities – the one at the Theresia is reportedly excellent.

Staying there

The walk to lifts from Saalbach's central hotels is minimal. Unfortunately Saalbach has seen a fair amount of expansion in recent years, and many of the cheaper hotels used by British tour operators tend to be situated in the least convenient part of the village. In Hinterglemm itself, position isn't so important. Most of the accommodation is near a lift.

HOW TO GO
Cheerful doesn't mean cheap

Chalets We are aware of a few 'club hotels' but Saalbach isn't really a chalet resort.
Hotels There are a large number of hotels in Saalbach, mainly 3-star and above. Most of the more expensive ones have excellent positions in the village centre, whereas the cheapest places tend to be along the road to Hinterglemm – or in Hinterglemm itself, which is rather less ritzy than Saalbach. Be aware that some central hotels are affected by disco noise.

Saalbach
((((4 **Alpenhotel** Luxurious, with a wealth of facilities, including an open-fire lounge, disco, pub and small pool.
((((4 **Berger's Sporthotel** Liveliest of the top hotels, with a popular daily tea dance, good bar and disco. Good pool.
((((4 **Kendler** Position second to none, right next to the Bernkogel chair. Classy, expensive, good food.
((((4 **Saalbacher Hof** Retains a friendly feel despite its large size.
(((3 **Haider** Best-positioned of the 3-stars, right next to the main lifts.
(((3 **Kristiana** Near enough to lifts but away from night-time noise. 'Excellent food.' Sauna, steam bath.
(((3 **König** Cheaper 3-star and more basic rooms, particularly well placed for nursery slopes.
Hinterglemm
((((4 **Theresia** Hinterglemm's top hotel, and one of the best for families; 'excellent, with great facilities', says a reporter. Out towards Saalbach, but nursery slopes nearby. Pool.
(((3 **Wolf** Small but well-equipped 4-star in the the nursery-sharing scheme. 'Especially good' food, excellent position. Pool.
((2 **Haus Ameshofer** Beside piste at Reiterkogel lift. 'Great value ski-in, ski-out B&B,' says a reporter.
((2 **Pension Spatz** Good value, friendly welcome, good position near the centre of the village.
Self-catering There's a big choice of apartments for independent travellers.

EATING OUT
Wide choice of hotel restaurants

Saalbach-Hinterglemm is essentially a half-board resort, with relatively few non-hotel restaurants. Peter's restaurant, at the top of Saalbach's main street, is atmospheric and serves excellent meat dishes cooked on hot stones. The Wallner Pizzeria on the main street is good value. The Auwirt hotel on the outskirts of Saalbach has a good à la carte restaurant.

APRES-SKI
It rocks from early on

Après-ski is very lively and can get very wild from mid-afternoon until the early hours. In Saalbach the rustic Hinterhagalm at the top of main nursery slope is packed by 3.30. When it closes around 6pm, the crowds slide down to Bauer's Skialm and try to get into the already heaving old cow shed to continue drinking and dancing. The

GETTING THERE

Air Salzburg, transfer 2hr. Munich, transfer 3½hr.

Rail Zell am See; hourly buses from station, transfer 40 min.

ACTIVITIES

Indoor Swimming pools, sauna, massage, solarium, bowling, billiards, tennis (Hinterglemm), squash

Outdoor Floodlit tobogganing, sleigh rides, skating, ice hockey, curling, 35km of cleared paths, paragliding

TOURIST OFFICE

Postcode A-5753
t +43 (6541) 680068
f 680069
contact@saalbach.com
www.saalbach.com

tiny Zum Turn (next door to the church and cemetery) is an atmospheric former medieval jail which also gets packed around 4pm with many who are still there at 11pm.

Later on The Pub on the main road out of town is packed with young Brits enjoying the karaoke. The Neuhaus Taverne and Crazy Bear have live music. Bobby's Bar is cheap, often full of British school kids, and has bowling. Kings Disco livens up after midnight. The Panther Bar has jungle decor, discreet music and well-heeled clientele. Zum Herrn'Karl, Hellis and Bergers are also popular. Arena disco has go-go dancers and is very popular.

In Hinterglemm there are a number of ice bars which are busy straight after the lifts close, including the Gute Stube of Hotel Dorfschmiede with 60s' music such as the Rolling Stones blasting out. The Tanzkimmel is an open, glass-fronted bar with a dance floor, next door to the Londoner, which is the biggest attraction later on – live and disco music, smart, friendly. Bla Bla is small, modern and smart, with reasonable prices. The Alm Bar has good music and some dancing.

Tour operator reps organise tobogganing, sleigh rides and bowling.

OFF THE SLOPES
Surprisingly little to do

Saalbach is not very entertaining if you're not into winter sports. There are few shops other than supermarkets and equipment places. Walks tend to be restricted to the paths alongside the cold cross-country trails or along the Saalbach toboggan run to Spielberghs. But there are excursions by bus and train (or car) to Kitzbühel and Salzburg.

Leogang 800m

Leogang is an attractive, although rather scattered, farming community-cum-mountain resort. The lack of any central focus has repercussions: many of the hotels are a long way from the main lifts, and the bus service is disappointingly infrequent.

Leogang is, however, a much less expensive alternative to Saalbach-Hinterglemm. It is also far quieter, smaller and less commercialised than its neighbours. Situated on the St Johann-Bischofshofen road, and having a mainline railway station, Leogang is also better placed for independent travel access and for taking day excursions. One visitor reported that the snow was better in Leogang than in the rest of the area.

The link with Saalbach is fairly reliable: the gondola towards Asitz is followed by a couple of short pistes and lifts, with all the slopes above a lofty 1590m. These pistes are red, but not difficult. Less experienced intermediates can amuse themselves on the blue slopes served by the first stage of the gondola.

Beginners have good nursery slopes, conveniently placed just above the village. If the snow is poor, the higher slopes are not too steep, though icy conditions can be a problem for novices.

Leogang is the best of the local villages for cross-country. There are 25km of trails, with a connection to Saalfelden, plus a panoramic high-altitude trail which links through to other resorts. Given good snow, trails are kept in fine condition.

The Leogang Altenberger school has a high reputation – 'excellent service and tuition; highly recommended'. There is a non-ski crèche, and children can start school at four years old.

Equity Total Ski and Snowboard run a catered chalet in a converted farmhouse in Hütten, a tiny hamlet west of Leogang, which is better positioned for the slopes and the gondola than the main village. Visitors report comfort and character with great catering and entertainment.

There are convenient hotels in each price category. The luxury Krallerhof has its own nursery lift, which can be used to get across to the main lift station. The 4-star Salzburgerhof is one of the best-placed hotels, within a two-minute walk of the gondola. The Stockinggut is a 3-star, within a reasonable walk of the main lift.

Restaurants are hotel-based. The Krallerhof has the excellent food you would expect. The much cheaper Gasthof Hüttwirt has a high reputation for wholesome Austrian home cooking.

The rustic old chalet Kralleralm is very much the focal tea-time and evening rendezvous.

Excursions to the pleasant nearby town of Saalfelden and the lovely city of Salzburg are the main attractions off the slopes. Other facilities include swimming and tennis.

St Anton 1305m

Non-stop on- and off- slope action and pretty village base

WHAT IT COSTS

(5)

HOW IT RATES

The slopes

Snow	****
Extent	****
Experts	*****
Intermediates	***
Beginners	*
Convenience	***
Queues	**
Restaurants	***

The rest

Scenery	***
Resort charm	****
Off-slope	***

MOUNTAIN FACTS

Altitude 1305m-2650m

Arlberg region

Lifts	85
Pistes	260km
Blue	25%
Red	50%
Black	25%
Artificial snow	37km

Recco detectors used

- + Extensive slopes for adventurous intermediates and experts
- + Heavy snowfalls, backed up by snowmakers, generally give good cover despite sunny slopes
- + Much-improved lift system has greatly reduced queuing problems
- + Very lively après-ski
- + Despite resort expansion, village retains distinct Tirolean charm

- − Slopes not ideal for beginners or timid intermediates
- − All the tough stuff is off-piste
- − Pistes can get very crowded
- − Some accommodation a long way out of centre
- − Surprisingly little to amuse off the slopes
- − Nightlife can get rowdy, with noisy drunks in the early hours

St Anton has, along with Wengen and Mürren, a strong British tradition. From the 1920s, successive generations learned to ski here, adopting the distinctive 'feet together' Arlberg style. Sir Arnold Lunn helped start the Kandahar race here in 1928, and the resort has remained popular with good British skiers ever since.

It has also become one of the world's Meccas for ski bums. That's a reflection of the wonderful, tough off-piste runs available in the bowls below the Valluga – the best that Austria has to offer. In good snow conditions they are superb. Sadly, conditions are often less than perfect except just after a fresh snowfall, because of their south-facing aspect. But if you are lucky with the snow you'll have the time of your life. There's a lot to offer adventurous intermediates too, both locally and at Lech and Zürs, a short bus-ride away.

There are lots of lively discos and bars, which keep going from 3pm to 2am. The resort is an ideal choice for the hard-drinking, disco-loving, keen-for-action holidaymaker who can stand the pace of getting to bed late and being up for the first lift – it's not for those who like a quiet life and gentle, uncrowded pistes.

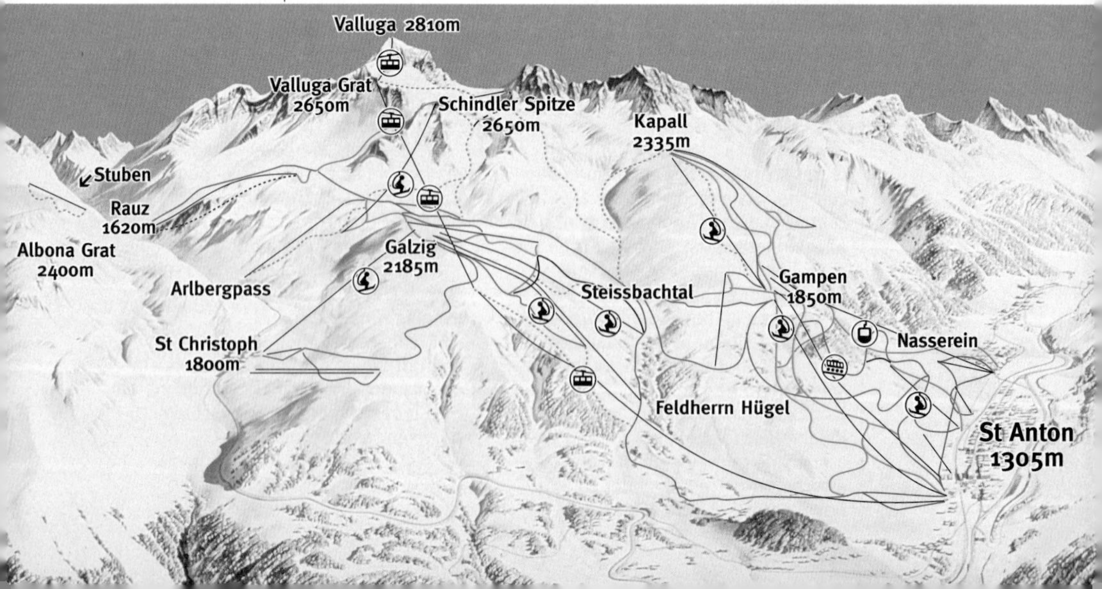

What's new

Big improvements have been made over the last few years in preparation for the Alpine Skiing World Championships to be held here from 28 Jan to 10 Feb 2001.

For 1999/2000 a hands-free electronic lift pass system was introduced where you keep your pass in your pocket.

1999/2000 also saw the new Fang four-seater chair go from slightly east of the central village up the local slopes. From the top of this you can get down to the village centre and central lifts or, on a new easy blue run, to Nasserein, where a new eight-person gondola up to Gampen will open for 2000/01 – this will transform the attraction of Nasserein as a place to stay.

The railway line and station will be moved to the outskirts of the town before the 2000/01 season, making it possible to ski right into the village centre.

boarding *Though steeped in skiing tradition, St Anton is moving with the times and improving facilities for boarders. Although we don't really recommend it to beginners, it is one of the best free-ride areas in the world, with lots of steep terrain and natural hits. There is a fun-park and 100m half-pipe on Rendl. There are still a few T-bars around but fast chair-lifts are now the main ways around the mountains. Tuition is provided by the ski schools and the Snowboard Academy (part of the Arlberg school). A book could be written about the almost legendary nightlife.*

The resort

St Anton is at the foot of the road up to the Arlberg pass, at the eastern end of a lift network that spreads across to St Christoph and above the pass to Rauz and Stuben. The resort is a long, sprawling mixture of traditional and modern buildings crammed into a narrow valley, between a busy road and mainline railway – but the railway is due to be moved before the start of the 2000/01 World Championship season, allowing the lower slopes to be extended right into the village centre.

It is an attractively bustling place, full of life, colour and noise. Although it is crowded and commercialised, St Anton is full of character, and its traffic-free main street retains Alpine charm and traditional-style buildings.

The resort's main slopes start with a central cable-car. This leads to the Valluga area. On the other side of the main road (served by free buses) a gondola goes to the Rendl area.

The mountains

St Anton vies with Val-d'Isère for the title of 'resort with most undergraded slopes'. There are plenty of red pistes which would be black in many other resorts, and plenty of blues which would be red. Strangely, there are no black pistes. There are very popular steep runs marked on the piste map but they are all given off-piste status. Some are classified as 'high-alpine touring routes' – this means they are not marked, not groomed, not patrolled and not protected from avalanche danger. There are also some 'ski routes'. These have some markers, are groomed occasionally in part, but are not patrolled and are protected from avalanches only in 'the immediate vicinity of the markers'.

The piste map says that high-alpine touring routes require 'extensive mountain experience' and 'are only recommended when accompanied by an authorised guide'. Ski routes are recommended only for people with

TVB ST ANTON AM ARLBERG

St Anton suits children better than you might think – and has two special kids' slopes ↓

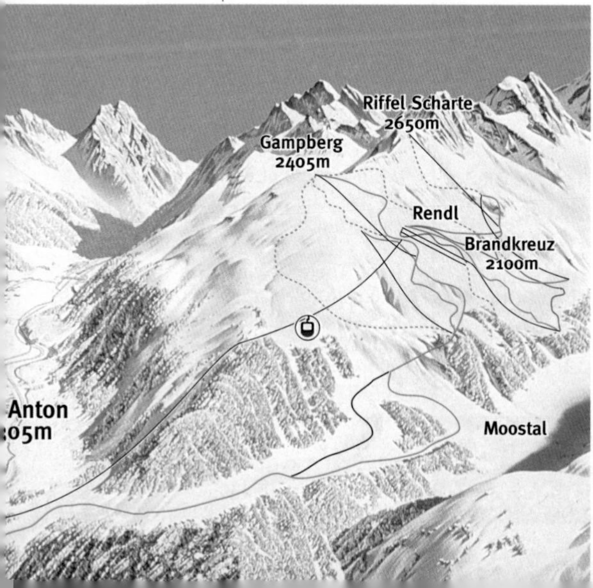

'Alpine experience or with an instructor'. And yet between them these grades of run cover most of the best runs for experts. And they are commonly used by holidaymakers without the services of an instructor or guide. One visitor commented, 'The lack of marked black runs is discouraging. When we were there the routes of the old black runs were clear and well used. It is entirely unreasonable to expect everyone to take guides on these routes, and it seems irresponsible to ignore the fact that people will go on them. They run the risk of alienating those who want to move off red runs but are not quite ready to take on anything and everything. On some of the ski routes there were snow-guns. This doesn't fit with the theory that you are on your own.' Another reporter tells a worrying tale of being badly lost on an avalanched ski route that was not marked as closed at the start.

The Arlberg region piste map seems rather inadequate; fortunately the on-mountain maps and signs are clearer. But this year some reporters have complained of poor piste grooming and one of a blue run that was closed part way down with no prior warning, forcing him to take novices down the only alternative – a steep ungroomed run. Reporters have found the local cable TV, showing the state of some of the pistes and queues, very useful.

If you want to go further afield, regular buses go to Zürs, Lech and the less-well-known Sonnenkopf area (which we had a rave review of), all covered by the Arlberg lift pass. Serfaus, Nauders, Ischgl and Sölden are feasible outings by car.

THE SLOPES

Large linked area

St Anton's slopes are made up of several sectors, all except one of which are linked, on a predominantly south-facing mountain.

From the centre, as alternatives to the cable-car, you have the choice of a four-person chair or a funicular up to **Gampen**. From there pistes lead back to St Anton and Nasserein, or in the opposite direction across to the links with the Valluga–Galzig area. Or you can go up higher to **Kapall** on the fast six-pack and head down unmarked routes – ending up at the same places.

For 2000/01 a gondola is due to go up from Nasserein to Gampen. And the Fang chair between Nasserein and St Anton feeds both the Nasserein and the town centre lifts. A run down to a four-person chair is the quickest link from Gampen to **Galzig**. This brings you out just above the mid-station of the cable-car up from St Anton. From here you can travel in most directions, including back to town, down to **St Christoph** (from where there's a high-speed quad back up) or back to Feldherrn Hügel. At peak periods the pistes down from Galzig are some of the most crowded we've come across.

From Galzig you can get up to St Anton's most famous slopes, the bowls below the **Valluga**, by taking the second stage of the cable-car or going up the Schindlergrat three-person chair, which delivers you to the same height (2650m) but on a different peak. There's a tiny third stage of the Valluga cable-car which takes you up to 2810m, but this is mainly for sightseeing. The only run down from there is off the back, off-piste to Zürs. You are not allowed to take skis or a board up the lift without a guide.

From both the second stage of the cable-car and the Schindlergrat chair, you can take the long, beautiful but very busy red run to Rauz, at the

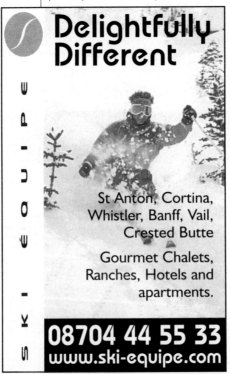

LIFT PASSES

2000/01 prices in schillings

Arlberg Ski Pass
Covers all St Anton, St Christoph, Lech, Zürs, and Stuben lifts, and linking bus between Rauz and Zürs.

Beginners Limited pass covering beginners' lifts.

Main pass
1-day pass 485
6-day pass 2230
(low season 2010)

Senior citizens
Over 65 male, 60 female: 6-day pass 1950

Children
Under 15: 6-day pass 1450

Short-term passes
Single ascent tickets on some lifts throughout Arlberg. Half-day tickets (adults 360) from noon, afternoon 'taster' tickets (205) from 3pm.

Notes 6-day pass prices are for Arlberg. 'Special' pass, available to adults and children staying in the Arlberg area (normal adult 6-day pass 2410). Main pass also covers Klösterle (10 lifts), 7km west of Stuben. Discounts during wedel, firn and snow crystal weeks.

western end of St Anton's own slopes. From Rauz you cross the road and go along to Stuben, where a slow two-stage chair-lift takes you to the quiet, mainly north-facing **Albona** area.

The final area, **Rendl**, is separate and reached by gondola from just outside town (there are free buses from the village, but it's an easy walk). Six lifts serve the west-facing runs at the top here, with a single north-facing piste returning to the gondola bottom station.

SNOW RELIABILITY

Generally very good cover

If the weather is coming (as it often is) from the west or north-west, the Arlberg gets it first, and as a result St Anton and its neighbours get heavy falls of snow. They often have much better conditions than other resorts of a similar height, and we've had great fresh powder here as late as mid-April in recent years. But many of the slopes face south or south-east, causing icy or heavy conditions at times. It's vital to time your runs off the Valluga to get decent conditions.

The lower runs are now well equipped with artificial snowmaking, which ensures the home runs remain open (but not necessarily enjoyable).

FOR EXPERTS

One of the world's great areas

St Anton vies with Chamonix, Val-d'Isère and a handful of others for the affections of experts. It has some of the most consistently challenging and extensive slopes in the world. The jewel in the crown is the variety of off-piste in the bowls beneath the Valluga – see feature panel below. Lower down, very difficult trails lead off in almost every direction from the Galzig summit. Osthang is an extremely tough, long mogul field that leads down to Feldherrn Hügel. Not much less challenging are trails down to Steissbachtal, St Christoph and past Maiensee towards the road. These lower runs can be doubly tricky if the snow has been hit by the sun.

The World Championship courses are between Kapall, Gampen and town, with a new finishing stadium which holds 10,000 people near the bottom of the Fang chair. There are countless opportunities for going off-piste in the Kapall–Gampen area, including the beautiful Schöngraben unmarked route to Nasserein.

The Rendl area across the road has plenty of open space beneath the top lifts and, with an accompanying guide, there is some delightful fun to be had off the back of this ridge.

The Albona mountain above Stuben has north-facing slopes that hold powder well and some wonderful, deserted off-piste descents including beautifully long runs down to Langen (where you can catch the train) and back to St Anton.

On top of all this, bear in mind that many of the red runs on the piste map are long and challenging too.

The ultimate challenge, though, is perhaps to go with a guide off the back of the third stage of the Valluga. The initial pitch is very, very steep (if you fall you die, type of pitch). But once you have negotiated that, the run down to Zürs is very beautiful and usually deserted.

THE VALLUGA RUNS

The off-piste runs in the huge bowl beneath the summit of the Valluga, and reached by either the Schindlergrat chair or the second stage of the Valluga cable-car, are justifiably world famous. In good snow, this whole area is an off-piste delight for experts.

Except immediately after a fresh snowfall, you can see tracks going all over the mountain – and some of the descents look terrifying. There are two main ski routes down marked on the piste map – both long, steep, often mogulled descents. The Schindlerkar gulley is the first you come to, and the steeper. For the wider, somewhat easier Mattun run, you traverse further at the top. Both these feed down into the Steissbachtal gulley where there are lifts back up to Galzig. The Schweinströge starts off in the same direction as the red run to Rauz but you traverse the shoulder of the Schindler Spitze and down a narrow gulley.

Our only reservation about this area is its sunny aspect. The snow can deteriorate very rapidly after a snowfall and so ice and slush are too often encountered.

↑ St Anton has a lot more steep off-piste slopes than it has groomed runs

TVB ST ANTON AM ARLBERG

FOR INTERMEDIATES

Some real challenges

St Anton is well suited to good, adventurous intermediates. They will be able to try the Mattun run from Vallugagrat (see page 149). The run from Schindler Spitze to Rauz is very long, tiring, varied (over 1000m vertical) and ideal for good (and fit) intermediates. Alternatively, turn off from this part-way down and take the – usually very crowded – Steissbachtal to the lifts back to Galzig.

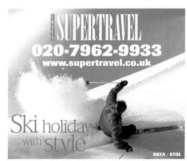

Selected chalets in St Antonn ADVERTISEMENT

THOMSON *www.thomson-ski.com* **T 0870 606 1470 F 020 8939 0402**

Luxury chalet offering a high level of comfort. Spacious bedrooms with en suite bathrooms – most have balconies. Sauna and relaxation area. Own minibus to transport you to and from the slopes.

Thomson offers a 4-star Premium Chalet Service including a (simple) cooked breakfast in addition to porridge, juice, cereals, fresh bread and preserves, yoghurt etc, daily packed lunch, afternoon tea and a three-course dinner with wine, after-dinner coffee, mints and liqueurs.

1700m from resort centre, 100m from closest ski bus stop, 900m from nearest lift, 600m from nearest slopes.

CHALET SATTELKOPF, ST ANTON→

The Kapall–Gampen section is also interesting, with sporty bumps among trees on the lower half. From Kapall to town (over 1000m vertical), following the men's downhill run is fun.

Less adventurous intermediates will find St Anton less to their taste. There are few easy cruising pistes. The most obvious are the short blues on Galzig and the Steissbachtal (aka 'Happy Valley'). These are reasonably gentle but get uncomfortably crowded, particularly at peak times. The blue to St Christoph is generally quieter. The narrowish blues between Kapall and Gampen can have some challenging bumps. Intermediates looking for easy cruising will find the best by taking the bus to Lech.

In the Rendl area a variety of trails suitable for good and moderate intermediates criss-cross, including a lovely long tree-lined run (over 1000m vertical from the top) back to the valley gondola station. This is the best run in the whole area when visibility is poor, though it has some quite awkward sections.

FOR BEGINNERS
Far from ideal
St Anton has supposedly better nursery slopes now, near the new Fang lift. But there are no easy, uncrowded runs for beginners to progress to. Experts and intermediates who are desperate to visit the Arlberg but are taking novices on holiday would be better off staying in Lech or Zürs and taking the free bus to Rauz when they want to try St Anton.

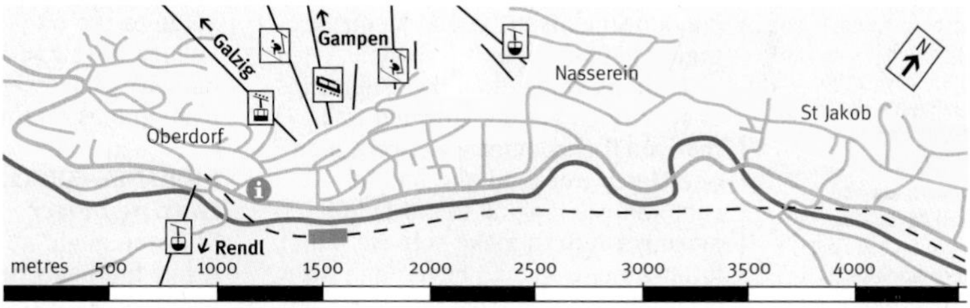

TVB ST ANTON AM ARLBERG

St Anton's traffic-free main street is very attractive ↘

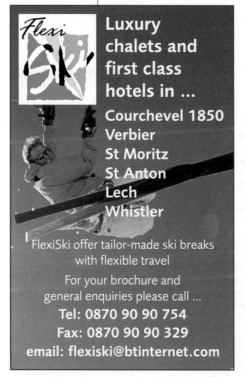

SCHOOLS/GUIDES

2000/01 prices in schillings

Arlberg
Manager Richard Walter
Classes 6 days
4½hr: 2½hr am and 2hr pm, from 9.30
6 full days 2390
Children's classes
Ages: 4 to 14
6 full days including lunch 3410
Private lessons
Half or full day
2550 for full day; each additional person 210

St Anton
Manager Franz Klimmer
Classes 6 days
4½hr: 9.30-noon and 1pm-3pm
6 full days 2580
Children's classes
Ages: 5 to 14
6 full days 1840
Private lessons
Half or full day
2650 for full day; each additional person 200

CHILDCARE

The kindergarten at the Kinderwelt (2526) takes toilet-trained children aged 30 months to 14 years, from 9am to 4.30. Ski tuition with the Arlberg ski school in a special snow-garden is available for children aged 4.

FOR CROSS-COUNTRY
Limited interest

There are a couple of uninspiring trails near town in the valley, another at St Jakob 3km away, and a pretty trail through trees along the Verwalltal to the foot of the Albona area. There is also a tiny little loop at St Christoph.

Snow conditions are usually good, but St Anton is not really a cross-country resort. Total trails 40km.

QUEUES
Improved, but still a problem

Queues are not the problem they once were after the replacement of several lifts by high-speed chairs. But they can still be tiresome in peak season and at weekends. There are useful 'singles lines' at some lifts which enable you to cut the queues if you don't mind who you ride with – with taped announcements in several languages urging people to fill the chairs.

Perhaps worse than the queues in busy periods are the crowded trails that you'll encounter – we were there one March weekend and had to continuously look all round before making a turn to make sure we didn't hit anyone; we could have done with wing mirrors. And even in January this year, the Steissbachtal was uncomfortably crowded.

MOUNTAIN RESTAURANTS
Plenty of choice

Look out for the little table-service huts, which have much more going for them than the characterless cafeterias. Two of the best are just above town, the Sennhütte and Rodelhütte. The Rendl Beach is also worth a visit. The S'Gräbli was highly recommended by a recent reporter, the Mooserwirt serves typical Austrian food, the Krazy Kanguruh burgers, pizzas and snacks. The goulash soup at the Taps Bar next to Krazy Kanguruh has been recommended, and the Kaminstube gets beautiful sunset views.

Lunching in St Christoph or Stuben is also a useful idea. The St Christoph choices include the atmospheric Hospiz Alm, where you can sit in a slide which delivers you to the lavatories (though we've had reports of poor restaurant service this year), the good value Almbar just above it and Traxl's ice bar at the Maiensee Hotel. In Stuben reporters say the views from the Albonagrathütte are worth the short walk to get to it, that the Albona is quiet and friendly and that there are a couple of cosy places in the village for a good, quiet lunch.

SCHOOLS AND GUIDES
Mixed reports

The relatively new St Anton school has brought much-needed competition to the Arlberg school. But this year we've had conflicting reports on the Arlberg school. 'Complete beginner group much too big despite our complaints and we learned more from our friends,' said one reporter. 'Superb teaching meant our novices had a great time and one was tackling red runs by the end of the week,' said another the following week. 'Arlberg school was excellent' and 'The Germans got all the attention, the English got cold and miserable' were two other comments.

Past reporters who have hired a guide to the off-piste at the top of the Valluga have had a great day. And we ourselves have skied with excellent off-piste guides on the main ski area.

FACILITIES FOR CHILDREN
Getting better

St Anton might not seem an obvious resort for family holidays, but the resort works hard to accommodate families' needs: the youth centre attached to the Arlberg school is excellent, and the special slopes both for tots (at the bottom) and bigger infants (up at Gampen) are well done.

Staying there

The resort is fairly sprawling but the attractive, traditional, traffic-free centre is fairly compact. Staying near the centre is best if you want to hit the nightlife regularly. For a quieter time the suburb of Nasserein will be a good base from this season, when it will be served by a new gondola up to Gampen. At night it is a short free bus-ride or 15-minute walk from the centre.

St Anton spreads up the hill to the west of the centre, towards the Arlberg pass. Places up here in and beyond Oberdorf can be 20 minutes' walk from the centre – but quite convenient for the slopes, if snow-cover is good.

HOW TO GO
Austria's main chalet resort

There's a wide range of places to stay, from quality hotels to cheap and cheerful pensions and apartments. What sets St Anton apart from other

GETTING THERE

Air Innsbruck, transfer 1½hr. Zürich, transfer 3hr.

Rail Mainline station in resort.

Austrian resorts for Brits is the number of chalets, which are fairly expensive, though few are particularly luxurious and many are well away from the centre up the hill or at Nasserein. There are chalets in the centre but they are virtually all apartment-based.

Hotels There is one 5-star hotel and lots of 4- and 3-stars and B&Bs.

((((5 **St Antoner Hof** Best in town, but its position on the bypass is less than ideal. Pool.

(((4 **Schwarzer Adler** Centuries-old inn on main street. Widely varying bedrooms.

(((4 **Alte Post** Atmospheric place on main street with lively après-ski bar. Highly recommended by a reporter.

(((4 **Neue Post** Comfortable if uninspiring 4-star at the centre of affairs, close to both lifts and nightlife.

(((4 **Kertess** Charmingly furnished, slightly further up the hill. Pool.

(((4 **Sport** Good central position, with varied bedrooms, good food. Pool.

((3 **Grischuna** Welcoming family-run place in peaceful position up the hill west of the town; close to the slopes, five minutes to the cable-car.

((3 **Goldenes Kreuz** A comfortable B&B hotel half-way to Nasserein, well positioned for cruising home.

Self-catering There are plenty of apartments available but package deals are few and far between.

STAYING DOWN THE VALLEY
Nice and quiet

Beyond Nasserein is the more complete village of St Jakob. It can be reached on snow, but is dependent on the free shuttle-bus in the morning.

Pettneu is a quiet village further down the valley, with slopes that most suit beginners. It's best for drivers.

EATING OUT
Mostly informal

You live fast and eat hard to make up for it in St Anton. Plain, filling fare is the norm, with numerous places such the Fuhrmannstube, Trödlerstube and the Reselehof and Alt St Anton in Nasserein serving healthy portions of traditional Austrian home-cooking. Dixies is highly recommended by a reporter for pizza, pasta, steaks and fish, and Bobo's serves good Mexican. A most atmospheric place for dinner is the wood-panelled Museum, where as well as enjoying (expensive) up-market food and wine, you can learn the history of the resort. The toboggan run is floodlit and lift-served a couple of nights a week, and it is great fun to stop off at the Rodelalm above Nasserein for traditional food, beer and schnapps. Booking is essential.

APRES-SKI
Throbbing till late

St Anton's bars rock from mid-afternoon until the early hours. A collection of bars on the slopes above town get packed by 3pm. The Krazy Kanguruh is probably the most famous. But, a bit lower down, the Mooserwirt and the S'Gräbli, opposite each other, are equally lively – live bands most days and dancing on the beams in ski boots. All this is followed by a trip down the piste in the dark. The bars in town are in full swing by 4pm too. Most are lively with loud music – only sophisticates looking for a quieter more relaxed time are less well provided for. The Underground bar has a great atmosphere and live music, but gets packed. The Hazienda and the Piccadilly pub are equally popular. Recent reporters enjoyed the atmosphere at Scotty's, Jacksy's, Amadaeus, Pub 37 and Funky Chicken. For late-night dancing Kartouche and the Stanton in the centre of town are the key places. The Drop In throbs into the early hours.

OFF THE SLOPES
Not very relaxing

St Anton is a sprawling resort, not especially attractive outside the centre, and with little to offer non-slope users. Many of the most attractive mountain restaurants are not readily accessible by lift for pedestrians. The centre is lively with a fair selection of shops. Getting by bus to the other Arlberg resorts is easy but buses tend to run only early morning and late afternoon, making excursions a long day. Lech would arguably be a better, if pricier, base, with more to do off the slopes. It's easy to visit Innsbruck by train.

St Christoph 1800m

A small, exclusive collection of hotels, restaurants and bars right by the Arlberg Pass with drag-lifts for local slopes and a high-speed quad chair-lift to the heart of St Anton's slopes. Home to Austria's elite academy for ski instructors. Good for a nice lunch. Expensive and deadly quiet to stay in. The most expensive hotel of all is the huge 5-star Arlberg-Hospiz.

ACTIVITIES

Indoor Swimming pool (also hotel pools open to the public, with sauna and massage), tennis, squash, bowling, museum, cinema in Vallugasaal

Outdoor 15km of cleared walks, natural skating rink (skating, curling), sleigh rides, tobogganing, paragliding

TOURIST OFFICE

Postcode A-6580
t +43 (5446) 22690
f 2532
st.anton@netway.at
www.stantonamarlberg.com

St Johann in Tirol 650m

Relax on easy runs with plenty of pit stops

WHAT IT COSTS

3

HOW IT RATES

The slopes

Snow	**
Extent	**
Experts	*
Intermediates	***
Beginners	****
Convenience	***
Queues	***
Restaurants	****
The rest	
Scenery	***
Resort charm	***
Off-slope	***

- ✚ Charming traffic-free centre, prettily lit in the evenings
- ✚ Lots of mountain restaurants
- ✚ Plenty of off-slope activities and things to do in the evening
- ✚ Easy to visit neighbouring resorts such as Kitzbühel
- ✚ Highly regarded for both ski and snowboard schools
- ✚ Few Brits by Tirol standards
- ✚ Good for beginners and early intermediates
- ✚ Good snow record for height and extensive snowmaking

- ▬ Very small area, with little to interest experts or keen piste-bashing intermediates
- ▬ Weekend crowds from Germany
- ▬ Can be especially busy when nearby resorts with less reliable snow are suffering

The charming, traffic-free main square and street, together with the easy, relatively snowsure slopes and the 14 cosy mountain huts, make St Johann an attractive place for beginners. It's also good for leisurely part-timers who like to spend as much time pottering about having drinks and lunch as they do actually cruising the slopes. But keener and more proficient skiers and boarders will soon get bored unless they are prepared to visit surrounding resorts such as Kitzbühel and the Ski Welt (all covered under the Kitzbüheler Alpen ski pass). There are a surprising number of lively bars in town too.

boarding *St Johann is home to some of the top boarders and it has a fun-park, half-pipe, jumps area and a carving course. But keen free-riders may find the small area limiting and want to visit nearby resorts. For beginners and intermediates the slopes are suitably gentle and the top-to-bottom gondola and number of chair-lifts mean drag-lifts are largely optional. Boarders are in a minority, but the nightlife is quite lively.*

What's new

A couple of years ago the resort made its main square and street car-free.

Nearly half the slopes are now covered by snowmaking.

Last season the resort started free weekly walking tours and next season will run snowshoe tours too.

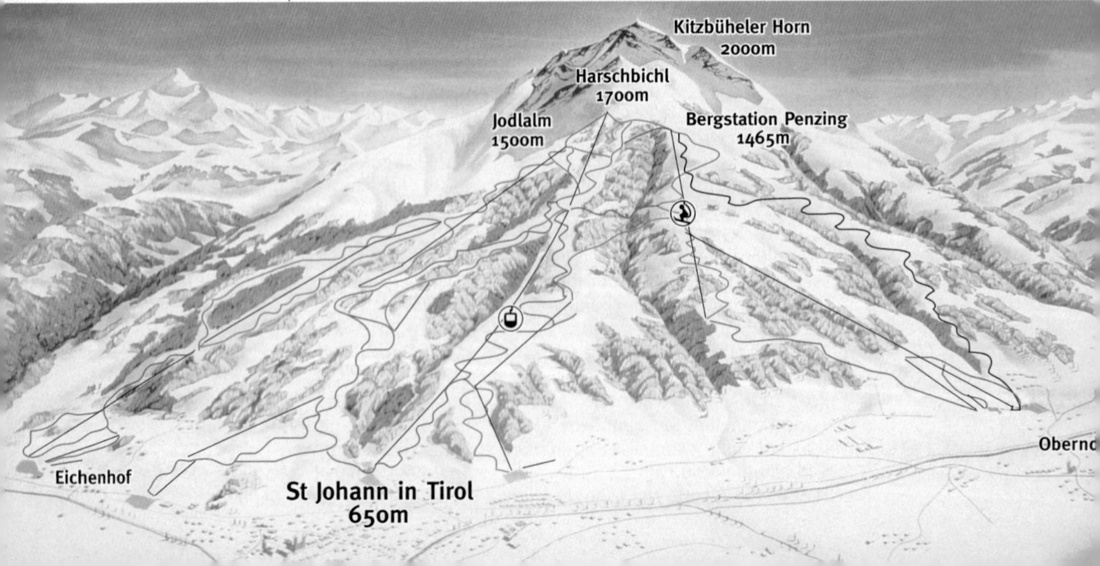

MOUNTAIN FACTS

Altitude	670m-1700m
Lifts	17
Pistes	60km
Blue	41%
Red	47%
Black	12%
Artificial snow	28km

LIFT PASSES

2000/01 prices in schillings

St Johann lift pass
Beginners Points card and half-day passes for nursery drags.
Main pass
1-day pass 360
6-day pass 1730
(low season 1500)
Children
Under 16: 6-day 865
Under 6: free pass
Short-term passes
Am till 12.30; pm from noon; 'late sleeper' from 11am; 'try out' from 2pm.
Alternative periods
5 in 6, 11 in 13 days.
Alternative passes
Schneewinkel – St Johann, Kirchdorf, Waidring, Fieberbrunn (adult 6-day 1890)
Kitzbüheler Alpen-skipass: 5 large areas – Schneewinkel, Ski Region Kitzbühel, Ski Welt, Bergbahnen Wildschönau and Alpbachtal (adult 6-day 2200).

The resort

St Johann is a sizeable town with a life other than as a resort. The compact centre is wedged between a railway track, main roads and converging rivers. The central area is attractive and traffic-free, with cobbled streets and traditional old wooden and painted buildings, and it is prettily lit at night. The five-minute walk from central hotels to the main lift involves negotiating the level crossing and walking beside a fairly busy road. But when you get there the main gondola does access the whole mountain.

St Johann has some sprawling suburbs. Lifts at the hamlet of Eichenhof to the east are convenient for the slopes, but it's a trek along a busy road to the centre of town. Lifts also start from Oberndorf, quite a way to the west.

The mountain

St Johann's small local slopes are on the north-facing side of the Kitzbüheler Horn – the 'back' side of Kitzbühel's 'second' and smallest mountain. It would be easy to link the slopes of the two resorts, but the local communities have never been able to come to a mutually acceptable arrangement. That said, it's only a 10-minute car or train ride to Kitz. The regional lift pass covers Kitzbühel and many other local resorts. And Leogang, Zell am See and Kaprun's glacier are all within reach.

THE SLOPES
Small and easy

The main access lift is a gondola which transports you to the top of the slopes at **Harschbichl** (1700m) with a mid-station at Angereralm. From the top, a choice of north-facing pistes lead back through the trees towards town. In general the slopes on the top half of the mountain are reds while those below the gondola mid-station are easy, wide blue runs. Two chair-lifts and the mid-station of the gondola allow you to 'yo-yo' the upper part of the mountain. There are more chairs and drags lower down. There is also a sunnier sector of west-facing pistes that can be accessed from the top or the mid-station and which lead down to a car park just above Oberndorf, served by an old, slow chair.

None of the runs is particularly challenging and average intermediates could cover the whole area in a day.

SNOW RELIABILITY
Better than its neighbours

St Johann is on by far the snowier side of the Kitzbüheler Horn – and gets more snow than neighbours such as Kitzbühel and the Ski Welt. This, together with its largely north-facing slopes, means that St Johann often has better conditions than its famous neighbours. When we were last touring this region, it certainly had much better snow than other nearby resorts

ST JOHANN TO

St Johann's gondola goes from top to bottom of its small mountain ↓

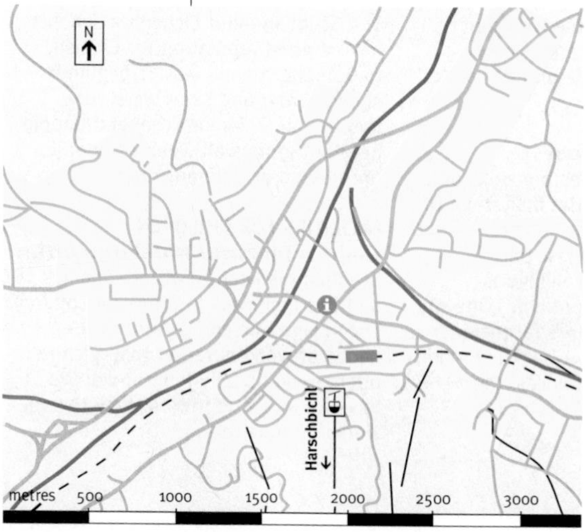

SCHOOLS/GUIDES

2000/01 prices in schillings

St Johann
Manager Ulli Arpe
Classes 6 days
4hr: 10am-noon and 1.30-3.30
6 full days 1560
Children's classes
Ages: from 4
6 full days including lunch 2100
Private lessons
Half-day
1100-1400; each additional person 200
Full-day
1950-2200; each additional person 300

Eichenhof
1999/2000 prices
Classes 6 days
4hr: 10am-noon and 1.30-3.30
6 full days 1390
Children's classes
Ages: from 4
6 full days including lunch 1930
Private lessons
Hourly or full day
500 for 1hr, for 1 to 2 people; each additional person 110
Full day
1650-2000; each additional person 300

CHILDCARE

Both ski schools have special areas for children aged 4 or more to take lessons, and can provide lunchtime care. The St Johann school's kindergarten takes younger children from 9.30 to 3.45. It has a fairytale playground and a Dwarfs' Express snowmobile lift.

The Eichenhof ski school cares for children under 4.

of comparable altitude. And now it has added substantial snowmaking, covering almost half the pistes and from top to bottom of the runs back to town and to Oberndorf.

Several nearby resorts, such as Waidring's Steinplatte, are fairly snowsure if St Johann is suffering. The glacier at Kaprun has guaranteed snow but gets very crowded when snow is scarce elsewhere. The Hintertux glacier and Obertauern are worth an hour's drive at such times.

FOR EXPERTS
Totally unsuitable

There is nothing here to challenge an expert. The long black run on the piste map is really a moderate red – and the snow suffers from the strong afternoon sun. Your best hope would be a solid week of snow, so you can practise powder technique.

FOR INTERMEDIATES
A small amount for all

The slopes are pleasantly varied, with something for everyone. Decent intermediates have a fairly direct-running piste between Harschbichl and town (runs 1b and 2b), and the black mentioned above. There are some easier red runs on the top part of the mountain, but the best of them (3a and 4b) are served by long drags or a slow, old chair. The Penzing piste (6a) is served by a high-speed quad chair. The less adventurous are better off getting off the gondola at the mid-station and enjoying variations of the wide gentle pistes down from there. As one confirmed St Johann fan says, 'The resort is good for people who don't want to ski much and aren't very confident – like my wife and her mate.'

FOR BEGINNERS
A great place to learn

The main nursery slopes are excellent. The slopes served by the first stage of the gondola make good runs to progress to – only the last part immediately above the village is uncomfortably steep for some. One of our most recent reporters (a beginner snowboarder, his wife a beginner skier) wrote: 'For complete novices, the mountain is excellent.'

CROSS-COUNTRY
Excellent valley trails

Given good snow, St Johann is one of the best cross-country resorts in Austria. A wide variety of trails totalling 75km fan out from the cross-country centre beyond the main road.

QUEUES
Good unless snow poor elsewhere

Queues are relatively rare except at weekends, during 'Fasching' week (mid-February) and any time Kitzbühel is struggling for snow, when the gondola can get long morning queues. The second stage of the Eichenhof drag will also get queues. But pistes becoming crowded is a bigger worry.

MOUNTAIN RESTAURANTS
Amazing array

With 14 restaurants spread over just 60km of piste, St Johann must have the densest array of huts of any sizeable resort in Europe. Needless to say, most are pleasantly uncrowded and competitively priced. Our favourite is the Angerer Alm, just above the gondola mid-station and dating from 1798. Anne-Marie Foidl, the young owner, serves excellent local food and has the most amazing wine cellar we have seen halfway up a mountain – a shrine to the grape, including 1905 wines from the Crimea, 1963 Mouton Rothschild, 1918 Madeira and so on (2000 bottles in total) – ask to see it. The Besgeigeralm is a lovely rustic restaurant on the Oberndorf side.

SCHOOLS AND GUIDES
Good attitude

The St Johann and Eichenhof schools have a good reputation for English, tuition and friendliness. A beginner snowboarder and skier were very impressed: 'They interchanged people between groups all week as people progressed at different rates.'

FACILITIES FOR CHILDREN
Good resort and hotel amenities

St Johann is keen to attract families and has first-class facilities for children. The village nursery, geared to the needs of workers rather than visitors, offers exceptionally long hours. We have no recent reports of how this all works in practice.

GETTING THERE

Air Salzburg, transfer 1½hr. Munich, transfer 2hr. Innsbruck, transfer 2hr.

Rail Mainline station in resort.

ACTIVITIES

Indoor Swimming, sauna, steam baths, solarium, 2 indoor tennis halls, massage, bowling

Outdoor Artificial skating rink, curling, sleigh rides, floodlit toboggan run, 40km cleared paths, ballooning, paragliding

TOURIST OFFICE

Postcode A-6380
t +43 (5352) 63335
f 65200
info@st.johann.tirol.at
www.st.johann.tirol.at

Staying there

Most accommodation is central, in or close to the traffic-free zone. But hotels beyond the railway track close to the lifts are best for the slopes.

HOW TO GO
Plenty of hotel packages

British tour operators concentrate on hotels plus a few pensions, but there are numerous apartments available.

Hotels All hotels are 3- or 4-star. The 4-stars are best placed for the slopes. There are dozens of B&B pensions.

(((4 **Brückenwirt** Smartest in town, but wrong side for the slopes.

((3 **Fischer** Central family-run 3-star.

((3 **Goldener Löwe** Vast, central 200-bed 3-star. It has widely differing rooms, the simplest offering excellent value.

((3 **Post** 13th century inn on the main street. 'By far the nicest.'

((3 **Park** Comfortable 4-star right next to gondola and school. 'Excellent.'

((3 **Sporthotel Austria** Ditto, with more amenities, including a pool.

(2 **Moser** Much smaller, cosier main-street hotel in the same price range as the Löwe's cheaper rooms.

(2 **Kaiserblick** A modest B&B in a quiet spot, yet close to amenities.

Self-catering The Alpenblick (expensive), Gratterer (mid-range) and Helfereich (very cheap) are some of the best-situated apartments.

EATING OUT
Large range of options

The restaurants stick mostly to good old-fashioned Austrian cooking. The Huber-Bräu is a working brewery where you taste local beers before moving on to good food – but it closes early. The Bären, hotels Post and Park, plus the Rettenbachstuberl specialise in tasty Tirolean dishes. The Lemberg, Lowengrill and the Crystal and Fischer hotels serve international cuisine as well as Austrian fare.

For a special meal, locals recommend the Ambiente. The Rialto does good pizza and the Hasianco both Mexican and pizza.

APRES-SKI
Plenty for all tastes

Ice bars and tea dancing greet you as you come off the slopes, and St Johann is lively without the rowdiness of some neighbouring Tirolean resorts. Max's ice bar, at the bottom of the main piste, has friendly service, music and a large umbrella. Popular Bunny's offers live music, as does Café Rainer. Almtränke is popular with locals, rustic, friendly and good for a quiet drink. Jagglebach, on the main street, is popular day and night. Platzl is a comfortable late-night bar with excellent service. Chez Paul is a wine bar. La Scala is the main disco, and Pub Max a teenage video bar.

Tour reps organise sleigh rides, tobogganing and Tirolean and nine-pin skittles evenings. The resort itself also puts on a show most evenings – ranging from snowboarding demonstrations and glühwein to festival hall concerts.

OFF THE SLOPES
A very good choice

There is plenty on offer, including an excellent public pool, indoor tennis, an artificial ice rink and 40km of cleared walks. There is also more worthwhile shopping in St Johann than is usual in a winter resort. Train excursions to Salzburg, Innsbruck, and to a lesser extent Kitzbühel, are interesting.

Waidring 780m

The nursery slopes are right in the centre of this quiet, unspoilt, friendly Tirolean village, making it ideal for beginners. The school has a good reputation. Beginners spend most of the week in the nursery area before graduating to the main slopes, the Steinplatte (10 minutes away by bus).

The Steinplatte has the best snow in the area and is wonderfully uncrowded on weekdays. A new jumbo gondola ensures minimal queueing even at weekends. Mountain restaurants are pleasant.

Buses go to St Johann and Fieberbrunn (both on the area lift pass) and to Ellmau and Kirchberg.

Cross-country skiers have 30km of dedicated trails.

The Waidringerhof is a central 4-star hotel with a pool.

Kirchdorf 640m

Kirchdorf is very similar to Waidring – quiet and traditional, with handy nursery slopes. It's five minutes by bus from St Johann, 20 from the Steinplatte, and a weekly pass includes a day in Kitzbühel. There's a specialist cross-country ski school and 80km of dedicated trails. Après-ski is livelier than in Waidring.

Schladming 745m

Pretty old town centre with extensive intermediate slopes

WHAT IT COSTS

(3)

HOW IT RATES

The slopes	
Snow	***
Extent	***
Experts	**
Intermediates	****
Beginners	****
Convenience	***
Queues	****
Restaurants	****
The rest	
Scenery	***
Resort charm	****
Off-slope	****

- ⊕ New lifts have linked extensive but previously fragmented slopes
- ⊕ Excellent slopes for intermediates
- ⊕ Extensive snowmaking operation and superb piste maintenance
- ⊕ Very sheltered slopes, among trees
- ⊕ Close to snowsure Obertauern and Dachstein glacier
- ⊕ Lots of good mountain restaurants
- ⊕ Charming town with friendly people and a life independent of tourism

- ⊖ Nursery slopes (at Rohrmoos) are inconvenient unless you stay beside them – and beginners are expected to pay for a full lift pass
- ⊖ Little for experts
- ⊖ The slopes lack variety – one mountain is much like the others
- ⊖ Most runs are north-facing, so can be cold and shady in early season

Schladming was transformed for the 1998/99 season by three new lifts and new pistes, which now link four previously fragmented mountains. There is now more than enough to keep a keen intermediate happy for a week without having to mess around catching buses, as you used to have to – and you really get a sense of travelling around. Taken together with Schladming's reliable snow record, impressive snowmaking system and pretty, traffic-free village centre, the resort deserves serious consideration. Even before it linked its mountains, Schladming received rave reviews from most of its customers.

Two of the big British tour operators now feature the resort in their brochures, and we predict that more will add it to their programmes over the next few years. So if you want to get there before the crowds, go now.

boarding *Schladming is popular with boarders. Most lifts on the spread-out mountains are gondolas or chairs, with some short drags around. There are two fun-parks/boarder-cross courses and two half-pipes, and the specialist school and Blue Tomato snowboard shop are run by former European and six-times Austrian champion boarder, Gerfried Schuller. The area is ideal for beginners and intermediates, except when snow is icy, though there is little to draw the expert boarder bar the between-the-trees powder. Nightlife is quite lively.*

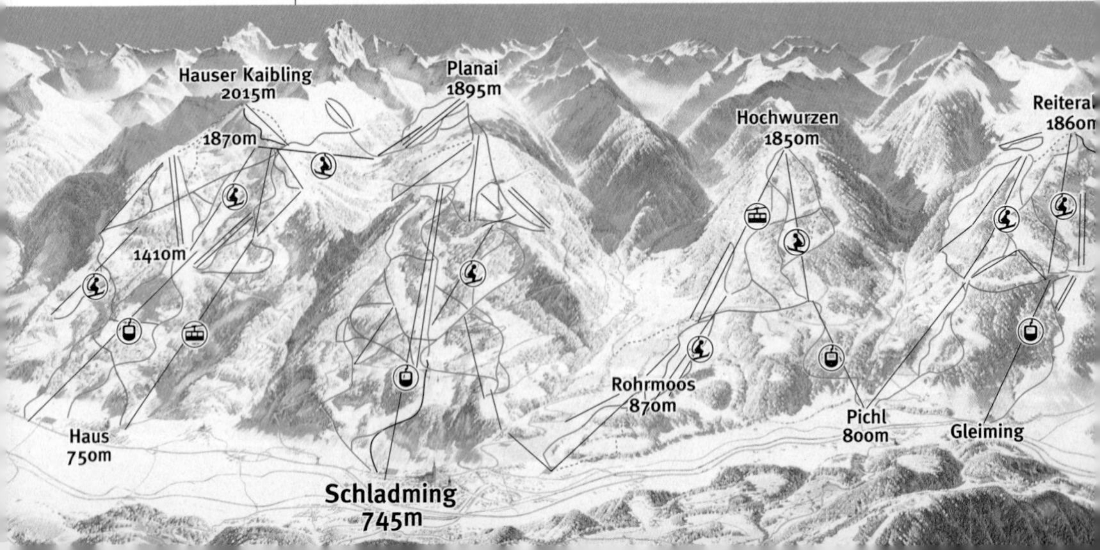

What's new

For the last two seasons Schladming's four local mountains have been linked by lifts and pistes – vastly increasing the attraction of the ski area. Before 1998/9 you had to catch buses if you wanted to use the slopes of two of the mountains. Now all of Schladming's pistes are linked and can be accessed using the gondola near the village centre.

For the 2000/01 season the old gondola from Haus will be replaced by a new eight-seater gondola, eliminating the queues here. And the slow double chair-lift from Rohrmoos on Hochwurzen will be replaced by a high-speed six-person chair.

MOUNTAIN FACTS

Figures relate to the whole Sportregion Schladming-Ramsau/ Dachstein area

Altitude	745m-2015m
Lifts	88
Pistes	167km
Blue	29%
Red	61%
Black	10%
Artificial snow	100%
Recco detectors used	

↑ Schladming is a sizeable town with a charming, traffic-free centre

SCHLADMING TO

The resort

The old town of Schladming has a long skiing tradition, having hosted World Cup races for years. It has a charming, traffic-free main square, which is prettily lit at night, and around which you'll find most of the shops, restaurants and bars (and some appealing hotels). The busy main road bypasses the town and is separated from it by a river. The main gondola to Planai starts close to the centre, and can now be used to access the 115km of linked pistes. The modern sports centre and tennis halls are near the Sporthotel, five minutes' walk from the centre. There is also accommodation out of town at Haus and Rohrmoos.

The mountains

The four main local hills have been linked and can be accessed from the gondola from the centre of Schladming or by lifts along the valley reached by car or a 'very efficient' ski-bus. Most pistes are on the wooded north-facing slopes above the main valley, with some going into the side valleys higher up. The runs are consistently easy reds, ideal for the intermediate majority but without much variety.

Your lift pass includes several other small areas, including the Dachstein glacier (a 45-minute bus-ride, with a handful of runs but superb views). The Top Tauern pass also covers resorts such as Flachau and Obertauern.

THE SLOPES
Four linked sectors

The gondola to **Planai** is just east of the town square. From here you can explore the local slopes, head east to **Hauser Kaibling,** or west to **Hochwurzen** and then on to **Reiteralm,** You have to get a lift down (and back up) through a tunnel decorated with Flintstones pictures between Planai and Hochwurzen. Many of the newly built pistes linking the other mountains are no more than access tracks or roads but they do give you a sense of travelling around adventurously. Hochwurzen and Reiteralm are more than big enough to keep intermediates interested for a few days, as are Planai and Hauser Kaibling together. Trying to cover all four areas in one day would be very ambitious, unless you set off at one end rather than the centre.

All the mountains have fairly similar terrain, with mainly red runs of much the same pitch down through heavily wooded north-facing slopes – we've had complaints of poor piste-side signing so it's difficult to remember where you are!

SNOW RELIABILITY
Excellent in cold weather

Schladming's impressive snowmaking operation makes it a particularly good choice for early holidays; and the

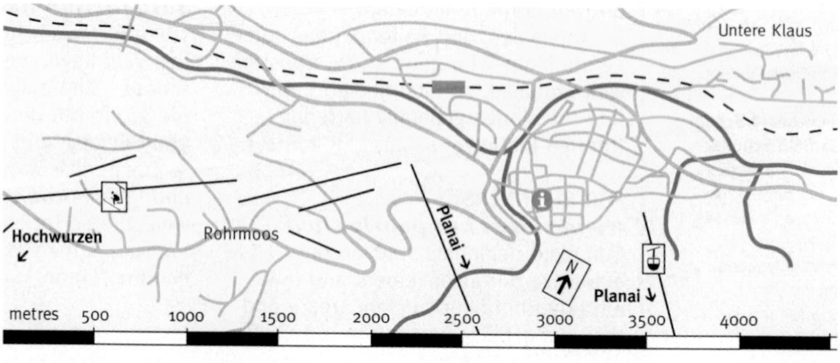

LIFT PASSES

2000/01 prices in schillings

Skiparadies Dachstein-Tauern
Covers all lifts in the Dachstein/Tauern region and ski-bus.

Main pass
1-day pass 420
6-day pass 2035
(low season 1935)

Children
Under 15 with parent: 6-day pass 1017
Under 5: free pass

Short-term passes
Half-day from 11am, noon and 1.30, 'trial' ticket valid for 2½hr.

Alternative periods
1½-day, 2½-day and 5 out of 7 days passes.

Notes Discounts for groups, families and senior citizens on request.

Alternative passes
Day passes for Ramsau/Dachstein (excluding the glacier), Galsterbergalm and Stoderzinken ski areas only; Top-Tauern Skicard covers Dachstein/Tauern, Obertauern, Lungau and Sportwelt Amadé.

SCHOOLS/GUIDES

2000/01 prices in schillings

Tritscher and Hopl-Planai

Classes 5 days
4hr: 2hr am and pm
5 full days: 1500

Children's classes
Ages: from 4
5 full days including lunch: 2000

Private lessons
1hr, 2½hr or 4½hr
475 for 1hr; each additional person 200

Snowboard School Gerfried Schuller

Classes 5 days
5 full days: 1700

Children's classes
Ages: from 5

Private lessons
1hr or 4hr
500 for 1hr; each additional person 100

northerly orientation of the slopes and superb maintenance help keep the slopes in better shape than in some neighbouring resorts. They claim 100 per cent artificial snow-cover, and certainly the main runs to the valley have full cover. Be wary of the bottom part of the World Cup downhill run back to town – it can get extremely icy (and was when we were last there). The best natural snow is usually found on Reiteralm and Hochwurzen.

FOR EXPERTS
Strictly intermediate stuff
Schladming's status as a World Cup downhill venue doesn't make it macho. The slopes are largely red runs, the steep black finish to the Men's Downhill course being an exception, and the moderate mogul slopes at the top of Planai another. Icy lower slopes can be a challenge. Hauser Kaibling's off-piste can be good, but it's rather limited. Excellent piste grooming and quiet slopes at off-peak times allow you to get up some speed – the Women's World Cup run is great fun.

FOR INTERMEDIATES
Red runs rule
The whole area is ideal for intermediate cruising. The majority of runs are graded red but it's often difficult to distinguish between blue and red in reality, leading to our main criticism of the area – lack of real variety. But for us that was more than made up for on our last visit by the great sense of travelling around that you can get now that all four mountains are linked up.

The open sections at the top of Planai and Hauser Kaibling have some more challenging slopes. And the two World Cup pistes, and the red that runs parallel to the Haus downhill course, are ideal for fast intermediates. Hauser Kaibling has a lovely meandering blue running from top to bottom for more moderate intermediates, and Reiteralm has some gentle blues with good snow. Runs are well groomed, so intermediates will find the slopes generally flattering (though the lower slopes can get icy).

FOR BEGINNERS
Good slopes but poorly sited
Complete beginners start on the extensive but inconvenient and low-altitude Rohrmoos nursery area – and they are expected to pay for a full lift pass. Another novice area near the top of Planai is more convenient for most people and has better snow.

FOR CROSS-COUNTRY
Extensive network of trails
Given sufficient snow-cover, there are 250km of trails in the region. The 1999 World Cross-country Championships were held at nearby Ramsau. There are local loops along the main valley floor and in the valleys between Planai and Hochwurzen. Further afield there are more snowsure trails at Stoderzinken, and the Dachstein glacier has small loops with spectacular views.

QUEUES
Only valley bottlenecks
The Planai gondola can suffer delays on peak-season mornings, but there are few other problems. The queues at Haus should be gone this season because of the new gondola there. Surprisingly, given its proximity to less snowsure resorts, Schladming does not suffer too badly from crowds when conditions are generally poor. Those in search of snow tend to go higher.

MOUNTAIN RESTAURANTS
Plenty of nice places
There are plenty of attractive rustic restaurants in all sectors, though Planai probably has the edge. Onkel Willy's is popular for its live music, open fire, indoor nooks and crannies and large terrace, Mitterhaus is good, and the Schladmingerhütte at the top of the Planai gondola has great food. The Knapplhof at Hauser Kaibling has many ski racing mementos on show as it's owned by the family of Helmut Höflehner (a former World Cup downhill star) – 'free schnapps' after lunch impressed one reporter. The hut near the base of the Hochwurzen gondola is recommended by a reporter.

SCHOOLS AND GUIDES
Satisfaction likely
There are two schools, and the reports this year have been on the Tritscher school – 'the only English speaker in the group but the instructor spoke good English and repeated everything'; 'a private lesson was money well spent and I shall do it again'. Boarders are well catered for by a specialist school. Ramsau is the best place to get cross-country tuition.

CHILDCARE

There is a nursery at Rohrmoos, which takes children from 18 months.

Children in ski school can be looked after all day.

GETTING THERE

Air Salzburg, transfer 1½hr.

Rail Mainline station in resort.

ACTIVITIES

Indoor Swimming, sauna, bowling, indoor tennis court, squash, museum
Outdoor Ice skating, curling, 8km floodlit toboggan run, sleigh rides, 50km of cleared paths in the Schladming and surrounding area, paragliding

TOURIST OFFICE

Postcode A-8970
t +43 (3687) 222680
f 24138
touristoffice@schladming.com
www.schladming.com

FACILITIES FOR CHILDREN
Rohrmoos is the place

The extensive gentle slopes that make up the suburb of Rohrmoos could have been designed to build up youngsters' confidence. Whether in the nursery or proper classes, this is where we would head with children. That's the theory; reports on the practice welcome.

Staying there

Much accommodation is central, which is where we'd recommend staying – just a few minutes' walk from the Planai gondola. Several reporters have said you don't need an alarm clock because the church bells start ringing at 7am! But some (cheaper) hotels and most apartments are on the outskirts.

Rohrmoos has doorstep slopes for beginners, peace and quiet, good-value hotels, but little to do in the evenings.

HOW TO GO
Packages means hotels

Packaged accommodation is in hotels and pensions, but there are plenty of apartments for independent travellers.
Hotels Most of the accommodation is in modestly priced pensions but there are also a few more upmarket hotels.
((((4 **Sporthotel Royer** Big, smart and comfortable, a few minutes' walk from the main Planai lift; but impersonal and attracts conferences.
(((3 **Alte Post** Characterful old inn with great position on the main square. Very good food, but some rooms are rather small by 4-star standards. 'Excellent value' says a recent reporter.
(((3 **Stadttor** Similarly priced, although less charming and well placed. 'Comfortable with excellent food,' says a reporter. Special deals for families.
(((3 **Neue Post** Large rooms, friendly, good food, on main square.
(((3 **Schladmingerhof** Bright, modern chalet in peaceful position, a bus-ride from centre in Untere Klaus.
Self-catering Ferienhaus Girik is the best-positioned apartment house in town, close to the gondola.

EATING OUT
Some good places

We had a delicious meal at Fritzi's gasthaus – which was allegedly offered a Michelin star but turned it down. Pumpkin soup and rösti and lamb fillet were superb. Reader recommendations include the Kirchenwirt hotel ('excellent home cooking'), Giovanni's (for pizza), Gasthof Brunner ('good value'), Talbackschenke ('good grills and atmosphere') and Lisi's. Hotels Neue and Alte Post are 'good but pricey'.

APRES-SKI
Varied and quite lively

The tea dance at the Tauernalm on Hochwurzen is great fun. Charley's Treff (with umbrella bar) opposite the Planai is lively as the slopes shut and has great photos of local hero Arnold Schwarzenegger inside. The Siglu (in a big plastic igloo-like bubble) rocks from 3pm until late.

We enjoyed the local brewpub Schwalbenbräu and Café Zauberkistl (which means Magic Box), where owner Magic Moritz is a champion table-magician and will amuse you with amazing tricks unless he has a gig (he also appears in some local hotels). Beizl is a smart, beautiful bar attracting a varied age group. Hangl Bar has wooden decor and middle-of-the-road music and occasional karaoke. The Pub has a nautical theme, loud music and a quiet room at the rear. La Porta gets very crowded and has live music. The Gondel Treff has an international football theme, big-screen TV for sports matches and gimmicks such as motorised lollipops. The Sonderbar is a central disco with a great DJ and three bars. Slopes and a toboggan run on Hochwurzen are floodlit (7.30 to 10).

OFF THE SLOPES
Good for all but walkers

Those not looking for on-slope action should still find adequate diversions. Some mountain restaurants are easily reached on foot or by lift. The town shops and museum are worth a look. Train trips to beautiful Salzburg are easy. Buses run to the old walled town of Radstadt. There's a public swimming pool and ice rink.

Haus 750m

Unlike Rohrmoos, Haus is a real village with a life of its own. It has a fair amount of accommodation plus its own schools and kindergartens.

The Hauser Kaibling lifts are a little out of town, but the user-friendly nursery area is more handily placed between town and gondola station.

Haus is a railway stop, so excursions are easy, but off-slope activities and nightlife are better in Schladming. Hotel prices are generally lower here than in Schladming.

Seefeld

1200m

Pretty all-round winter holiday resort with limited slopes

WHAT IT COSTS

3

HOW IT RATES

The slopes

Snow	**
Extent	*
Experts	*
Intermediates	**
Beginners	*****
Convenience	*
Queues	***
Restaurants	***
The rest	
Scenery	***
Resort charm	****
Off-slope	*****

What's new

For 1999/2000 there was a new six-seater chair-lift from the bottom of Rosshütte to halfway up the Härmelekopf peak. For 2000/01 it is planned to have another from part way down at Reither Joch Alm to the top.

'Play Castle Tirol' is a new multi-million pound leisure and entertainment complex for kids and teenagers on the edge of Seefeld, on the road to Garmisch.

MOUNTAIN FACTS

Altitude	1180m-2065m
Lifts	25
Pistes	30km
Blue	75%
Red	20%
Black	5%
Artificial snow	15km

TOURIST OFFICE

Postcode A-6100
t +43 (5212) 2313
f 3355
info@seefeld.tirol.at
www.seefeld-tirol.com

Seefeld rates highly for cross-country, and is also one of the best mountain resorts for off-slope activities – particularly curling, skating and swimming. For downhillers there are literally hundreds of better resorts in this book.

THE RESORT

Seefeld is a classic postwar Tirolean tourist development, built in a traditional chalet style. It is very well designed, with a large pedestrian-only central sector that is prettily lit at night and very pleasant to stroll around.

Seefeld sits on an elevated plateau, not far from Innsbruck, to which it is linked by rail. Ehrwald and Garmisch (over the border in Germany) are easy to reach, and car trips to the Stubai and Zugspitz glaciers are worthwhile.

THE MOUNTAINS

Seefeld's **slopes** consist of two main sectors, both on the outskirts and reached from most hotels by regular, free shuttle-bus. Gschwandtkopf is a rounded hill with 300m of intermediate vertical down two main slopes. Rosshütte is a more extensive but still very limited area – **snowboarders** will find a fun-park and half-pipe here. A funicular goes up to Rosshütte at 1800m, and a cable-car then goes up to 2100m. There is one main slope, also served by three drags. Runs go down from Rosshütte into the adjacent Hermannstal, with return by chair or the funicular. From Rosshütte another cable-car goes to the shoulder of Härmelekopf at 2050m, whence there is an excellent red run to the village. The bottom half of Härmelekopf can also be accessed by a new six-person chair and another six-person chair is due to run to the top for 2000/01.

With reasonable altitudes by Austrian standards and a serious snowmaking installation in both main sectors, **snow reliability** is not a serious problem. But most of the slopes are sunny in the morning or afternoon, affecting snow quality – particularly on Rosshütte.

The Rosshütte sector has some seriously steep off-piste challenges for **experts**. These are great for visitors coming from Innsbruck for the day, but no basis for a week's holiday.

Only the most timid of **intermediates** should think of coming here. Gschwandtkopf is tiny, and Rosshütte is a two-run area.

This is an excellent resort for **beginners** – the central village nursery slopes are broad and gentle; there is also a beginners' slope at Gschwandtkopf, but it gets very busy.

The excellence of Seefeld's **cross-country** trails is one of the reasons why Innsbruck has been able to hold the Winter Olympics twice. More recently, the Nordic World Championships have been held here. It is one of Europe's best resorts for cross-country, with 200km of trails.

Lift **queues** are rarely a problem.

Mountain restaurants are adequate, but many people lunch in the village.

Reports on the **ski school** say the instruction and standard of English are good; **children** are cared for all day, and there's a non-ski kindergarten.

STAYING THERE

The upmarket nature of the resort shows in the range of **hotels**. There are seven 5-star places, and almost 30 4-stars. On our last visit we stayed at the 4-star Hiltpolt – very comfortable with good food. Of the many pensions, Felseneck and Haus Kerber are recommended.

Most **restaurants** are hotel-based.There's a lively **après-ski** scene; many bars have live music (Chris Barber's jazz band was on when we were there). Graham's Pub has been recommended for its early evening music and happy hour. A few hotels have tea dancing. There's one of the few casinos in Austrian ski resorts. There's a new toboggan run in the Gschwandtkopf area with its own lift.

Seefeld has great **off-slope facilities** including tennis courts, saunas, skating rinks and 40 curling lanes. The superb pool has areas for non-swimmers and children and there's a brand new spa complex. It is also a very pleasant place to wander around with some good walks too. Lots of people potter around during the day and don't ski or snowboard.

Sölden 1380m

Good, extensive intermediate slopes with throbbing nightlife

Sölden has invested massively in new lifts to link its home slopes, which suit adventurous intermediates best, with snowsure runs on the Rettenbach glacier. The nightlife is noisy, drunken and wild – don't expect quaint Tirolean charm.

WHAT IT COSTS

4

HOW IT RATES

The slopes

Snow	****
Extent	***
Experts	**
Intermediates	****
Beginners	**
Convenience	***
Queues	**
Restaurants	***

The rest

Scenery	***
Resort charm	**
Off-slope	**

What's new

Sölden's glaciers – previously closed in winter – were opened up two years ago by an eight-seat gondola and two high-speed quads. A new fast quad from Giggijoch speeded up the link for 1999/2000. A further high-speed quad and a black run were also added.

2000/01 will see a new gondola on the Tiefenbach glacier and a six-pack from Langegg – the valley between the two main sectors – to Giggijoch.

MOUNTAIN FACTS

Altitude	1380m-3250m
Lifts	34
Pistes	141km
Blue	32%
Red	52%
Black	16%
Artificial snow	27km
Recco detectors used	

TOURIST OFFICE

Postcode A-6450
t +43 (5254) 5100
f 510520
info@soelden.com
www.soelden.com

THE RESORT

Despite its traditional Tirolean-style buildings and tree-filled valley, Sölden is a large, traffic-filled place which sprawls along both sides of a main road and river. It attracts a young, lively crowd – mostly Dutch and German. If you're looking for quiet evening ambience, stay in Hochsölden.

THE MOUNTAINS

Sölden's home **slopes** are made up of two similar-sized sectors separated by a small valley. High-capacity gondolas from either end of town take you up to Gaislachkogel and Giggijoch respectively. The two are linked from the central valley by chair-lifts. The Rettenbach and Tiefenbach glaciers are reached by a series of new lifts from above Giggijoch. Both main sectors have runs through trees to the village. There are **snowboard** fun-parks and half-pipes at Giggijoch and on the Rettenbach glacier.

Most of the area is over 2100m – a good height for Austria – so it is fairly **snowsure**, even without the glaciers.

Sölden has little to challenge **experts**. But there is a mountain guides' office in Sölden, and at the top of the valley is one of the Alps' premier touring areas.

Most of Sölden's main slopes are red runs for adventurous **intermediates**. There are several easy blacks, and the long, quiet piste down to Gaislachalm is ideal for high-speed cruising. Giggijoch and Rotkogl, above Hochsölden, are good if you prefer a more moderate pace, but Sölden is not really for timid types.

The **beginners'** slopes are situated inconveniently – just above the village at Innerwald – and prone to poor snow. Near-beginners can go up the Giggijoch gondola to two blue runs.

There are a couple of uninspiring **cross-country** loops by the river, plus a small area at Zwieselstein. The one factor in Sölden's favour is altitude.

Thanks to the upgrading of its lifts, Sölden has few **queues**.

The **mountain restaurants** tend to get very crowded and the quality of the food is nothing special.

We have few reports on the three competing **ski and snowboard schools** – except for observing small class sizes.

There is no proper day-care nursery for **children**, and kindergartens keep rather short hours. Children aged three and up can join the ski kindergarten.

STAYING THERE

The two main lifts are out at the edges of town so staying in the geographic centre is inconvenient. Sölden has some good **hotels**. The Central is the best and one of the biggest in town. The Villa Arno B&B, right on the piste above town, got a glowing report from a recent visitor. Self-catering **apartments** at the Posthausl are good quality. For peace and quiet, stay in Innerwald or Hochsölden.

For **eating out**, the good-value Café Hubertus does everything from snacks to full meals. The Nudeltopf and Café Corso vie for the title of 'best pizzas in town', and the Hotel Birkenhof's restaurant is pleasantly traditional. Hermann's, up the slopes at See, has been recommended for 'the best food and enormous portions'.

Sölden's **après-ski** is notorious, and the resort is full of bars, live bands and discos. It gets very loud and very rowdy. Even our keenest après-ski reporter was shocked on his last visit: 'Far too many drunken Dutch urinating and smashing glasses in the street. There is table dancing and striptease at Rodelhütte, and Lawine has great theme nights if you are into latex and leather.' Somewhat tamer are the nightly toboggan evenings, with drinking and dancing before an exciting 6km run back to town from the Gaislachalm mountain restaurant.

Given Sölden's size there is little to do **off the slopes**. Trips to Innsbruck and Igls are possible. Mountain bikes are available and there is a sports centre, swimming pool and ice rink.

Söll

700m

Small, lively village with large, easy ski and snowboard area

WHAT IT COSTS

3

HOW IT RATES

The slopes

Snow	**
Extent	****
Experts	*
Intermediates	****
Beginners	***
Convenience	**
Queues	***
Restaurants	**

The rest

Scenery	***
Resort charm	***
Off-slope	**

- ➕ Part of Ski Welt, Austria's largest linked ski and snowboard area
- ➕ Local slopes are the highest and steepest in the Ski Welt and north-facing so keep their snow well
- ➕ Massive recent investment in snowmaking has paid off
- ➕ Plenty of cheap and cheerful pensions for those on a budget
- ➕ Pretty village with lively après-ski

- ➖ Poor natural snow record
- ➖ Long walk or infrequent bus-ride to the lifts
- ➖ Little for experts or good intermediates
- ➖ Ski Welt slopes can get busy at weekends and in high season
- ➖ Local slopes are the most crowded in the Ski Welt
- ➖ Mostly short runs in local sector

Söll has long been popular with groups of British beginners and intermediates. Its pretty scenery, gentle slopes, small attractive traditional village, good-value accommodation and lively nightlife attract a mixture of young singles looking for a fun time and families looking for a quiet time. In the 1980s it gained notoriety as prime lager-lout territory; it still has some loud bars but has calmed down a lot. Many visitors find the village surprisingly small and are disappointed by the distance between it and the slopes (and by the bus service).

Its main drawback has always been snow. Because of its low altitude and sunny slopes, pistes have often been slushy or bare, not just in Söll but also throughout the extensive Ski Welt circuit it is part of. But this problem has been tackled by a massive investment in snowmaking and half of the Ski Welt's 250km of piste are now covered by snowmaking – more than in any other Austrian ski area. This ensures the region's main pistes and links stay open, though it can't prevent slush and ice developing.

When the snow is good Söll can be a great place for a holiday, cruising the attractive and undemanding pistes of Austria's largest linked area.

boarding *Söll is a good place to try out boarding: slopes are gentle and there are plenty of gondolas and chairs. For decent boarders it's more limited – the slopes of the Ski Welt are tame. But there is a fun-park and quarter-pipe near Hochsöll and lots of lively bars in the evening.*

What's new

The snowmaking capacity in the Ski Welt has been hugely increased in recent years. It now covers 125km of pistes (half the pistes in the Ski Welt) and is the largest snowmaking facility anywhere in Austria.

For 2000/01 the old single-seat chair to the Hohe Salve will be replaced by a fast eight-seater gondola from Hochsöll, giving much quicker access to the steepest runs and to the Hopfgarten and Brixen areas (via a link that will get new snowmaking for 2000/01 too).

In Hopfgarten, a queue-prone T-bar (a key link on the Ski Welt circuit) will be replaced by a high-speed six-seater chair.

The resort

Söll is a small, pretty, friendly village – much smaller than you might expect by its reputation; you can explore it in a few minutes and there aren't many shops. New buildings are traditional in design and there's a huge church near the centre. The pretty scenery adds to Söll's charm, and it benefits from being off the main road through the Tirol.

The slopes are a bus- or taxi-ride or a 15-minute walk from the centre, the other side of a busy road with a pedestrian tunnel underneath. The bus service has been criticised by most reporters as being too infrequent. Some accommodation is further away, though there is some near the lifts too.

The mountains

The Ski Welt may be the largest linked area in Austria, but that doesn't make it a Trois Vallées. It covers Hopfgarten, Brixen, Scheffau and Ellmau, but is basically a typically small, low, pastoral Austrian hill multiplied several times. One section is much like another, and most slopes best suit early to average intermediates. Runs are short and scenery attractive rather than stunning – although the panoramic views from the Hohe Salve are impressive on a clear day.

Westendorf is separate, but covered by the area pass. The Kitzbüheler Alpenskipass also covers many other resorts easily reached by car including

MOUNTAIN FACTS

Altitude	620m-1830m
Lifts	92
Pistes	250km
Blue	43%
Red	48%
Black	9%
Artificial snow	125km

LIFT PASSES

2000/01 prices in schillings

Ski Welt Wilder Kaiser-Brixental
Covers all lifts in the Wilder Kaiser-Brixental area from Going to Westendorf, and the ski-bus.

Beginners Points tickets (100 points 300). Most beginner lifts cost from 3 to 10 points.

Main pass
1-day pass 380
6-day pass 1890

Children
Under 16: 6-day pass 1070
Under 6: free pass

Short-term passes
Single ascent on some lifts, passes from 11am, noon 2pm to the end of the day.

Alternative periods
5 in 7 days, 7 in 10 days and 10 in 14 days.

Alternative passes
Söll pass available (6-day pass for adults 1310, for children 850) covers 12 lifts, 34km piste).
Kitzbüheler Alpen-skipass covers five large ski areas – Schneewinkel (St Johann), Ski Region Kitzbühel, Ski Welt Wilder Kaiser, Bergbahnen Wildschönau and Alpbachtal (adult 6-day 2200, children 1100).

Kitzbühel, Schneewinkel (includes St Johann, Fieberbrunn, Steinplatte, Waidring), Niederau and Alpbach – an impressive total of 260 lifts and 680km of pistes.

THE SLOPES
Short run network

A gondola takes all but complete beginners up to the shelf of Hochsöll, where there are a couple of short lifts and connections in several directions.

An eight-person gondola (new for the 2000/01 season) will take you to the high point of Hohe Salve. From here there are stunning views and runs down to Kälbersalve and Hopfgarten via Rigi. Rigi can also be reached by alternative chairs and pistes without going to Hohe Salve – to which it is itself linked by chairs. Rigi is also the start of runs down to Itter. From Kälbersalve you can head down south-facing runs to Brixen or up to Zinsberg and Eiberg and towards the north-facing runs in the Ellmau sector.

A quicker way to Ellmau without taking as many south-facing slopes is by taking a cable-car from Hochsöll.

The whole area is vast and will easily keep an early or average intermediate amused for a week.

We have had lots of criticism of the piste map by recent reporters: 'direction of runs/lifts and the links not clear'.

SNOW RELIABILITY
Artificial help saves the day

With a very low average height, and important links that get a lot of sun, the snowmaking that the Ski Welt has installed in recent seasons is essential. At 125km and covering half the area's pistes, it is one of Austria's biggest artificial snow installations. We were there in January 1999, before any major snowfalls, and snowmaking was keeping the links open well. It did not, however, prevent slush and icy patches forming – usually slush on south-facing slopes, ice on north-facing ones.

FOR EXPERTS
Not a lot

The black run from Hohe Salve towards Hochsöll and the black run alongside the Brixen gondola are the only challenging pistes. There are further blacks in Scheffau and Ellmau, but most experts will need to seek amusement off-piste – from Scheffau's Brandstadl down to Söll, for example.

FOR INTERMEDIATES
Mainly easy runs

With good snow, the Ski Welt is a paradise for early intermediates and those who love easy cruising. There are lots of blue runs and many of the reds in truth deserve a blue grading. It is a big area and you really get a feeling of travelling around – we skied it for two days in 1999 and felt we only scratched the surface. The main challenge you may find is when the snow isn't perfect – ice and slush can make even gentle slopes seem tricky. In general the most difficult slopes are those from the mid-stations to the valleys: the most direct of the runs between Brandstadl and Blaiken, the pistes down to Brixen and the red run from from Hochsöll back to Söll, for example. Higher up, the red from Hohe Salve to Rigi is a good cruise on relatively good snow.

FOR BEGINNERS
OK when snow is good

The big area of nursery slopes between the main road and the gondola station is ideal when snow is abundant – gentle, spacious, uncrowded and free from good skiers whizzing past. But it can get icy or slushy. In poor snow the Hochsöll area is used. Near-beginners and fast learners can get home to the bottom station when the narrow blue from Hochsöll is not too icy.

FOR CROSS-COUNTRY
Neighbouring villages are better

Söll has 35km of local trails but they are less interesting than those between Hopfgarten and Kelchsau or the ones around and beyond Ellmau. Lack of snow-cover is a big problem.

QUEUES
Much improved

Continued introduction of new lifts – most recently the new quad from Hochsöll towards Hohe Salve – has greatly improved this once queue-prone area, The Blaiken gondola is to be avoided on weekend mornings. However, most delays are directly related to conditions: when snow is in poor condition, the linking lifts to and from Zinsberg and Eiberg get busy.

MOUNTAIN RESTAURANTS
Good, but crowded

There are quite a few jolly little chalets dotted about, but they can get very busy. The atmospheric Stockalm (a

Next season the Hohe Salve (top of photo) will be accessed direct from Hochsöll by a new 8-seater gondola →

SÖLL TO

SCHOOLS/GUIDES

2000/01 prices in schillings

Söll-Hochsöll
Classes 5 days
2hr or 4hr: 10am-noon and 2pm-4pm
5 full days: 1430
Children's classes
Ages: 5 to 14
5 full days: 1380
Private lessons
Hourly or full day (4hr)
500 for 1hr; each additional person 180

Austria
1999/2000 prices
Classes 6 days
4hr: 10am-noon and 2pm-4pm
5 full days: 1300
Children's classes
Ages: 5 to 14
5 full days: 1260
Private lessons
Hourly or daily
480 for 1hr; each additional person 150

converted cow shed), Kraftalm and Grundalm are all near Hochsöll. The Alpenrose, near the top of Hohe Salve, has a good sun terrace, generous portions and reasonable prices. Further afield, the Neualm, halfway down to Blaiken, is one of the best huts in the Ski Welt. The nearby Brantlalm has been recommended for lovely views. The Jochstubn at Eiberg is self-service but has a good atmosphere and excellent Tiroler Gröstl. The Filzalm above Brixen is a good place for a quick drink on the way back from the circuit – don't miss the last lift connection. But our favourite is the Rübezahl above Ellmau – very rustic with wooden carvings, low doors, several rooms and excellent food.

SCHOOLS AND GUIDES
The usual reservations

The Austria school and the bigger Söll-Hochsöll school have fairly good reputations, though you may find over-large classes and poor spoken English. We have no recent reports, however.

FACILITIES FOR CHILDREN
Fast becoming a family resort

Söll has fairly wide-ranging facilities – the Söll-Hochsöll ski kindergarten, a Mini Club, which looks after children aged three to five who don't want to spend all day on the slopes, and a special kids-only drag and slope on the opposite side of the village to the main lifts. Reports welcome.

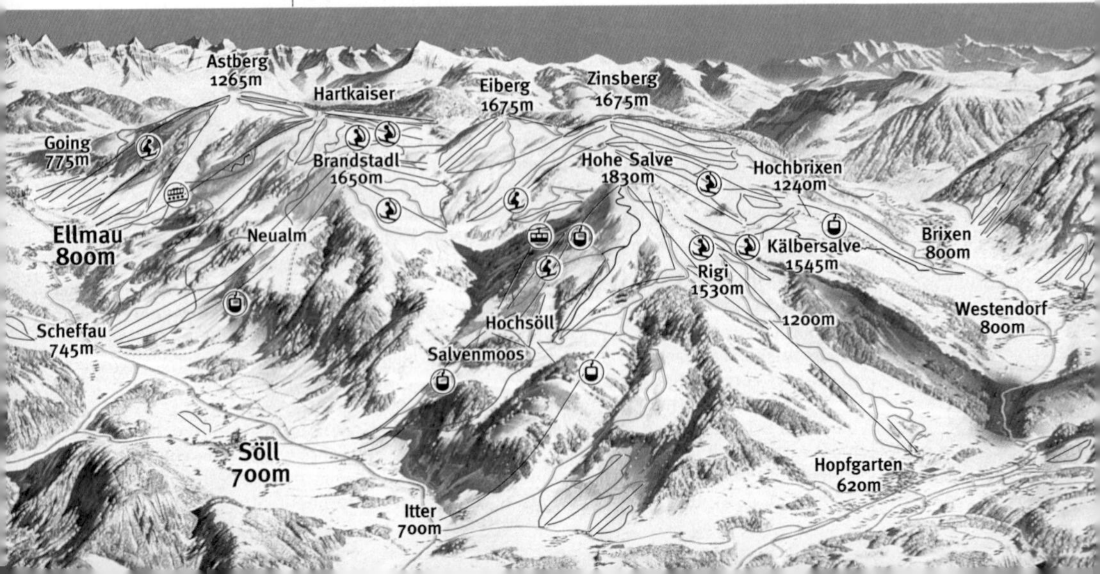

CHILDCARE

The ski schools take children from age 5 in special snow-gardens on the nursery slopes from 9.45 to 4pm. Once they progress to Hochsöll, care has to be arranged with the instructor.

Next to the main ski kindergarten, the Söll-Hochsöll school operates a Mini Club for children aged 3 to 5 from 9.45 to 4pm.

GETTING THERE

Air Salzburg, transfer 2hr. Innsbruck, transfer 1½hr.

Rail Wörgl (13km) or Kufstein (15km); bus to resort.

ACTIVITIES

Indoor Swimming, sauna, solarium, massage, bowling, squash
Outdoor Natural ice rink (skating, curling), sleigh rides, horse-riding, 3km floodlit ski and toboggan runs, paragliding, hang-gliding

TOURIST OFFICE

Postcode A-6306
t +43 (5333) 5216
f 6180
info@soell.com
www.soell.com

Staying there

There is some accommodation out near the lifts but most is in or around the village centre – a free ski-bus-ride from the slopes. Being on the edge of town nearest the lifts is the best for those who are prepared to walk to the slopes. The other side of town has the advantage that you can board the bus there before it gets too crowded. Be aware that some guest houses are literally miles from the centre and lifts, and that the ski-bus does not serve every nook and cranny of this sprawling community.

HOW TO GO
Mostly cheap, cheerful gasthofs

There is a wide choice of simple gasthofs, pensions and B&Bs, and an adequate amount of better-quality hotel accommodation – mainly 3-star. Söll is not a big catered chalet resort, but there are a couple of big 'club hotels' run by British tour operators.

Hotels

(((3 **Greil** The only 4-star – attractive place, but out of the centre on the wrong side for the lifts and pool.
(((3 **Postwirt** Attractive, central old 3-star with own bar and separate stube.
(((3 **Bergland** Small 3-star, well placed midway between the village and lifts.
(((3 **Theresa** Comfortable, 'superb' food, but a 10-minute walk out of the centre on the wrong side.
(((3 **Panorama** 3-star far from lifts but with own bus stop; wonderful views; pleasant rooms; best cakes around.
(((3 **Tulpe** Next to the lifts.
((2 **Feldwebel** Central 2-star.
((2 **Schirast** Next to the lifts.
((2 **Garni-Tenne** B&B gasthof between centre and main road.
Self-catering The central Ferienhotel Schindlhaus has nice accommodation, though the best apartments in town are attached to the Bergland hotel.

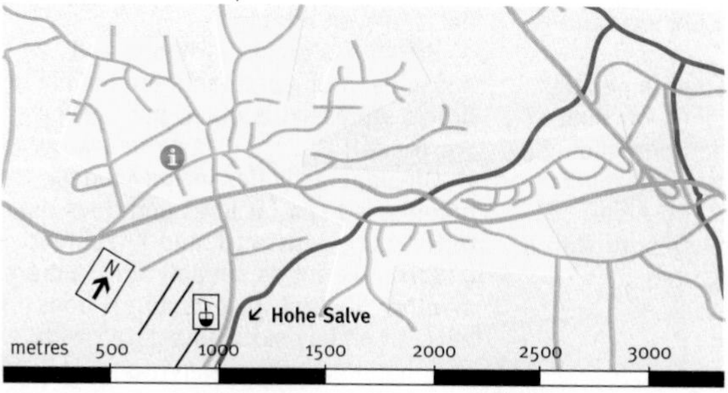

↑ The church in the centre of Söll is pretty, but you may curse its early morning bell ringing

SÖLL TO

EATING OUT
A fair choice

Some of the best restaurants are in hotels. The Greil and Postwirt are good but the Schindlhaus is said to be the best. Giovanni does excellent pizzas, while other places worth a visit include the Dorfstub'n and Venezia.

APRES-SKI
Still some very loud bars

Söll is not as raucous as it used to be, but it's still very lively and a lot of places have live music. Pub 15 is a bit of a sleazy remnant of the old days, but is lively. The Whisky Mühle is a large disco that can get a little rowdy, especially after other bars close. The Postkeller sometimes has a singalong. Buffalo's Western Saloon is new. There's a floodlit piste and separate toboggan run – both from top to bottom of the gondola. And for a romantic evening you can hire the Gerhard Berger VIP gondola, complete with leather upholstery, curtains and a champagne bucket.

OFF THE SLOPES
Not bad for a small village

You could spend a happy day in the wonderfully equipped Panoramabad: taking a sauna, swimming, lounging about. The large baroque church would be the pride of many tourist towns. There are numerous coach excursions, including trips to Salzburg, Innsbruck and even Vipiteno over in Italy.

Hopfgarten 620m

Hopfgarten is an unspoilt, friendly and traditional resort tucked away several kilometres from the busy Wörgl road. Most hotels are within five minutes' walk of the queue-free chair that accesses Rigi and Hohe Salve – the high point of the Ski Welt. The resort's great weakness is the poor snow quality on the south-west-facing home slope. The village is a good size: small enough to be intimate, large enough to have plenty of off-slope amenities.

When snow is good, the runs down to Hopfgarten and the nearby villages of Brixen and Itter are some of the best in the Ski Welt. But the fine, and relatively snowsure, runs above Scheffau are irksomely distant.

For a change of scene, and perhaps less crowded pistes, take a bus to Westendorf (see separate chapter) or Kelchsau, both on the Ski Welt pass.

There is a convenient beginner slope in the village, but it is sunny as well as low, so lack of snow-cover is likely to mean excursions up the mountain to the higher blue runs – at the cost of a lift pass.

Hopfgarten is one of the best cross-country bases in the area. There are fine trails to Kelchsau (11km) and Niederau (15km), and the Itter-Bocking loop (15km) starts nearby. Westendorf's trails are also close.

Partly because Hopfgarten seems to attract large numbers of Australians, English is widely spoken in the two schools.

Cheap and cheerful gasthofs, pensions and little private B&Bs are the norm here. The exceptions are the comfortable but rather expensive hotel Hopfgarten and Sporthotel Fuchs, both well placed for the main lift.

Après-ski is generally quiet, though a lively holiday can usually be ensured if you go with Aussie-dominated Contiki Travel. Though most of the restaurants are hotel-based, there are exceptions, including a Chinese and a pizzeria.

The village has off-slope amenities including swimming, riding, bowling, skating, tobogganing and paragliding. The railway makes trips to Salzburg, Innsbruck and Kitzbühel possible.

Hopfgarten is a family resort, with a nursery and ski kindergarten.

Itter 700m

Itter is a tiny village halfway around the mountain between Söll and Hopfgarten, with nursery slopes close to hand and a gondola just outside the village into the Ski Welt, via Hochsöll.

There's a hotel and half a dozen gasthofs and B&Bs. The school has a hire shop, and when conditions are good this is a good beginners' resort.

Brixen 800m

Brixen im Thale is a very scattered roadside village at the south-east edge of the Ski Welt, close to Westendorf. It may not be pretty, but it has a queue-free, high-capacity gondola and a chain of snowmakers on its main south-facing piste. This is some compensation for the inconvenience of the place: its main hotels are clustered around the railway station, a bus-ride from the lifts.

When snow-cover is good, Brixen has some of the best slopes in the Ski Welt. All three runs leading down under the gondola are fine runs in different ways: an unpisted route (fine if the snow is good) and a black and a red served by snowmaking. There's also a very small area of north-facing runs, including the nursery slopes, on the other side of the village at Kandleralm. The nursery slopes are secluded and shady, but meeting up with friends for lunch is a hassle – the area is an inconvenient bus-ride from the village.

A free bus runs to Westendorf every 45 minutes.

Snow permitting, Brixen is one of the best cross-country villages in the Ski Welt. There is a long trail to Kirchberg, and more leisurely loops that circumnavigate nearby Westendorf. A 5km loop up the mountain at Hochbrixen provides fine views and fairly reliable snow.

The ski school runs the usual group classes, and mini-group sessions for five to seven people.

Brixen has plenty of hotels and pensions, and restaurants are mainly in hotels. Après-ski is quiet, but livelier Westendorf is a short taxi-ride away.

Off-slope activities include tennis, hotel-based spa facilities and days out to Salzburg, Innsbruck and Kitzbühel.

Brixen is not as suitable for children as other Ski Welt resorts, but it does have an all-day ski kindergarten with optional lunchtime supervision.

Westendorf 800m

Lively, friendly resort with access to the Ski Welt

WHAT IT COSTS

3

HOW IT RATES

The slopes

Snow	**
Extent	*
Experts	*
Intermediates	**
Beginners	****
Convenience	***
Queues	****
Restaurants	***

The rest

Scenery	***
Resort charm	****
Off-slope	**

What's new

The amount of artificial snow in the resort was doubled a few seasons back and half the slopes are now covered, including the runs back to the village and the nursery slopes.

MOUNTAIN FACTS

Altitude	800m-1890m
Lifts	13
Pistes	45km
Blue	38%
Red	62%
Black	0%
Artificial snow	23km

TOURIST OFFICE

Postcode A-6363
t +43 (5334) 6230
f 2390
bergbahnen.westendorf@skiwelt.at
www.skiwelt.at/westendorf

Westendorf is part of the Ski Welt pass-sharing arrangement (along with Söll, Ellmau, Brixen and others) but not on the main circuit. Its own slopes are not uninteresting (except to experts), and its friendliness wins many repeat visitors.

THE RESORT

The village is a compact Tirolean charmer, complete with attractive onion-domed church and sleighs (it was awarded 'Europe's most beautiful village' in the European Floral Competition a couple of years ago). It attracts more Germans than Brits, and more Dutch than either.

THE MOUNTAINS

The local **slopes** form a small section of leisurely cruising. A two-stage gondola takes you to Talkaser (1760m), from where various north-west-facing runs go back to the resort. Short west- and east-facing pistes run below the two low peaks of Choralpe (1820m) and Fleiding (1890m), either side of Talkaser. A couple of red runs from Fleiding go down past the lifts to hamlets served by buses. There's a **snowboard** fun-park with a half-pipe. Entry into the main Ski Welt circuit is nearby using the gondola out of Brixen; there's a good bus service.

Westendorf's **snow reliability** is a bit better than some other Ski Welt resorts and over half its pistes are now covered by snowmaking.

Westendorf is far from suitable for **experts**; there is only one black run on the piste map, but some experts are happy pottering about off-piste and going to the main Ski Welt circuit. Leisurely **intermediates** have a fair number of pretty, quiet slopes. Most pistes are really of blue difficulty, even if officially graded red.

Early intermediates and confident **beginners** have nice runs both between the mid-station and village, and alongside the Choralpe chair. The extensive nursery slopes are Westendorf's pride and joy.

There are 30km of local **cross-country** trails but snow-cover is erratic.

Given good conditions, **queues** are rare, and far less of a problem than in the main Ski Welt area. If poor weather closes the upper lifts, queues do become long.

Of the **mountain restaurants**, Alpenrosenhütte is woody and warm, with good food; Brechhornhaus is quiet; Gassnerhof is good but you have to catch a bus back to town.

The three **ski schools** have quite good reputations, though classes can be over-large and may cram English and Dutch together. One recent reporter tells of her teenage son's 'excellent' private lesson with the Top school: 'He's been skiing since he was three, but this was a revelation.'

Westendorf sells itself as a family resort. Both the crèche and the ski kindergarten are open all day.

STAYING THERE

Staying in the centre puts you close to the village nursery slopes and a five-minute walk from the lifts to the main area on the edge of the village.

There are central 4-star **hotels** – the Jakobwirt and the 'excellent' Schermer – and a dozen 3-star ones, but most reporters stay in more modest guest houses. Pension Wetti is popular and away from the church bells. Pension Ingeborg is highly recommended and next to the gondola. The Schermerhof **apartments** are of good quality.

Most of the best **restaurants** are in hotels – the Schermer, Mesnerwirt, Post and Jakobwirt are good. The Wasselhof and Klingler have also been recommended. Booking ahead is advisable. A taxi to Berggasthof Stimlach is well worth it.

Nightlife is lively and jolly, but it's a small place with limited options. The Sportalm (on the slopes) is popular at end-of-play – it's only a short ski back into town. Gerry's Inn is about the liveliest bar – and the Dutch meeting place. The Village Pub, next to the hotel Post, is also very popular. The Wunderbar is great after dinner, with music. Also try In's Moment and the Mesnerkeller for live music. Discos liven up at weekends.

Off the slopes there are excursions by rail or bus to Innsbruck, Salzburg and Kitzbühel. Walks and sleigh rides are very pretty.

Wildschönau 830m

Niederau and neighbours – family resorts with friendly slopes

WHAT IT COSTS

(2)

HOW IT RATES

The slopes

Snow	**
Extent	*
Experts	*
Intermediates	**
Beginners	****
Convenience	***
Queues	****
Restaurants	**

The rest

Scenery	***
Resort charm	***
Off-slope	**

MOUNTAIN FACTS

Altitude	830m-1900m
Lifts	29
Pistes	50km
Blue	35%
Red	56%
Black	9%
Artificial snow	8km

Wildschönau ('Wild and Beautiful') is the dramatic-sounding brand name adopted by a group of attractive small resorts in the Tirol. Niederau is the main one – a spread-out little place, with a small but quite varied area of runs, that has a strong British following; good for families and beginners, so long as there is decent snow. Auffach is a higher area 7km away. On a col between the two is Oberau, with its own little nursery area. There is no denying that the slopes are limited, but the resorts suit families looking for a friendly, unsophisticated but civilised atmosphere. A faithful following of Brits returns each year.

THE RESORTS

The Wildschönau villages are good examples of what Austria does so well: unspoilt, hassle-free, family winter resorts in lovely valley settings and with traditional chalet-style buildings. Roads are quiet, except on Saturdays when day trippers come up from Innsbruck. Niederau is the largest resort: a cluster of restaurants and shops at the Markbachjoch gondola is the nearest thing to a focal point, but few hotels are more than five minutes' walk from a main lift. Oberau has almost as many guest beds and is the valley's administrative and cultural centre. It has its own small area of slopes and good bus connections. Auffach is the third largest village and has the valley's highest slopes.

THE MOUNTAINS

Niederau's **slopes** are spread over a broad, wooded mountainside which does not rise above 1600m. Access is via a chair or an eight-person gondola – these are just a few minutes' walk apart, in central Niederau. The Markbachjoch gondola goes up to a novices' plateau at 1500m and the area's steepest runs, back to the village. The chair doesn't go so high, but is followed by a steep drag to the high point of Lanerköpfl (1600m). A long black run leads back to the village. Beginner runs at the bottom of

WILDSCHONAU TO

When there's this much snow the area's gentle, wooded slopes are great for families and intermediates ↓

What's new

For 1999/2000 a new Ski & Board Arena opened in Niederau. This has a permanent race piste, speed skiing piste with timer and a boarder-cross course – all free to visitors. New snowmaking was installed at Auffach from above the mid-station right down to the village.

For 2000/01 a new hotel will be opened on Markbachjoch at Niederau with an après-ski bar.

the mountain are served by several short drag-lifts.

A reliable half-hourly bus (free) goes to Auffach. Its sunny area, consisting almost entirely of red runs, goes up to Schatzberg at 1900m, with a respectable vertical of 1000m. The main lift is a two-stage gondola and drag-lifts serve the top runs.

Oberau has its own nursery slopes, with a short black run above them. And there are further beginner slopes along the hillside at Roggenboden.

The valley has won awards for the quality of its piste grooming.

Snowboarders will find a half-pipe and a big fun-park at Schatzberg in Auffach and the new boarder-cross course at Niederau.

There are few **queues** in either area.

The low altitude means that **snow reliability** is relatively poor – and if you can't use all the runs back to Niederau, the piste area there is tiny. Auffach is a better bet, with most of its runs above mid-mountain. Snow-making has been increased in recent years and now covers the long red from the top of the Niederau gondola back to the base, the red from above the mid-station of the Auffach gondola to the base and some of the nursery slopes in Niederau and Oberau.

The Kitzbüheler Alpen ski pass gives you access to 680km of pistes in the Schneewinkel, the Kitzbühel ski region, the Ski Welt, the Alpbachtal area and Wildschönau.

The few black runs don't have much appeal for **experts**, though the Hochberg run deserves respect. More interesting perhaps, are the off-piste ski routes and tours – Stöck, beneath the Niederau gondola, and Gern which runs from the top of Schatzberg all the way down a deserted valley to the road, a little way from the outskirts of Auffach. A guide is recommended.

Good **intermediates** may find the ungroomed gulley black runs awkward and the area too small to keep them interested for more than a day or two – though the red runs do merit their status. Auffach has more intermediate terrain than Niederau and the long main piste, which runs from the top of Schatzberg to the village, is attractive.

Niederau seems suitable for **beginners**, with excellent nursery slopes at the foot and top of the mountain, but the low ones become cold when they lose the sun each afternoon, and there aren't many really easy long runs to go on to. Returning to the village from the upper slopes is mainly via black or red runs, making the gondola the most viable option for most beginners. Oberau is an attractive alternative base.

There are floodlit pistes at Niederau, Oberau and Roggenboden. The 30km of **cross-country** trails along the valley are good when snow is abundant.

Mountain restaurants are scarce but good, causing lunchtime queues as ski schools take a break – one reporter recommends eating slightly earlier to avoid the congestion. Many people lunch in the villages.

The **ski schools** have a good reputation but classes can be large.

The kindergarten and nursery take **children** from age two and Thomson and Neilson both run kids' clubs.

STAYING THERE

In Niederau the 4-star Sonnschein is reported to be the best hotel, with a pool open to the public. The Schneeberger and Staffler are well-placed 3-stars. The hotel Austria is another central recommendation with a pool. The Bergwelt is a good-value B&B. Haus Jochum is spacious, comfortable **self-catering** close to the Tennladen drag. The Vicky, with its Drift In bar, is now run by Thomson.

There are a number of attractive hotels and guest houses in Oberau and Auffach, many of which have pools. In Oberau the 3-star Kellerwirt is the oldest hotel in the valley, dating from 1200, and the 3-star Tirolerhof has a pool, sauna and steam room. There is more accommodation in the hamlets of Mühltal and Thierbach, but neither is as convenient for the main slopes.

Hotels Alpenland and Wastl-Hof in Niederau are good for **eating out**.

Niederau has a nice balance of **après-ski**, neither too noisy for families nor too quiet for the young and lively. Bobo's ice bar is popular at tea-time. Later, the Almbar is lively, as is the Cave-Bar under the Hotel Staffler. The other villages are quieter, once the tea-time jollity is over for the night. There are good tobogganing runs.

Off the slopes there are excellent sleigh rides, horse-riding, organised walks and the Slow Train Wildschönau – on wheels rather than rails. Try the trip to the unspoilt Kundl Gorge. Excursions to Innsbruck are possible.

TOURIST OFFICE

Postcode A-6311
t +43 (5339) 8255
f 2433
info@wildschoenau.com
www.wildschoenau.com

Zell am See 755m

Charming lakeside town, varied slopes and glacier option

WHAT IT COSTS

3

HOW IT RATES

The slopes	
Snow	**
Extent	**
Experts	**
Intermediates	***
Beginners	***
Convenience	**
Queues	**
Restaurants	***
The rest	
Scenery	***
Resort charm	***
Off-slope	****

What's new

Plans for 2000/01 are to have a winter garden at the Panorama-Pfiff restaurant and table-service will replace the self-service at Sonnkogel-Pfiff.

New for 1999/2000 were signs on the pistes, with directions, weather, waiting time for lifts and other info.

There was also a new half-pipe at Glocknerbahn, a new fun-park at Breiteck and new jumps at Hirschkogel.

Intersport shops are providing a new ski equipment and clothing hire service.

A newly organised Schmittenfriends club entitles you to discounts.

MOUNTAIN FACTS

Altitude	760m-2000m
Lifts	56
Pistes	130km
Blue	43%
Red	38%
Black	19%
Artificial snow	40km
Recco detectors used	

- ⊕ Pretty, tree-lined slopes with great views down to the lake
- ⊕ Lively, but not rowdy, nightlife
- ⊕ Charming old town centre with beautiful lakeside setting
- ⊕ Lots to do off the slopes
- ⊕ Huge range of cross-country trails
- ⊕ Kaprun glacier nearby
- ⊕ Varied terrain including a couple of steep black runs

- ⊖ Sunny, low slopes often have poor conditions despite snowmakers, which makes the area more limited
- ⊖ Trek to lifts from much accommodation, and sometimes crowded buses
- ⊖ Less suitable for beginners than most small Austrian resorts
- ⊖ The Kaprun glacier gets horrendous queues when it is most needed

Zell am See is an unusual resort – not a rustic village like most of its small Austrian competitors, but a lakeside town with a charming old centre that seems more geared to summer than winter visitors. It's a pleasant place, and – since a tunnel now takes through traffic to Schüttdorf – less plagued by traffic.

Zell's slopes have a lot of variety and challenging terrain for a small area, but not enough to keep a keen intermediate or better happy for long, especially if, as some reporters have found, there's a lack of snow. Zell is very near the Kaprun glacier, but so are many low-altitude resorts, all of which run buses there if snow is in short supply. The result can be horrendous queues.

Zell makes an attractive base for holidaymakers who enjoy travelling around. Having a car makes it easy to visit numerous other resorts – including Saalbach-Hinterglemm, Bad Gastein-Bad Hofgastein, Wagrain, Schladming and Obertauern.

boarding *Zell is well suited to boarders. There's a high proportion of chairs, gondolas and cable-cars and a fun-park and half-pipe. You'll also find plenty of life in the evenings. The Kaprun glacier also has a half-pipe and fun-park, with powder in its wide, open bowl. But it also has a high proportion of drag-lifts – some beginners we heard from 'had to do a lot of walking'.*

The resort

Zell am See is a long-established, year-round resort town set between a large lake and a mountain. Its charming, traffic-free medieval centre is on a flat promontory, and the resort has grown up around this attractive core. A gondola at the edge of town goes up one arm of the horseshoe-shaped mountain, but Zell's cable-cars are 2km away. Access by another gondola at Schüttdorf is 3km away. Most places to stay are a fair walk from the town gondola. Out by the cable-car station there is some accommodation, too.

You can also stay in Schüttdorf. Some of the accommodation here is close to the gondola (which goes directly to the highest part of the slopes), but the place is less appealing than Zell itself, especially for nightlife.

The mountains

Despite claims to the contrary, the extent of Zell's horseshoe of slopes is not large and the area is best suited to intermediates. The easiest runs are along the ridge, with steeper pistes heading down to the valley. Kaprun's snowsure glacier slopes are only a few minutes by bus; Saalbach and Bad Hofgastein are easily reached by bus and train respectively and, at a push, Wagrain, Schladming and Obertauern are car trips.

THE SLOPES
Varied but limited

The town gondola takes you to Mittelstation. From there it's either an easy or a steep run to the valley cable-car station. Or you can take a chair up to Hirschkogel to meet the gondola up

LIFT PASSES

2000/01 prices in schillings

Europa-Sportregion Kaprun-Zell am See
Covers all lifts in Zell and Kaprun, and buses between them.
Beginners Points card or limited pass.
Main pass
1-day pass 435
6-day pass 2050
(low season 1880)
Senior citizens
Over 65 male, 60 female: 6-day pass 1850)
Children
Under 15: 6-day pass 1200
Under 6: free pass
Short-term passes
Half-day pass from 11.30 for Zell only; reduces in price by the hour through the day.
Alternative periods
5 in 7 days and 10 in 14 days.
Notes Day pass valid at Zell am See only (28 lifts).

from Schüttdorf – which you can ride up further and then take a drag to the Schmittenhöhe top-station. This is also where the main valley floor cable-car brings you. A gentle cruise and a single short drag-lift moves you to Sonnkogel. Here several routes lead down to Sonnalm mid-station – where another cable-car from the valley arrives. A black piste runs from here to the valley floor. At the end of the day you can take a gentle piste from the top (Schmittenhöhe) cable-car back to town or ride one of the cars down.

SNOW RELIABILITY
Good snowmaking, but lots of sun

Zell am See's slopes get so much sun the snow can suffer as a result. Except for the Sonnkogel-Sonnalm area, lots of slopes are now well-covered by snow-guns, including the sunny home run to Schüttdorf. But though reporters have seen 'lots of snowmaking in evidence', slush, ice and closed runs have still marred their holidays. The Kaprun glacier is snowsure, but expect long queues there when snow is short elsewhere.

FOR EXPERTS
Several blacks, but still limited

Zell has more steep slopes than most resorts this size, but can't entertain an expert for a week. When we were last there it was fabulous speeding down the immaculately groomed black runs 13 and 14 – they were deserted first thing. However, as a recent reporter pointed out, 'they are more like French reds'. Off-piste opportunities are limited.

FOR INTERMEDIATES
Bits and pieces for most grades

Good intermediates have a choice of fine, long runs, but this is not a place for mileage. All blacks are within a brave intermediate's capability, and there's a lovely cruising run between Areit and Schüttdorf when conditions are good. Some Sonnkogel pistes are also suitable. The timid can cruise the ridge all day on quiet, attractive runs, or head past Mittelstation to Zell's cable-cars on an easy blue. Kaprun's snowsure glacier runs are also worth a visit 'especially piste 3 for early intermediates'.

FOR BEGINNERS
Two low nursery areas

There are small nursery slopes at the cable-car area and at Schüttdorf, both covered by snow-guns. Near-beginners and fast learners have plenty of short, easy runs at Schmittenhöhe, Breiteck and Areit. Some are used by complete beginners when snow conditions are poor lower down, but it means buying a lift pass.

↑ Schmittenhöhe with Kaprun's Kitzsteinhorn glacier in the distance

ZELL AM SEE TO

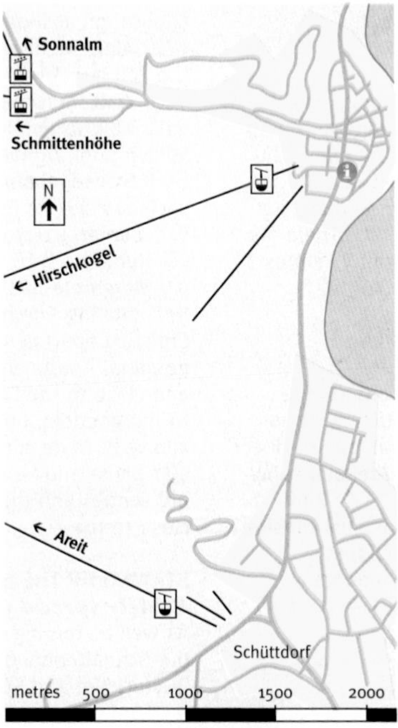

ZELL AM SEE TO

The pretty countryside is good for walks and, when the snow is good, for cross-country →

SCHOOLS/GUIDES

1999/2000 prices in schillings

Zell am See
Courses start Sunday and Monday
Classes 6 days 10am-noon and 1pm-3pm
5 full days: 1600
Children's classes
Ages: from 4
5 full days: 1600
Private lessons
Hourly or daily
550 for 1hr; each additional person 100

CHILDCARE

All the ski schools take children from age 4 and offer lunch-time care. The Areitbahn school runs a snow kindergarten and play room for children from age 3, from 9am to 4.30. This is up at Areit (handy for Schüttdorf residents).

The village nursery is Ursula Zink (56343), which takes children from age 3, from 9.30 to 3.30; younger children looked after on an hourly basis.

FOR CROSS-COUNTRY
Excellent if snow allows

The valley floor has extensive trails, including a superb area on the Kaprun golf course. At altitude there are just two short loops, one at the top of the Kaprun glacier, and the other at the top of the Zell gondola.

QUEUES
Not normally a problem

Zell am See doesn't have many problems except at peak times, when the Schmittenhöhe cable-cars are generally the worst hit. A recent visitor found that getting to Schmittenhöhe via the Sonnalm cable-car is quieter.

When snow is poor there are few daytime queues at Zell – many people are away queueing at Kaprun – but getting down by lift at the end of the day can involve delays.

MOUNTAIN RESTAURANTS
Plenty of little refuges

There are plenty of cosy, atmospheric huts. Among the best are Glocknerhaus, Kettingalm, Areitalm ('superb, freshly made strudel'), Pinzgauer and Brieteckalm. The Berghotel at Schmittenhöhe is good, but expensive. Its bar with loud music is lively (see Après-Ski). Over at the top of the Kaprun glacier the Aussichsrestaurant gets busy, but 'has wonderful views and quite good food'.

SCHOOLS AND GUIDES
A wide choice

There is a choice of schools in both Zell am See and Kaprun. A reporter found boarding lessons from the main Zell school to be 'well-organised', though classes were a bit large, and English not always spoken fluently. There are also specialist cross-country centres at Schüttdorf and at Kaprun.

FACILITIES FOR CHILDREN
Schüttdorf's the place

We have no recent reports on the childcare provisions, but staying in Schüttdorf has the advantage of direct gondola access to the Areitalm snow-kindergarten, and the Ursula Zink nursery is at Zeller-Moos, just outside Schüttdorf. There's a children's adventure park on the mountain.

Staying there

Choice of location is tricky, and we have three favourite strategies. Stay in a beautiful lakeside setting (which gets you on the shuttle-bus before it's too crowded); at the upper edge of the town centre (walking distance from the Zell gondola); or near the cable-car stations at the end of the valley.

Schüttdorf has easy access to the top of the mountain, but it is a characterless dormitory with little else going for it. Though closer to Kaprun, this is, perversely, a drawback unless you have a car. Trying to get on a glacier bus is tough, as they tend to be full when they leave Zell. Families wishing to use the Areitalm nursery and cross-country skiers stand to gain most from staying in Schüttdorf.

HOW TO GO
Choose charm or convenience

Lots of hotels, pensions and apartments.
Hotels A broad range of hotels (more 4- than 3-stars) and guest-houses.
(((4) **Salzburgerhof** Best in town – the only 5-star. Nearer lake than gondola, but has courtesy bus and pool.
(((4) **Tirolerhof** Excellent 4-star in old town. Good pool, hot tub and steam room. 'Food good, staff very friendly.'
(((4) **Eichenhof** On the outskirts of town, but popular and with a minibus service, great food and lake views.
(((4) **Alpin** Modern 4-star chalet next to the Zell gondola.
(((4) **Zum Hirschen** Comfortable, 4-star, easy walk to gondola. Sauna, steam, splash pool, popular bar.
(((4) **Schwebebahn** Attractive 4-star in secluded setting by cable-cars.
((3) **Berner** 4-star by the Zell gondola.
(2) **Hubertus** B&B near Zell gondola.
(2) **Margarete** B&B next to cable-car.
Self-catering The budget Karger Christine apartments are near the Zell gondola. Apartment Hofer is mid-range and close to the Ebenberg lift (linking to the gondola, but no boarders allowed). More comfortable are the 3-star Diana and Seilergasse (both in the old centre) and the Mirabell, which is close to the Zell gondola.

STAYING UP THE MOUNTAIN
Widely spread choices

As well as the big hotel at the top of the Schmittenhöhe cable-car, the Breiteckalm and Sonnalm mountain restaurants have rooms.

GETTING THERE

Air Salzburg, transfer 2hr. Munich, transfer 3hr.

Rail Station in resort.

ACTIVITIES

Indoor Swimming, sauna, solarium, fitness centre, spa, tennis, squash, bowling, museum, art gallery, cinema, library, massage, ice skating

Outdoor Riding, skating, curling, floodlit toboggan runs, plane flights, sleigh rides, shooting range, swimming (Kaprun), ice sailing, ice surfing, tubing

TOURIST OFFICE

Postcode A-5700
t +43 (6542) 770
f 72032
zell@gold.at
www.zellamsee.com

EATING OUT
Plenty of choice

Zell has more non-hotel places than is usual in a small Austrian resort. The Ampere is quiet and sophisticated; Guiseppe's is a popular Italian with excellent food; and Kupferkessel and Traubenstüberl both do wholesome regional dishes. There are Chinese restaurants in Zell and Schüttdorf. Car drivers can try the good value Finkawirt, across the lake at Prielau, or the excellent Erlhof.

APRES-SKI
Plenty for all tastes

Après-ski is lively and varied, with tea dances and high-calorie cafés, plus bars and discos a-plenty. When it's sunny Schnapps Hans ice bar outside the Berghotel at Schmittenhöhe really buzzes, with 'great music, a crazy DJ and dancing on tables and on the bar. All ages loved it.' The Diele disco bar rocks; Crazy Daisy on the main road has two crowded bars and 'the group loved it' says one reporter. Evergreen has a live band and 60s' and 70s' music. The Viva disco allows no under 18s – one reader proclaimed it 'excellent'. Or try the smart Hirschkeller, the cave-like Lebzelter Keller and the Sportstuberl with old ski photos on the walls.

OFF THE SLOPES
Spoilt for choice

There is plenty to do in this year-round resort. The train trip to Salzburg is a must, Kitzbühel is also well worth a visit and Innsbruck is within reach.

You can often walk across the frozen lake to Thumersbach, plus there are good sports facilities, a motor museum, sleigh rides and flights.

Kaprun 785m

Kaprun is a spacious and quite lively village with lots of Tirolean charm. There is a small area of slopes on the outskirts of the village at Maiskogel best suited to early intermediates, and a separate nursery area.

But most people will want to spend most of their time on the slopes of the nearby Kitzsteinhorn glacier or on Zell am See's slopes. Both are a busy bus-ride away.

The glacier is accessed by either an underground funicular or a gondola met by a quad chair. The main slopes are in a big bowl above served by several T-bars and a couple of chairs. Pistes are mainly gentle blues and reds with one tougher run from the very top at 3029m. The area above the top of the funicular is open for summer skiing and riding and is particularly good for an early pre-Christmas or late post-Easter break. Below the top of the funicular is an entertaining red run down to the bottom of the quad chair – our favourite run on the mountain. Snow is nearly always good – the drawback is the queues, which can be appalling when crowds are bussed in.

There are a couple of decent mountain restaurants – one at the funicular top station and another by the top of the gondola.

Off-slope activities are good, and include a fine sports centre with outdoor rapids. Nightlife is quiet, but the Baum and Nindl ('a good spot') bars are lively. Good restaurants include the Dorfstadl, the Bella Musica and the Schlemmerstuberl. The Orgler, Mitteregger and Tauernhof are among the best hotels. There are some catered chalets and chalet-hotels.

France

France overtook Austria as the most popular destination for British skiers and snowboarders some years ago, and it is by far the most popular country with our readers. It's not difficult to see why. France has the biggest linked ski areas in the world; for those who like to cover as many miles in a day as possible, these are unrivalled. Most of these big areas are also at high altitude, ensuring high-quality snow for a long season. French mountains offer a mixture of some of the toughest, wildest slopes in the Alps, and some of the longest, gentlest and most convenient beginner runs.

French resort villages can't be quite so uniformly recommended; but, equally, they don't all conform to the standard image of soulless, purpose-built resorts, thrown up without concern for appearance during the boom of the 1960s and 70s.

The French resorts we flock to are big names where prices are never going to seem low; but when the pound was down near 7 francs they seemed criminally high. As we go to press in June 2000, the pound is down from the heady heights it reached during the past season, but it is still above the magic 10 francs to the pound – a level at which most French resort prices seem bearable.

Towards the front of the book there is a special chapter on driving to the French Alps – something that increasing numbers of people like to do, especially if they are going self-catering.

ANY STYLE OF RESORT YOU LIKE

The main drawback to France, hinted at above, is the monstrous architecture of some of the purpose-built resorts. But not all French resorts are hideous. Certainly, France has its fair share of Alpine eyesores, chief among them Les Menuires, central La Plagne, Flaine, Tignes, Isola 2000 and Les Arcs. The redeeming features of places like these are the splendid quality of the slopes they serve, the reliability and quality of the snow, and the amazing piste-side convenience of most of the accommodation.

But the French have learnt the lesson that new development doesn't have to be tasteless to be convenient – look at Valmorel, Belle Plagne and Les Coches, for example, and the newer parts of Isola 2000 or Flaine. Val-Thorens, always one of the more acceptable new resorts, is being developed sensitively, too.

SNOWPIX.COM / CHRIS GILL

A classic purpose-built French resort: Val-Claret, part of Tignes ↓

If you prefer, there are genuinely old mountain villages to stay in, linked directly to the big lift networks. These are not usually as convenient for the slopes, but they give you a feel of being in France rather than a winter-holiday factory. Examples include Montchavin or Champagny for La Plagne, Vaujany for Alpe-d'Huez, St-Martin-de-Belleville for the Three Valleys and Les Carroz, Morillon or Samoëns (a short drive from the slopes) for Flaine. There are also old villages with their own slopes which have developed as resorts while retaining some or all of their rustic ambience – such as Serre-Chevalier and La Clusaz. Megève deserves a special mention – an exceptionally charming little town combining rustic style with luxury and sophistication.

And France has Alpine centres with a long mountaineering and skiing history. Chief among these is Chamonix, which sits in the shadow of Mont Blanc, Europe's highest peak, and is the centre of the most radical off-piste terrain in the world. Chamonix is a big, bustling town, where skiing and boarding go on alongside tourism in general. At the opposite end of the vacation spectrum is tiny La Grave, at the foot of mountains that are almost as impressive, but with only a few simple hotels.

France has advantages in the gastronomic stakes. While many of its mountain restaurants serve fast food, most also do at least a plat du jour that is in a different league from what you'll find in Austria or the US. It is generally possible to find somewhere to get a half-decent lunch and to have it served at your table, rather than queuing repeatedly for every element of your meal. In the evening, most resorts have restaurants serving good, traditional, French food as well

Get the price of this book back

and get the best booking service as well

You can reclaim the full price of Where to Ski and Snowboard when you book a 2000/2001 or a 2001/02 winter sports holiday. All you have to do is make your booking through the specialist travel agency Ski Solutions, and do a minute bit of form-filling. The price of the book will be knocked off your final holiday payment.

Ski Solutions is Britain's longest-established and most respected ski travel agency. You can buy whatever kind of holiday you want through it, so you're not losing out on breadth of choice.

Ski Solutions sells the complete range of package holidays offered by all the bonded tour operators in Britain, ranging from the smallest one-resort chalet operators (who otherwise sell directly by mail) to the mass-market operators who mainly sell through the brochure racks of high-street travel agents.

Ski Solutions can also tailor-make holidays for independent-minded travellers who want to go their own way – whether it's a long weekend in Chamonix or an 18-day tour of the best half-dozen resorts in the Rockies.

At the back of the book is a page comprising two vouchers. When you make your booking, tell Ski Solutions that you want to claim a refund, complete the vouchers and send one to Ski Solutions and one to Where to Ski and Snowboard (the addresses are on the vouchers). That's all there is to it.

This is what French purpose-built resorts are all about: snow. It doesn't get much better than this, at Val-Thorens →

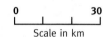

BASILE, MARK BUSCAIL / VAL-THORENS TO

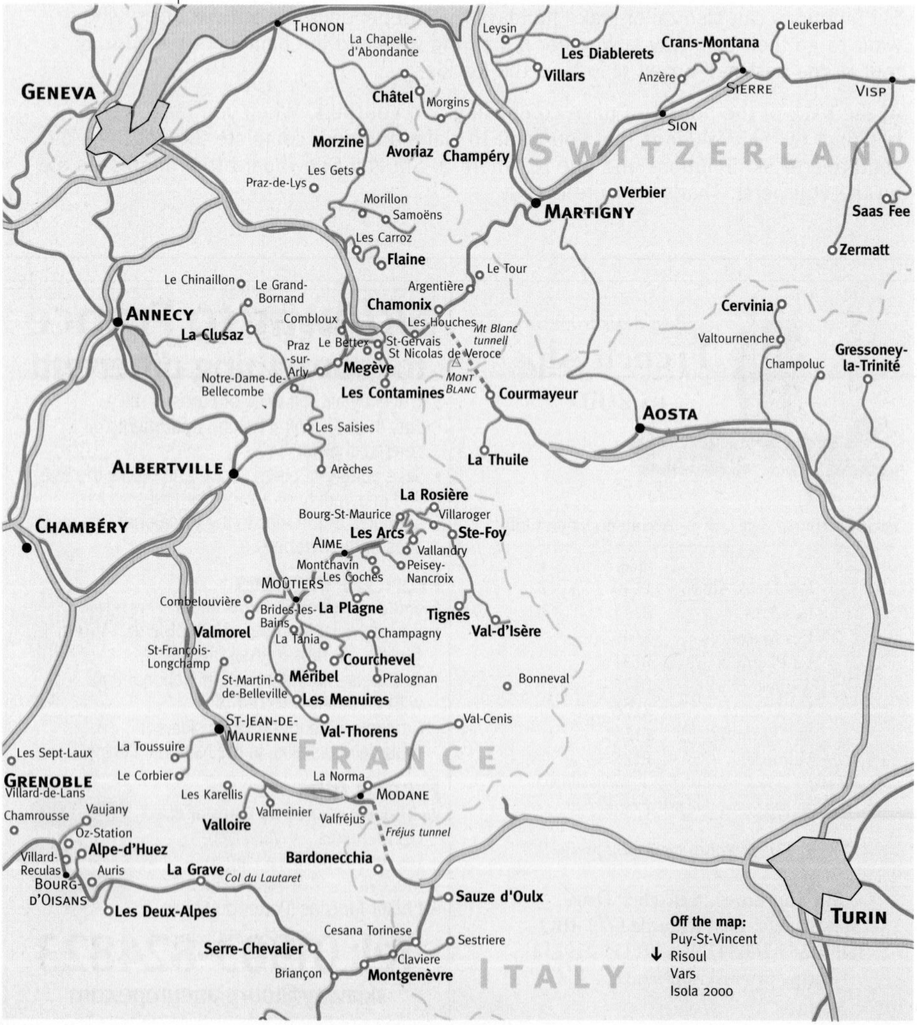

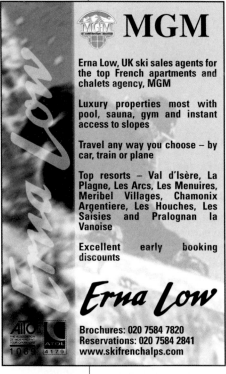

← Getting around the French Alps
Pick the right gateway – Geneva, Chambéry or Grenoble – and you can hardly go wrong. The approach to Serre-Chevalier and Montgenèvre involves the 2058m Col du Lauteret; but the road is a major one and kept clear of snow or reopened quickly after a fall.

as regional specialities. And the wine is decent and affordable.

Many French resorts (though not all) have suffered from a lack of nightlife, but things have changed in recent years. In resorts dominated by apartments with few international visitors, there may still be very little going on after dinner, but places like Méribel are now distinctly lively in the evening. (It should also be said that nightlife isn't important to many British holidaymakers. Most of our reporting readers say they can't recommend nightspots because all they want to do after dinner is to fall into bed.)

France is unusual among European countries in helping people decide which runs to try by using four grades of piste instead of the usual three – a system of which we heartily approve. The very easiest runs are graded green and, except in Val-d'Isère, they are reliably gentle. Blue, red and black follow. (Note that under Mountain facts in our major resort chapters, we lumped green and blue runs together to make the figures comparable to those for Swiss, Austrian and Italian resorts.)

Get next year's edition free

and help make it even better

There are too many resorts for us to visit them all every year, and too many hotels, bars, nightspots and mountain restaurants for us to see them all. So we are very keen to encourage more people to join our already healthy band of correspondents, who send in reports on their holiday experiences. To encourage readers, we'll be giving away 100 copies of next year's edition to the writers of the best reports.

There are five main kinds of feedback we need:
• what you particularly **liked and disliked** about the resort
• what aspects of the resort came as a **surprise** to you
• your suggestions for **changes to our evaluation** of the resort – changes we should make to the ratings, verdicts, descriptions etc
• your experience of **queues** and other weaknesses in the lift system, and of the **ski school** and associated childcare arrangements
• your feedback on other **individual facilities** in the resort – the hotels, bars, restaurants (including mountain restaurants), nightspots, equipment shops, sports facilities etc.

You can send your reports to us in two ways:
• by e-mail to reports@snow-zone.co.uk
• on paper, preferably word-processed – we can provide forms if you like.
Our address is at the front of the book.

Alpe-d'Huez 1860m

An impressive all-rounder; just a pity it faces south

WHAT IT COSTS

(5)

HOW IT RATES

The slopes	
Snow	****
Extent	****
Experts	****
Intermediates	****
Beginners	*****
Convenience	****
Queues	****
Restaurants	****
The rest	
Scenery	****
Resort charm	*
Off-slope	***

What's new

The 1km-long Signal run is now floodlit three nights a week. Snowmaking was extended in the Vaujany-Oz sector last season. More is planned for 2000/01.

Also for the coming season, a second stage is being added to the Marmottes gondola to replace the old Clocher chair, above the recently upgraded Lièvre Blanc chair – greatly improving access to some of the best red and black runs.

A two-seater chair will replace the tricky old Chatelard drag-lift.

The capacity of the Alpette gondola at Oz will be increased.

A lift from the Villard-Reculas car park to the new fast chair-lift is to be installed.

A new 3-star hotel is being constructed in Les Bergers – part of a new push to improve the standard of accommodation.

- ⊕ Extensive, high, sunny slopes, split interestingly into various sectors
- ⊕ Huge snowmaking installation to keep runs open despite the sun
- ⊕ Vast, gentle, sunny nursery slopes right next to the resort
- ⊕ Efficient, modern lift system, with very little queueing
- ⊕ Grand views of the peaks in the Ecrins national park
- ⊕ Some good, surprisingly rustic mountain restaurants
- ⊕ Short walks to and from the slopes
- ⊕ Good sports facilities
- ⊕ Pleasant alternative bases in outlying villages and satellites

- ⊖ In late season the many south-facing runs can be icy early in the day and slushy in the afternoon
- ⊖ Some main intermediate runs get badly overcrowded in high season
- ⊖ Many of the tough runs are very high, and inaccessible or very tricky in bad weather
- ⊖ Practically no woodland runs to retreat to in bad weather
- ⊖ Run gradings tend to understate difficulty
- ⊖ Messy, sprawling resort with a hotchpotch of architectural styles, no central focus and very little charm

There are few places to rival Alpe-d'Huez for extent and variety of terrain – in good conditions, it's one of our favourites. An important new lift will mean that experts will now be less dependent on the high, closure-prone Pic Blanc cable-car, and the scale of the snowmaking is increasingly impressive. But, in late season at least, ice can still make your mornings miserably hard work, however alluring the prospect of slushy moguls in the afternoons.

The village has few fans, but if you don't like the sound of it you always have the alternative of staying in rustic Vaujany (with its mighty cable-car) or Villard-Reculas, or more modern Oz and Auris – see the end of this chapter.

boarding *Alpe-d'Huez caught on to boarding early – it built a half-pipe in 1988. It then seemed to lose interest, but things have now picked up again: the fun-park at Lac Blanc, beside the low-speed nursery slopes, was improved for last season and there's now a permanent half-pipe, boarder-cross course and big air on the floodlit Signal run – plus a new fun-park at Auris. The extent and variety of the mountains mean that there's a lot of good free-riding to be had, and beginners will be pleased to hear that there are hardly any drag-lifts to contend with. Note the drawbacks listed above – the icy morning conditions and crowded pistes can be a nightmare. However, the off-piste is vast and varied and well worth checking out with a guide; the 5 Mountains school offers boarder tours. Planète Surf is the main snowboard shop in town and the Cactus Café is apparently a cool little hang-out.*

The resort

Alpe-d'Huez is a large village spread across an open mountainside, high above the Romanche valley, east of Grenoble. It was one of the venues for the 1968 Grenoble Winter Olympics, and then grew quickly in a seemingly unplanned way. Its buildings come in all shapes, sizes and designs – including a futuristic church (which hosts weekly organ concerts). It is a large, amorphous resort that lacks a definite centre. The nearest thing to a central focus is the main Avenue des Jeux in the geographic centre, where you'll find the swimming pool, ice skating and some of the shops, bars and restaurants. The rest of the resort spreads out in a triangle, with lift stations at two of the apexes.

Many reporters have remarked on

↑ Green runs stretch away from the top of the village – this is one of the great resorts for novices

SNOWPIX.COM / CHRIS GILL

the surprising friendliness of the place, and in terms of ambience, this once quiet, 'typically French' resort gets more animated and interesting each year. It now has an extremely good Palais des Sports, with lots of activities on offer. There are more bars and restaurants than you might expect from a high, purpose-built resort.

The bus service around the resort is free with one of the lift pass options, and there's a handy but slow bucket lift (with a piste beneath it), running through the resort. Slightly away from main body of the resort (and linked by chair-lift) are the 'hamlets' – apartment blocks, mainly – of Les Bergers and L'Eclose. There is accommodation down the hill in Huez, also linked by lift to the resort.

The mountains

Alpe-d'Huez ranks alongside giants like Val-d'Isère or La Plagne for extent and variety of its slopes. The piste grading is unreliable; although it occasionally overstates difficulty, it more often does the opposite – there are some red runs that deserve to be black, and a few blues that might be red.

THE SLOPES
Several well-linked areas

The slopes can be divided into four main sectors, with good connections between them.

The biggest sector is directly above the village, on the slopes of **Pic Blanc**. There is sport here for everyone, from excellent tough pitches at the top to vast, gentle beginner slopes at the bottom. The huge Grandes Rousses gondola, otherwise known as the DMC (a reference to its clever technology), goes up in two stages from the top of the village to 2700m. Above it, a cable-car goes up to 3330m on Pic Blanc itself, where the runs are genuinely black. A lower area of testing runs at Clocher de Macle, previously accessed by a slow chair, will now be served by the newly extended Marmottes gondola.

The Sarenne gorge separates the main resort area from **Signal de l'Homme**. A spectacular down-and-up fast chair-lift accesses this area from the Bergers part of the village. From the top you can take excellent north-facing slopes back down towards the gorge, or head south to Auris or west to the old hamlet of Chatelard. The return from here will now be by a new double chair-lift, replacing the famously tricky drag-lift.

On the other side of town from Signal de l'Homme is the small **Signal** sector, reached by drag-lifts next to the main gondola or by a couple of chairs lower down. Runs go down the other side of the hill to the old village of Villard-Reculas. Happily, a fast quad chair-lift has replaced another tricky drag-lift back from here. The 1km-long Signal blue run is now floodlit for two hours, three nights a week.

The **Vaujany-Oz** sector consists largely of north-west-facing slopes, accessible from Alpe-d'Huez via good red runs from either the mid-station or the top of the big gondola. At the heart of this sector is Alpette, the mid-

MOUNTAIN FACTS

Altitude	1120m-3320m
Lifts	85
Pistes	220km
Green/Blue	64%
Red	24%
Black	12%
Artificial snow	37km
Recco detectors used	

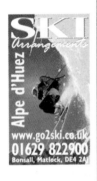

station of the two-stage cable-car from Vaujany. From here a disastrously sunny red goes down to Oz, and a much more reliable blue goes north to the Vaujany home slopes around Montfrais. The links back to Alpe-d'Huez are made by the top cable-car from Alpette, or a gondola from Oz.

Since a piste was created from below Alpette to Enversin, just below Vaujany, an on-piste descent of 2200m has been possible – not the biggest vertical in the Alps, but not far short. The area does offer the longest piste in the Alps – the 16km Sarenne on the back of the Pic Blanc (see page 188).

Outings by road are feasible to other resorts covered on a week's lift pass, including Serre-Chevalier, Les Deux-Alpes, Puy-St-Vincent and Montgenèvre. You can go to Les Deux-Alpes by helicopter for a modest fee.

SNOW RELIABILITY

Affected by the sun

Alpe-d'Huez is unique among major purpose-built resorts in the Alps in having mainly south- or south-west-facing slopes. The strong southern sun means that in late season conditions may alternate between slush and ice on most of the area. There are shady slopes above Vaujany and at Signal de l'Homme – and there is a small glacier area on the Pic Blanc, open in summer, but too small to be much of a snow guarantee in the winter. Overall, the orientation of the slopes is a real drawback of the area as a whole.

In more wintry circumstances the runs are relatively snowsure, and the natural stuff is backed up by very extensive snowmaking. This already covers the main runs above Alpe-d'Huez, Vaujany and Oz, and for 2000/01 a further huge investment is planned, adding almost 50 per cent to the installation. An impressive 700-odd snow-guns will now cover over 37km of runs.

FOR EXPERTS

Plenty of blacks and off-piste

This is an excellent resort for experts, with long and testing black runs (and reds that ought to be black) as well as serious off-piste options.

The slope beneath the Pic Blanc cable-car, usually an impressive mogul-field, is reached by a 300m tunnel from the back side of the mountain. The tunnel is being altered for this season, which should mean that the exit on to the slope is less awkward – the slope is of ordinary black steepness, but can be very tricky in the mornings because it gets a lot of sun. The run splits into three part-way down, with two of the variants leading to the Lac Blanc chair.

The long Sarenne run on the back of the Pic Blanc is described in the feature box over the page. There are several off-piste variants. There are also other very long off-piste descents over the bigger glaciers to the north and east, with verticals of 1900m to

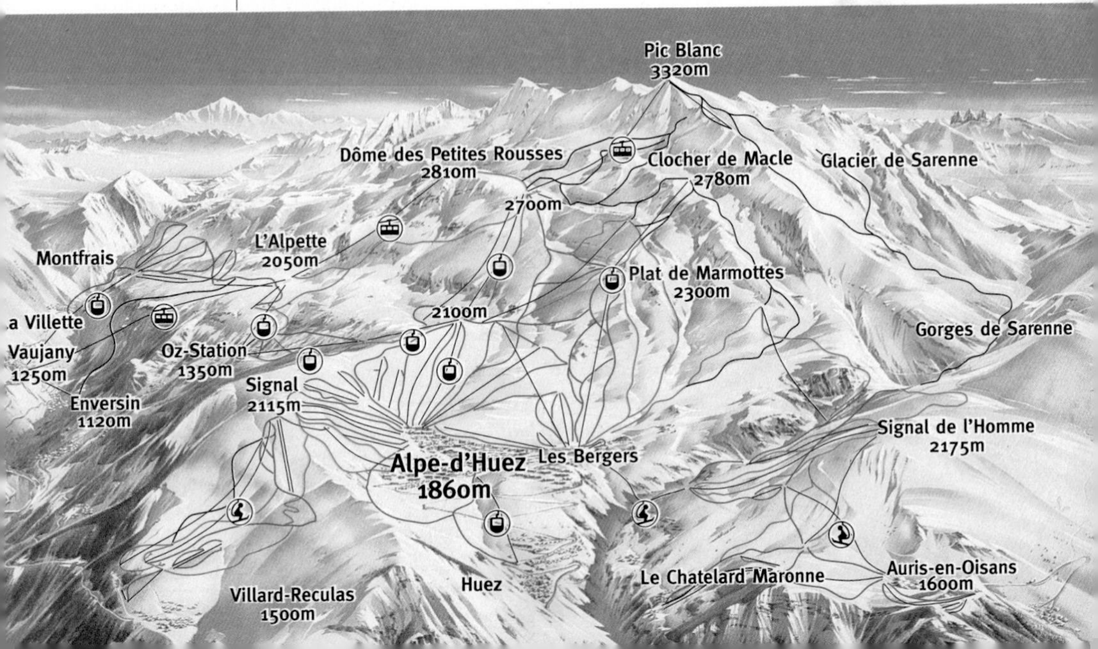

LIFT PASSES

2000/01 prices in francs

Grandes Rousses
Covers all lifts in Alpe-d'Huez, Auris, Oz, Vaujany and Villard-Reculas.

Beginners Daily lift passes for reduced areas. Beginner pass covers 11 lifts (59), Altitude 2000 covers 26 lifts (106)

Main pass
1-day pass 207
6-day pass 1070

Senior citizens
Over 60: 6-day pass 757
Over 70: free pass

Children
Under 16: 6-day pass 757
Under 5: free pass

Notes Pass for 6 days or more includes one day's skiing at each of the Grande Galaxie resorts (Les Deux Alpes, Serre-Chevalier, Puy-St-Vincent and the Milky Way) and free entrance to the sports centre.

Alternative passes
Passes for Auris only (15 lifts), Oz only (10 lifts), Vaujany only (10 lifts), Villard-Reculas only (8 lifts), Oz-Vaujany (19 lifts) and Moyenne Altitude (39 lifts). A 7-day pedestrian pass costs 380.

2200m, for which guidance is essential. Some end up in Vaujany, others in Clavans (where you need a taxi back), others in more remote spots where you need a helicopter back.

There is good off-piste in several other sectors, too – notably from Signal towards Villard-Reculas and Huez – and from Signal de l'Homme in various directions; the slopes above Auris are a particular favourite of locals. And there's abundant off-piste on the lower half of the mountain that is excellent in good snow conditions, including lovely runs through scattered trees at the extreme northern edge of the area above Vaujany.

Some of the upper red pistes are tough enough to give experts a challenge. These include the Canyon and Balme runs accessed by the Lièvre Blanc chair-lift from the gondola mid-station – runs which are unprepared and south-facing (late in the day, perhaps best tackled on a board), and steep enough to be graded black in many resorts. Above this, the brand new Marmottes II gondola (replacing the old Clocher chair for 2000/01) serves another series of steep black runs including the beautiful, long, lonely Combe Charbonniere.

FOR INTERMEDIATES
Fine selection of runs

Good intermediates have a fine selection of runs all over the area. In good snow conditions the variety of the runs is difficult to beat. Every section has some challenging red runs to test the adventurous intermediate. The most challenging are the Canyon and Balme runs, mentioned above. There are lovely long runs down to Oz and to Vaujany. The off-piste among the trees above Vaujany, mentioned earlier, is a good place to start your off-piste career in good snow. The Villard-Reculas and Signal de l'Homme sectors also have long challenging reds. The Chamois red from the top of the gondola down to the mid-station is beautiful but quite narrow, and miserable when busy and icy. Fearless intermediates should enjoy most of the super-long black runs from Pic Blanc.

For less ambitious intermediates, there are usually blue alternatives. The main Couloir blue from the top of the big gondola is a lovely run, well served by snowmakers, but it does get scarily crowded at times.

There are some great cruising runs above Vaujany; but it's not easy for early intermediates to get over to the Vaujany sector from Alpe-d'Huez. The blue down to the mid-station of the Vaujany gondola is picturesque and well served by snowmaking.

Early intermediates will also enjoy the gentle slopes leading back to Alpe-d'Huez from the main mountain, and the Signal sector.

FOR BEGINNERS
Good facilities

The large network of green runs immediately above the village is as good a nursery area as you will find anywhere – its only flaw is that it

THE LONGEST PISTE IN THE ALPS – AND IT'S BLACK??

It's no surprise that most ski runs that are seriously steep are also seriously short. Look at the exceptionally long runs in the Alps, and they tend to be graded blue, or red at the most. The Parsenn runs above Klosters, for example – typically 12km to 15km long – are manageable in your first week. Even Chamonix's famously long Vallée Blanche off-piste run doesn't include steepness in its attractions.

So you could be forgiven for being sceptical about the 'black' Sarenne run from the top of the Pic Blanc to the Sarenne gorge that separates the resort from the Signal de l'Homme sector. Even though the vertical is an impressive 2000m, a run 16km in length means an average gradient of only 11 per cent – typical of a blue run. Macho-hype on the part of the lift company, presumably?

Not quite. The Sarenne is a run of two halves. The bottom half is virtually flat (boarders beware) but the top half is a genuine black – a demanding and highly satisfying run (with stunning views) that any keen, competent skier will enjoy. The main challenge is the steep mogul-field starting just below the top lift station; after that, things are much gentler, even before you get to the really flat bit. The run gets a lot of sun, so pick your time with care – there's nothing worse than a sunny run with no sun.

SCHOOLS/GUIDES

2000/01 prices in francs

ESF

Classes 6 days
5½hr: 9.25-12.25 and 2.20-4.50
6 full days: 850
Children's classes
Ages: 4 to 16
6 full days: 830
Private lessons
Hourly
190 for 1hr, for 1 to 2 people

International

Classes 6 days
4½hr: 2½hr am, 2hr pm
6 full days: 1085
Children's classes
Ages: 3 to 12
6 full days: 910
Private lessons
Hourly
175 for 1hr, for 1 to 2 people

CHILDCARE

The main schools both run ski kindergartens.

The ESF Club des Oursons, at Les Bergers and near the main gondola (476 803182), takes children from age 4 during ski school hours. The Eterlous kindergarten (476 804327) has a private slope area and takes children aged 2½ to 11 all day.

The SEI (476 804277) runs the Baby-Club for children aged 2½ to 4, and the Club des Marmottes for those aged 4 to 12.

The Club Med nursery takes children from 4, with or without tuition.

carries a lot of through-traffic. A large area embracing half a dozen runs has been declared a low-speed zone protégée, but the restriction is not policed and so doesn't achieve much. Add to the quality of the slopes the convenience, availability of good tuition, a special lift pass covering 11 lifts and usually reliable snow, and Alpe-d'Huez is difficult to beat. There's another good beginners' area with gentle green runs at the top of the Vaujany gondola, and small slopes in Oz and Auris.

FOR CROSS-COUNTRY
High-level and convenient

There are 50km of trails, with three loops of varying degrees of difficulty, all at around 2000m and consequently relatively snowsure. All trails are within the Alpine domain and a cross-country user's pass costs about 180 francs.

QUEUES
Generally few problems

Even in French holiday periods, the modern lift system ensures there are few queues. Queues can sometimes build up for the gondolas out of the village, but the main gondola shifts its queue impressively quickly. With the recently installed Lièvre Blanc quad and the new Marmottes II gondola, one of the old troublespots has been eliminated. But this does mean that the Clocher de Macle area will no longer so secluded and enjoyable. The small Pic Blanc cable-car is still queue-prone and is often closed by bad weather. Although they may not cause queues, there are still lots of old drag-lifts dotted around the slopes. A much greater problem than lift queues over much of the area is that the main pistes can be unbearably crowded. The runs in the outlying satellites tend to be less crowded in peak periods.

MOUNTAIN RESTAURANTS
Some excellent rustic huts

Mountain restaurants are generally good – even self-service places are welcoming, and there are many more rustic places with table-service than you expect to find in French purpose-built resorts. One of our favourites is the Chalet du Lac Besson, a peaceful haven with good food on one of the cross-country loops north of the big gondola mid-station, and now accessed by a proper blue piste, the Boulevard des Lacs.

The pretty Forêt de Maronne hotel at Chatelard, below Signal de l'Homme, is delightful and has a good choice of traditional French cuisine. The Combe Haute, at the foot of the Chalvet chair in the gorge towards the end of the Sarenne run, is welcoming but gets very busy. A recent reporter recommends the Hermine, at the base of the Fontfroide lift, for basic but good-value food. The terrace of the Perce-Neige, just below the Oz-Poutran gondola mid-station, attracts crowds. The Plage des Neiges at the top of the nursery slopes is one of the best places available to beginners. The Bergerie at Villard-Reculas has good views and is highly recommended by reporters. The Alpette and Super Signal places are also worth a visit. Chantebise 2100, at the mid-station of the big gondola, offers slick and cheerful table service. The Cabane du Poutat, halfway down from Plat de Marmottes, is recommended for good food and service.

The restaurants in the Oz and Vaujany sectors tend to be cheaper. At Montfrais, Les Airelles is a rustic hut, built into the rock, with a roaring log fire, classical music and excellent, good-value food.

SCHOOLS AND GUIDES
Contrasting views of the schools

We lack recent reports, but over the years our reporters have favoured the International school, which limits classes to 10 and maintains high standards of spoken English. International Masterclass is an independent British-run outfit based in the International school offices that has been highly recommended by reporters, including repeat visitors. Reporters recommend booking in advance during high season. The Bureau des Guides also has a good reputation.

FACILITIES FOR CHILDREN
Mixed reports

We've had rave reviews in the past of the International school's classes for children ('started the week nervously snowploughing down greens, ended up skiing parallel down reds ... only three in the class'). Reports on the ESF, on the other hand, have been mixed.

GETTING THERE

Air Lyon, transfer 3hr. Geneva, transfer 4hr. Grenoble, transfer 1½hr.

Rail Grenoble (63km); daily buses from station.

ACTIVITIES

Indoor Sports centre (tennis, gym, squash, aerobics, climbing wall), library, cinema, swimming pool, billiards, bridge

Outdoor Artificial skating rink (skating and curling), 30km of cleared paths, outdoor swimming pool, hang-gliding, paragliding, all-terrain carts, quad-bikes

Staying there

Staying close to one of the gondolas is useful. Les Bergers, at the eastern entrance to the resort, is convenient for the slopes (it has its own nursery area) but is a trek from most of the other resort facilities. Being near the village bucket-lift is handy if you're not close to the slopes.

HOW TO GO

Something of everything

Chalets There are not many classic chalets in Alpe-d'Huez, but quite a few chalet hotels – hotels that have been taken over by UK chalet operators. Some could do with renovation.

Hotels There are more hotels than is usual in a high French resort, and a clear downmarket bias, with more 1-stars than 2- or 3-stars, and only one 4-star. As part of a shift in the balance, a new 100-bed 3-star hotel is to be built at Les Bergers. There is a huge Club Med at Les Bergers.

((((4 **Royal Ours Blanc** Central. Luxurious, with lots of warm wood. Good food. Superb fitness centre. It runs a free minibus to the lifts.

(((3 **Au Chamois d'Or** Good facilities, modern rooms (some with balconies), one of the best restaurants in town and well placed for main gondola.

(((3 **Cimes** South-facing rooms with balconies, excellent food; close to cross-resort lift and pistes.

(((3 **Grandes Rousses** Comfortable but a bit worn around the edges, friendly staff; close to pistes and lifts.

((2 **Beausoleil** The best-situated 2-star, offering good value.

((2 **Gentianes** Close to the Sarenne gondola in Les Bergers; a wide range of rooms, the best comfortable.

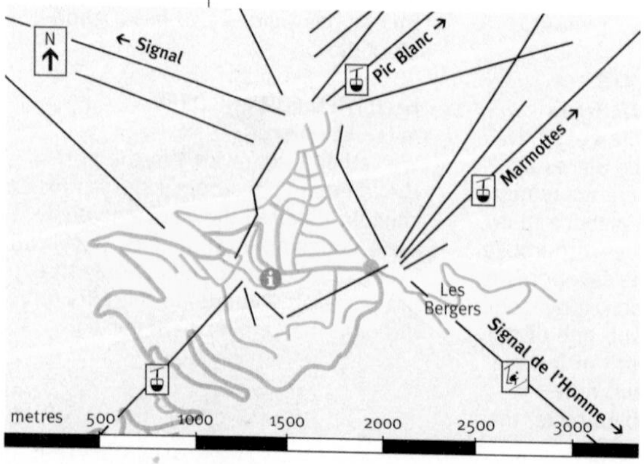

Self-catering There is an enormous choice of apartments available. Residence Les Bergers (formerly the Rocher Soleil apartments) is now owned by the Pierre et Vacances chain, and offers a high standard of accommodation with good facilities, near the Marmottes gondola.

EATING OUT

Good value

Alpe-d'Huez has dozens of restaurants, many of which are of high quality – and good value by French resort standards. The Crémaillère, on the road down to Huez, is highly recommended by a frequent visitor for its excellent food; it reportedly lays on a free taxi there and back. Au P'tit Creux gets a similarly positive review for excellent food, ambience and value. The 'outstanding' Génépi is a friendly old place with good cuisine. Au Vieux Guide also has admirable food, though the animal skins used for decor may be off-putting. The Pomme de Pin is also very popular. The Fromagerie and Edelweiss are others worth a try. The Origan and Pinocchio pizzerias serve good, wholesome Italian fare, the latter possibly having the best pizza in town.

APRES-SKI

Getting better all the time

Regular visitors tell us that you can count on a lively time in a number of bars, even in low season. Among these are likely to be the basement bars of chalet hotels run by British tour operators, notably Crystal's Vallée Blanche (the Roadhouse bar) and Neilson's Chamois (the Underground – an established favourite, and still popular). One expert complains that the bars are too widely dispersed, making pub crawls time consuming; but (in addition to the two above) he seems to have found his way to the Pacific ('friendly, pub-like') and Smithy's ('British hub, crowded, brilliant when there's a band').

The little Avalanche bar is popular with locals and visitors alike, and is often lively with good live music. The P'tit Bar de l'Alpe takes some beating for atmosphere, and also has live music. The Sporting is a large but friendly French rendezvous with a live band. The Ménandière is another popular place, often with live music, while the Alaska is recommended for being quiet and friendly. The Stage One and Igloo discos liven up whenever the French are in town en masse. The Igloo is especially popular with locals, is not too big and has loud music. English films are shown occasionally in the two cinemas, and the ice rink is open until 11pm.

OFF THE SLOPES
Good by purpose-built standards

There is a wide range of facilities, including a new indoor pool, older open-air pools, Olympic-size ice rink and splendid sports centre. There's also an ice driving school. Shops are numerous, but limited in range. The helicopter excursion to Les Deux-Alpes is amusing. It's a pity that the better mountain restaurants aren't easily accessible to pedestrians.

TOURIST OFFICE

Postcode 38750
t +33 476 114444
f 476 806954
info@alpedhuez.com
www.alpedhuez.com

Vaujany 1250m

Vaujany is a tiny rural village perched on the hillside opposite its own sector of the domain, above Montfrais. Thanks to hydroelectric riches, it has a giant 160-person cable-car (that whisks you into the heart of the Alpe-d'Huez lift system), a superb new sports centre, a huge snowmaking installation and apparently plans for a monorail within the village. Eventually, they are going to run out of things to buy.

As well as the cable-car there's a gondola to the bottom of the Montfrais runs and nursery slopes, with a mid-station at La Villette, an even smaller hamlet than Vaujany (just one tiny bar-restaurant). There's a run back to La

Villette, but you normally have to ride from there down to Vaujany. There are no village slopes, so even complete beginners have to ride the gondola.

What the piste map used to show as an itinerary route from the Montfrais area down to Enversin, below the village, is now the Fare black piste, ending at a short lift up to the village.

Vaujany gets some day visitors, but is generally a quiet spot. We've never seen the cable-car full. It has four simple hotels. The Rissiou is run by a British tour operator (Ski Peak) and is well situated for access to the cable-car. It has a popular bar (frequented by the locals), a pleasant dining room that serves excellent French cuisine (and good inexpensive wines), and fairly basic bedrooms. The staff are friendly and efficient. Ski Peak also has catered chalets in Vaujany and La Villette and some self-catering accommodation. A minibus service for guests is available.

The hotel Cîmes, over the road, is less rustic but useful for a change of bar scenery. The Etendard, by the lift station, is run by a Belgian tour operator and has a lively après-ski bar. There are two nightclubs. There's an open-air ice rink, well-stocked sports shop, small supermarket, a couple of restaurants and a few chickens wandering the streets. And there are some tasteful new developments up the mountainside.

Vaujany has its own ski school – reports have all been very positive. And there's a big, well-equipped day nursery by the lift station.

Oz-Station 1350m

Oz is a purpose-built little place close to the heart of the slopes, above the attractive original old village of Oz-en-Oisans. Its two large apartment blocks, which are the focus of the place, have been built in a sympathetic style, with much use of wood and stone. The village also benefits from being the only resort in the area with trees on all sides. It has the basics required of a tiny, family resort – good access to the slopes, ski school, sports shops, nursery slopes, a couple of bar-restaurants and a supermarket. A recent visitor detects that it is now 'taking off', with more facilities coming on-line, but another complains that there is still no nightlife for the teens and twenties. There is a choice of gondolas moving away in different directions, from where you can set off to all points in double-quick time. The main run home is liberally endowed with snow-guns, but needs to be.

Auris 1600m

Auris is a series of wood-clad, chalet-style apartment blocks with a few shops, bars and restaurants. Beneath it is the original old village, complete with attractive, traditional buildings, a church and all but one of the resort's hotels. This is a pleasant base for those with a car. They can nip up to the upper village to set off locally, and also have speedy access to the valley for excursions to neighbouring resorts such as Serre-Chevalier. The upper village is pleasantly set close to the thickest woodland in the area. It's a fine family resort, with everything close to hand, including a nursery and a ski kindergarten. There's also a ski school.

Unsurprisingly, evenings are quiet, with a handful of bar-restaurants to choose from. The Beau Site, which looks like an apartment block, is the only hotel in the upper village. A couple of miles down the hill, the attractively traditional Auberge de la Forêt and a selection of gîtes give you a feel of 'real' rural France. You can also stay round the hill, at Chatelard, in the cosy Forêt de Maronne.

Access to the slopes of Alpe-d'Huez is no problem, but there are plenty of local slopes to explore, for which there is a special lift pass. This covers 45km of piste for just over half the cost of the full area pass. Most of the sport is intermediate, though Auris is also the best of the local hamlets for beginners.

Villard-Reculas 1500m

Villard is a secluded village, complete with an old church, set on a small shelf wedged between an expanse of open snowfields above and tree-filled hillsides below. Following the installation of a fast quad chair up to Signal a couple of years back, the village is becoming more popular as an access point for day visitors, and is also beginning to find its feet as a 'resort'. Its 500 beds are mainly in self-catering apartments and chalets, though there is one 2-star hotel. The village also has a supermarket and a couple of bars and restaurants. Its local slopes have something for everyone, and there is now an ESF branch here. One surprise is the lack of snow-guns, often leaving the runs home icy and patchy.

Les Arcs 1600m-2000m

Purpose-built for a holiday on the slopes – and little else

WHAT IT COSTS

5

HOW IT RATES

The slopes	
Snow	****
Extent	***
Experts	****
Intermediates	****
Beginners	****
Convenience	****
Queues	***
Restaurants	**
The rest	
Scenery	***
Resort charm	*
Off-slope	*

What's new

For 1999/2000 Arc 2000 was linked to the bottom of the Aiguille Rouge cable by a new eight-person gondola, and there was a new ice rink at Arc 1800 and some new 'luxury' apartments in 1800.

There are plans to link the Les Arcs and La Plagne slopes by cable-car in the next couple of years, forming the world's third biggest linked ski area.

- + Very easy train access from UK
- + Easy access to the slopes from much of the accommodation
- + Excellent runs for all standards
- + Opportunity for skiing beginners to learn by the évolutif method
- + Few serious queues
- + Splendid views of Mont Blanc massif
- + Quite a few pretty tree-lined runs
- + Glowing recent reports of friendly locals – unusual for French resorts

- − Villages are purpose-built and lack traditional charm
- − Very quiet in the evenings
- − Few off-slope diversions
- − Some apartment buildings are quite a walk from lifts
- − Nearly all accommodation is in apartments; there's a lack of catered chalets and budget hotels – except down in Bourg-St-Maurice and other old valley villages

Les Arcs is a classic purpose-built French resort, with all the usual advantages and drawbacks. If a short walk from front door to lift base is your priority – and not village atmosphere or animation – put it on the short-list. A further attraction is that it is the only high-altitude French resort reachable by rail: the Eurostar and snowtrains to Bourg-St-Maurice connect with a funicular that takes you straight to Arc 1600. (For the two other Arcs it's a taxi, though.)

Les Arcs' terrain isn't in quite the same league as the Three Valleys, La Plagne or Val-d'Isère/Tignes for sheer extent, but within its slightly smaller area it contains an impressive variety, including some of the longest descents in the Alps. For a keen mixed-ability group, it is a strong candidate.

boarding *Les Arcs calls itself 'the home of the snowboard'. Local boy Regis Rolland played a big part in popularising the sport (not least with his 'Apocalypse Snow' movies), and the resort is constantly developing its boarding facilities. Some boarders are doubtless attracted by the budget self-catering accommodation, but also by the great mix of terrain served mainly by boarder-friendly lifts (though getting around can involve some long traverses). Arc 2000 and Vallandry have great smooth runs for beginners and carvers. There's a park and half-pipe, and a couple of specialist board schools and shops.*

The resort

Les Arcs is made up of three modern resort units, linked by road, high above the railway terminus town of Bourg-St-Maurice. The three villages have a lot in common: they are purpose-built, apartment-dominated places, offering doorstep access to the snow with no traffic hazards, but lacking Alpine charm, off-slope activities, and evening animation.

Much the largest of the three 'villages' is Arc 1800. It has three sections, though the boundaries are indistinct. Charvet and Villards are

SNOWPIX.COM / CHRIS GILL

← We've grown to like Les Arcs' varied slopes more and more – and even some apartments

MOUNTAIN FACTS

Altitude 1200m-3225m	
Lifts	76
Pistes	200km
Green/Blue	52%
Red	33%
Black	14%
Artificial snow	12km
Recco detectors used	

LIFT PASSES

2000/01 prices in francs

Massif Aiguille Grive-Aiguille Rouge
Covers all lifts in Les Arcs and Peisey-Nancroix, including funicular from Bourg-St-Maurice.

Beginners Five free lifts; one in 1600 and two each in 1800 and 2000.

Main pass
1-day pass 220
6-day pass 1065
(low season 710)

Senior citizens
Over 60: 6-day pass 905, low season 605
Over 75: free pass

Children
Under 14: 6-day pass 905 – low season 605
Under 7: free pass

Short-term passes
Half-day afternoon (adult 158). Half-day (am or pm) passes for each area (adult 118). Single and return tickets on most lifts for walkers.

Notes All passes over 1 day cover La Plagne and allow 1 day in La Rosière-La Thuile and Tignes-Val-d'Isère. 6-day pass and over allows one day each in the 3V, Pralognan-la-Vanoise and Les Saises. 5% reduction on presentation of previous season's pass.

Alternative passes
1- and 2-day passes (165, 305) are available; one covers Arc 2000 and Villaroger (21 lifts), the other Arc 1600 and 1800 (38 lifts).

dominated by apartment blocks the size of ocean liners. More pleasant on the eye is Charmettoger, with smaller, wood-clad buildings nestling among trees. The nearest thing 1800 has to a central focus is the Hotel du Golf, set more or less where Charvet meets Villards. The main village slopes and a couple of main lifts are just outside the door, and the village nursery and mini-club are nearby. The two arcades that house most of 1800's shops, bars and restaurants are either side. And it's the pivot of après-ski activity. For people self-catering, reports of the small supermarket are that it is 'expensive and not well stocked'.

Arc 2000 is just a few hotels, apartment blocks and the Club Med, huddled together in a bleak spot, with little to commend it but immediate access to the highest, toughest skiing.

Arc 1600 was the original Arc (it opened in December 1968) and remains our favourite. It has the advantage of being at the top of the Bourg-St-Maurice funicular, giving easy access from the UK by train and quick and easy access to civilisation. 1600 is set in the trees and has a friendly, small-scale atmosphere; and it enjoys good views along the valley and towards Mont Blanc. The central area is particularly good for families: uncrowded, compact, and set on even ground. But things are even quieter here at night than during the day.

There are a couple of alternative places to stay down in the valleys at either end of the ski area, well away from main purpose-built resorts – see the end of this chapter.

The mountains

Les Arcs' piste network is not huge. But its terrain is notably varied; it has plenty of runs suitable for experts as well as beginners and intermediates, and a good mixture of high, snowsure slopes and accessible low-level woodland runs ideal for bad weather.

THE SLOPES
Well planned, and varied

The slopes are very well laid out, and moving around is quick and easy. There are runs down into each of the villages, and Arc 2000 has runs descending below village level, to the lift-base, restaurant and car-park complex at Pré-St-Esprit, at about 200m lower. Each village has a number of lifts fanning out, and virtually any lift will do to gain height, after which there are countless runs criss-crossing the mountainsides to other sections.

Arc 1600 and Arc 1800 share a west-facing mountainside laced with runs leading down to one or other village. At the southern end are runs down through woods to Plan-Peisey and Vallandry, mountainside outposts above Peisey-Nancroix. This area is where the planned cable-car link to La Plagne will be.

From various points on the ridge above 1600 and 1800 you can head down into the Arc 2000 bowl. On the opposite side of this bowl, lifts take you to the highest runs of the area, from the Aiguille Rouge (3225m) and the Grand Col (2835m). As well as a variety of steep runs back to Arc 2000,

TEST YOUR NERVE ON THE FLYING KILOMETRE

One of the special features of Les Arcs is the 'flying kilometre' course, as used in the speed skiing event in the 1992 Albertville Olympics. The angle of the slope goes from 76° to 45° and it is 1.74km long. Various world speed records have been set here, on skis (current world record over 240kph – that's over 150mph), snowboards (world record over 195kph or 120mph) and mountain bikes (world record over 210kph or 130mph). But what makes the course especially interesting for holiday skiers is that you can have a go on it, though you won't go quite so fast. It takes barely 15 seconds but they are 15 seconds you will remember for life.

About 8000 people a year try it, and accidents are reassuringly rare (and rarely serious). You go from some way below the competition start at the top, and the stopping area is very wide, flat and (like the course itself) immaculately groomed. You get a mini-medal for averaging 90kph between the timing posts, a bronze medal for 110kph, silver for 130kph, and gold for 150kph; they say you're sure to get a bronze unless you resort to a snowplough. One run, including hire of helmet, goggles and special long, straight skis, costs FF50; an all-day pass is FF130.

SCHOOLS/GUIDES

2000/01 prices in francs

ESF

Classes 6 days
3hr: am or pm
6 half-days: 690

Children's classes
Ages: 3 to 14
6 half-days: 690

Private lessons
Hourly
190 for 1hr, for 1 or 2 people

CHILDCARE

The ESF branches in all three stations take children from 3. The International school's Club Poussin in 1800 starts at 4.

At Arc 1600 the Garderie at the Hotel de la Cachette (479 077050) runs three clubs for children from 4 months to 11 years, from 8.30 to 6pm, with ski lessons available.

At Arc 1800 various schemes running from 8.45 to 5.45 are offered by the Pommes de Pin (479 041530). The Nurserie takes children aged 1 to 3, the Garderie those aged 3 to 6, and children aged 3 to 9 can have lessons through the two clubs based at the Garderie.

At Arc 2000 Les Marmottons (479 076425) takes children aged 2 to 6 from 8.30 to 5.45, with lessons for those aged 3 to 6.

The Club Med (2000) has full childcare facilities – this is one of their 'family villages'.

the Aiguille Rouge is the start of a lovely long run (over 2000m vertical and 7km long) right down to the hamlet of Le Pré near Villaroger. You can also reach Le Pré from below Arc 2000, via a short drag-lift (although one reporter claimed it is often closed).

SNOW RELIABILITY

Good – plenty of high runs

A high percentage of the runs are above 2000m and a fair amount on north-facing slopes – though those above 1600 and 1800 get the afternoon sun. While the highest slopes from the Aiguille Rouge are more suitable for good skiers, there are easy north-facing runs starting from 2600m. There is limited artificial snow on some runs back to 1600, 1800 and Peisey.

FOR EXPERTS

Challenges on- and off-piste

Les Arcs has a lot to offer experts – at least when the high lifts are open (the Aiguille Rouge cable-car, in particular, is often shut in bad weather).

There are a number of truly black pistes above Arc 2000, and a couple in other areas. After a narrow shelf near the top, the Aiguille Rouge-Le Pré run is superb, with remarkably varying terrain throughout its vertical drop of over 2000m. There is also a great deal of off-piste potential, in various parts. There are steep pitches on the front face of the Aiguille Rouge, and secluded runs on the back side, towards Villaroger – the Combe de l'Anchette, for example. A short climb to the Grand Col from the chair-lift of the same name gives access to several routes, including a quite serious couloir and a more roundabout route over the Glacier du Grand Col. The wooded slopes above 1600 are another attractive possibility – and there are open slopes all over the mountain.

FOR INTERMEDIATES

Plenty for all standards

One strength of the area is that most main routes have easy and more difficult alternatives, making it good for mixed-ability groups. There are plenty of challenges, yet less confident intermediates are able to move around without getting too many nasty surprises. An exception is the solitary Comborcières black from Les Deux Têtes down to Pré-St-Esprit. This long mogul field justifies its rating and can be great fun for strong intermediates.

The woodland runs at either end of the domain, above Peisey and Le Pré, and the bumpy Cachette red down to 1600, are also good for better intermediates. Those who enjoy speed will like Peisey: its well groomed runs are remarkably uncrowded much of the time. Good intermediates can enjoy the Aiguille Rouge-Le Pré run (with red and blue detours available to avoid the toughest bits of the black piste).

The lower half of the mountainside is good for mixed-ability groups, with a choice of routes through the trees. The red runs down from Arpette and Col des Frettes towards 1800 are quite steep but usually well groomed.

Cautious intermediates have plenty of cruising terrain. Many of the runs around 2000 are rather bland and prone to overcrowding. The blues above 1800 are nice, though busy, motorways, while the easier of the pistes down to Plan-Peisey are pleasantly quiet.

FOR BEGINNERS

1800 best for complete novices

There are nursery slopes conveniently situated just above all three villages. The ones at Arc 1600 are rather steep for complete beginners, while those at 2000 get crowded with intermediate through-traffic at times. The sunny, spacious runs at 1800 are best. Fast learners can take the gondola up to Col de la Chal and enjoy good snow on the easy runs towards 2000.

FOR CROSS-COUNTRY

Very boring locally

Short trails, mostly on roads, close to all three villages, is all you can expect unless you travel down to the Nancroix valley's 40km of pleasant trails.

QUEUES

Few problems now

Reporters mentioned few queues this year. The new eight-person gondola seems to have solved the problems at Arc 2000 but it has also increased the sometimes lengthy waits for the Aiguille Rouge cable-car. The lifts above Plan-Peisey can get busy, too. At holiday times overcrowded pistes can be as big a problem as queues. The Grand Col quad chair-lift installed a few years ago has made this area rather congested. Several reporters have also mentioned that most chair-lifts are of the 'old slow variety'.

↑ The highest point of the slopes is the 3225m Aiguille Rouge, the start of a great 7km run down to the hamlet of Le Pré over 2000m below

SNOWPIX.COM / CHRIS GILL

MOUNTAIN RESTAURANTS
A good choice

L'Arpette has 'a wide choice of food and a salad buffet' as well as 'good crêpes'. L'Aiguille Grive, just above 1800, is a favourite with the ski instructors. The restaurant at Col de la Chal, at the top of the gondola, has fabulous views and the sun terrace of Chez Félix has good views of La Plagne. The Poudreuse, above the trees near the top of the Vallandry chair-lift, is one of the best, but gets busy. Blanche Muree is 'consistently excellent, with friendly service, good food and wine at sensible prices'.

The 500-year-old Belliou la Fumée at Pré-St-Esprit has a rustic atmosphere and good food. La Ferme and Aiguille Rouge down at Le Pré are both friendly and rustic, with good food. Chez Léa in Le Planay serves simple food in rustic surroundings.

It is easy to get back to the main villages for lunch where prices are generally lower. For a lovely typically French lunch in a rustic auberge take a five-minute taxi from Villandry to the l'Ancolie restaurant (tel 0479 079320).

SCHOOL AND GUIDES
Ski évolutif recommended

The ESF ski school is renowned for being the first in Europe to teach ski évolutif, where beginners learn parallel turns right from the start on short skis, gradually moving on to longer skis. The International school (Arc Adventure) has impressed reporters over the years – 'good instruction with English well spoken'. We continue to have glowing reports of the Optimum ski courses, using British instructors, based in a catered chalet in Le Pré (see p198).

FACILITIES FOR CHILDREN
Good reports

We have received good reports on the Pommes de Pin facilities in Arc 1800 – 'great care and attention', 'patient approach to teaching'. Comments on children's ski classes are favourable, too – 'nearly all instructors spoke English', 'classes went smoothly'.

Staying there

Les Arcs is essentially a convenience resort, and in 1600 and 2000 you need not worry much about where you are based. But self-caterers staying in 1800 should beware: some of its apartment blocks are a long walk from the snow. We have received glowing reports of smaller UK tour operators with catered chalets in the quieter, prettier villages of Le Pré (Optimum) and Le Villaret (Ski Hiver). Ski Olympic will have a brand new chalet-hotel in Villandry for 2000/01. We continue to receive reports of how friendly the locals are: 'welcoming staff in restaurants and bars', 'lift staff surprisingly friendly'.

HOW TO GO
Let the train take the strain

Daytime and overnight trains now run weekly from London direct to Bourg-St-Maurice, at the bottom of the funicular

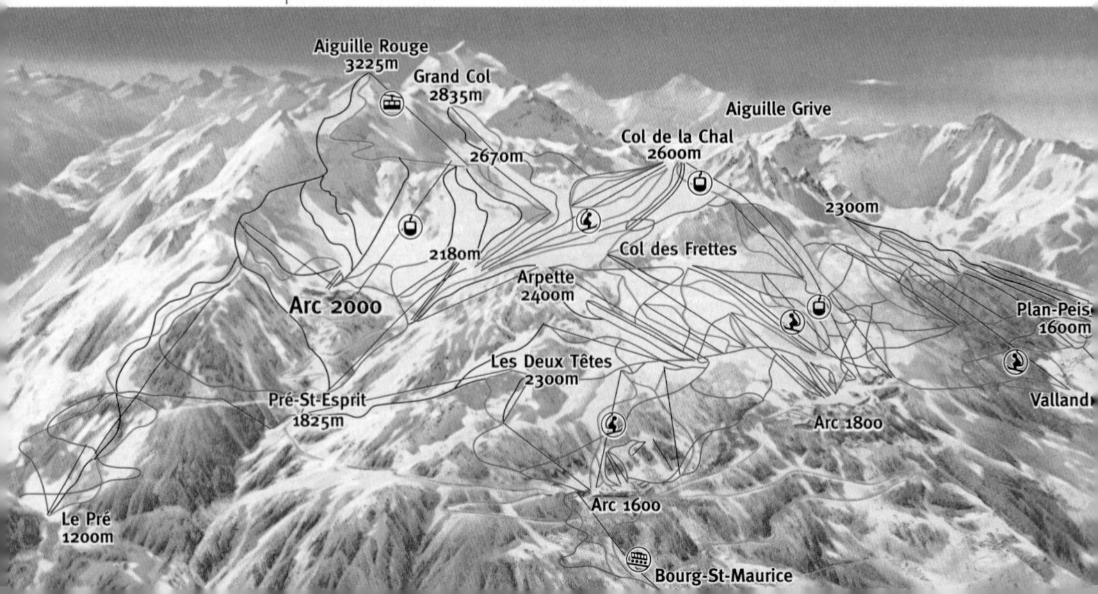

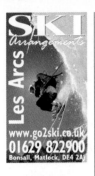

GETTING THERE

Air Geneva, transfer 3½hr. Lyon, transfer 3½hr. Chambéry, transfer 2½hr.

Rail Bourg-St-Maurice; frequent buses and direct funicular to resort.

UK Representative

Erna Low Consultants
9 Reece Mews
London SW7 3HE
t 020 7584 2841
f 020 7589 9531
info@ernalow.co.uk
www.ernalow.co.uk

up to 1600. There is no more convenient resort for train travel. Although all the big UK tour operators come here, their accommodation is limited – mostly apartments. There is a Club Med 'village' at Arc 2000.

Chalets There are hardly any catered chalet holidays in Les Arcs but there are in the lower villages (see p198).

Hotels The choice of hotels in Les Arcs is gradually widening, particularly at the upper end of the market. All-in packages of full-board accommodation and lift pass can be attractive.

(4) **Mercure** (1800) Recently built, and locally judged to be worth four stars rather than its actual three.

(3) **Golf** (1800) A super-pricey 3-star; the best in Les Arcs, with recently renovated rooms, sauna, gym, kindergarten and covered parking.

(3) **Village Club du Soleil** (1800) Good value family hotel, which takes children from three months.

(3) **La Cachette** (1600) Smartly renovated in the mid-1990s, with something of the style of an American resort hotel. But it was 'dominated by kids' said one reporter.

(2) **Aiguille Rouge** (2000) Daily free ski guiding.

Self-catering Over three-quarters of the resort beds are in apartments, mostly tight on space, so paying extra for under-occupancy is a sound investment. The luxury Alpages du Chantel apartments (new for 1999/2000 and bookable through Erna Low), above Charvet, are the best in town, with a pool, sauna and gym – and a lift to them is supposed to be in place for 2000/01. The Ruitor apartments are well equipped and set among trees between Villards and Charmettoger. L'Aiguille Grive has been recommended for spacious apartments and excellent slope access. The Nova residences in Villards, which house a kindergarten and mini-club, and the Pierre et Vacances places, the Arnoise and Grand Arbois, are about the best of the rest on the British package market.

EATING OUT

OK if you know where to go

A popular outing is to drive half-way down the mountain to the welcoming and woody Bois de Lune, at Montvenix, which has perhaps the best food in the area (booking advised – call 0479 071792). Down in Bourg-St-Maurice the restaurant of the Petite

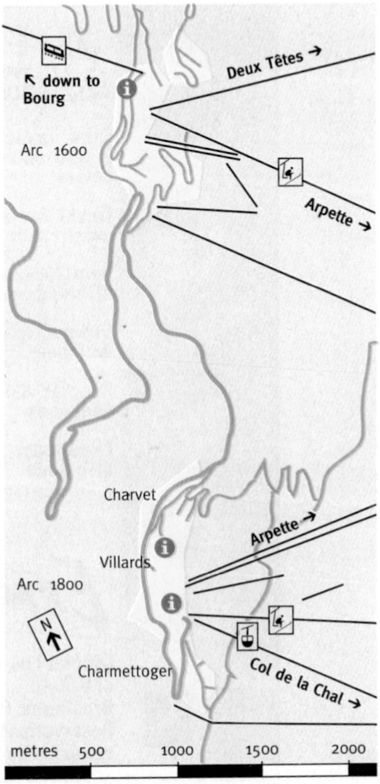

ACTIVITIES

Indoor Squash (3 courts 1800), Chinese gymnastics, saunas (1600, 1800), solaria, multi-gym (1800), cinemas, amusement arcades, music, concert halls, fencing (2000), bowling (1800)

Outdoor Natural skating rinks (1800 and 2000), floodlit skiing, speed skiing (2000), ski-jump, climbing wall (1800), organised snow-shoe outings, 10km cleared paths (1800 and 1600), hang-gliding, horse-riding, sleigh rides, helicopter rides to Italy, ice grotto, paint balling

TOURIST OFFICE

Postcode 73706
t +33 479 071257
f 479 074596
lesarcs@lesarcs.com
www.lesarcs.com

Auberge hotel is highly recommended by locals (book on 0479 073711). Back in Les Arcs, Le Petit Zinc restaurant in the Hotel du Golf has haute cuisine and high prices – we loved the Friday evening seafood buffet. The Gargantus in 1800 is a good informal place. Marmite and L'Equipage specialise in Savoyard dishes. Casa Mia does good pizza and pasta. Le Grenier des Arcs, in 1800, has been recommended for good food at modest prices.

APRES-SKI

Arc 1800 is the place to be

1800 is the liveliest centre. The Jo bar is open until the early hours and has a friendly, lively atmosphere. The Fairway disco keeps rocking until 4 most mornings. Red Hot Saloon attracts a younger crowd with bar games. The cinemas at 1800 and 1600 have English-language films once or twice a week. In 1600 the bar opposite (and belonging to) the Hotel La Cachette has games machines, pool and live bands, and can be quite lively even in low season. Nightlife in Bourg-St-Maurice has been described as 'non existent'.

OFF THE SLOPES

Very poor

Les Arcs is not the place for an off-the-slopes holiday. There is very little to do and it doesn't even have a swimming pool. A shopping trip to Bourg-St-Maurice (cheaper for buying ski equipment), preferably on Saturday for the market, and a few walks are the main options available.

Bourg-St-Maurice 840m

Bourg-St-Maurice is a real French town, with cheaper hotels and restaurants and easy access to other resorts for day trips. The funicular goes straight to Arc 1600 in seven minutes. Hostellerie du Pt-St-Bernard has been reported to be a reasonable 2-star hotel. You can leave your skis or board and boots at a ski shop next to the bottom of the funicular, run by a British couple.

Le Pré 1200m

A charming, quiet, rustic little hamlet with a chair-lift up towards Arc 2000. It has a couple of small bars and restaurants and is a short drive from Villaroger on the road between Bourg-St-Maurice and Val-d'Isère. British operator Optimum has a beautiful old chalet here that the owners Martin and Deirdre Rowe renovated and run themselves. We can personally vouch for fabulous food, free-flowing wine, jolly bar (run on an 'honour' system) and basic but adequate bedrooms; and the ski courses they run (Martin used to run the ski school in Andorra) have received rave reviews from reporters. But Le Pré is not suitable for beginners.

Peisey-Villandry 1550m

This small village of Peisey-Nancroix dates back to AD1000, and its most striking feature is the fine baroque church. The other, mostly old, buildings house a small selection of shops, restaurants and bars. The main tree-lined runs of Les Arcs start a five-minute gondola ride away, at Plan-Peisey-Vallandry.

Reporters recommend staying in Plan-Peisey or Villandry (Hotel Vanoise and Ski Hiver's chalets were praised) rather than 'shabby, claustrophobic Peisey-Nancroix'. They loved the pretty tree-lined easy red runs home. Villandry is developing rapidly as it will be the site for the cable-car link to La Plagne. Ski Olympic is building a new chalet-hotel here that will open for the 2000/01 season.

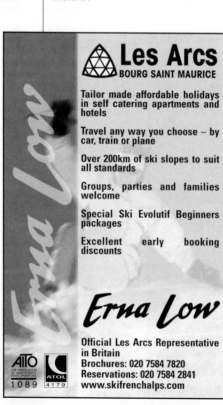

Avoriaz 1800m

The best base on the Portes du Soleil circuit for snow

WHAT IT COSTS

5

HOW IT RATES

The slopes	
Snow	***
Extent	*****
Experts	***
Intermediates	****
Beginners	****
Convenience	****
Queues	**
Restaurants	****
The rest	
Scenery	***
Resort charm	**
Off-slope	*

What's new

1999/2000 saw the introduction of a new hands-free lift pass system operated by an electronic card that you keep in your pocket. And a micro fun-park specially for snowboarding children was opened.

Recent years have seen substantial investment in high-speed chairs (including some six-seaters) which have greatly reduced lift queue problems.

For 2000/01 the gondola from Ardent to above Les Lindarets will be replaced by a higher-capacity one.

MOUNTAIN FACTS

Altitude	975m-2350m
Lifts	219
Pistes	650km
Green/Blue	51%
Red	40%
Black	9%
Arti. snow	522 acres
Recco detectors used	

- ⊕ Good position on the main Portes du Soleil circuit, giving access to very extensive, quite varied runs for all grades from novices to experts
- ⊕ Generally has the best snow in the Portes du Soleil
- ⊕ Accommodation right on the slopes
- ⊕ Resort level snow and ski-through, car-free village give Alpine ambience
- ⊕ Good children's facilities

- ⊖ Much of Portes du Soleil area is low for a major French area, with resulting risk of poor snow or bare slopes lower down
- ⊖ Still a couple of lift bottlenecks and (especially in local Avoriaz area) some crowded pistes
- ⊖ Non-traditional architecture, which some find ugly
- ⊖ Little to do off the slopes
- ⊖ Few hotels or chalets

For access to the impressive Portes du Soleil piste network, Avoriaz has clear attractions. In a low-altitude area where snow is not reliable, it has the best there is – on relatively high, north-facing slopes of varying difficulty, including some of the most challenging terrain in the Portes du Soleil.

But there are drawbacks. First, the character of the village: we don't mind sleeping in purpose-built resorts to get instant access to high-altitude snow, but there is no really high-altitude terrain here. The Portes du Soleil has several attractive low-altitude villages, and we'd rather be based in one. Secondly, cost: Châtel and Morzine are cheap by French standards; Avoriaz is not. Queues can be a nuisance, too, but they affect those exploring the Portes du Soleil from other bases as much as they affect those based in Avoriaz – more so, in fact.

boarding *Avoriaz has encouraged snowboarding ever since it first hit the slopes. The British championships have been held here and the first British chalet aimed specially at boarders opened just below here. Lifts have been upgraded, and now just a few (mainly avoidable) drags are left. There's an excellent 1.5km fun-park, half-pipe and slalom stadium just above the village – served by three lifts. There's a specialist snowboard school, a snowboard village for children aged 6 to 16 and a special micro fun-park for children. There's also a limited area pass for boarders. The blocks of self-catering accommodation may suit the budget boarder willing to pack people in. Nightlife revolves around the couple of bars that manage an atmosphere.*

The resort

Avoriaz is a purpose-built resort perched impressively above a dramatic, sheer rock face. Cars and coaches stop at the edge of town, and horse-drawn sleighs or snow-cats transport people and luggage to the accommodation. This can mean a lot of intrusive traffic, some of it fast moving. We've had reports that the problem with horse-mess has been reduced because the horses now have boxes beneath their backsides and staff on snowmobiles scoop up what escapes! A reporter advises using the underground car park to avoid a chaotic departure day if it snows (it took him three hours). The village is set on a considerable slope, but there are chair-lifts and elevators in buildings and moving around is no problem except when paths are icy.

Avoriaz usually has snow all over its byways, and being able to glide around town is convenient. Pistes, lifts and off-slope activities are close to virtually all accommodation.

The village is composed of angular, dark, wood-clad high-rise buildings, mostly apartment blocks. Reactions to the architecture vary but the place has

↑ The Portes du Soleil is an extensive intermediate circuit which crosses the Franco-Swiss border

SNOWPIX.COM / CHRIS GILL

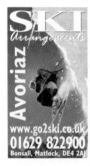

a distinct style, unlike the dreary cuboid blocks thrown up in the 1960s in Flaine and Les Menuires.

But the compact snow-covered village has a friendly Alpine feel despite the architecture. It is also pleasantly cosmopolitan. The evenings are not especially lively, but a reporter enjoyed the 'brilliant parade in half-term week, with a superb fire-eating display' a couple of years ago – 'though not as good this year' he says.

Avoriaz is above the valley resort of Morzine, to which it is linked by gondola (but not by piste). It also has good links to Châtel in one direction and Champéry in the other. Car trips are possible to Flaine and Chamonix.

The mountains

The slopes closest to Avoriaz are bleak and treeless, but snowsure. They suit all grades, from novice to expert and give quick access to the most challenging runs in the Portes du Soleil. The whole circuit can be done easily by intermediates of all abilities. It breaks down at Châtel, where there's a frequent shuttle-bus. The areas of Morzine and Les Gets are part of the Portes du Soleil network but are not on the core circuit. They are accessed from the far side of Morzine. A regular visitor praises the new Portes du Soleil piste maps introduced last season.

THE SLOPES
Short runs and plenty of them

The village has lifts and pistes fanning out in all directions. Staying close to Avoriaz assures the comfort of riding mostly chair-lifts – some other parts of the Portes du Soleil (especially on the Swiss side) have a lot of drags. Facing the village are the slopes of **Arare-Hauts Forts** and when the snow conditions allow there are long, steep runs down to Les Prodains.

The lifts off to the left go to the **Chavanette** sector on the Swiss border – a broad, undulating bowl. Beyond the border at the col is the infamous Swiss Wall – a long and impressive mogul slope with a tricky start, but not the terror it is cracked up to be unless it is icy (it gets a lot of sun). Lots of people doing the circuit (or returning to Champéry) ride the chair down. At the bottom of the Wall is the open terrain of Planachaux, above Champéry, with links to the even bigger open area around Les Crosets and Champoussin. There are several ways back from this sector, but the most amusing is the chair up the Wall, with a grandstand view of those struggling down beneath you.

Taking a lift up from Avoriaz (or traversing from some of the highest accommodation) takes you to the ridge behind the village, where pistes go down into the **Lindarets-Brocheaux** valley, from where lifts and runs in the excellent Linga sector lead to Châtel. Getting back is basically a matter of retracing your steps, although there are several options from Lindarets.

Morgins is the resort opposite Avoriaz on the circuit, and the state of the snow may encourage you to travel anti-clockwise rather than clockwise, so as to avoid the low, south-facing slopes down from Bec de Corbeau.

SNOW RELIABILITY
High resort, low slopes

Although Avoriaz is high, its slopes don't go much higher – and some parts of the Portes du Soleil circuit are much lower. Considering their altitude, the north-facing slopes below Hauts Forts hold their snow well. In general, the snow in Avoriaz is usually much better than over the border on the south-facing Swiss slopes.

SNOWPIX.COM / CHRIS GILL

It's no beauty; but it is convenient and has the best snow in the Portes du Soleil ↓

LIFT PASSES

2000/01 prices in francs

Portes du Soleil
Covers all lifts in all 12 resorts, and shuttle-buses.

Main pass
1-day pass 207
6-day pass 998

Senior citizens
Over 60: 6-day pass 798

Children
Under 16: 6-day pass 669
Under 5: free pass

Alternative passes
Pass covering the 39 lifts of Avoriaz only: 171 per day.
Beginner's pass covering more limited area: 110 per day.
Snowboarders pass covering fun-park and a few other areas: 124 per day; 6-day pass 570 (1999/2000 prices).

GETTING THERE

Air Geneva, transfer 2hr.

Rail Cluses (42km) or Thonon (45km); bus and cable-car to resort.

Piste maintenance is 'erratic and it is quite common for runs not to have been groomed overnight,' says a reporter. Snow-guns have been introduced in some places, including on some of the blacks and the great blue run from the top of the cable-car down to Les Prodains.

FOR EXPERTS
Several testing runs

The tough terrain is rather dotted about. The challenging runs down from Hauts Forts to Prodains (including a World Cup downhill course) are excellent. There is a tough red, and several long, truly black runs, one of which cuts through trees – particularly useful in poor weather. Two chair-lifts serve the lower runs, which snow-guns help to keep open. The Swiss Wall at Chavanette will naturally be on your agenda, and the Châtel sector is well worth the trip. The black runs off the Swiss side of Mossette and Pointe de l'Au are worth trying. It's not a great area for off-piste adventures, but there is plenty of snow just outside the pistes in all of these sectors.

FOR INTERMEDIATES
Virtually the whole area

Although some sections lack variety, the Portes du Soleil is excellent for all grades of intermediates when snow is in good supply. Timid types not worried about pretty surroundings need not leave the Avoriaz sector; Arare and Chavanette are gentle, spacious, above the tree-line bowls. The Linderets area and on down to Ardent is also easy, with pretty runs through the trees. Champoussin has a lot of easy runs, reached without too much difficulty via Les Crosets and Pointe de l'Au. Better intermediates have virtually the whole area at their disposal. The runs down to Pré-la-Joux and L'Essert on the way to Châtel, and those either side of Morgins, are particularly attractive. The long, sunny runs down to Grand-Paradis near Champéry are a must when snow conditions allow; they offer great views. Good intermediates may want to take on the Wall, but the chair to Pointe de Mossette from Les Brocheaux is an easier route to Champéry.

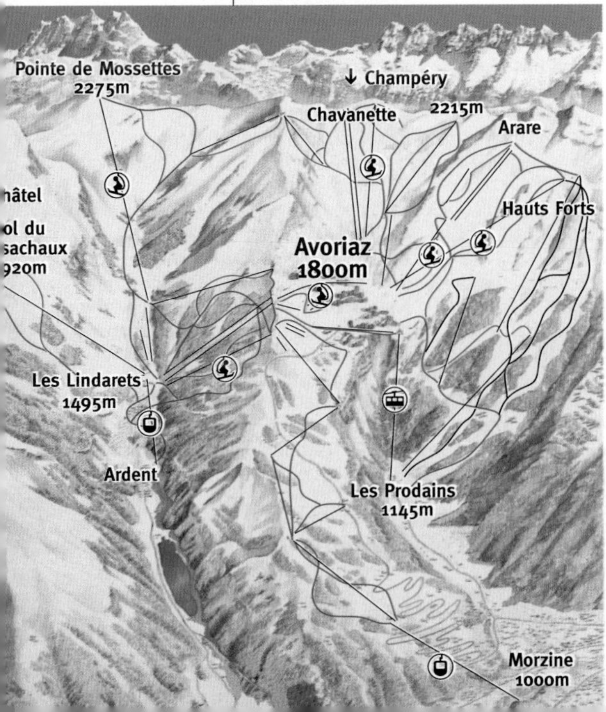

FOR BEGINNERS
Convenient and good for snow

The nursery slopes seem small in relation to the size of the resort, but are adequate because so many visitors are intermediates. The slopes are sunny, yet good for snow, and link well to longer, easy runs.

FOR CROSS-COUNTRY
Varied, with some blacks

There are 45km of trails, a third graded black, mainly between Avoriaz and Super-Morzine, with other fine trails down to Lindarets and around Montriond. The only drawback is that several trails are not loops, but 'out and back' routes.

QUEUES
Main problems now gone

The queues for the lifts to Arare and Chavanette have been more-or-less eliminated by new high-speed lifts. But

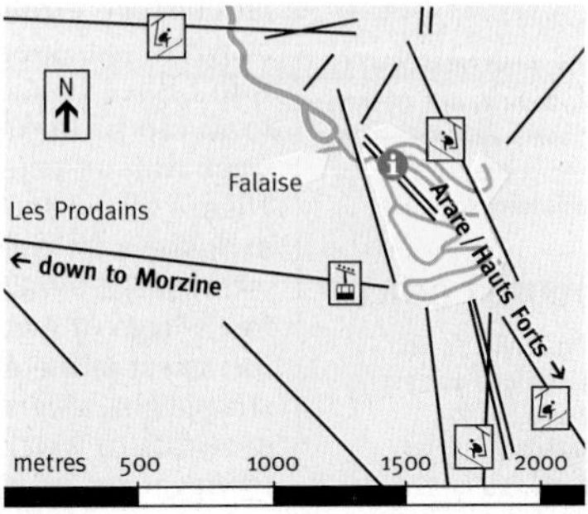

ACTIVITIES

Indoor Health centre 'Altiform' (sauna, gym, hot-tub), squash, Turkish baths, cinema, bowling
Outdoor Paragliding, hang-gliding, snow-shoe excursions, ice diving, floodlit tobogganing, dog-sleigh rides, walking paths, sleigh rides, skating, snow-scooter excursions, helicopter flights

SCHOOLS/GUIDES

2000/01 prices in francs

ESF
Classes 6 days
5hr: 2½hr am and pm
6 full days: 800
Children's classes
Ages: 4 to 11
6 full days: 690
Private lessons
1hr, 1½hr or 2hr
175 for 1hr, for 1 to 2 people; 230 for 3 to 6

L'Ecole de Glisse
Classes 6 days
2hr, am or pm
6 half-days: 560
Private lessons
1hr or 2hr
180 for 1hr; 340 2hr

CHILDCARE

Les P'tits Loups (450 740038) takes children aged 3 months to 5, from 9am to 6pm; indoor and outdoor games, and so on. You have to book in advance.

The Village des Enfants (450 740446) takes children aged 3 to 16, from 9am to 5.30.

The Club Med in Avoriaz is one of their 'family villages', with comprehensive childcare facilities.

TOURIST OFFICE

Postcode 74110
t +33 450 740211
f 450 741825
info@avoriazski.com
www.avoriazski.com

getting out of Les Lindarets towards both Châtel and Avoriaz at peak times can still mean a lengthy wait. Weekends can be particularly busy as people pour in to their holiday apartments. Crowds on the pistes (especially around the village) can be even worse than queues for the lifts, with care having to be taken to avoid collisions.

MOUNTAIN RESTAURANTS
Good choice over the hill

The charming, rustic chalets in the hamlet of Les Lindarets are one of the great concentrations of mountain restaurants in the Alps. A particular Lindarets favourite of ours is the Cremaillière which has wonderful chanterelle mushrooms. La Pomme de Pin is recommended by regular visitors to the resort for its warm welcome and friendly service. The rustic La Grenuille du Marais near the top of the gondola up from Morzine has good value food, good views and atmosphere. L'Abricotine, with table service, at Les Brocheaux, Le Yeti, at the top of town, and Chavanette at the top of the Swiss Wall have also been recommended.

SCHOOLS AND GUIDES
Try BASS

The ESF ski school has a good reputation, but classes can be large. The Avoriaz section of the British Alpine Ski School (BASS) is made up of British-qualified instructors with French qualifications too. It has been highly recommended, especially for 'quite excellent children's lessons. Bookings are taken at Le Tavaillon bar in the high street.' Emery is a specialist snowboard school.

FACILITIES FOR CHILDREN
'Annie Famose delivers'

The central Village des Enfants, run by Annie Famose, is a key part of the appeal of Avoriaz for many families. Its facilities are excellent – a chalet full of activities and special slopes complete with Disney characters. Children aged 3 to 16 can be looked after for a whole week without parental involvement. There's also a snowboard village exclusively for children aged 6 to 16, with special terrain, jumps etc. The car-free village of Avoriaz must be one of the safest in the Alps, but there are still sleighs, skiers, snowboarders and snowcats to watch out for. 'Great tobogganing for kids,' says a reporter.

Staying there

The main consideration when choosing where to stay in this steep village is your evening habits. By day you can get around using lifts, but at night you may have to walk home uphill (or nip in and out of apartment blocks using their internal lifts).

HOW TO GO
Self-catering dominates

Alternatives to apartments are few.
Chalets There are several available, comfortable and attractive but mainly designed for small family groups.
Hotels There is not much choice of hotels, but there is a Club Med village.
(3) **Dromonts** The original Avoriaz construction in the resort centre.
(3) **Hauts-Forts** Close to bottom of village, easy walk up in evening.
Self-catering Some of the better apartments are in the relatively new Falaise area, by the resort entrance and fairly convenient. But a reporter this year says the Saskia apartments in this area badly need refurbishment.

EATING OUT
Good; booking essential

There are more than 30 restaurants. The hotel Dromont's Bistro has some of the best French cuisine in town. L'Igloo is also good, but expensive. L'Ortolan, in the Elinka & Malinka complex, is friendly and good value. You can buy meal vouchers (£80 for adults, £40 for children) for seven evening meals in a range of five good restaurants. 'You choose from a restricted menu but it is excellent value for money,' says a reporter.

APRES-SKI
Lively, but not much choice

Nightlife lacks variety, but a few bars have a good atmosphere, particularly during happy hour. Le Choucas and The Place are lively and have bands, Le Tavaillon (popular with Brits because tour op reps meet there) has a football theme and Le Fantastique is worth a visit. Midnight Express club (free entry, pricey drinks) is popular.

OFF THE SLOPES
Not much at the resort

Those not interested in the slopes would be better off staying in Morzine, which has much more to offer, including shops and sports facilities.

Chamonix 1035m

High drama among Europe's highest peaks

WHAT IT COSTS

4

HOW IT RATES

The slopes

Snow	****
Extent	***
Experts	*****
Intermediates	**
Beginners	*
Convenience	*
Queues	**
Restaurants	***
The rest	
Scenery	*****
Resort charm	****
Off-slope	*****

- ⊕ A lot of very tough terrain, especially off-piste
- ⊕ Unforgettable cable-car ride to the Aiguille du Midi, leading to the most famous off-piste route of all – the Vallée Blanche
- ⊕ Amazing views of the Mont Blanc massif and its glaciers
- ⊕ Town steeped in Alpine traditions, with lots to do off the slopes
- ⊕ Well-organised and extensive cross-country trail system
- ⊕ Easy access by road, rail and air

- ⊖ Several separate mountains – a lot of driving or bussing required, and mixed ability groups are likely to have to split up
- ⊖ Pistes in each individual area are quite limited
- ⊖ Hardly any slope-side accommodation
- ⊖ Runs down to the valley floor are often closed due to lack of snow
- ⊖ Popularity means crowds and queues, and lots of road traffic
- ⊖ Bad weather can shut the best runs

Chamonix could not be more different from the the archetypal high-altitude French resort. It has no huge area of well-connected lifts and flattering pistes. Unless you are based next to one area and stick to it, you have to drive or take a bus each day to your chosen mountain – although the cable-car now linking Le Brévent to La Flégère has improved things a little. There is all sorts of terrain, but it offers more to interest the expert than anyone else, and to make the most of the area you need a mountain guide rather than a piste map. Chamonix is neither convenient nor conventional, but it is special.

The Chamonix valley cuts deeply through Europe's highest mountains and glaciers. The views are stunning and the runs are everything really tough runs should be – not only steep, but high and long. If you like manicured pistes accessed by slick lifts, stick to the Trois Vallées; if you like your snow and scenery on the wild side, give Chamonix a try. But be warned: there are those who try it and never go home – lots of them.

boarding *Chamonix is a place of pilgrimage for advanced boarders, but not the best place to learn. Head for Argentière and the Grands Montets for the hairiest action – the Helly Hansen-sponsored fun-park and half-pipe host regular competitions. There's also a natural half-pipe at Le Tour. Most of the ski areas are equipped mainly with cable-cars, gondolas and chairs, though there are quite a few drags at Le Tour. If you do the Vallée Blanche, be warned: the usual route is flat in places. If you're ready to tackle tougher off-piste, check out former British Champ Neil McNab's excellent Extreme Backcountry Camps (www.mcnab.co.uk). Staying in the town itself will certainly guarantee satisfactory nightlife.*

What's new

When we went to press it was highly unlikely that the Mont Blanc tunnel would open again before summer 2001 at the earliest. That means another season of lower pollution, to the relief of many of our reporters and Chamonix residents, who have been campaigning for a ban on freight traffic using the tunnel. It also means that day trips to Courmayeur are not a practical proposition.

For 1999/2000 a new green run, La Trappe, opened on La Flégère.

For 2000/01, a new mountain restaurant, La Bergerie, is to open at Planpraz, on Le Brévent, and there's a new parking area at Le Brévent.

The resort

Chamonix is a bustling town with scores of hotels and restaurants, visitors all year round and a lively Saturday market. The car-free centre of town is full of atmosphere, with cobbled streets and squares, beautiful old buildings and a fast-running river. Not everything is rosy: unsightly modern buildings have been built on to the periphery (especially near the Aiguille du Midi cable-car station), some of the lovely old buildings have been allowed to fall into disrepair, and at busy times traffic clogs the streets around the pedestrianised centre. But views of the mountains towering above town more than make up for these flaws. Vantage points in the town and, even better, on surrounding slopes offer an overwhelming spectacle. The town squares and pavement cafés are busy most of the day, and shoppers and sightseers sip their drinks and stare at the glaciers pouring down the

MOUNTAIN FACTS

Altitude	1035m-3840m
Lifts	49
Pistes	152km
Green/Blue	52%
Red	35%
Black	13%
Artificial snow	9km
Recco detectors used	

LIFT PASSES

2000/01 prices in francs

Cham'Ski pass
Covers all areas in the Chamonix Valley and the bus services between them, except Les Houches. Includes a day in Courmayeur.

Beginners Cham'Start 6-day pass covers all valley floor lifts (520), Cham'Baby 6-day pass covers the same for 4- to 11-year-olds (360). You can buy day extensions to higher lifts.

Main pass
1-day pass 241
6-day pass 999

Senior citizens
Over 60: 6-day pass 849 (15% off)

Children
12- to 15-year-olds: 6-day pass 849
Under 12: 6-day pass 699
Under 4: free pass

Notes 6-day passes include two ascents on the Grands Montets cable-car. Additional ascents cost extra (30 for 1 ascent, 480 for 20).

Alternative passes
Ski-pass Mont Blanc covers lifts in the 13 resorts of the Mont Blanc area (762km of piste) and Courmayeur in Italy (6 days 1200 for adults, 840 for children).

mountainsides. It all makes for a very agreeable and 'cosmopolitan' feel, as one visitor put it, though the 'dominant language is English'.

Chamonix's shops deal in everything from high-tech equipment to tacky souvenirs. But reporters often comment on the number and excellence of the former, and Chamonix remains essentially a town for mountain people rather than poseurs.

Strung out for 20km along the Chamonix valley are several separate lift systems, some with attached villages, from Les Houches at one end to Argentière and Le Tour at the other. Regular buses run to and from the lift stations but can get very crowded and aren't always reliable. Reader comments on getting around vary from 'bus service difficult to fathom' to 'not as much hassle as we had feared', but having a car is certainly useful. Then you can get easily to other resorts covered by the Mont Blanc pass, such as Megève and Les Contamines. Courmayeur in Italy is a long drive now the Mont Blanc tunnel is closed.

The mountains

Once you get over the initial impression that the place is hopelessly disconnected, you come to realise that Chamonix actually has a reasonable variety of slopes available. There is excellent tough terrain on the pistes at Les Grands Montets and Le Brévent and some classic off-piste routes, many over the glaciers that dominate much of the higher terrain. Some of these routes suit confident intermediates quite well while others are best reserved for the hardest of cores. Intermediates are best served at La Flégère and Le Tour (or at Les Houches, close to Chamonix but no longer sharing the valley lift pass).

THE SLOPES
Very fragmented

If you really like getting about, the Mont Blanc lift pass covers 11 resorts, 25 mountains, over 200 lifts and 700km of piste. It covers resorts far beyond the Chamonix valley – including St-Gervais, Megève, Les Contamines, and even Courmayeur in Italy.

The areas within the Chamonix valley – there are eight in total – are either small, low, beginners' areas or are much higher up on the valley side, with cable-car or gondola access from the valley floor. Keen expert reporters used to slope-side accommodation have been disappointed that this, combined with queues first thing, can mean a slow start in the mornings. The modern six-seater gondola for **Le Brévent** departs a short, steep walk from the centre of town, and the cable-car above takes you to the summit at 2525m. At **La Flégère**, like Le Brévent, the runs are mainly between 2000m and 2500m, and the views of Mont Blanc are worth the price of the lift pass. A new, fast chair recently replaced the old Trappe, and the 50-person cable-car linking La Flégère and Le Brévent makes this side of the valley more user-friendly – though reporters have said it's subject to frequent closure in high winds.

There have been improvements to the system at **Les Grands Montets** above Argentière, including increased snowmaking and remodelled runs, but much of the best terrain is still accessed by a cable-car of relatively low capacity. This costs extra to ride – though two free rides are included in a six-day pass – but still attracts queues.

Le Tour, already quite extensive, doubled in size recently with the addition of new runs – an 8km blue, a red and a black – above Vallorcine (which will eventually be linked by lift).

One of the valley-floor areas, Les Bosson, is open for floodlit skiing three nights a week.

To get the most out of each area use the local piste maps ('plastic and indestructible', raves one reporter) – the valley map is not sufficiently detailed. We are particularly impressed with the Grands Montets piste map. It includes brief descriptions of each run, with assessment of suitability for different standards of ability, a history of the area, advice on safety and a feedback form to send to the lift company – and all in English and other foreign-language versions.

Most of our reporters have been more impressed than they expected with the piste grooming, but not with the signposting of the runs, or with 'rather antiquated chairs and drags'.

SNOW RELIABILITY
Good high up; poor low down

The top runs on the north-facing slopes above Argentière are almost guaranteed to have good snow, and the season normally lasts well into May. The risk of finding the top lift

← La Flégère's sunny slopes have stunning views over the valley to the tumbling glaciers

SNOWPIX.COM / CHRIS GILL

shut because of bad weather is more of a worry (and is the excuse for not including the lift on the main pass). The Col de Balme area above Le Tour has a snowy location and a good late-season record. The largely south-facing slopes of Brévent and Flégère suffer in warm weather, and runs to the resort are often closed. There's snowmaking on the Bochard piste on Les Grands Montets as well as some of the smaller areas. Several of the beginners' areas need snow-cover down to the valley floor to be operational.

FOR EXPERTS

One of the great resorts

Les Grands Montets above Argentière is justifiably renowned for its extensive steep terrain. To get the best out of the area you really need to have a local guide. Without one you either stick to the relatively small number of pistes or you put your life at risk.

The Grands Montets cable-car takes you up to 3300m; if you've got the legs and lungs, climb the 121 steep metal steps to the observation platform above the station and take in the stunning views. (But bear in mind

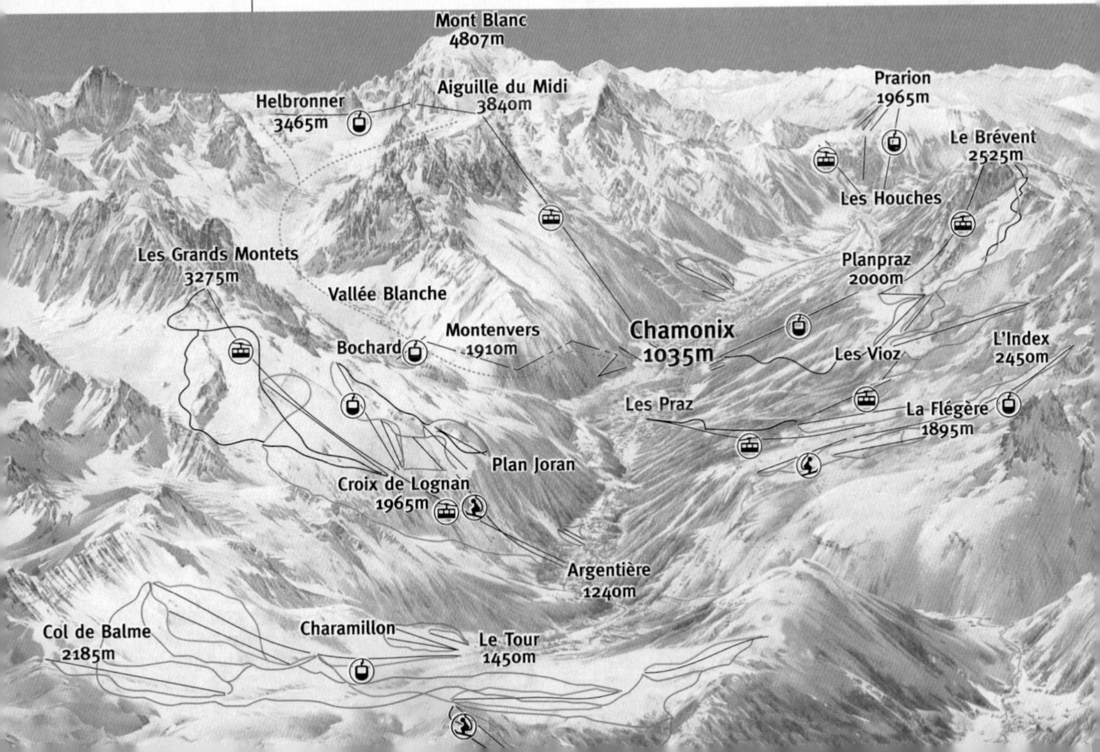

that it's a long way down again – 200 more steps once you are down to the cable-car before you hit the snow.)

The ungroomed black pistes from here – Point de Vue and Pylones – are long and exhilarating. The Point de Vue sails right by some dramatic sections of glacier, with marvellous views of the crevasses. The off-piste routes from the top are numerous and often dangerous; the Pas de Chèvre route is serious stuff, eventually joining the Vallée Blanche run. There are many routes down the Argentière glacier.

The Bochard gondola serves a testing red and a moderate black. Alternatively, head directly down the Combe de la Pendant bowl for 1000m vertical of wild, unpisted mountainside. The continuation down the valley side to Le Lavancher is equally testing; it suffers frequently from lack of snow on the steep bits.

At Le Brévent there's more to test experts than the piste map suggests – there are a number of variations on the runs down from the summit. Some are steep and prone to ice, and the couloir routes are very steep and very narrow. The runs in the sunny Col de La Charlanon are uncrowded and include one marked red run and lots of excellent off-piste if the snow is good.

At La Flégère there are several good off-piste routes – in the Combe Lachenal, crossed by the linking cable-car, for example – and a pretty tough run back to the village when snow-cover permits. Le Tour boasts little tough terrain on-piste but there are good off-piste routes from the high points to the village and over the back towards Vallorcine or into Switzerland.

FOR INTERMEDIATES

It's worth trying it all

For less confident intermediates, the best areas are at the two extreme ends of the Chamonix valley. The Col de Balme area above Le Tour is good for easy cruising and usually free from crowds. And the slopes of the separate Prarion-Bellevue system above Les Houches are mostly gentle tree-lined blue and red runs, very unlikely to intimidate anyone – a good area for building confidence.

More adventurous intermediates will also want to try the other three main areas, though they may find the Grands Montets tough going and crowded. The bulk of the terrain at Le

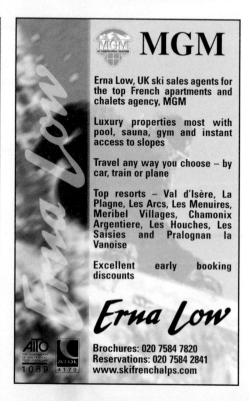

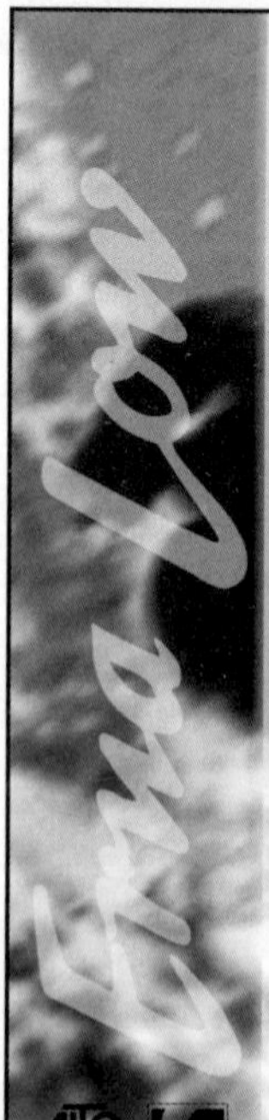

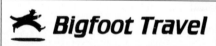

Brévent and La Flégère provides a sensible mix of blue and red runs; at Le Brévent the slopes have been redesigned to achieve this. If the weather is good take a guided trip down the Vallée Blanche, perfectly within a competent intermediate's capability.

A day trip to Courmayeur has traditionally made an interesting change of scene, especially when the weather's bad. But it's not practical while the Mont Blanc tunnel is closed.

FOR BEGINNERS
Best if there's snow in the valley
If there is snow low down, the nursery lifts at La Vormaine, Les Chosalets, Les Planards and Le Savoy are fine for teaching first-timers; learners will not be bothered by speed-merchants. The Planards and Glacier du Mont Blanc lifts both benefit from snowmaking and also provide some progression.

But the separation of beginners' slopes from the rest inhibits the transition to real runs, and makes lunchtime meetings of mixed groups impractical. Better to learn elsewhere, and come to Chamonix when you can appreciate the tough high-mountain terrain that is its hallmark.

FOR CROSS-COUNTRY
A good network of trails
Most of the 42km of prepared trails lie along the valley between Chamonix and Argentière. There are green, blue, red and black loop sections and the full tour from Chamonix to Argentière and back is 32km. All these trails are fairly low and fade fast in spring sun.

QUEUES
Fewer problems
There are still long queues for the top cable-car on Les Grands Montets. When they reach 30 minutes a booking system operates, so you can keep moving until it's your turn to ride.

At close of play, the lifts from the high-altitude areas to the valley floor get busy – especially the cable-cars.

In poor weather Les Houches is most likely to be open. The queues for the Bellevue cable-car can be bad.

CHILDCARE

The ESF runs ordinary classes for children aged 6 to 12. For children aged 4 to 6 there are lessons in a snow-garden. And children in either category can be looked after all day (and amused when not on the slopes) from 8.30 to 5pm.

The day-care centre at the Maison pour Tous (450 533668) takes children aged 18 months to 6 years from 7.45 to noon and 2pm to 5.30.

The Panda Club takes children aged 6 months to 12 years. There is a crèche in Chamonix that takes children from 6 months (450 558612). Older babies are taken here or to Argentière (450 540476), where the club has its own slopes, open to children aged 3 or more.

Some of the more expensive hotels will provide child-minding. Club Med has comprehensive in-house arrangements – their place here is one of their 'family villages', with a crèche taking babies from 4 months.

THE VALLÉE BLANCHE

This is a trip you do for the stunning scenery rather than the challenge of the run, which (although exceptionally long) is easy – well within the capability of the average intermediate, and not to be missed if you're there when conditions are right. But be prepared for extreme cold at the top, for flat and uphill sections on the way down, and for hordes of people – going early on a weekday gives you the best chance of avoiding the worst of the crowds. Go in a guided group – despite the ease of the runs, dangerous crevasses lurk to swallow those not in the know. Book your guide or sign up for a group trip the day before at the Maison de la Montagne or other ski school offices.

The cable-car is a stunning ride that takes you to 3790m. Across the bridge from the arrival station on the 'Piton Nord' is the 'Piton Central' and the highest point of the Aiguille du Midi. The view of Mont Blanc from the 3842 café a stair-climb higher should not be missed – and gives you the opportunity to adjust to the dizzying altitude. Afterwards a tunnel through the 'Piton Central' delivers you to the infamous ridge-walk to the start of the run. Many parties rope up for this walk and a fixed guide-rope provides further security. You may still feel envious of those strolling nonchalantly down in crampons; you may wish you'd stayed in bed.

After that the run seems a doddle; mostly effortless gliding down gentle slopes with only the occasional steeper, choppy section to deal with. So stop often and enjoy the surroundings fully. The views of the ice, the crevasses and seracs – and the spectacular mountains beyond – are simply mind-blowing.

There are variants on the classic route, all more difficult and more hazardous. The 'Vraie Vallée' is for experts only and the 'Envers du Plan' is a direct descent to the Refuge du Requin – a mountain hut where everyone takes a break and admires the Jardin des Seracs. Snow conditions may mean cutting short the full 24km route down to Chamonix, in which case the station at Montenvers (1910m) is the target, to catch a train. A short climb and gondola link the glacier to the station.

SCHOOLS/GUIDES

2000/01 prices in francs

ESF

In both Chamonix and Argentière

Classes 6 days
4hr: am and pm
6 full days: 880

Children's classes
Ages: 4 to 12
6 days: 9am-5pm, including supervised lunch: 1400-1600

Private lessons
1hr, 2hr, half- or full day
200 for 1hr, for 1 or to 2 people; 250 for 3 to 4 people

MOUNTAIN RESTAURANTS

Stunning views

The Panoramic at the top of Brévent enjoys the best views. The food's fine but the place is dull. Altitude 2000 provides table-service at rip-off prices. A recent reporter suggests you shun this 'grim experience' for 'a lovely, quiet, unpressurised lunch' at one of the small restaurants in the village by the Brévent lift. There's a straightforward self-service joint at La Flégère.

On the Grands Montets the Plan Joran serves good food and does table- and self-service. The restaurant at Lognan has been smartly renovated. The rustic Chalet Refuge du Lognan, off the beaten track overlooking the Argentière glacier, has marvellous food. Book in advance to guarantee a full menu.

The restaurants in the Prarion-Bellevue area at Les Houches are pleasant and good value.

SCHOOLS AND GUIDES

The place to try something new

The schools here are particularly strong in specialist fields – off-piste, glacier and couloir skiing, ski touring, snowboarding and cross-country. English-speaking instructors are plentiful. One second-week skier did report large classes and unimaginative teaching by the Evolution school though. At the Maison de la Montagne in Chamonix is the main ESF office and the HQ of the Compagnie des Guides, which has taken visitors to the mountains for 150 years.

Competition is provided by a number of smaller, independent guiding and teaching outfits, and there are many qualified British guides here.

FACILITIES FOR CHILDREN

Better than they were

The Panda Club is used by quite a few British visitors and reports have been enthusiastic. The Argentière base can be inconvenient for meeting up with children for the afternoons. The Club Med crèche seems to go down well too. Ski Esprit has three chalets here, with a nursery in the Cairn. Links with the ESF mean classes run just for Esprit children.

Beware of children being kept on the valley nursery slopes when they really should be getting some miles under their skis.

Staying there

The obvious place to stay is in Chamonix itself – it's central, has all the amenities going and some of the slopes are close at hand. For those who intend to spend most of their time in one particular area such as Argentière, Le Tour or Les Houches, staying near there obviously makes sense. Whatever the choice, no location is convenient for everything, so be prepared for some commuting – a car is a huge advantage, both for getting around the valley and for visiting other resorts on the Mont Blanc lift pass. The free ski-bus runs between Chamonix and the different local areas, and the Chamo'night bus runs through the evening.

The Mt Blanc massif certainly lives up to its name – and macho locals ski down it ➔

SNOWPIX.COM / CHRIS GILL

GETTING THERE

Air Geneva, transfer 1½hr. Lyon, transfer 3½hr.

Rail Station in resort, on the St Gervais-Le Fayet/Vallorcine line.

Direct TGV link from Paris on Friday evenings and weekends.

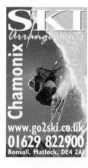

HOW TO GO

Any way you like

There is all sorts of accommodation, and lots of it.

Chalets Many are run by small outfits that cater for this specialist market. Quality tends to be high and value for money good. Collineige has a large selection – all very comfortable. We've had good reports of Bigfoot's chalets and 'Mercedes mini-vans to run you to and from the slopes'. Cheaper places are offered by HuSki (who also run a minibus service) and big tour operators such as Crystal and Inghams. Childcare specialist Ski Esprit has three places, including the excellent Cairn in Les Praz – built as a three-star hotel in 1992, and blessed with good bedrooms and bathrooms. New for 2000/01, Simply Ski has a centrally located catered chalet hotel, which is bookable for weekend breaks.

Hotels The place is full of hotels, many modestly priced, and the vast majority small, with fewer than 30 rooms. Hotel bookings for a day or two are easy to arrange since Chamonix's peak season is summer. There's a Club Med 'village'.

④ **Albert 1er** Smart, traditional chalet-style hotel with 'truly excellent food' (Michelin star, Gault-Millau rating). Recent visitors loved the new half-indoor, half-outdoor swimming pool.

④ **Auberge du Bois Prin** A small modern chalet with a big reputation; great views; bit of a hike to the centre; a shorter one to the Brévent lift.

④ **Mont Blanc** Central, luxurious.

④ **Jeu de Paume** (Lavancher) Alpine satellite of a chic Parisian hotel: a beautifully furnished modern chalet half-way to Argentière.

③ **Alpina** Much the biggest in town: modernist–functional place just north of centre.

③ **Labrador** (Les Praz) Scandinavian-style chalet close to the Flégère lift.

③ **Sapinière** Traditional hotel with good French food, run by long-established Chamonix family. Reasonable site on the Brévent side of town. Highly recommended by a recent visitor.

③ **Vallée Blanche** Smart low-priced 3-star B&B hotel, handy for centre and Aiguille du Midi cable-car.

② **L'Arve** By the river, just off main street; small newly decorated rooms.

② **Richemond** Now rather faded and old-fashioned, but with good public areas, table tennis and friendly staff.

② **Pointe Isabelle** Not pretty, but central location; friendly staff, good plain food, well-equipped bedrooms.

② **Roma** Simple but satisfactory B&B hotel in hassle-free location on south side of centre; friendly patron.

① **Faucigny** Cottage-style; in centre.

Self-catering Many properties in UK package brochures are typically in convenient but cramped and charmless

blocks in Chamonix Sud. The Balcons du Savoy look much better, are well situated and have use of a swimming pool, steam room and solarium. The Splendid & Golf apartments in Les Praz are charming and close to the Flégère cable-car. Erna Low have some luxury places available.

EATING OUT
Plenty of quality places

The good hotels all have good restaurants – the Eden at Les Praz and Bois Prin in Chamonix are first-rate – and there are many other good places to eat. The Sarpe is a lovely 'mountain' restaurant and The Impossible is rustic but smart and features good regional dishes. Recent visitors have especially recommended Le Panier des Quatre Saisons ('Excellent food at reasonable prices. Wonderful atmosphere') and Le Crochon ('Good Savoyard fare, plus some varied and innovative dishes'). The Monchu is also good for Savoyard specialities. There are a number of ethnic restaurants – Mexican, Spanish, Japanese, Chinese etc – and lots of brasseries and cafés.

APRES-SKI
Lots of bars and music

Many of the bars around the pedestrianised centre of Chamonix get busy for a couple of hours at sundown – none more so than the Choucas video bar. During the evening, The Pub, Wild Wallaby's, the Mill Street bar and the Bar du Moulin are busy. The Queen Vic gets the vote of one recent reporter for being 'nice and dark and dingy with a snug, pool table, good music and Beamish on tap'. There's a lively variety of nightclubs and discos. The Choucas (again), and Dick's Tea bar are popular. The Cantina sometimes has live music and is open late. There are plenty of bars and brasseries for a quieter drink too.

OFF THE SLOPES
An excellent choice

There's more off-slope activity here than in many resorts. Excursion possibilities include Annecy and Geneva, plus Courmayeur and Turin. The Alpine Museum is 'excellent and very interesting' and there are good sports facilities. The sports centre and 'excellent' swimming pool have been renovated after being damaged by floods a couple of years ago.

ACTIVITIES
Indoor Sports complex (sports hall, gym, table tennis), indoor skating and curling rinks, ice hockey, swimming pool with giant water slide, saunas, 6 indoor tennis courts, 2 squash courts, fitness centre, Alpine museum, casino, 3 cinemas, library, 10-pin bowling, climbing wall

Outdoor Ski-jumping, snow-shoe outings, mountain biking, hang-gliding, paragliding, flying excursions, heli-skiing, ice skating

TOURIST OFFICE
Postcode 74400
t +33 450 530024
f 450 535890
info@chamonix.com
www.chamonix.com

Argentière 1240m
The old village is in a lovely setting towards the head of the valley – the Glacier d'Argentière pokes down towards it and the Aiguille du Midi and Mont Blanc still dominate the scene down the valley. There's a fair bit of modern development but it still has a rustic appeal. Le Tour, just beyond Argentière, is quiet and picturesque.

A number of the hotels are simple, inexpensive and handy for the village centre – less so for the slopes – but the Grands-Montets is a large chalet-style building, right next to the piste and the Panda Club for children. The family-run Montana is recommended for 'lovely rooms, excellent food'.

Restaurants and bars are informal and inexpensive. The Office is the happening place in Argentière, from breakfast till late. The Savoy bar is the British/colonial ex-pat haunt.

Les Houches 1010m
Les Houches, 6km from Chamonix, is not on the valley pass, but is covered by the regional Mont Blanc pass. It's a pleasant village, sitting in the shade of the looming Mont Blanc massif – shady and cold in midwinter. There is an old core with a pretty church, but modern developments in chalet style have spread along the road up to Chamonix.

The area above Les Houches is served by a cable-car to **Bellevue** and a gondola to **Prarion**, the high-point at 1900m. Runs on the back of the mountain towards St-Gervais, and blue, red and black runs of 900m vertical down to Les Houches, make this the biggest single area of prepared runs in the Chamonix valley.

The almost entirely wooded slopes are popular when bad weather or the risk of avalanches closes other areas.

In good weather the slopes are quiet, and the views superb from the several attractive mountain restaurants. It is good for families, beginners and intermediates, with easy runs at the top of the mountain. Snow-cover on the lower slopes is not reliable, but there is a fair amount of snowmaking.

The village is quiet at night, but there are some pleasant bars and good restaurants. Recent visitors enjoyed staying in the Hotel du Bois, with its 'helpful staff and excellent restaurant' and 'a good local band in the bar on Saturday'. Buses run in and out of Chamonix all evening.

Châtel

1200m

A distinctively French base for touring the Portes du Soleil

WHAT IT COSTS

3

HOW IT RATES

The slopes

Snow	**
Extent	*****
Experts	***
Intermediates	****
Beginners	**
Convenience	**
Queues	***
Restaurants	***

The rest

Scenery	***
Resort charm	***
Off-slope	**

What's new

For 1999/2000 more snowmaking was installed at Super-Châtel and Linga. And there's now a hands-free electronic lift pass system, which means you can keep your pass in your pocket.

The high-speed quad chair from Pré-la-Joux to Plaine Dranse means fewer queues and faster access to Avoriaz.

Two new pistes off the Rochassons ridge have been created – both steep runs that are kept well groomed.

For 2000/2001 the chair from Les Combes to Cornebois will be replaced by a high-speed quad.

- ➕ Very extensive, pretty, intermediate terrain – the Portes du Soleil
- ➕ Wide range of cheap and cheerful, good-value accommodation
- ➕ Easily reached – close to Geneva, and one of the shortest drives from the Channel
- ➕ Pleasant, lively, French-dominated old village, still quite rustic in parts
- ➕ Local slopes relatively queue-free
- ➕ Good views

- ➖ Both resort and top of skiing are low for a French resort, with resulting risk of poor snow
- ➖ Bus or gondola ride to most snow-sure nursery slopes
- ➖ Queues can be a problem in parts of the Portes du Soleil circuit
- ➖ Congested village traffic, especially at weekends

Like neighbouring Morzine, Châtel offers a blend of attractions that is uncommon in France – an old village with plenty of facilities, cheap accommodation by French standards, and a large ski area on the doorstep. Châtel's original rustic charm has been largely eroded by expansion in recent years, but some of it remains, and the resort has one obvious advantage over smoother Morzine: it is part of the main Portes du Soleil circuit.

The circuit actually breaks down at Châtel, but this works in the village's favour. Whereas those doing the circuit from other resorts have the inconvenience of waiting for a bus mid-circuit, Châtel residents have the advantage of being able to time their bus-rides to avoid waits and queues. Those mainly interested in the local slopes should also consider Châtel. For confident intermediates, Châtel's Linga has few equals in the Portes du Soleil, while the nearby Torgon section has arguably the best views. The Chapelle d'Abondance slopes are pleasantly uncrowded at weekends. Châtel has become more beginner-friendly with nursery slopes at Super-Châtel and Pré-la-Joux, though these are a lift or bus-ride away.

boarding *Avoriaz is the hardcore boarder destination in the Portes du Soleil. But Châtel is not a bad place to learn or to go to as a budget option or as part of a mixed group of skiers and boarders. Most local lifts are gondolas or chairs and there's a fun-park, a half-pipe and a boarder-cross course at Super-Châtel. Also the Linga area is popular for varied terrain and off-piste possibilities. There are a couple of lively bars to spend the evenings in.*

The resort

Châtel lies near the head of the wooded Dranse valley, at the north-eastern limit of the French-Swiss Portes du Soleil ski circuit.

It is a much expanded and now quite large but nonetheless attractive old village. New unpretentious chalet-style hotels and apartments rub shoulders with old farmhouses where cattle still live in winter.

Although there is a definite centre, the village sprawls along the road in from lake Geneva, and the diverging roads out – up the hillside towards Morgins and along the valley towards the Linga and Pré-la-Joux lifts.

Lots of visitors take cars and the centre gets clogged with traffic during the evening rush-hour, and even more so at weekends. Street parking is difficult but there is a multi-storey car park. The other main French Portes du Soleil resorts – Avoriaz and Morzine – are quite easily reached on skis, but not by road.

A few kilometres down the valley is the rustic village of La Chapelle-d'Abondance (see end of chapter).

MOUNTAIN FACTS

Altitude	975m-2350m
Lifts	219
Pistes	650km
Green/Blue	51%
Red	40%
Black	9%
Art. snow	522 acres

Recco detectors used

LIFT PASSES

2000/01 prices in francs

Portes du Soleil
Covers all lifts in all 12 resorts, and shuttle-buses.

Main pass
1-day pass 207
6-day pass 998

Senior citizens
Over 60: 6-day pass 798

Children
Under 16: 6-day pass 669
Under 5: free pass

Short-term passes
Morning and afternoon passes for the Portes du Soleil (both 155), and for Châtel only (am or pm: both 118).

Alternative periods
5 non-consecutive days pass for Châtel only available (adult 714).

Alternative passes
Châtel pass covers 51 lifts in Châtel, Linga, Super-Châtel, Barbossine, Torgon and the link to Morgins (adult 6-day pass 748).

The mountains

The Portes du Soleil as a whole is classic intermediate terrain, and Châtel's local slopes are very much in character. Confident intermediates, in particular, will find lots to enjoy in the Linga and Plaine Dranse sectors.

THE SLOPES
The circuit breaks down here

Châtel sits between two sectors of the Portes du Soleil circuit – linked together by a frequent, free bus service. **Super-Châtel** is directly above the village – an area of easy, open and lightly wooded beginner slopes, accessed by a choice of gondola or two-stage chair from the top of the village. From here you can tour over to the quiet little Torgon sector or move clockwise around the Portes du Soleil circuit, crossing the Swiss border to Morgins and then Champoussin and Champéry, before crossing back into France above Avoriaz.

The **Linga** sector starts a bus-ride out of the village. For intermediates and better, Linga has some of the most interesting runs in the Portes du Soleil, the best of it leading back in the direction of Châtel. The quickest way of getting to the Avoriaz area is to stay on the bus at Linga and go to Pré-la-Joux. From here there is a high-speed quad direct to Plaine Dranse; then it's one more lift and run to Les Lindarets, where there is a choice of final lifts towards Avoriaz.

Although the Portes du Soleil piste map has recently been improved, reporters have commented on the need for better display signs to help orientate themselves.

SNOW RELIABILITY
The main drawback

The main drawback of the whole Portes du Soleil region is that it is low. So snow quality can suffer if it is warm. Châtel itself is at only 1200m (600m lower than Avoriaz) and some runs home can be tricky or shut, especially from Super-Châtel. But a lot of snowmaking has been installed recently at Super-Châtel and on the runs down from Linga and to Pré-la-Joux. These last two are mainly north-facing and generally have the best local snow – a regular visitor tells us there is usually good snow at Pré-la-Joux until May. But another told us of the snow being like a 'damp pudding' in March and pistes to Morgins and Les Lindarets being closed.

FOR EXPERTS
Some challenges

The best steep runs – on and off-piste – are in the Linga and Pré-la-Joux area. Beneath the Linga gondola and chair, there's a pleasant mix of open and wooded ground which follows the fall line fairly directly. And there's a genuine black mogul field between Cornebois and Plaine Dranse which has been described as 'steeper and narrower than the infamous Swiss Wall'. An unpisted trail from Super-Châtel towards the village is also fun. And the challenging Hauts Forts sector beyond Avoriaz is within reach. There's also a great off-piste route from Tête

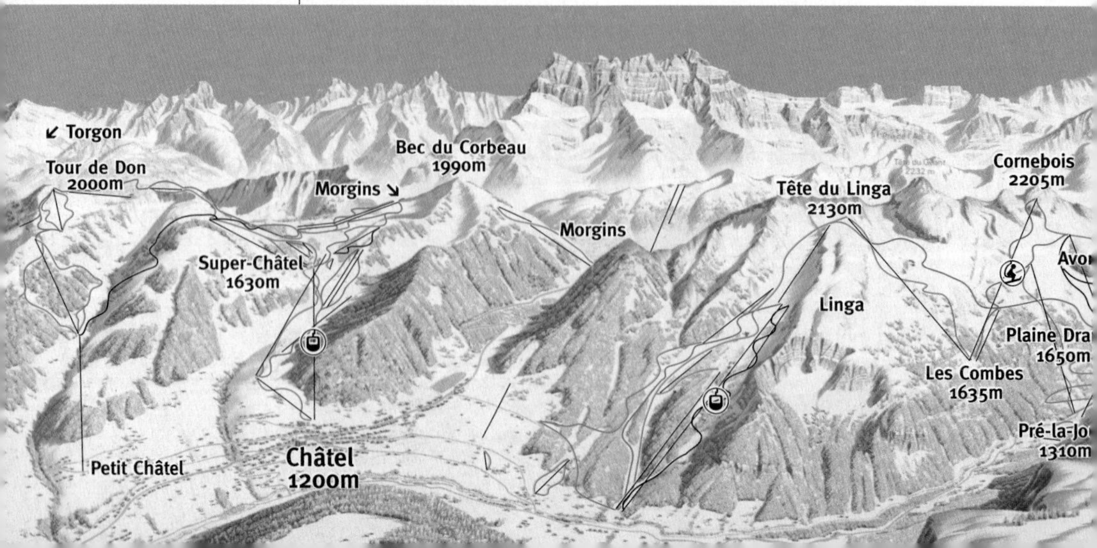

du Linga down the valley of La Leiche – but you'll need a guide.

Pierre Tardival's Extreme Clinics are held in Châtel and he doesn't seem to have any problem finding local, steep off-piste terrain (this is the man who climbed and skied Everest!).

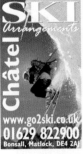

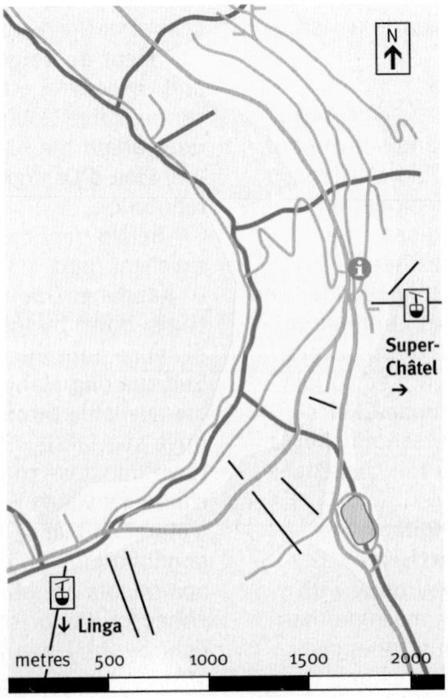

FOR INTERMEDIATES

Some of the best runs in the area

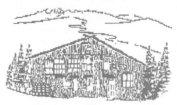

When conditions are right the Portes du Soleil is an intermediate's paradise. Good intermediates need not venture far from Châtel; Linga and Plaine Dranse have some of the best red runs in the whole area. But the Champéry-Avoriaz sector also beckons. The moderately skilled can do the whole circuit without any problems, and will particularly enjoy the runs around Les Lindarets and Morgins. Even timid types can do the circuit, provided they take one or two short-cuts and ride chair-lifts down trickier bits. The chair from Les Lindarets to Pointe de Mossette provides a red run into the Swiss area, which is a lot easier than the 'Swiss Wall' from Chavanette and also speeds up the whole journey round the circuit.

Leaving aside attempts to complete the whole circuit in both directions, there are rewarding out-and-back expeditions to be made clockwise to the wide open snowfields above Champoussin, beyond Morgins, and anticlockwise to the Hauts-Forts runs above Avoriaz.

FOR BEGINNERS

Getting better

With the opening of the beginners' area at Pré-la-Joux, beginners are no longer confined to the Super-Châtel or the low village nursery slopes. But you have to get the bus or a gondola to these more snowsure slopes.

J-F VUARAND / CHATEL TO

Châtel is a sprawling resort and you catch a bus between its two main ski areas →

SCHOOLS/GUIDES

1999/2000 prices in francs

ESF
Classes 6 days
2hr am or pm
6 half-days: 570
Children's classes
Ages: 5 to 16
6 half-days: 540
Private lessons
1hr or 1½hr
180 for 1hr, for 1 to 2; 3 to 4 people: 270

International
Classes 6 days
3hr: 9am-noon or 2pm-5pm; 2hr: noon-2pm
6 mornings: 640
Children's classes
Ages: from 8
6 afternoons: 690
Private lessons
1hr or 2hr
175 for 1hr, each additional person 15

Stages Henri Gonon
Courses can include 6 days' accommodation, pass and 5 half-days' tuition
Classes 5 days
3hr per day
5 days: 650
Children's classes
Ages: 5 to 16
5 days: 550
Private lessons
1hr
150 for 1 to 2 people

Other schools include: Francis Sports, Snow Ride and Virages.

CHILDCARE

The ESF's ski kindergarten is for children from age 4.

Le Village des Marmottons takes children from 2 to 8, from 8.30 to 5.30, with ski tuition for those aged 3 up.

Les Mouflets takes children from 10 months to 6.

Henri Gonon takes children over 8, as does the Ski and Surf International School.

Francis Sports caters for 3 to 8 year olds at the Pitchounes.

FOR CROSS-COUNTRY
Pretty, if low, trails

There are plenty of pretty trails along the river and through the woods on the lower slopes of Linga (42km), but snow-cover can be a problem.

QUEUES
Bottlenecks further afield

Queues to get to Avoriaz have been eased by the new high-speed quad at Pré-la-Joux. But there are still some bottlenecks further afield, which tend to be worse at weekends when a lot of locals hit the slopes (although reports this year have been good, with little queuing even during half-term). At Lindarets, in particular, there is often a lengthy wait for the chair-lift to the Rochassons ridge on the way back to Châtel and also for a lift up the other way towards Avoriaz. You can face queues to get down from Super-Châtel if the slope back is shut by poor snow.

MOUNTAIN RESTAURANTS
Some quite good local huts

There are atmospheric chalets to be found, notably at Plaine Dranse (Le Bois Prin, Chez Crépy, Tame aux Marmottes and Chez Dennis have all been recommended). The Perdrix Blanche down at Pré-la-Joux scarcely counts as a mountain restaurant, but is nevertheless an attractive spot for lunch. Super-Châtel is less well endowed with mountain restaurants but Portes du Soleil at the bottom of the Cocs drags is much better than the big place at the top of the gondola. The Escale Blanche is worth a visit.

SCHOOLS AND GUIDES
Plenty of choice

There are now six ski and snowboard schools in Châtel plus Ski McGarry, who have chalet accommodation as well as running ski courses. The International school has been recommended by a recent reporter and the Ski McGarry courses continue to receive glowing reports from several reporters. But those tempted to join the Pierre Tardival Extreme Clinics offered by the McGarry school should be sure they are up to the challenge.

FACILITIES FOR CHILDREN
Increasingly sympathetic

The Marmottons nursery (now with their own snowmaking machine) has good facilities, including toboggans, painting, music and videos, and children are reportedly happy there. There is also a crèche (Les Mouflets) in the centre of town. Francis Sports ski school have their own nursery area with a drag lift and chalet at Le Linga – 'very organised, convenient and reasonably priced'. The ESF have had good reports – 'small groups with excellent English spoken'.

Staying there

The town is spread out and there are lifts from both the centre and further out. A central position gives you the advantage of getting on the ski-bus to the outlying lifts before it gets very crowded, and simplifying après-ski outings. But there is accommodation near the Linga lift if that's the priority.

HOW TO GO
A wide choice, including chalets

Although this is emphatically a French resort, the days are long gone when packages from Britain were difficult to track down.

Chalets A fair number of UK operators have places here, including some Châtel specialists.

Hotels Practically all of the hotels are 2-stars, mostly friendly chalets, wooden or at least partly wood-clad. None of the 3-stars is particularly well placed. We've had a bad report on the hotel Amethyste: 'Cramped, basic, cold and very unfriendly.' Les Cornettes in La Chapelle (see below) is an interesting alternative.

(((3) **Macchi** Modern chalet, most central of the 3-stars.

(((3) **Fleur de Neige** Well-maintained and welcoming old chalet on edge of centre; Grive Gourmande restaurant does about the best food in town.

(((3) **Lion d'Or** Right in centre, good reputation.

((2) **Belalp** Very comfortable, with excellent food.

(1) **Kandahar** One for peace-lovers: a Logis, down by the river, a walkable distance from the centre.

Self-catering Many of the better places are available through Châtel- and self-drive specialists. The Gelinotte (out of town but close to the Linga lifts and children's village) and Les Erines (central and close to the Super-Châtel gondola) look good. The Flèche d'Or apartments are not so well positioned, either for lifts or shops. The Aveniers is right by the Linga gondola.

GETTING THERE

Air Geneva, transfer $1\frac{1}{2}$hr.

Rail Thonon les Bains (42km).

ACTIVITIES

Indoor Swimming pool, bowling, cinema, library

Outdoor Skating rink, horse-drawn carriage rides, helicopter rides, dog-sledding, snow-shoe excursions, farm visits, toboggan run, floodlit skiing at Linga

TOURIST OFFICE

Postcode 74390
t +33 450 732244
f 450 732287
touristoffice@chatel.com
www.chatel.com

EATING OUT

Fair selection

There is an adequate number and range of restaurants. Les Cornettes in La Chapelle-d'Abondance is one of our favourites – amazingly good value 'menus' with excellent food. The Vieux Four, in an old farm building, has a reputation for the best steaks in Châtel, but the restaurant's donkey which was behind a plate glass window has now disappeared (probably due to EU regulations). The Fleur de Neige hotel has a good restaurant and Le Fiacre is also popular. The Perrier serves Savoyard specialities. La Ripaille, almost opposite the Linga gondola, was highly recommended by a past reporter, especially for its fish.

APRES-SKI

All down to bars

Châtel is getting livelier, especially at weekends. The Tunnel bar, which used the be the Slalom, is very popular with the British and has a DJ or live music every night. The Isba bar is popular, too. La Godille – close to the Super-Châtel gondola and busy at tea-time – has a more French feel. The bar in the hotel Soldanelles is also pretty lively. Otherwise there's a bowling alley, and one of the cinemas shows English-language films on Wednesdays. The Dahu disco, on the road to Morgins, and the Jeans Club at the Super-Châtel bubble, are particularly busy at weekends. One reporter recommends the Saf disco in Morgins.

OFF THE SLOPES

Better to stay in Morzine

Those with a car have some entertaining excursions available: Geneva, Thonon and Evian. Otherwise there is little to do but take some pleasant walks along the river. The tourist office organises daily events for non-slope users. But those not keen on hitting the slopes would find more to do in Morzine. The Portes du Soleil as a whole is less than ideal for those not using the slopes who like to meet their more active friends for lunch: skiers and boarders are likely to be above some distant resort at lunchtime.

La Chapelle-d'Abondance

1010m

This unspoilt, rustic farming community, complete with old church and friendly locals, is 5km along a beautiful valley from Châtel. It's had its own quiet little north-facing area of easy wooded runs for some years, but has more recently been put on the Portes du Soleil map by a gondola and three chair-lifts that now link it to Torgon and, from there, Super-Châtel. This new section is only a spur of the Portes du Soleil circuit. But, taken together with Chapelle's own little area, it is worth exploring – good at weekends when Châtel gets crowded.

Nightlife is virtually non-existent: just a few quiet bars, a cinema and torchlit descents.

The hotel Cornettes is an amazing 2-star with 2-star rooms but 4-star facilities, including an indoor pool, sauna, steam room, hot-tubs, excellent restaurant and atmospheric bar popular with locals. Throughout there are showcases with puppets and dolls and eccentric touches, such as ancient old doors that unexpectedly open automatically. It has been run by the Trincaz family ever since it was founded in 1894. The Alpage and Chabi are other hotel options. The Airelles apartments have received a favourable report.

La Clusaz–Le Grand-Bornand 1100m

Great for late-booking Francophiles

WHAT IT COSTS

4

HOW IT RATES

The slopes	
Snow	**
Extent	***
Experts	***
Intermediates	****
Beginners	****
Convenience	***
Queues	***
Restaurants	****
The rest	
Scenery	****
Resort charm	****
Off-slope	***

What's new

In La Clusaz, last season saw a new gondola from the base of La Balme across to Cote 2000 on l'Aiguille – hugely improving the link between the two.

For 2000/01 the drag-lift at the top of l'Aiguille will be replaced by a quad chair-lift.

In Le Grand-Bornand, last season saw a new quad chair-lift and new black and red pistes in the Tolar area.

Snowmaking is improved at both La Clusaz and Le Grand-Bornand each year.

- + Mountain villages in a scenic setting, retaining traditional character
- + Extensive, interesting slopes – pistes best for beginners and intermediates
- + Very French atmosphere
- + Very short transfer time from Geneva and easy to reach by car from UK
- + Attractive mountain restaurants
- + Good cross-country trails
- + Slopes at La Clusaz and Le Grand-Bornand, linked by shuttle-bus

- − Snow conditions unreliable because of low altitude (by French standards)
- − Not many challenging pistes for experts – though there are good off-piste runs
- − Busy at weekends

Few other major French resorts are based around what are still, essentially, genuine mountain villages that exude rustic charm and Gallic atmosphere. Combine that with over 200km of largely intermediate slopes, above and below the tree line, spread over five linked sectors in La Clusaz and the separate Le Grand-Bornand area, and there's a good basis for an enjoyable, relaxed week.

The area's one big problem is its height, or rather the lack of it. Snowmaking has been installed in recent years and is continually increased, but it's still on a modest scale and of course makes no difference in mild weather. So prebooking a holiday here remains, as in other low resorts, a slightly risky business.

boarding *Snowboarding is popular in La Clusaz and, although there are still a lot of drag-lifts, most are avoidable. There are some good nursery slopes, served by chair-lifts, for beginners, and great cruising runs to progress to. La Balme is a great natural playground for good free-riders. There's a fun-park and a half-pipe on Etale and another in Le Grand-Bornand. During the week the resorts are fairly quiet, but La Clusaz livens up at the weekend.*

The resort

La Clusaz was once frequented almost entirely by the French. But it has developed into a major international resort – summer and winter. As one of the most accessible resorts from Geneva and Annecy, it's good for short transfers, but it does get crowded, and there can be weekend traffic jams.

The village is built beside a fast-flowing stream at the junction of a number of narrow wooded valleys, and has had to grow in a rather rambling and sprawling way, with roads running in a confusing mixture of directions. But, unlike so many French resorts, La Clusaz has retained the charm of a genuine mountain village. (It's the kind of place that is as attractive in summer as under a blanket of snow in winter.)

In the centre is a large old church, and other original old stone and wood buildings; and, for the most part, the new buildings have been built in chalet style and blend in well. Les Etages is a much smaller centre of accommodation above the main town, where two of the mountain sectors meet.

La Clusaz has a friendly feel to it. The villagers welcome visitors every Monday evening in the main square with vin chaud and a variety of local cheeses. There's a weekly market, tempting food shops and a wide choice of typically French bars.

For much of the season La Clusaz is a quiet and peaceful place for a holiday. But in peak season and at weekends the place gets packed out with French and Swiss families and the singles crowd.

Le Grand-Bornand, covered by the Aravis lift pass, is an even more charming village than La Clusaz, with even more sense that it remains a mountain community. This is partly because most of the development as a

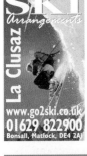

MOUNTAIN FACTS

La Clusaz

Altitude	1100m-2490m
Lifts	56
Pistes	132km
Green/Blue	71%
Red	24%
Black	5%
Artificial snow	34 guns
Recco detectors used	

Le Grand-Bornand

Altitude	1100m-2100m
Lifts	39
Pistes	80km
Green/Blue	70%
Red	25%
Black	5%
Artificial snow	50 guns
Recco detectors used	

LIFT PASSES

2000/01 prices in francs

Aravis pass
Covers La Clusaz and Le Grand-Bornand
Main pass
6 days 870 (760 low season)
Senior citizens
Over 60: 6 days 740
Over 75: free pass
Children
Under 16: 6 days 670
Under 5: free pass

La Clusaz pass
All lifts in La Clusaz.
Main pass
1-day pass 157
6-day pass 820
(low season 690)
Senior citizens
Over 60: 6-days 670
Over 75: free pass
Children
Under 16: 6-days 600
Under 5: free pass

Le Grand-Bornand pass
All lifts in Le Grand-Bornand.
Main pass
1-day pass 145
6-day pass 700
(low season 630)
Senior citizens
Over 60: 6 days 660
(low season 594)
Over 75: free pass
Children
Under 16: 6 days 580
Under 5: free pass

winter sports resort has gone on up the road at the satellite village of Le Chinaillon, which has been developed using chalet-style buildings. Le Grand-Bornand and La Clusaz are linked by a free 10-minute bus-ride and buses run every 30 minutes during the day. Le Grand-Bornand has quite extensive slopes and is well worth exploring for a day or two or considering as an alternative base.

If you are taking a car, you might also consider basing yourself at **St-Jean-de-Sixt** – a small hamlet midway between La Clusaz and Le Grand-Bornand, with a small slope nearby, mainly used for sledging.

The mountains

Like the village, the slopes at **La Clusaz** are rather spread out – which makes them all the more interesting (and scenic). There are five main areas, each connecting with at least one other. At **Le Grand-Bornand** the slopes spread out along the mountainside and can be accessed from either the village or Le Chinaillon up the road.

The Aravis pass, covering the lifts of both resorts, costs very little more than the La Clusaz pass, but a more substantial FF170 more than the Le Grand-Bornand pass.

THE SLOPES
Pretty and varied

Several points in **La Clusaz** have lifts giving access to the predominantly west- and north-west facing slopes of **L'Aiguille**. Links between this sector and the slightly higher and shadier slopes of **La Balme** area have improved massively in recent years: a long red piste has replaced the off-piste route from L'Aiguille towards La Balme, and last season a new gondola opened in the opposite direction, taking you up from the base of La Balme to Cote 2000 on L'Aiguille and cutting out the need to take a long, flat run back to La Clusaz. La Balme is a fairly substantial area with good lifts (a high-capacity gondola from the bottom linking to a quad chair); from the top there are wonderful views towards Mont Blanc.

Going the other way from L'Aiguille leads you to **L'Etale** via another choice of easy runs and the Transval cable-car, which shuttles people between the two areas. From the bottom of L'Etale, you can head back along another path to the village and the cable-car up to the fourth sector of **Beauregard** which, as the name implies, has splendid views and catches a lot of sunshine.

From the top of Beauregard you can link via another easy piste and a two-way chair-lift with the fifth area of **Manigod**. From here you can move on to L'Etale.

The main village at **Le Grand-Bornand** has two gondolas on the outskirts up to a gentle open area of easy runs (including nursery slopes) lying between 1400m and 1500m. Chairs fan out above this point, one going up to the 2100m high point of **Le Lachat,** where there are serious red and black runs. Other lifts and runs go across the mountainside to the slopes above **Le Chinaillon** (1300m). Here there is a broad, open mountainside with a row of chairs and drags serving blue and red slopes, and links to the rest of the domain – a wide area of blue and red runs.

SNOW RELIABILITY
Variable because of low altitude

Most of the runs are west- or north-west facing and tend to keep their snow fairly well, even though most of the area is below 2000m. The best snow is usually on the north-west-facing slopes at La Balme, where a lift takes you up to 2500m. La Clusaz itself is only just over 1000m and, in late season, the runs back can be dependent on artificial snow – of which there is now virtually blanket coverage. The main lifts to Beauregard and Crêt du Merle will carry people down as well as up. You can also ride the gondolas down to Le Grand-Bornand and the runs above Chinaillon have extensive snowmaking facilities.

FOR EXPERTS
Plenty to do, especially off-piste

The piste map doesn't seem to have a lot to offer, but the home resort of 1992 Olympic bumps champion Edgar Grospiron is not without challenges. Most of the sectors present off-piste variants to the pistes, and there are more serious adventures to undertake – all the more attractive for being ignored by most visitors.

The best terrain is at La Balme, where there are several fairly challenging pistes above mid-mountain. The black Vraille run, which leads to the speed skiing slope, is seriously steep. On the opposite side

SCHOOLS/GUIDES

1999/2000 prices in francs

ESF

Classes 6 days
4hr: 9.30-11.30, 2.45-4.45
5 full days: 800

Children's classes
Ages: 5 to 12
5 full days: 650

Private lessons
Hourly
190 for 1 to 3 people;
260 for 4 to 5 people

Sno Academie

1999/2000 prices in francs

Classes
3½ hr a day
5 days: 700

Private Lessons
1 or 2 people:
2hr 370
3 or 4 people:
2hr 450

CHILDCARE

The ESF runs a ski kindergarten for children aged 5 to 12, at normal class hours.

The two all-day kindergartens in La Clusaz operate 8.30 to 6pm. The Club des Mouflets (450 326950) offers creative activities and indoor games for non-skiing children aged 8 months to 4½ years (babies looked after in a special section). The Champions' Club (450 326950) takes from age 3½ to 6 for indoor and outdoor games, with the option of supervised skiing (with French instructors) for ages 3½ to 5.

In Le Grand-Bornand the kindergarten takes children from 3 months and the Chinaillon one from 8 months. Both offer all-day care.

of the sector, the entirely off-piste Combe de Bellachat can be reached.

The Noire run down the face of Beauregard can be tricky in poor snow. Elsewhere there are some very dark reds – the Tetras on L'Etale and Mur Edgar, below Crêt du Loup, for example. And L'Aiguille has a good off-piste run down the neglected Combe de Borderan.

In Le Grand-Bornand the steepest runs, including the black Noire du Lachat, go from the top of Le Lachat.

FOR INTERMEDIATES

Good if snow is good

Most intermediates will love La Clusaz if the snow conditions are good. Early intermediates will delight in the gentle slopes at the top of Beauregard and over on La Croix-Fry at Manigod, where there's a network of gentle tree-lined runs. And they'll be able to travel all over the area on the gentle, green linking pistes, where poling or walking is more likely to be a problem than any fears about steepness.

L'Etale and L'Aiguille have more challenging but wide blue runs.

More adventurous intermediates will prefer the steeper red slopes and good snow of La Balme and the linking run down the Combe du Fernuy from l'Aiguille.

Le Grand-Bornand is full of good cruising blue and red intermediate runs stretching in both directions above Le Chinaillon – well worth a visit for a day or two if you are staying in La Clusaz. Most visitors we hear from neglect Le Grand-Bornand and are missing out because of that.

FOR BEGINNERS

Splendid beginner slopes

There is a nursery slope at village level at La Clusaz, and a couple of others just above it, but the best nursery slopes are up the mountain at the top of the Beauregard cable-car and at Crêt du Merle. The Beauregard area has lovely gentle green runs to progress to, including one long run around the mountain right back to the village. There are also some greens at Le Grand-Bornand and St-Jean-de-Sixt.

FOR CROSS-COUNTRY

Excellent

The region has much better cross-country facilities than many resorts, with around 70km of loops of varying difficulty. One good area is near the Lac des Confins, reached by bus. There's also a lovely sunny area at the top of the Beauregard cable-car. At Le Grand-Bornand there are extensive trails in the Vallée du Bouchet and towards Le Chinaillon. And there are further trails at St-Jean-de-Sixt. All of these options are clearly laid out on an excellent special piste map.

QUEUES

Not a problem

Lift queues aren't a problem, except on peak weekends or if the lower slopes are shut because of snow shortage. The chair-lifts up the front face of L'Aiguille are the main weekend black spots – avoidable by taking other routes.

MOUNTAIN RESTAURANTS

High standard

Mountain restaurants are one of the area's strong points. There are lots of them and, for the most part, they are rustic and charming, and serve good, reasonably priced – often Savoyard – food. We have had excellent reports on the Télémark above the chair lift to l'Etale and Les Chenons at the bottom of La Balme. There are several other good restaurants higher up in the Aiguille sector, of which the Bercail is said to be the best. At night you can get to it by sledge or snowcat.

The restaurant at Beauregard by the cross-country trail is sunny and peaceful, with good views. The Relais de L'Aiguille at Crêt du Loup and Le Neve at Le Rosay on Le Grand-Bornand are also recommended. The Vieille Ferme at Merdassier (see Eating out) is also open at lunchtime.

SCHOOLS AND GUIDES

Mixed reports

There are tales of large classes and poor instruction in ESF group lessons, but we've heard from some satisfied customers too – especially those who took private lessons. According to reports, the smaller Sno Academie – with class sizes limited to eight – is much more reliable.

FACILITIES FOR CHILDREN

Good – in theory

We have had mixed reports about the kindergarten in La Clusaz and none about those in Le Grand-Bornand. Generally, however, the resorts are places where families can feel at home.

GETTING THERE

Air Geneva, transfer 1½hr. Lyon, transfer 2½hr.

ACTIVITIES

Indoor Various hotels have saunas, massage, hot-tub, weights rooms, aerobics, sun beds and swimming pools
Outdoor Ice skating, paragliding, micro-light flights, snow-shoe excursions, snowmobile rides, winter walks, horse-drawn carriage rides, quad-bikes, swimming pool.

Staying there

Le Grand-Bornand is a good choice if you want a quiet time in a very French atmosphere. La Clusaz is the place if you want a bit more life.

HOW TO GO
Decreasing choice of packages

Few of the big tour operators go to La Clusaz, but there's a fair choice of packages from smaller operators, some of whom go to Le Grand-Bornand too. The drive from the Channel and the transfer from Geneva airport are both among the shortest for any resort.

Chalets There are some chalets including some charmingly rustic ones.

Hotels Small, friendly 2-star family hotels are the mainstay of the area; luxury is not an option here.

(3) **Carlina** A reporter says it's the best, central with pool and grounds.

(3) **Beauregard** Comfortable; on the fringe of the village. Pool.

(3) **Alp'Hôtel** Comfortable modern chalet close to the centre, with one of the better restaurants. Pool.

(3) **Alpen Roc** Big but stylish, central and comfortable, although one reporter called his room 'very cramped'. Pool.

(3) **Saytels** Only 3-star in Le Grand-Bornand. Close to church.

(3) **Cimes** 3-star in Le Chinaillon.

(2) **Aravis** Traditional place with 'dated' rooms but 'great' food, in centre, close to lifts.

(2) **Chalet Alpage** Dinky chalet at foot of L'Etale slopes (bus stop outside) run by friendly British couple.

Self-catering There's quite a good choice, including self-catering chalets as well as apartments. Some are out of town and best for those with a car.

EATING OUT
Good choice

There's a wide choice of restaurants, some a short drive away, including the Vieux Chalet, which is one of our favourites – good food and service in a splendid, creaky old chalet. It has a nice sunny terrace for a lunchtime blowout too. The St Joseph at the Alp'Hotel is regarded as the best restaurant in La Clusaz. L'Ecuelle is the place to go for good seafood, or steak that you cook yourself on a little brazier on the table. La Cordee and L'Outa are simple places giving great value for money. At the other end of the price scale is the more formal Symphonie restaurant in the hotel Beauregard.

We're told some of the best food in the area is at the Ferme du Lormay in la Vallée du Bouchet, about 5km on from Le Grand-Bornand. But another

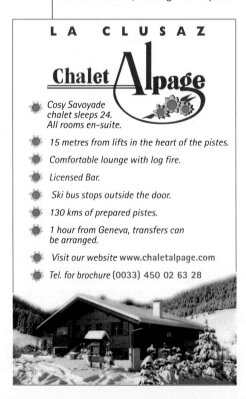

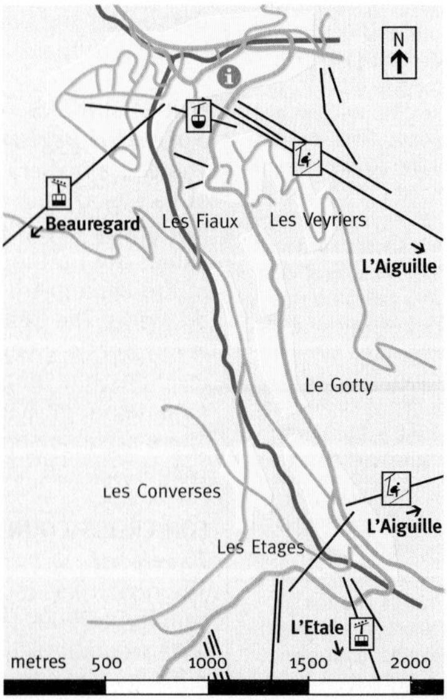

↑ Unlike so many French resorts, La Clusaz and Le Grand-Bornand retain the charm of being genuine mountain villages

LA CLUSAZ TO

TOURIST OFFICES

La Clusaz

Postcode 74220
t +33 450 326500
f 450 326501
infos@laclusaz.com
www.laclusaz.com

Le Grand-Bornand

Postcode 74450
t +33 450 027800
f 450 027801
infos@legrandbornand.com
www.legrandbornand.com

St-Jean-de-Sixt

Postcode 74450
t +33 450 027014
f 450 027878
infos@saintjeandesixt.com
www.saintjeandesixt.com

Vallées des Aravis

Postcode 74450
t +33 450 027874
f 450 023851
infos@aravis.com
www.aravis.com

reporter rates the Vieille Ferme at Merdassier his favourite place in the Alps – an old farm building with 'serious food, classy staff, perfect atmosphere'. Le Foly, overlooking the Lac des Confins, is a firm favourite with both tourists and locals alike.

APRES-SKI
La Clusaz getting livelier

These resorts have always seemed to us typically quiet French family places, with the difference that La Clusaz livens up at weekends. But reporters suggest that things are looking up. Les Caves du Paccaly, in the centre of La Clusaz, is a new place with woody decor and live music. Le Pressoir is a focal bar, popular for sports videos. Pub le Salto is run by an English couple and has Sky TV and draught Guinness. The Bali bar is a more French central recommendation. The Ecluse disco has a glass dance floor with a floodlit stream running beneath it. The Mezzaluna and Caffe Inn have DJs or live music, and Club 18 rocks, often with live bands.

OFF THE SLOPES
Some diversions

The villages are pleasant. It's easy for pedestrians to get around the valley by bus and to get up to several mountain restaurants for lunch. There are good walks along the valleys, and a day trip to the beautiful lakeside town of Annecy is possible.

STAYING UP THE MOUNTAIN
Cheap and panoramic

The Relais de l'Aiguille at Crêt du Loup has five adequate bedrooms that are about the cheapest in the resort. And there are no fewer than three places to stay at the top of Beauregard.

Les Contamines 1160m

An unusual blend of village charm and reliable snow

WHAT IT COSTS

4

HOW IT RATES

The slopes	
Snow	****
Extent	**
Experts	**
Intermediates	***
Beginners	***
Convenience	**
Queues	***
Restaurants	****
The rest	
Scenery	***
Resort charm	****
Off-slope	**

What's new

A new gondola on the back side of the mountain, from Belleville to La Ruelle, will replace the old chair-lift for 2000/01.

MOUNTAIN FACTS

Altitude	1165m-2485m
Lifts	26
Pistes	120km
Green/Blue	37%
Red	40%
Black	23%
Artificial snow	3km
Recco detectors used	

TOURIST OFFICE

Postcode 74170
t +33 450 470158
f 450 470954
Les.Contamines@wanadoo.fr
www.lescontamines.com

Les Contamines is a traditional, unspoilt village with pretty wooden chalets, impressive old churches, a weekly market in the village square and prices more typical of rural France than of international resorts. Its local slopes offer substantial, surprisingly snowsure, intermediate terrain – and spectacular views.

THE RESORT

The core of the village is compact, but the resort as a whole spreads widely, with chalets dotted over a 3km stretch of the valley, and the main access lift is 1km from the centre. A car is useful, but the Mont Blanc lift pass covers the local buses, as well as the lifts of Chamonix and Megève.

THE MOUNTAINS

From Le Lay a two-stage gondola climbs up to the **slopes**. Another gondola leads from a car park a little further up the valley. Above these, a sizeable network of open, largely north-east-facing pistes fans out, with lifts approaching 2500m in two places. You can drop over the ridge at Col du Joly (2000m) to a series of south-west-facing runs down to La Ruelle (1600m), with a single red run going on down to Belleville (1200m) and the road to the village of Hauteluce, 7km away. There is a **snowboard** fun-park and half-pipe.

Many of the shady runs on the Contamines side are above 1700m, and the resort has a justifiable reputation for good **snow conditions**, said to be the result of proximity to Mont Blanc.

The steep western section has black runs, which are enjoyable but not terribly challenging for **experts**. The main attraction is the substantial and varied off-piste terrain.

The black runs are manageable for good **intermediates**. Other runs are ideal for people of average ability, with some of the best from the gondola's top station to its mid-station. Given good snow, the south-facing runs down to La Ruelle are a delight.

In good snow, the village nursery area is adequate for **beginners**. There are other areas at the mid-station and the top of the gondola, but no long greens to progress to.

There are **cross-country** trails of varying difficulty totalling 26km.

Queues are not normally a problem, arising only if people are bussed in from other resorts with less snow.

There are quite a few lovely rustic **mountain restaurants**. La Ferme de la Ruelle is a jolly barn and Chalet du Col du Joly has great views. Best of all are two cosy chalets – Roselette and Bûche Croisée.

We have had mixed reports on the **ski school** – some parents thought their children's classes too strict and overcrowded. However, our most recent reports are positive. Excursions are offered, including a guided trip to the famous Vallée Blanche.

The village crèche is for **children** from one to seven years, the new all-day kindergarten for kids from two and a half up. Ski school starts at age four.

STAYING THERE

A couple of operators run catered **chalets** here, and there are a dozen modest **hotels**, the best of which is the 3-star Chemenaz at Le Lay; though convenient for the slopes, this uninspiring spot has few other merits.

There are various restaurants and crêperies in town for **eating out** – Le Husky, l'Auberge du Barattet and L'Op Traken are recommended. **Après-ski** is quiet, but there are several bars, some with live jazz on later, others that get a reasonable crowd at tea-time. There are also a couple of discos.

There are good walks and a natural ice rink, but St-Gervais (10 minutes by bus), Megève and Chamonix have more to offer **off the slopes**.

Courchevel 1300m-1850m

Gourmet skiing and boarding – and it needn't cost a fortune

WHAT IT COSTS

6

HOW IT RATES

The slopes	
Snow	****
Extent	*****
Experts	****
Intermediates	*****
Beginners	*****
Convenience	****
Queues	****
Restaurants	****
The rest	
Scenery	***
Resort charm	**
Off-slope	***

What's new

For 2000/01 the slow chair from Les Creux to La Vizelle will be replaced by a high-speed six-seater. The start of the Creux Noir chair will be moved up the mountain so the lift will be shorter and serve only the steeper upper slopes.

In 1650 the old access gondola is being replaced.

In La Tania extra cabins are being added to the gondola, and new snowmaking will keep the beautiful rolling blue run down to resort level in better condition.

New blasting equipment should get the highest slopes open sooner after a heavy snowfall.

And Courchevel is the only European resort we know to have daily hand-outs to show which runs were groomed overnight and what the weather forecast is for the next few days – an excellent service.

- ⊕ Extensive, varied local terrain to suit everyone from beginners to experts – plus the rest of the Three Valleys
- ⊕ Great easy runs for near-beginners
- ⊕ Lots of slope-side accommodation
- ⊕ Impressive, continuously updated lift system, particularly above 1850
- ⊕ Excellent piste maintenance, and widespread use of snowmakers
- ⊕ Wooded setting is pretty, and useful in bad weather
- ⊕ Choice of five very different villages
- ⊕ Some great restaurants, and good après-ski by French standards

- ⊖ Some pistes get unpleasantly busy
- ⊖ Rather soulless villages with intrusive traffic in places
- ⊖ 1850 has some of the most expensive hotels and bars in the Alps (prices in the other villages are much lower)
- ⊖ Little to do away from the slopes (during the day, at least)

Courchevel 1850 – the highest of the five components of this big resort – is the favourite Alpine hangout of the Paris jet set, who fly directly in to the mini-airport in the middle of the slopes. Its top hotels and restaurants are among the best in the Alps, and the most expensive. But don't be put off: a holiday here doesn't have to cost a fortune (especially in the lower villages), the atmosphere is not particularly exclusive, and the slopes are excellent. Courchevel is the most extensive and varied sector of the whole Three Valleys, with everything from long gentle greens to steep couloirs. Many visitors never leave the Courchevel sector; but there is good access to the rest of the Three Valleys, too.

Le Praz is an overgrown, but still pleasant village, La Tania and 1550 quieter and good for families, 1650 has more of an old village atmosphere than it seems from the drive through, and the posh bits of 1850 are stylishly woody. But overall the resort is no beauty. Well, nothing's perfect. Courchevel's long list of merits is enough to attract more and more Brits ('If I could only go to one resort, Courchevel would be the one.' says one enthusiastic reporter), but it remains much more French than Méribel, over the hill, as well as having better snow.

boarding *For an upmarket resort, Courchevel goes out of its way to attract boarders. There's a fun-park and a half-pipe just below 1850 and the Verdons terrain park (all for skiers as well as boarders) just above 1850. Except above 1650, it's easy to get around the Three Valleys using chairs and gondolas. The big snowboard hangout is 'Prends ta luge et tire toi', a combined shop/bar/Internet café in the centre of 1850.*

The resort

Courchevel is made up of five varied villages, most known by their altitudes. A road winds up the hill, linking Le Praz (1300), 1550 and 1650 to 1850; free buses run between the villages. La Tania is a few km along from Le Praz.

1850 is the largest village, and the focal point of the area. It has the main lifts to the Three Valleys connections and most of the nightlife and shops. It's conspicuously upmarket, with some very smooth hotels on the slopes just above the village centre and among the trees of Jardin Alpin. There's also a spreading area of smart private chalets. However, the centre of the village is a rather messy sprawl with a surprising amount of traffic and fumes.

While some readers 'couldn't afford a second week', others say, 'It's not as upmarket as it's made out to be.' You can pay through the nose to eat, drink

Courchevel's powerful lift system shifts you quickly around the mountain →

SNOWPIX.COM / CHRIS GILL

MOUNTAIN FACTS

Altitude 1300m-3200m	
Lifts	200
Pistes	600km
Green/Blue	49%
Red	37%
Black	14%
Artificial snow	90km
Recco detectors used	

LIFT PASSES

2000/01 prices in francs

Three Valleys
Covers all lifts in Courchevel, La Tania, Méribel, Val-Thorens, Les Menuires and St-Martin-de-Belleville.

Beginners 9 free lifts in the Courchevel valley.

Main pass
1-day pass 235
6-day pass 1160

Senior citizens
Over 60: 6-day pass 928
Over 70: 6-day pass 580
Over 75: free pass

Children
Under 16: 6-day pass 870
Under 10: 6-day pass 754
Under 5: free pass

Short-term passes
Half-day (from 12.30) for Courchevel valley (adult 145 and the 3 Valleys (adult 176).

Notes 6-day pass and over valid for one day each in Tignes-Val-d'Isère, La Plagne-Les Arcs, Pralognan-la-Vanoise and Les Saisies. Reductions for families.

Alternative passes
Vallée de Courchevel pass covers 67 lifts and 150km of piste around Courchevel and La Tania (adult 6-day 945. One-day extension for Three Valleys, 105).

and stay, but more affordable places are not impossible to find.

The main road cuts through **1650** but there's also an old village centre, lively bars and quietly situated chalets. Its local slopes (whose main access is an escalator-served gondola) are relatively peaceful. 1650 isn't the most convenient base for the rest of the Three Valleys, but a day trip to Val-Thorens is well within reach, and 1650 makes 'a pleasant beginning and end to the day'.

1550 is a quiet dormitory, a gondola ride from 1850. It has the advantage of having essentially the same position as 1850, with cheaper accommodation and restaurants. But it's a long trip to 1850 by road if you want to go there in the evening. Some accommodation is a fair distance from the gondola.

Le Praz (or 1300) was once a traditional village set amid woodland. Still attractive, its charm has been undermined by expansion triggered by the 1992 Olympics, including the Olympic ski jump. It's quiet, 'excellent for children', with good links to 1850, and has tree-lined slopes on its doorstep for bad weather days. Near-beginners face rides down as well as up: the pistes back to the village are red and black, and at this altitude snow conditions are often poor.

La Tania – off the small road linking Le Praz to Méribel – was built for the Olympics and has grown into a quiet, attractive, car-free collection of chalets and chalet-style apartments set among trees. A gondola leads to the slopes, and there are two wonderful sweeping intermediate runs down. They aren't ideal for progressing beginners, but the nursery slope is on your doorstep, and several visitors have commented that La Tania is 'very child friendly'.

The mountains

The local slopes are so well linked that Courchevel is essentially just one big network. The central 1850 area is suitable for all, wooded Le Praz suits experts best. La Tania has only intermediate pistes, while 1650 has mainly fairly easy slopes. Runs lead back to all the villages, but the runs to Le Praz are prone to close with lack of snow. Piste maintenance is superb and maps of which runs have been groomed are available at lift stations, snowmakers are abundant and the major lifts are modern, fast and comfortable – though there are a number of ancient drag-lifts, too. The area is also very well laid out. The main complaint we've had is that the slopes get busier than expected.

Many reporters recommend buying only a Courchevel pass ('I was still finding new runs after two weeks') and buying daily extensions when you want to try the rest of the Three Valleys. Champagny is an easy road outing, giving access to the La Plagne area.

THE SLOPES

Huge variety to suit everyone

A network of lifts and pistes spreads out from **1850**, which is very much the focal point of the area. The main axis is the Verdons gondola, leading to a second gondola to **La Vizelle** and a nearly parallel cable-car up to **La Saulire** (2740m). Both the high points give access to a wide range of intermediate and advanced terrain (including a number of couloirs), Méribel and all points to Val-Thorens. You can also get over to 1650 from here.

To the right looking up from 1850 the Chenus gondola goes towards a second departure point for Méribel, the **Col de la Loze**. Easy and intermediate runs go back to 1850, with more difficult runs in the woods above **La Tania** and **Le Praz** – splendid slopes when snow is in good supply.

To the left of the Verdons gondola is the Jardin Alpin gondola, which leads to some great beginner terrain, and serves the higher hotels and runs until 8pm. It also gives access to 1650.

1650 offers a good mix of beginner and intermediate slopes. Getting to and from Méribel and the rest of the Three Valleys involves slightly more effort than from the rest of Courchevel, since you have to go up and down another valley, but you can always catch the bus from 1850 if you run late on the way back.

SNOW RELIABILITY
Very good

The combination of Courchevel's orientation (its slopes are north- or north-east-facing), its height, an abundance of snowmakers and excellent piste maintenance usually guarantees good snow down to at least the 1850 and 1650 villages, and to Bouc Blanc (1680m), above La Tania. On countless visits we have found that the snow is usually much better than in neighbouring Méribel, which gets more sun.

FOR EXPERTS
Some black gems

There is plenty to interest experts, even without the rest of the Three Valleys.

The most obvious expert runs are the couloirs you can see on the right

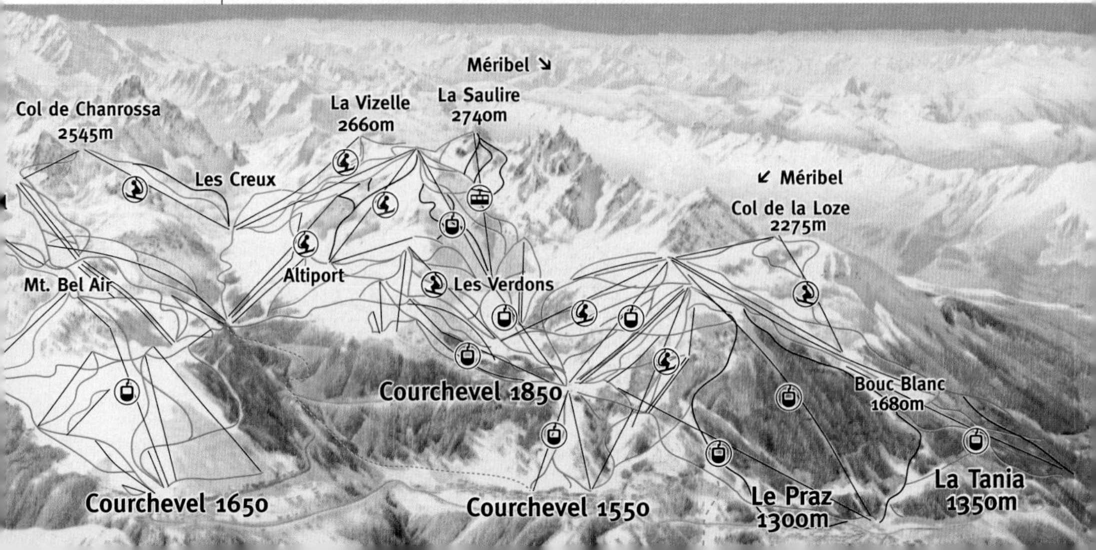

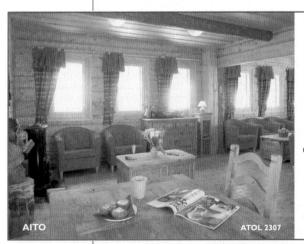

near the top of the Saulire cable-car. These are three of the steepest black pistes in Europe, with the Téléphérique couloir being seriously narrow as well. The Grand Couloir is the widest and easiest – but you have to traverse further along the narrow bumpy, precipitous access ridge to reach it.

There is a lot of steep terrain, on- and off-piste, on the shady slopes of La Vizelle, both towards Verdons and towards the link with 1650. Some of the reds on Vizelle verge on black steepness and the black M piste is surprisingly little used. If you love moguls, don't miss the top of the black Suisses. Chanrossa, which comes towards 1850 from the top of 1650 is quite difficult – the off-piste just next to it is tougher. For a change of scene and a test of stamina, a couple of long (700m vertical), genuinely steep blacks cut through the trees down to Le Praz.

There is plenty of off-piste terrain to try with a guide and a bit of climbing – high, north-facing slopes right at the top of the 1650 sector for example (the Vallée des Avals is a great run here). Also ask about the mysterious Hidden Valley in 1650, and the huge bowl accessed from the Creux Noir chair.

FOR INTERMEDIATES
Paradise for all levels

The Three Valleys is the greatest intermediate playground in the world, but all grades of intermediates will love Courchevel's local slopes too.

Above 1650 novices have the wonderful long runs of Pyramide and Grand Bosses. Gentle blues such as Biollay in 1850 are fine, gentle slopes, leading to the two easy home runs on either side of the Jardin Alpin.

Those of average ability can handle most red runs without difficulty. Our favourite is the long, sweeping Combe de la Saulire from top to bottom of the cable-car. Very pleasant first thing, when it's well groomed and free of crowds, it's a different story at the end of the day. Creux, behind La Vizelle, is another splendid, fast long red (it gets bumpy though, and crowded with ski school groups). Marmottes, especially if taken from its narrow start at the top of Vizelle, is more challenging.

The runs from Bouc Blanc through the trees towards La Tania are great – long, rolling cruises 'guaranteed to put a smile on your face'. The top of this section also has fine red runs down to 1850 and 1550, with easier blues alongside. Over at 1650, the reds on Mt Bel Air and Signal are excellent, if short, and rarely crowded.

FOR BEGINNERS
Great graduation runs

There are excellent nursery slopes above both 1650 and 1850. At the former, lessons are likely to begin on the short drags close to the village, but quick learners will soon be able to go from close to the top of the 1650 area all the way down to the village. The best nursery area at 1850 is at Pralong, above the village, near the airstrip. A green path links this area with chairs to 1650, so adventurous novices have the opportunity to move far afield. The Bellecôte green run down into 1850 is an excellent, long, gentle slope – but does get crowded. It is served by the Jardin Alpin gondola, and a drag which is one of 13 free

SCHOOLS/GUIDES

2000/01 prices in francs

ESF in 1850
Classes
6 full days:
Adults: 1250
Children: 980
Children's classes
Ages: from 3
1 full day: 290
Private lessons
2½hr morning, 2hr lunchtime, 2½hr afternoon, 7hr full day
1390 to 1650 for full day.

ESF in 1650
Classes 6 days
6 full days: 815
Children's classes
Ages: from 3
Private lessons
9.15-4.45
1,600 for full day

ESF in 1550
Classes 6 days
Adults: 1300
Children's classes
6 days, 1200. Ages from 3 to 5

ESF in La Tania (1999/2000 prices)
Classes 6 mornings
Adults: 800
Children's classes
6 days, 1100

Ski Academie
Classes 5 days
2½hr: am
5 mornings: 750
Children's classes
Ages: from 4
5 mornings: 650

Ski Supreme 1850
Classes 12hr course 895
Children's classes
12hr course 840
Private lessons
1hr 345

Le Ski School 1650
Classes 5 days
2hr: am
5 mornings: £85
Private lessons
2hr: £70 for 1 or 2 people, £14 per additional person. maximum 4 people

The Bel-Air restaurant at the top of the 1650 gondola has splendid views of La Vizelle →

SNOWPIX.COM / CHRIS GILL

beginner lifts in Courchevel. 1550, La Tania and Le Praz have small nursery areas, but most people go up to 1850 for its more reliable snow.

FOR CROSS-COUNTRY
Long wooded trails

Courchevel has a total of 66km, the most in the Three Valleys. Le Praz is the most suitable of the villages, with trails through the woods towards 1550, 1850 and Méribel. Given enough snow, there are also loops around the village.

QUEUES
Superb lift system copes well

Even at New Year and Easter, when 1850 in particular positively teems with people, queues are minimal, thanks to the excellence of the lift system. The Chenus, Verdons and Jardin Alpin gondolas have all had their capacity increased over the past few years, improving these old bottlenecks. However, as one reader points out, 'there can be a build-up at 1850 for the gondolas.' At such times 'it's best to avoid skiing back to 1850'. For example, try using the Plantrey chair, below 1850, or the Coqs chair, above it, to get over to Loze, Le Praz and La Tania. Queues for the huge Saulire cable-car have been all but eliminated by the upgrading of the parallel Vizelle gondola.

MOUNTAIN RESTAURANTS
Good but can be very expensive

Mountain restaurants are plentiful and pleasant by French standards, but it is sensible to check the prices and book for table-service restaurants.

The big Chalet de Pierres, on the Verdons piste just above 1850, is one of the highlights if you're inclined to extravagance – a comfortable, smooth place in traditional style, doing excellent food (including superb cakes) with high, high prices. Only a little way behind this for price comes the Cap Horn, near the airstrip. If you're feeling really flush, take a trip down to Bistrot du Praz at Le Praz for a blowout on a bad-weather day (treat yourself to the 'degustation de foie gras chaud'). The Bergerie on the Bellecôte piste is where the beautiful people hang out.

For a good-value lunch above 1850 try the busy self-service Altibar, with a fine terrace and good food, including 'wonderful fondue'. The Verdons is well placed for piste-watching and La Soucoupe is an atmospheric self-service place, now with table-service upstairs too. The Panoramic at the top of Saulire has a beautiful dining room for bad weather days. Behind the main lift station at 1850 the Telemark terrace is a great suntrap, with good pizzas.

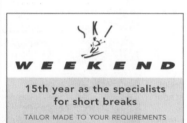

SIMPLY SKI *Chalet specialist*

T 020 8541 2209 *www.simplyski.co.uk*

Simply Ski offers a choice of nine chalets in Courchevel. Ranging from 8 to 21 beds, all are of a high standard and well located for enjoying the superb Three Valleys. In Courchevel 1850 we offer Chalets St Nicholas and St Christopher, ski in/ski out properties situated in the heart of the village, as well as a selection of chalet apartments in the popular Forum. Our chalets in picturesque Le Praz/Courchevel 1300 are ideal for families, offering easy access to our Crèche and Children's Club. All our chalets offer friendly and professional staff and cordon bleu cuisine. We also feature a range of chalets in Méribel and La Tania. Flexible travel options available.

CHALET SENECHAL →

SKI AMIS *Catered chalets*

T 01233 732187 *www.skiamis.com*

La Tania – Courchevel
Chalet Christine – 28 persons – en suite bedrooms
Chalet Balkiss – 14 persons – en suite bedrooms

- Superb chalets in snowsure resorts.
- 50m from the gondola, pistes and village.
- Resort services and free ski hosting.
- Excellent cuisine and a friendly personal service.
- Couples, families and groups welcome.
- Large, comfortable lounges with log fires, hi-fi and video.
- Ski room with boot warmers in each chalet.

La Plagne – Montalbert
Chalet Clyde – sleeps up to 11 adults and 6 children. Child-free weeks possible.

CHALET CHRISTINE ↑

SNOWLINE *www.snowline.co.uk*

T 020 8870 4807 F 020 8875 9236

For Courchevel skiing at a sensible price try one of Snowline's seven ski-in/ski-out chalets tucked into the woods above La Tania. A few minutes' skiing from Méribel and Courchevel, Snowline chalets offer unparalleled access to the vast Three Valleys area. They also offer cosy, timber beam comfort, open fires, fully en suite facilities, cable TV and individual boot warmers. Snowline chalet hosts are trained by a top London cookery school and, like the ski hosts, managers and drivers, really care about their guests. Holidays start from £379. Snowline also has nine chalets in Méribel.

CHALET ELLIOT, LA TANIA →

CHILDCARE

There are kindergartens in 1850 (479 080847) and 1650 (479 083369) which take children from age 2, until 5pm. The ESF branches in all main parts of the resort have ski kindergartens.

GETTING THERE

Air Geneva, transfer 3½hr. Lyon, transfer 3½hr. Chambéry, transfer 2½hr. Direct flights to Courchevel altiport from London at weekends only (contact tourist office for details). Also scheduled flights from Geneva to Courchevel.

Rail Moûtiers (24km); transfer by bus or taxi.

In 1650, Mont Bel-Air, at the top of the gondola, is excellent, with friendly table-service, and a splendid tiered terrace. Bouc Blanc above La Tania has table-service, good food and generally friendly staff, and Pub Le Lodge in La Tania itself has 'damn good chilli burgers', but 'grotty loos'. Down in 1550 try the Cortona – 'great pizza'.

SCHOOLS AND GUIDES

Size is everything

Courchevel's branches of the ESF add up to the largest ski school in Europe, with a total of almost 500 instructors. We've had bad reports on ESF 1850 in the past, but ESF La Tania is said to be 'excellent'. A Bureau des Guides runs all-day off-piste excursions.

Ski Academie, an independent group of French instructors, claims their dozen or so instructors speak 'fluent English'. 'Adequately clear English' would be nearer the mark, according to reporters.

Supreme in 1850 is owned and staffed by British instructors and we've had good reports: 'None of the follow-me approach that the ESF sometimes use.' Ski Cocktail ('excellent, with emphasis on fun') and Magic in Motion ('very good') run lessons from 1850 too.

Le Ski School is run in 1650 by British tour operator Le Ski. It uses mainly British instructors and can be booked through their UK office. 'Absolutely first-rate,' said a reporter – the school is doubling in size for 2000/01. Some of the instructors also work as New Generation. A reader enthuses: 'Young and highly motivated. Adapt teaching to the clients' needs, not ski school dogma.'

FACILITIES FOR CHILDREN

Lots of chalet-based options

There is an excellent ski kindergarten in 1850, which has generated positive reports from British families.

Several tour operators run their own crèches using British nannies – an alternative that many families have found attractive.

Staying there

1850 is the swanky place, with the best hotels and chalets, the biggest choice of restaurants and nightlife and the jet set. 1650 is better value, 1550 is quiet and good for families. Le Praz and La Tania are quiet and good value.

In all the resorts except Le Praz, there is lots of accommodation close to the lifts and runs. The prime place to stay is close to the main lift station at 1850, or on runs leading down to it.

HOW TO GO

Value chalets and apartments

Huge numbers of British tour operators go to Courchevel, with a wide choice of accommodation.

Chalets There are plenty of chalets available from dozens of UK tour operators, including some very comfortable ones and a few that are genuinely luxurious. As usual in a French resort with a stock of ageing hotel buildings, there are also some chalet hotels run by UK tour operators.

In 1850, FlexiSki has a new 10-person chalet, the newly refurbished Vizelle, on the Bellecôte piste. Scott Dunn has several upscale places. Ski Amis has the 28-bed all en suite Chalet

ACTIVITIES

Indoor Artificial skating rink, climbing wall, bridge, chess, squash, swimming and saunas (hotels), gymnasium, health and fitness centres (swimming pools, sauna, steam-room, hot-tub, water therapy, weight-training, massage), bowling, exhibitions (galleries in 1850 and 1650), cinema, games rooms, billiards, language courses

Outdoor Hang-gliding, paragliding, flying lessons, parachuting, floodlit skiing, ski jumping, snow-shoe excursions, dog-sledding, snowmobile rides, 35km cleared paths, 2km toboggan run, curling, ice-climbing, flight excursions

Christine in La Tania, joined by the equally special Balkiss for 2000/01. Simply Ski has highly regarded childcare in their fine Le Praz chalets. Lotus Supertravel has a number of luxurious 'superchalets' with upscale food and wines and free massages – we stayed in the splendid Chalet Founets. Thomson's recently refurbished flagship St Louis chalet hotel is in a great position just across from the Bellecôte piste. Crystal's club hotel New Solarium is set in the pretty Jardin Alpin. Finlays has one chalet in 1850 and four, including one new one for 2000/01, in 1550.

In 1650 Le Ski has 11 good value chalets, including the brand new Rikiki on the piste, and three fully en suite places in La Tania. Snowline has seven fine-sounding chalets in La Tania.

Hotels There are nearly 50 hotels in Courchevel, mostly at 1850 – including more 4-stars than anywhere else in France except Paris.

((((5 **Bellecôte** (1850) Our favourite among the more swanky places – it offers some Alpine atmosphere as well as sheer luxury.

((((5 **Mélezin** (1850) Superbly stylish and luxurious – and in an ideal position beside the bottom of the Bellecôte home slope.

((((5 **Carlina** (1850) Another luxury piste-side pad, next to the Mélezin.

((((5 **Byblos des Neiges** (1850) Next to stop on Jardin Alpin gondola; spacious public rooms, good pool.

(((4 **Grandes Alpes** (1850) On the piste right next to the main lifts.

(((4 **Rond Point** (1850) Relaxed family atmosphere and central position.

((3 **Croisette** (1850) Next to main lifts; recently taken over and refurbished. It contains the popular Le Jump bar.

((3 **Courcheneige** (1850) Pleasantly informal, large chalet in quiet position on the piste above the resort, with a popular lunchtime terrace.

((3 **Ducs de Savoie** (1850) Pleasant, wood-built; well placed in the trees for skiing to the door, but only five minutes' walk from the village.

((3 **Sivoliere** (1850) No beauty, but comfortable (though small sitting area) and pleasantly set among pines.

((3 **Golf** (1650) Rather impersonal 3-star, in a superb position on the piste next to the gondola station.

((3 **Ancolies** (1550) 'A real find,' said a past American visitor, impressed by the friendly staff and the excellent food.

(3) **Montana** (La Tania) 'Very good value', slope-side 3-star with sauna and fitness club. 'Friendly, English-speaking staff and excellent food.'
(2) **Peupliers** (1300) Well placed and cheap by local standards.
Self-catering There's a large selection of apartments, though high-season dates can sell out early. Some UK tour operators (including Erna Low) have places in the smart and central Forum complex in 1850. As with all French apartments, check room dimensions and book a place advertised for more people than there are in your party.

EATING OUT

Pick your price

There are a lot of good, very pricey French restaurants in Courchevel. Among the best, and priciest, are Le Chabichou and Le Bateau Ivre in 1850 – both with two Michelin stars. The 'friendly' Berçail also has a high reputation, notably for seafood. Other recommendations for Savoyard food include the cosy La Saulire (booking essential) and its sister restaurant La Fromagerie, the good-value L'Arbé, La Cloche ('good atmosphere') and Le Mazot – 'very traditional'. La Cendrée is a 'wonderful Italian'. The Smalto and Strada are good for pizza. Still in 1850, La Potinière does good, cheap pizzas, steaks and pasta. La Locomotive has a railway theme and a varied menu.

In 1550, L'Oeil du Boeuf is good for grills. La Cortona does good-value pizza.

The place for traditional French food in 1650 is the Montagne, while Le Petit

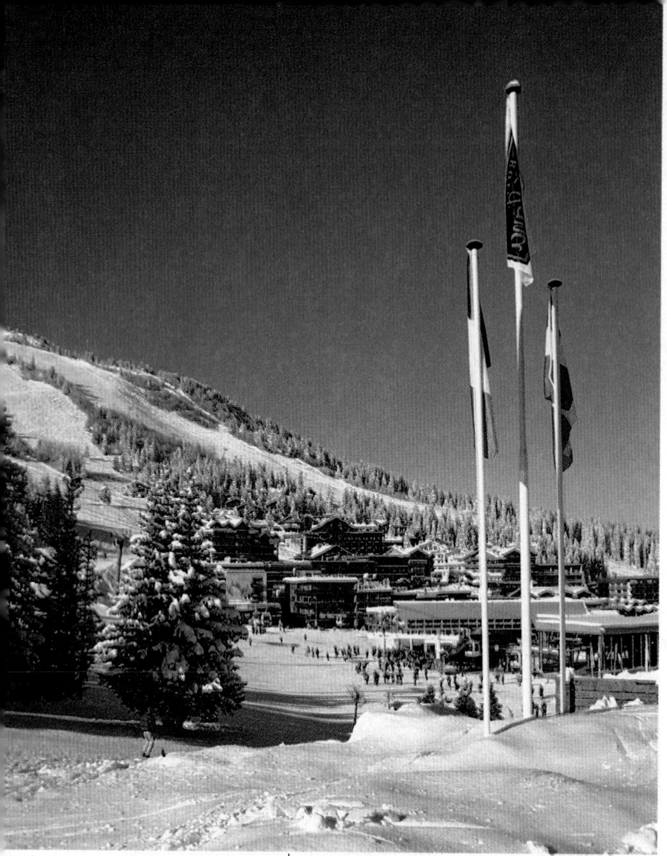

↑ The centre of 1850 has pistes down to it and lifts out of it in all directions

SNOWPIX.COM / CHRIS GILL

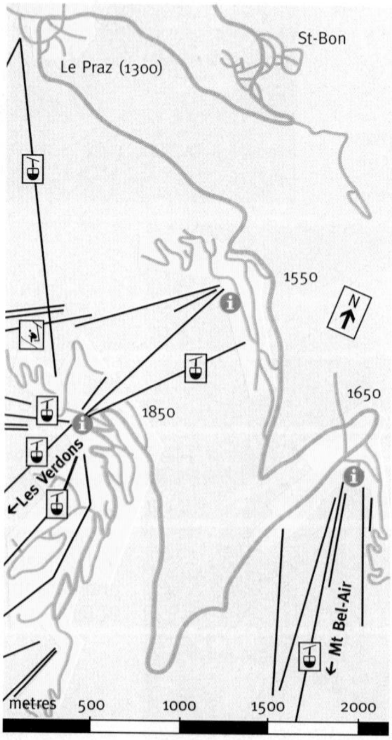

TOURIST OFFICE

Postcode 73122
t +33 479 080029
f 479 081563
pro@courchevel.com
www.courchevel.com
www.latania.com

Savoyard is the place for pizza. In Le Praz, Bistrot du Praz is pricey but excellent – see 'Mountain restaurants'. Le Yaca is also excellent.

In La Tania visitors have suggested La Ferme: 'very nice atmosphere, good food at reasonable prices'.

APRES-SKI
1850 has most variety

If you want lots of nightlife, it's got to be 1850. There are some exclusive nightclubs, such as La Grange and Les Caves, with top Paris cabaret acts and sky-high prices. The popular Kalico has DJs and cocktails and gets packed. The Bergerie does themed evenings – food, music, entertainment (but prices are high). The down-to-earth Bar L'Equipe seems to be readers' top nightspot.

El Gringo has theme nights. La Saulire (aka Jacques), Le Jump (packed at tea-time), Tee-Jay's and the cheap and cheerful Potinière are also popular.

Cinemas in 1850, 1650 and La Tania sometimes show films in English.

In 1650 Le Signal gets crowded as the slopes close and has great views at the back and strong Mutzig beer, but shuts at 9pm or so. Rocky's is very popular with Brits and has satellite TV and loud music. Au Plouc is a tiny, welcoming French bar. The Space Bar has pool, games and live music. Tour operator Le Ski is opening a bar for 2000/01 – which may well mean Le Signal becomes a lot quieter.

In 1550 the Chanrossa bar is British-dominated, with occasional live music, the Taverne 'French and friendly'.

In La Tania, Pub Le Ski Lodge is the hub, and in Le Praz it's the pizzeria tucked away in the shopping mall, with live music and modest prices. The Bang Bang Bar and the rustic Darbello have been recommended by reporters.

OFF THE SLOPES
1850 isn't bad

The Forum sports centre in 1850 includes a climbing wall in the shopping centre – good for spectating too. Shopping in 1850 includes Fat Face and White Stuff, and there are excellent markets at most levels. There's a fun ice-driving circuit and an ice-climbing structure. A pedestrian lift pass for the gondolas and buses in Courchevel and Méribel makes it easy for non-slope users to get around the area and meet companions for lunch on the slopes. And you can take joyrides from the altiport and try to spot friends below.

Les Deux-Alpes 1650m

Twin attractions of snow and fun

WHAT IT COSTS

(4)

HOW IT RATES

The slopes	
Snow	****
Extent	***
Experts	****
Intermediates	**
Beginners	***
Convenience	***
Queues	**
Restaurants	**
The rest	
Scenery	****
Resort charm	**
Off-slope	**

What's new

Last season saw a new blue run linking the Pied Moutet sector to the main slopes (via the Petite Aiguille chair-lift at the entrance to the resort. Snowmaking is to be installed on the new run for 2000/01.

Two new residences – le Flocon d'Or and Les Chalets d'Or – are being built for 2000/01.

SNOWPIX.COM / CHRIS GILL

There are sightseeing tours on the glacier, where the views are exceptional ↓

- ⊕ High, snowsure slopes, including an extensive glacier area
- ⊕ Varied high-mountain terrain, from motorway cruising to seriously steep blacks and off-piste slopes
- ⊕ Efficient, modern lift system
- ⊕ Excellent, sunny nursery slopes
- ⊕ Stunning views of the Ecrins peaks
- ⊕ Lively, varied nightlife
- ⊕ Wide choice of hotels

- ⊖ Piste network modest by French mega-resort standards – we're sceptical about the claimed 200km – and badly congested in places
- ⊖ Only one easy run back to the resort – a busy zig-zag path; others are red or black, and often ruined by sun
- ⊖ Virtually no woodland runs
- ⊖ Spread-out, traffic-choked resort
- ⊖ Few appealing mountain restaurants

We have a love-hate relationship with Les Deux-Alpes. We quite like the buzz of the town – arriving here is a bit like driving into Las Vegas from the Nevada desert – and we understand the appeal of its vibrant nightlife. We love the high-Alpine feel of its main mountain, and the good snow to be found on the north-facing runs in the middle of the mountain, above the icy home slopes and below the giant nursery slope that is the glacier. But we're very unimpressed by the extent of those slopes, and we hate the piste congestion that results when most of the town's 35,000 visitors are crammed on to them. Crowding apart, keen intermediates spoilt by high-mileage French mega-resorts (and not up to the excellent off-piste) will simply find the usable area of slopes rather small.

boarding *Les Deux-Alpes has been attracting snowboarders for years, and has built up a good reputation. There's a specialist school and beginners start on the slopes just in front of the resort, learning to use the many drags at this level early on. There's a fun-park with a boarder-cross, a half-pipe, music and a barbecue higher up the mountain in the Toura sector, where most of the lifts are chairs. This is relocated up to the glacier in the summer (access is by T-bar or funicular), which is where the Mondial du Snowboard competition is hosted each year. There's some excellent off-piste in the local area for free-riders and the link to La Grave offers some of the best off-piste terrain in the world for advanced riders – a guide is recommended. With cheap and plentiful accommodation, and noisy, lively nightlife in the bars and discos, it's a well-deserved reputation.*

MOUNTAIN FACTS

Altitude 1300m-3570m	
Lifts	59
Pistes	200km
Green/Blue	58%
Red	21%
Black	21%
Art. snow	59 acres
Recco detectors used	

LIFT PASSES

2000/01 prices in francs

Super ski pass
Covers all lifts in Les Deux-Alpes, entry to swimming pool and skating rink.

Beginners 4 free lifts; 'Première trace' pass covers 19 lifts.

Main pass
1-day pass 195
6-day pass 960
(low season 865)

Senior citizens
Over 60: 6-day pass 720 (low season 648)

Children
Under 13: 6-day pass 720 (low season 648)
Under 4: free pass

Short-term passes
Half day: from 2pm 118

Notes 6-day pass includes one day's skiing in Alpe-d'Huez, Serre-Chevalier, Puy-St-Vincent and the Milky Way.

Alternative passes
2 limited area passes: 'Ski sympa' covers 22 lifts (98 per day), 'Grand ski' covers 33 lifts (156 per day). Les 2 Alpes/La Grave (1999/2000 prices – 250 per day) or a FF50 supplement for this with a two-day or longer pass.

The resort

Les Deux-Alpes is a narrow village sitting on a high, remote col. Access is from the Grenoble-Briançon road to the north or by gondola from Venosc. The village is a long, sprawling collection of hotels, apartments, bars and shops, most lining the busy main street and the parallel street that completes the one-way traffic system. Although there is no centre as such, and lifts are spread fairly evenly along the village, a couple of focal points are evident.

The resort has grown haphazardly over the years, and there is a wide range of building styles, from old chalets through monstrous 1960s blocks to more sympathetic recent developments. France does have worse-looking resorts, though not many. Fans point out that it looks better as you drive out than as you drive in, because all the apartment buildings have their balconies facing the remote southern end of the resort.

The lively ambience helps to distract you from the look of the place. Bars and nightclubs that originally catered for young French weekenders now cater equally well for growing numbers of young Brits in search of fun. The place is popular with Italians too, especially at weekends and in summer.

The mountains

For a big resort, Les Deux-Alpes has a disappointingly small piste area, despite recent improvements. Although extremely long and tall (it rises almost 2000m) the main sector is also very narrow, with just a few runs on the upper part of the mountain, served by a few long, efficient lifts. Many of the higher runs are easy and crowded, and most of the red and black runs just above the resort are steep, and tricky in the poor snow conditions that often apply. The area has considerable attractions for experts (largely off-piste). For novices, there are very easy green runs on the glacier, as well as good village nursery slopes.

THE SLOPES
Long, narrow and fragmented

The western **Pied Moutet** side of Les Deux-Alpes is relatively little-used, although recent improvements in the lift system and more artificial snow-cover should serve to entice more people to the area. It is served by lifts from various parts of town but reaches only 2100m. As well as the short runs back to town which get the morning sun, there's an attractive, longer north-facing red run down through the trees to the small village of Bons. This is one of only two tree-lined runs in Les Deux-Alpes – the other going down to another low village, Mont-de-Lans, and reachable from either sector.

On the eastern side of the resort, the broad, steep slope immediately above it offers a series of relatively short, testing runs, down to the nursery slopes ranged at the bottom. Most of these runs are now classified as black, and rightly so: they are usually mogulled, and often icy when not softened by the afternoon sun.

The ridge of **Les Crêtes** above the village has lifts and gentle runs along it, and behind it lies the deep, steep Combe de Thuit. Lifts span the combe to the main mid-mountain station at 2600m, at the foot of the slopes on **La Toura**. The middle section of the mountain, above and below this point, is made up primarily of blue cruising runs and is very narrow. At one point, there is essentially just a single run down the mountain – a broad ledge skirting the Combe de Thuit back to Les Crêtes. There is now the alternative of taking the roundabout (ie partly flat) blue Gours run to the bottom of the combe, where a chair-lift takes you up to Les Crêtes. This pleasant run passes the base of the Fée chair, serving an isolated (and neglected) black run.

The top **Glacier du Mont de Lans** section, served by drag-lifts and the warmer underground funicular, has some fine, very easy runs which afford great views and are ideal for beginners and the less adventurous. You can go from the top here all the way down to Mont-de-Lans – a descent of 2268m vertical which, as far as we know, is the world's biggest on-piste vertical. A walk (or snowcat tow) in the opposite direction takes you over to the splendid La Grave area (a supplement is charged for the lifts).

The six-day pass covers a day in each of Alpe-d'Huez, Serre-Chevalier, Puy-St-Vincent and the Milky Way resorts from Montgenèvre to Sauze d'Oulx. All are easily reached by car, road conditions permitting. Helicopter trips to Alpe-d'Huez are good value at around FF350 return. One recent reporter describes it as a 'must'.

SNOW RELIABILITY
Excellent on higher slopes
The snow on the higher slopes is normally very good, even in a poor winter – one of the main reasons for Les Deux-Alpes' popularity. Above 2200m most of the runs are north-facing, and the top glacier section guarantees good snow. You should worry more about bad weather shutting the lifts, or extremely low temperatures high up, than about snow shortage. But the runs just above the village face west, so they get a lot of afternoon sun and can be icy at the beginning and end of the day. Artificial snow on some of the lower slopes helps keep them usable.

FOR EXPERTS
Off-piste is the main attraction
With good snow and weather conditions, the area offers wonderful off-piste sport. There are several good off-piste runs within the lift network, including a number of variations from underneath the top stage of the Jandri Express down to the Thuit chair-lift. The best-known ones are marked on the piste map. The Fée chair built a few years ago opened up new off-piste possibilities into the Combe de Thuit. There are also more serious routes that end well outside the lift network, with verticals of over 2000m.

The Super Diable chair-lift, from the top of the Diable gondola, serves the steepest black run around. The brave can also try off-piste variations here between the rocks.

If the conditions are right, an outing across the glacier to the largely off-piste slopes of La Grave is a must.

FOR INTERMEDIATES
Limited cruising
Les Deux-Alpes can disappoint keen intermediates. A lot of the runs are either rather tough – some of the blues could be reds – or boringly bland. The steep runs just above the resort put off many. As one of our reporters (who classes himself as an 'advanced' skier) said, 'I myself fell from top to bottom. I was lucky. A girl in a different group broke her back. You cannot afford to be complacent here.'

The runs higher up generally have good snow, and aggressive intermediates can enjoy great fast cruising, especially on the mainly north-facing pistes served by the chair-lifts off to the sides. You can often pick gentle or steeper terrain in these bowls as you wish, but avid piste-bashers will explore all there is to offer in a couple of days. Most of our reporters took the chance of excursions

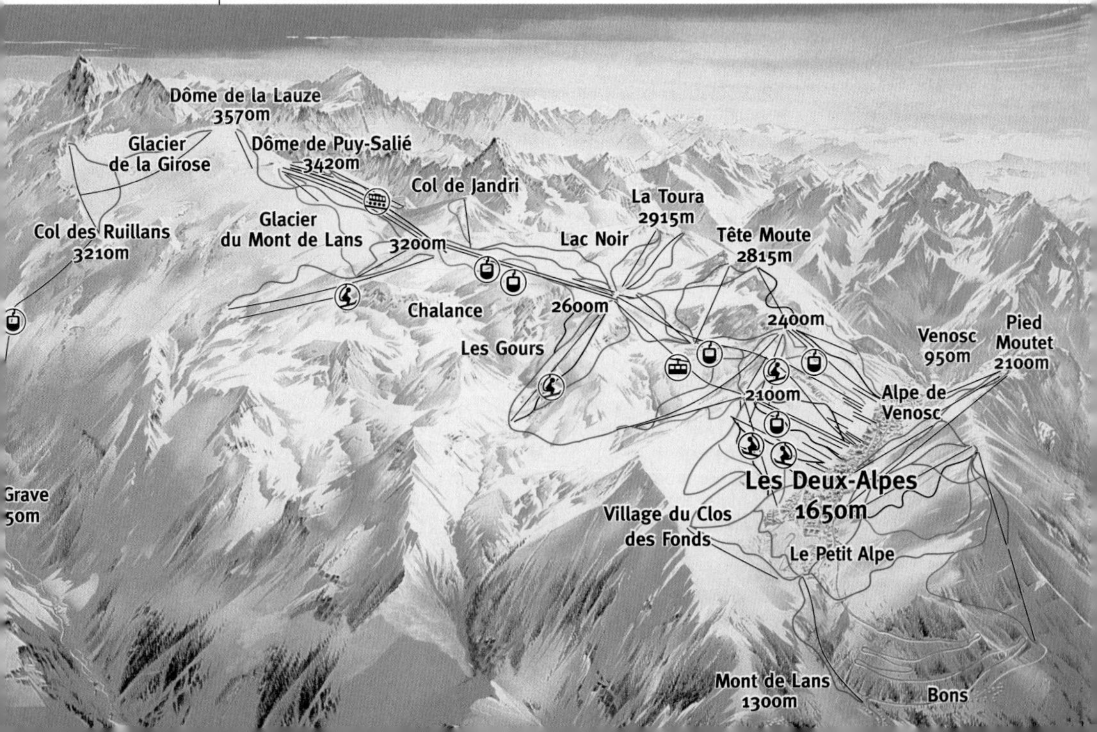

SCHOOLS/GUIDES

1999/2000 prices in francs

ESF
Classes 6 days
2¾hr: am; 2½hr: pm
6 mornings: 750
Children's classes
Ages: 6 to 12
6 mornings: 625
Private lessons
1hr over lunchtime or full day Sunday
190 for 1hr, for 1 to 3 people

International St-Christophe
Classes 6 days
2½hr: am or pm
6 mornings: 698
Children's classes
Ages: 6 to 12
6 mornings: 550
Private lessons
1hr over lunchtime
198 for 1hr, for 1 to 4 people

European Ski School
Classes 6 days
2hr: am or pm
Children's classes
Private lessons

CHILDCARE

Both ski schools run kindergartens on more-or-less identical terms – taking children aged 4 to 6 until 5pm. The ESF (476 792121) is slightly more expensive and does lunch only on request, but starts at 9.15 whereas the ESI de St Christophe (476 790421) starts at 9.30. The Crèche du Village offers an excellent service for babies from 6 months to 2 years, from 8.30 to 5.30.
The Garderie du Bonhomme de Neige is for children aged 2 to 6 years.
A list of babysitters is available from the tourist office.

to Alpe-d'Huez and Serre-Chevalier.

Less confident intermediates will love the quality of the snow and the gentleness of most of the runs on the upper mountain. Their problem might lie in finding the pistes too crowded, especially if snow is poor in other resorts and people are bussed in. At the end of the day, you can ride the Jandri Express down.

FOR BEGINNERS
Good slopes

The nursery slopes beside the village are spacious and gentle. The run along the ridge above them is excellent, too. The glacier also has a fine array of very easy slopes – but bear in mind that bad weather can close the lifts.

FOR CROSS-COUNTRY
Needs very low-altitude snow

There are three small, widely dispersed areas. La Petite Alpe, near the entrance to the village, has a couple of snowsure but very short trails. Given good snow, Venosc (950m), reached by a gondola down, has the only worthwhile picturesque ones. Total trail distance is 20km. You can ski the Mont de Lans glacier with a qualified guide.

QUEUES
Can be a problem

Les Deux-Alpes has a great deal of hardware to keep queues minimal. But the village is large, and queues at the mid-morning peak can be long for the Jandri Express and Diable gondolas. The Jandri queue moves quickly and, if you are headed for the top, it is worth using that lift to avoid further queues for the second stage. Problems can also occur when people are bussed in when snow is in short supply. At such times the lower slopes at Les Deux-Alpes are likely to be out of action too, causing even longer queues for the Jandri Express. The top lifts are prone to closure if it's windy, putting pressure on the lower lifts.

MOUNTAIN RESTAURANTS
On the up

There are mountain restaurants at all the major lift junctions, but they are generally pretty poor. La Pastorale, at the top of the Diable gondola, was for years the only recommendable place. But a few years ago the choice was doubled by the construction of the splendid Chalet de la Toura, in the middle of the domain at about 2600m, with a big terrace, a welcoming woody interior and efficient, if somewhat expensive, table-service throughout. And another new restaurant, the Refuge de la Fée, opened recently at the bottom of the new Fée lift. The Panoramique has been recommended.

SCHOOLS AND GUIDES
One of the better ESFs

The ski schools have a fairly good reputation for standards of tuition and English, although class sizes can be large. A recent report claims the European school was 'not very helpful'. Other specialised courses are available and include trips to other resorts.

FACILITIES FOR CHILDREN
Fine for babies

Babies can safely be entrusted to the village crèche. The kindergarten takes kids from two to six years, and there are chalet-based alternatives run by UK tour operators.

Staying there

Alpe de Venosc, at the southern end of town, has many of the nightspots and hotels, the most character, the fewest cars, the best shops and the Diable gondola up to the tough terrain around Tête Moute. More generally useful is the Jandri Express from the middle of the resort, where there is a popular outdoor ice rink and some good restaurants and bars. The village straggles north from here, becoming less convenient the further you go.

GETTING THERE

Air Lyon, transfer 3½hr. Grenoble, transfer 2hr. Chambéry, transfer 3hr. Geneva, transfer 4½hr.

Rail Grenoble (70km); 4 daily buses from station.

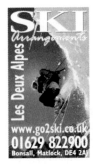

ACTIVITIES

Indoor 2 sports centres; Club Forme (squash, swimming pool, sauna, hot-tub), Tanking Centre (flotation chambers, physiotherapy, pressotherapy, sauna, hot-tub, Turkish baths)

Outdoor Ice skating, swimming pool, ice driving lessons, ice gliders (dodgems), snow-shoe excursions

TOURIST OFFICE

Postcode 38860
t +33 476 792200
f 476 790138
les2alp@les2alpes.com
www.2alpes.com

SNOWPIX.COM / CHRIS GILL

← The slopes of Pied Moutet don't get much traffic

HOW TO GO

Wide range of packages

Les Deux-Alpes has something for most tastes, including that rarity in high-altitude French resorts, reasonably priced hotels.

Chalets There are a number of catered chalet packages available from UK tour operators, but some use apartments.

Hotels There are over 30 hotels, of which the majority are 2-star or below.

((③ **Bérangère** Smartest in town, although dreary to look at, with an excellent restaurant and pool; on-piste, at less convenient north end of resort.

(② **Mariande** Highly recommended, especially for its 'excellent' five-course dinners. At Venosc end of resort.

(② **Chalet Mounier** Smartly modernised. Good reputation for its food, and well placed for the Diable bubble and nightlife.

(② **Souleil'or** Looks like a lift station, but pleasant and comfortable, and well placed for the Jandri Express gondola. The food and accommodation are 'fantastic' according to one reporter.

(② **Brunerie** 'Basic and cheerful', large 2-star with plenty of parking and quite well positioned.

Self-catering Many of the apartments are stuck out at the north end of the resort; it is well worth looking for more centrally situated ones.

EATING OUT

Plenty of choice

The village restaurants are much better than those up the mountain. The hotel Bérangère has an excellent restaurant and the Chalet Mounier has a high reputation. La Petite Marmite has good food and atmosphere at reasonable prices. Bel'Auberge does classic French and is highly recommended. La Patate and Crêpes à Gogo are recommended. Visitors on a budget can get a relatively cheap Italian meal at either La Vetrata or La Spaghetteria.

APRES-SKI

Unsophisticated fun

Les Deux-Alpes is one of the liveliest of French resorts, with plenty of bars, several of which stay open until the early hours. The Rodéo has a mechanical bucking bronco which attracts great numbers of rowdy après-skiers, many of them Brits. Mike's and the Windsor are other noisy British enclaves. Corrigans, Smokey Joe's and Le Baron are recommended. Bar Brésilien has 'great music and tremendous atmosphere – teeming with Brits and Italians'. The Avalanche is the most popular of the discos. There are quieter places around too – the 'cosy' Bleuets is recommended.

The resort has contrived a couple of ways of dining at altitude – you can snowmobile to the glacier and back, eating on the way (you're allowed one glass of wine), or at full moon you can ski or board back to town after dinner – that must be quite something.

OFF THE SLOPES

Not recommended

Les Deux-Alpes is not a particularly good choice for people not hitting the slopes. It is quiet during the day, the shopping is uninspiring and the village is rather cut off, with little public transport for excursions. The pretty valley village of Venosc is well worth a visit by gondola, and you can take a scenic helicopter flight to Alpe-d'Huez (though there's even less to amuse you there). For the active there are plenty of sports facilities. Only one of the decent mountain restaurants is easily accessible to pedestrians, and skiers or boarders will be very reluctant to descend the icy lower slopes to the village for lunch.

STAYING DOWN THE VALLEY

Worth considering

Close to the foot of the final ascent to Les Deux-Alpes are two near-ideal places for anyone thinking of travelling around to Alpe-d'Huez, La Grave and Serre-Chevalier, both Logis de France – the cheerful 13-room Cassini at Le Freney, and the even more appealing 10-room Panoramique, at Mizoën.

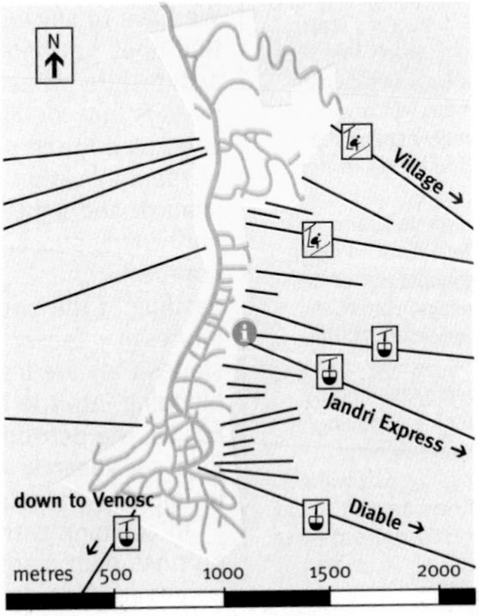

Flaine 1600m

Wonderful ski area; bleak buildings but cute alternatives

WHAT IT COSTS

3

HOW IT RATES

The slopes

Snow	****
Extent	****
Experts	****
Intermediates	*****
Beginners	*****
Convenience	*****
Queues	****
Restaurants	**

The rest

Scenery	****
Resort charm	*
Off-slope	*

What's new

Flaine's lift company has been taken over and the new owners are investing heavily.

1999/2000 saw three new chair-lifts in the Vernant bowl below Les Grands Vans – two high-speed six-seaters and one fixed grip quad. These improved connections between Flaine and the outlying villages enormously.

2000/01 sees the old slow chair-lift from Flaine Forêt to Les Grands Vans replaced by France's first high-speed eight-person chair, which will hugely speed the journey out of the village. There will also be more cabins on the Grandes Platières gondola out of the village, cutting the queues. In Morillon a four-person chair will be speeded up by adding a moving carpet to help loading. Sixt will get a new drag-lift to link the Cascades piste to its own small area of slopes.

- ➕ Big, varied area, with off-piste challenges for experts as well as extensive intermediate terrain
- ➕ Huge recent investment in new lifts
- ➕ Reliable snow in the main bowl
- ➕ Compact, convenient, mainly car-free village, right on the slopes
- ➕ Alternative of staying in traditional villages elsewhere in ski area
- ➕ Excellent facilities for children
- ➕ Scenic setting, and glorious views
- ➕ Very close to Geneva airport

- ➖ Bleak 1960s Bauhaus buildings are architecturally listed – but not to everyone's taste
- ➖ Main Flaine bowl has only a few short runs below the tree-line, so bad weather can be a problem
- ➖ Links from one area to another are prone to closure by high winds
- ➖ Not much nightlife
- ➖ Little to do off the slopes

So long as you don't care about the uncompromising architecture or narrow range of nightlife, Flaine has a lot going for it. Many visitors, especially those with children, love it – and many people who haven't tried it would enjoy it.

There is some very pleasant and convenient accommodation. If you want to spend a holiday with your kids, there is everything to help you – and the ski schools have improved in recent years. Flaine has slopes that intermediates will love, and lots of them; with its links to Samoëns, Morillon and Les Carroz, the Grand Massif lives up to its name. Flaine caters well for beginners too, with free access to nursery slope lifts. But there is also challenging terrain for experts – particularly for those prepared to take guidance and go off-piste.

boarding *Flaine suits boarders quite well – there's lots of varied terrain and plenty of off-piste with interesting nooks and crannies, including woods outside the main bowl. The key lifts are all now chairs or gondolas – with few unavoidable drag-lifts. There's a fun-park just below Les Grands Vans. The ESF runs a special 'Mini surf park' for kids, a great idea for a family-oriented resort like this. BlackSide is the local specialist shop, in the central Forum.*

The resort

We have to say we fall in the group that does not find Bauhaus architecture attractive. The concrete massifs that are Flaine's buildings were conceived in the sixties as 'an example of the application of the principle of shadow and light'. They look particularly shocking from the approach road – a mass of blocks nestling at the bottom of a the impressive snowy bowl. From the slopes they are less obtrusive, blending into the rocky grey hillside. For us, the outdoor sculptures by Picasso, Vasarely and Dubuffet do little to improve Flaine's austere ambience.

In common with other French Alpine purpose-built resorts, Flaine has improved its looks in recent years. The relatively new development of Hameau-de-Flaine is built in a much more attractive chalet style – but is inconveniently situated a good 15-minute walk or a short bus-ride from the slopes. Fortunately, the regular bus service is 'excellent'.

Flaine's planners made no mistakes with the layout. There is supermarket and speciality food shopping close to most of the accommodation; sports hire shops are a short hop away; the lifts are easy to get to, and trips to organise lift passes, school and so on are no problem. It is also easy to get to – only 70km from Geneva, and about 90 minutes from the airport.

There are two parts to the main resort. The hotels, and some apartments, are set in the lower part, Forum. The focus of this area is a

MOUNTAIN FACTS

Altitude	700m-2480m
Lifts	82
Pistes	265km
Green/Blue	39%
Red	46%
Black	15%
Artificial snow	5km
Recco detectors used	

snow-covered square with buildings on three sides, the open fourth side blending with the slopes. You have to watch out for skiers and boarders when you're strolling from one side to the other. Flaine Forêt, up the hillside and linked by lift, has its own bars and shops and most of the apartment accommodation.

There are children all over the place; they are catered for with play areas, and the resort is supposed to be traffic-free. This has become rather lax, in fact, and there is a fair amount of traffic; but the central Forum itself, leading to the pistes, is pretty safe.

There are long-term plans to expand Flaine's bed base significantly. Intrawest (a Canadian company which owns Whistler and several other resorts with attractive villages) is now part owner of Flaine so let's hope they bring their flair for attractive village development to France.

The mountains

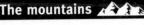

With its 265km of pistes, the Grand Massif claims to be the third largest resort in France (behind the Three Valleys and Espace Killy – the Franco-Swiss Portes du Soleil doesn't count). Certainly it is a genuinely impressive area, with plenty of scope for any standard of skier or boarder, provided you can get to all of it – the greater part of the domain lies outside the main Flaine bowl.

THE SLOPES
A big white playground

The day begins for most people at the **Grandes Platières** high-capacity stand-up gondola, which speeds you in a single long stage up the north face of the Flaine bowl to the 2480m high-point of the Grand Massif, and a magnificent view of Mont Blanc.

Most of the runs are reds (though there are some blues curling away to the right as you look down the mountain, and one direct black). There are essentially four or five main ways down the barren, treeless, rolling terrain back to Flaine, or to chairs in the middle of the wilderness going back to the summit.

On the far right, the easy 14km, picturesque Cascades blue run (one of the longest in the Alps) leads away from the lift system behind the Tête Pelouse and down to the outskirts of Sixt at 770m (giving a vertical drop of over 1700m). There is no lift back but there is a regular shuttle-bus service to the lifts at Samoëns or Morillon. Sixt has its own little west-facing area offering red and black slopes of 700m

SNOWPIX.COM / CHRIS GILL

Flaine's Bauhaus architecture is not to our taste but its interesting, varied and extensive slopes most certainly are ↓

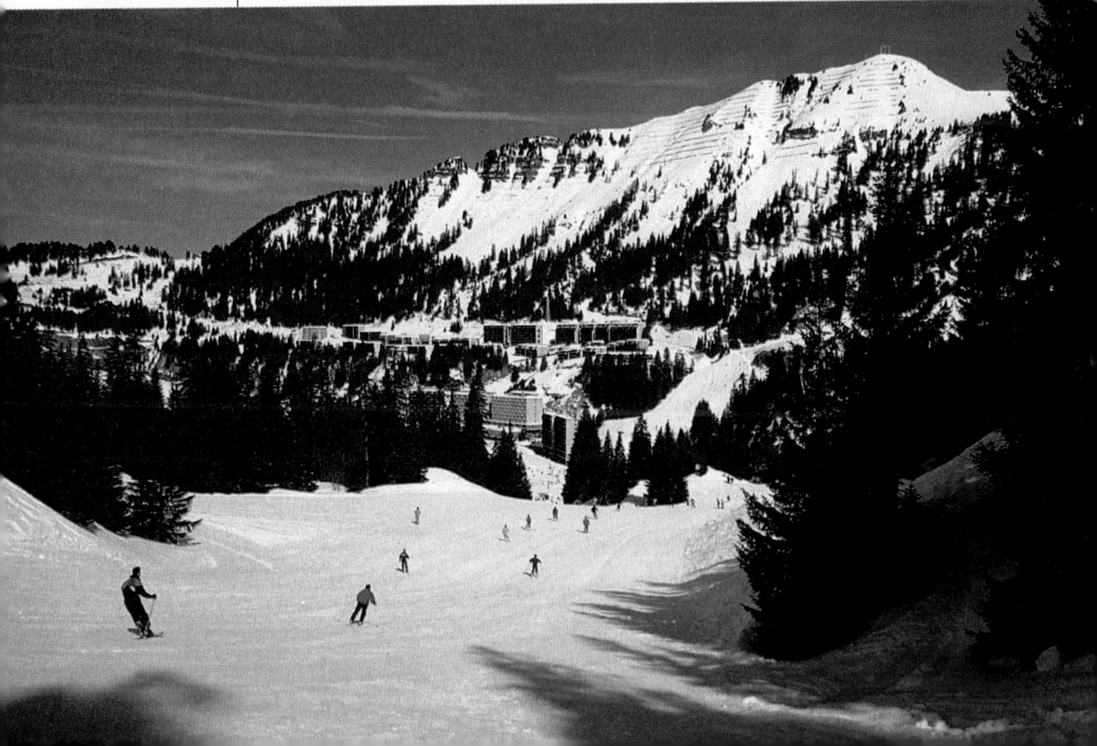

LIFT PASSES

2000/01 prices in francs

Grand Massif
Covers all the lifts in Flaine, Les Carroz, Morillon, Samoëns and Sixt.

Beginners Four free lifts. Ski pass for beginners covers 3 more lifts (about 82 per day for adults, 59 for children).

Main pass
1-day pass 193
6-day pass 970

Senior citizens
Over 60: 6-day pass 776 (20% off)
Over 75: free pass

Children
Under 12: 6-day pass 679 (30% off)
Under 5: free pass

Notes Discount on all ski-passes for 12- to 15-year-olds: 6-day 728 (25% off).

Alternative passes
Flaine area only (1-day pass 168 for adults, 118 for children).

vertical – linked to the Cascades run by drag-lift for the 2000/01 season.

On the other side of the Tête Pelouse, a broad cat-walk leads to the experts-only **Gers** bowl. At the bottom, a flat trail links with the Cascades run.

Back at Platières, the alternative is to head left down the long red Méphisto (many of the runs in this area have diabolic names – Lucifer, Belzebuth etc) to the **Aujon** area. This opens up another sector of the bowl, again mostly red runs but with some blues further down. The lower slopes here are used as slalom courses. This sector is also reachable by gondola or drag-lifts from below the resort.

The pistes in the Flaine bowl are mostly punchy medium-length runs. For a collection of longer cruises, head out of the bowl via the Grands Vans chair (a new high-speed eight-seater for 2000/01), reached from Forum by means of a slow bucket lift (aka télébenne or 'yogurt pots'). From the top, you go over the edge of the bowl and have a choice of three different resorts to head towards, each with its own lifts and runs. Getting around this bowl below Les Grands Vans was made much quicker last season by three new high-speed chair-lifts.

The lie of the land hereabouts is complicated, and the piste map does not represent it clearly. In good snow there is a choice of blues and reds winding down to **Les Carroz** (1140m) or **Morillon** (700m), the latter with a half-way point at 1100m. While there is a choice of blue, red and black runs on the top section above **Samoëns 1600,** the runs below here to Vercland are testing blacks and reds.

Arrival back in Flaine can cause a problem: some reporters have complained that it's difficult to get between the top of the resort and Forum. The trick is to loop round away from the buildings and approach from under the gondola – or catch the télébenne down.

It is possible to visit Chamonix and neighbouring resorts by road, or even to make a quick trip to Italy through the Mont Blanc tunnel (if it is open).

SNOW RELIABILITY
Usually keeps its whiteness

The main part of Flaine's slopes lie on the wide north- and north-west-facing flank of the Grandes Platières. Its direction, along with a decent height, means that it keeps the snow it receives. There is snowmaking on the greater part of the Aujon sector and on the nursery slopes. The runs towards Samoëns 1600 and Morillon 1100 are north-facing too, and some lower parts have snowmaking, but below here can be tricky or impossible. The Les Carroz runs are west-facing and can suffer from strong afternoon sun, but one of the runs has snowmaking. Recent reports have indicated a marked improvement in grooming.

FOR EXPERTS
Great fun with guidance

Flaine's family-friendly reputation tends to obscure the fact that it has some seriously testing terrain. But much of it is off-piste and, although some of Flaine's off-piste runs look like they can safely be explored without guidance, this impression is mistaken. The Flaine bowl is riddled with rock crevasses and potholes, and should be treated with the same caution that you would use on a glacier. There have been some tragic cases of off-piste skiers coming across nasty surprises, including a British skier falling to his death only yards from the piste.

All the black pistes on the map deserve their grading. The Diamant Noir, down the line of the main gondola, is a testing 850m descent, tricky because of moguls, narrowness and other people rather than because of great steepness; the first pitch down from the summit plateau is the most unnerving, with spectators applauding from the overhead chair-lift.

To the left of the Diamant Noir as you look down are several short but steep off-piste routes through the crags of the Grandes Platières.

The Lindars Nord chair serves a shorter slope that often has the best snow in the area, and some seriously steep gradients if you look for them.

The Gers drag-lift, outside the main bowl beyond Tête Pelouse, serves great expert-only terrain. The piste going down the right of the drag is a proper black, but by departing from it you can find slopes of up to 45°. To the left of the drag is the impressive main Gers bowl – a great horseshoe of about 550m vertical, powder or moguls top to bottom, all off-piste. You can choose your gradient, from steep to very steep. As you look down the bowl, you can see more adventurous ways into the bowl from the Grands Vans and Tête de Veret lifts.

SCHOOLS/GUIDES

2000/01 prices in francs

ESF
Classes 6 days
4hr: 10am-noon and 2.30-4.30
6 full days: 735
Children's classes
Ages: 3 to 12
6 full days: 610
Private lessons
1hr, 2hr or 6hr
200 for 1hr, for 1 to 2 people

International
Classes 6 days
3hr: 9.30-12.30
6 full days: 685
Children's classes
Ages: 6 to 12
6 full days: 625
Private lessons
1hr, 2hr or full day
190 for 1hr, for 1 to 2 people

Flaine Super Ski
Advanced skiers only
450 908288

Independent instructors
Hired by the day, hour or week; contact Guy Pezet
450 478454

There are further serious pistes on the top lifts above Samoëns 1600.

Touring is a possibility in the Desert de Platé area, behind the Grandes Platières, and there are some scenic off-piste routes from which you can be retrieved by helicopter – notably the Combe des Foges, next to Gers.

FOR INTERMEDIATES
Something for everyone

Flaine is ideal for confident intermediates, with a great variety of pistes (and usually the bonus of good snow conditions, at least above Flaine itself). The diabolically named reds which dominate the Flaine bowl are not really as hellish as their names imply – they tend to gain their status from short steep sections rather than overall difficulty, and they're great for improving technique. There are gentler cruises from the top of the mountain – Cristal, taking you to the Perdrix chair, or Serpentine, all the way home. The blues at Aujon are excellent for confidence-building, but the drag serving them is not.

The connections with the slopes outside the main bowl are graded blue but at least one blue-run reporter has found them tricky. Once outside the bowl, all intermediates will enjoy the long tree-lined runs down to Les Carroz, as long as the snow is good. You can choose between red routes or slightly easier blues, one of which goes under and over the road out of Flaine, allowing races with the coach drivers. The Morillon slopes are also excellent intermediate terrain.

FOR BEGINNERS
Very good

There are excellent nursery slopes right by the village, served by free lifts which make a pass unnecessary until you are ready to go higher up the mountain. There are no long green runs to progress to in the Flaine bowl – there is one above Morillon – but there are one or two gentle blues (see 'For intermediates').

CROSS-COUNTRY
Very fragmented

The Grand Massif claims 64km of cross-country tracks but only about 10km of that total is around Flaine itself. The majority is on the valley floor and dependent on low snow. There are extensive tracks between Morillon and Les Carroz, with some tough uphill sections. Samoëns 1600 has its own tracks and makes the best base for cross-country enthusiasts.

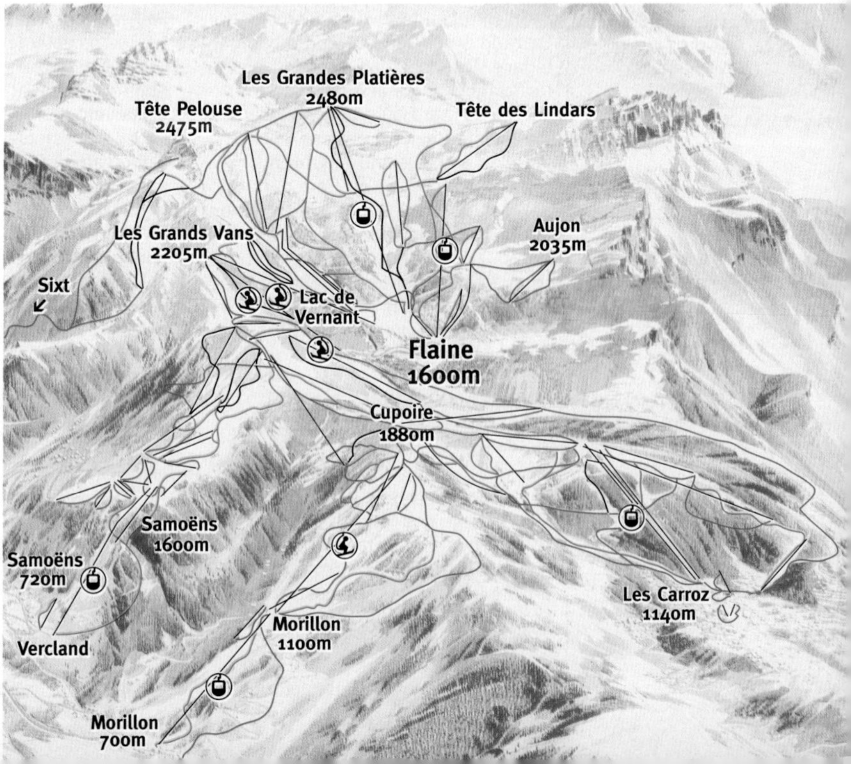

CHILDCARE

Both schools operate ski kindergartens. The ESF's Rabbit Club (450 908100) takes children aged 3 to 12, until 5pm. The SEI's Green Mouse Club (450 908441) takes children aged 3 to 12, until 5pm. Club Med Flaine (450 908166) has a nursery for babies aged from 4 months. The ESF's Rabbit Club will pick up children from Club Med for lessons, and deliver them at the end of the class. There is also an independent nursery, the Petits Loups (450 908782) for children aged from 6 months to 4 years.

GETTING THERE

Air Geneva, transfer 1½hr.

Rail Cluses (30km); regular bus service.

ACTIVITIES

Indoor Top Form centre (swimming pool complex with sauna, solarium, gymnasium, massage), arts and crafts gallery, cinema, auditorium, concerts, indoor climbing wall, cultural centre with library (some books in English)
Outdoor Natural ice-rink, snow-shoe excursions, hang-gliding, paragliding paraskiing, helicopter rides, snow scooters, high mountain outings, ice-driving car circuit

QUEUES
Few real problems

The massive recent investment in new lifts (see 'What's new') has eliminated the main trouble-spots. When the resort is full, the Grandes Platières gondola is prone to queues at the start of the day, but it is an efficient lift and the queue moves quickly – and more cabins are being added for this winter.

Reporters say other queues are rare, although some of the lifts are still somewhat antiquated, and the area does suffer a weekend influx – not surprising, given the ease of access.

MOUNTAIN RESTAURANTS
Back to base, or quit the bowl

In the Flaine bowl, there are few restaurants above the resort's upper outskirts. The Désert Blanc, at the top station, is a run-of-the-mill, two-room self-service snackery, with a terrace overlooking Mont Blanc. The Blanchot, at the bottom of the Serpentine run, is popular and rustic, with basic food.

At Forum level, across the piste from the gondola, is a pair of chalets containing the welcoming Michet, with very good Savoyard food and table service, and the self-service Eloge – friendly but with very limited food. Up at Forêt level, Chalet Bissac has a good atmosphere, traditional decor and excellent plain food. The nearby Cascade is self-service, with a good terrace. The Chalet L'Epicéa has a rustic atmosphere and rave reviews.

Outside the Flaine bowl, we loved the remote Chalet du Lac de Gers (book in advance and ring for a snowcat to tow you up from part way down the Cascades run) – simple food but splendid isolation and views of the frozen lake. Reporters recommend the Igloo above Morillon, the Chalet des Molliets beside the road up from Les Carroz and the Oreade at the top of the gondola from Les Carroz.

SCHOOLS AND GUIDES
Mixed reviews

The few reports we've had in recent years have been mixed; the ESF and International schools' class sizes can still be large and English patchy. 'Taught by three or four different instructors in the week', 'booked five private lessons and was sent to non-English speaker on first lesson!' There are several small specialist schools, of which Flaine Super Ski is one, and a group of independent instructors.

FACILITIES FOR CHILDREN
Parents' paradise?

Flaine prides itself on being a family resort, and the number of English-speaking children around is a bonus.

Club Med Flaine has good childcare facilities open to residents only. The Petits Loups nursery takes children from 6 months to 4 years. Some other accommodation units have kids' clubs.

Staying there

As a purpose-built resort, Flaine is convenient regardless of where you stay, except in Hameau-de-Flaine.

HOW TO GO
Plenty of apartments

Accommodation is overwhelmingly in self-catering apartments.
Chalets There are few catered chalet options, but they include a couple of attractively traditional Scandinavian-style huts in Hameau.
Hotels There are just two normal hotels plus a Club Med and Hotel Club de Flaine, all located around Forum.
(((3) **Totem** The smartest hotel and good value for money. Modern, stylish, great views of Aujon skiing.
((2) **Aujon** Large and impersonal, basic rooms, good food, good value, liked by most visitors.
Self-catering Most popular with Brits are the recently renovated Forêt and Grand Massif apartment buildings. Apartments are attractively woody inside and there are hotel facilities such as a restaurant, bar and kindergarten. But the best apartments, are out at Hameau.

EATING OUT
Not many stars

The Perdrix Noire in Forêt is a good bet – smart, busy but friendly. The Michet (see 'Mountain restaurants') is open in the evening. The Trattoria is a good Italian, Chez la Jeanne the best pizza restaurant. Chez Daniel offers a good range of Savoyard specialities.

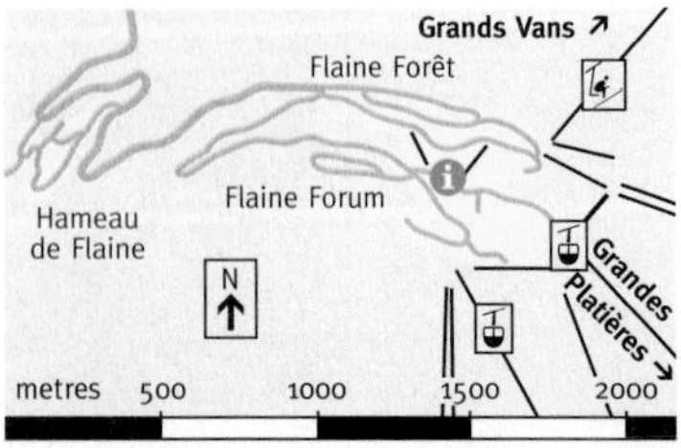

The Cîmes Rock is 'excellent, but it's best to go early because it gets very busy' (see below). .

APRES-SKI

Signs of life

Recent reports suggest that the après-ski scene is picking up. The resort is no longer limited to family groups, and some bars show signs of life.

The White Grouse pub is boisterous: extreme sports videos compete with rock music and punters trying to get pints in before the end of happy hour.

Later, the more French Cîmes Rock is liveliest, with bands or karaoke. The 'seedy' Diamant Noir pool hall is open late, the Chaintre disco later.

OFF THE SLOPES

Curse of the purpose-built

As with most purpose-built resorts, there are few walks, and no town to explore. Not recommended for people who don't want to hit the slopes. But there is a great ice-driving circuit where you can take a spin (literally) in your own car or, more sensibly, have a lesson in theirs (as we did). Snowmobile tours and the weekly torchlight descent are popular.

UK Representative

Erna Low Consultants
9 Reece Mews
London SW7 3HE
t 020 7584 2841
f 020 7589 9531
info@ernalow.co.uk
www.ernalow.co.uk

TOURIST OFFICE

Postcode 74300
t +33 450 908001
f 450 908626
flaine@laposte.fr
www.flaine.com

Les Carroz 1140m

This is a spacious, sunny, traditional, family resort where life revolves around the village square with its pavement cafés and interesting little shops. It has a 'lived-in' feel, with more animation than Flaine – 'a delight,' says a recent visitor, who recommends the hotel Arbaron for food, service and views.

The gondola and chair-lift go straight into the Grand Massif area, but there's a steep 300m walk up from the centre – the nursery drag is a help.

Apartments make up a high percentage of the beds available, but there are plenty of hotels.

The village centre has a pleasant atmosphere, and the ski school's torchlit descent is not to be missed – it starts off with fireworks and ends with vin chaud and live jazz in the square.

Samoëns 720m

This is the only resort in France to be listed as a 'Monument Historique'. Medieval fountains, rustic old buildings, an ancient church – it's all there, although one recent reporter feels that it doesn't add up to a more charming village than Les Contamines, say. Despite the village's recent growth on the outskirts, the traditional-style bars and restaurants still give you a feel for 'real' rural France. A reporter recommends the Pizzeria Louisiana for its wood oven pizzas and 'highly alcoholic' ice creams.

The slopes are a bus-ride away, but you can stay near the lift. The local terrain is generally testing and is, on the whole, best suited to confident skiers – though there is a good beginners' area at Samoëns 1600.

Morillon 700m

Not quite in the Samoëns league, but still a pretty rustic village, Morillon makes an excellent base, with an efficient gondola (and a road) up to the mid-mountain mini-resort of Morillon 1100. Up here there is a large and 'delightful' ski kindergarten plus good slopes for adult beginners.

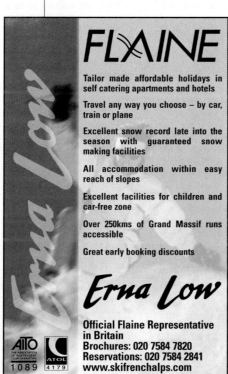

La Grave 1450m

A superb mountain for good skiers and free-riders

WHAT IT COSTS

(3)

HOW IT RATES

The slopes

Snow	***
Extent	**
Experts	*****
Intermediates	*
Beginners	*
Convenience	***
Queues	****
Restaurants	**

The rest

Scenery	****
Resort charm	***
Off-slope	*

What's new

La Grave does not change much, and that is half the charm of the place.

MOUNTAIN FACTS

Altitude	1400m-3550m
Lifts	4
Pistes	5km
Green/Blue	100%

(This figure relates to pistes; practically all the skiing – at least 90% – is off-piste)

Artificial snow	none

Recco detectors used

TOURIST OFFICE

Postcode 05320
t +33 476 799005
f 476 799165
o.t.la.meije@wanadoo.fr
www.lameije.com

La Grave enjoys legendary status among experts. It's a quiet old village with around 500 visitor beds and just one serious lift – a small stop-start gondola serving a high, wild and predominantly off-piste mountainside. The result: an exciting, refreshingly crowd-free area. Strictly, you ought to have a guide.

THE RESORT

La Grave is an unspoilt mountaineering village set on a steep hillside facing the impressive glaciers of majestic La Meije. It's rather drab, and the busy road through to Briançon doesn't help. But it still has a rustic feel, and prices in the handful of small hotels, food shops and bars are low by resort standards. Storms close the slopes on average two days a week – so a car is useful for access to other resorts.

THE MOUNTAIN

A slow two-stage 'pulse' gondola (with an extra station at a pylon halfway up the lower stage) ascends into the **slopes** and finishes at 3200m. Above that, a short walk and a drag-lift give access to a second drag serving twin blue runs on a glacier slope of about 350m vertical – from here you can ski to Les Deux-Alpes. But the reason that people come here is to explore the legendary slopes back towards La Grave. These slopes offer no defined, patrolled, avalanche-protected pistes – but there are two marked itinéraires of 1400m vertical down to the pylon lift station at 1800m. Top to bottom, the mountain offers a vertical of 2150m.

The Chancel route is mostly of red-run gradient; the Vallons de la Meije is more testing but not too steep. People do take these routes without a guide or avalanche protection equipment, but we couldn't possibly recommend it.

There are many more demanding runs away from the itinéraires, including couloirs that range from the straightforward to the seriously hazardous, and long descents from the glacier to the valley road below the village, with return by taxi, bus, or strategically parked car. The dangers are considerable, and guidance is essential. You can also descend southwards to St-Christoph, returning by bus and the lifts of Les Deux-Alpes.

The chances of powder **snow** on the high, north-facing slopes are good.

Only **experts** should contemplate a stay here – and then only if prepared to deal with bad weather by sitting tight or struggling over the Col du Lautaret to the woods of Serre-Chevalier. The itinéraires get tracked into a piste-like state, and adventurous **intermediates** could tackle the Chancel. **Beginners** tricked into coming here can go up the valley to Le Chazelet.

There are no special **snowboarding** facilities. There is a total of 30km of **cross-country** loops in the area.

There are short **queues** only at weekends – at the bottom station first thing, and at the mid-station later.

Surprisingly, there are three decent **mountain restaurants**; the best is the refuge on the Chancel itinéraire.

There are a dozen or so **guides** in the village, offering a wide range of services through their bureau.

Children's babysitting can be arranged through the tourist office.

STAYING THERE

There are several simple **hotels**. The Edelweiss is a comfortable, friendly 2-star with a cosy bar and restaurant. **Self-catering** accommodation is bookable through the tourist office.

Most people **eat** in their hotels, though there are alternatives. The standard tea-time **après-ski** gathering place is the central Glaciers bar, known to habitués as chez Marcel. O'Neill's Irish pub and Le Vieux Guide are busy later. The Candy bar is another option.

Isola 2000

2000m

Snow right on your doorstep, just above the Côte d'Azur

An EasyJet flight and a short (90km) drive from Nice makes Isola easy and cheap to reach, even for a weekend visit. It has slope-side accommodation and some snowsure slopes. Like many purpose-built French resorts, it has been extended in a sympathetic style but its original buildings are irredeemably block-like.

WHAT IT COSTS

(4)

HOW IT RATES

The slopes

Snow	***
Extent	**
Experts	**
Intermediates	***
Beginners	*****
Convenience	*****
Queues	***
Restaurants	**

The rest

Scenery	***
Resort charm	*
Off-slope	*

What's new

For 1999/2000 two new blue slopes were added. And for 2000/01 the fun-park will be improved.

MOUNTAIN FACTS

Altitude	1840m-2610m
Lifts	24
Pistes	120km
Green/Blue	54%
Red	35%
Black	11%
Artificial snow	13km

Recco detectors used

UK Representative

Erna Low Consultants. For details see La Plagne chapter.

TOURIST OFFICE

Postcode 06420
t +33 493 231515
f 493 231425
isola@cote-dazur.com
www.isola-2000.com

THE RESORT

Isola is one of the many small, high, purpose-built resorts in the French Alps, but it is further south than the rest, with access via Nice. On clear days, they say, you can see the sea.

Built by a British property company at the end of the 1960s, Isola aimed itself squarely at the family market. Front de Neige is a complex of block-like apartments, shops, restaurants, bars and a couple of hotels that makes up the core of the resort, with nursery slopes and lifts on the doorstep.

Various owners have since worked hard to glamorise the image of the resort with new hamlets of more luxurious, wood-clad apartment blocks.

THE MOUNTAINS

The piste map shows three areas of **slopes**, St-Sauveur, Pélevos and Levant. Really it is one linked area in a horseshoe shape around the resort. Due to the great base height of Isola – the lowest of the slopes is at 1840m – most of the runs are above the tree line. The gondola from the centre of the complex to Pélevos at 2320m gives access to The St-Sauveur sector too. Levant is linked but on the opposite side of the resort and reached directly by piste and chair-lift from the centre. There is a **snowboard** fun-park and half-pipe.

Isola can get different weather from other major French resorts. Sometimes it has masses of **snow** when the rest of the French Alps have none; at other times it misses out. Extra snowmaking was installed a couple of seasons ago. Regular visitors say that they never find all the lifts open, but there is always snow – and plenty of sun. The north-facing slopes of St-Sauveur and Pélevos keep their snow well.

Experts head for St-Sauveur, which has Isola's longest and most challenging runs, as well as its best off-piste runs. There are good reds and blacks here – and from the chair to Mont Mené. Heli-skiing is available too. The Pélevos area is an interesting cluster of red and blue runs where **intermediates** can take their pick of difficulty. The more adventurous can try the challenging St-Sauveur sector, with its choice of steep reds and blacks. The south-facing slopes below the Col de la Lombarde, in the Levant sector, are also intermediate.

There are excellent nursery slopes for **beginners** right in the heart of the resort, and an easy progression to greens, then blues, nearby.

There is a 4km loop just above the village, but little else to recommend Isola to **cross-country** enthusiasts.

The fast quad from the centre has done away with **queues** for the main gondola at peak times. Weekend day trippers from Nice can sometimes cause bottlenecks.

There is only a handful of **mountain restaurants**. The best is the excellent Génisserie at the foot of St-Sauveur.

The ESF **ski school** has a good reputation for its English and its tuition but, as ever, class size is variable.

Isola has an all-day crèche, and a snow-garden for **children** starting out. English is widely spoken.

STAYING THERE

Accommodation is largely in **self-catering** apartments, but there are several **hotels**. The 3-star Pas du Loup is next to the slopes and has been recommended by a reporter for its friendly welcome and helpful service. Of the two 4-stars, the small chalet-style Diva is luxurious and expensive.

With few UK operators serving Isola, the **après-ski** scene is quite staid. It picks up in high season and weekends, with visitors from the Riviera.

Despite its Aquavallée pool complex, sports centre and ice-driving circuit, Isola is hardly the place for someone not taking to the slopes. But trips to the Riviera and the casinos in Monte Carlo are easy.

Maurienne valley

Everything from cute old villages to 1960s monstrosities

WHAT IT COSTS

3

What's new

Valloire/Valmeinier

A new eight-person gondola, Crêt de la Brive, from the centre of Valloire up towards Crey du Quart, was installed last season. You still need to take a chair to get to the very top and the runs down into Valmeinier. Snowmaking has been extended in Valmeinier.

A new fast quad is being installed in Valmeinier – from Les Déserts up to Les Inversins (near the top of the Jeux chair) – and two runs down are being added. A blue run from Le Grand Plateau – Valloire's highest point – down into Valmeinier is planned.

Valfréjus

A new lift pass covering Valfréjus, Aussois and La Norma (165km) will be in operation for 2000/01.

Val-Cenis

Snowmaking was expanded last season – from the top of the gondola.

A new six-pack, replacing the Solert drag-lift, and a new two-seater chair-lift are planned for 2000/01 – the new lifts will access a new red and a blue piste, adding 5km more to the total piste area. A second snow park is also planned. A new public swimming pool and ice rink are being built in Lanslevillard.

Go to the southern extremity of the Val-Thorens piste network or set off ski-touring northwards from La Grave, and you come to the same place: the Maurienne valley – a great curving trench cut by a river appropriately called the Arc. This backwater has over 20 winter resorts, but only a handful have any international market – Valloire the best known among them. They range from pleasant old valley villages to convenience resorts purpose-built in the 1960s. About all they have in common is piste and lift networks that are rather limited in size and prices that are low by French standards. And participation in a special five-day pass deal that allows you a day each in any of the resorts. We gave it a try, with mixed results. The three resorts covered below left a favourable impression. The others are in our directory at the back of the book.

Many of these resorts are close enough to be linked together – and, in the boom years of the 1970s, grand plans were formulated to link Valfréjus with Valmeinier and Valloire to the west, and with Bardonecchia in Italy. For a while, Michelin maps showed a lift going right up to the Pointe du Fréjus on the Italian border; Valfréjus painted 'Bardonecchia' on its gondola cabins. But the lift was never built.

A trip to the Maurienne can also include a visit to Europe's highest resort and some of its best snow: Orelle (a non-village in the valley bottom) has a big gondola up to the Val-Thorens lift network.

Different though they are, in winter all of these resorts are of little appeal to anyone not intent on skiing or boarding.

VALLOIRE 1430m

Valloire is the best known of the Maurienne resorts internationally, and it offers the most extensive slopes, shared with the twin stations of Valmeinier 1500 and 1800. The village has a rustic French feel to it and retains a life as a farming community. The resort is quite a drive up from the valley. Despite considerable development, it has retained a feeling of 'real' France, complete with impressive old church, crêperies, fromageries, reasonable prices, villagey atmosphere and friendly locals (many, surprisingly, speaking some English).

The 150km of piste are spread over three similar-sized, lightly wooded areas: Sétaz – shady slopes, part open and part wooded, directly above the village and served by gondola to Thimel at mid-mountain; Crey du Quart – broad, open, west-facing slopes reachable from the village by chair-lift or a new gondola, or from Sétaz by chair-lift; and Valmeinier – mainly west-facing slopes in the next valley (beyond Crey du Quart), with just four main lifts. The slopes are almost entirely intermediate; Les Karellis (a 45-minute drive) is better for more taxing runs (and for superior snow and scenery). There are 40km of cross-country trails.

Reliable snow-cover is not a strong point. Despite snow-guns on many of the lower slopes, ensuring that most of the area is reliably accessible, some important links – notably the runs down to Valmeinier 1500 from Le Crey du Quart – can suffer from poor snow. The tree runs in the Sétaz area and the Valmeinier slopes hold their snow well. Grooming is said to be good.

There are plenty of intermediate options in all three sectors. The Crey du Quart section is particularly good for an easy day. Sétaz has several black runs, but they don't represent a challenge for experts – the mogul field down to Valmeinier 1500 is steeper.

The limited village nursery areas are adequate in low season when snow-cover is good. Otherwise, there are good nursery slopes up the mountain, at the top of the Sétaz gondola. But one report tells of beginners 'terrified' by the violent start of some drag-lifts on Crey du Quart.

There are few queues when snow-cover is good, but some bottlenecks when it isn't.

Mountain restaurants are in short supply but of good quality. The Thimel and Les Mérégers are recommended.

A recent report indicates that lack of

MOUNTAIN FACTS

Valloire/Valmeinier

Altitude	1430m-2600m
Lifts	36
Pistes	150km
Green/Blue	52%
Red	37%
Black	11%
Artificial snow	10km
Recco detectors used	

Valfréjus

Altitude	1550m-2735m
Lifts	12
Pistes	52km
Green/Blue	70%
Red	10%
Black	20%
Artificial snow	none
Recco detectors used	

Val-Cenis

Altitude	1400m-2800m
Lifts	22
Pistes	85km
Green/Blue	50%
Red	40%
Black	10%
Artificial snow	10km
Recco detectors used	

TOURIST OFFICES

Valloire

Postcode 73450
t +33 479 590396
f 479 590966
info@valloire.net
www.valloire.net

Valmeinier

Postcode 73450
t +33 479 595369
f 479 592005
info@valmeinier.com
www.valmeinier.com

Valfréjus

Postcode 73500
t +33 479 053383
f 479 051367
valfre@club-internet.fr
www.valfrejus.com

Val-Cenis

Postcode 73480
t +33 479 052366
f 479 058217
info@valcenis.com
www.valcenis.com

spoken English is a problem at the Valmeinier ski school. Whereas the Valloire school has been described as 'excellent', with 'good spoken English'.

There's a fair choice of hotel and apartment accommodation. The Grand (3-star) and Christiania (2-star) are the best hotels, and both are well placed.

Most of the restaurants are pizza and fondue joints. The Gastilleur has the best French cuisine in town. Après-ski is fairly quiet but picks up at the weekend. The Irish pub is 'packed, with a great atmosphere'.

VALFREJUS 1550m

Valfréjus is a small and unusual modern resort – built in the woods, with most of the slopes higher up above the tree line.

The resort is a compact and quite pleasant affair, built on a narrow, shady shelf, with woods all around. There are several apartment blocks grouped around the main lift station, and chalets dotted around the hillside.

There are runs of all grades back towards the village, but the focus of the slopes is Plateau d'Arrondaz, at 2200m, reached by gondola and a slightly lower chair-lift. Above here are steep, open slopes – genuine bumpy blacks, with excellent snow – on Punta Bagna (2735m), served by the second stage of the gondola, and gentler blue runs from Col d'Arrondaz (2455m). From both the top and the col there are also sunny intermediate runs on the back side of the hill, with chair-lifts back to both high points or the option of the glorious long blue Jeu run (with off-piste variations along the way) to the village – almost 1200m vertical.

Snow-cover in the main open area is pretty reliable, and there's a good chance of complete cover to village level even without artificial assistance. Within its small area, Valfréjus has something for everyone (there are nursery slopes both at mid-mountain and village level). Near-beginners might welcome more easy blues, but it would be a good place for a confident intermediate to get in some serious practice on good snow. Experts will relish the off-piste opportunities. Heli-skiing is available – dropping you off over the border in Italy.

There are good restaurants at both of the gondola stations – at the top, the Punta Bagna has superb views, and the Bergerie at the mid-station has table-service inside and out.

The best hotels are the 2-star Valfréjus and 2-star Auberge du Charmaix; both are central and have pleasant restaurants. Prices are modest, but if you want to pay even less, you could stay down in the railhead town of Modane.

The Chic-Choc serves decent Italian food and the Arolle is recommended.

Après-ski is limited – the Snow Club, the Bois Brûlé and the Rhumerie are the liveliest bars. The Javana is a new pub (replacing the Metal Café).

VAL-CENIS 1400m

Val-Cenis is a marketing concept rather than a place. It comprises two pleasant villages in the Haute Maurienne, the high and remote part of the valley.

Lanslebourg is a long, linear place, spreading along the Route Nationale 6 (a dead end in winter, when the road over the Col du Mont-Cenis is closed and becomes a piste). It's pleasant enough, but no great beauty. A few km up the valley, Lanslevillard is more captivating – off the road, randomly arranged, rustic, and split into three.

There are lifts up into the north-facing slopes from a number of points along the valley, including Lanslebourg and the two major bits of Lanslevillard. The main one, a gondola, starts between the two villages, on the fringes of Lanslevillard, and goes up to the main mid-mountain congregation area at 2100m, where there there is a rustic self-service restaurant.

There are intermediate runs heading more or less straight down through the woods to the valley, and easy ones winding down – including a splendid green following the hairpin road from the Col. Above mid-mountain is a good range of runs to suit every standard, served by chairs and drags. From the top station at 2800m, there is a good, mogulled black down the shady front face, a challenging red on the shoulder of the mountain and a sunny away-from-the-lifts black over to the Col, where a couple of drags serve a slightly separate area of red and blue runs. The lift pass also covers the 35km of slopes in Termignon-la-Vanoise (10 minutes by bus). All in all, a very enjoyable area for a short stay.

There are modest hotels in both villages, of which the best is the 3-star Alpazur. It does good food, and there is a reasonable range of modest eating-out alternatives. Après-ski is quiet.

Megève 1100m

One of the traditional old winter holiday towns

WHAT IT COSTS

5

HOW IT RATES

The slopes	
Snow	**
Extent	*****
Experts	**
Intermediates	****
Beginners	***
Convenience	**
Queues	****
Restaurants	*****
The rest	
Scenery	***
Resort charm	****
Off-slope	****

- ➕ Extensive slopes, with miles of easy pistes, ideal for intermediates
- ➕ Scenic setting, with splendid views
- ➕ Charming old village centre, with very swanky shopping
- ➕ Some lovely luxury hotels
- ➕ Sophisticated nightlife
- ➕ Gourmet mountain lunches in attractive surroundings
- ➕ Excellent cross-country trails, including some at altitude
- ➕ Mont Blanc lift pass covers many other worthwhile resorts nearby
- ➕ Great for weekends – cooperative hotels and close to Geneva
- ➕ If it snows, deserted mountains
- ➕ Plenty to do off the slopes

- ➖ With most of the slopes below 2000m there's a risk of poor snow, especially on runs to the village – although the grassy terrain does not need a thick covering and snowmaking has improved a lot
- ➖ Three separate mountains, two linked by lift but not by piste and the third not linked at all
- ➖ Not many challenging pistes – the few blacks are not extreme – but good off-piste potential

Megève is the essence of rustic chic. It has a medieval heart, but it was, in a way, the original purpose-built French ski resort – conceived in the 1920s as a French alternative to Switzerland's St Moritz. And although Courchevel took over as France's most fashionable winter sports resort ages ago, Megève's sumptuous hotels and chalets still attract plenty of 'beautiful people' with fur coats and fat wallets. Happily, you don't need either to enjoy it.

The risk of poor snow still makes us nervous about booking way ahead; but it is certainly true that a few inches of cover will do, and if you want a relaxing and indulgent holiday in France, Megève should certainly be on your shortlist.

boarding *Boarding doesn't really fit with Megève's traditional, rather staid, upmarket image. But there is a fun-park and a half-pipe on Mont Joux – and free-riders will find lots of untracked off-piste powder for a few days after new snowfalls. It's a good place to try boarding for the first time, with plenty of fairly wide, gentle runs and a lot of chair-lifts and gondolas; though there are a fair number of drag-lifts, they are generally avoidable. Nightlife tends to be rather sophisticated, but there are a few noisy bars as well.*

What's new

The new 'Evasion' Mont Blanc pass covers the whole Megève-St-Gervais ski area as well as nearby Les Contamines.

La Ferme de Mon Père is yet another new gastronomic restaurant.

Snowmaking is being installed on the Alpette piste for 2000/01. There will also be a new car park at Rochebrune.

Reconstruction work on the Mont Blanc Tunnel is supposed to start during the summer of 2000. However, it is still unclear when it will be properly open.

The resort

Megève is in a lovely sunny setting and has a beautifully preserved traditional medieval centre, which is pedestrianised and comes complete with open-air ice rink, horse-drawn sleighs, cobbled streets and a fine church. There are lots of smart food, clothing, jewellery, antique and gift shops.

The main Albertville–Chamonix road bypasses the centre, and there are expensive underground car parks. But the resort's affluent French and Swiss clientele arrives mainly by car and the resulting traffic and fumes can be a major problem – especially at weekends when the crowds arrive and at the end of the day when people are driving back from excursions.

The clientele are mainly well-heeled French couples and families, who come here as much for an all-round winter holiday and for the people-watching potential as for the slopes themselves. The nightlife is, as you'd expect for such a resort, lively and varied.

MOUNTAIN FACTS

Altitude	850m-2355m
Lifts	81
Pistes	300km
Green/Blue	45%
Red	41%
Black	14%
Art. snow	160 acres
Recco detectors used	

The mountains

Megève's slopes are predominantly easy intermediate cruising, much of it prettily set in the woods. But there are tough runs to be found, and large areas of off-piste that are neglected by most visitors. This is a great resort to head for if storms close down the slopes of Chamonix.

THE SLOPES
Pretty but low

There are three separate areas, two of them linked by cable-car (not by piste).

A gondola within walking distance of central Megève can get you to both areas, although its primary purpose is to give access to **Rochebrune**. This sector can also be reached directly by a small cable-car from the southern edge of town. From Rochebrune you can go up to Alpette (1870m), the starting point for Megève's historic downhill course. A network of gentle, wooded, north-east-facing slopes, served by drag-lifts and a high-speed quad, take you across to Cote 2000 – the sector's highest point, at 2015m.

From the lower slopes of Rochebrune the Rocharbois cable-car goes across the valley to **Mont d'Arbois**, Megève's largest and most varied area. The cable-car brings you to an area, also reachable by road, of chalets, hotels and lift stations at the foot of the sunny slopes above Megève. Mont d'Arbois is also accessed by another gondola starting at La Princesse, way out to the north-east of town. From the top, you can take north-east-facing slopes to Le Bettex and on down to St-Gervais at around 850m. Another two-stage gondola returns you to the top, with a mid-station at Le Bettex (1380m). You can work your way over to Mont Joux and up to the small Mont Joly area – Megève's highest slopes (2355m). And from there you can descend to the backwater village of St-Nicolas-de-Véroce (1150m); chair-lifts bring you back to Mont Joux.

Directly behind Mont Joly, further up the same valley as St-Nicolas-de-Véroce, is the substantial resort of Les Contamines. You can get to it off-piste and a proper lift-and-piste link is planned within the next two years, making an already big area enormous.

The third area, and much the quietest, is **Le Jaillet**, accessed by gondola from just outside the northern edge of town. From the top of the gondola (1580m) are predominantly easy, east-facing pistes. The high point is Christomet (1855m), served by a long chair-lift. In the other directions, a series of long, tree-lined runs and lifts serves the area above Combloux.

St-Gervais and Le Bettex are covered on the Megève lift pass. The Mont Blanc lift pass covers many other

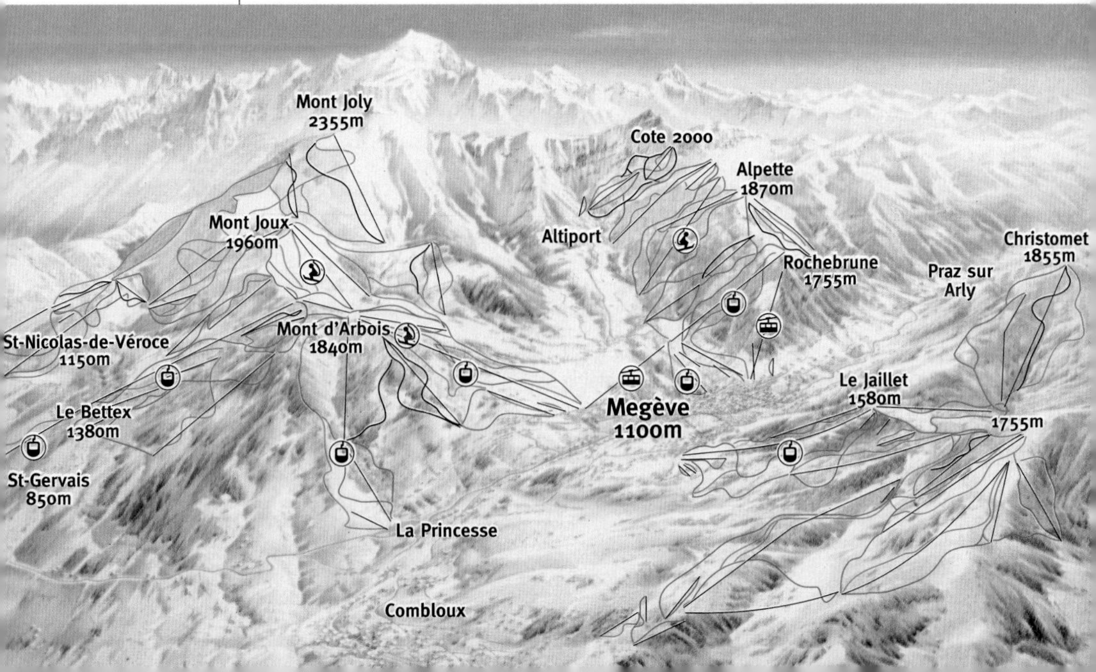

↑ Great views of Mont Blanc from many of the slopes

SERGE DESCHAMPS / ST GERVAIS TO

SCHOOLS/GUIDES

2000/01 prices in francs

ESF

Classes 6 days
4hr: 9.30-11.30 and 3pm-5pm
6 afternoons: 570

Children's classes
Ages: 5 to 12
6 afternoons: 510

Private lessons
Hourly or daily
210 for 1hr, for 1 to 2 people.
All-day classes are available.

1999/2000 prices in francs

International

Classes 6 mornings
2hr 10am-noon: 680

Children's classes
Ages: 4 to 12
6 full days 10am-noon, 3pm-5pm: 880

Private lessons
Hourly or daily
1 to 5 people: 1 hr 205

resorts, including Les Contamines, the Chamonix valley, and Courmayeur in Italy (see margin). Reporters have pointed out that piste grading is inconsistent and that less advanced skiers should not be too complacent.

SNOW RELIABILITY

The area's main weakness

The problem is that the slopes are low, with very few runs above 2000m, and partly sunny – the Megève side of Mont d'Arbois gets the afternoon sun. So in a poor snow year, or in a warm spell, snow-cover and quality on the lower slopes can suffer badly.

The good news is that the grassy slopes don't need much depth of snow, and that the resort has made great strides in tackling this weakness, expanding its snowmaking network to 160 snow-guns at the last count. Some runs are now entirely covered, including the long red Olympique run at Rochebrune. There is also a high standard of piste grooming.

FOR EXPERTS

Off-piste is the main attraction

The Mont Joly and Mont Joux sections offer the steepest slopes. The top chair here serves a genuinely black run, and the slightly lower Epaule chair has some steep runs back down and also accesses some good off-piste runs, as well as pistes, down to St-Nicolas.

The steep area beneath the second stage of the Princesse gondola can be a play area of powder runs among the trees. Cote 2000 has a small section of steep runs, including some off-piste.

A reporter tells of having fun on off-piste steeps from the Christomet and other chairs on Le Jaillet, too.

FOR INTERMEDIATES

Superb if the snow is good

Good intermediates will enjoy the Mont d'Arbois area best. The black runs below the Princesse gondola are perfectly manageable. The runs served by the Grand Vorasset drag and the most direct route between Mont d'Arbois and Le Bettex are also interesting. Similarly testing are the steepest of the Jaillet sector pistes above Combloux. The Christomet bowl is probably the best area for mixed abilities, with the same lift accessing three widely differing runs.

It's a great area for the less confident. A number of comfortable runs lead down to Le Bettex and La Princesse from Mont d'Arbois, while nearby Mont Joux accesses long, problem-free runs to St-Nicolas. Alpette and Cote 2000 are also suitable.

Even the timid can get a great deal of mileage in. All main valley-level lifts have easy routes down to them

LIFT PASSES

2000/01 prices in francs

Evasion Mont Blanc
Covers all lifts on Rochebrune, Cote 2000, Mont d'Arbois, Megève, St-Gervais, Mont Joux, St-Nicolas, Mont Joly, Le Jaillet and Combloux, Les Contamines, Bellevue.

Beginners Pay by the ride.

Main pass
1-day pass 188
6-day pass 890
(low season 801)

Senior citizens
Over 60: 6-day pass 801

Children
Under 13: 6-day pass 668
Under 5: free pass

Short-term passes
Half-day pass available in the afternoon.

Alternative passes
Mont Blanc pass covers all lifts in the 13 resorts of the Mont Blanc area (700km of piste and 190 lifts) and the buses between them, plus Courmayeur in Italy 6 days out of 6 (6 days 1200 for adults and 840 for children). Jaco pass valid for Le Jaillet, Christomet and Combloux.

CHILDCARE

There are three kindergartens dotted around the sprawling resort, all offering skiing. Age limits and hours vary. Caboche (450 589765) at the Caboche gondola station: ages 3 to 10, until 5pm. Meg'Loisirs (450 587784) is a comprehensive nursery: ages 1 to 6, until 6pm. Princesse (450 930086), out at the Princesse gondola: ages 2½ to 6, until 6pm.

(although the Milloz piste to the Princesse mid-station is a little steep). There are some particularly good, long, gentle cruises between Mont Joux and Megève via Mont d'Arbois. But in all sectors, you'll find easy, well-groomed blue runs.

FOR BEGINNERS
Good choice of nursery areas

There are beginner slopes dotted all around at valley level, and more snowsure ones at altitude on each of the main mountains. There are also plenty of very easy longer green runs to progress to.

FOR CROSS-COUNTRY
An excellent area

There are 75km of varied trails spread throughout the area. Some are at altitude (1300m–1550m), making lunchtime meetings with Alpine skiers or walkers simple. There is a special map for fondeurs, with run gradings.

QUEUES
Quiet during the week

Megève is relatively queue-free during the week, except at peak holiday time. It was described by a recent reporter as 'the quietest resort I have ever known'. But school holidays and sunny Sunday crowds can mean some delays. Queues are noticeably genteel, a far cry from the push and shove of more macho resorts. Overcrowded pistes at Mont Joux and Mont d'Arbois are a problem at busy periods. In our recent experience, anyone tough enough to venture out in falling snow gets the mountain to themselves.

MOUNTAIN RESTAURANTS
The long lunch lives

Megève is one of the great gourmet lunch destinations. Many of the 30 restaurants have table-service (at least as an option) and many of the terraces have magnificent views. Not surprisingly, they can be pricey.

The Mont d'Arbois area is particularly well endowed. There are two suave places still owned by the Rothschilds, original promoters of Megève, both popular with poseurs with small dogs and fur coats – the Club House and the Idéal Sports. The Igloo has both self-service and table-service sections with interesting food and wonderful views of Mont Blanc – recent reports of the self-service section are disappointing.

Above St-Nicolas are several little chalets offering great charm and good food at modest prices as well as glorious views.

At the base of the Mont Joux lift, Chez Marie du Rosay is recommended for good food and cheerful service. On the back side of the hill at Les Communailles, the Alpage was a key factor in one reader's decision to go back to Megève.

At the foot of the Cote 2000 slopes is a former farm, popular for its atmosphere, friendly service and good quality; Radaz, up the slope a little, enjoys better views and is similarly cosy, but the service was slack when we visited.

Alpette, atop the Rochebrune ridge, offers excellent all-round views outside, a comfortable lounge inside.

SCHOOLS AND GUIDES
Adventurous

The two schools both have broad horizons, offering expeditions to the Vallée Blanche and heli-skiing (in Italy) as well as conventional tuition. The International school advertises a wide range of different packages and excursions, and appears to be more popular with readers than its rival, the ESF. A recent reporter found the ESF children's classes to be inefficient, with impatient instructors.

FACILITIES FOR CHILDREN
Language problems

A comfortable low-altitude resort like Megève attracts lots of families who can afford day care. The facilities seem impressive – the kindergartens offer a wide range of activities as an alternative to the slopes. Lack of English-speaking staff (and companions) could be a drawback.

Staying there

Staying in the traffic-free centre of town gives you the best atmosphere and puts you within walking distance of the Chamois gondola. The bus services are not super-convenient.

HOW TO GO
Few packages

Relatively few British tour operators go to Megève, but there is an impressive range of accommodation.

Chalets A few UK tour operators offer catered chalets. For a cheap and very cheerful base, you won't do better

GETTING THERE

Air Geneva, transfer 1hr. Lyon, transfer 2½hr.

Rail Sallanches (13km); regular buses from station.

than Stanford's Sylvana – a creaky, unpretentious old hotel, reachable on skis, now run along chalet lines. Superb food when we visited.

Hotels Megève still attracts enough affluent visitors to sustain a range of exceptionally stylish and welcoming hotels. There are simpler places, too.

((((4) **Mont Blanc** Megève's traditional leading hotel – very elegant and fashionable. Right in the centre, and close to the main gondola.

((((4) **Chalet du Mont d'Arbois** Prettily decorated, former Rothschild family home, now a Relais & Chateaux hotel in a secluded position above town, near the Mont d'Arbois gondola.

((((4) **Fer à Cheval** French rustic-chic at its best, with a warmly welcoming wood-and-stone interior. Excellent food, and a fitness centre to redress the balance. Close to the centre.

(((3) **Coin du Feu** 'Very well managed' chalet midway between Rochebrune and Chamois lifts.

(((3) **Grange d'Arly** Wrong side of the road, but still quite close to the centre – a beautifully furnished chalet.

(((3) **Ferme Hôtel Duvillard** Smartly restored farmhouse, perfectly positioned for the slopes, at the foot of the Mont d'Arbois gondola.

((2) **Gai Soleil** Comfortable family-run place – five minutes' walk from the centre of town and the main gondola.

((2) **Mourets** 'Excellent, with superb food' but inconvenient location.

Self-catering There are some very comfortable and well positioned apartments available – not cheap.

EATING OUT

Very French

Megève naturally has lots of high-quality, expensive restaurants. The arrival of a couple of Michelin award winning chefs – Jacques Mégean and Marc Veyrat – over the last few seasons has raised the culinary standards even further, and may finally rectify the curious lack of any Michelin stars in the resort. Up to now, Michel Gaudin has probably been the best in town – with very good-value set menus. The restaurants in all the top hotels – eg the Fermes de Marie, Chalet du Mont d'Arbois, Mont Blanc and Mont Joly – are also excellent but much more expensive. Le Flocons de Sel, although quite pricey, is highly recommended for its quality and service. The Taverne du Mont d'Arbois is a lovely woody chalet at the foot of the Mont d'Arbois lifts.

Some reporters wish for more variety of cuisine. The Phnom-Penh is one of the few possibilities. Mama Mia is a popular Italian restaurant though recent reports are mixed. The Pallas is recommended for burgers and pizzas.

APRES-SKI

Plenty to try

Nightlife is lively, and less formal than it used to be. The Club de Jazz (aka Les 5 Rues) is something of an institution – a very popular jazz club-cum-cocktail bar, that gets some big-name musicians. The Chamois has been recommended. The Puck is an atmospheric locals' bar, while Harry's

ACTIVITIES

Indoor 'Palais des Sports' (climbing wall, swimming pool, sauna, solarium, skating, gym), judo, classical and contemporary dance classes, music lessons, bridge, tennis, bowling, archery, language classes, museum, library, cinemas, pottery, casino, concert and play hall, body-building hall, curling, tennis
Outdoor 50km of cleared paths, snow-shoe excursions, skating rink, riding, sleigh rides, plane and helicopter trips, paragliding, hot air ballooning, horse-riding, rock-climbing, ice driving, mountaineering

TOURIST OFFICE

Postcode 74120
t +33 450 212728
f 450 930309
megeve@megeve.com
www.megeve.com

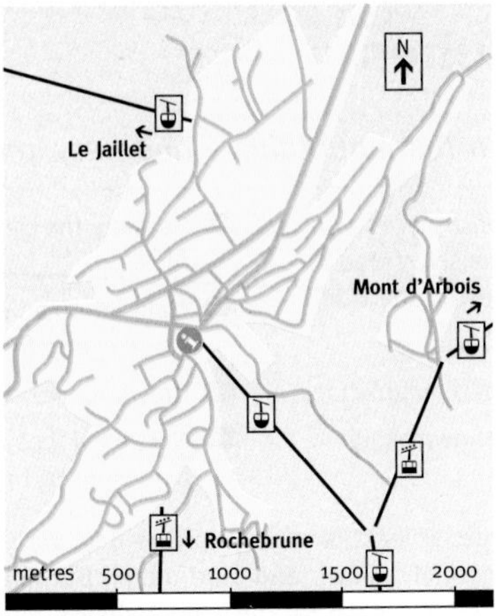

Bar is an informal rendezvous, popular for its wide range of beers, a weekly live band, karaoke and satellite TV. The Conga is another lively spot. The new casino opened a few seasons ago, further enhancing the resort chic.

OFF THE SLOPES
Lots to do

There is something for most tastes, with an excellent sports centre, a central outdoor ice rink, plenty of outdoor activities and a weekly market. Excursions to Annecy and Chamonix are possible. Walks are excellent, with 50km of marked paths, many at altitude. There is a special map of the paths, graded for difficulty. Meeting friends on the slopes for lunch is easy.

STAYING UP THE MOUNTAIN
Several possibilities

As well as mid-mountain Le Bettex (see St-Gervais), there are hotels further up on the slopes, near the summit of Mont d'Arbois. One is the 3-star Igloo (see 'Mountain restaurants'), another the 2-star Chez la Tante.

St-Gervais 850m

St-Gervais is a handsome 19th-century spa town set in a narrow river gorge, halfway between Megève and Chamonix, at the entrance to the side-valley leading up to St-Nicolas and Les Contamines. It has direct access to the Mont d'Arbois slopes via a 20-person gondola starting from just outside the town.

It's a pleasant place to explore, with interesting food shops and cosy bars. Among its diversions are thermal baths and an Olympic skating rink. Prices are noticeably lower than over the hill in Megève. Two hotels convenient for the gondola are the Hostellerie du Nerey, a pleasantly traditional 2-star, and the 3-star Carlina, best in town. At the gondola mid-station is Le Bettex (1380m), a small collection of hotels, private chalets and new apartments, conveniently situated for the runs but with little evening animation.

You can go up on the opposite side of St-Gervais on a rack-and-pinion railway which in 1904 was intended to go all the way to the top of Mont Blanc but actually takes you to the slopes of Les Houches (see Chamonix chapter). Given enough snow, you can descend to St-Gervais off-piste.

Its position makes St-Gervais a good base for touring the different resorts covered by the Mont Blanc regional lift pass.

Other resorts

Praz-sur-Arly and Notre-Dame-de-Bellecombe are much cheaper options for independent car travellers – they are not part of the Megève lift network. Praz (1035m) is a small, quiet place, but has hotels, restaurants, bars, sports club, ski school and ski kindergarten. It has a fair-sized slope of its own, with short, mainly easy, north-facing runs. (It is also covered on the Mont Blanc area pass.) Notre-Dame (1130m) is further along the road past Praz, a pleasant village with mainly apartment accommodation, simple hotels, and several bars and restaurants. It has its own varied, pretty area.

St-Nicolas-de-Véroce is part of the lift network, and has a handful of simple small hotels.

One reporter spent a very rewarding few days based at the hotel Terminus in Le Fayet, below St-Gervais, travelling to a different resort each day by coach.

Les Menuires 1850m

Lift your eyes to the mountains – and keep them there

WHAT IT COSTS

(4)

HOW IT RATES

The slopes

Snow	****
Extent	*****
Experts	****
Intermediates	*****
Beginners	***
Convenience	*****
Queues	****
Restaurants	***

The rest

Scenery	***
Resort charm	*
Off-slope	*

What's new

Snowmaking was further extended last season. The new Alpage restaurant, at the top of the Montaulever piste, also opened.

2000/01 will see the artificial snow network expand again. And two new luxury tourist residences in Bruyères and Reberty should also be ready.

- ⊕ Probably the cheapest place to stay in the famously extensive Three Valleys area – biggest in the world
- ⊕ Some great local slopes
- ⊕ Lots of slope-side accommodation
- ⊕ Extensive artificial snowmaking

- ⊖ Possibly the ugliest resort in the Alps
- ⊖ Main intermediate and beginner slopes get a lot of sun
- ⊖ No woodland slopes
- ⊖ Nursery slopes are busy as well as overexposed to the sun

Les Menuires is hideous, at least to our eyes. One day, we confidently predict, they'll simply knock most of it down and start again. But not everyone agrees – and it is certainly the bargain base for the Trois Vallées, with the bonus of immediate access to the excellent, challenging slopes on La Masse, rarely used by visitors from the other valleys.

boarding *Les Menuires gets a fair number of boarding visitors – not surprising since it gives relatively economical access to such a huge area of terrain. There is plenty here for every style of rider. Lots of chairs and gondolas in the massive lift system make for comfortable travel, but be warned – there are some flattish sections of piste to negotiate in places. And we'd certainly recommend beginners to go somewhere with more secluded nursery slopes and better snow. There's a fun-park with a half-pipe just above the main village.*

The resort

We concede that it's the original centre of the resort, La Croisette, that is particularly horrendous. Newer outposts of Reberty and Les Bruyères are better. The new outposts have their own shops and bars. The main centre has a claustrophobic indoor shopping complex. Some pleasant bar and restaurant terraces face the slopes.

The mountains

Les Menuires has two main attractions: La Masse, a challenging and neglected mountain; and the swift links to the rest of the Trois Vallées. It suits all standards except complete beginners.

THE SLOPES

A good base for the Trois Vallées

Les Menuires and St-Martin-de-Belleville share a local area with 160km of runs and 45 lifts. The west-facing slopes have the vast bulk of the runs. The main gondolas take you up to the **Mont de la Chambre** (2850m), from where you can head back south to Val-Thorens or east over the ridge to the Méribel slopes. Chairs and drags serve the local slopes, and you can work your way north to the charming old village of St-Martin-de-Belleville.

The north-east-facing slopes of **La Masse** (2805m) usually have excellent snow on the top half and are served by a two-stage high-capacity gondola.

Three Valleys lift passes for six days or more also give you a day in Val-d'Isère/Tignes, La Plagne or Les Arcs.

SNOWPIX.COM / CHRIS GILL

← Les Menuires' secret weapon – the neglected slopes of La Masse

MOUNTAIN FACTS

Altitude 1300m-3200m	
Lifts	200
Pistes	600km
Green/Blue	49%
Red	37%
Black	14%
Artificial snow	90km
Recco detectors used	

LIFT PASSES

2000/01 prices in francs

Three Valleys
See Méribel chapter.

Alternative passes
Vallée des Belleville pass covers 75 lifts and 300km piste in Val-Thorens, Les Menuires and St-Martin (adult 6-day 1080). Les Menuires and St-Martin pass covers 45 lifts and 160km of piste (adult 6-day 940).

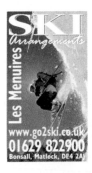

SCHOOLS/GUIDES

2000/01 prices in francs

ESF
Classes 6 days
5¼hr: 2¾hr am, 2½hr pm; half-day am or pm
6 full days: 950

Children's classes
Ages: up to 12
6 full days: 830

Private lessons
Hourly
190 for 1 or 2 people

SNOW RELIABILITY
Cover guaranteed but not quality

La Masse's height and orientation ensure good snow for a long season.

The opposite, west-facing slopes are supplied with abundant artificial snow (the resort boasts 315 snow-guns – 20km). But although cover there is guaranteed – so long as the weather is cold enough to make snow – the snow lower down is often icy or slushy.

FOR EXPERTS
Hidden treasures

La Masse has some of the steepest and quietest pistes in the Trois Vallées – most people doing the 'circuit' skip it. Long reds and a black come down beneath the top stage of the gondola. Other steep blacks, usually mogulled, are the Dame Blanche and Lac Noir.

From the top there are also some marvellously scenic off-piste runs, some sporadically marked as itinéraires, others requiring guidance. The wide, sweeping, but not too steep, Vallon du Lou goes towards Val-Thorens. Others go in the opposite direction to various villages from which you need transport back, but the Les Yvoses run takes you back into the Les Menuires lift system.

Easy access to the rest of the Trois Vallées means good skiers are spoilt for choice. Within an hour of leaving your door you can be on the steepest slopes of Méribel or Val-Thorens. Courchevel won't take much longer.

FOR INTERMEDIATES
600km of pistes to choose from

With good snow, you may find little reason for leaving the local slopes, which are virtually all blue and red. But because most slopes face west, the snow is often better elsewhere in the Trois Vallées. This is paradise for intermediates who like to travel. You can approach Méribel from five different peaks on the ridge. Even a second- or third-timer should have no problem cruising from valley to valley. In poor snow conditions the attractions of Val-Thorens become evident, and there's blue-run access via the Montaulever drag as well as red runs from the top of the mountain.

FOR BEGINNERS
Try elsewhere

Although there are wide and gentle slopes for beginners and a special beginner's lift pass, we think you'd be better off in a resort that has more of a real Alpine atmosphere and is easier on the eye. While others can get away from Les Menuires into beautiful Alpine scenery, beginners are stuck with it. The snow quality on the nursery slopes is a worry, and the blue slopes above the resort can get extremely crowded.

FOR CROSS-COUNTRY
Valley hike

There are 28km of prepared trails along the valley floor between St-Martin and halfway between Les Menuires and Val-Thorens.

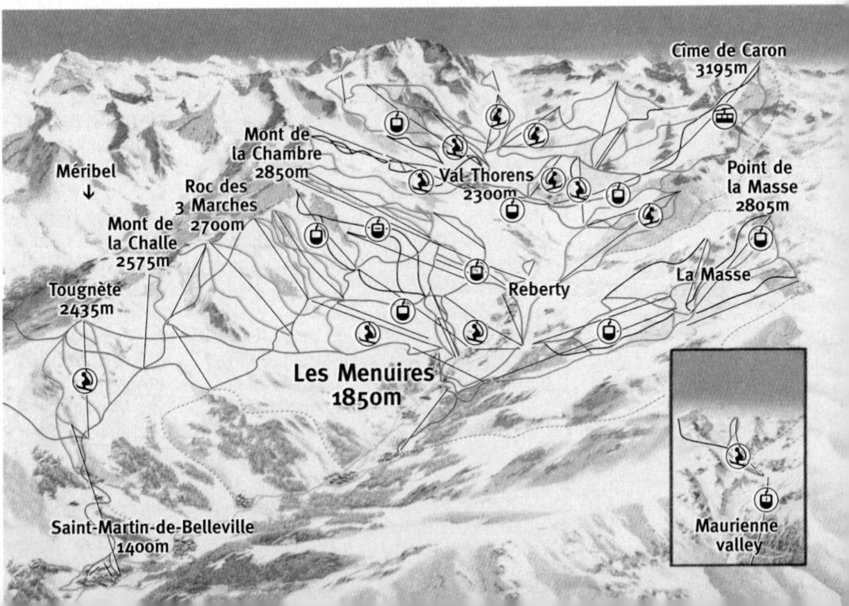

CHILDCARE

The ESF-run Village des Schtroumpfs (479 006379) takes children aged 3 months to 12 years. It has a nursery for babies, a Baby Club for toddlers and a leisure centre for older children, with activities and ski lessons for children aged 2½ or more.

At Reberty-les-Bruyères, the Marmottons offers similar facilities, but no nursery.

GETTING THERE

Air Geneva, transfer 3½hr. Lyon, transfer 3½hr. Chambéry, transfer 2½hr.

Rail Moûtiers (27km); regular buses from station.

ACTIVITIES

Indoor Library, games room, two cinemas, fitness centres
Outdoor Two outdoor heated swimming pools, microlight flights, hang-gliding, guided walks, snow-scooters, artificial skating rink, snow-shoe excursions, paragliding, guided tours

TOURIST OFFICE

Postcode 73440
t +33 479 007300
f 479 007506
lesmenuires@lesmenuires.com
www.lesmenuires.com

QUEUES
Can be bypassed

Queues are not much of a problem, provided the Mont de la Chambre gondola does not break down. A new fast quad at St-Martin helps the journey back from lunch there.

MOUNTAIN RESTAURANTS
Have lunch in St-Martin

The restaurant at the top of the first stage of the La Masse gondola is fairly pleasant. But a lot of people prefer to head for the restaurants of the old village of St-Martin-de-Belleville – Les Airelles is recommended by reporters. The Bouitte, in nearby St-Marcel, is a serious restaurant, and delightful for a blow-out. It's reachable off-piste, and they'll drive you to the lifts after lunch.

SCHOOLS AND GUIDES
Overcome language barrier

Reports tend to be positive, despite English not being widely spoken, and we have reports of children enjoying themselves in multinational classes.

FACILITIES FOR CHILDREN
All-embracing

This is very much a family resort, and the childcare arrangements seem well organised. The general view is that it is a good place for children to be introduced to the snow.

Staying there

Despite the fact that the resort is designed for convenient access to the slopes, you may wish to think about location. The central area around La Croisette is best for shops and après-ski. But the 'village' has several component parts with fewer facilities, and overall is well over 1km in length.

HOW TO GO
Budget packages

Some big UK tour operators go to Les Menuires. They have a fair selection of hotels and apartments. We know of no catered chalets. There is a Club Med above Reberty.

Hotels It comes as a slight surprise to find that there are some quite smart hotels here – although none above 3-star grading, and none with a pool.

(3) **Ours Blanc** Best in town: a wood-clad, chalet-style 3-star on the slopes above Reberty 1850.

(3) **Latitudes** 3-star on the lower fringe of Les Bruyères.

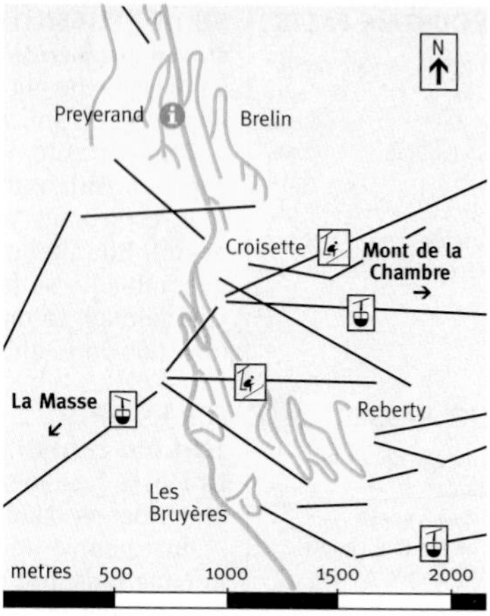

(2) **Menuire** Neat, well equipped place on southern fringe of the resort; but we have had some negative reports.

Self-catering Apartments are cheap but not usually cheerful. It's a classic French budget resort, so paying extra for under-occupancy is wise. L'Orée des Pistes and Residence Le Villaret are among the best. A recent report recommends Les Lauzes: 'excellent spacious apartment with spectacular views'.

EATING OUT
Good authentic French cuisine

Though some restaurants lack atmosphere, there's no shortage of good food. Savoyard specialities and 'real' French food are the order of the day. But there are alternatives, such as Italian and Tex-Mex. The restaurant in the Ours Blanc and the rustic Ruade are recommended by recent reporters.

APRES-SKI
Improving but still very limited

The young people who are attracted here by low prices have done their best to bring a spark of life to the nightlife scene, but it's still pretty quiet. The Challenge bar has live music and La Mousse is also popular. The Liberty and Passeport discos pick up later on at night.

OFF THE SLOPES
Forget it

Les Menuires is a resort for keen piste-bashers wanting to explore the world's most extensive slopes on a budget. It's not the place for those who do not take to the slopes themselves, though there are some pretty walks.

Méribel

1400m-1700m

The best-looking base for the wonderful Three Valleys

WHAT IT COSTS

6

HOW IT RATES

The slopes	
Snow	****
Extent	*****
Experts	****
Intermediates	*****
Beginners	***
Convenience	***
Queues	****
Restaurants	****
The rest	
Scenery	***
Resort charm	***
Off-slope	***

- ➕ In the centre of the biggest linked piste network in the world – ideal for intermediates who love covering the miles, but plenty for experts, too
- ➕ Modern, constantly improved lift system means little queueing and rapid access to all slopes
- ➕ Good piste grooming and snowmaking
- ➕ Village purpose-built in pleasing chalet-style architecture

- ➖ Main village spread out, straggling along a long, winding road, with much of the accommodation well away from the slopes
- ➖ Expensive
- ➖ Méribel-Mottaret satellite is rather lifeless
- ➖ Not the place to go for any sensation of being a traveller in France – too many Brits

For keen piste-bashers who dislike tacky purpose-built resorts, Méribel is difficult to beat. It is slap in the middle of the Three Valleys – the biggest interlinked winter sports area in the world. With 200 lifts and 600km of pistes, and endless off-piste possibilities, it is difficult to be bored in a fortnight here. Fans of Courchevel and Val-Thorens sniff at Méribel's local slopes, but since Mont Vallon and the top of the valley were opened up some years ago, Méribel can stand comparison on most counts.

You won't like it if you don't like sharing the slopes with hordes of Brits. And it's not cheap – it has had several luxurious hotels built and has moved much more upmarket recently It's now much more of a rival than it once was for traditionally swanky Courchevel. But don't be put off: we both love it (one of us learned to ski there) – and it has lots of all-inclusive tour operator-run chalets.

boarding *Méribel is increasingly boarder-oriented. The terrain locally and further afield has lots to offer, you rarely have to take a drag-lift, and there's one fun-park with half-pipe, two quarter-pipes and boarder-cross below the second stage of the Plattières gondola, and another park with quarter-pipe and trick course near the Arpasson drag above the Tougnète gondola mid-station. The resort hosts a number of big-air and boarder-cross competitions. Specialist shops include Board Brains, Exodus and the Quiksilver snowboard shop, and you're bound to feel at home in at least one of the lively Brit-dominated bars.*

What's new

For 1999/2000 there was a new black run at the top of the La Loze chair-lift. Building work continued at Méribel-Village, the original village, a fair way from the main resort but served by its own lift and piste. A new snowboard fun-park was built above the Tougnète gondola mid-station. And the valley finished a 10-year project of burying 15km of telephone and electricity cables underground and removing 300 pylons.

The resort

Méribel occupies the central valley of the Three Valleys system and consists of two main resort villages.

The original resort of Méribel-les-Allues (now simply known as Méribel) is built on a single steepish west-facing hillside with the home piste running down beside it to the main lift stations at the valley bottom. All the buildings are wood-clad, low-rise and chalet style, making this one of the most tastefully designed of French purpose-built resorts. A road winds up from the village centre at about 1400m to the Rond Point des Pistes at about 1650m, and goes on through woods to the outpost of the Altiport (an airport with snow-covered runway for little planes with skis) at around 1700m.

The resort was founded by a Brit, Peter Lindsay, in 1938, and has retained a strong British presence ever since. It has grown enormously over recent years, and although some accommodation is right on the piste, much of the newer building is more than a walk away. One clear exception is Belvédère, an upmarket enclave built on the opposite side of the home piste (there's a tunnel for road access). There are collections of shops and restaurants at a couple of points on the road through the resort – Altitude 1600 and Plateau de Morel. The hotels and apartments of Altiport enjoy splendid isolation in the woods, and

MOUNTAIN FACTS

Altitude 1300m-3200m	
Lifts	200
Pistes	600km
Green/Blue	49%
Red	37%
Black	14%
Artificial snow	90km
Recco detectors used	

LIFT PASSES

2000/01 prices in francs

Three Valleys
Covers all lifts in Courchevel, La Tania, Méribel, Val-Thorens, Les Menuires and St-Martin-de-Belleville.

Beginners Two free lifts in Méribel-Mottaret and two in Méribel; reduced price lift pass with beginners' lessons.

Main pass
1-day pass 235
6-day pass 1160

Senior citizens
Over 60: 6-day pass 928
Over 70: 6-day pass 580
Over 75: free pass

Children
Under 16: 6-day pass 870
Under 10: 754
Under 5: free pass

Short-term passes
Half-day passes (from 12.30) available for Vallée de Méribel (adult 145) and 3 Valleys (adult 176).

Notes 6-day pass and over valid for one day each in Tignes-Val-d'Isère, La Plagne-Les Arcs, Pralognan-la-Vanoise and Les Saisies. Reductions for families.

Alternative passes
Vallée de Méribel pass covers 150km of runs in Méribel and Méribel-Mottaret (adult 6-day 945). One day 3 Valley extension 108).

are convenient for some of the slopes.

The satellite village of Méribel-Mottaret was developed in the early 1970s. The original development was beside the piste on the east-facing slope, but in recent years the resort has spread up the opposite hillside and further up the valley. Both sides are served by lifts for pedestrians – but the gondola up to the original village stops at 7.30pm and it's a long, tiring walk up. Mottaret looks modern, despite wood-cladding on its apartment blocks. Even so, it's more attractive than many other resorts built for slope-side convenience. It has many fewer shops and bars and much less après-ski than Méribel, but reporters have found it makes a pleasant change, and enjoyed the convenience.

For the Olympics, a new gondola was built from Brides-les-Bains, an old spa town way down in the valley, which served as the Olympic Village for the games, up to Méribel-Centre. There's a mid-station at the old village of Les Allues – which, along with the newly linked-up Méribel-Village, is a possible place to stay.

The mountains

It's keen piste-bashers who will get the best out of what Méribel has to offer. There's endless cruising to be had, as well as challenging terrain. The lift system is generally very efficient and is planned to cut out walks and climbs. Piste grading is not always entirely reliable, however – reporters found 'some blues more difficult than some reds'.

To appreciate the merits of the whole Three Valleys region you'll need to read the entries for Courchevel, Les Menuires and Val-Thorens, too. Lift passes for six days or more also give you a day in Val-d'Isère-Tignes (an hour and a half away), La Plagne or Les Arcs (an hour or so away).

THE SLOPES
Highly efficient lift system

The Méribel valley runs north–south. On the eastern side, gondolas leave both Méribel and Mottaret for **La Saulire** at around 2700m. From here you can head back down towards either village or down the other side of the ridge towards Courchevel.

From Méribel a gondola rises to **Tougnète**, on the western side of the valley, from where you can get down to Les Menuires or St-Martin-de-Belleville. You can also head for Mottaret from here. From there, a fast chair then a drag take you to another entry point for the Les Menuires runs.

The Mottaret area has seen rapid mechanisation over the last decade. The **Plattières** gondola rises up the valley to the south, ending at yet another entry point to the Les Menuires area. To the east of this is the big stand-up gondola to the top of **Mont Vallon** at nearly 3000m. There are wonderful views from the top. A fast quad from near this area goes south up to **Mont de la Chambre,** giving direct access to Val-Thorens.

SNOW RELIABILITY
Pretty good piste-maintenance

Méribel's slopes aren't the highest in the Three Valleys, and snow conditions are often better elsewhere. The lower runs now have substantial snowmaking. We have always found the grooming good but some recent visitors have been less impressed. Lack of snow is rarely a problem, but ice or slush at the end of the day can be. And some busy routes 'get cut up quite quickly' and can be 'for rock-hoppers only'. The west-facing La Saulire side gets the afternoon sun, and conditions deteriorate here first – but then you can always go over to Courchevel. The north-west-facing slopes above Altiport generally have decent snow. At the southern end of the valley, towards Les Menuires and Val-Thorens, a lot of runs are north-facing and keep their snow well.

FOR EXPERTS
Exciting choices

The size of the Three Valleys means experts are well catered for. In the Méribel valley, head for Mont Vallon. The long, steep, mogulled Combe du Vallon run here is graded red, but often presents plenty of challenge. And there's a beautiful itinéraire (not marked on the piste map) in the next valley to the main pistes, leading to the bottom of the gondola.

The slopes down from the top of the Val-Thorens sector were all off-piste when we old hands first visited Méribel. Since the new lifts were installed up here, there are two pistes back from Val-Thorens, but still plenty of opportunity for getting off-piste in the wide open bowls.

A good mogul run is down the side

Mt Vallon is served by a powerful gondola and has wonderful, long runs down →

SNOWPIX.COM / CHRIS GILL

of the double Roc de Tougne drag-lift which leads up to Mont de la Challe. And there is a steep black run all the way down the Tougnète gondola back to Méribel. Apart from a shallow section near the mid-station, it's unrelenting most of the way.

At the north end of the valley the La Face run was built for the women's downhill in the 1992 Olympics. Served by a fast quad, it's a splendid cruise when freshly groomed, and you can terrify yourself just by imagining what it must be like to go straight down.

Nothing on the Saulire side is as steep or demanding as on the other side of the valley. The Georges Mauduit red run used to be black, however, and the red Pic Noir down from Col de la Loze is recommended by one visitor as a 'pleasant, long run, wonderful with good conditions'.

Throughout the area there are good off-piste opportunities. The ESF runs excellent-value guided groups.

FOR INTERMEDIATES
Paradise found

Méribel and the rest of the Three Valleys is a paradise for intermediates; there are few other resorts where a keen piste-basher can cover so many miles so easily. Virtually every slope in the region has a good intermediate run down it, and to describe them would take a book in itself.

For less adventurous intermediates, the run from the second station of the Plattières gondola back to Mottaret is ideal, and used a lot by the ski school.

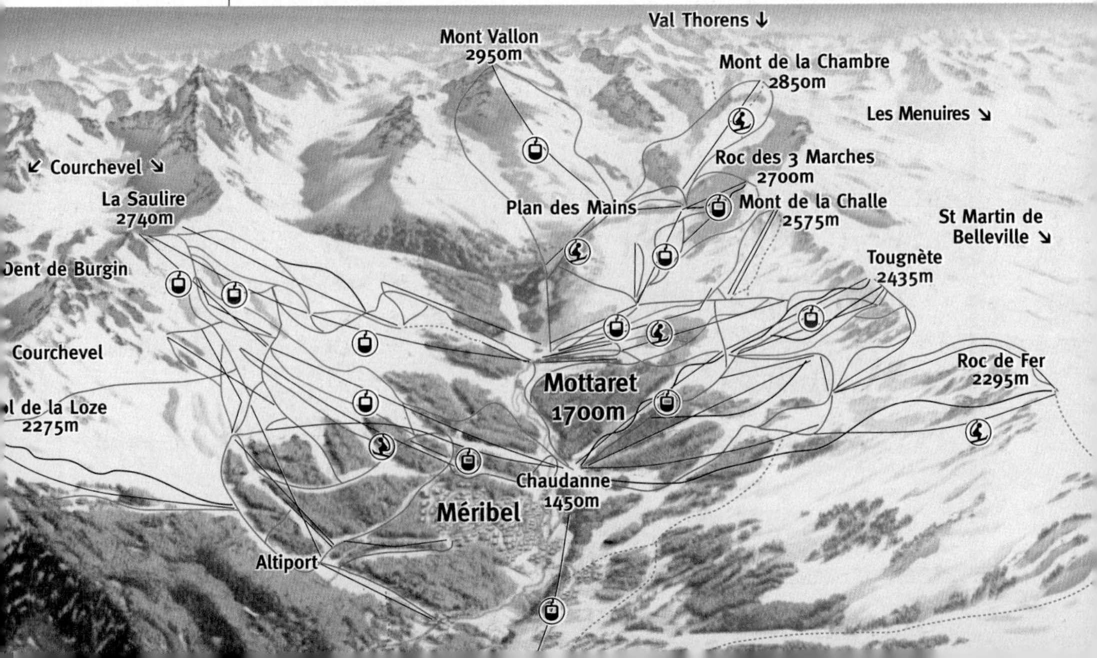

It is a gentle, north-facing, cruising run and is generally in good condition.

Even early intermediates should find the runs over into the other valleys well within their capabilities, opening up further vast amounts of intermediate runs. Go to Courchevel or Val-Thorens for the better snow.

Virtually all the pistes on both sides of the Méribel valley will suit more advanced intermediates. Most of the reds are on the difficult side.

FOR BEGINNERS
Not ideal

Méribel isn't ideal for beginners. The resort lacks good nursery slopes set apart from the main areas. There is a small one at Rond Point, mainly used by the children's ski school.

The best area for beginners is at Altiport, accessible direct from the village at Altitude 1600 by chair-lift. There is a gentle out-of-the-way area here that can be treated as a nursery slope. And, once you can tackle a drag-lift, you can get up to one of the best and most attractively situated green pistes we know, the Blanchot – long, gentle, wide and tree-lined, with little through-traffic.

FOR CROSS-COUNTRY
Scenic routes

The main area is in the woods near Altiport. There is about 17km of prepared track here, a pleasant introduction to those who want to try cross-country for the first time. There's also a loop around Lake Tueda, in the nature reserve, and for the more experienced an 8km itinéraire from Altiport to Courchevel.

QUEUES
Can still be long waits

Huge lift investment over the years has paid off in making the area virtually queue-free most of the time, despite the huge numbers of people. However, some readers have found 'long, long queues' and waited '30 minutes plus at Méribel-Mottaret', and been unhappy with the way the queues are managed. If you do come across a queue, there is generally an alternative route. For example, if you find a queue at Mottaret you can easily get over to Courchevel by descending to Méribel and taking a lift from there.

The Plattières gondola at Mottaret can get crowded at ski school time, when the schools gets priority.

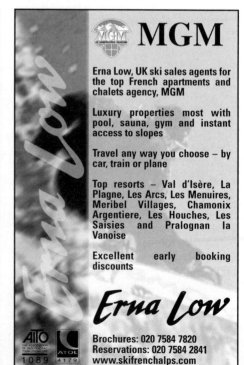

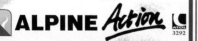

SCHOOLS/GUIDES

2000/01 prices in francs

ESF
in Méribel and Méribel-Mottaret
Classes 5 days
5hr: 9.30-noon and 2.15-4.45
5 full days: 1035
Children's classes
Ages: 5 to 13
5 full days: 828
Private lessons
1½hr 12.30pm to 2pm
300 for 1 to 2 people, 370 for 3 to 4 people
International section
In Méribel and Méribel-Mottaret
Classes 6 days
2½hr: 9.30-noon or 2.15-4.45
5 days: 635
Children's classes
Ages: 5 to 12
5 half days: 584

Ski Cocktail
(1999/2000 prices)
Classes 6 days
2hr am or 2hr pm
6 mornings: 845
Children's classes
Ages: 6 to 12
6 half days: 1395
Private lessons
2 hours 550, 3 hours 825, all day 1830

Magic in Motion
Classes 12 hours 880
Children's classes
Ages: from 6
32 hours 2100
Private lessons
2 hours 580, all day 1800

CHILDCARE

The ESF runs P'tits Loups kindergartens at both Méribel and Méribel-Mottaret, with snow-gardens (lifts, inflatable characters etc) for children aged 3 to 5. Open 9am to 5pm.

Les Saturnins in the Olympic Centre building in Méribel takes children aged 18 months to 3 years, offering indoor games and handicrafts, sledging and other outdoor activities.

MOUNTAIN RESTAURANTS
Lots of choice but watch the price

There is lots of choice, but most places get very busy. You might want to take lunch early or late. The Pierres Plates, at the top of the Saulire gondolas, has magnificent views and you can watch hang-gliders taking off, but the food is nothing special. Chardonnet, at the mid-station of the Mottaret gondola, has table-service and excellent food but is expensive. Rhododendrons, at the top of the Altiport drag, has a modern but atmospheric wooden dining room and 'reasonable, plentiful food'. The Altiport hotel has a great outdoor buffet in good weather and the 'best tarts in town' but, again, is expensive. Les Crêtes, below the top of the Tougnète gondola, is family-run, has good service and is one of smallest mountain restaurants in the Three Valleys. La Sitelle, above the first section of the Plattières gondola, has decent food and magnificent views towards Mont Vallon. Les Castors, at the main Méribel lift station, scarcely counts as a mountain restaurant, but earns praise for good, affordable food including 'exquisite' carbonara.

SCHOOLS AND GUIDES
No shortage of instructors

The three main schools all have plenty of English-speaking instructors.

The ESF is by far the biggest, with over 300 instructors. It has a special international section with instructors speaking good English. Recent reports have been mixed, but we've heard tales of instructors behaving more like guides, and abilities being too mixed within a class.

Ski Cocktail deals almost exclusively with the British market and believes its clients should 'have fun rather than learn to ski like racers'. But recent reports are mixed: one visitor was impressed that a beginner in his party 'managed a black by the end of the week', while another felt a 'too pushy' instructor was to blame for his wife being stretchered off the mountain during a lesson.

Magic in Motion continue to receive rave reviews. 'Classes small, English spoken well, we were all pleased with our progress', says one report.

Interesting alternative courses are on offer too. For example, the ESF runs off-piste guided tours, heli-skiing on the French/Italian border and 'Ski Discovery' tours of the Three Valleys.

FACILITIES FOR CHILDREN
Lots of choice

Despite our fat file of reports on Méribel, none deals first-hand with the resort's childcare facilities. Several chalet operators, like Meriski and Crystal, run their own crèches.

Staying there

Pick where you stay with care. For easy access to the piste, Mottaret is hard to beat, but even here there are better and worse spots.

For those who prefer chalets, a villagey ambience and a greater choice of shops, bars and restaurants, the best place is around or just above the village centre of Méribel. Check how far your accommodation is from the piste – lots of it is a long hike (and the resort is built on a hill). Hiring a ski locker, by the main piste area (above Jack's bar), is a convenient option. Local buses are free (though some readers complain they are inadequate), and many UK tour operators run their own minibus services to the lifts.

HOW TO GO
Huge choice but few bargains

Package holidays are easy to find, both with big UK tour operators and smaller Méribel specialists. There is a Club Med, occupying the swanky Aspen Park hotel at Rond-Point.

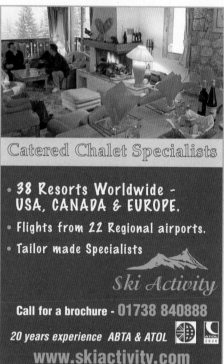

↑ The boss of Magic in Motion ski school (with the purple hair) guides a couple of novices towards Val-Thorens

SNOWPIX.COM / CHRIS GILL

GETTING THERE

Air Geneva, transfer 3½hr. Lyon, transfer 3½hr. Chambéry, transfer 2½hr.

Rail Moûtiers (18km); regular buses to Méribel.

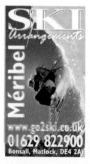

Chalets Méribel has more chalets dedicated to the British market than any other resort. Snowline now has eight here and Alpine Action has great locations and superb food. Ski Activity have six chalets, including a brand new five-bedroom, four-bathroom one, Dou du Pont, close to the ice rink and sports centre. In this sprawling resort it's no surprise that many of the best chalets are a long way from the lifts and the snow; Simply Ski's neat 12-person Montana is a notable exception, less than 100m from the Morel chair.

What really distinguishes Méribel is the range of luxurious chalets. Local specialists Meriski have 14, some numbering among our own favourites. If money is no object, try one of The Ski Company's four luxury chalets. Scott Dunn Ski has four individually designed, spacious chalets full of creature comforts. Drivers whisk guests to and from the slopes on demand.

There are not many 'jumbo' chalet hotels, but Mark Warner's Bellevue is one exception, handy for the Morel lift. For 2000/01 it has become 'adults only', and the operator has added the family-orientated 45-room Tarentaise to its programme, up in Mottaret.

Hotels Méribel has some excellent hotels, but they're not cheap.

((((5 **Antares** Best in town; beside the piste at Belvedere. Ambitious cooking. Pool, fitness room etc.

((((5 **Chalet** Luxurious, beautifully furnished wooden chalet at Belvedere, with lovely rooms and all mod cons – outdoor pool, fitness room etc.

((((4 **Grand Coeur** Our favourite almost-affordable hotel in Méribel. Just above the village centre. Welcoming, mature building with plush lounge. Magnificent food. Huge hot-tub, sauna, etc.

((((4 **Altiport** Modern and luxurious hotel, isolated at the foot of the Altiport lifts. Convenient for access to Courchevel, not for Val-Thorens.

((((4 **Mont Vallon** The best hotel at Mottaret, with a reputation for good food, and excellently situated for the Three Valleys pistes. Pool, sauna, hot-tub, squash, fitness room, etc.

((((4 **Chaudanne** One of the oldest Méribel hotels, renovated a few years ago, with a sports centre. However, a recent reporter found it to have 'tiny rooms, tacky decor and arrogant staff'.

(((3 **Adray Télébar** Welcoming piste-side chalet with pretty, rustic rooms, good food and popular sun terrace.

(2) **Roc** A good value B&B hotel, in the centre, with a bar-restaurant and crêperie below.

Self-catering There is a huge number of apartments and chalets to let in both Méribel and Mottaret. Take care to make sure that the place you book is conveniently situated and has enough space.

EATING OUT

Fair choice

There is a reasonable selection of restaurants, from ambitious French cuisine to relatively cheap pizza and pasta. For the best food in town, in plush surroundings, there is nothing to beat the top hotels – the Cassiopée in the Antares (with Méribel's one Michelin star), Grand Coeur ('So pleased we ate there several times'), Allodis and Chaudanne. Other recommendations include: Chez Kiki – 'good food and atmosphere'; Jardin d'Hiver – 'great char grills'; Les Castors – 'best French fare'; La Taverne – 'surprisingly good', the Tremplin – 'friendly service, booking essential', and the Cactus Café – 'good food and makes children welcome'.

Alternatives include the Galette, the Glacier, the Refuge, the Cava, Plantin and Cro Magnon, all popular for raclette and fondue. A reporter recommends the Crocodile in the Hameau at Mottaret. Scott's does good American-style food, and there's even a Pizza Express for the homesick.

At Les Allues, the Croix Jean-Claude serves (eventually) good-value French food in a pretty dining room.

ACTIVITIES

Indoor Parc Olympique Méribel (skating rink, swimming pool), Forme Méribel (spa, sauna, gym, bowling, billiards, climbing wall), library, bridge, fitness centres, hot-tub, 2 cinemas, concert hall

Outdoor Flying lessons and excursions, snow-mobiles, snow-shoe excursions, para-gliding, 20km of cleared paths, motor-trikes, sleigh rides

TOURIST OFFICE

Postcode 73551
t +33 479 086001
f 479 005961
info@meribel.net
www.meribel.net

APRES-SKI

Méribel rocks – loudly

Méribel's après-ski revolves around British-run places and some readers complain there's nowhere to go if you don't like loud pubs. The local clone of Dick's Tea Bar, the famous Brit-owned bar/club in Val-d'Isère, is now well established, but is remote from the slopes. At close of play it's the piste-side Rond Point that's packed – happy hour starts around 4pm – and has live music. Jack's, with a sun terrace, is also very popular, especially with resort staff and prices (even for holidaymakers) are said to be modest.

The ring of bars around the main square do good business at tea-time. La Taverne gets packed, but has a quieter downstairs bar. Just across the square is The Pub, with videos, pool and sometimes a band. The Capricorne attracts a cosmopolitan crowd and Le Refuge (down the road towards the lifts) is that rare thing in Méribel: a place where you'll be understood if you use your French.

Later on, live music brings in the crowds at The Pub, Artichaud (a bar/club hybrid) and Rond Point. There is late dancing at Scott's (next to The Pub) and, of course, there's Dick's Tea Bar (free entry and sub-disco drinks prices until 11.30). El Poncho's serves Mexican dishes and Desperado's (beer mixed with tequila).

In Mottaret the bars at the foot of the pistes get packed at tea-time – especially the terraces on a sunny day. The Rastro and DownTown are the most popular, though reporters inform us that Zig Zag has lower prices. Later on, Plein Soleil sometimes has live music, and the Rastro disco is the main venue for late revellers.

Both villages have a cinema which shows some films in English.

OFF THE SLOPES

Flight of fancy

Méribel is not really a resort for people who want to languish in the village but it is not unattractive. There's a good public swimming pool and an Olympic ice rink near the centre. You can also take joyrides in the little planes that operate from the Altiport. The pedestrian's lift pass covers all the gondolas and cable-cars in the Méribel and Courchevel valleys, and makes it very easy for pedestrians to get around the mountain and meet friends for lunch. The buses are free.

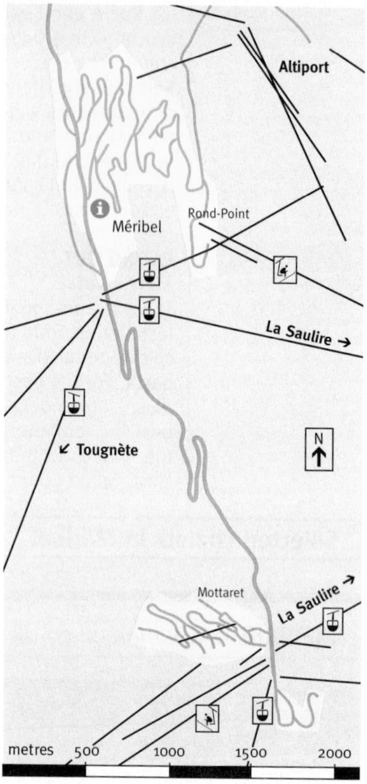

STAYING DOWN THE VALLEY

A few choices

If you want a quiet time, some UK tour operators have places in the old village of Les Allues, down the road from the resort and connected by the gondola up from Brides-les-Bains. There are a couple of bars and a good-value, well renovated hotel – the Croix Jean-Claude. Rooms are small, though.

Brides-les-Bains is an old spa town that served as the Olympic village in 1992 and is now turning itself into a winter as well as summer resort. It's cheap and has some simple hotels, all the necessary shops and a casino. But it's dead in the evening. And the long gondola ride to and from Méribel is tedious, cold and not included on your lift pass. If you are driving, it makes a good base for visiting other resorts.

The new development of Méribel-Village, is linked by chair-lift to the Altiport area with a blue run back and having a car is handy to reach nearby La Tania or Méribel proper. A recent reporter said: 'Not finished yet: no shop, no bar, no proper bus service. Impossible to get a taxi.' Let's hope it's better next season.

Montgenèvre 1850m

Not a pretty pass, but an admirably snowy one

WHAT IT COSTS

3

HOW IT RATES

The slopes	
Snow	****
Extent	****
Experts	**
Intermediates	****
Beginners	*****
Convenience	****
Queues	****
Restaurants	**
The rest	
Scenery	***
Resort charm	***
Off-slope	*

What's new

Cross-border links with Italy are improving: the Rocher de l'Aigle drag, to the border at Collet Vert, was replaced by a quad chair-lift a couple of years ago. And for 1999/2000 the Col Boeuf quad chair-lift from Clavière to Pian del Sole improved the return link back to France.

A new chair-lift from Clavière up to Col Saurel, in the Gimont valley, is planned for 2000/01. More artificial snowmaking is being installed as well.

- ➕ Good, convenient nursery slopes, with easy progression to longer runs
- ➕ Few queues on weekdays, unless people are bussing from other resorts with poor snow
- ➕ A lot of accommodation close to the slopes, and some right on them
- ➕ Good snow record, and local slopes largely north-facing – often the best snow in the Milky Way area
- ➕ Great potential for car drivers to explore other nearby resorts

- ➖ Poor base for exploring the Italian Milky Way resorts
- ➖ Slow lifts and short runs can be irritating
- ➖ Busy road lined by tatty bars reduces village charm and family appeal – crossing can be tricky
- ➖ Little to do off the slopes
- ➖ Little to challenge experts on-piste

Montgenèvre is set at one end of the extensive Milky Way network, reaching over to Sestriere and Sauze in Italy. It is not the ideal base for exploring the area – it's a time-consuming trek to much of the best terrain. This can be overcome by taking a car (also facilitating day trips to other French resorts such as Serre-Chevalier and La Grave). But Montgenèvre with its Monts de la Lune area is also worth considering on its own merits – including the slopes of Clavière, in Italy but only a few yards down the road. It's a convenient and pleasant village with a fair-sized area of intermediate slopes, particularly attractive to beginners and near-beginners wanting to do some longer runs on normally excellent snow.

boarding *There's plenty to attract boarders to Montgenèvre. There are good local beginner slopes and long runs on varied terrain for intermediates. The only real drawback is that many of the lifts in the area are drags, and you will have to use them to get around – getting over to Sestriere and back involves lots (and a flat green run to skate along as well). There's a fun-park on the lower slopes, and there are some excellent off-piste areas for more advanced boarders. Snow Box is the local specialist shop.*

SNOWPIX.COM / CHRIS GILL

The pass runs east-west; the village is on the sunny side of the road, the nursery slopes on the shady side →

MOUNTAIN FACTS

Altitude	1850m-2680m
Lifts	38
Pistes	100km
Green/Blue	42%
Red	39%
Black	19%
Artificial snow	10km
Recco detectors used	

The following figures relate to the whole Milky Way area

Altitude	1390m-2825m
Lifts	97
Pistes	400km
Blue	12%
Red	67%
Black	21%
Artificial snow	75km

The resort

Montgenèvre is a narrow roadside village set on a high pass only 2km from the Italian border. At first glance it appears a rather inhospitable place – a collection of tatty-looking bars and restaurants lining the side of the sometimes windswept and often busy main road over the col.

But appearances are deceptive. Tucked away off the main road is a charming old village, complete with quaint church and friendly natives. Being covered in snow for much of the season accentuates the charm factor, as do the pleasantly wooded mountains either side of the village. The slopes are convenient, despite the road. There is little walking to be done in this compact village, where most of the accommodation is less than five minutes from a lift. However, as the village expands, location is becoming more important. There is a free shuttle-bus. The underrated Chalvet area is on the same side of the road as the village. For their part, the cheap and cheerful cafés and bars add an animated atmosphere sometimes missing from French resorts. There is no bank, but there is a limited post office exchange service and now an automatic cash machine by the tourist office.

The mountains

Montgenèvre's local slopes are best suited to leisurely intermediates, with lots of easy cruising on blues and greens, both above and below the tree line. Intermediates who like to cover a bit of ground will want to cross into Italy to tour other Milky Way resorts (Sestriere and Sauze d'Oulx).

The best way to get to these other resorts and enjoy some time there is to travel by car. Serre-Chevalier and Puy-St-Vincent, with lift pass sharing arrangements, are also easily reached by car, and well worth an outing each. There's floodlit skiing on Wednesdays.

THE SLOPES

Slow going

The south-facing slopes of Le Chalvet lead straight up from the village. The major sector, the north-facing slopes of Les Anges and Le Querelay are across the main road from the village, with the nursery slopes at the bottom.

This sector has a high-altitude link via Collet Vert (reached by a quad chair) to the slopes above Clavière (covered on the Monts de la Lune lift pass) and so to the rest of the Milky Way. The alternative is to go via Clavière, reached either by plodding across valley-floor cross-country loops or by descending from Col de l'Alpet in

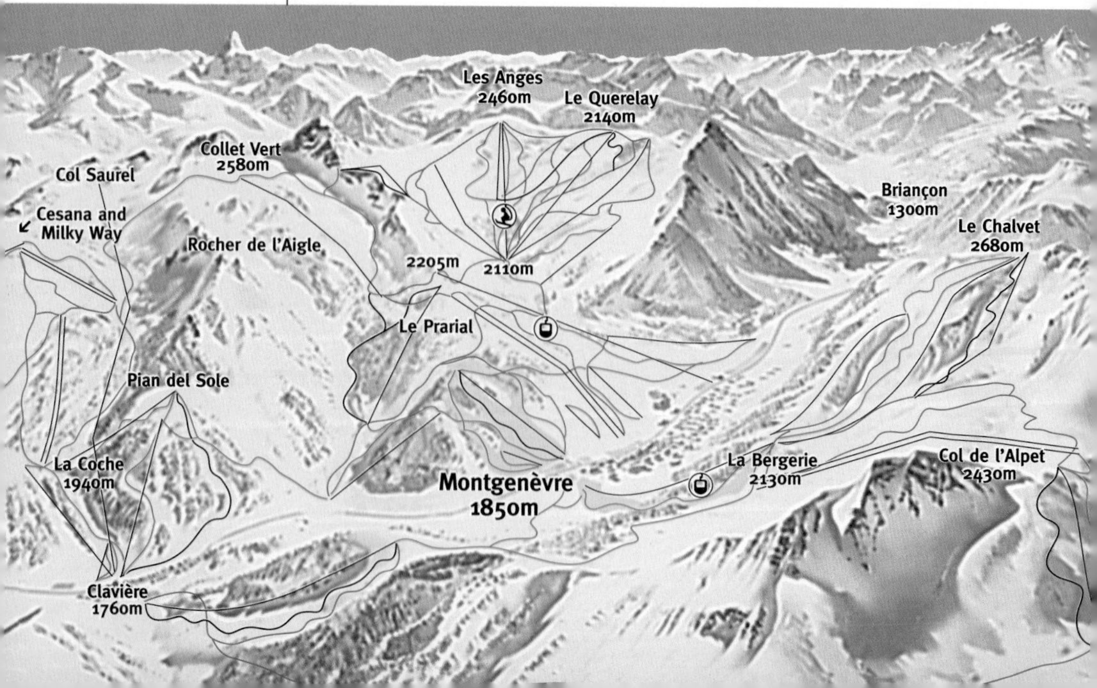

LIFT PASSES

2000/01 prices in francs

Montgenèvre
Covers Montgenèvre lifts only.

Beginners One free drag-lift. Points cards available. 'Petit Réseau' day pass covers 7 lifts (adult 97, child 78). Skiing by the hour is available (3-, 4- or 5-hour 'à la carte' passes).

Main pass
1-day pass 137
6-day pass 680

Senior citizens
Over 60: 6-day pass 585

Children
Under 12: 6-day pass 585
Under 6: free pass

Short-term passes
Single ascent for foot passengers of Le Chalvet or Chalmettes (adult 30).

Notes 6 day-pass and over allows free days at Alpe-d'Huez, Les Deux-Alpes, Puy-St-Vincent and Serre-Chevalier. Reductions for families. Extensions by the day to main pass for the Voie Lactée (adult 50).

Alternative passes
Montgenèvre-Monts de la Lune (Clavière) (adults 145 per day, children 116 per day). Voie Lactée (Milky Way) covers Montgenèvre, Clavière, Cesana, Sansicario, Sauze d'Oulx, Grangesises, Borgata, Sestriere – 400km (adults 245 per day).

the Chalvet area. The new Col Boeuf chair-lift out of Clavière has improved the return back into France.

Getting to and from the slopes of Sauze and Sestriere via Cesana and Sansicario is time consuming, involving a fair few slow chairs and drags. You may like the sensation of travel, or you may get the feeling you are doing too much clock watching to have any real fun. Access to Sestriere has in principle been improved by the reopening of a long red run from Monte Fraiteve. But it is sunny and not reliably open.

SNOW RELIABILITY

Excellent locally

Although it missed out entirely on the tragically heavy snowfalls two seasons ago, Montgenèvre has a generally excellent snow record, receiving dumps from westerly storms funnelling up the valley. The high, north-facing slopes naturally keep their snow better than the south-facing area but both have snowmaking on the main village-bound pistes. The slopes either side of the connecting Cesana valley are often bare, but chair-lifts make the link.

FOR EXPERTS

Limited, except for off-piste

There are very few challenging pistes in the Montgenèvre–Clavière–Cesana sectors. Many of the runs are overgraded on the map, none of the blacks being much more than a tough red. There is, however, ample opportunity for off-piste excursions, and heli-skiing on the Italian side when snow conditions are right.

The remote north-east-facing bowl beyond the Col de l'Alpet on the Chalvet side is superb in good snow and has black and red pistes, too.

On the major sector, both the runs from Collet Vert, on the Italian border at the top of the Rocher de l'Aigle chair-lift – one into Italy and one back into France – can be fun. The open section between La Montanina and Sagna Longa on the Italian side is another good powder area. Drivers should visit Sestriere for the most challenging runs.

FOR INTERMEDIATES

Plenty of cruising terrain

The overgraded blacks are just right for adventurous intermediates, though none holds the interest for very long. The pleasantly narrow tree-lined runs to Clavière from Pian del Sole, the steepest of the routes down in the Chalvet sector (including the lonely bowl mentioned for experts above) and the Montquitaine piste from that bowl to Clavière are all fine in small doses.

Average intermediates will enjoy the red runs, though most are short. The longest are down from the top of the Chalvet sector and the Collet Vert.

Getting to Cesana via the lovely sweeping red run starting at the top of the Serra Granet double-drag, and heading home from from Pian del Sole, is easier than the gradings suggest, and these can be tackled by less adventurous intermediates, who also have a wealth of cruising terrain high up at the top of the north-facing Anges and Querelay slopes above Montgenèvre. These are served by several upper lifts, but you have the option of continuing right down to the village. These long, gentle slopes are just as flattering as the famous motorways of Courchevel and Cervinia.

Further afield, the green down to Clavière from the top of the Gimont drags, on the Italian side, is a beautifully gentle cruise.

FOR BEGINNERS

Good for novices and improvers

There is a fine selection of convenient nursery slopes with reliable snow at the foot of the north-facing area. Progression to longer runs could not be easier, with a very easy blue starting at Les Anges (2460m), leading on to a green and finishing at the roadside 600m below.

FOR CROSS-COUNTRY

Having a car widens horizons

Montgenèvre is the best of the Milky Way resorts for cross-country enthusiasts, but it's useful to have a car. The two local trails, totalling 25km, offer quite a bit of variety, but a further 75km of track starts in Les Alberts, 8km away in the Clarée valley.

QUEUES

No problems most of the time

The slopes are wonderfully uncrowded during weekdays, provided surrounding resorts have snow. Some lifts become crowded at weekends and when nearby Bardonecchia is lacking snow. Links with Italy have improved and are improving still, but many of the lifts are old and slow. More of a problem, according to a recent reporter, is poor piste maintenance and signposting –

SCHOOLS/GUIDES

2000/01 prices in francs

ESF

Classes 6 half days mornings or afternoons
1 half day: 105
6 half days: 535

Children's classes
Ages: Up to 12
1 half day: 98
6 half days: 435

Private lessons
Hourly or daily
180 for 1hr; for 2-3 people 215

CHILDCARE

The Halte Garderie takes children aged 6 months to 6 years, from 9am to 5.30. Meals you provide can be administered.

The ESF's kindergarten takes children aged 3 to 5.

GETTING THERE

Air Turin, transfer 2hr. Grenoble, transfer 3hr. Lyon, transfer 4½hr.

Rail Briançon (15km) or Oulx (20km); 5 or 6 buses per day to Briançon from station.

ACTIVITIES

Indoor Library, cinema
Outdoor Natural skating rink, paragliding, snow-scooters, sledge runs, heli-skiing

TOURIST OFFICE

Postcode 05100
t +33 492 215252
f 492 219245
office.tourisme.montgenevre@wanadoo.fr
www.montgenevre.com

one of the signed runs from Collet Vert apparently leads you off piste. The hands-free electronic lift pass is a plus.

MOUNTAIN RESTAURANTS
Head for Italy
Restaurants are in very short supply locally. Most people travel back to the village for lunch. The Ca del Sol café-bar does a good pizza. There are several nice spots in Italy.

SCHOOLS AND GUIDES
Very varied reports
Over the years, comments on the school have varied greatly, from very good to very poor. They tend to push pupils hard, which suits some but not others. Recent reports are more positive.

FACILITIES FOR CHILDREN
Pity about the traffic
The intrusive main road apart, Montgenèvre would seem a fine family resort. Reports on the school's children's classes continue to be complimentary of both class size and spoken English.

Staying there

There are hotels, chalets and apartments available, all of which are cheap and cheerful places. Don't expect to find much luxury here. Location is becoming more important as the village expands – some of the newer accommodation is uphill, away from the slopes. But Montgenèvre is still reasonably compact.

HOW TO GO
Limited choice
UK tour operators concentrate on catered chalets, though some apartments are also available and a few operators also package hotels.
Chalets Several UK tour operators offer cheap and cheerful catered chalets.
Hotels There are a handful of simple places offering good value.

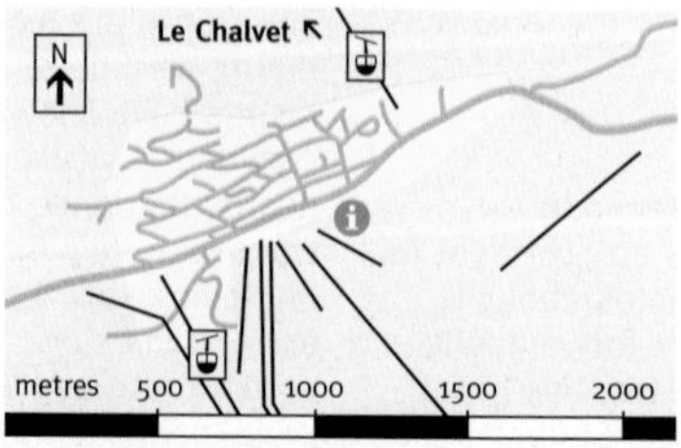

②② **Valérie** Central rustic old 3-star.
②② **Napoléon** 3-star on the roadside.
① **L'Alpet** Basic 2-star near the centre.
① **Chalet des Sports** About the cheapest hotel rooms in the Alps.
① **Le Boom** Cheap and cheerful place with tiny rooms near the village centre.
Self-catering Résidences La Ferme d'Augustin are simple, ski-to-the-door apartments on the fringes of the main north-facing slopes, five minutes' walk (across the piste) from town.

EATING OUT
Cheap and cheerful
There are a dozen places to choose from. The Ca del Sol and the Tourmente have been recommended by reporters. The Estable and Transalpin serve good-value traditional fare. Chez Pierrot and the Jamy have an authentic French feel. The 3-star Napoléon is the only hotel with a restaurant open to non-residents – a pizzeria. A trip to Clavière is worthwhile – reporters have testified to the excellence of the restaurants.

APRES-SKI
Mainly bars, but fun
The range is limited. Le Graal is a friendly, unsophisticated place; the Ca del Sol bar is a cosy place with an open fire. Pub Chaberton is also recommended. The little Blue Light disco is popular. The Refuge, La Crepouse, Les Rois Mages and the Jamy are the focal café-bars at tea-time.

OFF THE SLOPES
Very limited
There is a weekly market and you can walk the cross-country routes, but the main attraction is a bus-trip to the beautiful old town of Briançon. Excursions elsewhere are feasible only with a car.

STAYING IN OTHER RESORTS
Only for the dedicated
Cesana and Clavière are small villages with few facilities. Cesana is a 15-minute walk from its lifts. Clavière's nursery slope is small and steep but usually uncrowded and snow-reliable. There are longer runs suitable for progression. Both resorts are best for dedicated intermediates keen to make the most of the Milky Way slopes without much après-ski.

Morzine

1000m

A lively, year-round resort linked by lift to the Portes du Soleil

WHAT IT COSTS

4

HOW IT RATES

The slopes

Snow	**
Extent	*****
Experts	***
Intermediates	****
Beginners	***
Convenience	**
Queues	***
Restaurants	***

The rest

Scenery	***
Resort charm	***
Off-slope	***

What's new

1999/2000 saw the introduction of a new hands-free electronic lift pass system, so you can now keep your pass in your pocket.

A new childcare centre (Les Pingouins Malins) opened for those aged 4 to 12.

For 2000/01 the gondola up from Ardent to above Les Lindarets will be replaced by a higher-capacity one. In the local area, the Belvédère and Mouilles double chairs will be replaced by quads and the area at the top of the Pleney gondola will be rebuilt to make reaching the other lifts easier. More snowmaking will be installed on a main run down to town.

- ⊕ Part of the vast Portes du Soleil lift network
- ⊕ Larger local piste area than other Portes du Soleil resorts
- ⊕ Good nightlife by French standards
- ⊕ Quite attractive old town – a stark contrast to Avoriaz
- ⊕ One of the easiest drives from the Channel (a car is very useful here)
- ⊕ Few queues locally (but see minus points)

- ⊖ Takes a while to get to Avoriaz and main Portes du Soleil circuit
- ⊖ Bus-ride or long walk to lifts from much of the accommodation
- ⊖ Low altitude means there is an enduring risk of poor snow, though increased snowmaking has helped
- ⊖ Low altitude or inconvenient nursery slopes
- ⊖ Not a great resort for experts
- ⊖ Weekend crowds

Morzine is a long-established French resort, popular for its easy road access, traditional atmosphere and gentle tree-filled slopes, where children do not get lost and bad weather rarely causes problems. For keen piste-bashers wanting to travel the Portes du Soleil circuit, the main drawback to staying in Morzine is having to take a bus and cable-car or several lifts to get to Avoriaz and the main circuit. Morzine's local slopes can suffer from poor snow conditions.

Such problems can, however, be avoided by taking a car. A little-used gondola awaits at Ardent, a short drive from Morzine; from there, you can tour the circuit clockwise via Châtel, missing out Avoriaz (which is often crowded). If local snow is poor, a car means you have the alternative of visiting nearby Flaine, a resort far better than Avoriaz at coping with crowds looking for snow.

boarding *Avoriaz is the hard-core boarder destination in the Portes du Soleil and has an excellent 1.5km fun-park, half-pipe and slalom stadium. With interesting, tree-lined runs and few drag-lifts, the local Morzine slopes are good for beginners and intermediates. There are a few lively bars, of which the tiny Sherpa bar and Le Wallington are both popular with boarders.*

P JACQUES, FOC / MORZINE TO

Morzine is a large mountain town but its chalet-style buildings look charming under a blanket of fresh snow →

MOUNTAIN FACTS

Altitude	975m-2350m
Lifts	219
Pistes	650km
Green/Blue	51%
Red	40%
Black	9%
Art. snow	522 acres
Recco detectors used	

The resort

Morzine is a large, traditional, mountain town which sprawls amorphously on both sides of a river gorge and on several levels. Under a blanket of snow, its chalet-style buildings look charming, and in spring the village quickly takes on a spruce appearance.

The old centre is next to the river, but most resort amenities are clustered higher up around the Le Pléney lifts. Accommodation is widely scattered, and a good multi-route bus service links all parts of the town to outlying lifts, including those for Avoriaz.

Morzine is essentially a family resort, and village ambience tends to be fairly subdued. Our view that the resort suits car drivers is widely shared, and there are traffic problems.

The mountains

The local slopes suit intermediates well, with excellent areas for beginners and near-beginners too.

THE SLOPES
No need to go far afield

Morzine is not an ideal base for the Portes du Soleil circuit (described in the Avoriaz, Châtel and Champéry chapters). But it has an extensive local area, shared with Les Gets.

A cable-car and parallel gondola rise from the edge of central Morzine to **Le Pléney**, where numerous routes return to the valley, including a run down to Les Fys – a quiet junction of chairs which access **Nyon** and, in the opposite direction, the ridge separating Morzine from the **Les Gets** slopes. Nyon is also accessed by cable-car, situated a bus-ride out of Morzine, and is connected to the slopes of Les Gets higher up the valley that separates the two, with a lift up from Le Grand Pré to Le Ranfolly. The Nyon sector has two peaks – Pointe de Nyon and Chamossière – accessible from Nyon and Le Grand Pré respectively.

Connections between Pléney and

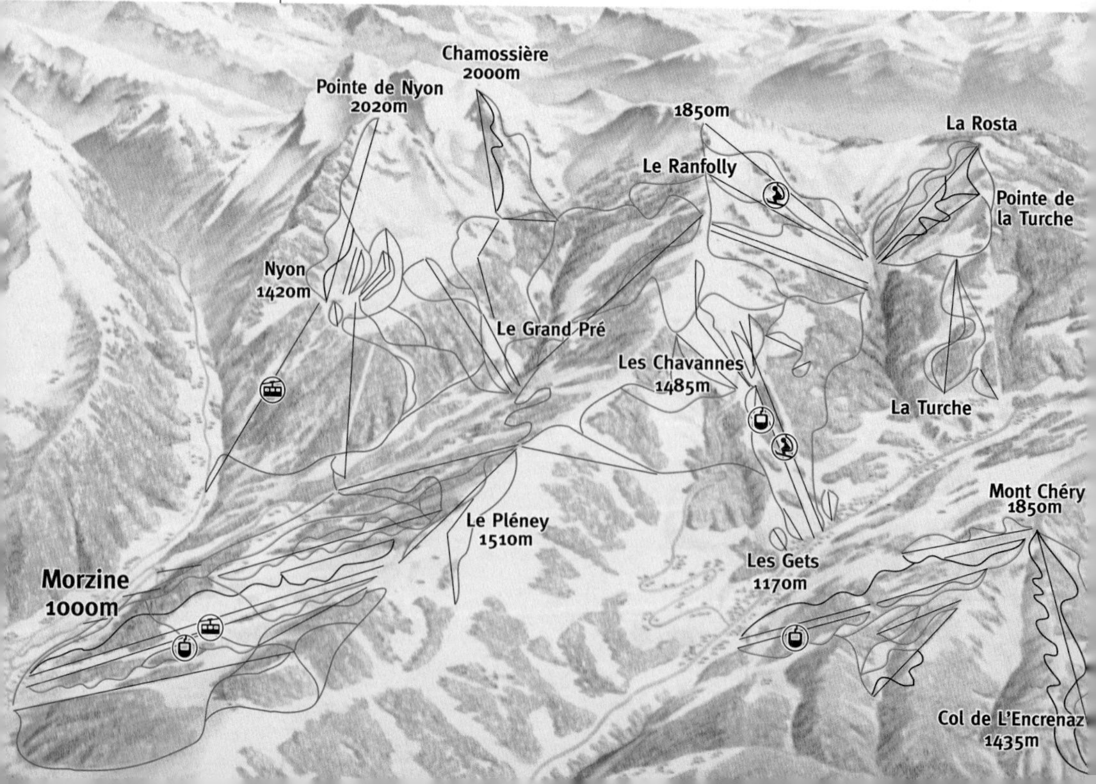

LIFT PASSES

2000/01 prices in francs

Portes du Soleil
Covers all lifts in 12 resorts, and shuttle buses.

Main pass
1-day pass 207
6-day pass 998

Senior citizens
Over 60: 6-day pass 798

Children
Under 16: 6-day pass 669
Under 5: free pass

Short-term passes
Half-day passes available for the Portes de Soleil (adult 155), Super-Morzine-Avoriaz (adult 137) and Morzine-Gets (adult 115).

Notes Discounts for groups of 13 or more and holders of the Carte Neige.

Alternative passes
Morzine-Les Gets pass covers 85 lifts (adult 6-day 760, child 570); 6-day pass including 5 days in Morzine-Les Gets and 1 day in Portes du Soleil (844 adults, 616 children).

Nyon are not easy for the uninitiated, owing to a poor piste map and signing. From Le Ranfolly you can descend directly to Morzine without using a lift. Access to Morzine from the slopes above Les Gets has been simplified; from the mid-mountain lift junction of Les Chavannes, you can descend to the Folliets chair-lift which takes you up to Le Pléney.

Beyond Les Gets is another small but worthwhile sector, on Mont Chéry. The short walk or 'petit train' shuttle through the village from the base of Chavannes takes about five minutes.

A third area starts at **Super-Morzine**, accessed from town by gondola – another handy 'petit train' shuttle service runs between this and the Le Pléney lifts. A series of pistes and lifts transports you to Avoriaz. This section is very much an access route, used mainly by Morzine clientele moving to and from Avoriaz. The alternative is a bus-ride or short drive to Les Prodains, from where you can get a cable-car to Avoriaz or a chair-lift into the **Hauts Forts** slopes above it.

By bus or car you can also get to Ardent, where a gondola accesses Les Linderets for lifts towards Châtel, Avoriaz or Champéry. The tree-lined slopes in this area are worth heading for in poor visibility. Car trips to Flaine and Chamonix are also feasible.

There is floodlit skiing twice a week.

SNOW RELIABILITY
Poor

Morzine has a very low average height, and when snow disappears from the valley, both of the main areas become very small and unconnected. There is some snowmaking, most noticeably on the runs linking Nyon and Le Pléney, and on red and blue runs back to town. The Les Gets area has recently benefited from extended snowmaking as well – but more is needed.

FOR EXPERTS
Limited on-piste

The run down from Pointe de Nyon is challenging, but for piste challenges the cable-car at Les Prodains is the place to head for, taking you up to Avoriaz. The Hauts Forts black runs, including the World Cup downhill course, are excellent. The above-the-tree-line slopes of Chamossière offer some of the best off-piste possibilities, and Mont Chéry is also well worth exploring. We've also had reports of great off-piste off the back of Col du Fornet down towards the Vallée de la Manche (but you'd need a guide).

FOR INTERMEDIATES
Something for everyone

Good intermediates will enjoy the challenging reds and blacks down from the Chamossière and Pointe de Nyon high points. Mont Chéry at Les Gets has some fine steepish runs which are worth heading for.

Those of average ability have a great number of runs to choose from, though most are rather short. Le Ranfolly accesses a series of good cruising runs on the Les Gets side of the ridge, and a nice piste back to Le Grand Pré. Le Pléney has a compact network of pistes that are ideal for groups with mixed abilities: mainly moderate intermediate runs, but with some easier alternatives for the more timid, and a single challenging route for the aggressive. Nyon's slopes are rather bitty for those not up to at least Chamossière runs.

Less experienced intermediates have plenty of options on Le Pléney, including a snow-gun-covered cruise from the summit back to the main lift station. Heading from Le Ranfolly to Le Grand Pré is another nice run. And the slopes down to Les Gets from Le Pléney is easy when conditions allow (the run is south-facing).

FOR BEGINNERS
Good for novices and improvers

The village nursery slopes are wide, flat and convenient, and benefit from snow-guns. Fast learners have the inconvenience that the slightly longer, steeper runs are over at Nyon. However, adventurous novices also have the option of easy pistes around Le Pléney. Near-beginners can get over to Les Gets via Le Pléney, and return via Le Ranfolly. The slopes at Les Gets suit near-beginners well.

FOR CROSS-COUNTRY
Good variety
There is a wide variety of cross-country trails, not all at valley level. The best section is in the pretty Vallée de la Manche beside the Nyon mountain up to the Lac de Mines d'Or where there is a good restaurant. The Pléney-Chavannes loop is pleasant and relatively snow-reliable. A network of trails runs between Super-Morzine and Avoriaz, and around Montriond lake.

QUEUES
Few problems when snow is good
Queues are not a problem in the local area. The Nyon cable-car and Belvédère chair-lift (Le Pléney) are weekend bottlenecks. Queues to and from Avoriaz are much improved in recent times, but are still bad when snow is in short supply.

MOUNTAIN RESTAURANTS
Within reach of some good huts
The nice little place at the foot of the d'Atray chair is perhaps the best of the local huts. Les Lindarets, Les Marmottes and Plaine Dranse are not too far and have some good restaurants. Pommes de Pin at the top of the télécabine d'Ardent is friendly with reasonably priced food. The Restaurant des Crêtes de Zore above Super-Morzine is good.

SCHOOLS AND GUIDES
British ski school here
The British Alpine Ski School, featuring BASI-qualified instructors, is based in Morzine and Les Gets and we have had good reports on the standard of tuition, although some reporters have complained about the children's classes and timetables being unreliable. It is used by several British tour operators. Reports on the ESF are generally quite good except for the usual complaints about class sizes.

FACILITIES FOR CHILDREN
Lots of possibilities
We have been quite impressed by the facilities of the Outa crèche, but have received reports of poor spoken English and low staff ratios. Ski Esprit's facilities are good, with in-chalet crèches, an afternoon Snow Club for children attending morning ski school and their own tuition scheme, using specially contracted instructors. Ski Famille and Ski Hillwood are other family specialists based in Les Gets.

SCHOOLS/GUIDES
2000/01 prices in francs
ESF
Classes 6 days
5hr: 9.30-noon and 2.30-5pm; 2½hr: am or pm
6 half-days: 570
Children's classes
Ages: Under 12
6 full days including lunch: 1300
Private lessons
Hourly
180 for 1 to 2 people

CHILDCARE
The Halte Garderie l'Outa (450 792600) takes children aged 2 months to 6 years, from 8.30 to 6pm. From age 3 they can have one-hour introductory lessons. Les Pingouins Malins takes children aged 4 to 12, with ESF instruction and lunch provided (1/2 or full days).

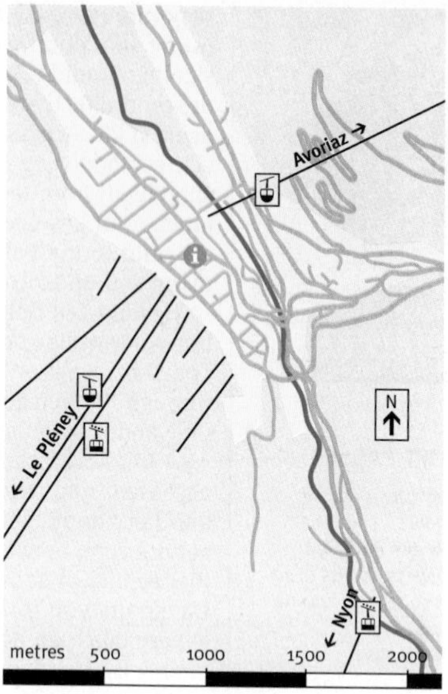

Staying there

As the extensive network of bus routes implies, Morzine is a town where getting from A to B can be tricky. It is well worth making sure that your accommodation is near the lifts that you expect to be using, which for most visitors means the gondola and cable-car to Le Pléney, gondola to Super-Morzine or cable-car to Avoriaz.

HOW TO GO
Good-value hotels and chalets
The tour operator market concentrates on hotels and chalets. Independent travellers have a wider choice, notably of apartments.
Chalets There's a wide choice, with something to suit all tastes and tour operators ranging from the smallest to the biggest. Position varies enormously: you can be in the centre of town or right on the edge of the slopes; many are on the outskirts, however, without either convenience.
Hotels The range of hotel accommodation is wider than it at first appears – the handful of 3-star hotels includes some quite smooth ones. But the core of the resort is its modest accommodation – dozens of 2-stars and quite a lot of 1-stars. If there is a resort with more hotels in the Logis de France group, we have yet to find it.
((((4) **Dahu** Best in town: upmarket 3-star, complete with elegant public areas and good restaurant and pool

GETTING THERE

Air Geneva, transfer 1½hr. Lyon, transfer 3½hr.

Rail Cluses or Thonon (30km); regular bus connections to resort.

ACTIVITIES

Indoor Skating, bowling, cinemas, massage, table tennis, fitness track
Outdoor Horse-riding, sleigh rides, snow-shoe classes, artificial climbing wall, tennis, paragliding

TOURIST OFFICE

Postcode 74110
t +33 450 747272
f 450 790348
touristoffice@morzine-avoriaz.com
www.morzine-avoriaz.com

complex. Some distance from all lifts and public buses except the Ardent route, but with private shuttle.
((((4 **Airelles** Central 3-star close to Pléney lifts and both Prodains and Nyon bus routes. Good pool.
((((4 **Champs Fleuris** Comfortable 3-star right next to Pléney lifts. Pool.
(((3 **Tremplin** Also next to the lifts; 'friendly staff, good food'.
(((3 **Bergerie** Rustic, old-fashioned chalet with a few rooms and many more studios, in centre. Friendly staff. Pool and gym.
((2 **Côtes** Simple, upwardly mobile 2-star, with more studios than rooms. Recently installed pool compensates for poor position on the edge of town.
((2 **Equipe** One of the better 2-stars, superbly placed next to the Pléney lift.
((2 **Alpen Sports** Friendly, family run hotel – 'excellent food and good value for money'.
Self-catering The Télémark apartments are of high quality, and are close to the Super-Morzine gondola. We're told that the apartments beside the Prodains cable-car are the best around.

EATING OUT
A fine choice
Morzine is scarcely a gourmet's resort, but by mountain resort standards it has a wide choice of good restaurants. The expensive La Chamade has high-quality French cuisine, Café Chaud is a popular and atmospheric place that does good fondue, Les Airelles has a fine restaurant (Les Jardins d'Ulysse), known for its hot buffets, and Le Dahu also has good food. The L'Etale (one reporter says 'La Luge dish is a must') is a cheap and cheerful pizza joint, bedecked in hundreds of different football scarves and serving local specialities. Reporters also recommend Clin d'Oeil, Le Don Camillo, the Gavottes and the Combe á Zore.

APRES-SKI
One of the livelier French resorts
Nightlife is good by French standards, though far from wild. Le Dixie is the most animated bar, with Eurosport, MTV, a great little cellar bar and occasional live music. Reporters say that at the Crépuscule 'dancing on the tables seems to be compulsory'. The tiny Sherpa, on the outskirts of town, is popular with resort staff. L'Opéra, Le Paradis du Laury's and Le Wallington (a ten-pin bowling alley-cum-disco-cum-pool-hall-cum-bar) are the only nightclubs. There are also two cinemas.

OFF THE SLOPES
Quite good; excursions possible
There is an excellent ice rink, which stages regular ice hockey matches and skating galas. Some of the hotels have pools which non-residents can pay to use. Buses run to Thonon, which is a useful shopping excursion, and car owners can drive to Geneva, Annecy or Montreux. There are lots of very pretty walks, and other activities include horse-drawn sleigh rides, horse-riding and paragliding.

Les Gets 1170m

Les Gets is not an ideal base for exploring the Portes du Soleil circuit, but its local slopes have a far larger, denser array of pistes than any of the resorts on the circuit, and are perfectly adequate for many intermediates. Decent children's facilities, pleasant trees, French ambience, convenience, nice village restaurants, fine nursery slopes and reasonable prices make Les Gets an excellent choice for families and many others. Several reporters have also mentioned that it feels tucked away and rather secretive. Weekend crowds are a drawback. Despite having a slightly higher elevation than Morzine, snow conditions can again be erratic. Happily, 50 new snow-guns were installed recently, improving cover back to the resort.

Les Gets is a little old village of mainly traditional chalet buildings, 6km from its larger neighbour, Morzine. Although the village has a scattered appearance, most of the facilities are conveniently close to the main lift station. It is on a through-road (Cluses–Morzine to Avoriaz), but traffic does not intrude too much, bypassing most of the village. There is a fair amount of nightlife but most places are quiet except at weekends when the atmosphere becomes more chic.

As well as the area shared with Morzine, Les Gets has slopes on Mont Chéry, accessed by gondola and parallel chair, with a further chair to the summit. The front slopes face south-east, bad news at this altitude; but the other two flanks are more shady. The black runs served by the Chéry Nord chair are steep in parts.

The village nursery slopes are quite good and are convenient for most accommodation, but there are better, more snowsure ones up the mountain at Chavannes. Progression to pistes is simple, with a very easy run between Chavannes and the resort, and a couple of nicely meandering routes from La Rosta. Easy pistes between Le Ranfolly and Les Chavannes, and down to La Turche, mean confident novices can get a lot of mileage in.

Cross-country skiers would be better off in Morzine, which has an excellent array of trails. But Les Gets has a good variety of loops on Mont Chéry and Les Chavannes – a total of 46km.

This year we've had mixed reports of the ESF, with tales of 'two instructors shouting at our 4-year-olds in French and 40 screaming children – our children lasted two mornings ... a dismal way of learning to ski' but also of children enjoying lessons with 'a great instructor'. Beginners should, if conditions are less than perfect, shop around for lessons at Chavannes.

The Ski Alpin pass covers all Les Gets, Nyon and Pléney lifts. The local ticket saves a fair bit on the cost of a Portes du Soleil pass, and is worth considering for the less experienced if snow conditions are good.

Many visitors stay in private chalets, quite a few of which are on the British market in catered form. Most are pleasant, comfortable, no-frills places. There are surprisingly few hotel beds and apartments available.

All the hotels are 3-star and below, mostly cheap and cheerful old 2-stars. The Crychar, 100m from central Les Gets at the foot of the slopes, is one of the best. The Ours Blanc and the Nagano are comfortable and central, and the former has 'good food and spacious well equipped rooms'. Hotel Marmotte has been reported to be 'wonderful, child friendly and helpful, although the pool is very grotty'. The hotel Bellevue at the bottom of the slopes is the natural rendezvous point.

Les Gets has a wide variety of places to eat. Most of the hotels have worthwhile restaurants. The Tyrol and the Schuss are good pizza places. The rustic Vieux Chêne is popular for its Savoyard specialities. The Flambeau and Tourbillon are also recommended.

Nightlife is quiet, particularly on weekdays. The Pub Irlandaise can get lively. Bar les Copeaux has been recommended. The Igloo and Havana Noche are popular discos. Prings, an English-owned pub, is often packed.

Les Gets has a well-equipped fitness centre with a pool, and an artificial ice rink. Outings to Geneva, Lausanne and Montreux are possible.

There is a non-ski nursery for children aged three months to two years, and two ski kindergartens. Ski Espace's 'Ile des Enfants' is reputedly the better of the two, and is open from 8am to 6pm, taking children from three years old. ESF's Club Fantaski has been criticised for inattentive supervision and having a roadside slope used by adults. Tour operators Ski Famille and Ski Hillwood have been recommended for their childcare.

La Plagne

1800m-2100m

A variety of villages spread across a vast playground

WHAT IT COSTS

(5)

HOW IT RATES

The slopes

Snow	****
Extent	****
Experts	***
Intermediates	*****
Beginners	*****
Convenience	*****
Queues	**
Restaurants	**

The rest

Scenery	****
Resort charm	*
Off-slope	*

What's new

For 1999/2000 a new snowboard park was created above Bellecôte and more snowmaking was put in at Montchavin and Montalbert. A new red run was cut through the forest above Montalbert and a new return run was created from Plagne Centre to Plagne 1800. Also new last season was the 3-star Terra Nova hotel in Plagne Centre.

For 2000/2001 the queue-prone Grande Rochette gondola from Plagne Centre is being replaced by a much more powerful lift. A 3-star hotel, Les Balcons, is opening in Belle Plagne. As are three luxury apartment blocks in Aime la Plagne, Plagne Villages and Plagne 1800.

There are plans to link the Les Arcs and La Plagne slopes by cable-car in the next couple of years.

SNOWPIX.COM / CHRIS GILL

Plagne 1800 is big on chalets →

- ⊕ Extensive intermediate slopes, plus plentiful off-piste terrain
- ⊕ Excellent nursery slopes
- ⊕ High and fairly snowsure – and blessed with some grand views
- ⊕ Purpose-built resort units are convenient for the slopes, and some are not unpleasant
- ⊕ Attractive, traditional-style villages lower down share the slopes
- ⊕ Wooded runs of lower resorts are useful in poor weather
- ⊕ Good cross-country trails

- ⊖ Few challenging pistes, few of any great length in the main bowl and several long flat sections
- ⊖ Still some serious lift bottlenecks in the high resorts
- ⊖ Lower villages can suffer from poor snow – Champagny especially
- ⊖ Unattractive architecture in some of the higher resort units
- ⊖ Not many green runs for nervous beginners to go on to – though some blues are very easy
- ⊖ Nightlife very limited

In terms of size, La Plagne's terrain and lift network ranks alongside those of Val-d'Isère/Tignes and the Trois Vallées, yet the resort doesn't enjoy the same status. What it lacks is the macho factor: it has very few black runs, and scores of blues. For most intermediates that is, of course, just the ticket – a friendly area, offering a real sensation of travel between the widely spread resort villages. (And in fact the place is fine for experts – just head off-piste.)

The resort is part-way through a major programme of investment in new lifts. That's very welcome, but it reflects the fact that the lift system is another weakness. The lifts to Roche de Mio and Bellecôte, in particular, are just inadequate, and there is no immediate sign of replacements.

boarding *La Plagne offers some pretty good terrain for all standards of rider – there's a good mix of long, easy runs and high, open slopes with some fantastic off-piste variations that should be done with a guide. Whether on- or off-piste, be prepared for some flat areas, though. There are two fun-parks – one at Dos Rond, above Montchavin-Les Coches and a new one at Plagne Bellecôte. The broad, gentle pistes are ideal for beginners and carvers (crowds permitting). Most lifts are gondolas or chairs, though there are still some difficult-to-avoid drag-lifts.*

The resort

La Plagne consists of no fewer than ten separate 'villages'; six are purpose-built at altitude in the main bowl, on or above the tree line and linked by road, lifts and pistes; the other four are dotted around outside the bowl.

Even the core resorts vary considerably in style and character. The first to be built, in the 1960s, was Plagne-Centre, at around 2000m – still the focal point for shops and après-ski. Typical of its time, it consists of big, ugly blocks and dark, depressing passageways that house a reasonable selection of shops, bars and restaurants. Some new developments just above Plagne Centre are more pleasing to the eye.

Above it, and linked by cable-car, is the even more obtrusive Aime-la-Plagne, with its monolithic hotel and apartment blocks ('the ugliest in the Alps', 'a carbuncle', say readers).

Below these two, and a bit of a backwater, is Plagne 1800, a more tasteful but rather amorphous chalet-style development.

A short walk above Plagne-Centre is La Plagne's newest incarnation, Plagne-Soleil, still small as yet, but with its own shops and some attractive new chalets – very convenient for the slopes. This area is officially attached to Plagne-Villages, which is a rather strung-out but otherwise attractive collection of small-scale apartments and chalets in traditional style, handy for the slopes but for nothing else.

The two other core resort units are a bus-ride away on the other side of a low hill. The large apartment buildings of Plagne-Bellecôte form a wall at the foot of the slopes down to it. Some way above it is traffic-free Belle-Plagne – as its name suggests, easy on the eye, with a Disneyesque neo-Savoyard look, and complete with entirely underground parking.

Accommodation in all these developments on the mountain is largely self-catering, and popular with French families, who pack the resort during peak season weeks. In low season it can be eerily empty. There are some hotels in Plagne-Centre and Belle-Plagne, where a new one is opening for 2000/01.

Then there are the lower resorts in the valleys – the old villages of Montchavin and Champagny, on opposite sides of the area, and the newly developed villages of Les Coches (near Montchavin) and Montalbert. For a description of each, see the end of this chapter.

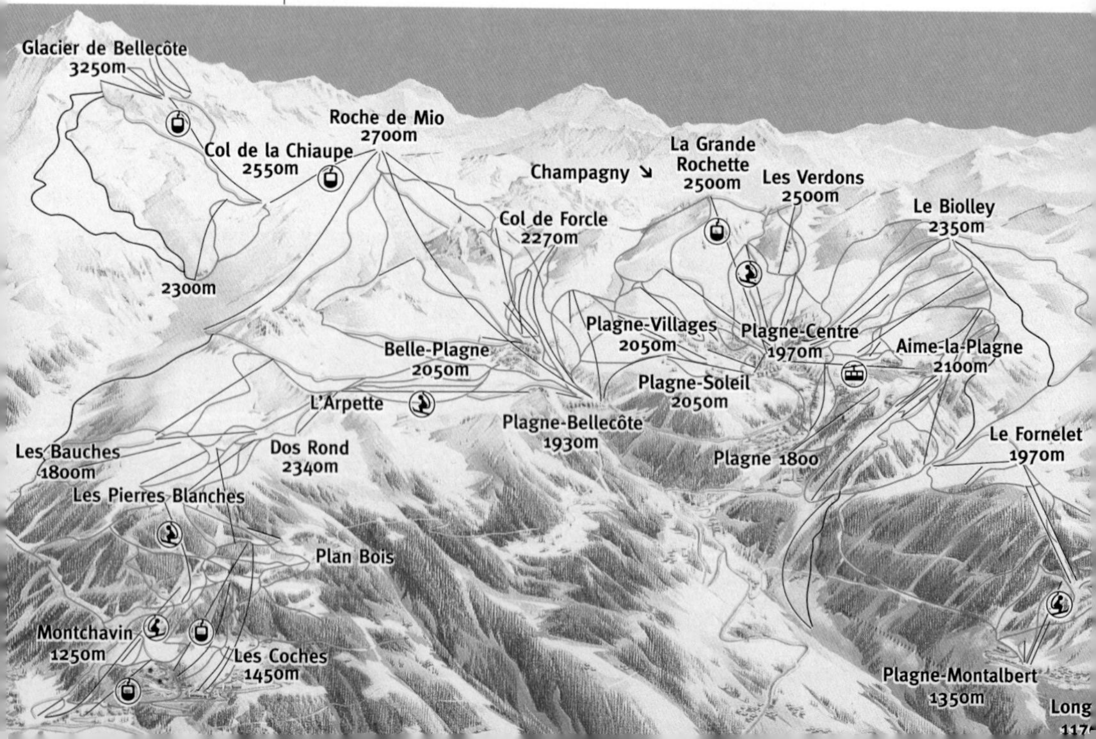

MOUNTAIN FACTS

Altitude	1250m-3250m
Lifts	110
Pistes	212km
Green/Blue	67%
Red	28%
Black	5%
Art. snow	50 acres
Recco detectors used	

The mountains

La Plagne is a great resort for all intermediates. There are wide motorways for early intermediates and long excursions for the more adventurous. Beginners are well catered for by the schools, which operate on easy, accessible nursery slopes. Experts mainly have to look off-piste for their thrills.

Day trips to Les Arcs are easy, trips to Val-d'Isère, Tignes or the Three Valleys more time-consuming.

THE SLOPES
Multi-centred; can be confusing

La Plagne boasts 212km of pistes over a wide area that can be broken down into seven distinct but interlinked sectors. From Plagne-Centre you can take a lift up to **Biolley**, from where you can head back to Centre, to Aime-la-Plagne or down gentle runs to **Montalbert**, from where you ride several successive lifts back up. But the main lift out of Plagne-Centre leads up to **Grande Rochette**. From here there are good sweeping runs back down and an easier one over to Plagne-Bellecôte, or you can drop over the back into the predominantly south-facing **Champagny** sector (from which a lift arrives back up at Grande Rochette and another brings you out much further east). From the Champagny sector there are great views over to Courchevel, across the valley.

From Plagne-Bellecôte and Belle-Plagne, a gondola heads up to **Roche de Mio**, where runs spread out in all directions. You can head back down towards La Plagne, or down towards Champagny in one direction and **Montchavin-Les Coches** in the other. Montchavin-Les Coches can also be reached by taking a chair from Plagne Bellecôte. From Roche de Mio you can also take a gondola down to Col de la Chiaupe (there are no runs in that direction) then up to the **Bellecôte glacier**, start of some of the steepest slopes in the area. In good snow there is an easy off-piste run from the foot of Bellecôte at 2300m to Les Bauches, and the Montchavin slopes. Otherwise, you have to return to Roche de Mio.

The special 'evasion' map identifies five circuits of varying difficulty.

SNOW RELIABILITY
Good except in low-lying villages

Most of La Plagne's runs are snowsure, being at altitudes between 2000m and 2700m on the largely north-facing open slopes above the purpose-built centres. The Bellecôte glacier drags are normally shut in winter.

Runs down to the valley resorts can cause more problems, and you may have to take the lifts at times. This is particularly true of the Champagny sector, where the two home runs are both south-facing and quickly lose their snow in warm weather. The runs down to Les Coches and Montchavin

SCHOOLS/GUIDES

2000/01 prices in francs

ESF
Schools in all centres. Prices do vary; those given here are for Plagne Centre
Classes 6 days
2½hr, 3hr, 5hr, 6hr, depending on centre and time of day and season
6 full days: 940
Children's classes
Ages: Up to 13 or 16 depending on village
6 full days: 825
Private lessons
1hr, 1½hr, 2hr
195 for 1hr

Eric Laboureix
Ski and mountain sports school in Belle-Plagne
Classes 6 days
am or pm
6 half days: 1020
Children's classes
Ages: Up to 14
6 full days: 1090
Private lessons
Hourly
200 for 1hr

Oxygène
Private school in Plagne-Centre
Classes 6 days
am or pm
6 full days: 990
Children's classes
Ages: Up to 14
6 full days: 990
Private lessons
Hourly
210 for 1hr

1999/2000 prices in francs

Evolution 2
Private school in Montchavin
Classes 5 days
5 days (3hr): 500
Children's classes
5 days (3hr): 430
Private lessons
Hourly
170 for 1hr

Antenne Handicap
Private lessons for the disabled
200 for 1h

are north-facing and have artificial snow – these, and a few runs around Montalbert and Plagne Bellecôte, are the main ones with artificial cover in the area, although the network is continually expanding. Grooming is patchy.

FOR EXPERTS
A few good blacks and off-piste

In theory there are two potentially great black runs from Bellecôte to the chair-lift back to the gondola at Col de la Chiaupe glacier – both beautiful long runs with a vertical of some 1000m that take you away from the lift system. In many visits, we've never found them open.

The long Emile Allais down from above Aime-la-Plagne through the forest, finishing at 1400m, is now graded black only at its final stage. With a couple of drag-lifts taking you back up, it is little used, which is surprising as it is north-facing and very enjoyable in good snow. The shorter Coqs and Morbleu runs in the same sector are seriously steep.

The long, sweeping Mont de la Guerre red run, with a 1250m vertical from Grande Rochette-Les Verdons to Champagny, is also a beautiful run in good snow – a rare event.

There are other good long reds to cruise around on. But experts will get the best out of La Plagne if they hire a guide and explore the vast off-piste potential. There are popular off-piste variants on the aforementioned black runs from Bellecôte down to Les Bauches (a drop of over 1400m). You can also head down off-piste to Peisey-Nancroix and take the lifts up to the Les Arcs slopes.

Another beautiful and out-of-the-way off-piste run from Bellecôte is over the Col du Nant glacier and down into the valley of Champagny-le-Haut.

Unfortunately, the glacier gondola can be closed by high winds or poor weather – and the black runs from the top are often closed because there's too much snow or too little.

In fresh snow, those who enjoy picking their way through woods in search of fresh light powder will not be disappointed by the forests above Montchavin and Montalbert.

FOR INTERMEDIATES
Great variety

Virtually the whole of La Plagne's area is a paradise for intermediates, with blue and red runs wherever you look. Your main choice will be whether to settle for one area for the day and explore it thoroughly, or just cruise around the pistes that form the main arteries of the network.

For early intermediates there are plenty of gentle blue motorway pistes in the main La Plagne bowl, and a long, interesting run from Roche de Mio back to Belle Plagne, Les Inversins, which includes a long, dark (and cold) tunnel. The blue runs either side of L'Arpette, on the Montchavin side of the main bowl, are glorious cruises. In poor weather the best place to be is in the trees on the gentle runs leading down to Montalbert. The easiest way over to Champagny is from

TRY THE OLYMPIC BOB-SLEIGH RUN

If the thrills and spills of a day on the slopes aren't enough, you can round it off by having a go on the 1992 Winter Olympics bob-sleigh run. The floodlit 1.5km run drops 125m, has 19 bends and you can go in a proper four-man 'taxi-bob' (FF460 in 1999/2000) or in a special driverless bob raft (FF190).

Most people, not surprisingly, take the cheaper option, and find the ride quite thrilling enough. The bob raft is padded and mounted on wide skids that keep the speed down to a mere 75–80kph; the ride takes around one and a half minutes.

With the taxi-bob, you are one of three passengers wedged in behind the driver. You reach a maximum speed of 100–105kph and the ride lasts about 50 seconds. The pressure in turns can be as high as 3g – be sure your physical state is up to it. You must be over 16. Additional insurance is available (yours may not be valid).

The bob raft is generally open to tourists from Tuesday to Sunday from 5pm to 7.30pm, while the taxi-bob runs only on Friday and Sunday from 3pm to 4.30pm. The course is open from Christmas to mid-March – though the season may be shorter if it's too warm. You can also watch the championship events that run regularly throughout the season.

the Roche de Mio area rather than from Grande Rochette.

Better intermediates have lots of delightful long red runs to try. Roche de Mio to Les Bauches is a drop of 900m (the second half of this run is marked as a black). There are challenging red mogul pitches down from the glacier to the mid-station of the gondola at Col de la Chiaupe. And the main La Plagne bowl has enjoyable reds in all sectors. The Champagny sector has a couple of tough reds – Kamikaze and Hara-Kiri – leading from Grande Rochette. The long Mont de la Guerre red is a satisfying run for adventurous intermediates.

FOR BEGINNERS
Excellent facilities for the novice

La Plagne is a good place to learn, with generally good snow and above-average facilities for beginners, especially children. Each of the main centres has nursery slopes on its doorstep. There's a free drag-lift in each resort as well. There are no long green runs to progress to, but no shortage of easy blues. One reporter felt that the runs back into Plagne 1800 were a bit difficult for novices.

CROSS-COUNTRY
Open and wooded trails

There are over 100km of prepared and marked cross-country pistes in La Plagne and its surrounding satellites. The most beautiful of these are the 30km of track set out in the valley around Champagny-le-Haut. Here, the pistes loop and wind through wild countryside, often in good, sunny conditions. The north-facing areas have more wooded trails that link the various centres. There is a 25km route above Montchavin-Les Coches and an 18km route above Montalbert. Plagne Bellecôte, Belle Plagne and Plagne Villages are similarly linked by a less arduous, 12km route. Each of the trails has a beginners' circuit. Access is free (except at Champagny).

QUEUES
Bottlenecks in high season

When the resort is full there can be big queues to get out of the high-altitude centres at the start of the day. The old gondola from Plagne-Bellecôte via Belle-Plagne to Roche de Mio is still a bad bottleneck, despite the alternative ways available. The higher gondola can also get oversubscribed when snow is

SNOWPIX.COM / CHRIS GILL

Belle-Plagne, in the centre, has a lot to recommend it as a base if nightlife isn't a priority ↘

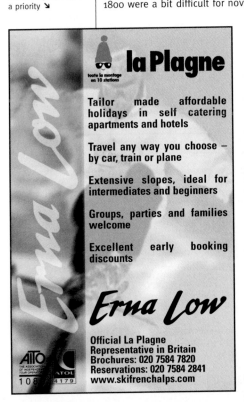

poor lower down. The queue-prone gondola from Plagne-Centre to Grande Rochette is being replaced for 2000/2001 – the new gondola will have double the capacity, which should do the trick. The old Colorado chair-lift next door to it is now a fast six-pack, but, frustratingly, it does not reach the ridge above Champagny. Two new six-packs on the top slopes of the Champagny sector have greatly improved the links on that side. The fast Arpette chair from Plagne-Bellecôte towards Montchavin still causes queues, and there are several other lifts that can generate queues that you can't avoid, once you've descended to them – at Plagne 1800 and Les Bauches for example. Crowds on the pistes are as much of a problem as lift queues, particularly above Bellecôte in the afternoon.

MOUNTAIN RESTAURANTS
An improving choice

Mountain restaurants are numerous, varied and seldom crowded, as many people prefer to descend to one of the resorts – particularly Champagny or Montchavin-Les Coches – at the end of the morning. Some pleasant new restaurants have been built both in the main bowl and on the Montchavin slopes. Le Val Sante at Les Bauches is recommended. Two great rustic restaurants in which to hole up in poor weather for a long lunch of Savoyard dishes are Le Sauget, above Montchavin, and Au Bon Vieux Temps, just below Aime-la-Plagne. Reservations may be required at either. Roc des Blanchets at the top of the Champagny gondola is also recommended – friendly staff, both table- and self-service, beautiful views over to Courchevel from the terrace and good basic cooking. The little Breton café at the bottom of the Quillis lift at the start of the Levasset piste and the Borseliers (lower down) have also been highly recommended. The Forperet at the start of the Gentil Montalbert run, above Montalbert, is also popular with reporters.

SCHOOLS AND GUIDES
Better alternatives to ESF

Each centre has its own ESF school, offering classes for all standards. Groups can be large in peak season. Instructors speak English of varying standard. Past reports on ESF tuition have generally been positive, but the consensus seems to be that the alternatives are preferable. The Oxygène school in Centre has impressed several reporters – and UK tour operators in Plagne 1800 – who find it more responsive than the ESF. One recent report has nothing but praise for the sympathetic instructors and management of El Pro in Belle-Plagne. We have had good reports on Evolution 2 (based in Montchavin) – 'wonderful', says the parent of one junior pupil. Antenne Handicap offers private lessons for skiers with any kind of disability.

CHILDCARE

There are ESF ski kindergartens in all the high resort units, generally taking children from age 3. The ESF also runs all-day nurseries in most of the villages, mostly taking children aged 2 to 6 (18 months to 3 years in Belle Plagne). In Centre, independent nursery Marie Christine does much the same.

The deal in the outlying satellite villages is similar, except that in Montchavin and Les Coches very young skiers are handled by the Nursery Club, the ESF taking over at age 4.

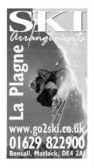

FACILITIES FOR CHILDREN
Good choice

Children are well catered for. The nursery at Belle-Plagne is 'excellent, with good English spoken'. The Club Med at Aime-la-Plagne is one of their 'family' villages. La Plagne and its satellites are fast becoming the chalet-crèche capital of the Alps – several UK operators run them.

Staying there

Slope-side accommodation is the norm in the high-altitude resorts; unless you miss a crucial linking lift, you can nearly always get home on the snow. There is, however, an efficient, free bus system linking the resorts, which runs until after midnight and might tempt you to explore the après-ski in different areas – the lifts between some of the villages also run late into the evening. Most people, however, are happy to use the après-ski facilities most immediately accessible.

Reporters have complained about the lack of easy access between the different levels in Belle Plagne – lots of long, tiring steps up to the 'upper sector'. Those who plan to use the facilities and bars in the evening would be advised to stay in the 'lower sector'. Another reporter found getting from one side of Plagne Centre to the other 'extremely tiring'.

HOW TO GO
Plenty of packages

For a resort that is very apartment-dominated, there is a surprising number of attractive chalets available through British tour operators. There are few hotels, but there are some attractive, simple 2-stars in the lower villages. There is a Club Med 'village' at Aime-la-Plagne. Accommodation in the outlying satellite resorts is described at the end of the chapter.

Chalets There's a large number available, though many are of a similar standard, type and position – fairly simple, small, and located in 1800.

Hotels There are very few, all of 2-star or 3-star grading. Probably the most comfortable place, if you're looking for a package, is Club Med, up at Aime-la-Plagne. A new hotel in Belle-Plagne, Les Balcons, will be ready for 2000/01.

(2) **Graciosa** Well-run 18-room hotel in Plagne-Centre.

(2) **Eldorador** Adequate hotel in Belle-Plagne – spacious rooms, generous buffet breakfast.

(2) **Terra Nova** Big, new, 120-room 3-star hotel in Plagne-Centre.

Self-catering La Plagne is the ultimate apartment resort, but many of the blocks are similar in standard. In-house communal facilities such as lounges, restaurants and the like are not as commonplace here as in most French purpose-built resorts. Fortunately, many tour operators have allocations in the above-average Pierre et Vacances apartments in Belle-Plagne.

EATING OUT
Emphasis on convenience

Throughout the resort there is a good range of restaurants, with something to suit most pockets and tastes, but the emphasis is on pizzeria-style dining, which suits the self-catering family. Some satellite villages cater more for the diner interested in the regional dishes: raclette and Savoyard fondue restaurants are popular (La Ferme in Plagne-Bellecôte is recommended as is the Chalet des Colosses).

Le Matafan in Belle-Plagne is popular with readers for its traditional French cuisine (at lunch as well as dinner). La Cloche and the Pappagone pizzeria have also been recommended. Hotel Les Glières, in Champagny, serves good Savoyard food in rustic surroundings.

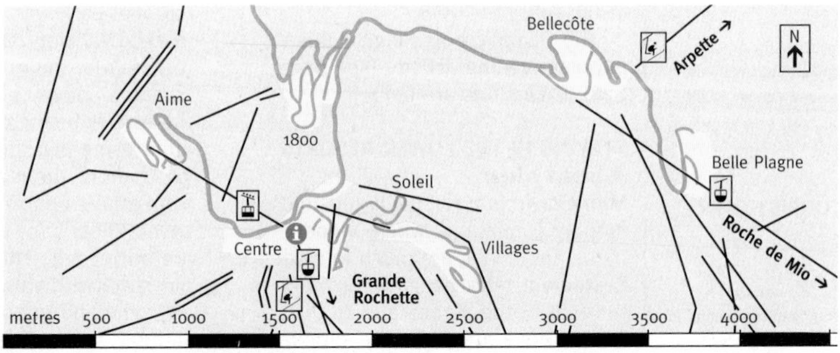

GETTING THERE

Air Geneva, transfer 3½hr. Lyon, transfer 3½hr. Chambéry, transfer 2½hr.

Rail Aime (18km) and Bourg-St-Maurice (35km) (Eurostar service to Bourg-St-Maurice and Aime available); frequent buses from station.

ACTIVITIES

Indoor Sauna and solarium in most centres, skating (Bellecôte and Aime-la-Plagne), squash (1800), fitness centres (Belle-Plagne, 1800, Centre, Bellecôte), cinemas, bowling

Outdoor Heated swimming pool (Bellecôte), bob-sleigh (La Roche), 30km marked walks, paragliding, skidoos, climbing, skating, hang-gliding, snow-shoe excursions

UK Representative

Erna Low Consultants
9 Reece Mews
London SW7 3HE
t 020 7584 2841
f 020 7589 9531
info@ernalow.co.uk
www.ernalow.co.uk

TOURIST OFFICE

Postcode 73211
t +33 479 097979
f 479 097010
ot.laplagne@wanadoo.fr
www.la-plagne.com

Au Bon Vieux Temps (see also under Mountain restaurants) at Aime-la-Plagne is open in the evening. One reporter, however, was not too impressed by the food at dinner. Other reader recommendations include La Métairie ('the most enjoyable we've encountered in the Alps'), in Plagne-Centre.

APRES-SKI
Bars, bars, bars

La Plagne has a wide range of après-ski amenities catering particularly for the younger crowd. Each centre produces a weekly events bulletin listing special forthcoming events, particularly those run by the hotel 'animateurs'. You can make use of a range of facilities, spread between the different stations, by taking the free shuttle-bus service between them. Most large hotels or apartment blocks have games rooms and other amenities. In Belle-Plagne, Mat's and the Cheyenne are the most popular bars. The King Café and Le Luna are the liveliest bars in Plagne-Centre, and sometimes have live music. The Couleur Café in Plagne 1800 is popular with the local staff. The Lincoln Pub in Plagne-Soleil is recommended. Plagne-Bellecôte is very limited at night, with only one real bar – Showtime. Neils (Plagne-Centre), Le Jet 73 (Plagne-Bellecôte) and Le Saloon (Belle-Plagne) are the main discos recommended by local chalet staff. Le Saloon requires you to change your francs into their own Saloon dollars to buy drinks – one reporter felt this was a real rip-off.

OFF THE SLOPES
OK for the active

As well as the sports and fitness facilities, winter walks along marked trails in the March and April sunshine are particularly pleasant. It's also easy to get up the mountain on the gondolas, which both have restaurants at the top.

The Olympic bob-sleigh run is a popular evening activity (see page 278). Excursions are limited.

STAYING IN THE LOWER RESORTS
A good plan

Montchavin is a relatively unspoilt old farming community where wooden barns and sheds are much in evidence. Restaurant terraces set in orchards at the foot of the slopes add to the scene. There are adequate shops, a kindergarten and a school. Reaching the La Plagne slopes involves four successive lifts (two fast chairs); but the local slopes have quite a bit to offer – the cheap local lift pass covers 30km of mostly easy, pretty, sheltered runs, well endowed with snowmakers, with nursery slopes at village level and up at Plan Bois. Those who do venture further afield can return from Roche de Mio (2700m) in one lovely long swoop (partly black). The more usual way home involves some of the trickiest blue runs we have encountered. Après-ski is quiet, but the village doesn't lack atmosphere and has a couple of nice little bars and a cinema. The Bellecôte is a modest hotel with a decent restaurant, the Boule de Neige.

Les Coches is only a walk away, and shares the same slopes. It is a sympathetically designed modern mini-resort that several reporters have liked for its 'small, quiet and friendly' feel and its traffic-free centre. It has its own school and kindergarten. One recent report was positive about the school: 'the ESF staff and instructor were very helpful and saved me from a potential divorce'. The Last One pub is good for après-ski. La Poze and la Taverne du Monchu are recommended restaurants.

Montalbert is a traditional but much expanded village with quicker access into the main area – though it's a long way from here across to the Bellecôte glacier. The local slopes are easy and wooded – a useful insurance against bad visibility. The Aigle Rouge is a simple hotel.

Champagny-en-Vanoise is a charming old village in a pretty, wooded setting. The south-facing local slopes mean you often have to get a gondola home at the end of the day, but Champagny is better placed than any of the other outlying villages for access into the main area and well placed for an outing by taxi or car to Courchevel or the beautiful Vanoise national park with its 500km of marked walking paths. There are routes from the gondola station to summits above Centre and Bellecôte, the former being a particularly speedy affair using just one further lift. Given good snow, there are lovely runs home from above Centre (2500m). There are several hotels, of which the two best are both Logis. The Glières is a rustic old hotel with varied rooms, a friendly welcome and good food. L'Ancolie is smarter, with modern facilities.

Portes du Soleil

What's new

The 1999/2000 season saw the introduction of a new hands-free lift pass system operated by an electronic card that you keep in your pocket.

The Portes du Soleil vies with the Trois Vallées for the title of World's Largest Ski Area, but its slopes are very different from those of Méribel, Courchevel, Val-Thorens and neighbours. The Portes du Soleil's slopes are spread out over a large area and most of them are part of an extensive circuit straddling the French–Swiss border; you can travel the circuit in either direction, with a short bus-ride needed only at Châtel. There are smaller areas to explore slightly off the main circuit. The runs are great for keen intermediates who like to travel long distances and through different resorts. There are few of the tightly packed networks of runs that encourage you to stay put in one area – though there are exceptions in one or two places. The area also has some nice rustic mountain restaurants, serving good food in pleasant, sunny settings.

The lifts throughout the area have been improved in recent years with several new high-speed chair-lifts eliminating some bad bottlenecks. But the slopes are low by French standards, with top heights in the range 2000m to 2300m and good snow is far from assured (though snowmaking has been expanded in recent years). When the snow is good you can have a great time racing all over the circuit (as we did in fresh powder on our last visit). But the slopes can get very crowded, especially at weekends and in the Avoriaz area.

Purpose-built **Avoriaz** (page 199) has the most snowsure slopes and is especially good for families, with a big snow-garden right in the heart of the car-free village. But its local slopes do get crowded and prices are rather high by local standards. The other French resort on the main circuit is **Châtel** (page 211). Given good snow, it has some of the best runs in the area. It is an old and quite characterful village, but it's a busy, traffic-jammed place. It has a couple of good beginner areas both at resort level and up the mountain. **Morzine** (page 269) is close to Avoriaz. It is linked by lift but there's no piste all the way back to town. It's a summer as well as a winter resort – a pleasant, bustling little town with good shops and restaurants, busy traffic and long walks to the lifts from much of the accommodation. The local slopes are extensive, and linked to those of the slightly higher, quieter, village of **Les Gets**. But they are low and good snow is certainly not assured. You can use Morzine as a base to ski the main Portes du Soleil circuit, but it's not ideal.

On the Swiss side **Champéry** (page 379) is a classic charming, attractive Swiss village – but just off the main circuit. You have to take a cable-car down from the main slopes as well as up to them, or a bus from a piste which ends out of town. It used to be popular with British tour operators but now few go there.

Champoussin and **Les Crosets** are purpose-built mini-resorts set on the very extensive open slopes between Champéry and Morgins, with fairly direct links over to Avoriaz. **Morgins**, in contrast to Champéry, has excellent village slopes – but they are low and very sunny, and although its more serious local runs are enjoyable and prettily wooded, they are also limited in extent.

On a spur off the main circuit are the resorts of **La Chapelle d'Abondance** (which has one of our favourite restaurants) in France and **Torgon** in Switzerland (which has splendid views over Lake Geneva). This area can be reached from above the Super-Châtel area and is usually quiet even when the rest of the circuit is packed.

Puy-St-Vincent 1400–1600m

Underrated little modern resort with some serious slopes

WHAT IT COSTS

3

HOW IT RATES

The slopes

Snow	***
Extent	**
Experts	***
Intermediates	***
Beginners	***
Convenience	*****
Queues	****
Restaurants	***

The rest

Scenery	***
Resort charm	**
Off-slope	*

What's new

A new drag-lift was installed and 10km of piste have been newly created – including the long Bois des Coqs red run from the top of the Lauzes drags down to 1600 – bringing the total up to 60km.

The gondola from 1600 to mid-mountain is being replaced by a fast quad for 2000/01.

MOUNTAIN FACTS

Altitude	1400m-2700m
Lifts	16
Pistes	60km
Green/Blue	50%
Red	42%
Black	8%
Artificial snow	7km
Recco detectors used	

TOURIST OFFICE

Postcode 05290
t +33 492 233580
f 492 234523
courrier@puysaintvincent.net
www.puysaintvincent.com

Puy-St-Vincent's ski area is not big by Alpine standards, but we like it a lot – more, to be honest, than we expected. It offers a decent vertical and a lot of variety, including steep stuff. There are excellent high-altitude cross-country trails, and the two purpose-built resort villages are not eyesores. People are friendly, and prices are low by French standards.

THE RESORT

Puy-St-Vincent proper is an old mountain village on the fringes of the Ecrins massif, not far south-west of Briançon. The modern resort of PSV is a two-part affair – the minor part, Station 1400, is just along the mountainside at 1400m; the major part, Station 1600, is a few hairpins (or a chair-lift ride) further up (yes, at 1600m). There are buildings in various styles dotted around the mountainside, but the main monolith at the foot of the lifts is unusual – boldly styled to resemble a mountain range, and largely finished in white. We and a recent reporter found PSV friendly ('even the lift operators') and well run.

THE MOUNTAINS

Within its small area, PSV packs in a lot of variety, with runs of all colours from green to black that justify their gradings. There are gentle **slopes** between the two villages, but most of the runs are above 1600. A new fast quad has replaced the gondola up to the tree line at around 2000m. Entertaining red runs go back down, and a green takes a less direct route. The main higher lift is a long chair to 2700m, serving excellent open slopes of red and genuine black steepness. The shorter Rocher Noir drag serves another steep slope, but also accesses splendid cruising runs that curl around the eastern edge of the area through the woods back to 1600. These runs are also accessed by a fast quad chair from just below 1600.

A short run above 1600 is floodlit in the early evening twice a week. **Snowboarders** have a floodlit fun-park with half-pipe at 1600, but are not allowed on the Rocher Noir drag-lift.

The six-day Galaxie pass covers a series of major resorts beyond Briançon. More to the point for most visitors, it also covers a day's skiing above the valley hamlet of Pelvoux, 10 minutes' drive away. It has blue, red and black runs, often used for race training, and a vertical of over 1000m served by a chair and a drag.

The slopes face north-east and are reasonably **reliable for snow**, with snowmaking on one run down to 1400 and on a couple of slopes above 1600.

The black runs are short but genuinely challenging for **experts**, and there are off-piste routes to be tackled with guidance. There are itinéraires outside the piste network, including one to the valley bottom – doubtless amusing in good snow.

Provided the limited extent doesn't worry you, it's an excellent area for **intermediates** who welcome a challenge – but there aren't many very easy runs. **Beginners** should be happy on either of the nursery slopes, and on the long green run from 2000m.

There are splendid **cross-country** routes between 1400m and 1700m, ranging from green to black difficulty.

There is a modern but pleasantly woody and reasonably priced **restaurant** at mid-mountain, but in good weather the sunny terraces at 1600 are the natural place to head for.

You have a choice of French and International **ski schools**. There are **nurseries** in both villages, and both schools run ski kindergartens.

STAYING THERE

Purpose-built and compact it may be, but 1600 (where most of the **accommodation** is located) is not perfectly laid out; beware walks to the lift. 1600 consists entirely of apartments; a reader recommends the Podium. There are some apartments down in 1400, and four cheap hotels.

The half-dozen bar-restaurants in each village meet both **eating out** and **après-ski** needs. The place is not quite devoid of things to do **off the slopes**, but not far off: snow-shoe expeditions and paragliding are about all there is.

Risoul 1850m

Villagey modern resort in an attractive southern setting

WHAT IT COSTS

3

HOW IT RATES

The slopes	
Snow	***
Extent	***
Experts	**
Intermediates	****
Beginners	****
Convenience	****
Queues	****
Restaurants	***
The rest	
Scenery	***
Resort charm	**
Off-slope	*

What's new

There were two new fast quads for 1999/2000.

For 2000/01 a new fast quad will improve the link from Clos Chardon to the Pic de Chabrières.

MOUNTAIN FACTS

Altitude	1660m-2750m
Lifts	56
Pistes	180km
Green/Blue	55%
Red	35%
Black	10%
Art. snow	520 acres

Recco detectors used

TOURIST OFFICE

Postcode 05600
t +33 492 460260
f 492 460123
o.t.risoul@wanadoo.fr
www.risoul.com

Reasonable prices, convenience, good snow, few queues and extensive slopes shared with Vars: Risoul has a lot going for it, particularly for intermediates, beginners and families. It is one of the more attractive purpose-built resorts.

THE RESORT

Risoul, purpose-built in the late 1970s, is a quiet, apartment-based resort, popular with families. Set among the trees, with excellent views over the Ecrins national park, it is made up of wood-clad buildings – mostly bulky, but with some concessions to traditional style. It has a busy little main street – surprisingly not traffic-free – and an array of restaurant terraces facing the slopes. Several reporters have commented on the friendliness of the natives. The village does not offer a very impressive array of resort amenities, and the lift network still has its weaknesses – but recent investment in fast chair-lifts has improved matters considerably. Airport transfers are long.

THE MOUNTAINS

The **slopes**, mainly north-facing, spread over several minor peaks and bowls, and connect with the sunnier slopes of neighbouring Vars via the Pointe de Razis (2570m) and the lower Col des Saluces. A new fast quad from Clos Chardon up to the Pic de Chabrières above Vars, the area's highest point at 2750m, will provide a third link for 2000/01. Together, they amount to one of the biggest domains in the southern French Alps – the combined area is marketed as the Forêt Blanche. The upper slopes are open, but those leading back into Risoul are attractively wooded, and good for bad-weather days. Recent improvements in the lift system mean that the link can now be made in both directions without having to ride any drag-lifts.

Risoul's slopes are all above 1850m and mostly north-facing, so despite its southerly position **snow reliability** is reasonably good. Snowmaking is fairly extensive and more is planned. Visitors recommend going over to the east-facing Vars slopes in the morning, when they get the sun, and returning to Risoul in the afternoon.

Risoul does not offer much to interest **experts**. The main top stations access a couple of steepish descents. There are some good off-piste opportunities if you have a guide.

The whole area is best suited to **intermediates**, with some good reds and blues in both the Risoul and Vars sectors. Almost all Risoul's runs return to the village, making it difficult to get lost in even the worst conditions. So intermediate children can be let off the leash without much worry.

Beginners have good, convenient, nursery slopes with a free lift, and a lot of easy pistes to move on to.

There are a couple of short **cross-country** loops, including a trail along the top ridge of the Alpine area.

There is a **snowboard** fun-park with a half-pipe near the village base.

Outside French school holidays, Risoul has impressively quiet slopes. **Queues** for the lifts out of the village in the morning can be quite long.

The **mountain restaurants** have increased in quantity and quality – the new Tetra is a stylish chalet; but most people return to the village terraces.

We have positive reports on both the ESF and Internationale **ski schools**.

Risoul is very much a family resort. It provides an all-day nursery for **children** over six months. Both ski schools operate ski kindergartens, slightly above the village, reached by a child-friendly lift. One parent reckons that many of the other drag-lifts have a dangerous 'whiplash' effect.

STAYING THERE

Most visitors stay in apartments – though there are a couple of decent **hotels**. **Chalets** are becoming more widely available from UK operators.

There's plenty of choice for **eating out**, from pizzerias to good French food, and it's mostly good value. More expensive is the Assiette Gourmande.

Après-ski is limited to a cinema and a few quiet bars. The best are the Licorne, Cimbro, Chérine, L'Ecureuil and Yeti – lively and full of Scandinavians. There is little to do **off the slopes** – excursions to Briançon are possible.

La Rosière 1850m

Pop over to Italy from the sunniest slopes in the Tarentaise

WHAT IT COSTS

(4)

HOW IT RATES

The slopes

Snow	***
Extent	***
Experts	**
Intermediates	***
Beginners	*****
Convenience	***
Queues	***
Restaurants	*

The rest

Scenery	***
Resort charm	***
Off-slope	*

What's new

For 1999/2000 a much-needed new mountain restaurant called La Traversette opened offering table-service.

A second ski school (Evolution 2) also opened, offering an alternative to the ESF.

MOUNTAIN FACTS

Altitude	1150m-2640m
Lifts	33
Pistes	140km
Green/Blue	45%
Red	37%
Black	18%
Artificial snow	22km
Recco detectors used	

Little-known La Rosière is worth considering for beginners, intermediates and families. Although purpose-built it's attractive, and cheaper than the big international resorts nearby. The slopes are sunny, but they get good snowfalls and are linked to La Thuile's north-facing slopes over the border in Italy.

THE RESORT

La Rosière has been built in traditional chalet style beside the road which zigzags its way up from Bourg-St-Maurice to the Petit-St-Bernard pass to Italy. In contrast to Les Arcs and La Plagne, across the valley, all the buildings are attractive, and many are dotted around discreetly in the woods. But there isn't much here except accommodation and a few shops. Expect peace, quiet and friendly locals, but not lively nightlife.

THE MOUNTAINS

The link with Italy means La Rosière has a big area of **slopes**. Its sunny home slopes are south-facing and offer great views over the valley to Les Arcs and La Plagne.

The chair and drag out of the village take you into the heart of the slopes, from where a series of drags and chairs, spread across the mountain, takes you up to **Col de la Traversette** (2400m). From there, you can get over the ridge and to the lifts which link with **Italy** at Belvedere (2640m). These top lifts are prone to being closed by wind or heavy snow. There is a **snowboard** fun-park and half-pipe.

Snow reliability is surprisingly good despite its south-facing direction, its relatively low height (most of the slopes are between 1850m and 2400m) and most of the area's artificial snow being on the Italian side.

Other than heli-skiing from just over the Italian border (it is banned in France) and guided off-piste, there is little excitement for **experts**. The steepest terrain is on the lowest slopes, down the Marcassin run to Le Vaz (1500m) and Ecudets or Eterlou to Les Ecudets (1150m).

For **intermediates**, La Rosière would be nothing special on its own, but there's lots to explore if you take into account its links to La Thuile. Apart from the lowest runs down to below the main village, the bottom half of La Rosière's slopes are mainly gentle, open, blue and green runs, ideal for early intermediates to brush up their technique. The top half of the mountain, however, below Le Roc Noir and Col de la Traversette, boasts steeper and more interesting red runs.

The red over the ridge from Col de la Traversette has good snow and views, but is narrow for its top section. Weaker intermediates can avoid it by taking the Chardonnet chair down.

For **beginners**, La Rosière has good nursery slopes and short lifts at the main slopes above the village and at the altiport.

La Rosière has three **cross-country** trails totalling 12km, set around the tree line in the altiport area.

Queues are not usually too much of a problem but it is much busier here than on the Italian side.

There are now two **mountain restaurants**: the self-service Plan du Repos and the new table-service La Traversette, both with big sunny terraces. There are a couple of bars near the top, which are fine for picnics.

We have no recent reports on either of the **ski schools**. **Children's** facilities include the snow garden of the Village des Enfants, and child specialist Ski Esprit has its own facilities.

STAYING THERE

The most convenient accommodation is in the main village near the lifts, or just below, in Le Gollet or Vieux Village. There is also accommodation by the other main lift up, in Les Eucherts. There are a few 2-star hotels and some ancient hamlets where you can rent gîtes, or you can stay in the valley below. British tour operators have some nice chalets on offer.

Après-ski is limited to a couple of bars in town, but there's a fair choice of **restaurants**. There is little **off-slope** entertainment, apart from scenic flights and a cinema. More walking paths have been added recently.

La Rosière gets good dumps of powder because of its position on the Col du Petit St-Bernard pass →

LA ROSIERE TO

TOURIST OFFICE

Postcode 73700
t +33 479 068051
f 479 068320
la.rosiere@wanadoo.fr
www.larosiere.net

Selected chalets in La Rosière

ADVERTISEMENT

SKI ESPRIT *The family ski specialist* **T 01252 618300** *www.ski-esprit.co.uk*

Ski Esprit offers seamless child care to families staying in their chalets, from qualified nursery care to exclusive ski lessons and activity clubs for children.

Chalets Grandes Alpes
with four chalet apartments:

- In-chalet nursery
- nearest lift 100m
- ski back to chalet
- family rooms
- sauna
- underground parking

CHALET GRANDES ALPES WITH FOUR CHALET APARTMENTS ↑

↑ LE BRACONNIER (20 GUESTS) - UNDER CONSTRUCTION

↑ LES LANDELIERES (20 GUESTS)

Chalets Romeo and Juliet – 10 guests each
These two apartments share dining and sitting rooms in the Chalet Romeo. They are separated by the building's internal staircase. Full child discounts if both apartments are taken with one booking.

Chalet Cleopatra – 10 guests
The location is close to our nursery and its facilities are used by nursery staff and children. Full child discounts for whole chalet bookings.

Chalet Valentine – 5/6 guests
This apartment has its own external entrance and is good for large families seeking exclusivity. The accommodation is only available for whole chalet bookings.

Other Ski Esprit chalets in La Rosière are Ferme d'Elisa (3 chalet apartments for 14 guests each and one for 12 guests) with a nursery and children's activity room, Le Braconnier (20 guests), Landelières (20 guests) and Chez Robert (12 guests).

Saint-Martin-de-Belleville 1400m

Explore the Three Valleys from a traditional old village

WHAT IT COSTS

4

HOW IT RATES

The slopes

Snow	***
Extent	*****
Experts	****
Intermediates	*****
Beginners	***
Convenience	***
Queues	****
Restaurants	****

The rest

Scenery	***
Resort charm	****
Off-slope	*

MOUNTAIN FACTS

Altitude	1300m-3200m
Lifts	200
Pistes	600km
Green/Blue	49%
Red	37%
Black	14%
Artificial snow	90km
Recco detectors used	

St-Martin is a traditional Savoyard village, with old church, small square and old wood and stone buildings, a few miles down the valley from Les Menuires. As a quiet, inexpensive base for exploration of the Three Valleys, it's very attractive. And it's an attractive spot to stop for lunch if you are cruising the slopes.

THE RESORT

In 1950 St-Martin didn't even have running water or electricity. Later, while new resorts were developed nearby, St-Martin remained a bit of a backwater, though it remained the administrative centre for the Belleville valley (which includes the resorts of Val-Thorens and Les Menuires). But in the 1980s chair-lifts were built, linking it to the slopes of Méribel and Les Menuires. The old village has been developed, of course, but the architecture of the new buildings fits in well with the old, and you can walk around it in a few minutes. The main feature of the centre remains the lovely old 16th century church – prettily floodlit at night. There are some good local shops and few 'touristy' ones. The guests are mainly Dutch, Scandinavian, German and British.

THE MOUNTAINS

Two chair-lift rides – the upper one now a fast quad – take you to a ridge from which you can access Méribel on one side and Les Menuires on the other. The whole of the Three Valleys can be easily explored from here.

Natural **snow reliability** is not the best in the Three Valleys – the local slopes face west and get the full force of the afternoon sun. But there is now snowmaking from top to bottom of the main run and more is planned.

The local slopes are pleasant blues and reds, mainly of interest to **intermediates** – including one of our favourite runs in the Three Valleys, the long, rolling, wide Jerusalem red. The whole of the Three Valleys is, of course, an intermediate's paradise.

Locally there are large areas of gentle off-piste for **experts** to explore, and access to La Masse for steep north-facing slopes is just one run away from the top of the local chairs.

St-Martin is not ideal for **beginners** – there's a nursery slope but no easy green runs to progress to.

Queues are not much of a problem – the local lifts can easily cope with the morning rush from the 1500 guest beds the village has. But we have had a recent report of 20-minute queues and 'queue rage' from some 'embarrassingly pompous Brits'.

What's new

A couple of years ago a delightful new blue piste back from the top of the Olympic Express from Méribel was created.

There are plans to build a two-stage gondola starting from the village and to replace the vicious drag-lift on the slope up from the church. But these won't happen until 2002 at the earliest.

TOURIST OFFICE

Postcode 73440
t +33 479 089309
f 479 089171
lesmenuires@lesmenuires.com
www.st-martin-belleville.com

New buildings blend in with old in tiny, picturesque St-Martin →

SNOWPIX.COM / CHRIS GILL

There are **cross-country** trails along the valley floor. The tourist office tells us there is now a fun-park for **snowboarders**.

There are three atmospheric old **mountain restaurants** on the main run down to the village. La Loe is said to be 'friendly and cheaper than most'. Brewski's (on the left, halfway down the local village slope with the drag-lift – watch for the signs) does good-value pub grub (pies are a speciality), has sunny terraces with views down the valley and is run by a couple of fun-loving kiwis – it attracts customers from all over the Three Valleys. La Bouitte in St-Marcel (an off-piste run away) is one of the best restaurants in the Three Valleys – a traditional, welcoming, rustic French auberge (but not cheap).

The **ski school** is said to teach in English because it is the common language of most guests. But a recent reporter said, 'They were kind and considerate to our children but my son struggled with French on his snowboard lesson.' We've had good reports of the **kindergarten**, which is housed in a new purpose-built building and takes children from three months.

STAYING THERE

New buildings have added more accommodation and blend in well with the original village. There are a few **hotels** – the Alp'Hôtel, Edelweiss and Saint Martin are all 3-stars.

Les Chalets de St Martin is the only British **chalet** operator in town – and has operated there ever since the first lift was built. It has catered chalets, all with en suite facilities, employs professional chefs and serves a variety of quality wines to match the food (the owner is a wine merchant). It also has a variety of self-catered chalets and **apartments** to rent. Cherferie is a British-run **chalet hotel** now operated by Ski Miquel, with well furnished en suite rooms of various sizes. The lively bar Brewski's (see above) is only a stone's throw away.

Après ski centres around two bars. The Pourquoi Pas? piano bar is delightfully cosy with a roaring log fire and comfortable easy chairs. Brewski's has wooden chairs and tables, a pool table, activities such as karaoke, sumo wrestling or live bands most nights and photos of old pop stars, such as Frank Zappa, Cream, the Beatles, Tina Turner and the Sex Pistols, on the walls. A rustic new restaurant called Le Montagnard opened last season and has been highly recommended by a reporter for good food, decor and atmosphere. There is not much else to do **off the slopes**.

Sainte-Foy-Tarentaise 1550m

Secret off-piste haven for those in the know

WHAT IT COSTS

4

HOW IT RATES

The slopes

Snow	***
Extent	*
Experts	****
Intermediates	***
Beginners	**
Convenience	***
Queues	*****
Restaurants	*

The rest

Scenery	***
Resort charm	***
Off-slope	*

What's new

The whole 'resort' is new and deserted. It's a wonder how it keeps going, considering how few lift tickets they sell.

MOUNTAIN FACTS

Altitude	1550m-2620m
Lifts	5
Pistes	25km
Green/Blue	23%
Red	54%
Black	23%
Artificial snow	none

TOURIST OFFICE

Postcode 73640
t +33 479 069519
f 479 069509
www.sainte-foy-tarentaise.com

This small area in the Tarentaise has been developed only since 1990. The millions who flock to the nearby mega-resorts of Val-d'Isère and Les Arcs never give it a thought. But those in the know are well rewarded. It's an uncrowded gem with some wonderful off-piste slopes for experts and intermediates.

THE RESORT

There isn't one; that's the charm of this place. It's ideal for getting away from the crowds when staying in one of the big resorts nearby. Ste-Foy is a tiny mountain hamlet set 8km off the main road between Val-d'Isère and Bourg-St-Maurice: turn off at Ste-Foy-la-Thuile. The largest building at the station houses the ticket office, cafés and the only equipment shop (Zigzags, which readers have roundly condemned for its shocking service).

THE MOUNTAIN

Off-piste guides from Val regularly bring clients to Ste-Foy's deserted **slopes**, which spread on both sides of three quad chairs, which rise, one above the other, from 1550m to the Col de l'Aiguille (2610m). There are never any queues. The top lift gives access to almost 600m of vertical above the tree line and to superb, long off-piste routes on the back of the mountain. The two lower chairs serve a number of pleasant green, blue and red runs through the trees and back to the base station. You don't come here for quality of grooming or modern lifts, but the words of one recent visitor may make you go: 'Most of my ski career I've been in Verbier, Zermatt and Vail. The skiing in Ste-Foy is better.'

The slopes face north or west. **Snow reliability** is good on the former but can suffer on the latter. But because of the lack of crowds you can expect to make fresh tracks days after the latest storm.

Experts can pass happy times on Ste-Foy's black and red runs, but it's the off-piste you come for, for which you need a guide. There are wonderful runs down through deserted villages to the road between Ste-Foy and Val-d'Isère and a splendid route off to the left which starts with a hike and takes you through trees and over a stream down to the tiny village of Le Crot.

Intermediates can enjoy 1000m vertical of uncrowded reds – ideal for confidence building and sharpening technique. The higher slopes are the more difficult – the red Aiguille run is a superb test for confident intermediates, who should also try some off-piste (with a guide). Keen piste-bashers may tire of the limited pistes in a day or two.

This isn't a resort for **beginners**, but there is a small drag near the base station. After that you can progress to a green run off the first chair – a pleasant, gentle track through trees – and a gentle blue off the second.

There are no prepared **cross-country** trails, but you can lay some original tracks through the woods.

There are two rustic **mountain restaurants** at the top of the first chair, Les Brevettes and Chez Leon, both converted from barns and serving good food. You need to book your plat du jour (the only thing on the menu) at the latter. There are a few bars and cafés near the ticket office and La Ruelle, near the bottom of the first chair, is a good, rustic bar-restaurant.

We've had good reports of **ski school**, especially for children, and there's a good chance classes will not be large. There is a crèche.

STAYING THERE

Hotel Monal, in the village of Ste-Foy in the valley below, is a basic auberge. Auberge sur la Montagne, just above the turn-off at Ste-Foy-la-Thuile, sleeps 20, has excellent food and atmosphere and is run by an English couple. Chalet Number One, in the nearby village of La Masure, is run by Brit snowboarder Lloyd Rogers, serving good food in rustic surrounding. Skiers welcome too! If you're spending the week, a car is a good idea, though there are buses. Most people stay in one of the major resorts and take a day trip to Ste-Foy. There may be a short-lived **après-ski** scene in one of the bars at the station, and the bar of the Monal can get lively. For eating out, book the excellent Chez Mérie, in the village of Le Miroir.

Serre-Chevalier 1350m-1500m

Surprise! Big, French, but full of character

WHAT IT COSTS

3

HOW IT RATES

The slopes	
Snow	****
Extent	****
Experts	***
Intermediates	****
Beginners	****
Convenience	***
Queues	***
Restaurants	***
The rest	
Scenery	****
Resort charm	***
Off-slope	**

What's new

For 2000/01 Serre-Chevalier will have a new high-speed six-seater chair from the base of Chantemerle towards the Prorel sector. The chair will serve a new blue run and meet the Aiguillette chair which takes you higher. There will also be more snowmaking and there is going to be a new Club Med.

For 1999/2000 the resort developed more special facilities for snowboarding and free-riding: a half-pipe, quarter-pipe, big air jump and a carving and snowblade area.

MOUNTAIN FACTS

Altitude	1350m-2780m
Lifts	74
Pistes	250km
Green/Blue	42%
Red	46%
Black	12%
Artificial snow	13km
Recco detectors used	

- + Fairly big, varied area, ideally suited to intermediate cruising
- + Interesting mixture of wooded runs (ideal for blizzards) and open bowls
- + One of the few big French areas based on old villages with character
- + Good-value and atmospheric old hotels, restaurants and chalets
- + Buses link all the villages, so you can end the day wherever you like
- + Lift pass covers several other major resorts easily reached by car

- − A lot of indiscriminate new building, which looks awful from the slopes
- − Still lots of slow, old lifts, including many drags, some vicious
- − Not many tough pistes
- − Serious queues in French holidays
- − Very misleading piste map
- − Limited nightlife
- − Busy road runs through the resort villages, with jams at times
- − Few off-slope diversions

Serre-Chevalier is less well known than most major French resorts. It deserves better. If you love old atmospheric French villages with traditional restaurants, hotels and crêperies, try it. It's one of the few resorts with the ambience you might choose for a summer holiday – a sort of Provence in the snow.

The slopes are equally likeable. Although there are runs on only one side of the long valley it is split into different segments, so you really feel you are travelling. In good snow conditions there are excellent off-piste opportunities to keep experts happy, as well as intermediates. What really sets the area apart from the French norm is the woodland runs, making Serre-Chevalier one of the best places to be when snow is falling – though there are plenty of open runs, too.

boarding *Serre-Che is a snowboarding hot-spot, popular mainly with advanced boarders because of the off-piste powder and because the resort has invested in loads of fun features. There's big air in Briançon, boarder-cross in Villeneuve and Chantemerle and a half-pipe in Villeneuve, all with sound-systems. The diverse pistes with open and tree-lined runs also suit intermediates, though there are annoying flat sections between some lifts and several tracks the less confident might find tricky. The main lifts are chairs and gondolas but there are a lot of difficult-to-avoid and violent drag-lifts. Evenings are fairly quiet but there's at least one lively bar in each centre.*

The resort

As one reporter puts it, Serre-Chevalier is 'much nicer than most French resorts'. Another marvels at the 'genuine friendliness of the locals'.

The resort is made up of a string of 13 villages set on a valley floor running roughly east–west below the north-facing ski slopes. The three main villages are Monêtier (Serre-Chevalier 1500) to the west, Villeneuve (1400) in the middle and Chantemerle (1350) to the east, spread over a distance of 5km and linked by regular buses. All the villages have charming old hamlets as well as modern development.

Monêtier is the smallest, quietest and most unspoilt of the main villages, with a Provençal feel to its narrow streets, stone buildings and small square with a fountain. New building, in sympathetic style, is on the other side of the main road, near the lifts.

Villeneuve has three major gondolas out of the village, plus the Casse du Boeuf high-speed quad, which takes you higher than any of them. The central area of new development near the lifts is fairly charmless. But the hamlet of Le Bez is peaceful and traditional. Across the main road and river is the old village of La Salle with stone houses, bars, hotels, restaurants and crêperies.

Chantemerle has some tasteless modern buildings in the centre and along the main road. The old sector is a couple of minutes' walk from the lifts with a lovely church and most of the restaurants, bars and small hotels.

Briançon is not strictly Serre-Chevalier but is linked to the same slopes and has a fair amount of accommodation. It feels like a town (in fact, it is the highest in France) not a mountain resort, and you can arrive there by direct train from Paris. The modern sector, around the lift station, has a wide selection of shops, bars, hotels and restaurants. The fortified old town with its narrow cobbled streets is worth a visit even if you're staying elsewhere.

The mountains

Serre-Chevalier's slopes are ideally suited to intermediates, with miles of easy cruising. Trees cover almost two-thirds of the mountain and pretty runs offer some of France's best wooded routes if the weather is poor.

Mixed ability groups are likely to find something to suit everyone, with the added advantage that it is easy to meet up for lunch. But the piste map is infuriatingly unclear and imprecise, and readers have found navigation is made even more challenging by 'particularly poor' signposting and the tendency of runs to 'change colour halfway down'.

The lift system is electronic and hands-free – you keep a card in your pocket. A six-day area pass covers a day in each of Les Deux-Alpes, Alpe-d'Huez, Puy-St-Vincent and the Milky Way. Several reporters have enjoyed a day out to Montgenèvre. You also get a day at La Grave at a preferential rate.

THE SLOPES
Interestingly varied and pretty

Serre-Chevalier's 250km of pistes are spread in four main sectors.

From **Monêtier** in the west, there's a choice of two chairs to mid-mountain. Two further lifts link with the other sectors. One goes to the highest point in Serre-Chevalier (2780m), and the other is the high-speed Eychauda quad, which takes you slightly lower. Heading on towards Villeneuve, the main link is a red piste which is more interesting than the narrow, flattish tracks you take in the other direction.

Villeneuve and **Chantemerle** are at the heart of Serre-Chevalier, and both

Prorel 2565m

L'Eychauda 266om

2575m

Tête de la Balme 2625m

Col de la Cucumelle 2500m

2780m

Serre-Chevalier 2490m

Tabuc

Bachas

Grand Alpe

Echallion

Frejus

Charvet

Serre Ratier 1905m

Goudissard

Le Bez

Peyra-Juana

Briançon 1325m

Chantemerle 1350m

Villeneuve 1400m

Le Freyssinet

Le Monêtier 1500m

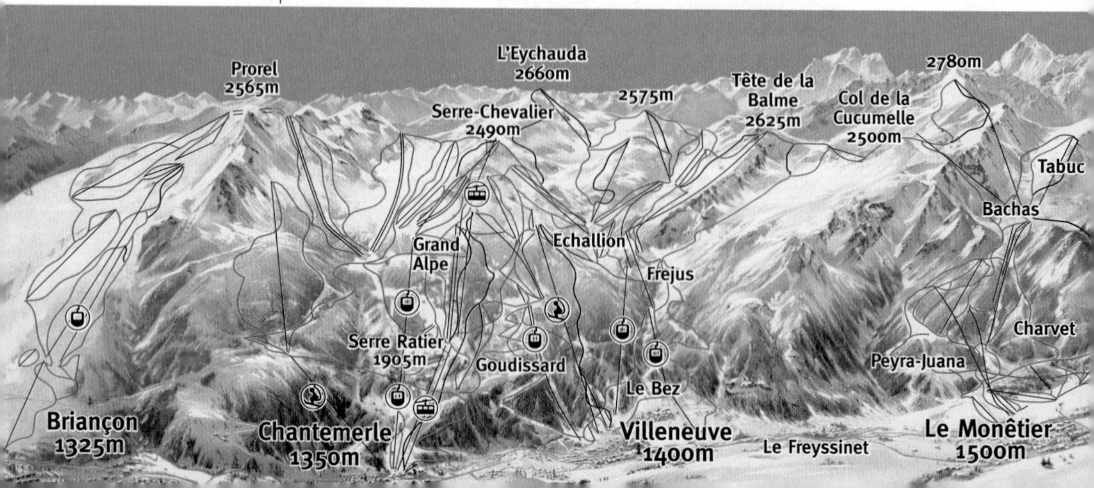

LIFT PASSES

1999/2000 prices in francs

Grand Serre-Chevalier
Covers all lifts in Briançon, Serre-Chevalier and Le Monêtier.

Main pass
1-day pass 191
6-day pass 970

Senior citizens
Over 60: 6-day pass 690
Over 70: free pass

Children
Under 12: 6-day pass 690
Under 6: free pass

Notes Passes of 6 days or more give one day in each of Les Deux-Alpes, Alpe-d'Huez, Puy-St-Vincent and Voie Lactée (Milky Way). Reductions for families.

Alternative passes
Passes covering individual areas of Serre-Chevalier. Adult 6-day pass: Briançon, 610, Le Monêtier 700, Villeneuve 740, Chantemerle, 693. Morning and afternoon passes. Night-skiing pass. Beginner's pass. Non-skier's pass.

have a choice of major lifts to the slopes. A network of chairs and drags makes it easy to get between them.

From the area above Chantemerle a pair of drags forms the link with **Briançon**. A long run with great views takes you to the edge of town and a gondola brings you back.

SNOW RELIABILITY
Good – especially upper slopes

Most slopes face north or north-east and so hold snow well, especially high up (most are above 2000m). The long runs to Briançon and Chantemerle have artificial snowmaking, as do sections above Monêtier and Villeneuve. Serre-Che's weather pattern is different from the northern Alps and it can get snow when there is none elsewhere (and vice versa – as happened last season).

FOR EXPERTS
Head off-piste

There are long black pistes down to Villeneuve, Chantemerle and Monêtier, but none is fearsomely steep. About the best is the lovely, varied and usually extremely empty Tabuc run which takes you through woods to Monêtier. This is generally narrow and in places genuinely steep, but levels out towards the bottom. A reporter recommends the blacks Cibouit and Col du Vent, above Bachas, if you're keen on moguls.

The top bowls above Villeneuve and Chantemerle have a few black runs. Isolée from the top of the Eychauda drag and the 'superb, long black' Casse du Boeuf are often praised.

But the main interest for experts is the off-piste, both above and through the trees. Highlights include: Tête de Grand Pré to Villeneuve (a climb from Cucumelle); off the back of l'Eychauda to Puy-St-André (isolated, beautiful, taxi-ride home); l'Yret to Monêtier via Vallon de la Montagnolle (steep at the start, very beautiful). And the off-piste Mecca of La Grave is nearby.

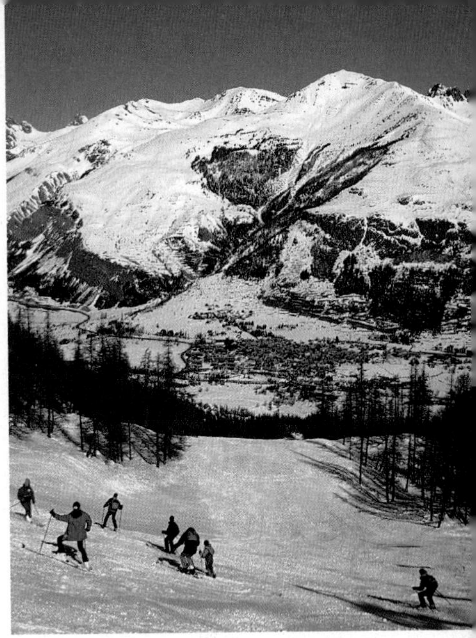

↑ Intermediates can get around the whole area, from Monêtier in the west to Briançon in the east

SNOWPIX.COM / CHRIS GILL

FOR INTERMEDIATES
Ski wherever you like

Serre-Chevalier's slopes ideally suit intermediates, who can buzz around without worrying about anything. You can really get a feeling of travelling by moving from sector to sector: 'I liked the fast journey from Monêtier to Briançon with no nasty surprises on the red runs,' commented one visitor. Looking at the piste map it might appear that red runs far outnumber blues. But most reds are at the easy end of the grading scale. Even nervous intermediates shouldn't have problems with them – especially in the light of the usually intensive grooming.

There's plenty for more adventurous intermediates, though. Many runs are wide enough for a fast pace. Cucumelle in the Fréjus sector is a favourite – a beautiful long red with a challenging initial section. In the bowls you can pick your own challenges. And many of

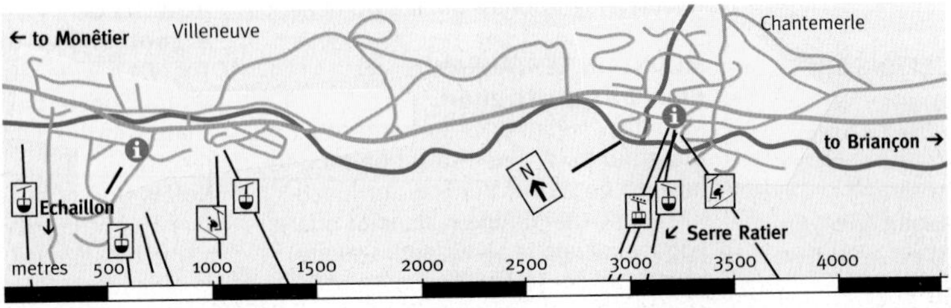

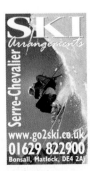

SCHOOLS/GUIDES

1999/2000 prices in francs

ESF In all centres
Classes 6 days, 5hr: 3hr am and 2hr pm; half-day am or pm
6 full days: 940
Children's classes
Ages: Up to 12
6 full days: 890
Private lessons
Hourly, 1 to 2 people 180/235

International
Group lessons, courses
Classes 6 days, am or pm, 6 mornings: 540
Children's classes
Ages: up to 12
6 mornings: 480
Private lessons
Hourly: 175/215

Génération Snow
Snowboard school
6 mornings: 790
Hourly: 265

Montagne Adventure
Off-piste, ski touring

Compagnie des Guides de l'Oisans
Off-piste, ski tours, ice climbing, snowshoes

Montagne à la carte
Off-piste, ski touring, heli-skiing, climbing, snowshoes

Montagne et Ski
Off-piste, ski touring, heli-skiing, snowshoes

David Legendre
Snowshoes

GETTING THERE

Air Turin, transfer $2^1/_2$hr. Grenoble, transfer $2^1/_2$hr. Lyon, transfer 4hr.

Rail Briançon (6km); regular buses from station.

the runs down to the valley, including the Olympique-Luc Alphand to Chantemerle and the Grande Gargouille towards Briançon, have steep pitches. The runs off the little-used Aiguillette chair in the Chantemerle sector are quiet, enjoyable fast cruises.

FOR BEGINNERS
Best at Villeneuve

All three main villages have nursery areas (at Chantemerle it's small, and you generally go up to Serre Ratier or Grande Alpe). Villeneuve has excellent green runs to progress to at the top of the Fréjus gondola. The Chantemerle sector is less suitable, but has some easy high runs, at Grande Alpe for instance, enjoyed by reporters. Both sectors have green paths winding down from mid-mountain. But they are narrow, and not enjoyable when the runs become rutted and others are speeding along. Monêtier's easy runs are at resort level, next to excellent nursery slopes, and the area has been recommended by beginners for 'better snow, fewer people and no drags'.

FOR CROSS-COUNTRY
Excellent if the snow is good

There are 45km of tracks along the valley floor, mainly following the gurgling river between Monêtier and Villeneuve and going on up towards the Col du Lautaret.

QUEUES
Avoid French school holidays

More than most resorts, Serre-Chevalier seems to fill up with French families during the February holidays, when there are serious queues everywhere. The Aiguillette chair in the Chantemerle sector is the place to escape to (though that may be more crowded this season because of the new high-speed chair to it from Chantemerle).

At other times an impressive range of big lifts means there are few problems from the valley. The electronic lift-pass system 'saves a lot of hassle', but old, slow lifts still cause queues. The Prorel double drag to Briançon is a bottleneck.

MOUNTAIN RESTAURANTS
Few, but quite good

Mountain restaurants are rather thin on the ground: 'We were disappointed to have to go out of our way for lunch.'

The big Grand Alpe restaurant offers good value, good views and a sunny aspect, as does Aravet 2000. But 'The small restaurant just down from the top of Prorel has the best views in the whole resort, and is very reasonable,' claims one visitor. We've had very variable reports on service and quality at Bachas, above Monêtier, which has a good sun terrace and views. Further down towards Monêtier, the Peyra Juana is 'excellent for service, food and value'.

At Serre Ratier, above Chantemerle, is an excellent self-service, with live entertainment. The welcoming Pi Maï in Fréjus, just off the Cucumelle run, does pricey table service but visitors 'thoroughly recommend' it.

SCHOOLS AND GUIDES
Nothing but praise

We have received a number of reports on the Ecole de Ski Buissonnière over the years – all of them full of praise. For example: 'We thoroughly enjoyed a two-hour introductory snowboarding class. Instructors speak good English and classes are small.'

FACILITIES FOR CHILDREN
Facilities at each village

We have had no very recent reports, but the Ecole de Ski Buissonnière (see above) also teaches children and has been praised in the past, as has Les Schtroumpfs in Villeneuve.

Staying there

The central resorts of Chantemerle and Villeneuve are more convenient for the main slopes than Monêtier and Briançon. And the link between the Monêtier and Villeneuve slopes relies on high chair-lifts that can be closed by wind. Buses do run along the valley, so location isn't crucial, but they stop early, so check times. There are also ski buses local to each area.

What makes Serre-Chevalier different is the old-world charm and French ambience of the traditional hamlets and villages. If you are a Francophile, go for one of the rustic areas, not a modern suburb.

HOW TO GO
A good choice of packages

There's a wide choice of packages from UK tour operators, several offering chalets in the different parts of the resort.

Hotels One of the features of this string of little villages is the range of attractive, modest hotels.
In Monêtier:

ACTIVITIES

Indoor Swimming pool, sauna, fitness centres, cinemas, bridge

Outdoor At Chantemerle: skating rink, paragliding, cleared paths, snow-shoe walks, snowmobiling. At Villeneuve: ice driving circuit, skating rink, horse-riding, sleigh rides, cleared paths, paragliding, snow-shoe walks, snowmobiling. At Monêtier: skating rink, cleared paths, hang-gliding, hot springs, snowshoe walks, ski joring.

CHILDCARE

Each of the three main villages has its own non-ski nursery that takes children all day (9am to 5pm) or for a half-day. At Villeneuve, Les Schtroumpfs (492 247095) caters for kids from age 6 months; meals not provided. At Chantemerle, Les Poussins (492 240343) takes them from age 8 months; meals provided. At Monêtier, Garderie de Pré-Chabert (492 244575) takes them from age 18 months (6 months out of school holiday times); meals not provided.

TOURIST OFFICE

Postcode 05240
t +33 492 249898
f 492 249884
contact@ot-serrechevalier.fr
www.serre-chevalier.com

(((3) **L'Auberge du Choucas** Smart wood-clad rooms, and a stone-vaulted restaurant with good food.
In Villeneuve:
((2) **Le Lièvre Blanc** Former coaching inn, with a large stone-vaulted bar. British owned with its own guide and hire shop.
((2) **Le Christiania** Traditional hotel on main road, crammed with ornaments.
((2) **La Vieille Ferme** Stylish conversion on the edge of the village.
((2) **Cimotel** Modern and charmless, with good-sized rooms and 'excellent' food. Near to the piste and a main lift.
(1) **Le Chatelas** Prettily decorated simple chalet by river (once a sawmill).
In Chantemerle:
((2) **Plein Sud** Modern; pool and sauna.
((2) **La Boule de Neige** Comfortable, friendly 2-star in the old centre.
(1) **La Ricelle** Charming, but tucked away in Villard-Laté on the other side of the valley from the slopes. Good food.
Self-catering Plenty of modern apartment blocks in Villeneuve, Briançon and Chantemerle. Few have charm.

STAYING UP THE MOUNTAIN
Worth considering

Chalet-hotel Serre Ratier, at the mid-station of the Chantemerle cable-car, does full board at reasonable rates.

EATING OUT
Unpretentious and traditional

In Monêtier, the Auberge du Choucas has sophisticated eating. The Alliey is a family restaurant with an excellent wine cellar. The Europe has 'excellent French cooking at reasonable prices'.

In the old part of Villeneuve, La Pastorale has an open-fire grill and good-value menu. The Marotte, a tiny stone building with classic French cuisine, has been highly praised. The Noctambule and La Refuge specialise in fondue and raclette. And there are good crêperies – try the Petit Duc, or La Manouille. Over in Le Bez, Le Bidule has 'first class food and service, at good value', while the Siyou in the old village of La Salle is good for 'local specialities at very reasonable prices'.

In Chantemerle, La Fourchette is recommended for local specialities. Le Couch'où is good value for fondue and raclette and has a pizzeria upstairs. The candlelit Crystal is the smartest, most expensive place in town. The Kandahar is a charming pizzeria and the rustic Ricelle offers amazing value.

APRES-SKI
Quiet streets and few bars

Serre-Chevalier isn't the place for wild nightlife, so a car is handy to try the scattered bar scene.

In Monêtier the 'basic but friendly' Le Pub is the place to go. In Villeneuve the Lièvre Blanc is popular with Brits; L'Iceberg is a pub-style bar frequented by teenagers. The Frog is cramped, but has 'good atmosphere'. In Chantemerle the Yeti and The Underground beneath it are focal. The Kitzbühel has a good atmosphere, particularly when sporting events are shown, and is 'not too full of fellow Brits'. After everything else has closed, a karaoke bar with 'an erratic door policy' may still let you in.

OFF THE SLOPES
Try the steam baths

Serre-Chevalier doesn't hold many off-slope attractions, and it's certainly not for avid shoppers, but Briançon is well worth a visit. Recent visitors enjoyed walking in the valley on 'well-prepared trails', and the indoor-outdoor thermal pool in Monêtier (reopened for 1999/2000) makes a great place to watch the sun go down. The swimming pool in the hotel Sporting in Villeneuve is open to non-residents.

Briançon 1325m

Briançon is linked by gondola to the Serre-Chevalier slopes. Its lovely 17th-century upper quarter is 'a delight', complete with impressive fortifications, narrow cobbled streets and typically French provincial restaurants, auberges and patisseries. And there are wonderful views from the top. However, the area surrounding the lift station is an ugly urban sprawl.

The east-facing local slopes (all intermediate) are sunny, but snow-guns ensure that the main pistes down to the gondola mid-station (1625m) stay open all season, and the run to town remains complete for much of it.

Packages are mostly geared towards car-driving self-caterers, but independent travellers have plenty of modestly priced hotels available.

Tignes 2100m

Great skiing and ... er, that's it

WHAT IT COSTS

6

HOW IT RATES

The slopes

Snow	*****
Extent	*****
Experts	*****
Intermediates	*****
Beginners	**
Convenience	****
Queues	****
Restaurants	**

The rest

Scenery	***
Resort charm	**
Off-slope	*

What's new

Major recent improvements include a road tunnel at Tignes-le-Lac so that the two sides of the lift system are no longer split by traffic. La Maison de Tignes, on the 'snow front' in Tignes-le-Lac, is an attractive new chalet housing all of the resort services.

For 1999/2000, two more covered six-packs improved mountain access from Le Lavachet. And two new underground car parks were opened. The Lavachet beginners' chair-lift was replaced by a drag. Several hotels and apartment blocks have been renovated.

A new 'hands free' electronic lift system is planned for 2001.

- + Good snow guaranteed for a long season – about the best Alpine bet
- + One of the best areas in the world for lift-served off-piste runs
- + Huge amount of terrain for all standards, shared with Val-d'Isère
- + Lots of accommodation close to the slopes (though there is also quite a bit that involves some walking)
- + Swift access to Val-d'Isère slopes

- − Resort buildings spoil the views from the slopes
- − Bleak, treeless setting – no woodland runs to retreat to on bad-weather days, and many slopes liable to closure after heavy snow
- − Still lots of long, slow chair-lifts
- − Poor mountain restaurants
- − Near-beginners have to go over to Val-d'Isère to find long green runs
- − Limited après-ski

The appeal of Tignes is simple: good snow, spread over a wide area of varied terrain. Tignes and Val-d'Isère together form the enormous Espace Killy – a Mecca for experts, and ideal for adventurous intermediates. And in many ways Tignes makes the better base: appreciably higher, more convenient, surrounded by better intermediate terrain, with quick access to the Grande Motte glacier.

Our preference is still to stay in Val, which is a more human place, a more rounded resort and a more central base for exploration of the whole area. But the case for Tignes is getting stronger as results flow from the resort's current campaign to reinvent itself in a generally less hostile form (Tignes is building its future, as the slogan goes). The road through Tignes-le-Lac was pushed underground a couple of years ago, so you no longer have to tangle with traffic to get from the western slopes to the eastern ones. Underground car parks are also encouraging development of the pedestrian-friendly feel that the resort is striving to achieve. Various buildings are getting a facelift to make the resort slightly easier on the eye. It all helps.

Although Tignes has invested in some impressive lifts accessing the Grande Motte and Val-d'Isère, enjoyment of the expansive western side of the Tignes bowl – and large areas of the Val sector, too – is limited by the time you spend riding slow chair-lifts.

SNOWPIX.COM / CHRIS GILL

Unlike many glaciers, the Grande Motte offers slopes of worthwhile gradient →

boarding *This is a big area, with a big boarder reputation. Snowsure (if a bit flat) boarding on the glacier gives way to steep tree-hopping above the lowest part, Tignes-les-Brévières. In between, the lift system relies more on chairs and gondolas than drags, and long, wide pistes to blast down, with acres of powder between them to play in. The glacier is a good place for near-beginners to practise. And there are a couple of specialist snowboard schools/shops. You can buy a specific pass for the fun-park and half-pipe. Hiring a guide and exploring the off-piste is recommended for good free-riders. Otherwise, check out the Val-d'Isère slopes for a change of scenery. There are a couple of bars worth going to – just follow the noise.*

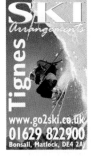

The resort

Tignes was created before the French discovered the benefits of making purpose-built resorts look acceptable. Later than most of its contemporaries, it has now woken up to the demand for traditional Alpine ambience. Traffic is now under control, with more space for pedestrians, and the main centres are certainly more pleasant as a result. (You may be less keen on these changes when you've lugged your luggage the 100m between your transfer bus and your hotel, of course.)

In the original and main village – Tignes-le-Lac – some of the smaller buildings in the central part, Le Rosset, are being successfully revamped in chalet style. But the place as a whole is dreary, and the blocks overlooking the lake from the quarter called Le Bec-Rouge will always be monstrous. Some attractive new buildings are being added on the fringes, in a suburb known as Les Almes.

The more modern subsidiary centres of Le Lavachet (close to Tignes-le-Lac) and Val-Claret (a couple of km up the valley, beyond the lake) are slightly more stylish, with a more welcoming ambience.

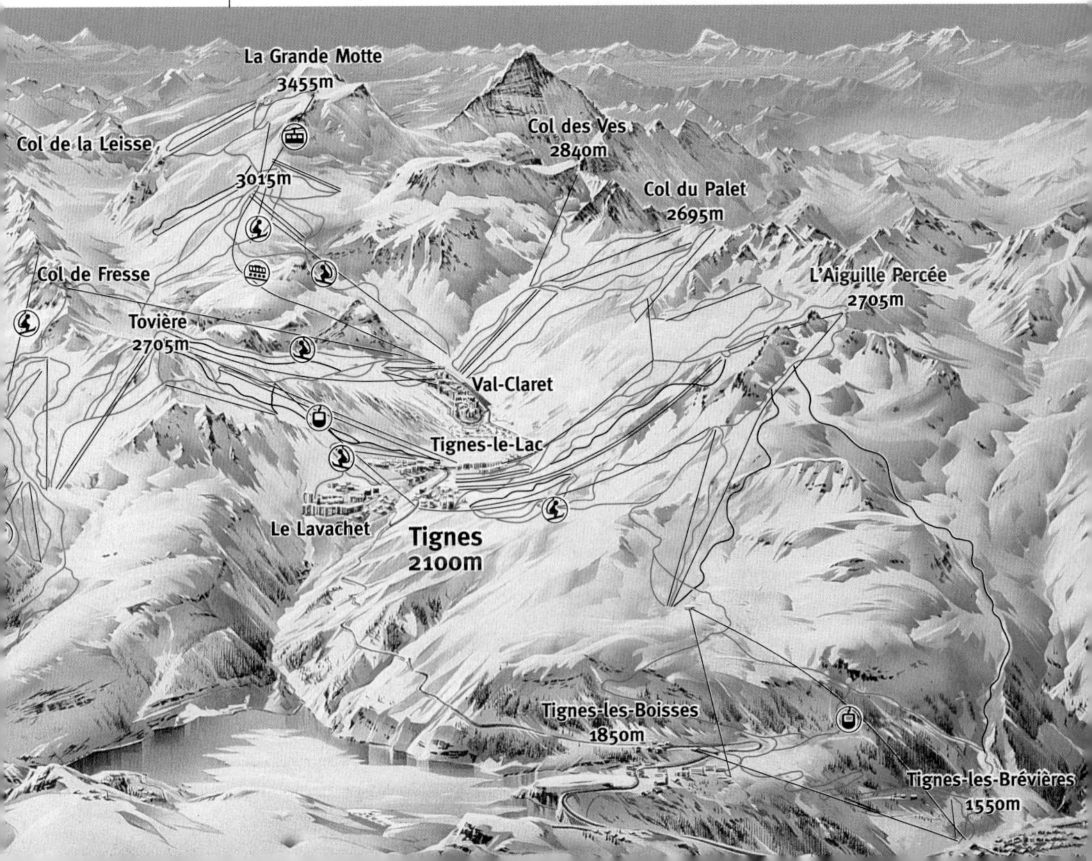

MOUNTAIN FACTS

Altitude	1550m-3455m
Lifts	97
Pistes	300km
Green/Blue	62%
Red	28%
Black	10%
Artificial snow	24km
Recco detectors used	

LIFT PASSES

2000/01 prices in francs
L'Espace Killy
Covers all lifts and resort buses in Tignes and Val-d'Isère.
Beginners Free lifts on all main nursery slopes; special beginners' half-day pass.
Main pass
1-day pass 228
6-day pass 1,070
Senior citizens
Over 60: 6-day pass 899
Over 75: free pass
Children
Under 13: 6-day pass 746
Under 5: free pass
Short-term passes
Half-day pass from 12.30 (adult 159, Super Tignes pass 143).
Alternative periods
14 non-consecutive days pass available.
Notes 2-day pass and over valid for one day in La Plagne-Les Arcs. 6-day pass and over valid for one day each in the Three Valleys, Pralognan-la-Vanoise, Les Saisies and Valmorel. On 3- to 15-day passes, pass reimbursed if all lifts are shut due to bad weather. Discount on new passes on presentation of previous season's pass. Extra discount for senior citizens aged 70 to 74.
Alternative passes
Super Tignes ski pass covers the lifts on the Tignes side of the Espace Killy only (adult 6-day 915).

Below the high valley of the main resort villages are two smaller settlements. Tignes-les-Boisses, quietly set in the trees beside the road up to the main Tignes villages, consists of a barracks and a couple of simple hotels. Lower Tignes-les-Brévières is a renovated old village at the lowest point of the slopes – a favourite lunch spot, and a 'friendly and unpretentious' place to stay.

A regular and efficient free bus service connects all the villages until midnight – though in the daytime the route runs along the bottom of Val-Claret, leaving residents of central Val-Claret with some hiking.

The mountains

The runs of the Espace Killy have few rivals for the attention of experts, thanks to almost limitless off-piste terrain. Intermediates, too, will have a great time here, with mile after mile of cruising runs. On the other hand, the Tignes bowl suffers from a complete lack of green runs for confidence-building, and arguably a shortage of genuinely testing red runs.

But the area's great weakness is that it can become unusable in bad weather. There are no woodland runs except immediately above Tignes-les-Boisses and Tignes-les-Brévières, and heavy snow produces widespread avalanche risk.

THE SLOPES
High, snowsure and varied

Tignes' biggest asset is the **Grande Motte** – and the runs from, as well as on, the glacier. Access is easy thanks to the underground funicular from Val-Claret, which whizzes you up to over 3000m in six minutes. There are chairs and drags to play on, as well as beautiful long runs back to the resort and a link over to Val-d'Isère.

The main lifts towards Val-d'Isère are efficient: a high-capacity gondola from Le Lac to **Tovière**, and a fast 'bubble' chair from Val-Claret to **Col de Fresse**. You can head back to Tignes from either: the return from Tovière to Tignes-le-Lac is via a steep black run, but there are easier runs to Val-Claret.

Going up the opposite side of the valley takes you to an area of drags and chair-lifts serving predominantly east-facing slopes split into two main sectors, linked in both directions – **Col du Palet** and **l'Aiguille Percée**. From the latter, you can descend to Tignes-les-Brévières, on blue, red or black runs (but beware the Chardons blue, which should be graded red); there's an efficient gondola back.

The Col des Ves chair-lift, at the south end of the Col du Palet sector, is not normally open until high season.

A six-day pass covers a day in some other resorts, including Les Arcs or La Plagne and the Three Valleys.

SNOW RELIABILITY
Difficult to beat

Tignes has all-year-round runs (barring brief closures in spring or autumn) on its 3455m Grande Motte glacier. And the resort height of 2100m generally means good snow-cover right back to base for most of the long season. The whole region, not just the glacier area, usually has good cover from November to May. The west-facing runs, especially those from Tovière to Val-Claret, suffer from the sun, although they now have serious snowmaking.

FOR EXPERTS
An excellent choice

It is the off-piste possibilities that make Tignes such a draw for experts. Go with one of the off-piste groups that the schools organise and you'll have a great time (snow permitting).

One of the big adventures is to head for Champagny (linked to the La Plagne area) or Peisey-Nancroix (linked to the Les Arcs area) – very beautiful runs, and not too difficult. Your guide will organise return transport.

Another favourite descent of ours is the Tour de Pramecou, from the Grande Motte glacier. After some walking and beautiful away-from-it-all runs, you end up on a steep, smooth north-facing slope which takes you back to Val-Claret. There are other descents across the glacier to the Leisse chair-lift.

The whole western side of the bowl has lots of off-piste possibilities. The terrain served by the Col des Ves chair is often excellent. To the left (looking up) there are wonderfully secluded, scenic and challenging descents. On the right, lower down, is a less heavily used and gentler area, ideal for off-piste initiation. To the north, there are excellent variants on the Sache run to Les Brévières (see below).

The ski schools and the guides' bureau offer the bizarre French form of heli-skiing: mountaintop drops are forbidden, but from Tovière you can ski down towards the Lac du Chevril to be retrieved by chopper. Or you can be dropped over the border in Italy.

The only serious challenge within the piste network is the long black run from Tovière to Tignes-le-Lac, with steep, usually heavily mogulled sections at the top and bottom; parts of this get a lot of afternoon sun. Our favourite black run is the Sache, from Aiguille Percée down a secluded valley to Tignes-les-Brévières.

FOR INTERMEDIATES
One of the best

For the keen intermediate piste-basher the Espace Killy is one of the top three or four areas in France, or the world.

Tignes' local slopes are ideal intermediate terrain. The red and blue runs on the Grande Motte glacier nearly always have superb snow. The glacier run from the top of the cable-car is a gentle blue. The Leisse run down to the chair-lift is now graded black and can get very mogulled but has good snow. The long red run all the way back to town is a delightful long cruise – though often crowded.

From Tovière, the blue 'H' run to Val-Claret is an enjoyable cruise and generally well groomed. But again, it can get very crowded. The direct way down from the top to Tignes-le-Lac is a steep black mogul field.

There is lots to do on the other side of the valley. We particularly like the uncrowded Ves red run reached by the low-capacity Col des Ves chair – the highest point of Tignes' non-glacier runs at 2840m. After an initial mogul field the run becomes an interesting undulating and curvy cruise, usually with good snow and a few moguls. The runs down from Aiguille Percée to Tignes-les-Boisses and Tignes-les-Brévières are also scenic and enjoyable. There are red and blue options as well as the beautiful Sache black run – adventurous intermediates shouldn't miss it. The runs down from Aiguille Percée to Le Lac are gentle, wide blues. The Bleuets blue from the top of the Aiguille Rouge chair is a more challenging alternative.

FOR BEGINNERS
Good nursery slopes, but ...

The nursery slopes of Tignes-le-Lac and Le Lavachet (which meet at the top) are excellent – convenient, snowsure, gentle, free of through-traffic and served by a slow chair and a drag (free). The ones at Val-Claret are much less appealing – steep and served by a free drag. You can also ride the first stage of the Bollin chair for free.

For long green runs you have to go over to the Val-d'Isère sector – easy enough, but you need an Espace Killy pass to use them, and you have to ride the gondola back down from Tovière. And in poor weather, the high Tignes valley is an intimidatingly bleak place – enough to make any wavering beginner retreat to a bar with a book.

FOR CROSS-COUNTRY
Interesting variety

The Espace Killy has 40km of cross-country trails. There are tracks on the frozen Lac de Tignes, along the valley between Val-Claret and Tignes-le-Lac, at Les Boisses and Les Brévières and up the mountain on the Grande Motte.

QUEUES
Very few

The queues here depend on snow conditions. If snow low down is poor, the Grande Motte funicular generates queues; the parallel high-speed chairs are often quicker. These lifts jointly shift a lot of people, with the result that the run down to Val-Claret can be seriously unpleasant. The worst queues now are for the cable-car on the glacier – half-hour waits are common.

Of course, if higher lifts are closed by heavy snow or high winds, the lifts on the lower slopes have big queues.

Queues can build up late in the day for the slow parallel chairs bringing Tignes residents back from the Val slopes to Tovière – the Borsat fast quad to Col de Fresse is quicker.

MOUNTAIN RESTAURANTS
Head out of the bowl

'We failed to find any nice ones,' says a reporter, echoing our own view that Tignes' mountain restaurants are inadequate, especially on the west side of the bowl. Here there is one cafeteria (with reasonable prices and good terrace views) at the Col du Palet mid-mountain lift junction and one pricey and crowded old hut – the Savouna – just above Tignes-le-Lac.

The opposite side of the bowl is slightly better equipped, with the atmospheric chalet at the top of Tovière and the newish but pleasantly woody Chalet du Bollin – just qualifying as a mountain restaurant, a

SCHOOLS/GUIDES

2000/01 prices in francs

ESF
Classes 5 days
6hr: 9am-noon and 1.45-4.45; 3hr: am or pm
5 full days: 990
Children's classes
Ages: 4 to 12
5 full days: 945
Private lessons
Hourly or daily
195 for 1hr, between noon and 2pm, 1520 for one day.

Evolution 2
(1999/2000 prices)
Classes 5 days
am or pm
5 half days: 720
Children's classes
Ages: 5 to 14
5 half days: 600
Private lessons
Hourly or daily
190 for 1hr

OTHER SCHOOLS

Tignes International
Snow Fun
Snocool
Kebra Surfing
Surf Feeling

CHILDCARE

The recently opened hotel Diva in Val-Claret (479 067000) has a nursery taking children from age 18 months.

The Marmottons kindergarten in Le Lac (479 065167) takes children from 2 to 8, with skiing with Evolution 2 instructors for those aged 3½ or more.

few metres above Val-Claret. Both offer table-service as well as self-service.

The big restaurant at the top of the Grande Motte funicular has great panoramic views from its huge terrace, which is traversed every few minutes by the next funicular-full of people. A recent reporter described the meals in the self-service section as 'nauseating'.

There are lots of easily accessible places for lunch in the resorts, many with terraces. One ski-to-the-door favourite of ours is the ground-floor restaurant of the hotel Montana, on the left as you descend from the Aiguille Percée. In Les Brévières, a short walk round the corner into the village brings you to places much cheaper than the two by the piste.

SCHOOLS AND GUIDES
Enormous choice
There are half a dozen schools, plus various independent instructors. The ESF and Evolution 2 are the main ones, with sections in the main resort centres. Evolution 2 has received the best reports recently – 'far superior to the ESF,' says one – with class sizes put at a maximum of eight and standards of English good. Based in Le Lac, Stages 2000 specialises in off-piste tuition; Association 9 Valleys does mostly inter-resort circuits and extreme skiing.

FACILITIES FOR CHILDREN
Mixed reports
In the past, we have had good reports on the Marmottons kindergartens, and on the 'experienced minders' of the Evolution 2 school in Le Lac. However, our most recent reporter was alarmed by the general lack of care and supervision he witnessed during his stay, and felt that the Marmottons kindergarten in Le Lac was poorly situated for child safety. Another report on the ESF kindergarten tells a familiar tale of indifference to infant suffering.

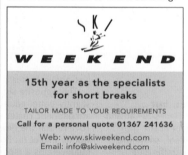

Staying there

Location isn't crucial, especially as Val-Claret, as well as Le Lac, now has swift access to the Val-d'Isère slopes. But Val-Claret is quite extensive – for real convenience, stay at the southern end. The new lifts out of Le Lavachet have made this a more attractive base. They are also very handy for those staying in Les Almes. The free bus service linking the main centres is efficient.

HOW TO GO
Unremarkable range of options
Although all three main styles of accommodation are available through tour operators, there isn't a lot of choice in any category, especially for those who like their creature comforts.
Chalets The choice of catered chalets is limited by comparison with Val-d'Isère and other major French resorts, and there are few specially notable ones. Ski Olympic's Chalet Rosset has been recommended by a reporter as an exception: 'Superb, with a lovely lounge with views, but a bit of an uphill plod at the end of the day.' Their Chardon is also rated 'excellent'. Crystal's hotel-style Curling, plumb in the centre of Val Claret, has neat public areas and spacious bedrooms (and see Après-ski section).
Hotels The few hotels are small and concentrated in Le Lac. Most are simple, and there is nothing really swanky.
(((3 **Campanules** Smartly rustic chalet (since its makeover) in upper Le Lac, with well equipped rooms and a good

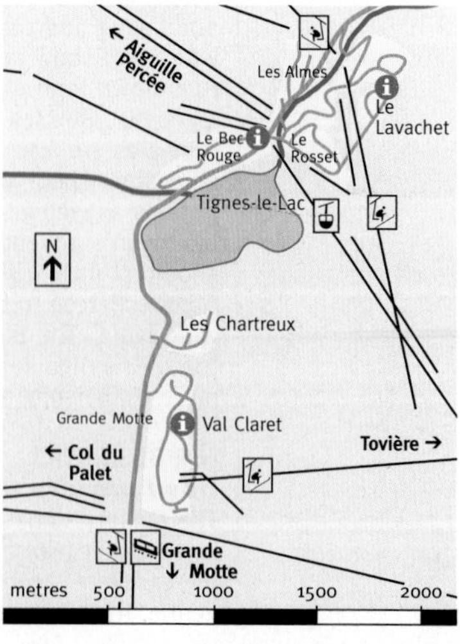

Tignes-le-Lac sits at the foot of steep slopes on its eastern side – the way home from Val-d'Isère is a serious black run ➔

SNOWPIX.COM / CHRIS GILL

GETTING THERE

Air Geneva, transfer 4hr. Lyon, transfer 4hr. Chambéry, transfer 3hr.

Rail Bourg-St-Maurice (30km); regular buses or taxi from station.

ACTIVITIES

Indoor 'Vitatignes' in Le Lac (balneotherapy centre with spa baths, sauna etc), 'Espace Forme' in Le Lac, 'Les Bains du Montana' in Le Lac, Fitness Club in Val-Claret (body-building, aerobics, squash, golf practice and simulation, sauna, hammam, Californian baths, hot-tub, swimming pool, massage), cinema, covered tennis court, bowling, climbing wall
Outdoor Natural skating-rink, hang-gliding, paragliding, helicopter rides, snow-mobiles, husky dog-sleigh rides, diving beneath ice on lake, heli-skiing, 'La Banquise' for children (ice skating, snow sliding, solarium, snow activities, climbing activities)

TOURIST OFFICE

Postcode 73321
t +33 479 400440
f 479 400315
information@tignes.net
www.tignes.net

restaurant, run by the friendly Reymond brothers.
(((3 **Village Montana** New, stylishly woody complex on the east-facing slopes above Le Lac, with suites and apartments as well as rooms. Outdoor pool, and spa treatments available. One recent reporter enthuses about the food but felt that the accommodation was fairly 'ordinary'.
((2 **Arbina** Well-run simple hotel close to the lifts in Le Lac, with lunchtime terrace, busy après-ski bar and one of the best restaurants in town.
((2 **Terril Blanc** Well run place next to the lake.
((2 **Neige et Soleil** Excellent family-run place in Le Lac – central, clean, cosy, comfortable, with good food.
((2 **Marais** Prettily furnished, simple little hotel in Tignes-les-Boisses.
Self-catering In upper Val-Claret, close to the Tovière chair, the Maeva 'Residence Le Borsat' apartments are about the best on offer – not too cramped, reasonably well equipped and with a communal lounge. The Chalet Club in Val-Claret is a collection of simple studios, but has the benefit of free indoor pool, sauna and in-house restaurant and bar.

EATING OUT
Good places dotted about
Each of the main centres has a range of restaurants, although the options in Le Lavachet are rather limited. Advance booking is recommended for many restaurants. Finding anywhere with some atmosphere is difficult in Le Lac, though the food in some of the better hotels is good – the Arbina and Campanules, for example. In Val-Claret the Bouf'Mich is a favourite ('terrific food, reasonable prices, helpful service, pretty interior'). The Ski d'Or is a swanky Relais & Châteaux hotel. Les Terrasses du Claret is recommended for large groups. Those on a budget here should try the Italian at the Pignatta. The Cordée in Les Boisses is recommended – unpretentious surroundings, great traditional French food, modest prices.

APRES-SKI
Early to bed
Tignes is rather quiet at night, though there is no shortage of bars, some doing food as well. Val-Claret has some early-evening atmosphere and happy hours are popular – the 'pub-like' Crowded House under Crystal's chalet hotel Curling gets most mentions, followed by the Wobbly Rabbit. Other recommendations include Grizzly's.

Le Lac is a natural focus for immediate après-ski drinks, but don't expect anything too riotous. The bar of the hotel Arbina is our kind of spot – adequately cosy, spacious enough to absorb some groups, friendly service.

The most animated bar in Le Lavachet is Harri's, though it's quite large and takes some filling before it warms up. The satellite TV here is popular.

Les Caves du Lac, Café de la Poste and Jack's are popular late night haunts.

OFF THE SLOPES
Forget it
Despite the range of alternative activities, Tignes is a resort for those who want to use the slopes, where anyone who doesn't is liable to feel like a fish out of water.

STAYING DOWN THE VALLEY
Only for visiting other resorts
See the Val-d'Isère chapter; the same considerations apply broadly here. But bear in mind that there are rooms to be had in simple hotels in Tignes-les-Boisses and Tignes-les-Brévières.

Les Trois Vallées

Despite competing claims, notably from the Portes du Soleil, the sheer quantity of lift-served terrain in the Trois Vallées puts it in a league of its own. There is nowhere like it for a keen skier or boarder who wants to cover as much mileage as possible while rarely taking the same run repeatedly. And it has a lot to offer everyone, from beginner to expert.

The runs of les Trois Vallées and their resorts are dealt with in five chapters. The four major resorts are Courchevel, page 223, Méribel, page 257, Les Menuires, page 254, and Val-Thorens, page 317. St-Martin-de-Belleville, a small village along the mountainside from Les Menuires, gets its own chapter on page 288.

None of the resorts is cheap. **Les Menuires** is the cheapest but it is also the ugliest. The slopes around the village get too much sun for comfort, but close by across the valley are some of the best (and quietest) challenging pistes in les Trois Vallées on its north-facing La Masse. Its near-neighbour, **St-Martin-de-Belleville**, is a small traditional village with good-value accommodation – and now with improved lift links into the rest of the area.

Up instead of down the Belleville valley from Les Menuires, at 2300m **Val-Thorens** is the highest resort in the Alps, and at 3200m the top of its slopes is the high point of the Trois Vallées. The snow in this area is almost always good, and it includes two glaciers where it's guaranteed. But the setting is bleak and the lifts are vulnerable to closure in bad weather. The purpose-built resort is very convenient. Visually it is not comparable to Les Menuires, thanks to the smaller-scale design and more thorough use of wood cladding, but it still isn't to everyone's taste.

Méribel is a two-part resort. The higher component, **Méribel-Mottaret**, is the best placed of all the resorts for getting to any part of the Trois Vallées system in the shortest possible time. It's now quite a spread-out place, with some of the accommodation a long way up the hillsides – great for access to the slopes, less so for access to nightlife. **Méribel** itself is 200m lower and has long been a British favourite, especially for chalet holidays. It is the most attractive of the main Trois Vallées resorts, built in chalet style beside a long winding road up the hillside. Parts of the resort are very convenient for the slopes and the village centre; parts are very far from either. A gondola leads up to Méribel from the old spa town of **Brides-Les-Bains** which has cheap accommodation but no piste back to it.

Courchevel has four parts. 1850 is the most fashionable resort in France, and can be the most expensive resort in the Alps (though it doesn't have to cost a fortune to stay there). The less expensive parts are Le Praz (aka 1300), 1550 and 1650. They don't have the same choice of nightlife and restaurants, and only 1550 enjoys the same central location in the lift system. Many people rate the slopes around Courchevel the best in the Trois Vallées, with runs to suit all standards. The snow tends to be better than in neighbouring Méribel, because many of the slopes are north-facing.

La Tania was built for the 1992 Olympics, just off the small road linking Le Praz to Méribel. It has now grown into a quiet, attractive, car-free collection of chalets and chalet-style apartments set among the trees and is popular with families. It has a good nursery slope but there are no very easy runs back to it.

Val-d'Isère

1850m

On- and off-piste playground with reliable snow

WHAT IT COSTS

(6)

HOW IT RATES

The slopes	
Snow	*****
Extent	*****
Experts	*****
Intermediates	*****
Beginners	***
Convenience	***
Queues	****
Restaurants	**
The rest	
Scenery	***
Resort charm	***
Off-slope	**

What's new

A new 'children's village' for 3- to 13-year-olds was opened last season.

2000/01 should see an end to the Pissaillas glacier access debacle. The defunct Cascade chair-lift is now being replaced by two quad chairs.

Further ahead, a new Funitel gondola on the Bellevarde Face will be in operation for 2001/02.

A new 'hands free' electronic lift system is also planned for 2001.

- + Huge area linked with Tignes, with runs for all standards
- + Some of the best lift-served off-piste runs in the world
- + High altitude means snow is more or less guaranteed
- + Wide choice of schools, especially for off-piste lessons and guiding
- + Wide range of package holidays and accommodation
- + For a high resort, the town is attractive, very lively at night, and offers a good range of restaurants
- + Piste grooming and staff attitudes have improved noticeably

- − Piste grading understates the difficulty of many runs – though moguls on greens now uncommon
- − You're quite likely to need the bus at the start or end of the day
- − Most lifts and slopes are liable to close when the weather is bad
- − Nursery slopes not ideal – and no easy return run to the village
- − Crowds on some runs
- − Still some lifts in need of upgrading
- − Seems at times more British than French – especially in low season
- − Disappointing mountain restaurants

Val-d'Isère is one of the world's best resorts for experts – attracted by the extent of lift-served off-piste – and for confident, mileage-hungry intermediates. But you don't have to be particularly adventurous to enjoy the resort, and the village ambience has improved greatly in recent years.

The list of drawbacks above looks long, but they are mainly petty complaints, whereas the plus-points are mainly things that weigh heavily in the balance, for us and for those who send us reports. The last of them – the clear recent improvements in piste grooming and lift staff attitudes – is as welcome as it is surprising. We await similar improvements in the local branch of the ESF.

boarding *Val-d'Isère is good for boarders, though Tignes is a more popular boarder destination. Most of the main lifts are cable-cars, chair-lifts and gondolas, with very few drag-lifts. But there are a few flat areas where you'll need to scoot or walk. Experts will revel in the off-piste. There's a fun-park with a half-pipe on Bellevarde, under the Mont Blanc chair-lift, and another at La Daille. There are several specialist snowboard shops and schools. The village nursery area is ideal for trying boarding for the first time and Le Fornet is good to progress to. Val's nightlife – with its huge selection of bars – is difficult to beat.*

The resort

Val-d'Isère spreads along a remote valley which is a dead end in winter. It is a classic ribbon development. As you drive in from La Daille – a convenient but hideous slope-side apartment complex – the apartments and chalets lining the road increase in density, and then give way to shops, bars, restaurants and hotels. As you approach the centre, the legacy of the 1992 Olympics becomes more evident: new wood- and stone-cladding, culminating in the tasteful pedestrian-only Val Village complex and the few remnants of the original old village.

There is a lot of traffic around, but the resort is working to get it under control and to make the centre more pedestrian-friendly – improvements to the main street include the reduction of traffic by tighter control of parking, and the installation of more greenery. Even now, many first-time visitors find the resort much 'prettier' than they expect a big-name high resort to be.

Beyond Val-d'Isère the valley road continues 3km to the old hamlet of Le Fornet – with its own cable-car, an attractive base for those in search of a quiet holiday.

↑ The Face de Bellevarde may not be the steepest of black runs, but it is an excellent slope

MARIO COLONEL / VAL-D'ISERE TO

MOUNTAIN FACTS

Altitude	1550m-3455m
Lifts	97
Pistes	300km
Green/Blue	62%
Red	28%
Black	10%
Artificial snow	24km
Recco detectors used	

The mountains

For experts, there are few areas to rival L'Espace Killy (the linked areas of Val-d'Isère and Tignes – see separate chapter). The main attraction is its splendid lift-served off-piste runs; there are challenges on-piste, but not many. Intermediates of all standards will find enough to keep them interested for several visits – though there are complaints about crowded high-season pistes. Despite the macho image, there are good areas for novices too. Several recent reporters have noted that piste grooming has improved – some feel that it is now too thorough, and that not enough bumps are being allowed to build up. A six-day lift pass gives a day's skiing in Les Arcs or La Plagne, plus the Trois Vallées – reachable by car. Other resorts nearby are Ste-Foy and La Rosière.

THE SLOPES
Vast and varied

Val-d'Isère's slopes divide into three main sectors. **Bellevarde** is the mountain which is home to Val-d'Isère's famous downhill course – the OK piste, which opens each season's World Cup Alpine circus in early December. You can reach Bellevarde by funicular from La Daille or by cable-car or fast chairs from Val. From the top you can get back down to the main lifts, play on a variety of drags and chairs at altitude or take a choice of lifts to the Tignes slopes.

Solaise is the other mountain accessible directly from the centre of Val-d'Isère. The Solaise cable-car was Val's first major lift – begun illicitly during the Occupation in 1940 and finished in 1942. The parallel Solaise Express fast quad chair-lift takes you a few metres higher. Once up, a short drag takes you over a plateau and down to a variety of chairs that serve this very sunny area of predominantly gentle pistes.

From near the top of this area you can catch a chair over to the third main area, above and below the **Col de l'Iseran**, which can also be reached by cable-car from Le Fornet in the valley. The chair-lift ride is spectacular or scary, depending on your head for heights: it climbs over a steep ridge and then drops suddenly down the other side. There is an alternative way over: a short and steep drag-lift takes you to a narrow tunnel through the ridge, leading to an awkward black run which is often closed. The runs at Col de l'Iseran are predominantly easy, with spectacular views and access to the region's most beautiful off-piste sections. The runs on the Pissaillas glacier beyond the col were accessed by snowcats and rope tows last season because of a disagreement between

AITO
ATOL 2307

3300m
Glacier de Pissaillas
Col Pers
Col de l'Iseran
2765m
2950m
2900m
Tignes
Col de Fresse
2770m
Tour Charvet
2325m
Le Manchet
1940m
Bellevarde
2705m
Solaise
2560m
Le Châtelard
Le Fornet
1930m
Le Laisinant
Val d'Isère
1850m
La Daille
1785m

LIFT PASSES

2000/01 prices in francs

L'Espace Killy
Covers all lifts and resort buses in Tignes and Val-d'Isère.

Beginners 7 free beginners' lifts on main nursery slopes.

Main pass
1-day pass 228
6-day pass 1,070

Senior citizens
Over 60: 6-day pass 899
Over 75: free pass

Children
Under 13: 6-day pass 746
Under 5: free pass

Short-term passes
Half-day pass from 12.30 (adult 159).

Alternative periods
14 non-consecutive days pass available.

Notes 6-day pass and over valid for one day each in the Three Valleys, Pralognan-la-Vanoise, Les Saisies and Ste-Foy. On 3- to 15-day passes, pass reimbursed if all lifts are shut due to bad weather. Discount on new passes on presentation of your lift pass for any one of the previous three seasons. Extra discount for senior citizens aged 70 to 74.

the resort and the Vanoise National Park authorities over the replacement of the defunct Cascade chair-lift. Normal service is expected to resume for 2000/01.

The local radio carries good weather reports in English as well as French.

SNOW RELIABILITY
Unbeatable

In years when lower resorts have suffered, Val-d'Isère has rarely been short of snow. Its height of 1850m means you can almost always get back to the village, especially because of the snowmaking facilities on the lower slopes of all the main routes home. But even more important is that in each sector there is lots to do above mid-mountain, between about 2300m and 2900m. Many of the slopes are north-facing (or northish) and plenty are between 2300m and 3000m, even ignoring the higher glacier skiing.

FOR EXPERTS
One of the world's best

Val-d'Isère is one of the top resorts in the world for experts. The main attraction is the huge range of beautiful off-piste possibilities – see feature panel on the facing page.

There may be better resorts for really steep pistes, but there is plenty to amuse the expert here, despite the small number of blacks on the piste map. Many of the red and blue runs are steep enough to get mogulled.

On Bellevarde the famous Face run is the main attraction – often mogulled from top to bottom, but not worryingly steep. Epaule is the sector's other black run – where the moguls are hit by long exposure to sun and can be slushy or rock-hard too often for our liking. There are several challenging ways down from Solaise to the village: all steep, though none fearsomely so. This has traditionally been classic bumps territory, but one recent reporter complains that the resort's new enthusiasm for grooming has extended even to these slopes.

FOR INTERMEDIATES
Quantity and quality

Val-d'Isère has even more to offer intermediates than experts. But the less experienced should be aware that many runs are under-graded. This remains a regular reporter complaint.

In the Solaise sector is a network of gentle blue runs ideal for building confidence. And there are a couple of beautiful runs from here through the woods to Le Laisinant, from where you catch the bus – these are ideal for bad weather, though prone to closure in times of avalanche danger.

Most of the runs in the Col de l'Iseran sector are even easier – ideal for early and hesitant intermediates. Those marked blue at the top of the glacier could really be graded green.

Bellevarde has a huge variety of runs ideally suited to intermediates of all standards. From Bellevarde itself there is a choice of green, blue and red runs of varying pitch. And the wide runs from Tovière normally give you the choice of groomed piste or moguls.

A snag for early intermediates is that runs back to the valley can be testing. The easiest way is to head down to La Daille, where there is a green run – but it should be graded blue (in some resorts it would be red), and it gets very crowded and mogulled at the end of the day. None of the runs from Bellevarde and Solaise back to Val itself is really easy.

The blue Santons run from Bellevarde takes you through a long, narrow gun barrel which often has people standing around plucking up courage, making things even trickier.

On Solaise there isn't much to choose between the blue and red ways down – and they're both narrow in places. At the top, there's no option other than the red run in full view of the lifts. Many early intermediates sensibly choose to ride the lifts down – take the chair for a spectacular view.

FOR BEGINNERS
OK if you know where to go

Val-d'Isère has a nursery slope right by the centre of town that is 95 per cent perfect; it's just a pity that the top of the slope is unpleasantly steep. The lifts serving it are free.

Once off the nursery slopes, there are some easy runs, but you have to know where to find them; many of the greens would be blue, or even red, in other resorts. One experienced local instructor admitted: 'We have to have plenty of green runs on the piste map, even if we haven't got many green slopes – otherwise beginners wouldn't come to Val-d'Isère.'

A good place for your first real runs off the nursery slopes is the Madeleine green run on Solaise – now served by a fast six-pack. The Col de l'Iseran runs are also gentle and wide, and not over-busy. There is good progression terrain on Bellevarde, too, but no genuinely easy way back to the valley.

FOR CROSS-COUNTRY
Limited
There are a couple of loops towards La Daille and another out past Le Laisinant. More picturesque is the one going from Le Châtelard (on the road past the main cable-car station) to the Manchet chair. But keen cross-country enthusiasts should go elsewhere.

QUEUES
Few problems
Queues to get out of the resort have been pretty much eliminated by the building of the funicular at La Daille and high-speed chair-lifts up the mountains as alternatives to the two main cable-cars.

To get to Tignes, it's quicker to take the high-speed quad to Col de Fresse than the slow and often busy Tommeuses chairs to Tovière. Returning from Val-Claret at the end of the day is now much quicker thanks to a high-speed, dual-loading, six-person chair-lift direct to Col de Fresse, with a run down to Bellevarde. Make sure you get into the correct queue: half the chairs stop part-way up the hill, serving runs back into Val-Claret.

The number of slow chair-lifts scattered about the area, particularly in Tignes, is a common complaint. Crowded pistes is another.

At the end of the day, there's usually a wait for the chair back from Col de l'Iseran to Solaise. But you can always descend to Le Fornet instead.

If you plan a return visit, keep your lift pass – those with a week's pass bought in the last three years are entitled to a 'loyal customer' reduction.

MOUNTAIN RESTAURANTS
Getting better
The mountain restaurants mainly consist of big self-service places with vast terraces at the top of major lifts.

La Fruitière at the top of La Daille gondola, kitted out with stuff rescued from a dairy in the valley, is about the

OFF-PISTE PARADISE

L'Espace Killy has some of the most extensive lift-served off-piste skiing in the world. Although the piste map no longer shows the classic off-piste runs, there are dozens waiting to be discovered and all with endless variations.

They are best explored with a professional guide because of the avalanche and other hidden dangers, such as cliffs to fall off and rivers to fall in. But many of the more popular runs are skied into an almost piste-like state soon after a fresh snowfall – here, again, a guide will be able to show you the less well known and less often skied routes.

Our favourite off-piste routes include:

– Col Pers, from the top of the glacier above Le Fornet. You traverse over to a big, wide, fairly gentle bowl with glorious views. There are endless variants on the way down. Most bring you out just below the source of the Isère river, where you drop into the very beautiful, narrow Gorges du Malpasset and ski on top of the frozen Isère back to the Le Fornet cable-car. This is a good area for spotting chamois grazing in the sun on the rocky outcrops above you.

– Tour de Charvet, from the top of the Grand Pré chair-lift in the Bellevarde sector. The easiest route starts with a long traverse in a huge bowl, before dropping into a narrow gorge which you ski along before the long run-out to the Manchet fast chair up to the Solaise sector.

– Tour de Pramecou, from the Grand Motte area in Tignes. After a long, flat section at the top and a couple of short climbs between downhill sections, you end up at the top of a long, steep, wide, north-facing slope (where the snow is usually excellent) and swoop down to the Carline piste back to the bottom of the Motte.

We recommend the Alpine Experience and Top Ski guided groups: you can join a group of your standard for off-piste skiing every morning (normally 9am until 1pm). Afternoons tend to be more conventional lessons to improve technique.

SCHOOLS/GUIDES

1999/2000 prices in francs

ESF
Classes 6 days
5½hr: 3hr am, 2½hr pm
6 full days: 1125
Children's classes
Ages: from 4
6 full days: 1035
Private lessons
1hr, mornings, afternoons, or whole day
200 for 1hr

Snow Fun
Classes 6 days
3hr am and 2½hr pm
5 mornings: 560
Children's classes
Ages: up to 13
6 full days: 990
Private lessons
Hourly or daily
185 for 1hr

Top Ski
Specialises in slalom, mogul and off-piste courses for small groups (max 6)
Classes 4 days
4hr: 9am-1pm; 2hr: 2pm-4pm
4 full days: 1440
Private lessons
am (8.45-1pm), pm (2pm-4.30) or full day (8.45-4.30)

Alpine Experience
Specialises in off-piste guiding and teaching for small groups (max 6)

best, serving generous portions of classic French food at reasonable prices. Service is friendly and the cheese trolley highly recommended. La Folie Douce is the more functional self-service section – again, popular with reporters. Other recommendations: Le Trifollet, about halfway up the La Daille gondola – table-service, great pizzas, terrace overlooking the men's downhill piste; Marmottes, in the middle of the Bellevarde bowl – big sunny terrace, self-service; the restaurants at the top of the Solaise Express and the Le Fornet cable-car ('excellent steak tartar'); and the 'tiny, happy' Bar de L'Ouillette, at the base of the Madeleine chair-lift.

Some of the best places for lunch are at valley level. Clochetons, near the cross-country course at Le Châtelard, is peaceful, with good views. There are a couple of restaurants on the lower slopes at La Daille that are reachable on snow and by pedestrians. Crêch'ouna, just across the slope from the funicular station at La Daille, is a charmingly rustic table-service place and now has an outside terrace too. Les Tufs, just below it, does good pizzas and Savoyard fare. One reporter recommends lunching at the Samovar hotel restaurant. Our favourite in Val-d'Isère is the big terrace of the Brussels, overlooking the nursery slopes. Bananas does good burgers, steaks and salads, and has a small terrace. When at Col de l'Iseran, one possible plan for lunch on a wintry day is to descend to the rustic Arolay at Le Fornet – good food, but 'rude service'. Lunch over in Tignes-les-Brévières is a popular option for those on a high-mileage mission.

SCHOOLS AND GUIDES
A very wide choice
There is a huge choice of schools and private instructors to choose from (over 15 in the resort brochure). We don't get many reports on the ESF adult classes; this year's are mixed, with one reporter in particular highly critical of his instructor's emphasis on psychology – not a common complaint with the ESF. We've heard from lots of satisfied Snow Fun pupils: their guides seem to 'know their snow'.

The pedestrian zone in the middle of the resort has been a great success →

CHRISTOPHE GUIBBAUD / VAL-D'ISERE TO

Several small outfits specialise in organising small groups to go off-piste – an excellent way to get off-piste safely without the cost of hiring a guide as an individual. Recent reports describe Evolution 2 as 'flexible and generally excellent', Alpine Experience as providing 'an interesting and exciting couple of days'. We have also had good reports on Ski Prestige and Top Ski. We've had great days ourselves with both Alpine Experience and Top Ski. In peak periods it's best to book in advance

Mountain Masters offers private on- and off-piste lessons. The Hors-Limites school is said to offer 'the best snowboard tuition in the Alps'.

All the schools have teachers who speak good English – in many cases it's their native language. Heli-trips can be arranged – you are dropped over the border in Italy because heli-drops are banned in France.

FACILITIES FOR CHILDREN

Good tour op possibilities

Many people prefer to use the facilities of UK tour operators such as Mark Warner. But there's a new 'children's village' for 3- to 13-year-olds, with supervised indoor and outdoor activities on the village nursery slopes. It's open daily from 8.30am to 6.30pm – reports welcome.

We have personal experience of the incompetence and indifference of the ESF's handling of children, reinforced this year by a report from the father of two children, aged 7 and 10, both of whom were placed in classes of French pupils and subsequently 'abandoned in mid-class' by their instructors.

CHILDCARE

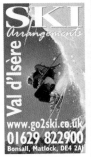

The new children's village, in the centre of town by the nursery slopes, takes children from 3 to 13, from 8.30 to 6.30.

The Petit Poucet (479 061397) in the Residence les Hameaux at Val takes children from age 2, from 9am to 5.30.

Both provide indoor and outdoor activities and delivery to and collection from ski school.

Snowfun's Club Nounours takes children aged 3 to 6 for lessons of 1hr 30 min, 2hr or 3hr. Older children can be left in classes all day.

The ESF runs a ski nursery for age 4 up, with rope tows and a heated chalet.

A list of babysitters is available at the tourist office.

Staying there

The location of your accommodation isn't crucial. Free shuttle-buses run along the main street linking the main lift stations. It is one of the most efficient bus services we've come across; even in peak periods, you never have to wait more than a few minutes. But in the evening frequency plummets and it may be quicker to walk. Dedicated après-skiers will want to be within walking distance of the town centre. The development up the side valley beyond the main lift station is mainly attractive; some places are a pleasant stroll from the centre, but the farthest-flung are a long slog – unless you're happy to pay for taxis, you need a car or a tour operator that provides transport.

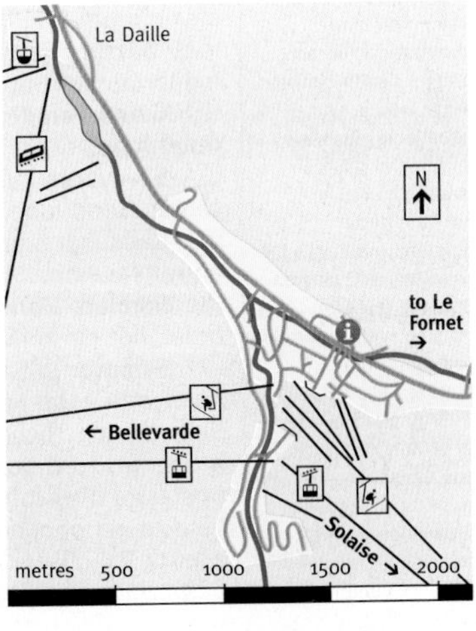

GETTING THERE

Air Geneva, transfer 4hr. Lyon, transfer 4hr. Chambéry, transfer 3hr.

Rail Bourg-St-Maurice (33km); regular buses from station.

ACTIVITIES

Indoor Swimming pool, sports hall (basketball, volleyball, table tennis, badminton, trampoline and gymnastics), library, bridge, health centres in the hotels Christiania, Brussels and Le Val d'Isère (sauna, hammam, hot-tub, body building, massages, solarium etc), cinema

Outdoor Walks in Le Manchet valley and Le Fornet, natural skating rink, hang-gliding, quad bikes, all-terrain karts, ice driving, snow-mobiles, paragliding, snow-shoe outings, heli-skiing, microlight trips, ice climbing

HOW TO GO

Lots of choice

More British tour operators go to Val-d'Isère than to any other resort except Méribel. The choice of chalets and chalet-hotels is vast. There is a Club Med 'village'.

Chalets There is everything from budget chalets to the most luxurious you could demand. The resort has a fair number of chalet operators who don't go anywhere else, including YSE and Val d'Isère Properties. Both of these include some luxury places in their portfolios, as do Scott Dunn Ski, Finlays, Supertravel and The Ski Company Limited, which has a group of luxury chalets out beyond the lift stations with fabulous views up the Manchet valley. Le Ski has four splendid new all-en-suite chalets on the edge of town, not far from YSE's lovely old Mountain Lodges, with another three being built for 2000/01.

There are lots of chalet hotels. Mark Warner has four, including the family-friendly, 'very good-value' Cygnaski, the nightlife hot spot Moris ('boisterous clients, helpful staff') and the smarter Val d'Isère ('well equipped and managed'), which enjoys free use of the adjoining village swimming pool.

The best-value chalets tend to be away from the centre, at Le Châtelard, Le Laisinant and Le Fornet.

Hotels There are about 40 to choose from, mostly 2- and 3-star, but for such a big international resort surprisingly few are notably attractive.

((((4 **Christiania** Recently renovated big chalet, probably best in town. Chic, with friendly staff. Sauna.

((((4 **Latitudes** Modern, stylish. Piano bar, nightclub. Leisure centre: sauna, steam room, whirlpool, massage.

((((4 **Blizzard** Renovated for Olympics. Indoor-outdoor pool. Convenient.

(((3 **Grand Paradis** Excellent position. Good food.

(((3 **Savoyarde** Rustic decor. Leisure centre. Good food. Rooms a bit small.

(((3 **Kandahar** Smart, newish building above Taverne d'Alsace on main street.

(((3 **Sorbiers** Modern but cosy B&B hotel, not far from centre.

(((3 **Samovar** In La Daille. Traditional hotel with good food.

Self-catering There are thousands of properties to choose from. UK operators offer lots of them, but they tend to get booked up early. Local agency Val-d'Isère Agence has a particularly good brochure.

EATING OUT

Plenty of good, affordable places

Restaurant standards are generally high. Although there are, among the 70-odd restaurants, some which specialise in Italian, Alsatian, Tex-Mex, even Japanese food, most offer good French dishes.

You can get a good meal for less than £15 in numerous pleasant places. The ever-popular Perdrix Blanche does everything from Savoyard to sushi – but recent reports suggest that the service (for Brits, at least) is not up to scratch. Better, perhaps, to head for the Taverne d'Alsace, another old favourite, with 'tasty traditional food and a good atmosphere'. Le Lodge delivers 'delicious, excellent-value meals'.

The Crêch'ouna, a little way up the slopes at La Daille (see Mountain restaurants), is worth an evening visit for its Alpine atmosphere. The Tufs just below it is also recommended, and will provide transport for groups. In the opposite direction, Clochetons at Le Châtelard is 'not cheap', but has 'excellent food and service'.

But our favourite – and that of many reporters – for a special night out is the Chalet du Crêt, off the main road on the edge of downtown Val, on the way to La Daille. Set in a 300-year-old stone-and-wood farmhouse, beautifully renovated by the Franco-British couple who run it, this place serves a fixed-price menu, with a magnificent hors-d'oeuvres spread to start with, a choice of main dish and dessert – and an excellent wine list. It's not cheap, but it's highly satisfying.

Those on tight budgets should try the pizzas in Chez Nano, next to Dick's Tea Bar, or the Pacific, next to the Moris pub, which serves generous portions of pasta and seafood. Several reporters have recommended Pizza Paolo, at the foot of the nursery slopes by the Bellevarde cable-car, for good value and service. The Melting Pot also gets rave reviews, especially for its 'authentic Sunday night curries'.

APRES-SKI

Very lively

Nightlife is surprisingly energetic, given that most people have spent a hard day on the slopes. There are lots of bars, many with happy hours followed by music and dancing later on.

La Folie Douce, at the top of the La Daille gondola, is popular at close of play, with music and dancing – you can ski down or ride the gondola. At La Daille you might then head for the Brighton Rock (run by First Choice). In downtown Val, Bananas, the Petit Danois, Café Face and the Moris pub (in the Mark Warner chalet) fill up as the slopes close, and Bar Jacques and the Perdrix Blanche bar are popular with locals. Later, the Pacific is a popular but dreary basement space with big-screen Sky TV – good for watching big sports events. The Aventure, next to Killy Sports, has household decor, including a fridge, a bath and a bed – it serves good food in a separate eating area. Victor's is a Swedish-run restaurant that turns into a bar later on – black-and-white decor and stainless steel loos. For a more Continental atmosphere, try Café des Sports or Boubou (which does tapas). The basement Taverne d'Alsace is quiet and relaxing. The famous Dick's Tea Bar seems now to be more popular with drunken young Swedes than with Brits. Club 21 is popular with the French and resort staff and stays open late, though it can be rather seedy, with topless dancers.

For those who like a quieter time, there are hotel bars, piano bars and cocktail lounges.

OFF THE SLOPES
Not much

Val is primarily a resort for those keen to get on to the slopes. The swimming pool has been renovated, but the other sports facilities are not particularly impressive. The range of shops is better than in most high French resorts. The best walks are up the Manchet valley. Lunchtime meetings present problems: the mountain restaurants easily accessible to pedestrians are few, and your friends are quite likely to prefer lunching miles away in places like Les Brévières.

STAYING DOWN THE VALLEY
Not a great idea

Val-d'Isère is a long way up its dead-end valley. If you're driving out to the Alps you could consider staying half an hour away in rustic Ste-Foy (which has its own delightful and deserted slopes), or even further away in Bourg-St-Maurice. But if you do that, you'll really want to consider exploring different resorts each day rather than just Val-d'Isère.

TOURIST OFFICE

Postcode 73155
t +33 479 060660
f 479 060456
info@valdisere.com
www.valdisere.com

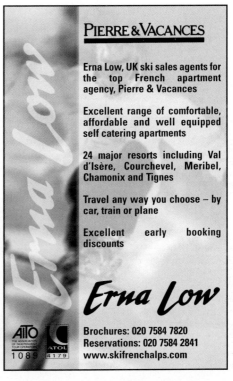

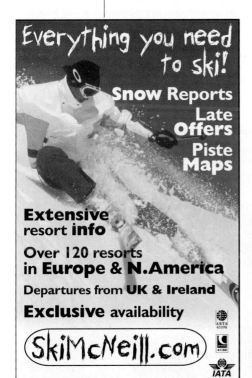

Valmorel 1400m

The purpose-built resort where they got it right

WHAT IT COSTS

(4)

HOW IT RATES

The slopes

Snow	***
Extent	***
Experts	**
Intermediates	****
Beginners	*****
Convenience	*****
Queues	****
Restaurants	**

The rest

Scenery	***
Resort charm	****
Off-slope	**

MOUNTAIN FACTS

Altitude	1200m-2550m
Lifts	55
Pistes	151km
Green/Blue	69%
Red	19%
Black	12%
Artificial snow	9km
Recco detectors used	

- ➕ Fairly extensive slopes provide something for everyone
- ➕ The most sympathetically designed French purpose-built resort
- ➕ Largely slope-side accommodation
- ➕ Beginners and children particularly well catered for
- ➕ One of the most accessible of the Tarentaise resorts
- ➕ Relatively cheap package holidays

- ➖ Few challenging runs
- ➖ Fairly low in altitude, so good snow not guaranteed
- ➖ Little variety in accommodation and in restaurants and bars
- ➖ A few fast quads have improved the lift system, but there are still a lot of slow lifts

Built from scratch in the mid-1970s, Valmorel was intended to look and feel like a mountain village: a traffic-free main street with low-rise hamlets grouped around it and along the lower slopes, and traditional Savoie stone and wood materials throughout. The end result is an attractive, friendly sort of place.

The slopes are extensive by most standards – though Valmorel can't rival its huge neighbours, the Three Valleys or Val-d'Isère-Tignes. But with good snow conditions and the whole system open, there's enough here to keep everyone except experts happy. As the snow conditions deteriorate, the variety of available runs reduces rapidly.

Unashamedly aimed at the middle ground (intermediates, families and mixed-ability groups), Valmorel does have considerable appeal because it has been so well put together.

boarding *Valmorel is a good place to try boarding for the first time – there's a separate beginners' slope and gentle runs to progress to served by chairs and gondolas. There's a fun-park and half-pipe when snow permits but few slopes (except off-piste) to challenge advanced boarders, who should look towards one of the bigger neighbours. Nightlife is far from throbbing in this family-oriented resort.*

JEANNE CATTINI

Purpose-built with style: Valmorel has convenience and charm ↓

What's new

For 2000/01 a new quad chair-lift Le Roset will go from go from the bottom of the Madeleine chair-lift up to the top of the Beaudin sector, replacing a shorter drag-lift and speeding up the return journey to Valmorel.

Last season a new drag-lift Le Peclet was built at the top of the high-speed quad out of the resort, taking you to the top of the Beaudin sector and speeding access to the Madeleine and Longchamp sectors.

Beautiful 'monumental' snow sculptures are planned for Christmas 2000 and a winter sports festival for February 2001.

The resort

Valmorel, a short drive from Moûtiers and the mega-resorts of the Three Valleys and La Plagne, is the main resort in 'Le Grand Domaine' – a ski area that links the Tarentaise with the Maurienne, by way of the Col de la Madeleine. Happily for Valmorel and its visitors, the place was built with more than just convenience in mind – it also manages to look pretty good.

Bourg-Morel is the heart of the resort – a traffic-free street where you'll find most of the shops, the restaurants, visitor information – just about everything – in a 200m stretch. It's pleasant and usually lively, with a distinctly family feel. And the slopes are right at hand, with the main pistes back to the resort and the chair-lift out meeting at the end of the street. Nearby is an information board showing lift and piste status and what's on locally.

Dotted around the hillside, but not very far from the centre, are the six 'hameaux' with most of the accommodation. Most is self-catering and of a reasonably high standard.

We've had a report of a jolly New Year's Eve in town, with lots of fireworks, a parade and torch jugglers. And beautiful snow sculptures are planned for Christmas 2000.

The mountains

Beginners and intermediates will take to Valmorel. Those looking for more of a challenge will find it more limited. Variety is provided by sectors of quite distinctive character, and the system is big enough to provide interesting, if hardly epic, exploratory trips to its farthest boundaries. There are still a few long, awkward drag-lifts, but most can be avoided with good planning. Piste grooming is said to be better in Valmorel than in Longchamp.

THE SLOPES

A big system in miniature

The 55 lifts and 151km of piste spread out in an interesting arrangement over a number of minor valleys and ridges either side of the Col de la Madeleine, with Valmorel at the eastern extremity of the system and runs coming down into the village on three sides.

The most heavily used route out of the village is via the high-speed Altispace covered quad, which takes you over the main pistes down to the resort. From the top a network of lifts and pistes takes you over to the **Col de la Madeleine** and beyond that to Lauzière (the highest point of the ski area at 2550m) or the slopes of **St-François** and **Longchamp** at the far western end of the area.

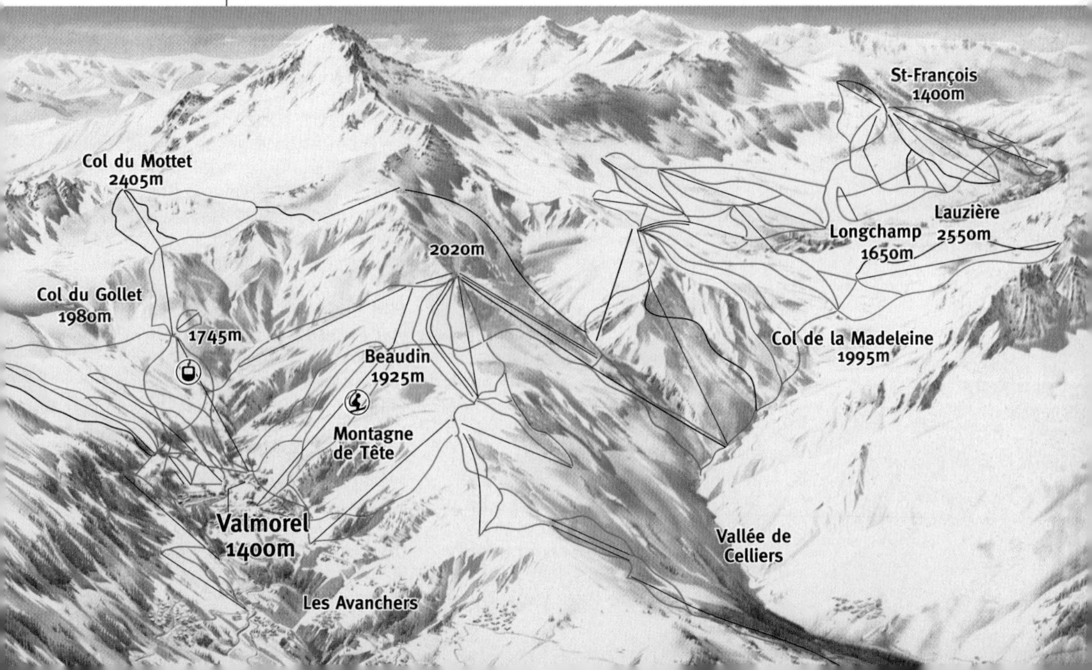

LIFT PASSES

1999/2000 prices in francs

Le Grand Domaine
Covers all lifts in Valmorel and St-François-Longchamp.

Beginners Limited area lift pass covers beginner lifts and runs.

Main pass
1-day pass 187
6-day pass 984
(low season 804)

Senior citizens
Over 60: 6-day pass 836

Children
8-13: 6-day pass 836
4-7: 640
Under 4: free pass

Short-term passes
Half-day from 11.30 (165) and 12.45 (140). Saturday morning until 1pm (140).

Alternative passes
Valmorel Domaine covers 37 lifts in Valmorel only (6 days 941 for adults, 800 for children aged 8-13, 612 for ages 4-7).

The Pierrafort gondola for the **Mottet** sector and the Crève-Cœur chair for the **Gollet** area take off from Hameau-du-Mottet at the top end of the village. Both have their own runs back towards the village, or the more experienced can work their way over to the Beaudin and Madeleine sectors (tough runs down only). There's an easy link in the other direction.

Adjacent to the village there are nursery areas with good easy runs.

All the mega-ski areas of the Tarentaise are within reasonable driving distance – the Trois Vallées, La Plagne, Les Arcs and even Val-d'Isère-Tignes. An off-piste tour through a number of these resorts starts from the Col du Mottet above Valmorel.

SNOW RELIABILITY
Sort of average

With a top station of 2550m and many of the runs below 2000m, good snow conditions are not guaranteed. Low runs are often closed, and even Lauzière, which has the system's high point but faces south, can suffer quite quickly during sunny spells. Mottet is north-facing and usually has the best snow.

Artificial snowmaking covers the nursery slopes and runs under the Altispace chair and the Pierrafort gondola down to village level.

FOR EXPERTS
Better than you might think

Although not renowned for its tough slopes, there are challenging runs. Gollet is usually a good place for moguls – plenty of them, but not too big and not too hard. We've done a great off-piste run from here with a guide, which started with a long traverse from the top of the drag-lift and ended right down in the village of Les Avanchers, way below Valmorel, passing through forests and over streams on the way.

There are steep black runs below the top section of the Mottet chair and some interesting off-piste variants. From the Riondet drag-lift to the north of here, there are a couple of fine runs (one off-piste) which generally have good snow down towards the Madeleine sector.

The Lauzière chair can seem a bit of a trek, but once there you'll probably find the area underused and a lot of fun, provided it hasn't suffered too much sun. There are three marked runs and plenty of acreage in which to pick your own route – there are some steep pitches and often some big bumps. You can also explore a lovely deserted north-facing off-piste run here if you hire a guide – we've found long stretches of great powder over a week after the last snowfall.

Touring is a popular activity in the region, and trips such as the Nine-Valley safari can be organised.

FOR INTERMEDIATES
Plenty to keep you busy

There's lots of scope, though a lot of people seem to mill around Beaudin and the Arenouillaz drag and Biollène chair – the adjacent runs are quite friendly. The runs into the Celliers valley are more testing, particularly the red and the black served by the Madeleine chair and the Grande Combe quad. Early intermediates will find them too difficult to cope with comfortably.

The main thoroughfare back to the village – from Beaudin along the line of the snow-guns – is graded blue then red, and the red stretch can be quite daunting at the end of the day. The artificial snow tends to pile up in surprisingly large heaps, as do tired beginners. After much use even the blue Les Traverses is not easy.

For a day out, the slopes around St-François-Longchamp are within easy striking distance, and form a big area of mainly broad, flattering runs.

The red route from the top of Mottet is outstandingly boring on the upper half – more push-and-walk than anything else – but the views are some compensation, and the lower half is much better.

The runs back to the village served by the Pierrafort gondola are graded blue but are long, interesting and in parts tricky. The adjacent Gollet slopes also provide plenty of scope for good intermediates to amuse themselves.

FOR BEGINNERS
An excellent choice

Valmorel suits beginners – there are dedicated learning areas right by the village for both adults (at Bois de la Croix) and children (in the snow garden of the children's club), and lots of expertise among the instructors.

The terrain does not allow extensive nursery areas in the valley, so progress from novice to beginner usually sees the children heading for the top of the Pierrafort gondola and adults for the

CHILDCARE

Saperlipopette (479 098445) provides care for children aged from 6 months to 7 years, from 8.30 to 5pm. Those aged 18 months to 3 are given 'a gentle and amusing first experience with the snow'. Those aged 3 to 7 have indoor activities as well as ski classes (divided into three levels), and there is a snow play area for those who do not wish to ski.

Beaudin sector. The lifts up to these areas can also be ridden down back into the village.

If the snow-cover is complete, there is a very pleasant green run through the trees down to Combelouvière.

FOR CROSS-COUNTRY
Inconvenient and not extensive

Valmorel is not for aficionados – more for those giving it a try. Trails adding up to 23km, at a number of locations in the valley (and so likely to have a limited season only), can be reached by special bus from Valmorel itself.

QUEUES
Much improved in recent years

Two main bottlenecks have been addressed recently by the Altispace and Grande Combe chairs, so getting onto the slopes in the morning, and over to the St-François and Lauzière side now presents few problems. The new Roset quad for 2000/01 should speed the return journey. All that remains is the queue at the double Frêne drag, which can't cope when everyone is returning to Valmorel.

MOUNTAIN RESTAURANTS
Fair to middling

There are half a dozen or so mountain restaurants in the area, none of them either appalling or wonderful. The Altipano at the top of the gondola has been recommended for good food and value for money and a sunny, peaceful terrace. Prariond, lower down, is livelier but more expensive, with good food and loud music. L'Arbet at the top of Lanchettes is reasonable value. The Banquise has been suggested as a good stopping point after a visit to the views and more challenging runs off Lauzière. Grolla at Combelouvière has 'good service and view.' One reporter lavishes praise on Le Grenier in Mottet.

SCHOOLS/GUIDES

2000/01 prices in francs

ESF

Classes 6 days
2½hr am or pm
6 half days: 623
Children's classes
Ages: 4 to 12
6 half days: 580
Private lessons
Hourly
185 for 1 or 2 people

SCHOOLS AND GUIDES
Good, especially for first-timers

We've had some good reports about the school over the years. Instructors generally speak good English and are enthusiastic and imaginative. Teaching for first-timers is a speciality of the resort, and likely to produce good results. A reporter told us of a visitor who had never skied before: 'He had one private lesson with the ESF, which he said was fine, and then managed to ski with his friends quite satisfactorily.'

FACILITIES FOR CHILDREN
Comprehensive, but book early

Saperlipopette is a comprehensive childcare facility, though past reports have varied from children loving it to being bored or distraught. We have no very recent reports. Children aged between four and eight taking ski lessons at the ski-school can also have lunch at Saperlipopette, being brought from or taken to their lesson by the staff. Advance booking is essential except for very quiet times.

Staying there

Valmorel is a traffic-free resort, with drop-off points for the accommodation. At the bottom end of Bourg-Morel is the base station of the Télébourg, a cross-village lift providing access to the 'Hameau-du-Mottet'.

Walking between the other hameaux and Bourg-Morel doesn't take long – but some of the pathways should be graded red. Hameau-du-Mottet probably wins the convenience contest – it is at the top of the Télébourg, and access to main lifts and from return runs is good. Hameau-du-Creve-Coeur was highly recommended by a reporter this year 'convenient for slopes and with own supermarket and boulangerie.'

A car is of no use in the resort but very handy for trips to other resorts.

One of our regular reporters stays down at Combelouvière, and finds it 'has almost as much ski-in, ski-out convenience as Valmorel, with a pleasanter run back home at the end of the day'. However, it's only a wise choice if you like quiet evenings.

HOW TO GO
Take a package for value

Self-catering packages are the norm.
Chalets There are some run by UK tour operators, but they tend to be catered apartments.
Hotels There are only three hotels.
(((3 **Planchamp** Best in town, family run, with a good French restaurant. Right on the piste.
((2 **Hotel du Bourg** Simple place in the middle of Bourg-Morel.
((2 **La Fontaine** Across the piste from the Planchamp. 'Good food, very good value, large rooms (for France),' says a reporter this year.
Self-catering Most people do – 8500 apartment beds are distributed throughout the six hamlets and they are generally well equipped. While it's

Pistes lead into and lifts go out of three sides of the village →

P JACQUES / SERVICE PRESSE JEANNE CATTINI

great having a view over the piste, the downside of certain locations in Mottet and Planchamp is the proximity of some very noisy snow-guns: the soundproofing is not quite good enough for light sleepers.

GETTING THERE

Air Geneva, transfer 3½hr. Lyon, transfer 3½hr. Chambéry, transfer 2½hr.

Rail Moûtiers (18km); regular buses from station.

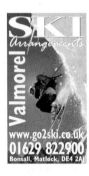

EATING OUT
Good enough but rarely thrilling

You can check out the menus of most of Valmorel's restaurants in 15 minutes of wandering up and down the main street. A pattern soon emerges – pizza, pasta, fondues and a smattering of Savoie fare. There are also couscous and galettes available. Not a huge variety but enough, and you're likely to get decent food and fair value. Many of the places need to be booked for any chance of a seat at a reasonable time.

The restaurant of hotel Planchamp is relatively upmarket with prices to match. The Petit Savoyarde is a mid-range place recommended by reporters. The Grenier in Mottet offers a bit of everything, is in a slightly different location and is highly recommended by a reporter who 'ate there every night but one' (and regretted their night off). Locals also recommend La Grange, the Perce Neige, La Cordee, the Ski Roc and Tex-Mex at Jimbololo. A pizza or shared fondue in the popular Pizzeria Chez Albert or Pizzeria du Bourg or a takeaway (they deliver) from the Casa Pizz' is good value.

ACTIVITIES

Indoor Cinema
Outdoor Snow-shoe outings, 12km of prepared walks, paragliding, horse-drawn carriage rides

APRES-SKI
Unexciting

Immediate après-ski is centred on the outdoor cafés at the end of Bourg-Morel and Le Grenier. Both are lively spots. The after-dark activities are, like everything else, concentrated around that main street. Café de la Gare has live music and Petit Prince and La Casbah are popular with locals, while the Perce-Neige frequently gets packed and boisterous. Cocktails can be enjoyed in more polished surroundings at the Shaker in hotel La Fontaine. There's one disco, Jeans, which is often neglected but occasionally buzzes.

You may catch an occasional musical event at the village hall, or a street parade (there's a Mardi Gras with medieval costumes and fireworks). A two-screen cinema and a wine-tasting evening are other possibilities.

TOURIST OFFICE

Postcode 73260
t +33 479 098555
f 479 098529
valmorel.la.belle@wanadoo.fr
www.valmorel-la-belle.com

OFF THE SLOPES
Pleasant but boring

It's not a great place to hang around if you're not using the slopes – unless you are happy spending time in cafés. There are some cleared walks around the village and at the top of all the main lifts and there's a pretty baroque church in Les Avanchers. Several mid-mountain restaurants are accessible to pedestrians, and it's also quite practical for friends using the slopes to return to the village for a lunchtime meet.

Snow-shoe treks and dog-sleigh trips can be organised – you can even learn to 'mush' the dogs.

STAYING DOWN THE VALLEY
Less than appealing

We have stayed at the Edelweiss down at Les Avanchers, which had decent French food, a rustic atmosphere and an eccentric patron. But there is little else there, and a reporter says the Cheval Noir is now closed and derelict.

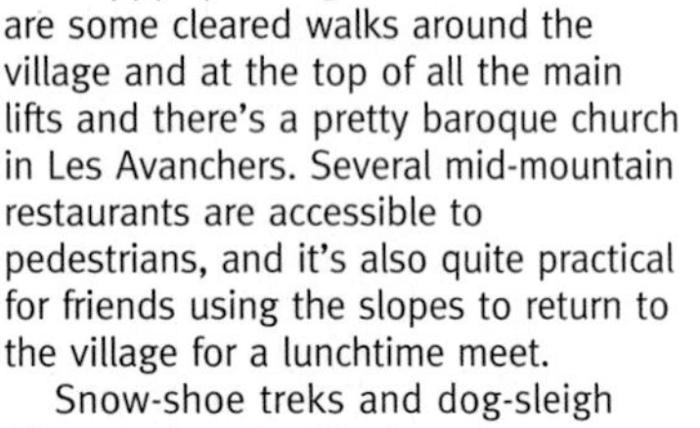

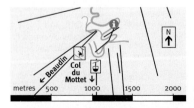

Val-Thorens 2300m

Europe's highest resort, with guaranteed good snow

WHAT IT COSTS

(5)

HOW IT RATES

The slopes

Snow	*****
Extent	*****
Experts	****
Intermediates	*****
Beginners	****
Convenience	*****
Queues	***
Restaurants	****

The rest

Scenery	***
Resort charm	**
Off-slope	**

MOUNTAIN FACTS

Altitude	1300m-3200m
Lifts	200
Pistes	600km
Green/Blue	49%
Red	37%
Black	14%
Artificial snow	90km
Recco detectors used	

- + Extensive local slopes to suit all standards, and good access to the rest of the vast Three Valleys
- + The highest resort in the Alps and one of the most snowsure, with north-facing slopes guaranteeing good snow for a long season, even off the glacier
- + Not as much of an eyesore as most high, purpose-built resorts
- + Compact village with direct slope access from most accommodation

- − Can be bleak in bad weather – not a tree in sight
- − Parts of the village are much less attractive to walk through in the evening than to ski past in the day
- − Not much to do off the slopes
- − Some very busy piste intersections
- − Still some queues – especially for the Cîme de Caron cable-car.

For the enthusiast looking for the best snow in the Alps, it's difficult to beat Val-Thorens – especially given that it's also one of the least unpleasant purpose-built resorts. But we still prefer a cosier base elsewhere in the Three Valleys. That way, if a storm socks in, we can play in the woods around Méribel or Courchevel; if the sun is scorching, we have the option of setting off for Val-Thorens. The formula doesn't work the other way round.

boarding *The best resort-level snow in Europe appeals to boarders as well as skiers – and pulls in considerable numbers. There are pistes to suit all abilities, and the good snow is great for beginners and carvers. There's plenty of off-piste choice for free-riders, though if you want trees you'll have to travel. The lifts are now mainly chairs and gondolas, though one or two drags remain. The fun-park towards the bottom of the Caron sector, served by a fast chair, now has a half-pipe and a sound-system, and hosts weekly competitions. Nightlife centres around bars and a couple of discos that, because of all the young people in the resort (especially Scandinavians), are usually noisy and entertaining.*

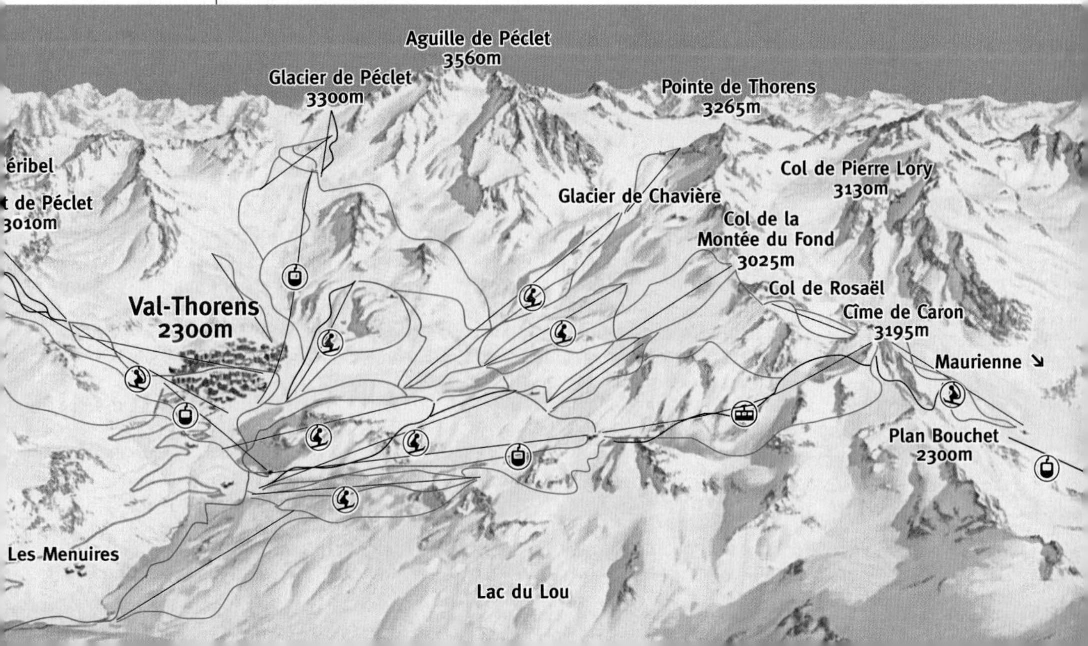

What's new

Last season two of the resort's four double-queue chair-lifts were equipped with additional chairs, increasing the frequency and shifting more people/hour.

An additional 31 snow-guns were installed, bringing the total to 148, and the gazex remote-control avalanche blasting system was extended.

For 2000/01 there will be a new boarder-cross course, and a 5km toboggan run down the length of the Péclet gondola.

SCHOOLS/GUIDES

1999/2000 prices in francs

ESF
Classes 6 days
3hr: am; 2½hr: pm
6 mornings: 730
Children's classes
Ages: 2½ to 12
6 mornings: 630
Private lessons
Hourly
175 for 1 to 2 people

Ski Cool
Classes 6 days
3hr, am or pm
6 mornings: 700
Children's classes
Ages: up to 12
6 mornings: 700
Private lessons
Hourly or daily
340 for 2hr, for 1 to 2 people

OTHER SCHOOLS

Ski Surf Nature
Pros Neige

GETTING THERE

Air Geneva, transfer 3½hr. Lyon, transfer 3½hr. Chambéry, transfer 2½hr.

Rail Moûtiers (37km); regular buses from station.

The resort

Val-Thorens is built high above the tree line on a sunny, west-facing mountainside at the head of the Belleville valley, surrounded by peaks, slopes and lifts. It is a classic purpose-built resort – compact, with lots of convenient slope-side accommodation. Seen from the slopes, it is not as hideous as many of its rivals. The buildings are mainly medium-rise and wood-clad, and some are distinctly stylish. The village streets are now supposedly traffic-free. Practically all visitors' cars are banished to garages, except on Saturday. But workers' cars still generate a fair amount of traffic, and many parts of the resort are designed with their 'fronts' facing the slopes, and their relatively dreary backs facing the streets. There are quite extensive shopping arcades, a fair choice of bars and restaurants, and a good sports centre.

The mountains

Take account of the height and the extent of its local slopes and the easy access to the rest of the Three Valleys, and the attraction of Val-Thorens becomes clear. The main disadvantage is the lack of trees. Heavy snowfalls or high wind can shut practically all the lifts and slopes, and even if they don't, poor visibility can be a problem.

THE SLOPES
High and snowsure

The resort has a wide piste going right down the front of it, leading down to a number of different lifts. The big **Péclet** gondola, with 25-person cabins, rises 700m to the Péclet glacier, with three red runs down. One links across to a wide area of intermediate runs served by lifts to cols either side of the **Pointe de Thorens**. From one of these you can descend into the 'Fourth Valley', the **Maurienne**; a chair serves red and blue slopes of 660m vertical.

The **Cîme de Caron** cable-car can be reached from the Pointe de Thorens area or by taking a gondola or fast chair from below the village. It rises 900m to the highest lift-served point in the Three Valleys, with red and black pistes down the front of the mountain.

The two Boismint chairs from the lowest part of the domain serve an underused area of intermediate runs.

Chair-lifts heading north from the resort serve sunny slopes above the village but also lead via the **Col de la Chambre** to the Méribel valley. Les Menuires can also be reached via these lifts; the alternative Boulevard Cumin along the valley floor is nearly flat, and can be hard work.

SNOW RELIABILITY
Difficult to beat

Few resorts can rival Val-Thorens for reliably good snow-cover, thanks to its altitude and generally north-facing slopes. Snowmaking now covers 20 per cent of the pistes, including the busy south- and west-facing runs on the way back from the Méribel valley.

FOR EXPERTS
Lots to do off-piste

Val-Thorens' local pistes are primarily intermediate terrain. The runs down from the Cîme de Caron cable-car are the most challenging. The fast Cascades chair serves a good steep run that quickly gets mogulled but is not currently on the piste map. The sunny Marielle run is one of the easiest blacks we've come across.

There are three good itinéraires. Two are on the Maurienne valley slopes. The long Lac du Lou itinéraire goes from the Cîme de Caron to the lower Boismint chair. There is also a great deal of unmarked off-piste terrain to explore, particularly on the north-facing slopes reached from the Col, Fond, Deux Lacs and Boismint chairs. It is rocky terrain with serious hazards.

FOR INTERMEDIATES
Unbeatable quality and quantity

The scope for intermediates throughout the Three Valleys is enormous. It will take a decent intermediate only 90 minutes or so to get to Courchevel at the far end, if not distracted by the endless runs on the way.

The local slopes in Val-Thorens are some of the best intermediate terrain in the region. Most of the pistes are easy reds and blues, made even more enjoyable by the excellent snow.

The snow on the red Col run is always some of the best around. The blue Moraine below it is gentle and popular with the schools. The runs on the top half of the mountain are steeper than those back into the resort. The Fond lifts serve a good variety of red runs. The Pluviometre from the 3 Vallées chair is a glorious

LIFT PASSES

2000/01 prices in francs
Three Valleys
Covers all lifts in Courchevel, La Tania, Méribel, Val-Thorens, Les Menuires and St-Martin-de-Belleville.
Beginners 4 free lifts in Val-Thorens.
Main pass
1-day pass 235
6-day pass 1160
Senior citizens
Over 60: 6-day pass 928
Over 70: 6-day pass 580
Over 75: free pass
Children
Under 16: 6-day pass 870
Under 10: 754
Under 5: free pass
Short-term passes
Half-day passes (from 12.30) available for Val-Thorens lifts (adult 140) and the 3 Valleys (adult 176).
Notes 6-day pass and over valid for one day each in Tignes-Val-d'Isère, La Plagne-Les Arcs, Pralognan-la-Vanoise and Les Saisies. Reductions for families.
Alternative passes
Vallée des Belleville pass covers 75 lifts and 300km piste in Val-Thorens, Les Menuires and St-Martin (adult 6-day 1080). Val-Thorens-only pass covers 30 lifts and 140km of piste: adult 6-day 855 (1999/2000 price).

CHILDCARE

Marielle Goitschel's Children's Village (479 000047) takes children aged from 3 to 16, from 9am to 5.30, 7 days a week. The ESF can provide all-day care and offers classes for children from age 2½. It also runs Mini Club crèches in two locations, at the top and bottom of the resort, taking children from age 3 months to 4 years.

varied red, away from the lifts. Adventurous intermediates shouldn't miss the Combe du Caron runs. The black run is not intimidating – it's very wide and usually has good snow.

FOR BEGINNERS
Good late-season choice

The slopes at the foot of the resort are very gentle and provide convenient, snowsure nursery slopes. There are no long green runs to progress to, but the blues immediately above the village are easy. The resort's height and bleakness make it cold in midwinter, and intimidating in bad weather.

FOR CROSS-COUNTRY
Try elsewhere

Val-Thorens is a poor base for cross-country, with only 4km of local trails.

QUEUES
Persistent at the Cîme de Caron

Recent reports suggest that there are few problems. But it is still common to wait 10 or 15 minutes for the Cîme de Caron cable-car, despite a scheme designed to speed up loading, and one March visitor found queues of 40 minutes plus, even in the mornings.

The Plein Sud six-pack chair-lift does a good job of getting the crowds on their way back to Méribel and Courchevel in the afternoon. The Côte Brune and Plan des Mains chairs, on the Mottaret side, are bottlenecks for Val-Thorens residents coming home.

When snow is in short supply elsewhere the pressure on the Val-Thorens lifts can of course increase.

MOUNTAIN RESTAURANTS
Lots of choice

For a high, modern resort, the choice of restaurants is good. We like the Chalet de Génépi, on the run down from the Moraine chair – great views, an open fire and a wide range of good dishes. The Bar de la Marine, on the Dalles piste, does excellent food, but service can be stretched. The Moutière, down from the chair of the same name, is one of the more reasonably priced of Val-Thorens' mountain huts (which are generally expensive). The Plan Bouchet refuge in the Maurienne valley is very popular and welcoming, but bar service can be slow. You can stay the night there, too. Chalet Plein Sud, below the chair of the same name, has excellent views but a 'rather limiting menu'. The big Chalet de Thorens has been praised for the its food and reasonable prices. Not surprisingly, lots of people lunch in the village.

SCHOOLS AND GUIDES
Good alternatives to ESF

Like so many branches of the ESF, this one is incompetently run. One reporter speaks of two classes saddled with 'rude, unhelpful and unsympathetic' instructors. More alarmingly, we have yet another report of an ESF instructor losing a child – an incident about which the ESF 'could not have been more arrogant and unconcerned'. In contrast, a reporter found Pros Neige classes 'really excellent – my wife's skiing changed dramatically'.

We've had good reports of private lessons with the ESF and other schools. The ESF have a Trois Vallées group for those who want to cover a lot of ground while receiving tuition – available by the day or the week, and can include off-piste. Ski Cool class sizes are guaranteed not to exceed 10. They also have off-piste courses. There are several specialist guiding outfits.

FACILITIES FOR CHILDREN
Not up to much

We have conflicting reports of the ESF Mini-Club crèche. Some reporters are happy with it; others describe it as 'complete chaos' and report having to rescue children abandoned on the slopes. Thomson's 'Kids Club' has been recommended.

Staying there

It's quite a complicated little village; since it's quite compact, it doesn't matter much where you stay. At its heart is the snowy Place de Caron, where pedestrians mix with skiers and boarders. Many of the shops and restaurants are clustered here, along with the best hotels, and the sports centre is nearby. The village is basically divided in two by a little slope with drag-lift that leads down to the main slope running the length of the village. The upper half of the village is centred on the Place de Péclet. A road runs across the hillside from here to the new chalet-style Balcons development. The lower half of the village is more diffuse, with the Rue du Soleil winding down from the dreary Place des Arolles bus station to the big Temples du Soleil apartments.

There aren't many snowier settings than this one →

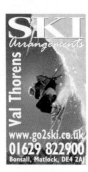

BASILE, MARK BUSCAIL / VAL-THORENS TO

ACTIVITIES

Indoor Sports centre (tennis, squash, climbing wall, roller skating, golf simulator, swimming pool, saunas, hot-tub, volleyball, weight training, table tennis, fitness, badminton, football), games rooms, music recitals, cinema, beauty centre
Outdoor Walks, snow-mobiles, paragliding, snow-shoe excursions

TOURIST OFFICE

Postcode 73440
t +33 479 000808
f 479 000004
valtho@valthorens.com
www.valthorens.com

HOW TO GO

Surprisingly high level of comfort

Accommodation is of a higher standard than many French purpose-built villages, with plenty of choice, too.
Chalets These are catered apartments, and many are quite comfortable.
Hotels There are plenty of hotels, mainly 3-stars.
((((5 **Fitz Roy** Swanky but charming Relais & Châteaux place with lovely rooms. Pool. Well placed.
(((4 **Val Thorens** Welcoming and comfortable; next door to the Fitz Roy.
((3 **Sherpa** Highly recommended for pleasant atmosphere and excellent, substantial food. Less-than-ideal position at the top of the resort.
((3 **Bel Horizon** Friendly, family-run 3-star, popular with reporters – 'cuisine wonderful'; south-facing rooms.
Self-catering The options include apartments of a higher standard than usual in France. The Temples du Soleil are recommended for good facilities.

EATING OUT

Surprisingly wide range

Val-Thorens has something for most tastes. The Fitz Roy and the Val Thorens hotels do classic French food. For something more regional, the best bets are the 'excellent' Vieux Chalet and the Chaumière. The Scapin is cosily done out in wood and stone, with 'good' food. Other reporters' recommendations include the Montana ('good food and service'), El Gringo's ('excellent but cramped Mexican'), Auberge des Balcons ('wonderful raclette'). The Galoubet has been praised for its steaks. The Blanchot is an unusually stylish wine bar with a simple but varied carte and of course an excellent range of wines. Several pizzerias are recommended, including that in the Temples du Soleil.

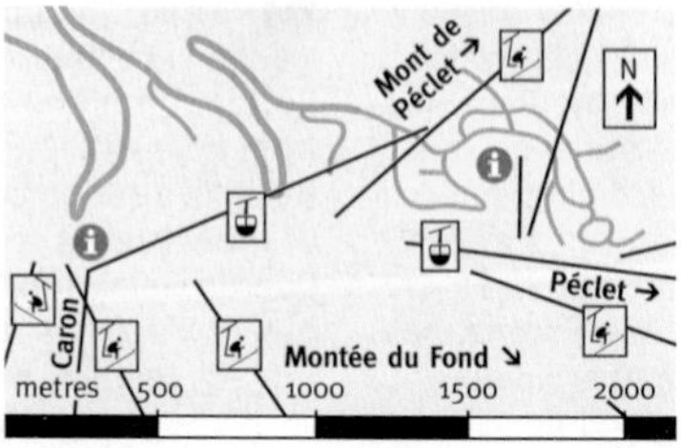

APRES-SKI

Getting there

Val-Thorens is surprisingly lively at night. The Red Fox up at Balcons is busy at close of play, with karaoke. At the opposite extreme the Sherlock Holmes in the Temples du Soleil is 'always lively'. The Frog and Roast Beef at the top of the village is a cheerful British ghetto with a live band at tea-time and half-price beer while it plays. The Underground nearby has an extended happy hour but 'descends into europop' when its disco gets going. Bloopers is another popular Scan-oriented bar-disco. The Malaysia cellar bar is recommended for good live bands, and gets very busy after 11pm. Quieter bars include O'Connells (run by a Dane, of course), the cosy Rhum (aka Mitch's) and the St Pierre.

OFF THE SLOPES

Forget it

There's a good sports centre, but the small pool can get a bit too crowded. You can get to some of the mountain restaurants by lift, and the 360° panorama from the top of the Cîme de Caron cable-car is not to be missed.

Vars 1850m

A less attractive alternative to Risoul – except for speed-skiers

WHAT IT COSTS

3

HOW IT RATES

The slopes

Snow	***
Extent	***
Experts	**
Intermediates	****
Beginners	***
Convenience	****
Queues	****
Restaurants	**

The rest

Scenery	***
Resort charm	**
Off-slope	**

What's new

There's a new fast quad from Ste-Marie to the top of the Olympic run – snowmaking down the whole length of the run is planned for 2000/01. Another fast quad – Platte de la Nonne, in Risoul – was also installed last season.

A new fast quad chair-lift from Clos Chardon on the Risoul side to the Pic de Chabrières will improve the links between the two resorts for 2000/01.

MOUNTAIN FACTS

Altitude	1660m-2750m
Lifts	56
Pistes	180km
Green/Blue	55%
Red	35%
Black	10%
Art. snow	520 acres
Recco detectors used	

TOURIST OFFICE

Postcode 05560
t +33 492 465131
f 492 465654
vars.ot@pacwan.fr
www.vars-ski.com

Vars is a purpose-built resort in the southern French Alps; its sunny slopes are linked to the shadier ones of Risoul to form a fair-sized area known as the Forêt Blanche, topped by the world's fastest speed-skiing course.

THE RESORT

Vars includes several small, old villages on or near the road running southwards towards the 2110m Col de Vars. But for winter visitors it mainly consists of purpose-built Vars-les-Claux, higher up the road. The resort has convenience and reasonable prices in common with Risoul, but is bigger and has far more in the way of amenities. There are a lot of block-like apartments, but Les Claux is not a complete eyesore, thanks mainly to surrounding woodland. There are two centres: the original and geographical one where the main gondola starts, with most of the accommodation and shopping, and Point Show – a collection of bars, restaurants and shops, 10 minutes' walk away at another main lift station. The resort is very French, and locals are friendly to those making some attempt at the native tongue.

THE MOUNTAINS

There are **slopes** on both sides of the village, linked by pistes and by chair-lift at the lower end of Les Claux. The wooded, west-facing Peynier area is the smaller sector, and reaches only 2275m – though there is a reasonable descent down to Ste-Marie at 1660m. The main slopes are in an east-facing bowl beneath the Pic de Chabrières (2750m) with direct links to the Risoul slopes at the top and at the Col des Saluces. The speed skiing course is at the top (you can have a go, via the ski school), with one or two black slopes nearby. Beneath it are easy runs, open at the top but descending into trees, with areas of red runs either side.

The main slopes get the morning sun, and are centred at around 2000m, so **snow reliability** is not that good, but snowmaking is widespread. Visitors recommend skiing the local slopes in the morning and then skiing on the Risoul side in the afternoon to get the best of the snow conditions.

There is little of challenge for **experts**, though the Crête de Chabrières top section accesses some off-piste, an unpisted route and a tricky couloir at Col de Crevoux. The Olympic red run from the top of La Mayt (2580m), on the other side of the Col des Saluces from Pic de Chabrières, down to Ste-Marie is a respectable 920m vertical.

Most of the area is fine for **intermediates**, with a good mixture of comfortable reds and easy blues, particularly in the main bowl.

Beginners have a nursery area close to central Vars, with lots of 'graduation' runs throughout the area. Quick learners will be able to get over to Risoul by the end of the week.

There's a fun-park with a half-pipe and boarder-cross for **snowboarders**.

There are **cross-country** trails that start at the edge of town, but those above Ste-Marie are more extensive.

Queues are rare outside the French holidays, and even then Vars is not overrun as some family resorts are.

There are nine **mountain restaurants** in all – Le Refuge on the Risoul side is recommended. A lot of people head back into Vars or into Risoul for lunch.

At the **ski schools,** lack of English-speaking tuition has been a problem in the past. The ski school runs a nursery for **children** from two years old. There is also a ski kindergarten. A list of babysitters can be obtained from the tourist office.

STAYING THERE

Les Claux is dominated by **apartment** accommodation. Le Caribou (with pool) is the smartest of the **hotels**. L'Ecureuil is an attractive, modern chalet (no restaurant). There are more hotels in the lower villages, including Ste-Marie.

The range of **restaurants** is impressive, with good-value pizzerias, crêperies and fondue places. Chez Plumot does proper French cuisine.

Après-ski is animated at tea-time, but less so after dinner, except at the weekend when the discos warm up.

Off-slope amenities are rather disappointing, given the size of Vars.

The French Pyrenees

It took us a long time to get round to visiting the resorts of the French Pyrenees – mainly because we had the idea that they were second-rate compared with the Alps. Well, it is certainly true that they can't compete in terms of size of ski area with the mega-resorts of the Trois Vallées and La Plagne. But don't dismiss them: they have considerable attractions, including price – hotels cost half as much as in the Alps, and meals and drinks are cheap.

We went with several preconceived ideas, not least that the Pyrenees are hills compared with the mountains of the Alps. Not true: the Pyrenees are serious mountains, and have dramatic picturesque scenery too. They are also attractively French. Unlike the big plastic mega resorts, many Pyrenean bases have a rustic, rural Gallic charm.

The biggest ski area is shared by **Barèges** and **La Mongie**. Between them they have 120km of runs and 50 lifts. The runs are best suited to intermediates, with good tree-lined runs above Barèges and open bowl skiing above La Mongie. The best bet for an expert is to try off-piste with a guide – one beautiful run away from all the lifts starts with a scramble through a hole in the rocks. There are atmospheric mountain huts dotted around the slopes. Barèges is a spa village set in a narrow, steep-sided valley, which gets little sun in midwinter. It's also the second oldest ski resort in France and the pioneer of skiing in the Pyrenees. Accommodation is mainly in basic 1-star and 2-star hotels. Its rather drab buildings and one main street grow on you, though there's little to do in the evenings other than visit the thermal spa and a restaurant (of which there are a good number serving solid local fare). La Mongie, on the other hand, is a purpose-built resort reminiscent of the Alps.

Cauterets is another spa town but a complete contrast to Barèges. It is much bigger (18,000 beds compared with 3500) and set in a wide, sunny valley. It is a popular summer destination, and even in March we were able to sit at a pavement café with a drink after dinner. It feels more like a town in Provence than a ski resort. Indeed, it wasn't until 1964 that skiing started here, when the cable-car to the slopes 850m above the town was built – you have to ride down as well as up. There are only 30km of slopes, set in an open, semi-circular bowl that can be cold and windy. A decent intermediate could cover all the runs in a day and there's little to challenge an expert. But Cauterets' jewel is its cross-country, set a long drive or bus-ride from town at Pont d'Espagne and served by a gondola. It is the start of the Pyrenees National Park and the old smugglers' route over the mountains between France and Spain. The 36km of snowsure cross-country tracks run up this beautiful deserted valley, beside a rushing stream and a stunning waterfall.

The other major Pyrenean resort is **St-Lary-Soulan**, a traditional village with houses built of stone, with a cable-car at the edge going up to the slopes, of which there are 80km, suiting mainly intermediates. There's a satellite called **St-Lary-Espiaube**, which is purpose-built and right at the heart of the slopes, up the road from the old village.

All the areas welcome snowboarders but Cauterets provides the most facilities and is the Pyrenees' leading boarding resort.

Italy

For a few years now, Italy has been a booming destination. Most people were attracted initially by price; in the mid-1990s, while the French franc, Austrian schilling and Swiss franc soared, the lira plummeted even more than the pound – so Italy became cheaper while other Alpine countries were finding themselves priced out of the market. Such variations are now supposed to be a thing of the past, since the lira has a fixed rate to the euro and should in due course disappear altogether. And it's clear that Italy isn't as cheap as it was – partly because Italian lift companies, hoteliers and restaurateurs cashed in on the boom. So Italy must compete with the other Alpine countries on the quality of the holidays it offers, not just their price.

Italy has some enduring attractions. Food and wine always were satisfying, the atmosphere always was jolly, the scenery always was splendid – in the Dolomites, simply stunning. But 10 or 20 years ago Italian lift companies had the reputation of being a bit of a joke.

Not any more. Now, lift systems are modern; snowmaking – which the Italians were early to catch on to – is very widespread, especially in the Dolomites; piste grooming is of a consistently high standard. The value side of the value-for-money equation is one you need not worry about.

Although there aren't huge numbers of them (on the international market, at least), Italian resorts vary as widely in characteristics as they do in location – and they are spread along the length of the Italian border, from Sauze and neighbours (just across the French border from Montgenèvre) all along the Swiss border to the Dolomites, an area that used to be part of Austria. There are high, snowsure ski-stations and charming valley villages, and mountains that range from one-run wonders to some of the most extensive domains in the world.

A lot of Italian runs, particularly in the north-west, seem flatteringly easy. This is partly because the piste grooming is immaculate, and also because piste grading seems to overstate difficulty. Nowhere is this clearer than in La Thuile (located in Italy, despite its French name). Its mountain connects (just) with that of La Rosière (across the valley from Les Arcs), and venturing from the Italian side to the French side is like moving from the shelter of harbour to the open sea. Red runs on the La Thuile side are virtually motorways; at La Rosière, they offer challenging moguls.

We have also been struck by the way Italian resorts continue to be weekend-oriented. Except in the Dolomites, which depend largely on German custom, resorts can be quiet as the grave during the week, especially in low season, and come to life on Friday night or Saturday morning when the weekenders from Italy's affluent northern plain arrive. If, like us, you quite like having the hotel bar to yourself (not to mention the pistes), this is a real advantage.

In general, Italians don't take their skiing or boarding too seriously. Some lifts may still close for lunch, and mountain restaurants are generally welcoming places serving satisfying food and wine, encouraging leisurely lunching. Pasta – even in the most modest establishment – is delicious. And eating and drinking on the mountain is still much cheaper than in other Alpine resorts.

DRIVING IN THE ITALIAN ALPS

There are four main geographical groupings of Italian resorts, widely separated. Getting to some of these resorts is a very long haul, and moving from one area to another can involve very long drives.

The handful of resorts to the west of Turin – Bardonecchia, Sauze d'Oulx, Sestriere and neighbours in the Milky Way region – are easily reached from France via two major routes: the Fréjus tunnel from Modane, or via the good road over the pass that the resort of Montgenèvre sits on.

Further north, and about equidistant from Milan and Turin, are the resorts of the Aosta valley – Courmayeur, Cervinia and La Thuile the best known among them. Since the construction of the Mont Blanc road tunnel from Chamonix in France, Courmayeur has been the easiest of all Italian resorts to reach from Britain. But as we go to press in mid-2000 it is still unclear when the tunnel will reopen following the disastrous fire in 1999; it could be a very long time. The Aosta valley can also be reached from Switzerland via the Grand St Bernard tunnel. The approach is high, and may require chains. The road down the Aosta valley is a major thoroughfare carrying heavy goods traffic, but the roads up to some of the other resorts are quite long, winding and (in the case of Cervinia) high.

To the east is a string of scattered resorts, most close to the Swiss border, many in isolated and remote valleys involving long drives up from the nearest Italian cities, or high-altitude drives from Switzerland. The links between Switzerland and Italy are more clearly shown on our larger-scale Switzerland map at the beginning of that

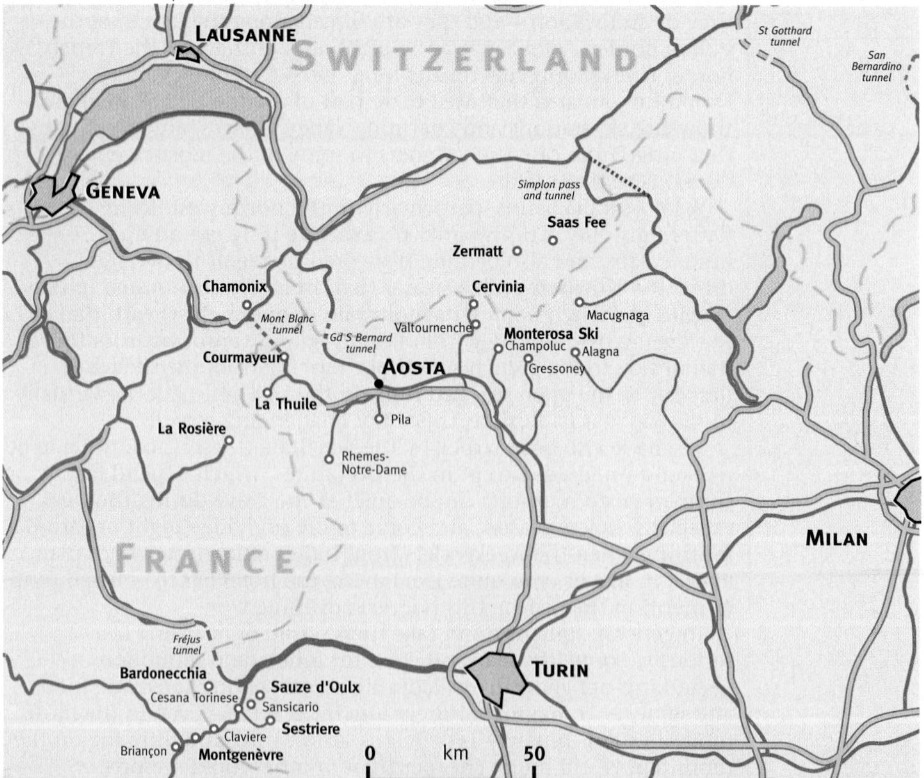

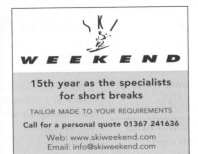

section. The major routes are the St Gotthard tunnel between Göschenen (near Andermatt) and Airolo – the main route between Basel and Milan – and the San Bernardino tunnel reached via Chur.

Finally, further east still are the resorts of the Dolomites. Getting there from Austria is easy, over the Brenner motorway pass from Innsbruck. But getting there from Britain is a very long drive indeed – allow at least a day and a half. We drove to Cortina for a week's holiday a few years back, and are not sure we'd want to do it again. Even though we believe driving is the best way of getting to the mountains, we wouldn't lightly drive there and back except as part of a longer tour. It's also worth bearing in mind that once you arrive in the Dolomites, getting around the intricate network of valleys linked by narrow, winding roads can be a slow business – not helped by impatient Italian driving.

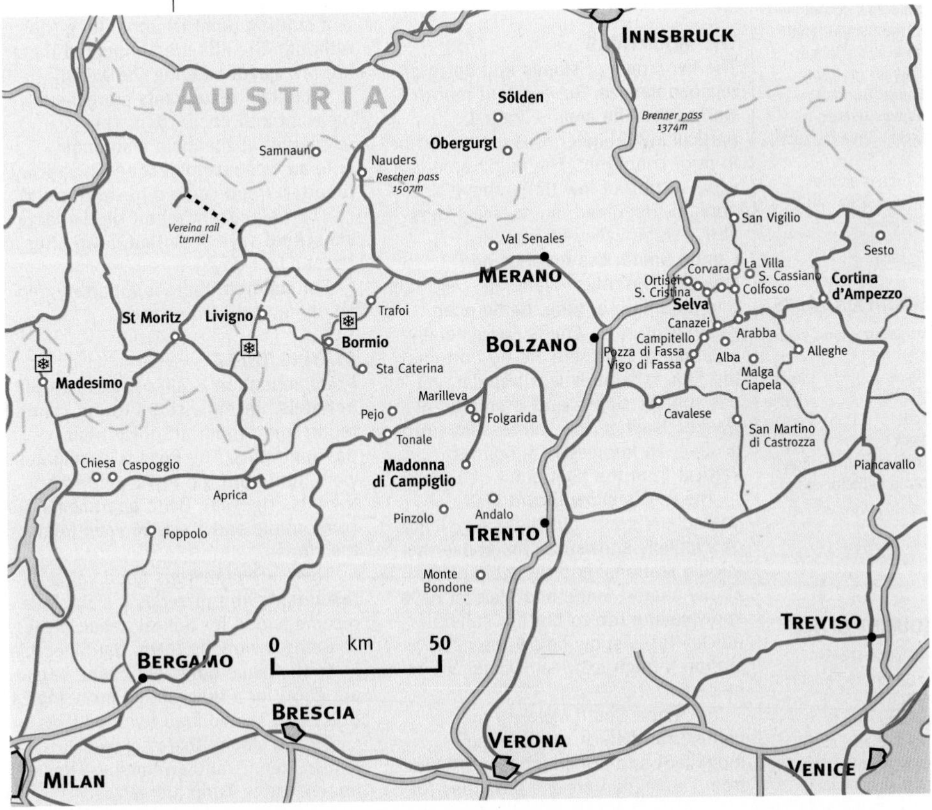

Bardonecchia

1310m

Plenty of leisurely cruises and a market-town flavour

WHAT IT COSTS

(2)

HOW IT RATES

The slopes

Snow	**
Extent	***
Experts	*
Intermediates	***
Beginners	**
Convenience	**
Queues	***
Restaurants	***

The rest

Scenery	***
Resort charm	*
Off-slope	**

What's new

1999/2000 saw the installation of two new drag-lifts: a short children's school lift at the Campo Smith base and a longer drag-lift up from Chesal (1800m), above Melezet, to Cresta Seba (2230m).

A further 3km of snowmaking was also installed.

MOUNTAIN FACTS

Altitude	1290m-2750m
Lifts	23
Pistes	140km
Blue	55%
Red	41%
Black	4%
Artificial snow	19km

Recco detectors used

TOURIST OFFICE

Postcode 10052
t +39 (0122) 99032
f 980612
bardonecchia@
montagnedoc.it
www.comune.
bardonecchia.to.it

A fairly extensive area worth considering as a base for touring other nearby French and Italian resorts. The local slopes, and the town itself, tend to be fairly quiet during the week, but lots of weekenders pour in from Turin.

THE RESORT

Bardonecchia is a sizeable old railway town, set in a beautiful, wide valley, at the entrance to the Fréjus road tunnel that links France and Italy. It has two separate areas of slopes either side of town, both a free bus-ride away. It offers cheap prices, moderate nightlife and moderately interesting slopes. The resort lacks classic mountain charm, but has traditional market-town character. But the frequent lack of resort-level snow and the intrusive railway rather detract. The Three Valleys can be reached via a gondola from Orelle on the French side of the Fréjus tunnel into the Val-Thorens area, and Valfréjus, Valloire, the Milky Way resorts (Sauze etc) and Serre-Chevalier are reachable by car.

THE MOUNTAINS

The two areas of **slopes** add up to a reasonable size. But a recent reporter warns that 'the area is limited, particularly if higher runs are closed or in poor condition'. The larger area is a wide section of low (little above 2000m), tree-lined, north-facing runs above three valley lift stations – Campo Smith, Les Arnauds and Melezet. The other – Jafferau – is a tall, thin mountain of long, partly open, west-facing runs. Chairs are generally antiquated and there are no bottom-to-top lifts. Jafferau is less popular, yet it has sunnier slopes and is emptier at weekends when the Torinese hit town. It offers an impressive 1460m of vertical from the high point of 2750m.

The area's **snow record** isn't particularly good, but there are plenty of relatively snowsure runs above the middle stations, and the main pistes above Campo Smith and Melezet have snowmaking top to bottom. Jafferau quickly loses snow below the mid-station though extra snowmaking has helped.

In Campo Smith-Melezet, the highest run (which can become mogulled) and a medium-length black from La Magnan are the best runs for **experts**. There is some off-piste in the trees when conditions allow. Jafferau has some good long red runs.

Virtually the whole 140km is suitable for **intermediates**. Above the mid-station, Jafferau has a network of fine runs for good intermediates. And there are lots of reds and leisurely cruising pistes in the other area – flying down the tree-lined red from the top station to Campo Smith is great fun.

Campo Smith and Melezet have nursery areas for **beginners**. For **boarders** there is a fun-park and half-pipe but there are a lot of awkward drag-lifts to cope with.

A varied, valley-level **cross-country** trail goes for miles in both directions from just above Campo Smith; Melezet is a starting point for other long trips.

Although the lifts are antiquated there are few **queues** during the week.

Mountain restaurants are generally pleasant and uncrowded. The restaurant at the main station at Jafferau was recommended by a recent reporter: 'food cooked fresh to order'.

The only recent report on the large **ski school** says 'it settled down after a chaotic first day'.

For **children**, there is a nursery and an all-day ski kindergarten.

STAYING THERE

Accommodation is almost exclusively in **hotels**. Recent visitors to the Tabor report good food but noise from passing trains. The Rosa is 10 minutes' walk from both the town centre and the lifts. The Gran Baita **apartments** are comfortable and a similar walk from the slopes.

There are numerous good-value **restaurants** and pizzerias – L'Etable is recommended for typical Italian dishes.

Being a working town, Bardonecchia lacks the usual **après-ski**. Some bars are good for a quiet drink, including La Botte and Nuovo Trau (with billiards).

Off the slopes there's a weekly market, tennis and swimming. Trips to more exciting Turin are easy.

Bormio

1225m

A tall, narrow mountain with a rather narrow appeal

WHAT IT COSTS

(2)

HOW IT RATES

The slopes	
Snow	***
Extent	**
Experts	*
Intermediates	***
Beginners	**
Convenience	***
Queues	***
Restaurants	****
The rest	
Scenery	***
Resort charm	****
Off-slope	****

What's new

1999/2000 saw the introduction of a new 'hands-free' lift pass system. The old single-seat Laghetti chair at Ciuk has been replaced by a new fast quad chair-lift.

Bormio has been chosen to host the Alpine skiing World Championships in 2005, 20 years after it first staged them. (The championships will be in St Anton in 2001 and St Moritz in 2003.)

MOUNTAIN FACTS

Figures relate to the Bormio, San Colombano and Santa Caterina areas only

Altitude	1225m-3010m
Lifts	36
Pistes	120km
Blue	36%
Red	48%
Black	16%
Artificial snow	47km
Recco detectors used	

- (+) Good mix of high, snowsure pistes and woodland runs with artificial snow, giving some excellent long runs when conditions are right
- (+) Worthwhile neighbouring resorts on the Valtellina lift pass
- (+) Attractive medieval town centre – quite unlike any other winter resort
- (+) Good mountain restaurants

- (–) Slopes all of medium steepness
- (–) Rather confined main mountain, with second area some way distant
- (–) Many slow lifts on the mountain, despite modern access lifts
- (–) Long airport transfers
- (–) Crowds and queues on Sundays
- (–) Central hotels inconvenient for the lifts and slopes

If you like cobbled medieval Italian towns and don't mind a lack of Alpine resort atmosphere, you'll find the centre of Bormio very appealing – though you're unlikely to be staying there. The slopes, too, suit a rather specific and perhaps rather uncommon breed of visitor: you need to enjoy red runs and very little else, but you need to be happy with a limited range of them – unless, that is, you're prepared to take the free bus out to the Val di Dentro-San Colombano area or make longer outings, to Santa Caterina or (further still) Livigno.

boarding *Bormio attracts some boarders, but it has no special appeal. The slopes are too steep to make first-time boarding enjoyable, and apart from some good long carving runs, there's little to attract experienced boarders either: no park or pipe; limited off-piste potential, little enthusiasm from the ski schools to teach boarding; and a mainly skier orientation on the slopes. At least the main area's lifts are mostly chairs, gondolas or cable-cars – though there are some drags. Nightlife is sedate and really gets going only at the weekend.*

The resort

Bormio is in a remote part of Lombardy, at the foot of the Stelvio pass, close to the Swiss and Austrian borders – and a tedious four hours from the airport. The 17th-century town centre is wonderfully preserved, with cobbled streets, markets and old facades for today's shops, restaurants and cafés. Bormio began life as a Roman spa, and still has thermal baths, but it's not as dreary and formal as many spas. It's positively colourful during the evening promenade, but it's not as lively as some Italian resorts, such as Courmayeur.

Between the town centre and the cable-car and gondola stations (over the river on the southern edge of town) is a characterless urban sprawl – mainly made up of hotels built for your convenience. Staying here saves most of a 15-minute walk or a bus-ride. The free shuttle-bus is reliable, but many people walk. There are more slopes well west of town, served by lifts at Oga, Le Motte and Val di Dentro.

The mountains

Bormio has good (but limited) slopes for confident intermediates who like long runs, with a nice mix of high, snowsure pistes and lower wooded slopes. Beginners, intermediates who prefer blue runs and experts are less well provided for.

Both the piste map and the piste marking need substantial improvement.

THE SLOPES
One-dimensional

The main slopes are tall (vertical drop 1800m) and narrow. Most pistes face north-west and head to town. The two-stage **Cima Bianca** cable-car goes from bottom to top (3010m) of the slopes via the mid-mountain mini-resort of **Bormio 2000**. An alternative gondola goes to **Ciuk** (1620m).

The San Colombano area above **Oga, Le Motte** and **Val di Dentro,** a short bus-ride out of Bormio, has grown to become a useful addition to the home slopes, and certainly merits one or more day trips. Half the runs

LIFT PASSES

1999/2000 prices in lire

Alta Valtellina
Covers all lifts in Bormio, Val di Sotto-Val di Dentro (San Colombano ski area), Santa Caterina (12km away) and Livigno (40km away), plus one free day in St Moritz.

Main pass
1-day pass 50,000
6-day pass 260,000 (low season 230,000)

Senior citizens
Over 65: 6-day pass 182,000

Children
Under 14: 6-day pass 182,000

Notes Day pass price covers Bormio and San Colombano lifts only.

Alternative passes
Up to 3-day pass for Bormio and San Colombano only (adult 3-day pass 145,000).

face east and are not high, but some face north. The mainly tree-lined pistes are very pleasant.

Day trips further afield add interest to Bormio. Santa Caterina (20 minutes by bus) and Livigno (90 minutes – good service, says a recent reporter) are covered by the Alta Valtellina lift pass. A six-day pass includes a day in St Moritz (three hours away).

SNOW RELIABILITY
Good above mid-station

Runs above Bormio 2000 are usually snowsure, and the snowmaking facility on the lower slopes is impressive. The high, shaded, north-facing slopes of Santa Caterina (1735m to 2725m) usually have good snow. Sadly, the glacial slopes of nearby Passo Stelvio aren't open in winter.

FOR EXPERTS
Rather limited

There are a couple of short black runs in the main area, and longer ones at Santa Caterina (the long black run down to Oga is now closed), but the main interest lies off-piste. Excursions from Cima Bianca to both east and west of the piste area are said to be feasible in good conditions – though the Ornella drag that allowed westward routes to be extended below Bormio 2000 has been removed.

FOR INTERMEDIATES
A few options for all grades

The Men's Downhill course used for the 1985 World Championships (and presumably to be used in 2005) starts with a steep plunge, but otherwise is just a tough red, ideal for strong intermediates. Stella Alpina, down to 2000, is another fairly steep piste.

Many runs are less tough – ideal for most intermediates. The longest is a superb top-to-bottom cruise. The outlying mountains are also suitable for early intermediates.

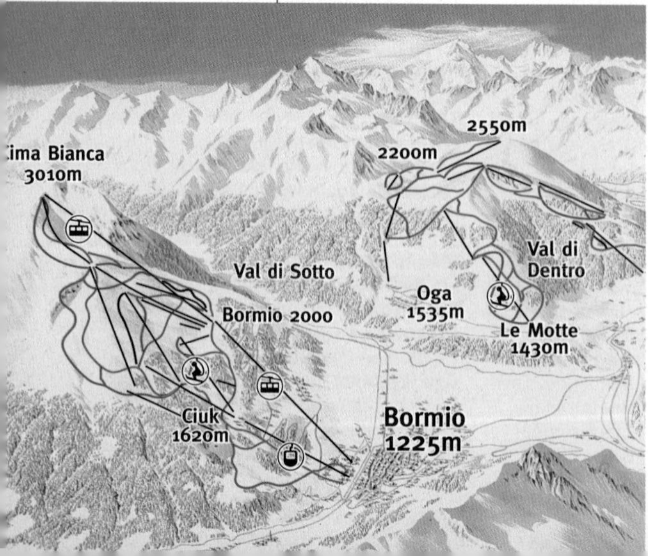

FOR BEGINNERS
Many better Italian resorts

The nursery slopes at Bormio 2000 offer good snow, but there are no very flattering longer pistes to move on to. Novices would be better off at nearby Santa Caterina or at Livigno.

FOR CROSS-COUNTRY
Go to Santa Caterina

There are some trails either side of Bormio, towards Piatta and beneath Le Motte and Val di Dentro, but cross-country skiers would be better off at snowsure Santa Caterina.

QUEUES
Much improved

Bormio has had a reputation for queues – though improvements to the lifts and the opening of Oga-Le Motte area have greatly improved matters. But both sections of the cable-car suffer delays in the morning peak period and on Sundays. And when the lower slopes are incomplete, queues form to ride the gondola down at the end of the day. Otherwise there are few problems outside carnival week.

MOUNTAIN RESTAURANTS
Good fare everywhere

The mountain restaurants are generally good for value and food. Even the efficient self-service at Bormio 2000 has a good choice of dishes. At La Rocca, above Ciuk, there is a welcoming chalet and a smart, modern place with table or self-service. Cedrone, at Bormio 2000, has a good terrace and a play area for children. The very welcoming table-service Baita de Mario, at Ciuk, is a great place for a long lunch. The San Colombano area has a couple of huts, one among trees on the run to Val di Dentro.

SCHOOLS AND GUIDES
Short lessons

There are half a dozen schools in Bormio itself, some with outposts at Bormio 2000 and one based at Ciuk. Most Brits get sent to Scuola Alta Valtellina by their tour operators. We

SCHOOLS/GUIDES

1999/2000 prices in lire

Nazionale
Classes 6 days
2hr: 11am-1pm
6 2hr days: 160,000
Private lessons
Hourly or daily
50,000 per hour; each additional person 10,000

OTHER SCHOOLS

Anzi
Bormio 2000
Capitani
Alta Valtellina
Sertorelli
Fondo Alta Valtellina

CHILDCARE

Children's ski classes are offered by some of the ski schools, but there are no special arrangements for all-day care, and no non-ski kindergartens.

GETTING THERE

Air Bergamo, transfer 4hr. Milan, 4hr.

Rail Tirano (40km); regular buses.

ACTIVITIES

Indoor Two museums, library, thermal baths, squash, swimming pool, sauna, massage, sports hall, skating rink
Outdoor Ski-bob, toboggan run, walks in the Stelvio National Park

TOURIST OFFICE

Postcode 23032
t +39 (0342) 903300
f 904696
aptbormio@provincia.so.it
www.provincia.so.it/aptvaltellina

have received good reports of their helpful and fun tuition. Classes are limited to half-day sessions.

FACILITIES FOR CHILDREN
Typically Italian – limited

There is no crèche or ski kindergarten. But the Nazionale, Sertorelli and Bormio 2000 schools, at least, seem to make some effort to cater for children. The latter has a roped-off snow garden at its mid-mountain chalet.

Staying there

Bormio is big enough for location to be of some importance. You choose between convenient locations on the lift side of the river and the vitality of the town. Several major hotels are on Via Milano, leading out of town, which is neither convenient nor atmospheric.

HOW TO GO
Probably on a hotel package

There are plenty of apartments, but hotels dominate the package market.
Hotels Most of Bormio's 40-plus hotels are 2-star and 3-star places, though there are a handful of 4-stars.
(4) **Palace** Only luxurious place in town, on the Via Milano. Pool.
(3) **Baita dei Pini** Best placed of top hotels: on the river, equidistant from lifts and centre. Excellent food, good facilities, fitness room and a piano bar.
(3) **Posta** In the pedestrian heart of the town, rated a 4-star but with some 'pretty basic' rooms. A recent report tells of incredibly friendly staff.
(2) **San Lorenzo** Friendly 3-star on edge of old town.
(2) **Ambassador Chalet** Welcoming place close to the gondola.
(2) **Derby** Large, attractive 3-star.
(1) **Piccolo Mondo** Small, basic but friendly B&B place with good breakfasts, close to Ciuk lift.
(1) **Dante** Good-value, central 2-star.

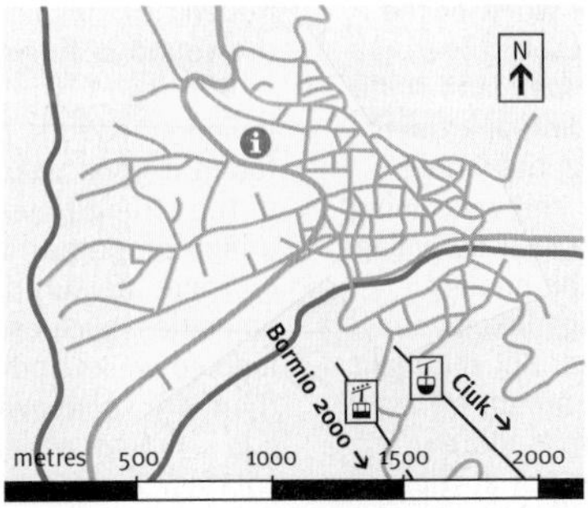

Self-catering The plain, modern Residence Jolly is close to the centre. The modern, well equipped Cristallo apartments have been recommended.

EATING OUT
Plenty of choice

There's a wide selection of restaurants. The atmospheric Taulà does excellent modern food with great service – worth the highish price. The Kuerc is also pricey but popular. The Vecchia Combo is also worth a try. There are excellent pizzerias, including the Jap – in a vault near the main square.

APRES-SKI
Tea-time promenading

The immediate après-ski scene starts on the mountain, perhaps at La Rocca. There are popular tea-time bars around the bottom lift stations, too. Clem's Pub, Gordy's, Mozart's and the Aurora piano bar are popular spots. Shangri-La is a friendly bar. The King's Club disco gets busy at weekends.

OFF THE SLOPES
Take in the thermals

Bormio's diversions include thermal baths, riding and walks in the Stelvio National Park. St Moritz and Livigno are popular excursions.

STAYING UP THE MOUNTAIN
Worth considering

The modern Girasole, at Bormio 2000, is simple but well run, with a warm welcome and lots of events. It comes recommended by a recent reporter, but a change of management is imminent.

BORMIO TO
The town enjoys a fine setting →

Cervinia 2050m

Mile after mile of high-altitude, snowsure cruising

WHAT IT COSTS

4

HOW IT RATES

The slopes	
Snow	*****
Extent	***
Experts	*
Intermediates	****
Beginners	*****
Convenience	***
Queues	***
Restaurants	***
The rest	
Scenery	****
Resort charm	**
Off-slope	*

- + Extensive mountain with miles of long, consistently gentle runs, usually with excellent snow
- + Ideal for early intermediates and anyone who isn't looking for steep challenges or nasty surprises
- + High, sunny and snowsure slopes amid impressive scenery
- + Link with Zermatt in Switzerland provides some spectacular views and good lunches

- − Very little to interest good or aggressive intermediates and above
- − Almost entirely treeless, with little to do in bad weather
- − Lifts prone to closure by wind, particularly early in the season
- − Village centre pleasant, but ugly buildings further out
- − Steep uphill walk to main lifts, followed by lots of steps in station
- − Few off-slope amenities

What brings people to Breuil Cervinia (as the resort now styles itself) in winter in the 20th century is what brought climbers to the original village of Breuil in the 19th century: altitude. For climbers it was a launch pad for assaults on the nearby Matterhorn (Monte Cervino). For winter sports, it offers an unusual combination: slopes that are gentle and extensive, sunny and snowsure.

For cruisers who like to cover the miles on flattering slopes with no worries about unexpected challenges, there is nowhere like it. But experts should steer clear: they'll find the slopes tame and the link with Zermatt disappointing because it doesn't access Zermatt's best slopes.

boarding *Cervinia has great slopes for learning to snowboard – gentle, wide and usually with good snow. And the main lifts around the area are chairs, gondolas and cable-cars, but there are a lot of drag-lifts as well. There's not much to interest better boarders – just as there's not much to interest better skiers. But there is a snowboarder-only piste and fun-park in the Cieloalto sector. Nightlife is fairly limited.*

What's new

For the 1999/2000 season the old cable-car from the resort to Plan Maison was renovated and two 85-person cabins fitted. This supplements the six-person gondola at peak periods.

At almost 3500m, the 'highest museum in Europe' was opened at Plateau Rosa.

The resort

Cervinia is at the head of a long valley up from the Aosta valley on the Italian side of the Matterhorn. The old climbing village developed into a winter resort in a rather haphazard way, and it has no consistent style of architecture. It's an uncomfortable hotchpotch, neither pleasing to the eye nor as offensive as the worst of the French purpose-built resorts. The centre is pleasant, compact and traffic-free. But ugly surrounding apartment blocks and hotels make the whole place feel less friendly and welcoming.

A lot of people stay near the village centre, at the foot of the nursery slopes. A series of drags takes you from here to the slopes. But the main gondola and cable-car are an awkward uphill walk away. There is more accommodation further out at the Cieloalto complex and on the road up to it – but some of the buildings are among the worst eyesores.

As well as the usual souvenir shops there are a few smart Italian clothes shops and jewellers. At peak periods, the resort fills up with day trippers and weekenders from Milan and Turin who bring cars and mobile phones, making parts of the village traffic- and fume-ridden at times and the hills alive with the sound of ringing.

The resort is relatively expensive by Italian standards, but reporters have found it good value recently because of the strong pound/weak lira. There is a high proportion of Brits.

There are surprisingly few off-slope amenities, such as kindergartens, marked walks and spa facilities. And there are some awkward walks and no bus – though some hotels have courtesy buses.

MOUNTAIN FACTS

Altitude 1525m-3480m	
Lifts	34
Pistes	120km
Blue	40%
Red	48%
Black	12%
Artificial snow	9km
Recco detectors used	

LIFT PASSES

1999/2000 prices in lire

Breuil-Cervinia
Covers all lifts on the Italian side of the border including Valtournenche.

Beginners Points tickets in Cretaz area only.

Main pass
1-day pass 53,000
6-day pass 270,000 (low season 206,000)

Senior citizens
Over 65: 6-day pass 214,000

Children
Under 12: 6-day pass 214,000
Under 6: free pass

Short-term passes
Half-day from noon for Cervinia. Single and return tickets on some lifts.

Notes Daily extension for Zermatt lifts around Klein Matterhorn and Schwarzsee (40,000).

Alternative passes
International pass which includes Zermatt: 6-day pass 312,000 or 234,000 for under 12s and over 65s (2000/01 price). Limited area passes for Carosello (4 lifts) and Cretaz (8 lifts). Day pass covering Cervinia, Zermatt and Valtournenche (70,000). Valle d'Aosta ski pass covers all lifts in Courmayeur, La Thuile, Gressoney, Alagna, Champoluc, Pila, Cervinia and Valtournenche (adult 6-day 274,000).

The mountains

Cervinia's main slopes are on a high, large, open and sunny west-facing bowl. It has Italy's highest pistes and some of its longest (13km from Plateau Rosa to Valtournenche – with only a short drag-lift part-way). Nearly all the runs are accessible to intermediates. The weather is more of a problem than steepness. If it's bad, the top lifts often close because of high winds. And even the lower slopes may be unusable because of poor visibility. There are few woodland pistes.

The slopes link to Valtournenche further down the valley (covered by the lift pass) and Zermatt over in Switzerland (supplement payable). Day trips by car are possible to Courmayeur, La Thuile and the Monterosa resorts of Champoluc (good off-piste) or Gressoney.

THE SLOPES
Very easy

Cervinia has the biggest, highest, most snowsure area of easy pistes we've come across. A gondola and a newly renovated cable-car leave from above the village centre, though it's a tiring, steep climb up to them – several reporters recommend the alternative route up using drag-lifts. The main lifts take you to the mid-mountain base of **Plan Maison** (2555m). From there a further gondola and cable-cars go up to **Plateau Rosa** (3480m) and a link with Zermatt.

Three successive high-speed quads also lead from Plan Maison to another link with Zermatt. From here you can ski back on Cervinia's easiest slopes to Plan Maison or right down to the village. The top runs here (and from Plateau Rosa to here) have been regraded from blue to red ('for marketing reasons', says one reporter) – but in truth they are very easy blues.

If you go right at Plateau Rosa you take the splendid wide Ventina run, which you can take all the way down to Cervinia (8km). Or you can branch off left down towards **Valtournenche**. The slopes here are served by a number of lifts above the initial gondola from Valtournenche to Salette at 2245m. The top of the Ventina run can be done several times by taking the giant 140-person cable-car. And there's a chair to play on – but no other lifts serve this sector and you can't get back to Plan Maison (though you can take the gondola down there, if you like).

There is also the small, little-used **Cieloalto** area, served by three lifts to the south of the cable-car at the bottom of the Ventina run. This has some of Cervinia's steeper pistes and can be very useful in bad weather as it has the only trees in the area.

The slopes just above the village are floodlit some evenings.

Several reporters have criticised the fact that old lift stations and pylons have been left on the slopes as eyesores after the lifts have been scrapped. And one complains that too many of the runs cross over each other and that they 'saw lots of accidents at these junctions'.

SNOW RELIABILITY
Superb

The mountain is one of the highest in Europe and, despite getting a lot of afternoon sun, can usually be relied upon to have good snow conditions. Lifts being closed due to wind is a bigger worry.

The village nursery slopes and the bottom half of the Ventina run have snowmaking facilities. But the run to Valtournenche below the top of the gondola doesn't – and has been closed on our last two visits in March.

FOR EXPERTS
Forget it

This is not a resort for experts. There are several black runs dotted about, but most of them would be graded red elsewhere.

This year we heard from a number of reporters who resorted to heading over to Zermatt daily for more challenging slopes (and better lunches – see below). But the Trockener Steg-Schwarzsee area of Zermatt closest to Cervinia has a great many easy runs and only a few challenging pistes. On a day trip, getting to and from the more challenging areas isn't practical.

FOR INTERMEDIATES
Miles of long, flattering runs

Virtually the whole area can be covered comfortably by average intermediates. And if you like wide, easy, motorway pistes, you'll love Cervinia: it has more long, flattering runs than any other resort. The high proportion of red runs on the piste map is misleading: most of them would be graded blue elsewhere. The easiest slopes are on the left as you look at the mountain. From top to bottom here there are gentle blue runs and almost equally gentle reds in the beautiful scenery at the foot of the south face of the Matterhorn.

The area on the right as you look at the mountain is best for adventurous intermediates. The Ventina run is a particularly good fast cruise. The long run down to Valtournenche is easy for most of its length. Good intermediates will be capable of the black runs.

The trip over to Zermatt will bring you first of all to even gentler motorways than on the Cervinia side, but then to some more challenging pistes around Schwarzsee.

There's also the bonus of even more spectacular scenery. The view of the Matterhorn from the Swiss side is the classic one you see in all the pictures (you wouldn't recognise it from the Cervinia side), and the view of the glacier when you ride the Klein Matterhorn cable-car to Europe's highest pistes is breathtaking. If you want to have a look at the village of Zermatt, allow plenty of time. The run down can be tricky, the lifts back time-consuming.

FOR BEGINNERS
Pretty much ideal

Complete beginners will start on the good village nursery slope, and should graduate quickly to the fine flat area around Plan Maison and its gentle green runs. Fast learners will end up going all the way from the top to the bottom of the mountain by the end of the week.

FOR CROSS-COUNTRY
Hardly any

There are a couple of short trails, but this is not a cross-country resort.

QUEUES
Can still be problems

Although much improved recently, there are still some antiquated lifts, and the system still has drawbacks. The two main access lifts to Plan Maison can get busy and the alternative is a roundabout series of drags and chairs. There can be queues for many lower lifts when the upper lifts are shut due to high wind.

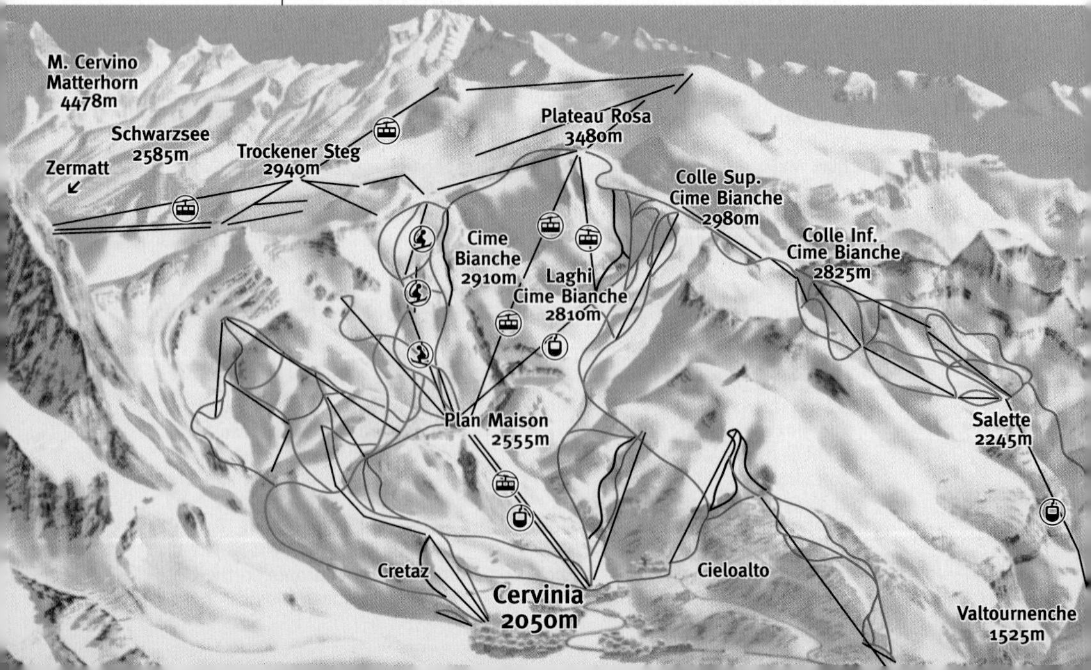

Cervinia's mountain restaurants are disappointing for an Italian resort →

SNOWPIX.COM / CHRIS GILL

↑ The mountains above Cervinia are beautiful, but parts of the village are a bit of an eyesore

SNOWPIX.COM / CHRIS GILL

CHILDCARE

The ski school runs a snow garden with mini-lift at the foot of the Cretaz slopes and one mini-lift in Plan Maison. Care arrangements 10am to 1pm. There is not a non-ski kindergarten.

SCHOOLS/GUIDES

1999/2000 prices in lire

Breuil

Classes 6 days
2hr 50min: 10am-12.50
6 days: 230,000

Children's classes
Ages: 5 to 7
(z6 days, 7hr a day): 720,000

Private lessons
Hourly
50,000 for 1 or 2 people; first additional person 10,000

MOUNTAIN RESTAURANTS
Disappointing for Italy

The food in mountain restaurants has disappointed recent reporters (some of whom have headed to Zermatt huts for a decent lunch), and the toilet facilities can be primitive. The restaurants are cheaper and less crowded on the Valtournenche side. The Motta, at the top of the drag-lift of the same name, has an excellent local speciality (Suppa di Valdostani – bread, cheese and vegetable soup). On the Cervinia side, the Igloo, at the top of the Bardoney chair just off the Ventina piste, is 'very English but the only decent mountain eatery in Cervinia',, says a reporter. 'Souvenirs from Brighton and enormous burgers and sandwiches' and 'a UK-style loo', say others. Baita Cretaz, near the bottom of the Cretaz pistes, is good value. The big self-service where the pistes for Cervinia and Valtournenche part is rustic, with lovely old photos and artifacts. The Stambucco self-service at Plan Maison has also been recommended.

SCHOOLS AND GUIDES
Getting better

Cervinia has two main schools, Cervino and Breuil. We've had decent reports this year: 'my son had a two-hour private snowboard lesson, which was great value; the instructor spoke perfect English' and 'my girlfriend said the school was erratic in its organisation but it was pleasant and the instructors spoke good English'. But earlier reporters said: 'mixed class with Italians; not good for instruction but good for international relations' and 'snowboarding lessons only for beginners and only in the afternoon'.

FACILITIES FOR CHILDREN
Do-it-yourself

Children's classes in the school is about it. The slopes, with their long gentle runs, should suit families.

Staying there

To avoid the awkward uphill walk to the main lifts, choose a hotel with its own shuttle-bus (there's no public bus service). Central hotels are quite convenient for the Cretaz drags, but not for the main gondola station.

HOW TO GO
Plenty of hotel packages

Most of the big tour operators come here, providing between them a wide selection of hotels, though other types of accommodation are rather thin on the ground.

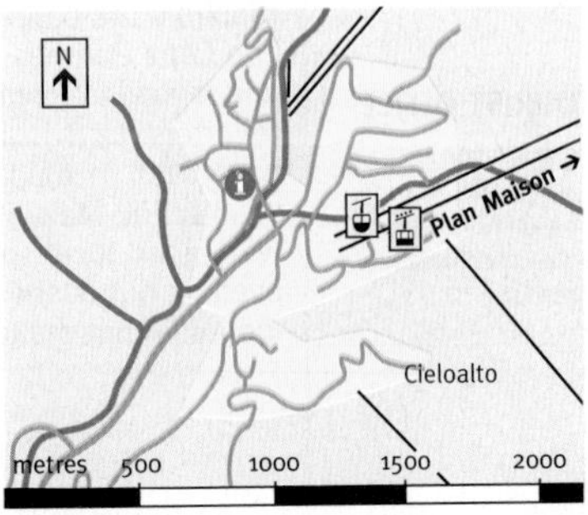

ACTIVITIES

Indoor Hotel with swimming pools and saunas, fitness centre, bowling

Outdoor Natural skating rink (until March), paragliding, hang-gliding, mountaineering, heli-skiing

GETTING THERE

Air Turin, transfer 2½hr. Geneva, transfer 2½hr.

Rail Châtillon (27km); regular buses from station.

TOURIST OFFICE

Postcode 11021
t +39 (0166) 949136
f 949731
breuil-cervinia@netvallee.it
www.cervinia.it

Hotels There are almost 50 hotels, mostly 2- or 3-star, with half a dozen 4-stars.

(((((5) **Cristallo** Luxury 4-star quite a way from town with pool, sauna, massage, great views. Free bus to lifts. Two opposing views from this year's reporters: 'did not live up to brochure description, pool taken over by the general public, disco shut, staff unfriendly, would never recommend it' and 'excellent, great food, good wines, good ski shop, free bus service worked well, skied back to hotel daily'.

((((4) **Hermitage** Small, luxurious Relais et Château just out of the village on the road up to Cieloalto. Great views, pool, free bus to lifts.

((((4) **Punta Maquignaz** Captivating chalet-style 4-star, in centre near Cretaz lifts.

(((3) **Sporthotel Sertorelli** Excellent food, large buffet breakfast, sauna and hot-tub. Ten minutes from lifts.

(((3) **Europa** Friendly and family run; near Cretaz lifts. Recommended by a reporter. Pool.

((2) **Astoria** Right by main lift station. Family run and simple. 'Excellent service, good food, room OK but a bit small, says a reporter this year.

((2) **Marmore** Friendly, family run, with 'quite good food'; on main street and an easy walk to the lift stations.

Self-catering There are many apartments in the resort, but few are available through British tour operators. The Cristallino apartments are fairly simple, but guests have use of the fine facilities of the Cristallo next door, including the free bus.

EATING OUT
Plenty to choose from

Cervinia's 50 or so restaurants allow plenty of choice.

The Chamoix and Matterhorn ('great T-bone steaks') are excellent, but quite pricey. The Grotta belies its name with good food. Casse Croute serves probably the biggest, and best, pizzas. The Copa Pan has a lively atmosphere and is again recommended by several reporters. La Bricole and La Nicchia have been recommended for grills and steaks. The Maison de Sausure does 'very good local specialities'. An evening out at the Baita Cretaz mountain hut makes a change.

APRES-SKI
Disappoints many Brits

Plenty of Brits come here looking for action but find there isn't much to do except tour the mostly fairly ordinary bars. The Copa Pan (see 'Eating Out') is lively, good value and serves generous measures. The Dragon Bar is popular with Brits and has satellite TV and videos. Lino's (by the ice rink) and Café des Guides (with mementos of the owner's mountaineering trips to the Himalayas, pints of gin and tonic and a happy hour) are recommended by reporters. The discos liven up at weekends, and according to one visitor, 'La Chimera is on the main street but the Garage is great and has minibuses that will pick you up and drop you home'. There are tour-rep-organised events such as snow-mobiling on the old bob-sled run, quiz nights, bowling and fondue nights.

OFF THE SLOPES
Little attraction

There is little to do. The pleasant town of Aosta is reached easily enough, but it's a four-hour round trip. Village amenities include pools, a fitness centre and a natural ice rink. The walks are disappointing. The mountain restaurants that are reachable by gondola or cable-car hold little interest for pedestrians.

STAYING UP THE MOUNTAIN
To beat the queues

Up at Plan Maison, the major lift junction 500m vertical above the resort, Lo Stambecco is a 50-room 3-star hotel ideally placed for early nights and early starts. Less radically, the Cime Bianche is a rustic 3-star chalet on the upper fringes of the resort (in the area known as La Vieille).

STAYING DOWN THE VALLEY
Great home run

Valtournenche, 9km down the road, is cheaper than Cervinia, has a genuine Italian atmosphere and a fair selection of simple hotels, of which the 3-star Bijou is the best.

A new gondola that opened in 1998 has cut the weekend waits. But the slow lifts above it mean it takes quite a time to reach Cervinia. The exceptionally long run back down, however, is a nice way to end the day – when it is all open. The main street through the village is very busy with cars going to and from Cervinia.

Cortina d'Ampezzo 1229m

Simply the world's most beautiful winter playground

WHAT IT COSTS

HOW IT RATES

The slopes

Snow	★★★
Extent	★★★
Experts	★★
Intermediates	★★★
Beginners	★★★★★
Convenience	★
Queues	★★★
Restaurants	★★★★

The rest

Scenery	★★★★★
Resort charm	★★★★
Off-slope	★★★★★

What's new

For the 1999/2000 season the quiet, very beautiful, outlying Cinque Torri area was transformed by the replacement of two ancient single-person chairs by a high-speed quad.

There are more distant plans for another high-speed quad to link the Cinque Torri with the Passo Falzarego slopes, cutting out the need for a shuttle-bus transfer.

Cortina has worked hard on much-needed snowmaking and now tells us that all pistes below 2300m (which is most) are covered by snow-guns. But it still has to be cold enough for them to be able to work.

The Marmolada glacier lifts will be included in the Dolomiti Superski pass for the 2000/01 season – rather than having to pay a supplement to use them.

➕ Magnificent Dolomite scenery – perhaps the most dramatic of any winter resort

➕ Marvellous nursery slopes and good long cruising runs, ideal for nervous intermediates

➕ Access to the vast area covered by the Dolomiti Superski pass

➕ Attractive, although rather towny, resort, with lots of upmarket shops

➕ Good off-slope facilities

➕ Remarkably uncrowded slopes

➖ Several separate areas of slopes, which are inconveniently spread around all sides of the resort and linked by buses

➖ Poor recent snow record

➖ Expensive by Italian standards

➖ Gets very crowded during Italian holidays

➖ Very little for experts

➖ Mobile phones and fur coats may drive you nuts

Nowhere is more picturesque than chic Cortina, the most upmarket of Italian resorts. Dramatic pink-tinged peaks rise sheerly from the top of the slopes, giving picture-postcard views from wherever you are.

Cortina's slopes are fine for its regular upmarket visitors from Rome and Milan, many of whom have second homes here and enjoy the strolling, shopping, people-watching and lunching as much as the odd leisurely excursion on to the slopes. For beginners and leisurely intermediates, the splendid nursery slopes and long, easy, well-groomed runs are ideal. For keen piste-bashers, Cortina's fragmented areas can be frustrating, especially if snow is scarce and the area is fragmented even more; but the access to the Sella Ronda and other Dolomiti Superski resorts, though time consuming, is some compensation – having a car is best for exploring. For experts, there are few tough runs, and the best of those are liable to poor snow conditions and closure because they face south.

boarding *Despite its upmarket chic, Cortina is a good resort for learning to board. The Socrepes nursery slopes are wide, gentle and served by a high-speed quad chair-lift. And progress on to the resort's other easy slopes is simple because you can get around in all areas using just chairs and cable-cars – though there are drags, they can be avoided. There is no half-pipe or fun-park and little off-piste to interest experienced boarders. And hardcore boarders might find the chic shops, beautiful people and expensive nightlife a bit hard to stomach.*

The resort

In winter, more people come to Cortina for the clear mountain air, the stunning views, the shopping, the cafés and to pose and be seen than for the winter sports – 70 per cent of all Italian visitors don't bother taking to the slopes. Cortina attracts the rich and wealthy from the big Italian cities, many of whom have second homes here. Fur coats, glitzy jewellery and mobile phones are everywhere.

The resort itself is a widely spread town rather than a village, with exclusive chalets scattered around the woods and the roads leading off into the countryside. The centre is the traffic-free Corso Italia, full of chic designer clothes and jewellery shops, art galleries and furriers – finding a ski shop can seem tricky. In early evening, the street is a hive of activity, with everyone parading up and down in their finery, window-shopping, people-watching and making calls on mobile phones. Seeing anyone dressed for the slopes at 5pm is a rarity, but the cobbles and picturesque church bell tower add to the Italian atmosphere. But all this glamour doesn't mean Cortina has to be expensive.

Surrounding the centre is a horrendous one-way system, often

MOUNTAIN FACTS

Altitude	1225m-2930m
Lifts	39
Pistes	120km
Blue	33%
Red	62%
Black	5%
Artificial snow	96km
Recco detectors used	

traffic-clogged and stinking of fumes – a nasty contrast to the stunning scenery everywhere else you look.

Unlike the rest of the Dolomites, Cortina is pure Italy. It has none of the Germanic traditions of Selva and the Sud Tirol, and doesn't attract many German visitors.

The mountains

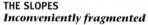

Cortina first leapt to fame as host of the 1956 Winter Olympics. At the time, it was very modern; now it feels dated. Its widely spread areas are nothing like the classic modern French purpose-built resorts. The lifts to the two main areas of slopes are a fair way from the centre, and at opposite sides of town. Other lifts are a lengthy bus-ride away.

If you fancy a trip further afield, **San Cassiano** is not far to the west, with links from there to **Corvara** and the other Sella Ronda resorts.

A car helps to make the most of other areas on the Dolomiti Superski pass. But the local bus service is good (though it could do with being more frequent), and tour operators offer day trips to other areas.

THE SLOPES
Inconveniently fragmented

All Cortina's smallish separate areas are a fair trek from the town centre. The largest is **Socrepes**, accessed by chair- and drag-lifts a bus-ride away. It links with **Tofana**, Cortina's highest area, also reached by two-stage cable-car from near the Olympic ice rink.

On the opposite side of the valley is the tiny **Mietres** area. Another cable-car from the east side of town leads to the

Faloria area, from where you can head down to the chairs that lead up into the limited but dramatic runs beneath the **Cristallo** peak.

Other areas are reachable by road. The cable-car from Passo Falzarego (2150m) up to Lagazuoi (2750m) accesses a beautiful red run to Armenterola which takes you away from all lifts and signs of civilisation and is called the Hidden Valley. On the way to Passo Falzarego is the tiny but spectacular Cinque Torri area. Its excellent, north-facing slopes are now accessed by a high-speed quad.

We've received praise for the excellent grooming and quiet slopes with few queues, but complaints about the piste map not showing some runs, poor piste marking, and World Cup races disrupting January skiing.

SNOW RELIABILITY
Lots of artificial help

Cortina has suffered from lack of natural snow for the last couple of seasons. The snowfall record is erratic – it can be good here when it's poor on the north side of the Alps (and vice

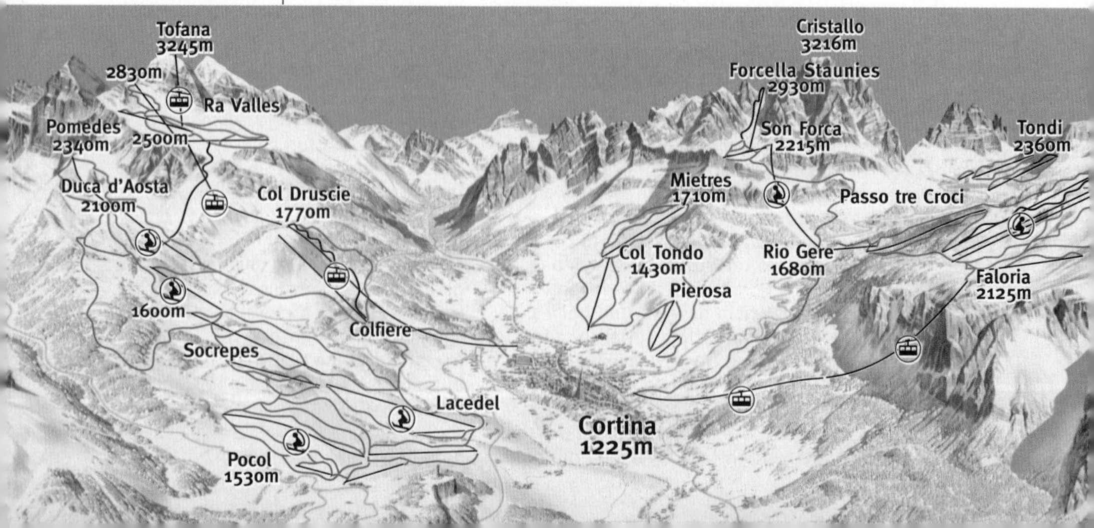

↑ Cortina's scenery is stunning, with dramatic peaks rising sheerly from the slopes

D G BANDION / CORTINA TO

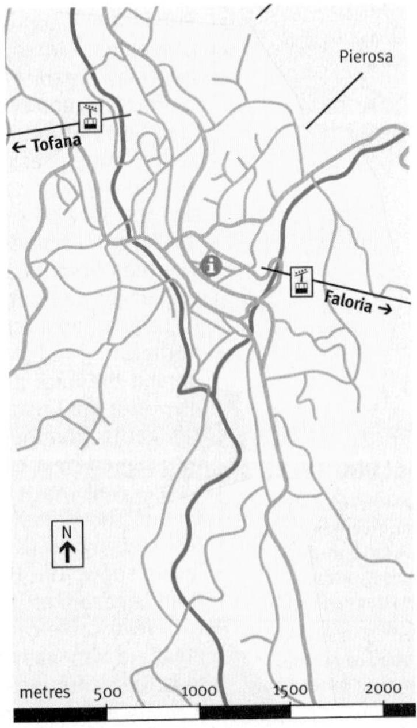

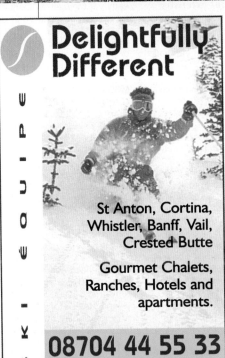

LIFT PASSES

2000/01 prices in lire

Dolomiti Superski
Covers 460 lifts and 1200km of piste in the Dolomites, including all Cortina areas.

Main pass
1-day pass 63,000
6-day pass 313,000
(low season 276,000)

Senior citizens
Over 60: 6-day pass 250,000

Children
Under 16: 6-day pass 219,000

Alternative pass
Cortina d'Ampezzo
Covers all lifts in Cortina, San Vito di Cadore, Auronzo and Misurina, and ski-buses.

Main pass
1-day pass 58,000
6-day pass 288,000
(low season 251,000)

Senior citizens
Over 60: 6-day pass 230,000

Children
Under 16: 6-day pass 200,000
Under 8: free pass

Notes Low season prices for all lift passes apply before Christmas, 7 Jan to 3 Feb and from 11 March

GETTING THERE

Air Venice, transfer 3hr (free transfer available for hotel guests; advance booking required).

Rail Calalzo (35km) or Dobbiaco (32km); frequent buses from station.

versa). But the resort has invested heavily in artificial snow and 80 per cent of the pistes are now covered, so cover should generally be good if it is cold enough to make snow. But last time we visited, the link between Tofana and Socrepes was closed because of lack of snow on a key south-facing slope – which made the areas even more fragmented.

FOR EXPERTS
Limited

The run down from the second stage of the Tofana cable-car at Ra Valles goes through a gap in the rocks, and a steep, narrow, south-facing section gives wonderful views of Cortina, deep down in the valley. It's often tricky because of poor snow conditions.

Cortina's other steep run goes from the top of the Cristallo area at Forcella Staunies. A chair-lift takes you to a steep, south-facing couloir, often shut due to avalanche danger or poor snow.

Other than these two runs (both shut on our last visit) there's little to keep experts happy for a week.

Heli-skiing is available.

FOR INTERMEDIATES
Fragmented and not extensive

If you like cruising in beautiful scenery and don't mind repeating runs, you'll get the most out of Cortina. But don't expect a huge linked area. If you have a car, it makes exploring the Sella Ronda areas and circuit more convenient – though tour operators generally organise weekly excursions.

The red runs at the top of Tofana are short but normally have the best snow. The highest are at over 2800m and mainly face north. But be warned: the only way down is by the tricky black run described above or cable-car. The reds from the linked Pomedes area are longer and offer good cruising.

Faloria has a string of fairly short north-facing reds – we loved Vitelli around the back away from all signs of lifts. And the Cristallo area that you can get to from here has just one long red, served by a high-speed quad.

It is well worth making the trip to Cinque Torri for wonderful, deserted fast cruising on usually excellent north-facing snow. The Hidden Valley run from Lagazuoi at the top of the Passo Falzerego cable-car to Armenterola is a must – a very easy red and one of the most beautiful runs we've come across. It offers isolation amid sheerly rising pink-tinged Dolomite peaks and frozen waterfalls. Make time to stop at the atmospheric Scotoni rifugio near the end, then it's a long pole, skate or walk to the welcome sight of a horse-drawn sled (with ropes attached) which tows the weary to Armenterola. Shared taxis take you back to Passo Falzerego (if you've time, try the slopes of Alta Badia, accessed from Armenterola).

FOR BEGINNERS
Wonderful nursery slopes

The Socrepes area has some of the biggest nursery slopes and best progression runs we have seen. Some of the blue forest paths can be icy and intimidating – including piste 160 to the Faloria cable-car. But you'll find ideal gentle terrain on the main pistes.

FOR CROSS-COUNTRY
One of the best

Cortina has 74km of trails, mainly in the woods towards Dobbiaco. There are also trails below the Cristallo area.

QUEUES
No problem

Most Cortina holidaymakers rise late, lunch lengthily and leave the slopes early – if they get on them at all. That means few lift queues and generally uncrowded pistes – a different world to the crowded Sella Ronda circuit. 'Lack of queues was one of the highlights of our holiday,' said one reporter.

MOUNTAIN RESTAURANTS
Good, but get in early

Lunch is a major event for many Cortina visitors. At weekends you often need to book or turn up very early to be sure of a table. Many restaurants can be reached by road or lift, and pedestrians arrive as early as 10am to sunbathe, admire the views and idle the time away on their mobile phones.

Although prices are high in the swishest establishments, we've found plenty of reasonably priced places, serving generally excellent food. In the Socrepes area, the Col Taron is highly recommended and the Pic de Tofana, Rifugio Pomedes and El Faral are also good. The Socrepes sector also has several hotels along the road at its edge – including the best restaurant in the resort, the Michelin-starred Tivoli.

At Cristallo the Rio Gere at the base of the quad chair and Son Forca, with fabulous views at the top of it, are both worth a visit.

SCHOOLS/GUIDES

2000/01 prices in lire

Cortina
Classes 6 days
2½hr: 9.30-noon; 2hr: noon-2pm
6 2½hr days: 310,000
Private lessons
Hourly
65,000 for 1hr; each additional person 17,000

Azzurra Cortina
Classes 6 days
3½hr: 9.15-1pm;
6½hr: 9.15-4pm
6 3½hr days: 725,000
Private lessons
Hourly
72,000 for 1hr; each additional person 22,000
Notes Prices lower pre-Christmas and from 11 March

CHILDCARE

There is non-skiing childcare, and schools offer all-day classes for children.

ACTIVITIES

Indoor Swimming pool, saunas, museums, art gallery, cinema, indoor tennis court, public library
Outdoor Rides on Olympic bob run, snow rafting down Olympic ski jump, crazy sledge for moonlit excursions, snow-shoe tours, all at Adrenalin centre; Olympic ice-stadium (2 rinks), curling, ice hockey, sleigh rides, horse-riding school, 6km walking paths, toboggan run, heli-skiing

TOURIST OFFICE

Postcode 32043
t +39 (0436) 866252
f 867448
cortina@dolomiti.org
www.sunrise.it/cortina

The restaurants at Cinque Torri, the Scoiattoli and the Rifugio Averau, offer fantastic views as well as good food, and, unusually, are non-smoking. Rifugio Lagazuoi, a hike up from the top of the Pazzo Falzerego cable-car, also has great views and no smoking.

SCHOOLS AND GUIDES
Mixed reports

Of the four ski schools, we've had mixed reports of the 'Cortina' school. One couple had good classes in English-speaking groups. But there were other reports of a group that included six Brits being taught mainly in Italian, and a tired intermediate asking for a short rest and being left stranded at the top of the mountain. The Gruppo Guide Alpine offers off-piste and touring.

FACILITIES FOR CHILDREN
Better than average

By Italian standards childcare facilities are outstanding, with a choice of all-day care arrangements for children of practically any age. Given the very small number of British visitors, you can't count on good spoken English. And the fragmented area can make travelling around with children difficult.

Staying there

There's a wide range of hotels in the centre and scattered in the outskirts. To get the most out of the town, staying in the centre is the best bet.

HOW TO GO
Now with more packages

Hotels dominate the market but there are some catered chalets.

Hotels There's a big choice, from 5-star luxury to 1-star and 2-star pensions.
((((5 **Miramonti** Spectacularly grand hotel, 2km south of town. Pool.
(((4 **Poste** Reliable 4-star, at the heart of the town.
(((4 **Ancora** Elegant public rooms, right on the traffic-free Corso Italia.
(((4 **Parc Victoria** Rustic 4-star with small rooms but good food, at the Faloria end of the town centre.
(((4 **Faloria** Newish, near ski jump, splendid pool, good food.
((3 **Olimpia** Comfortable B&B hotel in centre, close to Faloria lift.
((3 **Menardi** Welcoming roadside inn, a long walk from centre and lifts.
((3 **Villa Resy** Small and welcoming, just outside centre, with British owner.

Self-catering There are some chalets and apartments – usually out of town – available for independent travellers.

EATING OUT
Huge choice

There's an enormous selection, both in town and a little way out, doing mainly Italian food. The very smart and pricey El Toulà is in a beautiful old barn, just on the edge of town. Many of the best restaurants are further out – such as the Michelin-starred Tivoli, Meloncino, Leone e Anna, Rio Gere and Baita Fraina. Reasonably priced central restaurants include the Cinque Torri and al Passetto for pizza and pasta, and Mezcal which does drinks, snacks and Tex-Mex food, and often has dancing on the tables after midnight.

APRES-SKI
Lively in high season

Cortina is a lively social whirl in high season, with lots of well-heeled Italians staying up very late. Don't go on the early evening walkabout if fur coats and mobile phones annoy you.

Bar Lovat is one of several popular, high-calorie tea-time spots. Bar Cristallino is an elegant spot where young and old rub shoulders. There are three good wine bars. Enoteca has 700 different wines and good cheese and meats. Osteria has good rock music and local ham. Fe is a wine bar with good decor and is also busy later. The liveliest bar is the Clipper, with a bob-sleigh in the door, and lots of designer beer. A new pub opened last season, offering draught Guinness. Discos liven up after 11pm.

OFF THE SLOPES
A classic resort

Along with St Moritz, Cortina rates as one of the leading resorts if you're happier off the slopes. The setting is stunning, the town attractive, the shopping extensive, the mountain restaurants easily accessible by road (a car is handy). And there's plenty more to do: ice skating, dog-sledding, major ice hockey matches and an ice disco on the Olympic ice rink. You can have a run (with driver!) down the Olympic bob-sleigh run or try snow-rafting on the ski jump. There's horse jumping and polo on the snow occasionally. There are several museums and art galleries.

Trips to Venice are easily and inexpensively organised.

Courmayeur

1225m

A seductive village on the sunny side of Mont Blanc

WHAT IT COSTS

(4)

HOW IT RATES

The slopes	
Snow	****
Extent	**
Experts	***
Intermediates	****
Beginners	**
Convenience	*
Queues	****
Restaurants	****
The rest	
Scenery	****
Resort charm	****
Off-slope	***

What's new

When we went to press it was highly unlikely the Mont Blanc tunnel would open again before summer 2001 at the earliest. So access for the 2000/01 season will be quickest from Turin or Milan airports. From Geneva, the best route is through the Grand St Bernard tunnel. With the Mont Blanc tunnel closed, a day trip to Chamonix takes much longer.

For 1999/2000 a new blue piste was opened down to Dolonne, with buses back from there to town – so you no longer have to download on the cable-car.

For 2000/01 the Cresta d'Arp cable-car is said to be opening up for those without a guide, allowing them access to the off-piste runs from the top. And heli-skiing is due to start – from £70 a drop, including a guide.

- + Charming, traditional village, with car-free centre and stylish shops
- + Stunning views of Mont Blanc massif
- + Pleasant range of intermediate runs
- + Comprehensive snowmaking
- + Good mountain restaurants
- + Lively, but not rowdy, après-ski
- + Good base for heli-skiing

- − Lack of nursery slopes and easy runs for beginners to progress to
- − No tough pistes
- − Relatively small area, with mainly short runs; high-mileage piste bashers will get bored in a week
- − Slopes very crowded on Sundays
- − Tiresome walk and cable-car journey between village and slopes

Courmayeur is very popular, especially at weekends, with the smart Italian set from Milan and Turin. It's easy to see why: it's very easy to get to and certainly the most captivating of the Val d'Aosta resorts.

The scenery, the charm and the nightlife must influence the many Brits who go there, too. Certainly, the slopes themselves are unlikely to be the main draw, given their limited range of difficulty, inconvenient location across the valley from the village and, particularly, their limited size; a keen piste-basher will cover Courmayeur in a day. Now the Mont Blanc tunnel is closed you don't have the option of a quick trip to Chamonix. The resort could make a jolly week for those who want to party as much as hit the slopes. It also appeals to those with quite different ambitions who want to explore the spectacular Mont Blanc massif with the aid of a guide and other local peaks with the aid of a helicopter.

boarding *Courmayeur's pistes suit intermediate boarders, and most areas are easily accessible by novices as the main lifts are cable-cars, chairs and gondolas – but it's all a bit steep for beginners. The biggest draws for the more experienced are the off-piste routes. Guides take groups from the top of the main slopes, or on to the flanks of Mont Blanc. Like a lot of Italian resorts, Courmayeur has no fun-park or half-pipe; but it still manages to attract quite a few boarders, and you shouldn't find yourself in too much of a minority. Nightlife is lively in a stylish kind of way, and there's plenty of diversity in the bars.*

The resort

Courmayeur is a traditional old Italian mountaineering village that, despite the nearby Mont Blanc tunnel road (now deserted) and modern hotels, has retained much of its old-world feel.

The village has a charming traffic-free centre of attractive shops, cobbled streets and well-preserved buildings. An Alpine museum and a statue of a famous, long-dead mountain rescue hero add to the historical feel.

The centre has a great atmosphere, focused around the Via Roma. As soon as the lifts close, people pile into the numerous bars, which include some very civilised places. Others wander in and out of the many small shops, which include a salami specialist and a good bookshop. At weekends people-watching is part of the evening scene, as ski jackets are outnumbered by the fur coats of the Milanese and Torinese.

The village extends away from the centre in several directions, and its huge cable-car is right on the edge.

The mountains

The main slopes suit intermediates, but form a surprisingly small area for such a well known, large resort. The pistes are varied in character, if not in gradient, and pretty. Piste marking and maintenance could be improved.

THE SLOPES

Small but interestingly varied

The slopes are separate from the village: you have to ride a cable-car at the start and either take it down or

MOUNTAIN FACTS

Altitude	1295m-2755m
Lifts	25
Pistes	100km
Blue	40%
Red	50%
Black	10%
Artificial snow	18km
Recco detectors used	

take a bus from Dolonne at the end of the day. The cable-car, the only lift out of Courmayeur, transports you to the bottom of the slopes at Plan Checrouit (where you can store your equipment).

There are two distinct sections, both almost entirely for intermediates. The north-east-facing **Checrouit** area catches the morning sun, and has open, above-the-tree-line pistes. The 25-person, infrequently running Youla cable-car goes to 2625m, the top of Courmayeur's pistes. There is a further cable-car to Cresta d'Arp (2755m). This serves only long off-piste runs – and until now has been available only to those with a guide (for 2000/01, it is due to be open to everyone when avalanche risks are low).

Most people follow the sun over to the north-west-facing slopes towards **Val Veny** in the afternoon. These are interesting, varied and tree-lined, with great views of Mont Blanc and its glaciers. Connections between the two areas are good, with many alternative routes. The Val Veny slopes are also accessible by cable-car from Entrèves, a few miles outside Courmayeur.

A little way beyond Entrèves, up Val Ferret, is La Palud, where a cable-car

↑ Courmayeur's 27 mountain huts mean you are never far from a sunbathing opportunity

SNOWPIX.COM / CHRIS GILL

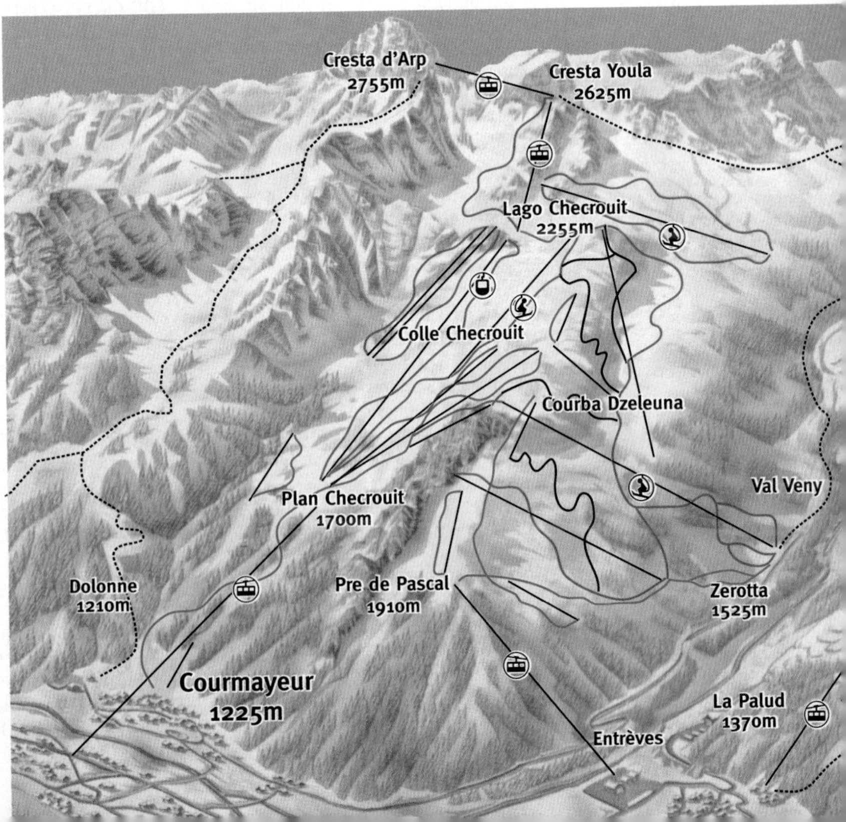

LIFT PASSES

1999/2000 prices in lire

Courmayeur Mont Blanc
Covers all lifts in Val Veny and Checrouit, and the lifts on Mont Blanc up to Punta Helbronner.

Beginners Free nursery lifts at Plan Checrouit and top of Val Veny cable-car (which can be paid for by the ride).

Main pass
1-day pass 55,000 (52,000 Mon to Fri, 45,000 after 3 April)
6-day pass 276,000 (low season 240,000)

Short-term passes
Single ascent on some lifts and half-day pass available.

Notes Passes of 6 or more days are valid for one day at Pila and Verbier and for two days in the resorts of the Mont Blanc region ski pass (incl Chamonix, Les Contamines, St Gervais, Mégève).

Alternative passes
Valle d'Aosta area pass covers all lifts in Courmayeur, Gressoney, Alagna, Champoluc, La Thuile, La Rosière, Pila, Cervinia and Valtournenche (adult 6-day 285,000). Mont-Blanc ski region pass covers all lifts in 13 resorts around Mont Blanc.

goes up in three stages to Punta Helbronner, at the shoulder of **Mont Blanc**. You can do the famous Vallée Blanche run to Chamonix from here – spectacularly scenic, and not difficult – without the horrific initial ridge walk you encounter on the Chamonix side. But it's a long way back with the Mont Blanc tunnel closed. Or you can tackle other off-piste runs on the Italian side of Mont Blanc. None of these glacier runs should be done without a guide.

La Thuile and Pila are an easy drive to the south, and Cervinia is reachable.

SNOW RELIABILITY
Good for most of the season

Courmayeur's slopes are not high – mostly between 1700m and 2250m. Those above Val Veny face north or north-west, so keep their snow well, but the Plan Checrouit side is rather too sunny for comfort in late season. There is snowmaking on most of the main runs, so good coverage in midwinter is virtually assured.

FOR EXPERTS
Off-piste is the only challenge

Courmayeur has few challenging pistes. The only black – the Competizione, on the Val Veny side – is not difficult, and few moguls form elsewhere. But if you're lucky enough to find fresh powder – as we have been several times – you can have fantastic fun among the trees.

Classic off-piste runs go from Cresta d'Arp, at the top of the lift network, in three directions – a clockwise loop via Arp Vieille to Val Veny, with close-up views of the Miage glacier; east down a deserted valley to Dolonne or Pré St Didier; or south through the Youla gorge to La Thuile.

On Mont Blanc, the Vallée Blanche is not a challenge (though there are more difficult variations, and the views are stunning), but the Toula glacier route on the Italian side from Punta Helbronner to Pavillon most certainly is, often to the point of being dangerous. There are also heli-drops available on a wide range of terrain.

FOR INTERMEDIATES
Ideal gradient but limited extent

The whole area is suitable for most intermediates, but it is small. The avid piste-basher will find it very limited.

The open Checrouit section is pretty much go-anywhere territory, where you can choose your own route and make it as easy or difficult as you like. The blue runs here are about Courmayeur's gentlest. On the Val Veny side, the red pistes running the length of the Bertolini chair are more challenging and very enjoyable. These pistes link in with the pretty, wooded slopes heading down to Zerotta.

The Zerotta chair dominates the area, with numerous alternatives starting at its top. It's a good area for mixed abilities, with runs of varying difficulty meeting up at several places on the way down to Zerotta.

The Vallée Blanche, although off-piste, is easy enough for adventurous, fit intermediates to try.

FOR BEGINNERS
Consistently too steep

Courmayeur is not well suited to beginners. There are several nursery slopes, but none is ideal. The area at Plan Checrouit gets crowded, and there are few easy runs for the near-beginner to progress to. The small area served by the short Tzaly drag, just above the Entrèves cable-car top station, is the most suitable beginner terrain, and it tends to have good snow.

FOR CROSS-COUNTRY
Beautiful trails

There are 35km of trails dotted around Courmayeur. The best are the four covering 20km at Val Ferret, to which there is a bus service. Dolonne has a couple of short trails.

QUEUES
Sunday crowds pour in

The lift system is generally excellent. The Checrouit and Val Veny cable-cars suffer queues only on Sundays, and even these can be beaten with an early start. Most patience is needed when waiting for the infrequently running Youla cable-car. Otherwise, no problems. Overcrowded slopes on Sundays, particularly down to Zerotta, are a greater problem.

MOUNTAIN RESTAURANTS
Lots – some of them good

The area is lavishly endowed with 27 establishments ranging from rustic on-piste huts to larger self-service places at main lift stations. Most restaurants do table-service of delicious pizza and pasta, but there are also snack bars selling more basic fare and relying on views and sun to fill their terraces. One of the better snack bars is Courba

SCHOOLS/GUIDES

2000/01 prices in lire

Monte Bianco
Classes 6 days
3hr: 10am-1pm
6 half-days: 250,000 (205,000 low season)
Children's classes
Ages: from 4
6 full days incl snack lunch: 500,000 (450,000 low season)
Private lessons
Hourly
70,000 for 1 person (50,000 low season); each additional person 6,000

CHILDCARE

The Kinderheim at Plan Checrouit (842477) takes children from the age of 6 months, from 9.30 to 4pm. Children taking lessons can be deposited at the ski school in Courmayeur at 9am, and they will be looked after for the whole day (lesson am, play pm). The Kinderheim at the Sports Centre takes children from the age of 3 months.

GETTING THERE

Air Turin, transfer 2hr.

Rail Pré-St-Didier (5km); regular buses from station.

Dzeleuna, at the top of Dzeleuna chair.

Several restaurants are excellent. Maison Vieille, at the top of the chair of the same name and run by the charming mountain man Giacomo, is our favourite – a welcoming rustic place with superb home-made pastas. Chiecco, next to the drag-lift with the same name at Plan Checrouit, is recommended for good food, atmosphere, friendly service and good views of struggling beginners. The pick of the restaurants at Plan Checrouit is the Christiania – book a table downstairs, where you can savour the superb food (especially excellent pizzas) in peace.

On the other side of the mountain in Val Veny is another clutch of places worth noting – La Zerotta, at the foot of the eponymous chair; the Petit Mont Blanc, nearby; the atmospheric Monte Bianco climbing refuge, along the mountainside; and the jolly Grolla, further along still.

SCHOOLS AND GUIDES
Classes not a strong point

We had a very enthusiastic report on the Mont Blanc ski school this year: 'We had the best instructor for ages – possibly ever.' There is a thriving guides' association ready to help you explore the area's off-piste; it has produced a helpful booklet showing the main possibilities.

FACILITIES FOR CHILDREN
Good care by Italian standards

The resort's childcare arrangements are well ahead of the Italian norm, but Courmayeur is far from an ideal resort for a young family.

Staying there

The cable-car station is on the southern edge of town, a fair distance from much of the accommodation. There is no shuttle-bus alternative to walking but you can leave your skis, boards and boots in lockers at the top – highly recommended by most reporters. There is another short walk from the top to the other lifts before you can get on the slopes.

Having accommodation close to the village cable-car is obviously advantageous. Parking at the cable-car is very limited, but drivers can go to Entrèves, a few kilometres away, where there is a large car park at the Val Veny cable-car. Buses, infrequent but timetabled, link Courmayeur with La Palud, just beyond Entrèves, for the Punta Helbronner–Vallée Blanche cable-car.

HOW TO GO
Plenty of hotels

Courmayeur's long-standing popularity ensures a wide range of packages (including some excellent weekend deals), mainly in hotels. Interski stay out of town and bus people in. One or two UK operators have catered chalets.

Hotels There are nearly 50 hotels, spanning the star ratings.

(((④ **Gallia Gran Baita** Luxury place with antique furnishings, panoramic views and 'superb food'. Pool. Shuttle-bus to cable-car.

(((④ **Pavillon** Comfortable 4-star near cable-car, with a pool. Friendly staff.

((③ **Auberge de la Maison** Relatively new small 3-star in Entrèves under same ownership as Maison de Filippo (see Eating Out).

((③ **Bouton d'Or** Small, friendly B&B near main square.

((③ **Berthod** Friendly, family-run hotel near centre.

((③ **Grange** Rustic, stone-and-wood farmhouse in Entrèves.

(② **Edelweiss** Friendly, cosy, good-value place close to the centre.

(② **Lo Scoiattolo** Good rooms, good food, shame about the position – at the opposite end of town to the cable-car.

Self-catering There is quite a lot available to independent bookers.

EATING OUT
Jolly Italian evenings

There is a great choice of restaurants, both in downtown Courmayeur and within taxi-range in neighbouring villages and valleys; there's a handy promotional booklet describing many of them (in English as well as Italian). The touristy but very jolly Maison de Filippo in Entrèves is famous for its fixed-price, 36-dish feast. Further out, at Val Ferret, Chalet Proment (Floriano's) is attractively rustic, but the latest reports say it has 'gone downhill'. We've been impressed by the traditional Italian cuisine of both Pierre Alexis and Cadran Solaire. The Tunnel pizzeria, Mont-Frety ('its antipasti is a must') and La Terrazza ('excellent pasta and very friendly, jolly service') have been recommended. Restaurants tend to be busy, so book well in advance.

ACTIVITIES

Indoor Swimming pool and sauna at Pré-St-Didier (5km), skating rink, curling, Alpine museum, cinema, library, sports centre with climbing, gym, indoor golf, squash, tennis
Outdoor Walking paths in Val Ferret, paragliding, snowbiking, dog-sledding

TOURIST OFFICE

Postcode 11013
t +39 (0165) 842060
f 842072
apt.montebianco@psw.it
www.courmayeur.net

APRES-SKI

Stylish bar-hopping

Courmayeur has a lively evening scene, centred on a series of bars in and around the main street. Our favourites are the Roma, the back room of the Caffe della Posta and the Bar delle Guide, all with comfy armchairs to collapse in. Ziggy's is also popular, and the Cadran Solaire is where the big money from Milan and Torino accumulates. The American Bar has excellent music, cocktails and wine. The Red Lion is worth a visit if you're missing English pubs. There is a disco or two.

OFF THE SLOPES

Much improved for sporty types

If you're not interested in hitting the snow you'll find the village pleasant. There are some interesting excursions – by cable-car up to Punta Helbronner and by bus to Aosta. It's easy to go up the main cable-car to Plan Checrouit to meet friends for lunch. There is a large sports complex with most facilities except a pool. Reporters found ice hockey matches very exciting to watch.

STAYING UP THE MOUNTAIN

Why would you want to?

Visiting Courmayeur and not staying in the charming village seems perverse – if you're that keen to get on the slopes in the morning, this is probably the wrong resort. But the Christiania at Plan Checrouit (see Mountain restaurants) has simple rooms; you need to book way in advance.

SNOWPIX.COM / CHRIS GILL

The big cable-car is the only way to travel between the slopes and the village centre ↓

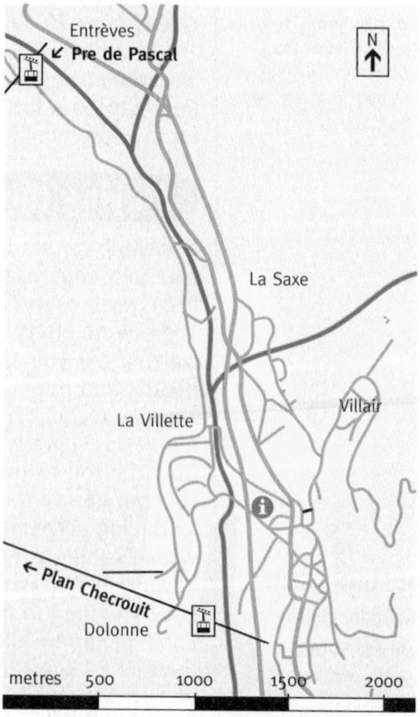

Livigno 1815m

Lowish prices and highish altitude – a tempting combination

WHAT IT COSTS

3

HOW IT RATES

The slopes

Snow	****
Extent	**
Experts	**
Intermediates	***
Beginners	****
Convenience	**
Queues	****
Restaurants	***
The rest	
Scenery	***
Resort charm	***
Off-slope	**

- ➕ High altitude plus snowmaking ensures a long season and a good chance of snow to resort level
- ➕ Large choice of beginners' slopes
- ➕ Modern and improving lift system, with few queues
- ➕ Cheap by the standards of high resorts, with the bonus of duty-free shopping – a great place to treat yourself to new equipment
- ➕ Cosmopolitan, friendly village with some Alpine atmosphere
- ➕ Long, snowsure cross-country trails

- ➖ No difficult pistes
- ➖ Long airport transfers
- ➖ Links across the valley depend on buses, overcrowded at peak times
- ➖ Village is very long and straggling, and appears a bit tatty at first sight
- ➖ Few off-slope amenities
- ➖ Bleak, windy setting – often resulting in upper lifts being shut
- ➖ Not many really comfortable hotels bookable through UK tour operators
- ➖ Nightlife can disappoint

Livigno offers the unusual combination of a fair-sized mountain, high altitude and fairly low prices. Despite its vaunted duty-free status, hotels, bars and restaurants are not much cheaper than in other Italian resorts, but shopping is – there are countless camera and clothes shops. As a relatively snowsure alternative to the Pyrenees or to the smallest, cheapest resorts in Austria, Livigno seems attractive. But don't overlook the long list of drawbacks.

boarding *Livigno attracts a fair number of boarders and young people generally. Freestylers are well catered for, with a 100m half-pipe and boarder-cross in the Mottolino area, a fun-park in the Sitas-Fontane sector, and a couple of parks for beginners. Intermediates and carvers will enjoy the longer, higher runs (with plenty of natural hits), accessed mainly by cable-cars and chairs. Unfortunately, the excellent beginner slopes are mainly served by drags. Galli's pub is the liveliest place to hang out.*

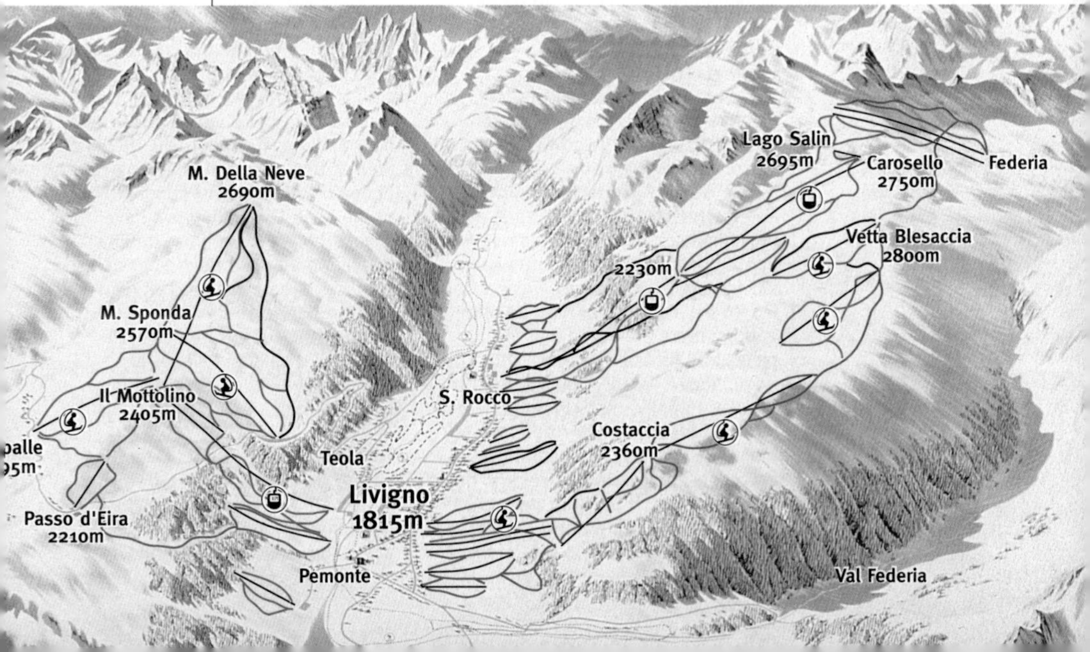

What's new

The antique chair-lift from Monte Sponda to the top of Monte della Neve is being replaced by a fast six-pack for 2000/01.

Plans to construct a lift from the new lift pass office up to the top of Monte della Neve still seem to be on the drawing board.

MOUNTAIN FACTS

Altitude	1815m-2800m
Lifts	31
Pistes	110km
Blue	42%
Red	46%
Black	12%
Artificial snow	30km
Recco detectors used	

LIFT PASSES

2000/01 prices in lire

Alta Valtellina
Covers all lifts in Livigno, Bormio (40km away), Val di Dentro (30km away) and Santa Caterina (50km away).

Main pass
1-day pass 52,000
6-day pass 265,000 £107
(low season 225,000)

Senior citizens
Over 60: 6-day pass 185,000

Children
Under 13: 6-day pass 185,000

Short-term passes
Afternoon pass for Livigno only.

Notes Day pass price is for Livigno lifts only. 6-day pass and over is valid for one day in St Moritz and Engadine.

Alternative passes
Livigno only pass for up to 2 days (adult 2-day 100,000).

The resort

Livigno is an amalgam of three villages in a wide, remote valley near the Swiss border – basically a string of hotels, bars and supermarkets lining a single long street. The buildings are small in scale and mainly traditional in style, giving the village a pleasant atmosphere. The original hamlet of San Antonio is the nearest thing Livigno has to a centre. Here, the main street and those at right angles linking it to the busy bypass road are nominally traffic-free; but this is Italy, so there is a petrol station right in the middle, spoiling the surroundings of the historic Alpina hotel. The road that skirts the 'traffic-free' area is constantly busy, and becomes intrusive in the northernmost hamlet of Santa Maria, 1km away. The third hamlet, San Rocco, is about 3km further south.

Lifts go to both sides of the valley slopes from the northern end of the resort, and you can get to the western slopes from San Rocco, too.

The mountain

The slopes appeal mainly to beginners and intermediates. They are extensive in comparison with many other cheap and cheerful destinations. The pass covers Bormio and Santa Caterina, an easy drive if the high pass is open, and a six-day pass covers a day in St Moritz – reached via a road tunnel.

THE SLOPES
Improved links

There are three areas, all of them suitable for moderate and leisurely intermediates, and two of them are reasonably well linked.

The ridge of **Mottolino** is reached by an efficient gondola from Teola, a tiresome walk or a short bus-ride from San Antonio. As well as north-west-facing runs back towards Livigno from Monte della Neve, the high point at 2690m, there are north-east-facing pistes and lifts on the other side of the ridge, above Trepalle, on the road to Bormio. Happily, the slow antique chair to from Monte Sponda to the top of Monte della Neve, which could leave you exposed and fiercely cold, is being replaced by a six-pack for 2000/01.

On the other side of the valley, closer to town, chairs in the middle of a row of nursery slopes take you up to **Costaccia** (2360m), where a long fast quad chair-lift goes along the ridge towards the **Carosello** sector. The linking runs between these sectors – particularly the one back from Carosello to the top of Costaccia – may involve energetic poling if the snow conditions and the wind are against you. Carosello is usually accessed by the optimistically named Carosello 3000 gondola at San Rocco, which goes up, in two stages, to 2750m. Most runs return towards the valley, but there are a couple on the back of the mountain, on the west-facing slopes of Val Federia – accessed by a double drag-lift.

Signposting is patchy and the piste map isn't always entirely accurate.

SNOW RELIABILITY
Very good, despite no glacier

Livigno's slopes are high (you can spend most of your time around 2500m), and with snow-guns on the lower slopes of Mottolino and Costaccia, the season is long.

FOR EXPERTS
Not recommended

The piste map shows a few black runs but these are not steep. There is off-piste to be done, but guidance would be needed and it wouldn't be cheap.

FOR INTERMEDIATES
Flattering slopes

Few pistes follow the fall line directly, so good intermediates looking for a challenge could be disappointed. Trying the off-piste may be the best option. The runs on the back of Carosello down to Federia are more challenging, and bumpy. Moderate intermediates have virtually the whole area at their disposal. The long run beneath the Mottolino gondola is one of the best. Leisurely types have several long cruises. Passo d'Eira-Teola, Monte della Neve-Sponda and Costaccia's easy runs are all enjoyable. The run beneath the Valandrea-Vetta chair, at the top of the Costaccia sector, is a splendid slope for confidence-building – 1.5km long, dropping only 260m.

FOR BEGINNERS
Excellent but scattered slopes

A vast array of nursery slopes along the sunny lower flanks of Costaccia, and other slopes around the valley, make Livigno excellent for novices –

although some of the slopes at the northern end are on the steep side. There are lots of longer runs suitable for fast learners and near-beginners.

CROSS-COUNTRY
Good snow, bleak setting
Long snowsure trails (40km in total) follow the valley floor, making Livigno a good choice, though the scenery is bleak. Staying in Santa Maria is best, being close to a nicer trail along the Val Federia. There is a specialist cross-country school, and the resort organises major cross-country races.

QUEUES
Few problems these days
Lift queues are not a problem apart from short delays for the Carosello gondola in peak season. Investment in fast new chairs at Carosello and Mottolino has rid the area of any long queues. A bigger problem is that strong winds often close the upper lifts, causing overcrowding lower down.

MOUNTAIN RESTAURANTS
More than adequate
Many reporters have commented on the consistent pleasures of the huts. Mottolino is the best bet for serious lunchers. The recently renovated refuge at the top of Mottolino is impressive with smart self- and table-service sections, a solarium and a crèche. And there are some more charming places lower down. The welcoming Tea del Vidal is at the base of the same sector. Costaccia's Tea del Plan is also pleasantly rustic and sunny, with good food. The self-service place at the top of Carosello is acceptable and Tea da Borch, in the trees lower down, serves great food in a Tirolean-style atmosphere, though the run down can be tricky. Lunch in the valley at the hotel Sporting (near the Carosello gondola station) is popular.

SCHOOLS AND GUIDES
Watch out for short classes
There are several schools. English is widely spoken, but recent reports are mixed. A common complaint is that most of the schools only offer short (two-hour) classes. One reporter notes that, due to local politics, the schools tend to stick to the specific areas in which they are based and are reluctant to ski the whole area. Reports certainly suggest that beginners spend too long on the nursery slopes.

FACILITIES FOR CHILDREN
Bring your own
The schools run children's classes, but (as so often in Italy) few have special arrangements for all-day care. Alì Babà's looks to be the best. We have one very positive report about the children's classes this year.

Staying there

In such a long village, with fragmented slopes, the location of accommodation can be important. Tour operator brochures are often a little vague. Beginners should avoid San Rocco (the Carosello end of town), because the school is a bus-ride away in San Antonio. The latter is the best all-round location now there is lift access via Costaccia to Carosello – though it is still quicker to take a bus out to the Carosello gondola. The local bus services, running on three colour-coded routes, are free but not very frequent. These are sometimes confusing, get overcrowded at peak times and stop early in the evening.

HOW TO GO
Lots of hotels, some apartments
Livigno has an enormous range of hotels and a number of apartments. There are some attractively priced catered chalets from UK operators.
Hotels Most of the hotels are small 2- and 3-star places, with a couple of 4-stars out of the centre.
((③ **Intermonti** Huge, modern 4-star with all mod cons (including a pool); some way from the village, on the slopes of Mottolino.
(② **Europa** One of the better 3-stars, within walking distance of the Mottolino gondola and village centre.
(② **Bivio** The only hotel in central Livigno with a pool.
(② **Steinbock** Nice little place, far from major lifts but only five minutes' walk from some nursery slopes.
(② **Teola** Quiet place, a little way up Mottolino slopes; recommended (despite small bedrooms) for good food and friendly staff.
(② **Larice** Stylish little 3-star B&B well placed for Costaccia lifts and slopes.
(② **Montanina** Good central 2-star.
(② **Gimea** Quiet B&B 300m from Carosello gondola.
(② **Camana Veglia** Charming old wooden chalet with popular restaurant, well placed in Santa Maria.
① **Silvestri** Well liked, reasonably handy

CHILDCARE
The Livigno school runs the Alì Babà kindergarten for children aged 3 and over. Lessons and lunches are available. The staff all speak English.

SCHOOLS/GUIDES
2000/01 prices in lire
Livigno Inverno/Estate
Classes 6 days
2hr: 9am-11am or 11am-1pm
6 2hr days: 135,000
Children's classes
Ages: from 4
6 2hr days
Private lessons
Hourly
50,000 for 1hr; each additional person 10,000

Azzurra Livigno
(1999/2000 prices)
Classes 6 days
2½hr: 10am-12.30pm
6 2½hr days: 160,000
Private lessons
Hourly
49,000 for 1hr

OTHER SCHOOLS

Livigno Italy
Livigno Soc Coop
Top Club Mottolino

GETTING THERE

Air Bergamo, transfer 5hr.

Rail Tirano (48km), Zernez (Switzerland, 28km); regular buses from station.

ACTIVITIES

Indoor Sauna, gym, body-building, games room, bowling, cinema
Outdoor Cleared paths, skating rink, snow-mobiles, horse-drawn sleigh rides, paragliding, mountaineering

TOURIST OFFICE

Postcode 23030
t +39 (0342) 996379
f 996881
info@aptlivigno.it
www.aptlivigno.it

LIVIGNO TO

Resorts this high and snowy aren't normally as competitive on price as Livigno ↓

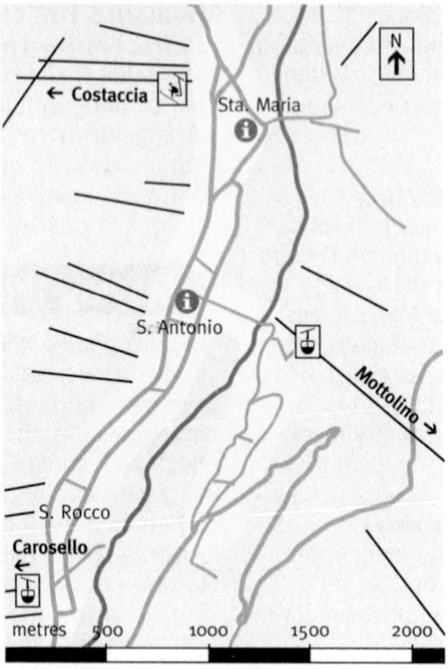

for lifts, schools and nightlife.
Self-catering All the big tour operators that come here have apartment options. Most are cheap and cheerful though some are more inconveniently situated than others.

EATING OUT
Value for money
Livigno has lots of traditional, unpretentious restaurants, many hotel-based. Hotel Concordia has some of the best cooking in town, and the Camana Veglia restaurant is superior to the hotel's 2-star rating. Mario's has one of the largest menus in town, serving seafood, fondue and steaks in addition to the ubiquitous pizza and pasta. The Bellavista is a charming little restaurant. Bait dal Ghet has excellent pizzas, the Rusticana wholesome, cheap food. Pesce d'Oro does 'high-quality Italian cuisine'.

APRES-SKI
Lively, but disappoints some
It's not that there isn't action in Livigno, but simply that the scene is quieter than some people expect in a duty-free resort. Also, the best places are dotted about, leaving the village lacking evening atmosphere. The San Rocco end of town is quiet. At tea-time many people return to their hotels for a quiet drink. But Tea del Vidal, at the bottom of Mottolino, gets lively. Galli's pub, in San Antonio (not to be confused with the Galli in San Rocco), is 'a full-on party pub', popular with Brits. After-dinner nightlife only gets going after 10pm. Galli's is again popular. Foxi's and Mario's are good video bars and the Kuhstall under the Bivio hotel has been recommended for its 'great atmosphere'. The Underground pub is a cheap and cheerful, noisy place. Kokodi and Cielo are the main discos.

OFF THE SLOPES
Disappointing but improving
Livigno does not have many off-slope amenities. Walks are uninspiring and there is no sports centre or public swimming pool. Trips to Bormio and St Moritz are popular things to do.

Madesimo 1545m

Respectable altitude, some traditional charm and low prices

WHAT IT COSTS

(2)

HOW IT RATES

The slopes

Snow	***
Extent	*
Experts	***
Intermediates	**
Beginners	***
Convenience	***
Queues	***
Restaurants	**

The rest

Scenery	***
Resort charm	**
Off-slope	*

What's new

Some serious money has been invested here of late. In 1996 an underground funicular from Campodolcino to Motta was opened, with four times the capacity of the original cable-car. And three covered fast quads were installed for 1999/2000 – two up to La Colmanetta above La Motta and another up to Montalto from the outskirts of town.

A snowtubing slope is being opened for 2000/01.

MOUNTAIN FACTS

Altitude	1545m-2880m
Lifts	15
Pistes	45km
Blue	29%
Red	54%
Black	17%
Artificial snow	25km
Recco detectors used	

TOURIST OFFICE

Postcode 23024
t +39 (0343) 53015
f 53782
aptmadesimo@provincia.so.it
www.madesimo.com

Madesimo's mountain is great for Italian weekenders. If you're planning a week, though, it's far from ideal: beginners will not find the progression to real runs easy, and others are likely to find the terrain limited.

THE RESORT

Madesimo sits in a remote, pretty side valley, a three-hour drive north from Bergamo that ends in a very dramatic hairpin-bend ascent. The village claims 17th-century origins and has old farm buildings housing restaurants to prove it. But the rest of the village is a piecemeal modern development. The delightful central church, narrow streets and little shops appear to be overlooked by an airport control tower (the hotel Torre).

THE MOUNTAIN

A two-stage cable-car is the primary lift to the **slopes**, with chair alternatives to the first section. Most runs return to the village, but the top station accesses pistes on the back side of the mountain. Or you can cut across the wide mountainside to the open slopes above Motta, now equipped with fast quads to deal with the weekend influx on the new funicular from the valley town of Campodolcino. The runs – facing almost east and west – get too much sun for **snow** to be very reliable.

Experts need the upper cable-car to be open for access to the famous Canalone, a long, sweeping run which is relatively shady and keeps its snow well – an easy black, now classed as an itinerary route. In theory there is also an itinerary of 1600m vertical to Fraciscio, next to Campodolcino.

The best **intermediate** runs also start from the top station, dropping over the back into the beautiful Val di Lei. The reds from the cable-car mid-station are very pleasant, passing through pretty woodland. The nursery slopes are fine, but **beginners** have few really easy pistes to graduate to: some of the blue runs are tricky.

There's a **snowboard** fun-park at Val di Lei. There's plenty of **cross-country** skiing dotted around the area, but you need a car to reach most of it.

There are weekend **queues** for the cable-car, but otherwise few lift delays.

The **mountain restaurants** are not particularly appealing.

The **ski school** has plenty of English-speaking instructors. The only **children's** facilities are in two of the hotels.

STAYING THERE

The village spreads for some way along both sides of a river, with the old centre and lifts on the eastern side, and many of the hotels and apartments on the other. The main lifts are at the southern end, the nursery slopes 500m away at the northern end.

A fair choice of **hotels** is available. The Emet is the only 4-star, but there are a number of 3-stars. The Cascata e Cristallo is a large, modern, multi-amenity place. The small modern Ferrè, with popular après-ski bar, is highly recommended by readers. The Andossi is attractive and friendly. You can also get **self-catering** apartments.

Eating out is one of Madesimo's delights. The Verosa is good value, atmospheric and popular for pizzas cooked over an open fire. Osteria Vecchia is a charming, traditional place. Dogana Vegia serves tasty specialities in a 17th-century building. The Cantinone, next to the hotel Andossi, is a smart white-walled bar-restaurant, with impressive wine list.

Après-ski is fairly quiet. There are several pleasant cafés for a tea-time cappuccino and cakes. The piano cellar bar in the Meridiana and the Ferrè are other focal spots.

There's not much to do **off the slopes** – walks and excursions.

Madonna di Campiglio 1520m

Extensive, easy slopes amid stunning scenery

WHAT IT COSTS

(4)

HOW IT RATES

The slopes

Snow	***
Extent	***
Experts	**
Intermediates	****
Beginners	****
Convenience	**
Queues	***
Restaurants	****
The rest	
Scenery	****
Resort charm	***
Off-slope	***

What's new

1999/2000 saw the opening of a 2km road tunnel bypassing the town centre and a new pedestrian-only zone. There was a new high-speed quad chair-lift at the Pinzola slopes, a few kilometres out of town. An electronic hands-free lift pass system was introduced, and new snowmaking installed.

For 2000/01 a new high-speed quad chair will go from the valley floor to the Pradalago area, easing queues at the junction with the slopes from Groste.

MOUNTAIN FACTS

Altitude	1550m-2505m
Lifts	51
Pistes	150km
Blue	44%
Red	40%
Black	16%
Artificial snow	71km
Recco detectors used	

TOURIST OFFICE

Postcode 38084
t +39 (0465) 442000
f 440404
info@campiglio.net
www.campiglio.net

Madonna is rather like Cortina – a pleasant Dolomite town with an affluent, almost exclusively Italian, clientele. In contrast Folgarida and Marilleva, with which Madonna shares its slopes, have a lot of British school and group visitors.

THE RESORT

Madonna is a spread-out, modern, but traditional-style town with a pedestrian-only centre, set in a prettily wooded valley beneath the impressive Brenta Dolomites. There is more development about 1km south, and a frozen lake between the two.

Madonna attracts an affluent, young, Italian clientele. It has almost as many 4-star hotels as 3-stars, and lots of smart shops. Many visitors potter about the village in the day, and promenading is an early evening ritual.

THE MOUNTAINS

The terrain is mainly intermediate, both above and below the tree line. There are three areas of linked **slopes** around Madonna – Cinque Laghi to the west, Pradalago to the north, and Passo Groste (the highest area, reaching 2505m) to the east. Pradalago is linked by lift and piste to Monte Vigo (2180m), where the slopes of Folgarida and Marilleva also meet. Purpose-built Pinzola is near Madonna and has a separate area of 30km of slopes.

Although many of the runs are sunny, they are at a fair altitude, and there has been hefty investment in snowmakers. As a result, **snow reliability** is reasonable.

Madonna's status as a World Cup racing resort should not lead **experts** to expect a lot. But the 3-Tre race course and the Spinale Direttissima are steep. Pista Nera, in the Folgarida section, can be a challenging mogul field. There is good off-piste.

Cinque Laghi, Madonna's racing mountain, is ideal for good **intermediates**. Early or timid intermediates will love the area and have no difficulty exploring most of the network, though the connection to Folgarida is a bit trickier. Groste and Pradalago have long, easy runs, though the former can get crowded.

It's a good resort for **beginners**, provided they don't mind using the erratic bus service out to the excellent nursery slopes at Campo Carlo Magno.

The World **Snowboarding** Championships are being held here in January 2001, so facilities for boarders are obviously excellent.

There are 30km of pretty **cross-country** trails through the woods.

Few **queues** develop except at the lift that links to Marilleva. The new lift to Pradalago from the Groste sector should solve the problems there.

The **mountain restaurants** are a highlight: good food, atmosphere and views. Cascina Zeledria, a little off-piste, will tow you back to the piste by snowcat and is recommended by a reporter, as is Bosh.

There are several **ski schools**, but some instructors don't speak English. The Nazionale and Rainalter schools have both been recommended.

STAYING THERE

The bus service is not free and doesn't run at night. There is a wide choice of **hotels**. The 3-star Christiania B&B and the 4-star Spinale are convenient. The luxury 4-star Lorenzetti is on the edge of town but with free transport. Some self-catering is sold by tour operators.

There are around 20 **restaurants** to choose from, mainly serving Italian dishes. Belvedere, Le Roi and Stube Diana are recommended.

Après-ski is quiet. Bars include the lovely Franz-Joseph Stube, Prince Pub, Bar Suisse and Bar Dolomiti. Des Alpes is the smartest club, with live music.

Off the slopes, window-shopping, skating and walking are popular.

Monterosa Ski 1640m

Extensive, attractive slopes, especially off-piste

WHAT IT COSTS

3

HOW IT RATES

The slopes

Snow	***
Extent	***
Experts	**
Intermediates	****
Beginners	**
Convenience	****
Queues	****
Restaurants	**

The rest

Scenery	****
Resort charm	***
Off-slope	*

What's new

For 1999/ 2000, there was a new chair-lift in Antagnod and more snowmaking.

For 2000/01, there are plans to replace the old cable-car from Alagna and install a new chair-lift. There will also be a new lift in the Gressoney area.

And Antagnod and Gressoney will both get new snow-parks for children.

MOUNTAIN FACTS

Altitude	1200m-3350m
Lifts	40
Pistes	200km
Blue	33%
Red	62%
Black	5%
Artificial snow	50km

Recco detectors used

TOURIST OFFICE

Postcode 11020
t +39 (0125) 303111
f 303145
kikesly@tin.it
www.monterosa-ski.com

Monterosa Ski is Italy's little-known and much less extensive answer to the Three Valleys. The pistes are mostly easy (and at present link only two of the three valleys, in fact), but they offer the same feeling of travelling around, amid impressive scenery – and there's excellent off-piste.

THE RESORTS

The main resorts on the UK package market are Gressoney, in the central valley, and Champoluc, to the west. Gressoney-la-Trinité is a quiet, neat little village a bus-ride from the outpost of Stafal at the head of the valley. Gressoney-St-Jean, a more substantial village (with shops) 5km down the valley, has its own good, if somewhat limited, slopes. Champoluc is a quiet, straggling village with little except a handful of hotels and shops. The main resort in the east valley is Alagna. Trips to Cervinia, La Thuile and Courmayeur are possible by car. Buses covered by the lift pass run frequently from La Trinité to Stafal and St Jean.

THE MOUNTAINS

The **slopes** of Monterosa Ski are relatively extensive, and very scenic. The pistes are almost all easy (and very well groomed), and the lifts are a mixture of slow, old ones and modern, high-speed chairs. The terrain is undulating and fragmented; runs are attractively varied, but many lifts serve only one or two pistes. The piste map is badly printed and unclear.

There are lifts out of La Trinité, but the main linking lifts are at the head of the valley, at Stafal. La Trinité's local slopes are centred on the sunny shelf of Gabiet (2300m). Chairs and drags serve the area below it, and above it a long 12-person gondola goes up to Passo dei Salati (3000m). From here, a well-used off-piste run makes the link to the Alagna valley. You can descend to Orsia, or Stafal (both in the Gressoney valley) with lifts up to the Colle Bettaforca (2705m), the link with the Champoluc valley. Champoluc's lifts are a fair walk or bus-ride from most hotels. Antagnod is a separate area of gentle slopes, good for families.

There are no special facilities for **snowboarders**. The **snow reliability** is good, thanks to altitude and extensive snowmaking. It ensured good piste cruising for reporters even during last season's Italian snow drought.

For **experts**, there's great off-piste from the high-points of the lift system in all three valleys, and some excellent heli-drops. Alagna is a cult area for expert off-piste. A guide is essential. Apart from that there's one black of 700m vertical and a testing black in Gressoney-St-Jean. At Alagna there is a long black run (roughly 7km for only 850m vertical) from the top of the cable-car at Punta Indren (3260m).

For **intermediates** who like to travel on easy, undemanding pistes, the area is great, with long runs from the ridges down into the valleys. There isn't much for more demanding intermediates.

The lower slopes at La Trinité are adequate for **beginners**, but the sunny area at Crest (1950m) in Champoluc and St Jean's nursery slopes are better.

There are long **cross-country** trails around St Jean, and shorter ones up the valley; Brusson, in the Champoluc valley, has the best trails in the area.

Only at weekends, when the hordes from Turin arrive, are there any **queues**. The **mountain restaurants** are good and cheap. The Chamois at Punta Jolanda, Bedemie on the way down to Gressoney from Gabiet, Del Ponte above Gabiet, Vieux Crest, above Champoluc, and the Guglielmina, Lys and Gabiet refuges are recommended.

We have had decent reports on the **ski schools** and an excellent one of the Gressoney mountain guides. There is a mini-club for **children** at St Jean.

STAYING THERE

If you want to be by the slopes and don't mind isolation, **accommodation** at Stafal is an option – but the Monboso has changed hands and is now 'awful'. At La Trinité reporters recommend the Jolanda Sport and the Dufour, by the slopes. At Champoluc the Castor is 'an absolute gem' and runs a mini-bus to the slopes.

Après-ski is very quiet and only picks up at weekends. Go elsewhere for **off-slope activities**.

Pila

1800m

Secret, snowsure slopes above cute, ancient town

WHAT IT COSTS

3

HOW IT RATES

The slopes	
Snow	***
Extent	**
Experts	**
Intermediates	****
Beginners	***
Convenience	***
Queues	****
Restaurants	***
The rest	
Scenery	***
Resort charm	***
Off-slope	**

What's new

For 1999/2000 there was a new fun-park for boarders and skiers, a new floodlit piste and a timed run.

MOUNTAIN FACTS

Altitude	1550m-2710m
Lifts	13
Pistes	70km
Blue	12%
Red	74%
Black	14%
Artificial snow	8km
Recco detectors used	

TOURIST OFFICE

Postcode 11100
t +39 (0165) 521148
f 521437
info@pila.it
www.pila.it

Pila is virtually unknown outside Italy. It offers a worthwhile surprise to those who pay it a visit. A fair-sized area of well-groomed, snowsure slopes rises around a purpose-built resort, linked by gondola to an old Roman town below.

THE RESORT

Pila is a modern, car-free, purpose-built, ski-in ski-out resort. It is high for an Italian resort at 1800m and its architecture is a mix of chalet-style buildings and large apartment blocks typical of a French resort. There are genuinely old buildings dotted around the area as well as new constructions.

Below the resort at 1370m, and connected by an 18-minute gondola ride or an 18km drive on a winding road, is the regional capital of Aosta, which was founded by the Romans in 25BC, and the city's historical guide lists 25 'important' historical buildings. The centre is traffic-free, with cobbled streets and alleys lined with shops and cafés (catering largely for local rather than tourist trade), a huge church and a central square.

The whole area is virtually unknown on the international market and the vast majority of visitors are Italian. Other resorts in the Aosta valley, such as Courmayeur, La Thuile and Cervinia, are within easy day-trip distance for those with a car and are covered by the Aosta valley lift pass.

THE MOUNTAINS

The terrain is an interesting mix of mainly red-graded **slopes** above and below the tree line, with stunning views from the top (2750m) from Mont Blanc in the west to the Matterhorn and Monte Rosa in the east. Chair-lifts and a cable-car fan out from the village and there are runs for all standards. It's a good resort for snowboarding, with mainly chair-lifts, wide pistes, good off-piste and a fun-park.

Most of the slopes are north- or north-east facing and above 2000m, so **snow reliability** is good. There's an increasing amount of artificial snow and grooming is rated 'top-notch'.

Experts will find Pila's slopes limited. There are steep pistes and mogul fields at the top and some good off-piste. But not huge amounts.

But the slopes are ideal for all standards of **intermediate** with great cruising on mainly red runs. A keen piste-basher could cover all the runs in a day or two, but there is more variety here than in nearby Courmayeur.

It's a good resort for **beginners**, with a nursery area right on your doorstep and wide, easy, well groomed runs to progress to.

There are only 8km of prepared **cross-country** trails but these are at altitude and so snowsure.

Except at weekends, when Italians in the know pour on to the slopes, there are few **queues**.

There are several good **mountain restaurants**. Our favourite was the rustic Lo Bautson (which means cow shed) – where the Penne all'Arrabiata was one of our best ever.

The only **ski school** reports we've had are of the Interski operation, which features mainly British instructors – satisfied customers only.

STAYING THERE

The choice is between staying in the resort and in Aosta. The former is more convenient for the skiing, the latter for old-town atmosphere, visiting other resorts and price. Most of the resort **hotels** and apartments are right on the slopes, and there are several pizza and pasta **restaurants** as alternatives to those in the hotels and apartments. **Après-ski** is quiet during the week, but at weekends the karaoke at the Bar Brimod and the KU disco liven up.

In Aosta most **hotels** are 3-star, near the centre and an easy 10-minute walk from the gondola. We stayed in the reasonable 4-star Europe. There's also a Holiday Inn. There's a good choice of **restaurants** which cater mainly for locals. **Après-ski** largely means bars (there are English and Irish pubs), but there are a couple of discos. And there's a casino in nearby St Vincent.

Off the slopes, Aosta is a far more interesting base than Pila for people not intending to hit the slopes. It has lots of shops, sights, bars and streets to wander around. And there are ice hockey matches to watch.

Sauze d'Oulx 1510m

'Suzy does it' still, but with more dignity than in the past

WHAT IT COSTS

3

HOW IT RATES

The slopes	
Snow	**
Extent	*****
Experts	**
Intermediates	****
Beginners	**
Convenience	**
Queues	***
Restaurants	***
The rest	
Scenery	***
Resort charm	**
Off-slope	*

- ⊕ Extensive and uncrowded slopes, great intermediate cruising
- ⊕ Linked into Milky Way network
- ⊕ Mix of open and tree-lined runs is good for all weather conditions
- ⊕ Entertaining nightlife
- ⊕ Some scope for off-piste adventures
- ⊕ One of the cheapest major resorts there is – and more attractive than its reputation suggests

- ⊖ Still lots of old lifts, making progress around the slopes slow
- ⊖ Erratic snow record – and still far from comprehensive snowmaking
- ⊖ Crowds at weekends
- ⊖ Brashness and Britishness of resort will not suit everyone
- ⊖ Very few challenging pistes
- ⊖ Mornings-only classes, and the best nursery slopes are at mid-mountain
- ⊖ Steep walks around the village, and an inadequate shuttle-bus service

If you're looking for a cheap holiday in a major resort with extensive slopes, you should have Sauze on your shortlist. In the 1980s it was prime lager-lout territory; but it always was a resort of two halves – young Brits on a budget alongside mature second-home owners from Turin – and these days the two halves seem to be much more in balance, especially at weekends. It still has lively bars and shops festooned in English signs, but sober Brits like you and us need not stay away. We like it more than we expect to – as do many reporters.

We are slightly haunted, though, by the memory of the bare slopes of our first visit, in the mid-1980s. Last season's thin cover brought it all back: Sauze is a resort that needs comprehensive snowmaking, and doesn't yet have it.

boarding *Sauze has good snowboarding slopes – it's got local tree-lined slopes (with space in the trees, too), high, undulating, open terrain, and links to other resorts in the Milky Way. But although it has a fair number of chair-lifts, there are also lots of drags – a serious drawback for novice riders. There's no park or pipe, but the amount and variety of terrain makes up for this. Sauze's mainly young visitors ensure lively, entertaining nightlife.*

SAUZE D'OULX TO

Yes, they are carrying their skis: this is not one of Sauze's most modern lifts but it is one of the main ways up the mountain ↓

What's new

Turin has been chosen to host the 2006 Olympic Winter Games; most of the Alpine events will be held at Sansicario and Sestriere, and freestyle competitions at Sauze d'Oulx.

Three fast quad chairs are now dotted around the slopes, including the main lift up to Sportinia. A fast quad has replaced the double drag-lift out of Sansicario towards Sauze d'Oulx. The old Basset drag, up to Col Basset, is now a quad chair-lift.

The snowmaking network is now automated, and there is more cover on the Soleil Boeuf slopes above Sansicario.

The resort

Sauze d'Oulx sits on a gentle mountain shelf facing north-west across the Valle di Susa. It's not immediately obvious, but Sauze has an attractive old core, with narrow, twisting streets and the occasional carved stone drinking fountain; houses have huge stone slabs serving as roof slates.

Most of the resort, however, is modern and undistinguished, made up of block-like hotels, relieved by the occasional chalet, spreading down the steep hillside from the foot of the slopes to the village centre and beyond. Despite the shift in clientele, the centre is still quite lively at night; the late-closing bars are usually quite full, and the handful of discos do brisk business at the weekend, at least.

Out of the bustle of the centre, where most of the bars and nightclubs are located, there are quiet, wooded residential areas full of secluded apartment blocks, and a number of good restaurants are also tucked out of the way of the front line. Chair-lifts go from the top of the village and from two points on its fringes. There's also a chair from nearby Jouvenceaux.

Traffic roams freely through the village, which can be congested morning and evening as cars vie for convenient parking spaces or the quickest way out of town. The roads become slushy and dirty during the day and icy and treacherous at night – hazardous, as there are few pavements. Buses (not covered by the lift pass) run around the resort, but the service is inadequate. Most reporters complain of them being too infrequent and too small, and therefore crowded. The service around lunch-time is particularly poor, and the service to Jouvenceaux stops inconveniently early, at 5.30pm. Although the buses do stop at predetermined points, there are no signs to show where they are.

Sauze is surrounded by trees, and on a good day the views across the Valle di Susa, to the towering mountains forming the border with France, can be impressive.

The mountains

Sauze's mountains provide excellent intermediate terrain. The piste grading fluctuates from year to year, if you believe the resort's map – and we're never sure we've caught up with the latest changes from blue to red and red to blue. But most reporters agree that many runs graded red or even black should really be graded blue; challenges are few and far between. (The same might be said of the whole extensive Milky Way area, of which Sauze is one extreme.)

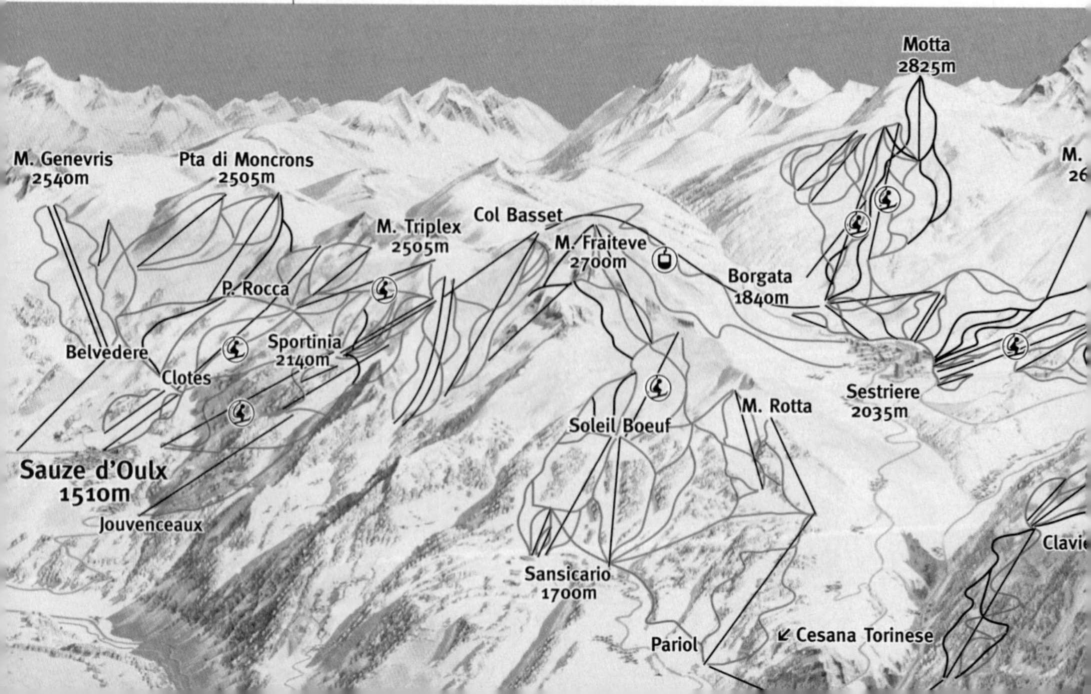

MOUNTAIN FACTS

Figures relate to the whole Milky Way area

Altitude	1390m-2825m
Lifts	97
Pistes	400km
Blue	12%
Red	67%
Black	21%
Artificial snow	75km

LIFT PASSES

1999/2000 prices in lire

La Via Lattea
Covers all lifts in Sauze d'Oulx, Sestriere, Sansicario, Cesana and Clavière.

Beginners Points book (80 points 140,000), with lifts costing from 1 to 12 points.

Main pass
1-day pass 49,000
6-day pass 265,000
(low season 215,000

Senior citizens
Over 60: 6-day pass 247,000

Children
Under 13: 6-day pass 247,000
Under 8: free pass

Short-term passes
Some single ascent passes and afternoon pass.

Notes Includes one free day in each of: Alpe-d'Huez, Les Deux Alpes, Serre-Chevalier and Puy-St-Vincent. One day extension for Montgenèvre (24,000). One day extension for Pragelato and Bardonecchia available.

Alternative passes
La Via Lattea VIP card also covers Montgenèvre and Pragelato.

THE SLOPES
Big and varied enough for most

Sauze's local slopes are spread across a broad wooded bowl above the resort, ranging from west- to north-facing. The main lifts are chairs, from the top of the village up to **Clotes** and from the western fringes to **Sportinia** – a sunny mid-mountain clearing in the woods, with a ring of restaurants and hotels (see Staying up the mountain) and a small nursery area.

The high point of the system is **Monte Fraiteve**. From here you can travel west on splendid broad, long runs to **Sansicario** – and on to chair-lifts near **Cesana Torinese** that link with **Clavière** and then **Montgenèvre**, in France, the far end of the Milky Way (both are reached more quickly by car).

You normally get to **Sestriere** from the lower point of Col Basset, on the shoulder of M Fraiteve. The alternative of descending the sunny slope from M Fraiteve itself has been reinstated after a few years of closure; but snow here is not reliable, which we're told is why the old lift from Sestriere up this slope was removed some years ago.

As in so many Italian resorts, piste marking, direction signing and piste map design are not taken particularly seriously.

The slopes of Montgenèvre and Sestriere are dealt with in separate chapters. If you have a car, you can go beyond Montgenèvre to Briançon, Serre-Chevalier and Bardonecchia.

SNOW RELIABILITY
Can be poor, affecting the links

The area is notorious for erratic snowfalls, and last season saw the area receive very little snow. Another problem is that many of the slopes get a lot of afternoon sun. At these modest altitudes, late-season conditions are far from reliable. Reporters have found icy, bare slopes at vital link points earlier in the season, too – particularly from M Fraiteve. There's snowmaking on a couple of slopes, notably the key home run from P Rocca via Clotes to the village, and more is in the pipeline.

FOR EXPERTS
Head off-piste

Very few of the pistes are challenging. The best slopes are at virtually opposite ends of Sauze's local area – a high, north-facing run from the shoulder of M Fraiteve, and the sunny slopes below M Moncrons. The main interest is in going off-piste. There are plenty of minor opportunities within the piste network, but the highlights are long, top-to-bottom descents of up to 1300m vertical from M Fraiteve, ending (snow permitting) at villages dotted along the valleys. The best-known of these runs (which used to be marked on the piste map) is the Rio Nero, down to the road near Oulx. When snow low down is poor, some of these runs can be cut short at Jouvenceaux or Sansicario.

FOR INTERMEDIATES
Splendid cruising terrain

The whole area is ideal for confident intermediates who want to clock up the kilometres. For the less confident, the piste map doesn't help because it picks out only the very easiest runs in blue – there are many others they could manage. The Belvedere and Moncrons sectors at the east of the area are served only by drags but offer some wonderful, uncrowded high cruising, some of it above the tree line.

The long runs down to Sansicario and down to Jouvenceaux are splendid, confidence-boosting intermediate terrain. Getting back to Sauze involves tackling some of the steepest terrain in the area – the black run from M Fraiteve to the Col Basset lifts at Malafosse. This presents a problem for many intermediates and is a serious shortcoming in the circuit. The run down to Sestriere gets a lot of sun but is worth it for the somewhat more challenging intermediate terrain on the opposite side of the valley. If conditions are too poor, you can always ride the gondola down.

At the higher levels, where the slopes are above the tree line, the terrain often allows a choice of route. Lower down are pretty runs through the woods, where the main complication can be route-finding. The mountainside is broken up by gullies, and pistes that appear to be quite close together may in fact have no easy connections between them.

FOR BEGINNERS
There are better choices

Sauze is not ideal for beginners: its village-level slopes are a bit on the steep side and the main nursery area is up the mountain, at Sportinia. Equally importantly, the mornings-only classes don't suit everyone.

CHILDCARE

The village kindergarten, Dumbo (0347 6913531), has English and Italian staff and takes children aged from 6 months to 6 years, from 8.30 to 5pm. You have to provide lunch, but it can be heated up.

SCHOOLS/GUIDES

1999/2000 prices in lire

Sauze Sportinia
Classes 6 days
3hr: 10am-1pm
6 3hr days: 250,000
Children's classes
Ages: from 6
6 3hr days: 250,000
Private lessons
Hourly
50,000 for 1hr

Sauze d'Oulx
Classes 6 days
3hr: 10am-1pm
6 3hr days: 220,000
Children's classes
Ages: from 6
6 3hr days: 220,000
Private lessons
Hourly
52,000 for 1hr

Sauze Project
Italian-speaking only school.

FOR CROSS-COUNTRY
Severely limited, even with snow

There is very little cross-country skiing, and it isn't reliable for snow.

QUEUES
Slow lifts the biggest problem

There can be 10-minute waits at Sportinia when school classes are setting off or immediately after lunch, but otherwise the system has few bottlenecks. The main problem with the network is that, despite the recent introduction of three high-speed quads, most of the lifts are ancient and rather slow. Amazingly, they haven't yet replaced the old lift to Clotes shown on page 353, which requires you to carry your skis and hit the ground running at the top. Although it links to a fast quad which takes you the rest of the way to the top, this lift is still hugely inadequate for such an important link, making the uplift seem interminable. Breakdowns on elderly drag-lifts may also be a nuisance.

MOUNTAIN RESTAURANTS
Some pleasant possibilities

Restaurants are numerous and generally pleasant, though few are particularly special (and a recent Sestriere-based reporter was unimpressed). One place that's certainly worth picking out is the hotel Capricorno, at Clotes – one of the most civilised and appealing lunch-spots in the Alps. It is not cheap, though. There are more modest mid-mountain restaurants across the mountainside, with the main concentration at Sportinia, where service is friendly (though plastic cutlery detracts from the experience). The Capannina and the Belvedere are popular. A reporter described the Ciao Pays, at the top of the Clotes chair-lift, as 'the real thing', and others have recommended the Chalet Clot Bourget.

SCHOOLS AND GUIDES
Tuition variable, large classes

We always used to get good reports about the schools here, but more recent reporters have found a lack of good English spoken and large classes. Some found the tuition satisfactory, others were disappointed. Classes are only half a day, but last three hours. Reporters on the school in Sansicario have found the instruction enthusiastic and useful, with good spoken English.

FACILITIES FOR CHILDREN
Tour operator alternatives

Although there is a resort kindergarten, you might want to look in to the crèche facilities offered by some of the major UK tour operators in the chalets and chalet hotels that they run here – Crystal and Neilson, for example.

Staying there

Most of the hotels are reasonably central, but the Clotes lift is at the top of the village, up a short but steep hill, and the Sportinia chair is an irritatingly long walk beyond that. There is a shuttle-bus, but it is infrequent and gets very crowded in the morning.

HOW TO GO
Packaged hotels dominate

All the major mainstream operators offer hotel packages here, but there are also a few chalets.

Hotels Simple 2-star and 3-star hotels form the core of the holiday accommodation, with a couple of 4-stars and some more basic places.

(((3 **Capricorno** Small, charming; at Clotes (see Staying up the mountain).

(((3 **La Torre** Cylindrical landmark 200m below centre. Excellent rooms and buffet-style food; free wine; mini-buses to lifts.

((2 **Hermitage** Neat chalet-style hotel in about the best spot for the slopes – beside the home piste from Clotes.

((2 **Stella Alpina** Right at the foot of the slopes, just below the Clotes chair-lift. Well run – friendly and lively (and home to the popular New Scotch Bar).

((2 **Gran Baita** Comfortable place in quiet, central backstreet, with excellent food and good rooms, some with spectacular sunset views from their balconies.

((2 **Biancaneve** Pleasant, with smallish rooms. Close to the centre.

((2 **Des Amis** Down in Jouvenceaux, but close to bus stop; small, simple hotel run by Anglo-Italian couple.

Self-catering There are apartments and chalets available, some through UK tour operators.

EATING OUT
Caters for all tastes and pockets

Typical Italian banquets of five or six courses can be had in the upmarket Don Vincenzo and Il Cantun restaurants. The Italian chef at the Del Falco cooks a particularly good three-course 'skiers' menu'. In the old town,

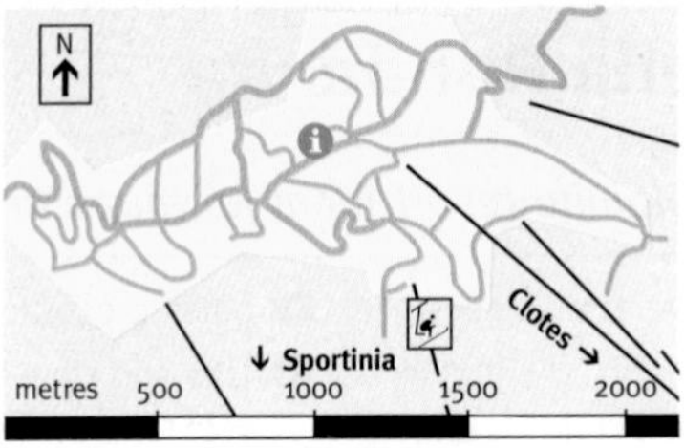

ACTIVITIES

Indoor Bowling, cinema, sauna, massage
Outdoor Artificial skating rink, torchlit descents, heli-skiing, ice climbing, snow-shoeing

GETTING THERE

Air Turin, transfer 2hr.
Rail Oulx (5km); frequent buses.

TOURIST OFFICE

Postcode 10050
t +39 (0122) 858009
f 850700
sauze@montagnedoc.it
www.montagnedoc.it

Del Borgo serves perhaps the best pizza in town, and has a very friendly atmosphere – though Kaly's pizzeria is recommended for 'that 5am snack'. Near Del Borgo is La Griglia, which is full of character and does a good steak. Il Lampione is the place to go for 'pub grub' – good-value Chinese, Mexican and Indian food. We have a report that Sugo's provides delicious, filling and economic fare. Le Pecore Nere has also received good reviews. A number of reporters have suggested booking restaurants in advance to avoid disappointment.

APRES-SKI
Suzy does it with more dignity

Once favoured almost solely by large groups of youngsters, some of whom were very rowdy, the number and atmosphere of Sauze's bars now impress reporters young and old.

The Assietta terrace is popular for catching the last rays of the sun at the end of the day. The more discerning then move on to the excellent New Scotch Bar, while nearby the once-famous Andy Capp's Pub still attracts punters looking for a 'home from home'. Il Lampione, in the old town, is highly recommended for crêpes.

After dinner, more places warm up. One of the best is the smart, atmospheric cocktail bar Moncrons, which holds regular quiz nights. We also like the late-night Osteria, under Andy Capp's, which is popular with Italians and workers. The Cotton Club provides good service, directors' chairs, video screen and draught cider. The Rock Café has as many Italian clients as Brits. Upstairs is popular with an older crowd, and downstairs has karaoke. Paddy McGinty's is especially popular with resort staff and has a lively atmosphere. Gran Trun has live music and reminded us of a Majorcan barbecue venue, with bottles on the wall and white stucco decor. The Derby is nice for a quiet drink in a relaxed setting. Of the discos, Il Bandito is a walk away, and popular with Italians. Schuss runs theme nights and drink promotions – entrance is normally free.

Tour reps organise activities, including torchlit descents, bowling and 'broomball' on the ice rink.

OFF THE SLOPES
Go elsewhere

Sauze is not a particularly pleasant place in which to while away the days if you don't want to hit the slopes. Shopping is limited, there are no gondolas or cable-cars for pedestrians and there are few off-slope activities. Turin or Briançon are worth a visit.

STAYING UP THE MOUNTAIN
'You pays your money ... '

In most resorts, staying up the mountain is an amusing thing to do and is often economical – but usually you pay the price of accepting simple accommodation. Here, the reverse applies. The 4-star Capricorno, up at Clotes, is one of the most comfortable hotels in Sauze, certainly the most attractive and by a wide margin the most expensive. It's a charming little chalet beside the piste, with a smart restaurant and terrace (a very popular spot for a good lunch on the mountain) and only eight bedrooms.

Not quite in the same league are the places up at Sportinia. Crystal is running a couple of them now as jumbo chalets. The company also has a smaller chalet here. Reporters who stayed here enjoyed the isolation and easy access to the slopes – but you can't get down to town after 4pm, making it more suitable for groups providing their own entertainment or those for whom nightlife matters little.

Sansicario 1700m

If any resort is ideally placed for exploration of the whole Milky Way, it is Sansicario. It is a modern, purpose-built, self-contained but rather soulless little resort, mainly consisting of apartments linked by monorail to the small shopping precinct. The 45-room Rio Envers is a reasonably comfortable, quite expensive hotel. Visitors recommend the Chalmettes for its views and food at lunch-time, and the Enoteca in the evening for fondue and grappa. The whole place will doubtless get a bit of a boost from the 2006 Olympics – downhill and super G races will be held here.

Selva/Sella Ronda 1565m

Spectacular Dolomite resort ideal for intermediates

WHAT IT COSTS

4

HOW IT RATES

The slopes

Snow	****
Extent	*****
Experts	***
Intermediates	*****
Beginners	****
Convenience	***
Queues	***
Restaurants	****

The rest

Scenery	*****
Resort charm	***
Off-slope	***

What's new

The Sella Ronda lift system has been radically improved in recent years.

For 2000/01 two new quad chairs are due to replace old ones towards Corvara from Arabba, speeding up the anti-clockwise Sella Ronda circuit. And a new gondola will replace an old single-person chair in Colfosco. In Canazei, two chairs on Belvedere are being upgraded: to a six-pack and a quad.

For 1999/2000 gondolas replaced the cable-cars from Ortisei to Seceda and Alpe di Siusi.

There's still room for improvement, however – we have reports of 45-minute waits for the Fodom chair up to Passo Pordoi, for example.

The Marmolada glacier lifts will be included in the Dolomiti Superski pass for the 2000/01 season – rather than having to pay a supplement to use them.

- ⊕ Vast network of connected slopes – suits intermediates particularly well
- ⊕ Stunning, unique Dolomite scenery
- ⊕ Superb snowmaking and grooming
- ⊕ Jolly mountain huts with good food
- ⊕ Many new lifts with only a few bad Sella Ronda circuit bottlenecks left now
- ⊕ Good nursery slopes
- ⊕ Excellent value

- ⊖ Small proportion of tough runs
- ⊖ Lifts and slopes can be crowded, especially on Sella Ronda circuit
- ⊖ High proportion of short runs, not so many long ones
- ⊖ Rather unattractive, straggly village, with little 'ski-in, ski-out' convenience
- ⊖ Erratic snow record; slopes vulnerable to warm weather
- ⊖ Main language is German, which detracts from jolly Italian feel

The Sella Ronda has been revolutionised over the last few years by heavy investment in both the lift system and artificial snowmaking. Both are now among the best and most extensive in Europe. Add extraordinarily picturesque Dolomite scenery, a lift pass that covers over 460 lifts and 1200km of runs, cheap Italian prices and jolly mountain refuges, and you have a compelling case for visiting.

Only experts who find a lack of challenging runs frustrating will be disappointed with the slopes. If what you want is a feeling of travelling around great scenery, there's little to beat the Sella Ronda – a trip around the Gruppo Sella massif, easily covered in a day by an average intermediate. On the way round you will hit many separate local slopes worth exploring – but also crowds and queues.

If you don't want to stay in Selva, there are plenty of smaller, quiet, attractive places on the circuit to base yourself in.

boarding *Selva is one of the few Italian resorts to build a half-pipe and fun-park; but they are away from the main pistes, by the chair-lift leading to the summit of the Seceda. Reporters have mentioned another, on the Sella Ronda circuit at Pordoi. The main lifts out of Selva are all gondolas or chairs and you can do the Sella Ronda clockwise using only one drag – the anti-clockwise route has more. The area mainly suits beginners and intermediates, with little to challenge experts. And there are some frustratingly flat sections where you have to scoot or walk. There are enough lively bars to have a good time in the evenings.*

The resort

Selva is a long roadside village, almost merged with the next village of Santa Cristina. It suffers from traffic but has traditional-style architecture and an attractive church. And it enjoys a lovely setting under the impressive pink-tinged walls of the Gruppo Sella massif and Sassolungo. The area is famed for wood carvings – you'll see them all over.

Despite its World Cup fame (as Val Gardena, the name of the valley) and animated atmosphere, Selva is neither upmarket nor brash. It's a good-value, lively but civilised family resort.

Gondolas rise in two directions. One east from the top of the nursery slopes towards Colfosco and Corvara and the clockwise Sella Ronda route. The other takes you south from the village to Ciampinoi and the anti-clockwise route.

The free buses that run around are usually packed. Some reporters prefer to share cheap taxis. Others suggest a beer or two before going back to the chalet, to let the scrum subside.

For many years the area was under Austrian rule, and reporters admire the Tirolean charm of the resort. German is the main language, not Italian, and most visitors are German, too. Selva is also known as Wolkenstein and the Gardena valley as Gröden. The local dialect is Ladino, which has resisted being absorbed into German or Italian.

MOUNTAIN FACTS

Altitude	1235m-2520m
Lifts	82
Pistes	175km
Blue	30%
Red	60%
Black	10%
Artificial snow	120km
Recco detectors used	

The mountain

The slopes cover a vast area, all amid stunning scenery and practically all ideally suited to intermediates who don't mind shortish runs. Set off for the day to explore a local area that takes your fancy. Or do the Sella Ronda circuit – see page 361. But there are different piste maps for different areas, and a common complaint is that they are inadequate. Piste marking and signing also come in for some flak. The useful contour map of the whole Sella Ronda circuit is by far the best map to use if you are doing the circuit.

It's an easy road trip to Cortina, covered by the Dolomiti Superski pass.

THE SLOPES
High mileage piste excursions

A gondola and parallel-running chair go up from Selva to **Ciampinoi**, from where several pistes, including the famous World Cup Downhill run, spread out across the mountain and lead back down to Selva, **Santa Cristina** and **Plan de Gralba**. From Plan de Gralba, you can head off towards **Passo Sella**, **Canazei** and the rest of the Sella Ronda.

Across the valley from the Ciampinoi gondola is a chair that links with the Dantercëpies gondola. This accesses the Sella Ronda in the opposite direction or you can return to Selva on the Ladies Downhill. From the top you head down to **Colfosco**, then lifts link with **Corvara**, and you go on to **Arabba** and the rest of the Sella Ronda.

There are several linked areas that are not directly on the Sella Ronda circuit that are worth exploring. The biggest is the **Alta Badia** area to the west of Corvara, from which you can get down to **San Cassiano** and **La Villa**.

Local to Selva is the **Seceda** area, accessed by a gondola a bus-ride from town. You can head back down to the bottom of here or to **Ortisei**. And from Ortisei a cable-car goes up the other side of the valley to **Alpe di Siusi** and its virtually flat plateau of easy runs, cross-country and walks.

CORVARA TO

You'll find stunning scenery and delightful rifugios everywhere – shame about the local dress sense though ↓

SNOW RELIABILITY
Excellent when it's cold

The slopes are not high. There's very little above 2200m; most are between 1500m and 2000m. And natural snowfalls are erratic – the last two seasons have been especially poor. But we have experienced excellent pistes here in times of severe natural snow shortage – the area has invested heavily in snowmaking and now has one of the largest capacities in Europe, covering 120km of runs. Most areas have snow-guns on the main runs to the resorts, and almost all Selva's local pistes are well endowed. Good piste grooming adds to the effect.

Problems arise only in poor snow years when temperatures are too high to make snow. But the Marmolada glacier near Arabba is open most of the winter. A recent reporter found the snow excellent, but it 'was worth going to for the spectacular views rather than for the typically boring glacier slopes. The lifts are clearly ancient ... and we were astonished at the lack of infrastructure – no loo, restaurant, or panorama map of peaks'.

FOR EXPERTS
A few good runs

In general experts may find the region too tame, especially if they're looking for lots of steep challenges or moguls.

Arabba has the best steep slopes (and snow). North-facing blacks and reds from Porta Vescovo back to Arabba are served by an efficient high-capacity gondola and are great fun. The Val Gardena World Cup piste, the 'Saslonch', is one of several steepish runs between Ciampinoi and both Selva and Santa Cristina. Unlike many World Cup pistes it is kept in racing condition for Italian team practices, but it is open to the public much of the time. It's especially good in January, when it's not too crowded. The unpisted trail down to Santa Cristina,

LIFT PASSES

2000/01 prices in lire

Dolomiti Superski
Covers 460 lifts and 1200km of piste in the Dolomites, including all Sella Ronda resorts.

Main pass
1-day pass 63,000
6-day pass 313,000
(low season 276,000)

Senior citizens
Over 60: 6-day pass 250,000

Children
Under 16: 6-day pass 219,000

Alternative pass
Val Gardena pass covers all lifts in Selva Gardena, S Cristina, Ortisei and Alpe di Siusi, and ski-bus between Selva and Ortisei.

accessed from the the Florian chair on Alpe di Siusi, is not difficult, but pleasantly lonely.

Overall, off-piste is limited because of the sheer-drop nature of the tops of the mountains in the Dolomites, but for the daring there is excitement to be found with a guide. The run from Sass Pordoi (the highest point around at 2950m) to Colfosco ends in a spectacular narrow descent through the Val de Mesdi. For the not so daring, a trip in the terrifying cable-car is worth it for the view.

FOR INTERMEDIATES

A huge network of ideal runs

The Sella Ronda region is famed for easy slopes. For early or timid intermediates, the runs from Dantercëpies to Colfosco and Corvara, and over the valley from there in the Alta Badia, are superb for cruising and confidence-boosting. They're easy to reach from Selva, but returning from Dantercëpies may be a little daunting. Riding the gondola down is an option.

Nearer to Selva, the runs in the Plan de Gralba area are gentle. The Alpe di Siusi runs above Ortisei are rather flat, but a recent visitor found this area 'a much underrated winter wonderland. It took our breath away for scenery and quiet, good blue runs'.

Average intermediates have a very large network of suitable pistes, though there are few long runs. The beautiful swoop down the far side of the Seceda massif from Cuca to Ortisei is a favourite with recent reporters. The Plan de Gralba area runs either side of the Florian chair on Alpe di Siusi, and the main pistes to San Cassiano and La Villa in the Alta Badia area are other recommended cruises.

Several reporters also enjoyed the area above Canazei, below the Belvedere: 'Well served with efficient lifts, and good snow. The red to Lupo Bianco is an especially beautiful run through the trees.'

The runs back down to the valley direct from Ciampinoi are a bit more challenging, as are the descents from Dantercëpies to Selva. And of course

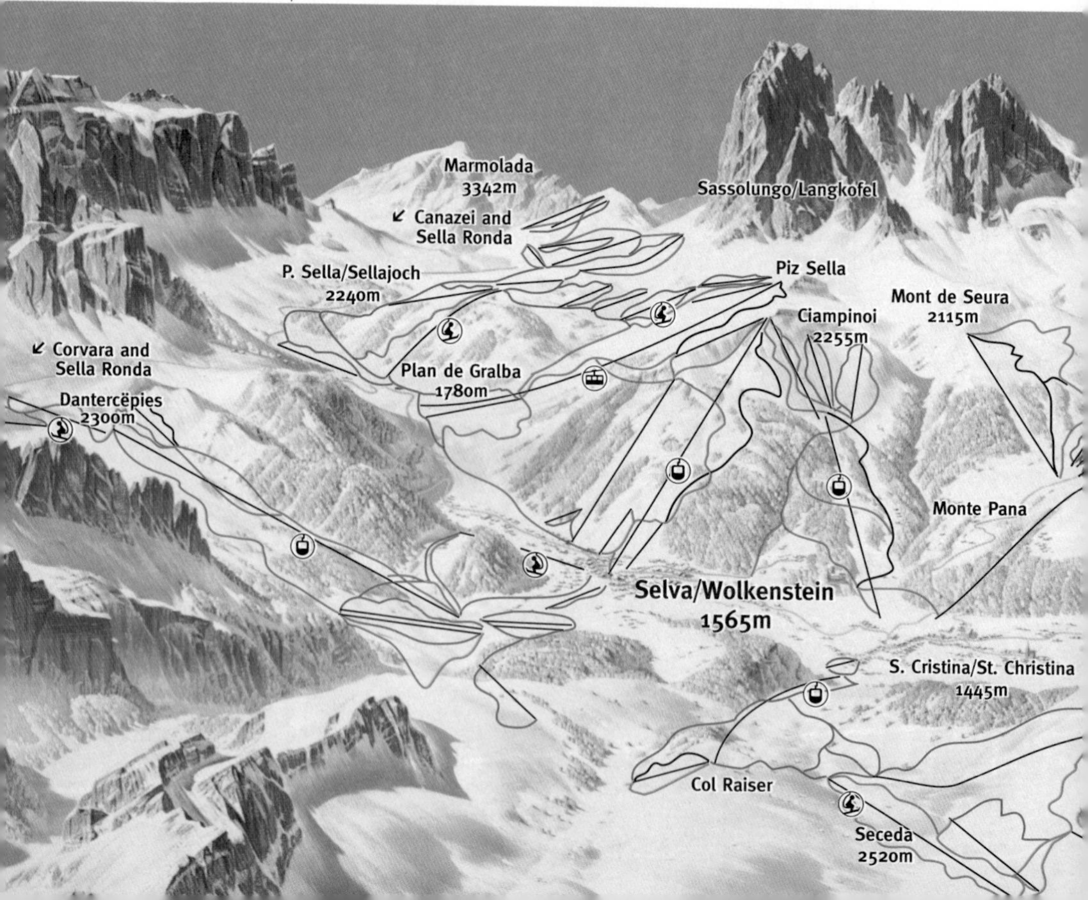

most intermediates will want to do the Sella Ronda circuit at least once during a week – see feature panel.

The spectacular 'Hidden Valley' is also worth a visit. It's reached via a cable-car at Lagazuoi to which you get a bus or shared taxi from Armentarola. See the Cortina chapter for details.

FOR BEGINNERS
Great slopes, but ...
Near-beginners have numerous runs, and the village nursery slopes are excellent – spacious, convenient, and kept in good condition. There are splendid gentle runs to progress to. Visiting beginners have thoroughly recommended the area in the past. However, we have varying reports about the school – see 'Schools and Guides' section.

FOR CROSS-COUNTRY
Beautiful trails
There are over 70km of trails all enjoying wonderful scenery. The 12km trail up the Vallunga-Langental valley is particularly attractive, with neck-craning views all around. The largest section of trails (40km) has the

THE SELLA RONDA

The Sella Ronda is one of the world's classic circuits for intermediates and above. The journey around the Sella massif, among spectacular Dolomite scenery, is easily managed in a day by even an early intermediate. We've done it in just three and a half hours plus some diversions and hut stops.

The slopes you travel along are almost all easy and take in Colfosco, Corvara, Arabba and Canazei. You can do the circuit clockwise by following very clearly marked orange arrows and direction boards or anti-clockwise by following the green boards. We prefer the clockwise route which is slightly quicker and avoids a tedious series of drag lifts from Colfosco towards Selva. Reporters agree this way is also better for interesting slopes. There's a good free map of the Sella Ronda available, complete with contour lines so you get a good idea of how the land lies. You can also buy a bigger scale one for around 7000 lire.

The whole journey involves around 23km of skiing or boarding and around 14km of lift riding. The lifts take a total of about two hours (plus any queuing). But be warned: it can be crowded (both on the pistes and on the lifts) on busy days, with hordes of people having the same idea as you. 'It's a bit of a slog,' said one reporter. Set out early and, if possible, choose low season or a Saturday.

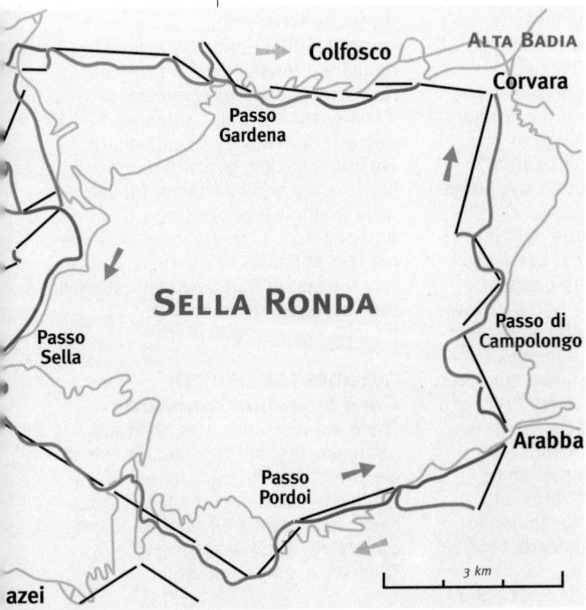

Another reporter found the circuit 'boring, but a good way to get to other areas'. To make the journey more enjoyable we suggest experts take time out for some diversions.

The long runs down from Ciampinoi to Santa Cristina and Selva, from Dantercëpies to Selva, from the top of the Boe gondola back down to Corvara and the runs from the top of the Arabba gondola are particularly entertaining. Take in all those in a day round the circuit and you'll have had a good day!

Intermediates could take time out to explore the off-the-circuit Alta Badia area. Groups of different standards can do the circuit and arrange to meet along the way. There are plenty of welcoming rifugios at which to take a break.

SCHOOLS/GUIDES

1999/2000 prices in lire

Selva Gardena
Classes 6 days
6 3hr days: 230,000
Children's classes
Ages: 4 to 12
6 6hr days: 365,000 (includes lunch)
Private lessons
Hourly
55,000 for 1hr for 1 person; each additional person 10,000

Ortisei
Classes 6 days
4 6hr days: 200,000
Children's classes
Ages: from 3
5 6hr days: 355,000
Private lessons
Hourly
55,000 for 1hr for 1 person; each additional person 10,000

S Cristina
Classes 6 3hr days: 215,000
Children's classes
Ages: from 2½
6 4hr days: 230,000
Private lessons
Hourly
54,000 for 1hr for 1 person; each additional person 10,000

CHILDCARE

The ski schools run a kindergarten for children aged 1 to 4, with skiing available for the older children. Those attending proper ski school classes can be looked after all day.

advantage of being at altitude, running between Monte Pana and Seiseralm, and across Alpe di Siusi.

QUEUES
Much improved: a few problems

New lifts have vastly improved the area and bottlenecks are no longer as common, except in peak periods. That said, we still get complaints about parts of the Sella Ronda circuit. And you may find the crowds on the pistes worse than the queues for the lifts.

In busy periods the chair-lifts from Arabba in both directions have been a problem (though the proposed new lifts towards Corvara should ease the anti-clockwise queues), as have the long, cold drag-lifts from Colfosco to Selva. And recent reporters were surprised to find the slow T-bar from Campolongo to Bec de Roces still chugging along.

MOUNTAIN RESTAURANTS
One of the area's highlights

Our reporters are unanimous in their praise for the mountain huts – there are lots of them all over the area, and virtually all of them offer good food, atmosphere and value for money, plus you can find live music for a lunchtime bop if required.

In Val Gardena the Panorama is a small, cosy, rustic suntrap at the foot of the Dantercëpies drag. On the way down to Plan de Gralba from Ciampinoi, the Vallongia Rolandhütte is tucked away on a corner of the piste. In the Plan de Gralba area the top station of the cable-car does excellent pizza slices; the Comici is atmospheric with a big sun terrace. Further west the Sangon, above Col Raiser, 'has bags of atmosphere. It's cosy on bad days, and it's lovely to sit out on the terrace in the sun'.

The triumvirate of little huts in the Colfosco area – Forcelles, Edelweiss and Pradat – are all very pleasant.

At Alta Badia the Piz Sorega above San Cassiano gets very busy. Nearby Las Vegas is smaller and more atmospheric – lots of stuffed creatures, if you like that sort of thing. Pride of place must go to Trappers' Home – a Wild West mountain hut with totem pole, teepee, country music and a Harley Davidson in the basement. Chertz above Passo di Campolongo has great views of Marmolada (and a beautiful big St Bernard).

Around Arabba Bec de Roces and Col de Burz are both suntraps. The rifugio at the top of the Porta Vescovo lifts has been recommended as 'modern, clean, bright, efficient and with excellent food'. Capanna Bill, on the long run to down Malga Ciapela, has stunning views of the Marmolada glacier.

On Alpe di Siusi the rustic Sanon Refuge gets a good review, particularly since 'the barman came out to serenade us with his Tirolean accordion'. And the Wilhelms Hutte at the top of the Florian chair has 'superb views under Sassopiatto'.

Above Canazei there are at least six huts dotted around the Belvedere bowl. Lower down, Lupo Bianco is a notable rendezvous point and suntrap. As well as restaurants, there are lots of little snow bars for a quick grappa.

SCHOOLS AND GUIDES
Mixed views

If you are lucky enough to be in a suitable group, Selva has a good reputation for standards of tuition. However, one visitor commented, 'Classes were too big. Although instructors were very friendly and English speaking, overall I didn't improve my skiing.' Others, though, were 'well pleased', as 'class numbers dropped from 11 to 7'. Some beginners felt lost in a class of 15 where English was the last of four languages spoken, but subsequently enjoyed private lessons.

FACILITIES FOR CHILDREN
Good by Italian standards

There are comprehensive childcare arrangements, but German and Italian are the main languages here and English is not routinely spoken. That said, in the past we have had reports of very enjoyable lessons and of children longing to return.

→ Marks out of 10 for Dolomite scenery? We'd give it 10 – simply the best

CANAZEI TO

GETTING THERE

Air Verona, transfer 3hr; Bolzano, transfer 45min; Innsbruck, transfer 3hr.

Rail Chiusa (27km), Bressanone (35km), Bolzano (40km); frequent buses from station.

Staying there

Selva is the biggest and liveliest of the places to stay right on the Sella Ronda circuit. Ortisei is the administrative centre of the Val Gardena – pretty, and more of a complete community – but it is not so convenient for the slopes. For a brief description of the other villages on or near the circuit, see the end of this chapter.

In Selva itself, the most convenient position is near one of, or between, the two main gondolas. There is a free, regular bus service throughout the valley until early evening, but reporters say this can get very oversubscribed.

HOW TO GO
Not many Brits

Selva and the Sella Ronda area have made a recent comeback in British tour operators' programmes – but there are still relatively few Brits around. There is a fair choice of catered chalets, and some of the properties are good quality, with en suite bathrooms.

Hotels There are 10 4-stars, over 30 3-stars and numerous lesser hotels. Few of the best hotels are well positioned.

(((3 **Gran Baita** Large, luxurious sporthotel, with lots of mod cons including indoor pool. A few minutes' walk from centre and lifts.

(((3 **Aaritz** Best-placed 4-star, opposite the gondola, and with an open fire.

((2 **Astor** Family-run chalet in centre, below nursery slopes. Good value.

((2 **Continental** 3-star situated right on the nursery slopes.

((2 **Olympia** Well positioned 3-star.

((2 **Solaia** 3-star chalet, superbly positioned for lifts and slopes.

Self-catering There are plenty of apartments to choose from – some more convenient than others. We have had excellent reports of the Villa Gardena and Isabelle apartments over the years (the latter are attached to the Gran Baita hotel).

EATING OUT
Plenty of good-value choices

Selva offers the best of both Austrian and Italian food at prices to suit all pockets. The higher-quality restaurants are mainly hotel-based. The Antares and Laurin have especially good menus while the Olympia is renowned for its fondues. The Bellavista is recommended for good pasta and Costabella for 'excellent Tirolean specialities'. Da Rino has 'excellent pizza and good wine'.

APRES-SKI
Above average for a family resort

Nightlife is lively and informal, though the village is so scattered there is little on-street atmosphere. La Stua is an après-ski bar on the Sella Ronda route, with accordion music later on. The Igloo at Plan de Gralba is also 'good fun for those first few beers before heading back to Selva in virtual darkness'. For a civilised early drink try the good value ski-school bar at the base of the Dantercëpies piste. Or the Costabella is cosy, serving good gluwein. Café Mozart on the main street is highly recommended for ice cream and cakes.

Ardent après-skiers should visit the Posta Zirm in Corvara. 'The ski-boot tea

ACTIVITIES

Indoor Swimming, sauna, solaria, bowling alley, squash, artificial skating rink, ice hockey, museum, indoor golf, concerts, cinema, billiards, tennis, climbing wall, fitness centre
Outdoor Sleigh rides, torch-light descents, snow-shoeing, toboggan runs, mountain biking, paragliding, horse-riding, extensive cleared paths around Selva Gardena and above S Cristina and Ortisei

TOURIST OFFICE

Postcode 39047
t +39 (0471) 792277
f 792235
info@val-gardena.com
www.val-gardena.com

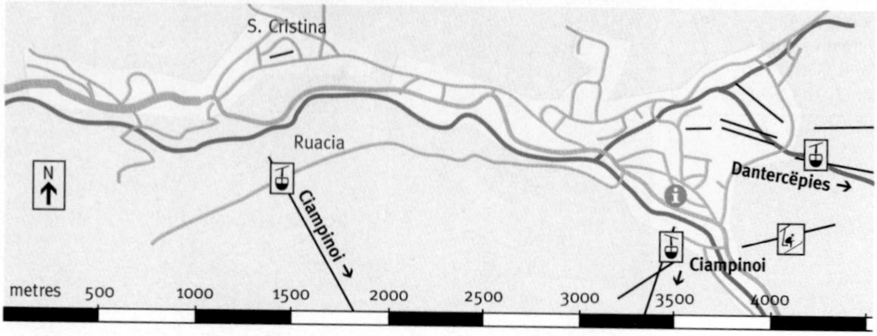

dance was excellent,' recommends one reporter. 'Do try the champagne cocktails.' Tour operators often organise transport back to other resorts.

For thigh slapping in Selva later on, the Laurinkeller has good atmosphere though it's 'quite expensive', while the Luislkeller gets 'a very rowdy German and Scandinavian clientele'.

La Bula 'has live music every night, and gets quite lively later'. The next-door hotel Stella's disco has a 'good crowd and is well used by Brits'.

OFF THE SLOPES
Good variety

There's a sports centre, lovely walks and sleigh rides on Alpe di Siusi; and snow-shoeing around Chertz is reputed to be good. The charming town of Ortisei is well worth a visit for its large hot-spring swimming pool, shops, restaurants and lovely old buildings.

Pedestrians can reach numerous good restaurants, nicely scattered around the mountains, by gondola or cable-car. Car drivers have Bolzano and Innsbruck within reach and tour operators do trips to Cortina.

Ortisei 1235m

Ortisei is a market town with a life of its own, but its local slopes aren't on the main Sella Ronda circuit. It's full of lovely buildings, pretty churches and pleasant shops. The lift to the south-facing slopes is very central, but to start on the north-facing Alpe di Siusi slopes you have to negotiate the busy road that skirts town. The nursery area, school and kindergarten are at the foot of these slopes, but there's a fair range of family accommodation on the piste side of the road. The fine public indoor pool and ice rink are also here. The quickest way to get to Selva and the Sella Ronda circuit is by bus or car.

There are hotels and self-catering to suit all tastes and pockets and many good restaurants, mainly specialising in local dishes. Après-ski is quite jolly, and many bars keep going till late.

For some alternative nightlife, one reporter says, 'Ice hockey matches at the ice stadium were a great night out, and you can eat in the restaurant while watching the match.'

Corvara 1570m

Corvara is the most animated Sella Ronda village east of Selva, with plenty of hotels, restaurants, bars (including the popular Posta Zirm – see Après-ski, above) and sports facilities.

It's well positioned, with village lifts heading off to reasonably equidistant Selva, Arabba and San Cassiano. The main shops and some hotels cluster around a small piazza, but the rest of the place sprawls along the valley floor.

Colfosco 1645m

Colfosco is a smaller, quieter version of Corvara, 2km away. It has a fairly compact centre with a sprawl of large hotels along the road towards Selva. It's connected to Corvara by a horizontal-running chair-lift. In the opposite direction, a series of drag-lifts head off to the Passo Gardena and on to Selva.

Several large hotels between them provide plenty of services.

San Cassiano 1530m

San Cassiano is a pretty little village, set in an attractive, tree-filled valley. It's a quiet, slightly upmarket resort, full of well-heeled Italian families and comfortable hotels, but little else. The local slopes, the Alta Badia, though sizeable and fully linked, are something of a spur of the main Sella Ronda. Adventurers who want to do the circuit will find it a tiresome business.

The best hotel in town is the 4-star Rosa Alpina. The tea dance in Corvara's Posta Zirm is a must if you want something lively. Stop there at the end of the day, taxi home afterwards. Later nightlife is very limited. The Rosa

Alpina has dancing and there's a bowling alley. Walking in the pretty scenery is the main off-slope activity. Swimming is the other. There is no nursery or ski kindergarten.

La Villa 1435m

La Villa is similar to neighbouring San Cassiano in most respects – small, quiet, pretty, unspoilt – but it is slightly closer to Corvara, making it rather better placed for the main Sella Ronda circuit. There is a home piste that features on the World Cup circuit, and village amenities include a pool, bowling and skating on a frozen lake.

Canazei 1440m

Canazei is a sizeable, bustling, pretty, roadside village of narrow streets, rustic old buildings, traditional style hotels and nice little shops, set in the Sella Ronda's most heavily wooded section of mountains. It has reasonably animated nightlife and plenty going on generally – and has been highly recommended by the many reporters who've visited over the past few years.

It is not an ideal choice for British families because of the busy road and lack of English spoken in the school and nursery facilities. 'One instructor took all the English visitors,' said one reporter, 'and was excellent.' Well, that may be okay if everyone is the same standard, but what if they aren't?

A 12-person gondola is the only mountain access point, but it shifts the queues (which can be long) quickly. A single piste back to the village is linked to runs returning from both Selva and Arabba, but it is often closed. The village nursery slope is good but inconveniently located and is unlikely to be used after day one. The local Belvedere slopes are uniformly easy and dotted with mountain restaurants.

There are no luxury hotels, but the rather grand 3-star Dolomiti in the middle of town is one of the original resort hotels. The chalet-style Diana is charming and five minutes from the village centre. The Astoria has a pool and minibus transfers to and from the gondola. There are a fair number of catered chalets run by UK tour operators.

There are numerous restaurants. The Stala, Rosticceria Melester and Te Cevana are all worth a try. For early après-ski the La Stua dei Ladins serves good local wines on candlelit tables. The Husky, Roxy and Montanara bars and the Black Cat and Deodat discos are all worth a visit.

Off the slopes the walks are beautiful and the clothes shopping worthwhile. There's a pool, sauna, Turkish baths and skating in neighbouring Alba. Children have an all-day nursery and ski kindergarten.

Campitello 1445m

Smaller and quieter than next door Canazei and still very unspoilt. By Sella Ronda standards, the village is nothing special, particularly when there's little snow – which is much of the time – but it's still pleasant.

It's remarkably quiet during the day, having no slopes to the village. A cable-car takes you up into the Sella Ronda circuit. If you don't wish to return by lift, take the piste to Canazei and catch a bus.

The Rubino is an elegant 4-star hotel with a pool and well placed close to the cable-car. The Park Diamant is a new 4-star next door and under the same management. Campitello is quite lively – we've had trouble getting near the bar of the throbbing Da Giulio in the early evening. Neighbouring Pozza has ice skating and floodlit slopes. There are no children's facilities.

Arabba 1600m

Arabba is a small, traditional, still uncommercialised village. But the lifts into the Sella Ronda in both directions make it very convenient. It is more of a serious skier's and boarder's destination than its sunny, family-oriented neighbours. The high north-facing slopes have the best natural snow and steepest pistes in the Dolomites. The nearby Marmolada glacier is open most of the winter and guarantees good snow.

The 4-star Sport is the best hotel, and reporters recommend the large, 3-star Porta Vescovo: 'Excellent hotel, wonderful food, nicely furnished rooms and a well-equipped fitness centre.' It has the only pool in town. Apartment-conversion chalets and self-catering accommodation are available.

Venues for eating out are limited. 7 Sass and Ru De Mont are cheap and cheerful pizzerias.

The après-ski is also limited – but cheap. Bar Peter and hotel bars are the focal points. The Delmonego family's bar-caravan, at the bottom of the piste, is the tea-time rendezvous.

Sestriere 2000m

Modern resort with access to the Milky Way

WHAT IT COSTS

3

HOW IT RATES

The slopes	
Snow	***
Extent	****
Experts	***
Intermediates	****
Beginners	***
Convenience	****
Queues	***
Restaurants	**
The rest	
Scenery	***
Resort charm	*
Off-slope	*

What's new

Turin has been chosen to host the 2006 Olympic Winter Games; Sestriere will host many of the Alpine events.

The Combetta and Garnel drags are being replaced by chairs for 2000/01.

SNOWPIX.COM / CHRIS GILL

The village is very sunny. So are the slopes of Monte Fraiteve, behind it; they are not reliably skiable, but the red run down is being reopened, and a new chair-lift for quicker access to the Milky Way is planned ↓

Sestriere was built for snow – high, with north-west-facing slopes – and it has very extensive snowmaking, too. So even if you are let down by the notoriously erratic snowfalls in this corner of Italy, you should be fairly safe here – certainly safer than in Sauze d'Oulx, over the hill.

THE RESORT

Sestriere was the Alps' first purpose-built resort. It sits on a broad, sunny and windy col at 2000m. Neither the site nor the village, with its large apartment blocks, looks very hospitable, though the buildings have benefited from recent investment, and they'll doubtless get more in the run-up to the Olympics. There are some interesting buildings, but much of the village still seems rather scruffy.

THE MOUNTAINS

Sestriere is at one extreme of the big Franco-Italian Milky Way area. The local **slopes** have two main sectors: Sises, directly in front of the village, and more varied Motta, above Borgata – to the north-east and 225m higher.

Drag- and chair-lifts predominate on the local north-west-facing slopes. Access to Sansicario and the rest of the Milky Way is via the gondola from Borgata to Col Basset, at the top of the Sauze d'Oulx area, and a drag-lift back up to Monte Fraiteve. Snow permitting, the return to Sestriere is via a long red from the top of the gondola at Col Basset – or the newly restored red run down from Monte Fraiteve (see left). But it more often depends on riding the gondola down.

With most of the local slopes facing north-west and ranging from 1840m to 2820m, and an extensive snowmaking network covering most of the Sises sector and half of Motta, **snow-cover** is usually reliable for most of the season. The notoriously erratic snowfalls in the Milky Way left the whole area seriously short of snow last season. Thanks to the extensive snowmaking, Sestriere coped better than the other resorts in the area, but one reporter complains that the guns weren't used in late March despite freezing conditions.

There is a fair amount to amuse **experts** – steep pistes served by the drags at the top of both sectors, and off-piste slopes in several directions from here and Monte Fraiteve.

Both sectors also offer plenty for confident **intermediates**, who can also explore practically all of the Milky Way areas, conditions permitting.

The terrain is good for **beginners**, with several nursery areas and the gentlest of easy runs down to Borgata. However, one reporter points out that there is a lack of easy intermediate runs to progress to.

There are two **cross-country** loops covering a total of 10km, and there is now a **snowboard** fun-park.

The lifts are mainly modern, but **queues** for the main lifts occur at the weekends and holidays. The lifts from Borgata to Sestriere are a bottleneck at the end of the day. One reporter complained of queues when poor weather closed the gondola link to Sauze. Another commented on the poor signposting.

MOUNTAIN FACTS

Figures relate to the whole Milky Way area

Altitude	1390m-2825m
Lifts	97
Pistes	400km
Blue	12%
Red	67%
Black	21%
Artificial snow	75km

TOURIST OFFICE

Postcode 10058
t +39 (0122) 755444
f 755171
sestriere@montagnedoc.it
www.montagnedoc.it

The local **mountain restaurants** could only be described as 'fair' – the one at Sises is best – but there are better ones further afield.

Lack of spoken English can be a problem with the **ski schools**. There are no special facilities for **children.**

STAYING THERE

Sestriere is not the most convenient of purpose-built resorts, but location is not crucial. Borgata is less convenient for nightlife and the shops and a recent report suggests that buses to and from Sestriere are infrequent. Most **accommodation** is in apartments, but there are a dozen hotels, mostly of 3-star or 4-star status. Just out of the village (but not far from a lift) is the luxurious Principi di Piemonte. The Savoy Edelweiss is a central, attractive 3-star. The distinctive round towers in the centre are the Club Med quarters.

There are plenty of **eating out** options. Try Lu Peirol for home-made ravioli and atmosphere. Tre Rubineti has been highly recommended for 'outstanding Italian cooking' and an enormous wine list.

Après-ski is lively at weekends: the Black Sun piano-bar-cum-disco and the Tabatà club are great fun, and the Prestige and Palace are two of the many little bars that liven up. The Pinki is perhaps the best of the bars that double as eateries, with lots of low sofas in the classic Italian style. There's quite a bit to do **off the slopes**, but it isn't a very attractive place, despite some smart shops.

La Thuile 1450m

Little-known resort with extensive slopes and link with France

WHAT IT COSTS

(3)

HOW IT RATES

The slopes

Snow	****
Extent	***
Experts	**
Intermediates	****
Beginners	****
Convenience	***
Queues	****
Restaurants	*
The rest	
Scenery	***
Resort charm	***
Off-slope	**

MOUNTAIN FACTS

Altitude	1150m-2640m
Lifts	33
Pistes	140km
Green/Blue	45%
Red	37%
Black	18%
Artificial snow	22km
Recco detectors used	

What's new

The link with France was vastly improved a few seasons back, when the Col de la Traversette drag-lift on the French side was replaced by a quad chair with a moving carpet. The resort has continued to improve the lift network: the Argillien Express was installed two seasons ago and the new Fourclaz fast quad was put in for 1999/2000.

More snowmaking was installed on the runs accessed by the Argillien Express last year and more snow-guns are planned for 2000/01.

- ⊕ Fair-sized area with good lift system linked to La Rosière in France
- ⊕ Excellent beginner and easy intermediate slopes
- ⊕ Unusual mix of purpose-built accommodation at foot of slopes and more villagey atmosphere of the old town, a 10-minute walk away

- ⊖ All the seriously tough pistes are low down, and most of the low, tree-lined runs are tough
- ⊖ Mountain restaurants are generally disappointing
- ⊖ Not the place for lively après-ski

La Thuile deserves to be better known on the British market. The slopes best suit beginners and intermediates not seeking challenges, but are not devoid of interest for experts, particularly if the snow conditions are good – there is the choice of venturing off-piste above the Petit St Bernard pass (closed in winter) or trying the short but serious blacks through the trees above the village.

The Petit St Bernard and the slopes around it get good snow, and you'll doubtless want to venture over the border to France. But be warned: these days, Italian grooming is better than French, and Italian piste grading often overstates difficulty. Moving from corduroy-smooth red runs to serious moguls can be a bit of a shock to the system.

boarding *These are great slopes for learning to board. You can confine yourself to riding chair-lifts and the gondola, and most of the slopes are very easy with good snow. The standard of English for instruction could be a problem. For more experienced boarders there are some great tree runs, and the link with France offers some good off-piste possibilities. Though there are no specific facilities for boarders, there is a lot of good free-riding to be had, as well as some good long carving runs. The nightlife is pretty quiet during the week.*

The resort

La Thuile is a resort of parts. At the foot of the lifts is a modern complex, with places to stay, a leisure centre, bars, shops and restaurants. This looks and feels like a typical French purpose-built resort such as La Plagne or Tignes, but with a distinctly Italian atmosphere – and on a much smaller scale. The modern-resort feel is reinforced by the lifts: a fast chair or gondola takes you up the mountain, and there are more high-speed chairs to the top.

Cross the river and things are very different. La Thuile started life as a mining town but then large parts of it fell into disrepair until the slopes were developed. Much of the old village has been restored and new buildings tastefully added. But parts are still in ruins, with a 'ghost town' feel to them. There are reasonable restaurants and bars but not many entertaining shops.

The mountains

For a little-known resort, La Thuile has surprisingly extensive slopes. And it is normally very uncrowded, with quiet pistes and hardly any lift queues. Many runs are marked red, but deserve no more than a blue rating. The lift system is excellent in general. Electronic 'hands-free' passes are available if you pay a supplement on the ticket price. The slopes can be very cold, especially early in the season.

The slopes link with La Rosière, over the border in France. Courmayeur is easily reached by car, and Cervinia is about an hour away.

THE SLOPES
Big and gentle

The lifts out of the village take you to **Les Suches** (2200m), with black runs going back down directly to the village through the trees, and reds taking a more roundabout route. From here

LIFT PASSES

2000/01 prices in lire

Dominio Internazionale
Covers all lifts in La Rosière and La Thuile.

Beginners One baby-lift in village. Points tickets (50 points 78,000).

Main pass
1-day pass 54,000
6-day pass 260,000
(low season 234,000)

Children
Under 12: 6-day pass 202,000
(low season 180,000)
Under 6: free pass with every purchase of an adult pass of the same length

Short-term passes
Half-day pass (adult 38,000), passes for 2hr (31,000) or 3hr (40,000).

Alternative periods
6-day (non-consecutive) pass available (adult 317,000).

Alternative passes
Valle d'Aosta pass covers La Thuile, Courmayeur, Gressoney, Champoluc, Alagna, Cervinia, Valtournenche and Pila (adult 6-day 300,000).

chairs and drags take you to the top of the mountain and a number of different gentle bowls accessed from **Chaz Dura** (2580m). You can also drop down over the back from here to the Petit St Bernard road.

The link to **La Rosière** in France is via Belvedere (2640m) and the Col de Traversette (2385m). In contrast with La Thuile the French slopes are largely south-facing. Although the runs in France tend to be steeper, the snow in Italy tends to be better.

SNOW RELIABILITY
Good

Most of La Thuile's slopes are north- or east-facing and above 2000m, so the snow generally keeps well. There's also a decent amount of snowmaking, both above the tree line and on the runs home. You can check the conditions at Les Suches via a camera and screens around the resort.

FOR EXPERTS
Rather limited

The only steep pistes are those down through the trees from Les Suches back to the resort. The steepest of these, the Diretta, is serious stuff.

The best of the rest, for experts, is the area above the Petit St Bernard road, where there is some genuinely black terrain and plenty of off-piste. You'll find many red runs overgraded.

Heli-lifts are available. One of the best, to the Ruitor glacier, has a 20km run into France ending at La Rosière.

FOR INTERMEDIATES
Something different

La Thuile has some good intermediate runs, and its link with La Rosière in France adds adventure. However, timid intermediates are best off staying on home ground: the start of the route back from La Rosière is a short but tricky red, and most of La Rosière – particularly the top half of the mountain – is fairly challenging. One reporter warns of an essential drag link back being too difficult for young kids.

On the Italian side, the bowls above Les Suches have many gentle blue and red runs, ideal for cruising and practising. There are also long reds through the trees back to the resort.

The red runs on the other side of the top ridge, down towards the Petit St Bernard road, offer a greater challenge for more adventurous intermediates. But La Thuile's slopes suit less ambitious intermediates best.

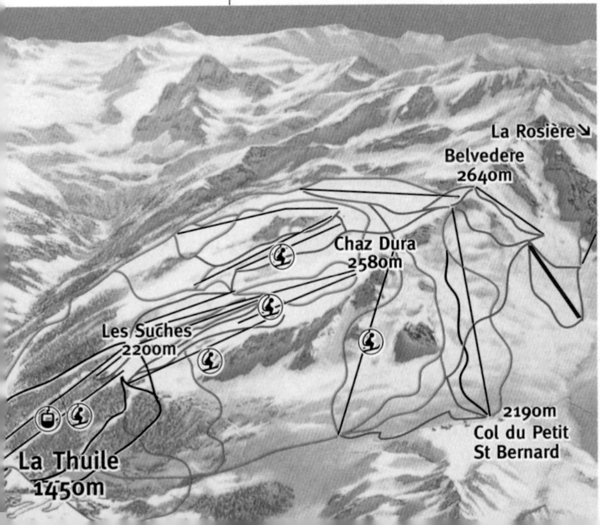

FOR BEGINNERS
Good, but slopes can be crowded

There are nursery slopes at village level and up at Les Suches. There's a good gentle green run above Les Suches to progress to, and some shallow blues. But nothing is segregated from the main slopes. Some reporters enjoyed the less crowded slopes above the Belvedere lift more. But remember that the runs down to the resort are red and black – so taking the gondola back down is the only real option.

FOR CROSS-COUNTRY
Varied choice

La Thuile has four loops of varying difficulty on the valley floor, adding up to 20km of track.

QUEUES
Very rare

The resort has a very effective lift system for the number of visitors, starting with a gondola and parallel fast chair up to Les Suches. There are short queues at peak weekends.

MOUNTAIN RESTAURANTS
On the up?

We were disappointed by the mountain restaurants when we last visited, and recommend heading back to the resort; one possibility is Rascard, just off the nursery slope (take the drag-lift up), but there are others in the Planibel complex – see 'Eating out'. Although there are several ristorantes on the piste map, most served little more than sandwiches and snacks. If you are

SCHOOLS/GUIDES

1999/2000 prices in lire

La Thuile
Classes 6 days
2½hr: 10am-12.30;
6 2½hr days: 193,000
Children's classes
Ages: from 5
6 2½hr days: 193,000
Private lessons
1hr
56,000 for 1 person

CHILDCARE

There is a free non-skiing kindergarten for children from 4 to 12 years.

GETTING THERE

Air Geneva, transfer 2½hr., transfer, 2½hr, Turin.

Rail Pré-St-Didier (10km); regular buses to resort.

ACTIVITIES

Indoor Two swimming pools, amusement arcade, gymnasium, solarium, sauna, squash
Outdoor heli-skiing

TOURIST OFFICE

Postcode 11016
t +39 (0165) 884179
f 885196
lathuile@lathuile.net
www.lathuile.net

going to Italy for the pasta, you'd be better off going elsewhere. But recent reports have been more positive. Recommendations include the Foyer, near the top of the Combes chair and the Off Shore at the bottom of the Belvedere chair for good-value Italian food. One reporter enthuses about the basic Riondet, on the 11km red run from Chaz Dura back to town.

SCHOOLS AND GUIDES
Good but foreign

Reporters we've heard from praise the school for reasonably sized classes and fair instruction. Their reservation is that some of the instructors don't speak good English. A recent reporter had two days of 'excellent' off-piste tuition.

FACILITIES FOR CHILDREN
OK when they're older

There's a Miniclub for children from 4 to 12 but we haven't received any recent reports on this, The ski school starts at five years – and, in the past, we've heard of youngsters who've had a good time.

Staying there

The modern Planibel complex at the foot of the lifts is most convenient for the slopes. But many people find this rather soulless and prefer to stay in the old town over the river (served by a regular free bus service) or in one of the more traditional buildings nearer the slopes.

HOW TO GO
Some choice of packages

The number of tour operators going to La Thuile is increasing.

Hotels Choice is between the swanky but characterless 4-star Planibel, a few 3-stars and simpler places.

(4) **Planibel** American-style 'resort hotel' with all mod cons, including a pool and underground parking. Right at the base of the lifts. Recent reports suggest that the hotel needs some refurbishment.

(3) **Eden** Comfortable modern hotel in traditional wood and stone style. Very close to lifts and the Planibel.

(2) **Chalet Alpina** Simple place with the atmosphere of a catered chalet, on the outskirts of the resort.

Self-catering The Planibel apartments receive much praise from reporters. They're spacious, well equipped, handy for the slopes and great value. Not

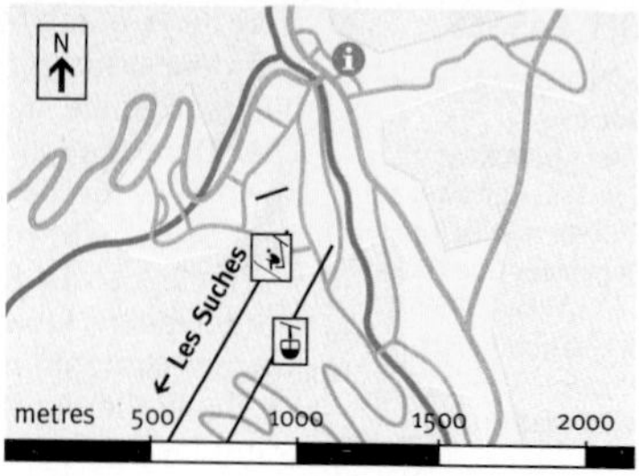

surprisingly, they book out early. Our most recent report on these is also positive, though it points out that some of the apartments are in need of a bit of upgrading.

EATING OUT
Limited, but consistently good

La Thuile doesn't have a lot of restaurants, but we've received positive reports on most of them. At Rascard, we had superb home-made pasta with wild boar bolognese. The Bricole is highly recommended by recent reporters for excellent traditional food at reasonable prices. La Fordze is also recommended. The modern Lunch and Dinner spaghetteria in the Planibel hotel complex, at the foot of the slopes, was also recommended by our most recent reporter – 'wished we'd gone there earlier in the holiday'. La Raclette does good cheese dishes such as fondue. The always-busy Lo Créton and Grotta vie for the title of Best Cheap and Cheerful Pizza and Pasta place. Booking is advisable. According to one report, the restaurant at the Piccolo San Bernardo hotel doesn't take credit cards – be warned.

APRES-SKI
Early to bed

The main bar to fill up after the lifts close is the Buvette. The Bouchon in the Planibel is a piano bar, which is open until late. The Rendezvous bar has karaoke but the Bricolette and Bricole are more atmospheric. The Bricole and Fantasia discos warm up at the weekend.

OFF THE SLOPES
Limited options

The Planibel complex has decent leisure facilities and a good pool, but there are few attractive walks or shops. Excursions to Courmayeur can be organised. It's easy for pedestrians to ride up the gondola for lunch.

Switzerland

Switzerland is home to some of our favourite resorts. For sheer charm and spectacular scenery, the 'traffic-free' villages of Wengen, Mürren, Saas-Fee and Zermatt take some beating. Many resorts have impressive slopes too – including some of the biggest, highest and toughest runs in the Alps, as well as a lot of reassuring intermediate terrain. For fast, efficient, queue-free lift networks, Swiss resorts rarely match French standards – but the real black spots are gradually disappearing. And there are compensations: the world's best mountain restaurants, for example. People always seem to associate Switzerland with high prices. Barring some catastrophic accident to the Swiss franc, prices are never going to be low, but usually they are not greatly different from prices in major French resorts; and what you get for your money is first class.

While France is the home of the purpose-built resort, Switzerland is the home of the traditional mountain village that has transformed itself from farming community into year-round holiday centre. Many of Switzerland's most famous mountain resorts are as popular in the summer as in the winter, or more so. This creates places with a much more lived-in feel to them, and a much more stable local community. Many are still run and dominated by a handful of families who were lucky or shrewd enough to get involved in the early development of the area.

This has its downside as well as advantages. The ruling families are able to stifle competition and prevent newcomers from taking a slice of their action. Alternative ski schools, competing with the traditional school and pushing up standards, are much less common than in other countries, for example.

Switzerland is associated with high living, and the swanky grand hotels of St Moritz, Gstaad, Zermatt and Davos are beyond the dreams of most ordinary holidaymakers. And even in more modest resorts, nothing is cheap. But the quality of the service you get for your money is generally high. Swiss hotels are some of the best in the world. The trains run like clockwork to the advertised

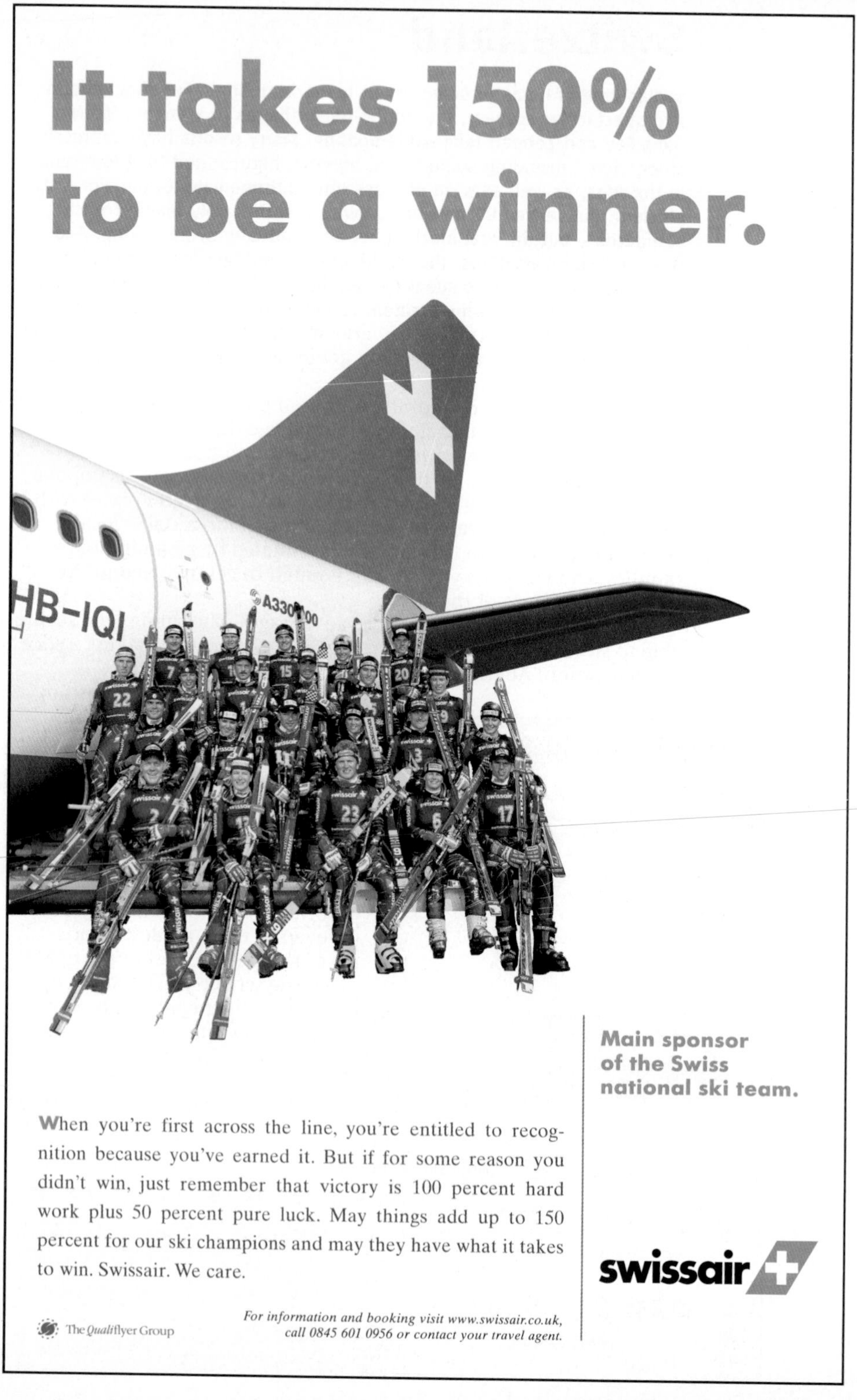
It takes 150%
to be a winner.
HB-IQI
A330-200
Main sponsor
of the Swiss
national ski team.
When you're first across the line, you're entitled to recognition because you've earned it. But if for some reason you didn't win, just remember that victory is 100 percent hard work plus 50 percent pure luck. May things add up to 150 percent for our ski champions and may they have what it takes to win. Swissair. We care.
swissair
The Qualiflyer Group
For information and booking visit www.swissair.co.uk, call 0845 601 0956 or contact your travel agent.

timetable (and often they run to the top of the mountain, doubling as ski-lifts). The food is almost universally of good quality and much less stodgy than in neighbouring Austria. In Switzerland you get what you pay for: even the cheapest wine, for example, is not cheap; but it is reliable – duff bottles are very rare.

Perhaps surprisingly for such a long-established, traditional, rather staid skiing country, Switzerland has gone out of its way to attract snowboarders by developing the facilities they look for.

GETTING AROUND THE SWISS ALPS

Over the page are road maps of Switzerland. Access to practically all Swiss resorts is fairly straightforward when approaching from the north – just pick your motorway. Many of the high passes that are perfectly sensible ways to get around the country in summer are closed in winter, which can be inconvenient if you are moving around from one area to another. There are car-carrying trains linking the Valais (Crans-Montana, Zermatt etc) to Andermatt via the Furka tunnel and Andermatt to the Grisons (Flims, Davos etc) via the Oberalp pass – closed to road traffic in winter but open to trains except after very heavy snowfalls.

St Moritz is more awkward to get to than other resorts, as well as being further away. The main road route is over the Julier pass. This is normally kept open, but at 2284m it is naturally prone to heavy snowfalls that can shut it for a time. The fallback is the car-carrying rail tunnel under the Albula pass. A major new rail tunnel opened in November 1999, offering an alternative route. The Vereina tunnel runs for 19km from Klosters to a point near Susch and Zernez, down the Inn valley from St Moritz.

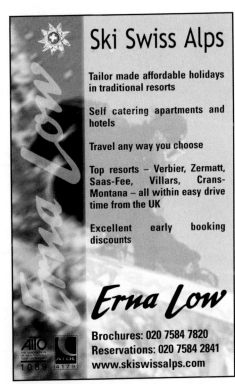

These car-carrying rail services are painless unless you travel at peak times, when there may be long queues – particularly for the Furka tunnel from Andermatt, which offers residents of Zürich the shortest route to Zermatt and the other Valais resorts. Another rail tunnel service that's very handy is the Lötschberg tunnel, linking Kandersteg in the Bernese Oberland with Brig in the Valais. Apart from helicopters, there's no quicker way from Wengen to Zermatt.

There is a car-carrying rail tunnel linking Switzerland with Italy – the Simplon. But most of the routes to Italy are kept open by means of road tunnels. See the Italy introduction on page 323.

To use Swiss motorways (and it's difficult to avoid doing so if you're driving serious distances) you have to buy a windscreen sticker (costing SF40 last time we asked). They are sold at the border, and are for all practical purposes compulsory.

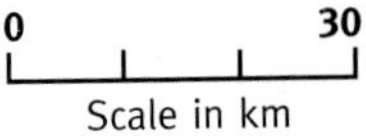

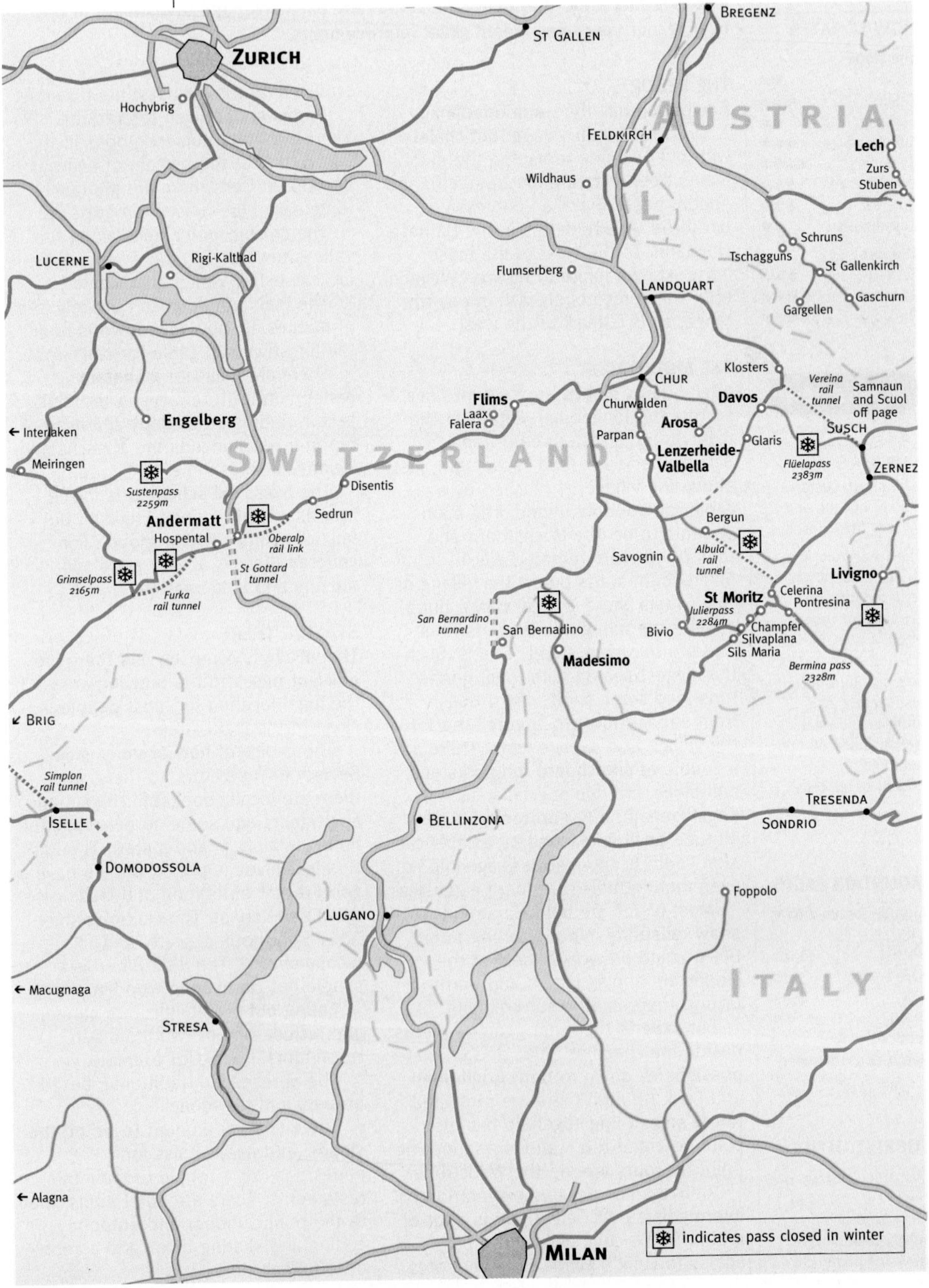

Adelboden 1355m

Chocolate-box village with fragmented slopes

WHAT IT COSTS

(3)

HOW IT RATES

The slopes	
Snow	**
Extent	***
Experts	**
Intermediates	***
Beginners	****
Convenience	***
Queues	***
Restaurants	**
The rest	
Scenery	***
Resort charm	****
Off-slope	****

What's new

Until two years ago, Adelboden's slopes had a sixth sector – Fleckli; but the one lift was then closed.

The T-bar from Aebi to Sillerenbühl was replaced by a new six-pack for 1999/2000. A new 'hands-free' lift pass system was also introduced last season. And artificial snowmaking was installed on the Aebi and Chuenisbergli runs.

MOUNTAIN FACTS

Altitude	1070m-2355m
Lifts	50
Pistes	160km
Blue	48%
Red	44%
Black	8%
Artificial snow	8km
Recco detectors used	

TOURIST OFFICE

Postcode CH-3715
t +41 (33) 673 8080
f 673 8092
info@adelboden.ch
www.adelboden.ch

Adelboden is unjustly neglected by the British market: for intermediates who find relaxing, pretty surroundings more important than convenience for the slopes it has a lot of appeal. The slopes are extensive, and investment in lifts over recent years has meant great improvements.

THE RESORT

Adelboden has the traditional image of a Swiss mountain village: old chalets with overhanging roofs line the quiet main street (cars are discouraged), and 3000m peaks make an impressive backdrop. Adelboden is in the Bernese Oberland, to the west of the much better-known Jungfrau resorts (Wengen etc). These resorts are within day-trip range, as is Gstaad to the west.

THE MOUNTAINS

Adelboden's **slopes** are split into five sectors (no longer six). Lifts near the main street access three of them. Schwandfeldspitz (aka Tschenten), just above the village, is reached by a cable-car–gondola hybrid. The main gondola to nearby Höchsthorn and then on to more remote Geils-Sillerenbühl starts below the village at Oey (where there is a car park), but a connecting mini-gondola starts from close to the main street. This is much the biggest sector, with long, gentle runs (and some short, sharp ones) from 2200m down to 1350m – back to the village and over to Lenk. There are a couple of **snowboard** fun-parks and half-pipes and two specialist schools. Engstligenalp, a flat-bottomed high-altitude bowl is reached by a cable-car 4km south of the resort; Elsigenalp is even more remote, but more extensive.

Most pistes are below 2000m – so **snow reliability** is not a strong point. But it could be worse, most of the slopes are above 1500m and north-facing. There is little snowmaking.

For **experts** there are genuine blacks beside the chairs at Geils, and off-piste possibilities down to both Adelboden and Lenk (though there are protected forest areas). Engstligenalp has off-piste potential too – and is a launching point for tours around the Wildstrubel.

All five areas deserve exploration by **intermediates**. At Geils there is a lot of ground to be covered – and trips across to Lenk's gentle Betelberg area (covered by the lift pass) are possible.

Beginners are well catered for. There are good nursery slopes in the village and at the bottom of nearby sectors. At Geils there are gloriously long, easy blue runs to progress to.

The **cross-country** trails along the valleys towards Engstligenalp and Geils are extensive, varied and scenic.

The main gondola isn't entirely free of **queues**. If snow low down is poor, the Engstligenalp cable-car can't cope.

There are pleasant **mountain restaurants** with terraces in the Geils sector. Aebi is particularly charming. A reporter recommends the Metschstand: 'Sunny, small, simple, but good.'

The Swiss **ski school** gets mixed reports – 'caring, good English', but 'mix of abilities within group'. For **children** there is a 'very good' ski nursery and kindergarten.

STAYING THERE

The village is compact, and there are efficient buses to the outlying areas; the ideal location for most people is close to the main street.

The choice of **how to go** is wide. Several UK operators go there, and there are locally bookable chalets and apartments and some 30 pensions and hotels (mainly 3- and 4-star). The Park Hotel Bellevue is pricey, but we have a good report of its food and facilities (pool and sauna). The central 3-star Adler Sporthotel is pretty and recommended. The little Bären is a simple but captivating wooden chalet.

Eating out possibilities are varied, and include one or two mountain restaurants – Aebi, for example.

The **après-ski** is traditional, based on bars and tea rooms.

There is a fair amount to do **off the slopes**, and easy access for pedestrians to a couple of mountain restaurants. There are hotel pools open to the public, indoor and outdoor curling and skating rinks, and a couple of toboggan runs.

Andermatt

1445m

An old-fashioned resort with some great off-piste

WHAT IT COSTS

3

HOW IT RATES

The slopes

Snow	****
Extent	*
Experts	****
Intermediates	**
Beginners	*
Convenience	***
Queues	**
Restaurants	*

The rest

Scenery	***
Resort charm	****
Off-slope	**

What's new

As well as the local Andermatt Gotthard lift pass, there is now the option of the Gotthard-Oberalp pass, which includes Sedrun and Disentis. But it's pricey – about 25 per cent more than the local pass.

Hands-free electronic passes are now available.

MOUNTAIN FACTS

Altitude	1445m-2965m
Lifts	13
Pistes	56km
Blue	29%
Red	42%
Black	29%
Artificial snow	none
Recco detectors used	

TOURIST OFFICE

Postcode CH-6490
t +41 (41) 887 1454
f 887 0185
info@andermatt.ch
www.andermatt.ch

Andermatt used to be a firm favourite with the British, but as other areas developed it got left behind and the village became a bit of a backwater. Its lift system is limited – but gives access to some great, steep off-piste slopes.

THE RESORT

Andermatt is quite busy in summer and gets weekend business, but at other times seems deserted apart from the soldiers whose barracks are here. It is quietly attractive, with wooden houses lining the dog-leg main street that runs between railway and cable-car stations. The railway is the only link in winter with the Grisons to the east and the Valais to the west – trains carry cars.

THE MOUNTAINS

A two-stage cable-car from the edge of the village serves magnificent, varied **slopes** on the open, steep and usually empty slopes of Gemsstock. Across town is the gentler Nätschen/ Gütsch area. And a bus or train-ride along the valley is Winterhorn (above Hospental). There is also an isolated nursery slope further along at Realp.

Andermatt has a justified reputation for **reliable snow**. The Gemsstock cable-car takes a while to get going after a heavy snowfall.

It is most definitely a resort for **experts**. The top Gemsstock cable-car serves two main slopes: the north-facing bowl beneath it is a glorious, long black slope (about 800m vertical), usually with excellent snow, in which there is usually one marked run down, and countless off-piste routes; the Sonnenpiste, once again properly graded red after a spell as a black, is a fine open run curling around the back of the mountain to the mid-station. From mid-mountain to the village there is a black run, not too steep but heavily mogulled. There are guides for off-piste adventure, and heli-trips. Both Nätschen and Winterhorn have black pistes and off-piste areas.

Intermediates needn't be put off the Gemsstock: the Sonnenpiste can be tackled, and there is a pleasant red at mid-mountain, served by a drag-lift. Winterhorn's modest lift system offers all standards of piste down the 900m vertical, while Nätschen's south and west-facing mountain is perfect for confidence-building.

The lower half of Nätschen has a good, long, easy run back to the village. But essentially this is not a resort for **beginners**.

There are **snowboard** facilities (park and pipe) on Nätschen and on the Gemsstock. And there is a 20km **cross-country** loop along the valley.

Although the Gemsstock cable-car has been upgraded, it can still generate morning **queues** in the village and at mid-mountain when conditions are attractive. The few **mountain restaurants** are basic.

The good work of the Swiss **ski school** is overshadowed by the excellent Alpine Adventures Mountain Reality, an off-piste guiding outfit run by the famous Alex Clapasson (who also happens to run the lift company).

There are no special facilities for **children**; but there are slopes they can handle at Nätschen and the Swiss school takes children's classes.

STAYING THERE

Andermatt's **accommodation** is in cosy 2- and 3-star hotels. Gasthaus Sternen, in the centre, is an attractive old chalet with a lively restaurant and bar. The 3-star Sonne, between the centre and the lift, is welcoming and comfortable. The neighbouring 2-star Bergidyll is a British favourite. Alpenhotel Schlüssel is new, with spacious rooms. **Après-ski** revolves around cosy local bars, and finishes early during the week – Café Gotthard and the terrace at the Drei Könige & Post hotel are recommended. There's little to do **off the slopes**.

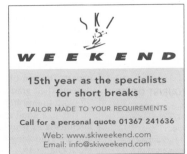

Arosa

1800m

Classic all-round winter holiday resort

The classic image of a winter sports resort is perhaps an isolated, snow-covered Swiss village, surrounded by big, beautiful mountains, with skating on a frozen lake, horse-drawn sleighs jingling through the streets and people in fur coats strolling on mountain paths. Arosa is just that. It's a pity that many of its comfortable hotels date from the time when pitched roofs were out of fashion.

WHAT IT COSTS

4

HOW IT RATES

The slopes

Snow	***
Extent	**
Experts	*
Intermediates	***
Beginners	****
Convenience	***
Queues	****
Restaurants	****

The rest

Scenery	***
Resort charm	**
Off-slope	****

What's new

For 2000/01 a new quad chair-lift will replace two existing slow chairs from mid-mountain to near the top of the Weisshorn.

MOUNTAIN FACTS

Altitude	1800m-2655m
Lifts	14
Pistes	70km
Blue	38%
Red	57%
Black	5%
Artificial snow	8km

Recco detectors used

TOURIST OFFICE

Postcode CH-7050
t +41 (81) 378 7020
f 7021
arosa@arosa.ch
www.arosa.ch

THE RESORT

High and remote, Arosa is in a sheltered basin at the head of a beautiful wooded valley, in contrast to the open slopes. It's a long, winding road or splendid rail journey from Chur. Obersee, at the centre, is drab, though its lakeside setting adds charm. The rest of Arosa is scattered, with a hill separating Obersee from the older, prettier Innerarosa – which has a chair, a drag and (away from the village) a gondola. Arosa is quiet; its relaxed ambience attracts an unpretentiously wealthy clientele of families and older people, with very few Brits. Some accommodation is a long walk from the lifts, but there's a good, free bus.

THE MOUNTAINS

For such a well known resort, Arosa's **slopes** are modest and lack challenges. The slopes are spread widely over two main sectors. The **Weisshorn** faces mainly south and south-east. Tschuggen, halfway to the Weisshorn peak, is the major lift junction, reachable from both Obersee and Innerarosa. An inconveniently sited gondola below Innerarosa is the main access to the east and north-east-facing slopes of the **Hörnli** sector. Drags and chair-lifts allow you to travel either way between the two sectors.

There is a **snowboard** park and a half-pipe and specialist school (Bananas). You can get to Davos-Klosters, Flims and Lenzerheide by road and the latter off-piste.

Arosa has relatively good **snow reliability**. The best south-facing pistes are above 2000m, and the shadier Hörnli slopes hold their snow well.

Arosa isn't the resort for a keen **expert**. The two black runs don't deserve their grading, but you can ski off-piste to and from Lenzerheide.

This is a good area for **intermediates** who want to take it easy and aren't looking for high mileage or much challenge.

For beginners the Tschuggen nursery slopes are excellent and usually have good snow, but they get a lot of through traffic. Innerarosa has a quieter but more limited area usually reserved for children.

Although it lacks the sheer length of trails of many resorts, Arosa (with 25km) has some of the best and varied **cross-country** loops in the Alps.

With many part-timers, Arosa does not suffer **queues**. There can be waits for the Weisshorn cable-car, though a recent reporter had no problems.

The **mountain restaurants** are okay, but there are too few of them. Consequently they get crowded. Carmennahütte is the best, while Tschuggenhütte is a rustic little refuge with a nice sun terrace.

There's a big **ski-school** and a lot of demand for private lessons from the affluent Arosa guests. Arosa seems a good choice for a family holiday, and several hotels have kindergartens for the **children**.

STAYING THERE

The village is a spread-out place, but where you stay is not that important as there is an excellent shuttle bus. Innerarosa has the advantage of lifts to both sectors. Arosa is a **hotel** resort, with a high proportion of them 3- and 4-stars. A reporter says the Belvedere is 'very friendly and handy for the cable-car'. Most restaurants are hotel-based. For a true gourmet experience, the tiny wood-panelled Zum Wohl dining room in the unprepossessing Hotel Anita is an expensive treat that has to be booked. **Après-ski** is quite lively. The Carmenna hotel by the ice rink has well priced drinks and live jazz. Later the popular bar of the Eden hotel has live music. There are plenty of **off-slope** alternatives. You can get a pedestrian's lift pass, and many mountain restaurants are reachable via 35km of cleared, marked walks. Sleigh rides in the mountains are beautiful.

Champéry 1050m

Picture-postcard village, with access to the Portes du Soleil

WHAT IT COSTS

(3)

HOW IT RATES

The slopes

Snow	**
Extent	*****
Experts	***
Intermediates	****
Beginners	**
Convenience	*
Queues	****
Restaurants	***

The rest

Scenery	****
Resort charm	****
Off-slope	***

What's new

1999/2000 saw the introduction of a new hands-free lift pass system operated by an electronic card that you keep in your pocket.

5km of floodlit skiing (twice a week) was opened between Champéry and Les Crosets.

Mitchell's bar and restaurant, on the road up from the cable-car station, is an excellent new stop-off at the end of the day.

MOUNTAIN FACTS

Altitude	975m-2350m
Lifts	219
Pistes	650km
Blue	51%
Red	40%
Black	9%
Art. snow	522 acres
Recco detectors used	

- ⊕ Charmingly rustic mountain village with impressive views of the Dents du Midi range
- ⊕ Cable-car takes you into very extensive Portes du Soleil slopes, linking with Avoriaz and Châtel in France as well as other Swiss resorts
- ⊕ Quiet, relaxed place – yet plenty to do off the slopes
- ⊕ Easy access for independent travellers whether travelling by rail or road

- ⊖ Local slopes suffer from the sun – facing south-east
- ⊖ No runs back to the village – and sometimes none back to the valley
- ⊖ Beginners face hassle and expense getting up to Planachaux, which is not as gentle as it could be
- ⊖ Not many tough slopes nearby

With good transport links and sports facilities, Champéry is great for part-timers, or for families looking for a quiet time in a lovely place, especially if they have a car. It also deserves consideration if you want to explore the Portes du Soleil from a base strong on character rather than convenience. The north-facing slopes of Avoriaz, across the French border, are fairly easy to get to – and we have found fresh powder there when Champéry's lower slopes were bare and its upper ones slushy. It's one of the least attractive resorts for beginners, though.

boarding *Champéry is not the best choice in the Portes du Soleil for a beginner boarder – the local slopes are a cable-car ride away and aren't great when you get to them. And progress onto more difficult terrain and the rest of the Portes du Soleil circuit means learning to navigate drag-lifts early on. Intermediate and advanced riders will find a lot of decent-free-riding opportunities (providing the conditions are good) on both the local Swiss slopes and the rest of the extensive Portes du Soleil network. There's a fun-park in Les Crosets and a half-pipe in Morgins. The terrain-park in Avoriaz is definitely worth checking out. Nightlife is fairly quiet – Mitchell's and La Crevasse are the best bet later on.*

The resort

Set beneath the dramatic Dents du Midi, Champéry is the stuff of picture postcards. The main street is lined with old wooden chalets housing most of the hotels, bars and restaurants, liberally adorned with Swiss flags.

An attempt has been made to provide the facilities demanded by today's holidaymakers without spoiling the old-world charm. Down a steepish hill, away from the main street, are the cable-car, sports centre and a convenient new terminus for the narrow-gauge railway.

The village has a friendly, relaxed atmosphere; it would be ideal for families if it wasn't separated from its slopes by a steep, fragmented mountainside. You can get back to Grand Paradis, 2km up the valley, on snow (assuming there's enough cover).

The mountains

Champéry's local slopes are as friendly and relaxing as the village, at least for intermediates. It is far from ideal for absolute beginners. Experts can cover vast amounts of ground on the Portes du Soleil piste circuit, which takes in the French resorts of Avoriaz and Châtel as well as the Swiss ones of Champoussin, Les Crosets, and Morgins – also easily reached by car, as are the off-piste possibilities of Verbier and Chamonix. Very well lit slopes linking with Les Crosets are open some evenings.

THE SLOPES
Extensive and sunny

The village of Champéry is not quite part of the main Portes du Soleil circuit but its slopes are – the sunny bowl of **Planachaux**, way above the village,

LIFT PASSES

2000/01 prices in Swiss francs

Portes du Soleil
Covers all the lifts in 12 resorts.

Beginners Points card (adult 50-point card 30).

Main pass
1-day pass 50
6-day pass 241

Senior citizens
Over 60: 6-day pass 193

Children
Under 16: 161
Under 6: free pass

Short-term passes
Half-day pass from noon (adult 38).

Notes Reductions for families and groups.

Alternative passes
Half-day (to and from noon), 1- and 2-day passes available for 35 lifts and 100km of piste in Champéry, Les Crosets, Champoussin, Morgins and Torgon: adult 1-day 37 (1999/2000 prices).

with a couple of runs leading down to the valley at **Grand Paradis**, a short bus-ride from Champéry.

There are no pistes to Champéry itself, though on rare occasions local conditions allow off-piste trips. Planachaux is rather featureless, and most people quickly move on – at least as far as next-door Les Crosets. You can explore the Portes du Soleil by travelling west towards Avoriaz or north-east to Champoussin, Morgins and Châtel.

There are three ways to get to Avoriaz – via a chair-lift from the eastern side of the Planachaux bowl to Chavanette (over the infamous 'Swiss Wall' mogul field) or via one of two lifts from Les Crosets.

Queues form at some lifts, and the run home is often either closed or made awkward by poor snow. Getting to the top of the Champéry cable-car to ride down is a roundabout business.

The easy Champoussin runs are best reached by chair-lift (a walk across the Les Crosets car park) to Pointe de l'Au. Then a network of short runs and lifts goes to Champoussin and Morgins.

For more on the Portes du Soleil area, see the chapters on Avoriaz, Châtel and Morzine in France.

SNOW RELIABILITY
Better in France

The snow on the north-facing French side of the area is usually better than on the sunnier Swiss side to the south. And getting to Avoriaz's north-facing slopes when conditions are poor can be unpleasant for early intermediates.

Champéry has just 14 mobile snow-guns to cover the area it shares with Les Crosets. This isn't enough.

FOR EXPERTS
Few local challenges

Champéry is not well placed for reaching the tough runs of the Portes du Soleil. The Swiss Wall, on the Champéry side of Chavanette, is an intimidatingly long, steep slope, but not nearly as terrifying as its various names suggest; the main difficulty is at the very top, which can be icy when snow is in short supply or may have moguls the size of small cars when it is in abundance.

There's a limit to how many times you will want to battle the Wall, and it's quite a trek to the Hauts Forts above Avoriaz – the main black-run sector in the Portes du Soleil.

There's lots of scope for off-piste at Chavanette and on the broad slopes of Les Crosets and Champoussin.

FOR INTERMEDIATES
Wonderful if snow is good

Confident intermediates have the whole of the Portes du Soleil at their disposal. But there are plenty of possibilities to enjoy without straying across the border.

The runs home to Grand Paradis are as good as any when the snow conditions allow, and enjoyable by all intermediates. It's not worth dwelling too long around the bland Planachaux area, but Les Crosets is a junction of

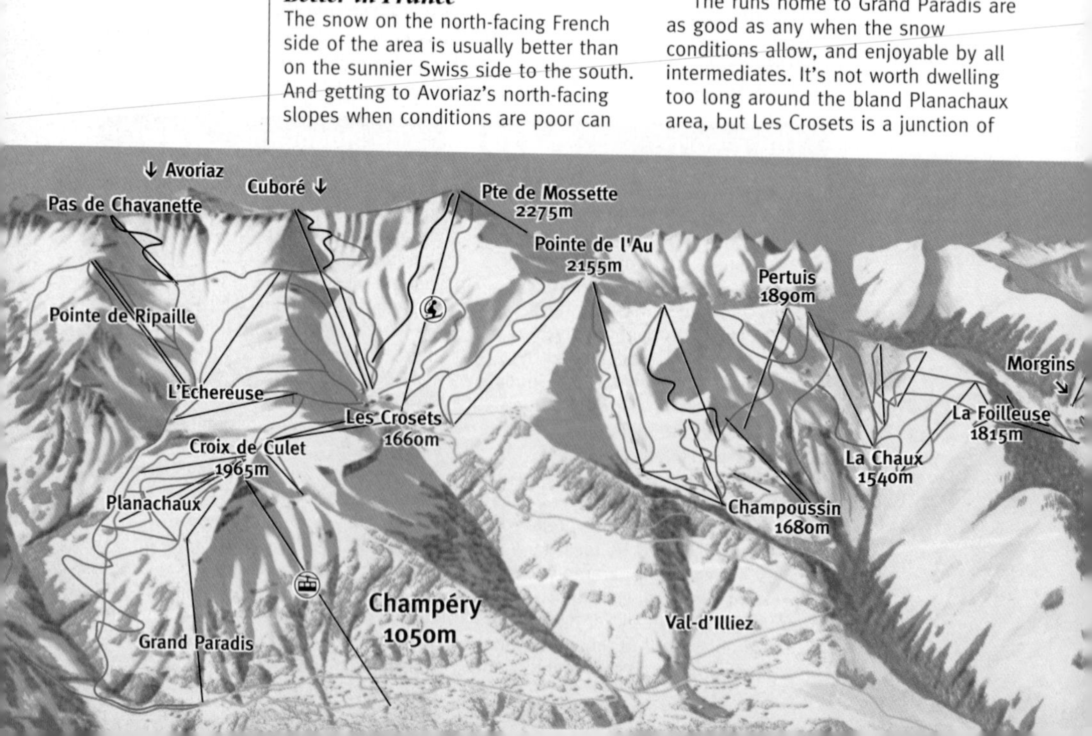

SCHOOLS/GUIDES

1999/2000 prices in Swiss francs

Swiss
Classes 5 days 3hr: 9.30-12.30
5 half-days: 130
Children's classes
Ages: from 3 to 7
5 days including lunch: 250
Private lessons
1½hr, 3hr, or 6hr
75 for 1½hr for 1 person or 90 for 2 people

CHILDCARE

The ski school runs a ski kindergarten for children aged 3 to 7, from 9.30 to 4.30.

The tourist office publishes a list of babysitters and home-based child minders.

several fine runs.

The pistes down from Pointe de Mossette and Grand Conche are good direct runs ideal for competent, or simply confident, intermediates. The runs back from Pointe de l'Au also hold the interest. Champoussin has a network of short, easy pistes ideal for leisurely cruising. With lots of ungroomed areas to the sides of many runs, the area is great for those venturing off-piste for the first time.

Those 'doing the circuit' tend not to spend time on these slopes, leaving them nicely uncrowded for residents. Beyond, the runs down to Morgins are delightful tree-lined meanders – the place to go in poor visibility.

FOR BEGINNERS
Go elsewhere if you have a choice

Despite its good school, Champéry is far from ideal for beginners. An expensive cable-car ride takes novices to the steepish Planachaux runs, on the shortest of which they receive tuition. Beginners with a car can reach the far more suitable Champoussin slopes reasonably quickly.

FOR CROSS-COUNTRY
Very poor

A 10km loop is advertised, but it's very unreliable for snow and also not well maintained. 4km of trails are floodlit each evening until 10pm.

QUEUES
Few local problems

The cable-car comfortably copes with the village's quite low demand. When snow is good, weekend and special holiday crowds can be a problem – hence the car park opposite the cable-car station – but Avoriaz's queues are a greater concern, and we've had reports that the pistes are becoming more crowded, especially around Les Crosets – the chair-lift back up to Planachaux was the only real bottleneck our reporter experienced during the New Year period. If the snow is good enough, you can avoid any end-of-play queues for the cable-car down by taking the Grand Paradis run to the valley floor and getting the regular free bus back into town.

MOUNTAIN RESTAURANTS
Wide choice, some highlights

The local area is very good in terms of numbers of mountain restaurants. Chez Coquoz at Planachaux has been recommended for its good cheesy specialities and traditional atmosphere.

The tiny Lapisa on the way down to Grand Paradis is delightfully rustic with piped accordion music and home-made meats and cheese – they will tow you back up by snowmobile if there's not enough snow to ski on down.

Chez Gaby, above Champoussin, has been recommended.

Further afield, the refuges at Les Lindarets are worth heading for (see Avoriaz chapter).

SCHOOLS AND GUIDES
No worries

The few (now rather ancient) reports that we've had on the school are free of criticism and tell of a surprising number of instructors who speak good English.

FACILITIES FOR CHILDREN
Not a lot

The tourist office provides a list of babysitters and home-based child minders. The Swiss ski school kids' club accepts children from three to seven years.

VICTORIA LONG / CHAMPERY TO

The cable-car goes up over essentially unskiable terrain, but there is a run back to village level further up the valley ↓

GETTING THERE

Air Geneva, transfer 2hr.

Staying there

Although it's a small village, most hotels are some way from the cable-car station on the outer fringes – so the shuttle-bus is quite important. It is fairly efficient; but having your own transport is an advantage (especially for quick access to nearby resorts).

HOW TO GO
Limited packages available

Champéry is one of the easiest resorts to get to – by car, train or plane.

There's a limited range of hotels and catered chalets available through tour operators – though the number of operators featuring Champéry has fallen in recent years.

Hotels There's are no luxury hotels but a reasonable choice from 3-star down and prices are low by comparison with many smarter Swiss resorts.

(((3 **Champéry** Biggest and best 3-star in town, but hardly in the luxury bracket – a pleasantly comfortable chalet on the main street.

(((3 **Suisse Golden Tulip** Rival adjacent 3-star.

(((3 **National** Classic Swiss villa-style hotel on the main street, with neatly renovated bedrooms; 'friendly staff and lovely breakfast'.

((2 **Beau Séjour** Comfortable, traditional 3-star at the southern end of the main street.

((2 **Alpes** Creaky old chalet in a slightly inconvenient position. Good food, but rather sparse rooms.

Self-catering Some apartments are available to independent travellers.

EATING OUT
A fair choice

Two of the best places are just outside the village. Cantines des Rives, on the other side of the valley, is a taxi-ride away. It's a beautiful traditional chalet specialising in fondue and raclette. Similarly distant is the Grand Paradis. It serves excellent, if pricey, local specialities. The stuffed animals decorating the place may be off-putting for some.

There are impressive, pricey gourmet restaurants in the Hotel Suisse Golden Tulip. Good, less expensive places are the restaurants of the Hotel des Alpes and Hotel National. Our most recent reporter was thoroughly disappointed by his meal at the Vieux Chalet. For a less formal ambience it's best to try the local specialities of the Farinet (closed last season but reopened this summer) or the 'excellent' restaurant in the Hotel du Nord. Mitchell's is a popular new bar and restaurant with a great atmosphere in a cool modern setting.

Twice a week when the slopes are floodlit, the restaurant at the top of the cable-car is open in the evening.

APRES-SKI
Something for everyone

Champéry has a convivial atmosphere at tea-time, but things are fairly sedate later in the evening.

Mitchell's, up the hill from the cable-car station, is the place to head for at close of play – big sofas, fireplace, good music and a great atmosphere. The Pub gets busy before the little Crevasse disco downstairs gets going at around midnight. It's frequented mostly by resort workers.

The pleasantly informal bars in the hotel Suisse Golden Tulip are cosy little places. The Bar des Guides is a pre-dinner watering hole with interesting relics and photographs of pre-war skiing. The Mines d'Or cellar bar is mainly frequented by instructors and is good for a mellow late drink.

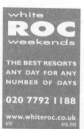

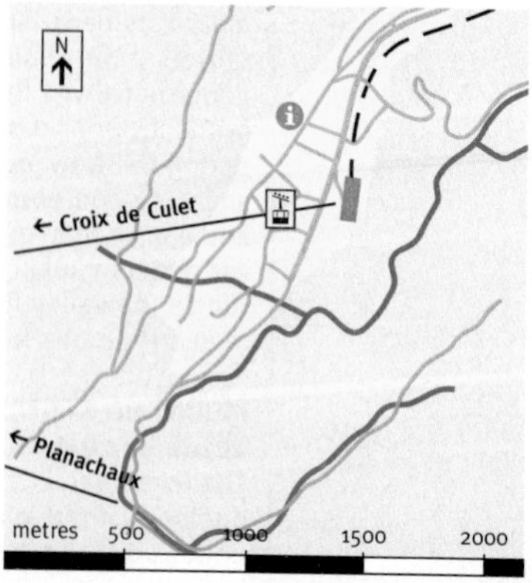

ACTIVITIES

Indoor Swimming pool, ice skating and curling rink, Sunfit fitness centre (sauna, solarium, body building, physiotherapy)
Outdoor Paragliding, cleared walking paths, bungee jumping

TOURIST OFFICE

Postcode CH-1874
t +41 (24) 479 2020
f 479 2021
champery-ch@portesdusoleil.com
www.champery.ch

The Farinet is a spacious cellar nightclub with upstairs restaurant, which is good fun when there are enough people to give it atmosphere – mostly at weekends.

OFF THE SLOPES
Excellent for the energetic

The Portes du Soleil has a general drawback for pedestrians, in that anyone on the the slopes other than beginners is very unlikely to want to hang around (or return to) the local area for lunch. But, that aside, Champéry is very attractive for the those who don't insist on a lot of animation in the village.

Walks, particularly along to Val d'Illiez, are very pleasant, and the narrow-gauge railway allows excursions to Montreux, Lausanne and Sion.

There is a good range of activities and a decent sports centre.

Les Crosets 1660m

Les Crosets has a prime position on the Portes du Soleil, with good runs and snow all round and quick access to Avoriaz, Champéry, Champoussin and Morgins. But there's not much there – it's little more than a multi-lift station and car park, with a couple of restaurants and hotels, a few chalets and apartments, a disco-bar and floodlit slopes open twice a week and linked to Champéry.

Hotel La Télécabine here is a homely place, run by an English woman and her French husband-chef, which serves delicious food in a lovely rustic dining room. It also has a ski shop and big self-service lunch-time restaurant for non-residents. It would be a good base for those looking for a quiet time and slopes on the doorstep.

Champoussin 1680m

Champoussin is, theoretically at least, a good choice for a family looking for a small, quiet, user-friendly base – no through traffic, convenient for the slopes, enough altitude to have snow in the village often, no noisy late-night revellers, rustic-style buildings and the comfortable Royal Alpage Club hotel (two restaurants, pool, gym, disco).

Barring one very negative report on Champoussin some years ago (problems with the hotel, school and Miniclub) most reports are very positive – praising the friendliness of the natives, the atmosphere, the 'stupendous views of the Dents du Midi', the proximity to the slopes, the child-friendly attitude of the Alpage hotel and the progress children made in the multi-lingual Miniclub.

Our most recent reporter was also enthusiastic about the resort and the ski school classes. Fellow guests had apparently enthused about the children's Miniclub. The report does, however, complain about there being only one, basic, supermarket. There's not a lot to do off the slopes – a car is recommended for a change of scene.

Morgins 1350m

Morgins can disappoint visitors attracted by visions of a quiet little Swiss village. The reality is a fairly scattered resort where some accommodation is a fair walk from one or both of the Portes du Soleil lifts. Although reasonably attractive and friendly, the village is not in the same league as Champéry for charm, though it does attract a fair proportion of repeat visitors.

The bland local slopes lead visitors to look further afield. But an irritating series of short lifts and lack of public transport to Châtel slow you down, making it best suited to those with a car. You can drive to Les Crosets for the highest and best of the Swiss Portes du Soleil slopes, or to the lifts at Châtel.

Those expecting typical Swiss efficiency are also surprised to find poor local piste grooming and marking. Cross-country enthusiasts have 20km of pleasant trails. A recent report describes the Swiss ski school as 'very satisfactory and well organised'.

The large Bellevue is a modern hotel, but built in traditional style, and has been praised by reporters in the past for its friendliness and comfort. The cheaper Pension de Morgins is also recommended. Ski Morgins has a number of catered chalets – the rustic Chalet Mesange has a central location, near the main lifts.

There are a couple of worthwhile bars and restaurants – the T-Bar attracts a lively young crowd and gets very busy later on. The Crystal Pub and the terrace bar at the Pension de Morgins have been recommended. The Yucatan is popular for late-night drinks. Off-slope amenities include indoor tennis, horse-riding and a natural ice rink. If you have a car, nearby Châtel offers more in the way of entertainment.

Crans-Montana 1500m

Sun-soaked slopes with stunning views and big town base

WHAT IT COSTS

3

HOW IT RATES

The slopes

Snow	**
Extent	***
Experts	**
Intermediates	****
Beginners	***
Convenience	**
Queues	***
Restaurants	***

The rest

Scenery	****
Resort charm	**
Off-slope	****

What's new

Floodlit skiing has been expanded to the 3.5km Grand Signal run.

A new 6km toboggan from Petit Bonvin to Aminona opened for 1999/2000.

The drag and chair-lift up from Plumachit have been removed, so you now have to hike back up the hill from the restaurant. The long drag up from Arnouvaz to Cry d'Er has also been removed.

The separate lift companies have merged, and a single lift ticket for the whole area – including the glacier – is being introduced for next season.

- ➕ Large piste area suitable for all, except if you prefer black runs
- ➕ Splendid wooded setting with magnificent panoramic views
- ➕ Fair number of woodland slopes – good for bad weather
- ➕ Modern, well-designed lift system, with few queues
- ➕ Golf course provides excellent, gentle nursery slopes
- ➕ Very sunny slopes (but see right)
- ➕ Excellent cross-country trails

- ➖ Snow badly affected by sun except in early season
- ➖ Large town (rather than village) composed partly of big chalet-style blocks but mainly of dreary cubic blocks – and therefore entirely without Alpine atmosphere
- ➖ Bus or car rides to lifts from much of the accommodation
- ➖ Not many challenging pistes

When conditions are right – clear skies above fresh, deep snow – Crans-Montana takes some beating. The mountains you bounce down with the midday sun full on your face are charmingly scenic, the slopes broken up by rock outcrops and forest. The mountains you gaze at – Zermatt's Matterhorn just discernible among them – are mind-blowing. When conditions are right, mountain-lovers may forgive Crans-Montana anything – in particular, its inconvenient, linear layout and the plain, towny style of its twin resort centres.

Sadly, conditions are more often wrong than right. Except in the depths of winter, the strong midday sun quickly bakes the pistes. For someone booking six months ahead, this is enough to keep Crans-Montana off the shortlist. For those who can time a visit according to the weather – and are more interested in impressive distant views than cosy immediate surroundings – the resort is worth serious consideration.

SNOWPIX.COM / CHRIS GILL

The glorious views across the Rhône valley are one of the main attractions →

boarding *Despite Crans-Montana's staid, middle-aged image, boarding is very popular. There are plenty of broad, smooth pistes, lots of underexploited off-piste, and good specialist facilities. Aminona is a good area for experienced boarders and has a fun-park, and there's a half-pipe in the more central Cry-d'Er area. There are a number of specialist shops: the Pacific Surf shop is home to the Stoked snowboard school. The main lifts are chairs and gondolas, and the drag-lifts are usually avoidable with good planning. It is a good place for beginner and intermediate boarders – and, of course, slush is not such a problem for novice boarders to navigate as it is for novice skiers! But avoid the ice first thing in the morning. Nightlife tends to be a fairly civilised affair, though; the George & Dragon can get quite lively and has a 'typical' pub atmosphere.*

The resort

Crans-Montana celebrated 100 years as a resort in 1993, but is far from being a picturesque Swiss chocolate-box village. Set on a broad shelf facing south to the great mountains across the Rhône valley, it is really two villages, their centres a mile apart and their fringes now merging. Strung along a busy road, the resort's many hotels, villas, apartments and smart shops are mainly dull blocks with little traditional Alpine character.

Fortunately, the resort's many trees help to screen the buildings, and make some areas positively attractive. And its wonderful setting means you get a lot of sun as well as superb views. There are several lakes and two golf courses, one home to the Swiss Open.

The resort is reached by good roads, and by a fast funicular railway up from Sierre to Montana. It depends heavily on summer conference business, which sets the tone even in winter. Hotels tend to be comfortable but formal, village facilities varied but daytime-oriented, and visitors middle-aged and dignified. In the evenings there's little Alpine-village atmosphere.

Gondolas go up to the main slopes from both villages. Crans is the more upmarket, with expensive jewellery

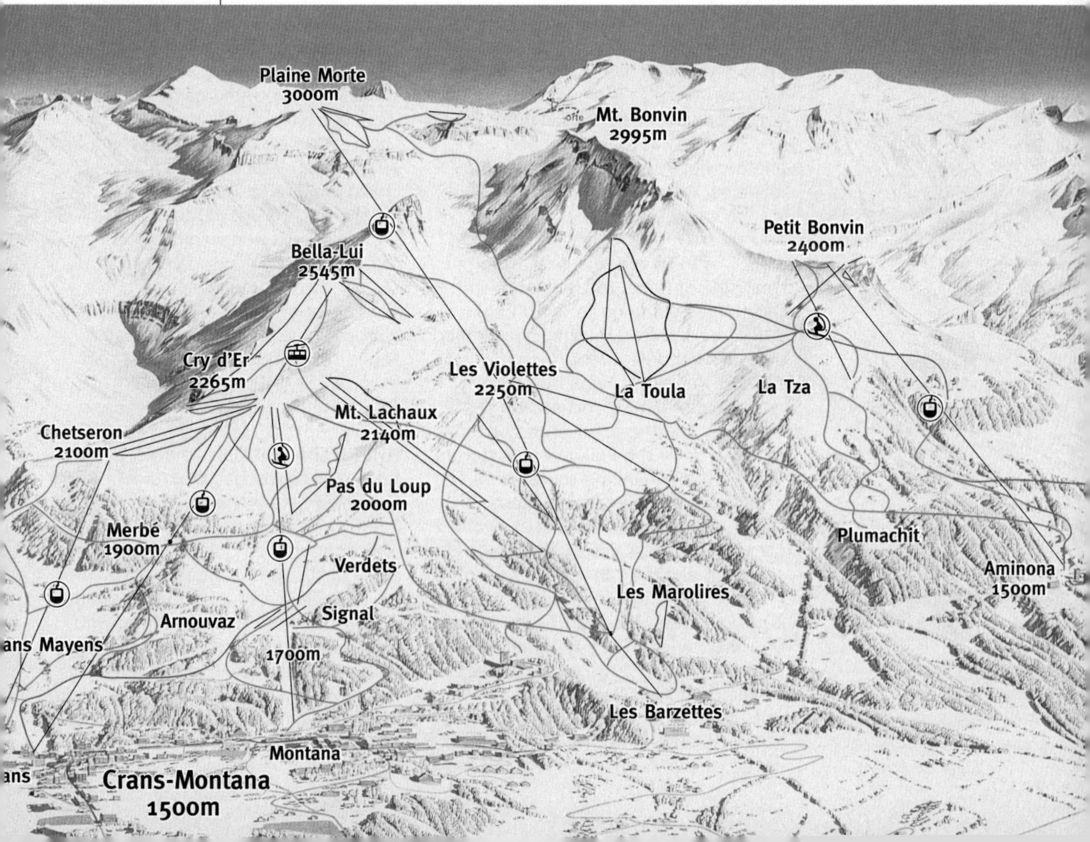

shops, a casino, and a high fur-coat count. It is well situated for the pretty golf course area, which has baby lifts for complete beginners, a cross-country trail and lovely walks. Montana has somewhat cheaper restaurants and bars. There are other gondola base stations and places to stay further east: at Violettes in Les Barzettes (the lift from here connects directly to the top glacier lift and is the fastest way to the top) and at Aminona.

The mountains

Although it has achieved some prominence in ski-racing, Crans-Montana has slopes that suit intermediates well, with few challenges and no nasty surprises. Beginners are well catered for.

THE SLOPES
Interestingly fragmented

Crans-Montana's 160km of piste are spread over three well-linked areas, all equally suitable for intermediates of varying abilities and persuasions.

Cry d'Er is the largest sector – an open bowl descending into patchy forest, directly above Montana. Cry d'Er itself is the meeting point of many lifts and the starting point of the cable-car up to the sector high point of Bella-Lui (2545m). Cry d'Er is served directly by two gondolas – a newish eight-person one from just above Crans, and another from just above central Montana, which has a useful mid-station where beginners can get off and access high-altitude nursery slopes. A third gondola goes from the west side of Crans to Chetseron, with a drag above going on to Cry d'Er.

The next sector, reached by another powerful gondola directly from Les Barzettes (labelled 'Violettes' on the resort piste map), is focused on Les Violettes, starting point of the jumbo gondola up to the Plaine Morte glacier. There are three linking routes from Cry d'Er to the **Violettes-Plaine Morte** sector. The highest, starting at Bella-Lui (or, strictly, at Col du Pochet, a short run and drag beyond) used to be off-piste but is now an official red run. Bella-Lui is also the start of the Men's Downhill course (Piste Nationale) that goes past Cry d'Er to Les Barzettes.

The third **Petit Bonvin** sector is served by a gondola up from Aminona at the eastern end of the area. This is linked to Les Violettes by red and blue runs passing the drag and chair-lift at La Toula.

Reporters complain of confusion caused by poor signing.

Anzère is nearby to the west, though the slopes aren't linked. You can make expeditions to Zermatt and Verbier by road or rail.

SNOW RELIABILITY
The resort's main drawback

Crans-Montana's slopes go up to glacier level at 3000m, but this is misleading; the runs on the Plaine Morte glacier are very limited and, excellent though it is, the solitary run down from there does not make this a snowsure area as a whole. Few of the other slopes are above 2250m, and practically all get a lot of direct sun. Late in the season, at least, this makes for slush in the afternoons, rock-hard ice in the mornings, and a tendency for snow to disappear. There is now snowmaking on the main runs down from both Violettes and Cry d'Er to Montana, from Cry d'Er to Crans and the bottom part of the run from Chetseron. We applaud these efforts; but it is a losing battle.

FOR EXPERTS
Lacks challenging pistes

There are few steep pistes. The only moguls worthy of the name are on the short but often quiet slopes at La Toula. There's plenty of off-piste in all sectors, but particularly beneath Chetseron and La Tza; guides are usually easy to book. The off-piste tour from Plaine Morte to Aminona is recommended.

The Piste Nationale course is far from daunting taken at 'normal' speed, but has some enormous jumps just above Les Marolires. The direct run from La Tza to Plumachit is fairly testing in places, especially when icy.

FOR INTERMEDIATES
Lots of attractive, flattering runs

Crans-Montana is very well suited to intermediates. Pistes are mostly wide and, although red dominates the map, many of the red runs don't justify the grading. They also tend to be uniform in difficulty from top to bottom, with few nasty surprises for the nervous. Avid piste-bashers enjoy the length of many runs, plus the fast lifts and good links that allow a lot of varied mileage.

The 11km run from Plaine Morte to Les Barzettes starts with superb top-of-

MOUNTAIN FACTS

Altitude	1500m-3000m
Lifts	35
Pistes	160km
Blue	38%
Red	50%
Black	12%
Artificial snow	17km
Recco detectors used	

LIFT PASSES

2000/01 prices in Swiss francs

Crans-Montana-Aminona
Covers all lifts in Crans-Montana and Aminona and the ski-bus.

Beginners Points card

Main pass
1-day pass 52
6-day pass 239

Senior citizens
Over 65 (men)
62 (women): 6-day pass 225 (15% off)

Children
Under 16: 6-day pass 143 (40% off)
Under 6: free pass

Short-term passes
Half-day from 11.15 (adult 40) or 12.30 (adult 34); 2hr afternoon pass from 2pm (adult 30).

Alternative periods
8 non-consecutive days (adult 346).

SCHOOLS/GUIDES

2000/01 prices in Swiss francs

Swiss
Classes 6 days
3hr: 9.30-12.30
6 days: 170
Children's classes
Ages: from 3
9.30-12.30 or 9.30-4
Half day 45
1 day with meal 80
Private lessons
Hourly
60 for 1hr

Swiss
Classes 6 days
3hr: 9.30-12.30
6 days: 170

Ski & Sky
Private lessons
Hourly
60 for 1hr

Stoked Snowboard
Classes Half day: 50

CHILDCARE

The Montana ski school runs a kindergarten with skiing available up at Signal and the Crans school on the golf course for children aged 3 to 6, from 9.30 to 4.30.

There are several other kindergartens. In Montana, Fleurs des Champs takes children aged 3 months to 7 years; and Zig-Zag takes children from 2 to 6 years.

the-world views and powder snow, and finishes among pretty woods. But many people love the top half so much ('my favourite run in Europe') they do it repeatedly, curtailing their descent halfway down at either the Barmaz or Cabane de Bois chair-lifts to Les Violettes, for quicker access to the top gondola. Because of the gondola's high capacity the run can get crowded.

The short runs from Bella-Lui to just below Cry d'Er have some of the best snow and quietest slopes in the area, and provide fine views of awesome Montagne de Raul. The Piste Nationale is a good test of technique, with plenty of bumps but also lots of room. The quietest area, and good for groups of varying intermediate standards, is the Petit Bonvin sector.

FOR BEGINNERS
Plenty to offer the first-timer

There are three excellent nursery areas, with slopes of varying difficulty. Complete beginners have very gentle slopes on the golf course next to Crans. Cry d'Er has an area of relatively long, easy runs, with up-the-mountain views and atmosphere as well as better snow. But the runs aren't just for beginners, and you do need a full lift pass. The Verdets-Grand Signal run is steeper, and the drag-lift can get terribly icy. Near-beginners can try the little run up at Plaine Morte.

FOR CROSS-COUNTRY
Excellent high-level trails

There are 40km of cross-country trails altogether. There are some pretty, easy trails (skating-style as well as classic) on and around the golf course. But what makes Crans-Montana particularly good for cross-country is its high-level route, in and out of woods, across the whole mountainside from Plans Mayens to beyond Aminona. 10km of trails at Plaine Morte are open when the lower trails are closed.

QUEUES
Few problems

The resort's big recent investment in new gondolas – notably the jumbo 'Funitel' gondola from Les Violettes to the Plaine Morte glacier slopes in the mid-1990s and the new lift out of Crans – has greatly alleviated any queue problems – though bottlenecks can occur at the Nationale drag-lifts. Recent reporters say you rarely wait longer than five minutes – except occasionally if snow lower down is in poor condition. More of a problem can be bottlenecks on some pistes, including the top glacier run. The resort does not get weekend crowds.

MOUNTAIN RESTAURANTS
A good choice

There are 20 mountain restaurants listed on the piste map and many of them offer table-service. The Merbé, at the Crans-Cry d'Er gondola mid-station, is one of the most attractive in the sector, with table-service of good food in a pleasant setting just above the tree line. It does get very busy, however, and advance bookings are recommended. Bella-Lui's terrace (with service) offers good views. The Chetseron eatery has fine views and allows picnics if you buy a drink.

Petit Bonvin, at the top of the Aminona sector, has self-service and table-service sections, with superb views. The table-service restaurant at Plumachit, towards the bottom of the sector, has a large sun terrace in a pretty setting and is recommended by reporters (again, book ahead) – unfortunately, the lifts back have been removed so you now have to hike uphill for 10 minutes before descending to Aminona. There is not much choice in the Violettes sector, but we had a good meal on the table-service terrace of the main restaurant (also with a picnic area). And the small self-service Cabane des Violettes, 50m below this, gets rave reviews for food and views (be there early for a seat on the terrace).

SCHOOLS AND GUIDES
Good reports

Both local branches of the Swiss school have mainly attracted favourable comments over the years. Last year we received a bad report of the Montana school: 'Poor, poor, poor! No real tuition and they didn't find us any nice snow. Only good point was free wine at the drinks break.' But our only report this year suggests a return to form. Cry d'Er is a common rendezvous spot. Private lessons are easily booked, for both on- and off-piste.

FACILITIES FOR CHILDREN
Adequate, but few reports

The resort facilities for children seem to be adequate, especially in Montana, but we have no recent reports.

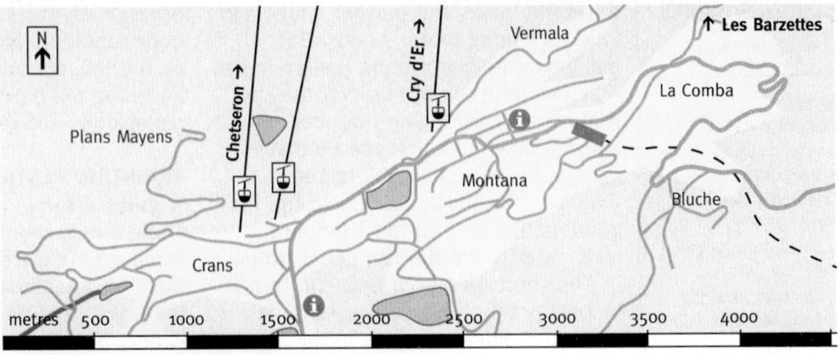

GETTING THERE

Air Sion, transfer 30min. Geneva, transfer 3hr.

Rail Sierre (15km), Sion (22km); regular buses to resort.

ACTIVITIES

Indoor Hotel swimming pools, tennis, bowling, bridge, chess, golf simulator, squash, concerts, cinemas, casino, curling, ice skating, galleries
Outdoor Toboggan run, ski-bob, horse-riding, ice skating, paragliding, balloon flights

TOURIST OFFICE

Postcode CH-3962
t +41 (27) 485 0404
f 485 0460
info@crans-montana.ch
www.crans-montana.ch

Staying there

Crans-Montana is quite sprawling. A free shuttle-bus links the villages and satellite lift stations during the day. At peak times the frequency is inadequate and the buses can get very crowded – one reporter recommends taking a car. The main Crans and Montana gondola stations are above the main road and a tiring walk. Many people store their equipment at lift stations overnight.

HOW TO GO

Much more choice on your own

There is a wide choice of hotels and apartments, and some are available through UK tour operators.

Hotels This conference resort has 53 mainly large, comfortable, expensive hotels. Most have three or more stars.

(5) **Crans-Ambassador** Huge luxury place with 'superb food, good leisure facilities'. Near Montana gondola.

(4) **Aïda Castel** Beautifully furnished in chic rustic style. Between the two resort centres. Outdoor pool.

(4) **Le Green** Well placed near the Crans lifts; small, modern and chic.

(3) **La Forêt** Highly recommended. Almost at Les Barzettes, with minibus to lifts. Pool and splendid views.

(3) **National** Perfectly placed for the Crans-Cry d'Er gondola; 'quiet, comfortable, good food'.

(3) **Curling** Comfortable, near centre of Montana and with bus stop outside.

(3) **Robinson** B&B only; well placed near the National, in Crans.

Self-catering There are many apartments available, particularly to independent travellers.

EATING OUT

Plenty of alternatives

There is a good variety of restaurants from French to Lebanese. Almost all the cheaper ones are in Montana. The Dent Blanche has been recommended for fondues. We had a good, simple Italian meal at Il Padrino in Crans. La Nouvelle Rotisserie is reputed to be excellent (the same owner as the wonderful La Poste – now closed). The Gréni is a welcoming restaurant on the western fringe of Montana. The Cervin up at Vermala is unusually rustic.

APRES-SKI

Can be ritzy, but otherwise quiet

Crans-Montana visitors tend to prefer quiet meals and drinks to raucous nightlife. Amadeus 2006 and Chez Nanette are tents on Cry d'Er serving close-of-play vin chaud. The George & Dragon in Crans is one of the liveliest, most crowded bars with 'the cheapest beer in town'. Reporters recommend Bar 1900, La Grange, Le Constellation and Indiana Café. The outdoor ice rink in Montana is 'fun' on Friday and Saturday evenings. The cinema has films in English. Bridge is played in the hotels Royal and Aïda.

OFF THE SLOPES

Excellent, but little charm

There are plenty of off-slope activities including lovely walks. Swimming is available in several hotels. Sierre is easily reached for shopping, and the larger Sion is only a few minutes further. Montreux is within reach. Mountain restaurants are mainly at gondola and cable-car stations.

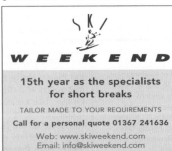

Davos

1550m

A big town surrounded by a great Alpine playground

WHAT IT COSTS

5

HOW IT RATES

The slopes

Snow	****
Extent	*****
Experts	****
Intermediates	*****
Beginners	**
Convenience	**
Queues	**
Restaurants	***

The rest

Scenery	****
Resort charm	**
Off-slope	*****

What's new

Sadly, plans for the long-overdue replacement of the ancient Parsennbahn funicular have been cancelled. This is the key lift from town to the main slopes (and down again) and horrendous queues can form each way – it will remain one of the worst bottlenecks in the Alps. Further up the mountains, things are better, with new high-speed quad chair-lifts replacing T-bars most years (including one on Jakobshorn for 1999/2000).

There is a new carving course underneath the Parsennhütte cable car.

Parking charges have been introduced at all ski areas.

It is hoped that all hotels in Davos will offer Internet access by December 2000.

There is a new booking system which links all hotels in Davos (+41 (81) 415 2121).

- + Very extensive slopes
- + Some superb, long and mostly easy runs away from the lifts
- + Lots of off-piste, with lots of marked itineraries and some short tours
- + Good cross-country trails
- + Excellent sports facilities, pretty walks, good range of shopping
- + Some captivating mountain restaurants above Klosters
- + Klosters is attractively villagey

- − Dreary block-style buildings of Davos spoil the views
- − Davos is a huge, city-like resort, rather plagued by traffic and lacking Alpine atmosphere
- − The slopes are spread over five or six essentially separate areas
- − Some access lifts are old and out-of-date, with long queues – especially the main funicular from Dorf
- − Only one piste (black) back to Davos Dorf, which finishes 500m from town

Davos was once hugely popular with Brits, but has fallen out of favour and is now dominated by Germans. Few resorts in the world have more extensive slopes, or offer more for all standards. But the area has its drawbacks: it is split into several unlinked sectors, and relatively ancient and queue-prone lifts access many of them. Those prepared to accept such drawbacks normally do so as the price of staying in a captivating Alpine village. But Davos is far from that.

Whether you forgive the flaws and fall for the resort depends on how highly you value three plus-points: the distinctive, long intermediate runs of the Parsenn area; being able to visit a different sector every day; and the considerable off-piste potential. We like all three, and we always look forward to visiting.

But you don't have to stay in Davos to enjoy its slopes: Klosters offers a much more captivating alternative. Despite royal connections, it is not exclusive – on the contrary, it has exceptionally welcoming places to stay. But it is less well placed than Davos for exploring all the mountains.

boarding *Although the nursery slopes are not ideal, the long easy runs of the Parsenn are good for near-beginner boarders and you can avoid drags if you plan your runs. But intermediate and advanced boarders will get the most out of Davos's vast terrain and off-piste potential. The established boarder mountain is the Jakobshorn, with its half-pipe, fun-park, boarder-cross course and funky Jatz Bar nearby. The Rinerhorn and Pischa each have a fun-park. There are several cheap and cheerful hotels specially for boarders, including the 180-bed Bolgenhof hotel (new for the 1999/2000 season) near the Jakobshorn, the Snowboardhotel Bolgenschanze and the Snowboarder's Palace.*

SWISS-IMAGE / DAVOS TOURISMUS

Davos is a big town, with Europe's worst lift queues to get up (and down) the mountain →

The resort

Davos is set in a broad, gently sloping valley, with its slopes either side. Arguably it was the very first place in the Alps to develop its slopes. The railway up the Parsenn was one of the first built for skiers (in 1931), and the first drag-lift was built on the Bolgen nursery slopes in 1934. But Davos was already a health resort; many of its luxury hotels used to be sanatoriums.

Sadly that's just what they look like. There are still several specialist clinics and these, along with hosting conferences (including the World Economic Forum) and top international sporting events, are what the town of Davos has become well known for. It is also a popular destination for athletes wanting to train at high altitude.

It has two main centres, Dorf and Platz, about 2km apart. Easiest access to the slopes is from Dorf to the main Parsenn area, via the funicular railway, or from Platz to the Strela and Jakobshorn areas. Davos shares its slopes with the royals' favourite resort of Klosters, down the hill.

MOUNTAIN FACTS

Altitude	810m-2845m
Lifts	54
Pistes	320km
Blue	30%
Red	50%
Black	20%
Artificial snow	17km

Recco detectors used

The mountains

The slopes here have something for everyone, though experts and nervous intermediates need to choose their territory with care. Trips are possible by car or rail to St Moritz (the Vereina rail tunnel offers access to the Engadine area without having to negotiate the snowy Flüelapass) and Arosa, and by car to Flims-Laax and Lenzerheide.

THE SLOPES
Vast and varied

If you wanted you could hit a different mountain in Davos every day for a week. In practice, the minor areas tend to be neglected by most visitors – and are therefore much quieter.

The ancient Parsennbahn funicular from Davos Dorf takes you to the major lift junction of Weissfluhjoch (2665m), at one end of the **Parsenn**. At the other is Gotschnagrat, reached by cable-car from Klosters. Between the two is the wide, open Parsenn bowl. From Davos Platz, a funicular takes you up to Schatzalp, at the base of the **Strela** area. Follow this with a long, two-person chair, a cable-car and finally a T-bar, and you will eventually gain access to the Weissfluhjoch.

Across the valley, **Jakobshorn** is reached by cable-car from Davos Platz; this is the main snowboarders' hill. **Rinerhorn** and **Pischa** are reached by bus or (in the case of Rinerhorn) train.

Beyond the main part of Klosters, a gondola goes up from Klosters Dorf to the sunny, scenic **Madrisa** area.

Lift passes are monitored electronically, without the need to take them out of your pocket. But you'll need your receipt if you want free use of the local buses or trains.

There is a small floodlit slope area at the Jakobshorn.

SNOW RELIABILITY
Good, but not the best

Davos is high by Swiss standards. Its mountains go respectably high too – though not to glacial heights. Not many of the slopes face directly south, but not many face directly north either Snow reliability is generally good higher up but can be poor lower down – you may have to take the lifts down to both Davos and Klosters after using the Parsenn slopes. Snowmaking has been added on some lower runs.

FOR EXPERTS
Plenty to do, on- and off-piste

A glance at the piste map may give the misleading impression that this is an intermediate's resort. In fact several black runs have been been regraded to off-piste itineraries (marked on the map but not prepared or controlled). These and official black runs are largely in the wooded lower slopes, which means good visibility when snow is falling – the Meierhofer Tälli run to Wolfgang is excellent – but rough going when snow is thin. Two exceptions are the trio of runs at the southern extremity of the Strela area, and the runs from Gotschnagrat directly towards Klosters – around the infamous Gotschnawang slope. The Wang run is a seriously steep ski route (and rarely open, in our experience). Drostobel is less scary, though the overall gradient is little different.

The main appeal of the area to experts, however, is the excellent off-piste and short tours – as a recent expert reporter confirms. But another reporter complains of a lack of moguls due to too much grooming!

Arosa can be reached much more quickly on snow than by road or rail, but requires a return by rail via Chur. From Madrisa you can make tours to

LIFT PASSES

2000/01 prices in Swiss francs

Top Card
Covers all Davos and Klosters, the railway in the whole region and buses between the resorts.

Beginners Single and return tickets on main lifts in each area.

Main pass
1-day pass 55
6-day pass 273 (low season 218)

Senior citizens
Over 65 (male), 62 (female): 6-day pass 218

Children
Under 16: 1-day pass 33; 6-day pass 164
Under 6 (with adult): free pass

Notes
A confusing array of passes are available for individual areas (Parsenn, Schatzalp, Jakobshorn, Rinerhorn, Gotschna and Madrisa) and combined areas, from a half day to 15 days, (although some areas are from a minimum of 2 days). Several reporters have complained that not all passes are available at each base station. For instance if you're staying in Klosters and want to buy a Parsenn pass (which covers Gotschna, Schatzalp and Pischa) you'll have to travel to Davos to buy it.

Gargellen in Austria's Montafontal. This means an exhausting one-hour walk on skins or snow-shoes on the way back.

FOR INTERMEDIATES
A splendid variety of runs

For intermediates of any temperament, this is a great area. There are good cruising runs on all five mountains, so you would never get bored in a week. This variety of different slopes taken together with the wonderful long runs to the valleys makes it a compelling area with a unique character.

The epic runs to Klosters and other places (described in the feature box) pose few difficulties for a confident intermediate or even an ambitious near-beginner (one of the editors did the run to Klosters on his third day on skis and some of our reporters did the run to Küblis on their second holiday). And there are one or two other notable away-from-the-lifts runs to the valley. In particular, you can travel from the top of Madrisa back to Klosters Dorf via the beautiful Schlappin valley.

FOR BEGINNERS
Platz is the more convenient

The Bolgen nursery slope is adequately spacious and gentle, and a bearable walk from the centre of Platz. But Dorf-based beginners face more of a trek out to Bünda – unless staying out at the hotel of the same name.

There is no shortage of easy runs to progress to, spread around all the sectors. The Parsenn sector probably has the edge, with long, early intermediate runs in the main Parsenn bowl, as well as in the valleys down from Weissfluhjoch.

FOR CROSS-COUNTRY
Long, scenic valley trails

Davos has a total of 75km of trails running in both directions along the main valley and reaching well up into Sertigtal, Dischmatal and Flüelatal. There is a cross-country ski centre and special ski school on the outskirts of town.

QUEUES
Still a problem in the valley

The ancient Parsennbahn railway is a relic of the past. It generates some of the longest lift queues remaining in the Alps – a 90-minute wait is not unheard of at busy times. And when snow is poor you have to queue to come down as well. So we are very disappointed that its planned replacement has been cancelled. In Klosters, queues for the Gotschna cable-car have been much reduced by a doubling of its capacity, but can still be a problem at weekends. One of our editors, who visited Davos at New Year, found the queues at all the areas unbearable – and took up snow-shoeing instead. Once you manage to get up the mountain, queues for the higher lifts are not too bad.

THE PARSENN'S SUPER-RUNS

The runs from Weissfluhjoch that head north, on the back of the mountain, make this area special for many visitors. The pistes that continue to Schifer and then to Küblis, Saas and Serneus, and the one that curls around the mountain to Klosters, are graded red but are not difficult. What marks them out is their sheer length (10–12km) and the sensation of travel they offer.

Until the late 1980s, only the very top 2.5km and 400m vertical of this enormous snow field could be done over and over; once below Kreuzweg, you had to go down to the valley and catch the train home. Usually, you did it towards the end of the day, dawdling in the rustic restaurants in the woods on the lower reaches. The long Schiferbahn gondola changed all that – you can now 'yo-yo' 1100m vertical as often as you like. Some long-standing visitors regret the change, but there is the added advantage that the lower runs, below the Schifer gondola station, are quieter – especially if you do them early in the day rather than as your last run.

The longest runs are the marked but unpatrolled routes to Fideris and Jenaz, the latter being 18km from Weissfluhjoch, according to official figures. But these are often closed because of shortage of snow low down. Start at the Weissfluh summit and you can add another kilometre, as well as another 200m vertical. But these are not continuous runs: they require skins or snow-shoes for a couple of short ascents, and payment for the use of the lifts at Fideriser Heuberge on the way.

CHILDCARE

The ski school runs the Pinocchio nursery at Bünda, on the outskirts of Davos Dorf, taking children from age 3, from 8.30 to 4.30. Children can stay in the nursery, play on skis or take ski school classes.

The kindergarten at Pischa takes children from age 3, 10am to 4pm.

A common complaint is that there is no crèche in town and babysitters are hard to find.

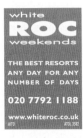

SCHOOLS/GUIDES

2000/01 prices in Swiss francs

Classes
4hr: 2hr am and pm
5 full days: 210

Children's classes
Ages: 4 to 16
5 full days: 210

Private lessons
Half day or full day
175 for half day or 280 for full day

MOUNTAIN RESTAURANTS
Stay low down

The main high-altitude restaurants are dreary self-service affairs, but the Strelapass hut is recommended as particularly enjoyable on a warm sunny day, with good views and 'excellent' food (although it's a five-minute climb). There are other compelling places – notably the rustic Conterser Schwendi and Serneuser Schwendi in the woods on the way down to the Klosters valley from the Parsenn (both serve great rösti). These are fun places to end up as darkness falls – Klosters Schwendi, at least, sells wax torches to illuminate your final descent to the village. The Skilife, down from Totalp, is self-service, has very loud pop music and is popular with hordes of school children. The Jatzhutte near the boarders' fun-park on Jakobshorn is wild – with changing scenery such as mock palm trees, parrots and pirates.

The Munggaloch bar (at the mid-station of the Parsenn) – is convenient if you're waiting for the queue to disperse to go down in the funicular. And the station restaurants at Saas and Küblis are pleasant places to wait.

SCHOOLS AND GUIDES
Don't count on English

The Davos Swiss ski school has been renamed the Swiss Snowsportschool to emphasise the variety of instruction available (including skiing, boarding, carving, snowblading). Given the small number of British visitors that Davos attracts, it's not surprising to find that classes are often German-dominated. A Davos regular has said that the school is well organised, but that the instructors vary widely. There is an alternative ski school called New Trend and a choice of three schools for snowboarding.

FACILITIES FOR CHILDREN
Not ideal

Davos is a rather spread-out place in which to handle a family – and indeed the school's nursery is in a slightly isolated spot, at Dorf's Bünda nursery slope, inconvenient for dropping off and picking up. A recent reporter tells us the school is 'well organised, but even good instructors forget at times that your child doesn't speak German'.

Staying there

Davos is a big, spread-out resort and although transport is good, with buses around the town as well as the railway linking Dorf and Platz to Klosters and other villages, location is important. Dorf has direct but queue-prone access to the Parsenn; Platz has lifts to Jakobshorn and Strela, the big sports facilities, the smarter shopping and more evening action.

HOW TO GO
Hotels dominate the packages

Although most bed space in Davos is in apartments, hotels dominate the UK package holiday market.

Hotels A dozen 4-star places and about 30 3-stars form the core of the Davos hotel trade, though there are a couple of 5-stars and quite a few cheaper places, including B&Bs.

(((((5 **Flüela** The more atmospheric of the two 5-star hotels, in central Dorf, and quite well placed to beat the Parsenn queues. Pool.

((((4 **Golfhotel Waldhuus** As convenient for winter langlaufers as for summer golfers. Quiet, modern, tasteful. Pool.

((((4 **Davoserhof** Best in town. Small, old, beautifully furnished, with excellent food; well placed in Platz. But will be under new management for 2001.

(((3 **Parsenn** Right opposite the Parsenn

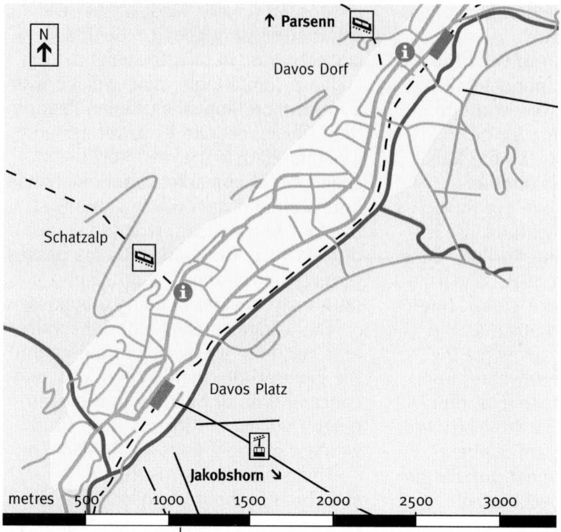

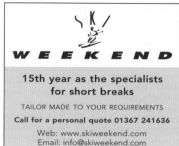

GETTING THERE

Air Zürich, transfer 2hr by car, 3hr by rail or bus.

Rail Stations in Davos Dorf and Platz. 20 minutes from Davos to Klosters.

railway in Dorf. What was an attractive chalet has been marred by the big new McDonald's on the ground floor.

(3) **Bahnhof Terminus** Friendly, three restaurants including a great Chinese, good sauna, right by bus stop in Platz.

(2) **Alte Post** Traditional and cosy; in central Platz. Popular with boarders.

(2) **Hubli's Landhaus** 5km out at Laret, towards Klosters. Quiet country inn with sophisticated, expensive food.

(1) **Snowboarder's Palace** Close to Schatzalp lift, offers good-value dormitory accommodation.

STAYING UP THE MOUNTAIN
The quieter option

The 3-star Berghotel Schatzalp, on the tree line about 300m above Davos Platz and reached by funicular (free to guests), is a converted sanatorium made famous by Thomas Mann's novel *The Magic Mountain*. The Strela slopes just above have something for everyone, and there is a nursery slope right next to the hotel. Schatzalp is also the start of one of the resort's toboggan runs.

EATING OUT
Wide choice, mostly in hotels

Most of the better restaurants are in hotels. The Davoserhof's two restaurants are among the best in town, both for food and ambience. There is a choice of two good Chinese restaurants – the lavish Zauberberg in the Europe and the Golden Dragon in the Bahnhof Terminus.

Good-value places include the Pizzeria Al Ponte, La Caretta (good for home-made pasta) and the small and cosy Gentiana (with an upstairs stübli). An evening excursion for dinner out of town is popular. Schatzalp (reached by a funicular), the Hauser in Sertig and Landhaus in Frauenkirch have all been recommended.

APRES-SKI
Lots on offer, but quiet clientele

There are plenty of bars, discos and nightclubs, and a large casino in the hotel Europe. But we're not sure how some of them make a living – Davos guests tend to want the quiet life. At tea-time high calories are consumed at

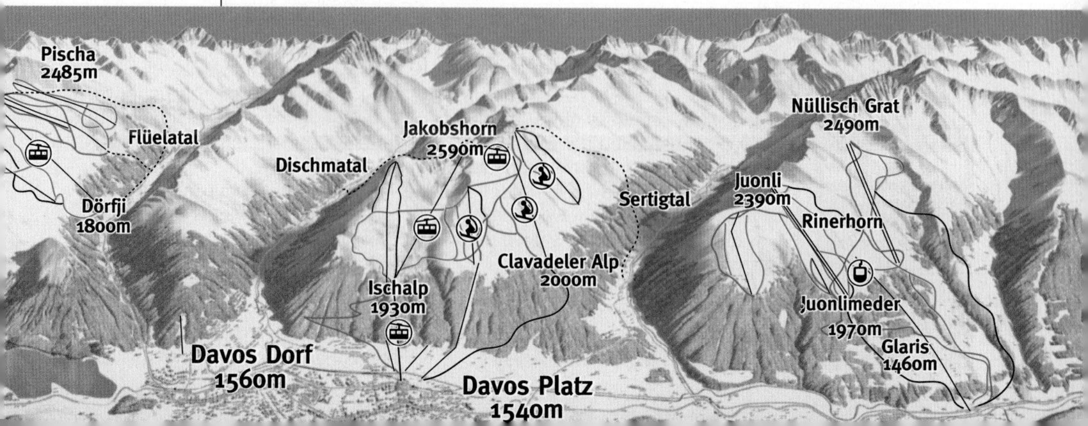

ACTIVITIES

Indoor Artificial skating rink, fitness centre, tennis, squash, swimming, sauna, cinema, museums, galleries, libraries, massage, badminton, golf-driving range

Outdoor Over 80km of cleared paths (mostly at valley level), snow-shoe trekking, full-moon skiing, toboggan run, snow volleyball, natural skating rink, curling, horse-riding, mule-trekking, sleigh rides, hang-gliding, paragliding

TOURIST OFFICE

Postcode CH-7270
t +41 (81) 415 2121
f 415 2100
davos@davos.ch
www.davos.ch

cafés Weber and Schneider. Scala has a popular outside terrace.

The liveliest place in town is the rustic little Chämi bar (popular with locals). It's one of the few spots to retain a spark of life late in the evening. The Schützen – where Ranch meets Jungle decor – is another interesting place; there is live music, and it is also popular with locals. The Ex Bar is a smart mixture of Parisienne Brasserie with a touch of Pancho Villa and attracts a mixed age group. One reporter tells of a bar known as the 0815 which sells large beers for the price of a small beer elsewhere, but 'has sticky carpets and several drunks'.

Nightclubs tend to be sophisticated, expensive and lacking atmosphere during the week. The most popular are the Cabanna, the Rotliechtli, Cava Grischa, Millennium! Bar Senn and for live music Grand-Café.

Bolgenschanze and Bolgen are popular boarder hang-outs.

OFF THE SLOPES

Great apart from the buildings

Provided you're not fussy about building style, Davos can be unreservedly recommended for off-slope fun. The towny resort has shops and other diversions, and transport along the valley and up onto the slopes is good – though the best of the mountain restaurants are well out of range for pedestrians. The sports facilities are excellent; the natural ice rink is said to be Europe's biggest, and is supplemented by artificial rinks, both indoor and outdoor.

Spectator sports include speed skating as well as hockey (most noteworthy is the Spengler Cup held in December). And there are lots of walks up on the slopes as well as around the lake and along the valleys.

Klosters 1190m

In a word association game, Klosters might trigger 'Prince of Wales'. The world's TV screens have shown him skiing there countless times. In 1988 he was almost killed there in an off-piste avalanche that did kill one of his companions, and now the enlarged cable-car to Gotschna – which takes you to the Parsenn area shared with Davos – is named after him.

Don't be put off. We don't know why HRH likes to ski in Klosters particularly, but it is certainly not because the place is the exclusive territory of royalty. Most of the really smart socialising goes on behind closed doors, in private chalets.

It's a comfortable, quiet village with a much more appealing Alpine flavour than Davos, despite its lower altitude. Klosters Platz is the main focus – a collection of upmarket, traditional-style hotels around the railway station, at the foot of the steep, wooded slopes of Gotschna. The road to Davos passes through, and traffic is a problem (although they are building a bypass).

The village spreads along the valley road for quite a way before fading into the countryside; there's then a second concentration of building in the even quieter village of Klosters Dorf, from where a gondola goes up to Madrisa.

There is a choice of ski and snowboard schools, and Klosters is well known for excellent mountain guides. There are some nursery lifts at valley level, but the sunny slopes of Madrisa are more appealing.

Klosters' upmarket image is reinforced by the upmarket UK tour operators that go there – The Ski Company Ltd and Powder Byrne.

There are some particularly attractive hotels. The central Chesa Grischuna is irresistible, combining traditional atmosphere with modern comfort – and a lively après-ski bar.

The less central Wynegg (renowned for its excellent chinoise fondue) is a favourite with British visitors, with good-value bedrooms. The Sport hotel in Dorf has also been recommended.

The huts in the woods above the village attract lots of people on their last run of the day, and the Conterser Schwendi serves excellent food. In the village, the Chesa Grischuna is a focus of activity from tea-time onwards, with its piano bar, bowling and restaurant.

Gaudy's at the foot of the slopes is a popular pit stop after skiing, as is the lively bar at the four-star Alpina and the Wynegg. Top of the price bracket for eating out is the Walserhof, while Alberto's is the best pizzeria in town.

In the late evening the bar of the hotel Kaiser is popular. The Casa Antica is a small but popular disco. The Kir Royale, under the hotel Silvretta Park, is bigger and more brash. The Funny Place, under the Piz Buin, is more grown-up and expensive.

Klosters is an attractive base for walking and cross-country skiing, but has little else off the slopes. Some hotels have pools and there is curling.

Engelberg 1050m

One of the biggest verticals in the Alps

WHAT IT COSTS

3

HOW IT RATES

The slopes	
Snow	***
Extent	**
Experts	***
Intermediates	***
Beginners	**
Convenience	*
Queues	***
Restaurants	***
The rest	
Scenery	***
Resort charm	***
Off-slope	***

What's new

The new 'Ice Flyer' high-speed six-seater chair-lift (with protective bubble) replaced the upper drag-lift on Titlis for 1999/2000.

2000/01 will see the drag-lift across the frozen lake at Trübsee replaced by a new chair-lift.

MOUNTAIN FACTS

Altitude 1050m-3020m	
Lifts	23
Pistes	82km
Blue	31%
Red	67%
Black	2%
Artificial snow	2km
Recco detectors used	

TOURIST OFFICE

Postcode CH-6390
t +41 (41) 639 7777
f 639 7766
tourist.center@engelberg.ch
www.engelberg.ch

Engelberg makes a great weekend retreat for the residents of Lucerne, less than an hour away. Despite impressive and distinctive mountains towering 2000m above the village, it attracts few foreign visitors – partly, we guess, because its slopes are rather inconveniently fragmented.

THE RESORT

Engelberg is a long-established, year-round resort – bustling, towny and home to an impressive 12th-century monastery – surrounded by spectacular mountains. Much of the old-world charm of the original village has been diluted by modern development, but away from the town the valley is very scenic. Engelberg is rather isolated from other resorts, but you can get to Andermatt and to the Jungfrau region.

THE MOUNTAINS

The **slopes** are in contrasting sectors on either side of the village. For the main sector, a regular, free shuttle-bus takes you across the valley, where a two-stage gondola or a funicular and then cable-car take you up to the shelf of Trübsee (1800m). From here a two-stage cable-car rises to Stand and then on to Titlis at over 3000m, the second stage having the novelty of revolving cabins for optimal scenery-gazing. Below the summit is a new six-pack and a drag-lift serving red and black slopes; descent to Stand (2430m) is via a single steep piste, with an easier red from there down to Trübsee. Across the frozen lake, a separate set of lifts serve good red runs above and below Jochpass (2205m). There is a roundabout run back to the valley.

The Brunni area, accessed by a cable-car from the edge of town, has a small network of sunny pistes between Schonegg (2040m) and Ristis (1600m), and a run back to town when snow conditions permit.

High, north-facing Titlis is **snowsure** (the glacier is open all year round). The Brunni sector is much less reliable.

For **experts**, the big attraction is off-piste – the famous Laub. This steep wall drops 1000m from the shoulder of Titlis – superb when conditions are right, dangerous when they aren't. The pistes generally suit confident **intermediates**, though they are not very extensive; there are not many really easy slopes. There are nursery slopes in various places, but they mainly involve lift-rides – the resort is not ideal for **beginners**.

The resort attracts quite a few **snowboarders**; there's a fun-park and half-pipe at Jochpass. Engelberg is good for **cross-country**, with 39km of trails amid lovely scenery at Trübsee and along the valley.

Queues and overcrowded pistes are likely at weekends and holiday times – a recent reporter describes 10-minute queues at most of the lifts one March weekend.

Mountain restaurants are plentiful. Most are friendly and inexpensive by Swiss standards. The Titlis restaurant is good (though not its snack bar), and the cosy Berghotel Trübsee-Hof has a vast sun terrace overlooking the frozen lake. Reporters have enjoyed the traditional, friendly Untertrübsee.

Unusually, the Swiss **ski school** has competition – the Neue Schischule, plus several specialist boarding schools. There is a **kindergarten** and the Edelweiss, Trübsee and Regina Titlis hotels have supervised crèches.

STAYING THERE

Most package **accommodation** is in hotels, with chalets and apartments to rent locally. The elegant 3-star Hess has nice rooms and good food. Among the other 3-stars, Edelweiss is poorly placed but has good children's facilities, and the Crystal and Engelberg are central. The 3-star Berghotel Trübsee-Hof is up at Trübsee.

Eating out is mostly in hotels, though there are alternatives. The Engelstübli is recommended for tasty, inexpensive food.

Après-ski is good, particularly at weekends, with lots of live music. The Alpenclub and Bänklialp have extensive folklore programmes. The Casino appears to have a lively bar.

Engelberg has plenty to do **off the slopes**, with good sports facilities, a monastery tour, glassworks and trips to Lucerne and Zürich.

Flims

1100m

A splendid, spacious area that deserves to be better known

WHAT IT COSTS

4

HOW IT RATES

The slopes

Snow	***
Extent	****
Experts	***
Intermediates	*****
Beginners	****
Convenience	***
Queues	***
Restaurants	***

The rest

Scenery	***
Resort charm	***
Off-slope	***

What's new

For 1999/2000 a new beginners' lift was built at Nagens.

A new 'slope system' was introduced (shown on the ski school map) which indicates areas for beginners, all-rounders (groomed slopes for carving), free-riders (slopes with waves, dips and jumps) and backcountry areas (off-piste slopes).

New Technology Centres now offer a complete package of ski clothing and equipment rental by the day – turn up in your city clothes and get everything you need for SF115 a day, including lift pass and even a shower after you finish.

- (+) Extensive, varied slopes suitable for all but experts
- (+) Impressive lift system
- (+) Virtually queue-free on weekdays
- (+) Fair number of slopes above 2000m, partly offsetting effects of their sunny south-east orientation
- (+) Lots of wooded runs for bad-weather days
- (+) Just 90 minutes from Zürich airport

- (–) Sunny orientation can cause icy or slushy pistes and shut lower runs
- (–) Buses or long walks to lifts from much of the accommodation
- (–) Very subdued in the evenings
- (–) Village very spread out, which detracts from its charm
- (–) Weekend crowds
- (–) Local dialect has unfortunate name for 'peak' – they call it 'crap'

Flims/Laax has an impressive 220km of mainly intermediate pistes. The resort is very popular with weekenders and has invested in some large-capacity lifts, including a 3-stage gondola from Flims, a jumbo gondola from Laax and several high-speed chair-lifts. It can be very quiet during the week, and it is virtually unknown outside the Swiss and German markets. It deserves better. Don't be put off by the unfortunate (for English-speakers) local name for 'peak', which is 'crap'. All the mountain-tops are called crap, a top après-ski venue is the Crap Bar and the tourist office has used the slogan 'Flims is crap' in promotions.

There are very long runs from the tops of three different interconnected mountains, amid stunning scenery – all ideal for adventurous intermediates. And there's plenty to play around on in all areas. The two main drawbacks are its sunny orientation, which can soon spoil the snow on the lower part of the mountain (especially later in the season), and the lack of any sense of real Alpine charm in any of the alternative places to stay. They aren't ugly – just lacking in the chocolate-box charm you might look for in Switzerland.

boarding *Flims/Laax is a snowboard hot spot. Crap Sogn Gion is a popular meeting point, with plenty of loud music from the outdoor Rock Bar and the No-Name Café, which overlooks two of four half-pipes on the mountain. The slopes are well suited to beginners and intermediates as well as experts. As the slopes close, the Crap Bar (includes Internet terminals and a games machine room called Laax Vegas) at Murschetg is popular with boarders. The Arena in Flims is good for live gigs. The Rider's Palace in Laax and Mountain Hostel have great value accommodation (from SF30 per person per night for a six-bed room). Flims/Laax also hosts various international snowboarding events.*

SWISS-IMAGE / MOUNTAIN MARKETING AG

The village is spread out with no real focus beneath an impressively large area of intermediate slopes →

MOUNTAIN FACTS

Altitude	1100m-3020m
Lifts	28
Pistes	220km
Blue	29%
Red	45%
Black	26%
Artificial snow	13km
Recco detectors used	

The resort

Flims is made up of two parts over a kilometre apart on a sunny, wooded mountain terrace. Dorf sprawls along a busy main road lined with shops, hotels, restaurants, bars and the main lift station, but has no real centre. Waldhaus is a sedate, sophisticated huddle of hotels quietly set among trees. Both parts look traditional, with wooden chalet-style buildings.

The slopes spread across the mainly south-east-facing mountain to another lift base-station at Murschetg (1.5km from Waldhaus), an outpost of Laax. From here there's an efficient jumbo gondola and less efficient cable-car – this is the easiest entry point for those with cars. There's also a high-speed quad at Falera, 5km from Waldhaus.

Most hotels are a bus-ride from the slopes but a combination of resort, hotel and post buses works well.

The mountains

Flims has extensive, underrated, varied slopes: some long runs and some high peaks (which are exposed and can be very windswept), including a small glacier area. Because of its sunny aspect, the lower runs can deteriorate quickly and it can be difficult to get back to Flims on snow (although there is some snowmaking). In poor visibility there are plenty of tree-lined runs. Trips are possible to Lenzerheide, Davos–Klosters and Arosa.

THE SLOPES
Impressive and well planned

There are essentially four sectors, each suitable for all grades but expert. The slopes are well planned, and moving around them is straightforward but can involve a lot of traversing.

The gondola from Flims has two mid-stations, the first at Plaun, where you change cabins or catch a high-speed six-person chair to **Crap Sogn Gion** at the heart of the Laax slopes. From here you can go down towards Murschetg, Laax or Falera or catch a cable-car up to **Crap Masegn**. This area is the biggest section of slopes.

If you take the next stage of the gondola there's another mid-station at Scansinas before you hit the top at Nagens (2130m) – alighting at either of these will allow you to get over to **La Siala** (via drag-lifts if you choose the Scansinas option). From La Siala (2810m) there's a red run to the high **Vorab glacier** (which reaches 3020m).

There is also a link via a two-way, two-stage gondola (which can be closed by wind) between the Vorab glacier and Crap Masegn. And there's a slope linking Crap Masegn with Plaun.

The **Cassons** sector above Flims Dorf is the smallest, particularly when runs to the village are incomplete. The peak (2675m) is reached via two chairs and a cable-car. It is linked via piste and lift to Nagens and Grauberg.

The piste map shows each type of lift and the time it takes to ride – an excellent idea that makes meeting others on time very easy.

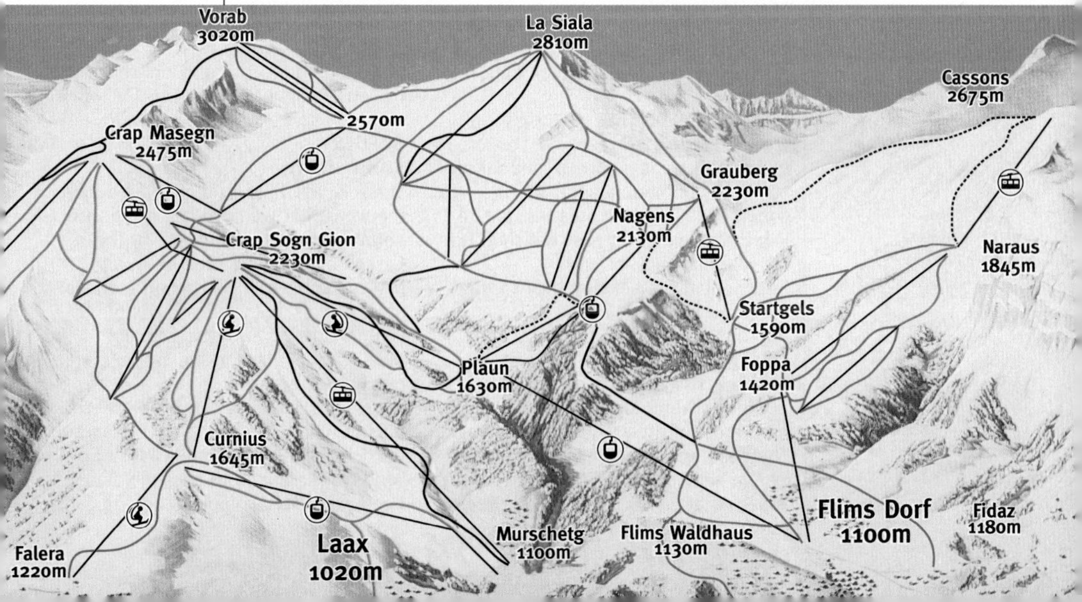

LIFT PASSES

1999/2000 prices in Swiss francs

Alpine Arena
Covers all lifts and buses between Flims, Laax and Falera.

Main pass
1-day pass 54 Mon-Fri, 59 Sat-Sun
6-day pass 296

Senior citizens
Over 65 (male), 62 (female): 6-day pass 250

Children
Under 16: 6-day pass 156
Under 6: free pass

Short-term passes
Half day from 12.15 (adult 46).

Alternative periods
Passes for 6 non-consecutive days (adult 324).

Notes Discount for 16- to 20-year-olds (6-day pass 250).

Top Ski Pass A season pass which covers Flims, Laax, Falera, Davos-Klosters, St Moritz and Arosa (in 1999/2000 it cost 990).

SNOW RELIABILITY
Good higher up

The upper runs are generally snowsure. But due to the sunny aspect, the runs back to Flims itself can suffer. There is snowmaking on three main runs from Crap Sogn Gion, including the splendid black race course run right down to Murschetg. There is also snowmaking from Segnes-Hütte to Flims and on the bottom part of the run to Alp Ruschein.

FOR EXPERTS
Bits and pieces

There is a fair amount to challenge, but it's rather dotted about, with the added frustration that some of it is on short sections of otherwise easy pistes. The toughest run is the steep, unpisted Cassons black, reached by a steep climb from the top of the cable-car. Other off-piste trips from this summit might look tempting, but don't even think about it without a guide.

One of the great pleasures of the whole area is the men's World Cup Downhill course from Crap Sogn Gion to Murschetg. It's so long (1000m vertical) and pretty that doing it repeatedly using the Murschetg cable-car doesn't get boring – and it's not so vulnerable to the sun now that it has snowmakers. The Nagens–Startgels run is short but steep. The Grauberg cable-car is used as a link between areas but its own ski area is usually very quiet and definitely worth exploring.

The off-piste is generally between pistes. Ruschein, at the western end of the area, is the best sector. And the long Sattel piste from Vorab – see below – is a good, beautiful starting point. Note that many of the black runs are really no more than 'dark red'.

FOR INTERMEDIATES
Paradise for all

In general this is a superb area for all standards of intermediate. When conditions allow, the area just above Flims is splendid for easy cruising. But the real highlight for early intermediates is heading over to the Vorab glacier and back on blue and red runs. On the way back you can take the cable-car from Grauberg to Startgels to avoid some awkward runs.

More adventurous intermediates have most of the area to choose from. There's a wonderful descent of over 1700m vertical on reds and blues if you start at La Siala and go all the way down to Flims. The easier of two unpisted runs from Cassons is a lovely trip along the shoulder of the mountain into a valley and on to Startgels – but check snow conditions first. The run from Crap Sogn Gion to Larnags via Curnius is also great fun.

Good intermediates will enjoy the superb and beautiful Sattel black run from the glacier to Ruschein at the extreme west of the area. It starts with a challenging mogul field but develops into a fast cruise and is one of the longest, most beautiful runs around.

The Crap Sogn Gion to Plaun routes are interesting, being quite steep and sheltered – and are some of the few runs not to directly face the sun.

Less confident intermediates should note that some easy runs have short steep sections (normally marked black on the map). The links from Nagens towards Flims can be intimidating.

FOR BEGINNERS
Plenty of options

There's a good nursery area in Dorf, and alternatives at Startgels and Nagens if snow is poor. The Foppa and Naraus areas have good confidence-building runs to move on to. Getting the bus to the lovely easy runs above Falera is another option for those just off the nursery slopes. There's plenty of tuition in English.

FOR CROSS-COUNTRY
One of the best

An excellent choice. There are 70km of beautiful, well marked, mainly forest trails. Loops range from 3km to 20km. The cross-country ski school, centred at Waldhaus, has a good reputation and organises group classes. 3km of trail are floodlit. The only drawback is the possibility of poor snow.

QUEUES
Some delays

There is generally little queuing during the week, but we have had a report of 30-minute and longer waits for the Cassons, Crap Sogn Gion and Crap Masegn cable-cars. The resort is busier at weekends, with coach loads of day visitors arriving at Murschetg. But delays out of Flims in the morning are rare. The chair towards La Siala can generate queues, as can the slow two-person Alp Ruschein chair and some of the T-bars. Lifts closing because of wind (especially up to Cassons) has been a common complaint among reporters.

GETTING THERE

Air Zürich, transfer 1½hr.

Rail Chur (22km); regular buses to resort.

SCHOOLS/GUIDES

1999/2000 prices in Swiss francs

Swiss
Classes 5 days
4hr: 2hr am and pm
5 full days: 320
Children's classes
Ages: up to 12
5 full days: 320 with lunch
Private lessons
Half or full day
170 for half day

CHILDCARE

The ski school runs ski kindergartens (Dreamlands) taking children from age 3 – in Flims, Laax and Falera from 9am to 4.30.

Several hotels claim special facilities for children – the Park Hotel Waldhaus has its own crèche.

MOUNTAIN RESTAURANTS
Good, wide selection

Mountain restaurants are numerous and generally good. The large cafeterias at Curnius, Sogn Gion and Vorab are clean, efficient and serve good wholesome food. Nagens has another good high-altitude place with great views, a sun terrace and live music, but the nicest refuges are lower down. The Spaligna below Foppa and the Startgels Hütte above Foppa are good. We had a great lunch (with electronic ordering) in the rustic Tegia by the Murschetg gondola mid-station at Larnags. The Runcahöhe where the Stretg piste flattens out and crosses the path down from Startgels is another good cosy cabin. For a more expensive menu the restaurant at Crap Masegn is highly recommended.

SCHOOLS AND GUIDES
Plenty of English tuition

The school has a good reputation and standards of English are reported to be good too. They offer Early Bird specials on empty pistes followed by breakfast – a great North American concept not generally available in Europe. Also available is free-riding coaching and off-piste guiding.

FACILITIES FOR CHILDREN
Good Dreamland centres

Children aged three and over (both skiers and non-skiers) can be looked after at one of three Dreamland centres in Flims Dorf, Laax Murschetg and Falera. One reporter even enjoyed watching the cartoons they showed the children at a restaurant one snowy day! For children under three the resort can recommend qualified nannies for childcare.

Staying there

Although it might seem best to stay near the lifts in Dorf, in practice most of the better hotels in Waldhaus (and the remote bits of Dorf) run efficient courtesy buses to and from the slopes. These satisfy most guests, especially as there's not much to tempt you into town after dinner (only a 10-minute walk, says one fit reporter).

Also consider staying in Laax, Murschetg or rustic Falera – all have speedy access to the heart of the Laax slopes.

HOW TO GO
Few tour operators

Only a handful of tour operators feature Flims.

Hotels Flims has over 30 hotels. The majority are either 3-star or simple B&B places (the latter get booked up long in advance). Of six top hotels, five are in Waldhaus. Grading of hotels is accurate – you get what you pay for.

((((5) **Park** Enormous and very comfortable, but rather institutional, 5-star in wooded grounds at Waldhaus. Efficient courtesy bus. Pool.

(((4) **Adula** Big 4-star in Waldhaus, highly recommended by recent reporters. Good pool. 'Superb food and service,' says reporter.

(((4) **Sunstar Surselva** Part of the reliable Sunstar chain but run in a rather more institutionalised way than most. Quiet situation in Waldhaus with excellent new spa facilities.

((3) **Grischuna** Pretty little 3-star just outside Dorf and close to the lifts.

((3) **Cresta** Rave review by reporter. 'Helpful staff, fabulous spa facilities and food, unpretentious family hotel.'

((3) **Curtgin** Attractive, quiet place on edge of town, quite near the lifts.

((3) **Albana Sporthotel** Modern 3-star beside lifts, with focal après-ski bar.

((3) **Waldeck** Neat 3-star place in Waldhaus, with pleasant restaurant.

(1) **Rider's Palace** Limited space at a bargain price. Laax base station.

Self-catering Minerva in Waldhaus has by far the nicest of the limited apartments available.

EATING OUT
Varied options

Most Flims restaurants are in hotels. The National, by the bus station, has good fish dishes. The Meiler hotel restaurant also has a good reputation. For something a bit different, go up to the Spaligna mountain restaurant and use the toboggan run to get home. Little China is a good Chinese, and the Alpina Garni (Waldhaus) is very good value, does good pizzas and is 'busy and fun', says a recent reporter.

APRES-SKI
Not a strong point

Flims is very quiet après-ski. The Spaligna trip mentioned under Eating out is the highlight of the week. The Iglou bar at the base of the gondola is packed when the slopes close, as is the Stenna-Bar, opposite, which has has a tea dance. Just across the road

ACTIVITIES

Indoor Large public swimming pool and over 20 hotel pools (many open to the public), saunas, 4 indoor tennis courts, covered hall with ice-skating and 4 curling rinks, fitness centres (including Prau La Selva), table tennis, whirlpool, solarium
Outdoor 60km of cleared paths, riding, natural skating rinks, curling, sleigh rides, toboggan runs, skibob, paragliding, hot-air ballooning, hang-gliding, snow-shoeing, helicopter flights and night skiing

TOURIST OFFICE

Postcode CH-7017
t +41 (81) 920 9200
f 920 9201
tourismus@alpenarena.ch
www.alpenarena.ch

the Albana Pub is popular with a young crowd. Later, the focal spot is also in Dorf, at the hotel Bellevue's Caverna, an atmospheric old wine vault. The Angel is a new late-night club. The Park hotel is the centre of limited action in Waldhaus, having an old cellar with entertainer, and the Chadafo bar with dancing to live music. At Murschetg, the Crap Bar is lively when the slopes close and Casa Veglia has live bands and dancing.

OFF THE SLOPES
Lots to do

There are plenty of things to do. The enormous sports centre has a huge range of activities, including shooting – and 'guest cards' from hotels and the tourist office provide a discount. Flims also has some of the best and most extensive (60km) marked walks of any winter resort, some into and through the ski areas. Historic Chur is a short bus-ride away. Other good trips are to the impressive church at Zillis, and to the Rhine canyon, which is nature at its best. The Glacier Express train from Chur to Andermatt takes you through some wonderful scenery.

STAYING UP THE MOUNTAIN
Space station St John

Even though there are entire resorts that are higher, the prospect of staying 1100m above Murschetg, in the ultra-modern 3-star Crap Sogn Gion, is an exciting one. It has all mod cons, including a pool. You can also stay above Flims in the more traditional Berghaus Nagens – it has dormitories as well as comfortable double rooms.

Laax 1020m

Laax is a quiet, spacious old farming community which has retained a lot of its original character; but most of its modern development has taken place a short bus-ride away at Murschetg. This modern, functional complex has been built at the base of the lifts. Though the oldest house in Laax dates from 1615, and the setting is pleasant enough, the old village is no more than routinely charming.

The Murschetg jumbo gondola shifts the morning crowds quickly, the alternative cable-car less so.

A fine cross-country trail network of 60km starts near Laax.

Laax has its own school and ski kindergarten, run by the former star downhill racer Conradin Cathomen.

The Vallarosa and Signina are Murschetg 4-stars. The 4-star Arena Alva is a more attractive building in the old village, with its own transport to the lifts. We've enjoyed staying at the charming, central old Posta Veglia, with its lively stubli and piano bar, and at the traditional Larisch, set well back off the busy bypass. A good central B&B is the Cathomen.

Restaurants are mostly hotel-based. The Laaxer Bündnerstuben in the Posta Veglia is best for a meal in traditional surroundings. The limited nightlife scene centres around the Bistro Bar in the Capricorn hotel, live music in the Vallarosa Bar or Laaxerhof, and, again, the Posta Veglia. At Murschetg the Crap Bar gets packed when the lifts close – popular with snowboarders.

Falera 1220m

Along the road from Flims, beyond Laax, lies the rustic village of Falera, a quiet traffic-free little place, with two old churches. Sitting on a sunny plateau, it has good views over three valleys. Two successive fast quad chairs take you to the heart of the slopes, so Falera is quite an attractive base if you want a quiet time.

Accommodation is mostly in apartments. But La Siala is a large 4-star hotel with pool and sauna and its Spielkeller is the only real nightspot.

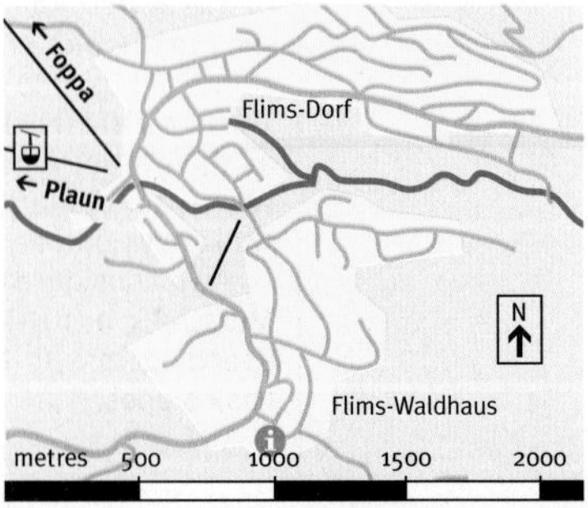

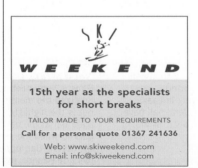

Grindelwald 1035m

Traditional mountain town in spectacular scenery

WHAT IT COSTS

3

HOW IT RATES

The slopes

Snow	**
Extent	***
Experts	**
Intermediates	*****
Beginners	***
Convenience	**
Queues	**
Restaurants	***

The rest

Scenery	*****
Resort charm	****
Off-slope	****

What's new

Two new fast quad chairs were installed for 1998/99 – the Grindel, on the First slopes, and the Gummi, speeding up movement from Männlichen to Kleine Scheidegg.

- ➕ Dramatically set in magnificent scenery directly beneath the towering north face of the Eiger
- ➕ Lots of long, gentle runs, ideal for intermediates, with links to Wengen
- ➕ Pleasant old village with long mountaineering history, though the tourist trade now sets the tone
- ➕ Fair amount to do off the slopes, including splendid walks and recently expanded toboggan runs

- ➖ Village gets very little midwinter sun
- ➖ Few challenging pistes for experts
- ➖ Inconvenient for visiting Mürren
- ➖ Snow-cover unreliable
- ➖ Major area accessed by slow gondola, queue-prone especially at weekends, and very slow and infrequent trains – life revolves around timetables

For stunning views from your hotel window and from the pistes, there are few places to rival Grindelwald, and two of them are just over the hill. The village is nowhere near as special as Wengen or Mürren, but staying here does give you direct access to Grindelwald's own First area. But you can spend hours queueing for, waiting for or sitting in the gondola or trains up into the Kleine Scheidegg area shared with Wengen. (The gondola ride takes over half an hour.) Grindelwald regulars accept all this as part of the scene, and some elderly skiers even find it adds to the holiday by enforcing a slow pace.

boarding *This isn't prime boarder territory. The facilities on the Männlichen disappeared a couple of seasons ago, presumably through lack of support. But there's a fun-park and a half-pipe at Oberjoch on First. Intermediates will enjoy the area most – the beginners' slopes can be bare, while experts will hanker for the steep, off-piste slopes of Mürren. Nightlife caters mainly for the more affluent, middle-aged visitors.*

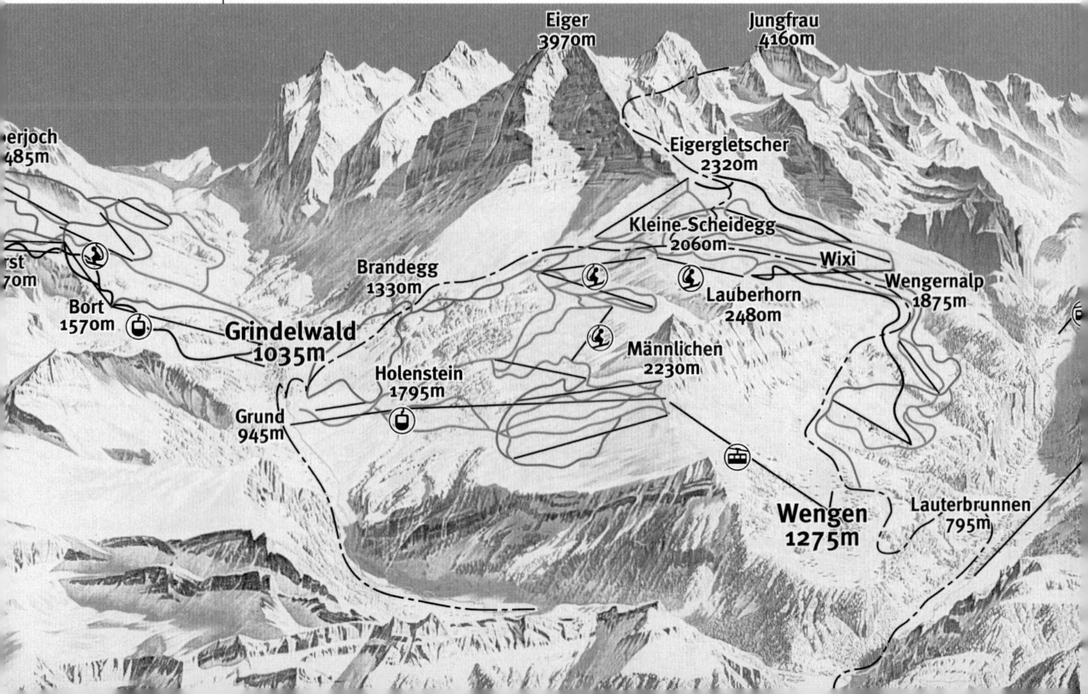

MOUNTAIN FACTS

Altitude	945m-2970m
Lifts	45
Pistes	205km
Blue	30%
Red	50%
Black	20%
Artificial snow	30km
Recco detectors used	

LIFT PASSES

2000/01 prices in Swiss francs

Jungfrau Top Ski Region
Covers all lifts in Wengen, Mürren and Grindelwald, trains between them and Grindelwald ski-bus.

Beginners Points card (adult 100 points 48, lifts cost 4 to 10 points).

Main pass
1-day pass 52
6-day pass 254

Senior citizens
Over 62: 6-day pass 229 (10% off)

Children
Under 16: 6-day pass 127 (50% off)
Under 6: 25

Short-term passes
Single ascent tickets for most lifts. Half-day pass available for each of First, Kleine Scheidegg-Männlichen and Mürren-Schilthorn (adult 40).

Alternative periods
3 days in 7 pass available (166).

Notes Day pass price for Kleine Scheidegg-Männlichen area only (102km of piste, 21 lifts), as Jungfrau Top Ski Region pass is only available for 2 days or over. Discounts for teenagers 16 to 20 (6-day 203) and groups.

Alternative passes
1- and 2-day passes available for each of First, Mürren-Schilthorn and Kleine Scheidegg-Männlichen (adult 2-day 95).

The resort

Grindelwald is set either side of the road along the foot of a narrow valley. Buildings are primarily traditional Swiss chalet-style. Towering mountains rise steeply from the valley floor, and the resort and main slopes get very little sun in January.

At weekends the train and gondola to the main area can get very crowded with coachloads of day visitors.

Grindelwald can feel very jolly at times, such as during the ice-carving festival in January, when large and beautiful tableaux are on display along the main street. The village is livelier at night than the other Jungfrau resorts of Wengen and Mürren. There's live music in several bars and hotels, but it isn't a place for bopping every night until dawn.

The mountains

The major area is shared with Wengen and is described in more detail in that chapter (page 431). The slopes are best for intermediates and can be marvellous in fresh snow.

Trips to other resorts are not very easy, but you can drive to Adelboden. Getting to the tougher, higher slopes of Mürren is a lengthy business unless you've got a car.

THE SLOPES
Broad and mainly gentle

From Grund, near the western end of town, you can get to **Kleine Scheidegg** by cog railway, or to **Männlichen** by gondola. On return to the resort you need a bus or an infrequent train to get back from Grund to the village centre. The slopes of the separate south-facing First area are reached by a three-stage gondola starting a bus-ride east of the centre. From all over the slopes there are superb views, not only of the Eiger but also the Wetterhorn and other peaks.

SNOW RELIABILITY
Poor

Grindelwald's low altitude – the slopes go down to below 1000m and few are above 2000m – and few snowmakers mean this is not a resort to book up months in advance. And it's not the place for a late-season holiday. First is sunny, and so less snowsure that the main area.

PISTES PATROLS RESTORED

On our last trip to this area we noticed a statement on the main mountain map board at Kleine-Scheidegg saying that several pistes in the area were not swept by patrollers at the end of the day. This disgraceful departure from universally accepted standards was not even indicated on the printed piste maps. One of the editors of this guide owes his life to the fact that he was rescued from a Swiss piste by an end-of-day patrol, so we're keen on them. We protested to the Jungfrau lift company, and as a result 'all blue, red, black slopes and the sledge runs will be swept by piste patrols at the end of the day in the whole ski area of Kleine Scheidegg-Männlichen from next winter season on'. If you see such notices at Kleine Scheidegg or anywhere else, let us know.

FOR EXPERTS
Very limited

The area is quite limited for experts. The black run on First beneath the gondola back to town is quite tough, especially when the snow has suffered from too much sun – late in the season, the run is one of the first to close. See also the Wengen chapter.

Heli-trips with mountain guides are organised if there are enough takers.

FOR INTERMEDIATES
Ideal intermediate terrain

In good snow, First makes a splendid intermediate playground, though the general lack of trees makes the area less friendly than the larger Kleine Scheidegg-Männlichen area, and most of the lifts are T-bars. The runs to the valley are great fun, but naturally popular in the afternoon. Nearly all the runs from Kleine Scheidegg are long blues or gentle reds – including an easy scenic blue run all the way down to the village. On the Männlichen there's a choice of gentle runs down to the mid-station of the gondola up from Grindelwald Grund. If conditions permit, you can get right down to the bottom on easy red runs ('barely deserving the grade' says a reporter, despite one run having been marked black in earlier years!).

For tougher pistes, head for the top of the Lauberhorn lift and then runs to

SCHOOLS/GUIDES

2000/01 prices in Swiss francs

Swiss
Classes 5 days
4hr: 10am-noon and 2pm-4pm
5 full days: 214
Children's classes
Ages: 3 to 14
5 full days: 214
Private lessons
2½hr or 5hr
170 for 2½hr
288 for 5hr

CHILDCARE

The ski school takes children from age 3, and they can be looked after at lunchtime in the Children's Club kindergarten at the Bodmi nursery slopes. This takes children from age 3, from 9.30 to 4pm. It apparently ceases to function if snow shortage closes the nursery slopes.

Children's ski races every Thursday are organised by the Grindelwald ski school.

GETTING THERE

Air Zürich, transfer 3hr. Bern, transfer 1½hr.

Rail Station in resort.

ACTIVITIES

Indoor Sports centre (swimming pool, sauna, solarium, table tennis, fitness room, climbing room, games room), indoor skating rink, curling, bowling, cinema
Outdoor 80km of cleared paths, train rides to Jungfraujoch, tobogganing, snow-shoe excursions, sleigh rides, paragliding, heli-skiing and boarding, open-air ice skating, snowrafting, glacier tours, devalkarts

Kleine Scheidegg, or to Wixi (following the start of the downhill course). You could also try the north-facing run from Eigergletscher to Salzegg, which often has the best snow late in the season.

FOR BEGINNERS
In good snow, wonderful

The nursery slope is friendly and scenic, just above the village, but in late season it can suffer from the sun and low altitude. There are splendid longer runs served by the railway to Kleine Scheidegg, notably the blue Mettlen-Grund run (22), right from the top to the bottom.

FOR CROSS-COUNTRY
Good but shady

There are over 30km of prepared tracks. Almost all of this is on the valley floor at around 1000m, so it's very shady in midwinter and may have poor snow later in the season.

QUEUES
Can be dreadful at peak times

The queues for the gondola and train at Grund can be very bad in high season, especially when weekend visitors pour in. The popular Oberjoch chair-lift is a bottleneck. Queues for the rest of the upper lifts build up only when snow is short lower down.

MOUNTAIN RESTAURANTS
Wide choice

See the Wengen chapter for restaurants around Kleine Scheidegg and down towards Wengen. Brandegg, on the railway, is recommended for its 'wonderful' apple fritters. Berghaus Bort does very good rösti, but the 'best rösti anywhere' is at the Jägerstubli, 500m up the road from the Aspen, off the Rennstrecke piste.

SCHOOLS AND GUIDES
One of the better Swiss schools

A recent report declares the Swiss school 'very good'; spoken English is normally excellent. It now has some competition in the form of private lessons from the Buri Sport school.

FACILITIES FOR CHILDREN
Good reputation

A past reporter who put four children through the Grindelwald mill praised caring and effective instructors, and a recent reporter rates them 'brilliant'. The First mountain restaurant runs a day nursery, which is a neat idea.

Staying there

The most convenient place to stay for the slopes is at Grund. But this is out of the centre and rather charmless.

There's a wide range of hotels in the heart of the village, handy enough for everything else, including the First area, at the foot of which are nursery slopes, ski school and kindergarten.

HOW TO GO
Limited range of packages

The hotels UK tour operators offer are mainly at the upper end of the market, but traditional little B&B pensions and self-catering apartments are widely available to independent bookers.

Hotels One 5-star, a dozen 4-stars, and a good range of more modest places.
((((5) **Regina** The one 5-star. Big and imposing; right next to the railway station. Nightly music in the bar. Pool.
((((4) **Belvedere** Family-run, recently renovated, close to station with a 'wonderful' pool.
((((4) **Schweizerhof** Beautifully decorated 4-star chalet at west end of centre, close to station. Pool.

THE JOURNEY TO THE TOP OF EUROPE

From Kleine Scheidegg you can take a train through the heart of the Eiger to the highest railway station in Europe – Jungfraujoch at 3454m.

The journey itself is a bit tedious – you're in a tunnel most of the time. You stop part way up to look out of a viewing gallery carved into the sheer north face of the Eiger, with magnificent views down the valley and over to Männlichen. At the top is a big restaurant complex. There's a fascinating 'ice palace' carved in the glacier with beautiful ice sculptures and slippery walkways, an outdoor 'plateau' to wander around and a panoramic viewing tower called the Sphinx.

The return trip cost SF47 in 1999/2000 if you had a Jungfrau lift pass for three days or more, but around three times that if you didn't. So it's much more attractive to skiers and boarders. Watch out for the altitude. At almost 3500m the air is thin, and we met people having breathing and balance problems.

No, it's not the Eiger: the Wetterhorn dominates the views from the First area, and also looks mighty fine from this slope below Kleine Scheidegg →

SNOWPIX.COM / CHRIS GILL

TOURIST OFFICE

Postcode CH-3818
t +41 (33) 854 1212
f 854 1210
touristcenter@grindelwald.ch
www.grindelwald.ch

(4) **Bodmi** Little chalet right on the village nursery slopes.
(3) **Hirschen** Excellent family-run 3-star in central position at foot of nursery slopes.
(3) **Fiescherblick** Hospitable chalet on eastern fringe of village, five minutes from the First gondola.
(3) **Derby** Popular, modern 3-star next to station, with 'first-class' service, good food and great views.
(2) **Tschuggen** Modest chalet in central position below nursery slopes.
(1) **Hotel Wetterhorn** Cosy, simple chalet way beyond the village, with great views of the glacier.
Self-catering One independent reporter recommended the apartments of the hotel Hirschen for comfort and space.

EATING OUT
Hotel based

There's a wide choice of good hotel restaurants, but cheaper pizzeria-style places are in short supply. The Latino does home-made Italian cooking.

Among the more attractively traditional places are: the Gepsi in the Eiger; Schmitte in the Schweizerhof; Challi-Stübli in the Kreuz; and the Alte Post. The Fiescherblick's 'brilliant but expensive' Swiss Bistro restaurant is repeatedly recommended. The Kirchbuhl and Oberland are good for vegetarians, the Bahnhof in the Derby for fondue and raclette. Hotel Spinne covers many bases – it has the Mercato for Italian, Mescalero Keller for Mexican, a Chinese and the candlelit Rôtisserie for a special romantic meal. Hotel Belvedere has a gourmet French restaurant. There's even a Japanese restaurant, the Samurai.

APRES-SKI
Relaxed

A jolly way to end the day is to have a drink or two at Kleine Scheidegg before skiing home. Nightlife is not the special subject of our reporters, but we can say that there are at least three discos and a handful of bars that aim to keep going late. There's also a cinema, plus ice hockey and curling matches to watch. There's an excellent sports centre with pool. Tobogganing and tubing are organised on First, and Thursday to Friday a 'Sledge Express' train takes people up to Brandegg/Alpiglen for fondues and tobogganing.

OFF THE SLOPES
Plenty to do, easy to get around

There are many cleared paths with magnificent views, especially around the First area – and there's a special (though expensive) pedestrian bus/lift pass. A trip to Jungfraujoch is spectacular (see previous page), and excursions by train to Interlaken are easy, and Bern possible. Tobogganing has recently undergone a bit of a renaissance, with runs up 15km on First (Europe's longest) and 30km of runs in total. Helicopter flights from Männlichen are recommended.

STAYING UP THE MOUNTAIN
Several possibilities

See the Wengen chapter for details of rooms at Kleine Scheidegg. The Berghaus Bort, at the gondola station in the middle of the First area (1570m), is an attractive alternative.

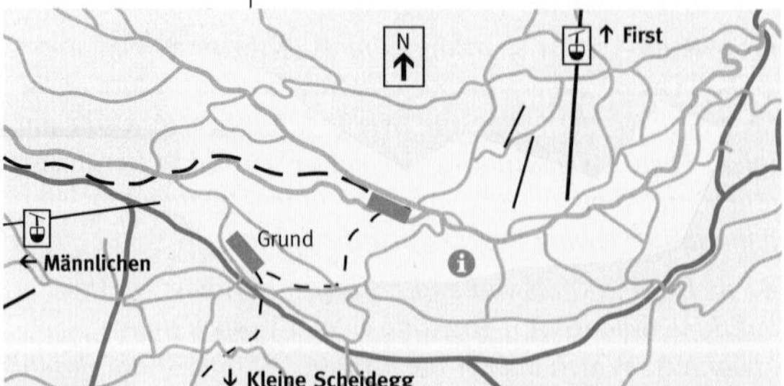

Gstaad

1050m

Surprisingly unpretentious, with extensive, pretty slopes

WHAT IT COSTS

5

HOW IT RATES

The slopes

Snow	*
Extent	****
Experts	**
Intermediates	***
Beginners	***
Convenience	*
Queues	***
Restaurants	***

The rest

Scenery	***
Resort charm	****
Off-slope	****

What's new

Last season the Col du Pillon cable-car to the glacier was hugely improved. For 2000/01 the revamp of the restaurant at the top should be complete. The drags up Eggli from outside Saanen are to be replaced by a chair.

MOUNTAIN FACTS

Altitude	950m-3000m
Lifts	69
Pistes	250km
Blue	48%
Red	36%
Black	16%
Artificial snow	8km

TOURIST OFFICE

Postcode CH-3780
t +41 (33) 748 8181
f 748 8183
gst@gstaad.ch
www.gstaad.ch

Gstaad is renowned as a jet-set resort, but for 'ordinary' holidaymakers, too, it is civilised, crowd-free and rustic, with beautiful scenery, quality hotels and excellent off-slope facilities. However, it's not convenient, snowsure or cheap.

THE RESORT

Gstaad is a traditional, year-round resort in a spacious, sunny setting surrounded by a horseshoe of wooded mountains. The main street, lined with hotels, smart shops and cafés, has a pleasant and relaxing feel now that it it's traffic-free. The Montreux-Oberland-Bernois (MOB) railway station is only yards away, and accesses numerous surrounding villages and lift stations.

THE MOUNTAINS

There are four main areas of **slopes,** covered by a single map that is a confusing mess. Three are accessed via lifts dotted around the fringes of Gstaad and served by a regular shuttle-bus service. Wasserngrat (to the east of the village) and Wispile (to the south) are both small areas with one or two main lifts and runs alongside them. Eggli (to the west) is more complex, and leads via the valley of Chalberhöni to the crags of Videmanette, and down to the lovely French-speaking village of Rougemont.

The fourth and largest sector is not directly accessible from the village, but the lift stations at Saanenmöser and Schönried are no more inconvenient than Gstaad's local lift stations, given a train timetable. Schönried also has a separate sunny area of slopes on the opposite side of the valley.

The Glacier des Diablerets is covered by the local area pass but is 15km away to the south, with lifts at Reusch and Col du Pillon. There are excellent runs below glacier level, but the glacier itself is limited.

There are **snowboard** fun-parks and facilities in two or three sectors.

A lack of altitude means that **snow-cover** can be unreliable except on the glacier, but most of the slopes are roughly north-facing and there is now quite a lot of snowmaking.

Few runs challenge **experts**. Black runs rarely exceed red difficulty, and some should be blue. There are off-piste possibilities – steep ones on the wooded flanks of Wispile and Eggli.

Given good snow, this is a superb area for **intermediates**, with long, easy descents in the major area to the villages dotted around its edges. The run to Rougemont from the top of the Eggli sector is lovely. The adventurous should take a trip to the Diablerets glacier for the splendid shady red run down the lift-free Combe d'Audon.

For **beginners**, nursery slopes at the bottom of Wispile are adequate, and there are plenty of runs to progress to.

The 100km of **cross-country** trails are very pretty, but virtually all are low down and can suffer from poor snow.

Time lost on buses or trains is more of a problem than **queues**, except at peak times and weekends.

Mountain restaurants are plentiful, and most are attractive, if pricey.

English is more widely spoken by the **ski school** than in many other Brit-free zones. It has a good reputation, too. The **kindergarten** offers limited hours.

STAYING THERE

Gstaad is certainly exclusive, with over three-quarters of its accommodation in private chalets and apartments. The remainder of the beds are in 3-star **hotels** and above. The 5-star Palace is extravagantly swish, in secluded grounds. The Bernerhof and Christiana are recommended 4-stars. The Olden and Rössli occupy charming, central, chalet-style buildings. There is a wide choice of **self-catering** available locally.

Restaurants are mainly hotel-based, and pricey. The rustic Chlösterli – a massive 350-seat establishment a short drive out – is a popular place to eat and dance. Hotel Rössli is reasonably priced and the locals' bar in the Olden has filling, value-for-money meals. In season **nightlife** is lively both at tea-time and later on.

Gstaad's **off-slope** activities are wide-ranging. The tennis centre and swimming pool complex are impressive, and there are 50km of pretty cleared walks. Getting around is easy, and excursions to Montreux and Interlaken are possible.

Mürren 1650m

Stupendous views, an epic run, and a chocolate-box village

WHAT IT COSTS

3

HOW IT RATES

The slopes

Snow	***
Extent	*
Experts	***
Intermediates	***
Beginners	**
Convenience	***
Queues	***
Restaurants	**

The rest

Scenery	*****
Resort charm	*****
Off-slope	***

What's new

For 1999/2000 the ancient funicular up to Allmendhubel was replaced by a smart new one with revamped stations at the top and bottom. The Allmendhubel restaurant was also renovated.

- ➕ Tiny, charming, traditional 'traffic-free' village, with narrow paths and chocolate-box chalets
- ➕ Stupendous scenery, best enjoyed on the challenging run from the panoramic Schilthorn
- ➕ Good sports centre
- ➕ Good snow high up, even when the rest of the region is suffering

- ➖ Extent of local pistes very limited no matter what your level of expertise
- ➖ Lower slopes can be in poor condition and are served by some awkward T-bars
- ➖ Quiet, limited nightlife
- ➖ Like all other Swiss 'traffic-free' villages, Mürren is gradually admitting more service vehicles

Mürren is one of our favourite resorts – for a short visit, at least. There may be other Swiss mountain villages that are equally pretty, but none of them enjoys views like those from Mürren across the deep valley to the rock faces and glaciers of the Eiger, Mönch and Jungfrau: simply breathtaking. And then there's the Schilthorn run, which draws us back like a magnet whenever we're driving through the Oberland.

Our visits are normally one-day affairs; holidaymakers, we concede, are likely to want to explore the extensive intermediate slopes of Wengen and Grindelwald, across the valley. And you have to accept that getting there takes time.

It was in Mürren that the British more or less invented modern skiing. Sir Arnold Lunn organised the first ever slalom race here in 1922. Some 12 years earlier his father, Sir Henry, had persuaded the locals to open the railway in winter so that he could bring the first winter package tour here. Last winter, we had the great pleasure of a chat in the bar of the hotel Eiger with Sir Arnold's son Peter, who first skied here in November 1916 and now skis here with his children and grandchildren. Mürren's that kind of place.

boarding *Like other Swiss resorts, Mürren has a traditional image, but it is trying to move with the times and offer a more snowboard-friendly attitude. This may be at odds with the resort's usual clientele, but they build a half-pipe every season, and the major lifts are cable-cars and chair-lifts (though there are some key drag-lifts too). The terrain above Mürren is suitable mainly for good free-riders – it's steep, with a lot of off-piste routes. Intermediates will find the area tough and limited, but nearby Wengen is ideal and is much better for beginners. At night, Mürren is quiet, with not much scope for raving.*

The resort

Mürren is set on a shelf 800m above the Lauterbrunnen valley floor, across from Wengen, and can be reached only by cable-car from Stechelberg or funicular and then railway from Lauterbrunnen. Once you get there you can't fail to be struck by Mürren's tranquillity and beauty. The tiny village is made up of paths and narrow lanes weaving between tiny wooden chalets and a handful of bigger hotel buildings. The roofs and paths are normally snow-covered, giving the village a really traditional Alpine feel.

Two further stages of the cable-car take you up to the high slopes of Birg and the Schilthorn, nearby lifts go to the main lower slopes, and a newly modernised funicular halfway along the village accesses the other slopes.

Although in our summary above we protest against the gradual 'traffic' increase, Mürren still isn't plagued by electric carts and taxis as most other traditional 'traffic-free' resorts now are.

It's not the place to go for lively nightlife, shopping or showing off your latest gear to admiring hordes. It is the place to go if you want tranquillity and stunning views.

MOUNTAIN FACTS

Altitude	945m-2970m
Lifts	45
Pistes	205km
Blue	30%
Red	50%
Black	20%
Artificial snow	30km

Recco detectors used

LIFT PASSES

2000/01 prices in Swiss francs

Jungfrau Top Ski Region
Covers all lifts in Wengen, Mürren and Grindelwald, trains between them and Grindelwald ski-bus.

Beginners Points card (adult 100 points 48, lifts cost 4 to 10 points).

Main pass
1-day pass 52
6-day pass 254

Senior citizens
Over 62: 6-day pass 229 (10% off)

Children
Under 16: 6-day pass 127 (50% off)
Under 6: 25

Short-term passes
Single ascent tickets for most lifts. Half-day pass for Mürren-Schilthorn (adult 40).

Alternative periods
3 days in 7 pass available (166).

Notes Day pass price for Mürren-Schilthorn area only (53km of piste, 12 lifts), as Jungfrau Top Ski Region pass is only available for 2 days or over. Discounts for teenagers 16 to 20 (6-day 203) and groups.

Alternative passes
1- and 2-day passes available for Mürren-Schilthorn (adult 2-day 50) and Kleine Scheidegg-Männlichen (adult 2-day 95).
4-, 5- and 6-day passes available for non-skiers (adult 6-day 189)

The mountain

Mürren's slopes aren't extensive. But it has something for everyone, including one of our favourite runs. And those happy to travel to Wengen-Grindelwald will find plenty of options. These resorts are covered by the Jungfrau pass and easily if not quickly reached.

THE SLOPES
Small but interesting

There are three connected areas around the village, reaching no higher than 2145m. The biggest is **Schiltgrat**, served by a fast quad chair behind the cable-car station. You can also get there from the top of the modernised funicular, which goes from the middle of the village to the nursery slope at **Allmendhubel** – from where a run and a drag-lift take you to the slightly higher **Maulerhubel**. Runs go down from here to the Winteregg stop on the railway, too. These lower slopes take you up to around 2000m.

Much more interesting are the higher slopes reached by cable-car. The first stage takes you to Birg at 2675m, and the **Engetal** area, where an old T-bar serves short, steep, shady slopes. Two chair-lifts below the Engetal now serve some snowsure intermediate slopes. But plans for a third chair, up to Birg, have been shelved. To get back to the Birg cable-car station and avoid the tricky run down to the village, you face an annoying walk up from these chairs to the old T-bar.

The final stage of the cable-car takes you up to the 2970m summit of the **Schilthorn** and the Piz Gloria revolving restaurant, made famous by the James Bond film *On Her Majesty's Secret Service*. In good snow you can go all the way from here (via the Engetal and the Maulerhubel drag-lift) to Lauterbrunnen at 795m – a distance of almost 16km and a vertical drop of 2175m. The Inferno race (see box below) takes place over this course, conditions permitting. But below Winteregg it's all boring paths.

The Jungfrau piste map doesn't deal with Mürren's slopes at all well. The one used in the Mürren brochures (on which our own is based) is better.

SNOW RELIABILITY
Good on the upper slopes

The Jungfrau region does not have a good snow record – but Mürren always has the best snow in the area. When Wengen-Grindelwald (and Mürren's lower slopes) have problems, the Schilthorn and Engetal often have packed powder snow because of their height orientation – north-east to east. Piste grooming seems haphazard, except at Winteregg.

FOR EXPERTS
One wonderful piste

The run from the top of the Schilthorn starts with a steep but not terrifying slope, in the past generally mogulled but now often groomed. It flattens into a schuss to Engetal, below Birg. Then there's a wonderful, wide run with stunning views over the valley to the Eiger, Mönch and Jungfrau. Since the chair-lifts were built here you can play on these upper runs for as long as you like. Below the lifts you hit the Kanonenrohr (gun barrel). This is a very narrow shelf with solid rock on one side and a steep drop on the other – protected by nets. After an open slope and scrappy zig-zag path, you arrive at the 'hog's back' and can descend towards the village on either side of Allmendhubel.

From Schiltgrat a short, serious

THE INFERNO RACE

Every January 1800 amateurs compete in the spectacular Inferno race. Conditions permitting, and they usually don't, the race goes from the top of the Schilthorn at 2970m right down to Lauterbrunnen at 795m – a vertical drop of 2175m and a distance of almost 16km. The racers start in pairs at 30-second intervals and the fastest finish the course in around 15 minutes, but anything under half an hour is very respectable. And this includes a short climb at Maulerhubel. Apart from seven gates, you can choose your own route down the mountain.

The race was started by Sir Arnold Lunn in 1928 when he and his friends climbed to the top of the Schilthorn, spent the night in a mountain hut and then raced down in the morning. For many years the race was organised by the British-run Kandahar Club, and there is still a strong British presence among the competitors.

SCHOOLS/GUIDES

1999/2000 prices in Swiss francs

Swiss
Classes 6 days
2hr: 9.45-11.45
6 days: 136
Children's classes
2hr. Ages: from 4
6 days: 136
Private lessons
Half day (2hr) or full day (5hr)
from 100 for 2hr

CHILDCARE

The ski school takes children from age 4.

For the last few years there has been non-skiing childcare in the sports centre. But lack of demand has meant that it may not be available in the coming seasons. The tourist office suggest you contact them for the latest situation.

mogul run – the Kandahar – descends towards the village, but experts are more likely to be interested in the off-piste runs into the Blumental – both from here (the north-facing Blumenlucke run) and from Birg (the sunnier Tschingelchrachen) – or the adventurous runs from the Schilthorn.

FOR INTERMEDIATES
Limited, but Wengen nearby

Keen piste-bashers will need to make a few trips to the long cruising runs of Wengen-Grindelwald. The best easy cruising run in Mürren is the blue down to Winteregg, which is north-facing. The reds on the other low slopes can get mogulled, and snow conditions can be poor. The area below the Engetal normally has good snow, and you can choose your gradient from easy to quite testing.

FOR BEGINNERS
Not ideal, but adequate

The nursery slopes at Allmendhubel, at the top of the funicular, are on the steep side. And there are not many easy runs to graduate to – though the blue down the Winteregg chair is easy, and the Schilt-Apollo blue served by the long Gimmeln drag and the less tiring Schiltgrat chair is ideal.

FOR CROSS-COUNTRY
Forget it

There is one small cross-country loop above the village in the Blumental, and extensive loops along the valley floor from Lauterbrunnen or Stechelberg. But snow is unreliable at valley height. There are many better resorts for cross-country enthusiasts.

QUEUES
Generally not a problem

Mürren doesn't get as crowded as Wengen and Grindelwald, except on sunny Sundays. There can be queues for the cable-cars – usually when snow shortages bring visitors from less fortunate resorts. The top stage has only one cabin. The new Allmendhubel funicular goes at twice the speed of the old one.

MOUNTAIN RESTAURANTS
Disappointing at altitude

Piz Gloria revolves once an hour, displaying a fabulous 360° panorama of peaks and lakes. Don't expect particularly good food, or a small bill. By the 'new' Engetal chair-lifts, the Schilthorn Hutte is small and rustic.

Lower down, the Suppenalp in the Blumental is rustic and quietly set, does 'excellent food' but gets no sun

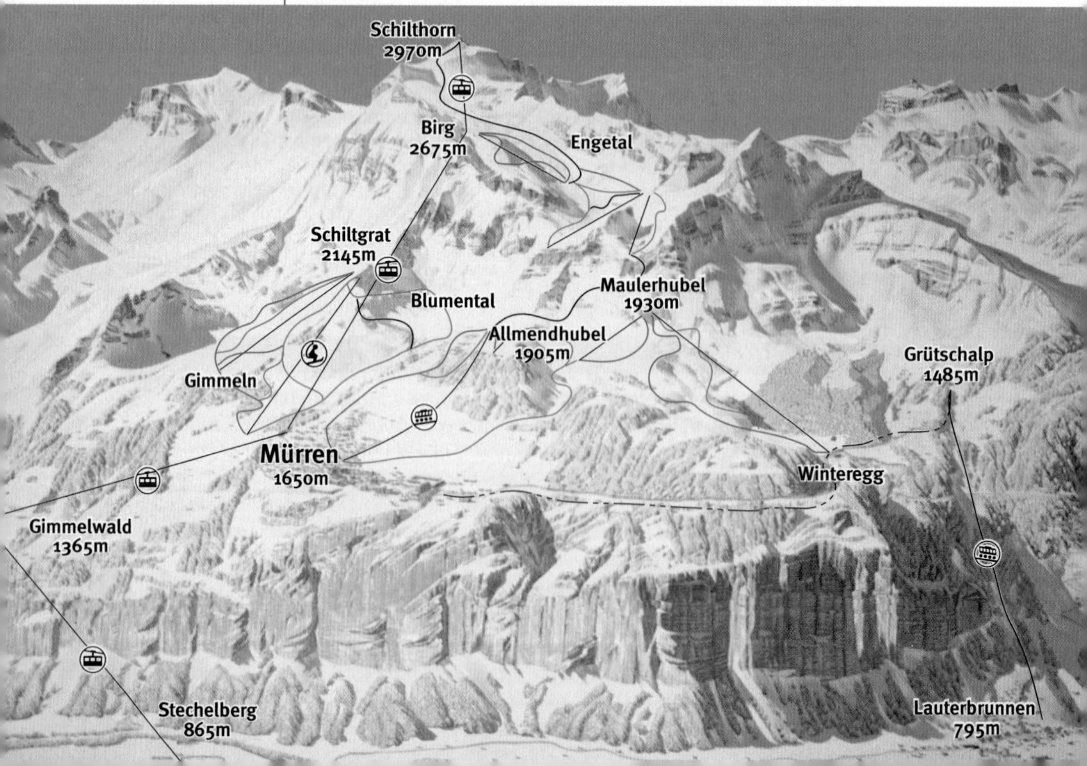

It wasn't easy to get a view of Mürren that manages to exclude the famous peaks of Eiger, Mönch and Jungfrau, all of which are off to the right. But our picture does include Wengen's Lauberhorn →

SNOWPIX.COM / CHRIS GILL

GETTING THERE

Air Zürich, transfer 3½hr. Bern, transfer 1½hr.

Rail Lauterbrunnen; transfer by mountain railway and tram.

ACTIVITIES

Indoor 'Alpine Sports Centre Mürren' swimming pool, whirlpool and children's pool, library, children's playroom, gymnasium, squash, sauna, solarium, steam bath, massage, fitness room
Outdoor Artificial skating rink (curling, skating), toboggan run to Gimmelwald, 15km cleared paths

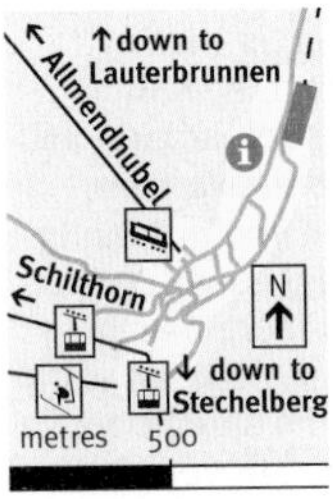

TOURIST OFFICE

Postcode CH-3825
t +41 (33) 856 8686
f 856 8696
info@muerren.ch
www.muerren.ch

in January. Sonnenburg is sunnier. Gimmeln is a self-service place with a large terrace, famous for its apple cake. Winteregg does something similar, as well as 'the best burger east of the Rockies'. Both have little playgrounds to amuse kids.

SCHOOLS AND GUIDES
Small, not perfectly formed

Recent reports speak of good progress for beginners, but also of one English speaker who had a rather lonely week in a group with six Germans – the kind of thing that happens in a small resort.

FACILITIES FOR CHILDREN
Adequate

There is a baby slope with rope tow behind the central hotel Jungfrau. And there may be a club at the sports centre where two-year-olds and above can be looked after – see margin.

Staying there

Mürren is so small that location is not a concern. Nothing is more than a few minutes' walk.

HOW TO GO
Mainly hotels, packaged or not

A handful of operators offer packages to Mürren.
Hotels There are fewer than a dozen hotels, ranging widely in style.
((((4 **Palace** Victorian pile near railway station – recently renovated.
((((4 **Eiger** Plain-looking 'chalet' blocks next to railway station, widely recommended; good blend of efficiency and charm; good food; pool.
(((3 **Alpenruh** Attractively renovated chalet next to the cable-car station.
(((3 **Edelweiss** Small square block, friendly, excellent food and facilities.
((2 **Alpenblick** Simple, small, modern chalet near railway station.
Self-catering There are plenty of chalets and apartments in the village for independent travellers to rent.

STAYING DOWN THE VALLEY
A cheaper option

See the Wengen chapter for options in Lauterbrunnen and Interlaken. If you want to use both Wengen and Mürren, Lauterbrunnen in particular is a good budget place to stay. It has a resort (rather than a town) atmosphere and access to and from both main resorts until late (also covered by your lift pass).

EATING OUT
Mainly in hotels

The rustic Stägerstübli is the main alternative to hotels – a bar as well as restaurant. The locals eat in the little diner at the back. The food at the Eiger hotel is good, and the Bellevue and Alpenruh get good reports.

APRES-SKI
Not devoid of life

The Eiger Bar (in the Eiger guest house, not the hotel) is the Brits' meeting place. The tiny Stägerstübli is cosy, and the place to meet locals. Other activities are hotel-based. The Palace's Balloon bar is an attempt at a trendy cocktail bar; it also has a weekend disco, the Inferno. The Bliemli Challer disco in the Blumental caters for kids, the nightly Tachi disco in the Eiger for a more mixed crowd.

OFF THE SLOPES
Tranquillity but not much else

Other than admiring the peace of the village and stunning beauty of the views, there isn't a lot to amuse people who don't want to hit the slopes. But there is a very good sports centre, with a splendidly set outdoor ice rink. And it's easy to make excursions by car or train to Interlaken and to Bern (Switzerland's ancient capital).

It's no problem for friends to return to the village for lunch. The only problem with meeting at the top of the cable-car is the expense.

Saas-Fee 1800m

Beautiful, car-free village with slopes on top of the world

WHAT IT COSTS

4

HOW IT RATES

The slopes

Snow	*****
Extent	**
Experts	***
Intermediates	****
Beginners	*****
Convenience	***
Queues	***
Restaurants	***
The rest	
Scenery	****
Resort charm	*****
Off-slope	****

What's new

For 1999/2000, the ancient two-person Plattjen gondola was replaced by a fast, new six-person one.

There's a new family offer for 2000/01 – children aged up to 16 will ski for free if two adults buy a 6-day or 5-days-in-7 pass.

- ⊕ Spectacular setting amid high peaks and glaciers
- ⊕ Traditional, 'traffic-free' village
- ⊕ Good percentage of high-altitude, snowsure slopes
- ⊕ Powerful lift access to highest slopes for year-round skiing
- ⊕ Good facilities – even a slope where skis and snowboards are banned

- ⊖ Disappointingly small area of slopes, with mainly easy runs
- ⊖ Glacier stifles off-piste potential
- ⊖ Much of the area is in shadow in midwinter – cold and dark
- ⊖ Bad weather can shut the slopes
- ⊖ Parts of the village are inconvenient for the slopes – quite a bit of walking involved

Saas-Fee is one of our favourite places. It oozes Swiss charm and the setting is stunning – spectacular glaciers and 4000m peaks surround the place.

If only the skiing matched the scenery and the charm! For many intermediates it does, but good skiers are likely to get bored quickly with the limited extent and challenges of the slopes. The extensive glacier slopes are gentle and easy – and the glacier itself severely restricts the area's development. The tight ring of high peaks can also make the village dark and cold in midwinter, which is good for the snow, not so good for those wanting to sit on restaurant terraces or those on the beginner slopes. But Saas-Fee's snow reliability is unbeatable, especially if you're taking a late holiday. With much of the area above 2500m, snow conditions are often excellent when many other resorts are struggling to keep runs open. The question is: can you put up with a limited choice of runs and the occasional lunchtime shiver in exchange for perfect packed powder?

boarding *Saas-Fee encourages boarding in a big way. In summer, in particular, its glacier slopes are dominated by boarders. Facilities include an 80m half-pipe, a fun-park and a boarder-cross with just about every conceivable obstacle. The nearby Maste 4 snow-bar is the place for a break. While the gentle glacier slopes are ideal for learning, only main access lifts are boarder-friendly (gondolas, cable-cars and a funicular); nearly all the rest are drags. There's a specialist school, Paradise, and the local Swiss ski school takes boarding seriously. Expert free-riders may be frustrated by the limits imposed on off-piste riding by the glacier. But nightlife doesn't disappoint – the Popcorn board shop and bar is popular.*

The resort

Like nearby Zermatt, Saas-Fee is car-free (there are car parks at the resort entrance) but rather plagued by electric vehicles. On most other counts, Saas-Fee and its more exalted neighbour are a long way apart in style. Saas-Fee still feels like a village, with attractive old chalets, cow sheds and narrow streets.

There are some very smart hotels (plus many more modest ones) and plenty of good eating and drinking places. But there's little of the glamour and greed that, for some, spoil Zermatt – and even the electric taxis here are driven at a more considerate pace.

The village may be chilly in January, but when the spring sun is beating down, Saas-Fee is a quite beautiful place in which to just stroll around and relax, admiring the impressive view.

Depending on where you're staying and which way you want to go up the mountain, you may do more marching than strolling. It's a long walk (or costly taxi) from one end of the spread-out village to the other, though your hotel may a run courtesy bus to and from the lifts. Three major lifts start from the southern end of the village, at the foot of the slopes, and lots of the hotels and apartments are 1km or more away. The modern Alpin Express starts below the centre, though, quite near the entrance to the resort.

The village centre has the school and guides' office, the church and a few more shops than elsewhere, but doesn't add up to much of a focus. On a sunny day, though, the restaurant terraces fronting the nursery slopes at the far end of the village are a magnet, with breathtaking views up to the horseshoe of 4000m peaks – you can see why the village is called 'The Pearl of the Alps'.

MOUNTAIN FACTS

Altitude	1800m-3620m
Lifts	27
Pistes	100km
Blue	25%
Red	50%
Black	25%
Artificial snow	10km
Recco detectors used	

The mountain

The area has been steadily improved by the installation of new lifts, but the slopes are still a bit fragmented. Many visitors complain about this, and about the number of cold drag-lifts. But the reason for these complaints is also Saas-Fee's strong point – its snowsure glacier slopes. The glacier can move downhill by 100m a year and drag-lift pylons can be moved to cope, but chair-lifts are not practicable.

The upper slopes are largely gentle and easy, while the lower half of the mountain, below the glacier, is steeper and rockier. For many people, though, there are simply not enough kilometres of piste. But Saas-Almagell, Saas-Balen and Saas-Grund are not far away, and you can buy a lift pass that covers all four resorts and buses between them.

Day trips to Zermatt, Grächen and Crans-Montana are realistic options.

Saas-Fee is one of the leading resorts for mountaineering and ski-touring. Several nearby peaks can be climbed and the extended Haute Route from Chamonix ends at Saas-Fee.

LIFT PASSES

1999/2000 prices in Swiss francs

Saas Fee area
Covers all lifts in Saas Fee only.

Beginners Village area pass covers 5 beginners' lifts. 1-day 15, 6 days 90

Main pass
1-day pass 58
6-day pass 270

Children
Under 16: 6-day pass 162
Under 6: free pass

Short-term passes
Single and return tickets on most main lifts. Half-day pass from noon (adult 46).

Notes Discount for groups of 20 or more.

Alternative passes
Separate passes for each of the other ski areas in the Saastal (Saas-Grund, Saas-Almagell, Saas-Balen). Pass for all four villages in the Saastal also available, and includes ski-bus between them. 6-day pass, 294.

THE SLOPES
A glacier runs through it

The main **Felskinn-Längfluh** area can be reached in three ways. The efficient 30-person Alpin Express jumbo gondola takes you to Felskinn at 3000m, starting across the river from the main village between the main slopes and the perimeter car parks. It has a mid-station at Maste 4 (where you have to change cabins).

The Felskinn cable-car, starting a short drag-lift away from the foot of the main pistes and nursery slopes at the southern end of the village, also takes you to Felskinn.

From Felskinn, the Metro Alpin (an underground funicular) hurtles to the thin air at 3500m Mittelallalin. From below here the top two drag-lifts access the high point of 3620m.

From near the drag-lift to the Felskinn cable-car, a gondola leaves for Spielboden. This is met by a cable-car which takes you up to Längfluh.

Felskinn and Längfluh are squeezed out to opposite fringes of an off-limits glacier area. A very long drag-lift from Längfluh takes you to a point where you can get down to the Felskinn area. These two sectors are served mainly by drag-lifts, and you can get down to the village from both.

A recently installed smart and 'very efficient' six-person gondola takes you from near the Spielboden gondola up to Saas-Fee's smallest area, **Plattjen**. It has some of Saas-Fee's best steep black slopes (though being low down they can get icy) as well as quite tricky reds and some easy cruising.

EUROPE'S HIGHEST LUNCH?

There is something beautifully Swiss about the idea of a revolving restaurant – and, sure enough, all three pivoting pubs in the Alps are to be found in Switzerland. 'Customers complaining that they're not getting a share of the views? We can't have that – and we can't expect them to switch tables. Only one thing for it: we'll have to spin the whole restaurant about once an hour.' Actually, of course, they don't spin the whole restaurant: the bit of floor with the tables on it revolves while the stairs stay put (along with the windows and the window sill – and any gloves you thoughtlessly put down on it).

Two years after Saas-Fee built the Alps' highest funicular railway in 1984, it crowned that achievement with what is certainly the world's highest revolving restaurant – a good 500m higher than the one on Mürren's Schilthorn, the Piz Gloria of the James Bond movie On Her Majesty's Secret Service *fame – and possibly Europe's highest eatery of any kind.*

We don't rate the views from Mittelallalin particularly highly. But it's an amusing novelty that most visitors enjoy trying once. If you're going, do it properly and reserve a table next to the windows – phone 957 1771.

SNOW RELIABILITY
Good at the highest altitudes
Most of Saas-Fee's slopes face north and many are above 2500m, making this one of the most reliable resorts for snow in the Alps. The glacier is open most of the year. Visitors tell us that the substantial recent investment in snow-guns still doesn't completely ensure good coverage on the rocky lower slopes, though piste grooming is 'excellent'. Conversely, after heavy snowfalls you may find yourself limited to the nursery area for a while.

FOR EXPERTS
Not a lot to keep your interest
There is not much steep stuff, except on the bottom half of the mountain where the snow tends not to be as good. The highest drag-lift on the left near Felskinn serves two short, steep blacks and one easy one. The slopes around the top of Längfluh often provide good powder and there are usually moguls above Spielboden. The blacks and trees on Plattjen are worth exploring. The glacier puts limits on the local off-piste even with a guide – crevasse danger is extreme. But there are extensive touring possibilities, especially late in the season.

FOR INTERMEDIATES
Great for gentle cruising
Saas-Fee is ideal for early intermediates and those not looking for much of a challenge. For long cruises, head for Mittelallalin. The top of the mountain, down as far Längfluh (the bottom of the long drag) in one direction, and as far as Maste 4 (the end of the first stage of the Alpin Express) in the other, is ideal, with usually excellent snow. Gradients range from gentle blues to slightly steeper reds which can build up smallish bumps.

Recent visitors loved the 'beautiful, wide blue and red cruising runs accessed by the drag between Maste 4 and Felskinn'.

The 1800m vertical descent from Mittelallalin (via Felskinn or Längfluh) to the village is a great test of stamina – or, if you choose, an enjoyable long cruise with plenty of view stops. The lower runs have steepish, tricky sections and can have poor snow, especially if it isn't cold enough to make snow – timid intermediates might prefer to take a lift down from mid-mountain.

Plattjen has a variety of runs, all of them fine for ambitious intermediates and often underused.

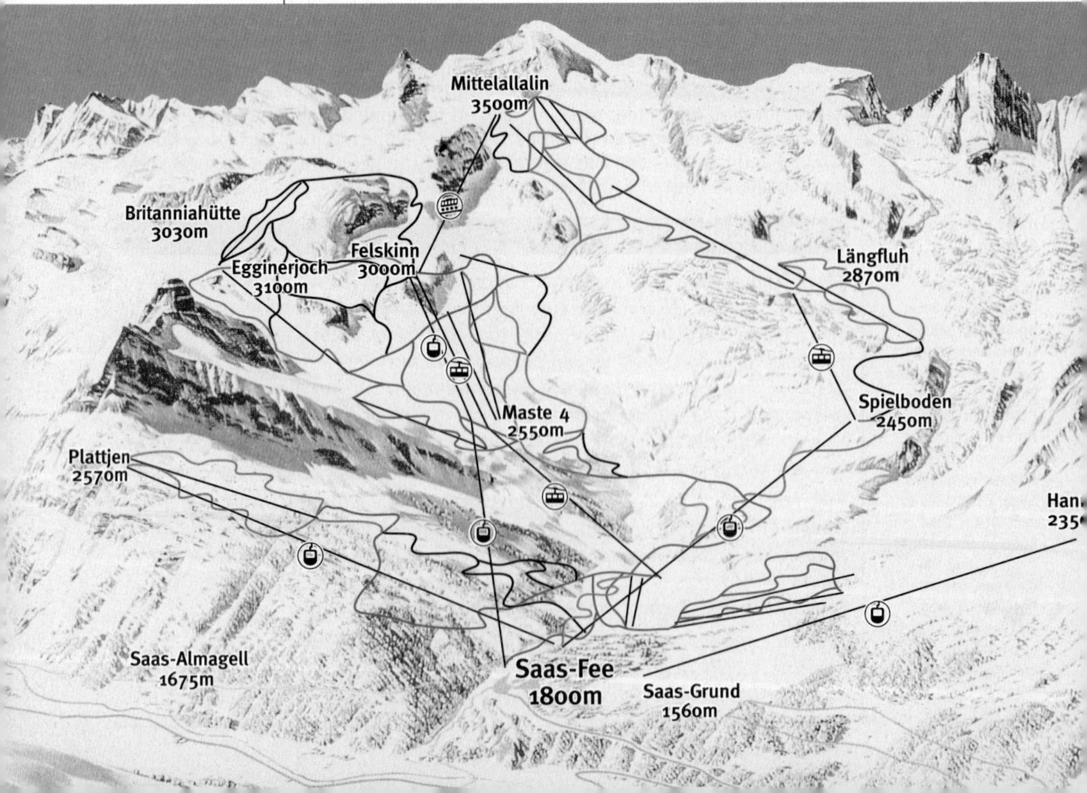

SCHOOLS/GUIDES

1999/2000 prices in Swiss francs

Swiss
Classes 5 days
3hr: 10am-1pm, 45
5 days (15hr): 168
Children's classes
Five day ski courses including lunch, from age 3, 300, from age 4, 390
Private lessons
Hourly or daily
56 for 1hr for 1 to 2 people

FOR BEGINNERS
Usually a nice place to start

There's a good, large, out-of-the-way nursery area at the edge of the village, though we've had reports of icy mornings, rocks and slush. Those ready to progress can head for the gentle blues on Felskinn just above Maste 4 – it's best to return by Alpin Express. There are also gentle blues at the top of the mountain, from where you can head down to Längfluh. Again, use the lifts to return to base.

A useful beginners' pass covers all the short lifts at the village edge, for those not ready to go higher.

FOR CROSS-COUNTRY
Good local trail and lots nearby

There is one short (8km) pleasant trail at the edge of the village. It snakes up through the woods, providing about 150m of climb and nice views. There are more options in the valley.

QUEUES
Hardly any

Lift improvements seem to have done their job – recent reporters rarely had to wait: 'Considering it was half-term, and the weather wonderful with excellent snow, we were relieved at how little we had to queue.' Queues are likely to be worst at weekends, if snow is poor elsewhere.

MOUNTAIN RESTAURANTS
Fair choice but not like Zermatt

The restaurants at the main lift stations are functional. The best places are slightly off the beaten track: the Berghaus Plattjen (just down from Plattjen) and the Gletscher-Grotte, halfway down from Spielboden (watch for the path from the piste). Both have good food in old huts. If you're up for a trek, the Britanniahütte is a real mountain refuge, with atmosphere and views. The new restaurant at the top of Plattjen has 'friendly service and the best rösti in the resort'. At Spielboden there's 'good food', a terrace and views of tricky slopes. At Längfluh the large terrace has views of huge crevasses. Maste 4 has 'cheap and very good' pizza. Back in the village, the sunny, piste-side terrace of the Waldesruh Hotel serves 'wonderful' rösti and the terrace of the Belmont is a popular sunbathing spot.

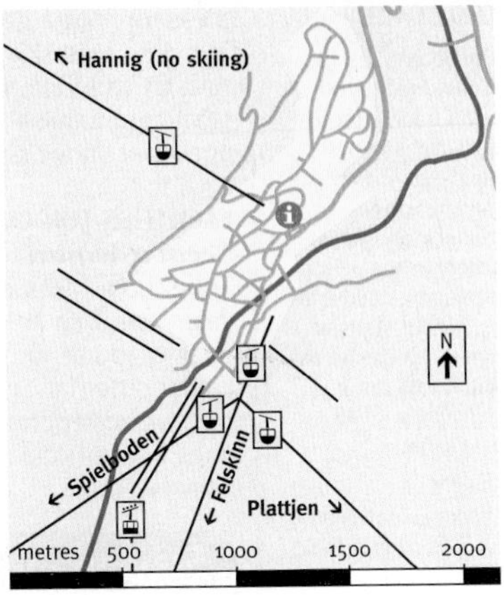

SCHOOLS AND GUIDES
Good reports

For skiing, it's the Swiss school or nothing. In the past we've received complaints of 'arrogant attitude', but this year's reporters seem better

SNOWPIX.COM / CHRIS GILL

The pretty, car-free village sits at the foot of a horseshoe of 4000m peaks. They call it 'The Pearl of the Alps' →

CHILDCARE

The Bären-Klub (Bears Club) kindergarten takes infants for full days or half days. From age 3, they can go here in the morning and to ski school in the afternoon. Full junior ski school starts at age 4. Lunchtime care and meals can be provided with all programmes.

There's also a children's day centre for kids aged 2 to 6 in Saas Grund.

GETTING THERE

Air Sion, transfer 1hr, Geneva, 3½hr, Zurich 4hr, Milan 3hr.

Rail Brig (38km); regular buses from station.

ACTIVITIES

Indoor Bielen Leisure centre (swimming, hot-tub, steam bath, whirlpool, solarium, sauna, massage, tennis, gym), cinema, museum, concerts, badminton

Outdoor 20km cleared paths, natural skating rink (skating, curling, ice hockey), toboggan run, paragliding

TOURIST OFFICE

Postcode CH-3906
t +41 (27) 958 1858
f 958 1860
to@saas-fee.ch
www.saas-fee.ch

pleased: 'Had a good private lesson and felt I was skiing better afterwards.' And for children: 'Most classes quite small and English spoken.' There's a specialist snowboard school – Paradise.

FACILITIES FOR CHILDREN
Seem adequate

The school takes children from three years old. One solution for younger ones is to use an in-house kindergarten at one the hotels – we've had recent reports of two 'excellent' ones in the Hotel Alphubel the Hotel Schweizerhof.

Staying there

Staying near a main lift makes most sense. If you do end up at the wrong (north) end of the village – and most budget accommodation is there – ease the pain by storing kit near the lifts.

HOW TO GO
Check the location

Quite a few UK tour operators sell holidays to Saas-Fee, offering an excellent range of hotels. But there are surprisingly few chalet holidays.

Hotels 50-plus hotels so lots of choice.

((((5 **Fletschhorn** Elegant chalet in woods, with original art and individual rooms, long way from the village and lifts, but fabulous food (Michelin star).

(((4 **Walliserhof** Excellent 4-star. Superb, friendly welcome and service, delicious dinners, champagne breakfast. Spa.

(((4 **Schweizerhof** Stylish place in quiet position just above the centre. 'Fantastic food, friendly staff, excellent kindergarten.' Pool.

((3 **Beau-Site** 'First-rate' but quiet 4-star in central, but not convenient, position. Good food. Pool.

((3 **Saaserhof** Modernised old chalet in good position, just over river from the nursery slopes. Sauna, whirlpool.

((3 **Ambassador** Modern chalet, well placed close to the nursery slopes.

((3 **Alphubel** At the wrong end of town, praised by reporters for its own 'brilliant nursery', which is also used by guests in sister hotel, the Waldesruh.

((3 **Waldesruh** Strongly recommended by a reporter: 'Best situation in Saas-Fee for the Alpin Express. Sauna, steam and jacuzzi for a small charge.'

((3 **Hohnegg** A rustic alternative to the Fletschhorn, in a similarly remote spot; only eight rooms.

(2 **Belmont** The most appealing of the hotels looking directly on to the nursery slopes.

Self-catering Most apartments featured by UK operators are at the north end of the village, remote from the slopes, but they are generally spacious and well equipped. Independent travellers can choose better situated apartments.

EATING OUT
No shortage – some high class

Gastronomes will want to head for the Michelin-starred Fletschhorn (see Hotels) – expensive but excellent. Our favourite is the less formal Waldhaus Bodmen along a path into the woods. It has great food (from rösti to fillet steak) and rustic ambience. We had a delicious Thai meal in one of the Walliserhof's several restaurants. Boccalino is cheap and does pizzas – book or get there early. The Roadhouse does hamburgers and other snacks. Alp-Hitta specialises in rustic food and surroundings. The hotel Dom's restaurant specialises in endless varieties of rösti. Arvu-Stuba, Zur Mühle, La Gorge, Feeloch, Skihütte and La Ferme have all been recommended.

APRES-SKI
Excellent and varied

Late afternoon, Nesti's ski-bar, Zur Mühle and the little snow-bars such as Black Bull, near the lifts, are all pretty lively, especially if the sun's shining. Later on, Nesti's and the Underground keep going till 1am. Popcorn is packed and praised for 'lively atmosphere, brilliant music and catering for all ages'. The Arts Club is smarter and more sophisticated, with live music. The Metro Bar is like being in a 19th century mine shaft; Why Not pub is popular; The Metropole has the Crazy Night disco and three other bars.

OFF THE SLOPES
A mountain for pedestrians

There is a whole mountainside, the Hannig, where eating, drinking, walking, tobogganing and paragliding take priority, and skiers and boarders are banned. In the village, the splendid Bielen leisure centre boasts a 25m pool, indoor tennis courts and a lounging area with sunlamps. There's also the 'interesting' Saas museum and the Bakery Museum, where children can make bread. Don't miss the largest ice pavilion in the world, which is carved out of the glacier at Mittelallalin and includes a wedding chapel.

St Moritz 1770m

Luxury living – on and off the flatteringly easy slopes

WHAT IT COSTS

6

HOW IT RATES

The slopes

Snow	****
Extent	*****
Experts	****
Intermediates	****
Beginners	**
Convenience	**
Queues	**
Restaurants	****

The rest

Scenery	****
Resort charm	*
Off-slope	*****

What's new

The Vereina rail Tunnel, opened last season, bringing Klosters and Davos within 1½hr of St Moritz.

There are plans to develop the nearby Upper Engadine regional airport to allow scheduled and charter flights to operate from here.

Further snowmaking facilities are planned in time for the World Alpine Ski Championships, to be held in St Moritz in 2003.

- + Beautiful panoramic scenery
- + Off-slope activities second to none – including the Cresta Run, horse-racing and lots of varied festivals
- + Extensive, largely intermediate slopes
- + Fairly snowsure, thanks to altitude and extensive snowmaking
- + Good après-ski, for all tastes
- + Good mountain restaurants, some with magnificent views
- + Painless rail access via Zürich

- – Some hideous block buildings
- – A sizeable town, with little traditional Alpine character
- – No proper nursery slopes at resort level – except at Celerina
- – Several unlinked mountains, with a bus, train or car needed to most
- – Runs on two main mountains all fairly easy and much the same
- – Difficult road access and long overland airport transfers
- – Expensive

St Moritz is Switzerland's most famous 'exclusive' winter resort: glitzy, pricey, fashionable and, above all, the place to be seen – it's the place for an all-round winter holiday with an unrivalled array of different diversions, including such whacky pursuits as polo, golf and cricket on snow and gourmet and music festivals. The slopes on the two main mountains are almost uniformly easy intermediate – we don't rate it highly for complete beginners, and experts must be prepared to venture off-piste. But for langlaufers, it is superb.

The town of St Moritz itself is surprisingly unattractive. It is far removed from the chocolate-box image of the Swiss mountain resort, all wooden huts and cows with bells round their necks. Here, many of the buildings resemble council flats (extremely neat and clean ones – this is Switzerland, after all).

St Moritz itself may be unattractive to look at, but its setting is spectacular – beside the lowest in a long chain of lakes at the foot of the 4000m Piz Bernina. This is one of those areas where our progress on the mountain is regularly interrupted by the need to stand and gaze. It may not have quite the drama of the Jungfrau massif, or the Matterhorn, or the Dolomites, but its wide and glorious mountain landscapes are equally special. And the langlauf, walking and other activities on the frozen lake give it a real 'winter wonderland' feel.

boarding *Despite the high prices and its glitzy image, the terrain in St Moritz turns out to be quite favourable and the resort produces a special boarders' booklet with recommended 'secret spots'. The main boarding domain is above the town on Corviglia, which has a half-pipe and fun-park in the Signal area. Only the Corvatsch area has links that rely on drags – otherwise, most lifts are chairs, gondolas, cable-cars and trains. The extent of well-groomed cruising runs should appeal to any hard-booter, and there are several specialist snowboard shops. At night, there are a few places you don't have to wear a dinner jacket to get in.*

The resort

St Moritz has two distinct parts. Dorf is the fashionable main part, on a steep hillside above the lake. It's a busy, compact town with two main streets lined with boutiques selling Rolex watches, Cartier jewellery and Hermes scarves, a few side lanes and a small main square. A funicular takes you from Dorf to the main slopes of Corviglia, also reached by gondola from down the road at Celerina, and by cable-car from Dorf's other half, the spa resort of St Moritz Bad, spread around one end of the lake.

Everything in Bad is less prestigious. Many of the modern

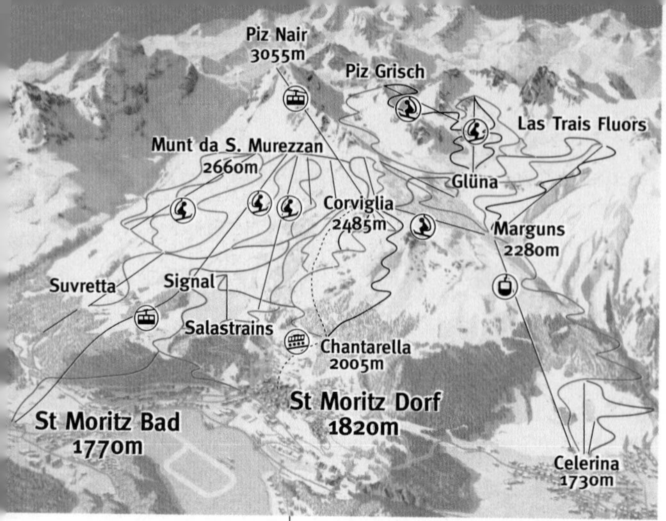

MOUNTAIN FACTS

Altitude 1730m-3300m	
Lifts	55
Pistes	350km
Blue	16%
Red	71%
Black	13%
Artificial snow	18km
Recco detectors used	

buildings are uncompromisingly rectangular and spoil otherwise superb views. In winter the lake is used for eccentric activities including horse and greyhound racing, show jumping, polo, 'ice golf' and even cricket. It also makes a superb setting for walking and cross-country skiing.

Other downhill slopes, at Corvatsch, are reached via lifts at Surlej, on the fringe of Silvaplana, and Sils Maria. Cross-country skiing is the main activity around the outlying villages of Samedan and Pontresina.

The town clientele is typified by the result of the annual Cresta Run race, which finishes at Celerina. In the top 29 on one of our recent visits were three Lords, one Count, one Archduke and a Baronet – but the race was won by a Swiss, without a title.

The mountains

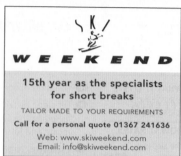

Like the resort, most of the slopes are made for posing. There are lots of long and generally wide flatteringly well-groomed runs, with varied terrain. There's an occasional black run, but few are seriously steep. But there is tough off-piste, and it doesn't get tracked out as it does in more macho resorts. Beginners' slopes are few and far between. Trips to other resorts such as Klosters, Davos (both around 90 minutes by train or car) and Livigno (an hour by car) are also possible.

THE SLOPES
Big but broken up

There are several distinct areas which add up to a substantial 350km of pistes. The main slopes, shown on our piste maps, are nearby Corviglia–Marguns and Corvatsch–Furtschellas, a bus-ride away (although you can get back to Bad on snow). Diavolezza, Piz Lagalb, Alp Languard and a few more distant bits and pieces make up the

rest. Some of these areas are well worth an outing. It helps to have a car, although the free bus service is reported to be efficient.

From St Moritz Dorf a two-stage monorail train goes up to **Corviglia**, a fair-sized area with slopes facing east and south. The peak of Piz Nair, reached from here by cable-car, splits the area – the sunny runs towards the main valley, and less sunny ones in the bowls to the north. From Corviglia you can head down (snow permitting) to Dorf and Bad, and via the lower lift junction of Marguns to Celerina.

From Surlej, a few miles from St Moritz, a two-stage cable-car takes you to up to the north-facing slopes of **Corvatsch**. From the mid-station at Murtèl you have a choice of red runs to Margun-Vegl and Alp Margun. From the latter you can work your way over to **Furtschellas**, also reached by cable-car from Sils Maria. Runs go down to Sils Maria and Surlej, and to Bad.

Diavolezza (2980m) and Lagalb (2960m), the main additional areas, are on opposite sides of the road to the Bernina pass to Italy, less than half an hour away by bus. **Diavolezza** has excellent north-facing pistes of 900m vertical, down under its big 125-person cable-car, and a very popular off-piste route, off the back of the mountain, across a glacier and down a valley beneath Piz Bernina to Morteratsch. **Lagalb** is a smaller area with quite challenging slopes, with an 80-person cable-car serving the west-facing front slope of 850m vertical.

SNOW RELIABILITY
Reasonable

This corner of the Alps has a rather dry climate, but the altitude means that any precipitation is likely to be snowy. There is snowmaking in every sector: several easy slopes around Corviglia are covered, as is an excellent 800m vertical red run on Corvatsch (Murtèl to Surlej), much of the 900m vertical face of Diavolezza and part of Lagalb.

FOR EXPERTS
Dispersed challenges

If you're looking for challenges, you're liable to find St Moritz disappointing on-piste. Red runs (many of which are no more than blues) far outnumber the black, and mogul fields are few and far between. The few serious black runs are dotted about different sectors.

The blacks at Lagalb and Diavolezza are the most testing pistes. The direct

SNOWPIX.COM / CHRIS GILL
St Moritz is worth a visit for the magnificent scenery as much as the skiing ↓

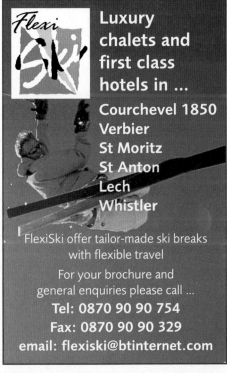

LIFT PASSES

2000/01 prices in Swiss francs

Upper Engadine
Covers all lifts in St Moritz, Celerina, Surlej, Sils Maria, Maloja, Lagalb, Diavolezza, Pontresina, Punt Muragl, Samedan, Müsella and Zuoz, and the swimming pools in St Moritz and Pontresina.

Main pass
1-day pass 60
6-day pass 282

Children/ teenagers
Age 16-20: 6-day pass 254
Under 16: 6-day pass 141
Under 6: free pass

Short-term passes
Half-day pass from 11.45 (adult 49).

Notes Discount for groups of 15 or more. Ski pass also valid in Gstaad Superski region, and gives one day's skiing in Livigno.

Alternative passes
Half-day and day passes for individual areas within the Upper Engadine.

Minor run down the Lagalb cable-car has 850m vertical of non-stop moguls.

There are plenty of opportunities to venture a little way off-piste in search of challenges – there is an excellent north-facing slope immediately above the Marguns lift junction, for example. Experts often head for the tough off-piste runs on Piz Nair or on the Corvatsch summit. More serious expeditions can be undertaken – such as down the splendid Roseg valley from Corvatsch. The off-piste potential is all the better for being relatively little exploited.

FOR INTERMEDIATES
Good but flattering

St Moritz is great for intermediates. Most of the pistes are easyish reds that could well have been graded blue.

One of the finest runs is the Hahnensee, from the northern limit of the Corvatsch lift system at Giand' Alva down to St Moritz Bad – a black-graded run that is of red difficulty for most of its 6km length and 900m vertical drop. It's a five-minute walk from the end of the run to the cable-car up to Corviglia.

Diavolezza is mostly intermediate. There is an easy open slope at the top, served by a fast quad chair, and a splendid long intermediate run back down under the lift. The popular off-piste run to Morteratsch requires a bit of energy and nerve. After a gentle climb, you have to cross the glacier on a narrow ledge, with crevasses waiting to gobble you up on the right should you slip. When we last did it, there were ice-picks and shovels at intervals along the path, put there by the enterprising proprietors of the beautifully laid out, welcoming ice bar which greets you at the end of the 30-minute slog. After that, it's downhill through the glacier all the way – with splendid views. Lagalb has more challenging pistes.

FOR BEGINNERS
Not much to offer

St Moritz is not ideal for beginners. It sits in a deep, steep-sided valley, with very little space for nursery slopes at the lower levels. Beginners start up at Salastrains or Corviglia, or slightly out of town, at Suvretta. Celerina has good, broad nursery slopes at village level. Progression from the nursery slopes to intermediate runs is rather awkward, as these invariably include the odd difficult section.

FOR CROSS-COUNTRY
Excellent; go to Pontresina

The Engadine is one of the premier regions in the Alps for cross-country, with 150km of trails of all levels, amid splendid scenery and with pretty reliable snow. The famous Engadine Ski Marathon takes place here every March, with over 12,000 racers taking part. Pontresina is a great location for cross-country and has good skating and curling rinks and swimming pools. There are floodlit loops too.

QUEUES
Crowds can be a problem

St Moritz has invested heavily in new lifts in recent years. High-speed quad chairs with bubble covers are now common on Corviglia and six-seat chairs are beginning to appear. But the area as a whole is over-dependent on cable-cars – most not of huge capacity – both for getting up the mountain from resort level and for access to the peaks from mid-mountain. Queues can be the result, though our reporters have had good experiences lately – the enlarged cable-car from Surlej to Murtèl is a big improvement.

THE CRESTA RUN

No trip to St Moritz is really complete without a visit to the Cresta Run. It's the last bastion of Britishness (until recently, payment had to be made in sterling) and male chauvinism (women have been banned since 1929 – unless you can secure an invitation from a club member for the last day of their season).

Any adult male can pay around £200 for five rides on the famous run (helmet and lunch at the Kulm hotel included). Watch out for the Shuttlecock corner – that's where most people come off, and the ambulances ply for trade. You lie on a toboggan (aptly called a 'skeleton') and hurtle head-first down a sheet ice gully from St Moritz to Celerina. David Gower, Sandy Gall and many others are addicts. Fancy giving it a go?

GETTING THERE

Air Zürich, transfer 4hr.

Rail Mainline station in resort.

SCHOOLS/GUIDES

2000/01 prices in Swiss francs

St Moritz
Classes 6 days
4hr: 10am-noon and 1.30-3.30
6 full days: 250
Children's classes
Ages: from 5
6 full days: 250
Private lessons
Half-day (2hr) or full-day (5hr)
160 for half-day

Suvretta
1999/00 price
Small groups of 4 to 6 people
Classes 6 days
2hr, 3hr, 4hr or full-day (5hr)
1/2 day: 38

CHILDCARE

The St Moritz ski school operates a pick-up service for children. Both schools provide all-day care.

Children aged 3 or more can be looked after in hotels – there are nurseries in the Carlton, the Parkhotel Kurhaus and the Schweizerhof, open from 9am to 4.30 or 5.30.

MOUNTAIN RESTAURANTS
Some special places

Mountain restaurants are plentiful, and include some of the most glamourous in Europe. Prices can be high, and reservations are advisable, especially if you want to sit in particular spots. But there are plenty of cheaper places too.

On Corviglia, the gourmet highlight is the Marmite; but it is outrageously expensive. And don't expect Alpine charm: it is housed in the Corviglia lift station, known locally as the highest post office in Switzerland because of its bright yellow paint. Much better for charm is the Paradis, with glorious panoramic views from the terrace, and the Lej de la Pesch behind Piz Nair.

On the Corvatsch side, we've heard good reports about the self-service restaurant at the top, while Fuorcla Surlej is a delightfully secluded spot, as is Hahnensee, on the lift-free run of the same name down to St Moritz Bad – a splendid place to pause in the afternoon sun on the way home. On stormy days, the most captivating place is the extremely rustic Alpetta, at Alp Margun (table-service inside).

The hotel-restaurant up at Muottas Muragl, between Celerina and Pontresina, is well worth a visit. It has truly spectacular views overlooking the valley, as well as good food. But the best time to go is at sunset.

Morteratsch restaurant (at the end of the off-piste run from Diavolezza) is splendid – sunny, by the cross-country area and tiny railway station and with excellent, good-value food.

SCHOOLS AND GUIDES
Internal competition

The St Moritz and Suvretta schools are branches of the national Swiss school. They also run The St Moritz Experience, a school specialising in powder. We lack recent reports on them. They also offer free 'ski safaris' every Thursday – something we've only come across in North America before. Some of the posh hotels have their own instructors, for private lessons only.

FACILITIES FOR CHILDREN
Hotel-based nurseries

Children wanting lessons have a choice of the two schools, but others must be deposited at one of the hotels with nurseries: the Parkhotel Kurhaus close to the cable-car in Bad, and the Schweizerhof up in Dorf. Club Med has its usual good facilities.

Staying there

For high society you will want to stay in Dorf. You can find convenient accommodation in either part of the resort. Bad has the advantage that you can get back to it from Corvatsch and Corviglia. Dorf has a better choice of bars and restaurants. Celerina is another option.

HOW TO GO
Several packaged options

A fair number of tour operators package the resort but a lot of people make their own arrangements. There is a branch of Club Med – its all-inclusive deal cuts the impact of high prices.

Hotels Over half the hotels are 4-stars and 5-stars – the highest concentration of high-quality hotels in Switzerland.

We don't actually like any of the famous 5-star places, but if forced to choose would prefer the glossy, secluded Carlton or the even more secluded Suvretta House to the staid Kulm or the Gothic Badrutt's Palace.

((((4 **Crystal** Big 4-star in Dorf, as close to the Corviglia lift as any, recently refurbished. But restaurant service 'indifferent/poor' says a reporter.

((((4 **Schweizerhof** 'Relaxed' 4-star in central Dorf, five minutes from the Corviglia lift, with 'excellent food and very helpful staff'.

((((4 **Albana** 4-star in Dorf, with walls adorned by hundreds of big game trophies bagged by proprietor's family.

(((3 **Monopol** Good value (in St Moritz terms) 4-star in centre of Dorf. Excellent buffet breakfasts. Pool and sauna recently renovated.

(((3 **Nolda** One of the few chalet-style buildings, close to the cable-car in St Moritz Bad.

EATING OUT
Mostly chic and expensive

It's easy to spend £50 a head eating out in St Moritz – without wine – but you can eat more cheaply. We liked the excellent Italian food at the down-to-earth, atmospheric Cascade in Dorf and the three restaurants in the Chesa Veglia. Hauses and the Veltlinerkeller are recommended by locals. But the best food is supposed to be out at Champfer, at Jöhri's Talvo.

On a clear day, try an evening up the funicular at Muottas Muragl for a splendid sunset followed by dinner in the hotel's unpretentious restaurant.

ACTIVITIES

Indoor Curling, swimming, sauna, solarium, tennis, squash, museum, health spa, cinema (with English films), aerobics, beauty farm, health centre, Rotary International club
Outdoor Ice skating, sleigh rides, ski jumping, toboggan run, hang-gliding, golf on frozen lake, Cresta run, 150km cleared paths, greyhound racing, horse-riding and racing, polo tournaments, cricket tournaments, ski-bob run, paragliding, curling

TOURIST OFFICE

Postcode CH-7500
t +41 (81) 837 3333
f 837 3377
information@stmoritz.ch
www.stmoritz.ch

APRES-SKI
Caters for all ages

There is an enormous variety of après-skiing age groups in St Moritz. The fur coat count is high – people come to St Moritz to be seen.

At tea-time, if you can tear yourself away from the mountain bars, the key venue is the famous Hanselmann's, for 'fabulous tea and strudels'.

Pit Stop is the favourite hang-out for boarders, with minimalist decor and a concrete floor. The three bars in the Schweizerhof are all popular after dinner: the Muli Bar has a country and western theme and live music, the Stubli has louder music and a younger crowd, the Piano Bar is for the chic with jacket and tie. The Cresta Bar, at the Steffani, is popular with the British, while the Cava below it is louder, livelier and younger. It is also amusing to put on a jacket and tie and explore the Palace and Kulm hotels and bars.

The two most popular discos are Vivai (expensive) at the Steffani and Kings at the Palace (even more expensive; jackets and ties required).

OFF THE SLOPES
Excellent variety of pastimes

Even if you lack the bravado or masculinity for the Cresta Run, there is lots to do. In midwinter the snow-covered lake provides a playground for bizarre events (see earlier in chapter) but in March the lake starts to thaw. There's an annual 'gourmet festival', with chefs from all over the world.

Some hotels run special activities, such as a curling week, health spa week or even rock and roll courses.

Other options are hang-gliding, indoor tennis and even trips to Italy (Milan is four hours away by car). The public pool in Bad is worth a visit.

St Moritz has a reputation for being sunny – 322 sunny days a year, says the tourist board – so there are many outside eating facilities, even at resort level. Try the Sunny Bar of the Kulm hotel, south-facing and overlooking the lake. Many Cresta riders lunch there.

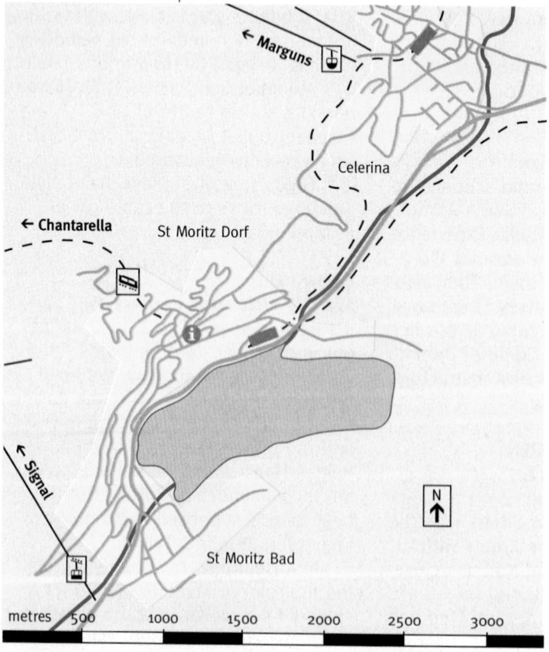

STAYING UP THE MOUNTAIN
Excellent possibilities

Next door to each other at Salastrains, just across the mountainside from Chantarella, are two chalet-style hotels, the 3-star hotel Salastrains, with 60 comfortable beds, and the slightly simpler and much smaller Zuberhütte. Great views, and no queues.

Celerina 1730m

At the bottom end of the Cresta Run, Celerina is an unpretentious, villagey if rather quiet resort, with good access to Corviglia. It is a sizeable village with a lot of second homes, many owned by Italians (the upper part is known as Piccolo Milano). There are also some appealing small hotels – as well as a couple of bigger 4-stars.

Pontresina 1805m

Pontresina is small and sedate and an excellent base for the extensive cross-country skiing on its doorstep.

It's a sheltered, sunny village with essentially a single narrow street of traditional old buildings, spoilt somewhat by the sanatorium-style of architecture that blights this whole area. All downhill skiing involves a bus- or car-ride. Five minutes away towards Celerina is the Muottas Muragl area, where a funicular railway serves a tiny mountain-top area with marvellous views and a single long run to the bottom station. Pontresina's own hill, Languard, has a single long piste.

Much is made of Pontresina being a cheaper place to stay than St Moritz, but cheaper doesn't mean cheap. There is another Club Med here.

Dining is mostly hotel-based and nightlife is very quiet.

Verbier 1500m

Paradise for nightlife-loving powder hounds with cash

WHAT IT COSTS

5

HOW IT RATES

The slopes

Snow	***
Extent	*****
Experts	*****
Intermediates	***
Beginners	**
Convenience	**
Queues	***
Restaurants	***

The rest

Scenery	****
Resort charm	***
Off-slope	***

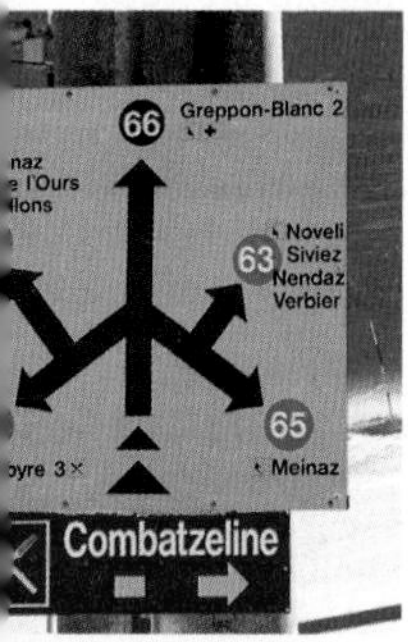

- ➕ Extensive, challenging slopes with a lot of off-piste potential
- ➕ Lively nightlife
- ➕ Wide range of chalet holidays
- ➕ Hardly any drag-lifts
- ➕ Fewer queues than there used to be
- ➕ Sunny, panoramic setting, and great views from the highest slopes
- ➕ Good advanced-level tuition
- ➕ Much improved piste grooming in recent seasons

- ➖ Overcrowded pistes in certain areas
- ➖ Sunny lower slopes will always be a problem, even with snowmaking
- ➖ Still some serious queues
- ➖ Piste map and direction signposting still inadequate
- ➖ Busy traffic (and fumes) in centre
- ➖ Some long walks/rides to lifts
- ➖ The Four Valleys network is no rival for the Three Valleys
- ➖ Pretty expensive

There is no doubt that Verbier is trying hard to retain its international visitors, improving over the last few years its grooming, snowmaking, ski school and lifts – most recently with the overdue replacement of the Tortin gondola. But major grouses remain. Some are down to the organisation of the resort – the kind of piste signposting shown on the left would be comical if it were not infuriating – but others have their roots in the lie of the land.

For experts prepared to hire a guide in order to explore off-piste, Verbier is one of the big names. With its 4 Valleys lift network and a claimed 400km of pistes, Verbier would seem at first sight to rank alongside the French mega-resorts such as Courchevel or La Plagne for piste skiers, too. But it doesn't; the 4 Valleys is an inconveniently sprawling affair, while Verbier's local pistes are surprisingly confined. Of course, piste skiers can have a satisfying holiday here – but you can do that in scores of resorts from Alpbach to Zell am See. Whether they can match Verbier's famously vibrant nightlife is another question.

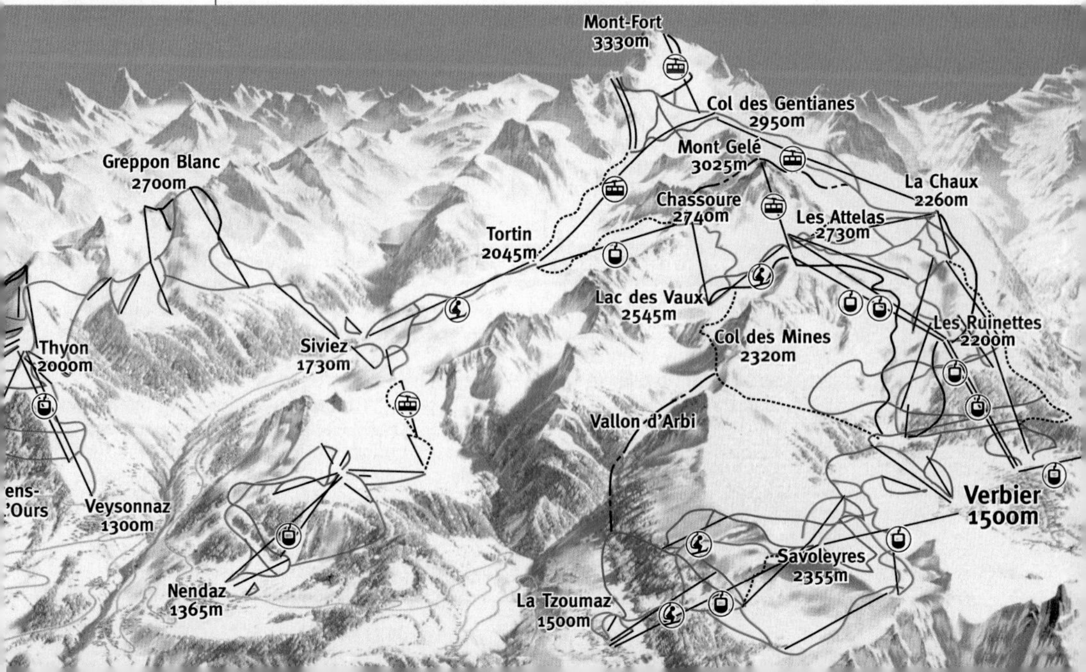

What's new

In 1998 the notorious old Tortin gondola was finally replaced by a new eight-seater one – tripling the capacity and with the possibility of quadrupling it, if need be. This has successfully rid the Alps of one of its worst queues.

In 1999 the Lac des Vaux area got a fast quad chair up to Attelas, dealing with another bottleneck.

Work on the proposed upgrade of the three-stage gondola from Le Châble to Attelas, via Verbier and Ruinettes, has been postponed for this year. The first two stages should be complete for 2001/02 while the third and final stage will be ready for the following year.

MOUNTAIN FACTS

Altitude	1400m-3330m
Lifts	100
Pistes	410km
Blue	32%
Red	42%
Black	26%
Artificial snow	50km
Recco detectors used	

boarding *As with its skiing, Verbier is one of Europe's best off-piste and extreme boarding resorts for those able and willing to pay for a guide or join a group. The main area is served by gondolas, cable-cars and chairs, with no drag-lifts at all. There are two fun-parks (the Swatch-sponsored boarder-cross course at La Chaux and another one at La Tournelle) and a half-pipe at Gentianes. Less experienced boarders should try Savoleyres, though there are a few drag-lifts. To see some real experts in action, hang around the resort in late March, when the world's best congregate here for the Red Bull Xtreme contest, on the cliff-like north face of the Bec des Rosses. There is a specialist snowboard school and a couple of specialist snowboard shops. And then there's the nightlife, which gets pretty wild at times.*

The resort

Verbier is an amorphous sprawl of chalet-style buildings, without too much concrete in evidence, and with an impressive setting on a wide, sunny balcony facing spectacular peaks. It's a fashionable, but informal, very lively place that teems with a youngish, cosmopolitan clientele. But it's no longer exclusive. The resort attracts a broad range of British holidaymakers, and there are plenty of Scans too.

Most of the smart shops and hotels (but not chalets) are set around the Place Centrale and along one street, sloping up to the main lift station at Medran 500m away, with another street sloping down, out of town. Much of the nightlife is here, too, though bars are rather scattered.

More chalets and apartments are built each year – which means building sites spoil the views in places – with much of the recent development inconveniently situated along the road to the secondary Savoleyres lifts, about a mile from Medran. There's an efficient free bus service. Parking is tightly controlled; your chalet may not have any, which means a hike from the free parking at the Sports Centre or paying for garage space.

The mountains

Verbier is at one end of a long, strung-out series of interconnected slopes, optimistically branded the 4 Valleys and linking Verbier to Nendaz, Thyon, Siviez and Veysonnaz. A second and much smaller area, Savoleyres, links Verbier to La Tzoumaz. Other small areas reached by bus are covered by the lift pass, including Bruson – also reached by riding a gondola down to Le Châble and taking a bus from there. Chamonix and Champéry are within reach by car.

THE SLOPES
Very spread out

Savoleyres is the smaller area, mainly suited to intermediates and reached by a gondola from the north-west end of town. This area is underrated and generally underused. It has open, sunny slopes on the front side, and long, pleasantly wooded, shady runs on the back. When conditions are good you can get back to Verbier on south-facing slopes, but even in January these deteriorate quickly.

You can take a catwalk across from Savoleyres to the foot of Verbier's main slopes. These are served by lifts from Medran, at the opposite end of town. Two gondolas rise to **Ruinettes** and then on to **Attelas**. From Attelas a small cable-car goes up to Mont-Gelé, for steep off-piste runs only. Heading down instead, you can go back westwards to Ruinettes, south to La Chaux or north to Lac des Vaux. From here chairs go back to Attelas, and to Chassoure, the top of a steep and wide off-piste mogul field, north-east-facing and leading down to **Tortin**, with a new gondola coming back up.

La Chaux is served by two slow chair-lifts and is the departure point of a jumbo cable-car up to Col des Gentianes and the glacier area. A second, much smaller cable-car then goes up to **Mont-Fort,** the high point of the 4 Valleys at 3330m. From the glacier is another off-piste route down to Tortin, a north-facing run of almost 1300m vertical. A cable-car returns to Col des Gentianes.

Tortin is the gateway to the rest of the 4 Valleys. From there you head down to **Siviez**, where one chair goes off into the long, thin **Nendaz** sector and another heads for the **Thyon** and **Veysonnaz** sectors, reached by a couple of lifts and a lot of catwalk skiing. Both these sectors suit intermediates best.

LIFT PASSES

2000/01 prices in Swiss francs

4 Valleys/Mont-Fort
Covers all lifts and ski-buses in Verbier, Mont-Fort, Bruson, Champex-Lac, La Tzoumaz, Nendaz, Veysonnaz and Thyon.

Beginners Station pass covers six beginner lifts.

Main pass
1-day pass 58
6-day pass 292

Senior citizens
Over 65: 6-day pass 175

Children
Under 16: 6-day pass 175

Short-term passes
Half-day pass from 11am (adult 53) or 12.30 (adult 46).

Notes Reductions for families and groups. Children up to 6 years free; 17-20 years 15% off.

Alternative passes
Limited passes for Savoleyres-la Tzoumaz, Bruson, and Verbier only.

Allow plenty of time to get to and from these remote corners – you don't want to be stranded in the wrong valley. It's an expensive taxi-ride.

SNOW RELIABILITY

Improved snowmaking

The slopes of the Mont-Fort glacier always have good snow. The runs to Tortin are normally snowsure too. But nearly all of this is steep, and much of it is formally off-piste. Most of Verbier's main local slopes face south or west and are below 2500m – so they can be in poor condition at times. Snowmaking on the lower slopes has improved a lot in recent years. The north-facing slopes of Savoleyres and Lac des Vaux are normally much better.

FOR EXPERTS

The main attraction

Verbier has some superb tough slopes, many of them off-piste and needing a guide. The very extreme couloirs between Mont-Gelé and Attelas and below the Attelas gondola are some of the toughest of all. There are safer, more satisfying off-piste routes from Mont-Gelé to Tortin and La Chaux.

There are hardly any conventional black pistes, and where they exist they are often indistinguishable from nearby reds. The front face of Mont-Fort is a conspicuous exception: a wonderful tough mogul field, all of black steepness but with a choice of gradient from seriously steep to intimidatingly steep. Occasionally you can get from Mont-Fort all the way to Le Châble off-piste. You can also head off-piste down to Siviez via one of two spectacular couloirs off the back of Mont-Fort. The North Face of Mont-Fort is one of the hottest of expert runs.

There is often off-piste powder around the north-facing slope from Gentianes to Tortin – and those willing to shoulder their skis and walk up a steep slope near the start (apparently now known as the Highway to Heaven rather than the Stairway, on account of its popularity) are rewarded by usually good powder in a quiet valley parallel to the main run. Attelas is the start of shorter runs towards the village.

A couple of long, but easy, off-piste routes go from Lac des Vaux via Col des Mines. One is a popular route back to Verbier, the other a very beautiful run through Vallon d'Arbi to La Tzoumaz. They are not always open: a piste-basher needs to form a ledge across a steep slope to the Col –

FINDING YOUR WAY AROUND THE SLOPES OF VERBIER

It isn't easy. The main area is complicated, and difficult to represent on a single map. So the lift company, Téléverbier, has dropped its hopeless map and produced a booklet of maps dealing separately with each sector. This, too, is hopeless.

They have based the Verbier map on an aerial photo. It looks lovely. But using a photo for a piste map means you can't cheat, and distort the mountains so as to show how runs and lifts connect. Both Lac des Vaux and Tortin are impossible to understand from this map. Savoleyres is covered by two maps, both hopeless.

Direction signposting on the mountain is equally frustrating. There are two problems. One is a strange faith in the kind of 'motorway' signs shown on page 421. We and our readers find these impossible to relate to the real choices of route. The second is that although the signs religiously use piste numbers there are no such numbers on the piste map. So how do you connect the two?

Navigation is further complicated by confusion over where it is prudent to go. For years now, runs that once were black pistes have been defined as 'itinéraires à ski' (eg both runs down to Tortin) or 'itinéraires de haute-montagne' (eg the Col des Mines run home from Lac des Vaux). We've long campaigned for these runs to be restored to piste status, but at least their non-piste status needs to be clear.

With patience, you can work out than neither is patrolled, and possibly deduce that 'itinéraires de haute-montagne' are 'not protected against mountain dangers' (ie avalanches) and should be tackled only in the company of an experienced mountaineer or a guide. But it is far from clear.

No other resort finds all this so difficult to resolve. All it takes is a modest budget, some awareness of visitors' needs and half a brain. What does Téléverbier lack?

otherwise the traverse is scary.

The World Cup run at Veysonnaz is a steepish, often icy, red, ideal for really speeding down. There is also an entertaining off-piste run from Greppon Blanc at the top of the Siviez–Thyon sector down to Leteygeon. An hourly bus (covered by the lift pass) brings you back to Thyon. There are 'memorable' heli-trips.

FOR INTERMEDIATES
Go to Savoleyres

Many keen piste-bashing intermediates find Verbier disappointing. The intermediate slopes in the main area are concentrated between Attelas and the village, above and below Ruinettes, plus the little bowl at Lac des Vaux and the sunny slopes served by the chairs at La Chaux. This is all excellent and varied intermediate territory, but there isn't much of it – to put it in perspective, this whole area is no bigger than the slopes of tiny Alpbach – and it is used by the bulk of the visitors staying in one of Switzerland's largest resorts. So it is often very crowded, especially the otherwise wonderful sweeping red from Attelas to Ruinettes served by the big gondola. Even early intermediates should taste the perfect snow on the glacier (provided you don't mind T-bars). The red run back to La Chaux is not too difficult, but it does have a high-mountain feel and it's no disgrace to ride the cable-car down instead.

Intermediates should make much more use of the Savoleyres area. This has good intermediate pistes, usually better snow and far fewer people (especially on Sundays). It is also a good hill for mixed abilities, with variations of many runs to suit most standards of intermediate.

The area as a whole presents some difficulties for early intermediates, as the editorial daughter, Laura (aged 8), found last season. There is excellent easy blue-run skiing at La Chaux, but there is no easy way back to Ruinettes from there. From Savoleyres there is an easy way across to Medran but, last season at least, there was no easy way down to that link from the top of Savoleyres. In both cases, we had to take quite testing red runs. Laura managed it, but in a properly run resort the difficulties would have been foreseen and sorted out.

FOR BEGINNERS
Progression is the problem

There are sunny nursery slopes close to the middle of the village and at Les Esserts, at the top of it. These are fine provided they have snow (they have a lot of snowmakers, which helps). The problem is what you do after the nursery slopes. There are easy blues on the back side of Savoleyres, and at La Chaux, but they are not easy to get back from (see above).

FOR CROSS-COUNTRY
Surprisingly little on offer

Verbier is limited for cross-country. There's a 4km circuit in Verbier, 4km at Ruinettes-La Chaux and 30km down at Le Châble/Val de Bagnes.

↑ There's a wild, high-mountain feel about the whole area around Col des Gentianes – this is the bowl leading down to La Chaux, underneath the jumbo cable-car, with the Cabane du Mont-Fort set in splendid isolation

SNOWPIX.COM / CHRIS GILL

SCHOOLS/GUIDES

1999/2000 prices in Swiss francs

Swiss Ski School
Classes 6 days
2½hr: 9.15-11.45 or 2pm-4.30
6 half-days: 141
Children's classes
Ages: 3 to 12
6 half-days: 168
Private lessons
Hourly, half- or full-day
120 for 2hr for 1 to 2 people

OTHER SCHOOLS

Fantastique
Adrénaline

QUEUES
Not the problem they were

It's clear that Verbier's queue problems have been greatly eased by recent investment. The jumbo gondola to Attelas has virtually eliminated queues at Ruinettes, but it has increased the overcrowding on the pistes back down. The mega-queues at Tortin for Chassoure are a thing of the past, thanks to the new eight-seater gondola. The new fast chair at Lac des Vaux has greatly eased the bottleneck there. But the cable-car from Tortin to Gentianes can produce queues, and the Mont-Fort cable-car above it can still generate very long ones.

Queues at the main village lift station at Medran persist, especially when day visitors are filling one of the gondolas by boarding down in the valley at Le Châble. There are plans to improve the three-stage Le Châble-Attelas gondola – work has been postponed for this year, but the first two stages should be complete by 2001/02.

Crowds are less of a problem at Savoleyres unless bad weather elsewhere forces people into the area.

MOUNTAIN RESTAURANTS
Disappointing in main area

There are not enough huts, which means queues and overcrowding in high season. Savoleyres is the best area. The hotel by the Tzoumaz chair takes some beating for value and lack of crowds. Also worth trying are Chez Simon ('simple and cheap'), Le Mayen (beneath the Combe 1 chair) and the rustic Marmotte ('wicked, excellent rösti'), just below the Sud drag. Le Sonalon, on the fringe of the village beneath the gondola, is 'excellent, with great views', but reached off-piste.

In the main area, the rustic Chez Dany at Clambin, on the off-piste run down from the La Chaux area, is about the best, and gets packed despite being a bit tricky to get to at times. Carrefour is popular and well situated at the top of the village, above the golf course. The restaurants at Ruinettes – table-service upstairs – have big terraces with splendid views. L'Olympique at Attelas is a good table-service restaurant.

The Cabane du Mont-Fort is a proper mountain refuge off the run to La Chaux from Col des Gentianes (see photo); great views, but very busy.

SCHOOLS AND GUIDES
Good reports

Verbier is an excellent place for advanced skiers, in particular, to get tuition. Several reporters are complimentary about the off-piste lessons with the Swiss ski school. More than 20 guides are available for heli-trips, which include trips to

Zermatt and the Aosta valley. The Vallée Blanche at Chamonix and a trip to Zinal are cheaper excursions. Verbier is also quite big on snowboard and telemark tuition. The consensus is that the Swiss school's standards have improved generally, partly thanks to the replacement of some old-timers by keen new recruits. Of the others, the Adrénaline international school gets rave reviews, particularly for its private lessons.

CHILDCARE

The ski school's Kids Club kindergarten, on the slope at Les Moulins, has its own drag-lift and takes children from aged 3 from 8.30 to 5pm.

The Schtroumpfs non-ski kindergarten (771 6585), close to the middle of the resort, takes children of any age up to 4 years (older ones by arrangement), from 8.30 to 5.30.

FACILITIES FOR CHILDREN
Wide range of options

The Swiss school's facilities in the resort are good, and the resort attracts quite a lot of families. The playground up at La Chaux has also received favourable reports. Although it is not used exclusively by the school, space on the bus back is limited, and priority is given to school groups. The possibility of leaving very young babies at the Stroumpfs nursery is valuable. British families have the option of travelling with family-oriented chalet operators – Ski Esprit and Mark Warner both have crèches, and Simply Ski has a nanny service you can arrange in advance.

There are considerable reductions on the lift pass price for families on production of your passports.

Staying there

Staying at the top of the resort, close to the Medran lift station, is convenient for the slopes and sufficiently distant from nightlife to avoid late evening noise. But in practice most people just get used to using the free buses, which are pretty efficient and run until 7pm; there are several routes running around the network of busy streets (congested at weekends). Some areas have quite an infrequent service. We are told that from 7pm to 8.30 there is a special taxi service that will drop you at any of the usual bus stops within the resort for five francs per person. If nightlife is not a priority, staying somewhere near the upper fringes of the village will mean that you can almost get back on skis.

GETTING THERE

Air Geneva, transfer 2hr.

Rail Le Châble (7km); regular buses to resort or gondola.

HOW TO GO
Plenty of options

Verbier is the chalet-party capital of the Alps. Given the size of the place there are surprisingly few apartments and pensions available, though those on a budget have inexpensive B&B options in Le Châble. Hotels are expensive in relation to their grading. Given a sleeping bag you can bed down at the sports centre for about £10 a night, including use of the pool.

Chalets There are chalets available for most tastes. Small ones, of the kind that you might take over for a family or small group of friends, are particularly common – for a cosy, creaky, traditional place, we like Simply Ski's chalet Marzuolus. There are also large chalets good for groups, places handy for the slopes, and others slap bang in the centre of Verbier's lively nightlife. There are not, however, many luxury options on the UK package market. The only chalet we've seen with all en-suite rooms is The Ski Company Ltd's chalet Goodwood, which is in a league of its own – electric everything, beautifully furnished, and in a prime spot near the square. Flexiski's chalet Bouvreuil is tastefully furnished with rustic antiques and plush sofas, and well positioned three minutes from the lifts. Ski Verbier is recommended by a reporter for its 'great' properties, especially the modern Antika apartment – central location, unobstructed views.

Hotels There are half a dozen 4-star places, a dozen 3-star and a handful of simpler places.

(4) **Rosalp** The place to stay if you can afford it, not least for the food in Roland Pierroz's Michelin-starred restaurant, which is the best you'll find in a Swiss resort. Good position midway between centre and lifts.

(4) **Montpelier** Very comfortable 4-star, but out of town (a courtesy bus is provided).

(4) **Vanessa** Central 4-star with spacious apartments as well as rooms.

(4) **Rois Mages** Smart little B&B hotel in secluded setting, up near the Savoleyres lift.

(3) **Rotonde** Much cheaper, well positioned 3-star between centre and lifts; some budget rooms.

(3) **Chamois** 3-star close to lifts.

(3) **Poste** Well placed 3-star midway between centre and lifts; the only hotel pool. Some rooms rather small.

(3) **de Verbier** Central 3-star, popular with tour operators and their clientele; renowned for good food; atmospheric and traditional, with helpful owners and staff.

(2) **Farinet** Central 3-star hotel, now

ACTIVITIES

Indoor Sports centre (swimming, skating, curling, squash, sauna, solarium, steam bath, hot-tub), cinema, ice hockey, indoor golf

Outdoor Ski-bob, 20km cleared walking paths, paragliding, hang-gliding, mountaineering, sledging

British-owned, with a focal après-ski bar on its elevated terrace.

Self-catering Apartments through tour operators are very thin on the ground. Self-caterers usually book direct. The comfortable Richemont and Troika apartments are close to the nursery slopes, a trek from the main lifts. The similar standard Blizzard is midway between Place Centrale and lifts.

The Vieux Valais apartments have a position second to none for the slopes, next to the main lift station. Close to the town centre are the simple Carina places. The La Bagnardise apartments on the quiet, convenient Chemin de Vernes get a good report.

EATING OUT

Very big choice

There is a very wide range of restaurants. Hotel Rosalp is clearly the best (and most expensive) in town, and among the best in Switzerland, with an awesome wine cellar to match its excellent Michelin-starred food – splash out on the seven-course Menu Gastronomique if you can afford it. The Pinte bistro in the hotel basement is a less pricey option – worth trying out.

The Grotte à Max does a vast variety of rösti plus unusual meats such as ostrich and kangaroo. The popular King's bar developed a restaurant a couple of years back, and its innovative food ('not a fondue in sight') and wide-ranging wine list quickly gained a reputation. An equally refreshing newcomer is the stylish Millénium, above the Toro Negro steak-house.

The Farinet restaurant is atmospheric and has good food at affordable prices. For Swiss specialities, try the Relais des Neiges, Robinsons, Le Caveau, Vieux-Verbier by the Medran lifts or Les Esserts by the nursery slopes. Two-star hotel Chalet Phénix has a decent Chinese restaurant. Le Fer à Cheval is a very popular and lively place for pizza and other simple dishes. Arguably the best-value Italian food in town is at Al Capone's out near the Savoleyres gondola. The Spaghetteria and Café Hacienda are other inexpensive places. Harold's is Verbier's burger joint.

You can snowmobile up to Chez Dany or La Marmotte for an evening meal, followed by a torchlit descent.

APRES-SKI

Throbbing but expensive

It starts with a 4pm visit to the Offshore Café, for people-watching (you may be happy to know that it is, at last, licensed to sell alcohol). Au Mignon at the bottom of the golf course has become popular since it was smartened up and given a large sun deck. Then if you're young, loud and British it's on to the Pub Mont Fort – there's a widescreen TV for live sporting events. The Nelson is popular with locals. The Farinet is particularly good in spring, its live band playing to the audience on a huge, sunny terrace – there's now a conservatory-type cover over it when it's cold. Au Fer à Cheval is a fun place full of locals and regular Verbier-ites.

After dinner the Pub Mont Fort is a very lively pick-up joint, popular with Brits and locals alike (the shots bar in the cellar is worth a visit). Crock No Name has good live bands or a DJ and is entertaining for its cosmopolitan crowd. Murphy's Irish pub in the Garbo hotel is popular, with a good resident DJ. The much-loved King's is a quiet candlelit cellar bar with 60s decor – 'hip crowd, good music'. Bar New Club is a sophisticated piano bar, with comfortable seating and a more

↑The restaurants around the Medran lift station in the village do good business at lunch time, whatever the weather

M SHAPIRO / VERBIER TO

discerning clientele. Jacky's is a classy piano bar frequented by big spenders on their way to the Farm Club – an outrageously expensive nightclub which inexplicably is very popular, especially with balding geriatrics with much younger girls in tow (tables are difficult to book). It's packed with rich Swiss paying SF200 for bottles of spirits on Fridays and Saturdays and has more Brits on Tuesdays (chalet girls' day off on Wednesdays!).

More within the pocket of most Brits is the noisy, glitzy Marshalls Club, which sometimes has live music. Taratata is a friendly club that seems to be growing in popularity. Scotch is the cheapest disco in town and popular with teenagers and snowboarders. Big Ben is another cheaper place, popular with youngsters.

The nursery slope at Les Esserts is floodlit for tubing etc on Saturday and Sunday evenings.

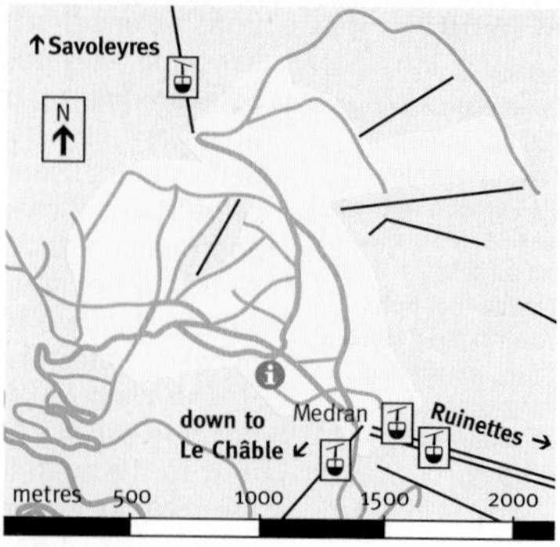

OFF THE SLOPES

No great attraction

Verbier has an excellent sports centre and some nice walks, but otherwise very little to offer if you don't want to hit the slopes. Montreux is an enjoyable train excursion from Le Châble, and Martigny is worth a visit for the Roman arena and museums. Various mountain restaurants are accessible to pedestrians. Both toboggan runs – on the shady side of Savoleyres and from Ruinettes – are an impressive 10km long.

STAYING IN OTHER RESORTS

A lot going for them

There are advantages to staying in the other resorts of the 4 Valleys. For a start, you can avoid the worst of the morning queues if you set off early, spend the day in the Verbier area and wave to the crowds on your way home.

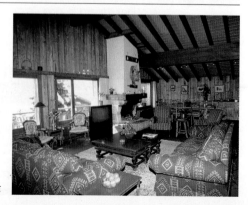

Secondly, they are substantially cheaper for both accommodation and incidentals. What you lose is the Verbier ambience and its range of restaurants, bars and nightlife.

Nendaz is a sizeable and quite rounded resort, described below.

Veysonnaz and Thyon are both small resorts, with mainly apartment accommodation. Veysonnaz is by far the more attractive – an old village complete with church. It has adequate bars, cafés and restaurants, a disco, sports centre with swimming pool, and school and guides. Thyon is a functional, ugly, purpose-built place.

Le Châble is a village a gondola-ride below Verbier. As changing gondola cars is not necessary for moving on to Ruinettes and Attelas, access to the slopes can be just as quick (or even quicker) from the queue-free valley. Le Châble is particularly convenient for those travelling by train, and for drivers who want to visit other resorts.

TOURIST OFFICE

Postcode CH-1936
t +41 (27) 775 3888
f 775 3889
verbiertourism@verbier.ch
www.verbier.ch

Nendaz 1400m

Nendaz is a big resort with over 17,000 beds and handily placed for exploring all of the 4 Valleys. But it is virtually unheard of on the British market, with only one British tour operator going there, Nendaz specialist Snow Plus. It deserves more attention, especially if you want to use Verbier's slopes but avoid the Sloanes and other Brits it attracts.

Nendaz is cheaper than Verbier and has a 12-person gondola straight to the top of its local north-facing slopes at Tracouet (2200m). Here there are good, snowsure nursery slopes plus blue and red intermediate runs back to town through the trees. There is also a snowboard fun-park and 17km of cross-country tracks.

Intermediate and better skiers and boarders can head off down the back of Tracouet to a cable-car which takes you to Plan de Fou at 2430m. From there you can go down to Siviez and the links to Tortin, Mont Fort and the local Verbier slopes in one direction and Thyon and Veysonnaz in the other.

It has a central and convenient location in the 4 Valleys and allows you to avoid most of the worst queues. Coming back to Nendaz you have to use an unpisted ski route but intermediates can take the Plan de Fou cable-car down instead. Or you can take a shuttle-bus between Nendaz and Siviez.

Nendaz itself is a large place on a shelf above and with great views of the Rhône valley. Accommodation is mainly in apartments but there are a few friendly and traditional hotels. Most of the resort is modern but built in traditional chalet-style and the original old village of Haute-Nendaz is still there, with its narrow streets, old houses and barns, and baroque chapel dating from 1499.

Off the slopes, Nendaz has plenty of shops, bars and restaurants and four discos. It has 70km of winter walks, an open air ice rink, a fitness centre and squash courts.

It is also just 25 minutes from Sion airport in the Rhône valley or 177km from Geneva airport, so it makes a good weekend destination.

Tour operator Snow Plus offers free car hire for groups of four or more and three days of free guiding with hand-picked Swiss qualified instructors. It also organises heli-skiing on the Rosablanche glacier for skiers of at least red run standard or on more difficult slopes for those who want them. And next season it will be organising some special heli-skiing weekends. It can fix hotel, apartment or chalet holidays.

Villars

1300m

Let the train take the strain

With its mountain railway and gentle low-altitude slopes, Villars is the kind of place that has been overshadowed by modern mega-resorts. But for a relaxing and varied family holiday the attractions are clear – and improved lifts and links with Les Diablerets have added to the appeal.

WHAT IT COSTS

4

HOW IT RATES

The slopes	
Snow	**
Extent	**
Experts	**
Intermediates	***
Beginners	****
Convenience	***
Queues	***
Restaurants	***
The rest	
Scenery	***
Resort charm	****
Off-slope	****

What's new

A six-seat chair from to Grand Chamossaire was built last year.

For 2000/01 there will be a new chair on the far side of Meilleret.

MOUNTAIN FACTS

Altitude	1130m-3000m
Lifts	46
Pistes	125km
Blue	40%
Red	50%
Black	10%
Artificial snow	17km

TOURIST OFFICE

Postcode CH-1884
t +41 (24) 495 3232
f 495 2794
information@villars.ch
www.villars.ch

THE RESORT

Villars sits on a sunny shelf at 1300m, looking across the Rhône valley to the mountains of the Portes du Soleil. A busy high street lined with all sorts of shops gives Villars the air of a pleasant small town; all around are chalet-style buildings, with just two or three block-like large hotels.

There is now an improved link with Les Diablerets, and outings to Leysin and Champéry are possible by rail or road. Many other resorts (such as Verbier) are within driving distance.

THE MOUNTAINS

The railway up from Bex goes on up to the **slopes**, terminating at Bretaye (1800m); a gondola from the other end of the village goes to one of the high points of the slopes, Roc d'Orsay.

The col of Bretaye has intermediate slopes on either side, with a maximum vertical of 300m back to the col and much longer runs back to the village. To the east, easier open slopes (very susceptible to sun) go to La Rasse (1350m) and the link to the otherwise separate Les Chaux sector – also served by a gondola up from a large car park above Gryon. A chair-lift beyond Bretaye now provides a two-way link with Les Diablerets.

Low altitude and sunny orientation mean that Villars' **snow reliability** is not good, though new mobile snowmakers have helped.

The main interest for **experts** is in exploring off-piste. There is plenty of worthwhile terrain reachable from the Charmet chair, for example.

For **intermediates** the local slopes offer a good range of variety, and the improved link with Les Diablerets opens up a lot of terrain.

Beginners will feel comfortable on the village nursery slopes, and riding the train to Bretaye. There are gentle slopes here, too, but also lots of people charging about a crowded area.

There are **snowboard** fun-parks at both Bretaye and Les Chaux.

The **cross-country** trails up the valley past La Rasse are long and pretty, and there are further loops in the depression beyond Bretaye.

It is mainly at weekends that **queues** appear for the lifts at Bretaye.

The **mountain restaurants** are often over-busy. The Golf Club is pricey but gets excellent reports, as does the Col de Soud ('best rösti ever'); Lac des Chavonnes (open weekends and peak periods) is worth the walk involved.

Villars' Ecole Moderne (still using the ski évolutif method) and the Swiss **ski school** both get positive reports. Riderschool is a specialist snowboard outfit. The Bureau des Guides organises heli-trips. Both ski schools run **children's** classes. There is also a non-ski nursery for children up to six.

STAYING THERE

Although the town of Villars is quite compact, the gondola is a shuttle-bus-ride from the centre (buses reliable but busy at times), and many **hotels** are between the two lifts. The hotel du Golf is a favourite 3-star ('great, family tries hard'). The 4-star Eurotel Victoria lacks character, but has huge rooms.

For many visitors, **eating out** means regional specialities in the neo-rustic Vieux Villars. Charlie's, the Central and the Mini-Pub are popular **après-ski** bars. El Gringo and Fox are the discos.

There's plenty to keep you active **off the slopes**: tennis courts, walks, swimming, skating and curling; or trips on the train – to Lausanne for instance.

Wengen 1275m

Charm, stunning views and extensive intermediate terrain

WHAT IT COSTS

3

HOW IT RATES

The slopes	
Snow	**
Extent	***
Experts	**
Intermediates	****
Beginners	***
Convenience	***
Queues	***
Restaurants	****
The rest	
Scenery	*****
Resort charm	*****
Off-slope	****

What's new

The exceptional snowfalls of 1999 led to serious avalanches, one of which hit the Männlichen cable-car station at the top of the village. The station was rebuilt for 1999/2000 in a much more convenient position, close to the main street. The cabins are unchanged in capacity, but now run at higher speed and so shift more people per hour.

By Christmas 2000 the hotel Victoria Lauberhorn will have been rebuilt, with a new swimming pool.

- ✚ Some of the most spectacular scenery in the Alps
- ✚ Traditional, 'traffic-free' Alpine village, reached only by cog railway
- ✚ Lots of long. gentle runs, ideal for intermediates, linked to Grindelwald
- ✚ Rebuilt cable-car now an attractive alternative to trains up to the slopes
- ✚ Nursery slopes in heart of village
- ✚ Calm, unhurried atmosphere

- − Limited terrain for experts
- − Despite some artificial help, snow conditions unreliable – especially on sunny home run and nursery slope
- − Trains to slopes from here and from Grindelwald are slow and infrequent – life revolves around timetables
- − Getting to Grindelwald's First area can take hours
- − Subdued in the evening, with little variety of nightlife

Given the charm of the village, the friendliness of the locals and the drama of the scenery, it's easy to see why some people – including numbers of middle-aged British people who have been going for decades – love Wengen. But non-devotees should think carefully about the lack of challenge, the unreliable snow and the dependence on cog railways before signing up.

The last of these drawbacks is slightly less serious than it was. The avalanches of 1999 had one happy outcome: the new station of the Männlichen cable-car has been built in the heart of the village, where it is not only less vulnerable to avalanche but also much more convenient. Of course, the cable-car is now more popular, and gets queues. So those willing to gear their holiday activities to timetables – or to accept half-hour waits for trains – will still mainly rely on the railway. The rest of us will go probably elsewhere.

boarding *Wengen seems to have reversed its marketing policy of trying to attract snowboarders. A couple of seasons ago it had a special 'Snow Valley' fun area and half-pipe for boarders by the Wixi chair. But last year it was not rebuilt. And the Männlichen fun-park was converted to a carving slope. But it is not a bad place for gentle boarding. The nursery area is not ideal, but beginners have plenty of slopes to progress to, with lots of long blue and red runs served by the train and chair-lifts. Getting from Kleine Scheidegg to Männlichen means an unavoidable drag-lift though. Experts will tire quickly of the area, and hanker after the steeper slopes of Mürren.*

The resort

Wengen is set on a shelf high above the Lauterbrunnen valley, opposite Mürren, and reached only by a cog railway, which carries on up the mountain as the main lift. Wengen was a farming community long before skiing arrived; it is still tiny, but it is dominated by a sizeable hotel, mostly of Victorian origin. So it is not exactly pretty, but it is charming and relaxed, and almost traffic-free. The only traffic is electric hotel trucks, which gather at the station to pick up guests, and a few ordinary petrol-engined taxis.

The main street is the hub of the village. Lined with chalet-style shops and hotels, it also has the ice rink and village nursery slopes. The nursery slopes double as the venue for floodlit ski-jumping and parallel slalom races.

The views across the valley are stunning. They get even better higher up, when the famous trio of peaks comes fully comes into view – the Mönch (Monk) protecting the Jungfrau (Maiden) from the Eiger (Ogre).

The main way up the mountain is the regular, usually punctual trains to Kleine Scheidegg, from the southern end of the village. The alternative cable-car is a much quicker way to some of the slopes, and to Grindelwald, and now starts very conveniently close to the main street.

The cog railway is still the main way up the mountain. Punctual it may be; crowd-free it ain't →

SNOWPIX.COM / CHRIS GILL

The mountains

MOUNTAIN FACTS

Altitude	945m-2970m
Lifts	45
Pistes	205km
Blue	30%
Red	50%
Black	20%
Artificial snow	30km
Recco detectors used	

Although it is famous for the fearsome Lauberhorn Downhill course – the longest and one of the toughest on the World Cup circuit – Wengen's slopes are best suited to early intermediates. There are no seriously steep pistes and the scariest part of the Downhill course, the Hundschopf jump, is shut to holidaymakers. Most runs are gentle blues and reds, ideal for cruising. The slopes are shared with Grindelwald in the next valley, and on that side there are some long and beautiful runs down to the village. But the lower parts of these often suffer from poor snow conditions, and there is hardly any snowmaking on the Grindelwald side.

You can get to Mürren by taking the train down to Lauterbrunnen, and a funicular and connecting train up the other side. The Jungfrau pass covers all of this.

THE SLOPES
Picturesque playground

Most of the slopes are on the other side of the mountain from Wengen. From the railway station at **Kleine**

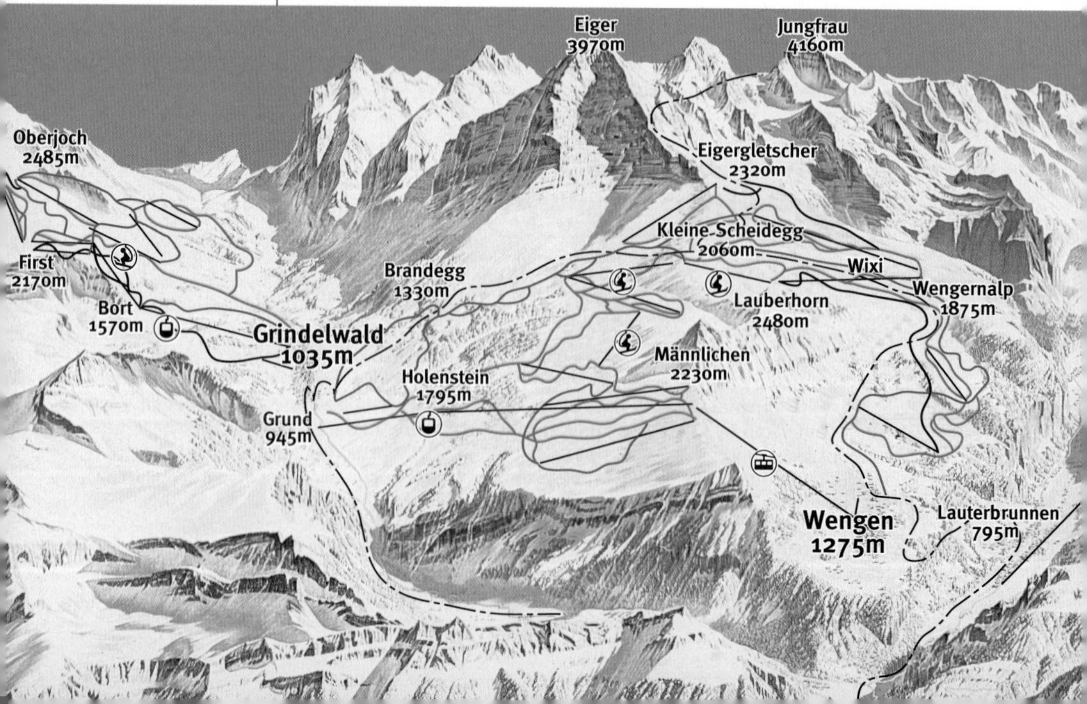

LIFT PASSES

2000/01 prices in Swiss francs

Jungfrau Top Ski Region
Covers all lifts in Wengen, Mürren and Grindelwald, trains between them and Grindelwald ski-bus.

Main pass
1-day pass 52
6-day pass 254

Senior citizens
Over 62: 6-day pass 229 (10% off)

Children
Under 16: 6-day pass 127 (50% off)
Under 6: 25

Short-term passes
Single ascent tickets for most lifts. Half-day pass for First (adult 40), Kleine Scheidegg-Männlichen (adult 40) and Mürren-Schilthorn (adult 40).

Alternative periods
3 days in 7 pass available (166).

Notes Day pass price for Kleine Scheidegg-Männlichen area only (102km of piste, 21 lifts), as Jungfrau Top Ski Region pass is only available for 2 days or over. Discounts for teenagers 16 to 20 (6-day 203) and groups.

Alternative passes
1- and 2-day passes available for First (adult 2-day 95), Mürren-Schilthorn (adult 2-day 95) and Kleine Scheidegg-Männlichen (adult 2-day 95).
4-, 5- and 6-day passes available for non-skiers (adult 6-day 189)

THE BRITISH IN WENGEN

There's a very strong British presence at Wengen. Many Brits have been returning to the same rooms in the same hotels in the same week, year after year, and treat the resort as a sort of second home. There is an English church with weekly services, and a British-run club, the DHO (Downhill Only) – so named when the first Brits persuaded the locals to keep the summer railway running up the mountain in winter so they would no longer have to climb up in order to ski down again. That greatly amused the locals, who until then had regarded skiing in winter as a necessity rather than a pastime to be done for fun. The DHO is still going strong and organises regular events throughout the season.

Scheidegg (2060m) you can head straight down to Grindelwald or work your way across the mountain with the help of a couple of lifts to the top of the **Männlichen** (2230m). This area is served by drag- and chair-lifts, and can be reached directly from Wengen by the improved cable-car.

There are a few runs back down towards Wengen from the top of the **Lauberhorn** (2480m), but below Kleine Scheidegg there's really only one.

SNOW RELIABILITY
Why not use the guns?

Most slopes are below 2000m, and at Grindelwald they go down to less than 1000m. Very few slopes face north and Wengen's snowmaking facilities are not up to protecting them. The real shame is that the snowmaking that exists isn't always used when it's needed.

All this can mean problems, and while we've found wonderful snow a couple of times in late March, we've also struggled to find decent snow to ski on in January.

FOR EXPERTS
Few challenges

Wengen is quite limited for experts. The one genuine black run in the area takes you from Eigergletscher to Wixi. For most of its length, the Lauberhorn Downhill course is merely an intermediate red run. The main challenges are off-piste runs such as Oh God from near Eigergletscher to Wixi and White Hare from under the north face of the Eiger. There are a number of off-piste runs from the Jungfraujoch late in the season.

For more challenges it's well worth going to nearby Mürren, an hour away by train and funicular. Heli-trips with mountain guides are organised if there are enough takers.

FOR INTERMEDIATES
Wonderful if the snow is good

Wengen and Grindelwald share superb intermediate slopes. Nearly all are long blue or gentle red runs – see Grindelwald chapter. The run back to Wengen is a relaxing end to the day, as long as it's not too crowded.

For tougher pistes, head for the top of the Lauberhorn lift and then runs to Kleine Scheidegg, or to Wixi (following the start of the Downhill course). You could also try the north-facing run from Eigergletscher to Salzegg, which often has the best snow late in the season.

FOR BEGINNERS
Not ideal

There's a nursery slope in the centre of the village – it's convenient, but the snow is unreliable. A small part of it is

SNOWPIX.COM / CHRIS GILL

Looking down from Männlichen, it's surprising that the avalanches of 1999 didn't do more damage than they did ↓

SCHOOLS/GUIDES

1999/2000 prices in Swiss francs

Swiss
Classes 6 days
3hr: am
6 half days: 210
Children's classes
Ages: 4 to 12
6 half days: 210
Private lessons
2hr, 3hr or 5hr
135 for 2hr

CHILDCARE

The kindergarten on the first floor of the Sport Pavilion takes children aged 2 to 7, from 8.30 to 5pm, Sunday to Friday. Children can be taken to and from lessons with the ski school, which starts at age 4.

A couple of 4-star hotels have their own kindergartens.

GETTING THERE

Air Zürich, transfer 3½hr. Bern, transfer 1½hr.

Rail Station in resort.

PISTES PATROLS RESTORED

On our last trip to this area we noticed a statement on the main mountain map board at Kleine-Scheidegg saying that several pistes in the area were not swept by patrollers at the end of the day. This disgraceful departure from universally accepted standards was not even indicated on the printed piste maps. One of the editors of this guide owes his life to the fact that he was rescued from a Swiss piste by an end-of-day patrol, so we're keen on them. We protested to the Jungfrau lift company, and as a result 'all blue, red, black slopes and the sledge runs will be swept by piste patrols at the end of the day in the whole ski area of Kleine Scheidegg-Männlichen from next winter season on'. If you see such notices at Kleine Scheidegg or anywhere else, let us know.

now served by a moving carpet lift, ideal for children. There's a beginners' area at Wengernalp, but to get back to Wengen you either have to climb up to the train or tackle the run down, which can be tricky. There are good, long, gentle slopes to progress to.

FOR CROSS-COUNTRY
There is none

There's no cross-country skiing in Wengen itself. There are tracks down in the Lauterbrunnen valley, but the snow there is unreliable.

QUEUES
Improving, but a long way to go

There can be some horrific bottlenecks in peak periods, and daily scrums to board the trains that the school uses. Weekend invasions can increase the crowds. Particular black spots are the train and the appallingly slow four-seat gondola from Grindelwald, which takes over half an hour to reach Männlichen.

Queues up the mountain have been alleviated a lot in the last few years. Three of the drag- and chair-lifts have been replaced by fast quad chairs – though plenty of old lifts remain.

MOUNTAIN RESTAURANTS
Plenty of variety

A popular but expensive place for lunch is Wengernalp, where the rösti is excellent and the views of the Jungfrau are superb. The highest restaurant is at Eigergletscher. If you get there early on a sunny day, you can nab a table on the narrow outside balcony and enjoy magnificent views of the glacier. The station buffet at Kleine Scheidegg gets repeated rave reviews, so it's not surprising that it also gets packed. The Grindelwaldenblick is a worthwhile trudge uphill from Kleine Scheidegg, with great food and views of the Eiger. For restaurants down towards Grindelwald, see that chapter.

SCHOOLS AND GUIDES
Healthy competition

A reporter says, 'The Swiss school is definitely trying harder than a few years ago.' The tuition and the standard of English are usually good. The independent Privat school has been recommended for private lessons.

Snowboarders are well served. And guides are available for heli-trips and powder excursions.

FACILITIES FOR CHILDREN
Apparently satisfactory

Our reports on children's facilities are from observers rather than participants, but are all favourable. It is an attractive village for families, with the baby slope in the centre. The train gives easy access to higher slopes.

Staying there

Wengen is small, so location isn't as crucial as in many other resorts. The main street is ideally placed for the station. The hotels on the home piste are convenient for the slopes. Those who don't fancy a steepish morning climb should avoid places set well below the station.

HOW TO GO
Wide range of hotels

Most accommodation is in hotels. Plenty of tour operators organise hotel packages here.

There is only a handful of catered chalets (and no especially luxurious ones). Self-catering apartments are few, too. There is a Club Med.

Hotels There are about two dozen hotels, mostly 4-star and 3-star, with a handful of simpler places.

((((4) **Wengener Hof** No prizes for style or convenience, but recommended for peace, helpful staff and spacious, spotless rooms with good views.

((((4) **Sunstar** Modern hotel on main

ACTIVITIES

Indoor Swimming pool (in Beausite Park and Sunstar hotels), sauna, solarium, whirlpool, massage (in hotels), cinema (with English films), billiards

Outdoor Skating, curling, 50km cleared paths, toboggan runs, paragliding, glacier flights, sledging excursions, hang-gliding

TOURIST OFFICE

Postcode CH-3823
t +41 (33) 855 1414
f 855 3060
information@wengen.com
www.wengen-muerren.ch

street. Comfortable rooms; lounge has a log fire. Live music some nights. Pool with views. Food very good. Friendly.

((((4 **Regina** Quite central. Smart, traditional atmosphere. 'Best food in Wengen.' Carousel nightclub.

((((4 **Silberhorn** Comfortable, modern 4-star in excellent central position, with choice of restaurants.

((((4 **Caprice** Small, smartly furnished chalet-style hotel across the tracks from the Regina. Kindergarten.

(((3 **Bellevue** Some way out, but does have the best views as well as 'friendly staff and excellent food'.

(((3 **Alpenrose** Long-standing British favourite; eight minutes' climb to the station. Small, simple rooms, but good views; 'first-class' food; friendly staff.

(((3 **Eiger** Very conveniently sited, right next to the station. Focal après-ski bar. Rebuilt with comfy modern rooms.

(((3 **Falken** Further up the hill. Another British favourite, known affectionately as 'Fawlty Towers'.

Self-catering The hotel Bernerhof's decent Residence apartments are well positioned just off the main street, and hotel facilities are available to guests.

EATING OUT
Lots of choice

Most restaurants in the village are in the hotels. They offer good food and service, and are open to non-residents. Recent recommendations include the Eiger, with a traditional restaurant and a stube with Swiss and French cuisine, the Sunstar ('high quality, not such high prices') and the Bernerhof ('good-value honest cooking'). The little hotel Hirsch has 'the best steaks'.

There's no shortage of fondues in the village. Several bars do casual food, including good-value pizza at Sina's. You could book a table at Wengernalp's excellent restaurant – the last train back to Wengen leaves at 11.45pm. If you feel daring, you could come back on skis or on a toboggan.

APRES-SKI
It depends on what you want

People's reactions to the après-ski scene in Wengen vary widely, according to their expectations and appetites. If you're used to raving in Kitzbühel or Les Deux Alpes, you'll rate Wengen dead, especially for young people. If you've heard it's dead, you may be pleasantly surprised to find that there is a handful of bars that do good business both early and late in the evening. But it is only a handful of small places. The traditional Tanne (happy hour 6 to 8) and the funky Chilli's are almost opposite on the main street, and generally lively. Sina's, a little way out by Club Med, does 2-for-1 drinks 4 to 6, and usually has live music. The stube at the Eiger and the tiny, 'always welcoming' Eiger Bar are popular at the end of the day, especially with Germans and Scans.

There is a disco in the Silberhorn hotel, and Sina's has disco nights. There is dancing and live music in some hotels. The cinema often shows English-language films.

OFF THE SLOPES
Good for a relaxing time

Wengen is a superb resort for those who want a completely relaxing holiday, with its unbeatable scenery and pedestrian-friendly trains and cable-car (there's a special, though expensive, five-day pass). There are some lovely walks, ice skating and a curling club. Excursions to Interlaken and Bern are possible by train, as is the trip up to the Jungfraujoch (see the Grindelwald chapter). Helicopter flights from Männlichen are recommended.

STAYING UP THE MOUNTAIN
Great views

You can stay at two points up the mountain reached by the railway: the pricey Jungfrau at Wengernalp and at Kleine Scheidegg, where there's a choice of rooms in the big Scheidegg-Hotels or dormitory space above the Grindelwaldblick restaurant and the station buffet. The big restaurant at Männlichen also has rooms.

STAYING DOWN THE VALLEY
The budget option

Staying in a 3-star hotel like the Schützen or Oberland in Lauterbrunnen will cost about half as much as similar accommodation in Wengen. The train from Wengen runs until 11.30pm and is included in your lift pass. Staying in Lauterbrunnen also improves your chances of getting a seat on the train to Kleine Scheidegg rather than joining the scrum at Wengen. Lauterbrunnen is also much better placed for Mürren.

You can save even more by staying in Interlaken. Choose a hotel near Interlaken Ost station, from which you can catch a train to Lauterbrunnen (22 minutes) or Grindelwald (36 minutes). Driving can take longer at weekends.

Zermatt 1620m

Magical in many respects – both on and off the slopes

WHAT IT COSTS

5

HOW IT RATES

The slopes

Snow	****
Extent	****
Experts	*****
Intermediates	****
Beginners	*
Convenience	*
Queues	***
Restaurants	*****

The rest

Scenery	*****
Resort charm	*****
Off-slope	****

What's new

For the 1999/2000 season a new electronic 'hands-free' lift pass system was introduced, enabling you to keep your lift pass in your pocket.

A new fun-park and ice cave were built in the Klein Matterhorn area.

'Into the Hotel' is a new luxury 5-star built on top of huge rocks and with many amazing features.

- ⊕ Wonderful, high and extensive slopes for experts and intermediates, with three separate and interestingly different areas
- ⊕ Spectacular high-mountain scenery, dominated by the Matterhorn
- ⊕ Charming, if rather sprawling, old mountain village, largely traffic-free
- ⊕ Reliable snow at altitude
- ⊕ World's best mountain restaurants
- ⊕ Extensive helicopter operation
- ⊕ Nightlife to suit most tastes
- ⊕ Smart shops
- ⊕ Linked to Cervinia in Italy

- ⊖ Getting to main lift stations may involve a long walk, crowded bus or expensive taxi-ride
- ⊖ Ski school has poor reputation
- ⊖ Beginners should go elsewhere
- ⊖ One-way link only between Klein Matterhorn and the other two areas
- ⊖ Getting up the mountain and around the different areas can be slow
- ⊖ Recent complaints about poor piste maintenance and long lift queues
- ⊖ Annoying electric taxis detract from the otherwise relaxed, car-free village ambience

You must try Zermatt before you die. Few places can match its combination of excellent advanced and intermediate slopes, reliable snow, magnificent scenery, Alpine charm and mountain restaurants with superb food and stunning views.

Many people complain that the car-free village is spoiled by intrusive electric carts and taxis; some complain about the time it takes to get to the top of the mountain; others say that the atmosphere is of Swiss efficiency and international tourism rather than mountain-village friendliness. But friendliness and service have definitely improved in the last few years and there's a magical feel to both the village and the mountains.

Zermatt's flaws are minor compared to its attractions, which come close to matching perfectly our notion of the ideal winter resort. It is one of our favourites.

boarding *Boarders in soft boots have one big advantage over skiers in Zermatt – they have much more comfortable walks to and from the lift stations at resort level! The slopes are best for experienced free-riders, because the tough piste and off-piste action is what Zermatt is really about – there's a fun-park and half-pipe too. The main lifts are boarder-friendly: train, funicular, gondolas and cable-cars. The resort is not ideal for learning to board, just as it isn't ideal for first-time skiers. The evenings have something for everyone.*

The resort

Zermatt started life as a traditional mountain village, developed as a mountaineering centre in the 19th century, then became a winter resort too. Summer is still as important as winter here.

Be warned: Zermatt is big business and most restaurants and hotels are owned by a handful of families. Many of the workers are brought in from outside Switzerland – but that is probably one of the reasons many reporters have remarked on the increased friendliness and improved service in recent years.

The village sprawls along a narrow valley either side of a river, with mountains rising steeply on each side. It is a mixture of chocolate-box chalets and more modern buildings – most in traditional style. You arrive by mountain railway from Täsch, where cars have to be left. The main street runs past the station and is lined with large luxurious hotels and smart shops.

Zermatt doesn't have the relaxed, quaint feel of some other car-free resorts, such as Wengen and Saas-Fee.

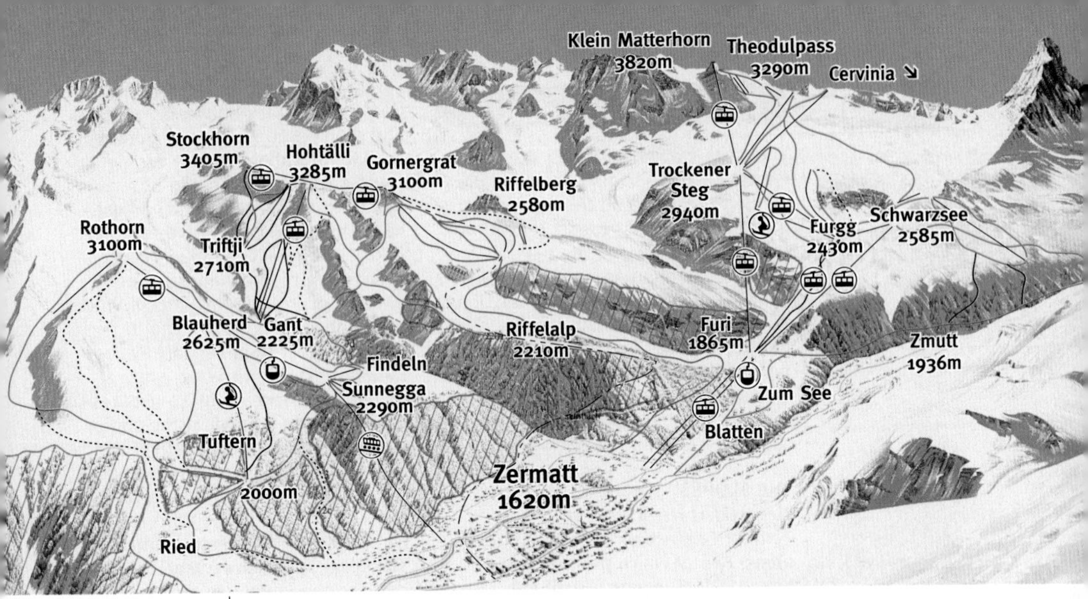

That's partly because the electric vehicles buzzing around are more intrusive and aggressive, and partly because the clientele is more overtly upmarket and part of the jet set, with large contingents from the US.

For a resort with such good and extensive slopes, there's a remarkably high age profile. Most visitors seem to be over 40, and there's little of the youthful atmosphere you get in rival resorts with comparable slopes, such as Val-d'Isère, St Anton and Chamonix.

The main street, with the station square near one end, is the focal point of village life. The cog railway to the Gornergrat area leaves from opposite the main station, and the underground funicular to the Sunnegga area is just a few minutes' walk away. The gondola to the Klein Matterhorn (and the link to Cervinia) is a 15-minute trek from here.

The school and guides office (a splendid new wood-and-glass building), the tourist office and many hotels, restaurants, shops, bars and nightspots are on, or a short stroll from, the main street. There's another main street along the side of the river. To each side are narrow streets and paths, many of which are hilly and treacherous when icy.

SNOWPIX.COM / CHRIS GILL

The Matterhorn dominates the view everywhere in Zermatt ↓

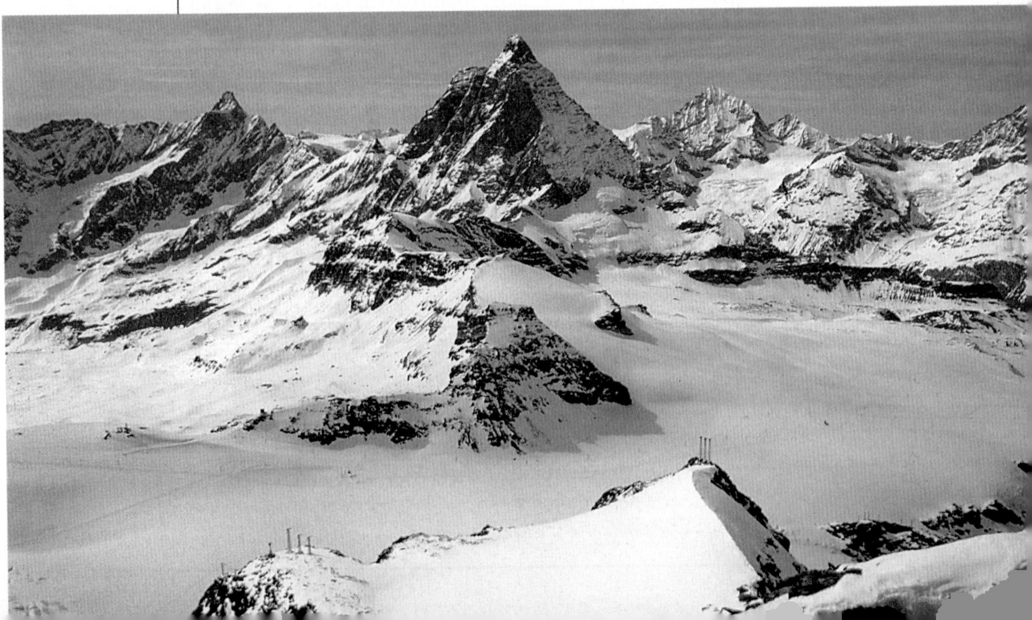

MOUNTAIN FACTS

Altitude	1620m-3820m
Lifts	74
Pistes	245km
Blue	33%
Red	44%
Black	23%
Artificial snow	43km
Recco detectors used	

The mountains

There are slopes to suit all standards except absolute beginners, for whom we don't recommend the resort. For intermediates and experts Zermatt has few rivals worldwide. There are marvellously groomed cruising trails, some of the best moguls around, long, beautiful scenic runs out of view of the lift system, exciting heli-trips and off-piste possibilities if you hire a guide, as well as the opportunity to get down into Italy for the day and lunch on pasta and chianti.

THE SLOPES
Beautiful and varied

Zermatt consists of three separate areas, two of which are now well linked. The **Sunnegga-Blauherd-Rothorn** area is reached by the underground funicular starting about five minutes' walk from the station. This shifts large numbers rapidly but can lead to queues for the subsequent gondola – you can take a run down to a high-speed quad alternative.

From the top of this area you can make your way – via south-facing slopes served by snowmakers – to Gant in the valley between Sunnegga and the second main area, **Gornergrat-Hohtälli-Stockhorn**. A new 125-person cable-car opened a couple of seasons ago linking Gant to Hohtälli in just seven minutes – a vast improvement on the two gruelling steep T-bars which were the only links before. A gondola makes the link back from Gant to Sunnegga. Gornergrat can be reached direct from Zermatt by cog railway trains which leave every 24 minutes and take 30 or 40 minutes to get to the top – arrive at the station early to get a seat on the right-hand side and enjoy the stupendous views.

From Gornergrat, there's a piste to Furi to link up with the third and highest area, **Klein Matterhorn-Trockener Steg-Schwarzsee**. But you can't do the journey in the opposite direction: once on the Klein Matterhorn, moving to a different mountain means heading down and getting from one end of the village to the other to catch a lift up. The Klein Matterhorn gives access to Cervinia – you need to buy an 'international pass' or pay a daily supplement to your Zermatt lift pass and the high lifts are

THE WORLD'S BEST MOUNTAIN RESTAURANTS

We once met a man who had been coming here for 20 years simply because of the mountain restaurants. The choice is enormous (the tourist information says 35, but it seems more). Most have table-service, nearly all of those we've tried have excellent food and many are in spectacular settings. It is impossible to list here all those worth a visit – so don't limit yourself to those we mention. It is best to book.

The restaurants at Fluhalp and Grünsee have beautiful isolated situations and good food (and live music at Fluhalp). The large terrace of the restaurant at Sunnegga offers decent food and a great view of skiers and the mountains. Up at Rothorn, the restaurant has excellent food – we had wonderful lamb – and views. Down at Findeln are several attractive rustic restaurants, including Findlerhof (aka Franz & Heidy's) and Chez Vrony ('unbeatable on a snowy day'). And the restaurant at Tuftern sells good Heida white wine from the highest vineyard in Europe – just down the valley at 1200m.

At Furi, the Restaurant Furi itself, Aroleid above it and Simi's on the road below all have large sun terraces and good food. The hotel at Schwarzsee is set right at the foot of the Matterhorn, at over 2500m, with staggering views of the mountain and the Trockener Steg slopes, and it serves endless variations of rösti. Round the back from here Stafelalp is charmingly situated and does good rösti. Up above Trockener Steg Gandegghutte has stunning views of the glacier. On the way back to the village below Furi, Zum See now has the enviable reputation of serving the best mountain food in Zermatt, and Blatten is good too.

The Kulmhotel, at 3100m at Gornergrat, has both self-service and table-service restaurants with amazing views of lift-free mountains and glaciers.

Wherever you go, don't miss the local alcoholic coffee – in its many varieties!

LIFT PASSES

1999/2000 prices in Swiss francs

Area Pass
Covers all lifts on the Swiss side of the border.

Main pass
1-day pass 62
6-day pass 306

Senior citizens
Over 65 (male), 62 (female): 6-day pass 230

Children
Under 16: 6-day pass 153
Under 9: free pass

Short-term passes
Single ascent tickets for most lifts.

Notes Daily supplement available to cover all lifts in Cervinia and Valtournenche (31).

Alternative passes
Passes for any period available for each area of Zermatt (Gornergrat-Stockhorn, Sunnegga-Rothorn, Trockener Steg-Klein Matterhorn-Schwarzsee), and combinations of areas. Pass available for Zermatt, Cervinia and Valtournenche (1-day: 62; 6-day: 340).

sometimes shut because of high winds.

There are pistes back to the village from all three areas – though some of them can be closed or tricky due to poor snow conditions at times.

SNOW RELIABILITY

Good high up, poor lower down

Zermatt has rocky terrain and a relatively dry climate. But it also has some of the highest slopes in Europe, and quite a lot of snowmaking.

All three areas go up to over 3000m, and the Klein Matterhorn cable-car is the highest in Europe, ending at over 3800m and serving a summer glacier. There are loads of runs above 2500m, many of which are north-facing, so guaranteeing decent snow except in freak years.

Artificial snowmaking machines serve some of the pistes on all three areas, from around 3000m to under 2000m. But the runs back to the village can still be patchy and we've had complaints of poor snow maintenance and hazard marking.

FOR EXPERTS

Good – with superb heli-trips

If you've never been, Zermatt has to be on your shortlist. If you have been, we're pretty sure you'll want to return.

If you love long, fluffy mogul pitches, the slopes at Triftji, below Stockhorn, are the stuff of dreams. From the top of the Stockhorn cable-car there's a run down to the T-bar that serves another two steep 2km runs – one each side of the lift. The whole mountainside here is one vast mogul field – steep, but not extremely so. Being north-facing and lying between 3400m and 2700m, the snow is usually the best around, which makes the huge moguls so forgiving that even we can enjoy them. The snag in early season is that this whole area is unlikely to open until well into January, and possibly later.

You can continue down from here to Gant and catch the gondola up to Blauherd. On that mountain there are a couple of wonderful off-piste 'downhill routes' from Rothorn, which have spectacular views down towards the village and over to the Matterhorn.

On the Klein Matterhorn, the best area for experts is Schwarzsee, from where there are several steep north-facing gullies through the woods. Unfortunately, you can't try these repeatedly without taking the beautiful, but slightly boring, track down to Furi and catching the cable-car up again.

There are marvellous off-piste possibilities from the top lifts in each sector, but they aren't immediately obvious to those without local knowledge. They are also dangerous because of rocky and glacial terrain.

We don't recommend anyone going off-piste without a guide. You can join daily ski touring groups but there aren't standard off-piste groups as there are in resorts such as Val-d'Isère and Méribel. You have to hire a guide privately for a full day, and that's expensive unless you have a fair-sized group. The Ski Club of Great Britain usually hires a guide for off-piste skiing once a week – we joined that in 1999 and had a great day.

Zermatt is the Alps' biggest heli-trip centre; the helipad resembles a bus station at times, with choppers taking off every few minutes. There are only three main drop-off points, so this can mean encountering one or two other groups on the mountain, even though there are multiple ways down. From all three points there are routes that don't require great expertise. The epic is from the Monte Rosa, at over 4000m, down through wonderful glacier scenery to Furi – but take care when you reach the almost vertical, icy end of the glacier (you may be roped down if there isn't much snow).

FOR INTERMEDIATES

Mile after mile of beautiful runs

Zermatt is ideal for adventurous intermediates. Both the blue and the red runs tend to be at the difficult end of their grading. There are some very beautiful reds down lift-free valleys from both Gornergrat and Hohtälli to Gant – we love these first thing in the morning, before anyone else is on them. A variant to Riffelalp ends up on a narrow wooded path with a sheer cliff and magnificent views to the right.

On Sunnegga, the 5km Kumme run, from Rothorn to the bottom of the Patrullarve chair, also gets away from the lift system and has an interesting mix of straight-running and mogul pitches. On Klein Matterhorn, the reds served by the Hörnli and Garten drags and the fast four-person chair from Furgg are all long and gloriously set at the foot of the Matterhorn.

For the less adventurous intermediate, the best areas are the blues on Sunnegga and above

Riffelberg on Gornergrat, and the runs between Klein Matterhorn and Trockener Steg. Of these, the Riffelberg area often has the best combination of good snow and easy cruising, and is popular with the school. Sunnegga gets a lot of sun, but the artificial snow means that the problem is more often a foot or more of heavy snow near the bottom than bare patches.

On the Klein Matterhorn, most of the runs, though marked red on the piste map, are very flat and represent the easiest slopes Zermatt has to offer, as well as the best snow. The problem here is the possibility of bad weather because of the height – high winds, extreme cold and poor visibility can make life very unpleasant. To get to Cervinia, you set off from Testa Grigia with a choice of two routes – even an early intermediate should find the easier 10km route (on the left as you look at the Cervinia piste map) down to the village manageable. The red Ventina run is a delightful cruise for better intermediates.

Beware of the run from Furgg to Furi at the end of the day, when it can be tricky and very crowded.

FOR BEGINNERS
Learn elsewhere

Zermatt is to be avoided by beginners. The easiest slopes are outlined above. And there's no decent nursery slope area. Unless you have a compelling reason to start in Zermatt, don't.

FOR EVERYONE
A spectacular cable-car ride

The Klein Matterhorn cable-car is an experience not to miss if the weather is good. The views down to the glacier and its crevasses, as the car swings steeply into its hole blasted out of the mountain at the top, are stupendous. When you arrive, you walk through a long tunnel, to emerge on top of the world for the highest piste in Europe – walk slowly, the air is thin here and some people have altitude problems. The top drag-lifts here are used in summer but normally shut in winter.

FOR CROSS-COUNTRY
Fairly limited

There's a 4km loop at Furi, 3km near the bottom of the gondola to Furi, and 12 to 15km down at Täsch (don't count on there being snow). There are also some 'ski walking trails' – best tackled as part of an organised group.

QUEUES
Some bottlenecks, and slow lifts

Zermatt used to have one of the worst reputations for queues in the Alps. Many major problems have now been eliminated but there can still be a lengthy scrum for the gondola out of town towards Klein Matterhorn at the start of the day, followed by long waits for two successive cable-cars before you reach the top – one recent reporter complained the whole journey took two and a half hours. Buses back to town from the Klein Matterhorn area at the end of the day are also

SCHOOLS/GUIDES

1999/2000 prices in Swiss francs

Swiss

Classes 5 days
4hr: 2hr am and pm
5 full days: 180 to 220

Children's classes
Ages: 4 to 12
5 full days including lunch: 255

Private lessons
1hr, half- or full-day
1hr: 80 for 1 or 2 people
full day: 290 for 1 or 2 people; each additional person 15

CHILDCARE

There are nurseries in two upmarket hotels. The one in the Nicoletta (967 0151) takes children aged 2 to 8, from 9am to 5pm. The Kinderclub Pumuckel at the Ginabelle (966 5000) takes children from 30 months, from 9am to 5pm, and ski tuition is available on the spot. The Kinderparadies (967 7252) takes children from 2 to 3 months from 9am to 5pm and in the evening looks after 4 to 9 year olds from 5pm to 10pm. Private babysitters are available, too.

Ski school lessons start at age 4.

oversubscribed: 'we scrummed down for 30 minutes one day', said the same disgruntled reporter. The other main problem is the Gornergrat train, where many people get standing room only.

But one of the things we love about Zermatt is that you can start out early – the lifts start at 8am. Catch an early lift and you can have a great time on deserted slopes for at least two hours.

SCHOOLS AND GUIDES
Poor reputation

The school has a poor reputation and a recent reporter said: 'Awful – in three days, the instructor taught our early intermediate no technique, spoke no English and used the follow-me method the whole time.' Another praised the half-day private lessons his wife had: 'Excellent English and her skiing improved dramatically.' There's a separate Stoked snowboard school.

FACILITIES FOR CHILDREN
Good hotel nurseries

The Nicoletta and Ginabelle hotels have obvious attractions for families who can afford them (though their nurseries are open to others). Despite our exceptionally fat file of reports on Zermatt, we have no first-hand reports on them. For children of ski-school age the resort is difficult to recommend.

Staying there

Choosing where to stay is very important in Zermatt. The solar-powered shuttle buses are crowded, but at least they are now large, free to lift-pass holders and more frequent than they used to be. Walking from one end of the village to the furthest lifts can take 15 to 20 minutes and can be unpleasant because of icy paths.

The best spot for most people is near the centre and the Gornergrat and Sunnegga railways. Some accommodation is inconveniently situated, up the steep hill across the river from the centre. Recent Winkelmatten visitors say it's not as isolated as we said in the previous edition – you can ski back to it from all areas and the bus to town is reliable.

Getting up to the village from Täsch is no problem. The trains run on time and have automatically descending ramps that allow you to wheel luggage trolleys on and off. You are met at the other end by electric and horse-drawn taxis and hotel shuttles.

HOW TO GO
A wide choice, packaged or not

Chalets Several operators do have places here, many of the most comfortable contained in sizeable blocks of apartments.

Hotels There are over 100 hotels, mostly comfortable and traditional-style 3-stars and 4-stars, but including some luxurious and pricey and some more affordable places.

((((5) **Into the Hotel** Latest fashionable place to open, with amazing gimmicks such as revolving beds, a suite with hinged roof and open air hot-tub, glass-floored night club, huge pool. Pricey.

((((5) **Mont Cervin** Biggest in town. Elegantly traditional. Central. Good pool.

((((5) **Zermatterhof** Traditional 'grand hotel' style with piano bar and pool.

(((4) **Alex** Close to station. Welcoming; charmingly decorated. Good facilities, including a pool. Reporters love it.

(((4) **Ambassador** Peaceful position on northern fringe, near Gornergrat station. Large pool; sauna.

(((4) **Monte Rosa** The original Zermatt hotel, towards southern end of village – full of climbing pictures and mementos, but well modernised. The Whymperstube is named after the British conqueror of the Matterhorn, who stayed here.

(((4) **Ginabelle** Smart pair of chalets, over the river, not far from Sunnegga lift; great for families – on-the-spot ski nursery as well as day care.

(((4) **Nicoletta** Bright, modern chalet quite close to centre, with nursery.

(((4) **Sonne** Nicely decorated in traditional style, in quiet setting away from main street; 'Roman Bath' complex.

((3) **Butterfly** 'Small, friendly, close to and as well furnished as the Alex but much better food,' says a recent reporter.

((3) **Julen** Charming, modern-rustic chalet over the river, with Matterhorn views from some rooms.

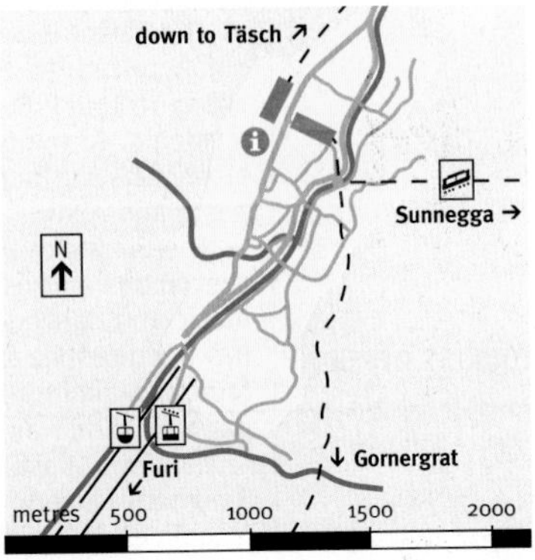

GETTING THERE

Air Geneva, rail transfer 4hr. Zürich, rail transfer 5hr.

Rail Station in resort.

ACTIVITIES

Indoor Sauna, tennis, hotel swimming pools (some open to public), salt water pool, keep-fit centre, squash, billiards, curling, bowling, gallery, excellent Alpine museum, cinema, indoor golf
Outdoor Skating, curling, sleigh rides, 30km cleared paths, helicopter flights, paragliding, cycling, ice diving

TOURIST OFFICE

Postcode CH-3920
t +41 (27) 967 0181
f 967 0185
zermatt@wallis.ch
www.zermatt.ch

(2) **Atlanta** No frills, but good food; close to centre, with Matterhorn views from some rooms.
(2) **Alpina** Modest but very friendly, and close to centre.
Self-catering There is a lot of apartment accommodation in the village, but not much of it finds its way to the UK package market – so it sells out early.

STAYING UP THE MOUNTAIN
Comfortable seclusion

There are several hotels at altitude, of which the pick is the Riffelalp at the first stop on the Gornergrat railway, due to reopen for 2000/01 after building a huge extension. At the top of the railway, at 3100m, is the Kulmhotel Gornergrat – a rather austere building with basic accommodation.

STAYING DOWN THE VALLEY
Attractive for drivers

In Täsch, where visitors must leave their cars, there are five 3-star hotels, costing less than half the price of the equivalent in Zermatt. The Täscherhof is next to the station; the City and Bellevue close by. It's a 13-minute ride from Zermatt, with trains every 20 minutes for most of the day; the last train down is 11.10pm.

EATING OUT
Huge choice at all price levels

There are 100 restaurants to choose from, ranging from top-quality haute cuisine, through traditional Swiss food, Chinese, Japanese and Thai to egg and chips and even a McDonald's.

In 1998/99 'Enzo, Vrony' opened (Enzo used to own Zermatt's best mountain restaurant). It has superb food and unique decor (combining new with old), with the kitchen in full view in the centre. Booking is essential.

The Mazot is also highly rated and highly priced. All the top hotels have classy restaurants open to non-residents. At the other end of the scale, Café du Pont has good-value pasta and rösti.

The Schwyzer Stübli has local specialities and usually live Swiss music and dancing. The Bahnhof Buffet has been rebuilt and serves reasonable food in a dining room built like a panoramic railway carriage.

Da Mario, Casa Rustica and The Spaghetti Factory were all recommended this year by readers.

APRES-SKI
Lively and varied

There's something for almost every taste, with a good mix of sophisticated and informal fun, though it certainly helps if you have deep pockets.

On the way back to the village from the Klein Matterhorn there are lots of restaurants below Furi for a last drink and sunbathe – and delicious fruit tarts at Zum See. On the way back from Sunnegga, Othmar's Hutte is popular and the Olympia Stübli often has live music. Near the church at Winkelmatten, the Sonnenblick is 'a great place to watch the sun set'. In town, there are fewer places than you might expect to have an end-of-the-day glühwein or hot chocolate. The Papperla is one of the most popular (it's busy after dinner, too). Elsie's bar, renowned for its snails, oysters and champagne, is atmospheric and gets packed both early and late. The North Wall is popular with seasonal workers. Promenading along the main street is popular.

Later on, the hotel de la Poste complex is popular for eating, drinking, dancing and jazz. There is something for everyone in this remarkable establishment, from a quiet, comfortable bar (David's Boathouse) to a lively disco-bar (Le Broken); Pink Elephant has live music (jazz, Irish etc).

Grampi's has dancing and is worth a visit. Z'Alt Hischi is an atmospheric bar for a quiet drink. The Hexenbar is a similarly cosy place. The hotel Alex appeals to over-30s for eating, drinking and dancing, with 'middle-of-the-road music and candlelit tables'.

The Vernissage is our favourite bar in town for a quiet evening drink. It is an unusual and stylish modern place, with the projection room for the cinema built into the upstairs bar and displays of art elsewhere. And try a cocktail at Into the Hotel to see the design and beautiful people.

OFF THE SLOPES
Considerable attractions

Zermatt is an easy place to spend time (and money). And if lunch up the mountain appeals, this is nearly as good a resort for pedestrians as it is for those on boards. The Alpine museum is recommended – as is a helicopter trip around the Matterhorn. You can also try the ice diving (they provide a wetsuit) at Trockener Steg.

United States

Until this year, virtually all the reports we received on US resorts had one thing in common: wholehearted praise for the US skiing experience. In general, people are captivated by it and by the contrasts with European resorts. Nearly everyone is struck by the high standards of service and courtesy you receive, by how few people there are on the runs, by the immaculate piste grooming that happens every night and by the top-quality accommodation. Depending on the resort you choose, you may also be struck by the superb quality of the snow, the cute Wild West ambience and how easy it is to visit other nearby areas. But don't fall into the trap of lumping all US resorts together – they differ enormously. There are distinct disadvantages of US skiing, too. And this year, for the first time, we have picked up early signs that America may be losing its edge on service (perhaps because the low level of US unemployment means recruiting staff is now more difficult).

It was snow that first took the British to America in large numbers, during the Alpine snow droughts of the late 1980s. The super-high Rockies had the reputation of getting limitless quantities of super-light snow. The reputation went slightly beyond the reality, but in practice it doesn't matter; most American resorts receive serious amounts of snow (25ft in a season is perfectly normal). And most resorts have serious snowmaking facilities too. What's more, they use them well – they lay down a base of artificial snow early in the season, rather than using snow-guns to patch up shortages later on.

This is partly a reaction to the pattern of natural snowfall. A lot of the Rockies' snow arrives relatively late in the season – something that seems to be increasingly true in the Alps, but not traditionally what we expect. In January, or even February, you may encounter signs saying: 'Caution: Early Season Conditions Apply'. What they mean is that you may occasionally encounter a rock.

Piste grooming is taken very seriously – most American resorts set standards that Alpine resorts are only now beginning to attempt to match. Every morning you can expect to step out on to perfect 'corduroy' pistes. But this doesn't mean that there aren't moguls – far from it. It's just that you get moguls where the resort says you can expect moguls, not where you're expecting an easy cruise. Indeed many resorts have now taken to grooming half the width of some runs and leaving the other half mogulled – so you can choose your terrain. Most runs are delightfully deserted compared with Europe.

American resorts are well organised in lots of other respects, too. Many offer free guided tours of the area. Lift queues are short, partly because they are highly disciplined, and spare seats on chair-lifts are religiously filled, with the aid of cheerful, conscientious attendants. Piste maps and boxes of tissues are freely available at the bottom of most lifts. Mountain 'hosts' are on hand to advise you about the best possible routes to take. School standards are uniformly high – with the added advantage of English being the native language. And facilities for children are impressive too – our reporters are universally glowing in their praise about children's ski school classes.

US resorts have the reputation of not providing opportunities for off-piste, but this seriously misrepresents the position. It's true that areas practically always have a boundary, and that venturing beyond it is discouraged or forbidden. But within the area there is often challenging terrain that is very much like being off-piste in an Alpine

↑ Like so many American resorts, Aspen has great, steep, ungroomed slopes within the area boundary

SNOWPIX.COM / CHRIS GILL

resort – with the important advantage that it is much safer because it's patrolled and checked for avalanche risk. Increasing numbers of resorts are adding areas that you have to hike too – and the effort is rewarded by delightful isolation. Last winter your editors delighted in such terrain in Winter Park, Aspen and Telluride. And we enjoyed lift-served untracked powder in the trees in Vail's new Blue Sky Basin and in newly reopened Berthoud Pass – see the Winter Park chapter.

There are drawbacks to the US as well, though. One is that many resorts (including big names) have areas that are very modest in extent compared with major Alpine areas. But many US resorts are very close to each other – so if you are prepared to travel a bit, you won't get bored. A more serious problem as far as we are concerned (and many of our reporters agree with us) is that the day is ridiculously short. The lifts often shut at 3pm or 3.30, even late in the season. That may explain another major drawback for those who like a good lunch on the mountain – the dearth of decent mountain restaurants. Monster self-service cafeterias doing pizza, burgers and other fast foods are the norm – so that people can spend as much time on the slopes and as little time eating as possible. Small

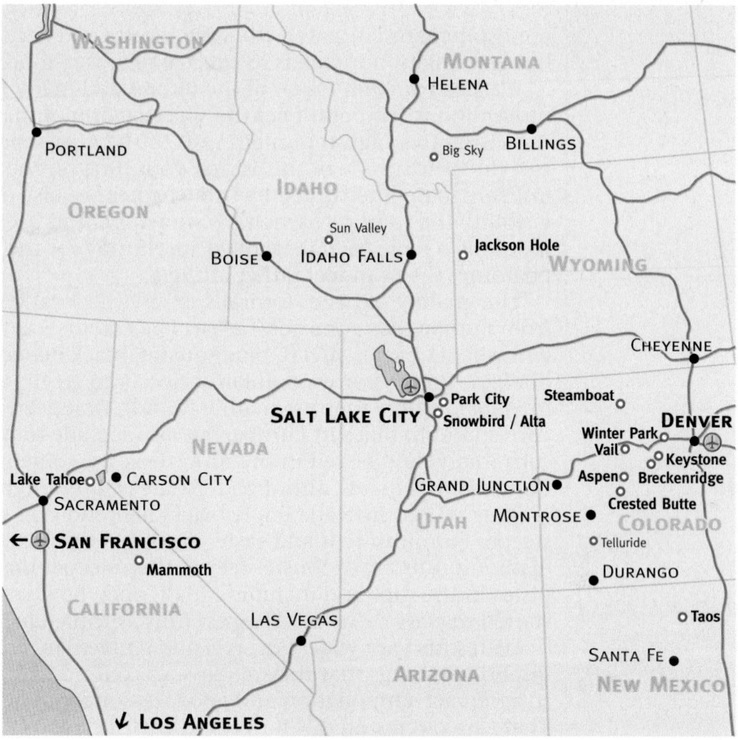
Washington
Montana
Helena
Portland
Billings
Big Sky
Idaho
Oregon
Sun Valley
Jackson Hole
Boise
Idaho Falls
Wyoming
Cheyenne
Park City
Steamboat
Salt Lake City
Snowbird / Alta
Denver
Winter Park
Vail
Keystone
Nevada
Aspen
Breckenridge
Lake Tahoe
Carson City
Grand Junction
Sacramento
Crested Butte
Utah
Montrose
Colorado
San Francisco
Telluride
Mammoth
Durango
California
Taos
Las Vegas
Santa Fe
Arizona
New Mexico
Los Angeles

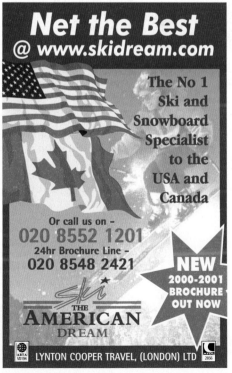

atmospheric restaurants with table-service and decent food are rare – but growing in number as resorts try to attract more European guests.

It's also true that much of the terrain and many of the runs are monotonous. You don't get the spectacular mountain scenery and the distinctive high-mountain runs of the Alps – most are below the tree line (the upside of this is that your time on the slopes is very unlikely to be interrupted by bad weather because of the good visibility the trees give when it's snowing). And because most of the mountains have been developed specifically for the skiing and boarding, they can feel rather artificial.

The grading of pistes (or trails, to use the local term) is different from Europe. Red runs don't exist. The colours used are combined with shapes: green circles, blue squares, black diamonds (single and double). Greens correspond fairly closely to greens in Europe (that is, in France, where they are mainly found). American blues largely correspond to blues in Europe, but also include tougher intermediate runs that would be red in the Alps; these are sometimes labelled as double-blue squares, although in some resorts a hybrid blue-black grading is used instead. Single-black-diamond runs correspond to steeper European reds and easier European blacks. Double-black-diamond runs are seriously steep – often steeper than the steepest pistes in the Alps and including high, open bowls. A few resorts have started to class their very steepest runs as triple-black-diamonds.

US resorts vary widely in style and convenience. But two important things that they all have in common are good-value, spacious accommodation and good, reasonably priced restaurants. There are old restored Wild West towns such as Telluride, Crested Butte and Aspen, genuine cowboy towns such as Jackson Hole, purpose-built monstrosities such as Snowbird, and even neon-lit, skyscraping gambling dens such as Heavenly. The most important difference in terms of the on-slope experience is between the east and the west. While resorts in New England can expect slush, ice and very variable weather and snow conditions, resorts in the west generally have much better snow and more consistently cold winter temperatures. Western American resorts are also more geared up for visitors staying a week and generally have a resort feel to them, while most New England resorts target skiers coming from the big cities for a day or a weekend and have less (or no) resort ambience.

In the end, your reaction to skiing and snowboarding in America may depend mainly on your reaction to America. If repeated cheerful exhortations to have a nice day wind you up, perhaps you'd better stick to the Alps. If you like the idea that the customer is king, give America a try. But if it's service you want, our advice is to go quickly. Last season we picked up dissatisfaction with American service for the first time. We heard from reporters who said their hotel room was dirty and the restaurant staff rude. We came across lift queues that weren't being properly organised and were in danger of becoming a European-style free-for-all because of 'shortage of staff'. And we encountered lifties who didn't even reply when you thanked them – unheard-of surliness compared with previous visits. When we quizzed the authorities about this they blamed low unemployment and too many vacancies they couldn't fill.

But all this is quibbling a bit. In general, you'll still find American service streets ahead of European. We love American skiing and wouldn't miss our annual visit for anything.

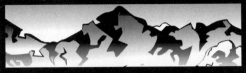

California

California? It means surfing, beaches, wine, Hollywood, Disneyland and San Francisco cable-cars. But it also has the highest mountains in continental USA and some of America's biggest winter resorts, usually reliable for snow from November to May (one often remains open until the Independence Day holiday, the 4th of July). What's more, winter holidays in California are tremendous value for money.

Holidays here are cheap because winter is low season for much of the accommodation and for scheduled flights from Britain into Los Angeles and San Francisco. There is huge capacity available for the massive summer tourist trade and hotel owners and airlines are happy to offer cut-price deals to keep a contribution coming in towards their overheads. A couple of years back we met a British family who had been on four holidays in bargain-basement Bulgaria. They had decided to try California for a change because it wasn't much more expensive. Not surprisingly, they loved it.

California's mountains get a lot of snow. In five out of the last six years, Californian resorts have recorded the deepest snow-cover in North America. In 1997/98, Kirkwood near Lake Tahoe was a powder hound's paradise with at least six inches of fresh snow on the mountain no fewer than 78 days – that's roughly half the days in the season. In 1998/99 it received almost 600in of snow (though that was the one year when one or two resorts elsewhere got more) and last season 520in. A common allegation is that the snow that falls in California is wet 'Sierra Cement'. Our fat file of reports from visitors has some complaints about that – especially late in the season – but most people have found the snow just fine – as we have.

Heavenly, Squaw Valley and Mammoth, in particular, are impressive mountains, with something for all standards of skier or boarder. Our main reservation has been the character of the resorts themselves; they don't have the traditional mountain-town ambience that we look for in the States. That's partly because this is California, the automobile state: the resorts were not originally designed with walking in mind, which has made them rather soulless. When you go skiing, you drive to the lifts, which have little village development at their bases. When you go out to eat, you drive to your restaurant of choice. In compensation, Heavenly, at least, offers uniquely big-time entertainment in its casinos. And the scenery, particularly around Lake Tahoe, is simply stunning – much more spectacular than you find in most US winter resorts.

But things are changing, with several new 'pedestrian villages' being developed. A new slope-side mini-village is already forming at Mammoth and construction of the Village at Mammoth, a new resort centre to be linked to the slopes by gondola, is due to start next year. Next season at Heavenly, there will be a direct gondola link up to mid-mountain from South Lake Tahoe – the first stage in development of the new Heavenly Village. Work on the Village at Squaw Valley is also expected to begin this year.

If you go to California, consider a two-centre holiday – taking in both Lake Tahoe and Mammoth. We recommend having a hire-car, especially in the Lake Tahoe region. There is public transport, but having a car gives you much more flexibility to explore the 14 nearby ski and snowboard areas at your own pace. Mammoth is a few hours' drive from the Lake Tahoe resorts.

Heavenly

1995m

Knockout lake views, and gambling until dawn

WHAT IT COSTS

5

HOW IT RATES

The slopes	
Snow	****
Extent	***
Experts	***
Intermediates	****
Beginners	****
Convenience	*
Queues	****
Restaurants	*
The rest	
Scenery	****
Resort charm	*
Off-slope	**

What's new

In late 1997 Heavenly was bought by The American Skiing Company, which now owns nine US resorts. Plans were already in place to build a gondola from downtown South Lake Tahoe up to the slopes, and that gondola – running up to a new lodge near the bottom of the Tamarack chair – will be open for 2000/01. Subject to final approvals, there will also be two new chair-lifts at the top of the gondola, plus three new trails.

Work on a 34-acre pedestrian village around the new gondola base is under way, with the ASC's signature Grand Summit Resort hotel at its heart.

Direct jet services to South Lake Tahoe airport from LA recommenced last year.

- + Amazing views across Lake Tahoe and arid Nevada
- + Fair-sized mountain which offers a sensation of travelling around – common in the Alps, not in the US
- + Lots of easy off-piste among trees
- + Some serious challenges for experts
- + Numerous other worthwhile areas within driving distance
- + Very good value package deals
- + A unique après-ski scene
- + Impressive snowmaking facilities

- − The base-town of South Lake Tahoe is quite unlike a traditional resort, and not attractive – though things are changing with construction of a new resort village near the existing downtown area
- − Very little traditional après-ski activity – though this may soon change as well
- − If natural snow is in short supply, most of the challenging terrain is likely to be closed

A resort called Heavenly invites an obvious question: just how close to heaven does it take you? Physically, close enough: with a top height of 3060m and vertical of 1065m, it's the highest and biggest of the resorts clustered around scenic Lake Tahoe (see page 455 for the others). Metaphorically, it's not quite so close. The slopes have something for all standards, and having another dozen resorts within easy reach by car means that an interestingly varied holiday is assured. But anyone who (like us) is drawn to the place by its amazing views across the lake is likely to be dismayed by the appearance and atmosphere of the town of South Lake Tahoe, at the foot of the slopes.

Even the powerful American Skiing Company may have trouble arranging the demolition of the casino-hotels that interfere with the views from the mountain. But it is making great strides in turning South Lake Tahoe into a more attractive destination: the shabby Park Avenue area has been flattened to make way for a new 34-acre resort village with luxury accommodation, shops, restaurants, bars and an ice-rink – all built in a more sympathetic style. And a new eight-seat gondola will run the two-and-a-half miles from here to the slopes this season.

boarding *Lake Tahoe is quickly becoming known as the snowboarding hub of North America and, as you would expect, boarders are very well catered for at Heavenly. There are good fun-parks and half-pipes on both the California and Nevada sides. The off-piste in trees and double-black-diamond bowls make a great playground for good free-riders. Beginners and intermediates will enjoy great cruising runs and the easy-to-ride chair-lifts. There are a couple of specialist board shops in South Lake Tahoe, but quite an absence of lively boarder-friendly bars.*

The resort

Heavenly is at the south end of Lake Tahoe, on the borders of California and Nevada, east of San Francisco. Heavenly's base-town – South Lake Tahoe – is unlike any other resort we know. The Stateline area at its centre is dominated by a handful of monstrous hotel-casinos (located just inches on the Nevada side of the line). These brash but comfortable hotels offer good-value accommodation (subsidised by the gambling) and big-name entertainment as well as slot machines, roulette wheels, craps and endless card games. They are a conspicuous part of the amazing lake views from the lower slopes (though not from above mid-mountain, nor on the Nevada side). The area around the casinos is strangely devoid of 'downtown' atmosphere (never mind mountain resort atmosphere); there are few bars or shops, and the centre is bisected by US Highway 50. The rest of the town consists of low-rise motels, stores, wedding chapels and so on, spreading for miles along this busy, pedestrian-hostile highway; many are rather shabby, though this is partly camouflaged by the tall trees that surround most of them. The Heavenly Village project – a new, sympathetically designed resort village just on the California side of the stateline – will greatly improve the town's appeal as a base for a holiday.

The construction of a gondola direct from the Heavenly Village site to the slopes might be taken to mean that in future it won't be so important to have a car. But it will still be valuable. Many of the best bars and restaurants are tucked out of the way. Most of SLT's accommodation will still be a drive from the slopes. And you need a car to explore the wider Lake Tahoe area.

The main town is surprisingly downmarket. The casinos have some swanky restaurants, but basically exist to allow gambling-starved Americans to feed their quarters into slot machines. The accommodation away from the centre is not particularly smart. But most of it conforms to American norms, and (except at weekends) all of it is under-used in winter, which is one reason why you can get cheap deals.

You reach the slopes from any of the four base stations, which can easily be reached by road. The new Heavenly Village will ultimately be the main base area. California Lodge, up a heavily wooded slope a mile out of South Lake Tahoe, beside a huge car park, will remain the main base for people staying outside the downtown area. Boulder and Stagecoach base lodges lie around the mountain in Nevada. There is an 'excellent' free shuttle bus service to the three out-of-town bases.

The mountain

Most of Heavenly's slopes suit intermediates down to the ground but there are also good beginner slopes at the California base, and some splendid easy runs to progress to. Experts can find genuine challenges at the two extremes of the area – as well as lots of fun in acre upon acre of easy off-piste wooded terrain. Keep in mind that there are other worthwhile areas within easy reach by car or bus (or paddle steamer!). You'll want to try at least a couple during your stay, as well as Heavenly – see page 455.

Recent visitors enjoyed Kirkwood and Alpine Meadows but warn: 'After two visits to Tahoe we are yet to ski Squaw Valley. Roads are often closed because of snow.' The Hornblower boat shuttle across the lake to Squaw Valley and Alpine Meadows is a pleasant alternative to driving.

THE SLOPES
Interestingly complex

Heavenly's mountain is quite complicated, and getting from A to B requires more careful navigation than is usual on American mountains.

There is a fairly clear division between the California side (the lifts and runs directly above South Lake Tahoe) and the Nevada side (above Stagecoach Lodge and Boulder Lodge).

Directly above California Lodge is a steep slope of around 520m vertical, with broad black pistes down the fall line and the narrower Roundabout blue trail snaking down. A mid-sized cable-car and the recently upgraded Gunbarrel fast quad go up to the first ridge. These can be ridden down again by novices. Short, easy runs go from the ridge down into a narrow wooded valley, the starting point of the blue Roundabout run. Various lifts here serve easy green and blue runs, and give access to the main bowl on the California side, above the Sky Deck restaurant. The blue and black runs here are served by three chair-lifts, including the Sky fast quad. The new gondola station will be hereabouts.

There are two routes to the Nevada side of the area – via the Sky chair and Skyline Trail catwalk, or via the six-seater Tamarack chair.

On this side there are three main bowls. The central one, above East Peak Lodge, is an excellent intermediate area served by two fast quad chairs, with a downhill extension of the bowl served by the Galaxy chair. On one side of this central bowl is the steeper, open terrain of Milky Way Bowl, leading to the seriously steep Mott and Killebrew canyons, served by the Mott Canyon chair. On the other side is the North Bowl, with lifts up from Nevada's two base lodges.

There are no really easy runs on the Nevada side, apart from limited nursery slopes at the base.

MOUNTAIN FACTS

Altitude	1995m-3060m
Lifts	31
Pistes	4800 acres
Green	20%
Blue	45%
Black	35%
Art. snow	500 acres

LIFT PASSES

2000/01 prices in dollars

Heavenly
Covers all lifts on Heavenly mountain.
Beginners 3-day learn to ski packages include lift pass and rental (adult 233).
Main pass
1-day pass 57
6-day pass 306
Senior citizens
Over 65: 6-day pass 144
Children
13 to 18: 6-day pass 246
Under 13: 6-day pass 144
Under 5: free pass
Short-term passes
Half-day passes available from 12.30 to 4pm (adult 42)
Notes Passes of three days or more allow one non-skiing day; 6-day pass valid for 7 days, with one non-skiing day.

SNOW RELIABILITY
No worries

Heavenly suffered from drought in the early 90s. That, no doubt, prompted it to install a very impressive snowmaking system that now covers 69% of the trails and ensures that most sections are open most of the time. In recent years Californian resorts have consistently recorded some of the deepest snow cover of any North American resorts; and when we last visited most of the snow-guns were invisible – entirely buried underneath natural snow.

FOR EXPERTS
Some specific challenges

Although the area as a whole suits intermediates better, there are genuine challenges for the more advanced. The runs under the California base lifts – including The Face and Gunbarrel (often used for mogul competitions) – are of proper black steepness, and very testing when the snow is hard. Ellie's, at the top of the mountain, may offer continuous moguls too.

The really steep stuff is on the Nevada side. Milky Way Bowl offers a fairly gentle introduction to this terrain. At the extremity of the bowl the seriously steep Mott and Killebrew canyons have roped gateways. The less expert are steered to lower gates.

All over the mountain, there is excellent off-piste terrain among widely spaced trees, which offers tremendous fun when the conditions are right.

FOR INTERMEDIATES
Lots to do

Heavenly is excellent for intermediates, who are made to feel welcome and secure by excellent piste grooming and signposting. The California side offers a progression from the relaxed cruising of the long Ridge Run, starting right at the top of the mountain, to more testing blues dropping off the ridge towards the Sky Deck restaurant. The confident intermediate may want to spend more time on the Nevada side, where there is more variety of terrain. Recent visitors enjoyed 'fast blues off the Dipper Express chair'. You should also head for some of the long, quite testing runs down to the base stations and to the Galaxy chair.

It's a pity that there is only the one Roundabout intermediate way back to California Lodge.

ACTIVITIES

Indoor 6 casinos, 6 cinemas, cheap factory shops, ice skating, bowling, gyms, spas, Western museum
Outdoor Boat cruises, snowmobiling, horse-drawn sleigh rides, horse riding, ice skating, hot springs, ghost town tours

FOR BEGINNERS
An excellent place to learn

The California side is more suited to beginners, with gentle green runs served by the Pioneer drag-lift and the Powderbowl chair-lift at the top of the cable-car. There are good nursery slopes at base lodge level.

FOR CROSS-COUNTRY
A separate world

The Spooner Lake Cross Country Area located close to Tahoe is an extensive meadow area of over 100km in 21 prepared trails. There are ample facilities for both instruction and rental. Organised moonlit tours are a popular alternative to the noise and bright lights of the casinos.

QUEUES
Some at weekends

Lift lines are generally not a problem, except during some weekends and public holidays when the entire Tahoe area is swamped with weekenders and day trippers. The key lifts moving people out from the base lodges are fast, reliable and comfortable – and of course will be less busy when supplemented by the new gondola.

MOUNTAIN RESTAURANTS
Several options, none exciting

Two restaurants can be recommended on the California side. At The Top of the Tram is a table-service restaurant (Monument Peak) which makes up for its simple food with a calm atmosphere and the famous lake view (reservations necessary). The Sky Deck at the heart of the California slopes has an excellent barbecue, where Californian rock music blasts and cool dudes hang out.

In Nevada, East Peak Lodge has a terrace and barbie, plus interesting views over arid Nevada, but it gets hideously overcrowded when the weather drives people indoors. There's an Italian-themed place at Stagecoach Lodge, and a Tex-Mex at Boulder.

STEVE BARKER / HEAVENLY SKI RESORT

The view of the lake from the mountain is pretty spectacular, even with the intruding casino-hotels of South Lake Tahoe ↓

SCOTT MARKEWITZ / HEAVENLY SKI RESORT

The Nevada side of Heavenly has some seriously challenging terrain – provided there's enough snow ↓

SCHOOLS/GUIDES

2000/01 prices in dollars

Perfect Turn Clinics 7 days
2¾hr: from 10am or 1pm
5 half days: 185

Children's clinics
Ages: 4 to 13
5 5hr days including pass, rental and lunch: 493

Private clinics
1hr, 2hr, 4hr and 6hr
85 for 1hr

CHILDCARE

Heavenly's state-of-the-art Day Care Center opens at 8.30 to care for children between the ages of 2 months and 4 years. A full day costs $75. Book ahead.

Children between 4 and 13 can enrol in the Perfect Kids programme. It offers skiing from age 4 and a snowboarding option from 8 upwards. It is an all-inclusive day of supervision, lessons, lunch, lift access, equipment and snacks. The programme is based at California Lodge (which includes an indoor play area) or at Boulder Lodge. There are also 'Tag-along' private lessons where a parent can observe their child's progress.

GETTING THERE

Air San Francisco, transfer 3½hr. Reno, transfer 75 min. South Lake Tahoe, transfer 15 min.

TOURIST OFFICE

Postcode NV 89449
t +1 (775) 586 7000
f 588 5517
info@skiheavenly.com
www.skiheavenly.com

SCHOOLS AND GUIDES

Good system

The American Skiing Company's Perfect Turn ski and ride programmes build on your strengths rather than focusing on your weaknesses. As well as normal lessons they offer a variety of special classes – carving, mogul and women-only clinics, for example. Free guided demos on the latest skis are also possible. There are free daily guided tours of the mountain.

FACILITIES FOR CHILDREN

Comprehensive

The recently opened Day Care Center in the California Lodge has attracted particular praise from one reporter: 'This was an excellent facility – very convenient and very professionally run. I would thoroughly recommend it.'

Staying there

Give careful consideration to your plans for evenings as well as daytime. If you have a car, your options are numerous; for example, you could base yourself out at one of the Nevada lift stations, and drive when you want entertainment. Night owls can scarcely do better than to stay in a casino.

HOW TO GO

Hotel or motel?

Accommodation in the South Lake Tahoe area is abundant and ranges from the glossy casinos to small, rather ramshackle motels. Hotel and motel rooms are easy to find midweek, but can be sold out at busy weekends.
Chalets UK tour operators run some good catered chalets, including some lakeside ones.
Hotels Caesars, Harrah's, Horizon and Harveys are the main casino hotels, in descending order of price. Rooms booked on the spot can be quite expensive; packages are good value.
((((4 **Embassy Suites** Luxury one-bedroom suites in a new, traditional-style building next to the casinos.
((2 **Tahoe Chalet Inn** Clean and friendly, close to casinos. Back rooms (away from busy highway) preferable.
((2 **Best Western Timber Cove Lodge** Bland but well run, with lovely lake views from some rooms.
Self-catering Plenty of choice. Some are available from tour operators. We've had a rave report about The Ridge Tahoe condos near Stagecoach Lodge: 'Luxury accommodation. The bathroom was big enough for waltzing.' There's an indoor/outdoor pool, hot-tub and a private gondola to whisk you to the slopes.

EATING OUT

Good value

The casino hotels offer fantastic value in their buffet-style all-you-can-eat dining. They have some more ambitious 'gourmet' restaurants too – some high enough up their tower blocks to give superb lake views. Caesars casino has an in-house branch of Planet Hollywood. The sprawling resort area offers a great choice of international dining, from cosy little pizza houses to large, traditional American diners, Mexican tequila-and-tacos joints, and English and Irish pubs. Visitors' suggestions include Paul Kennedy's steakhouse, and Fresh Ketch at Tahoe Keys Marina for 'wonderful fresh fish and harbour views – though don't expect snazzy presentation'. The new Riva Grill is also recommended. The Tudor Pub is better than it sounds.

APRES-SKI

Extraordinary

What makes the area unique is the casinos on the Nevada side of the stateline. These aren't simply opportunities to throw money away on roulette or slot machines: top-name entertainers, pop and jazz stars, cabarets and Broadway revues are also to be found in them – designed to give gamblers another reason to stay. We saw a great show by acrobats and trapeze-artists on our last visit. Turtles, at the Embassy Suites, is the place for a bop to the latest hits.

A more unusual way to spend the evening is to dance and dine your way across the lake aboard an authentic paddle steamer.

OFF THE SLOPES

Luck be a lady

You're in luck if gambling is your weakness. Or then again, perhaps not. If you want to get away from the bright lights, try a boat trip on Lake Tahoe, snowmobiling a short drive from South Lake Tahoe, or a hot-air balloon ride.

Pedestrians can use the existing cable-car or the new gondola to take a walk at altitude and view the lake and mountains below. When the sun is shining, it is a pleasant way to while away an afternoon.

Lake Tahoe 1890m

Slopes everywhere you look and magnificent lake views

WHAT IT COSTS

5

What's new

Squaw installed two six-packs last season and there's another for 2000/01. Work on the new alpine village is under way.

Accommodation in Kirkwood is up by 70% and three new lifts, including a fast quad, will open up 125 acres of expert terrain for 2000/01.

A new chair-lift will open 200 acres of new expert terrain in Northstar next year.

MOUNTAIN FACTS

Alpine Meadows

Altitude	2085m-2630m
Lifts	12
Pistes	2000 acres
Green	25%
Blue	40%
Black	35%
Art. snow	185 acres
Recco detectors used	

Kirkwood

Altitude	2375m-2985m
Lifts	12
Pistes	2300 acres
Green	15%
Blue	50%
Black	35%
Art. snow	55 acres

Northstar-at-Tahoe

Altitude	1930m-2625m
Lifts	12
Pistes	2420 acres
Green	25%
Blue	50%
Black	25%
Art. snow	200 acres

Squaw Valley

Altitude	1890m-2760m
Lifts	30
Pistes	4000 acres
Green	25%
Blue	45%
Black	30%
Art. snow	360 acres
Recco detectors used	

Set high in the mountains 200 miles east of San Francisco, on the borders of California and Nevada, Lake Tahoe has the highest concentration of resorts in the US, with 14 downhill and seven cross-country centres. It is a very beautiful region, ideal for driving around on a tour, visiting a different area each day – though the major mountains are worth devoting several days to.

THE RESORTS

The resorts of the Lake Tahoe region are mostly not fully fledged resorts in the European sense. Some have no accommodation, others a little. Most of the areas attract weekend or day trippers from the local area, or from the big west-coast cities. There are lots of B&Bs and motels dotted around the lake, and a couple of quite pleasant small towns.

Then there is South Lake Tahoe, at the foot of the Heavenly slopes (the biggest resort in the area), which is a quite unpleasant small town (see Heavenly chapter). It has boomed on the back of gambling, which is a big industry on the Nevada side of the stateline that cuts through the region and through Lake Tahoe itself. (The impact on Tahoe City, on the stateline at the north end of the lake, has been much less pronounced.)

The next biggest resort is Squaw Valley, about a 90-minute drive from South Lake Tahoe. It has some accommodation and very little nightlife – but resort developer Intrawest begins the construction of an alpine village at the resort base in mid-summer 2000.

THE MOUNTAINS

The choice of **slopes** around the lake is enormous, with more than enough to keep even the keenest skier or boarder happy for a couple of weeks. With a car you can make the best of the weather, heading for sheltered areas when a storm socks in, for example.

Snow reliability hasn't been a problem in the last few years – which have seen massive falls. The area also has huge amounts of artificial snowmaking capacity, so lack of snow shouldn't be a problem.

Heavenly, at the southern end of the lake, has the greatest vertical drop of the region, with slopes to suit all standards and splendid lake views. See the Heavenly chapter for details.

Nearby **Sierra-at-Tahoe** is a smaller, tree-lined area – more sheltered, so useful in bad weather.

Kirkwood, also at the south end of the lake, is renowned for its powder, steep runs and uncrowded slopes. It also has fine intermediate groomed trails and is currently developing a mountain village with accommodation and resort facilities. The lift system is also being developed – three new lifts, one of them opening up 125 acres of seldom used expert terrain, are being installed for 2000/01.

The major resort at the north end of the lake is **Squaw Valley**, with 4000 acres of open, above-the-tree-line bowls on six linked mountains. It is unusual in having no named runs at all. Instead of graded runs, it has green, blue and black lifts. The possibilities for experts here are phenomenal, with lots of steep slopes, chutes and big mogul fields – many extreme skiing and boarding movies are made here. But it is good for intermediates, with lovely long groomed runs including a top-to-bottom three-mile cruise, and a superb beginner area at altitude. Squaw is a big snowboarding centre and at night a fun-park, half-pipe and run (for skiers too) down from mid-mountain is floodlit. Massive recent investment has resulted in a very slick lift system, including North America's first twin-cable mega-gondola (as in Verbier and Crans-Montana). Construction of the new 13-acre Intrawest 'Village at Squaw Valley' gets under way this summer.

Alpine Meadows has the longest season and some of the most varied terrain in the Tahoe region – snow conditions can still be good in July some years. This area is excellent for all standards, with green runs and nursery slopes at the bottom, top-to-bottom blues and some varied blacks, including high bowls and tree-covered

TOURIST OFFICE

Alpine Meadows

Postcode CA 96145
t +1 (530) 583 4232
f 583 0963
info@skialpine.com
www.skialpine.com

Kirkwood

Postcode CA 95646
t +1 (877) 547 5966
f 258 8899
kwd-info@
ski-kirkwood.com
www.skikirkwood.com

Northstar-at-Tahoe

Postcode CA 96160
t +1 (530) 562 1010
f 562 2215
northstar@
boothcreek.com
www.skinorthstar.com

Squaw Valley

Postcode CA 96146
t +1 (530) 583 6985
f 581 7106
squaw@squaw.com
www.squaw.com

terrain. The mountain has slopes facing in all directions, giving good conditions whatever the weather.

Northstar-at-Tahoe is a fairly small, almost entirely easy-to-intermediate mountain close to Squaw. Although there are black runs marked on the trail map, none is seriously steep and the nine or so blacks on the back-side (served by a single fast quad) vary little in character and are really good long advanced intermediate cruises. A new chair-lift for 2000/01 will open up 200 acres of expert terrain on Lookout Mountain. Previously, this has been accessible only by snowcat. Again, the whole area is very sheltered and good for bad-weather days. There's a pleasant shopping, restaurant and bar area at the bottom of the mountain.

Those are the six areas we'd most recommend visiting. But there are eight other areas in the Tahoe region in case you get bored, most of which are marked on our map. A regular visitor to the region who is particularly keen on the north shore recommends Diamond Peak for its 'breathtaking views and fab restaurant', Mount Rose for its 'great snow always and carving runs', and both for quiet slopes and zero lift queues. There are also **cross-country** possibilities at most of the downhill areas as well as in dedicated cross-country areas.

Queues are rare in all the areas, except at peak weekends when people pour in from San Francisco and Los Angeles. We have few reports of the **schools** or facilities for **children**, but one regular visitor assures us that they are of the utmost quality.

STAYING THERE

We'd recommend spending a few days at each end of the lake.

At the southern end the main options are the brash and rather tacky town of South Lake Tahoe (see the chapter on Heavenly), or the quiet mountain village at Kirkwood.

At the northern end there's more choice, Squaw Valley has a handful of hotels. The Lodge at Squaw Creek, in an isolated position with its own lift into the slopes and a piste back down, is a huge, luxurious place that attracts big conferences and seminars. Squaw's cable-car runs in the evenings to serve the floodlit slopes and the dining facilities at High Camp. This is an incredible mid-mountain complex, with several restaurants and bars, outdoor pool, ice skating, tennis and bungee jumping. The new resort village at the base will massively increase Squaw's attraction for a week's stay.

Northstar has very convenient hotel rooms and condominiums. It would be a good family choice for a quiet stay.

An alternative is to stay in the small town of Tahoe City, right on the lake, a short drive from both the Squaw Valley and Alpine Meadows areas and a little bit further from Northstar. It has a fair number of hotels and bars, and some good restaurants.

Our specialist Tahoe reporter also recommends Incline Village (which comes a close second to Tahoe City for choice of bars and restaurants) for its 'country charm and ambience, and friendly people'. The visitor centre can fix you up with an inexpensive condo on the spot, without advance booking (this is low season, remember). Incline Village is handy for Diamond Peak and Mount Rose, a bit of a drive from Squaw and Alpine Meadows, but under an hour from Heavenly. Could be the ideal compromise.

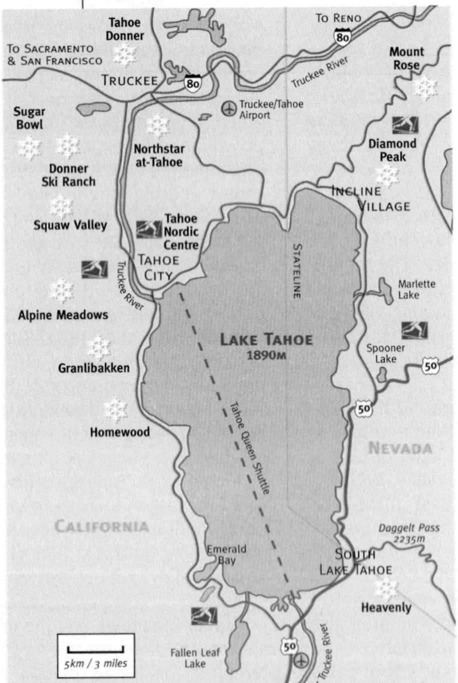

Mammoth Mountain 2430m

Californian sun and snow with extensive, varied terrain

WHAT IT COSTS

(5)

HOW IT RATES

The slopes	
Snow	****
Extent	***
Experts	****
Intermediates	****
Beginners	****
Convenience	**
Queues	****
Restaurants	*
The rest	
Scenery	***
Resort charm	**
Off-slope	*

- ⊕ One of North America's biggest and best mountains, with steep bowls at the top and easy/intermediate cruises lower down, in the trees
- ⊕ Can get a lot of snow – and there's extensive snowmaking
- ⊕ Deserted slopes during the week
- ⊕ Good children's facilities
- ⊕ Excellent daytime bus service
- ⊕ Lots of recent resort improvements

- ⊖ Mammoth Lakes is a rather straggling place with no focus, where it helps to have a car
- ⊖ Most accommodation is miles from the slopes – though this is changing
- ⊖ Weekend crowds from Los Angeles
- ⊖ Runs not clearly marked on map or mountain, especially high up
- ⊖ Wind can close high lifts, and upper runs can be icy and windblown

Mammoth lives up to its name, more or less. It may not be giant in Alpine terms, but it is much bigger than most resorts in the US, and big enough to provide a week's amusement for most people. It has everything from steep, high, experts-only chutes and bowls (with magnificent views) to long, easy cruising runs in the trees. What it lacks, more than anything else, is a real village at the base.

Enter Intrawest, owner of Whistler and now of various key plots of land here, plus a majority share in Mammoth Mountain. Intrawest is investing heavily in transforming the resort infrastructure and creating 10,000 more guest beds over the next decade – and opened the first stage of a new slope-side development at Juniper Springs last season. Plans for a new pedestrian village centre, to be linked to the mountain by gondola, will take longer to realise. For now, the mountain is the attraction. But it is quite a mountain.

boarding *Mammoth initially set out to attract boarders to its sister mountain June, where there's a good fun-park and half-pipe. But Mammoth itself now has three impressive 'Unbound' terrain parks and half-pipes for different standards. The main one is served by the high-speed Thunder Bound Express lift, with the Quarter Pipe Cafe half-way up the slope. The rest of Mammoth's slopes are ideal for all standards, with some excellent free-riding in the high bowls and perfect beginner and intermediate runs below. All but one tiny lift are chairs or gondolas. There are some good bars in town, lively at weekends.*

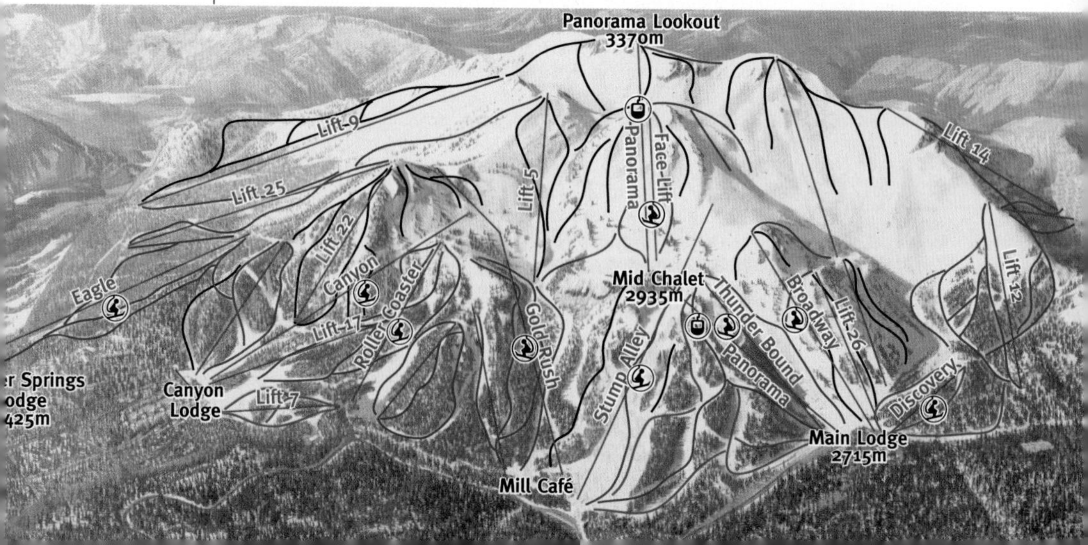

What's new

The first stage of a slope-side mini-village developed by Intrawest opened for 1999/2000 with the new Juniper Springs Lodge. Further developments are under way here. For 2000/01 the two lifts up from this point, chairs 15 and 24, will be replaced by the Eagle chair – the first fast six-seater here.

Work on a new pedestrian village at the core of Mammoth Lakes, eventually with a gondola link to the slopes at Canyon Lodge, is now to start in 2001.

Upgrading of the Panorama gondola to an eight-seater was completed for last season. The new base station houses the Woolywood kids' school and skier services. And the Discovery fast quad replaced two old chairs serving the beginner slopes at the Main Lodge.

Following the 62-acre extension of snowmaking to the Canyon Lodge area last year, an additional 100 acres in the Juniper Springs area is being added for 2000/01.

Planned to open last season as the Top of the World, the Parallax restaurant will open at the top of the gondola for fine dining for 2000/01.

MOUNTAIN FACTS

Altitude	2430m-3370m
Lifts	27
Pistes	3500 acres
Green	30%
Blue	40%
Black	30%
Art. snow	450 acres
Recco detectors used	

The resort

Most people stay in Mammoth Lakes, a small year-round resort town four miles from the main lift base. There is no 'downtown' area: hotels, bars, restaurants and little shopping centres are dotted along Main Street, the very wide highway running through the resort, and Old Mammoth Road at right angles to it. The buildings are generally rustic in style, and are set among trees, so although Mammoth Lakes may be short on resort ambience it has a pleasant enough appearance. Even McDonald's has been tastefully designed. The 'village' is usually under a blanket of snow, which also helps.

There is also accommodation at the main base area at the Mammoth Mountain Inn complex, along with some restaurants. And along the road up to the slopes lie several hotels and condos. Shuttle-buses run efficiently on several routes serving the lift bases, but they are limited after 5.30pm and a car is useful, especially for getting to June Mountain for a change of scenery.

The five- or six-hour drive up from Los Angeles, along a very good road, is spectacular. You pass through the San Bernardino mountains and Mojave Desert before reaching the Sierra Nevada range, of which Mammoth is part. Light aircraft can fly into Mammoth Lakes' own airport.

The mountain

Although Mammoth is one of the US's largest areas, its claim to have 150 trails should not be taken too seriously. The slightest variant of a run is given a separate name. Nevertheless, the 27 lifts access an impressive area suitable for all standards. The highest runs are almost exclusively steep bowls and chutes, most of which are for experts only. In general, the lower down you go the easier the terrain.

Finding your way around is something else. The lifts are mainly known by numbers, allocated as they were built, so the system has no geographic logic: chair 17 is between chairs 7 and 8 and below chair 22, and so on. New lifts are now being given names, though, which is starting to make things easier. However, the trail map still shows trails by means of symbols and names, not continuous lines, so it's difficult to see where a particular run takes you. On the lower part of the mountain this doesn't matter a lot: head downhill, and you'll eventually come to a lift. But higher up there are real dangers, especially in poor visibility.

Though Intrawest is now the majority owner, Dave McCoy, who built the first lift here in the 1940s, still has the final say about mountain development. People told him it was too high, too remote and too stormy here to make it as a resort, so he is naturally proud that he has seen the inhospitable mountains developed into a top American resort.

THE SLOPES
It's all here

There are three major lift-stations along the foot of the slopes, which mainly face north-east. An isolated fourth base – Juniper Springs – is growing in importance.

Main Lodge has the biggest choice of lifts. The newly upgraded two-stage Panorama gondola goes via Mid Chalet, the site of a huge restaurant, right to 3370m. The views are great, with Nevada to the north-east and the jagged Minarets to the west.

From the top, there are essentially three ways down. The first, on which there are countless variations, is down the front of the mountain, which ranges from steep to very steep – or vertical if the wind has created a cornice, as it often does. The second is off the back, down to **Chair 14 Outpost**, whence chairs 14 or 13 bring you back to lower points on the ridge. The third is to follow the ridge down to the Main Lodge area – a route that can hardly be detected on the idiotically unhelpful trail map. This route brings you past an easy area served by chair 12, and a very easy area by the new Discovery fast quad.

Mid Chalet can also be reached using the Stump Alley fast chair from **The Mill Café**, on the road up from town. Other lifts from here, including the fast Gold Rush quad, take you into the more heavily wooded eastern half of the area. This has long, gentle runs served by lifts up from **Canyon Lodge** and the new **Juniper Springs Lodge** and seriously steep stuff as well as some intermediate terrain on the subsidiary peak (nameless, of course) served by lifts 25 and 22.

A separate ski area called **June Mountain** is 30 minutes' drive away and is covered by the lift pass.

LIFT PASSES

2000/01 prices in dollars

Mammoth Mountain
Covers all lifts at Mammoth.

Beginners 69 a day learn-to-ski packages include pass, lessons and rental.

Main pass
1-day pass 54
6-day pass 281

Senior citizens
Over 65: 6-day pass 140

Children
Under 13: 6-day pass 140
Under 7: free pass

Short-term passes
Scenic Mammoth Gondola ride (adult 16); afternoon pass (adult 43)

Notes Main pass also covers the eight lifts at June Mountain. 13-18-year-olds get a discount on pass. Passes of over 2 days allow for one non-skiing day – 5-day pass is valid for 6 days, with one non-skiing day.

SCHOOLS/GUIDES

2000/01 prices in dollars

Mammoth Mountain

Classes 7 days
3hr: 10am-1pm
5 full days: 180

Children's classes
Ages: 4 to 14
5 full days including lunch: 380

Private lessons
1hr, 3hr or 6hr
65 for 1hr; each additional person 12

SNOW RELIABILITY
A long season

Mammoth has an impressive snow record – an annual average of 380in, which puts it in the second rank, ahead of major Colorado resorts and about on a par with Jackson Hole (but a long way behind Alta and Snowbird). Thanks to both its height and an ever-expanding array of snow-guns, it enjoys a long season – opening as late as 4 July in many years. But we and reporters have found that the upper mountain can get icy and windswept.

FOR EXPERTS
Some very challenging terrain

The steep bowls that run the width of the mountain top provide wonderful opportunities for experts. There are one or two single-diamond slopes, but most are emphatically double-diamond runs requiring a lot of bottle. The snow up here can suffer from high winds and it can be difficult to find your way – marking is virtually non-existent, so take great care.

The steep chutes either side of lift 22 are also very challenging, and being relatively sheltered are often open in bad weather when the top is firmly shut. Above Main Lodge is another steep area ideal for advanced skiers.

Many of the lower trails are short, but you can go virtually from top to bottom all day entirely on black runs.

FOR INTERMEDIATES
Lots of great cruising

Mammoth's piste maintenance is generally good, and many slopes that might become intimidatingly mogulled are kept easily skiable. And there is plenty for all standards of intermediate.

Some of the mountain's longest runs, served by chairs 9 and 25, are ideal for good intermediates. And a couple of lovely, fairly steep, tree-lined pistes run from the top of the Goldrush chair down to The Mill Café.

The tree-lined runs above Juniper Springs Lodge are flattering, and there are several motorway cruises – notably the slopes converging on The Mill Café.

A reporter recommends the quiet little bowl at the western extremity of the slopes down to Chair 14 Outpost: 'The whole group enjoyed runs like Arriba, Surprise and Oops.'

The less adventurous have some good, wide runs through trees in the triangle between Main Lodge, The Mill Café and Mid Chalet.

FOR BEGINNERS
Good tuition

'Excellent for beginners,' says one visitor. 'Good nursery slopes and lots of marvellous improving slopes, such as Sesame Street West, Lower Road Runner and Bridges.' Excellent tuition, fine piste grooming and snow quality usually make progress speedy.

FOR CROSS-COUNTRY
Very popular

Two specialist centres, Tamarack and Sierra Meadows, provide tuition and tours (the Sierra Meadows trails aren't groomed). There are 70km of trails in all, including some through the pretty Lakes Basin area, and lots of scenic ungroomed tracks through woods.

QUEUES
Weekend invasions

During the week the lifts and slopes are usually very quiet, with no queues. But even the efficient lift system can struggle when 15,000 visitors arrive from LA on fine weekends. That's the time to try June Mountain. Mind you, as one reporter put it, 'The weekend rush was like a quiet day in the Alps.'

MOUNTAIN RESTAURANTS
Lots of new venues

The giant functional cafeteria at Mid Chalet used to be the only on-mountain option. But for 2000/01 the new Parallax restaurant, at the top gondola station, will offer fine dining and views at Mammoth's highest point. Not surprisingly, many people eat at the bases, where there are several more civilised options. The Mill Café boasts 'gourmet sandwiches'. Or choose from Mexican, Italian, Asian and more at the revamped Canyon Lodge. Sun decks and music are the norm. There are outdoor BBQs at Juniper Springs Lodge and Chair 14 Outpost. There's also a new sun deck at the Yodler at Main Lodge. A recent reporter recommends the Mountainside Grill at the Mountain Inn.

SCHOOLS AND GUIDES
Excellent reports

Mammoth has a high reputation for tuition. Our most recent reporter rated his three-hour advanced class 'excellent'. And we have reports of beginners making 'excellent progress' as well. There are also some special camps (eg steep terrain and racing) for experts, and for seniors and women.

CHILDCARE

Children's classes are handled by the Woollywood Ski and Snowboard School in the Panorama gondola building, which 'interfaces' with Small World Child Care (934 0646) based at the nearby Mammoth Mountain Inn. Small World Child Care takes children from newborn to age 12, from 8am to 5pm.

GETTING THERE

Air Los Angeles, transfer 5hr. Reno, transfer 3hr. Mammoth Lakes, transfer 20 minutes.

ACTIVITIES

Indoor Mammoth museum, art galleries, theatre, mini golf
Outdoor Snowmobiling, ski touring, bob-sleigh, dog-sledding, ice skating, tobogganing, sleigh rides, hot air balloon rides, snow-shoe tours

TOURIST OFFICE

Postcode CA 93546
t +1 (760) 934 0745
f 934 0616
woolly@mammoth-mtn.com
www.mammothmountain.com

FACILITIES FOR CHILDREN
Family favourite

Mammoth is keen to attract families. The children's Woollywood school, now based in the new Panorama gondola station, works closely with the nearby Small World childcare centre. We've had glowing reports; one reporter noted the 'family feel of the resort'.

Staying there

Staying near Main Lodge or at the new condo complexes at Canyon Lodge or Juniper Springs Lodge is pretty convenient for the slopes. But there's still a greater choice of bars and restaurants in central Mammoth Lakes, and the efficient bus service means getting to the slopes is easy.

HOW TO GO
Good value packages

A good choice of hotels (none very luxurious or expensive) and condos. The condos tend to be out of town, near the lifts or on the road to them.
(4) **Mammoth Mountain Inn** Motel/hotel/condo complex at Main Lodge. Comfortable, spacious bedrooms. Rather gloomy public rooms.
(3) **Quality Inn** Good main street hotel with a big hot-tub. Bus stop outside.
(3) **Alpenhof Lodge** Comfortable and friendly, in central location. Shuttle-bus stop and plenty of restaurants nearby.
(3) **Austriahof** Ski-out location near Canyon Lodge, recommended by a reporter despite modest-sized rooms.
(3) **Jagerhof Lodge** British-run, friendly; praised by past reporters. At the edge of town on bus route.
Self-catering The new Juniper Springs Lodge opened for 1999/2000, with a new fast chair for mountain access. Close to the Canyon Lodge base-station, the 1849 Condominiums are spacious and well equipped. The Mammoth Ski and Racquet Club, a 10-minute walk from the same lifts, is very comfortable.

INTRAWEST

The Mammoth Mountain Inn is isolated out at the Main Lodge area, but very convenient for the slopes ↓

EATING OUT
Outstanding choice

There are over 50 restaurants in town, dotted around over a wide area, catering for most tastes and pockets. We've had delicious dinners at Nevados and Skadi (both 'modern American' food). Other good places are the atmospheric Slocums and lively Whiskey Creek. The Yodler does good hearty food at the Main Lodge area. Roberto's offers Mexican food; the Shogun Japanese (and karaoke). The Mogul, Alpenrose, Giovanni's, Berger's, Mountainside Grill, Angel's, Ocean Harvest and Grumpy's have all been recommended. For delicious breakfasts and pastries try Schat's Bakery.

APRES-SKI
Lively at weekends

The liveliest immediate après-ski spot is the Yodler, at the Main Lodge base – a chalet transported from Switzerland (so they say). Nightlife in town is essentially bars, which come to life at weekends (one reporter warns that during the week they'll be pushing you out at 12.30am). Whiskey Creek is the liveliest. It has live bands and gets packed. Slocums is popular with locals while Gringo's does great margaritas.

OFF THE SLOPES
Mainly sightseeing

The main diversion is sightseeing by car (preferably 4WD), which can be spectacular. Sights include the pretty Mono Lake and the beautiful Yosemite and other National Parks. What you can do will depend on the weather, but there's always the gold-mining ghost-town of Bodie to visit. There are some diverting clothes shops (including factory stores). The town of Bishop, 40 minutes' drive south of Mammoth is recommended for a day out – restaurants, shops and other attractions.

Colorado

Colorado was the first US state to market its resorts internationally and is still the most popular American destination for UK visitors. And justifiably so: it has the most alluring combination of attractive resorts, slopes to suit all standards and excellent, reliable snow – dry enough to justify its 'champagne powder' label.

Colorado has amazingly dry snow. Even when the snow melts and refreezes, the moisture seems to be magically whisked away, leaving it in soft powdery condition. The snow is good even in times of unusual snow shortage; in December 1998, when very little snow had fallen, we had a great week cruising on magical man-made snow.

Now that BA has a non-stop scheduled flight from London to Denver, Colorado resorts are more easily accessible again. There has been talk of a United Airlines non-stop flight – but as we go to press, authority for the route has not been granted. The best alternative for some resorts is to fly in to Eagle Vail via another gateway airport. The cheapest options, however, take longer and involve arriving at Denver after a change of plane elsewhere in the US.

Colorado resorts vary enormously, both in the extent and variety of slopes and in the character of the villages themselves. Some resorts have easy access to other major mountains nearby, while others are rather isolated. The clientele varies as well. You are much less likely to bump into fellow Brits in Telluride or Copper Mountain than Breckenridge and Vail. Wherever you go, you can count on terrain for every standard, a very warm welcome and great service.

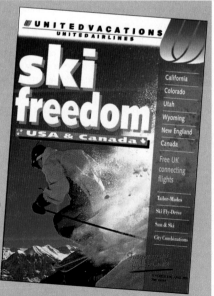

Aspen

2420m

The definitive American resort

WHAT IT COSTS

6

HOW IT RATES

The slopes

Snow	*****
Extent	****
Experts	*****
Intermediates	*****
Beginners	*****
Convenience	**
Queues	****
Restaurants	****

The rest

Scenery	***
Resort charm	****
Off-slope	****

- ✚ Endless slopes to suit all standards, with a vertical drop at Snowmass of 1342m – biggest in the US, and respectable by Alpine standards
- ✚ Notably uncrowded slopes, even by American standards
- ✚ Attractive, characterful, old mining town, with lots of smart shops
- ✚ Lively, varied nightlife and a great range of restaurants in the town
- ✚ Now has about the best 'gourmet' mountain restaurants in the States
- ✚ Large amounts of slope-side accommodation at Snowmass
- ✚ Aspen Skiing Company combines dynamism with responsibility – high standards of environmental care

- ━ Four mountains are widely separated (though there's efficient, free transport between them)
- ━ Some accommodation in Aspen town is a long walk or a bus-ride from the local lifts
- ━ Can be very expensive (although certainly doesn't have to be)

What's new

For 2000/01 there will be a new kids' ski school lift and and intermediate boarder-cross course at Snowmass. At Highlands, more terrain is to be opened in Highland Bowl (the G Zones) and phase two of the new base area will be complete, with a new bar and restaurant, and Ritz Carlton club.

1999/2000 saw several developments at Highlands: a new high-speed quad replaced three existing lifts; new terrain was opened in Highland Bowl; and the Cloud Nine 'bistro' was opened. The Sundeck restaurant at the top of Aspen Mountain was completely rebuilt. At Snowmass, a new tubing hill was opened on Assay Hill.

Aspen is our favourite American resort. We reached that view two editions back, and another tour of Colorado by both editors in March 2000 simply confirmed it. Convenience-freaks will find it a bit of a nightmare, but that really is the only serious drawback, and nowhere else comes close to matching the combination of plus-points listed above. If you're thinking America, put Aspen at the top of your shortlist and be prepared to let it stay there.

Worried by the film-star image? Forget it. Yes, the resort has many rich and famous guests, with their private jets parked at the local airport, and for connoisseurs of cosmetic surgery it can be a fascinating place. But most celebs are keen to keep a low profile – we've never spotted one – and like all other 'glamorous' ski resorts Aspen is actually filled by ordinary holidaymakers.

boarding *Aspen has great snowboarding for every standard. Although Aspen Mountain still bans snowboarding, the other three mountains welcome it wholeheartedly – there's a special three-mountain ride-guide leaflet – and facilities have greatly improved recently. All three mountains are worth visiting – they are all served almost entirely by chairs or gondolas, and all have special boarder facilities – but it's Snowmass, with three man-made half-pipes and five terrain-parks, as well as lots of natural boarder-friendly terrain, that has set about establishing itself as the greatest snowboarding mountain in the Rockies. Some of the bars can be quite entertaining at night.*

The resort

In 1892 Aspen was a booming silver-mining town, source of one-sixth of the USA's silver, with 12,000 inhabitants, six newspapers, an opera house and a red-light district. But Aspen's fortunes took a nose-dive when the silver price plummeted in 1893, and by the 1930s the population had shrunk to 700 or so. Handsome Victorian buildings – such as the Wheeler Opera House and the Hotel Jerome – had fallen into disrepair. Development of the skiing started on a small scale in the late 1930s. The first lift (then the world's longest chair-lift) was opened shortly after the Second World War, and Aspen hasn't looked back since. Now, the historic centre – with a typical American grid of streets – has been beautifully renovated to form the core of the most fashionable ski town in the Rockies. There's a huge variety of shops, bars, restaurants and galleries – some amazingly upmarket. Spreading out from this centre, you'll find a mixture of developments, ranging from the homes of the super-rich on the outskirts to the mobile homes for the workers who now find it too expensive to buy or rent in Aspen.

Although the town is busy with traffic, pedestrians seem to have priority in much of the central area.

Twelve miles away is Snowmass, with its own mountain and modern accommodation right on the slopes.

Day trips to other resorts are rather a long slog, but a two-centre holiday is easily arranged. Winter Park in particular is trying to promote them.

MOUNTAIN FACTS

Altitude	2400m-3815m
Lifts	44
Pistes	4780 acres
Green	13%
Blue	44%
Black	43%
Art. snow	566 acres
Recco detectors used	

The mountains

Aspen has lots for every standard; you just have to pick the right mountain. All of them have regular free guided tours, given by excellent amateur ambassadors, and other guest services on the slopes such as drinks, biscuits and suncream. The ratio of acres to visitor beds is high, and the slopes are usually blissfully uncrowded.

THE SLOPES
Widely dispersed

There are four mountains, only one accessible directly from Aspen town. Each is big enough to keep you amused for a full day or more, but Snowmass is in a league of its own – almost five miles across, with over 60 per cent of Aspen's total skiable acreage and the biggest vertical in the US (1342m). Getting around between the areas by free bus is easy, and for $3 you can have your equipment ferried from one mountain to another overnight. (Pay more, and you can get your edges and bases serviced, too.)

The Silver Queen gondola takes you from the edge of town to the top of **Aspen Mountain** in 14 minutes. A series of chairs serves the different ridges – Gentleman's Ridge along the eastern edge, the Bell in the centre, and Ruthie's to the west – with gulches in between. In general, there are long cruising blue runs along the valley floors and short steep blacks down from the ridges. There are no green runs at all. And boarding is banned.

Snowmass is a separate resort some 12 miles west of Aspen, opened in 1967. Chair-lifts fan out from the purpose-built village at the base towards four linked sectors – Elk Camp, High Alpine, Big Burn and Sam's Knob. Since 1995 there has also been access to the Elk Camp sector via the Two Creeks lift base, which is much nearer to Aspen, and has free slope-side parking. Many of the Snowmass runs are wide, sweeping cruisers. But it also has some of the toughest terrain.

Buttermilk is the least challenging mountain. The runs fan out from the top in three directions. The West Buttermilk and Main Buttermilk areas are almost all gentle; Tiehack, to the east, is a bit more demanding – ideal for an intermediate keen to progress.

Aspen Highlands was, until 1993, separately owned. Since then, Aspen Skiing Company has transformed the mountain, replacing a network of slow lifts with three fast quad chairs. Broadly, the mountain consists of a single ridge, with easy and intermediate slopes along the ridge itself and steep black runs on the

GET THE BEST OF THE SNOW, ON- AND OFF-PISTE

Aspen offers several special experiences for small numbers of skiers or riders.

Fresh Tracks *The first eight skiers to sign up each day get to ride the gondola up Aspen Mountain at 8am the next morning, and to get first tracks on perfect corduroy or fresh powder. Free!*

Off-piste Tours *On Fridays, backcountry guides lead expert skiers and riders (no more than four per guide) around the famous double-black terrain of Highlands (eg the Y Zones) and Snowmass (eg Hanging Valley). 9am–2.30pm, $99.*

Powder Tours *Spend the day exploring the backcountry beyond Aspen Mountain, with a 10-passenger heated snowcat as your personal lift. Away from the lifts and other people, your two guides search out untracked snow – there's 1500 acres to choose from. You're likely to squeeze in about 10 runs in all. At midday, you break for lunch at an old mountain cabin. Full day, $240 (1999/2000).*

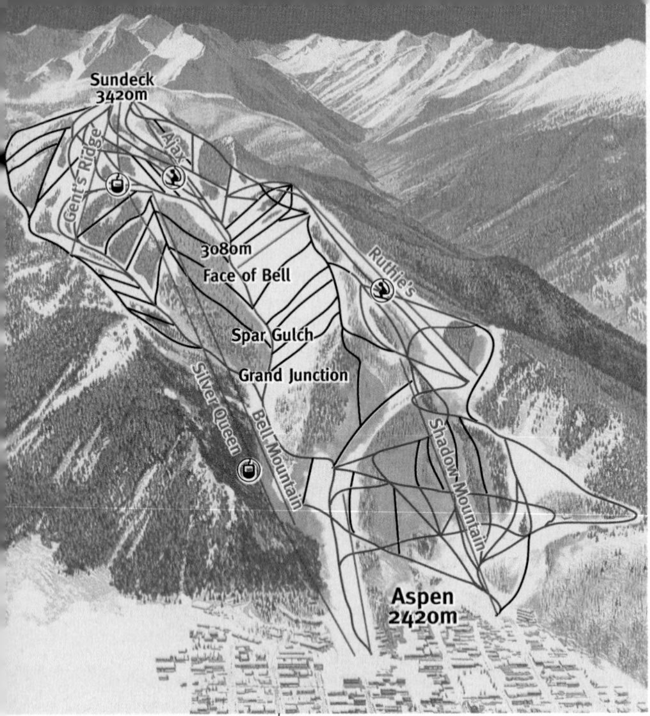

SNOW RELIABILITY

Rarely a problem

Aspen gets an annual average of 300in of snow on the major mountains – not in the front rank, but not far behind. In addition, all areas except Snowmass have substantial snowmaking. Immaculate grooming adds to the quality of the pistes.

FOR EXPERTS

Buttermilk is the only soft stuff

There's plenty to choose from – all the mountains except Buttermilk offer lots of challenges. If it suits your timing, consider joining a Friday guided group as an introduction to the best of Snowmass or Highlands (see p463).

Aspen Mountain has a formidable array of double-black-diamond runs. From the top of the gondola, Walsh's, Hyrup's and Kristi are double-diamonds on a lightly wooded slope that link up with Gentleman's Ridge and Jackpot to form the longest black run on the mountain. A series of steep glades drop down from Gentleman's Ridge. The central Bell ridge has less extreme single-diamonds on both its flanks – see photo. On the opposite side of Spar Gulch are another row of proper double-blacks collectively called the Dumps, because waste was dumped here in the silver-mining days. Last but not least, the lower slopes directly above the town have several seriously steep slopes.

At Snowmass, our favourite area is around the Hanging Valley Wall and Glades – beautiful scenery and

flanks – very steep ones at the top. And beyond the lift network are the Y Zones and Highland Bowl, where gates give access to a splendid open bowl of entirely double-black gradient. The views from the upper part of Highlands are the best that Aspen has to offer – the famous Maroon Bells that appear on countless postcards. A new base lodge incorporating underground parking opened at Highlands last season, and construction continues.

Aspen Mountain's Face of Bell is great terrain for those who like their slopes black but not too black, and their trees widely spaced. The chair-lift is Ajax →

SNOWPIX.COM / CHRIS GILL

wonderful tree-covered slopes, and steep enough everywhere to satisfy the keenest – well worth the short hike. The other seriously steep area is the Cirque. The Cirque drag-lift takes you well above the tree-line to Aspen's top altitude of almost 3815m. The Headwall is open and not terrifyingly steep, but there are also narrow, often rocky, chutes – Gowdy's is one of the steepest in the whole area. All these runs funnel into a pretty, lightly wooded valley. Other less extreme areas to check out include the mogul slopes served by the High Alpine and Sheer Bliss chairs. And most of the runs from Sam's Knob.

At Highlands there are challenging runs from top to bottom of the mountain. Highland Bowl, beyond the top lift, is superb in the right conditions: a big open bowl with pitches from a serious 38° to a terrifying 48° – facts you can check in the very informative Highlands Extreme Skiing Guide leaflet. If you're lucky, the ski patrol may be running snowcat rides to the first access gate of Highland Bowl; otherwise, it's a 20-minute hike. More of this terrain – the G Zones – is due to open for 2000/01. Within the lift system, the Steeplechase area consists of a number of parallel natural avalanche chutes, and their elevation means the snow stays light and dry. The Olympic Bowl area on the opposite flank of the mountain has great views of the Maroon Bells peaks and some serious moguls. The Thunderbowl chair from the base serves a nice varied area that's often underused.

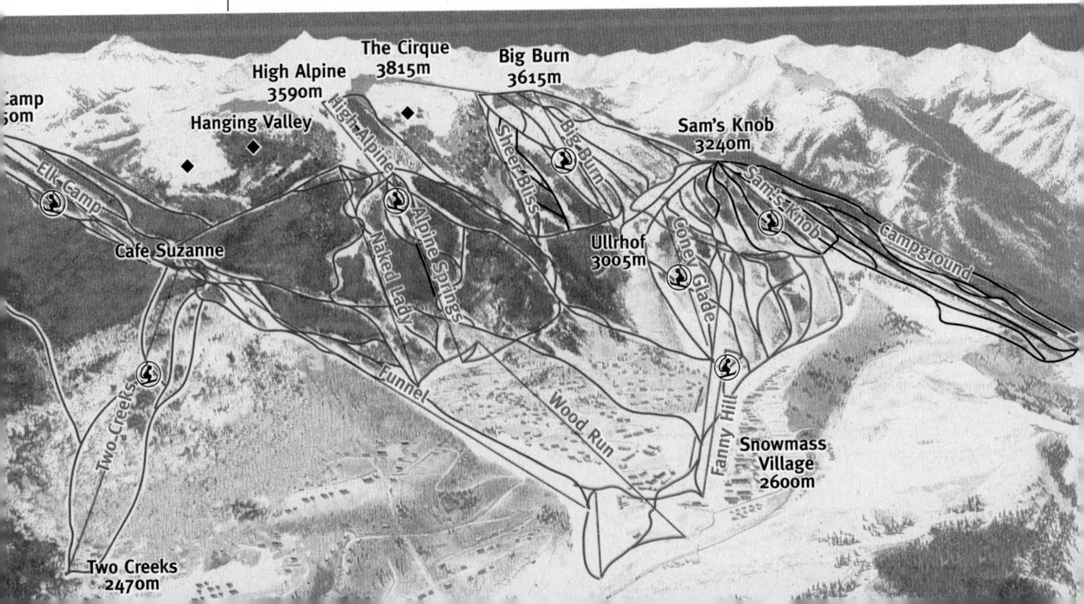

LIFT PASSES

1999/2000 prices in dollars

Four Mountain Pass Covers Aspen Mountain, Aspen Highlands, Buttermilk and Snowmass, and shuttle-bus between the areas.

Beginners Included in price of beginners' lessons; 219 for 3-day learn-to-ski or snowboard lessons and rental.

Main pass
1-day pass 63+ (depends on season and snow conditions)
6-day pass 330 (low season 239)

Senior citizens
Over 65: 6-day pass 306
Over 70: season pass 99

Children
Under 12: 6-day pass 231
Under 7: free pass

Advance purchase
Big savings can be made if you buy lift passes well in advance – cheaper adult passes, or a free child pass for each adult pass bought through certain tour operators.

GETTING THERE

Air Aspen, transfer ½hr. Eagle, transfer 1½hr. Denver, transfer 4hr.

Rail Glenwood Springs (70km).

FOR INTERMEDIATES
Grooming to die for

Snowmass is the best mountain for intermediates and the Big Burn is definitely the first place to head for. The huge lightly-wooded area is a cruising paradise. The runs merge into each other, though there's a satisfying variety of terrain and some trees to add interest – and the tempting Powerline Glades for the adventurous. The easiest intermediate slopes are reached from the Elk Camp lift. There's a choice of runs from the top, through spruce trees, and long runs all the way down to Two Creeks – Long Shot is a glorious three-mile run, lost in the forest, and well worth the short hike up to get to the start. In the centre of the area, the two chair-lifts below High Alpine serve yet more intermediate slopes – a little trickier and more varied. The Sam's Knob sector offers slightly more advanced challenges, including some regularly groomed single-black runs. Finally, Green Cabin, at the top of the High Alpine lift, is a magical intermediate run cruising from top to bottom of the mountain, with spectacular views.

Most intermediate runs on Highlands are concentrated above the mid-mountain Merry-Go-Round restaurant, many (including the very popular Scarlet's Run) served by the new Cloud Nine fast quad chair. But there are good slopes higher up and lower down – don't miss the vast, neglected expanses of Golden Horn, on the eastern limit of the area.

Aspen Mountain has its fair share of intermediate slopes, but they tend to be tougher than on the other mountains. Copper Bowl and Spar Gulch, running between the ridges, are great cruises early in the morning but can get crowded later. Upper Aspen Mountain, at the top of the gondola, has a dense network of well-groomed blues. The unusual Ruthie's chair – a fast double, apparently installed to rekindle the romance that quads have destroyed – serves more cruising runs and the popular Snow Bowl, a wide, open area with moguls on the left but groomed on the right and centre.

Buttermilk has a lot going for it. The Main Buttermilk runs offer good, easy slopes to practise on. And good intermediates should be able to handle the relatively easy black runs in the Tiehack area and progress to the tougher blacks on other mountains.

FOR BEGINNERS
Can be a great place to learn

Buttermilk is a great mountain for beginners. West Buttermilk has beautifully groomed, gentle runs. The easiest slopes of all, though, are at the base of the Main Buttermilk sector – on Panda Hill. The easiest beginner slope at Snowmass is the wide Assay Hill, at the bottom of the Elk Camp area. Right next to Snowmass Village Mall is the Fanny Hill fast quad and beginners' run. Further up, from Sam's Knob, there are long, gentle cruises.

Despite its macho image, Highlands boasts the highest concentration of green runs in Aspen.

FOR CROSS-COUNTRY
Backcountry bonanza

There are 80km of groomed trails between Aspen and Snowmass in the Roaring Fork valley – the most extensive maintained cross-country system in the US. And the Ashcroft Ski Touring Centre maintains around 30km of trails around Ashcroft, a mining ghost-town. Take the opportunity of eating at the Pine Creek Cookhouse: excellent food and accessible by ski, board or sledge only. In addition, there are limitless miles of ungroomed trails. Aspen is at one end of the famous Tenth Mountain Division Trail, heading 230 miles north-east almost to Vail, with 13 huts for overnight stops.

QUEUES
Few problems

There are rarely major queues on any of the mountains. At Aspen Mountain, the gondola can have delays at peak times, but you have alternative lifts to the top. Snowmass has so many alternative lifts and runs that you can normally avoid any problems. But some long, slow chairs can be cold in mid-winter, and the home slope gets very busy. Aspen Highlands is almost always queue-free, even at peak times. The two lifts out of Main Buttermilk sometimes get congested.

MOUNTAIN RESTAURANTS
Good by American standards

Aspen has some good mountain restaurants by American standards – and they're getting better.

On Aspen Mountain the new Sundeck at the top has quite a stylish self-service section with a good range of food, but the table-service Benedict's restaurant is unappealing

SCHOOLS/GUIDES

1999/2000 prices in dollars

Aspen Skiing Company
Snowmass and Buttermilk for all abilities; Aspen Mountain and Aspen Highlands for intermediate and advanced only
Classes 5 days
5hr: 10am-3pm; 2½hr: 10am-12.30 or 12.45-3.15
5 full days: 299
Children's classes
Ages: 7 to 12
Private lessons
half or full day
439 for full day
299 for half day
(you are allowed up to 5 people in your class)
Other options
Beginner's Magic
3 full days incl lift pass: 219
Small group lessons
99 for full day
Mountain Explorers
(incl video, race training)
3 full days: 239
Off-piste tours
99

CHILDCARE

The childcare possibilities are too numerous to list in detail.

There's a children's 'learning center' at Buttermilk with a special children's shuttle-bus from Aspen. The Powder Pandas classes there take children aged 3 to 6. At Snowmass, the Big Burn Bears ski kindergarten takes children from age 3½, and children aged 6 weeks to 3½ have the Snow Cubs playschool. The Nighthawks programme looks after children aged 3 to 10 from 4pm to 11pm.

There are several all-day non-skiing crèches.

(unless the terrace is in operation). Sadly the swanky lunch club that shares the new building is strictly for members, and the price of admission is stratospheric. The mid-mountain restaurant formerly called Ruthie's is now Gwyn's; as well as a self-service section it has an exceptionally civilised table-service restaurant with excellent food and good views over Aspen.

At Snowmass, Gwyn's High Alpine is an elegant restaurant serving excellent food. The best views are from Sam's Knob, where there is a self-service and a new and impressive Italian table-service restaurant, Finestra.

At Highlands the big news for serious lunchers is the opening in 1998 of the Cloud Nine 'Alpine bistro' – about the nearest thing you will find in the States to an Alpine chalet with Alpine views, but with better food – thanks, ironically, to an Austrian chef (see photo). The Merry-Go-Round has the biggest terrace in the valley.

On Buttermilk the mountaintop Cliffhouse is known for its 'Mongolian Barbecue' stir-fry bar and great views.

SCHOOLS AND GUIDES
Special programmes

There's a wide variety of specialised instruction – bumps, powder, mountain exploration groups, backcountry groups, and so on. A reporter raves about the semi-private lessons, with maximum four pupils per group On Snowmass and Aspen Mountain there are performance centres where your alignment is tested and adjusted, and you can test any number of skis.

FACILITIES FOR CHILDREN
Choice of crèches

There is no shortage of advertised childcare arrangements. We have no recent first-hand reports, but reporters' observations were that, as usual in the US, all the kids were having the time of their lives. And past reports have always been first-class. Young children based in Aspen town are taken from the gondola building each morning around 9am by the Max the Moose bus to Buttermilk's very impressive Fort Frog – a wooden frontier-style fort, with lookout towers, flags, old wagons, a jail, a saloon and a native American teepee village – and delivered back at 4pm. Snowmass has its own facilities. The Kids' Trail Map is a great way to get them used to finding their way around using maps.

Staying there

Aspen town is the liveliest place to stay, and near the gondola is the most convenient location. Buses for the other areas also leave from nearby. Snowmass offers ski-out convenience at 95 per cent of its properties, and buses from Aspen run until 1am or later.

HOW TO GO
Accommodation for all pockets

Aspen town and Snowmass between them have beds for some 16,000 guests in a mixture of hotels, inns, B&Bs, lodges and condos.
Chalets Several UK tour operators have chalets here – some very luxurious.
Hotels There are places for all budgets.
⑤ **St Regis** Opulent city-type hotel, near the gondola. Fitness centre, outdoor pool, whirlpool spas, sauna.
⑤ **Little Nell** Stylish modern hotel right by the gondola, with popular bar. Fireplaces in every room, outdoor pool, hot-tub, sauna and more.
⑤ **Jerome** Step back a century: Victorian authenticity combined with modern-day luxury; pool, hot-tub. Several blocks from the gondola.
④ **Sardy House** Elegantly furnished, intimate little hotel 10 minutes from the gondola, with comfortable modern extension. Small outdoor pool, hot-tub.
④ **Lenado** Smart modern B&B place with open-fire lounge and individually designed rooms – we loved it.
④ **Silvertree** Large slope-side hotel at Snowmass. Pools, hot-tubs.
③ **Innsbruck Inn** Consistently liked by reporters. Tirolean-style hotel, 10 minutes from lifts.
③ **Stonebridge Inn** Good-value hotel close to Snowmass slopes; nice restaurant, pool, hot-tub.
③ **Hotel Aspen** Best 'moderate' place in town, 10 minutes from the gondola; comfortable motel-style rooms, pool, hot-tubs, après-ski buffet.
② **Skier's Chalet** Closest 'economy' lodging to the lifts.
Self-catering The standards here are high, even in US terms. Many of the smarter developments have their own free shuttle-buses. The Gant is luxurious, with impressive communal facilities, and close to the gondola. Chateau Roaring Fork and Eau Claire, four blocks from the gondola, are spacious and well-furnished. with the largest outdoor pool in Aspen. There are some luxurious houses on offer.

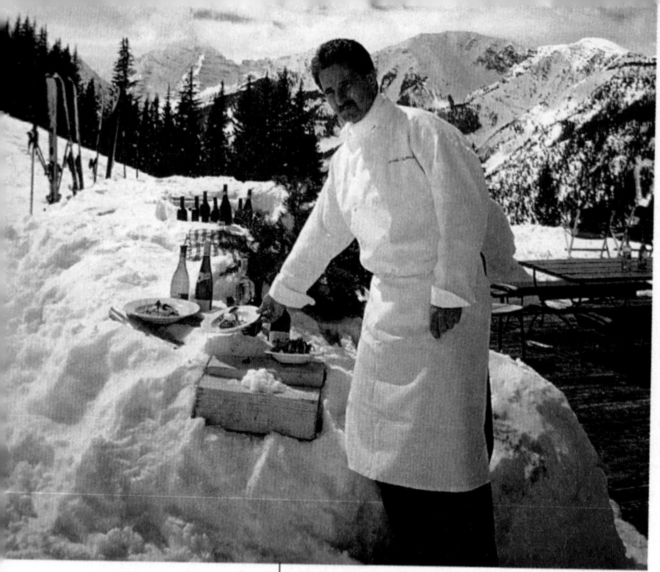

↑ How unAmerican can you get? Aspen Highlands' funky little Cloud Nine 'bistro' does exceptional food, thanks to Austrian chef Andreas Fischbacher, as well as exceptional views of the Maroon Bells from its terrace

SNOWPIX.COM / CHRIS GILL

EATING OUT
Dining dilemma

You can dine in whatever style you like in Aspen town. As you'd expect, there are excellent upmarket places, but also plenty of cheaper options.

Piñons serves innovative American food in South-Western surroundings. Syzygy is a suave upstairs place with live jazz from 10pm. On our last visit we particularly enjoyed the 'fierce American food' at Jimmy's. Conundrum (modern American food, expensive) and Pacific (seafood) are top-notch. Poppie's Bistro Cafe is famous for its breads and puddings. L'Hostaria, The Mother Lode, Campo de Fiori and Farfalla are good Italians. Cache Cache does good-value Provençal.

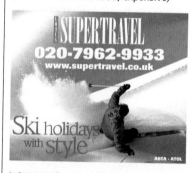

Cheaper recommendations include: Boogie's (a 50s-style diner, great for families), Hard Rock Cafe, Main Street Bakery, Mezzaluna, O'Leary's, Red Onion, Rusty's Hickory House and the Skier's Chalet steak house. At Snowmass, the choice is adequate. Condo-bound families can get pasta delivered from Mangia, Mangia literally by the bucketful.

APRES-SKI
Party time (later)

As the lifts shut, a few bars at the bases do reasonable business. At Snowmass, the slope-side Cirque Cafe has live bands most days. In Aspen a favourite spot for grown-ups is the bar of the Little Nell (which also has live jazz later on). But it's after dinner that Aspen town livens up.

Many of the restaurants are also bars – Ajax , Jimmy's (spectacular stock of tequila), Mezzaluna, O'Leary's, Red Onion, for example. The J-bar of the Jerome hotel still has a traditional feel. Shooters is a splendid country-and-western dive with pool, line-dancing, sometimes live music. Maxfield's is a popular pool bar. For pool in more suave circumstances, there's Aspen Billiards adjoining the fashionable Cigar Bar, with its comfortable sofas (and smoking permitted!). The Tippler is a quite spacious disco with great 70s nights on Tuesdays. The Double Diamond has live bands most nights (from 11pm). Popcorn Wagon is the place for munchies after the bars close at 2am. You can get a week's membership of 426, a club appealing to 30-somethings. Old timers like us prefer to get an evening's use of the Caribou club for the price of dinner.

OFF THE SLOPES
Silver service

Aspen has lots to offer, especially if you've got a high credit card limit. There are literally dozens of galleries, as well as the predictable clothes and jewellery shops. Just wandering around town is pleasant. It's a shame that all the best mountain restaurants are awkward for pedestrians to get to. Most hotels have excellent spa facilities. There's tubing at Snowmass.

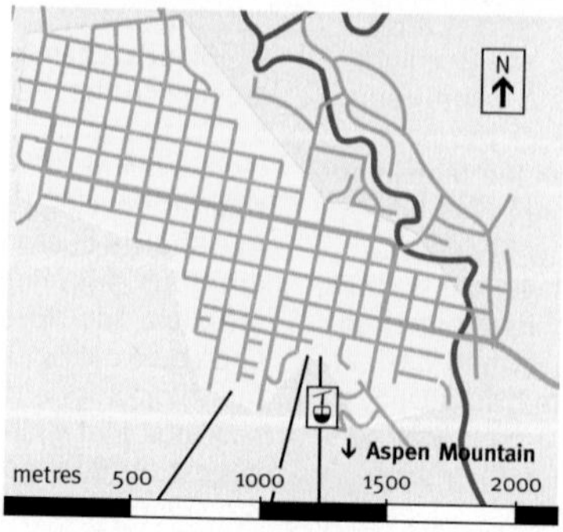

ACTIVITIES

Indoor Aspen Athletic Club (racquetball, swimming, free weights, aerobics classes, sauna, steam, hot-tubs), skating
Outdoor Ballooning, paragliding, snowcat tours, snow-shoe tours, sleigh rides, dog-sledding, snowmobiles, tours of mines

TOURIST OFFICE

Postcode CO 81612
t +1 (970) 925 1220
f 920 0771
intlres@skiaspen.com
www.aspensnowmass.com

Breckenridge 2925m

Popular introduction to Colorado

WHAT IT COSTS

6

HOW IT RATES

The slopes	
Snow	*****
Extent	**
Experts	****
Intermediates	****
Beginners	****
Convenience	***
Queues	****
Restaurants	**
The rest	
Scenery	***
Resort charm	***
Off-slope	***

- ➕ Varied local mountains, with something for all standards
- ➕ Good snow record and lots of artificial help
- ➕ Shared lift pass with nearby Keystone and Arapahoe Basin and not-so-nearby Vail and Beaver Creek
- ➕ Efficient lifts mean few queues
- ➕ Lively bars, restaurants and nightlife by US standards
- ➕ Based on restored Victorian mining town, with many new buildings in attractive 19th-century style
- ➕ One of the nearest major resorts to Denver, so relatively short transfer

- ➖ The local area is rather small, with few long runs
- ➖ At this extreme altitude there is an appreciable risk of sickness for visitors coming straight from lower altitudes (the village is situated at 3000m and the highest lift-accessed terrain is around 4000m)
- ➖ The pseudo-Victorian style gets a bit overblown in places, and there are some out-of-place modern buildings that detract from its charm
- ➖ Main Street is just that – always busy with traffic

Breckenridge is very popular with first-time visitors to Colorado. It's easy to see why: it is one of the closest resorts to Denver Airport, has slopes for all standards, usually excellent dry snow, good facilities for families, relatively lively nightlife and good-value slope-side accommodation. Add to that the image of a restored Wild West mining town and you have a very compelling package.

It is true that the slopes do not cover a huge area (even by US standards) and that the town is rather spoiled by out-of-style buildings in parts and a rather Disneyesque feel to other parts. But it has skiing and boarding for all standards, and there are lots of other areas to try on day trips, some covered by a shared lift pass (Vail, Beaver Creek, Keystone and Arapahoe Basin), some not (such as Copper Mountain) – much more than you could cover in a week or 10 days.

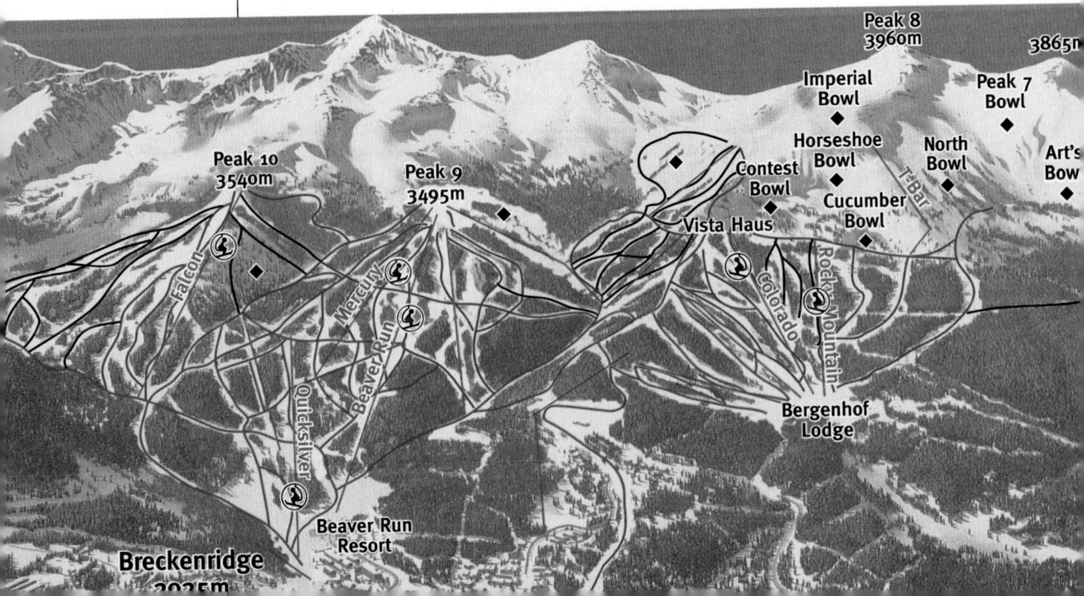

What's new

The 1999/2000 season saw the first double-loading high-speed six-person chair in the US replace the Quicksilver high-speed quad. Costing $4 million it has an ultimate capacity of carrying 4,200 people an hour.

Breckenridge was also the first US resort to invest in a super Dragon 2000 – which cuts the deepest, widest half-pipes possible.

A vast new indoor ice skating rink opened in the summer of 2000, along with new conference facilities.

The Bell Tower Mall at the foot of Peak 9 has been demolished and is being replaced with a complex of shops and timeshare condos called Main Street Station.

MOUNTAIN FACTS

Altitude	2925m-3960m
Lifts	23
Pistes	2043 acres
Green	14%
Blue	26%
Black	60%
Art. snow	516 acres
Recco detectors used	

boarding *Breckenridge is pretty much ideal for all standards of boarder and plays host to several major US snowboarding events. Beginners have ideal nursery slopes and easy greens to progress to and intermediates have great cruising runs, all served by chairs. For good boarders there's one of the best fun-parks in the US on Peak 9, with a series of great jumps and obstacles and an enormous championship half-pipe (with a 'moving carpet' to get you back up) on Peak 8. The powder bowls at the top of Peaks 7 and 8 make for awesome riding – unfortunately accessed only by an awkward T-bar. Nearby Arapahoe Basin is another area for hardcore boarding in steep bowls and chutes.*

The resort

Breckenridge was founded in 1859 and became a booming gold-mining town in the latter part of the century. The old wooden and clapboard buildings have been well renovated and form the bottom part of Main Street. Over 250 restored Victorian buildings are included in what is Colorado's largest national historic district. New shopping malls and buildings have been added in similar style – though they are obvious modern additions.

The town centre is attractively lively in the evening, with over 100 restaurants and bars. Christmas lights and decorations remain throughout the season, giving the town an air of non-stop winter festivity. This is enhanced by a number of real winter festivals such as Ullr Fest – a carnival honouring the Norse God of Winter – and Ice Sculpture championships, which leave sculptures for weeks afterwards.

Hotels and condominiums are spread over a wide, wooded area and are linked by regular shuttle buses. Breckenridge boasts more slope-side accommodation than any other Colorado resort.

The mountains

There are four separate peaks, linked by lift and piste. Boringly, they are named Peaks 7, 8, 9 and 10 – going from right to left as you look at the mountain. Though there's something for all standards, the keen piste-basher will want to explore other resorts too. Breckenridge and Keystone were bought in 1996 by the owners of Vail and Beaver Creek (around an hour away); a multi-day lift ticket covers these four resorts and Arapahoe Basin, also nearby but no longer under common ownership. Copper Mountain is not covered by the same ticket. All six of these resorts are linked by regular buses (free except for a $10 return fare for Vail and Beaver Creek – or $5 with the free Peaks Card available from main lift stations). Steamboat and Winter Park are both less than two hours' drive away.

THE SLOPES
Small but fragmented

Two high-speed chair-lifts go from the top end of town up to **Peak 9**, one accessing mainly green runs on the lower half of the hill, the other mainly blues higher up. From there you can get to **Peak 10**, which has a large number of blue and black runs served by one high-speed quad.

The other flank of Peak 9 takes you to a lift up into the **Peak 8** area – tough stuff at the top, easier lower down. The base lifts of Peak 8 at the Bergenhof can also be reached by the town shuttle-bus or the Snowflake lift from the edge of town. From the top T-bar of Peak 8, you can traverse to the all-black **Peak 7** slopes and back bowls which have no lifts of their own – you go back to the base of Peak 8.

At the end of the day three trails lead back down to town from Peak 8 – Sawmill to the main Peak 9 lifts, Snowflake to the edge of town and Four O'Clock down towards the centre. A regular free shuttle runs around the resort to the Peak 9 and Peak 8 lifts.

SNOW RELIABILITY
Excellent

With the village at almost 3000m (the highest of the main North American resorts), the slopes going up to almost 4000m and a lot of east and north-east-facing slopes, Breckenridge boasts an excellent natural snow record. That is supplemented by substantial artificial snowmaking mainly intended for pre-Christmas use. We have visited on pre-Christmas trips for the last two years (both very bad years for early snow) and found plenty of good cruising on man-made snow in mid-December on both occasions.

LIFT PASSES

1999/2000 prices in dollars

Breckenridge-Keystone
Covers all lifts in Breckenridge, Keystone and Arapahoe Basin. Multi-day passes also cover Vail and Beaver Creek.

Beginners
3 beginners' lifts. Beginners and novices have a reduced area pass in ski school.

Main pass
1-day pass 53
6-day pass 264

Senior citizens
Over 64: 6-day pass 222
Over 70: free pass

Children
Under 13: 6-day pass 114
Under 6: free pass

Alternative periods
Passes of 2 days and over allow one non-skiing day, eg 6-day pass valid for a 7-day period, with one non-skiing day.

Notes Discounts for groups of over 20. If you buy a lift pass in advance for the 2000/01 season through a UK tour operator, a 6-day adult pass will cost 210.

SCHOOLS/GUIDES

1999/2000 prices in dollars

Breckenridge

Classes 7 days
5hr: 9.45-12.15 and 1.30-4pm; 2½hr: am or pm
2 full days: 130

Children's classes
Ages: 3 to 12
6 full days 378 (including lunch for 3 to 5 year-olds)

Private lessons
1hr, 3hr or 6hr – prices are per instructor regardless of 1 to 6 persons.
1hr: 115; 3hr: 260
6hr: 425.

FOR EXPERTS

Quite a few short but tough runs

A remarkable 60 per cent of Breckenridge's runs are classified as 'most difficult' (single-black-diamond) or 'expert' (double-black-diamond) terrain. That's a higher proportion than the famous 'macho' resorts, such as Jackson Hole, Taos and Snowbird. But remember that Breckenridge is not a big area by European standards, so most experts there for a week or more will want to spend some of their time exploring the other nearby resorts.

Peak 7 is an entirely off-piste area, which is reached by traversing or hiking up from the top of the T-bar. It has great steep runs with good snow on north-east-facing slopes. Peak 8 has some good open terrain in Horseshoe and Contest bowls, where the snow normally remains good and you can hike up to Imperial Bowl and Lake Chutes, where the steepest slopes are.

We particularly liked the back bowls of Peak 8. This is basically terrain among a thin covering of trees and bushes. Lots of runs, such as Lobo, Hombre, Amen and Adios, are marked on the trail map. But in practice you can easily skip between them and invent your own way down. It's picturesque and not too steep. Steep black mogul fields lead down under chair 4 to the junction with Peak 9.

Peak 9 itself has nothing to offer experts except very steep blacks from the top down under chair E on the North Face. These have had very patchy snow covering on each of our visits, conditions which probably account for their fearsome names such as Devil's Crotch and Satan's Inferno.

Peak 10 offers much more interest. Off to the right of the chair, at the edge of the area, is a network of interlinking black mogul runs by the side of the downhill course – consistently steep and bumpy. To the left of the chair is a lovely, lightly wooded off-piste area called The Burn.

FOR INTERMEDIATES

Nice cruising, limited extent

Breckenridge has some good blue cruising runs for all standards of intermediate. But dedicated piste-bashers will find it limited and will want to visit the other nearby resorts.

Peak 9 has the easiest terrain. It is nearly all gentle, wide, blue runs at the top and almost flat, wide, green runs at the bottom. Timid intermediates will find it reassuring to see the ski patrol enforcing slow speed skiing in narrow and busy areas. Peak 10 has a couple of more challenging runs graded blue-black, such as Crystal and Centennial, which make for good fast cruising.

Peak 8 has a choice of blues down through trails cut close together in the trees. We particularly liked the quiet Claimjumper, which is visited less than the others because of its position at the far northern end of the area, next to the boundary. More adventurous intermediates will also like to try some of the high bowl runs (see 'For experts'). And Keystone, Vail, Beaver Creek and Copper Mountain all offer miles of excellent intermediate terrain.

FOR BEGINNERS

Excellent

The bottom of Peak 9 has a big, virtually flat area and some good gentle nursery slopes. There's then a good choice of green runs to move on to. Beginners can try Peak 8 too, with another selection of green runs and a choice of trails back to town.

FOR CROSS-COUNTRY

Specialist centre in woods

Breckenridge's Nordic Center is prettily set in the woods between the town and Peak 8 (and is served by the shuttle-bus). It has 38km of trails.

QUEUES

Not normally a problem

Breckenridge's six high-speed chair-lifts (three on Peak 9, two on Peak 8 and one on Peak 10) make light work of peak-time crowds. We've never come across serious queues, and neither have our reporters, except at exceptional times, such as President's Day weekend.

MOUNTAIN RESTAURANTS

Improving

Breckenridge is making an effort to improve on the standard US cafeterias serving burgers, pasta and chillies.

Ten Mile Station, situated between Peaks 9 and 10, is the newest and best (it opened last year), with a heated outdoor deck as well as indoor facilities. Border Burritos (in the Bergenhof at the base of Peak 8) has been recommended by reporters. Spencer's at Beaver Run does a good all-you-can-eat breakfast and lunch menu. Vista Haus, at the top of Peak

↑ There they are: Breckenridge's three main peaks, as seen from Keystone's Outback

KEYSTONE PHOTO / BOB WINSETT

8, has a couple of restaurants, but it's a shame the Italian table-service Piz Otto's has closed down.

SCHOOLS AND GUIDES
Excellent reports

Our reporters are unanimous in their praise for the school: classes of five to eight; doing what the class, not the instructor, wants; special clinics on, for example, bumps or powder.

FACILITIES FOR CHILDREN
Excellent facilities

We have had several reports on the children's ski school and the crèche, every one bubbling with enthusiastic praise. Typical comments: 'the instructors make the classes FUN', 'excellent teaching, combining serious coaching with lots of fun', 'our boys enjoyed every minute of it', 'kids got a daily report card which they liked', 'so much more positive than in Europe'.

CHILDCARE

At each major lift base there is a resort-run Children's Center (970 453 3258), with a complex array of options for all-day care from 8.30 to 4.30. Children aged 6 to 14 go into ordinary children's school, but all-day care is available at Kid's Castle meeting areas at each lift base.

At Beaver Run there is also an independent childcare option called Kinderhut for six week to six year-olds (970 453 0379). Their hours are 8.15 to 4pm and from Tuesday to Friday they are also open from 6pm to 10pm.

Staying there

Breckenridge is quite spread out. Although there is a lot of slope-side accommodation, there is also a fair amount away from Main Street and the lift base-stations. Free shuttle-buses serve most of the area well, but less reliably in the evening than the day. The area between the base of Peak 9 and Main Street is the best location if you plan to go out in the evening.

HOW TO GO
Lots of choice

A lot of tour operators feature Breckenridge in their programmes and it's easy to arrange your own holiday there too – Resort Express run a regular and efficient transfer service from Denver Airport.

Chalets Several tour operators have very comfortable chalets, both in and out of town – there is more choice than in any other US resort. We were very impressed by a stay at Chalet Whispering Pines (run by Kokopelli chalets and sold through American Dream).

Hotels There's a good choice of style and price range.

((((4) **Great Divide** Used to be the Hilton but now owned by Vail Resorts. Prime location, good bar, vast rooms, recently renovated and very popular with Brits. Pool, tubs.

((((4) **Lodge at Breckenridge** Stylish luxury spa resort set out of town among 32 acres, with great views. Private shuttle-bus. Pool, tubs.

((((4) **Little Mountain Lodge** Luxury B&B near ice rink. Highly recommended.

(((3) **Beaver Run** Huge resort complex with 520 spacious rooms. Many reporters stay here and nearly all rave about its position right by one of the main lifts up Peak 9. Pool, hot-tubs.

(((3) **Williams House** Beautifully restored, charmingly furnished four-room B&B on Main St.

((2) **Fireside Inn** Dormitory-style rooms.

GETTING THERE

Air Denver, transfer 2½hr.
BA has direct flights from London to Denver.

ACTIVITIES

Indoor Sports clubs, swimming, sauna, massage, hot-tubs, cinema, theatre, art gallery, library, indoor miniature golf course
Outdoor Horse- and dog-sleigh rides, fishing, snow-mobiles, toboggans, scooters, mountain biking, snow-shoeing, ice skating, hot air balloon rides

TOURIST OFFICE

Postcode CO 80424
t +1 (970) 453 5000
f 453 3202
international@vailresorts.com
www.breckenridge.com

Historic part of town. Tub.
① **Breckenridge Wayside Inn** Friendly budget place out of town. Tub.
Self-catering There is a huge choice of condominiums, many set conveniently along the aptly named Four O'Clock run. Comfortable, well equipped and conveniently located condos include Liftside Inn, Wedgewood Lodge, Tannhaüser, Pine Ridge, River Mountain Lodge, Sundowner, Wedgewood, Tyra Summit and Wildwood. The Beaver Run resort has self-catering and hotel accommodation.

STAYING DOWN THE VALLEY
Good for exploring the area
Staying in Frisco makes sense for those touring around or on a tight budget. It's a small town based on a Victorian settlement, where the stage-coach used to stop. There are cheap motels (including the old stagecoach stop, now the Frisco Inn), some B&B places and a Best Western hotel.

EATING OUT
Over 100 restaurants
There's a very wide range of eating places, with pretty much everything you'd expect, from typical American food to 'fine-dining', and almost every ethnic cuisine you could wish for.

The Brewery is famous for its enormous portions of appetisers such as Buffalo Wings – as well as its splendid brewed-on-the-spot beers. We particularly liked the Avalanche beer.

We also liked Poirier's Cajun Café and the sophisticated food at both Café Alpine and Pierre's Riverwalk Café. Sushi Breck has also had good reviews. Downstairs at Erics has good pizzas and burgers in a sports bar atmosphere. Mi Casa has good cheap Mexican food and margaritas. The Hearthstone has been recommended for 'lovely food in good surroundings'.

APRES-SKI
The best in the area
There's a lively atmosphere as soon as you come off the slopes, but things quieten down later. The Breckenridge Brewery, Shamus O'Toole's and Tiffany's are popular hangouts. The Gold Pan saloon dates from gold rush days, and is reputedly the oldest bar west of the Mississippi. Cecelia's has good cocktails. The Underworld part of Downstairs at Eric's is a trendy disco bar. But one of the locals' best kept secrets is Mount Java – a relaxed cafe-cum-bookshop with Internet access, serving excellent coffee and snacks. More unusually, an Oxygen bar, where you can snort different flavours of oxygen, has opened in Lacima's Mall.

OFF THE SLOPES
Pleasant but quiet
Breckenridge is a pleasant place to wander around with plenty of souvenir, clothing and gift shops (though a lot sell similar things). Silverthorne (about 30 minutes away and connected by a free bus service) has excellent serious shopping at bargain factory outlet stores such as Levi, Timberland, Gap and Ralph Lauren. But those staying for a week and not using the slopes would find Breckenridge pretty limited.

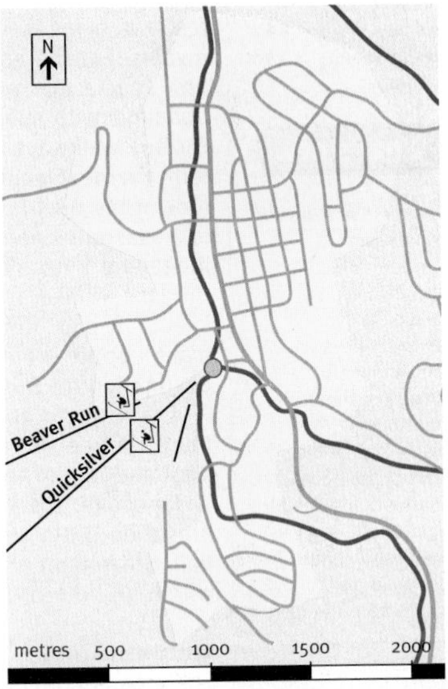

BOB WINSETT
Breck's Victorian-style Main Street looks kinda pretty when there's snow around (and you can't see the busy main road) ➔

Copper Mountain 2960m

Great slopes for all standards above a born-again resort

Copper's slopes are some of Colorado's best. From this season there should be a resort centre to match the quality of the slopes. Phase 2 of Copper's transformation from carbuncle to flower of the Rockies should be complete.

WHAT IT COSTS

6

HOW IT RATES

The slopes

Snow	*****
Extent	**
Experts	****
Intermediates	****
Beginners	****
Convenience	****
Queues	****
Restaurants	*

The rest

Scenery	***
Resort charm	**
Off-slope	*

What's new

Copper is now owned by Intrawest, a company which is also involved in resorts such as Whistler, Keystone and Mammoth. It has set about transforming the resort and by the start of the 2000/01 season there should be a whole new car-free resort centre designed 'to incorporate the rustic natural elements surrounding Copper'. We look forward to seeing it.

In previous years new high-speed lifts were also installed.

MOUNTAIN FACTS

Altitude	2925m-3765m
Lifts	21
Pistes	2433 acres
Green	21%
Blue	25%
Black	54%
Art. snow	380 acres

TOURIST OFFICE

Postcode CO 80443
t +1 (970) 968 2882
f 968 2711
international@ski-copper.com
www.ski-copper.com

THE RESORT

Copper Mountain was built as a functional, purpose-built resort, high on convenience, low on charm – rather like the French resorts of the 1960s. Because of that it has never taken off on the international market.

But it has always had one of Colorado's best ski areas. And the resort is being transformed by its new owners. For the 2000/01 season four new spectacular wood-and-stone-clad buildings with shops, restaurants and car-free walkways and squares will form the new heart of Copper, at the foot of the main lift out. This follows last season's opening of a new base lodge and a luxury condo building in the East Village, from which a high-speed six-pack departs. All this should make Copper a much more attractive destination for British visitors.

The resort is good for families and there's a fine sports club, with a huge pool and indoor tennis.

Keystone, Breckenridge and Arapahoe Basin are all nearby, and Vail, Steamboat and Winter Park are within an hour or two.

THE MOUNTAIN

The **area** is quite sizeable by American standards, and has great runs for all ability levels. As you look up at the mountain, the easiest runs are on the the right-hand side and the terrain gradually gets steeper the further left you go. The Super Bee six-seat chair from Copper Station gives fast access to Spaulding and Resolution Bowls. And two high-speed quads whizz you up from the main centre to the tree line, from where numerous runs head back towards the base. Further lifts serve the resort's open bowls above, including the Excelerator high-speed quad, which links in to the top of the Super Bee.

Height and an extensive snowmaking operation give Copper an early opening date to the season and excellent **snow reliability.**

There is a lot of good **expert** terrain, especially in the steep and wild Copper Bowl on the back side of Copper's mountain and in the bump runs through the trees in Spaulding Bowl.

Good **intermediates** will find long steep runs in the Copper Peak section on the left of the mountain. The slightly less proficient can enjoy gentler runs on the middle section of mountain, while early intermediates have gentle cruising terrain in the Union Peak area on the right.

The nursery slopes are excellent for **beginners**, and there are plenty of very easy green runs to graduate to.

Snowboarders are spoilt for choice with separate expert and intermediate terrain parks, a competition half-pipe and a mini-pipe.

For **cross-country**, there are 25km of trails through the woods.

Copper is popular with day visitors from Denver but **queues** are rare because of the efficient lift system.

The **mountain restaurants** offer a standard selection of American fare.

The **school** has a fine reputation, especially for teaching children. And there are adult snowboarder courses run by the renowned Delaney brothers (advance booking needed).

The Belly Button **childcare** facility takes children from two months old.

STAYING THERE

The new accommodation opening for this season looks splendidly luxurious with spectacular architecture, outdoor hot-tubs, etc. **Après-ski** has been lively when the lifts close (because of the day skiers) but quiet later on. What happens now the resort has expanded remains to be seen. Of the existing **restaurants**, Pesce Fresco does seafood and pasta, O'Shea's burgers and Rackets in the sports club more sophisticated food. Evening sleigh rides take people out to Western-style tented dinners. **Off-slope activities** centre around the sports club. A multi-screen cinema is nearby.

Crested Butte 2855m

Surprises galore in a Jekyll and Hyde resort

WHAT IT COSTS

6

HOW IT RATES

The slopes	
Snow	****
Extent	**
Experts	****
Intermediates	***
Beginners	****
Convenience	***
Queues	*****
Restaurants	*
The rest	
Scenery	***
Resort charm	****
Off-slope	**

- ➕ Known for its 'extreme' terrain
- ➕ Enough non-extreme but steep runs to keep experts happy
- ➕ Excellent for beginners and for near-beginners, with long easy runs
- ➕ Charming, tiny, restored Victorian mining town with good restaurants
- ➕ Alternative convenient resort village nearby, with more shops and restaurants being built
- ➕ Excellent school, with special courses for the disabled
- ➕ Attractive scenery for Colorado

- ➖ Limited for confident intermediate piste-bashers
- ➖ Old town is 10 minutes from resort village by shuttle-bus
- ➖ Out on a limb, away from mainstream Colorado resorts
- ➖ Only one satisfactory mountain restaurant

Among experts who are at home on steep, unprepared runs – and 'extremists' who like their mountains as steep as possible – Crested Butte enjoys cult status, thanks to the extent and gradient of the slopes on the outer fringes of the area. Meanwhile, the commercial success of the place depends on beginners and timid intermediates, for whom the long, groomed slopes of the main area are ideal. These two groups can safely include Crested Butte on their shortlists. But avid piste-bashers should stay away – there isn't enough suitable terrain. That's a shame because the cute old town is one of our favourites for atmosphere.

boarding *Boarders with a taste for powder will love Crested Butte, as much of its area is unpisted and 'extreme'. It is also very pro-boarding, and attracts many to its mountain, not least for the extreme snowboarding competitions. The resort runs half-pipe workshops. Beginners will find a large section of easy, long, wide green runs down to the base station. Unfortunately, there's little suitable terrain for progressing riders. The mountain is covered by chairs and is easy to get around – though the extreme area can be reached only by drag-lifts. The Colorado Boarder is a highly regarded specialist snowboard shop. The town has a couple of lively bars but is not bursting with nightlife.*

What's new

For 2000/01 274 extra acres are due to be added to the Extreme Limits by reopening Teocalli Bowl. This area is accessed from the High Lift at the top of the resort and has been closed for five years because of patrolling problems – which have now been solved.

The Crested Butte Marriot Resort hotel at the foot of the slopes has closed down and will reopen for the 2000/01 season as a Club Med village.

The resort

Crested Butte is a small resort in a remote corner of Colorado, well away from the Denver–Breckenridge–Vail mainstream. It takes its name from the local mountain – an isolated peak (a butte, pronounced 'beaut') with a distinctive shape. Crested Butte started life as a coal-mining town in the late 1800s; it is now one of the most attractive resorts in the Rockies – just a few narrow streets with beautifully restored wooden buildings and sidewalks, and the tiniest imaginable town jail, straight out of a Western. Elk Avenue, the main street, is a five-minute stroll from top to bottom, and is lined with interesting bars, restaurants and shops. There's even a classic general store.

The bars and restaurants are varied in price and character. But wherever you go you'll find genuinely friendly and hospitable locals. And mingled with them you'll find a fair share of down-to-earth celebrities.

The resort village of Mount Crested Butte, linked by regular free shuttle-buses, is a huge contrast to the town of Crested Butte. Nearly all the buildings are modern and characterless, and the two main hotels have adopted Club Med and Sheraton chain identities. There is a cluster of bars and restaurants at the foot of the slopes, around the large Club Med village.

MOUNTAIN FACTS

Altitude	2775m-3620m
Lifts	14
Pistes	1434 acres
Green	15%
Blue	44%
Black	41%
Art. snow	300 acres

Recco detectors used

SCHOOLS/GUIDES

2000/01 prices in dollars

Crested Butte
Classes 7 days
2½hr workshops: 9.45-12.15 and 1.15-3.45
70 per session.
Group lessons: 9.45-12.15
4 2½hr days: 165
Children's classes
Ages: 3 to 12
5 5½hr days including rental, pass and lunch: 360
Private lessons
2hr, 3hr or 6hr
150 for 2hr; each additional person 35

Never-ever lessons (aged 13 and up): 17

Reductions for over 65s (50% for group, 25% for private)

The mountain

It's a small area, but it packs in an astonishing mixture of perfect beginner slopes, easy cruising runs and expert terrain. The only people it might not suit are piste-bashing intermediates who like different groomed runs all the time and experts who don't fancy seriously steep terrain.

THE SLOPES
A Jekyll and Hyde mountain

Two high-speed quad chairs leave the base. The Silver Queen takes experts to black runs and links with lifts to the steepest runs. The Keystone lift takes you to the easiest runs. Intermediates can access cruising blue runs from either of these two lifts.

SNOW RELIABILITY
Excellent – usually

Crested Butte claims to benefit from snowstorms approaching from several directions, and it has a substantial snowmaking installation which covers groomed runs from most lifts. We've usually had superb snow here.

FOR EXPERTS
Some cult terrain

For those who like steep, ungroomed terrain, Crested Butte is idyllic – see below. Though there are also some steep black runs, for the average black-run mogul lover the resort is much more limited. And be warned: the Extreme Limits needs a lot of snow cover, and it is not unusual for it to be closed until the third week in January.

Also, the Irwin Lodge up the road

THE EXTREME LIMITS

Crested Butte's Extreme Limits makes up over half its terrain, though you wouldn't dream it, looking up from the groomed trails. Two drag-lifts access all this. The North Face button-lift, which takes only a couple of minutes to ride, is like Dr Who's Tardis. You get to the top and 225 acres of the Extreme Limits, hidden from the blue runs below, stretches before you, beyond a sign which says: 'This terrain is the steepest lift-served terrain in North America. Experts only'. There are cliffs to leap off if you want them, but good skiers and boarders can have the time of their lives on seriously steep but prettily wooded and safe terrain – there are free guided tours of the North Face twice a day. The newer High Lift opens up more extreme slopes that until a few years ago could only be reached by long climbs, including the 274-acre Teocalli Bowl, due to reopen for 2000/01.

LIFT PASSES

2000/01 prices in dollars

Crested Butte Mountain Resort
Covers all lifts in Crested Butte only.

Beginners Beginners' lessons in ski school includes lift pass.

Main pass
1-day pass 53
6-day pass 265

Short-term passes
Half-day pass available (adult 36).

Alternative periods
All lift passes of 4 days and over allow for one day off, eg 4 days' skiing in 5, or 6 in 7.

Notes Free lift passes for early and late weeks of season (26/11/00 to 16/12/00 and 1/4/01 to 8/4/01), with reductions on ski hire and lodgings. Children under 13 pay their age for each day's skiing. Seniors 65 to 69 pay half price, and over 70s go free.

runs a snowcat skiing and riding operation on its virgin powder slopes – see 'Staying up the mountain'.

FOR INTERMEDIATES
Not a lot

Good intermediates are likely to find the area limited unless they enjoy perfecting their technique on the same few runs each day. Mind you, a recent reporter was in raptures despite the limitations: 'If I'm in powder I'm in paradise, if it be green, blue or black.'

For early, unsure intermediates, Crested Butte has attractions. The east-facing runs down the Paradise, Teocalli and East River lifts are all wide, fairly gentle, well groomed and normally uncrowded cruising runs that can be taken fast or slow. Each has several run variations to choose from, ending up back at the same lifts.

A particularly gentle and uncrowded area is served by the Gold Link lift, isolated from the rest of the slopes.

FOR BEGINNERS
Excellent

There are excellent nursery slopes near the village. After that you'll be taking the Keystone chair-lift up to a choice of several long, easy green runs leading back down again. Or you can stop off part-way down to catch the Painter Boy lift. This has green runs down again or you can use it to head for the easy blues down the Gold Link lift.

FOR CROSS-COUNTRY
Looks good

There are 30km of cross-country trails near the Nordic Ski Center in the old town of Crested Butte, and backcountry tours are available in Elk Mountain and the Gunnison National Forest.

QUEUES
No problem

Queues are virtually non-existent – the only complaint we've heard is that Saturdays can get crowded when the lift passes are free at the beginning and end of season!

MOUNTAIN RESTAURANTS
Only one worth visiting

Most people go back to the base for lunch – not a hardship. The restaurant at the base of the Paradise lift is fairly civilised, though. There's Bubba's table-service restaurant as well as the large self-service and outdoor barbecue areas. At the other restaurant, at the base of the Twister lift, the food is primitive, 'though fine for a burger or snack'. Many callers bring their own.

SCHOOLS AND GUIDES
A major asset

The school has an excellent reputation. and offers specialised workshops (including All-Terrain, Ski Board, Half Pipe and Telemark) as well as normal group and private lessons. You can also ski for the day with ex-Olympic and World Extreme Champion skier Kim Reichhelm (who also runs her Women's Ski Adventures from here).

There are free daily mountain tours for intermediates or better, and the school has a high reputation for teaching people with disabilities.

FACILITIES FOR CHILDREN
Comprehensive

Crested Butte takes childcare seriously, and parents have praised the teaching and the separate children's area.

SNOWPIX.COM / CHRIS GILL

The dictionary says a butte is 'an isolated hill with steep sides and a flat top'. But this is a crested butte ↓

CHILDCARE

The Children's Center in the Whetstone building at the foot of the slopes offers a comprehensive range of care for non-skiing children aged 6 months to 7 years, from 8.30 to 4.30. There are separate skiing lessons for children aged 3 to 4, 5 to 7, and 8 to 12.

For more adventurous 8 to 15 year olds, there are 'Rip Sessions'. And mini-boarders aged 8 to 12 can take a Shred Bears class.

GETTING THERE

Air Gunnison, transfer ½hr. Denver, transfer 4½hr.

ACTIVITIES

Indoor Racquetball, swimming, hot-tubs, weight-training, aerobic classes, saunas
Outdoor Snowcat skiing, snowmobiling, sleigh rides, ballooning, winter horse riding, mountain barbecues, snow-shoe tours

TOURIST OFFICE

Postcode CO 81225
t +1 (970) 349 2286
f 349 2250
info@cbmr.com
www.crestedbutteresort.com

Staying there

Most accommodation is at the resort village. You can stroll to the lifts from some of it; but from many condos you are dependent on the bus. There is some accommodation in the town.

HOW TO GO
Plenty of choice

Most tour operators with serious US programmes include Crested Butte.
Hotels You have a broad range of options, from international-style comfort to homely character.
(3) **Sheraton Crested Butte Resort** Restored log and stone lobby. Indoor/outdoor pool and outdoor hot-tub with great views.
(2) **Nordic Inn** B&B. The oldest hotel in the mountain village, a short walk from the lifts. 'Full of character, charming hosts', outdoor hot-tub and large rooms.
(2) **Manor Lodge** Comfortable modern hotel close to the lifts, with live entertainment most evenings.
(2) **Crested Butte Lodge** More modern, nearer the centre, with an indoor pool, sauna and outdoor hot-tub.
(2) **The Inn at Crested Butte** 'Scandinavian-style' non-smoking hotel on the edge of the old town, with good views. Outdoor hot-tub.
(2) **Elk Mountain Lodge** Renovated miners' hotel in old town with good rooms. B&B only.
Self-catering There are thousands of apartments available, mainly in the village. Crested Mountain apartments are perhaps the most convenient and have pool, hot-tubs, saunas and friendly service. The Buttes, The Gateway and The Plaza are also recommended. The Three Seasons condos have plenty of mod cons but are some way from the lifts.

EATING OUT
Better than you'd expect

For such a small place Crested Butte has a surprisingly high number of decent restaurants – nearly all of them in the old town. Top of the pile is undoubtedly Soupcon, a tiny place in an old log cabin just off the main street, serving refined French food. Le Bosquet and Timberline run it close, and The Bacchanale is a good Italian. The Idle Spur is the statutory micro-brewery, doing satisfying food as well as beers. In the resort village, the WoodStone Grille prides itself on the presentation as well as the quality of the food. You can also take a sleigh ride up to Bubba's on the mountain.

APRES-SKI
Lively bars

The old town of Crested Butte has plenty of diversions, provided you're not looking for great sophistication or variety. Kochevar's is an amusing Wild West saloon, complete with shuffleboard (American-style shove-ha'penny). Recent visitors also recommend The Wooden Nickel and The Powerhouse. At the resort village, Rafters usually has a lot going on, and Casey's has ski movies and nightly drinks specials.

OFF THE SLOPES
Limited

Charming though it is, Crested Butte won't keep non-skiers/boarders amused for very long. Even shopping is limited, though it does have galleries, a theatre and a cinema.

STAYING UP THE MOUNTAIN
A wilderness retreat

For experts, cross-country skiers, snowmobiling and those who simply like to get away from it all, Crested Butte has something special.

Irwin Lodge is a great wooden barn of a place in a remote backcountry area, reached in winter only by snowcat or snowmobile. It has an outdoor hot-tub, great views and fairly simple rooms above a huge communal sitting room with open fire. Most people go there for the guided powder opportunities, with uplift by snowcat. For details call 00 1 970 349 2773.

Keystone

2835m

Pampered cruising in the trees

WHAT IT COSTS

6

HOW IT RATES

The slopes	
Snow	*****
Extent	**
Experts	***
Intermediates	****
Beginners	****
Convenience	**
Queues	****
Restaurants	***
The rest	
Scenery	***
Resort charm	**
Off-slope	**

- ➕ Good mountain for everyone but the double-diamond diehard; extensive, immaculately groomed intermediate slopes are a particular strength
- ➕ Huge night-skiing operation – almost half the runs are floodlit and open until 9pm
- ➕ Lots of other nearby resorts, and a shared lift pass with Breckenridge, Vail and A-Basin
- ➕ Efficient lift system – few queues
- ➕ Luxurious condominiums set in woods (with good-value rates)
- ➕ Very impressive childcare facilities

- ➖ Very quiet in the evenings
- ➖ Very high – altitude sickness can be a problem for some visitors
- ➖ Few slope-side properties, and most involve bus-rides to and from lifts
- ➖ Resort lacks village atmosphere except in the newish River Run development
- ➖ Poor shops for self-catering
- ➖ Limited choice of restaurants by usual US resort standards

Keystone's slopes are impressive from many points of view. If there was a village at the foot of them like Vail or Breckenridge, Keystone's stable-mates, it would be easily recommendable. But what Keystone offers at present is less compelling. River Run – a joint venture with Whistler's Canadian owner, Intrawest – is developing into something like a recognisable resort village, but it still has some way to go before a week of evenings spent there could be called an attractive prospect. And the appeal of Keystone's other 'neighborhoods' – all less entertaining, all but one further from the lifts – is difficult to see.

Perhaps it is price: you may find some of Keystone's lodgings offer exceptional value. Hire a car to simplify shopping, and plan on eating in more than out.

boarding *Until the 1996/97 season, snowboarding was banned at Keystone. Then they invested $2.5 million in facilities – these include the 20-acre Jawhacker terrain-park and adjoining Area 51 half-pipe, on the front side of Keystone Mountain – floodlit to make the biggest night-snowboarding operation in Colorado (you can actually ride from 8.30am to 9pm – if you've got superhuman stamina and are mad enough, that is). Keystone as a whole is ideal for beginners and intermediates, with mainly chair-lifts and gondolas, good beginner areas (there are a couple of easily avoidable drag-lifts here) and superb cruising runs. Experienced riders will love The Outback and the bowls and chutes of nearby A-Basin, a favourite area with hardcore boarders. Evenings are quiet and devoid of traditional snowboard hang-outs.*

What's new

2000/01 will see a new six-pack on the back side of Keystone Mountain – speeding up the return from North Peak.

Free mountain passports – allowing free access to a number of activities – will be issued with every room reservation.

A new five-day pass offer gives you another another five days' skiing free if you book a second holiday.

The resort

Keystone is a sprawling resort of condominiums spread over wooded countryside at the foot of Keystone Mountain, beside Snake River and the highway to Loveland Pass. As yet it has no clear centre, but is notionally divided into six 'neighborhoods', with regular buses between them. Some consist of little more than groups of condos, while others have shops, restaurants and bars (though no supermarkets or liquor stores – they are out on the main highway).

At River Run, at the base of the main gondola, an attractively designed, car-free development is taking shape that is destined to become the new focal point of the resort. A second lift base area half a mile to the west, Mountain House, is much less of a village. Another mile west is Keystone Village, set around the picturesque lake – a huge natural ice rink in winter. These and two other 'neighborhoods' are shown on our resort plan; Ski Tip (with famous Lodge) is off to the east.

MOUNTAIN FACTS

Altitude	2835m-3720m
Lifts	22
Pistes	1861 acres
Green	13%
Blue	36%
Black	51%
Art. snow	859 acres

LIFT PASSES

1999/2000 prices in dollars

Vail Resorts
1- or 2-day pass valid in Breckenridge and A-Basin as well as Keystone. Passes for 3 days or more also valid for Vail and Beaver Creek.

Beginners Beginners and novices have a reduced area pass in ski school.

Main pass
1-day pass 53
6-day pass 264

Senior citizens
Over 65: 1-day pass 37
Over 70: free pass

Children
Under 13: 1-day pass 21
Under 5: free pass

Alternative periods
Passes of 2 days and over allow one non-skiing day, eg 6-day pass valid for a 7-day period, with one non-skiing day.

BEN BLANKENBURG

If the daylight hours aren't enough, Keystone is the place for you ↓

The mountains

Keystone's terrain has expanded rapidly in the last few years and by US standards now offers extensive intermediate slopes and some challenging steeper stuff.

High-speed quad chairs are becoming more the norm – the latest replacement is the Santiago, which takes you from the bottom of Keystone Mountain up to North Peak.

Keystone and Breckenridge (visible from the slopes – see Breckenridge chapter) were bought in 1996 by Vail Resorts, the owner of Vail and Beaver Creek (around an hour away). Lift tickets between the four resorts are interchangeable, and there is bus transport between them ('Having a car is pointless,' says one reporter). Copper Mountain is nearby and Arapahoe Basin (or A-Basin as it is known locally) a few minutes by road, but both are separately owned. Your lift ticket covers a trip to A-Basin, but not to Copper. In contrast to Keystone's superb modern lifts, A-Basin is still served by a series of slow old chairs.

THE SLOPES
A keen intermediate's dream

Three tree-lined, interlinked mountains form Keystone's local slopes. The only one directly accessible from the resort is **Keystone Mountain**, from Mountain House or River Run. The front face of the mountain has Keystone's biggest network of lifts and runs by far, mainly of easy and intermediate gradient. From the top you can drop over the back down to Keystone Gulch, where there are lifts back up to Keystone Mountain and on to the next hill, **North Peak.** Or you can ride the Outpost gondola directly to the top of North Peak. From North Peak you can get back to the bases of both Keystone Mountain and the third peak, known as **The Outback**, served by another high-speed quad chair-lift.

SNOW RELIABILITY
Not a natural strength

Keystone's annual snowfall is low by Colorado standards – 230in, whereas many other resorts get 300in or more. But shortage of snow is rarely a problem, not least because Keystone has one of the world's biggest snowmaking systems as back-up.

One of the main reasons for the snowmaking is to help form an early-season base. Keystone traditionally vies with Killington to be the first US resort to open its runs for the season – normally in October. There have even been snow-guns installed in the new fun-park, for early-season riding.

A-Basin has no need for artificial snow. It has the highest lift-served terrain in the US, at almost 4000m, and the base-station is at an impressive 3290m. The slopes are normally open well into June.

FOR EXPERTS
Some steeps, no super-steeps

Keystone has a reputation for great groomers, but it also has a lot of steeper ungroomed terrain (though none of it gets a double-diamond grading).

Windows is a 60-acre area of experts-only glade runs on Keystone Mountain's back side, opened in 1998. The trail map identifies around 10, but on the ground they are not clearly defined. All three mountains have some good mogul runs, such as

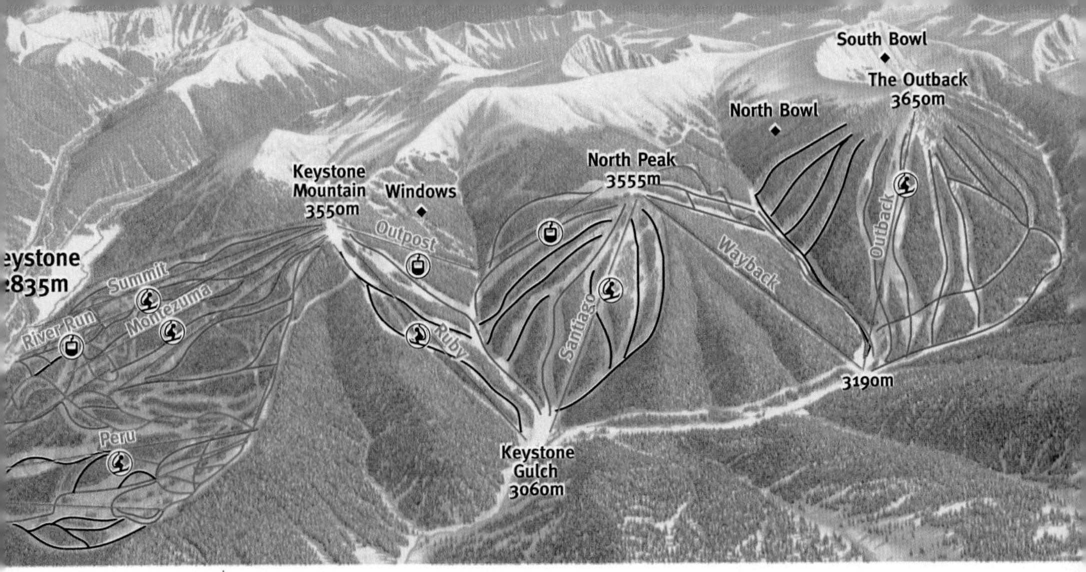

Ambush and Geronimo, and there are splendid glade runs on both North Peak and The Outback. Traversing from the top of the lift on The Outback takes you to open and glade runs in the North Bowl and the South Bowls, which are basically ski-anywhere areas.

Arapahoe Basin, down the road, is a good place for those looking for more of a challenge. The East Wall here has some splendid steep chutes. And the opposite side of the bowl is riddled with steep bump runs – although none of the runs is particularly long.

Copper Mountain and Breckenridge have some good challenging terrain, for those prepared to travel around.

FOR INTERMEDIATES

A cruiser's paradise

Keystone is ideal for intermediates. The front face of Keystone Mountain itself is a network of beautifully groomed blue and green runs through the trees. Enthusiastic piste-bashers will love it.

The Outback and North Peak also have easy cruising blues, and The Outback has some of the steepest blue runs, including a couple of blue-blacks through the trees that are pretty much off-piste and unmarked.

On top of that, Vail, Beaver Creek and Copper Mountain all have some great intermediate terrain.

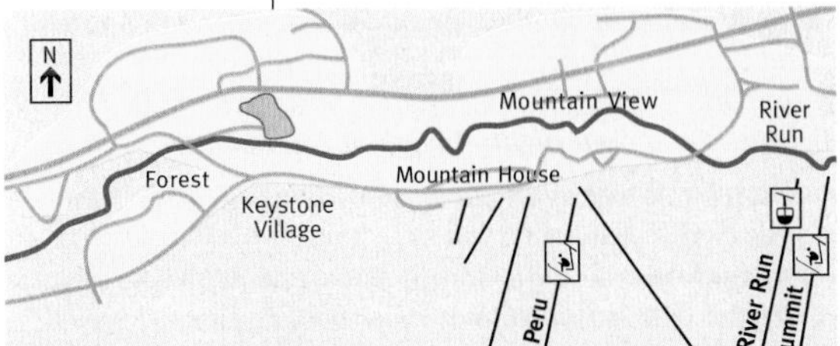

FOR BEGINNERS

Nice gentle greens

There are good nursery slopes (floodlit in the evening) at the top and bottom of Keystone Mountain, which also has

DAVE NAGEL

River Run has some way to go before it can be counted a complete resort village, but it's already the best place to stay in Keystone →

SCHOOLS/GUIDES

1999/2000 prices in dollars

Keystone

Classes 7 days
2½hr: 10.30-1pm or 1.30-4pm; 2hr evening: 4.30-6.30
66 per session for beginners and 96 for intermediates, including lift ticket and equipment; for advanced 56 excluding lift ticket and equipment

Children's classes
Ages: 3 to 14
Full day including lunch and ski-pass: 80

Private lessons
1hr, 1½hr, 2hr, 3hr or 6hr
125 for 1½hr

CHILDCARE

The Children's Center at the base of the mountain caters for children aged 2 months to 12 years and is open from 8am to 9pm. They can also provide evening babysitting in your own room. From age 3, children can join in the Snowplay programmes.

The school's Mini Minor's Camp takes children aged 3 to 4, the Minor's Camp those from 5 to 12.

some excellent long green runs to progress to – one of them, Schoolmarm, goes right from top to bottom of the mountain. There's another long green on North Peak, accessible by gondola.

FOR CROSS-COUNTRY
Extensive facilities

The special Cross-Country and Touring Center between Keystone and A-Basin is served by a shuttle-bus. There are 29km of groomed trails. And 57km of unprepared trails take you through spectacular scenery in the Montezuma area, with great views of the Continental Divide. Some trails lead to old mining ghost-towns. The Cross-Country and Touring Center runs guided tours, including a Full Moon evening tour.

QUEUES
Not a problem

Keystone has an efficient, modern lift system, and, except at the morning peak, there are few queuing problems.

MOUNTAIN RESTAURANTS
A resort of extremes

There are two mountain restaurant complexes. Summit House at the top of Keystone Mountain has a food court, a pizza place and a bar, all inclined to get over-busy – 'Eat at the base,' says a reporter. The Outpost Lodge at the top of North Peak is beautifully designed in wood, with high ceilings, picture windows and a big terrace. Its Timber Ridge food court is strictly for refuelling, but the table-service Alpenglow Stube (see below) is something else. It has a luxury atmosphere rarely found in mountain restaurants, even in Europe – but it is of course expensive. There's a simple cabin and outdoor grill at Keystone Gulch, at the foot of North Peak.

SCHOOLS AND GUIDES
Advanced classes a bargain

As well as the normal lessons, there are bumps, bowls and trees classes, courses run by Olympic medallists Phil and Steve Mahre, special carving ski clinics and snowboarding lessons designed specially for experienced adult skiers. Recent reporters have been very impressed by these advanced classes, partly because they found themselves in tiny groups or even getting one-to-one tuition.

FACILITIES FOR CHILDREN
Excellent

Childcare facilities are excellent, with programmes tailored to specific age groups, and nursery care going on into the evening. Children have their own teaching areas, with 'magic carpet' lifts. There are also three fun themed areas for kids and their minders to explore. One reporter complains that kids' classes are all-day, with no half-day option.

Staying there

The most convenient places to stay are near the Mountain House or River Run lifts. But all the accommodation is well served by free shuttle-buses.

HOW TO GO
As you please

It's easy to fix your own lodgings, and regular shuttles operate from Denver airport, but packages can offer very attractive prices. There are hotels but most accommodation is in condominiums.

Hotels There isn't a great choice but they're all of a high standard.

((((4) **Chateaux d'Mont** Luxury condo-hotel near the lifts; only 15 suites, with private hot-tubs and other luxuries.

GOURMET NIGHT SKIING

Keystone has the biggest floodlighting operation in the US, covering Keystone Mountain top to bottom. When the light begins to fade, the floodlights come on and you can carry on skiing or riding up to 9pm. A gondola, high-speed quad and drag-lift serve 17 green and blue runs (longest top-to-bottom trail over three miles long) and a 20-acre terrain park. Cruising through falling snow illuminated by the bright lights can be delightful. On a clear night, though, it can be bitter.

You can combine the action with dinner on the mountain. The Alpenglow Stube, at the top of North Peak (reached by gondola), stays open until 8.15pm to serve haute cuisine with a Colorado flavour for pedestrians, skiers and snowboarders. Slippers are provided. A cheaper option is next door's Der Fondue Chessel which features fondue, raclette and 'Bavarian' music and dancing.

GETTING THERE

Air Denver, transfer 2hr.

ACTIVITIES

Indoor Swimming, hot-tubs, tennis
Outdoor Floodlit ice skating, sleigh and stagecoach rides, snowmobiling, horse-riding, tubing, dog-sledding, evening gondola trips

TOURIST OFFICE

Postcode CO 80424
t +1 (970) 496 6772
f 453 3202
international@vailresorts.com
www.keystoneresort.com

(((4 **Keystone Lodge** Large, recently renovated hotel in Keystone Village. All rooms have mountain views. Pool and fitness centre.
(((3 **Inn at Keystone** Modern, comfortable, resort-owned hotel. Hot-tubs with great views. Liked by reporters who stayed there.
(((3 **Ski Tip Lodge** Former stagecoach halt and home of Keystone's founder, Max Dercum, who restored and extended it and used broken ski tips found on the slopes as door handles – hence the name. Atmospheric old rooms, bar and lounge with log fires. Well out of town by the cross-country centre and some new development. Good restaurant.
Self-catering All the condominiums we've seen or heard about are large and luxurious – and we've stayed in some fabulous ones with nice touches such as log fires and two-storey floor-to-ceiling windows. There are hundreds of well-appointed condos, most with use of a pool and hot-tub. There are lots at the River Run development. The Lakeside condos (near the lake!) come complete with all mod cons and facilities. The equally comfortable and well positioned Frostfire condos have fewer amenities, but each unit has an en suite whirlpool bath. Cinnamon Ridge at Mountain View, Slopeside at Mountain House and Flying Dutchman in the Forest 'neighborhood' are other recommended places.

STAYING DOWN THE VALLEY
Possible, good for exploring

A few years ago a couple of reporters stayed in **Silverthorne**. The Days Inn was thought comfortable but basic. The Alpen Hutte was friendly and had its own private bus transfer. **Frisco** is a good centre for visiting other nearby resorts – reporters recommend the Alpine Inn, Lake Dillon Lodge and Hotel Frisco.

EATING OUT
Not the widest choice

You can have your evening meal up the mountain. The Summit House, at the top of the gondola on Keystone Mountain, remains busy at the end of the normal day because of the floodlit sessions at night. There's live country and western entertainment and simple food – hamburgers, ribs and so on. The Outpost, on North Peak, is a hive of dining activity including the Alpenglow Stube (see facing page).

There are some good upmarket places at valley level too. We've eaten well at the Ski Tip Lodge by the cross-country track (the menu changes daily) – a charming former stagecoach halt. The Keystone Ranch, well outside the resort, serves six-course dinners in a building based on a 19th-century homestead. The Garden Room of Keystone Lodge overlooks the lake.

River Run and Keystone Village each offer half a dozen options, including steak houses and pizza places. But there isn't the range of mid-market restaurants that makes eating out such a pleasure in many American resorts – and it's in the nature of the place that the restaurants are dotted around in different parts of the resort. Paisano's is an 'excellent' Italian at River Run, where there are also two taverns. The cosy Snake River Saloon in the Mountain View neighbourhood is recommended for grills. The Bighorn Steakhouse in Keystone Lodge is well worth avoiding – lousy service in a dreary room.

APRES-SKI
Pretty quiet in the evenings

Immediately after coming off the slopes, it can be quite lively. The Summit House at the top of the gondola has live music and caters for people using the slopes at night as well as après-skiers. The Kickapoo Tavern at River Run has a sunny deck and eight Colorado microbrews on tap and Montezuma has rock 'n roll. Some of the eateries double as bars with live music. The Snake River Saloon has a happy hour, 5–7pm, and is thoroughly recommended by a reporter: 'Brilliant restaurant and lively bar – including a fire-eating barman.' Ida Belle has ragtime music and a miners' tavern decor; and Dillon Inn has Country and Western.

However, places empty out quite early and Keystone isn't really the place for late-night revellers.

OFF THE SLOPES
OK if you want a peaceful time

Keystone makes it easy for pedestrians to get around the mountain, with both mountain restaurant complexes easily accessible by gondola. It's also easy to get to Breckenridge and Vail.

There are plenty of other activities, including skating on the frozen lake (the largest outdoor maintained rink in the US) and indoor tennis.

Steamboat

2100m

Powder glade expansion above a cowboy town

WHAT IT COSTS

6

HOW IT RATES

The slopes

Snow	****
Extent	***
Experts	***
Intermediates	****
Beginners	*****
Convenience	***
Queues	****
Restaurants	***

The rest

Scenery	***
Resort charm	**
Off-slope	**

- ➕ Now a fair-sized mountain, with a decent amount of black-diamond terrain to go with its excellent beginner and early intermediate runs
- ➕ Famed for its gladed powder terrain
- ➕ Plenty of slope-side lodging
- ➕ Town of Steamboat Springs has some Western character – though it's less of a wild cowboy town than the hype leads you to expect
- ➕ Good snow record combined with modest altitude – sickness problems are very unlikely

- ➖ Old town is a couple of miles from the slopes, and the resort as a whole sprawls over a large area
- ➖ Modern resort 'village' at the foot of the slopes is rather a mess, with some big eyesore buildings
- ➖ Mountain lacks distinctive character
- ➖ Not enough tough blue/easy black runs to amuse keen intermediates for a week
- ➖ Not a huge amount of double-black stuff – and most of it involves hiking
- ➖ Green runs tend to be winding catwalks rather than proper runs

Steamboat's brochures routinely feature horse-riding, Stetson-wearing, lasso-wielding cowboys. There are working cowboys around, but as Steamboat the ski resort has grown it has rather swamped Steamboat Springs the cattle town – without itself developing much of a village atmosphere.

Steamboat's mountain may not be a match in extent and challenge for some Colorado neighbours – experts and keen piste-bashers going for a week or more might do well to plan a two-centre holiday. But Steamboat is one of the best resorts for powder fun among the trees. Recent expansions have added to its appeal in this respect – and there are 500 acres more to come.

boarding *Steamboat is ideal for first-time boarders – there's a special learning area, ideal gentle slopes to progress to and you can get all over the mountain using chair-lifts and the gondola. The snowboard school even offers another lesson free if you can't ride from the top of the beginners' area after the first. Steamboat is also great for experienced boarders, with two fun-parks (The Beehive, especially for kids, and the excellent Mavericks) and the competition-standard Dude Ranch half-pipe. And riding the glades in fresh powder is unbeatable. There's also a choice of specialist snowboard shops, a special ride guide piste map and benches and tools at the top of lifts.*

What's new

Steamboat's terrain has expanded a lot in recent years – first into Morningside Park and then into the Pioneer Ridge area, where the first lift was opened for 1998/99. Another lift and another 500 acres of terrain are to follow, but not yet.

The dynamic American Skiing Company bought Steamboat in 1997. The company's signature Grand Summit hotel at the base, originally planned for last season, is sure to open for 2000/01.

CYNTHIA HUNTER / STEAMBOAT

Rolling hills, with trails cut through the forest: classic Colorado terrain →

The resort

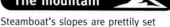

The resort is a 20-minute bus-ride from the old town of Steamboat Springs – a long drive or short flight from Denver. Near the gondola station there are a couple of shop- and restaurant-lined multi-level squares leading to the one main street; the buildings are all modern, but with plenty of wooden facades. Some of the accommodation is up the sides of the piste, but the resort also sprawls across the valley.

The old town can be a bit of a disappointment after the hype of the brochures. It may be a working cattle town – it's certainly a great place to buy a Stetson (at the famous FM Light & Son) – but the Wild West isn't much in evidence except in January when the Cowboy Downhill brings cowhands into town to compete in a fun slalom, lassoing and saddling competition.

The main (and almost only) street in the old town is very wide, with multiple lanes of traffic each way – it was built that way to allow cattle to be driven through town. It is lined with bars, hotels and shops, built at various times over the last 120 years, in a wide mixture of styles, from old wooden buildings to modern concrete plazas.

The town got its name in the mid-1800s, when trappers going along by the Yampa river heard a chugging they thought was a steamboat. It turned out to be the bubbling of a hot spring.

MOUNTAIN FACTS

Altitude	2100m-3220m
Lifts	20
Pistes	2939 acres
Green	13%
Blue	56%
Black	31%
Art. snow	438 acres

The mountain

Steamboat's slopes are prettily set among the trees, with views down to the rolling hills below. It claims to be one of Colorado's biggest areas, and with its recent ongoing expansion it is. There's now more terrain for better skiers in particular – but even when the expansion is finished it still won't rival places such as Aspen and Vail.

With an Early Bird pass ($9) you can ride the gondola at 8am, have a buffet breakfast at Thunderhead and get fresh tracks when the slopes open at 8.30.

There are various complimentary guiding deals. Mountain hosts do tours of blue and black runs daily at 10.30. Olympic medallist Billy Kidd takes

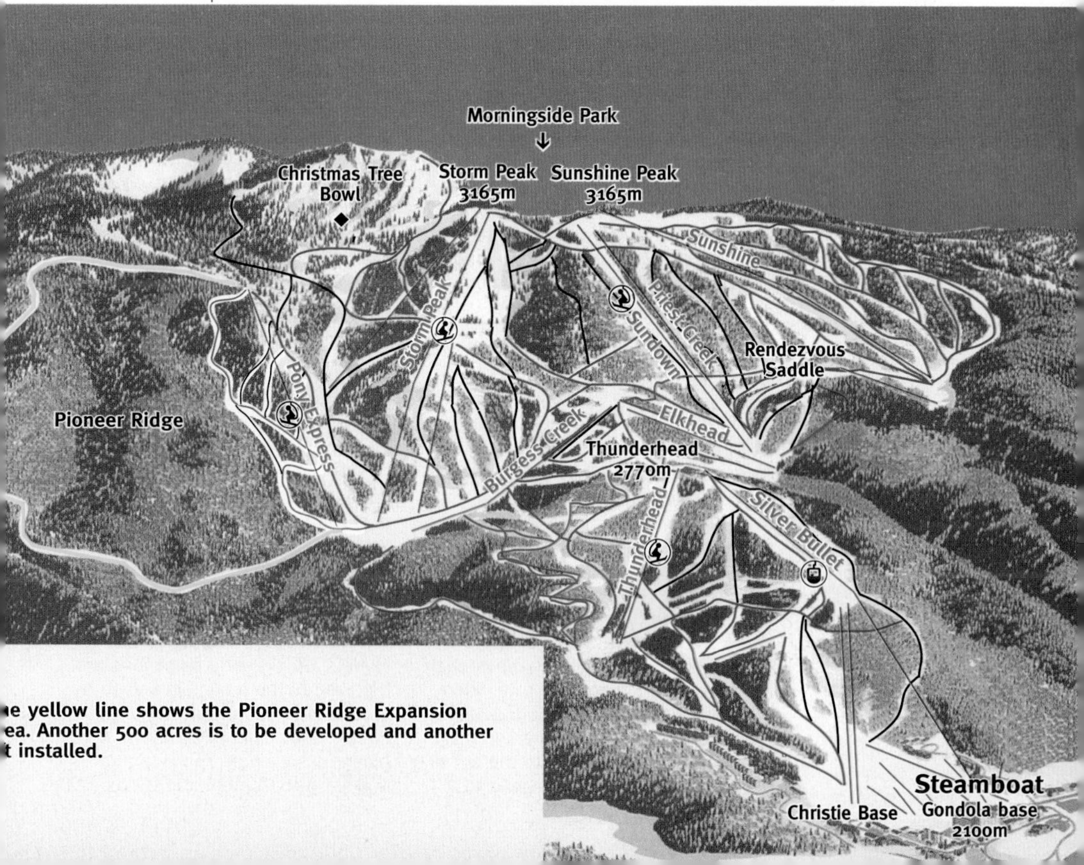

e yellow line shows the Pioneer Ridge Expansion ea. Another 500 acres is to be developed and another t installed.

LIFT PASSES

1999/2000 prices in dollars

Steamboat
Covers all lifts at Steamboat only.

Beginners One free lift at base (Preview); day pass for beginners covers two extra lifts (adult 35).

Main pass
1-day pass 54
6-day pass 282
(low season 252)

Senior citizens
Over 65: 6-day pass 210
Over 70: free pass

Children
Under 13: 6-day pass 180 – but can be free, see Notes below

Short-term passes
Afternoon passes from 12.15 (adult 43) and from 2pm (adult 30). Single ascent on Silver Bullet Gondola for non-skiers only (adult 16).

Alternative periods
3-day pass is valid for 4 days with one non-skiing day. Passes of 4 days and over allow two days' non-skiing, so 4 days' skiing in 6, 6 in 8.

Notes Children up to 12 ski free when parents buy full lift pass and stay for 5 days or more (one child per parent). Discounts for groups.

groups down the mountain most days at 1pm. There are nature ski tours three times a week. And five days a week at 9am local guides lead groups of over-50s on a 'mellow cruise' of groomed runs.

Holiday visitors generally overlook Steamboat Springs' little local hill, Howelsen. As well as a row of ski jumps, it has a modest area of pistes, and they are open most evenings.

If you have a car, Vail-Beaver Creek, Copper Mountain, Keystone, Arapahoe Basin, Breckenridge and Winter Park are all less than a two-hour drive.

THE SLOPES
Five different flanks

The slopes divide naturally into five sectors, and most have runs to suit all abilities. The gondola from the village rises to **Thunderhead**. From here you can choose the runs back to the village and a variety of chairs. Or you can go down to the left to catch a chair up to **Storm Peak** or to the new **Pioneer Ridge** area. From Storm Peak you can drop over the back into the not-quite-so-new, very pretty and generally quiet **Morningside Park** area. If you turn right from Thunderhead you can catch a chair up to **Sunshine Peak.**

SNOW RELIABILITY
Good despite 'low' altitude

Steamboat is relatively low by Colorado standards; it goes from 2100m to 3220m. So its highest slopes are below the height of the base of Arapahoe Basin. Despite this it has an excellent snow record, with an annual average of 334in – more than most of the higher resorts. This is where they invented the term Champagne Powder™. And there is now snowmaking from top to bottom of the mountain.

FOR EXPERTS
Powder glades are the highlight

The main attraction of Steamboat for experts is the challenging 'off-piste' terrain in the forest glades. The trees are particularly wonderful after a fall of fresh powder.

A great area is on Sunshine Peak below the Sundown Express and Priest Creek lifts. You simply take off through the aspens and choose a route where the trees are spaced as you like them – wide or narrow. Of the marked black runs in this area, the two to the left of the lifts as you go up – Closet and Shadows – are only loosely pistes: the trees have just been thinned out a bit. On the right of the lift as you go up are some clearer marked black runs.

Morningside Park and Pioneer Ridge also have excellent gladed terrain, without any scary gradients.

The scary gradients are reached via the lift back from Morningside – the three numbered Chutes are easily accessed, and a short hike gets you to the tree skiing of Christmas Tree bowl.

Most other marked blacks are easy for good intermediates, but they make great fast runs if they've been groomed. If it's bumps you're after, try the series of bump runs off Four Points that let you tackle moguls all day – including Nelson's, named after local hero Nelson Carmichael, bronze medallist at the Albertville Olympics.

Steamboat Powder Cats run snowcat skiing tours over 15 square miles of backcountry.

FOR INTERMEDIATES
Some long cruises

Much of the mountain is ideal intermediate territory, with long cruising blue runs such as Buddy's Run, Rainbow and Ego on Storm Peak and High Noon and One O'Clock on Sunshine Peak. Some black runs, such as West Side and Lower Valley View, also make good, challenging intermediate runs when the bumps have been groomed out of them.

Morningside Park is a great area for playing on easy black as well as blue slopes. And don't ignore Thunderhead either – there are a lot of good runs that it's easy to miss out on if you always head for the top of the mountain.

The runs on Sunshine at the far right-hand side of the area are very gentle – Tomahawk and Quickdraw are marked blue but are perfectly possible for those who normally stick to green.

The main problem for keen intermediates will be the limited extent of the area – not really enough to keep you interested for a week unless you enjoy repeating the same runs.

FOR BEGINNERS
Excellent learning terrain

There's a big, gentle nursery area at the base of the mountain served by several lifts. You progress from this to the Christie chairs to a variety of gentle green runs such as Yoo Hoo and Giggle Gulch. A green run winds all the

CHILDCARE

The Kids' Vacation Center is run by the resort in the lower gondola station. The Kiddie Coral nursery takes children aged 6 months to 6 years, all day. Those aged 2 can opt for the Buckaroos programme with a one-hour private lesson (ski rental not included). Older children go on to the Sundance Kids group classes.

The school has Rough Rider and Desperados programmes for children up to 15, with their own skiing skills playground area and lunchtime supervision.

The Adventure Club at Night offers evening childcare in the Vacation Center for ages 4 to 12, from 6pm to 10pm. Reservations necessary.

way down from Thunderhead, but there is rather a shortage of 'proper' green runs up the mountain for those not ready for the psychological leap to the easy blues on Sunshine.

FOR CROSS-COUNTRY
Plenty out of town

There's no cross-country in Steamboat itself but a free shuttle service takes you to the Touring Center, where there are 30km of groomed tracks and lessons available. There are also Forest Service trails around Rabbit Ears Pass – many quite testing, apparently.

QUEUES
Can be problem in the morning

There may be irritating queues for the gondola at the start of the day; at least they are well organised. New fast quad chairs have cut out the worst bottlenecks up the mountain, though there can still be queues for the slow Sunshine lift serving the easiest top-of-the-mountain runs.

MOUNTAIN RESTAURANTS
Good by US standards

There are two main restaurant complexes on the mountain, both of which include good table-service restaurants. At Thunderhead there's a choice of the big BK Corral self-service food court, a barbecue on the sun deck, or table-service in the pub-style Stoker bar or more elegant Hazie's restaurant. At Rendezvous Saddle there's a slightly smaller alternative, which has a two-floor self-service section including a pizza bar, another sun deck and barbecue and Ragnar's table-service Scandinavian restaurant. You can book for Ragnar's and Hazie's. There's also a snack bar and sun deck at Four Points.

SCHOOLS AND GUIDES
Lots of variety

The programme includes special workshops such as powder, bumps and style clinics. There are also special Billy Kidd Performance Camps, run by the 1964 Olympic silver medal winner. Our latest reports on the school, which are not very recent, have been generally positive, but we have had one complaint about the familiar American problem of 'a different instructor every day'. The Guided Demo Center at the top of the gondola provides not only the latest skis to test but instructors to help you get the best out of them, for $10/hr.

SCHOOLS/GUIDES

1999/2000 prices in dollars

Steamboat
Classes 5 days
2hr 30min: 11.15am-1.45pm
5 half days: 172
Children's classes
Ages: 6 to 15
5 5hr days including lunch: 295
Private lessons
1hr, 2hr, 3hr or full-day
80 for 1hr

FACILITIES FOR CHILDREN
Kids Go Free

Steamboat has a Kids Go Free scheme – free lift pass for one child of up to age 12 per parent buying a pass for at least five days. The school has a variety of courses for different standards and age groups. 'Our two boys in the Desperados ski week had the time of their lives and their skiing improved dramatically,' said one past reporter. Childcare arrangements are comprehensive, including evening entertainment or excursions from 6pm.

Staying there

Our preference is to stay on the slopes and make occasional excursions to Steamboat Springs. If you have a car, you can compromise and stay between the two – the worst of both worlds.

HOW TO GO
Plenty of packages

A fair number of UK tour operators have Steamboat in their programme. There's accommodation for all tastes, including more downmarket places than is the US norm.

Chalets There are some catered chalets run by UK tour operators. A reporter recommends Skiworld's Christie Haus.

Hotels The smarter hotels out at the resort have less character than some of the in-town options.

((((4) **Grand Summit** New 330-room resort-owned condo-hotel close to the lift base, due to open in 2000. Plans include a luxury spa.

((((4) **Best Western Ptarmigan Inn** Ideally situated just above the gondola station and right on the piste, with an outdoor pool and hot-tub, a sauna and good après-ski bar with a happy hour.

((((4) **Sheraton** Big, comfortable but impersonal hotel well placed near the gondola, with a pool and hot-tub.

(((3) **Harbor** The oldest hotel in the old town. Rooms vary in size and style; sauna, steam room and two hot-tubs.

((2) **Bristol** Traditional little hotel on main street of old town, with 'small but fairly priced' rooms.

((2) **Alpiner Lodge** Bavarian style economy option in old town.

((2) **Rabbit Ears Motel** Recommended by a reporter: 'Excellent. Family run with comfortable rooms.'

Self-catering There are countless apartment developments, many with good pool/tub facilities and shuttle-buses. The ones we have seen have all

GETTING THERE

Air Yampa Valley regional airport, transfer ¾hr. Denver, transfer 3½hr.

ACTIVITIES

Indoor Ice skating, hot-tubbing, swimming pools, tennis, gym, weights room, climbing wall, museum

Outdoor Ice driving school, dog-sledding, snowmobiling, ballooning, hot springs, dinner sleigh rides, horse-riding, skating, ice and rock climbing, fly-fishing, snowcat skiing, tubing

TOURIST OFFICE

Postcode CO 80487
t +1 (970) 879 6111
f 879 7844
steamboat-info@steamboat-ski.com
www.steamboat-ski.com

been impressive, but the best were the Bear Claw condos – wonderfully spacious and individually furnished, set at the top of the nursery slope. Other recommendations include Timber Run, a short shuttle-ride from the centre with multiple hot-tubs; The Lodge at Steamboat, close to the gondola station; Thunderhead Lodge & Condominiums; and the aptly named Ski Inn. Storm Meadows condos at Christie base are 'wonderful'.

EATING OUT
Huge variety

There's a wide choice of places to suit all pockets – over 70 bars and restaurants. Pick up a dining guide booklet to check out menus.

Steamboat specialises in mountain-top dining, in three restaurants accessed via the gondola to Thunderhead. Five nights a week the Western BBQ does an all-you-can-eat buffet, with country and western music and dancing. Or you can have a gourmet treat at Hazie's, where the menu goes somewhat upmarket from lunchtime. Three nights a week you can take a sleigh hauled by a snowcat to Ragnar's at Rendezvous Saddle for a Scandinavian meal with live music.

In the resort, the Slopeside Grill has a good selection of pizza and pasta dishes and doubles as a bar, with live music some nights. Dos Amigos and La Montana are recommended Mexicans.

Down in the valley you can take horse-drawn sleigh rides to other dinner options, such as down Walton Creek canyon, to eat in heated tents with Western music.

In downtown Steamboat Springs try L'Apogee for fine French-style food, or the cheaper Harwig's Grill on the same premises. The Steamboat Yacht Club on the river bank is recommended for seafood and views of ski-jumping. Antares is deservedly popular for its excellent international cuisine. The Steamboat Brewery has a wide-ranging menu as well as its own beers. For more traditional American fare try the popular Old West Steakhouse – 'very charming, reasonably priced, great food' – or the Old Town Pub, dating from 1904. Cantina is recommended for Tex-Mex and Cugino's for Italian. For a real budget buy, head for the barbecue food at the Double Z.

APRES-SKI
Fairly lively

Restaurants apart, the old town is quiet in the evening. The Old Town Pub has live music at weekends. The Tap House is 'a must for Brits missing their soccer', with 30 TVs as well as the best draft beer choice in town.

The base lodge area is livelier. Popular places at close of play are the Slopeside Grill and the Inferno, in the gondola square, both with live music and a happy hour. The Inferno is the place for dancing to loud live music – and on Sundays it has a very popular 'Disco Inferno' night. Dos Amigos and the Tugboat Tavern are popular bars for drinks by the pitcher. The Ptarmigan Inn offers a rather more sophisticated atmosphere.

Evening activities include watching floodlit ski-jumping in the old town and tubing on the floodlit nursery slope at the main ski area.

OFF THE SLOPES
Lots to do

Getting up to Thunderhead restaurant complex is easy for pedestrians. Visiting town is, too. And you can go and relax in outdoor Strawberry Park Hot Springs six miles from town. The snowmobiling terrain around Rabbit Ears Pass looks great to our untutored eye. The ice rink is Olympic size.

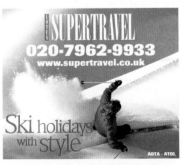

CYNTHIA HUNTER / STEAMBOAT

Two key ingredients in the Steamboat recipe – Champagne Powder™ and pleasantly spaced trees ↓

Telluride 2660m

Cute old town, impressive little mountain

WHAT IT COSTS

6

HOW IT RATES

The slopes

Snow	****
Extent	**
Experts	****
Intermediates	***
Beginners	*****
Convenience	****
Queues	*****
Restaurants	*

The rest

Scenery	****
Resort charm	****
Off-slope	**

What's new

For the 2000/01 season, the smart Club St Sophia will open at the top of the gondola, offering lunch and dinner.

For 1999/2000 two new fast quads were installed. At the top of the area, Lift 6 was upgraded to a triple chair, realigned to cut down the hike to the steeps of Gold Hill.

Approval has been given for a major expansion into Prospect Bowl, adding about 70% to the existing terrain with five new lifts – due for 2001/02.

MOUNTAIN FACTS

Altitude	2660m-3625m
Lifts	12
Pistes	1050 acres
Green	21%
Blue	47%
Black	32%
Art. snow	204 acres

Recco detectors used

TOURIST OFFICE

Postcode CO 81435
t +1 (970) 728 3041
f 728 6475
skitelluride@telski.com
www.telski.com

High-mileage piste-bashers will find Telluride's mountain rather small, but it has something for everyone (not least for experts) and it's growing. We have great affection for the place – the dramatic San Juan mountains set the resort apart from others in the Rockies, and the town has lots of character.

THE RESORT

Telluride is an isolated resort in south-west Colorado. The town first boomed when gold was found – some say its name is a shortened version of 'To hell you ride', but in fact it's more probably due to the presence of tellurium in the rock. Now it looks like a typical small Wild West town from the movies – except that the main street is busy with pickup trucks, not horses. The slopes and lifts start right on the edge of town. Up on the slopes, Mountain Village is a model American leisure resort with modern buildings, including The Peaks, a huge hotel. A free gondola (running through the evening as well as in daytime) links the two.

THE MOUNTAINS

The **slopes** feature some fearsomely steep terrain, and also ideal beginner and intermediate areas; it's quantity that's lacking, not quality.

Three chair-lifts serve the steep wooded slopes directly above the town, and give access to the bowl beyond it. This has steep slopes at the top (some reached by hiking from the top lift towards Gold Hill), intermediate slopes in the middle and gentle beginner terrain at the bottom, below Mountain Village. The world's longest fast quad chair serves the long, easy runs of a separate mountain.

Snowboarders have one of the best fun-parks in the south-west of the US.

Snow reliability is good. Telluride has a high average snowfall and lots of well-placed snowmaking.

The double-black bump runs directly above the town made the area's reputation for **experts** – 960m of vertical. There are also great, steep gladed runs at the top of the main bowl, some served by Lift 6, others involving hiking.

The **intermediate** runs are mainly served by Lift 4 from Mountain Village and Lift 5 slightly higher up. It's nicely varied terrain, but there's not a lot of it. From the top of the mountain, there are some glorious scenic cruises. There is one easy way back to town – the winding blue Telluride Trail.

There are ideal **beginner** runs in the Meadows below Mountain Village, and splendid long greens and blues served by the long, fast Lift 10 chair.

The scenic beauty of the area makes it splendid for **cross-country** – the Telluride Nordic Center runs over 40km of trails, plus various adventure trips.

Queues are rarely a problem – there are no weekend crowds, and the lift system in increasingly impressive.

Up to now the **mountain restaurants** have been fairly primitive and entirely self-service affairs. Gorrono Ranch, just above Mountain Village, has a big outside terrace with a barbecue, and a separate bar in an old cabin. But Club St Sophia will change all this (see left).

As well as the usual, **ski schools** offer special mogul tuition and free mountain orientation tours daily.

There is thorough provision for **children**. The Adventure Club provides indoor and outdoor play before and after lessons.

STAYING THERE

The resort is offered by only a few US specialist operators. Thanks to the gondola link between the town and Mountain Village, it doesn't much matter where your **accommodation** is. Most hotels are in the town, but the biggest, plushest and priciest is The Peaks in Mountain Village. The New Sheridan is one of the town's oldest hotels. Skyline Guest Ranch is a lovely old house with excellent food, a few minutes' drive from Mountain Village.

There are also plenty of self-catering condos and houses to rent.

There is a cosmopolitan choice of **eating out**, from French to Tex-Mex. Harmon's is one of the best. There's a lively bar-based **après-ski** scene too. Leimgruber's is popular in the early evening, but closes early. Several other bars are lively into the early hours. There's quite a lot to do **off the slopes**.

Vail-Beaver Creek 2500m

Luxury living and the US's biggest and ever-improving area

WHAT IT COSTS

6

HOW IT RATES

The slopes

Snow	*****
Extent	****
Experts	****
Intermediates	*****
Beginners	*****
Convenience	***
Queues	***
Restaurants	**

The rest

Scenery	***
Resort charm	****
Off-slope	***

- ➕ Biggest area in the US – great for confident intermediates
- ➕ Vail's Back Bowls are a big area of treeless terrain – unusual in the US
- ➕ Fabulous new area of ungroomed, tree-lined slopes opened last season
- ➕ Beaver Creek's slopes are blissfully quiet and very varied
- ➕ Largely traffic-free resort villages, with great bus service
- ➕ Lively après-ski for a US resort

- ➖ Vail's slopes can be crowded by American standards, with lift queues even in low season
- ➖ The famous Back Bowls may be closed in early season
- ➖ Tirolean-style Vail Village and exclusive Beaver Creek are far from the Wild West atmosphere you might look for on a trip to the US
- ➖ Expensive, especially Beaver Creek
- ➖ Disappointing mountain restaurants

Blue Sky Basin, Vail's controversial new area of mostly ungroomed slopes with skiing and riding through the trees, opened ahead of schedule last season – after protests and sabotage by environmentalists. We loved it when we skied it last March and it has transformed Vail's attraction for good skiers and riders.

Vail mountain alone is the biggest in the US. And when you add on nearby Beaver Creek, Bachelor Gulch and Arrowhead, owned by the same company, it offers a huge amount of terrain. The resorts cultivate an exclusive image – and accommodation and eating out can be pricey. But what matters more to our enthusiastic reporters is the resorts' convenience, civilised atmosphere and great snow. Most of the terrain is ideal for novices and intermediates. Experts will also find runs to interest them in Vail's largely ungroomed Back Bowls and Blue Sky Basin and on the mogul fields of Beaver Creek. While Vail is busy and bustling, Beaver Creek is a haven of peace – both on and off the slopes.

We always enjoy visiting Vail and Beaver Creek, despite the lack of a Wild West atmosphere that you get in other US resorts based on old mining or cowboy towns. Vail and Beaver Creek are more Walt Disney than John Wayne.

boarding *This slick pair of resorts are wooing boarders with excellent facilities and a positive attitude – there's even a special snowboard trail map showing which runs free-riders and free-stylers should head for. With beautifully groomed, gentle slopes and lots of high-speed chairs, these are great areas for beginners, but there's plenty of terrain for experts too. Both resorts have fun-parks with half-pipes including the new Chaos Canyon adventure zone which opened last season. There are specialist board shops in both villages and good tuition. Vail has livelier bars and nightlife than Beaver Creek.*

What's new

The big news for the 1999/2000 season was the opening of 520 acres of largely ungroomed terrain in the new Blue Sky Basin area, a season ahead of schedule. This was served by two new high-speed quads. See feature box later in this chapter.

The 2000/01 season will see another high-speed quad and another 125 acres of terrain open in Blue Sky Basin.

Two Elk restaurant, which had been burned down by people who had environmental objections to the new development, was rebuilt and reopened for the 1999/2000 season.

In Beaver Creek, 100 acres of new gladed terrain, new children's trails and new terrain parks were opened.

The resort

Standing in the centre of Vail Village, surrounded by chalet-style buildings and bierkellers, you could be forgiven for thinking you were in a top Austrian resort. And that's just what Vail's founder, Pete Seibert, intended back in the 1950s. But Vail Village is now just part of an enormous resort, stretching for miles along the valley – most of it in anonymous modern style.

Beaver Creek, developed by the owners of Vail in the 1980s, is ten miles to the west. It is unashamedly exclusive, with a choice of top-quality hotels and condos right by the slopes. It centres on a large pedestrian square featuring escalators to the slopes, exclusive shops, exquisite bronze statues and an open-air ice rink. Arrowhead is linked to Beaver Creek and is a secluded area of luxurious chalets.

MOUNTAIN FACTS

Beaver Creek

Altitude	2255m-3490m
Lifts	13
Pistes	1625 acres
Green	34%
Blue	39%
Black	27%
Art. snow	580 acres

Vail

Altitude	2475m-3525m
Lifts	33
Pistes	5289 acres
Green	18%
Blue	29%
Black	53%
Art. snow	380 acres

Recco detectors used

The mountains

Even leaving aside Beaver Creek, Vail has the biggest area of slopes in the US, with immaculately groomed trails and ungroomed powder skiing in open bowls and among the trees. And Beaver Creek, Bachelor Gulch and Arrowhead offer the nearest thing you'll find in the US to the linked lift networks of the Alps. There isn't the sheer extent of terrain that you find in the biggest Alpine areas – but with the addition of Blue Sky Basin, it's not far off.

There are runs to suit every taste, from beginner or nervous intermediate to powderhounds and mogul freaks. The resort stands out for our reporters' enthusiasm for it. The main criticism is that some of the runs (especially black diamonds) are overgraded. And while Vail's slopes can be crowded by US standards, Beaver Creek and Blue Sky Basin are delightfully deserted. Vail's slopes are patrolled by yellow-jacketed 'speed patrollers' who stop slope users skiing or riding recklessly quickly.

The Vail and Beaver Creek areas are completely separate but linked by bus and covered on the same lift pass. They also feel very different. Beaver Creek is inexplicably overlooked by many people staying in Vail. They're making a big mistake, in our view.

Both areas have 'new technology centers' at mid-mountain where you can test the latest equipment.

THE SLOPES
Something for everyone

The slopes above **Vail** can be accessed via three main lifts. From right next to Vail Village, the Vista Bahn fast chair goes up to the major mid-mountain focal point, Mid-Vail (3095m); from Lionshead, the Eagle Bahn gondola goes up to the Eagle's Nest complex (3155m); and from the Golden Peak base area just to the east of Vail Village, the Riva Bahn fast chair goes up towards the Two Elk area.

The front face of the mountain is largely north-facing, with well-groomed trails cut through the trees. At altitude the mountainside divides into three bowls – Mid-Vail in the centre, with Game Creek to the south-west and Northeast Bowl to the, er, north-east. Lifts reach the ridge at three points, the highest at 3430m, all giving access to the **Back Bowls** (mostly ungroomed and treeless) and through them to the new **Blue Sky Basin** area (mostly ungroomed and with skiing and riding through the trees).

The slopes immediately above **Beaver Creek** (where the men's downhill and super giant slalom were held in the 1999 World Championship) divide into two sectors, each accessed by a fast quad chair. The major sector is centred on Spruce Saddle, with lifts above it reaching 3485m. The other is lower and smaller and forms the link with **Bachelor Gulch** and **Arrowhead**. Up the valley a little, and between these two sectors, is Grouse Mountain, with seriously steep slopes. British

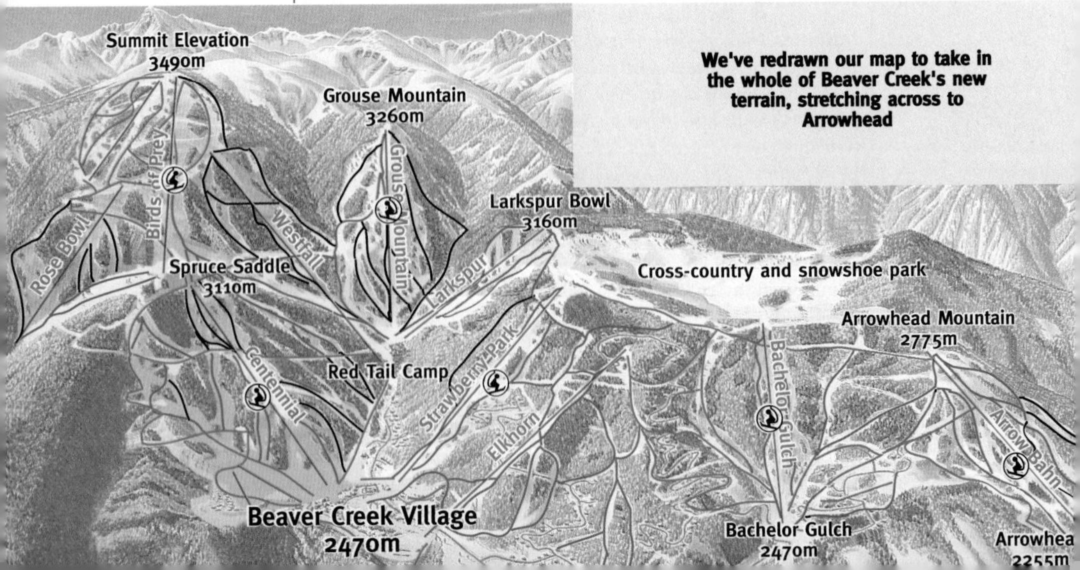

We've redrawn our map to take in the whole of Beaver Creek's new terrain, stretching across to Arrowhead

guests can ski the Beaver Creek area once a week with Martin Bell, formerly Britain's best-ever downhiller, now UK Ski Ambassador to Vail Resorts and a charming guy.

Other resorts within a two-hour drive include Breckenridge and Keystone (both owned by Vail Resorts and covered by multi-day lift passes), Aspen, Steamboat and Copper.

SNOW RELIABILITY

Excellent, except in the Bowls

As well as an exceptional natural snow record, Vail and Beaver Creek both have extensive snowmaking facilities, normally needed only in early season. Although snow in the Back Bowls is often poor because of its largely south-facing aspect, Blue Sky Basin is largely north-facing and sheltered from sun by

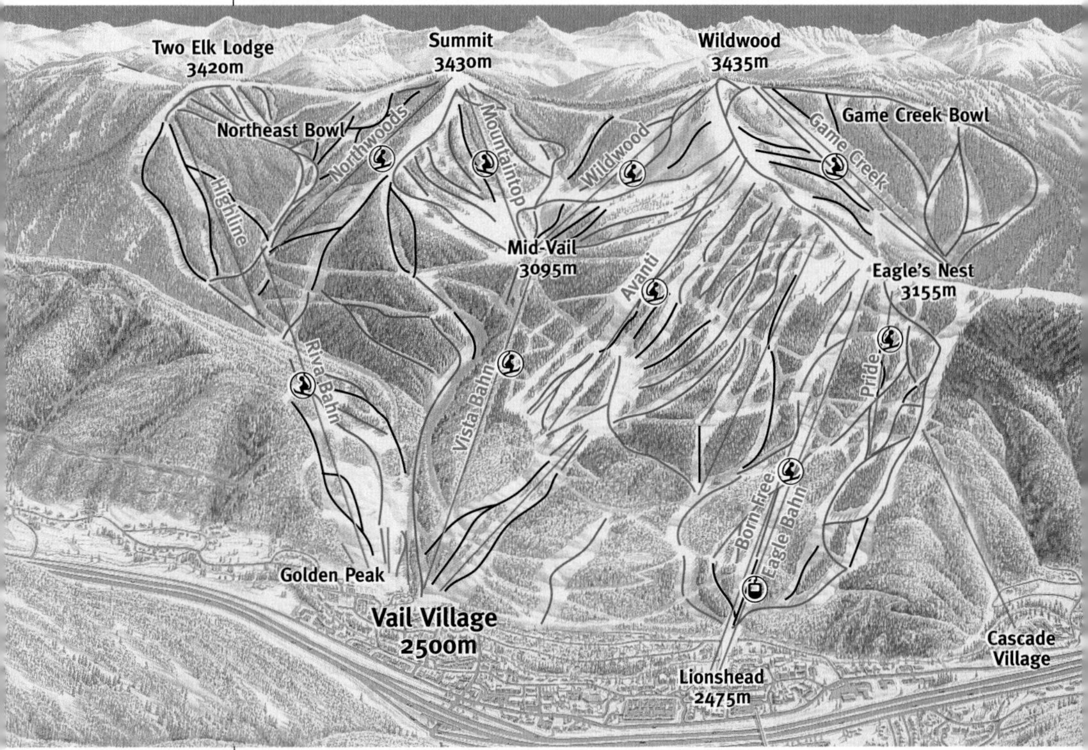

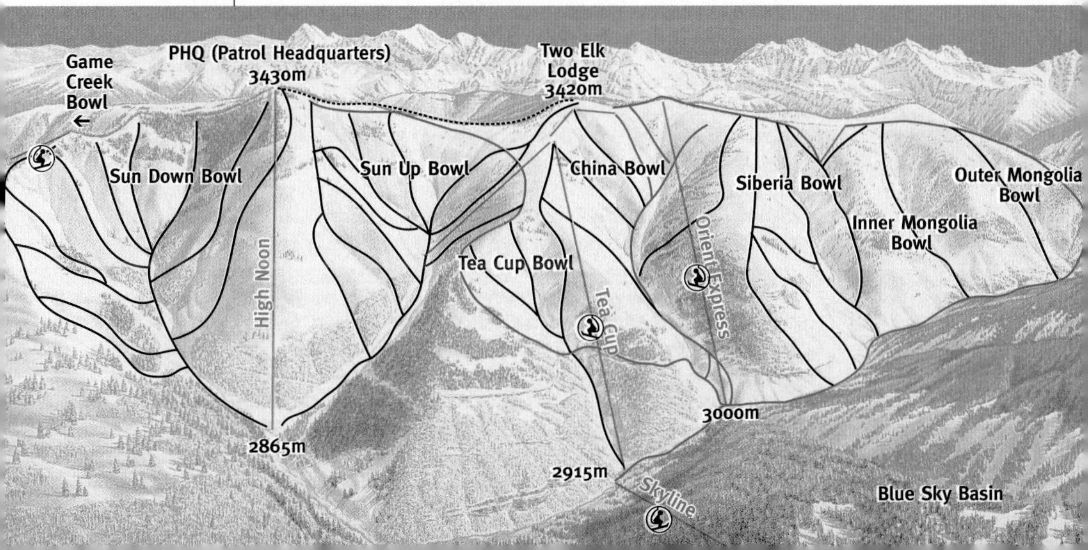

LIFT PASSES

1999/2000 prices in dollars

Vail and Beaver Creek
Covers all Vail and Beaver Creek lifts, and ski-bus around resort. Multi-day passes also cover Breckenridge, Keystone and Arapahoe Basin.

Beginners 1 day 95 for learn-to-ski course including lift pass

Main pass
1-day pass 59 to 61
6-day pass 330 to 342

Senior citizens
Over 65: 6-day pass 312
Over 70: free pass

Children
Under 13: 1-day pass 37

Short-term passes
Return trips on some lifts for foot passengers only. Half-day pass from noon available.

Notes
If you buy a lift pass in advance through certain UK tour operators, a 6-day adult pass for 2000/01 will cost 210.

trees – so the snow quality can be expected to be excellent, with powder lasting for days after the latest fall. The Grouse Mountain slopes in Beaver Creek can suffer from thin snow cover (some locals call it Gravel Mountain).

FOR EXPERTS

Transformed by Blue Sky Basin

Vail's Back Bowls are vast areas, served by three chair-lifts and a couple of short drag-lifts. You can go virtually anywhere you like in their 2734 acres, trying the gradient and terrain of your choice. There are interesting tree-lined areas as well as the more common tree-free mogulled slopes. But the Bowls are not particularly steep, and they have disappointed some of our more dare-devil correspondents. But Blue Sky Basin, which opened last season, has some great adventurous runs in the trees – see below.

On the front face there are some genuinely steep double-black-diamond runs which usually have great snow; they are often mogulled but sometimes groomed to make wonderful fast cruising. The Highline lift on the extreme east of the area serves three. And Prima Cornice, served by the Northwoods Express is one of the steepest runs on the front side.

If the snow is good, try the backcountry Minturn Mile – you leave the ski area through a gate in the Game Creek area for a European-style off-piste run starting with a powder bowl and finishing on a path by a river – ending up in the atmospheric Saloon (see Après-ski).

Beaver Creek probably has more intimidatingly steep double-diamond runs than Vail. In the Birds of Prey area and Grouse Mountain areas most runs are long, steep and mogulled from top to bottom. The Larkspur Bowl area has three short steep mogul runs.

Beaver Creek is a great place to ski fast on perfectly groomed trails, thanks to the lack of crowds. Even by American standards, Beaver Creek's runs are often deserted.

FOR INTERMEDIATES

Ideal territory

The majority of Vail's front face is great intermediate territory, with easy cruising runs. On the western side of the area, especially, there are excellent long, relatively quiet blues – Born Free and Simba both go from top to bottom. Game Creek Bowl, nearby, is excellent too.

As well as tackling some of the easier front-face blacks, intermediates will find plenty of interest in the Back Bowls. Some runs are groomed, making it easy for groups of mixed ability to take different routes and ride the lifts together. Several of the runs are graded blue, including Silk Road which loops around the eastern edge of the domain, with wonderful views. More adventurous intermediates can branch out to try some of the unpisted slopes, many of which can make the ideal introduction to powder. They will also enjoy Blue Sky Basin – choose the more open runs to start with.

Beaver Creek is an intermediate's dream. There are marvellous long,

BLUE SKY BASIN

This is the biggest new development in any Colorado ski area for years – and the prospect of it caused outrage among environmental groups, some of whom burned down the Two Elk mountain restaurant, the ski patrol HQ and some lift stations in protest. The first 520 acres of it, served by two high-speed quads, opened in January 2000. We skied it in March and loved it. Exclusively for adventurous intermediate and advanced skiers and riders, the area is almost entirely ungroomed and the runs are among the trees – some widely spaced, some very tight. Few of the runs are very steep but are made tricky by having to avoid the trees. The main trails are marked by ribbons hanging off the trees but really it is go-anywhere terrain on snow that will generally be much better and more powdery than in the Back Bowls because of the shelter given by the trees and the generally north-facing aspect. The easiest runs are Cloud 9 in Pete's Bowl (named after Vail's founder Pete Seibert) and The Divide followed by In the Wuides in Earl's Bowl (named after Earl Eaton, who discovered Vail's terrain). The lack of crowds, excellent snow, uncrowded slopes and delightful terrain of Blue Sky Basin have transformed Vail's attraction for good skiers and we can't wait to go back.

SCHOOLS/GUIDES

1999/2000 prices in dollars

Vail and Beaver Creek
At four locations – Vail Village, Lionshead, Golden Peak and Beaver Creek
Classes 7 days
5hr: 9.45-3.45 with 1hr lunch; 3hr 15mins: 12.30-3.45
Vail 1 day: 70 to 80
Beaver Creek 1 day: 85 to 95
Children's classes
Ages: 3 to 14
6½hr day including rental, lift pass, lunch
Vail 1 day: 80 to 90
Beaver Creek 1 day: 86 to 96
Private lessons
1hr, 2hr, half- and full-day
1hr: 110, for 1 to 6 people
half-day: 295, for 1 to 6 people

CHILDCARE

School tuition is based at Children's Ski Centers located at Golden Peak and Lionshead in Vail, and at Beaver Creek resort. There are separate programmes to suit children of different ages and competence – Mini-Mice for children aged 3, Mogul Mice and Superstars for those aged 4 to 6.

Small World Play Schools, located at Golden Peak in Vail and at Beaver Creek, provide day care for children aged 2 months to 6 years, from 8am to 4.30.

quiet, cruising blues almost everywhere you look, including top to bottom runs with a vertical drop of just over 1000m. The Larkspur chair and the chairs going west from the village serve further cruising runs – and lead to yet more ideal terrain served by the Bachelor Gulch and Arrowhead fast chairs.

FOR BEGINNERS
Difficult to beat

There are excellent nursery slopes at both Vail and Beaver Creek, at resort level and at altitude. And there are plenty of easy longer runs to progress to, including runs from top to bottom of the mountains.

FOR CROSS-COUNTRY
Some of the best

Vail's cross-country areas are at the foot of Golden Peak and at the Nordic Center on the golf course. At Beaver Creek there's a splendid, extensive, mountain-top network of tracks at McCoy Park, reached via the Strawberry Park lift from the resort.

QUEUES
Can be bad in Vail

Vail has some of the longest lift queues we've hit in the US, especially at weekends because of the influx from Denver. As usual in the US, they move quickly (rarely exceeding 15 minutes). The worst queues are at Mid-Vail and in the Back Bowls. Beaver Creek, on the other hand, is virtually queue-free – it is amazing that more people don't go there from Vail.

MOUNTAIN RESTAURANTS
Surprisingly poor

Vail's mountain restaurants are not bad by US standards, but for such an up-market resort they are surprisingly poor. The most exclusive place is the members-only Game Creek Club. There are couple of table-service places at Eagle's Nest – it's best to reserve. The self-service places get very crowded, especially Two Elk (the nicest).

At Beaver Creek, Spruce Saddle at mid-mountain is a large, spectacular log and glass building and the main place for lunch. Red Tail Camp does decent barbecues. Rendezvous Bar and Grill in the village at the bottom of the main slope is very civilised with good food. Gundy's Camp at Bachelor Gulch is the locals' favourite. Beano's, Zach's and Allie's Cabins are all beautifully built members-only clubs at lunchtime.

SCHOOLS AND GUIDES
Among the best in the world

The Vail-Beaver Creek school has an excellent reputation. All the reports we've had of it have again been glowing. Class sizes are usually small – as few as four is not uncommon. Having tried three different instructors, we can vouch for the high standard. There are specialist half-day workshops in, for example, bumps and powder and adventure tours of Blue Sky Basin. You can sign up on the mountain.

FACILITIES FOR CHILDREN
Excellent

The comprehensive arrangements for young children look excellent, and we've had good reports on the children's school. At both Vail and Beaver Creek there are splendid children's areas with adventure trails and themed play areas.

Staying there

Vail is vast, with a free and efficient bus-service. The most convenient – and expensive – places to stay are in mock-Tirolean Vail Village near the Vista Bahn fast chair or in functional Lionshead, near the gondola.

But there is a lot of accommodation further out – the cheapest tends to be across the main I-70 freeway, but lacks the real Vail atmosphere.

Beaver Creek can be reached by a shuttle bus from Vail. It is an unashamedly upmarket resort with a fair choice of luxurious, expensive hotels, all within an easy walk of the slopes. Nightlife and choice of bars and restaurants is much more limited.

HOW TO GO
Package or independent

There's a big choice of packages to Vail and a smaller one to Beaver Creek. It's easy to organise your own visit, with regular airport shuttles.
Chalets Vail offers the widest choice of catered chalets in the US, through a wide range of UK tour operators. Many are out of the centre at East Vail or West Vail or across the busy freeway.
Hotels Vail has a fair choice of hotels, ranging from luxurious to budget. In the more upmarket Beaver Creek you can go completely overboard.
At Vail:
((((5) **Vail Cascade** One of the best in town. A resort within a resort – lots of facilities and a chair-lift right outside.

GETTING THERE

Air Eagle, transfer 1hr. Denver, transfer 2½hr.

SNOWPIX.COM / CHRIS GILL

There it is folks – Vail's latest addition in the distance. In our view it transforms the attraction of the resort for good skiers and riders ↓

(((((5) **Sonnenalp Bavaria Haus** Very smart and central. Large spa and splendid piano bar-lounge. The other Sonnenalp place – Swiss Haus – isn't so special.

(((((5) **Lodge at Vail** Owned by Vail Resorts, right by the Vista Bahn in Vail Village. Some standard rooms small. Huge buffet breakfast. Outdoor pool.

(((3) **Vail Village Inn** Condo and hotel complex. Good position. Outdoor pool.

(((3) **Chateau Vail (Holiday Inn)** Not quite as central. Adequate comfort, with a pool.

At Beaver Creek, there are lots of luxury places. To pick just two:

(((((5) **Inn at Beaver Creek** Luxury pad with ski-in/ski-out convenience. Pool.

(((((5) **Hyatt Regency** Much better than your standard Hyatt, with impeccable service. Lively bar.

Self-catering For those who want lots of in-house amenities, the Racquet Club at East Vail is superb. The Mountain Haus has high-quality condos in the centre of town. There are plenty of cheaper options, and several tour operators have allocations conveniently close to the Lionshead gondola.

STAYING UP THE MOUNTAIN

Great if you can afford it

Trappers Cabin above Beaver Creek and Game Creek chalet above Vail are luxurious private enclaves up the mountain, which a group can rent by the night (from $600 each). You ski in at the end of the day to a champagne welcome, soak in an outdoor hot-tub and enjoy a gourmet dinner. The cabin-keeper then leaves, returning in the morning to prepare breakfast.

STAYING ALONG THE VALLEY

Cheaper but quiet

Staying out of central Vail is certainly cheaper but not so lively. If you rent a car, staying out of town and visiting nearby resorts makes for an interesting holiday. East Vail and West Vail both have reasonably priced lodging. Another budget option is to stay in Avon at the foot of the approach road up to Beaver Creek. It's not a very atmospheric town but it does have a number of reasonably priced hotels and motels. The Eagle River Inn in Minturn in 1998 is a stylish B&B.

EATING OUT

Endless choice

Whatever kind of food you want, Vail has it. But most of it is not cheap. 'All restaurants require a fat wallet' and 'high standards but at New York prices' are typical comments from reporters.

Recommended fine-dining options in Vail include the Wildflower, in the Lodge, Ludwig's, in the Sonnenalp Bavaria Haus, the Left Bank and La Tour. The Saddleridge, in Beaver Creek, offers a marvellous night out. It is a luxurious wooden building packed with photos and Wild West artefacts, including old six-shooters and General Custer's hat. The Mirabelle, at the bottom of the access road, is also rather special. The sleigh ride to Beano's Cabin in Beaver Creek makes a good evening out.

For a budget option we liked the Hubcap Brewery in Vail Village, with local ales and filling American food.

Recommendations from readers this year include May Palace (Chinese) in

The north-facing black runs on Vail's front face keep their snow well and are great fun in powdery conditions →

SNOWPIX.COM / CHRIS GILL

ACTIVITIES

Indoor Athletic clubs and spas, massage, museum, cinema, theatre, tennis courts, artificial skating rink, library, galleries

Outdoor Hot-air ballooning, skating, ice hockey, sleigh rides, fishing, mountaineering, snowmobiles, snow-shoe excursions, snowcat tours, dog-sledding, paragliding. Tubing hill, ski biking, sledding at Vail

TOURIST OFFICE

PO Box 7, Vail, CO 81658
t +1 (970) 496 6772
international@vailresorts.com
www.vail.com
www.beavercreek.com

West Vail, Blu's (good value), Los Amigos, Russells and Toscanini (in Beaver Creek).

APRES-SKI

Vail lively, Beaver Creek quiet

In Vail, Trail End Bar at Lionshead is convenient for the end of the day and has live music. Garfinkel's has a DJ and happy hour. The Red Lion in the village centre is popular, with big-screen TVs and huge portions of food. The George tries to be an English-style pub. The Ore House serves 'mean margaritas and very hot chicken wings.'

The Swiss Chalet attempts to recreate European 'gemütlichkeit'; King's Club is the place to go for high-calorie cake, and becomes a piano bar later; Louie's has live jazz; and Los Amigos and the Hubcap Brewery are other lively places at four o'clock.

You can have a good night out at Adventure Ridge at the top of the Eagle Bahn gondola. As well as bars and restaurants, there's ice skating, tubing, snowmobiling, snow-shoeing, snowbiking, and a Communications Center where you can send e-mails, access the Internet or set up a video conference with the office back home.

Later on, Club Chelsea has 80s' disco sounds, Garton's is popular, with a suspended floor that moves with the dancing, the Bully Ranch at the

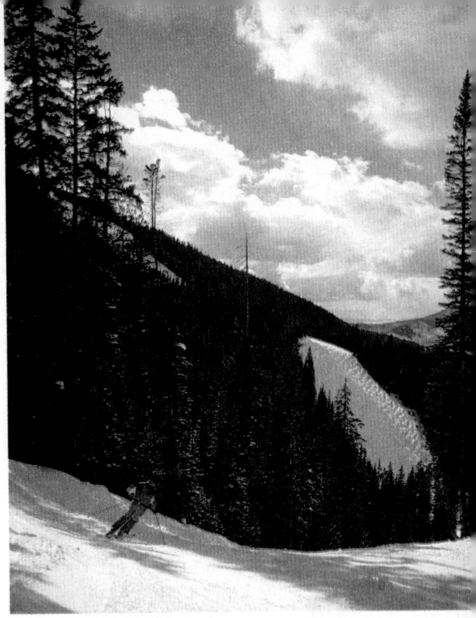

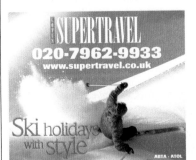

Sonnenalp is famous for its 'mudslide' drinks, Nick's is a snowboard hangout, Vendettas does good pizza and beer.

Out of town in Minturn, the Saloon is worth a trip – genuine old-west style with photos of famous skier patrons on the wall. It serves mean margaritas and large quantities of good-value American and Mexican food.

Beaver Creek has a couple of bars (of which readers liked the Rendezvous best) but is generally fairly quiet.

OFF THE SLOPES

A lot to do

Getting around on the free bus is easy and there are lots of activities to try. Snowshoeing has become very popular and there are some dedicated trails. An early morning balloon ride was highly recommended by a reporter. A trip to the factory outlets at Silverthorne is a must for shopaholics who can't resist bargains from Timberland, Nike, Levi's, Tommy Hilfiger, Fila and the like.

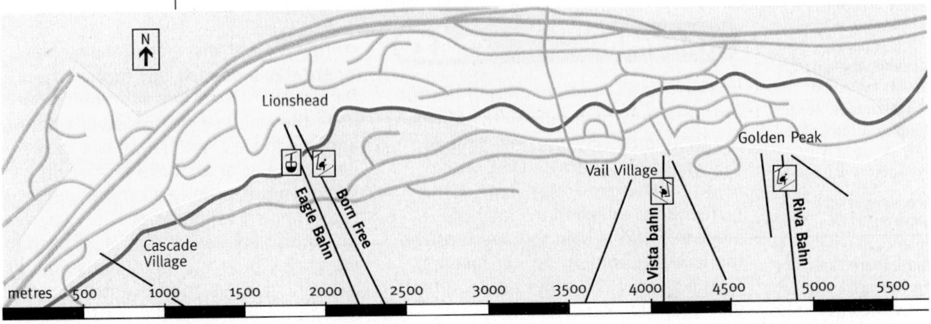

Winter Park 2745m

Colorado's best-kept secret, now becoming better known

WHAT IT COSTS

5

HOW IT RATES

The slopes	
Snow	*****
Extent	***
Experts	****
Intermediates	****
Beginners	*****
Convenience	***
Queues	****
Restaurants	***
The rest	
Scenery	***
Resort charm	**
Off-slope	*

- ➕ The best snowfall record of all Colorado's major resorts
- ➕ Slopes to suit all standards, from superb beginner terrain to countless testing mogul slopes
- ➕ Great expert terrain and great untracked snow at Berthoud Pass
- ➕ Quiet on weekdays, and impressive lift system copes with weekends
- ➕ Leading resort for teaching people with disabilities to ski and ride
- ➕ Good views by US standards
- ➕ Largely free of the inflated prices and glitz you expect in a resort

- ➖ Also largely free of the the range of restaurants and shops you expect in a resort
- ➖ Town is a bus-ride away from the slopes – though there is now the option of staying in the expanding development at the main lift base
- ➖ The nearest big resort to Denver, so can get crowded at weekends – mainly a problem on runs close to the base, and in hire shops

Winter Park was developed to amuse the residents of Denver, only a 90-minute drive away, and still belongs to the city. So we were slightly surprised by what we found when we first visited a few years ago: a mountain (if not a resort) of world class. If variety of shops and restaurants is not important to you, and value for money and snow are more important than glamour, the place should be high up on your Colorado shortlist. Especially now that the development of a new pedestrian village at the foot of the slopes is well under way.

For good skiers and riders, Winter Park's secret weapon is actually another 'resort' a few miles away – Berthoud Pass. It has no lodgings and only two chair-lifts, but they serve large amounts of wild terrain, the snow approaches Utah's exalted standards, and no one goes there. Yet.

boarding *The great boarder facilities on Winter Park Mountain make it a favourite with many riders. The half-pipe, just above Snoasis, is great for both experts and novices. Mad Hatters and The Rolls fun-parks have enough jumps, ramps, winding gullies and tabletops to satisfy any big-air thrill seeker. Special 'Terrain Park Ambassadors' are often available to demonstrate tricks. There is some great advanced and extreme boarding terrain. Winter Park is also an ideal beginner and intermediate boarder area, with excellent terrain for first steps on a board, a good school and a network of lifts that is entirely chairs. Though there's no longer a ride guide to the mountain, signposts indicate the most boarder-friendly routes to take. The bars get crowded and lively at weekends – and boarders tend to hang out at Slade's Underground downtown.*

What's new

Last season the first phase of Winter Park's new slope-side village opened, including the smart Zephyr Mountain Lodge condos. For 2000/01 a total of 11 new shops and restaurants will open.

The slow Eskimo triple chair from Snoasis to the top of Winter Park Mountain was replaced by a fast quad in 1999.

The resort

Winter Park started life around the turn of the century as a railway town, when Rio Grande railway workers climbed the slopes to ski down. One of the resort's mountains, Mary Jane, is named after a legendary 'lady of pleasure' who is said to have received the land as payment for her favours.

The railway still plays an important part in Winter Park's existence, with a station right at the foot of the slopes where trains deposit day trippers from Denver every Saturday and Sunday.

In the last year or two, stylish hotel and condo accommodation has been developed at or near the foot of the slopes, most recently a car-free mini-resort known variously as The Village or Winter Park Resort. But most of the accommodation is a shuttle-bus-ride away in spacious condos dotted around either side of the road through

MOUNTAIN FACTS

Altitude	2740m-3675m
Lifts	22
Pistes	2886 acres
Green	9%
Blue	35%
Black	56%
Art. snow	294 acres

LIFT PASSES

1999/2000 prices in US dollars

Winter Park Resort
Covers all lifts in Winter Park, Mary Jane, Vasquez Ridge, Vasquez Cirque and Parsenn Bowl areas.

Main pass
1-day pass 52
6-day pass 228
(low season 180)

Senior citizens
Over 61: 6-day pass 162
Over 70: free pass

Children
Under 14: 6-day pass 90
Under 6: free pass

Short-term passes
Half-day passes up to or from 12.15 (adult 33)

Alternative periods
Passes of 2 days and over allow one non-skiing day, eg 6-day pass valid for 7 days with one day off. 8- and 9- day passes allow 2 non-skiing days.

Notes Special rates for disabled skiers.

downtown Winter Park – US highway 40, which continues to the nearby town of Fraser. There are also motels, bars and restaurants along the road, and at night Winter Park resembles an established ski resort town – but in the daytime it's clear that the place doesn't amount to much. Confusingly, an area between the mountain and the town is known as Old Town.

Shuttle buses run regularly between the town and the lift base, and the hotels and condos also provide shuttle services. But a car does simplify day trips to Denver or to other resorts – within a two-hour drive are Steamboat, Breckenridge, Copper Mountain, Keystone and Vail, and experts should not miss Berthoud Pass (see p502).

The locals are very friendly and helpful – typical small-town America.

The mountains

Winter Park has a mountain that's big by US standards, and an excellent mix of terrain that suits all standards. 'I would recommend it to anyone visiting Colorado for the first time,' says a reporter, and we're inclined to agree.

THE SLOPES
Interestingly divided

There are five very distinct, but well-linked, areas – each with its own special character. From the main base, a high-speed quad takes you up the original **Winter Park** mountain to the Sunspot restaurant area at 3260m. From there, you can descend in all directions. Runs lead back towards the main base and over to the **Vasquez Ridge** area on the far right. This is served by a high-speed quad which allows you to use that area continuously or get back to the Winter Park mountain. Both areas are mainly beginner and intermediate terrain.

From the top of Winter Park mountain you can get to **Mary Jane** mountain (3415m), which has much tougher runs. Mary Jane is served by six lifts, including four from its own separate base area. From the top you can head up to **Parsenn Bowl** (3675m) via the double Timberline chair, which has intermediate and advanced terrain, above and in the trees. From here, conditions permitting, you can hike for up to half an hour to access the advanced and extreme slopes of **Vasquez Cirque**. A long ski-out takes you to the bottom of Vasquez Ridge and the Pioneer Express lift.

SNOW RELIABILITY
Among Colorado's best

'Copious amounts of beautiful, dry powder,' enthuses a reporter. Winter Park's position, close to the watershed of the Continental Divide, gives it an average yearly snowfall of over 350in – the highest of any major Colorado resort. As a back-up, artificial snowmaking covers a high proportion of the runs on Winter Park mountain.

FOR EXPERTS
Some hair-raising challenges

Mary Jane has some of the steepest mogul fields, chutes and hair-raising challenges in the US. The fearsome runs of Mary Jane's back side are accessed by a control gate off a long black run called Derailer. Hole in the Wall, Awe Chute, Baldy's Chute and

NATIONAL SPORTS CENTER FOR THE DISABLED

If you are able-bodied, the most striking and humbling thing you'll notice as you ride your first chair-lift is the number of people with disabilities hurtling down the mountain faster than many of us could ever hope to. There are blind skiers, skiers with one leg, no legs, paralysis – whatever their problem, they've cracked it.

That's because Winter Park is home to the US National Sports Center for the Disabled (NSCD) – the world's leading centre for teaching skiing and snowboarding to people with disabilities. As well as full-time instructors, there are 1,000 trained volunteers who help in the programme. People are placed with instructors trained to teach people with their particular disability – more than 40 disabilities are specially catered for.

If you are disabled and want to learn to ski or snowboard, there's no better place to go. It's important to book ahead so that a suitable instructor is available. The centre can help with travel and accommodation arrangements:

NSCD, PO Box 36, Winter Park, CO 80482, USA. Tel: 00 1 970 726 1540.

Jeff's Chute are all steep, narrow and bordered by rocks. More manageable are the wider black mogul fields such as Derailer, Long Haul and Brakeman. There are good blue/black runs on Mary Jane's front side and some good challenges on Winter Park Mountain.

When it's open, Vasquez Cirque has excellent ungroomed expert terrain with long views. But to get to the best of it you have to earn your turns with a 20- to 30-minute hike around the cirque, and you don't get much vertical before you hit the forest. One way to explore the area is on the Improvement Center's three-hour Cirque Adventure Tour.

FOR INTERMEDIATES
Choose your challenge
From pretty much wherever you are on Winter Park mountain and Vasquez Ridge you can choose a run to suit your ability. Most are well groomed every night giving you perfect early morning cruising on the famous Colorado 'corduroy' pistes.

For bumps try Mary Jane's front side, where 'the blue/blacks are particularly enjoyable'. Parsenn Bowl has grand views and some gentle cruising pistes as well as more challenging ungroomed terrain. It's an intermediate paradise and an ideal place to try your hand off-piste.

FOR BEGINNERS
The best we've seen
Discovery Park is a 25-acre dedicated area for beginners, reached by a high-speed quad and served by two more chairs. As well as a nursery area and longer green runs, it has an adventure trail through trees and a special terrain park. Once out of the Park, there are easy runs back to base.

FOR CROSS-COUNTRY
Lots of it
There are several different areas, all with generally excellent snow, adding up to well over 200km of groomed trails, as well as backcountry tours.

QUEUES
Rarely a problem
During the week the mountain is generally quiet, though there may be a crowd waiting for the opening of the Zephyr Express from the main base. At weekends the Denver crowds arrive – even then the network of more than twenty lifts (including eight fast quads) makes light work of the crowds.

The Crooked Creek saloon at Fraser, with Winter Park trails in the background. Motto: Eat until it hurts; drink until it feels better →

BYRON HETZLER / WINTER PARK RESORT

CHILDCARE

The ski school runs special classes for children aged 3 to 13 and provides lunch. The Children's Center has a non-skiing programme for children aged 2 months to 5 years. The Children's Center is open 8am to 4pm. Lessons are 10am to 3pm.

SCHOOLS/GUIDES

2000/01 prices in dollars

Intermediate and advanced classes
6 days
2½hr: from 9.30 or 12.45
6 2½hr days: 222

Beginner classes
6 days
2½hr: from 9.30 or 12.45
6 2½hr days: 120

Children's classes
Ages: 3 to 13
6 full days including pass and lunch: 395

Private lessons
1½hr, 3hr or 6hr
100 for 1½hr, for 1 or 2 people

National Sports Center for the Disabled
Special programme for disabled skiers and snowboarders

Private lessons
3hr or 6hr, with pass and special equipment
40 for 3hr; 80 for 6hr

MOUNTAIN RESTAURANTS
Some good facilities

The highlight is the Lodge at Sunspot, at the top of Winter Park mountain. This wood and glass building has a welcoming bar with a roaring log fire, a table-service restaurant and very good self-service. The Club Car at the bottom of Mary Jane is good and Snoasis is self-service – you can order fresh pizza here by phoning from the mountain.

SCHOOLS AND GUIDES
A good reputation

Recent visitors have been 'impressed by the standard of instructors'. There is a comprehensive range of ski and snowboard programmes, including innovative ideas such as Family Private, if different standards want to learn together, and Quick Tips, a 'quick fix' video analysis with suggestions for improvement (only $5).

FACILITIES FOR CHILDREN
Some of the best

The Children's Center at Winter Park base area houses day-care facilities and is the meeting point for children's classes, which have their own areas, including 'magic carpet' lifts. We lack recent reports.

BYRON HETZLER / WINTER PARK RESORT

← The trail map gives a fair idea of how the land really lies →

GETTING THERE

Air Denver, transfer 1½ hr.

Rail Leaves Denver Sat and Sun at 7.15am and returns at 4.15pm. Journey time 2 hr.

ACTIVITIES

Indoor Cinema, swimming pool, roller skating, casino trips, amusement arcade, health club, comedy club, aerobics, racquetball
Outdoor Dog-sledding, sight-seeing flights, snow-shoe excursions, sleigh rides, 'tubing', ice skating, snowmobiling, snowbiking, snowcat tours, ice fishing, visits to hot springs

TOURIST OFFICE

Postcode CO 80482
t +1 (970) 726 5514
f 726 1572
wpinfo@mail.skiwinterpark.com
www.winterparkresort.com

Staying there

Most accommodation is down in town, but the choice at or near the base has improved a lot.

HOW TO GO
Fair choice
Several UK operators offer Winter Park.
Chalets Several operators offer them.
Hotels There are a couple of outstanding hotel/condo complexes.
((((4) **Iron Horse Resort** Slope-side, comfortable; but some way from lifts.
((((4) **Vintage** Closest hotel to lifts (also has some apartments); good facilities.
(((3) **Mountain Lodge** Across the valley from the lifts; pleasant atmosphere, with micro-brewery above the bar.
Self-catering There are a lot of comfortable condo complexes, including the slope-side Zephyr Mountain Lodge, new for 1999/2000.

EATING OUT
A fair choice
There's a fair choice of restaurants. Recent reporters are keen on the long-established Deno's – seafood, steaks etc. Try the Crooked Creek Saloon at Fraser for atmosphere and typical American food (see photo); Smokin' Moe's for ribs; the Divide Grill for pasta, seafood and grills; The Shed for Mexican and Fontenot's for Cajun.

APRES-SKI
If you know where to go ...
It's easy to get the impression that nothing is going on, but all you need is guidance. Start with the Black Diamond Nightlife Tour Map, which also gets you two-for-one drink deals. At close of play, there's action at the Derailer Bar at the main lift base and the Club Car at the bottom of Mary Jane. Later on, try The Slope (in Old Town) for live music and dancing or Adolph's, just across the road. Downtown, Rome on the Range is great for country and western dancing. The Shed can be lively. The Crooked Creek is popular with locals.

OFF THE SLOPES
Mainly the great outdoors
Most of the diversions involve getting about on snow in different ways. Not a spot for self-indulgence.

DON'T PASS ON BERTHOUD PASS

The drive to Winter Park from Denver – unusually for an American resort – involves a winding climb. It takes you to the summit of Berthoud Pass (3450m), where there is a small car park – usually near-empty – and a couple of chair-lifts. Press on over the pass to your destination, right? Wrong. Well, wrong if you press on and don't come back during your stay. And if you like deep untracked snow.

You've heard of heli-skiing and cat-skiing. Well, Berthoud offers something damn-near as good: bus-skiing. The chair-lifts – a triple and a quad – lift you a modest 200m vertical above the pass, but you descend to much lower points on highway 40, where beaten-up buses (with classic 60s pop playing) pick you up.

There are runs of every standard, but in practice this is a mountain for good skiers and riders. The slopes down to the road are steep, and sometimes very steep. The runs back to the summit of the pass are easier, but hardly any of them are groomed, and they can be quite tricky if there is a substantial snowfall. And there often is: Berthoud is on the Continental Divide, and claims for its annual snowfall range from 400in to 500in a year. This is Jackson Hole/Alta territory.

The terrain and the snowfall are two key elements. The third is the lack of people. There is a limit of 400 day passes, and there are about 200 season pass holders. In practice, it's normal to have between 100 and 200 people on the slopes, which cover 1100 acres. That's something in the order of 10 acres each. Enough?

In the base lodge, as well as a ski shop there is the highest pub in North America and a pleasant table-service restaurant – so a day here can be quite a civilised affair. And it won't cost a lot: the price of a day pass is low, and depends on the snow – $34 if there's 4in of fresh powder, $30 if there's no fresh for two days. Winter Park's passes are flexible (eg 5 days out of 6) so it's easy to slot in a day at Berthoud. But you may want to make it more than one.

Utah

'The Greatest Snow on Earth' – that's what Utah claims. (Until recently it made the claim on every car number plate, but it now seems to be targeting broader markets.) It's a debatable claim: the Colorado resorts say that their famous powder is drier, and have figures to prove it. What they can't dispute is that some Utah resorts do get huge dumps of snow – up to twice the amount, over the season, that falls on some big-name Colorado resorts. In any case, by Alpine standards the snow here is wonderful stuff. If you like the steep and deep, the pilgrimage to Utah is one you shouldn't put off much longer.

There are differences in snowfall. The biggest dumps are reserved for Snowbird and Alta, close together in Little Cottonwood Canyon; combined with some super-tough terrain, the snow record of these small resorts makes them the powder capitals of the world. Alta (page 505) is the cult powder skiers' resort, but Snowbird (page 515) is the more established international destination.

Brighton and Solitude in neighbouring Big Cottonwood Canyon get almost as much snow, and have the advantage that the snow doesn't get skied out within hours of opening time. A couple of years back, your editors at last got around to skiing the Utah Interconnect – a day-long off-piste tour from Park City to Snowbird, taking in Brighton and Solitude. It was a memorable day – largely because of the fabulous skiing we had in Solitude. The two resorts don't figure on the international market for the very good reason that they have hardly any accommodation, but they are well worth a visit. Sadly, there is no lift-pass-sharing deal, so to try both in a day would involve a day pass plus an afternoon pass.

Brighton (2670m, vertical 530m, 7 lifts, 64 runs, 850 acres), right at the end of the end of the canyon, gets almost as much snow as Alta and Snowbird – which may help to explain why Utah's first ski-lift was built here, in 1936. There are a lot of trails packed into quite a small area here. Two of the three major lifts – including the area's one fast quad – serve mostly easy-intermediate slopes, but the Great Western slow quad goes over a more testing slope that represents the resort's full vertical of 530m, and the separate Mount Millicent area has some good steep slopes, both in and out of bounds. There are several accommodation options, including the slope-side Brighton Lodge and various cabins and chalets.

Solitude (2435m, vertical 625m, 7 lifts, 63 runs, 1600 acres) gets slightly less snow but covers a much bigger area, even without counting the excellent out-of-bounds terrain that you can get to from the top lift. Basically, the slopes here get steeper as you go up the mountain – except that the area's one fast quad, Eagle, serves a slightly separate ridge that is almost entirely blue in gradient, and starts slightly down the valley from the main base. We haven't yet had a chance to explore the entirely black 400 acres of Honeycomb canyon, reached from the top lift. Accommodation is in one hotel – the 46-room Inn at Solitude – or a small condo development.

The 2002 Winter Olympics will be based in **Salt Lake City**, so you'll be hearing a lot about Utah in the next couple of years. But don't expect to hear much about the resorts of the Cottonwood Canyons: they don't have the infrastructure to cope with Olympic events, and the road to Snowbird and Alta in particular is prone to closure because of avalanche risk.

↑ This is about all there is to Solitude

SNOWPIX.COM / CHRIS GILL

Park City (page 508), the main 'destination' resort of the area, is hosting – in partnership with next-door Deer Valley (page 507) the lion's share of the events. But it's unknown Snowbasin that gets the prestige downhill and super-G events. Snowbasin is a quite extraordinary resort, for which we predict a great future, so we have now given it a proper chapter (page 513). Right now, it has the distinction of being the only resort in these pages with absolutely no visitor beds. You can stay nearby in the sprawling city of Ogden, which is hosting the curling events.

The other Utah resort that gets a bit of international attention – not least because it's owned by Robert Redford – is **Sundance** (1860m, 655m vertical, 4 lifts, 41 runs, 450 acres). It's a small, narrow mountain but the vertical is respectable, the setting beneath Mt Timpanogos is spectacular and there is terrain to suit all standards. The lower mountain is easy-intermediate, served by a quad chair, the upper part steeper: one triple chair serves purely black slopes, the other blue and black trails. Bearclaw's Cabin, at the top of it, is said to be the only mountaintop restaurant in Utah – though it's about to be joined by one at Snowbird. There are beautifully furnished 'cottages' to rent, and grander chalets.

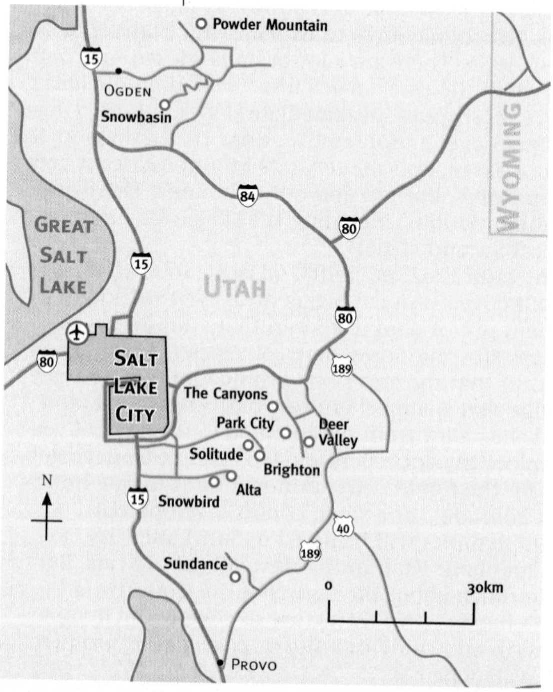

An unusual and interesting holiday exploring the Utah powder can be had by staying in Salt Lake City. The resorts are all within day-trip driving distance, accommodation and car hire are cheap, and the town has the kind of nightlife that only a real American town can offer. What are you waiting for?

Alta 2605m

Cult resort with phenomenal snowfalls

WHAT IT COSTS

6

HOW IT RATES

The slopes

Snow	*****
Extent	*
Experts	*****
Intermediates	***
Beginners	***
Convenience	****
Queues	***
Restaurants	**

The rest

Scenery	****
Resort charm	**
Off-slope	*

What's new

Big news: Alta has a new lift, and it's a detachable – but it's not a fast quad. Last season the Sunnyside lift from Albion Base was upgraded to a mid-speed double.

The Alf Engen ski school now offers combined classes in which parents learn techniques to help their child's skiing progress.

In the pipeline are a new Watson Shelter and some trail modification.

MOUNTAIN FACTS

Altitude	2605m-3245m
Lifts	13
Pistes	2200 acres
Green	25%
Blue	40%
Black	35%
Art. snow	50 acres

Recco detectors used

TOURIST OFFICE

Postcode UT 84092
t +1 (801) 359 1078
f 799 2340
info@altaskiarea.com
www.altaskiarea.com

Alta is famous for remarkable amounts of powder snow arriving with great regularity, for a stubborn refusal to develop or modernise the area and for one of the cheapest lift passes around. The resort is limited but the slopes are classy, and preserved for skiers – snowboarding is banned.

THE RESORT

Alta sits at the craggy head of Little Cottonwood Canyon, 2km beyond Snowbird and less than an hour's drive from downtown Salt Lake City. The peaceful location was once the scene of a bustling and bawdy mining town. The 'new' Alta is a strung-out handful of lodges and parking areas, and nothing more; life revolves around the two separate lift base areas – Albion and Wildcat – linked by a bi-directional rope tow along the flat valley floor.

THE MOUNTAINS

Alta's **slopes** haven't changed much in the last 20 years and are served by mainly slow double and triple chairs. As Alta's mayor explained to us: 'Alta's philosophy is old-fashioned quality. Keeping slow, old chair-lifts means you never have too many people on the slopes, so you have a quality skiing environment.'

The dominant feature of the terrain is the steep end of a ridge that separates the area's two basins. To the left, above Albion Base, the slopes stretch away over easy green terrain towards the black runs of Point Supreme and Devil's Castle; to the right is a more concentrated bowl with blue runs down the middle and blacks either side. These two sectors are linked at altitude, and by a flat rope tow along the valley floor.

The quantity and quality of snow that falls here, and the northerly orientation of the slopes, put Alta right in the top drawer for **snow reliability**.

Small though it is, Alta has cult status among local **experts**, who flock to the high ridges after a fresh snowfall. There are dozens of steep slopes and chutes throughout the area.

Adventurous **intermediates** do pretty well at Alta, too – there's good variety in the runs and the easier blacks offer a gradual progression. Piste-bashers hungry for mileage will find it limited.

Timid intermediates and **beginners** will be happy on the Albion side, where the lower runs are broad, gentle and well groomed.

There's little provision for **cross-country** skiing; but it does go on, and the surrounding backcountry offers adventures for those with guidance.

Queues are not unknown at Alta – the snow record, easy access from Salt Lake City and the slow, old chair-lifts see to that – especially in spring and on sunny weekends. At least the lift company limits the tickets sold.

There's a **mountain restaurant** in each sector of the slopes – Collins Grill on the Wildcat side has civilised table-service – and several places in the valley are open for lunch.

The famous Alf Engen **ski school** naturally specialises in powder lessons – though all the regular classes and clinics are also available. The ski school organises **children's** lessons. Day care for those over 3 months old is available at the Children's Center in the Albion ticket building.

STAYING THERE

There are about a dozen places to stay – simple **hotels and apartments**. None of the hotels is luxurious in US terms. Most get booked up well in advance by repeat visitors. Unusually for America, most lodges (as they call themselves) work on a half-board basis with dinner included. The Alta Lodge is one of Alta's oldest, and feels rather like an over-crowded chalet-hotel in the Alps. Rustler Lodge is more luxurious, with a big outdoor pool, but impersonal. The comfortable, modern Goldminer's Daughter and the basic Peruvian Lodge are cheaper. The former contains the main après-ski congregation bar.

Eating out in Alta is unusual: eating in is the routine. **Après-ski** is in the lodges and rarely goes beyond a few drinks and possibly a sports film. Nor are there many **off-slope alternatives** other than a trip to Salt Lake City.

The Canyons 2075m

Potentially the biggest mountain in the US

WHAT IT COSTS

6

HOW IT RATES

The slopes

Snow	****
Extent	***
Experts	***
Intermediates	***
Beginners	***
Convenience	****
Queues	****
Restaurants	***

The rest

Scenery	***
Resort charm	**
Off-slope	**

What's new

1999/2000 saw the completion of the first stage of the resort village with the opening of the Grand Summit hotel and Sundial Lodge condos. A new four-person chair-lift opened up Peak 5 (300 acres of new terrain), at the southern end of the slopes.

2000/01 sees the opening of an eighth mountain and 300 acres of new terrain, accessed by a new quad chair-lift. More accommodation, restaurants and bars are also being built.

MOUNTAIN FACTS

Altitude	2075m-3045m
Lifts	14
Pistes	3900 acres
Green	14%
Blue	46%
Black	40%
Art. snow	150 acres

Recco detectors used

TOURIST OFFICE

Postcode UT 84098
t +1 435 649 5400
f 649 7374
info@thecanyons.com
www.thecanyons.com

The Canyons is the new kid on the Park City block. Formerly a small locals' area known as Park West and then Wolf Mountain, it was taken over and renamed by the American Skiing Company in 1997. They have ambitious plans to make the slopes the biggest in the US, and have already doubled the area and installed eleven new lifts. They are now building a slope-side resort village. We're keeping a close eye on it, with visits in 1999 and 2000, and so should you.

THE RESORT

When we visited in March 1999 there wasn't a resort – just a muddy car park and building site. On our return in March 2000, the car-free village was really taking shape (see margin). But at present most people will still visit The Canyons from a base in Park City.

THE MOUNTAINS

Red Pine Lodge at the heart of the **slopes** is reached by an eight-person gondola. From here you can move in either direction across a series of ridges – and the valleys between them that give The Canyons its name. These ridges range from Peak 5 and Ninety-Nine-90 (named after its height of 9990ft, or 3045m) to the south to Murdock Peak to the north. 2000/01 sees the opening of an eighth mountain peak, south of Peak 5, as the resort continues to expand south towards Park City. Runs come off both sides of each ridge, meaning that they generally face north or south (see snow reliability below). Most runs finish in the valley floors with some long, relatively flat run-outs. Five of the major lifts are high-speed quads, all put in along with the gondola since 1997. It's a great area to **snowboard** in, with lots of natural hits and half-pipes, Utah's biggest terrain park and half-pipe. Canis Lupis (aka James Bond trail) is a mile-long tight, winding natural gully with high banked walls and numerous obstacles – like riding a bob-sleigh course. For beginners and intermediates there's easy cruising served by chair-lifts. Complimentary mountain tours are offered twice daily.

Snow reliability is not the best in Utah. The Canyons gets as much snow on average as next-door Park City and Deer Valley. But although the north-facing slopes are normally in good condition, the south-facing ones suffer in sunny late-season conditions.

There is steep **expert** terrain all over the mountain. We particularly liked the north-facing runs off Ninety-Nine-90, with steep double-black-diamond runs plunging down through the trees to a pretty but almost flat run-out trail. Go south at the top of the lift and (when the gate is open) you can legally enter the backcountry – with the right kit and guidance, of course. There are lots of groomed blue runs for **intermediates** on all the main sectors except Ninety-Nine-90. Some are quite short, but you can switch from valley to valley easily for added interest, and you can contrive some longer runs. There's a good area just for **beginners** near Red Pine Lodge. But the run you progress to gets very crowded with through-traffic. There are also beginner slopes at the bottom – quieter, but less appealing due to the building work. **Lift queues** don't seem to be a problem.

Of the **mountain restaurants**, the central Red Pine Lodge is a large, new, attractive log-and-glass building with a busy self-service cafeteria and a table-service restaurant. The Lookout Cabin has wonderful views and excellent table-service food and is recommended by recent reporters. Sun Lodge, with sun decks, was new for 1999/2000.

The **ski school** uses the American Skiing Company's Perfect Turn formula, which focuses on an individual's strengths and builds on them (rather than correcting faults). There's day care for **children** from 18 months.

STAYING THERE

At the moment, the luxurious Grand Summit hotel and the Sundial Lodge condos are the only **accommodation** options in the village. The Grand Summit contains several **après-ski** bars and the Cabin **restaurant** serving eclectic American cuisine. Staying in Park City is much more attractive.

Deer Valley 2075m

The ultimate upmarket ski resort

WHAT IT COSTS

6

HOW IT RATES

The slopes

Snow	****
Extent	**
Experts	***
Intermediates	****
Beginners	****
Convenience	****
Queues	****
Restaurants	****

The rest

Scenery	***
Resort charm	***
Off-slope	**

What's new

There's a new family ski area served by a new three-seater chair on Empire Canyon. A fast quad has replaced the old triple chair-lift from the base lodge to Silver Lake Lodge. The Homestake chair from there back to Bald Eagle (and so to the base area) is now a quad.

Snowmaking is being increased for 2000/01, and a new race course and expert trail are planned. A new day lodge at the bottom of the Empire and Ruby lifts will be ready for 2001/02.

MOUNTAIN FACTS

Altitude	2000m-2920m
Lifts	19
Pistes	1750 acres
Green	15%
Blue	50%
Black	35%
Art. snow	500 acres

Recco detectors used

TOURIST OFFICE

Postcode UT 84060
t +1 (435) 649 1000
f 645 6939
marketing@deervalley.com
www.deervalley.com

Deer Valley prides itself on pampering its guests. Free valet ski storage, gourmet dining, immaculately groomed slopes, limits on numbers of skiers on the mountain, no snowboarding. But there's more to it than that – it has some remarkably good slopes, with interesting terrain for all standards.

THE RESORT

Just a mile from the end of Park City's Main Street, Deer Valley is the 'dude' capital of Utah – famed for the care and attention lavished on both slopes and guests. Valets will unload your equipment before you park your car – it's very obviously aimed at people who are used to being pampered and can pay for it. Luxurious private chalets are dotted around the slopes. The hotels and eating places are particularly upmarket.

There is not much of a village to stroll around. There are a few shops, hotels and restaurants at Silver Lake Lodge (mid-mountain but accessible by road) but for any real animation you need to head for Park City's Main Street – easily reached by free buses.

THE MOUNTAINS

The slopes are varied and interesting. Deer Valley's reputation for immaculate grooming is justified, but there is also a lot of exciting tree skiing and some steep mogul runs too. There is a special experts' trail map with a bit of extra information on the chutes, bowls and glades. Snowboarding is banned.

Two high-speed quads take you up to Bald Eagle Mountain, just beyond which is the mid-mountain focus of Silver Lake Lodge. You can ski from here to the isolated Little Baldy Peak, served by a gondola and quad chair-lift, with mainly easy blue and green runs to serve property being developed there. But the main skiing is on three linked mountains above Silver Lake Lodge. From left to right these are Bald Mountain, Flagstaff Mountain and Empire Canyon. Empire was new for 1998/99 and is serviced by a fast quad – the top of which is just a few metres from the runs of the Park City ski area. If you were extravagant enough to buy lift passes for both areas, you could duck the fence and treat them as one.

Snow reliability is excellent, as you'd expect in Utah, and there's plenty of snowmaking back-up too.

Despite its image of pampered luxury there is excellent **expert** terrain on all three main mountains, including fabulous glade skiing as well as defined chutes and open bowl slopes. And because the place doesn't attract many hot-shots the snow doesn't get skied out quickly.

There are lots of groomed blue runs for **intermediates** all over the mountain. It is also good for **beginners** – there are nursery slopes at Silver Lake Lodge as well as the base, and gentle green runs to progress to on all the mountains.

Queues are not something that Deer Valley wants its guests to experience, so it limits the number of lift tickets sold. For **cross-country** facilities, see the Park City chapter.

There are attractive wood-and-glass **mountain restaurants** run by the resort at both Silver Lake Lodge and the base lodge, with free valet ski storage. The food is fine (though pricey) but the self-service crush doesn't fit in with Deer Valley's image. We recommend pampering yourself by eating table-service at the Stein Eriksen Lodge or the Goldener Hirsch.

The **ski school** is doubtless excellent, though we have no reports. Deer Valley's **Children's Center** gives parents complimentary pagers in case their little darlings have a problem.

STAYING THERE

The Stein Eriksen Lodge and Goldener Hirsch at Silver Lake Village are two of the plushest **hotels** in any ski resort – the Stein Eriksen has luxury cabins and a spa built in the grounds. There are many luxury **apartments** to rent.

The Lounge of the Snow Park Lodge at the base area is the main **après-ski** venue, with live music. In the evening there's a choice of gourmet **restaurants** of which the Mariposa is the best. The Seafood Buffet and McHenry's grill are also recommended.

Park City 2105m

An entertaining base for excursions into Utah's deep powder

WHAT IT COSTS

6

HOW IT RATES

The slopes

Snow	****
Extent	***
Experts	****
Intermediates	****
Beginners	****
Convenience	***
Queues	****
Restaurants	**

The rest

Scenery	***
Resort charm	***
Off-slope	***

What's new

Developments for 1999/2000 included the remodelling of the Summit House restaurant, a 'Skiosk' for on-mountain snacks, a new ski/board demo centre at the top of the Bonanza chair and additional glading in McConkey's Bowl and Ski Team Ridge.

In preparation for the 2002 Olympics, a new base lodge – Legacy Lodge – opened in May 2000. The building reflects the area's mining history and houses a food court restaurant and ski and board rental facilities.

An Olympic half-pipe and increased snow-making capacity are other improvements due to be completed during 2000.

- + Increasingly touristy Wild West-style main street, convenient for slopes
- + Lots of bars and restaurants make nonsense of Utah's image as a puritanical Mormon state
- + Well maintained slopes, good snow record, and lots of snowmaking
- + Good lift system including four fast six-packs – more than any other resort in the world
- + Good base for visiting other major Utah resorts – especially Deer Valley next door and The Canyons down the road a few miles

- − Rest of town doesn't have same charm as main street – lots of recent building has created an enormous sprawl (and building continues)
- − The blue and black runs tend to be rather short – most lifts give a vertical of around 400m
- − Although the snowfall record is impressive by normal standards, it comes nowhere near that of Alta and Snowbird, a few miles away
- − Lack of spectacular scenery

You'll be hearing a lot about Park City in the next couple of years. For the 2002 Olympics, it is hosting the giant slalom and the snowboarding events, and next-door Deer Valley is hosting the slalom and freestyle events. The bob-sleigh, luge and Nordic events will take place down the road in the new winter sports park.

For a holiday, Park City has clear attractions, particularly if you ignore its sprawling suburbs and stay near the centre to make the most of the lively bars and restaurants in its beautifully restored and developed main street. But the place really comes into its own as a base for a more wide-ranging holiday taking in other resorts as well. Deer Valley is separated from Park City's slopes by a fence, and by separate ownership with quite different objectives. All that is required to link them is the removal of the fence – a situation that seems bizarre to Europeans. The Canyons isn't quite so close, although at its present rate of expansion it soon will be. Both are excellent mountains, well worth exploring. And then there are the famously powdery resorts of Snowbird and Alta, less than an hour away by bus or car. All four are covered in separate chapters.

SNOWPIX.COM / CHRIS GILL

Any half-competent off-piste skier staying in Park City should look into doing the Interconnect day-tour, via Solitude to Alta and Snowbird (see page 510) →

boarding *Boarding was banned on Park City's slopes until a couple of years ago – and still is on Deer Valley's slopes. But Park City has now fully embraced boarding, with a great fun-park and Olympic standard half-pipe – floodlit at night. It has wonderful free-ride terrain, its higher lifts giving access to some great powder bowls. Beginners have their own excellent area, good easy cruising and a lift system which is entirely chair-lifts. Intermediates have to put up with fairly short cruising runs. The town has plenty of bars to keep you going.*

The resort

Park City is in Utah's Wasatch Mountains, 45 minutes by road from Salt Lake City. It was born with the discovery of silver in 1872. By the turn of the century it boasted a population of 10,000, a red-light district, a Chinese quarter and 27 saloons. Careful restoration has left the town with a splendid historic centre-piece in Main Street. The old wooden sidewalks and clapboard buildings are now filled with a colourful selection of art galleries, shops, boutiques, bars and restaurants – though it is getting rather touristy, with some tacky shops. New buildings have been tastefully designed to blend in smoothly. But away from the centre the resort lacks charm, sprawls over a wide area and is still expanding.

There is a lift up to the slopes from the heart of the town, but the main lift base area is Resort Center, on the fringes with modern buildings and its own bars, restaurants and lodgings.

Deer Valley and The Canyons are almost suburbs of Park City, but all three retain quite separate identities. They are linked by free shuttle-buses, which also go around town. Roads to other Utah ski areas are good.

The mountain

The greater part of the area consists of blue and black trails cut through the trees on the flanks of rounded mountain ridges, with easier runs running along the ridges and the gullies between. The bite in the system is in the lightly wooded bowls and ridges at the top of the resort's slopes. It was only last season that Park City started using double-diamond gradings to identify this terrain as 'experts only'.

THE SLOPES
Bowls above the woods

A fast six-seat chair-lift whisks you up from Resort Center, and another beyond that up to Summit House, the

MOUNTAIN FACTS

Altitude	2100m-3050m
Lifts	14
Pistes	3300 acres
Green	18%
Blue	44%
Black	38%
Art. snow	475 acres
Recco detectors used	

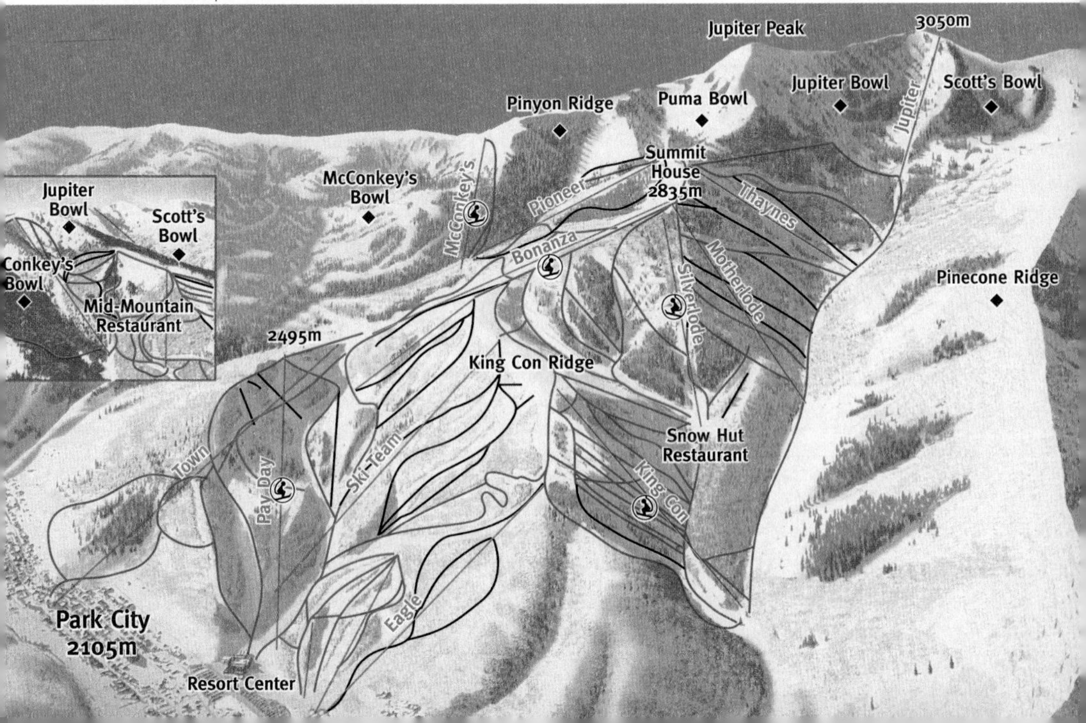

LIFT PASSES

1999/2000 prices in dollars

Park City
Covers all lifts in Park City Mountain Resort, with free ski-bus.

Beginners Beginners' courses (1, 3 or 5 day) includes 1-day free ski pass on First Time Lift.

Main pass
1-day pass 59
6-day pass 282

Senior citizens
Over 65: 1-day 30
Over 70: free pass

Children
Age 7-12: 6-day pass 126
6 and under: free

Short-term passes
Half-day passes from 1pm (adult 42). Night skiing pass 4pm-9pm (22).

Notes All multi-day passes are good for one week, allowing for days off. Reductions for groups and students.

Alternative passes
Multi-area passport is available through UK tour operators.

main mountain restaurant.

Most of the easy and intermediate runs lie between the Summit House and the base area, and spread along the sides of a series of interconnecting ridges. Virtually all the steep terrain is above Summit House in a series of ungroomed bowls, and accessed by the new McConkey's six-pack and the old Jupiter double chair which takes you to a high point of 3050m.

There are a few old wooden mine buildings left dotted around the slopes, which add extra atmosphere. Daily mountain tours of the historical sites are offered free of charge – as are the daily black-diamond tours for advanced skiers.

A floodlit run – the longest in the Rockies – is available until 9pm, together with a floodlit half-pipe.

SNOW RELIABILITY

Not quite the Greatest on Earth

Utah resorts make a lot of fuss about the quality and quantity of their snow. Park City's record doesn't match those of Alta and Snowbird, but an annual average of 350in is still impressive, and ahead of most Colorado figures. And there's artificial backup on about 15 per cent of the terrain.

FOR EXPERTS

Lots for hikers

There is a lot of excellent expert terrain at the top of the lift system. We particularly like the prettily wooded McConkey's Bowl, now served by its own six-pack and offering a range of pitches including gladed terrain. The old Jupiter lift accesses the higher bowls, which include some serious terrain – with narrow couloirs, cliffs and cornices – as well as easier wide-open slopes. The Jupiter bowl runs are accessible directly, but there is a much greater amount of terrain accessible by traversing and hiking – turn left for West Face, Pioneer Ridge and Puma Bowl, right for Scotts Bowl and the vast expanse of Pinecone Ridge, stretching literally for miles down the side of Thaynes Canyon.

Lower down, the side of Summit House ridge, serviced by the Thaynes and Motherlode chairs, has some little-used black runs, plus a few satisfying trails in the trees. There's a zone of steep runs towards town from further round the ridge. And don't miss Blueslip Bowl near Summit House – so called because ski company employees who skied it in the past when it was out of bounds were handed a blue slip which meant they were fired.

Good skiers (no snowboarders, due to some long flat run-outs and hikes) should not miss the Utah Interconnect. For bigger budgets, Park City Powder Guides offer heli-skiing on 20,000 acres of private backcountry land.

FOR INTERMEDIATES

Many better places

There are blue runs served by all the main lifts, apart from Jupiter. The areas around the King Con high-speed quad and Silverlode high-speed six-pack have a dense network of great (but fairly short) cruising runs. There are also more difficult trails close by, for those looking for a challenge.

But the keen intermediate piste-basher who might be happy at Vail, Snowmass or Heavenly won't be so happy here. There are few long, fast cruising runs – most trails are in the

THE UTAH INTERCONNECT

Good skiers should not miss this excellent guided backcountry tour that runs four days a week from Park City to Snowbird. (Three days a week it runs from Snowbird, but only as far as Solitude.) When we did it we got fresh tracks in knee-deep powder practically all day. After a warm-up run to weed out weak skiers, you head up to the top of the Jupiter chair, go through a 'closed' gate in the area boundary and ski down a deserted, prettily wooded valley to Solitude. After taking the lifts to the top of Solitude we did a short traverse, then down more virgin powder towards Brighton. After more powder runs and lunch back in Solitude, it was up the lifts and a 30-minute hike up the Highway to Heaven (see photo, page 508) to north-facing, tree-lined slopes and a great little gulley down into Alta. How much of Alta and Snowbird you get to ski depends on how much time is left.

The price (about $125) includes two guides – one leading, another at the rear – lunch, lift tickets for all five resorts you pass through and transport home.

SCHOOLS/GUIDES

1999/2000 prices in dollars

Park City
Classes 5 days
3hr: 9.30-12.30 or 1pm-4pm; 3 3hr days: 165
Children's classes
Ages: 7 to 12
Half day 65
Full day 83 (incl lunch)
5 consecutive days 365
Private lessons
1hr, 2hr, half- or full-day
95 for 1hr; 230 for half day; additional cost for more than one person

CHILDCARE

The ski school's Kinderschule takes children aged from 3 to 6, from 8.30 to 4.30, mixing tuition with other activities.

There are several different nurseries in the town.

ACTIVITIES

Indoor Park City Racquet Club (4 indoor tennis courts, 2 racquetball courts, heated pool, hot-tub, sauna, gym, aerobics, basketball), Prospector Athletic Club (racquetball courts, weights room, swimming pool, aerobics, spa, massage and physical therapy, whirlpool, sauna), art galleries, concerts, theatre, martial arts studio, bowling
Outdoor Snowmobiles, ballooning, sleigh rides, ski jumping, ice skating, bob-sleigh and luge track, sports and recreation opportunities for disabled children and adults

1km to 2km region and many have long, flat run-outs. The Pioneer and McConkey's chair-lifts are off the main drag and serve some very pleasant, often quiet runs. One reporter complains of too many ungroomed mogul runs, 'leaving a choice of ultra-easy cruising or bump-running, with little in between'.

Intermediates will certainly want to visit The Canyons and Deer Valley for a day or two (see separate chapters) and may be tempted further to try the famous Alta/Snowbird powder.

FOR BEGINNERS
A good chance for fast progress

Novices get started on short lifts and a dedicated beginners' area near the base lodge. The beginners' classes graduate up the hill quite quickly, and there's a good, very gentle and wide 'easiest way down' – the three-and a half-mile Home Run – clearly marked all the way from Summit House. It's easy enough for most beginners to manage after only a few lessons. The Town chair can be ridden down.

FOR CROSS-COUNTRY
Some trails; lots of backcountry

There are prepared trails on both the Park City golf course, next to the downhill area, and the Homestead Resort course, just out of town. They charge $6 to $10 a day for use of their trails. There is also lots of scope for 'backcountry' trips.

QUEUES
Peak period problems only

Lift queues aren't normally a problem with all the high-speed six-seat chairs in the area. But it can get pretty crowded (on some trails as well as the lifts) on busy weekends.

MOUNTAIN RESTAURANTS
Standard self-service stuff

There are three proper restaurants, all of reasonable quality. The Mid-Mountain Lodge is a 19th-century mine building which was heaved up the mountain to its present location near the bottom of Pioneer chair. The food is standard self-service fare. The Summit House is café-style – good for chilli, pizza, soup etc. The Snow Hut is a smaller log building and usually has an outdoor grill. The new skiosk is an on-mountain yurt (a kind of tent) serving snacks, halfway down the Bonanza chair-lift. There's quite a choice of restaurants back at the base area including the food court at the new Legacy Lodge.

SCHOOLS AND GUIDES
Thorough, full of enthusiasm

The school offers programmes such as women's camps, mountain adventure and carving clinics, as well as the usual group and private lessons. The school offers beginners a guarantee: success on your first day or the next lesson is free.

FACILITIES FOR CHILDREN
Well organised; ideal terrain

There are a number of licensed carers who operate either at their own premises or at visitors' lodgings. The ski school deals with children under the umbrella of a separate Kinderschule. Book in advance.

Staying there

If you're not hiring a car, pick a location that's handy for Main Street and either the Town chair or the free shuttle-bus. The bus goes around town and to the Resort Center; it's frequent and runs until late. A trolley-bus runs along Main Street. Regular buses serve Deer Valley and The Canyons. A car would be useful for longer outings.

HOW TO GO
Packaged independence

Park City is the busiest and most atmospheric of the Utah resorts, and a good base for visiting the others.
Hotels There's a wide variety, from typical chains to individual little B&Bs.
((((4 **Silver King** Deluxe hotel/condo complex at base of the slopes, with indoor-outdoor pool.
((((4 **Radisson Inn Park City** Excellent rooms and indoor-outdoor pool, but poorly placed for nightlife (out of town and on main road).
((((4 **Yarrow** Recently renovated with big welcoming lobby, outdoor pool and hot-tub. Free shuttle to slopes.
((((4 **Washington School Inn** 'Absolutely excellent' historic inn in a great location near Main street, with free wine and snacks creating a thriving après-ski social scene.
(((3 **Best Western Landmark Inn** Way out of town near The Canyons and factory outlet mall. Free bus to slopes.
(((3 **Old Miners' Lodge** A 100-year-old building next to the Town lift, restored and furnished with antiques.

GETTING THERE

Air Salt Lake City, transfer ½hr.

TOURIST OFFICE

Postcode UT 84060
t +1 (435) 649 8111
f 647 5374
info@pcski.com
www.parkcitymountain.com

(2) **Chateau Apres Lodge** Close to the slopes: comfortable, faded, cheap.
(2) **1904 Imperial Inn** Quaint B&B at the top of Main Street.
Self-catering There's a big range available. The Townlift studios near Main Street and Park Avenue condos are both modern and comfortable and the latter have outdoor pool and hot-tubs. Silver Cliff Village is adjacent to the slopes and has spacious units and access to the facilities of the Silver King Hotel. Blue Church Lodge is a well-converted 19th-century Mormon church with luxury condos and rooms.

EATING OUT
Book in advance

There are over 100 restaurants to suit all tastes and pockets. But they all get busy, so book in advance. Zoom is the old Union Pacific train depot, now a trendy restaurant owned by Robert Redford. The Riverhorse is in a beautiful, high-ceilinged first-floor room with live music. Chimayo has great south-west cuisine. The Juniper at the Snowed Inn has won awards. Chez Betty is small, sophisticated and has perhaps the best food in town – pricey though. Cheaper places include the Claimjumper and the US Prime Steakhouse ('best steak ever'), Cisero's and Grappa (Italian), Jambalaya (Cajun), Wasatch Brew Pub (good value), Baja Cantina (Mexican).

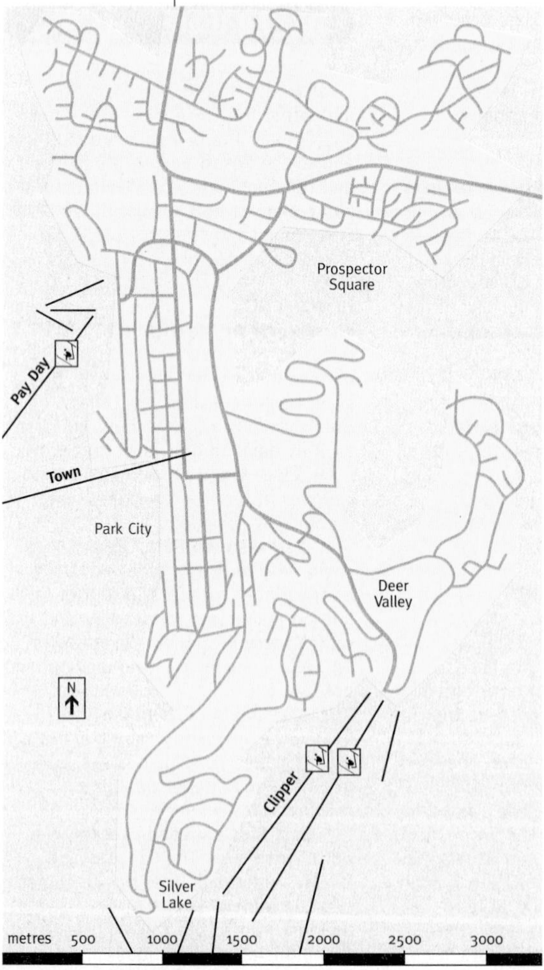

APRES-SKI
Better than you might think

Although there are still some arcane liquor laws in Utah, provided you're over-21 and have your ID handy the laws are never a serious barrier to getting a drink. At the bars and clubs that are more dedicated to drinking (ie don't feature food but do serve spirits) membership of some kind is required. This may involve handing over $5 to cover two weeks' membership – one member can then introduce numerous 'guests' – or else there'll be some old guy at the bar already organised to 'sponsor' you (sign you in) for the price of a beer.

As the slopes close the Pig Pen in the new lodge is the place to head for at the Resort Center – but you can of course make directly for Main Street. The Wasatch Brew Pub makes its own ale and has a good supper menu. The Claimjumper, JB Mulligans and the scruffy Alamo are lively places and there's usually live music and dancing at weekends. Harry O's and Cisero's nightclub are good too.

OFF THE SLOPES
Should be interesting

There's a factory outlet mall near The Canyons, and you can go on a silver mine tour locally. Scenic balloon flights and excursions to Nevada for gambling are both popular. Snowmobiling is big. In January there's Robert Redford's Sundance Film Festival.

There are lots of shops and galleries in town, and the museum and old jail house are worth a visit. Salt Lake City has some good concerts and shopping and a few points of interest, many connected with its Mormon heritage.

You might like to learn to ski-jump at the Utah Winter Sports Park down the road, and you can have a go on the Olympic bob track for a small fee.

Snowbasin 1785m

Coming shortly to a screen near you

WHAT IT COSTS

5

HOW IT RATES

The slopes

Snow	*****
Extent	***
Experts	****
Intermediates	****
Beginners	**
Convenience	*
Queues	*****
Restaurants	*

The rest

Scenery	****
Resort charm	**
Off-slope	*

What's new

A big snowmaking system was installed in 1999, with over 520 guns covering 580 acres, which immediately puts Snowbasin alongside Sun Valley as having one of America's biggest installations. An advanced remote-control avalanche detonation system was installed.

By January 2001 the new base lodge buildings will be complete, with bars and restaurants seating 550 people.

By the time of the Olympics in 2002, there will be two fair-sized mountain lodges, at the top of the two gondolas.

Snowbasin? You haven't heard of it – but you will by 2002. The four Olympic downhill events (men's and women's downhills, plus the downhill elements of the combined) and the two super giant slaloms are to be held here. It's a great hill, and it gets great snow (usually). All it needs is a great village.

THE RESORT

There is no resort, in the European sense of a village with accommodation. There will be one day: the mountain is in the same ownership as Sun Valley, and big investment in hotels and other accommodation is expected over the next few years. But for now you have to stay elsewhere. One choice is Ogden, the nearby city that is hosting the curling events, and drive up to the slopes. Ogden has an up-and-coming 'historic district' as well as the usual car-oriented urban sprawl. It's also possible to stay nearer the mountain in (or close to) Huntsville – a spacious backwater town beside a reservoir on the floor of a high basin, surrounded by mountains. But we guess most people will make the trip here from Salt Lake City, which from October 2000 when a new highway is completed will be only 40 miles away.

THE MOUNTAINS

Snowbasin's **slopes** (shown over the page) are impressive. This is not one of those Olympic hills that make a good race course but a lousy basis for a holiday. There is a lot of terrain, it is pleasantly varied and it is served by nine lifts including a fast quad chair and two gondolas, all three installed in 1998. And there are other attractions. Not the least is the amazing view from the top across the Great Salt Lake and surrounding plain. Another is the excursion to cutely named Powder Mountain, a few miles away across the other side of the Huntsville basin. This has (as you might hope) a reputation for powder. But it's a simple resort and a not very challenging hill, mainly of interest to locals.

A new base lodge is under construction, and should be complete early in 2001. From the main base, the Middle Bowl gondola goes up to the top of the complex Middle Bowl, which has lots of different slopes and gullies presenting different challenges. The John Paul fast quad chair, on the extreme right, serves great black slopes, on- and off-piste, with just one blue alternative way down. Above it, a small cable-car goes up to Allen's Peak and the start of the downhill race course.

Snowbasin's **snow reliability** is not quite in the Alta league, but at 400in the average snowfall here is way ahead of Vail and the rest. To make sure that the racing is not disrupted, Snowbasin also has a huge snowmaking system.

Given good snow, this is a great mountain for **experts**. All the lifts serve worthwhile terrain – even Strawberry has some severe chutes reached by hiking or traversing from the top, but most of the steep stuff is at the other end of the area. The cable-car serves a short black slope that was mogulled when we were there but will be glass-smooth when it serves as the start of the Olympic downhill race course. The course has been designed by Bernhard Russi – who else? It drops 844 metres and is already claimed to be a modern classic. The parts of it that were open when we visited in 1999 were certainly impressive. Between the race course and the area boundary is a splendid area of off-piste wooded glades and gullies. This is where most good skiers and riders will want to spend their time, riding the fast John Paul chair.

It's also a good mountain for **intermediates**, particularly those keen to tackle deep snow when it arrives. Strawberry accesses mainly long open blue runs but also leads to a lightly wooded steeper slope at the extremity of the area. Middle Bowl is great terrain for the adventurous.

A place like this can't seriously be recommended for **beginners** from afar, but there is a nursery slope, and longer green runs for progression.

We saw no evidence of **cross-country** skiing trails.

Given the lift system, we can't see any **queues** arising for some years.

MOUNTAIN FACTS

Altitude	1785m-2675m
Lifts	9
Pistes	3200 acres
Green	13%
Blue	49%
Black	38%
Art. snow	580 acres
Recco detectors used	

There are no **mountain restaurants** yet, but there will be soon – see What's New.

There is a **ski school** doing private and group lessons, and the new base buildings now under construction will include special facilities for **children**.

STAYING THERE

Ogden has various standard-issue **hotels** and motels, including a couple of all-suite places, a Holiday Inn and a huge Marriott.

Huntsville has a small hotel, the Jackson Fork Inn, and a couple of small B&Bs – the Heritage Inn and the Valley House Inn. The 'town' has Utah's oldest tavern (opened 1879), the Shooting Star – a splendidly authentic, scruffy relic of times past. On the walls are not only a stuffed moose and an elk but a stuffed St Bernard dog – apparently a beast of record-breaking enormity. The place is equally famous for its offensively huge Starburgers, which come with sausage as well as multiple burger patties etc. Nearby, for something of a contrast, is Holy Trinity Abbey, a Cistercian monastery selling stoneground bread and honey.

TOURIST OFFICE

Postcode UT 84317
t +1 (801) 399 1135
f 399 1138
info@snowbasin.com
www.snowbasin.com

SNOWPIX.COM / CHRIS GILL

A short hike from the lifts gives access to some seriously steep chutes →

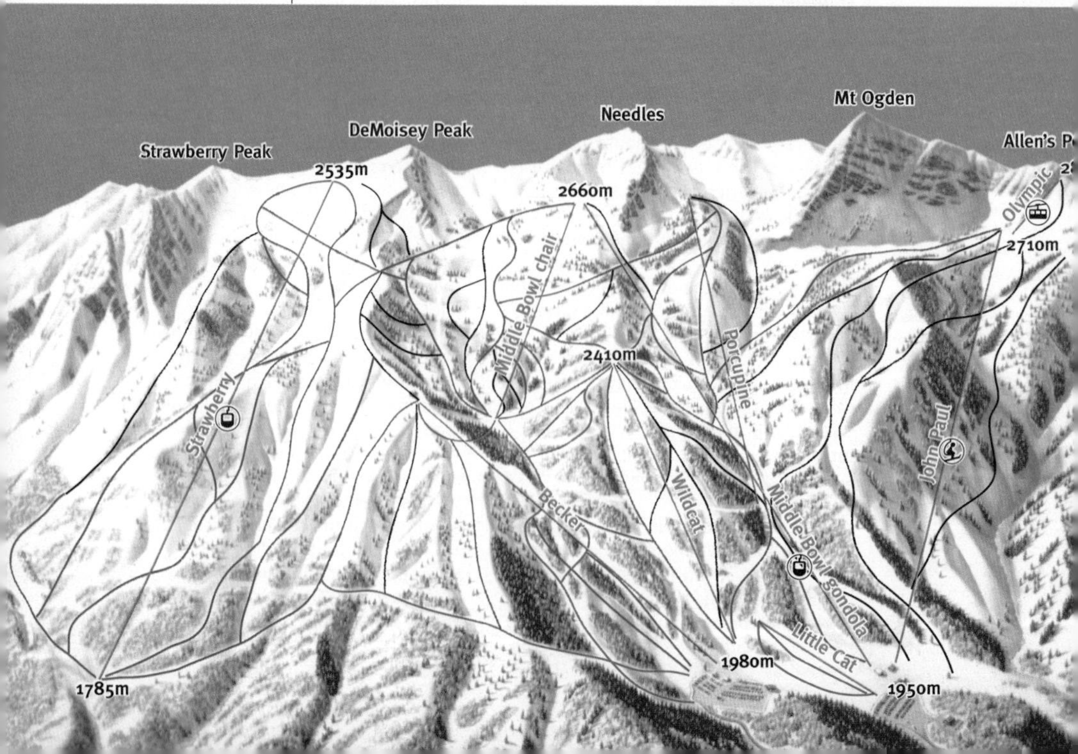

Snowbird 2470m

Alta-style snow, with city-style lodgings

WHAT IT COSTS

6

HOW IT RATES

The slopes

Snow	*****
Extent	*
Experts	*****
Intermediates	***
Beginners	**
Convenience	*****
Queues	**
Restaurants	*

The rest

Scenery	***
Resort charm	*
Off-slope	*

What's new

For the 1999/2000 season a new fast quad chair-lift in Mineral Basin on the back of the mountain opened up 500 acres of terrain previously served by snowcat tours. This is the first stage of a five-year expansion plan that includes another lift in Mineral Basin, which would allow for a link to Alta, the upgrading of the Little Cloud lift to a high-speed quad, more snowmaking and a restaurant and shop at the top of the cable-car.

Also new for last season was a new terrain park and half-pipe in Gad Valley.

MOUNTAIN FACTS

Altitude	2410m-3355m
Lifts	10
Pistes	2500 acres
Green	25%
Blue	30%
Black	45%
Art. snow	100 acres
Recco detectors used	

+ Quantity and quality of snow unrivalled except by next-door Alta – and fully justify Utah's reputation
+ Fabulous ski-anywhere slopes, with steep and not-so-steep options, despite its small area
+ Luxurious accommodation with excellent facilities
+ Slopes-at-the-door convenience
+ Access to other Utah resorts (so long as access road open)

− Area is small and particularly limited for those who want to stick to groomed trails
− Tiny, claustrophobic resort
− Uncompromising modern architecture
− Main cable-car generates queues, despite its impressive size
− Snowbird is very prone to avalanches, which can close the road and keep you safely indoors
− Very quiet at night

There can be few places where nature has combined the steep with the deep better than at Snowbird, and even fewer places where there are also lifts to give you access. So despite the notably charmless appearance of the purpose-built 'base village' and the limited extent of the slopes – particularly confining for keen intermediates who are not yet comfortable off-piste – it remains one of the top US locations for hotshots. For visitors from Britain it is the main destination in Little Cottonwood Canyon although Alta is, if anything, more compelling (see separate chapter), and anyone staying in Snowbird will certainly want to explore next door. There is no shared lift pass, but buying passes by the day does not add much to the cost.

boarding *Unlike Alta next door, Snowbird's whole mountain is now open to snowboarders. Ask any Utah boarder where the best place to ride is and you'll get the same answer, 'the Bird's the word'. Competent free-riders will have a wild time in Snowbird's legendary powder and there was a new terrain park and half-pipe for 1999/2000. However, Snowbird's attractions would be wasted on beginners. And the nightlife's deadly dull.*

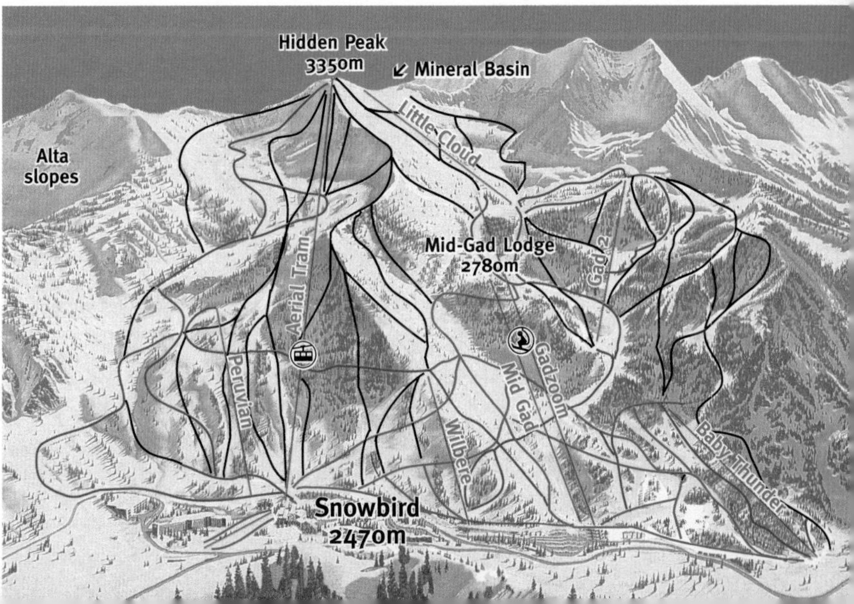

LIFT PASSES

2000/01 prices in dollars

Snowbird
Covers lifts and aerial tram in Snowbird.

Beginners Chickadee chair pass (10 per day).

Main pass
1-day pass 54
6-day pass 282

Senior citizens
Over 65:
1-day pass 41

Children
Under 12: 10 per child per day (up to 2 children per adult)

Short-term passes
Half-day (am or pm) pass available (adult 37)

Alternative passes
Day and half-day passes for chair-lifts only (45 per day for adults, 30 for seniors, free for two children under 12 with an adult)

The resort

Snowbird lies 40km south-east of Salt Lake City in the Wasatch mountains, some 10km up Little Cottonwood Canyon – just before Alta. The setting is rugged and rather Alpine – and both the resort and (particularly) the approach road are prone to avalanches and closure: visitors are sometimes confined indoors for safety. The resort buildings are mainly block-like and dull – but they provide high-quality lodging and are convenient for the slopes.

The resort area and the slopes are spread along the road on the south side of the narrow canyon. The focal Snowbird Center is towards the eastern, up-canyon end; much of the rest consists of car-parking areas.

The mountain

Snowbird's mountain is a small one by Alpine standards, but it manages to pack in runs of all standards.

THE SLOPES
Looming above the resort

The north-facing slopes rear up from the edge of the resort. Five access lifts are ranged along the valley floor, the main one being the 125-person cable-car from Snowbird Center (the Aerial Tram), which takes eight minutes to get up to Hidden Peak at 3350m. The toughest terrain is on the flanks of the ridge beneath the line of the tram. To the west of the tram, in Gad Valley, there are runs ranging from very tough to nice and easy – and six of the nine chair-lifts (all slow doubles, except the Gad 1 fast quad). Mineral Basin, on the back of Hidden Peak, has opened up 500 acres of terrain for all standards.

Free guided tours of the mountain are available twice daily. The First Tracks programme allows you to ride the Tram to the top at 8am so as to be first up on the mountain. Numbers are limited: book ahead.

SNOW RELIABILITY
Exceptional

With Little Cottonwood Canyon's huge snowfalls, with north-facing slopes and all runs above 2400m, snow reliability is very good. Snowbird and Alta typically average about twice the snowfall of most Colorado resorts – and appreciably more than the Park City area.

FOR EXPERTS
Steep and deep – superb

Snowbird was created for and still appeals mainly to experts, with a lot of tough terrain. The trail map is liberally sprinkled with double-black-diamonds, and some of the gulleys off the Cirque ridge – Silver Fox and Great Scott, for example, are exceptionally steep and frequently neck-deep in powder. At the edge of the area, High Baldy is an expert area that leads to an off-piste route over to next-door Alta. Lower down the mountain lurk the bump runs, including Mach Schnell – a great run straight down the fall line through trees. There is some wonderful ski-anywhere terrain in the bowl beneath the high Little Cloud chair, and the Gad 2 lift opens up some attractive tree runs at the western extremity. Mineral Basin has added some more expert terrain – single-diamond runs either side of the new lift, and seriously steep double-diamonds reached by traversing. Backcountry tours are available, and Wasatch Powderbird Guides offer heli-skiing and boarding .

FOR INTERMEDIATES
Quality, not quantity

The winding Chip's Run on the east side of the Cirque ridge provides the only comfortable route down from the top of Hidden Peak for intermediates – at 5km, it's Snowbird's longest run, and enjoys good views towards the top of the canyon. Certain blue and green trails (including Chip's) are designated family runs. For adventurous intermediates wanting to try powder skiing, the bowl below the Little Cloud lift is a must – you'll rarely find better powder than this. There are some testing runs through the trees off the Gad 2 lift. There are also some nice long cruises in Mineral Basin now.

FOR BEGINNERS
Better than you'd expect

Beginners have the Chickadee lift right down in the resort – ideal for getting started – and then there's a small network of suitable trails on the lower slopes of Gad Valley. Big Emma is a lovely, wide, smooth trail.

FOR CROSS-COUNTRY
Go elsewhere

There are no prepared cross-country trails at Snowbird. All-terrain skiers can hike into the backcountry, but for loops you need to go elsewhere.

SCHOOLS/GUIDES

2000/01 prices in dollars

Snowbird
Classes 5 days
Half- (pm only) or full-day
5 5½hr days: 335
Children's classes
Ages: 3 to 15
5 full days including lunch: 370
Private lessons
1hr, 3hr or 6hr
75 for 1hr, for 1 or 2 people, 100 for 3-6 people

CHILDCARE

The Camp Snowbird day camp, in the Cliff Lodge, takes children from 3 to 12, from 8am to 5pm. The nursery takes infants from 6 weeks to 3 years and should be booked in advance.

The Chickadees ski classes start at age 3.

GETTING THERE

Air Salt Lake City, transfer ½hr.

ACTIVITIES

Indoor Snowbird Canyon Racquet Club (tennis, racquetball, squash, climbing wall, aerobics, weight training, fitness room), hot-tubs, The Cliff Spa (fitness room, aerobics, beauty centre, sauna, steam room, solarium), conference centre, art gallery
Outdoor Swimming pools, hot-tubs, ice skating, tubing, snow-shoeing

TOURIST OFFICE

UT 84092-9000
t +1 (801) 742 2222
f 933 2298
info@snowbird.com
www.snowbird.com

QUEUES
Avoid the tram

At Snowbird nearly everyone wants to use the tram – for much of the season queues of up to 40 minutes are common. The Gadzoom fast quad and the Little Cloud chair above it – sadly, also rather queue-prone – get you almost as high as the tram.

MOUNTAIN RESTAURANT
Note the use of the singular

Choosing a mountain restaurant for lunch doesn't take long: it's the Mid Gad self-service cafeteria – or 'fuel stop', to use the resort's own description – or else it's back to base.

SCHOOLS AND GUIDES
Something for everyone

The ski school offers a progressive range of lessons and speciality clinics – such as women-only clinics, over-50s lessons, bumps and diamonds lessons, and experts-only programmes ('a life-altering experience').

FACILITIES FOR CHILDREN
All ages well cared-for

The 'kids ski free' programme allows two children (12 and under) to ski for free with each adult buying an all-day lift ticket. There are occasional evening distractions like parties, games and movies to keep the kids happy.

Staying there

All the lodgings and restaurants are within walking distance of each other. The tram station is central and the Gad lifts can be reached on snow. There are shuttle bus services linking the lodgings, the lifts and the car parks, and a regular service up to Alta.

HOW TO GO
Package or independent

Salt Lake City airport is close, and well set up to handle independent travellers. There are several companies offering frequent transfers. If you plan to visit several other resorts, you'll want to hire a car, and it's worth considering Salt Lake City as a base – not least because avalanche danger can close Little Cottonwood Canyon after heavy snowfalls, in which case you won't be able to tour around.

A few UK tour operators feature accommodation in Snowbird – mostly rooms in Cliff Lodge, the huge luxury hotel and restaurant complex just up the nursery slopes from the Snowbird Center. There's a rooftop pool and hot-tub, sauna, steam room, gym and treatment rooms for massage and beauty treatments. Prices here are understandably high, but if you can bear to share a four-bed 'dorm' room they're great value, considering the facilities you can use. There are other lodges, and smaller condominium blocks. A number of UK holidaymakers combine a stay in Snowbird with a stay in Park City.

EATING OUT
A reasonable choice

Generally eating out revolves around Cliff Lodge and Snowbird Center – both house a number of restaurants. It's advisable for at least one member of a party to pay a few dollars to join the Club at Snowbird (guests at the Cliff Lodge are automatically registered) as most of the better restaurants are classed as private clubs. The Aerie and the Wildflower are quite upmarket venues, the Mexican Keyhole Junction and the Forklift are easier on the pocket and better for families.

APRES-SKI
Very quiet weekdays

Après-ski in Snowbird tends to be a bit muted, especially during the week. The Tram Club under the tram itself was rocking with live music as the slopes closed when we were there. The Keyhole Cantina also has a good atmosphere at end-of-play. A sunset swim and a few cocktails at the rooftop pool in Cliff Lodge is reputed to be the best way to meet the in-crowd. It's quite feasible to head into downtown Salt Lake City for the occasional big night out on the town – lots of live bands and so on.

OFF THE SLOPES
Head down-canyon

People not using the slopes will be bored at Snowbird once they've tried the Cliff Spa and its treatments. The spa also offers Movement Energy Therapy (MET) classes (yoga etc). You could head towards the city – the Racquet Club down the valley is owned by Snowbird and has superb tennis facilities, and there are some attractions downtown, particularly around Temple Square. And there are various natural wonders, including the Great Salt Lake itself and, further afield, the Utah National Parks.

The Rest of the West

This section covers a varied group of isolated resorts in different parts of the great Rocky Mountain chain that stretches the length of the United States from Montana and Idaho down through Wyoming and Colorado to New Mexico. Each has its own unique character – and each is well worth knowing about.

Sun Valley, Idaho, was America's first purpose-built resort, developed in the 1930s by the president of the Union Pacific Railway. It quickly became popular with the Hollywood jet set and has managed to retain its stylish image and ambience over the years. It hasn't become a big international destination, because of its rather isolated location, limited hotel accommodation and poor reputation for snow – although this has largely been rectified by the huge snowmaking installation. But if you want to indulge yourself a little and be pampered, bear it in mind – it has one of our favourite luxury hotels.

If you don't mind a bit of a cross-state drive, you might combine a visit to Sun Valley with a visit to the famously snowy resorts of Utah (see previous section) or to Jackson Hole in Wyoming – another resort with an impressive snow record. Jackson is the nearest there is to a resort with a genuine Wild West cowboy atmosphere. The old town is lined with wooden sidewalks and there are lively saloons, where modern-day working cowboys drink, play pool and dance to country music. The mountain is a 15-minute drive away and offers some of America's most extreme terrain, with steeps, jumps and bumps to suit all – a sharp contrast to the tame, immaculately groomed runs typical of many US resorts. It does have easier runs, but that's not why most people go there.

A little way north of both Sun Valley and Jackson, just inside Montana, is Big Sky, not to be confused with Big Mountain at the far northern end of the state, or indeed Big White, over the Canadian border in British Columbia. Big Sky has one of the biggest verticals in America (1275m) thanks to its Lone Peak cable-car, going way above the tree line to 3400m. Its extensive slopes have something for everyone, from extreme steeps at the top to countless gentle cruises at the bottom. But there's not much to do here except ski and board.

Taos, New Mexico, is the most southerly major resort in America, and because of its isolation is relatively unknown on the international market. There's a tiny resort development at the foot of the slopes, which are set high above the traditional adobe town of Taos, 18 miles away in the arid valley. The area was developed in the 1950s by a European and is still family-run, with a friendly feel to it. It is one of the few resorts still to ban snowboarders from its slopes, which have many very challenging runs, including some very long, steep mogul fields.

Big Sky 2285m

Vast and empty slopes for all standards

WHAT IT COSTS

6

HOW IT RATES

The slopes	
Snow	****
Extent	***
Experts	*****
Intermediates	****
Beginners	****
Convenience	****
Queues	*****
Restaurants	*
The rest	
Scenery	***
Resort charm	**
Off-slope	**

What's new

For 1999/2000 two new lifts were added – one serving local accommodation, the other opening up 200 acres of new terrain and four new trails.

The new 10-storey Summit hotel-condominium opened in March 2000, with easy access to the main lifts and slopes back to the door.

MOUNTAIN FACTS

Altitude	2125m-3405m
Lifts	18
Pistes	3500 acres
Green/Blue	10%
Red	47%
Black	43%
Artificial snow	10%

Recco detectors used

TOURIST OFFICE

Postcode MT 59716
t +1 (406) 995 5000
f 995 5001
info@bigskyresort.com
www.bigskyresort.com

Big Sky is renowned for its powder, steeps and big vertical, and has lots of blissfully empty gentler slopes. There's no real village, just a very small collection of shops, restaurants and accommodation units – and nightlife is limited to say the least. If that's what you want, it's fine – we have one reporter who has been four times, last time with a varied group of ten, who all loved it.

THE RESORT

Big Sky, now over 25 years old, has started to attract a few international visitors who have heard of its huge snowfalls and deserted slopes.

The resort is set amid the wide open spaces of Montana, one hour's drive from the airport town of Bozeman. At the foot of the slopes is Mountain Village – the obvious base, with some slope-side condominiums and lodges. Despite efficient free buses, condos dotted around a golf course 10km east at Meadow Village hold little appeal.

Bridger Bowl is less than two hours' drive away, and makes a worthwhile outing – a broad, lightly wooded mountain of 600m vertical.

THE MOUNTAINS

The **slopes** cover a big area spread over two linked mountains, with long runs for all standards. Lone Mountain dominates. Half a dozen chairs and a gondola serve the wooded lower half of the mountain (with a vertical of about 500m). The Lone Peak chair adds another 250m of blue-run slopes and leads to the Lone Peak Tram – a tiny 15-person cable-car to the top, which serves great experts-only terrain all around the top bowl.

Andesite mountain is a much more modest wooded hill of 400m vertical.

Snowboarders have a terrain park and half-pipe on Andesite.

Snow reliability is good; snowfall averages 400 inches, which puts Big Sky ahead of most Colorado resorts and alongside Jackson Hole. The grooming is good, too.

The terrain accessed from the Tram is great for **experts**, including narrow couloirs and wide powder fields. Castro's Shoulder is the steepest route at 50°. There are good black slopes lower down, around the tree line.

There is lots of cruising terrain for **intermediates** – the shady runs on Andesite from the Ramcharger chair are splendid, but practically all the lower lifts serve worthwhile blue runs.

For **beginners** it's excellent, with a nursery area at the base and long greens on both mountains.

There is 65km of **cross-country** trails at Lone Mountain Ranch.

Queues are non-existent unless high winds close the upper lifts, and the runs seem deserted. There are 3500 skiable acres, and on a busy day they sell 1500 lift tickets; do the sums.

There is one tiny **mountain restaurant** doing fast food. You can head back to base to eat.

The **ski school** received excellent reviews: 'my grandson aged six loved it'; 'both the beginner and the intermediate in my group had only two in their classes'.

Handprints nursery in the slope-side Snowcrest lodge takes **children** from age six months ('it was perfection – four to an adult,' says a reporter).

STAYING THERE

There are many **self-catering** condos. Huntley Lodge (highly recommended by a reporter), Shoshone and the new slope-side Summit are the most convenient **hotels,** with good facilities.

For **après-ski** Chet's bar has live music, pool and poker games, Lolo's has cheap drinks and attracts a young boarding crowd, Scissor Bill's is popular as the slopes close.

Given a car, your **eating out** options extend to about 20 restaurants and bars. Huntley Lodge does a great buffet breakfast, Twin Panda serves Chinese at the base, First Place, Café Edelweiss and Rocco's in Meadow Village have had good reports. The lively Corral and 320 Ranch at Gallatin Canyon were recommended.

The main things to do **off the slopes** are snowmobiling, horse riding, sleigh rides, visit Yellowstone national park and go shopping in Bozeman.

Jackson Hole 1925m

Wild West cowboy town close to wild, exciting slopes

WHAT IT COSTS

6

HOW IT RATES

The slopes

Snow	****
Extent	***
Experts	*****
Intermediates	**
Beginners	***
Convenience	***
Queues	***
Restaurants	*

The rest

Scenery	***
Resort charm	****
Off-slope	***

- ⊕ Big, steep mountain, with some real expert-only terrain and one of the US's biggest verticals (1260m)
- ⊕ Jackson town has an entertaining Wild West ambience and lots of shops geared to summer tourists
- ⊕ Unspoilt, remote location with some impressive scenery nearby
- ⊕ Excellent snow record
- ⊕ Even more snow (and astonishingly empty slopes) 90 minutes away at Grand Targhee – with snowcats
- ⊕ Low altitude, so no altitude sickness
- ⊕ Good variety of cross-country terrain
- ⊕ Cheap lodgings (winter is off-peak)
- ⊕ Plenty to do off the slopes
- ⊕ Airport is only minutes from town

- ⊖ Intermediates lacking the confidence to tackle black runs (often with deep snow) will be more-or-less confined to the minor Apres Vous mountain
- ⊖ Inadequate mountain restaurants
- ⊖ The cable-car serving the top runs still generates long queues
- ⊖ Low altitude, and slopes face roughly south-east, so snow can be poor on the lower slopes
- ⊖ Jackson town is 15 minutes from the mountain, although Teton Village offers accommodation at the base
- ⊖ Getting there from the UK involves two or three flights

What's new

Ten more acres of snowmaking were installed on Apres Vous mountain for 1999/2000, taking the total up to 160 acres. And Delta Airways now runs a new daily service to Jackson from Salt Lake City. But perhaps the biggest news for last season was the opening up of 2500 acres of backcountry terrain in the Teton National Park and Bridger Teton National Forest. The terrain is accessed through six gates.

A new chair-lift replaces the old drag at the base of the Hobacks for 2000/01. More lodging facilities are on the way.

For those who like the idea of steep slopes smothered in deep powder or plastered with big bumps, Jackson Hole is Mecca. Like many American mountains, Jackson has double-diamond steeps that you can't find in Europe except by going off-piste with a guide. What marks it out from the rest is the sheer quantity of black-graded terrain, and the scale of the mountain.

Utah devotees will tell you that the snow here isn't as light as at Alta/Snowbird; but it's light enough, and falls in quantities somewhere between those found in Colorado and those famously found in Utah – the average annual total is around 400in, but in recent seasons it has been around or above the 500in mark.

With its wooden sidewalks, country-music saloons and pool halls, tiny Jackson is a determinedly Western town – great fun, if you like that kind of thing. We do.

boarding *Jackson Hole is a cult resort for expert snowboarders, just as it is for expert skiers. The steeps, cliffs and chutes make for a lot of high-adrenalin thrills for competent free-riders. There's a fun-park and a half-pipe near the Apres Vous chair (these are to be relocated for next season), and Dick's Ditch is a natural pipe. It's not a bad resort for novices either, with the beginner slopes served by a high-speed quad. Intermediates not wishing to venture off the groomed runs will find the resort a bit limited. There are some good snowboard shops, including the Hole-in-the-Wall at Teton Village. The nightlife in the bars around the town square is reasonably lively.*

The resort

The town of Jackson sits at the south-eastern edge of Jackson Hole – a high, flat valley surrounded by mountain ranges, in the north-west corner of Wyoming. This is real 'cowboy' territory, and the town strives to maintain its Wild West flavour, with traditional-style wooden buildings and sidewalks, and a couple of 'cowboy' saloons. Jackson gets many more visitors in summer than winter (thanks to the nearby national parks), which accounts for the many clothing and souvenir shops, alongside the more upmarket galleries appealing to affluent second-home owners. But in winter it's basically a ski town with a Western feel.

The slopes, a 15-minute drive north-east, rise abruptly from the flat valley floor. At the base is Teton Village – a small purpose-built collection of lodgings, shops and restaurants in a pleasantly woody setting, some neo-Alpine but increasingly in local style.

The mountains

Jackson Hole has long been recognised as one of the world's most compelling resorts for advanced and expert skiers. With recent improvements to the lifts and some of the buildings at Teton Village, the resort may seem less of a cult destination for hard-core experts and more of a conventional resort, with something for everyone. Don't be fooled: the beginner slopes are fine, but intermediates wanting to build up confidence should look elsewhere.

THE SLOPES
One big mountain, one small one

Trail gradings are accurate at Jackson: our own small map doesn't distinguish black from double-black-diamond runs, but the distinction matters once you are there – 'expert only' tends to mean just that. Some of the double-black runs are simply steep; but there are also cliffs, bumps, jumps and couloirs, including the infamous Corbet's.

One big mountain makes Jackson Hole famous – **Rendezvous**. The summit, accessed by a mid-sized cable-car (the Tram), provides a 1260m vertical drop – exceptional for the US. And the vertical is usable: conditions and thighs permitting, you can go from top to almost bottom on black slopes.

To the right looking up is **Apres Vous** mountain, with half the vertical and mostly much gentler runs, accessed by the short Teewinot and the longer Apres Vous fast quads.

Between these two peaks is a broad mountainside split by gulleys, accessed since 1997 by the **Bridger gondola**. This opened up new terrain, and gives speedy access to the Thunder and Sublette quad chairs serving some of the steepest terrain on Rendezvous.

Hosts offer complimentary tours of the mountains, starting from the Host building at 9.30am. And at 1.30pm on weekdays you can usually take a tour with Olympic gold medallist Pepi Stiegler – Jackson's director of skiing.

Snow King is a separate area right next to Jackson town. You can get hourly passes, and locals (who call it the Town Hill) use it in their lunch-hour. In the evening it's partly floodlit. It looks small but at the top it's satisfyingly steep, and the vertical measures a respectable 480m.

Grand Targhee, famous for its powder snow, is within 90 minutes' drive – buses run daily. See page 525.

SNOW RELIABILITY
Steep lower slopes can suffer

The claimed average of 402in of 'mostly dry powder' snow is much more than most Colorado resorts claim – and for a core three-month season conditions are likely to be reasonable. But the base elevation here is relatively low for the Rockies, and the slopes are quite sunny – they basically face south-east. If you're unlucky, you may find the steep lower slopes like the Hobacks in poor shape, or even shut. Happily, much of the best expert terrain is relatively shady. And snowmaking covers top-to-bottom runs from the gondola and on Apres Vous.

FOR EXPERTS
Best for the brave

For the good skier or boarder who wants challenges without the expense of hiring a guide to go off-piste, Jackson is one of the world's best resorts – maybe even the best.

Rendezvous mountain offers virtually nothing but black and very black slopes, and the Tram ride up is accompanied by suitably stern warnings about experts-only terrain.

The routes down the main Rendezvous Bowl are not particularly fearsome; but some of the alternatives are. Go down the East Ridge at least once to stare over the edge of the notorious Corbet's Couloir. The Tram passes right above it, providing a great view of people throwing themselves off the lip. It's the jump in that's special; the word is that the slope you land on is a mere 50° to the horizontal.

Below Rendezvous Bowl, the wooded flanks of Cheyenne Bowl offer serious challenges, at the extreme end of the single-black-diamond spectrum. If instead you take the ridge run that skirts this bowl to the right, you get to the Hobacks – a huge area of open and lightly wooded slopes, gentler than those higher up, but still black.

Corbet's aside, most of the seriously steep slopes are more easily reached from the slightly lower quad chairs. From Sublette, you have direct access

MOUNTAIN FACTS

Altitude	1925m-3185m
Lifts	10
Pistes	2500 acres
Green	10%
Blue	40%
Black	50%
Art. snow	160 acres

Recco detectors used

LIFT PASSES

2000/01 prices in dollars

Jackson Hole
Covers all lifts and includes 'Tram'.

Main pass
1-day pass 56
7-day pass 329

Senior citizens
Over 65: 7-day pass 165

Children
15 to 21: 7-day pass 247
Under 14: 7-day pass 165

Short-term passes
Afternoon pass from 12.30 (adult 41)

Notes 5-year-olds and under have free use of some lifts.

ALPENHOF LODGE

TETON VILLAGE • JACKSON HOLE • WYOMING

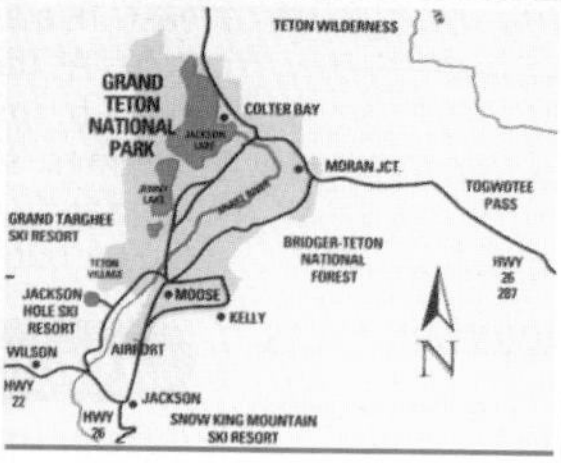

There are many places around the world offering exciting holiday pursuits, but few can compare with one spectacular destination – Jackson Hole, Wyoming, a secluded valley dramatically enveloped by a commanding parade of palatial mountains.

Throughout the seasons Jackson Hole plays host to visitors from around the world. Its superb location only a breath away from Grand Teton National Park, Yellowstone National Park, the National Elk Refuge and two magnificent wilderness areas make this an unforgettable place to visit.

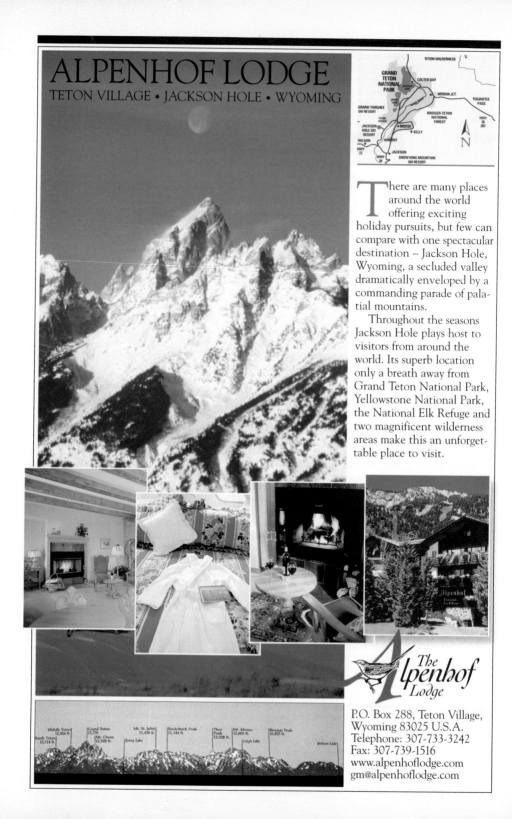

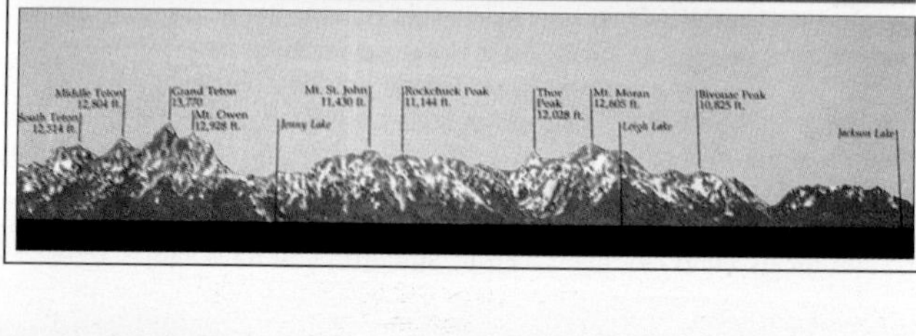

The Alpenhof Lodge

P.O. Box 288, Teton Village, Wyoming 83025 U.S.A.
Telephone: 307-733-3242
Fax: 307-739-1516
www.alpenhoflodge.com
gm@alpenhoflodge.com

The Tram rises 1260m from Teton Village to the summit of Rendezvous →

BOB WOODALL / WADE MCKOY / JACKSON HOLE SKI RESORT

to the short but seriously steep Alta chutes, and to the less severe Laramie Bowl beside them. Or you can track over to Tensleep Bowl – pausing to inspect Corbet's from below – and on to the less extreme (and less chute-like) Expert Chutes, and the single black Cirque and Headwall areas (some hiking required for the latter). Casper Bowl – accessed through gates only – is recommended for untracked powder stashes. Thunder chair serves further steep, narrow, north-facing chutes.

Again, the lower part of the mountain here offers lightly wooded single-black slopes.

The gondola serves terrain not without interest for experts. In particular, Moran Woods is a splendid under-utilised area. And even Apres Vous itself has an area of serious single blacks in Saratoga bowl.

There are some heli-trip operations and with the new open-boundary policy, some serious backcountry touring in the Teton National Park.

FOR INTERMEDIATES
Exciting for some

There are great cruising runs on the front face of Apres Vous, and top-to-bottom blues from the new gondola also offer quite gentle runs. But they don't add up to a great deal of mileage, and you shouldn't consider Jackson unless you want to tackle the blacks. It's then important to get guidance on steepness and snow conditions. The steepest single blacks are steep; intimidating when mogulled and fearsome when hard. The daily grooming map is worth consulting.

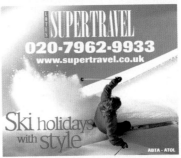

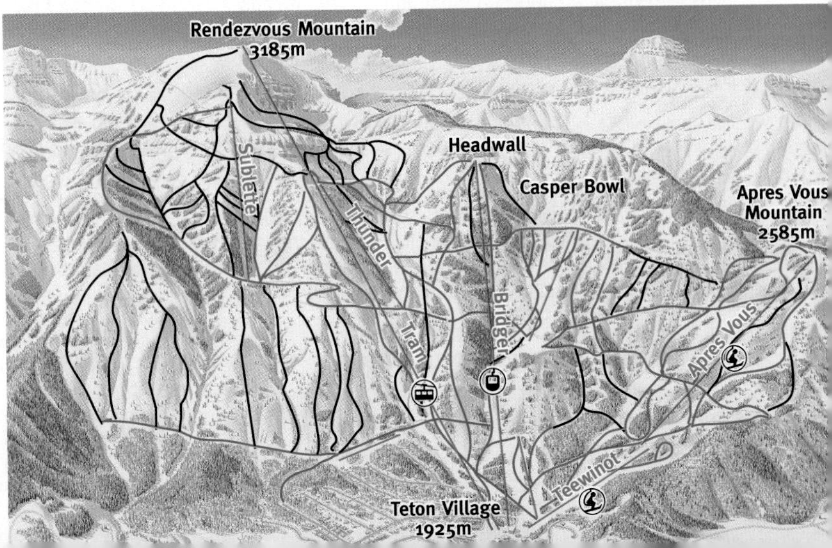

FOR BEGINNERS
Fine, up to a point
There's a choice of two lifts – the Eagle's Rest and Teewinot chairs – and four or five broad, gentle runs – fine for getting started. The progression to the blue Werner run off the Apres Vous chair is gradual enough – but what then? Most of the blues on the trail are traverses and the exceptions will not help build a novice's confidence.

FOR CROSS-COUNTRY
Lots of possibilities
There are three centres in the valley, offering trails of various lengths and difficulty. The Spring Creek Nordic Center has some good beginner terrain and offers moonlight tours. The Nordic Center at Teton has 17km of trails and organises trips into the National Parks.

QUEUES
Avoidable queues for the Tram
The Bridger gondola has relieved some of the pressure on the 30-year-old Tram. But the Tram is still the quickest way up Rendezvous, still the only way to the very top and still not able to keep up with demand; there may be queues all day.

MOUNTAIN RESTAURANTS
Head back to base
There's only one real restaurant on the mountain – at the base of the Casper chair-lift; it does a good range of self-service food, but gets very crowded. There are simple snack-bars at four other points on the mountain. At the base, Nick Wilson's in the Clocktower, the Alpenhof restaurant and the Mangy Moose ('great atmosphere, friendly service') are favourites.

SCHOOLS AND GUIDES
Learn to tackle the steeps
The school handles any standard of skier and rider, and there are also special Mountain Experience classes on steep and deep slopes. On certain dates, special 'Wild West adrenalin camps' are available, featuring steep skiing and boarding, racing, all mountain, freestyle and women's camps.

FACILITIES FOR CHILDREN
Just fine
The area may not seem to be one ideally suited to children, but in fact there are enough easy runs and the 'Kids' Ranch' care facilities are good.

Staying there

For convenience, choose Teton Village. There's a wider choice of lodgings in Jackson – and lots of other attractions. Most of the lodging in town is within a five-minute walk of the town square – though some is a mile or two out. The public bus service to the mountain ($2 single) is reported to be irregular and slow, and not all hotel courtesy bus services are reliable.

HOW TO GO
In town or by the mountain
Hotels From economy motels to expensive hotels and lodges, there's something to suit most tastes – though nothing really luxurious. There are quite a few small, characterful B&Bs. Because winter is low season, prices are low.
(((④ **Alpenhof** Our favourite (and our readers') in Teton Village. Tirolean-style, with a warm atmosphere. Getting a facelift for 2000/01, first phase of an ambitious development plan. Rooms of varying standard and price – the best very comfortable and attractive. Good food. Pool, sauna, hot-tub.
(((④ **Wort** Brick-built hotel right in the centre of town, above the lively Silver Dollar Bar. 'Very comfortable.' Hot-tub.
(((④ **Rusty Parrot Lodge** A stylish place in Jackson town, with a rustic feel and handcrafted furniture. Hot-tub.
(((④ **Renaissance Resort Hotel** At Teton Village – the reincarnated Sojourner. It is now smartly welcoming as well as comfortable and convenient, with new spa facilities for 2000/01.
(((④ **Spring Creek Ranch** Exclusive retreat midway between town and slopes; cross-country on-hand. Hot-tub.
(((④ **Huff House Inn** Charming old inn – the best of Jackson's many luxury B&B places.
(((④ **Painted Porch** Gorgeous B&B full of antiques.
((③ **Lodge at Jackson Hole** Western-style place on fringe of Jackson town. Comfortable mini-suite rooms, and free breakfast/après-ski munchies. Pool, sauna, indoor and outdoor hot-tubs.
((③ **Parkway Inn** Friendly, family-run place in Jackson town; nice pool.
(② **Trapper Inn** Friendly, good value, a block or two from Town Square, near bus stop; hot-tubs.
Self-catering There is lots of choice at Teton Village, within and around Jackson and at more isolated locations.

SCHOOLS/GUIDES

1999/2000 prices in dollars

Jackson Hole
Classes 3 days
3 half-days am or pm: 130
3 full-days 10am-3.30 with a lunch break: 155
Half-day: 50
Full-day: 60
Children's classes
Ages: 3 to 14
3 or 5 full days including lunch: 185 or 290 (full-day: 70)
Private lessons
For 1 to 5 people
2hr, 3hr, 4hr, or 6hr: 175, 250, 295, 395 respectively

CHILDCARE

The Kids' Ranch (739 2691) in the Cody House at Teton Village takes children aged 2 months to 5 years, from 8am to 5pm, with indoor and outdoor games and one-to-one ski lessons from age 3. Kids use the Fort Wyoming snow-garden, with 'magic carpet' lift.

GETTING THERE

Air Jackson, transfer ½hr.

ACTIVITIES

Indoor Art galleries, ice skating, cinemas, swimming, theatre, concerts, wildlife art museum

Outdoor Snowmobiles, mountaineering, horse riding, snow-shoe hikes, snowcat tours, floodlit skiing, heli-skiing, sleigh rides, dog-sledding, walks, wildlife safaris and tours of Yellowstone National Park

TOURIST OFFICE

Postcode WY 83001
t +1 (307) 733 7182
f 733 1286
info@jacksonhole.com
www.jacksonhole.com

EATING OUT

It's a pleasure in Jackson

Teton Village has pizza, Mexican, a steakhouse and a number of hotel restaurants. Most people favour the Mangy Moose – good value, good fun. In Jackson there are lots of places to try (but book ahead). The cool art-deco Cadillac Grille does good food – in the attached bar as well as the restaurant. The Range is excellent for trendy American regional cuisine. The Blue Lion is small, cosy and casually stylish. The 'saloons' do hearty meals, and a reporter reckons the Million Dollar does 'the best steaks and ribs in town'. A good budget place is the Snake River brew-pub – not to be confused with the pricey, over-rated Snake River Grill. The 'Greek-inspired' food at the cute log-cabin Sweetwater is recommended. There's also Italian (Anthony's, 'cosy and friendly' Nani's), Cajun, Chinese (Lame Duck), Indian, Tex-Mex and sushi (Masa Sushi).

APRES-SKI

Amusing saloons

For immediate après-ski festivities at Teton Village, the biggest draw is the Mangy Moose – a big, happy, noisy place, often with good live music. In sharp contrast is the calmly welcoming Dietrich's bar, at the Alpenhof.

In Jackson there are two famous 'saloons'. The Million Dollar Cowboy Bar features saddles as bar stools and a stuffed grizzly bear, and is usually the liveliest place in town, with good food and live music some nights. The Silver Dollar around the corner is more subdued; there may be ragtime playing as you count the 2032 silver dollars inlaid into the counter. The Rancher is a huge pool-hall. The Shady Lady saloon at Snow King sometimes has live music – country and western of course. The Virginian saloon is a quieter watering hole.

For a night out of town, join the local ravers at the Stagecoach Inn at Wilson, especially on Sundays.

OFF THE SLOPES

'Great' outdoors diversions

The famous Yellowstone National Park is 100km to the north. You can tour the park by snowcat or snowmobile, but you'll be roaring along the snowy roads in the company of several hundred other snowmobiles – 'more like a Grand Prix than a wilderness', as a recent reporter puts it. There is much more rewarding snowmobiling to be done elsewhere, eg at Goosewing Ranch and along the Gros Ventre river – much quieter and more wildlife.

The National Elk Refuge, next to Jackson and across the road from the National Museum of Wildlife Art, has the largest elk herd in the US. In town there are some 40 galleries and museums and a number of outlets for Indian and Western arts and crafts. There is, believe it or not, a branch of Ripley's Believe It or Not®.

A DAY OUT IN GRAND TARGHEE 2440M

We'd recommend any adventurous visitor to make the hour-and-a-half trip over the Teton pass to sample Grand Targhee's fabled powder. The average snowfall here is over 500in – 25 per cent greater than Jackson, and on a par with Utah's best. Locals call it Grand Foggee, because there is often low cloud even when it's not snowing. This may be just as well, because the slopes generally face south-west, which is about the worst orientation in the book for sun damage.

On the main Fred's Mountain, the 1500 acres of slopes are blissfully empty. A central fast quad serves a wide area of open and lightly wooded blue and black runs with a respectable 670m vertical. Off to the left, a slow quad chair serves an excellent area of short green runs, and beyond that a longer slow double serves another splendid area of tough blues and easy blacks – deserted when we visited.

Next-door Peaked Mountain offers slopes that are similar in extent but accessed only by snowcats, so at any one time there will be no more than 20 or 30 people on the slopes. There is a slightly greater vertical of 860m, and the lower half of the mountain is more heavily wooded.

Daily buses to Targhee pick up at various points around town and Teton Village. A combined bus/lift ticket costs just over $50. The snowcat operation costs $240 a day, $175 a half-day. You can take an instructor along, for a premium.

Sun Valley 1755m

Stylish resort with slopes to flatter its rich and famous guests

WHAT IT COSTS

6

HOW IT RATES

The slopes	
Snow	***
Extent	***
Experts	***
Intermediates	****
Beginners	***
Convenience	**
Queues	****
Restaurants	****
The rest	
Scenery	***
Resort charm	***
Off-slope	***

What's new

Sun Valley's owner Earl Holding has invested millions in high-speed lifts, new runs, a huge computer-controlled snowmaking system and the plushest on-slope restaurant complexes and base lodges. Currently he is ploughing money into his new baby, Snowbasin in Utah, which will host the downhill events in the 2002 Olympics. So Sun Valley development is on hold.

MOUNTAIN FACTS

Altitude	1755m-2790m
Lifts	13
Pistes	2067 acres
Green	38%
Blue	45%
Black	17%
Art. snow	600 acres

TOURIST OFFICE

Postcode ID 83340
t +1 (208) 726 3423
f 726 4533
ski@sunvalley.com
www.sunvalley.com

Millions of dollars have been spent in recent years building new facilities to maintain Sun Valley's reputation as America's original luxury purpose-built winter sports resort. For a peaceful, relaxing time, it's hard to beat.

THE RESORT

Sun Valley is based around the old mining village of Ketchum. It was built in the 1930s by Averell Harriman, President of the Union Pacific Railway, and became a favourite with stars such as Clark Gable and Judy Garland. Its current owner, Earl Holding, has pumped millions of dollars into the mountain to restore it to state-of-the art luxury and Sun Valley now attracts stars like Clint Eastwood and Arnie Schwarzenegger. The town of Ketchum retains its old-world charm and has atmospheric bars, restaurants and shops. But it's not cheap: 'More expensive than Aspen. I didn't buy, but I enjoyed looking in the high-quality shops,' says a reporter.

THE MOUNTAINS

The main **slopes** of Bald Mountain (known locally as Baldy) are accessed from one of two luxurious base lodge complexes at River Run and Warm Springs, a shuttle bus-ride from most accommodation. Of the 13 lifts, seven are high-speed quads. One reporter complained of 'dangerous icy pistes that should have been closed, and pistes crossing each other, causing more collisions than I have seen anywhere'. The separate Dollar Mountain has good beginner terrain.

Snowboarding is now allowed on almost all the mountain and the chair-lifts make getting about easy.

The resort has an erratic natural **snow reliability** record, so it has installed 600 acres of snowmaking, covering over 70 per cent of the groomable runs.

There are a few tough runs and bowls for **experts**, but nothing beyond single-black-diamond pitch, including the two most famous mogul runs, Exhibition and Limelight. Heli-skiing is available locally. Most of the terrain is ideal for **intermediates**, with lots of runs at a similar consistent pitch. There are good blue bowl runs with great views from the top ridge as well as groomed cruisers through the trees.

Both Baldy and Dollar are good for **beginners**, with very gentle, long green runs to progress to. The ski school and kids' programmes cater for **children**.

Forty kilometres of prepared **cross-country** skiing trails start at the Nordic Center by the Sun Valley Lodge, and there are more along the valley.

Queues are rarely a problem, with Sun Valley's network of high-speed quads whisking people around.

The **mountain restaurants** and base lodges have to be seen to be believed. They are way ahead of most US on-slope facilities, with floor-to-ceiling windows, beautiful wooden decor, heated terraces so snow instantly melts, and marble public loos with gold-plated taps. At the end of the day one reporter enjoyed 'the piano and violin players and people-watching at the River Run base'.

STAYING THERE

One of our favourite **hotels** in any resort is the stylish Sun Valley Lodge, part of the original development. As well as magnificent rooms, there are a big outdoor ice rink and a pool, and the corridors are lined with photos of film-star guests. Hemingway wrote *For Whom the Bell Tolls* here. But there are plenty of cheaper options, including motels and **self-catering**.

There are over 80 restaurants for **eating out** and Sun Valley was rated number one in the US by readers of *Gourmet* magazine. We enjoyed excellent food at the relaxed Evergreen Bistro and had a great breakfast at The Knob Hill Inn. A reporter recommends Chandlers. Atmospheric **après-ski** places include the Sawtooth Club (popular with locals), Whiskey Jaques for live music and dancing, and the Pioneer Saloon, popular for its prime rib and Clint Eastwood spotting.

You can have a fine time relaxing **off the slopes**, including sleigh rides, walking, ice skating, swimming and strolling round the galleries and shops. There's a special snow-shoe trail too.

Taos 2800m

New Mexico adds spice to the slopes and resort

WHAT IT COSTS

6

HOW IT RATES

The slopes

Snow	****
Extent	**
Experts	*****
Intermediates	***
Beginners	**
Convenience	***
Queues	****
Restaurants	*

The rest

Scenery	***
Resort charm	***
Off-slope	**

What's new

By the start of the 2000/01 season Taos will have completed a three-year project to upgrade its snow-making operation – over 98 per cent of intermediate runs will be covered.

For the 1999/2000 season it improved its Children's Centre.

There are rarely new lifts at Taos, but part of the attraction of the place is that it doesn't want to overdevelop its mountain, and it chooses to keep some of the best skiing for those willing to hike to get to it.

MOUNTAIN FACTS

Altitude	2800m-3600m
Lifts	12
Pistes	1100 acres
Green	24%
Blue	25%
Black	51%
Art. snow	496 acres
Recco detectors used	

- ➕ Some very steep, challenging terrain
- ➕ Intermediates and beginners surprisingly well catered for
- ➕ Small, intimate resort nestled in the splendour of New Mexico's Rockies
- ➕ Two contrasting bases
- ➕ One of the best schools in the US

- ➖ Taos town a long drive from the resort
- ➖ Some of the best runs are a long hike from the top lifts
- ➖ Relatively small area of slopes
- ➖ Very little accommodation in the resort itself

Taos is unlike any other US resort. It is set high above an arid New Mexico valley, 18 miles from the adobe town of Taos, home to many famous artists and writers over the years, including D H Lawrence. Its culture and food is southern, and it makes a good contrast with the Colorado resorts, a five- or six-hour drive away – you could consider it as part of a two-centre holiday.

The slopes are different, too. If you are after the steep and deep, Taos has some of the best in North America. Many runs are made deliberately awkward to reach to keep the numbers using them low and the quality of the snow high.

boarding *Taos is one of the few resorts that bans snowboarding, and shows no sign of changing its mind. The resort says it bears no ill will towards boarders, it's just passionate about skiing: 'So quit whining and ski it!'*

The resort

Not far from Santa Fe in New Mexico, Taos Ski Valley is the most southerly mainstream resort in North America. It could be on a different planet from the town of Taos, some 18 miles away through red-brown desert scenery.

The resort is little more than a handful of lodges, built in chalet style – and a huge car park. It was founded in 1955 by Ernie Blake, and the resort is still family-run.

Taos town, in contrast, is sizeable, and rich in cultural influences – native American, Spanish and classic South-Western. It's full of art galleries, museums, restaurants and bars, as well as hotels and B&Bs.

The mountain

The first thing to strike you at Taos Ski Valley is Al's Run, a mogul pitch of formidable steepness rising sheerly out of the resort. Ernie Blake put up a sign saying 'Don't panic! You're looking at 1/30 of Taos Ski Valley. We have many easy runs too'. They do, but it is still best for experts – Slim, a spreadeagled, lifelike dummy, warns you to be careful on this steep terrain.

THE SLOPES
Small but expandable

There are runs on three separate flanks of the mountain. Two chairs take you up – one a high-speed quad. All the lifts give you a choice of green, blue and black runs. Many of the toughest runs, however, can be reached only via a lengthy climb.

SNOW RELIABILITY
Enviable

Because of its southerly position Taos has a different weather pattern from Colorado. Last season was very bad for snow, but the snow record is generally good – one 1998 visitor told us, 'In my 16 days seven feet of snow fell.' Snow-guns cover over 98 per cent of beginner and intermediate terrain.

FOR EXPERTS
Hike to the heights

Al's Run is the most obvious challenge, but the bottom section is often shut.

The best terrain is an energetic hike from the top of the mountain. Highline Ridge and West Basin Ridge both have a collection of very steep and narrow chutes through the trees and rocks.

The other major challenge is a 75-minute-plus hike to Kachina Peak for magical off-piste bowls and powder. If you don't want to hike, chairs 2 and 6 take you to 'the best double-black-diamond tree runs in the world'. There is also excellent back-country terrain.

FOR INTERMEDIATES
Good but limited cruising
There are always easy-cruising alternatives to the steeps, but they are limited. Try the lovely long blues at the western end of the slopes, and to the east those accessed by the Kachina lift. Adventurous intermediates will enjoy the open Hunziker Bowl. A reporter suggests Papa Bear for a 'taste of a not-too-steep bump run' – but also warns that 'some pitches on the blues are narrow and steep'.

FOR BEGINNERS
Good facilities
Strawberry Hill at the base is devoted to novices, and there are easy green tracks all over the mountain.

FOR CROSS-COUNTRY
No facilities
But those with a guide can head off into parts of the National Forest.

QUEUES
Imposed limits
Taos has to restrict the number of people on the mountain to 4800. Queues are rare except at the bottom lifts at peak times – such as when all the ski school lessons set off on Sunday and Monday.

MOUNTAIN RESTAURANTS
Head back to base
There are just two restaurants, neither selling the world's greatest food. But the Phoenix has a good sun deck. For a decent lunch, head back to the resort. The large terrace of the hotel St Bernard is a favourite spot, with barbecue, music and lots of atmosphere.

SCHOOLS AND GUIDES
Simply the best?
Many consider the school at Taos to be one of the best: 'Dynamic, fun – they do push you, but they're also patient.' The aim is to push everyone as far and as fast as possible – but also to have fun. In addition to straight group classes and private lessons you can arrange whole-week packages and special workshops – there are women's and over-50s' ski weeks, for example.

FACILITIES FOR CHILDREN
Childcare from 6 weeks old
The resort takes childcare as seriously as it takes tuition, with programmes tailored to different age groups.

Staying there

Choose between limited Taos Ski Valley, cultural but distant Taos town, or one of the many lodges in between. You need a car if you stay out of the resort.

HOW TO GO
Little choice
Very few UK tour operators feature Taos. But any US specialist could put a package together for you.
Hotels There are no luxurious hotels, but lots of more modest places.
At Taos Ski Valley:
((((4 **Inn at Snakedance** Original Taos hotel, with panoramic, glass-walled bar, large sun terrace and spa facilities.
(((3 **St Bernard** At the base of Al's Run; 'rustic and full of character', fine food, après-ski scene. Also has condos.
In Taos town itself:
((((4 **Historic Taos Inn** Indian-influenced hotel with excellent restaurant and stylish Adobe Bar. Outdoor pool, hot-tub.
(((3 **Sagebrush Inn** Adobe built in 1929. Excellent food, nightly entertainment, tennis, pool, hot-tubs.
Self-catering There's a wide selection of condos. The Quail Ridge Inn Resort between Taos and the slopes is a large, comfortable adobe-style complex. There are hot-tubs and an outdoor pool.

EATING OUT
Spoilt for choice if you drive
At the resort, you'll find a couple of places to try out New Mexico dishes as well as more traditional US fare.

In Taos town you'll find south-western food, seafood and steaks. The Historic Taos Inn has good food.

APRES-SKI
A quiet time
Some hotels and bars have live music, but you don't come here to rave.

OFF THE SLOPES
Stay in Taos
In Taos there's ice skating, swimming, clothes and jewellery shopping, the art museum and a walking tour. Trips to historic, pretty Santa Fe, and to Taos Pueblo – home of the Tiwa Indians for nearly 800 years – are recommended.

TOURIST OFFICE
Postcode NM 87525
t +1 (505) 776 2291
f 776 8596
tsv@skitaos.org
www.skitaos.org

New England

You go to Utah for the deepest snow, to Colorado for the lightest powder and swankiest resorts, to California for the mountains and low prices. You go to New England for ... well, for what? Extreme cold? Rock-hard artificial snow? Mountains too limited to be of interest beyond New Jersey? Yes and no: all of these preconceptions have some basis, but they add up to an incomplete and unfair picture.

Yes, it can be cold: one of our reporters recorded –27°C, with wind chill producing a perceived temperature of –73°C. Early in the season, people wear face masks to prevent frostbite. It can also be warm – another reporter had a whole week of rain that washed away the early-season snow. The thing about New England weather is that it varies. Not as much as in Scotland, maybe, but the locals' favourite expression is 'If you don't like the weather in New England, wait two minutes'. But we got routine winter weather on both our visits – one in January, one in February.

Certainly, New England doesn't get much super-light powder or deep snow to play in. But the resorts do have big snowmaking installations, designed to ensure a long season and to help the slopes to 'recover' after a thaw or spell of rain. They were the pioneers of snowmaking technology; and 'farming' snow, as they put it, is an art form and a way of life – provided the weather is cold enough. And they make and groom their snow to produce a superb surface. Many of the resorts get impressive amounts of natural snow, too.

Sure, the mountains are not huge in terms of trail mileage. But several have verticals of over 800m (on a par with Colorado resorts such as Keystone) and most have over 600m (matching Breckenridge), and are worth considering for a short stay, or even for a week if you like familiar runs. For more novelty, a two- or three-centre trip is the obvious solution. You won't lack challenge – most of the double-black runs are seriously steep. And you won't lack space: most Americans visit over weekends, which means deserted slopes on weekdays – except at peak periods such as New Year and during the President's Day holiday, in late February. It also means the resorts are keen to attract long-stay visitors, so UK package prices are low.

But the big weekend and day-trip trade also means that few New England resorts have developed atmospheric resort villages – just a few condos and a hotel, maybe, with places to stay further out geared to suit car drivers who ski, eat, sleep, ski, go home.

But New England is easy to get to from Britain – a flight to Boston, then perhaps a three-hour drive to your resort. And there are some pretty towns to visit, with their clapboard houses and big churches. You might also like to consider spending a day or two in Boston – one of America's most charming cities. And you could save a lot of money on normal UK prices by having a shopping spree at the factory outlet stores that abound in New England.

We cover four of the most popular resorts on the UK market in the separate chapters that follow. But there are many other small areas too. And if you are going for a week or more, we recommend renting a car and visiting a few resorts rather than sticking to just one area. In the rest of this introduction, we outline the attractions of the main possibilities.

From Killington (by far the biggest resort), you can go south to a range of smaller resorts. **Okemo** competes with Smugglers' Notch for the family market. Okemo mountain has southern Vermont's biggest vertical (655m) and longest trail (over 7km). The slopes, on several flanks of a single peak, are largely intermediate or easy – though there are a dozen black runs and a couple of short double-black-diamonds. Boarders are well catered for, with an extensive park leading into a half-pipe. There is almost 100 per cent snowmaking cover – and the product is said to be the best in the east.

Mount Snow is another one-peak resort, with a long row of lifts on the front face serving easy and intermediate runs of just over 500m vertical, and a separate area of black runs on the north face – including one short but serious double-black. (The sister resort of Haystack, a short drive away, has more steep slopes in its Witches area.) Mount Snow claims its 900m-long snowboard park is the biggest in the east.

Stratton offers something like the classic Alpine arrangement of a village at the foot of the lifts. It's a smart, modern development with a pedestrian shopping street. The slopes – mostly easy and intermediate, with some blacks and some short double-black pitches – is spread widely around the flanks of a single peak, served by modern lifts including a 12-person gondola and a fast six-seat chair. Stratton calls itself the 'snowboarding capital of the east', claiming the best terrain park, half-pipe, instruction and (of course) attitude.

You may find more interest in **Sugarbush**, to the north of Killington on the way to Smugglers' Notch. Sugarbush, midway

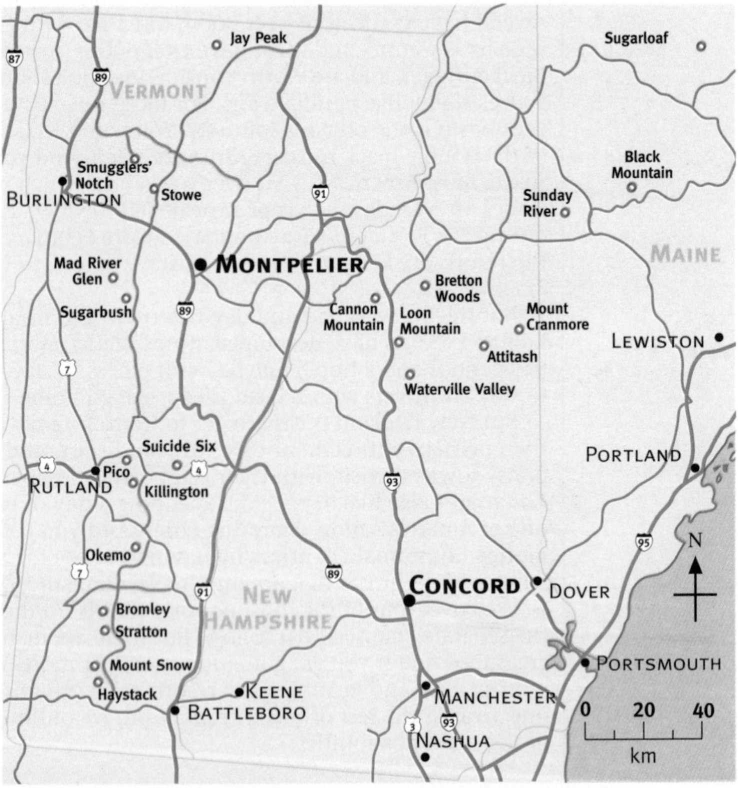

between Killington and Stowe, is a fast-developing resort with one of the larger ski areas (111 trails). The main sector is an extensive bowl below Lincoln Peak, with lifts up to six points on the rim; a long up-and-over chair-lift links the Mt Ellen area – smaller, but with more altitude and more vertical (808m). The easy skiing is confined to the lower slopes; higher up, the direct runs are seriously steep. There are snowboard parks in both areas. Most of the accommodation is in the historic village of Waitsfield, but the American Skiing Company is building a village at the base.

Mad River Glen next door is a cult resort with locals, with some tough ungroomed terrain, a few well-groomed intermediate trails and old-fashioned lifts – it still has a single-person chair-lift.

Further north, near the Canadian border, is **Jay Peak**. It gets busy at weekends (with Canadian as well as American visitors) but is quiet in the week. It has Vermont's only cable-car which takes you to the summit and views of four US states plus Canada. It gets a lot of snow for New England and has some good runs for advanced skiers and adventurous intermediates.

Sugarloaf in Maine already has a much better developed village than most small New England resorts. But the mountain is small and a keen piste-basher could ski it out in a day or two. Very popular with day and weekend skiers and boarders, it was very noticeable on our visit how safety conscious the local slope-users were. There was a higher proportion of people wearing protective helmets here than any other resort we have visited. We estimate well over 50 per cent were helmeted – and these included all age groups, from children to octogenarians. Even teenage and twenty-something skiers and boarders were comfortable in their helmets – a sign of things to come in Europe perhaps? Sugarloaf is another resort that is now owned by the American Skiing Company (Killington, Mount Snow, Sugarbush, Sunday River and Attitash Bear Peak are its other New England resorts) – and it has a Magnificent Seven pass which covers seven days at all its resorts.

New Hampshire has several small resorts dotted along the Interstate 93 highway. **Bretton Woods** is one of the smaller areas, 460m vertical on a single mountain face, but is highly rated, particularly by families, who relish the top-to-bottom easy trails. There is a good mix of terrain, and snowmaking is comprehensive. Snowboarders have a park and a half-pipe. There are a few places to stay near the base, with more five miles away at Twin Mountain.

Cannon is a ski area and nothing more – lifts from two base areas close to I-93 converge on the summit 650m above, serving mainly intermediate slopes; there are quite a few black runs, but no double-blacks and not much that is genuinely easy. It's only a few minutes' drive to Franconia in one direction and Lincoln in the other.

Loon is a small, smart, modern resort just outside the sprawling town of Lincoln. The mountain (640m vertical) is mostly of intermediate difficulty, though some fall-line runs merit their black grading. There is a long snowboard park.

Waterville Valley is a compact area with runs dropping either side of a broad, gentle ridge rising 615m above the lift base. There are a couple of short but genuine double-black-diamond mogul fields, but most of the slopes are intermediate. Boarders are well catered for. The village is a Disneyesque affair a couple of miles away down on the flat valley bottom.

Killington 670m

Good slopes, great après-ski, shame about the place

WHAT IT COSTS

5

HOW IT RATES

The slopes	
Snow	***
Extent	**
Experts	***
Intermediates	***
Beginners	****
Convenience	*
Queues	****
Restaurants	*
The rest	
Scenery	***
Resort charm	**
Off-slope	*

- ➕ The biggest mountain in the east, matching some Colorado resorts
- ➕ Lively après-ski, with lots of bar-restaurants offering happy hours and late-night action
- ➕ Terrain to suit everyone, from long, easy trails to serious challenges
- ➕ Excellent nursery slopes
- ➕ Comprehensive snowmaking
- ➕ Good care and tuition for children, although it's not a notably child-oriented resort

- ➖ No real resort village – hotels, condos and restaurants are widely spread around the base of the mountain and along the 5-mile access road; you don't absolutely need a car, but it helps
- ➖ The trail network is complex, on-mountain marking is poor and there are lots of trail-crossings
- ➖ Terminally tedious for anyone who is not a skier or boarder
- ➖ This is New England: the snow can deteriorate or disappear

It's difficult to ignore Killington. It claims to have: the largest mountain in the east, whether gauged in trail length, accessible area, vertical drop or top altitude; the most quad chairs in the east; the world's biggest snowmaking installation and the east's largest grooming fleet, and as a result the longest season in the east (it tries to be the first resort in America to open in October, but often shuts again shortly after); America's longest lift and longest trail – a winding 16km for a drop of 945m (a gradient just steep enough to keep you moving); and allegedly New England's steepest mogul slope – Outer Limits, 800m long for a drop of 370m (a gradient steep enough to keep you moving all the way to the bottom if you fall). All quite impressive by local standards.

They've now built the Grand Resort Hotel and Conference Center at the main lift base, allowing them to claim the largest conference facilities in Vermont. They plan to build a slope-side village here too, but until that happens, the place will lack anything resembling a village – a serious drawback for many visitors (from Europe, at least). But we kinda like the place. Once you get used to driving everywhere, it ceases to be a problem. And the vibrant nightspots weigh in the balance, even for us: in the early evening they're jolly places to eat, even if you're visiting with kids. The main problem is the unpredictable weather.

boarding *A cool resort like Killington has to take boarding seriously, and it does. There are three half-pipes – two served by a rope tow lift – two fun-parks and a boarder-cross course. There's floodlit riding on Wednesdays and Saturdays. And there are terrain features scattered around the area. There's a Ride Guide to take you to the best slopes, and parts of the mountain have been reshaped to cut out some of the unpleasant flats on contouring green runs. Several big-name board events are held here. For less competent boarders, there are excellent beginner slopes, and plenty of friendly high-speed (ie slow-loading) chair-lifts – and the Perfect Turn Discovery Center caters just for beginners.*

What's new

Killington has grand plans for a resort village at Snowshed (the main lift base) near the new Grand Resort Hotel and Conference Center – work is due to start in summer 2001.

It also plans to link Pico – 'Killington's 7th mountain' – with the main area of slopes but this is taking a back seat to the resort village project.

The resort is also installing yet more snowmaking, following a couple of very bad seasons for natural snow and warm weather.

The resort

Killington is an extraordinary resort, especially to European eyes. Most of its hotels and restaurants are dotted along a five-mile approach highway, with just a small part of the accommodation concentrated in developments close to the slopes. The nearest thing you'll find to a focus is the occasional set of traffic lights, though there is a concentration of buildings along a two-and-a-half mile stretch of the road. The resort caters mainly for day, weekend and short break slope-users who drive in from the big cities (including a lot of New Yorkers). Here the car is king.

MOUNTAIN FACTS

Altitude	325m-1295m
Lifts	32
Pistes	1160 acres
Green	29%
Blue	33%
Black	38%
Art. snow	864 acres

LIFT PASSES

1999/2000 prices in dollars

Killington Mountain Pass
Covers all lifts in the Killington and Pico ski resort area.

Beginners See Schools/Guides

Main pass
1-day pass 56
6-day pass 270

Senior citizens
Over 64: 6-day pass 168

Children
Under 6: free
6-12: 6-day pass 168
13-18: 6-day pass 240

The mountains

Killington has a densely woven mesh of runs that offers something for everyone. To some extent the terrain on its six sectors suits different standards – the bottom part of Skye Peak is all beginner slopes, Rams Head is all easy-intermediate, Bear Mountain has mainly more advanced stuff. But there are also areas where a mixed ability group would be quite happy and there are easy runs from top to bottom of each peak.

Killington has also created areas which are called Fusion Zones – thinned-out forest areas, where you pick your own line of where to go. These areas are neither groomed nor patrolled – and they come in blue and single- and double-black-diamond grades. We found them great fun.

The piste map is one of the largest and most fact-packed we've ever come across. But this makes it unwieldy and awkward to handle and one reporter says 'they blow out of peoples' hands and all over the trails'. Some runs of all levels are left to form bumps; there is half-and-half grooming on selected trails; and terrain features – ridges, bumps, quarter-pipes – are created.

THE SLOPES
Complicated

The runs spread over a series of wooded peaks, all quite close together but giving the resort a basis for claiming to cover six mountains – or seven with nearby Pico. A huge number of runs and impressive number of lifts are crammed into a modest area. The result is a very complex network of runs.

Killington Base area has chairs radiating to three of the six peaks – **Skye**, **Killington** (the high-point of the area) and **Snowdon**. Novices and families head for the other main base area, which has two parts: Snowshed is at the foot of the main beginner slope, served by several parallel chairs; just across the road up to Killington Base is Rams Head, where there's a Family Center at the foot of the entirely gentle **Rams Head** mountain.

The two remaining peaks are behind Skye Peak; they can be reached by trails from Killington and Skye, but each also has a lift base accessible by road. **Bear Mountain** is the expert's hill, served by two quad chairs from its mid-mountain base area. The sixth 'peak', **Sunrise**, is a slight blip on the mountainside, the arrival point of a long triple chair from the Sunrise base area in the valley, beside the main road. Not far away is another main-road access lift, the Skyeship gondola, up to Skye Peak, with cabins that are heated and wildly decorated. It makes a good access point for those staying at the end of the resort access road.

Pico is a few minutes' drive from the Killington Road junction on US Route 4. The mountain doesn't have much challenge, but suits intermediates well. One reporter said, 'Pico is so quiet mid-week that they sometimes close it – we were unable to ski it because of this.'

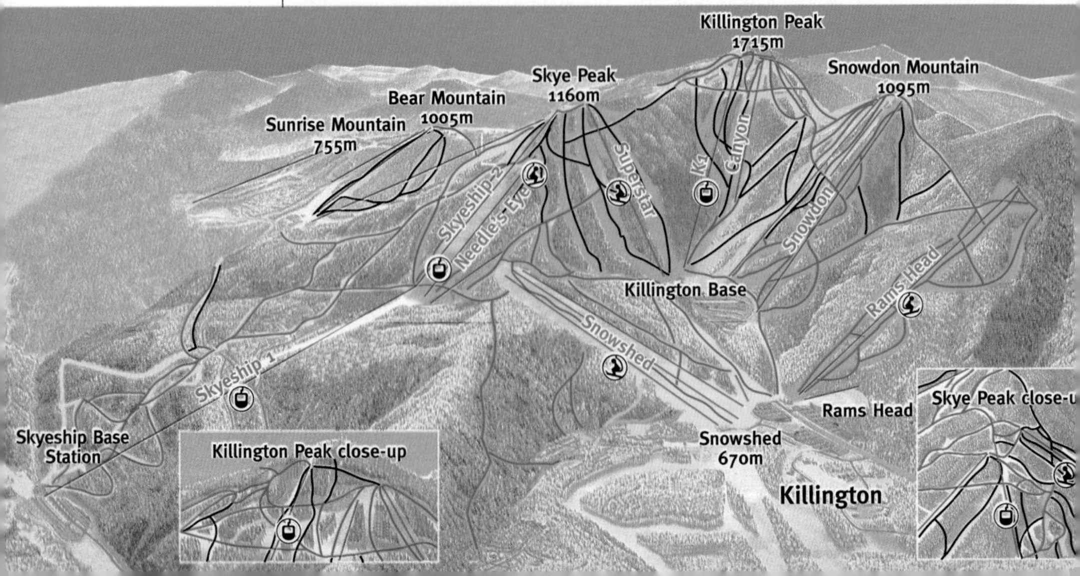

SCHOOLS/GUIDES

1999/2000 prices in dollars

Perfect Turn clinics
7 days
2hr: from 9.30, 10.15, or 1.30: 31

Learn to ski clinics
(incl lift pass, equipment and use of Discovery Centre)
1 day: 60
3 days: 139

Children's classes
Ages: 4 to 6 (incl lift pass)
half day: 8.30-12 or 12.30-4: 59
full day: 89
Ages: 7 to 12 (excl lift pass)
half day: 9.30-11.30 or 1-3: 71
full day: 101

Private lessons
1hr, 2hr, half- or full-day
75 for 1hr (115 for 2 people)
195 for half-day of 3hr (270 for 2 people)

SNOW RELIABILITY
Good if it's cold

Killington has a huge snowmaking system. But even that is no good if it is too warm to operate it.

Bad weather can ruin a holiday even in mid-season. One reporter this year says, 'Last year there was new snow each night and lots of soft powder. We went back the same time this year (8 March) and they were experiencing the hottest temperatures on record – people were skiing in shorts and T-shirts and there was little snow on the ground. A lot of runs were closed and even green runs were icy.' A February visitor told of 'everything from frostbite warnings to pouring rain'.

FOR EXPERTS
Some challenges

The main areas that experts head for are Killington Peak, where there is a handful of genuine double-diamond fall-line runs under the two chair-lifts, and Bear Mountain. Most of the slopes here are single blacks but Outer Limits, under the main quad chair, is a double-diamond claimed to be 'the steepest mogul slope in the east'. But we suspect there are steeper runs at Stowe and Smugglers' Notch. There are two or three worthwhile blacks on Snowdon, too. The Fusion Zones on Skye and Snowdon are well worth seeking out. But one reporter thought many of the black runs overgraded: 'Some would be red in Europe and comfortably skied by an intermediate.'

FOR INTERMEDIATES
Navigation problems?

There are lots of easy cruising blue and green runs all over the slopes, except on Bear Mountain, where the single blacks present a little more of a challenge for intermediates. Snowdon is a splendid area for those who like to vary their diet. There's a blue-graded Fusion Zone on Rams Head. Finding your way around the complicated network of trails may be tricky, though. One reporter liked Pico a lot but complained that the blue run down was more difficult than some blacks.

FOR BEGINNERS
Splendid

The facilities for complete beginners are excellent. The Snowshed slope is one vast nursery slope served by three chair-lifts and a very slow drag-lift. Rams Head also has excellent gentle slopes. The ski school runs a special, purpose-built Discovery Center just for first-time skiers and boarders – they introduce you to the equipment, show you videos and provide refreshments.

FOR CROSS-COUNTRY
Two main options

Extensive cross-country loops are available at two specialist 'resorts' – Mountain Meadows down on Route 4, and Mountain Top Ski Touring, a short drive away at Chittenden.

QUEUES
Weekend crowds

Killington gets a lot of weekend and public holiday business, but at other times the slopes and lifts are likely to be quiet. One New Year reporter told of 'a madhouse with overcrowded slopes, and a 20-minute crawl up the access road'. Lift capacity is huge, so overcrowded slopes are more of a problem than lift queues.

NATHAN BILOW

You might be lucky enough to get powder like this, but hardpack and ice are more common ↓

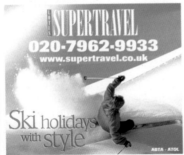

GETTING THERE

Air Boston, transfer $2^{1}/_{2}$hr.

ACTIVITIES

Indoor Killington Grand Resort Hotel has massage, fitness centre, outdoor pool, hot-tub, sauna, aerobics. Cinemas and bowling at Rutland
Outdoor Skating, floodlit tubing and snowboarding, sledding, sleigh rides, cross-country, snowshoe tours

CHILDCARE

A Family Center at Rams Head was built a few years ago. The Friendly Penguin nursery takes kids from age 6 weeks to 6 years – reservations required. Outside the door is the Snow Play Park, with magic carpet lift and handle tow-lift. There are ski classes for several age groups.

TOURIST OFFICE

Postcode VT 05751
t +1 (802) 422 3333
f 422 4391
info@killington.com
www.killington.com

MOUNTAIN RESTAURANTS
Bearable base lodges

There are only two real mountain restaurants. We have mixed reports on the one at the top of Killington Peak, in what was the top station of the old gondola. Max's Place, on Sunrise, has 'table service burgers, pasta, salad etc, and is highly recommended to escape the squalor of the other on-mountain eating places', says a reporter. Each of the lift base stations has some sort of eatery, of which the one at Killington Base Lodge is the least dreary.

SCHOOLS AND GUIDES
In search of the Perfect Turn

The philosophy of the Perfect Turn school is to build on your strengths rather than correct your mistakes, and it seems to work for most people. There is a special Discovery Center for beginners, where you start and finish in a dedicated beginners' building with easy chairs, coffee, videos and help with choosing and fitting your equipment. But, unusually, the school gets a bad report this year: 'Inconsistent because you don't get the same instructor each day and on our last day they took us down a black mogul run that nobody could cope with, which shattered my confidence.'

FACILITIES FOR CHILDREN
Fine in practice

There is a Family Center at the Rams Head base, which takes kids from 6 weeks and will introduce them to skiing from age 2 years.

Staying there

Killington is one of the most spread-out resorts we have come across, with lots of its accommodation literally miles from the lift bases. Provided you're renting a car, this isn't that much of a hassle. Staying near the end of the access road is convenient for the Skyeship gondola and Pico.

HOW TO GO
Wide choices

There is a wide choice of places to stay. As well as hotels and condos, there are a few chalets.

There are a few places near the lifts, and reachable on snow – the Killington Grand Resort hotel (complete with pool and other spa facilities) and some condos at Snowshed, for example. Further out, The Cortina Inn ('20 mins away, pool, excellent food, but poor soundproofing'), Red Rob Inn ('pool, good restaurant, a cut above the usual motel style'), Inn of the Six Mountains ('more facilities, higher price, good food') and Telemark Village condos ('at end of access road') have all been recommended by recent reporters.

EATING OUT
You name it

There are all sorts of restaurants spread along the Killington Road, from simple pizza or pasta through to 'fine dining' places. They get very busy at weekends and many don't take reservations. Many of the nightspots mentioned below serve food for at least part of the evening.

The local menu guide is essential reading. Claudes Choices and the the Cortina and Red Rob Inns have been recommended by recent reporters.

APRES-SKI
The beast of the east

Killington has a well-deserved reputation for a vibrant après-ski scene; many of its short-stay visitors are clearly intent on making the most of their few days (or nights) here.

Although there are bars at the base lodges, keen après-skiers head down Killington Road to one of the lively places dotted along its five-mile length. From 3pm it's cheap drinks and free munchies, then in the early evening it's serious dining time, then later on the real action starts (and admission charges kick in). Most of the places mentioned here would also rate a mention in Eating Out.

The train-themed Casey's Caboose is said to have the best 'wings' in town. Charity's is another lively bar, with an interior apparently lifted from a turn-of-the-century Parisian brothel. The Wobbly Barn is a famous live-music place that rivals Jackson's Mangy Moose for the position of America's leading après-ski venue. The Pickle Barrel caters for a younger crowd, with theme nights and loud music. The Outback complex has something for everyone, from pizzas and free massages to disco and live bands.

OFF THE SLOPES
Rent a car

If there is a less amusing resort in which to spend time not skiing or boarding, we have yet to find it. Make sure you have a car, as well as a book.

Smugglers' Notch 315m

Fine fun for families

WHAT IT COSTS

(5)

HOW IT RATES

The slopes

Snow	***
Extent	*
Experts	***
Intermediates	***
Beginners	****
Convenience	*****
Queues	****
Restaurants	*
The rest	
Scenery	***
Resort charm	**
Off-slope	*

MOUNTAIN FACTS

Altitude	315m-1110m
Lifts	9
Pistes	1000 acres
Green	22%
Blue	53%
Black	25%
Art. snow	139 acres

What's new

There was a new lift in Morse Bowl for 1999/2000. This accesses a new beginner area with five trails and a new lodge at the base. The Fun Zone is a new family adventure centre offering various facilities and activities. The Science of Nature is a new programme, intended to teach kids more about the winter environment. The Sycamores is a smart new condo development next to the Meadowlark trail, a few minutes from the village centre.

A new water reservoir will increase the snowmaking capacity by 66% for 2000/01. The snow-gun network is being extended.

Smuggs hits the family target squarely, with a constant round of early-evening activities, sympathetic instructors, comprehensive childcare, a 'petting zoo' with sheep and goats, a generally child-friendly layout and some long, quiet, easy runs. There are challenging slopes, too, but it's a small domain and mileage-hungry intermediates should go elsewhere (as should nightbirds).

THE RESORT

Smugglers' Notch is about the nearest thing you'll find in the US to a French-style purpose-built family resort – except that it doesn't look so bad. The village isn't genuinely traffic-free – you may have to tangle with traffic to get to the childcare centre, even – but it comes close, and once installed in your condo you can happily do without a car. Those not afflicted with children could find the family orientation of the resort a bit overpowering: you may find it's difficult to get away from Billy Bob Bear and pals.

The resort is energetically managed and produces a constant flow of developments designed to tighten its grip on the market. Yet again it has been voted 'North American family resort of the year' by at least one American skiing publication – and a recent British reporter calls it 'the best family resort I have been to'.

THE MOUNTAIN

Smuggs has varied and satisfying **slopes**, spread over three hills – Morse, above the village, with the new Morse Bowl area off to the left, and Madonna and Sterling off to the right, reached by green links. There are some real challenges as well as easy cruising, and a worthwhile vertical of 800m. It's blissfully quiet on the mountain except at weekends and holidays. It's undeniably a small area, though. You can get to Stowe's Spruce Peak by an intermediate trail from the top of Sterling, and some but not all lift passes include a day in Stowe.

The amount of snowmaking is gradually increasing, and **snow reliability** is already good.

It's a great area for **beginners**. One of the chair-lifts out of the village runs at half speed, and the runs it accesses are of an ideal gradient. Morse Bowl adds another tailor-made novice area. And the higher lifts take you to long easy runs that even 'never-evers' can tackle during their first week.

There are **intermediate** runs of every grade; there just aren't many of them. The link with Stowe adds variety.

There are challenges for **experts**. We were impressed by the two or three double-diamond runs on Madonna, and they have recently opened The Black Hole – the only triple-diamond run in the east, they say, and certainly the only one we have encountered. You can go off-piste in the trees anywhere within the resort boundary – but these areas are not patrolled.

Smuggs encourages **snowboarding**, and has a couple of impressive fun-parks and a half-pipe. Evening beginners' lessons are available three times a week.

The 23km of **cross-country** trails may be a bit limited for expert skiers.

We encountered no **queues**, and away from weekends we'd be surprised if anyone else did.

There are no real **mountain restaurants**, but there is a new warming hut with snacks at the top of the Prohibition Park half-pipe and the new lodge at Morse Bowl serves food. Most skiers go back to base for lunch.

The **ski school** (or 'Snow Sport University') is 'outstanding' according to a recent report and has often been voted the best in North America. It

THE CHILD'S VIEW

Smuggs is a great place for children who like to ski. It has lots of little special trails for younger children like Laura, who was four years old when we went there, and fairly difficult runs for older children like me (I was eight). There are two ski clubs to look after children of different ages. My teachers were very friendly and they take you on slopes that are just right.
By Alex Gill

Editorial offspring Laura Gill successfully negotiates the end-of-week slalom for junior beginners – a festive occasion at Smuggs, even on a grey day →

SNOWPIX.COM / CHRIS GILL

guarantees that you will learn to ski or board, or improve your technique. Among its bright ideas are private lessons for a parent and child, with the idea that the parent learns how to help the child develop while having fun.

Smuggs aims to be simply the best for **children**. The mountain is child-friendly, offering excitement with safety – with a special jolly kids' trail map. There's a terrain park for kids, and little forest glades where even tinies can be taken 'off-piste'. Alice's Wonderland Child Enrichment Center is a comprehensive nursery. The school arrangements are very good, too, with childcare before, between and after skiing sessions, and carriage to the kids' chair-lift by horse-drawn sleigh. See special report on previous page.

STAYING THERE

There are no **hotels** in the resort itself – though there are some within driving distance. There are lots of comfortable condos on or near the slopes, and none is very far from the snow.

There are a couple of **restaurants** in the resort, including the cosy Hearth and Candle, and others a short drive down the road to the outside world – we and the kids enjoyed an outing to Banditos. Babysitters can be arranged.

The adult **après-ski** possibilities are about the most limited we have come across. We hear good reports of the teen centre, and our kids loved the diversions laid on for them.

There is very little to do **off the slopes**. Organised day trips to Vermont or Montreal are possible.

TOURIST OFFICE

Postcode
VT 05464-9537
t +1 (802) 644 8851
f 644 2713
smuggs@smuggs.com
www.smuggs.com

SMUGGLERS' NOTCH RESORT

Kids love getting off the main trails into the trees ↓

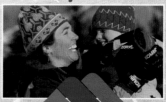

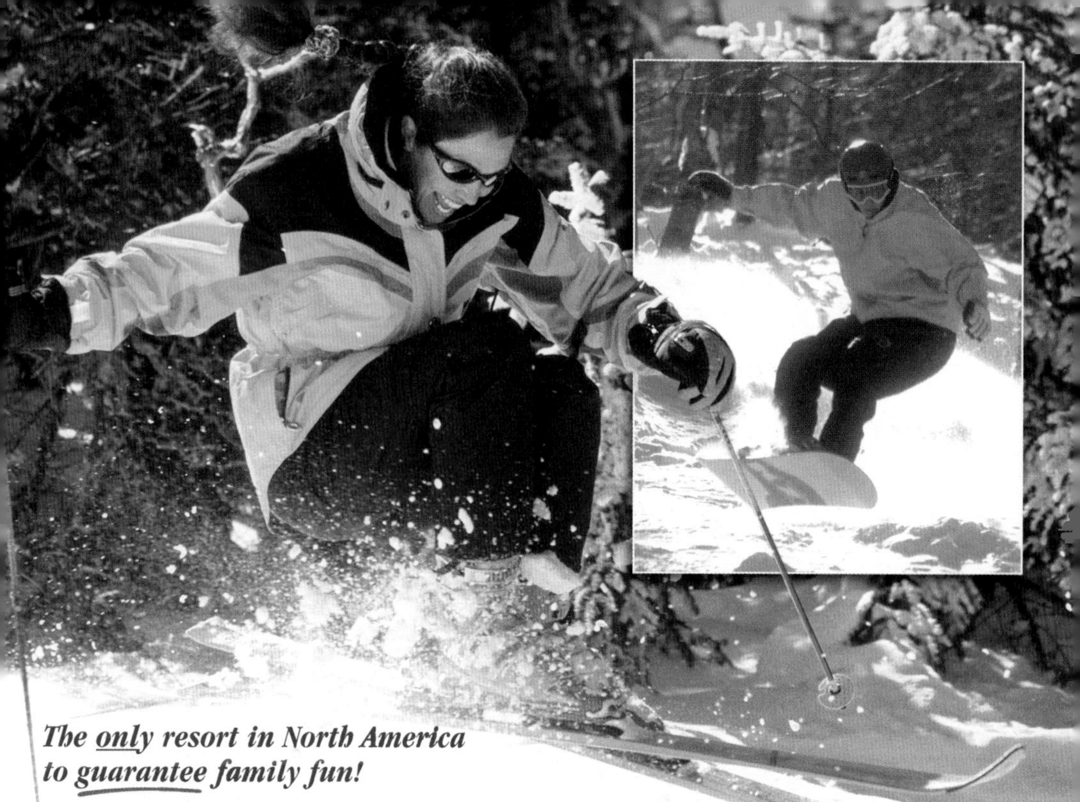

Stowe 475m

Charming Vermont town, small but serious mountain

WHAT IT COSTS

5

HOW IT RATES

The slopes	
Snow	***
Extent	*
Experts	***
Intermediates	****
Beginners	****
Convenience	*
Queues	****
Restaurants	**
The rest	
Scenery	***
Resort charm	****
Off-slope	*

What's new

The Stowe Toys Demo Center was opened last season – guests can test out the latest equipment and get advice from professional instructors.

There are long-term plans for a $150 million expansion project, which would include a lift link between Mount Mansfield and Spruce Peak – and perhaps upgraded chair-lifts on Spruce Peak itself.

MOUNTAIN FACTS

Altitude	390m-1110m
Lifts	11
Pistes	480 acres
Green	16%
Blue	59%
Black	25%
Art. snow	350 acres

TOURIST OFFICE

Postcode VT 05672
t +1 (802) 253 3500
f 253 3406
info@stowe.com
www.stowe.com

Stowe is one of New England's cutest little towns, its main street lined with dinky clapboard shops and restaurants. Its mountain, six miles away, is modest in size, but has everything from great cruising to fearsome mogul-fields. And it is now linked by trails and lifts to Smugglers' Notch next door.

THE RESORT

Stowe is a classic little New England town – a real community and a popular spot for tourists year-round, with bijou 'specialty' shops lining its sidewalks. You could find no sharper contrast to the other New England resorts we feature in this edition. The slopes of Mount Mansfield, Vermont's snow-capped (though mainly wooded) highest peak, are a 15-minute drive away and much accommodation is along the road out to it. There's a good day-time shuttle-bus service but a car is recommended for flexibility.

THE MOUNTAIN

The **slopes** are in three sectors, two linked by blue runs mid-mountain and green ones at the base, the third (Spruce Peak) a short shuttle-ride away (there are plans for a lift link, but it's not imminent).

The main sector, served by a trio of chair-lifts from Mansfield Base Lodge, is dominated by the famous Front Four – a row of seriously steep double-black-diamond runs. But there is plenty of intermediate and easy stuff, too.

A fast eight-seat gondola serves the next sector: easy-intermediate runs with one black alternative – plus the short but very steep Waterfall, under the gondola at the top.

The third area, Spruce Peak, has the main nursery area at the bottom, with a slow chair-lift to mid-mountain and another beyond that. 'Possibly the slowest chairs in the world,' says a reporter. The top of this sector links with Smugglers' Notch, over the hill (see the previous chapter).

Snow reliability is helped by snowmaking on practically all the blue (and some black) runs of the main sectors, and on lower Spruce Peak.

For **experts,** the Front Four and their variants present a real challenge. For **intermediates**, the usual New England reservation applies: the terrain is limited in extent; there's also a severe shortage of ordinary black runs. For **beginners**, the nursery slopes and long green runs are great. 'Spruce Peak is one of the best beginner/early skier areas we've seen,' says a report.

Stowe attracts many **snowboarders** and has two fun-parks and a half-pipe. It has excellent **cross-country** centres dotted around the landscape (including the musically famous Trapp Family Lodge), with lots of connected trails – 35km of groomed and 40km of back country trails.

The area is largely free of **queues** mid-week but we've had reports of 25-minute queues at weekends.

Of the **mountain restaurants,** Cliff House, at the top of the gondola, is a lofty room with table-service and good food and views. Midway Café near the base of the gondola has a BBQ deck and table-service inside. The Octagon Web Café, on the main sector, is a small cafeteria where you can send free e-mails to friends back home. There are excellent **children's** facilities.

STAYING THERE

Stowe is a long-established tourist town, with more 3- and 4-diamond **hotels** and **restaurants** than any other place in New England except Boston. There are hotels in and around Stowe itself and various points along the road to the slopes, some with Austrian or Scandinavian names and styles. Ye Olde England Inne is recommended by reporters (despite the appalling name). Stowehof Inn and Green Mountain Inn are also recommended. There are restaurants of every kind. The Cliff House at the top of the gondola is open for dinner.

Après-ski is muted – Stowe reportedly goes to bed early. There's a good cinema with new releases.

Stowe is a pleasant town in which to spend time **off the slopes** – at least if you like shopping. A trip to the Burlington shopping mall is recommended.

Sunday River 245m

The biggest snowmaking system in New England

WHAT IT COSTS

5

HOW IT RATES

The slopes	
Snow	***
Extent	**
Experts	**
Intermediates	****
Beginners	****
Convenience	***
Queues	****
Restaurants	***
The rest	
Scenery	***
Resort charm	**
Off-slope	*

What's new

For the 1999/2000 season a new terrain-park called Nebula opened on Aurora Peak. It is designed for expert skiers and riders looking to catch big air and perform aerial tricks. 150 new 'tower' snow-guns were also installed.

For 2000/01 there will be a top-to-bottom terrain-park and a third half-pipe, as well as more snowmaking.

MOUNTAIN FACTS

Altitude	245m-955m
Lifts	18
Pistes	655 acres
Green	25%
Blue	35%
Black	40%
Art. snow	603 acres

TOURIST OFFICE

Postcode ME 04217
t +1 (207) 824 3000
f 5110
snowtalk@sundayriver.com
www.sundayriver.com

Sunday River was one of the pioneers of snowmaking, and over 90 per cent of its trails are served by it. So the snow should be as good here as anywhere in the east. The terrain is varied and quite extensive. But it lacks village ambience.

THE RESORT

Sunday River is where the American Skiing Company (which owns eight other US resorts) started and where it still has its HQ. Despite this, there isn't really a slope-side village yet – there are various developments scattered around the slopes – so there isn't much village ambience. Bethel is the nearest small town, a 10-minute drive away; it's a pleasant place with a few shops and a handful of restaurants and bars. The resort attracts quite a lot of British school groups, especially at half-term and Easter.

THE MOUNTAINS

The **slopes** range over about 5km from east to west and across eight different peaks. It does feel like a reasonably extensive network of trails and glades – 126 at the last count – and there are numerous base areas, parking lots and accommodation units dotted around. The White Cap base marks the eastern extremity of the system and is handy for the Grand Summit hotel, the half-pipe and other evening activities. The peaks around the main base areas are fairly packed with lifts and trails. The Jordan Grand hotel is at the western limit of the system, and in general the western sector (Aurora, Oz and Jordan Bowl) has far fewer lifts and runs and a more remote and backwoods feel. Indeed, 40 per cent of the trails are graded black.

Snow reliability is good: a decent natural snow record is backed up by a high-capacity, high-tech system for making and grooming artificial stuff.

Experts will enjoy the challenge of the narrow, often mogulled double-blacks on White Cap and Barker Mountain, and there is excellent glade skiing on Aurora, Oz and Jordan Bowl.

It's generally a good resort for **intermediates** who will enjoy cruising around on a series of nice rolling blues (often deserted in mid-week), and there are also some not too fearsome glades to tempt the bold. South Ridge is a well-organised area for **beginners**, with good, easy runs to progress to.

Snowboarders will find a competition standard half-pipe and other terrain-parks in which to amuse themselves and the half-pipe is floodlit for evening use. In and around Bethel there are three **cross-country** centres with a total of around 140km of trails.

When we were there in mid-week **queues** were non-existent – indeed most lifts and slopes were deserted. Even on busy weekends you should be okay if you stick to the four high-speed quads. There are no real **mountain restaurants**, but there are good, civilised table-service places at the Jordan Grand and Grand Summit hotels as well as the usual self-service places.

The Grand Summit and South Ridge Centre house the main **children's** facilities. There's also a family entertainment centre called the Nite Cap, which has skating, a tubing hill and a games arcade, plus the half-pipe. **Ski school** is not a term they use at Sunday River but there is a series of 'Perfect Turn' clinics available. A reporter who took a group of 40 school children said the ski instructors were 'overstretched at half-term but still superb, and one even bought his class baseball caps'.

STAYING THERE

The main slope-side **hotels** are the new Jordan Grand and the Grand Summit. There's also a dorm as well as normal rooms at the Snow Cap Inn. And in and around Bethel are numerous inns, lodges, motels and B&Bs. There are slope-side condos.

Après-ski in Sunday River is quiet. Bumps pub often has live bands. A recent reporter recommends the Foggy Goggle bar, which also has live music, and the Matterhorn Steak Bar in Bethel (large steaks, local beers, good atmosphere). There are two brew pubs.

Off the slopes, apart from the likes of snowmobiling, tubing, ice-fishing and swimming, there are a few antique and craft shops. And there's a good Laser Quest games place in Bethel.

Canada

Ten years ago hardly any British skiers went to Canada. It simply wasn't on the map as a winter sports destination. How times have changed. Now more of us go to Canada for a skiing or boarding holiday than go to America or even to Switzerland. It's easy to see why: they get lots and lots of snow, prices are great value (both for packages and for eating and drinking when you get there), the people are friendly and helpful and the scenery can be spectacular.

A couple of seasons ago we drove from Whistler to Banff, calling in at lots of smaller resorts on the way. The whole trip took two weeks and for eight consecutive days in the middle it snowed. It snowed and snowed and snowed. It made driving from resort to resort tricky as we insisted on driving at night after getting in a full day on the slopes. But the skiing was spectacular – day after day of dry, light powder. Wow ... To be honest, after about four or five days of snow we craved some sunshine. And some views – at every resort we arrived at in the interior of British Columbia our mountain guide would point out into the clouds and say, 'If only you could see, over there is a spectacular view of the Monashees.' We never did see them. We asked a local on a chair-lift in Red Mountain, 'Do you ever get any sun round here?' To which he replied with incredulity, 'Hell ... what do you want sun for? Ruins the snow.' Well, he has a point.

If you want snow, western Canada is the place. The weather on our trip was not unusual. In an average year Whistler, for example, gets 10 metres of snow and it snows (or rains at resort level!) for half the days in the season. That makes for superb conditions on the slopes. When you reach Banff-Lake Louise you might not get quite the same frequency of snow but it stays in great condition because it is further inland, the air is drier and temperatures colder. You get a better chance of blue skies there – but also a higher chance of a day or two of very low temperatures of –20°C or less.

So you go to western Canada for the skiing not the sunbathing and posing you can hope to do in the Alps in a week of fine weather. If you prefer long lunches on warm, sun-drenched mountain restaurant terraces, stick to March in the Alps. If you want a good chance of hitting powder and polishing up your powder technique, put Canada high on your list of possible destinations.

If you really want untracked powder and are feeling flush, there is nothing to beat Canada's amazing heli- and snowcat skiing operations. The main difference is that the former is faster paced and more expensive than the latter. But with both you are taken to the middle of nowhere in a deserted mountain wilderness and then let loose with a guide who takes you down untracked slopes to another spot in the middle of nowhere, where you are picked up and taken to the top of another mountain and another untracked run. And so it goes on! You can do it by the day but the hedonistic luxury option is to book a few days or a week in a luxury lodge run by the heli-skiing or snowcat operation, eating gourmet dinners and stepping out of the door each morning straight into the chopper or snowcat.

If you can't afford the £3000 plus a week that this would cost, you can always try a day for £200 plus. But if you resist heli-skiing or snowcat heaven, you'll find a holiday in Canada can be very cheap. Package prices start at around £400 for a week to western Canada and around £350 for a week in the east. These prices are made possible by cheap direct and charter flights to the key airports and the use of accommodation in resorts where winter is low-season compared with summer. And once you get there you'll find the cost of eating and drinking out very cheap compared to the Alps.

Another difference you'll notice compared to the Alps is the people. For a start they speak English (very useful, especially for ski or board lessons). But more importantly they are friendly and have the American service culture that 'the customer is king'. You'll find mountain hosts to show you around the slopes, immaculately groomed runs, civilised lift queues, lots of fast quad chair-lifts, piste maps available at the bottom of most lifts, and cheerful, helpful staff.

In the west you'll also find spectacular scenery (when the clouds clear) to rival that of the Alps and far superior to anything you'll find in the US. You'll also find an amazing variety of wildlife, especially in Banff-Lake Louise, Jasper and the interior of British Columbia. Herds of elk and big-horn sheep roam the streets and road sides. You might even see a moose or a bear.

For us, the main attraction of eastern Canada is that the resorts are in the heart of the province of Québec, where the French influence is predominant – language, cuisine and culture are all dominated by French-Canadians and it makes for a unique ambience. Québec is now attracting a fair number of British winter visitors, including school groups. It also has the attraction of a shorter flight time but the disadvantage of extremes of weather.

As well as downhill skiing and snowboarding, Canada is famous for a wide variety of other activities such as snowmobiling, cross-country skiing, dog-sledding, snow-shoeing and ice fishing.

Western Canada

Western Canada is the main draw for visitors from Britain. It has fabulous scenery, good snow and a wonderful sense of the great outdoors. The big names of Whistler and Banff-Lake Louise capture most of the British market at present, but there are lots of worthwhile smaller resorts that more adventurous travellers are now starting to explore. We recommend renting a car and combining two or more of these resorts, perhaps with a couple of days on virgin powder served by helicopters or snowcats as well. You'll have the holiday of a lifetime. Smokers should be warned that BC has banned smoking in all public buildings (ie restaurants etc).

The map over the page shows the area we're covering here. Two of the smaller resorts where we reckon you're most likely to want to stay for a bit now get their own detailed reports.

Fernie Alpine Resort (page 556) – previously Fernie Snow Valley – is three-and-a-half hours from Calgary and three hours south of Banff. It has a deserved reputation for great powder, and now that it's in the same ownership as Lake Louise and has doubled its terrain, installed two new lifts and started building a resort village with luxury slope-side accommodation, you can expect to hear a lot more about it. As well as the main lift-served slopes, there's the attraction of an excellent snowcat operation at Island Lake Lodge, nearby.

Panorama (page 559) is two hours south-west of Banff, with a big vertical drop and an impressive range of slopes. Intrawest (which also owns Whistler and Tremblant) has built an attractive purpose-built village right at the foot of the slopes, with slope-side hot tubs and condos and an attractive base lodge. Panorama is also home to RK Heli-Ski, which offers one-day heli-trips for intermediates.

Kimberley Alpine Resort is another new addition to the portfolio of Resorts of the Canadian Rockies, owners of Lake Louise. It is about 90 minutes from Fernie and three hours from Banff and offers a mix of blue and black runs and a vertical of 700m, five minutes' drive from downtown Kimberley itself. The town of Kimberley has a 'Bavarian theme' and Canada's largest cuckoo clock (thanks to a rather unusual attempt by tourist authorities in the 1970s to boost visitor numbers). The base at the Kimberley ski area is going through a major $200 million transformation. A whole new village is being built at the bottom of a new high-speed quad. This includes a day lodge, a massive children's facility, and a Marriott-run hotel. Log and stone construction makes this village area an impressive sight.

Kimberley's main attraction to date has been exceptional snow. The slopes lie in a perfect catchment area for powder, and snow stays light and dry for days especially in the plentiful quiet and gladed black runs. Kimberley's terrain was doubled a few seasons ago when owner Charlie Locke took an old Lake Louise chair-lift and opened up a raft of new runs. Another expansion is on the drawing board.

A new place to appear on the map is **Kicking Horse Mountain,** formerly known as Whitetooth and renamed in April 2000. These slopes above the town of Golden are 90 minutes' drive from Lake Louise and perfect for a day trip or a few days at this stage. Until now a small area with a lone rinky-dink double chair-lift, Kicking Horse's new European owners have big plans for the area: no less than a 1200m long gondola to be completed by the 2000/01 season, six more chair-lifts, a flash eatery at the gondola top station and more than a smattering of condos and chalets clustered at the base. Quite a change from the current base area with its shabby cafeteria and ski shop/ski hire/ski school housed in a trailer. Property values in Golden jumped 20 per cent overnight after the April announcement.

Spectacular views of the Rocky, Selkirk and Purcell mountain ranges will be found at the gondola summit as well as awesome ridgeline skiing off the Dogtooth range. This will complement the wide green and blue and few black runs already carved out lower down. Kicking Horse has serious cred among avid skiers who have been settling in Golden in droves over the past two years, their aim being to hike and ski the powdery fields above the current chair-lift. The area is renowned for its big snowfalls. Golden is home to a helicopter skiing operation, and from 2001 Kicking Horse will be open seven days a week instead of the current four.

The other resorts you might think of taking in on a tour of BC are further west, in the 'interior'. There is some great terrain and great snow out here, and the slopes are deserted on weekdays.

Red Mountain is up there with Fernie in our estimation, but suffers from its isolated location midway between Vancouver and Calgary. But if you find yourself in Spokane (Washington) one winter, head north. There are green and red runs, but it's the black and double-black stuff that is the real attraction, coupled with superb powder. We loved the terrain here – mostly in trees, with gradients as steep as you can handle. Granite Mountain is a conical peak with more-or-less separate faces of blue, black and double-black steepness, and a total vertical of 880m – all served by a couple of triple chairs. Next-door Red Mountain itself is half the size and has only a lone double chair, but is no less interesting. There's accommodation close to the slopes or a couple of miles away in Rossland, an unpretentious little town that has bred countless Canadian ski racers. No wonder.

Whitewater, nearby on Highway 6, is well worth a look in and an absolute must after a storm. Tucked even further into the ranges than Red Mountain, Whitewater's bottomless powder elicits rave responses from those in the know. Accommodation is found in the charming historic town of Nelson on the West Arm of the Kootenay Lake – cute bed and breakfasts, hotels and good restaurants.

Then, west again, there is a cluster of resorts around the Okanagan valley. Probably the least compelling is **Apex**, a family-oriented resort with a modern mini-resort at the foot of its slopes and good views from the top, 610m higher.

Big White is BC's highest ski area, peaking at 2318m, and the next biggest after Whistler, with over 100 runs and 2000 skiable acres. Like Red Mountain, it has a reputation for powder although, like Red, it claims an average of 'only' 300in. The place also has a reputation for freezing fog, which converts its hilltop trees into 'white ghosts'. The slopes – open at the top, descending through glade areas to dense forest – have something for everyone, but our favourites are the single blacks served by the Gem Lake fast quad – 2.5km long and 700m vertical. The purpose-built slope-side village is small, but developing fast. It has a splendid base lodge, and a very impressive childcare centre. Restaurants include a Japanese one and the atmospheric Snowshoe Sam's.

Silver Star, above the town of Vernon, is a newly developed 'gaslight-era' 1890s-style village right on the slopes. The wooded mountain has two separate but linked faces; the south face around the village has mainly easy and intermediate slopes served mainly by a fast quad of 480m vertical; the back north face is a splendid wooded bowl of easy runs along the rim and black and double-black trails dropping into the middle to meet the 630m-vertical fast quad.

Sun Peaks, near Kamloops, was known as Tod Mountain. Now $100 million of investment has created a cute, car-free, Tirolean-style slope-side village and good intermediate and beginner terrain to go with the steeps that used to dominate. Olympic gold medallist Nancy Greene is the energetic director of skiing, and she and her husband run a hotel by the slopes. The resort claims the biggest vertical in the BC interior, with 880m; the mountain is open at the top and densely wooded lower down, with a balance of blue and black runs at top and bottom and a couple of areas of genuinely double-black stuff. Novices are safely tucked away on their own hill.

Jasper, in Alberta, is a spectacular three-hour drive from Lake Louise along the Columbia Icefields Parkway, past glaciers, frozen waterfalls and lakes in the Banff and Jasper National Parks – one of the most beautiful drives in the world. The town itself is tiny and in the National Park itself, which is teeming with wildlife, including herds of elk and long-horned sheep. The ski area of Marmot Basin is a 30-minute drive – small but with runs for all standards. Go to Jasper for an all-round winter holiday, not just for skiing or riding.

Western Canada is also home to the world's most famous **heli-skiing** operations, where you can stay for a week in a luxurious lodge and be whirled up to virgin powder for several runs a day – at a cost of £2500 or more (plus flights from the UK). Mike Wiegele and CMH are two of the most famous, both operating out of interior British Columbia. Tyax Lodge Heli-Skiing, 60 miles north of Whistler, is a similar operation. Or you can try heli-skiing for a day from many resorts – a much more affordable option. An even cheaper alternative is snowcat skiing where you ride up the mountain in a much more relaxed fashion in a converted snowcat.

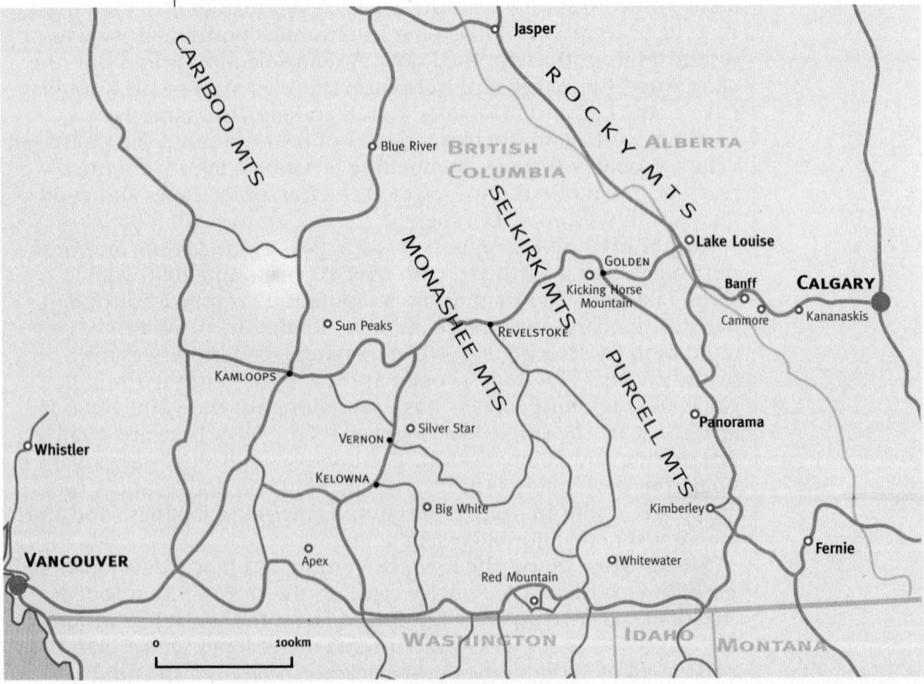

Banff-Lake Louise

1340m-1645m

Winter wonderland with wildlife

WHAT IT COSTS

4

HOW IT RATES

The slopes	
Snow	****
Extent	****
Experts	****
Intermediates	****
Beginners	***
Convenience	*
Queues	****
Restaurants	**
The rest	
Scenery	****
Resort charm	***
Off-slope	****

- ➕ Spectacular high-mountain scenery – quite unlike the Colorado Rockies
- ➕ Three widely separated mountains add up to a lot of terrain
- ➕ Excellent snow record at Sunshine
- ➕ Lots of wildlife around the valley
- ➕ Some extraordinary hotels
- ➕ Lots of touristy shops
- ➕ Great value for money at current favourable exchange rate

- ➖ Separate mountains are a long way apart, though buses are good and there's the scenery to enjoy
- ➖ Can be very cold in early season – and lifts offer no protection
- ➖ Quite a few slow chair-lifts
- ➖ Lack of traditional ski resort atmosphere
- ➖ Mediocre mountain restaurants
- ➖ Can seem over-full of Brits

The British now go to Banff and its neighbouring resorts in unbelievable numbers, making up 40 per cent of all winter holidaymakers (if you leave out weekenders). Price has been a key factor in getting us to make the trip. Winter is low season in the spectacular and unspoilt Banff National Park, so room prices are low; add cheap charter flights to Calgary, and the result is very tempting package prices. But that's only half the story: most visitors are delighted with what they find, and keen to go back.

It's not difficult to see why. The landscape is one of glaciers, jagged peaks and magnificent views, and the valleys are full of wildlife that you'll never see in Europe. The slopes have something for everyone, from steep couloirs to gentle cruising. The snow is some of the coldest, driest and most reliable you'll find anywhere in the world and there's a lot of it (at Sunshine Village, at least). And there are the standard Canadian assets of people who are friendly and welcoming, and low prices for meals and other on-the-spot expenses.

For us, these factors count for more than the drawbacks. But then we, luckily, have not encountered the extremely low temperatures (–30°C is not unusual) that have left some early-season reporters feeling less convinced.

SNOWPIX.COM / CHRIS GILL

Downtown Banff – tourist shops by the score, and Norquay in the background ↓

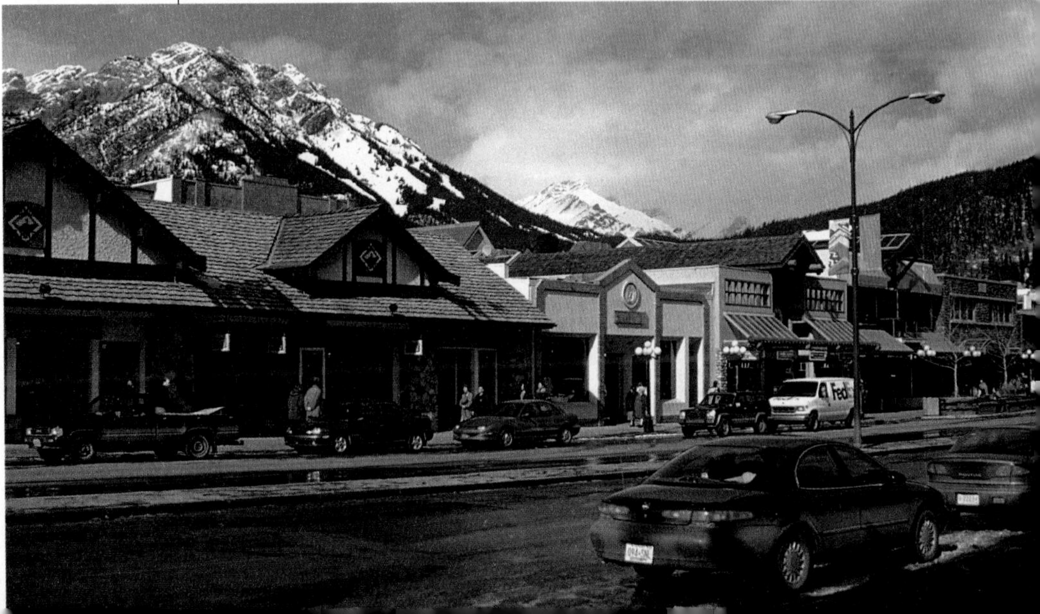

boarding *Boarders will feel at home in Banff-Lake Louise. All three mountains have good fun-parks and half-pipes and all have some excellent free-riding terrain for experienced riders. Norquay offers a snowboard park lift ticket for those wishing to use only the park and pipe and Lake Louise now boasts the largest terrain park in North America. We have had mainly positive reports about the tuition. Beware green trails, however, as they can be really flat and require some walking. Banff is the best spot for lively nightlife.*

What's new

1999/2000 saw Lake Louise's snowmaking system (already huge) further enhanced. And the terrain park was expanded as well.

Sunshine Village further improved its snowboard facilities last year and also expanded its expert terrain with the reopening (after 14 years) of the extreme Delirium Dive, on the north face of Lookout.

At Norquay, the old Cascade double chair was upgraded to a quad for 1999/2000 and the Sundance drag was replaced by a magic carpet lift for 1999/2000. Some new beginner terrain was also added.

For 2000/2001, Lake Louise will add another fast quad chair from the base. As we went to press, Sunshine Village was still awaiting approval for its plans to replace the Wheeler chair and Fireweed T-bar.

The resort

Banff (1340m) is a big summer resort that happens to be within driving distance of three separate ski and snowboard areas. Norquay is a small area overlooking the town. Sunshine Village, 20 minutes away, is a bigger mountain; despite the name, it's not a village (nor is it notably sunny) – it has just one small hotel at mid-mountain. Lake Louise is another half-hour away, and is a resort in its own right – but most of its visitors (and most of its workers) are based in Banff.

Banff is spectacularly set, with several towering peaks rising up around its outskirts (see picture on page 547). There is lots of wildlife around, at least when the weather is right; don't be surprised to find a herd of elk or long-horned sheep outside your hotel. And in spring there may be bears along the highways.

Banff town has grown substantially since 1990, when it became independent of the Banff National Park authority. But it still consists basically of one long main street and a small network of side roads built in grid fashion, lined by clothing and souvenir shops aimed mainly at summer visitors. The buildings are low-rise, and not unpleasant individually – some are attractively wood-clad. But the town lacks genuine charm; it's a tourist town, not another Aspen or Telluride.

Lake Louise is a resort of parts. First, there's the lake itself, in a spectacular mountain setting beneath the 3564m Victoria Glacier. Tom Wilson, who discovered it in 1882, declared, 'As God is my judge, I never in all my exploration have seen such a matchless scene.' Neither have we – it is simply stunning. And it can be appreciated from many of the rooms of the monster Chateau Lake Louise hotel on the shore. Then there's Lake Louise 'village' – a shapeless little collection of hotels, condominiums, petrol station, supermarket, liquor store and few shops, a couple of miles away down in the main valley, close to the railway and highway from Banff to Jasper. Finally, a mile or two across the valley is the lift base station (1645m).

A car can be helpful here, especially in cold weather. The buses to these areas (free to Tri-area lift pass holders) are frequent and generally reliable, although a recent reporter points out that, depending on the number of pickups, the bus rides can take twice as long as advertised.

The mountains

We may not seem very keen on the villages, but we approve of the mountains. Taking the slopes of Lake Louise and Sunshine Village together, the area is big, and the views are the most spectacular that the Rockies have to offer. Both major areas have slopes to suit every level of skill, but are particularly interesting for those looking for a challenge. There are dozens of black-diamond runs, and considerable numbers of double-blacks, especially at Lake Louise.

There are free guided tours of all three mountains.

THE SLOPES

A lot of moving around to do

The biggest of the three areas is **Lake Louise** (claimed to be one of the biggest in North America in terms of acreage of slopes, though it certainly isn't in terms of marked pistes).

Two successive high-speed quads take you to the top of the main mountain. From here, as elsewhere, there's a choice of green, blue or black runs to other lifts. The tree line comes about halfway up the top lift, but there are alternative lifts that stop a bit lower, so you can stay in the trees in bad weather. From mid-mountain, a drag-lift (a rare thing here) takes you to the high-point of the area (2640m), at the shoulder of Mount Whitehorn.

From the top there's a stunning view of some of the high peaks of the Continental Divide, including Canada's uncanny Matterhorn lookalike, Mount Assiniboine.

MOUNTAIN FACTS

Altitude	1635m-2730m
Lifts	28
Pistes	7530 acres
Green	22%
Blue	43%
Black	35%
Art. snow	1700 acres

NORQUAY MOUNTAIN FACTS

Altitude	1635m-2135m
Lifts	5
Pistes	160 acres
Green	20%
Blue	36%
Black	44%
Art. snow	145 acres

SUNSHINE MOUNTAIN FACTS

Altitude	1660m-2730m
Lifts	12
Pistes	3170 acres
Green	20%
Blue	50%
Black	30%
Art. snow	none

LAKE LOUISE MOUNTAIN FACTS

Altitude	1660m-2670m
Lifts	11
Pistes	4200 acres
Green	25%
Blue	45%
Black	30%
Art. snow	1555 acres

Recco detectors used

From either the top chair or the drag you can go over the ridge and into Lake Louise's treeless back bowl runs. The bowl is predominantly north-facing and so keeps its snow well.

From the bottom of the bowl runs you can take a lift back to the top again or up to the separate **Larch** area, served by a fast quad chair. With a vertical of 465m it's not huge, but it has pretty wooded runs of all standards. From the bottom you can return to the top of the main mountain via the Ptarmigan chair or take a long green path back to the main base area.

The slopes of **Sunshine Village** are slightly higher than those of Lake Louise. More importantly, they are on the Continental Divide and as a result get more snow. The main slopes are not visible from the base station: you ride a long dog-leg gondola, first to the base of the recently developed Goat's Eye Mountain, and then on to Sunshine Village itself. Most of the slopes here are above the tree line. Although there is a wooded sector served by the second section of the gondola and a couple of chairs, in bad weather you're better off elsewhere.

Goat's Eye is served by one lift, a fast quad chair rising 580m. Although there are some blue runs, this is basically a black mountain, with some genuine double-blacks at the extremities. There has been talk of building an additional fast quad up the middle of the slopes to a point more or less on the tree line; this would make the area more useful in bad weather, but is still awaiting approval.

Lifts fan out in all directions from Sunshine Village, with short runs back from Mount Standish and longer ones from Lookout Mountain.

Many people ride the gondola down at the end of the day. But the 2.5km green run to the bottom is a pretty cruise. If you go down while the lifts are running you can take the Fireweed lift to cut out a flat section, but the run gets busy and is much more enjoyable if you delay your descent a bit.

Norquay is much the smallest area. But it's worth a visit, especially in bad weather – it has wooded slopes to suit all standards served by a row of five lifts. One trail is floodlit at weekends.

Some reporters feel that runs on all three mountains are undergraded, though we didn't.

The small resorts of Nakiska and Fortress are within range – see p555.

SNOW RELIABILITY
Excellent

Sunshine Village claims '100 per cent natural snow,' a neat reversal of the usual snowmaking hype. Certainly, the lack of snowmaking there has never been a problem in our experience. 'Three times the snow' says another Sunshine slogan – a cryptic reference to the fact that the average snowfall here is 360 to 400 inches (depending on which figures you believe) – as good as anything in Colorado, and rivalling Jackson Hole – compared with a modest 140 inches on the front face at Lake Louise and 120 inches on Norquay. But we're told the Sunshine figures relate to Lookout, and that Goat's Eye gets less. There is snowmaking on 40 per cent of the pistes at Lake Louise, and 90 per cent at Norquay. So all in all, lack of snow is unlikely to be a problem.

FOR EXPERTS
Widespread pleasure

All three areas have satisfying terrain for good skiers and boarders.

At Lake Louise there are countless steep slopes. On the front face, as well as a score of marked black-diamond trails in and above the trees, there is the alluring West Bowl, reached from the Summit drag – a wide open expanse of snow outside the area boundary. (Because this is National Park territory, you can in theory go anywhere. But outside the boundaries there are no patrols and of course no avalanche control. A guide is essential. Inside the boundaries there are also areas permanently closed because of avalanche danger.) Going over to the back bowls opens up countless black mogul/powder runs. Last season the avalanche-prone Whitehorn 2 area directly behind the peak (marked 'Occasional Openings' on the trail map) was opened, providing our Ozzie editor with what she calls 'some of the most exciting in-bounds skiing in North America' – a row of extreme chutes, almost 1km long.

The Top of the World quad takes you to the very popular Paradise Bowl, served by its own triple chair – one run is marked on the map but there are endless variants. From the Summit drag you can access wide open slopes that take you right away from all signs of lifts. Again, there are endless variations. On the 'end' of the mountain, between the front and back faces, is the area served by the Ptarmigan quad chair. This seriously steep slope provided many of the logs for the new base lodge, and offers great glade terrain as a result. The Larch area has some steep stuff in the trees, and open snowfields at the top for those with the energy to hike up above the lift.

Sunshine has plenty of open runs of genuine black steepness above the tree line on Lookout, but the recently added Goat's Eye Mountain has made this area much more compelling. It has opened up a great area of expert double-black-diamond trails and chutes, both above and below the tree line – one reporter enjoyed the area so much that he and his party kept 'going back again and again'. There are short, steep runs on Mount Standish, too. One particular novelty is a pitch, near the mid-station, known as the Waterfall run – because you do actually ski down over a snow-covered frozen fall.

Real experts will want to get to grips with the recently reopened Delirium Dive on Lookout Mountain's north face – only to be attempted with full avalanche kit (a guide is also recommended). We haven't yet had a chance to try this, but at 40° pitch and 585m vertical it sounds impressive.

Norquay's two main lifts give only 400m vertical, but both serve black slopes and the North American chair accesses a couple of double-diamond runs that justify their grading.

Heli-skiing is available from bases outside the National Park in British Columbia – roughly two hours' drive.

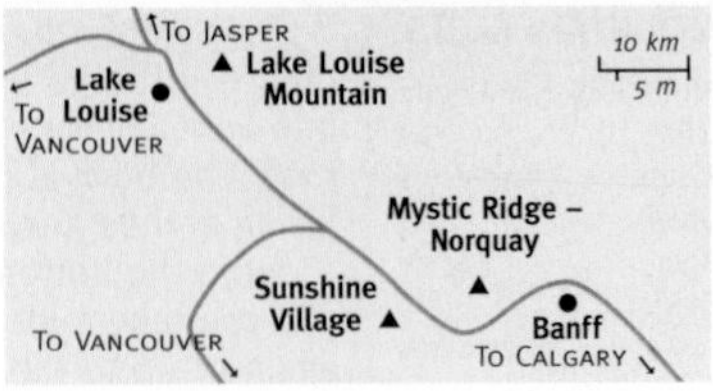

FOR INTERMEDIATES

Ideal runs wherever you go

In all three areas, at least one third of the runs are classified as intermediate. One thing that characterises both Lake Louise and Sunshine is that there is a wide choice of runs from the top of virtually all lifts. Wherever you look there are blue and green ways down – some of the greens as enjoyable (and pretty much as steep) as the blues.

On Louise, Meadowlark is a beautiful tree-lined run from the top of the Eagle chair to the base area. Juniper and Juniper Jungle are wonderful cruising runs on the western side. The Larch area has some short but enjoyable intermediate terrain. And the adventurous should try the blue-graded Boomerang which starts with a short hike from the top of the highest lift, the Summit drag. On many runs one side is groomed, the other left to develop moguls.

On Sunshine, we particularly like the World Cup Downhill run, from the top of Lookout to the mid-mountain base. Don't ignore the Wawa T-Bar, which gives access to the often quiet Wawa Bowl and Tincan Alley. Or the delightful wooded area beneath the second stage of the gondola.

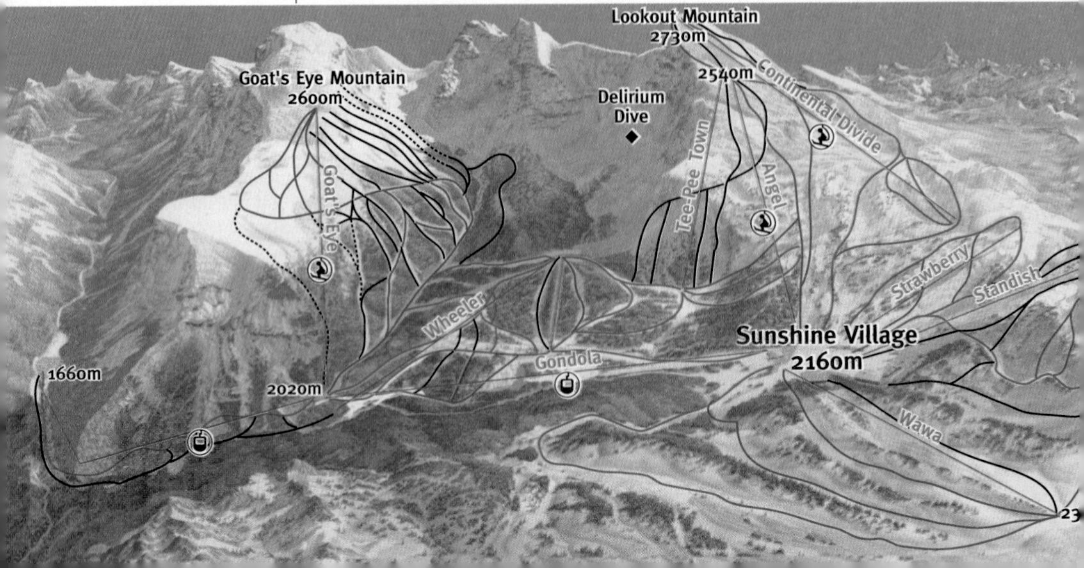

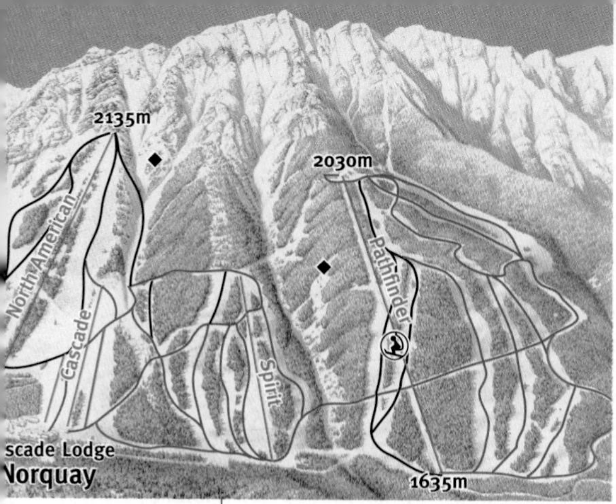

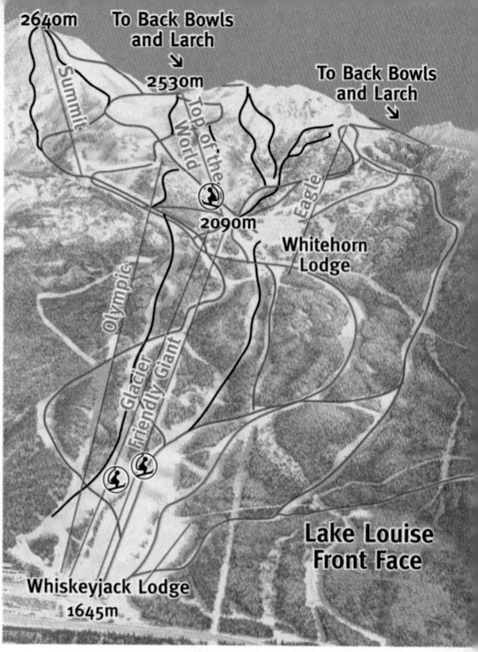

The Pathfinder fast quad at Norquay serves a handful of quite testing tree-lined blues and a couple of sometimes-groomed blacks.

FOR BEGINNERS
Excellent terrain

Louise has a good nursery area near the base, served by a short T-bar; Sunshine has a good area by the mid-mountain base, which is served by an even shorter hand-tow. And Norquay has a small nursery area but no real runs for progressing beginners.

In all areas there are great runs to progress to. Recommended on Louise are the gentle, wide Wiwaxy (designated a slow skiing zone, so there are no lunatics bombing past you) and the slightly more difficult Deer Run or Eagle Meadows on the upper mountain. There are even greens round the back bowls and in the Larch area – worth taking for the views.

Sunshine has the beginners-only Meadow Park among other user-friendly greens.

This may not seem the ideal destination for a mixed party of beginners (who may want to stay in one place) and more experienced friends (who are likely to want to visit all three areas). But the Club Ski and Club Snowboard deal may solve the problem (see Schools and guides).

FOR CROSS-COUNTRY
High in quality and quantity

It's a good area for cross-country. There are trails near Banff, around the Bow River, and on the Banff Springs golf course. But the best area is around Lake Louise. Altogether, there are around 80km of groomed trails within Banff National Park.

QUEUES
Not unknown

Half of the area's visitors come for the day from nearby cities such as Calgary – so it's fairly quiet during the week. The gondola up to Sunshine is rarely free of morning queues, and recent reports speak of waits of up to 90 minutes in February; a parallel six-pack will relieve the pressure, eventually. Lake Louise is so sure of its lift system that it offers vouchers, to be used within the year, if you have to queue for over ten minutes. A new chair on the front side is being installed for 2000/01 to be on the safe side. But a recent reporter encountered weekend queues of up to ten minutes on the back of Lake Louise, not the front.

More of a problem than queues is the cold. Temperatures as low as –30°C are not unusual in mid-winter. At these temperatures, you might hope to find more chairs with shields, and gondolas. Reporters recommend investigating local conditions before picking your mountain, as the weather can be drastically different at each one.

A number of readers have found the trail marking a bit vague, with trail markers too widely spaced.

MOUNTAIN RESTAURANTS
Not a highlight

All three mountains have eating facilities – both at the base area and up the mountain at Lake Louise and Sunshine Village. But most are

LIFT PASSES

2000/01 prices in Canadian dollars

Tri-area lift pass
Covers all lifts and transport between Banff, Lake Louise and Sunshine Village.

Beginners First time ski packages including rental, pass and tuition available

Main pass
1-day pass
6-day pass 336

Children
Under 13: 6-day pass 114

Short-term passes
Half-day pass for individual areas of Lake Louise, Sunshine Village or Banff Mount Norquay.

Notes Tri-area only available for 3 days or more.

Alternative passes
Day passes for individual areas of Lake Louise, Sunshine Village or Banff Mount Norquay, with reductions for senior citizens (over 65, and over 55 at Norquay), teenagers (13-17) and students with ID (13-25).
The Canadian Rockies Super Pass (about $55 per day) covers eight Alberta and BC ski resorts: Lake Louise, Sunshine Village, Norquay, Fernie, Kimberley, Fortress, Nakiska and Panorama.

CHILDCARE

The nursery at Lake Louise takes children aged 18 days to 6 years, from 8am to 4.30. The ones at Sunshine Village and Norquay's Cascade Lodge take children aged 19 months to 6 years, from 9am to 4pm. In all three, children aged 3 or more can take short ski lessons.

cafeteria-style and serve the usual basics: burgers, sandwiches, soups.

On Louise, Temple Lodge, near the bottom of the Larch lift, is built in rustic style with a big terrace; it can get very crowded, but options include a calm table-service restaurant with the option of a well-priced buffet (buffalo stew a speciality). Whitehorn Lodge, at mid-mountain on the front face, has excellent views from its balcony. The new Lodge of the Ten Peaks at the base is a hugely impressive log-built affair; there are several different eating options (ranging from dreary self-service to comfortable dining rooms and lounges) here and at Whiskeyjack. Beavertails, at the Gazebo, is popular with reporters for a quick lunch, though it can get very crowded.

Sunshine Village has a choice of eating places at its mid-mountain base. The recently renovated Day Lodge has improved its choice of food. Mad Trapper's Saloon is a jolly western-style place in Old Sunshine Lodge, serving different food on its two levels. The Sunshine Inn hotel has the best food – table-service snacks in the Chimney Corner Lounge or a full lunch in the Eagle's Nest Dining Room. The Java Hut, at the bottom of Goat's Eye Mountain, has been recommended.

At the base of Norquay, the big new timber-framed Cascade Lodge is excellent – it has great views and a table-service restaurant upstairs as well as a self-service cafeteria.

SCHOOLS/GUIDES

1999/2000 prices in Canadian dollars

Club Ski and Club Snowboard
3 days of guided tuition of the three areas

Club Ski classes
4½hr per day
3 full days: 149

Club Ski Junior
Age 6 to 12
4½hr per day
3 full days 149

Club Snowboard classes
3hr per day
3 full days 139

SCHOOLS AND GUIDES
Some great ideas

Each mountain, like many of the big hotels, has its own school. Recognising that visitors wanting lessons won't want to be confined to just one mountain, the resorts have organised an excellent Club Ski and Club Snowboard Program – three-day courses starting on Mondays and Thursdays that take you to all three mountains, offering a mixture of guiding and instruction – including free video analysis, a fun race and a group photo. We'd recommend this to anyone who wants to see the whole area while improving their technique. Reporters who've tried it rave about it: 'absolutely brilliant' and 'improved more in three days than in a week anywhere else'. All standards are catered for, including beginners.

'The best tuition we've encountered' is how a recent reporter described his 'bumps' lesson at Lake Louise. Another took a day's tuition at Norquay with great success.

FACILITIES FOR CHILDREN
Good for non-skiers

There are none of the snow-garden facilities that are common in the Alps, but all three areas have crèches where children can be looked after. One reporter who used all three said: 'I'd recommend all three and advise booking in advance at Lake Louise.'

Staying there

Wherever you stay (except at mid-mountain on Sunshine) it will be a drive or bus-ride to the slopes. Lake Louise village is the nearest place to major slopes. The sports shop in the little mall here gets repeated recommendations. But don't expect any resort ambience or much nightlife. Some of the Banff lodgings (even on the main Banff Avenue) are quite a distance from downtown, but there's a good bus service.

HOW TO GO
Superb-value packages

A huge amount of accommodation is on offer – especially hotels and self-catering, but also a few catered chalets run by British tour operators. We have an enthusiastic report ('wonderful views, excellent food, great hot-tub') on the Timberline Inn, reachable on skis from Norquay and now run as a kind of chalet hotel by Crystal.

Hotels Summer is the peak season here. Prices halve for the winter – so you can stay in luxury at bargain rates. In or near Banff:

((((4 **Banff Springs** A turn-of-the century, castle-style Canadian Pacific property, well outside town. It's virtually a town within itself – it can sleep 2,000 people, has over 40 shops, numerous restaurants and bars, a nightclub and a huge indoor pool. There's also a superb health club and spa for which there's a charge. The reception area is undergoing reconstruction which means some facilities will be unavailable for a while.

(((3 **Banff Caribou Lodge** On the main street, slightly out of town. It has a variety of wood-clad, interestingly and individually designed rooms, a sauna and hot-tub complex and a good restaurant and bar. Repeatedly recommended by reporters.

GETTING THERE

Air Calgary, transfer 1½hr.

(((3 **Rimrock** Spectacularly set, out of town towards Sulphur Mountain, with great views and a smart health club. Luxurious but impersonal.
((2 **Inns of Banff** About 20 minutes' walk from town centre; recommended by reporters for its large rooms, room service and fitness facilities.
((2 **Banff Park Lodge** In the town itself. Large and central, with hot-tub, steam room and indoor pool.
((2 **Banff King Edward** An old hotel recently renovated. Right in the town centre, set above shops; recommended by reporters for large rooms and being surprisingly quiet for its position.
At Lake Louise village:
((((4 **Post** A member of the Relais & Châteaux chain, with the best cuisine in the area, wood-panelled rooms and even a few log cabins in the grounds. Indoor pool, hot-tub and steam room. Go for a room facing away from the railway to avoid the worst of the hooting trains during the night.
((2 **Lake Louise Inn** The cheaper option in the village, still with pool, hot-tub and sauna. 'Comfortable rooms' and an efficient shuttle-bus, but 'disappointing restaurants'.
At Lake Louise itself:
(((3 **Chateau Lake Louise** With stunning views over frozen Lake Louise, this 500-room Canadian Pacific-owned hotel has recently undergone a multi-million dollar restoration and has a choice of restaurants and a health club with indoor pool, steam room and hot-tub. Unless you have a car, you're pretty well stuck here in the evenings. Gets lots of Japanese visitors.
((2 **Deer Lodge** A simpler, cheaper option with a rooftop hot-tub.
Self-catering The biggest complex is the Banff Rocky Mountain Resort, set in the woods on the edge of town, which has a wealth of in-house facilities including indoor pool, squash and hot-tubs. Reporters have also recommended the Douglas Fir resort for families – though 'a bit out of town' – and Woodland Village.

EATING OUT

Lots of choice in Banff

The best cuisine in the region is in the Post hotel restaurant at Lake Louise. The Outpost (also in the Post hotel) is recommended for good inexpensive pub food. Chateau Lake Louise has two Alpine-style restaurants – the Walliser Stube, serving fondue and cured meats, and the Edelweiss, for more formal dining. It also has the Poppy Room, for family-style food and some other options. In (or near) Lake Louise village, the Station Restaurant is repeatedly recommended for food, service, value and cosy atmosphere (it's in the brilliantly converted old station building); also the Baker Creek Bistro.

But there's much more choice in Banff, with over 100 different restaurants, from McDonald's to fine dining in the Banff Springs hotel. Reporters are enthusiastic about lots of places but complain about them being busy and many places not taking bookings. Many places do huge portions that you can share. Regular recommendations include Earl's (burgers and ethnic dishes, very popular and lively), Melissa's (steaks), Balkan (Greek), Joe Btfsplk's (a classic 1950s diner with jukebox), Magpie and Stump (Mexican, with Wild West decor), Giorgio's (Italian), Silver Dragon (Chinese), Sukiyaki (Japanese), Rose & Crown (pub grub), Hard Rock Café (burgers), Bumper's (huge portions of ribs), the Keg (steaks, two branches – one in town and one in Caribou Lodge), the Pines (excellent Canadian cuisine) and Coyotes (Californian cuisine).

APRES-SKI

Liveliest in Banff

One of the drawbacks of the area is that teatime après-ski is limited because the villages are a drive from the slopes. But Mad Trapper's Saloon at the top of the Sunshine Village gondola is popular at the close of play happy hour (with endless peanuts). And at Lake Louise, the Whiskeyjack Lodge is a popular après-ski spot – especially at weekends, when there's live music. There are also weekly dinners with live entertainment at the mid-mountain Whitehorn Lodge, followed by a torchlit descent on a perfectly groomed green run – hugely popular with British visitors.

In Banff, things liven up later. Wild Bill's has live country and western music and line dancing. The Rose & Crown has live music and gets crowded. The Works and the Barbary Coast nightclubs are popular, as is Melissa's on a Tuesday night. And Outabounds attracts a young lively crowd. The St James Gate Irish pub is very popular with reporters for its great atmosphere, good-value food and wide

ACTIVITIES

Indoor Film theatre, museums, galleries, swimming pools (one with water slides), gym, squash, racquetball, weight training, bowling, hot-tub, sauna, mini-golf, climbing wall

Outdoor Swimming in hot springs, ice skating, heli-skiing, horse-drawn carriage rides, sleigh rides, dog-sled rides, snowmobiles, curling, ice hockey, ice fishing, helicopter tours, snowshoe tours

TOURIST OFFICE

Postcode ToL oCo
t +1 (403) 762 4561
f 762 8185
info@skibanfflake louise.com
www.skibanfflake louise.com

range of beers.

Lake Louise is much quieter. The Glacier Saloon, in Chateau Lake Louise, with traditional Wild West decor, often has live music until late. Explorer's Lounge, in the Lake Louise Inn, has nightly entertainment. The Post hotel's Outpost Pub is recommended.

OFF THE SLOPES
Beautiful scenery

If you enjoy walking, the area has a lot of attractions. You can go snow-shoeing and on organised ice canyon walks. There are museums to visit such as the Whyte Museum of the Canadian Rockies, the Natural History Museum, the new Canadian ski museum and the Buffalo Nation's Luxton Museum of the Indians of the Northern Plains. And, of course, there's the wildlife and the natural hot springs.

There are sleigh rides, dog-sledding, skating and tobogganing. Lake Louise has ice skating and broomball games.

Reporters are impressed by the sheer quantity of shops ('a shopaholic's dream') and many have commented on the friendly atmosphere – 'the friendliest place on the planet'.

STAYING UP THE MOUNTAIN
Worth considering

At Sunshine Village, the Sunshine Inn is the only slope-side hotel. It is well run, has a good atmosphere, a big outdoor hot-tub, good food and small but attractive rooms with excellent views. Unlike every other hotel in the area, it closes in summer, and its winter rates are as high as any.

VISITING OTHER RESORTS
The road to Jasper is stunning

An attractive option is to spend a couple of days in Jasper – see introduction to Western Canada, page 544. The three-hour trip on the Columbia Icefields Parkway, through the Banff and Jasper National Parks, is a stunningly beautiful drive.

Day trips to other resorts are worth the effort if on an extended stay. Panorama is a couple of hours away to the south-west (see separate chapter, page 559). On the way to Calgary are Nakiska, about an hour's bus ride, and Fortress, a further half-hour away. The bus is scheduled to run twice a week, and it's possible to spend the morning in one and then take the bus to the other in the afternoon. Nakiska, made famous by the 1988 Calgary Olympics, is a small area of runs cut through woods. 'Empty, with excellent grooming,' says a reporter. Fortress, in stark contrast, is primitive and wild – set at the base of dramatic sheer cliffs. 'Superb powder, great fun.'

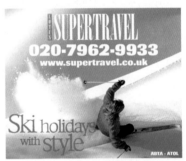

SNOWPIX.COM / CHRIS GILL

More snowy than sunny, and nothing like a village, but this is Sunshine Village ➔

Fernie

1070m

Lots of snow, and lots of steeps

WHAT IT COSTS

5

HOW IT RATES

The slopes

Snow	****
Extent	***
Experts	*****
Intermediates	**
Beginners	****
Convenience	****
Queues	****
Restaurants	*

The rest

Scenery	****
Resort charm	**
Off-slope	**

What's new

1998/99 saw the completion of a huge expansion project that doubled the skiable terrain. Two new lifts opened up three new bowls – Siberia, Timber and Currie.

Last season, the new mountain village started to take shape with the opening of three new condo-hotels, plus shops restaurants and crèche.

For 2000/01 the Bear T-bar will be replaced by a fast quad, improving access to both Lizard and Cedar Bowls.

MOUNTAIN FACTS

Altitude	1070m-1925m
Lifts	9
Pistes	2500 acres
Green/Blue	30%
Red	40%
Black	30%
Art. snow	25 acres
Recco detectors used	

- ⊕ Good snow record, with less chance of rain than at Whistler, and less chance of Arctic temperatures than at Lake Louise
- ⊕ Great terrain for those who like it steep and deep, with lots for confident intermediates and beginners, too
- ⊕ Great snowcat operation nearby at Island Lake Lodge
- ⊕ Good on-slope accommodation becoming increasingly available in small, friendly mountain resort

- ⊖ Despite installation of fast quads in 1998 and 2000, the lift system still has weaknesses, with hikes and traverses to some of the best terrain
- ⊖ After a dump it can take time to make the black bowls safe and groom the blue cruisers
- ⊖ Only one basic mountain pit-stop
- ⊖ Mountain resort is still small, with very limited evening options, and town of Fernie (a short drive away) is not particularly appealing either
- ⊖ Not much to do off the slopes

Fernie has long had cult status among Alberta and BC skiers for its consistently steep and even fall lines and superb natural snow, but it is only now finding an international market. In 1998 the slopes were doubled in area and the operation was bought by Charlie Locke, owner of Lake Louise. Since then, there has been a lot of investment in the development of the village at the foot of the slopes. Some visitors would rather see more investment in the mountain, to cut down the amount of hiking and traversing, and to speed up reopening after a serious snowfall. We see their point, but most reports we get are dominated by excitement at Fernie's combination of snow and terrain. 'It was love at first ski!' says one highly experienced reporter. We admit we felt the much the same.

boarding *Fernie is a fine place for boarders. Lots of natural gullies, hits and endless off-piste opportunities – including some fantastic adrenalin-pumping tree-runs and wide open knee-deep powder bowls – will keep free-riders of all standards grinning from ear to ear. There's also a good terrain park and half-pipe for free-stylers. Snowcat rides are available to take you to some excellent untouched powder. There are a couple of pretty good bars in the town, and Frozen Ocean and Board Stiff are the main board shops.*

The resort

Fernie Alpine Resort is a rapidly growing and increasingly attractive village at the lift base a little way up the mountainside from the flat Elk valley floor. The accommodation at the resort is mushrooming, and there is more in the little town of Fernie, a couple of miles away in the valley.

The town is named after William Fernie – a prospector who discovered coal here and triggered a boom at the turn of the century. Much of the town was destroyed by fire in 1908 but some downtown stone and brick buildings survived and are still there. We thought it a nondescript spot, but reporters who have spent more time there liked its friendly atmosphere.

The mountains

Fernie's 2500 acres pack in a lot of variety, from superb green terrain at the bottom to ungroomed chutes that will be satisfyingly steep to anyone but the extreme specialist. Quite a few of the runs have the rare quality of consistently steep pure fall lines, says our resident expert.

THE SLOPES
Bowl after bowl

What you see when you arrive at the lift base is a trio of impressive mogul slopes towering above you. The Deer chair approaches the foot of these slopes, but goes no further. You get to them by traversing and hiking from the main Lizard Bowl, on the right. This is

LIFT PASSES

1999/2000 prices in Canadian dollars
Main pass
1-day pass 46
Senior citizens
Over 65: 38
Children
Under 13: 15
Under 6: free pass
Short-term passes
Half-day pass from noon (adult 38)
Notes
Mighty Moose lift passes available for beginners: 15

SCHOOLS/GUIDES

1999/2000 prices in Canadian dollars
Fernie
Classes
1¾hr: 10am and 1.30pm
½ day: 27
Multi ½ days: 23
Children's classes
Ages 3 to 4 and 5 to 12
Multi full day: 38
Private lessons
Hourly: 50 (22 for each additional person)

CHILDCARE

The resort day care centre takes children of all ages. It is open daily from 9am to 4pm.

GETTING THERE

Air Calgary, transfer 3½hr.

a broad snowfield of blue gradient, reached by a series of lifts: a slow quad, a fast quad (replacing the old T-bar this season) and finally the short Face Lift – a dreadful rope tow. It is also the main way into lift-free Cedar Bowl (where a recent reporter came across a moose) and to Snake Ridge beyond it. There is a mini-bowl between Lizard and Cedar, served by the 500m vertical Boomerang chair.

The Timber Bowl fast quad chair gives access to Siberia Bowl and the lower part of Timber, but for access to the higher slopes and to Currie Bowl you must take the White Pass Quad. A long traverse from the top gets you to the steeper slopes on the flanks of Currie that are otherwise reached by hiking from the main Lizard Bowl.

There are excellent hosted tours of the area twice a day.

Outings to Kimberley are possible; a coach does the trip on Thursdays.

SNOW RELIABILITY
A key part of the appeal

Fernie has an excellent snow record – with an average of 350 inches per year, better than practically all of Colorado. There is no snowmaking, and the altitude is modest – rain is not unknown, and in warmer weather the lower slopes can suffer.

FOR EXPERTS
Wonderful – deep and steep

The combination of heavy snowfalls and abundant steep terrain with the shelter of trees makes this a superb mountain for good skiers. There are about a dozen identifiable faces offering genuine black or double-black slopes, each of them with several alternative ways down. The bowls accessed by the two new lifts have some serious double-diamonds, but are mainly genuine single-diamonds.

There are also backcountry routes you can take with guidance.

FOR INTERMEDIATES
Far from ideal

Although there are intermediate runs both low down and high up, they don't add up to a lot of mileage and are liable to present some difficulties after a heavy snowfall.

FOR BEGINNERS
Excellent

The lower mountain is a beginner's delight with lots of wide, smooth trails to gain confidence on. And there are long winding green trails back down to the base from all the higher lifts. There are green trails running out from Siberia and Currie bowls, but you have to ski blues to get to them.

FOR CROSS-COUNTRY
Some possibilities

There are 15km of trails marked out in the forest adjacent to the resort, and the Fernie golf and country club allows enthusiasts on to their white greens.

QUEUES
Not usually a problem

Unless there is a weekend invasion from Calgary, queues are rare. The replacement of the Bear T-bar by a fast quad will deal with the queues that did build there, but is likely to increase pressure on the already inadequate Face Lift tow. If heavy snow keeps part of the mountain closed, there can be queues for other sectors.

MOUNTAIN RESTAURANTS
What mountain restaurants?

Bear's Den at the top of the Elk chair is an open air fast-food kiosk. So it's back to base for lunch.

SCHOOLS AND GUIDES
'Lessons for all abilities'

Recent reports have praised the ski school and its small classes. 'First Tracks' gets you up the mountain at 8am for two hours.

FACILITIES FOR CHILDREN
They exist

There's a new resort day care centre in the Cornerstone Lodge.

Staying there

You're going for the snow, so our advice would be to stay on or close to the hill. But it's cheaper to stay in the town, where there is a wider choice of restaurants, bars and other diversions, and a much wider choice of shops.

HOW TO GO
More packages

Fernie is increasingly easy to find in tour operator brochures.

Hotels and condos
As the resort develops the choice is widening and shifting upmarket.

((((4) **Lizard Creek Lodge** New luxury ski-in/ski-out condo hotel. Spa, pool and hot tub. Highly recommended.

ACTIVITIES

Indoor Museum, galleries, aquatic centre, saunas, bowling, fitness centre, ice skating, cinema, curling
Outdoor Sleigh rides, snowmobiling, dog-sledding, snow-shoe excursions

TOURIST OFFICE

Postcode VoB 1M1
t +1 (250) 423 4655
f 423 6644
info@skifernie.com
www.skifernie.com

(((3 **Cornerstone Lodge** New condo hotel in the village core.
(((3 **Polar Peak Lodges** Chalet-style condos a walk from the slopes.
(((3 **Griz Inn** Condo-hotel with good facilities. Pool.
((2 **Wolf's Den Lodge** Comfortable but simple, conveniently close to lift.
((2 **Timberline Village** Very comfortable condos a shuttle-ride from the lifts.

EATING OUT
Not a highlight

At the base, Gabriella's Little Italy is repeatedly recommended. The Lizard Creek Lodge is now regarded as having the best dining anywhere in the area. Kelsey's is more casual and offers good large servings. The Powderhorn in the Griz Inn does 'good, reasonably priced' food. In Fernie, the restaurants at the Royal and Grand Central hotels are recommended, as is Rip and Richard's Eatery – 'great' south-western food and a lively atmosphere. Some alternatives: the Old Elevator has a pleasantly traditional atmosphere; Jamocha's has everything from three meals a day to live music at night; JV's Pantry does prime ribs and pasta dishes. The Whistle Stop in the Art Station is a wholefood place.

APRES-SKI
Have a beer

The Grizzly bar at the base is lively at close of play. The Powderhorn, in the nearby Griz Inn, is good for a relaxed drink. During the week, the bars are pretty quiet later on. In town, the bar of the Royal hotel is popular with locals. Other recommendations are the Park Place Lodge Pub and the bar in the Grand Central hotel.

OFF THE SLOPES
Get out and about

There is a heritage walking tour of historic Fernie. The old railroad station is now the Art Station. Shopping is fairly limited. The main diversion is the great outdoors.

RIDE THE SNOWCATS AT ISLAND LAKE LODGE

Any good skier who relishes off-piste should consider treating themselves to three or four days staying at Island Lake Lodge. (You can do single days without accommodation, but only on a standby basis.) The Lodge is a cosy chalet 10km from Fernie, amid 7000 acres of spectacular bowls and ridges. It has 36 beds, and four snowcats to act as lifts. In a day you might do eight powder runs averaging 500m vertical, taking in all kinds of terrain from gentle open slopes to some very Alpine adventures – maybe not as exciting as heli-skiing, but in its way just as rewarding. Three-day packages cost around £700. There are other snowcat operations in the region, less well-known and so less likely to be booked solid.

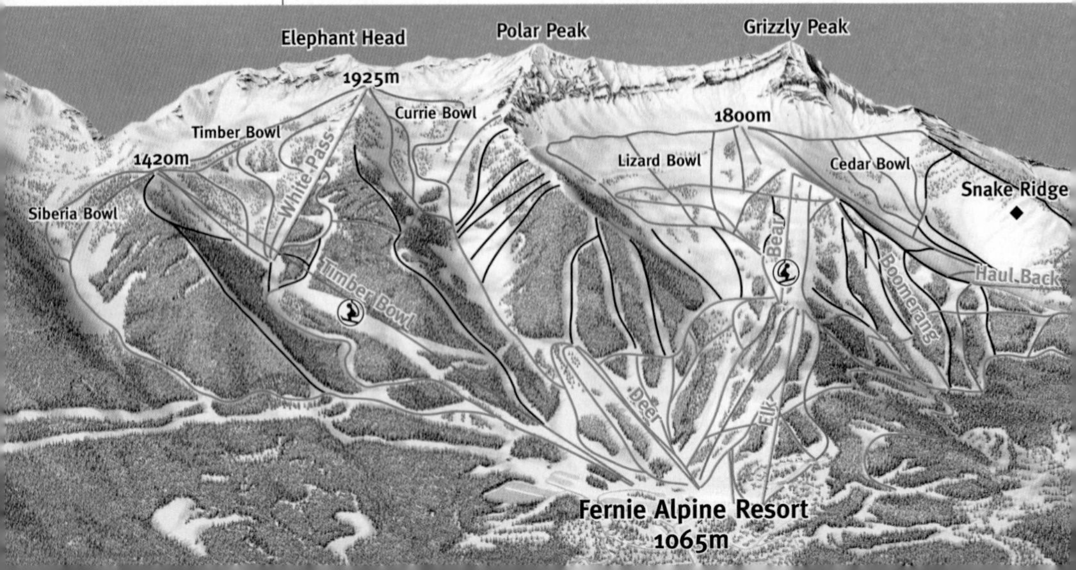

Panorama

1160m

Vertically challenging and fast developing

WHAT IT COSTS

5

HOW IT RATES

The slopes

Snow	***
Extent	**
Experts	****
Intermediates	***
Beginners	****
Convenience	***
Queues	****
Restaurants	*

The rest

Scenery	***
Resort charm	**
Off-slope	*

What's new

For 2000/01 about 1000 acres of new terrain called Taynton Bowl should be open, adding 50% to the existing acreage. The new Panorama Springs Slopeside condo-hotel is set on the nursery slopes, next to the 6000 sq ft outdoor Panorama Springs Hot Pools complex, which is free to Panorama lodging guests.

There is a new eight-person gondola connecting the lower and upper village and new advanced terrain in Canadian Bowl.

MOUNTAIN FACTS

Altitude	1160m-2380m
Lifts	10
Pistes	2000 acres
Blue	20%
Red	55%
Black	25%
Artificial snow	40%

TOURIST OFFICE

Postcode VoA 1To
t +1 (250) 342 6941
f 342 3395
paninfo@panoramaresort.com
www.panoramaresort.com

You can expect to hear more and more about Panorama. Its dynamic owner, Intrawest, has big plans for it, and the mountain has great potential. Its vertical drop of 1220m is one of the biggest in North America, and less than a third of the available terrain is in use at present. Like Fernie's, the slopes are less good for the intermediate piste-basher than for the novice and the expert; unlike Fernie's, they are not known for remarkable snowfalls. Heli-skiing by the day from the fringe of the village is an unusual attraction.

THE RESORT

Panorama is a small (but growing) purpose-built resort above the lakeside town of Invermere in eastern BC, about two hours' scenic drive south-west of Banff. Recently, more accommodation has been built at the foot of the main slopes but a lot is in a 'lower village' now linked by a short gondola.

THE MOUNTAIN

The **slopes** basically follow three ridges, joined at top and bottom. At the top, between the left and central ridges, is the double-black-diamond Extreme Dream Zone. A fast quad goes over gentle slopes to mid-mountain. Above this a double-chair followed by two T-bars opens up intermediate and expert slopes. From the very top there are long runs down the two outer ridges as well as the central one. Those on the left arrive back at the base. Those on the right bring you to a triple-chair up to mid-mountain, which also serves its own bunch of runs. Either way the whole vertical is usable.

Snowboarders will love the extensive powder bowls and tree runs, and the Show Zone fun-park and pipe.

Snow reliability could be better – the annual snowfall is less than half of the Fernie/Whistler figure. But snowmaking covers 40% of the area, and most slopes are not over-sunny.

There are genuine black runs dotted all over the mountain, but also some areas of special interest for **experts**. One is the Extreme Dream Zone – seriously steep trails complicated by cliffs as well as tight trees, accessed by a gateway at the very top. On the extreme right of the mountain is a quite different area of gentler glades, where you can pick the density of trees and steepness of slope to suit yourself. And RK Heli-Skiing operates from a base on the outskirts of the village.

For adventurous **intermediates** the terrain is excellent, but for the less experienced it may be uncomfortably challenging. The View of 1000 Peaks (now re-graded black) and Schober's Dream are beautiful and long for North America (up to 3.5km) – and in places quite challenging. The blues in the centre of the area are excellent, but don't add up to a lot. A recent reporter complained of erratic piste grading and sparse signage.

Beginners have a couple of nursery lifts and access to good, longer runs.

There is a fair network of **cross-country** trails; the golf-course club-house becomes the Nordic Centre.

There can be **queues** for the chair from mid-mountain and T-bars above, though the trails are usually deserted.

There are no real **mountain restaurants**. But there's a good coffee shop and the Ski Tip daylodge at the base is an excellent modern affair.

The Bilodeau **School of Skiing and Snowboarding** (SOS) was 'universally agreed as superb by all who tried it', says a recent reporter.

Wee Wascals is the childcare centre, taking **children** from 18 months.

STAYING THERE

There's an increasing choice of **hotels and condos**. The better places are the newer ones up on the nursery slope level – Ski Tip (recommended by a reporter) and Tamarack Lodges, Pine Inn (though 'soulless' says a reporter) and the new Panorama Springs.

Eating out options are mainly in the lodges – we enjoyed the Toby Creek restaurant, and the Starbird Steak House does a good buffet breakfast.

Après-ski revolves around the lively Kicking Horse bar in the Pine Inn and the Jackpine pub in the Horsethief Lodge. There's not much to do **off the slopes** without making excursions.

Whistler 675m

North America's biggest mountain set in Alpine-style scenery

WHAT IT COSTS

6

HOW IT RATES

The slopes

Snow	****
Extent	****
Experts	*****
Intermediates	*****
Beginners	****
Convenience	****
Queues	***
Restaurants	**

The rest

Scenery	***
Resort charm	***
Off-slope	**

- ⊕ North America's biggest mountain, both in area and vertical (1610m)
- ⊕ Good slopes for all standards, with an unrivalled combination of high open bowls and woodland trails
- ⊕ Good snow – 360 inches a year
- ⊕ Despite ever-increasing bed-base, still plenty of room on the mountain
- ⊕ Almost Alpine scenery, unlike the rounded Rockies of Colorado
- ⊕ Attractive modern village at the foot of the slopes, car-free in the centre, with lively après-ski
- ⊕ Good range of restaurants and bars (though not enough of them)
- ⊕ Easy access from the UK – non-stop flights to Vancouver, short transfer
- ⊕ Excellent heli-operation nearby

- ⊖ Proximity to the ocean means a high risk of British-style cloudy weather and, with the low altitude, heavy snowfalls on the mountain can mean rain at resort level
- ⊖ Two separate mountains are linked only at resort level
- ⊖ Some runs are busy by North American standards
- ⊖ Lift queues are beginning to be a bit of a problem
- ⊖ Mountain restaurants are mostly functional (and overcrowded)
- ⊖ Getting busier all the time – and the shortage of restaurant seats both for lunch on the mountain and dinner in the village is getting silly

Provided you go to Whistler expecting clouds and prepared for rain at the base, you'll love it. And you may be lucky: some reporters come back with a tan, and question our emphasis on the weather. But in three visits we've had only one blue-sky day. We don't care: Whistler's combination of wonderful varied and extensive terrain, big vertical, good snow and good lifts is unrivalled, and for a purpose-built resort the village is attractive. Most readers love it, too. Extracts from this year's crop of ecstatic reports: 'This place has everything.' 'Words cannot express it.' 'Awesome!' 'World-class.' 'One of the best.' 'Alpine paradise.' And perhaps most telling of all: 'This was my second year running at Whistler; to my surprise, I was still impressed by the whole experience.'

boarding *Both mountains are excellent for every standard of boarder, from beginner to expert. All the main lifts are chairs and gondolas and there is terrain for all – from gentle green runs to wide open bowls and heart-stopping cliff drops and chutes. The newly expanded Whistler Mountain terrain-park and half-pipe is a good place to hone your skills before moving on to the more difficult park on Blackcomb. The resort regularly hosts some big snowboard events so it's not uncommon to see pro riders here. There are T-bars up on the Glacier, but the discomfort is worth it for the powder! It's a popular area with snowboarders and is well known for its summer boarding camps.*

What's new

1999/2000 saw the installation of two fast quad chairs on Whistler mountain in parallel with the gondola, bringing Whistler's total number of fast lifts up to 15. A small new restaurant was opened near the top, and additional gladed runs cut beneath the higher chair-lift. Whistler Mountain's Nintendo 64 terrain-park was doubled in size to 26 acres.

Intrawest plans to invest $130 million at Whistler Creek over the next three years, with three condo-hotels, restaurants and shops. The first phase for 2000/01 will involve replacement of the old base lodge and will include a new Dusty's bar and grill.

The resort

Whistler Village sits at the foot of its two separate mountains, Whistler and Blackcomb, a scenic 75-mile drive inland from Vancouver on Canada's west coast. Whistler started as a locals' ski area in 1966 with a few ramshackle buildings in what is now called Whistler Creekside. Whistler Village was developed in the late 1970s, and Blackcomb village, spreading up the lower slopes of Blackcomb mountain, in the 1980s. Whistler has now annexed its smaller neighbour, and Blackcomb village, a 10-minute walk away, is now called the Upper Village.

Both centres are traffic-free. The architecture is varied and, for a purpose-built resort, quite tasteful.

There are lots of chalet-style apartments built on the hillsides. The centres have individually designed wooden and concrete buildings, blended together in a master plan and built around pedestrian streets and squares. There are no monstrous high-rise blocks, but there are a lot of large five- or six-storey hotel and apartment buildings. Whistler Village has the main concentration of bars, restaurants and shops, and the two main gondolas (one going up each mountain). Upper Village is much smaller and quieter, with a limited range of shops and restaurants. Its huge Chateau Whistler hotel, built in true Canadian Pacific style, dominates the views of the village from the mountain. Whistler North, a longer walk from the lifts, is a recent development.

Creekside, a 10-minute bus-ride from the main Whistler Village, is rather out on a limb, with limited bars and restaurants. However, a five-year development project is well under way.

There is a free bus service between Whistler and Upper Village, but if you're staying centrally, it's just as quick to walk between the two. Accommodation further out involves paying for bus rides or taking taxis (which are inexpensive).

It is a very cosmopolitan resort, with many visitors from Japan and Australia as well as Europe and the US.

The mountains

The area has acquired a formidable reputation among experts, and that reputation is well deserved. But both mountains also have enormous amounts of well-groomed intermediate cruising terrain. Together they have over 200 marked trails, and they form the biggest area of slopes, with the longest runs, in North America.

THE SLOPES
The best in North America

Whistler mountain is accessed from Whistler Village by a two-stage, 10-person gondola which rises over 1100m from the village to the Roundhouse Lodge, the main mountain base at 1850m. There is now the alternative of fast quad chairs, though they take you to a slightly lower point.

Runs back down through the trees fan out in all directions from the top of the gondola – cruises to the Emerald and Big Red fast chairs on the flanks, steeper stuff to the gondola mid-station (1005m).

From Roundhouse you can see the jewel in Whistler's crown – the magnificent above-the-tree-line bowls below the peak. These offer some groomed trails, but are mostly go-anywhere terrain for experts. They are served by two fast quads.

A six-person gondola from Creekside also accesses Whistler mountain.

Access to **Blackcomb** from Whistler Village is by an eight-seater gondola, followed by a fast quad chair. From the Upper Village you take a fast quad, and then another, to the main Rendezvous restaurant. From the arrival points you can go left for great cruising terrain and lifts up into the Horstman Glacier area, or right for steeper slopes or the 7th Heaven fast chair. The 1610m vertical from the top of this chair to the base is the largest in North America (and big even by Alpine standards). From the top you can instead go over into the glacier area. A T-bar from the Horstman Glacier brings you (with a short hike) to the Blackcomb Glacier in the next valley – a beautiful run which takes you right away from all lifts.

Fresh Tracks is a deal that allows you to ride up Whistler mountain (at extra cost) at 7.30, have a buffet breakfast at the top and hit the slopes as soon as they open – very popular with our reporters. And Blackcomb has floodlit beginner slopes a couple of nights a week. Free guided tours of each mountain are offered twice a day.

SNOW RELIABILITY
Excellent at altitude

Snow conditions at the top are usually excellent – the place gets around 350in of snow a year, on average. But because the resort is low and close to the Pacific, the bottom slopes can be wet or unskiable, and sometimes people 'download' in the gondolas from the mid-stations because of poor snow, especially in late season.

FOR EXPERTS
Few can rival it

Whistler Mountain's bowls are enough to keep experts happy for weeks. Each of them has endless possible variations, with chutes and gullies of varied steepness and width. The biggest challenges are around Glacier, Whistler and West Bowls, with runs such as The Cirque and Doom & Gloom

MOUNTAIN FACTS

Altitude	650m-2285m
Lifts	33
Pistes	7071 acres
Green	18%
Blue	55%
Black	27%
Art. snow	530 acres
Recco detectors used	

You can't count on sunshine, but there was this day in 1998 ... Both mountains have glorious open bowls above the forest – this is Blackcomb's 7th Heaven, seen from Whistler's Harmony →

SNOWPIX.COM / CHRIS GILL

– though you can literally go anywhere in this high and wide area.

Blackcomb has challenging high slopes, too; they aren't as extensive as Whistler's, but they are possibly even more testing. From the top of the 7th Heaven lift you can traverse across to Xhiggy's Meadow, where there are good sunny bowl runs. Or if you're feeling brave, you can go in the opposite direction and drop over the ridge into the extremely steep chutes down towards Glacier Creek, including the infamous 41° Couloir Extreme. Or you can hike up from the Glacier Express lift to Spanky's Ladder to get to the serious steeps of Sapphire, Garnet, Diamond and Ruby bowls.

On both mountains there are challenging trails through the trees. On Blackcomb, a particular attraction is the 'gladed' (thinly wooded) runs on both faces of the hill. For the adventurous, there are newly cut trails to explore below Whistler's West Bowl down to Creekside – outside the area boundary at present, so rescues are expensive.

If all this isn't enough, there's also local heli-skiing available by the day.

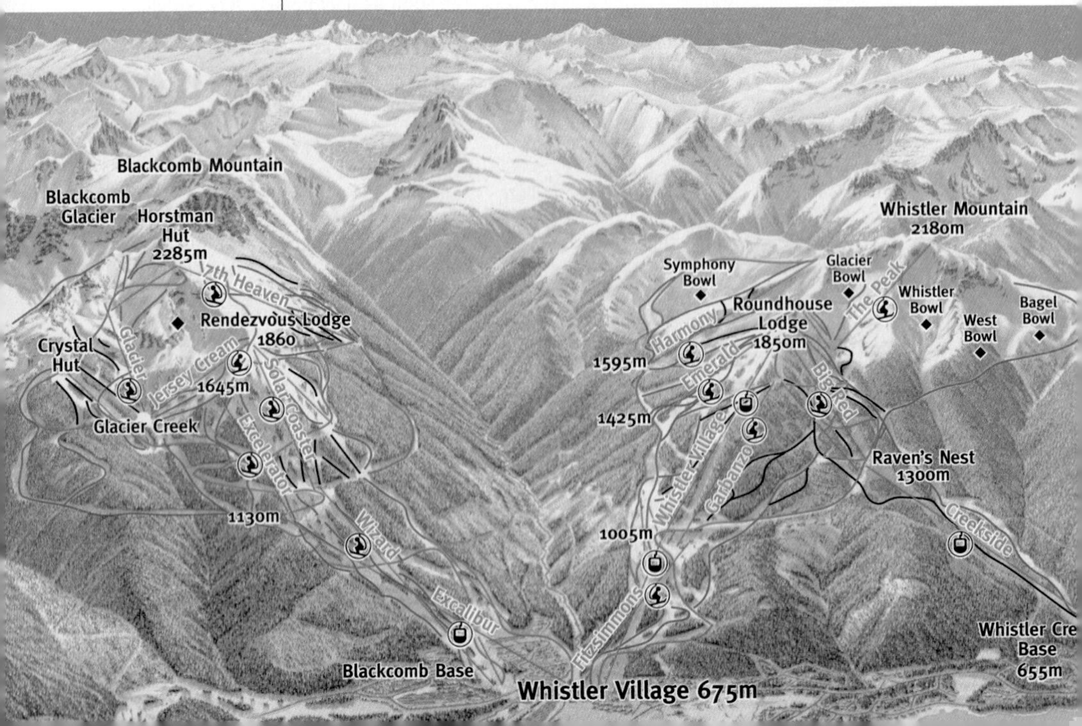

LIFT PASSES

1999/2000 prices in Canadian dollars

Dual Mountain Lift Ticket
Covers all lifts on both Whistler and Blackcomb mountains.

Main pass
1-day pass 59
6-day pass 324

Senior citizens
Over 65: 6-day pass 275

Children
Age 7-12: 6-day pass 162
Under 7: free pass

Short-term passes
Half-day pass

Notes Dual mountain pass of 5 days or over gives one non-skiing day; 6-day pass valid for 7 days with one day non-skiing. Further discounts for 13- to 18-year-olds, and groups of over 25.

FOR INTERMEDIATES

Ideal and extensive terrain

Both mountains are paradise. In good weather, good intermediates will enjoy the less extreme variations in the bowls on both mountains.

One of our favourite intermediate runs is the Blackcomb Glacier from the top of the mountain to the bottom of the Excelerator chair about 1200m below. This 5km run away from sight of all lifts starts with a two-minute climb up from the top of the Showcase T-bar. You drop over the ridge into a wide, wide bowl – the further you traverse, the shallower the slope.

You are guaranteed good snow on the Horstman Glacier runs, too, with typically gentle top-of-the-mountain glacier runs. Lower down there are large numbers of perfectly groomed cruising runs through the trees – ideal for when the weather is bad.

On Whistler Mountain, there are easy blue pistes in Symphony, Harmony and Glacier bowls, which allow even early intermediates to try the bowls for themselves, always knowing there's an easy way down. The Saddle run from the top of the Harmony Express lift is a favourite with many of our reporters. The blue path round the back from the top of The Peak chair, which skirts West Bowl, has beautiful views over a steep valley and across to the rather phallic-shaped Black Tusk mountain.

Lower down the mountain there is a vast choice of groomed blue runs with a series of efficient fast chairs to bring you back up to the top of the gondola. It's a cruiser's paradise – especially the aptly named Ego Bowl. A great run to take at the end of the day is the Dave Murray Downhill all the way from mid-mountain to the finish at Whistler Creek. Although marked black on the map, it's a wonderful fast and varied cruise when it has been groomed.

SCHOOLS/GUIDES

1999/2000 prices in Canadian dollars

Whistler and Blackcomb
Guided instruction with Ski Esprit course
Classes 3 or 4 days
Full day from 9.45
3 days: 249
4 days: 289
Children's classes
Ages: 3 to 12
5 6hr days including lunch: 349
Private lessons
Half day: 305
Full day: 469

FOR BEGINNERS
Great if the sun shines

Whistler has excellent nursery slopes by the mid-station of the gondola – and Blackcomb down at the base area. Both also have facilities higher up.

On Whistler, after progressing beyond the nursery slopes, Upper Whiskey Jack is a gentle first run from the top of the gondola. You can return to its start by various chair-lifts or continue right down to the base area on simple greens. There is a variety of other easy green and blue runs.

On Blackcomb, Green Line runs right from the top of the mountain to the bottom. The top part is particularly gentle, with a couple of steeper pitches lower down.

Our main reservation is – you guessed – the weather. Beginners don't get a lot out of heavy snowfalls, and might be put off by rain.

FOR CROSS-COUNTRY
Picturesque but low

There are over 28km of cross-country tracks, starting in the valley by the frozen river, on the path between Whistler and Blackcomb, and heading off towards the Lost Lake. And there is more cross-country around the golf courses. But all this is at low altitude, so conditions can be unreliable. Keen cross-country merchants can catch the train to better areas.

QUEUES
An increasing problem

Reports suggest that Whistler is becoming a victim of its own success. Even with 15 fast lifts – more than any other resort in North America – the mountains are far from queue-free. There is a cute system for displaying waiting times at strategic points, but most people would prefer negligible waiting times. Some reporters have signed up with the ski school in order to get lift priority. The new fast chairs in parallel with the Whistler gondola have helped, but queues still arise at the base in the morning, especially for the Blackcomb gondola. On high season weekends the base queues can be 'horrendous'. Creekside is much less of a problem. Some of the chairs up the mountain also produce queues – Harmony is a particular problem, but several on Blackcomb can build queues, too.

MOUNTAIN RESTAURANTS
Not a highlight

The main restaurants sell decent good-value food but are charmless self-service refuelling stops involving repeated queueing. Although huge, they are not huge enough. They now employ 'seat-seekers' to find spaces, but success is not guaranteed. In previous years, reporters have stressed the need to lunch early to beat the crowds. That no longer works – 'they're packed by 11.30am'.

Blackcomb has the better restaurants. Rendezvous is mainly a big (850-seat) self-service place, but also has Christine's, a table-service restaurant which is the best on either mountain and has an award-winning wine list. Glacier Creek Lodge, at the bottom of the Glacier Express lift, is the best self-service place – an attractive building with good food and a wide choice including stir-fry, pasta and salad bars. But even this huge place (1496 seats) gets 'incredibly busy'. Crystal Hut at the top of the Crystal Ridge chair (recommended by recent reporters, especially for 'Belgian' waffles) and Horstman Hut at the top of the mountain are tiny Alpine-style huts with great views.

Whistler's main place is the massive (1740-seat) Roundhouse Lodge, at the top of the gondola; Steeps Grill is its table-service refuge from the self-service zoo. Raven's Nest, at the top of the Creekside gondola, is a small and friendly deli/café. Jack's Junction is a new 'funky, rustic wood restaurant' near the top of the new Garbanzo chair-lift. You can of course descend to one of the bases – Dusty's at Creekside is recommended.

SCHOOLS AND GUIDES
A great formula

The main multi-day classes for non-beginners, called Ski Esprit and Ride Esprit, run for three or four days and combine instruction with showing you around the mountains – with the same instructor, European-style. Many of our reporters have joined these groups (usually small), and all the reports we get are enthusiastic: 'Excellent – we improved dramatically during the four days,' was one typical comment.

As well as standard lessons, there are specialist courses, clinics and snowboard classes.

CHILDCARE

Whistler Kids takes non-skiing children aged 3 months to 3 years, as well as acting as the base for ski tuition.

Whistler Kids offers various skiing and snowboarding programmes to children of all ability levels, aged 3 to 17. The Kids' Adventure Camp is a 5-day camp for 3 to 12 year olds. Ride Tribe is the teen programme for ages 13 to 17.

Après-ski programmes – with a 'Kids' Night Out' – are offered during the season.

GETTING THERE

Air Vancouver, transfer 2hr.

ACTIVITIES

Indoor Ice skating, museum, tennis, hot-tubs
Outdoor Flightseeing, heli-skiing, snow-shoe excursions, snowmobiling, paragliding, fishing, horse-riding, sleigh rides, guided tours

TOURIST OFFICE

Postcode VoN 1B4
t +1 (604) 932 3928
f 932 7231
reservations@tourismwhistler.com
www.whistler-blackcomb.com

FACILITIES FOR CHILDREN
Comprehensive

The facilities are as impressive as usual in North America. Blackcomb's base area has a special slow-moving Magic Chair to get children part-way up the mountain. Whistler's gondola mid-station has a splendid dedicated kids-only area. Our main reservation about taking young children here would be the risk of bad weather.

Staying there

The most convenient place to stay is Whistler Village, where you can go straight up either mountain by gondola. A lot of chalets and apartments are an inconvenient walk or bus-ride from the villages and slopes. Creekside, though convenient for Whistler's slopes, is less so for Blackcomb and is very quiet.

A number of recent visitors have found the central area around Village Square very noisy in the early hours.

Smoking has now been banned in all public buildings in BC.

HOW TO GO
High quality packages

A lot of British tour operators go to Whistler, some using charter flights to Vancouver. They offer a wide range of comfortable accommodation, including some catered chalets – though some operators are apparently meeting difficulties because of restrictions on the use of private homes.

Hotels There is a very wide range.

((((5) **Chateau Whistler** The top hotel, modern but in traditional Canadian Pacific château-hotel style, right at the foot of Blackcomb mountain. It has an indoor-outdoor pool, exercise machines etc. The premium-price Entree Gold floor is particularly cosseting, with its private lounge-breakfast room.

(((4) **Pan Pacific Lodge** New luxury all-suite place, perfectly positioned at Whistler Village base. Pool/sauna/tub.

(((4) **Lost Lake Lodge** 'Excellent' place with studios and suites, out by the golf course. Pool/tub.

(((4) **Crystal Lodge** 'Comfortable, friendly, conveniently placed' in Whistler Village, with 'good buffet breakfast'. Pool/sauna/tub.

((3) **Glacier Lodge** In Upper Village. Pool/tub.

Self-catering There are plenty of spacious, comfortable condominiums in both chalet and hotel-style blocks.

EATING OUT
High quality and plenty of choice

There is no shortage of good places to eat. Reporters are enthusiastic about the range, quality and value for money. You have to book well ahead: there simply aren't enough restaurant seats to meet the demand (although most of the bars serve decent food, too). But some of the cheaper places won't accept bookings for small groups, which means you're in for long waits.

At the top of the market, Umberto's Trattoria in Whistler Village is highly regarded for classy Italian cuisine. One reporter reckons the less pricey La Bocca is as good. The Rimrock Café at Creekside serves 'the best seafood we have ever eaten'.

In the middle of the market, Whistler Village places with good reports include Araxi (Italian/Pacific), the Keg (steak and seafood), Teppan Village (Japanese), Mongolie (Asian), Citta's (American), Kipriaki Norte (Greek). Crab Shack, near the Coast Whistler hotel, is recommended by several reporters for its good-value seafood. Two strong recommendations in Village North: the Brewhouse has 'great atmosphere, friendly staff' (American food) and Caramba does 'good Mediterranean food at reasonable prices'.

There are plenty of budget places, including the bars mentioned under après-ski. The Old Spaghetti Factory is popular for good-value fuel.

APRES-SKI
Something for most tastes

With over 50 bars, night-clubs and restaurants, Whistler is very lively in the evening – including the early evening. A favourite bar at close of play is the 'extremely lively' Longhorn at Whistler, with a huge terrace that is packed in spring; inside, the place rocks till after midnight. The Dubh Linn Gate Irish pub has 'live music and a great atmosphere'. Black's is better for a quiet drink. Merlin's is the focus at Blackcomb base, and Dusty's is the place to go at Creekside – good beer and nachos and loud music.

Buffalo Bill's is lively and loud later on. The Cinnamon Bear in the Delta Resort hotel, a sports bar with some live music, is also recommended. The Alpenrock House is a bizarre entertainment hall with all sorts of games (from glow-in-the-dark bowling to virtual reality), restaurants and bars

– all in a neo-Swiss setting.

The Mallard bar in Chateau Whistler and the Crystal Lodge piano bar are popular for a more relaxed time.

Later on, Tommy Africa's is good for a bit of a rave and vies with the Savage Beagle and Maax Fish for the younger clubbing crowd.

OFF THE SLOPES
Not ideal

Whistler is a long way to go if you don't plan to go skiing or riding. Meadow Park Sports Centre has a full range of sports and fitness facilities. There are also a number of luxurious spa facilities. Excursions to Squamish (famous for its eagles) are easy. The day trip to Vancouver is recommended.

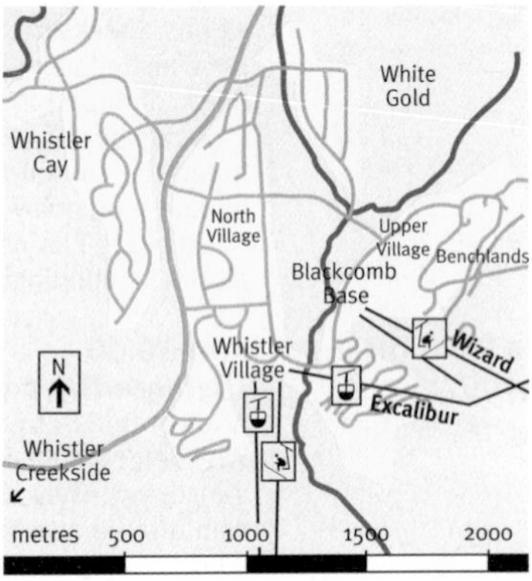

PAUL MORRISON / WHISTLER RESORT ASSOCIATION

← For a modern purpose-built resort Whistler Village is easy on the eye

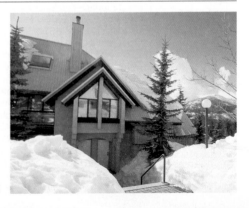

Eastern Canada

What's new

Mont-Ste-Anne and Stoneham in Québec have been bought by the company that owns Lake Louise, Fernie and several other resorts in Canada's west. The company has grand plans, which include 'making Québec city the destination of choice for skiers in eastern North America'.

It has already introduced a three-area lift pass covering its own two resorts plus Le Massif. And it plans to build more slope-side accommodation, open more après-ski venues and expand the ski areas.

For us the main attraction of skiing or riding in eastern Canada is the French culture and language that are predominant in the province of Québec. It really feels like a different country from the rest of Canada – as indeed many of its residents want it to become. It is also only a six-hour flight from the UK, compared with ten for Canada's west. Tremblant is the main destination resort and is one of the cutest purpose-built resorts we've seen. The other main base is Québec city, which dates from the 17th century and is full of atmosphere and Canadian history. The slopes of the main resorts are small both in extent and in vertical drop, and the weather can be perishingly cold in early and mid-winter. But at least this means that the extensive snowmaking systems that all the resorts have can be effective for a long season. Be prepared for variable snow conditions and don't go expecting light, dry powder – if that's what you want, head west.

There are lots of ski and snowboard areas in Ontario – Canada's most populated province – but most of them are tiny and cater just for locals. For people headed on holiday for a week or more, eastern Canada really means the province of Québec. Québec – and its capital, Québec city – are heavily dominated by the French culture and language. Notices, menus, trail maps and so on are usually printed in both French and English. Many ski area workers will be bilingual or just French-speaking. And French cuisine abounds.

The weather is very variable, rather like New England's – but it can get even colder. Hence the snow, though pretty much guaranteed by snowmaking, can vary enormously in quality. When we were there in April we were slush skiing in Tremblant one day and rattling along on a rock hard surface in Mont-Ste-Anne the next.

The main destination resort is **Tremblant** (see separate chapter), about 90 minutes' drive from Montreal. Other areas near here popular with locals include **Mont Blanc** (with only 300m of vertical, hardly a competitor to the Franco-Italian version) and the **Saint-Sauveur** valley (five areas, each with around 200m of vertical and with interchangeable lift passes).

The other main place to stay for easy access to several ski resorts is **Québec city**. Old Québec, at the city's heart, is North America's only walled city and is a World Heritage site. Within the city walls are narrow, winding streets and 17th and 18th century houses. It is situated right on the banks of the St Lawrence river. In February there is a famous two-week carnival, with an ice castle, snow sculptures, dog-sled and canoe races, night parades and grand balls. But most of the winter is low season for Québec city, with good-value rooms available in big hotels. Because of this, the area is popular with British school groups, especially in late season.

There are several ski and snowboard areas close to Québec city – and there's now a joint pass which covers the three main areas. A car is handy but there are buses to some areas.

The biggest and most varied area (though easily skied in a day by a good skier) is **Mont-Ste-Anne**, 30 minutes away and with some accommodation of its own. A gondola takes you to the top, and slopes lead down the front (south) and back (north) sides. There are intermediate cruising runs on both sides and some steep blacks (including World Cup runs) through the trees on the front among its 63km of trails. There are some easy top-to-bottom runs and good nursery slopes at the base. The views from the front over the ice-flows of the St Lawrence are spectacular. Five nights a week 14 trails are floodlit until 10pm. Over 80 per cent of the runs are covered by snowmaking. It also has the largest cross-country centre in Canada, with 223km of trails. In the spring you can stop by the Taffi hut and try fresh maple toffee, made to order.

Stoneham is the closest resort to Québec city, around 20 minutes away. It also has its own small village with accommodation and an impressive base lodge with bar, restaurant and big wooden deck. Après-ski in the lodge can be lively, and there is sometimes live music. It is a small area, with only around 30km of runs spread between three faces and a vertical of 420m. But it is very sheltered in a sunny setting protected from wind. It suits families well, with mainly intermediate and beginner terrain. It also has the biggest night skiing operation in Canada with two of the three faces lit top-to-bottom, and 95 per cent of the area has snowmaking.

Le Massif is around an hour away from Québec city and is a cult area with locals. Just metres from the St Lawrence, the views of the ice-flows are stunning, and you feel you are heading straight down into them when you are on the pretty, tree-lined trails. The area is in a UNESCO World Biosphere Reserve, and although it has only three lifts it has the largest vertical drop in the east. There are a couple of steep double-black-diamond runs and some good, well-groomed black and blue cruising runs. But it suits experts and good intermediates best – beginners and timid intermediates would be better off elsewhere.

Tremblant 265m

Charming new village below surprisingly small area of slopes

WHAT IT COSTS

(5)

HOW IT RATES

The slopes

Snow	****
Extent	**
Experts	***
Intermediates	***
Beginners	****
Convenience	****
Queues	***
Restaurants	**
The rest	
Scenery	***
Resort charm	****
Off-slope	***

What's new

For 1999/2000, 20% was added to the slopes by opening a new face of the mountain called Versant Soleil (which means 'sunny side') of mostly advanced and intermediate terrain including 15 new trails plus gladed runs, served by a fast quad. For 2000/01 a new beginner run will go from top to bottom of the north side and snowmaking will be improved. A new slope-side Westin Resort hotel and a new conference centre will be open.

MOUNTAIN FACTS

Altitude	265m-915m
Lifts	12
Pistes	79km
Green	20%
Blue	25%
Black	55%
Art. snow	440 acres

TOURIST OFFICE

Postcode JOT 1ZO
t +1 (819) 681 2000
f 5990
info_tremblant@intrawest.com
www.tremblant.ca

Tremblant is eastern Canada's main destination resort and attracts quite a lot of Brits. But for keen piste bashers the limited slopes don't really do justice to the cute and lively little village, which has been built in traditional style.

THE RESORT

Tremblant has been transformed in recent years from a day or weekend ski area for locals to being eastern Canada's leading ski resort and cutest resort village. Intrawest (which also owns Whistler and several other North American resorts) has developed a charming purpose-built village in the same traditional style as the original old village. Pastel coloured buildings line narrow, cobbled traffic-free streets and squares, with lots of galleries, boutiques, patisseries and cafés. It has a very French feel to it and large ski-in, ski-out hotels and condos blend in unobtrusively, as does a £2 million Acquaclub pool complex built to resemble a lake set in a forest.

THE MOUNTAINS

A heated gondola takes you to the top of the **slopes**, from where there are good views over the village and a 14km lake on the so-called south side and over National Park wilderness on the north side. The north side is really north-east facing and gets the morning sun – a high-speed quad brings you back and there are two other chairs to play on. The Edge lift accesses another summit, serving mainly expert terrain. Back on the south side (really south-west facing and so good for the afternoon sun) you can go right back to town on blue or green runs, or use two high-speed quads to explore the top and bottom halves. The new Versant Soleil area is more directly south-facing and has one top-to-bottom blue run with all the rest being black runs and tree runs.

Snow reliability is good and over 70 per cent of the terrain is covered by snowmaking – claimed to be 'the most powerful in North America'.

Over half the runs are graded as suitable for advanced or **expert** skiers and riders. But we found a few of the blacks rather overgraded. There are steep top-to-bottom bump runs on the north side and great tree runs off the Edge lift. The new Versant Soleil area has more black runs and some tough runs in the trees. The south side has some shorter challenging runs.

Both north and south sides have good **intermediate** cruising and we found the north side rather less crowded. There are blue-graded runs in the trees as well as on groomed trails. **Beginners** are best off sticking to the south side, where there are nursery slopes and good runs to progress to. The slopes are good for **snowboarding** with mostly chairs and a good fun-park and half-pipe on the top half of the north side (new for last season).

There are around 100km of **cross-country** trails.

At weekends there can be **queues** but they tend to move quickly. We found crowds on the main run back to the village more of a problem. The main Grand Manitou **mountain restaurant** has good views back over town and decent food but can get crowded. Many people go back to town for lunch – Le Shack and La Forge were recommended by reporters. The **ski school** offers a wide variety of options and a reporter recommends the 90-minute Super Group 3 (maximum of three people). Another said, 'Ski school brilliant, couldn't recommend more highly – for both children and adults.' **Children** from age one can be looked after during the day and until 9.30pm.

STAYING THERE

Many of our reporters stayed at the luxurious Chateau Mont Tremblant **hotel** and recommend it highly. Others stayed at the Plaza condos – 'comfortable', 'spacious', 'central', 'virtually ski to the door'. There's a decent variety of **restaurants** and bars for **après-ski** – there was live music in the main square when we were there in April. **Off the slopes**, you can go ice skating, snowmobiling, dog-sledding (though one April visitor complained that these weren't available in late season and was disappointed by the Acquaclub) and visit Montreal.

WHAT IT COSTS

(2)

What's new

1999/2000 saw a huge investment in three high-speed six-person chairs, two high-speed quads, an eight-seater gondola, three drag lifts, ten new runs and two new restaurants in the Soldeu-El Tarter-Canillo ski area alone. This is now linked by lift and piste to Pas de la Casa's ski area. Between them the two resorts now have 186km of pistes – comparable with some big-name Alpine resorts such as Kitzbühel, Wengen-Grindelwald and Les Deux Alpes. But this is mañana territory. They spend all this money on new lifts and then can't agree lift pass sharing arrangements. Last season, there was no joint lift pass for the area. And at the time we went to press there was no agreement for 2000/01 either – let's hope there is by the time the season starts.

For the 2000/01 season a new gondola is due to link two other areas – Pal and Arinsal, giving a combined total of 63km of slopes. They have shared a joint lift pass for some years.

Andorra

- ➕ Excellent choice for beginners and early intermediates, with resorts that offer good tuition, good piste grooming and mountains that won't frighten
- ➕ Lots of efficient, modern new lifts
- ➕ Lively nightlife with cheap drinks and generous measures of spirits
- ➕ Resorts close enough to each other – and some are now linked – so you can sample at least one other during a week
- ➕ Cheap packages; duty-free prices in resort

- ➖ Fairly limited slopes, with little to challenge experts
- ➖ Most resorts have little in the way of charm, and Soldeu and Pas de la Casa are sited on the busy main road through the country
- ➖ Nightlife tends to revolve around booze and clubs – not much variety and can get rowdy at night

More than most winter sports countries, Andorra invites generalisations. Because it's such a small country, all the resorts are remarkably similar, having almost all the same pluses and minuses. Low prices (including duty-free goods), ugly villages, lively bars and clubs, good ski schools, fairly reliable snow, young clientele, a lot of Brits, mainly easy, well-groomed and often busy slopes with plenty of snowmaking facilities and mediocre mountain restaurants are all fairly typical of Andorran resorts across the board.

There's an immediate temptation to compare Andorra to eastern Europe. Some of the above pluses and minuses would be appropriate to Borovets and company, too. But Andorra really is in a slightly different league. It is more expensive (though still cheap by Alpine standards), has much better lifts and other resort infrastructure, much livelier nightlife, attracts a mostly young and lively clientele rather than families, and has more reliable snow. In recent years there has been substantial investment in efficient, modern lifts and this year's reporters have been extremely complimentary about the new lifts and the high standard of piste maintenance and grooming.

Andorra is attracting many British visitors from Austrian and Italian resorts, partly because of its price advantage but also because of its reliable snow record. Its situation close to both the Atlantic and Mediterranean oceans together with the high altitude of its resorts means it usually gets substantial natural snowfalls. It has also invested heavily in snowmaking. This combination means you can book Andorra months in advance with some confidence. And an early reservation is necessary: late bookers can have difficulty finding an Andorra package.

Package holiday prices are low, as are prices once you arrive, notably for drinks and extras such as tuition and equipment hire. But some reporters have been disappointed to find duty-free luxury goods not the super-bargain they had expected. As for nightlife, it is very lively, with lots of throbbing bars, cheap drinks and bar staff who half-fill glasses with spirits – there are no official measures. Rowdy bar crawls of young Brits are a common sight (and sound) but if you get bored with bar-hopping, there's little else.

The sight of cranes is not uncommon, as the Andorrans rush to build hotels, slopes and ski lifts as fast as they can to keep up with the mostly British demand. Adjacent resorts have begun to link their areas together, meaning bigger ski areas and a bit more variety. Pas de la Casa's and Soldeu's slopes were linked by lift and piste last season. But there was no joint lift pass; and by the time we went to press there was no agreement for the coming season either. Arinsal and Pal in the west are due to be linked by a new gondola for the 2000/01 season – and have had a joint lift pass for some years.

To ski or ride the slopes of all five resorts in a week is easy if you have a car or tour operator transport and stay in one of the towns in the middle of Andorra such as Canillo, Encamp, Andorra la Vella, La Massana or Ordino. The quickest way into the Soldeu and Pas de la Casa slopes in this case is via the powerful gondola from Encamp. These central towns also offer an antidote to the booze-fuelled nightlife of the mountain resorts and far more off-slope facilities. The local bus service is slow but straightforward.

boarding *As with most places that draw a young crowd, boarding has a big following in Andorra. Most of the resorts now boast fun-parks and half-pipes amongst their facilities, and many areas are installing more chairs and gondolas. Tuition is excellent, and there is a lively après-board scene, with good cheap bars and pumping clubs.*

Arinsal 1550m

Lots of young people come here for the nightlife, and Arinsal does not disappoint. The numerous lively bars and discos are not as rowdy as in nearby Soldeu. But there is little to do apart from bar-hopping and clubbing, and the spread-out nature of Arinsal itself means there is little village atmosphere and a lot of cold walks between 'happening' places.

The local slopes are quite limited and have been difficult to recommend to anyone except beginners. But the new link with Pal should change that.

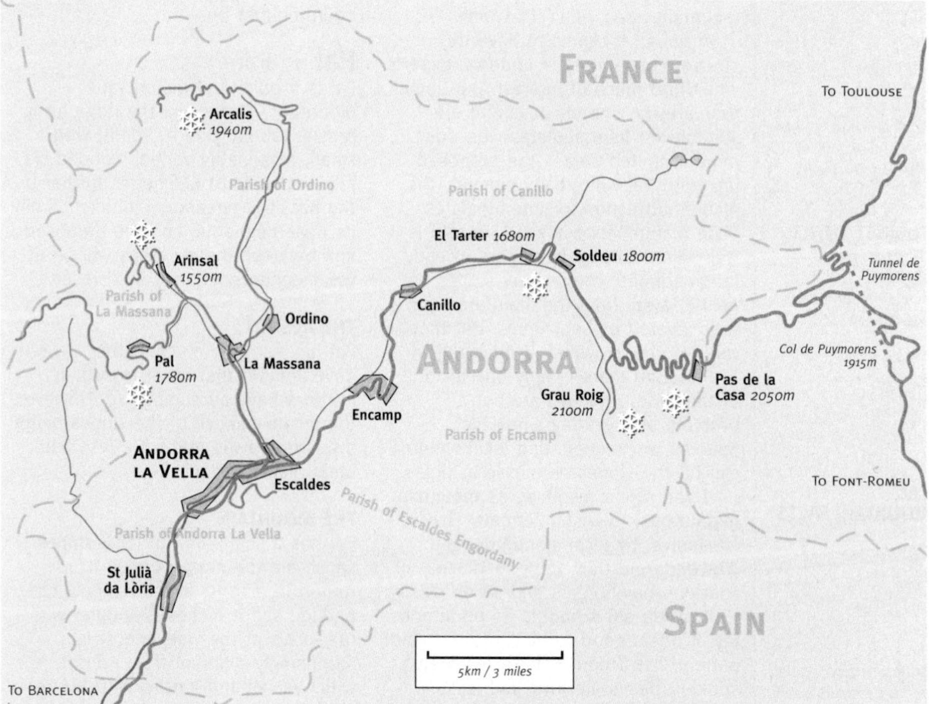

ARINSAL HOW IT RATES

The slopes

Snow	***
Extent	*
Experts	*
Intermediates	**
Beginners	***
Convenience	***
Queues	***
Restaurants	*

The rest

Scenery	***
Resort charm	*
Off-slope	*

What's new

For 1999/2000 Arinsal built a new fun-park and enlarged both its half-pipe and its beginners' slopes at Prat de la Coma.

More snow-making was also installed.

For 2000/01 Arinsal and Pal are due to be linked by a gondola, increasing the area's attractiveness hugely.

MOUNTAIN FACTS

Altitude	1550m-2560m
Lifts	14
Pistes	28km
Green/Blue	45%
Red	31%
Black	24%
Artificial snow	5km

Recco detectors used – helicopter based

TOURIST OFFICE

t +376 737020
f 836242
emap@andornet.ad
www.arinsal.ad

PAL MOUNTAIN FACTS

Altitude	1780m-2360m
Lifts	14
Pistes	35km
Green/Blue	35%
Red	60%
Black	5%
Artificial snow	10km

Recco detectors used – helicopter based

THE RESORT

Arinsal is a little village of Catalan slate and grey stone, near the head of a narrow valley north of Andorra la Vella. It has seen rapid development in recent years, giving the place a building-site appearance. The gondola, from the village centre to the mid-station, installed for 1998/99 put an end to the trek to the inconveniently situated chair-lift – a kilometre out of town and a fair walk or bus-ride from most of the accommodation. Arinsal is dominated by British holidaymakers.

THE MOUNTAIN

The very small local area is a narrow, east-facing coomb of mainly open **slopes**, suitable for beginners, children and unadventurous intermediates. Almost all the runs lead straight back towards the mid-station area, ideal for parents to keep a watchful eye on children. But for 2000/01 the slopes are due to be linked to those of Pal, which will add size and much needed variety to the resort, including some more challenging and relatively snowsure tree-lined runs.

With most runs above 1950m and a fair number of guns, **snow reliability** is relatively assured. Most lifts above the mid-station are drags, keeping the mountain open when it's windy.

Although it claims to have the steepest black runs in Andorra, **experts** won't find much of interest. But some runs are not entirely easy and are suitable for **intermediates** who don't mind a limited area – the proposed link with Pal will greatly enhance the resort's attraction for intermediates. Piste maintenance is good. Arinsal is well-suited to near-**beginners** or early intermediates. The nursery slopes are gentle, away from the main area and well covered by snow-guns. But they can get very crowded at peak times.

Although there is only one lift out of the centre, **queues** are not a problem on weekdays; however, Spanish weekenders and local children can hit the slopes en masse at times.

If you rate a resort by its **mountain restaurants**, this isn't Zermatt. They're expensive, by local standards, and crowded. And they serve mediocre snacks – hamburgers and so on.

Arinsal's **ski school** is its pride and joy. It offers good technical tuition and patient instruction. English is widely spoken; prices are low; and lessons are fun. Class sizes can, however, be very large in peak season. There is a ski kindergarten and a non-skiing crèche for younger **children**.

STAYING THERE

Arinsal is essentially a cheap and cheerful small hotel resort.

The Crest is perhaps the best **hotel** in Arinsal, and has the advantage of being next to the chair-lift; it offers half-board or B&B terms. The studio-style rooms are geared towards families, sleeping up to five. Hotel-restaurant Micolau and the Solana have good food but simple rooms. Apartments are generally of a higher standard than the hotels.

There is a fair range of **restaurants** for a small resort. Cisco's is a lively restaurant/bar serving Mexican food, Borda specialises in Catalan dishes and La Calisa has Spanish cooking.

For **après-ski**, Arinsal has very animated bars and discos, but if you tire of these, there isn't much else to do – a fondue evening is the best bet. Prices are low, but not as low as many expect of Andorra. Red Rock is a focal spot, popular for its large measures, videos and burgers.

Arinsal has few facilities for those **off the slopes**. The main thing to do is to shop in la Vella, half an hour away by infrequent bus.

Pal 1780m

Pal is a quiet and picturesque mountain village over the ridge from Arinsal (about 5km by road), with a small, reasonably varied, wooded ski area a couple of kilometres further up the hill. It is remarkably different from its near-neighbour, and the proposed link between the ski areas will be a great enhancement for both resorts.

THE RESORT

Pal has escaped much of the development that other resorts in Andorra have succumbed to. However, the inconvenience of the slopes being a bus-ride away make it a less than ideal place to stay.

THE MOUNTAIN

Pal has a small area of local **slopes** which are the most wooded of the Andorran resorts, and the ample car-parking space makes it popular with the locals at the weekend. It is surprisingly different from Arinsal, which is tall and narrow with no trees; Pal is short and wide, and covered

What's new

For 1999/2000 Pal opened the new area of Seturia with two red runs and one blue, served by a new high-speed quad chair and 28 new snow-guns.

Two cafeterias at the foot of the slopes were doubled in size.

For 2000/01 Pal and Arinsal are due to be linked by a new gondola.

TOURIST OFFICE

t +376 737000
f 835904
emap@andornet.ad
www.pal.ad

with greenery. So the scheduled link with Arinsal will create an interesting area with a fair amount of variety.

The local slopes can be accessed from any of the car parks on the road that skirts them; most lifts seem to have one at the end of them. There is a main base lodge which has a couple of shops and a restaurant, and is attractively set amongst trees. **Snow reliability** is fair, with snow-guns on the nursery slopes. The high altitude and north-facing slopes help to give a reasonably long season.

The only thing to attract **experts** will be fresh snowfall, when access to off-piste through well-spaced trees is best. Tree cover is so sparse in other Andorran resorts that Pal is the only option for this. **Intermediates** should go high, where well-bashed reds come down from the summit to the mid-station area. There are a couple of quite steep reds leading off to the Coll de la Botella, one of which can grow moguls. **Beginners** start off on the very gentle slopes just in front of the base lodge, and progress to the short blues that are accessed by longer lifts starting from the same spot.

Queues are not generally a problem, and mid-week the slopes are often deserted. As with Arinsal and Arcalis, the weekenders really do make their presence felt mid-season. By the end of the season the Spanish are already making for the seaside!

There are a few **mountain restaurants**: La Caubella at the base lodge is modern with a sun terrace, and the huts at Pla de la Cot and Coll de la Botella are basic and uninspiring but reasonable for drinks and snacks.

The Pal **ski school**, like the one in Arinsal, has good class sizes and instruction, but there are few English-speaking instructors. There is a ski kindergarten and a crèche for **children**.

STAYING THERE

We have had no reports from anyone who has stayed in the village itself, as its development as a package destination has been overlooked by tour operators in favour of the Brit-dominated Arinsal. There is a regular bus service between the two resorts, which is covered by the joint lift pass. Buses to la Massana and Andorra la Vella are also available, if somewhat more erratically timetabled. There is little scope in the village for **après ski** or **off the slopes** alternatives.

Arcalis 1940m

As the most remote resort in Andorra, it's easy to assume Arcalis is not a worthwhile day-trip. But that would be a shame, as the variety of the terrain is better than most of the other resorts, even if the extent is not up to much. Unfortunately, a day-trip is all it would be – with no accommodation for 15km, it's a long trek.

THE RESORT

With no village at the resort, it does at least mean that Arcalis has not suffered the affliction of the usual collection of hotels and apartments 'thrown up' on the mountainside, as with other resorts in Andorra.

This lack of development may be due to Arcalis's publicly owned status – most Andorrans seem rather proud of the place. It also has some nice touches; it has the nicest base lodge in Andorra, and even a couple of sculptures nestling in amongst the landscape.

The resort is very popular with weekenders, both from Andorra and Spain, and the ample car parking on the approach road soaks them up.

THE MOUNTAIN

The **slopes** are made up of two valleys which join with a central ridge, creating a horseshoe shape. To the left of the ridge is the main valley, the Cercle d'Arcalis, which is bowl-shaped and is well populated on its left flank with trees. It also contains most of the lifts, which fan out from the base lodge. The ridge provides a couple of steep, sheltered, north-facing pistes back into the right of the bowl, and access to the south-facing runs off the side. These are long blues and reds which run down the second valley, the Cercle de la Coma, which is tree-free. These runs return to the base station around the end of the ridge.

Snow reliability is good. Artificial snow covers the base area and some pistes leading into it. The height of the area, which starts a good 400m higher than Arinsal, also adds to the length of the season.

Of all the resorts in western Andorra, Arcalis has the most to offer **experts**. The black run that leads from the ridge back down towards the base is steep, and often mogulled, while the red run it connects to starts from the top of the main chair, going

ARCALIS MOUNTAIN FACTS

Altitude	1940m-2600m
Lifts	14
Pistes	26km
Blue	54%
Red	38%
Black	8%
Artificial snow	8km

Recco detectors used – helicopter based

What's new

For 1999/2000, a new quad chair opened up a new area at Creussans with a 2km blue run, and a self-service restaurant was expanded. There will be more snowmaking for 2000/01.

TOURIST OFFICE

t +376 850121
f 850440
ito@andorra.ad
www.andorra.ad/comuns/ordino

PAS DE LA CASA HOW IT RATES

The slopes	
Snow	***
Extent	***
Experts	*
Intermediates	***
Beginners	****
Convenience	****
Queues	***
Restaurants	***
The rest	
Scenery	**
Resort charm	*
Off-slope	*

What's new

For 1999/2000 the area at Pla de les Pedres was enlarged with a new high-speed six-pack. This meets the new lift up from Soldeu and forms the new link between the areas. (but there was no joint lift pass last season).

Snowmaking has been increased and a new beginners' area formed at the Funicamp mid-station. And there are new drag-lifts here and at Cubil. The beginners' area in Pas de la Casa has also been expanded and the snowmaking capacity increased.

11km of new slopes (five blue, three red) have opened.

For 2000/01 a high-speed six-pack and a quad chair will replace five existing drag-lifts.

MOUNTAIN FACTS

Altitude	2050m-2640m
Lifts	33
Pistes	100km
Blue	25%
Red	55%
Black	20%
Artificial snow	22km

Recco detectors used – helicopter based

TOURIST OFFICE

t +376 801060
f 801070
pasgrau_reserves@andornet.ad
www.pasdelacasa.ad

through a spectacular gulley before widening out. There is also plenty of space between runs for off-piste forays, especially in the Cercle de la Coma. Arcalis is well-known for heli-skiing; the mountains facing the area are favoured by the guides.

Intermediates are well catered for, with smooth, long blues and reds being the main feature of Arcalis's slopes. These head through the trees in the Cercle d'Arcalis, and a couple of variations of wide, open runs on blues and reds down through the Cercle de la Coma. The **beginners'** slopes are conveniently located near the base lodge, with a couple of drag-lifts leading to some longer blue runs.

Queues are not a problem; midweek you can explore the resort and see hardly anyone. At the weekend the area is much busier, especially in good weather, but the approach road/car park has lifts at a number of different places, and with recent investment in high-speed chairs there shouldn't be a long wait at the bottom.

The base station has a restaurant and facilities. Other **mountain restaurant** choices are limited; there is a snack bar at the top of the main lift, and a good – but rather busy at weekends – self-service restaurant in the Cercle de la Coma.

We have no reports on the **ski school**, but it seems well run, with a good range of options. There is a day nursery for children aged 1 to 5, and a ski kindergarten for 5 to 12-year-olds.

STAYING THERE

With no accommodation at the slopes, there is no option but to stay elsewhere – Ordino is a small town 15km down the valley, and the closest accommodation base (the pool there is worth a visit). La Massana is 2.5km further on.

Pas de la Casa 2050m

Even before the link with Soldeu, Pas de la Casa had the biggest ski area and highest lift-served terrain in Andorra. Now the two resorts have a combined 186km of pistes – that's about the same as some big-name Alpine resorts such as Kitzbühel, Wengen-Grindelwald and Les Deux Alpes. With a convenient, if charmless resort base, and cheap and plentiful accommodation, it is proving to be a popular package destination.

THE RESORT

Sited right on the border between Andorra and France, Pas de la Casa is a sizeable collection of concrete-box style apartment blocks and hotels, indicative of the rapid development Andorra saw in the late 60s and early 70s. At least some thought has gone into its development, with most accommodation conveniently placed near the main slopes. The town centre boasts plenty of cheap shops and bars, as well as a sports centre. Reporters complain that it's starting to look a little tatty and run-down, and being on the main road into Andorra, it suffers from traffic pollution. Pas de la Casa is less Brit-dominated than other Andorran resorts and attracts some French and Spanish families.

THE MOUNTAINS

The local **slopes** are on a high, treeless, north/south ridge, with Pas de la Casa on the east side, Grau Roig on the west. To the south of Grau Roig, towards the head of the valley, is Mont Malús, a small wooded area served by a drag with a couple of pretty reds and a black run through the trees. To the west of Grau Roig, a quad chair goes up to a ridge from which pistes lead into the next valley and lifts from there up to the Colada d'Enradort (2447m) and the Funicamp top station – connected to the village of Encamp by a 6km gondola. 6km of new runs, down to the gondola mid-station are now in place. The link with Soldeu also starts here.

Heavy investment in artificial snowmaking equipment, coupled with the area's height, has meant a very good **snow reliability** record and a season that often stretches into late April. Piste marking seems to have improved slightly, although some of the reds and blacks are over-rated.

Experts will find little to challenge them, but the black runs heading back to the resort, including the Slalom, are of a steep pitch and can be mogulled, though they are groomed before the bumps grow very large. The black run down from the top of the Mont Malús drag is a good one.

The slopes cater for aspiring **intermediates** far better, with plenty of top-to-bottom reds and blues on the main ridge, though the criticism that they are a little bland, being of consistent gradient most of the way down, is not wholly unjustified.

SOLDEU
HOW IT RATES

The slopes	
Snow	***
Extent	**
Experts	*
Intermediates	***
Beginners	****
Convenience	***
Queues	***
Restaurants	*
The rest	
Scenery	***
Resort charm	*
Off-slope	*

What's new

The long-awaited link with Pas de la Casa opened in 1999/2000, via the Solana section, which boasts 11 km of new pistes, two new six-seater chairs and a quad. But there was no joint Soldeu/Pas de la Casa lift pass.

Access to the slopes is now via a gondola, and there's a bridge to the bottom of the new Sport Village hotel, making it possible to ski right back to the village and the gondola.

A new six-seater chair goes from Pla Riba Escorxada to Tossa dels Espiolets.

An eight-seater gondola links Canillo and El Forn.

Pla des Espiolets, above Soldeu, has a new restaurant.

Planned for 2000/2001 is a gondola, two quad chairs and a restaurant at Canillo with new access to the slopes.

MOUNTAIN FACTS

Altitude 1680m-2560m	
Lifts	29
Pistes	86km
Green/Blue	50%
Red	25%
Black	25%
Artificial snow	25km
Recco detectors used – helicopter based	

There are two areas for **beginners**, though the one in Grau Roig is of little use to people staying in Pas de la Casa. The area on the resort side of the mountain is a short but inconvenient bus-ride out of town, though there are plenty of gentle slopes in the main area to progress to.

Snowboarding is popular with the young crowd that Pas de la Casa attracts, and there is a small, lift-served board-park and half-pipe on the Grau Roig side of the mountain.

Queues occasionally build up, mainly at the resort base in the mornings, where a high-speed quad gets through them reasonably efficiently. Over the other side, in the Grau Roig sector, high-speed chairs have eliminated most problems.

The **ski school** has an excellent reputation, with good English spoken.

There's floodlit skiing every Wednesday night on the Font Negre.

STAYING THERE

There's a wide choice of apartments and **hotels** on offer, and even a few chalets and chalet hotels. The main thing to watch out for is the location, as some is not in town but higher up on the col over to Soldeu, about 5km out of the resort.

The **après-ski** scene and **eating out** tend to gel into one: there are numerous bars, restaurants and nightclubs. The tour operators take over one bar (the Marselles) as a focal point for British activity. In the popular Milwaukee bar and, later on, the Billboard club, there's more of an international flavour. The Safari bar is quieter. **Off-the-slopes** activity is limited to shopping, the leisure centre, or taking a trip to Andorra la Vella.

Soldeu 1800m

Soldeu has a lot in common with other resorts in Andorra – low prices, great ski school, grim-looking village, lively bar-based nightlife. However, its local slopes are some of the best in the region. And thanks to the new link with Pas de la Casa/Grau Roig the ski area has more than doubled in size to 186km, as mentioned earlier.

THE RESORT

The village is a small, though ever-growing, ribbon of ugly modern buildings along a busy road, most of them hotels and bars. Other than sleeping, eating, drinking, and getting on to the slopes there is nothing to do, and poor transport facilities make excursions difficult. The new gondola and ski bridge across the river have improved access to the slopes.

THE SLOPES

The main local **slopes** are shared with El Tarter. There are few challenges and the runs are most suited to timid or early intermediates. A chair-lift rises over wooded, north-facing slopes to Espiolets, a broad, extensive nursery area. From here, a short gentle run to the east takes you to a lift up to Solana (2440m), the area that gives access to Grau Roig and then Pas de la Casa, and has new chairs to aid the passage. It has also recently created five new blue runs and three red, adding a further 11km. A longer, gentle run in the opposite direction takes you to the foot of the open bowl of Riba Escorxada and the arrival point of the lift up from El Tarter. Lifts ascend to both Solana and the high-point of Llosada (2560m), with blue, red and green runs down. All main routes have very easy options, so all but complete beginners can get around the area. A new six-seater chair links El Tarter's Pla Riba Escorxada with Soldeu's Tossa dels Espiolets, giving easier access in both directions.

Soldeu enjoys fairly **reliable snow**. Most slopes are north-facing, with artificial snow on the descents to Soldeu. The snowmaking is expanded each year, but should runs to the village be incomplete, the area as a whole is not unduly affected. It's a limited area for **experts**. There are short off-piste trails down the bowl beneath Llosada, and sometimes you can play in powder among the trees above El Tarter. The most direct of the wooded runs down to El Tarter and Soldeu are suitable for good **intermediates**, while those of moderate ability will enjoy the relatively long pistes from Llosada. Timid skiers have gentle cruises throughout the area. Riba Escorxada is a fine section for mixed ability groups, and the new link to Canillo/El Forn and newly created runs there allow for more cruising mileage. A new building here includes a ski school and restaurant.

This is a good resort for **beginners**. It is relatively snowsure, and there are numerous easy pistes to move on to. The Espiolets nursery area and playground has recently been

TOURIST OFFICE

t +376 890500
f 890509
soldeu@soldeu.ad
www.soldeu.ad

expanded by 50 per cent, and two new rope tows have been added. A bar, cafeteria, and nursery are soon to be located inside a new building there.

There's a well-equipped fun-park and half-pipe for **snowboarders**, which is easier to get to due to a new six-seater chair.

Despite some new lifts, the lift system is antiquated and inefficient in places, and free of **queues** on weekdays only because of the high proportion of beginners. When there is an influx at weekends, there can be waits up the mountain.

The **mountain restaurants** are poor and busy. The one at the top of the El Tarter chair is the best of a bad bunch.

The **ski school** has an excellent reputation for standards of English, quality of tuition and friendliness. **Children** aged three to ten can attend a non-ski nursery. Children's ski school starts from six years old, but lunchtime supervision is not available.

STAYING THERE

The central 4-star Sporthotel, Sport Village (no ski room, though, says a reporter) and Piolets hotels are the best **hotels** in Soldeu – tastefully designed in local stone and stained pine and boasting excellent sports facilities. The popular Naudi offers good value provided you stay in the main hotel, not the more basic annexe. The Edelweiss apartments are spacious and generally pleasant, and well placed opposite the Sporthotel, the facilities of which are available.

Though standards are not particularly high, there is plenty of choice of places for **eating out**. The Pussycat and El Squirol (Indian) are recommended as is El Mosquit in El Tarter. The Duc hotel restaurant has arguably the best food in town.

Although **après-ski** is lively, it consists mainly of bars and rep-organised outings. The Sol Y Nieve bar at the foot of the slopes starts things off, while later on the Edelweiss, Bruxelles, Piccadilly and Bonnel bars are all popular. Aspen is the main snowboard hang-out. The Naudi has a quieter locals' bar. The El Duc is the best disco. Expect noise from late-night revellers on the streets.

There is little to amuse **non-skiers** apart from a very smart sports centre in Canillo with lots of facilities (closed in the afternoons). The big hotels have excellent sports facilities.

La Massana

La Massana is a small town, on the junction of two valleys, one that leads to Pal (9km) and Arinsal (5km), and the other to Arcalis (18km). The valley leads on down to the capital of Andorra la Vella (6km), and there are regular buses in all directions. There is plenty of reasonable accommodation, and the nightlife is much more sedate than the likes of Arinsal – reporters have recommended the 'cheap and cheerful' Pascol bar, the Viking (with disco) and the Pizzeria Vesuvi. A recent reporter praised the Snowcoach programme based here, which busses you to a different resort each day.

Andorra la Vella

For anyone not using the slopes, the lack of facilities in the resorts is a major drawback. The main alternative is to travel to Andorra la Vella – or, if the skiing is less important to you than the facilities, stay here and travel to the resorts. The new Funicamp 24-person gondola goes from Encamp, just up the road from Andorra la Vella to the heart of the Soldeu/Grau Roig/ Pas de la Casa area and takes just 14 minutes. Buses run to it from Andorra la Vella and Escaldes.

There are plenty of high-quality, if relatively expensive, hotels. Andorra la Vella is not a big place, and most hotels are within easy walking distance of the centre of the town.

The town itself has many attractions. The duty-free shopping could fill a page, but probably the most interesting place is Caldea spa. The interior is laid out in a 'Hanging Gardens of Babylon' style, and the facilities are very impressive – indoor-outdoor pools, with fountains and waterfalls, saunas, hot-tubs, Turkish baths, hydrotherapy, sunbeds, massage ... even a grapefruit bath!

There is plenty of choice when it comes to dining out. Andorrans love seafood, and the traditional Catalan restaurants delight in providing it, which seems odd in the mountains; it is delivered fresh from the coast daily. Nightlife is also well catered for – there are plenty of bars and nightclubs, and most stay open until 4am. However, the clientele is generally a more sophisticated bunch, mainly Andorrans and Spaniards, and the 'drink-until-you-drop' attitude of the mountain resorts is rare.

Spain

The Spanish Pyrenees were a popular British budget destination a decade ago, but then Andorra and eastern Europe succeeded in capturing much of the Spanish trade. It's easy to see why this happened. The mass-market resorts often struggled for snow and, even when conditions were good, there was a tendency for high winds to close the lifts. Although prices were low, they were lower elsewhere, and Spain also gained a reputation for poor hotels, ancient equipment and so on.

But it's dangerous to generalise about Spanish resorts – note that we have avoided adding our usual ⊕ and ⊖ points – and there is more to the country than its downmarket image suggests. There are now some well equipped Pyrenean resorts with fine, snowsure slopes that compare favourably with mid-sized places in the Alps. Two resorts are certainly not downmarket – Sierra Nevada and Baqueira-Beret are both frequented by the king of Spain. Winter sports are becoming more popular with the prosperous Spanish themselves, and as a result many of the smaller resorts are continually improving.

Furthermore, the general ambience of Spanish resorts is attractive – not unlike that of Italy. There's plenty of animation, with eating, posing and partying taken seriously. Large families often lunch together, creating much merriment while huge amounts of food are consumed. Dinner starts late after such a blowout so, in turn, nightlife doesn't get going before many a British punter has retired, disgruntled at the lack of action.

Sierra Nevada (2100m) – also known as Sol y Nieve – in the extreme south of Spain suffers from extremely unpredictable weather conditions. The much-fêted 1995 World Championships had to be cancelled at the eleventh hour due to a lack of snow-cover, with high temperatures rendering the resort's state-of-the-art snowmaking installation useless (fortunately better conditions permitted the Championships to take place in 1996).

The resort's natural snow arrives via completely different weather patterns from those supplying the Alps and the Pyrenees; in 1990, when the Alps were disastrously snowless, Sierra Nevada had the best conditions in Europe.

The mostly intermediate slopes are very exposed to the elements. When the wind blows, as it does, the slopes close, and the strong sun makes the pistes either icy or soft in late season. On a good day, however, visitors are treated to a fantastic view from the top of the highest point at Veleta, across the Med, all the way to the Atlas mountains in Morocco.

The resort is very ugly but user-friendly, and its restaurants, bars and shops are nicely gathered around a central square. Granada's proximity means good outings but overcrowding at weekends and holidays. Hotels are comfortable and good value, and appear in a handful of UK tour operator brochures.

Baqueira-Beret (1500m) is the best of the Pyrenean resorts (see next page for a full report).

Candanchu/Astún (1500m), with 105km of piste, is probably the biggest resort you have never heard of. It has a wide range of accommodation set in some of the Pyrenees' most stunning scenery, and a local reputation for tough runs.

The smaller Pyrenean resorts are best toured by car: spend a day in each and drive to more sheltered places if the wind blows.

The best-known, **Formigal**, appears in a few tour operator brochures and is working hard to improve its standing as a winter resort. There has been recent expansion and a number of lift improvements. It has a good ski school but the 56km of pistes are windswept.

Nearby **Panticosa** is a charming old village with sheltered but limited slopes that have recently doubled in size to 34km of pistes.

The 44km of runs at **La Molina** and its purpose-built satellite **Supermolina** (1700m) are now linked to those of **Masella**, over the mountain, via a new gondola and six-pack. The whole area, Alp 2500, now extends over 100km.

Baqueira-Beret 1500m

Spain's leading winter resort – fit for their king

Baqueira is in a different league from other resorts in the Spanish Pyrenees – a smart family-oriented resort with a wide area of slopes that gives a real feeling of travel. It attracts an almost entirely Spanish clientele (which regularly includes the Spanish royal family) so don't count on English being spoken.

WHAT IT COSTS

(2)

HOW IT RATES

The slopes

Snow	***
Extent	***
Experts	***
Intermediates	****
Beginners	**
Convenience	***
Queues	***
Restaurants	**

The rest

Scenery	***
Resort charm	**
Off-slope	*

What's new

A fourth high-speed chair (a six-pack) opened last year on Beret along with a 30% increase in snowmaking.

For 2000/01 a new chair and pistes and more snowmaking are proposed (but not definite) for Beret – the first stage of an ambitious plan for 12 new lifts and 35km of new pistes, which is being opposed by environmental groups.

MOUNTAIN FACTS

Altitude	1500m-2510m
Lifts	23
Pistes	77km
Green/Blue	43%
Red	48%
Black	9%
Art. snow	30km

TOURIST OFFICE

Postcode 25530
t +34 973 644455
f 973 644488
(new numbers imminent but not available when we went to press)
baqueira@baqueira.es
www.baqueira.es

THE RESORT

Baqueira was purpose-built in the 1960s and has its fair share of drab, high-rise blocks; however, some very attractive, newer developments are being built using local stone, and there are some attractive villages slightly further afield. The resort is user-friendly, with all the essentials catered for. Ski Miquel has long been the only UK tour operator here. They cater for non-Spanish-speakers by offering their own chalet hotel and tame instructors.

THE MOUNTAINS

There is an extensive area of long, mainly intermediate, runs with efficient modern lifts. The treeless **slopes** are split into three distinct but well-connected areas; Baqueira, Beret and Bonaigua. From the base station at Baqueira, a fast quad takes you up to the nursery slopes at 1800m. Fast chairs go on up to Cap de Baqueira. From here there is a wide variety of long runs, served by chairs and drags. Those at the extremities of the slopes link with the smaller area of Bonaigua, on the back of the hill, or with Beret, along the mountainside – a series of more-or-less parallel chairs serving mainly blue and red runs of about 400m vertical, and a longer black run, from the high point at 2510m. The lift bases at Beret, Orri and Bonaigua are accessible by road.

There's a new permanent half-pipe for **snowboarders** at Beret.

Mainly north- and north-west-facing slopes above 1800m and extensive artificial backup make the area fairly **snowsure** despite its latitude.

Experts will find few on-piste challenges, but there's plenty of terrain off-piste if you hire a guide. The infamous Escornacrabes itinerary, from the top of Cap de Baqueira, is steep and narrow. Cheap heli-lifts are available.

It's excellent for **intermediates**, with lots of varied blues and some classic long red runs such as Mirador. The route to Bonaigua is enjoyable and holds a few interesting surprises. Less daring intermediates will enjoy the long blue from the Dossau ridge to Beret, and the Argulls valley runs.

There are some good nursery runs for **beginners**, but on the main mountain progression is not easy, as some of the blues can be a bit tricky; there are gentler blue runs at Beret, but you'd need to take a taxi to them.

There is 7km of **cross-country** skiing between Orri (along the road from Baqueira) and Beret.

The network of modern lifts means few **queues** most of the time. But at peak times, when French and Spanish holidaymakers flood into the resort, some waits can be 10 minutes.

Mountain restaurants are cheap and charmless, but with good-value food and pleasant terraces. One reporter said the restaurant at 2200m was best. The castle at Cap del Port is recommended. Tapas back in the village is a good option, especially at the Tamarro: 'worth going just for this'.

The **school** gets good reports, though lack of English-speaking instructors may be a problem.

English is unlikely to be spoken in the **kindergartens**.

STAYING THERE

Most of the **accommodation** is in hotels. The 4-star Montarto and the 3-star Tuc Blanc and Val de Ruda hotels are recommended, as is the 4-star Parador in Arties. We have good reports of Ski Miquel's chalet hotel Salana. Self-catering is available.

There is no shortage of bars and **restaurants** in the area, and reporters have enjoyed the tapas. There are lots of pubs and discos in the valley for **après-ski**. Baqueira is small and there is not much to do **off the slopes**. Pool and spa facilities are available in hotels, but not much else. A trip to Viehla, 15km away, is possible.

Bulgaria

WHAT IT COSTS

①

- ⊕ Still very cheap, despite growth of economy
- ⊕ A completely different winter holiday, with the chance to experience a fascinating, although depressed, culture
- ⊕ Good ski schools

- ⊖ Basic hotels and low standards of comfort and food, in particular
- ⊖ Archaic airports, airline and coaches can cause long travel delays (Plovdiv airport is a disaster)
- ⊖ Not particularly snowsure, and little artificial backup
- ⊖ Poor piste and lift maintenance
- ⊖ Limited off-slope facilities
- ⊖ Problems with theft of equipment

Bulgaria attracts holidaymakers on a tight budget: the basic flight-and-hotel-package, equipment hire, school and lift pass are all very cheap. Drawbacks include limited slopes, old lifts, and mountain food that has you reaching for the Mars bars. But there are compensations: many reporters have been struck by the friendliness of the people, the ski schools are excellent, the tour operator-organised nightlife is good fun, and from Borovets an excursion to Sofia is recommended.

The resorts also try hard to provide the sort of amenities 'westerners' require from a holiday resort. Many of the hotels have the potential to be perfectly adequate places to stay, and Bulgaria, like the rest of eastern Europe, is struggling to raise standards. But progress is slow. Keen piste-bashers, gourmets, posers, and those wanting creature comforts should look elsewhere or be prepared for a culture shock.

The flow of readers' reports has dried up over the last couple of seasons, but we have trawled the Internet for holiday reports in order to gauge visitors' reactions to the resorts. Most reports – at least from absolute beginners – are extremely positive, enthusing about the standard benefits mentioned above, but others tell worrying tales of burgled rooms and stolen ski equipment (mainly in Borovets). And those who have skied elsewhere tend to be more critical.

Bulgaria's two main resorts are some way apart, served by different airports, with similarly short transfer times (less than two hours). They are similar places in some ways; both have good tuition and poor mountain restaurants. But the two areas suit people of different levels of ability.

Pamporovo (1650m) is by far the better bet for beginners and early intermediates, with mostly easy runs. Others are likely to find 17.5km of mainly short runs too limited. But the slopes are pretty and sheltered, with pistes, starting at a high point of 1925m, cutting through pine forest. Getting around is easy, with no bottlenecks or hazards, and getting lost is difficult even in the worst weather. The Lodge is reported to be the best bet for a meal on the slopes. Beginners should book a 'learn to ski' package through their tour operator. It's a good deal, saving up to 80 per cent of the cost of booking extras locally. Despite having to ride a bus to the slopes, families praise Pamporovo. Not only are the slopes suitable but the English-speaking crèche is well regarded, and the purpose-built village has 'everything to hand'. The ski schools are repeatedly praised by reporters – instructors are patient, enthusiastic and speak good English, and class sizes are usually quite small. The Snow Shack is recommended for snowboard hire and tuition. Hotel Pamporovo was new for 1999/2000 and offers the best accommodation in the resort. It's close to the village centre, and facilities include an indoor swimming pool, a hot-tub and a gym. More basic, but entirely adequate, are the Perelik (also with a pool) and

Mourgavets – both are in the heart of the village. The food is monotonous, though the buffets offer a fair choice. The nightlife is fairly lively, although limited to a handful of bars and discos – BJ's, the White Hart and the Havana club are the most popular. The organised evening events are recommended by several reporters. Late-season snow-cover is unreliable.

Borovets (1300m) is one of the few eastern European resorts to meet the needs of those on a budget seeking reasonable slopes, pretty scenery, and convenient village lifts.

The resort is little more than a small collection of large, ugly, modern hotels, with bars, restaurants, shops etc housed within them. The beautiful wooded setting of the place provides a degree of Alpine-style charm, and trees do hide some of the worst architectural excesses. One cluster of large hotels surrounds the main village lift (a gondola) up to two of the three ski sectors. A couple of minutes' walk takes you to the top of the resort, where an enormous hotel overlooks the remaining village lifts.

The 40km of piste are spread over three sectors, two of which are loosely connected. The two largest have fairly steep and awkward slopes. The gondola rises over 1000m to service both the small, high, easy slopes of the Markoudjika sector (up to 2700m), and the mainly long, steepish Yastrebets pistes that lead back to the same lift station. A little drag-lift and path connect the two. The third Baraki sector is accessed by several lifts. Runs are short, with a range of just 550m up to a top station at 1850m. The runs are best suited to good intermediates. Less confident skiers may find the mainly tough red runs a bit intimidating and experts will find little of real challenge. Although many visitors to the resort are first-timers, the slopes are not particularly suitable for novices. The nursery slopes are conveniently positioned at the foot of the Baraki section, but are inadequate. The excellence of the ski school, known for caring, patient, fun tuition, is some compensation (though we have come across reports of poor organisation causing first-day delays). Markoudjika is good for near beginners, but progress beyond that means going straight on to reds.

Borovets has enjoyed some excellent snowfalls in recent years though reliable cover is by no means guaranteed. The area as a whole is markedly reduced when runs to the village are bare. At such times (as in peak periods, when the resort is full), queues can be dreadful – 'unruly and pushy' – and skiers bussed in from lower-lying Pamporovo compound the problem. Reporters recommend an early start (before 9am) to avoid the worst of the gondola queues – the main bottleneck. Lifts also have a tendency to shut 'for maintenance'. Erratic grooming and poor signing are other common complaints.

Mountain restaurants are mostly basic little snack bars with limited seating, serving large portions of very simple fare. Lunchtime queues can be more time-consuming than lift delays and you need to be wary of your equipment. You might find that, unbeknown to to you, your kit has been 'guarded' for a small fee.

Reports of the ski kindergarten have been complimentary, although supervision is suspect. The non-ski nursery is situated in hotel Rila.

The hotel Rila gets low marks for everything (especially food), and reports suggest a fairly high incidence of burgled rooms. The Samokov is much more popular and its pool is a major asset in a resort with few off-slope facilities. The Breza and Edelweiss get reasonable reviews. There is an attractive Scandinavian-style development out in the forest. Eating-out options are fairly limited. Recommended restaurants include Krima, The Bulgarian Dish, Ela Tavern and Franco's. Reporters are enthusiastic about the nightlife. Events organised by tour operator reps include folklore evenings and a visit to a local village for dinner. The Black Tiger pub (with karaoke) and Bonkers have been recommended.

Excursions to the Rila monastery by coach and to Sofia by coach or helicopter are interesting.

Vitosha (1810m) is no more than a few widely scattered hotels with very limited, bland runs and a top elevation of 2290m. The hotels are fairly dour, and most are a bus-ride from the lifts. The resort is just over 20km from the centre of Sofia, allowing for short transfers and easy excursions, but the slopes get overrun at weekends. The slopes are north-facing and Vitosha's main saving grace is its snow record.

Romania

+ Extremely cheap
+ Interesting excursions and friendly local people
+ Good standard of affordable tuition

− Primitive facilities
− Uninspiring food
− Limited slopes with few real challenges

WHAT IT COSTS

①

Like Bulgaria, Romania sells mainly on price. On-the-spot prices, in particular, are very, very low. Provided you have correspondingly low expectations – and provided you go to Poiana Brasov and not Sinaia – you'll probably come back content. If you have any interest in good living, and particularly good lunching, stay away. It's a place for beginners and near-beginners – the slopes are limited in extent and challenge, but the tuition is good (and cheap, of course).

There is another possible dimension to a holiday here, which is the experience of visiting (and supporting) an interesting and attractive country with a traumatic recent history. Reporters have commented on the friendliness of the people, and most recommended exploring beyond the confines of the resorts. Bucharest is 'not to be missed'.

It's some years since we visited the country. The abiding impression we brought back then was one of resources stretched to their limits. To judge by the few reports we have received, post-revolutionary Romania has, sadly, not made much progress.

Romania's two main resorts are in the Carpathian mountains, about 120km north-west of the capital and arrival airport, Bucharest. They are very different places, but have one or two things in common apart from low prices: patient tuition, with excellent spoken English, and small classes; and very basic mountain restaurants, with extremely primitive loos that, according to one past reporter, would 'shock the toughest of characters'.

The main resort is **Poiana Brasov** (1020m), near the city of Brasov. It is purpose-built, but not designed for convenience: the hotels are dotted about a pretty, wooded plateau, served by regular buses and cheap taxis. There is nothing resembling a real village – the place has the air of a spacious holiday camp.

The main slopes (approximately 17km of pistes in total) consist of decent intermediate tree-lined runs of about 750m vertical, roughly following the line of the main cable-car and gondola, plus an open nursery area at the top. There are also some nursery lifts at village level. A black run takes a less direct route down the mountain, which means that on average it is gentler than the red run under the lifts; it has one steepish pitch towards the end. The more adventurous would need to seek opportunities to go off-piste. The resort gets weekend business from Brasov and Bucharest, and the main lifts can suffer serious queues as a result.

The recently refurbished Bradul and Sport hotels are handy for the lower nursery slopes and for one of the cable-cars. The Alpin gets good reports and the Ciucas is a 'good, basic' place with satellite TV. Après-ski revolves around the hotel bars and discos and can be quite lively at times. The two nightclubs put on cheap cabarets. Off-slope facilities are limited; there is a good-sized pool, and bowling. A trip to the Carpathian Stag in Brasov for an evening of wine tasting in the wine cellars, dinner and a folklore show is recommended. An excursion to nearby Bran Castle (Count Dracula's home) is also popular.

One or two companies offer holidays in **Sinaia** – a small town on the busy road from Bucharest to Brasov. When we visited it some years ago we were impressed by the modest intermediate slopes, on largely treeless hills next to the town. The town was a rather depressing place, and reporters since have been shocked and saddened by the evident poverty. But a new 4-star hotel and new chalets may help to attract your much-needed cash.

Slovenia

WHAT IT COSTS

(2)

- ⊕ Good value for money
- ⊕ Beautiful scenery
- ⊕ Good beginners' slopes and tuition
- ⊕ Good off-slope diversions and excursions

- ⊖ Limited, easy slopes on the whole
- ⊖ Antiquated lifts
- ⊖ Not particularly inspiring cuisine

Slovenia offers good value for money 'on the sunny side of the Alps'. A handful of UK tour operators run packages to some of the better-known resorts. An alternative would be to arrange an independent trip to the mountains combined with a break in the vibrant city of Ljubljana. Kranjska Gora and Bohinj are the best-known resorts, popular with economy-minded British and Dutch visitors, and with visitors from neighbouring Italy and Austria, giving quite a cosmopolitan feel to the resorts.

Slovenia is a small country bordering Italy to the west and Austria to the north. It was the first state to break away from former Yugoslavia and has managed to escape the turmoil that engulfed the Balkans. The economy is improving steadily, and there is a positive feel to the resorts – along with a warm and hospitable welcome.

The main resorts are within two and a half hours by bus of the capital, Ljubljana.

The ski areas are generally small, with fairly antiquated lifts but few queues. The mountain restaurants are mainly unappealing, while the ski schools are of a high standard and cheap, with good English encountered by our most recent reporter. Hotel star ratings tend to be a trifle generous, but high standards of service and hygiene are observed. Snow reliability is not particularly good, but some resorts have artificial cover.

Kranjska Gora (810m), a few kilometres from the Austrian and Italian borders, is the best-known resort on the British market. The pretty village is dominated by the majestic Julian Alps. The Lek, Kompass and Larix hotels – with pools – are the best placed for slope-side convenience.

There are 30km of mainly intermediate slopes, rising up to 1570m. The only challenging slopes are a couple of short, demanding runs in the Podkiron area and the World Cup slalom run. For those wanting a change of slopes, trips to Arnoldstein in Austria are available. Snow reliability is not good, despite artificial backup and a northerly exposure. The lift system is rather antiquated (three-quarters of the 20 lifts are T-bars), but at least queues are rare. Mountain restaurants are poor and most people choose to lunch in the village. There are 40km of cross-country trails. There is a good selection of bars and discos for Austrian-style après-ski – Brincelj, No.1 and Prisank's are recommended.

Bled, with its beautiful lake and fairly lively nightlife (the Kilkenny Pub and Dioneiz have been recommended), is an ideal base for visiting the surrounding resorts – three small local areas of mainly undemanding slopes. The Grand Hotel Toplice and the Park are the best hotels.

Vogel (1540m), in the beautiful **Bohinj** basin – 20km from Bled – has the best slopes and conditions in the area. The 36km of slopes are reached by a cable-car up from the valley. There's a collection of small hotels and restaurants at the base. Pistes of varying standards run from the high point at 1800m back into a central bowl with a small beginner area. For a change of scene, **Kobla**, with 20km of wooded runs is a short bus-ride away.

Kanin (2200m), near the village of **Bovec**, 17km from Italy, offers the only high Alpine skiing – 14km of pistes between 980m and 2300m.

Slovenia's second city, **Maribor** (325m), in the north-east, is 6km from its local slopes – the biggest ski area in the country, with 40km of mainly advanced and intermediate runs. Accommodation is cheap and there are several atmospheric old inns serving good, Hungarian-influenced food.

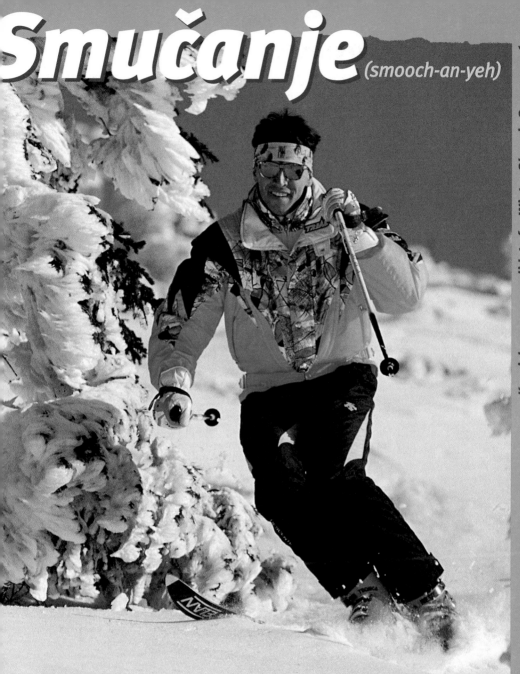

WHAT IT COSTS

4

Norway

- ⊕ Probably the best terrain and facilities in Europe for serious cross-country skiing
- ⊕ The home of telemark – plenty of opportunities to learn and practise
- ⊕ Complete freedom from the glitziness often associated with downhill resorts, and from the ill-mannered lift queues of the Alps
- ⊕ Quiet atmosphere that suits families and older people
- ⊕ Impressive snowboard parks
- ⊕ Usually reliable snow conditions throughout a long season

- ⊖ Very limited downhill areas – small, and mostly with few challenges
- ⊖ Mountain restaurants are little more than pit stops
- ⊖ Prohibitively high prices (because of high taxes) for alcoholic drinks
- ⊖ Unremarkable scenery – even 'Alpine' Hemsedal resembles the Pennines more than the Alps
- ⊖ Après-ski is either deadly dull or irritatingly rowdy
- ⊖ Short daylight hours in midwinter
- ⊖ Highly changeable weather
- ⊖ Limited off-slope activities

Norway and its resorts are very different from the Alps, or indeed the Rockies. Some people find the place very much to their taste. For cross-country there is nowhere like it; and for downhillers who dislike the usual resort trappings, and prefer a simpler approach to winter holidays, it could be just the place. For families with young children, in particular, the drawbacks are less pronounced than for others; you'll have no trouble finding junk food for the kids to eat – the mountain restaurants serve little else.

Speaking for ourselves, any one of the first three ⊖ points we've listed above would probably be enough to put us off; when these are combined in a single destination – and when you add in the other negative points – you can count us out.

From the 1960s to the 1980s, Norway's popularity with British skiers declined steadily, until the country was attracting only 1500 or so – about one-tenth of the peak number. So in 1988 the tourist agencies launched an initiative to reverse the trend. Aided by the Alpine snow shortages at the turn of the decade and the award of the 1994 Olympic Winter Games to Lillehammer, the campaign has been a success. Bookings from the UK have grown appreciably.

There is a traditional friendship between Norway and Britain, and we think of Norwegians as welcoming people, well disposed towards British visitors. We have to say that our visits have left us underwhelmed by the warmth of welcome. But at least English is widely spoken – universally spoken, in our experience.

For the Norwegians and Swedes, skiing is a weekend rather than a special holiday activity, and not an occasion for extravagance. So at lunchtime they tend to haul sandwiches out of their backpacks, and in the evening they cook in their apartments. Don't expect a wide choice of restaurants.

The Norwegians have a problem with alcohol. Walk into an après-ski bar at 5pm on a Saturday and you may find young men already inebriated – and by that we mean not merry but incoherent. And this is despite – or, some say, because of – prohibitively high taxes on booze. Restaurant prices for wine are ludicrous, and on our recent visit we were unable to check out shop prices because the resort (Hemsedal) had no state-controlled liquor store. Our one attempt at self-catering (well, OK, our one takeaway meal) was an unusually sober affair as a result. Crystal, cutely, offers free wine with dinner in some of its hotels.

Other prices are generally not high by Alpine standards, and those for ski equipment rental and ski school are relatively low.

Cross-country skiing comes as naturally to Norwegians as walking; and even if you're not that keen, the fact that cross-country is normal, and not a wimp's alternative to 'real' skiing, gives Norway a special appeal. Here, cross-country is both a way of getting about the valleys and a way of exploring the hills. Although you can plod around short valley circuits as you might in an Alpine resort, what distinguishes Norway for the keen cross-country skier is the network of long trails across the gentle uplands, with refuges along the way where backpackers can pause for refreshment or stay overnight. This network of mountain huts offers cheap, if basic, accommodation which can turn touring into a week-long adventure away from the crowds. Several tour operators now offer ski-touring packages, or they can be arranged on the spot.

More and more Norwegians are taking to telemarking (a bit like cross-country, with a free-heel binding, but with broader skis) for both downhill and backcountry skiing trips.

Snowboarding is very popular, particularly with local youths who swarm on to the slopes and impressive fun-parks at weekends.

For downhill skiing, the country isn't nearly so attractive. Despite the fact that it is able to hold downhill races, and despite the successes of its Alpine racers during the 1990s, Norway's Alpine areas are of limited appeal.

The most rewarding resort for downhillers is **Hemsedal,** which we cover in detail on the next page.

The site of the 1994 Olympics, the little lakeside town of **Lillehammer** (200m), is not actually a downhill resort at all. There is plenty of cross-country terrain around, but the nearest downhill runs are 15km north at Hafjell (230m). This is a worthwhile little area, with a vertical of 830m, 10 lifts, and pistes totalling 25km with a longest run of 4.5km. The Olympic slalom events were held here; but the planned women's downhill and super-G races were moved elsewhere after the racers judged the course too easy. They went to Kvitfjell, about 35km further north, developed specially for the men's downhill and super-G. It's steeper but smaller – 20km of pistes.

Norway's other internationally known resort is **Geilo** (800m) – a small, quiet, unspoilt community on the railway line that links Bergen, on the coast, to Oslo. It provides all the basics of a resort – a handful of cafés and shops clustered around the railway station, 10 hotels more widely spread around the wide valley, children's facilities and a sports centre.

Geilo is a superb cross-country resort. As the Bergen–Oslo railway runs through the town it is possible to go for long tours and then catch the train back at the end of the day.

But Geilo is very limited for downhillers. The 29km of piste are spread over two small hills – one, Vestlia, a bus-ride away from Geilo, with a good, informal hotel and restaurant at its foot – offering a maximum vertical of 380m and a longest run of 2km. None of the runs is really difficult.

Clearly the best hotel, and one of the attractions of staying in Geilo, is the Dr Holms Hotel – smartly white-painted outside, beautifully furnished and spacious inside. This is the centre for après-ski, but prices are steep. All the other hotels we have seen can be safely recommended. The resort is quiet at the end of the day, but the main hotels often provide live entertainment.

A long way north of the other resorts is **Oppdal** (550m), with more downhill runs than any of its rivals (about 80km). The total vertical is about 750m, but this is misleading as most of the runs are short.

There are almost equally extensive slopes at **Trysil** (600m), off to the east on the border with Sweden, and the runs are longer (up to 4km and 650m vertical). The runs here are all around the conical Trysilfjellet, some way from Trysil itself – though there is some accommodation at the hill.

In complete contrast to all of these resorts is **Voss** (50m), a sizeable lakeside town quite close to Bergen and the sea. A cable-car links the town to the slopes on Hangur and Slettafjell, with a total of 40km of pistes. Snow reliability can be poor. There are plenty of excursion possibilities, in particular the spectacular Flåm railway, which plunges down the side of a mountain to fjord (sea) level. From there you can take a boat trip to link up with a bus back to Voss. Nearby Bergen is a pleasant city that is worth a visit.

Hemsedal

650m

Norway's best Alpine resort

WHAT IT COSTS

4

HOW IT RATES

The slopes

Snow	****
Extent	*
Experts	**
Intermediates	****
Beginners	***
Convenience	*
Queues	****
Restaurants	*

The rest

Scenery	**
Resort charm	**
Off-slope	*

What's new

The resort was taken over last season and is now owned by the same company that owns Åre and Sälen, in Sweden.

2000/01 will see an expansion in the snowmaking network and 90 new ski-in/ski-out apartments. More dining facilities at the base are also planned.

MOUNTAIN FACTS

Altitude	650m-1450m
Lifts	16
Pistes	30km
Green	52%
Blue	24%
Black	24%
Art. snow	12km

Recco detectors used

TOURIST OFFICE

Postcode N-3561
t +47 32055030
f 32055031
hemsedal@hemsedal.net
www.hemsedal.com

Hemsedal's craggy terrain, 810m vertical, proper black runs and worthwhile off-piste terrain are reminiscent of a small-but-serious Alpine resort. The snow is good, and the season long. But the village has little to offer.

THE RESORT

Hemsedal is both an unspoilt valley and a village, also referred to as Trøym and Sentrum ('Centre'), which amounts to very little – a couple of hotel/apartment buildings, a handful of shops, a bank (with ATM) and a petrol station. Though there has been talk of a lift from Trøym to the slopes, for now the lift base is a mile or two away, across the valley. A walkable distance from the lifts is a cluster of self-catering apartments. A ski-bus links these points, and others in the valley, but it's inadequate in every way; really, the place is geared to visitors arriving by car or by coach. Most of them come at weekends.

THE MOUNTAINS

Hemsedal's **slopes** pack a lot of variety into a small space and, with no less than four fast chairs to play on, you can pack a lot of runs into the day. The lift pass also covers smaller Solheisen, a few miles up the valley, and you can get a ticket that also covers Geilo, an hour away. There's a **snowboard** fun-park and half-pipe.

The combination of northerly latitude and reasonable altitude makes for impressive **snow reliability**. It's a good bet for a late holiday; the season runs until the first weekend in May.

There is quite a bit to amuse **experts** – two or three black pistes of 450m vertical served by a fast triple chair from the base, and wide areas of gentler off-piste terrain served by drags above the tree line.

Mileage-hungry piste-bashers will find Hemsedal's 30km of runs very limited, but other **intermediates** will find good variety in the blue and red runs, and the easier blacks.

Absolute **beginners** might find the nursery slope rather steep. There are splendid long green runs (up to 6km), but they get a lot of traffic, some of it irresponsibly fast. Some long blues and reds also suit near-beginners.

The steep mountainsides that make this a worthwhile Alpine resort mean that it is not classic Norwegian **cross-country** skiing terrain. But by Alpine standards there is still lots to do, both in the valley and at altitude, and a few miles down the valley at the Gravset cross-country centre.

Hemsedal is Norway's premier downhill resort, and is only a three-hour drive from Oslo. Good weekend weather fills the car parks, leading to **queues** for the main access lifts, and possibly for others. But midweek it is quiet. The upper lifts are very exposed, and are easily closed by bad weather.

There's one functional self-service **mountain restaurant** doing dreary fast food, plus two or three kiosks with picnic benches. Most Norwegians take their own picnics.

Our one reporter on the ski school was not particularly impressed, except by the spoken English. The children's facilities at the lift base are good, with day care for those over 3 months old. The admirably gentle kids' nursery slope is inconveniently set, well below the main lift base.

STAYING THERE

Most of the accommodation is in **apartments**, varying widely in convenience for the lifts. The Alpin apartments near the lift base are simple but satisfactory, provided you don't fill all the beds. The adjacent Tinden ones are quite smart; Neilson offer a couple as catered **chalets**. The best **hotel** is the Skogstad in central Hemsedal – comfortable, but noisy at weekends. Other hotels along the valley are used by UK tour operators.

There are few options for **eating out** – when Norwegians go self-catering, they cater for themselves.

Après-ski is minimal in the early and middle parts of the week, rowdy at weekends and holidays.

There are some **off-slope alternatives** including sleighs drawn by horses or dogs. The pool at the hotel Skogstad is open to the public.

Sweden

WHAT IT COSTS

(4)

- ✚ Snowsure from December to May
- ✚ Unspoilt, beautiful landscape
- ✚ Uncrowded pistes and lifts
- ✚ Vibrant après-ski and nightlife scene
- ✚ Good range of non-skiing activities

- ⚊ Limited challenging downhill terrain
- ⚊ Small areas by Alpine standards
- ⚊ Lacks the dramatic peaks and vista of the Alps
- ⚊ Short days during the early season

Sweden's landscape of forests and lakes and miles of unspoiled wilderness is entirely different from the Alps' grandeur and traffic-choked roads. Standards of accommodation, food and service are good and the people welcoming, lively and friendly. There are plenty of off-slope activities but most of its downhill areas are limited in size and challenge. Sweden is likely to appeal most to those who want an all-round winter holiday in a different environment and culture from a normal Alpine resort. Don't be put off by the myths that Sweden is expensive, dark and cold – see below.

Holidaying in Sweden is a completely different experience, culturally as well as physically, from a holiday in the Alps. The language is generally incomprehensible to us and, although virtually everyone speaks good English, the menus and signs are often written only in Swedish. The food is delightful, especially if you like fish and venison.

One of the myths about Sweden is that it is expensive for British pockets. Sweden is significantly cheaper than neighbouring Norway, especially for alcohol, and prices are pretty much on a par with the main Alpine countries.

Another myth is that it is dark. It is true that the days are very short in of December and early January. But from early February the lifts generally work from 9am to 4.30pm and by March it is light until 8.30pm. And most resorts have floodlit pistes for night skiing.

On the down side, downhill slopes are generally limited in both challenge and extent and the lift systems tend to be dominated by T-bars. But there is lots of cross-country and backcountry skiing. Snowboarding is also popular, with parks and pipes in most resorts.

There is plenty to do off the slopes: snowmobile safaris onto deserted plateaux, ice fishing, ice climbing, dog-sled rides, and of course saunas galore – as well as visiting a local Sami (the politically correct name for Lapp) village. And resorts are very family-friendly.

The main resort with the most varied terrain is **Åre** (see separate chapter).

Salen is Scandinavia's largest resort – and is really six resorts and four sets of slopes with 144km of piste and a well-developed lift system. Most slopes are very gentle, suiting beginners and early or timid intermediates best. There are 31 black runs listed, including the locally notorious 'Wall' in Hundfjället.

Vemdalen has two separate areas of slopes 18km apart by road. Björnrike is great for families, beginners and early intermediates, with 8 lifts and 15km of mainly gentle pistes. The Country Club hotel is right on the slopes and built in modern Scandinavian style. Vemdalsskalet has more advanced intermediate terrain, served by 10 lifts and 13km of pistes. The Högfjällshotell at the base is large, dates from 1936 and prides itself on its lively après-ski.

Riksgransen, 250km north of the Arctic Circle, is an area of jagged mountain peaks and narrow fjords. The season starts in mid-February and ends in June – when you can be on the slopes under the midnight sun. There are only six lifts and 21km of piste. But there is some good off-piste and midnight heli-skiing.

Björkliden, also above the Arctic Circle, is famous for its subterranean skiing inside Scandinavia's largest cave system. You need to go with a guide.

Ramundberget is a good, small, quiet family resort with ski-in, ski-out accommodation. It gets large amounts of snow and its 22km of pistes are mainly easy or intermediate cruising runs. There is a special children's area with its own lift.

Åre

380m

Sweden's best slopes strung out along a frozen lake

WHAT IT COSTS

(4)

HOW IT RATES

The slopes	
Snow	***
Extent	**
Experts	**
Intermediates	****
Beginners	****
Convenience	***
Queues	****
Restaurants	***
The rest	
Scenery	***
Resort charm	***
Off-slope	***

What's new

Duved is now connected to its slopes by a drag-lift from the village to a high-speed six-seat chair-lift which takes just five minutes to get to near the summit.

There was a new kindergarten last winter for children from age 2.

There was also a new 1.4km boarder- and skier-cross course and more snow-guns were installed.

MOUNTAIN FACTS

Altitude	380m-1275m
Lifts	44
Pistes	97km
Green/Blue	57%
Red	35%
Black	8%
Recco detectors used	

TOURIST OFFICE

Postcode
Box 53, 830 13
t +46 (647) 17720
f 17712
info@areresort.se
www.areresort.se

Åre has the biggest area of linked slopes in Sweden and some of its most challenging terrain. But it suits beginners, intermediates and families best. It has a dinky little town centre and a long area of slopes set along a frozen lake.

THE RESORT

Åre is a small town made up of old, pretty, coloured wooden buildings and some larger, modern additions. When we were there the main square had a roaring open fire to warm up by. As well as accommodation in town, there is lots spread out along the valley, with a concentration in the Duved area. All the slopes and accommodation are set on the shore of a huge, long lake, frozen in the winter months.

THE MOUNTAINS

The terrain is mainly green and blue tree-lined **slopes**, with a couple of wind-swept bowls above the trees. There are two main areas. The largest is accessed by a funicular from the centre of town or a chair or cable-car a short climb above it. This takes you to the hub of a network of runs and T-bars that stretches for 10km from end to end. The cable-car is often shut because it goes to the top of the above-the-tree-line slopes (known as the 'high zone'), which often suffers from howling gales. A gondola also accesses the high zone from a different point. You can get back on-piste right into the town square. A separate area of slopes is above Duved, the other main bed base, now served by a high-speed chair. There are four floodlit slopes, each open on a different night.

Snow reliability is good from November to May. More of a problem is the wind, which can blow fresh snow away. It also means that artificial snow is often made wet so that it doesn't blow away – it then compacts to a hard, icy surface (and certainly had when we tried the Olympia night skiing area – the top part was sheet ice).

Experts will find Åre's slopes limited, especially if the 'high zone' is closed. If it is open, there is a lot of off-piste available, including an 8km run over the back accessed by a snowcat service in high season. On the main lower area the steepest (and iciest when we were there) pistes are in the Olympia area. There are also steep black and red runs back to town.

The slopes are ideal for most **intermediates** with pretty blue runs through the trees. Because they tend to be more sheltered, the blue runs also often have the best snow. You can get a real sense of travelling on the main area – from hill to hill and valley to valley. There are good facilities for **beginners**, both on the main area and at Duved.

The area has an amazing 300km of **cross-country** trails, both on prepared tracks and unprepared trails marked with red crosses. Some trails are floodlit in the evening.

In high season there can be **queues** for some lifts, especially in the central area immediately above Åre. There are some good **mountain restaurants**. Our favourite was the rustic Buustamons, tucked away in the woods near Rödkulleomradret. The **ski school** has an excellent reputation – and this, the easy terrain and excellent childcare facilities make it a good area for families and **children**. There are special children's areas and under 11s get free lift passes if wearing helmets.

STAYING THERE

The main central **hotels** are the delightful old Åregarden and the simpler Diplomat Ski Lodge. The big Sunwing is right on the slopes, but a bit out of town. The Renen in Duved is very popular with families. There are plenty of cabins and apartments. Our favourite **restaurant** was Sames, with excellent Swedish food. There are plenty of alternatives. **Après-ski** is amazingly lively – the Sunwing is packed from 3pm onwards and the Diplomat is the liveliest place in town (both have live bands). Later on, the Diplomat, the Country Club and Bygget all have live bands and there are plenty of bars for a quiet drink.

Off the slopes, there is lots to do including dog-sled and reindeer-sled rides, tobogganing on a floodlit run, ice skating, snowmobiling, ice fishing, ice driving and ice climbing.

Scotland

- ➕ The resorts are easy to get to from northern Britain
- ➕ It is possible to experience perfect snow and stirring skiing
- ➕ Decent, cheap accommodation and good-value packages are on offer
- ➕ Mid-week is rarely crowded
- ➕ There are extensive ski-touring and ski-mountaineering possibilities
- ➕ Few travel hassles
- ➕ Lots to do off the slopes

- ➖ Weather is extremely changeable and sometimes vicious
- ➖ Snowfall is erratic, and has been poor in several recent seasons
- ➖ Slopes are limited; runs tend to be short
- ➖ Queueing can be a problem – though usually only at peak times and if some lifts are closed
- ➖ Little ski village ambience and few memorable mountain restaurants

Scotland is different. If you want reliable snow, perfect pistes, blue skies, sunshine and charming mountain restaurants, forget it. Conditions in Scotland are unpredictable, to say the least. If you are willing to take a chance, or if you live nearby and can go at short notice when things look good, fine. But don't look on it as a replacement for your usual week in the Alps. If you try it, you'll either love it or hate it; but at least you'll know. And you'll have something to talk about in the pub.

What's new

The long-awaited funicular railway at Cairngorm is now under construction and should be ready for 2001/2002. Various facilites have been relocated to accommodate the building work.

The ski area at the Nevis Range doubled in size thanks to the addition of three new lifts (two chairs and a T-bar) several years ago. Snowboarding facilities were expanded last season and guided tours in the back corrie are planned for 2000/01.

The Lecht's snowmaking network has been extended recently. A new three-person chair-lift is being installed next season and will access a new snowtubing run.

Scotland's five ski areas are surprisingly different from one another, although they do share some characteristics. Snow conditions and the weather can vary dramatically – especially from west to east; up-to-date and accurate information on conditions and the latest weather forecast are particularly important for those contemplating a trip at short notice. Conditions can be testing. Rain, gales, icy slopes, slush, fog, rocks and heather are not unheard of, but those who ski regularly in Scotland tend to finish up as strong, versatile skiers. Some of the resorts have artificial snowmaking and this is being increased in places.

For novices who are really keen to learn – and who are prepared for the possibility of less than ideal conditions – Scotland could make sense, especially if you live nearby. One option is to book instruction via one of the excellent outdoor centres, many of which also provide accommodation and a wide range of other activities. Otherwise, the tuition at the resorts themselves, with BASI and BSA qualified instructors, is also very good.

For intermediates, a tour by car that takes in the five main areas is an amusing way to spend a week if you are lucky with the weather. Most of the slopes in most of the areas fall somewhere around the intermediate level. But all areas, apart from the Lecht, offer the occasional piece of tough or very tough skiing. Much of the terrain is suitable for ski touring and ski mountaineering; Cairngorm especially is something of a centre of expertise for mountain activities.

Snowboarding is popular in Scotland and most of the resorts have some special snowboard-friendly features, but conditions are not always conducive to maintaining these fun-parks and half-pipes in good nick. Fortunately, the natural terrain is very good for free-riding when the conditions are right.

Apart from weather, Scotland's style, ambience and attitude is not to everyone's taste. All these elements are better than they were – the relatively new Nevis Range area has probably had a lot to do with that – but Aviemore is still ugly, Fort William is hard to like, and cosy, charming café-bars and restaurants are still too few in number. Licensed restaurants have appeared at the slopes in the last few years, bringing not just alcohol but also much better catering. The limited facilities at the base areas (none has accommodation) mean that après-ski there is poor. By 5pm almost everybody has gone. There is nightlife, of course – there are reasonable pubs

CAIRNGORM MOUNTAIN FACTS

Altitude	550m-1100m
Lifts	17
Pistes	2085 acres
Green	32%
Blue	32%
Red	32%
Black	4%
Artificial snow	none

Cairngorm Chairlift Company

Postcode PH22 1RB
t +44 (1479) 861261
f 861207
cairngorm@sol.co.uk
www.aviemore.org/cairngorm

NEVIS RANGE MOUNTAIN FACTS

Altitude	650m-1220m
Lifts	12
Pistes	1560 acres
Green	20%
Blue	34%
Red	31%
Black	15%
Artificial snow	none

Tourist Office

Postcode PH33 6SW
t +44 (1397) 705825
f 705854
nevisrange@sol.co.uk
www.nevis-range.co.uk

and bars – but it's like Scotland not Switzerland.

Cairngorm is the biggest and best-known resort in Scotland. Aviemore is the main centre (with a regular shuttle-bus link to the slopes) but a significant amount of Cairngorm business also comes in from other villages in the Spey valley.

The slopes, which lie between 550m and 1100m, are accessed from car parks about a mile apart at the base of two corries – Coire Cas (the main area) and Coire na Ciste (a narrow gulley with the toughest skiing in it). The two sectors come together at the Ptarmigan beginners' area just below the summit of Cairn Gorm. There are chair-lifts operating from both base areas and, as the snowline recedes up the hill, they provide access to the skiing. Construction of a new funicular from the main car park (655m) up to Ptarmigan at 1100m is now under way – the funicular will replace the Car Park and White Lady chair-lifts and will mean a warm, sheltered ride on bad-weather days, when high winds might well have caused the chair-lifts to close. The project will be ready for 2001/20002.

There are mountain restaurants at each of the base areas, at the Shieling (midway up Coire Cas) and at Ptarmigan, at the very top.

There's a fun-park for snowboarders, the condition of which is heavily dependent on the snow conditions. Free guided tours of the mountain start from the Day Lodge twice daily.

There's no accommodation at the ski area. The Stakis Coylumbridge, the nearest hotel, offers good-value packages. The Red Macgregor Hotel is centrally located in Aviemore and there are many more attractive options in and around the town. Chalets, cottages, houses and caravans (and even the occasional castle) are available to rent on a self-catering basis – the Highlands of Scotland tourist board provides a comprehensive list. For the après-ski late in the evening, Cafe Mambo, Chevvy's, the Winking Owl and Crofter's Show Bar are the most popular nightspots. A recent reporter recommends the restaurant at the Cairngorm Hotel.

Nevis Range is the newest and the highest Scottish resort and it occupies the north-facing slopes of Aonach Mor (Gaelic for Great Ridge) – Britain's eighth highest peak, at 1220m – and is in close proximity to the Ben itself. The resort opened in 1989 and in the mid-1990s invested in three new lifts – two chairs and a T-bar (with names like Braveheart and Rob Roy one senses something of a nationalist pride about the place) – which have opened up the north-east-facing corries in the Coire Dubh area and doubled the amount of available slopes to 1560 acres. The additional area also holds its snow well because of its orientation. A new beginners' area was also built higher up the mountain, which has more reliable snow than the original, low nursery slopes. There is a 75m dry ski slope in the middle of the actual slope area – the tow for this is open throughout the season and allows access to the upper slopes in poor conditions, when the Snowgoose chair may be closed by high winds. There's a fun-park under the Snowgoose and other snowboard features are built when the weather allows it.

A long gondola ride in comfortable six-seater cabins is something of a novelty in Scotland and a fair indicator of the relative sophistication of the facilities here. The chair-lift – a few minutes' walk from the gondola station – arrives at an altitude of 900 metres and is crucial to keeping skiing going late in the season – the upper runs are expected to last until late May.

When the sun shines and the views of Ben Nevis and Carn Mor Dearg are at their most spectacular, intermediates should head for the summit and take it all in – it's superb. The main mountain restaurant, the self-service Snowgoose Restaurant and Bar, shares a building with the gondola top station and is frequently the most popular location on the mountain. Gondola trippers as well as skiers hang out here looking for warmth.

Fort William is only a 15-minute drive from the skiing. The town provides everything that the visitor needs; some hotels arrange transport to the slopes. There are many B&Bs and hotels in and around Fort William that offer accommodation – the Milton hotel has great leisure facilities. Self-catering units are plentiful. The Nevisport bar and the Chekka are popular nightspots. The Grog & Gruel is known for good-value pub fare, and the Crannog is recommended for top quality seafood.

GLENCOE MOUNTAIN FACTS

Altitude	305m-1110m
Lifts	7
Pistes	494 acres
Green	25%
Blue	25%
Red	38%
Black	12%
Artificial snow	none

Glencoe Ski Centre

Postcode PA39 4HZ
t +44 (1855) 851226
f 851233
glencoe@sol.co.uk
www.ski.scotland.net

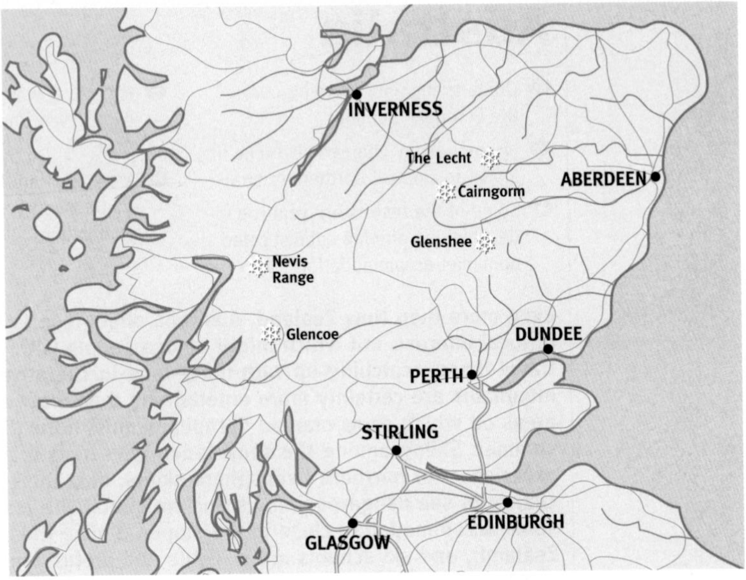

THE LECHT MOUNTAIN FACTS

Altitude	610m-825m
Lifts	13
Pistes	600 acres
Green	15%
Blue	50%
Red	25%
Black	10%
Artificial snow	15 acres

The Lecht Ski Area

Postcode AB36 8YP
t +44 (1975) 651440
f 651426
thelecht@sol.co.uk
www.lecht.co.uk

GLENSHEE MOUNTAIN FACTS

Altitude	610m-1070m
Lifts	26
Pistes	2000 acres
Green	26%
Blue	34%
Red	34%
Black	6%
Artificial snow	5 acres

Glenshee Ski Area

Postcode AB35 5XU
t +44 (1339) 741320
f 741665
glenshee@sol.co.uk
www.ski.scotland.net

Glencoe's slopes lie between 305m and 1110m, on the Meall A Bhuiridh mountain at the edge of Rannoch Moor and just east of Glen Coe – a moody and magnificent setting if ever there was one. The base area is a car park and a few buildings housing the Log Cabin restaurant, ticket office and a museum. The Access lift, a double chair, rises to the Plateau tow, which opens up the main nursery area and provides access to the other tows (and one chair) and the bulk of the slopes, including the Fly Paper black run – Scotland's steepest piste. The only on-mountain café, the Plateau, is up here. The upper slopes enjoy good snow-cover, often for a season that lasts from December to May.

The area is popular with snowboarders thanks to some good natural terrain full of bumps, jumps and gullies that make up for the lack of a fun-park.

The only hotel nearby is the isolated Kings House Hotel a mile away. It also has a bunkhouse and an area for tents.

Glenshee has expanded into a system that now boasts 26 lifts and has comfortably the biggest area – spread out over three valleys – and uplift capacity of the Scottish resorts. There are two big on-slope café/restaurants and another big café at the base station car park. Most of the slopes, which lie between 610m and 1070m, are suitable for intermediates and beginners. There's some good natural snowboard terrain for free-riding and a reasonable fun-park as well.

It remains primarily a venue for day trippers because of the lack of a major accommodation centre, though there are hotels, hostels and B&Bs in the area – lists can be provided by the local tourist board.

The Lecht is largely a beginners' area, 32 miles from Aviemore. The slopes (610m–820m) are on the gentle east-facing side of a high pass with a series of parallel drag lifts and runs just above the car parks. The main area includes five beginner tows and six others, each with a run or two back down towards the road. With a maximum vertical of only around 200m, runs are short. There is a floodlit dry ski slope on the mountainside which ensures some evening skiing and a bit of summer business. There's also a fun-park with a half-pipe for snowboarders. Refreshments are supplied by the Day Lodge at the base station, and a snack bar.

The nearest place to stay, Tomintoul, is six miles away from the slopes. It is a typical Highland village with a few hotels and B&Bs, but the nearest accommodation is at the Allargue Arms in Corgarff, three miles from the slopes.

Australia

- ⊕ Offers skiing and boarding during the European summer
- ⊕ In one holiday you can also take in a visit to tropical northern Australia
- ⊕ Some of the resorts are year-round destinations offering sophisticated upmarket accommodation

- ⊖ It's a long way from anywhere except New Zealand and south-east Asia
- ⊖ Mountains are rather low, and lift/trail networks are small by Alpine standards

Even more than New Zealand, Australia offers resorts that are basically of local interest, but which might amuse people with other reasons to travel there – catching up with those long-lost relatives, say. The mountains are certainly more entertaining than most of the glacier areas on which snow-starved Europeans must normally rely in the summer. Skiing among the snow-laden gum trees is also a unique experience for northern hemisphere skiers, plus there is often the chance to see kangaroos, emus and wombats. The resorts mainly offer some accommodation close to the slopes (unlike those in New Zealand), and ski schools are sizeable and professional.

The major resorts are concentrated in the populous south-east corner of the country, between Sydney and Melbourne, with the largest in New South Wales (NSW), in the National Park centred on Australia's highest mountain, Mt Kosciusko (2230m), about six hours' drive from Sydney. Skiing has been going on here since the early years of the century – as in the next-door state of Victoria, where there are several resorts within three or four hours' drive of Melbourne. Visitors to Tasmania may want to check out the possibilities there.

The season generally runs from early June to mid-October, but may be extended at either end if snow conditions allow.

The big news in Australian skiing is the construction of a commercial airport just 20 minutes' drive from Mount Hotham in Victoria. Qantas started twice-weekly flights in 2000, effectively making the resort the closest to a major city: 90 minutes from Sydney, under an hour from Melbourne. Mount Hotham doubled its terrain two years ago, putting it on a par with NSW's Thredbo.

Mount Hotham now competes with the prestigious and long-established alpine village of **Thredbo** in NSW. Thredbo hosted the only World Cup race event held in Australia thanks to its size and vertical of 670m.

Thredbo is rather like a small and quite smart French purpose-built resort – user-friendly, and mostly made up of modern apartments (and lodges run by clubs). But there are many more bars than you would find in the French equivalent. There is an Austrian flavour to some of the lodges and bars, due to the early influx of Europeans. It's a steep little place, with stiff climbs to get around from one part to another. Road access is easy, but the toll is high. It costs $A60 just to enter the park. Once you're there it's $A73 a day to ski, the same as its long-standing rival Perisher Blue.

The slopes, prettily wooded with gum trees, rise up across the valley from the village, served by a regular shuttle-bus through the resort. The runs are well laid out, with better connections between slopes than in many areas – and the resort as a whole gives the impression of good organisation. The dozen lifts include four fast quad chairs, and the trails include Australia's highest (2035m) and longest (6km). While the blacks are not difficult, they offer some variety, and on the higher lifts there are off-piste variants.

Since 1987 $A100 million has been poured into Thredbo by its owners. The result is an abundance of luxurious apartments, an attractive pedestrian mall with good shopping and some high-class restaurants both on and off the mountain. There is also an impressive four-year-old Australian Institute of Sport training complex open to the public, with an Olympic-size pool, waterslide, traverse climbing wall, squash and tennis courts, gym, and basketball courts. On the hill a 700m bob-sleigh track for the public is popular all year round. You can take the Crackenback gondola to the mountain top for dinner.

On the other side of the mountain range is the **Perisher Blue** resort complex, with a pass covering 51 lifts – more than anywhere else in Australia – but a vertical of less than 400m. The main area is Perisher/Smiggins, where lifts and runs – practically all easy or intermediate – range over three lightly wooded sectors. The resort is reachable by road, but is also served by the Skitube, a rack railway that tunnels its way up from Bullocks Flat and goes on to the second area, **Blue Cow/Guthega**, where the slopes offer more challenges. Perisher Blue has been doing its best to catch up to Thredbo by upgrading hotels and building more facilities, but it remains spread out and does not have the cosy village atmosphere which Thredbo fans adore. On the other hand, Perisher Blue has more ski-in ski-out accommodation. Its main advantage over Thredbo is its snow, thanks to its position further within the mountain ranges and its altitude: Perisher Blue's lifts start at about the same elevation as Thredbo's mid-station.

Many people also stay in apartments or hotels in the lakeside town of Jindabyne, a half-hour drive from both Thredbo and Perisher, or in cosy chalets along the Alpine Way, which leads to Thredbo.

From Perisher, a snowcat can take you on an 8km ride to the isolated chalets of Australia's highest resort, **Charlotte Pass** (1760m), with five lifts but only 200m vertical. People visit the Pass more for its charm than the skiing, although it is a favourite with families. The major hotel is the historic and turreted Kosciusko Chalet, a good spot for romantic weekends.

In Victoria, resorts are not as high as in NSW but many have good snow due to being set well within the ranges. The aforementioned **Mount Hotham** has a reputation for powder snow. The 11 lifts serve a complete range of runs with plenty of variety. The longest run is 2.5km and there is more consistently steep terrain here than at any other area in Australia.

Mount Hotham is unique among the Australian fields in that the village is built along the top of a ridge, with the slopes below it. The focus of the village is Mount Hotham Central, comprising apartments, shops and a choice of eateries, including several excellent restaurants catering to the rising champagne factor in the village. Mount Hotham skiers can also stay 15 minutes' drive away at Dinner Plain, a settlement of architect-designed chalets set prettily among gum trees. There are a few restaurants and bars here, and many cross-country trails.

There is also a 10-minute helicopter link from Mount Hotham to another resort nearby (and covered by the same lift pass), **Falls Creek**, that costs all of $A59. Falls Creek is the most alpine of Australia's resort, completely snow-bound in winter. Guests not arriving by chopper are taken by snowcat to their ski-in ski-out lodge. There are 18 lifts, though the area is smaller than Mount Hotham's.

New for 2000 was snowcat skiing on Australia's steepest accessed mountain, Mt McKay. This is the country's only true expert terrain, featuring narrow chutes, large boulders and majestic views. Snow mobiling and dog-sleigh rides are also possible.

The other Victorian resort of note is **Mt Buller**. This place is to Melbourne what Cape Cod is to Manhattan – a magnet for old money and a place to be seen. Drive time from Melbourne is just three hours. Big-time entrepreneurs have poured millions into infrastructure surrounding Mt Buller's isolated peak, creating a proper resort village with a luxury hotel, and even a university campus. Draped around the mountain are 25 lifts – the largest network in Victoria, including 13 chair-lifts. There's also a tubing hill, snow-shoeing, cross-country, telemarking lessons and tobogganing.

Mt Buffalo is worth visiting mainly to stay in the historic Mt Buffalo Chalet with its dramatic views over the craggy Victorian alps. The slopes, a short drive away, are in an alpine basin surrounded by boulders, with five lifts almost purely for beginners.

New Zealand

- ⊕ For Europeans, good for a combined holiday to the southern hemisphere and more interesting than summer skiing on glaciers
- ⊕ For Australians, conveniently close, with flights from Sydney
- ⊕ Huge areas of off-piste terrain accessible by helicopter on the South Island
- ⊕ Some spectacular views

- ⊖ It's a long way from anywhere except Australia
- ⊖ Limited mountain facilities – mountain restaurants are mostly basic pit stops
- ⊖ Generally long drives from accommodation up to the ski areas
- ⊖ Highly changeable weather
- ⊖ No trees, so skiing in bad weather virtually impossible

The number of keen skiers and boarders from New Zealand found kicking around the Alps gives a clue that there must be some decent slopes back home – and indeed there are. The resorts are rather different from those of the Alps or the Rockies, and the networks of lifts and runs are rather limited by those exalted standards. However desperate you are for snow during the northern summer, we wouldn't advise travelling halfway round the world from Europe or the US just to get access to the likes of Coronet Peak, Mount Hutt or Whakapapa. But the heli-skiing around the Mt Cook region on the South Island is definitely worth writing home about. For Europeans already spending a lot to travel to New Zealand, the extra cost of a day or two's heli-drops is well worth while. New Zealand's ski resorts could make an interesting part of a wider-ranging visit to the country, and may be the best option you have if you're starting from somewhere nearer. From Australia, there are now direct flights into Queenstown each Saturday, so you can be skiing within half a day of leaving Sydney.

There are exceptions but, broadly speaking, the system in New Zealand is that you stay in towns at fairly low altitude – usually below the snow line – and drive up each day to a base lodge where there will be a simple restaurant, equipment hire and one or two shops as well as the main lifts, but usually no accommodation.

There are resorts on both North Island and South Island. The main concentration on South Island is around the lakeside town (and year-round resort) of Queenstown, covered in detail in a separate chapter starting on page 597. Queenstown has become known as the adrenalin capital of New Zealand – and probably the world – by offering a range of dangerous (or at least thrilling) activities, of which the best known is bungee jumping. Most are available in winter as well as summer.

In what follows, we describe the most prominent resorts (apart from Queenstown and its two local mountains), but there are a number of other possibilities. The main commercial ones are described briefly in our directory at the back of the book, but there are also other ski-fields run by clubs. By all means inquire about what's available on the club field front, but don't expect groomed trails or other luxuries: club fields are pretty primitive, involving stiff walks to get to the base and crude rope tows when you get there. You even have to bring your own food and drink. If you must visit any club field, Craigieburn on the South Island, near Mt Hutt, wins the vote for the most impressive terrain out of the selection.

Any of the major resorts is worth a day or two of your time if you're in the area and the conditions are right. But if your credit card is also in good condition, don't miss the heli-skiing; even if you're no expert off-piste, with powder skis it's a doddle, and tremendously satisfying. There are several companies operating on South Island, based in Queenstown, Wanaka

WHAKAPAPA MOUNTAIN FACTS

Altitude	1625m-2300m
Lifts	20
Pistes	1360 acres
Blue	25%
Red	50%
Black	25%
Art. snow	some

TOURIST OFFICE

t +64 (7) 892 3738
f 892 3732
snow@whakapapa.co.nz
www.whakapapa.co.nz

and Methven. Methven Heli Ski arguably has the most impressive terrain on offer, operating in steep and spectacular ranges surrounding New Zealand's highest peak Mt Cook. Harris Mts Heli-Ski, operating out of Queenstown and Wanaka, caters mainly for the large Japanese market, and the three-run days are generally very easy skiing with long waits in between lifts. The other major Queenstown operation, Southern Lakes Heli-Ski, is more amenable to exciting skiing. Try to leave the arrangements loose, to cope with the highly changeable weather. A heli-ski day NZ style usually starts with a 7.30am phone call to those who've booked letting them know if the weather's suitable.

An alternative adventure is to fly by plane to ski 10km down the length of the Tasman Glacier. Be aware that this is quite a costly venture for a gentle schuss down a very mild slope, with few areas to lay real turns. The main drawcard of the Tasman is the immense grandeur of the place, along with the ski-plane flights over stunning blue ice-flows and the close proximity of Mt Cook. The Tasman is also one of the few glaciers in the world where it is possible to walk through the eery ice-blue glacial caves – quite a surreal experience.

As in the northern hemisphere, the season doesn't really get under way until about midwinter – mid or late June – and runs until some time in October. Mount Hutt aims to open first, in mid-May, and disputes the longest-season title with Whakapapa, which generally stays open until mid-November.

Snowboarding is very popular in New Zealand, and most of the major resorts have special terrain parks including half-pipes, as well as boarding classes and hire equipment.

Whakapapa (pronounced Fukapapa) is on the slopes of the active volcano Mt Ruapehu, which has occasionally erupted in recent years, leaving the slopes black with volcanic ash. Until the late 1990s the volcano had not caused havoc since the 1950s when an eruption washed away a bridge.

Mt Ruapehu is in the middle of the North Island and within four hours' drive of both Auckland and Wellington. Whakapapa, New Zealand's largest ski field, is located on the north-facing slopes with a top height of 2300m and a vertical of 675m served by 20 lifts including one fast quad. Terrain is typified by large, wide open cruisers plus challenging off-piste. Next to the base lodge is an extensive beginner's area, Happy Valley, with half a dozen rope tows and snowmaking that allow this particular section to open early in the season. The resort's lifts and runs range across craggy terrain made especially interesting because of the unpredictable twists, turns and drops of the solidified lava on which it sits. There is a mix of deep gullies, superb natural half-pipes for snow boarders and narrow chutes. There is a handful of mountain restaurants.

Accommodation is 6km away at Whakapapa village, with the best

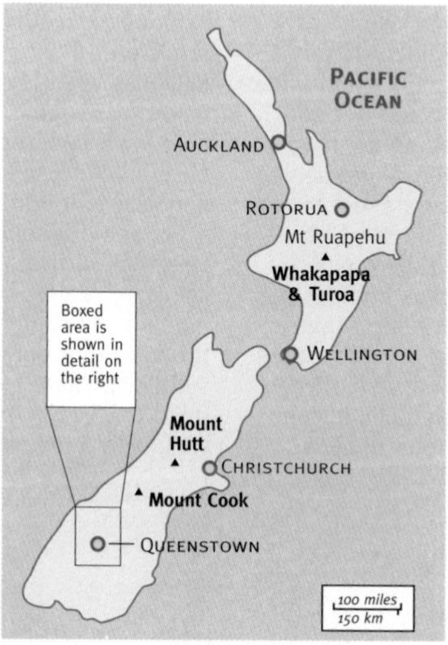

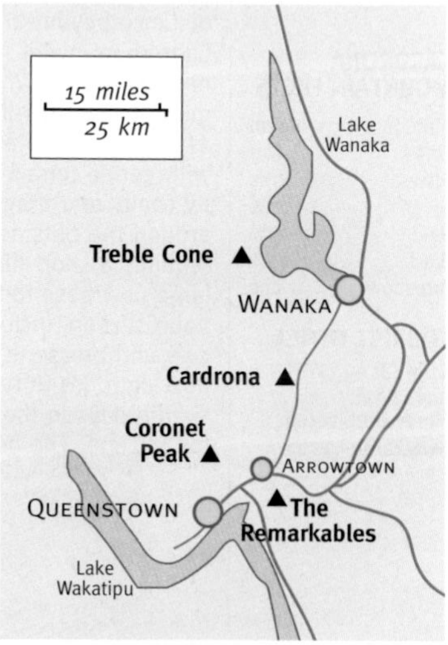

MOUNT HUTT MOUNTAIN FACTS

Altitude	1420m-2075m
Lifts	10
Pistes	902 acres
Green	25%
Blue	50%
Black	25%
Art. snow	103 acres

TOURIST OFFICE

t +64 (3) 308 5074
f 308 5076
marketing@nzski.com
www.nzski.com

TREBLE CONE MOUNTAIN FACTS

Altitude	1200m-1860m
Lifts	5
Pistes	1359 acres
Green	15%
Blue	45%
Black	40%
Art. snow	125 acres

TOURIST OFFICE

t +64 (3) 443 7443
f 443 8401
tcinfo@treblecone.co.nz
www.treblecone.co.nz

CARDRONA MOUNTAIN FACTS

Altitude	1505m-1895m
Lifts	7
Pistes	790 acres
Green	20%
Blue	55%
Black	25%
Art. snow	none

TOURIST OFFICE

t +64 (3) 443 7411
f 443 8818
info@cardrona.com
www.cardrona.com

middle-of-the-road property being a motel named the Skotel. A complete anomaly in this area of rustic lodges is the Chateau, a hotel in the grand style of the 1920s, with overly high ceilings, sweeping drapes over picture windows, a marble foyer and formal dining room with grand piano.

Worth knowing about is the hike to Mt Ruapehu's fizzing Crater Lake. Ask ski patrol for directions or better still talk them into taking you on a guided trip. This involves about a half-hour hike up from the top of the highest T-bar, and then a long traverse across a large flat tundra-like area. A few lefts and rights and you are staring into the mouth of a volcano. Awesome views and neighbouring volcanos give this area an other-worldly feel.

On the south-western slope of Mt Ruapehu (reachable on snow by going off-piste from Whakapapa after a stiff climb) is **Turoa** (now under the same ownership as Whakapapa) – smaller, but with an impressive 722m vertical – the biggest in Australasia. The longest run is 4km. There's plenty of scope off-piste away from the gentle intermediate runs, plus the chance to ski on the Mangaehuehu Glacier. Accommodation is 20 minutes away in Ohakune.

The South Island has 15 ski areas, including five club fields. **Mt Hutt**, an hour west of Christchurch in the northern part of the island, has a 672m vertical and some of the country's most impressive, consistently steep, wide-open terrain – all within view of the Pacific Ocean. On a clear day you can even see the sandy beaches in the distance beyond the patchwork Canterbury plains. The lift system is half the size of Whakapapa's and a few more faster chair-lifts would not go astray. The main area is an open bowl with gentle terrain in the centre served by chairs and drags and steeper terrain around the outside, some of which requires a short hike to the top. A large new base lodge was built for the 2000 season, including a big carpeted café and brasserie, plus a well stocked hire shop. Mt Hutt Helicopters offers six-run days in the mountains beyond for $NZ600. The helicopter departs from the heli-pad right in the car park – just wander up to the heli hut and book in. There is no accommodation on-mountain – most people stay in the quiet little town of Methven, where there are several truly comfortable up-market B&Bs as well as motels and apartments. The very British South Island capital of Christchurch, an hour and a half away, is also an option for accommodation.

About six hours' drive south of Christchurch is the quiet lakeside town of Wanaka, which is also 90 minutes from Queenstown, and there are two resorts accessible from here.

Treble Cone, 20km from Wanaka, has more advanced slopes than any other NZ ski area, plus the advantage of a better lift system including the first six-seater chair-lift in the southern hemisphere. There are two well maintained intermediate trails, one 3.5km the other 2km. Both on the main flank and off to the side in Saddle Basin there are long natural half-pipes which are great fun when snow is good, as well as smooth, wide runs for cruising. Treble Cone is reached by a long and winding dirt track that adds to the excitement. The ski field offers stunning views across Lake Wanaka, its shores usually free of snow, with snowcapped Alpine-style peaks in the distance. There's an adequate café at the lift base.

Cardrona, 34km from Wanaka, is famous for its dry snow. The terrain is noted for its well-groomed, flattering cruisers. But there are some serious if short chutes, and the middle basin, Arcadia, hosts the New Zealand Extreme Skiing Championships. The total vertical is a modest 390m. Millions have been poured into the resort by its family owners over the past few years, resulting in a large base area focused around an impressive, if odd, clock tower. There's a bar and brasserie-style restaurant, large hire facility and a licensed childcare centre, plus several neat and modern self-contained apartments at the base (but bring all your own supplies). There are four half-pipes for boarders. Learners are looked after well, with three magic carpet lifts.

Queenstown 310m

A lively base for sampling a range of resorts

HOW IT RATES

The slopes

Snow	**
Extent	*
Experts	***
Intermediates	***
Beginners	***
Convenience	*
Queues	***
Restaurants	*
The rest	
Scenery	****
Resort charm	**
Off-slope	*****

- + For Europeans, more interesting than summer skiing on glaciers
- + For Australians, conveniently close, with flights from Sydney
- + Huge areas of off-piste terrain accessible by helicopters, with excellent snow at the right time
- + Lots to do off the slopes, especially for adrenalin junkies
- + Lively town, with lots going on and good restaurants
- + Grand views locally, and the spectacular 'fjord' country nearby

- − Slopes (in two separate areas locally) are a drive from town
- − Limited lift-served slopes in each area
- − It's a long way from anywhere except Australia
- − Mountain restaurants are little more than pit stops
- − Highly changeable weather
- − No trees, so skiing in bad weather virtually impossible

If you want a single destination in New Zealand – as opposed to visiting a few different mountains on your travels – Queenstown is probably it, especially if you can cope with the cost of a few heli-drops. Although the resorts of North Island are impressive, the Southern Alps are, in the end, more compelling – and their resorts are free of volcanic interruptions. Mount Hutt may be a slightly more impressive area than either of Queenstown's local fields – Coronet Peak and The Remarkables – but it's a rather isolated field. From Queenstown you have a choice of the two local fields plus the option of an outing to Treble Cone and Cardrona. The best way to take them in would be to plan on a night or two in Wanaka, an hour or two away (see Introduction to New Zealand).

boarding *Boarding is popular in New Zealand, and although the two mountains close to Queenstown don't seem to have quite such a hold on the boarding market as Cardrona (see New Zealand introduction), they have everything you need, including equipment, tuition and new terrain-parks and half-pipes. You needn't go anywhere near a drag-lift, and there are no flats to worry about except on the lowest green run at The Remarkables.*

What's new

The snowmaking network in both Coronet Peak and the Remarkables has been extended.

The NZ Superpass is a card that gets you discounts on lift passes and other activities.

The resort

Queenstown is a winter-and-summer resort on the shore of Lake Wakatipu. (There is a map of the area in the introductory chapter.) Although the setting is splendid, with views to the peaks of the aptly named Remarkables range beyond the lake, the town itself is no beauty – it has grown up to meet tourists' needs, and has a very commercial feel. In recent years much effort has been put into smartening up the town, with such additions as the classy new Steamer Wharf complex by the lake and new luxury accommodation. It has a lively, relaxed feel, and makes a satisfactory base, with some good restaurants, plenty of entertaining bars and lots of touristy clothes shops.

The mountains

There are four lift-served mountains – all small by Alpine standards – that you can get to from Queenstown. The two described here – Coronet Peak and The Remarkables – are close by. The others – Cardrona and Treble Cone – are a more serious drive away, and best visited from Wanaka (see New Zealand introduction). At each base area you'll find a mini-resort – a ski school, a ski rental shop, a functional self-service restaurant, but no accommodation except at Cardrona.

All these areas have something for all standards of skier or boarder, with off-piste opportunities as well as prepared and patrolled trails. These areas use the American green/blue/black convention for run gradings.

↑ The Remarkables look more remarkable from Queenstown than from the ridge above Sugar Bowl

SNOWPIX.COM / CHRIS GILL

THE REMARKABLES MOUNTAIN FACTS

Altitude	1620m-1980m
Lifts	5
Pistes	543 acres
Green	30%
Blue	40%
Black	30%
Art. snow	25 acres

TOURIST OFFICE

t +64 (3) 442 4615
f 442 4619
admin@theremarkables.co.nz
www.nzski.com

CORONET PEAK MOUNTAIN FACTS

Altitude	1210m-1650m
Lifts	7
Pistes	690 acres
Green	20%
Blue	45%
Black	35%
Art. snow	200 acres

TOURIST OFFICE

t +64 (3) 442 4620
f 442 4624
admin@coronetpeak.co.nz
www.nzski.com

THE SLOPES
Not the height of convenience

The Remarkables, true to their name, are a dramatic range of craggy peaks visible across the lake from some parts of Queenstown. The slopes are tucked in a bowl behind the peaks, a 40-minute drive from town.

Two chairs go up from the base. The slow Alta lift serves easy runs and accesses the higher Sugar Bowl chair, which serves mainly long, easy runs plus a couple of black chutes. The Shadow Basin chair accesses steeper terrain, including three hike-accessed, expert-only chutes that drop down to Lake Alta, and the Homeward Run – a broad, fairly gentle, unprepared slope down to the resort access road, where a shuttle-truck takes you back to the base. The Remarkables is also home to New Zealand's first snowcat operation in the bowls behind the main slopes.

Coronet Peak, about 25 minutes' drive from Queenstown is a far more satisfying resort, especially for intermediates and above. Again, there are three main chair-lifts, one a fast quad that accesses practically all the runs. The main mountainside is a pleasantly varied intermediate slope, full of highly enjoyable rolling terrain that snowboarders adore, though it steepens near the bottom. The main enjoyment comes from venturing off-piste all over the place. A fourth lift, a T-bar, serves another mainly intermediate area to one side. There are also drags for beginners. Night skiing runs from July to September on Fridays and Saturdays.

SNOW RELIABILITY
Good at Coronet

The New Zealand weather is highly variable, so it's difficult to be confident about snow conditions. Coronet tends to receive sleet and/or rain even when it's snowing in The Remarkables. But Coronet Peak has snowmaking on practically all its intermediate terrain.

FOR EXPERTS
Challenges exist

Both areas have quite a choice of genuinely black slopes. Coronet's Back Bowls is an experts-only area, and The Remarkables' Shadow Basin chair serves some excellent slopes.

FOR INTERMEDIATES
Fine, within limits

There's some very enjoyable intermediate skiing in both areas – appreciably more at Coronet, where there are also easy blacks to go on to. But remember: these are very small areas by Alpine standards.

FOR BEGINNERS
Excellent

There are gentle areas at both areas served by rope tows, and longer green runs served by chairs. And many other diversions if you decide it's a drag.

CHILDCARE

At both areas there is a Skiwiland Club for children aged 4 to 6 with morning and afternoon sessions. The Queenstown Crèche can take younger children all day. There is a licensed crèche at the Remarkables, taking children from 2 to 4.

SNOWPIX.COM / CHRIS GILL

The lack of snow at village level is normal, not only here but at Wanaka and elsewhere in NZ ↓

FOR CROSS-COUNTRY
Unremarkable
There is a short loop around a lake in the middle of The Remarkables area, but the only serious cross-country area is the elevated plateau of Waiorau Snow Farm, near Cardrona.

QUEUES
It depends
Coronet and The Remarkables can suffer a little from high-season crowds – there are certainly enough beds locally to lead to queues at peak times. But they aren't a major worry.

MOUNTAIN RESTAURANTS
Er, what mountain restaurants?
Both areas have a simple cafeteria at the base, and Coronet has a brasserie, but nothing up the mountain.

SCHOOLS AND GUIDES
All the usual classes
The schools are well organised, with a wide range of options, including 'guaranteed' beginner classes.

FACILITIES FOR CHILDREN
Look good
Childcare looked OK to us.

Staying there

Some hotels are quite some way from central Queenstown – inconvenient for après-ski unless there's a shuttle-bus.

HOW TO GO
Stay out of town?
The hotels range from the very simple to the glossily pretentious Millennium. Aim to get a room with a view across Lake Wakatipu and the mountains – the view is worth the extra dollars. There are lots of big, smart but rather impersonal places built to meet the big summer demand for beds in this popular lakeside resort. One of the most welcoming places – with more of a 'ski-lodge' atmosphere – is Nugget Point, a few miles out.

EATING OUT/APRES-SKI
Lots of choice
Queenstown is a lively little town, with a good range of bars and clubs that stay open late with disco or live music. There are over 100 restaurants – Chinese, Italian, Malaysian, Lebanese ... you name it. The Moa is a particularly stylish bar-restaurant, with

live music sometimes. Solero Vino has delicious Mediterranean food and a rustic bar, and McNeill's is an excellent brew-pub housed in a stone cottage. The Bunker does excellent local cuisine such as Bluff oysters and lamb. At the other end of the scale, pizza-lovers crowd into The Cow, a cosy barn-like place where you sit on logs around a fire waiting for tables or takeaways. Lone Star offers big servings of satisfying American-style food. A small upmarket casino opened in 1999 in the plush Steamer Wharf, which also holds a classy cigar bar and good duty free.

OFF THE SLOPES

Scare yourself silly

There are lots of scary things to do – see below. Just to the west is New Zealand's spectacularly scenic 'fjord country', and you can go on independent or guided walks. By all reports, the Milford Sound sightseeing flights by plane or helicopter are to be preferred to the slow, lumbering bus-ride from Queenstown – but be aware that the weather can ruin your plans. Arrowtown is interesting for a quick visit – a cute, touristy old mining town where you can kit yourself out to go panning for gold. The Winter Festival, held in mid-July, is an annual 'action-packed week of mayhem on the mountain and in the town'.

GET THAT ADRENALIN RUSH

The streets of Queenstown are lined by agencies offering various artificial thrills.

AJ Hackett's bungee jump at Kawarau Bridge is where this crazy activity got off the ground – you plunge towards the icy river, but are pulled up short by your bungee cord and lowered into an inflatable boat.

The Shotover Jet Boat experience is less demanding. You get chauffeured at high speed along the rocky river in a boat that can get along in very shallow water, execute high-speed 360° turns and pass very close to cliffs and trees. It's probably more fun in summer than in temperatures of –10°C.

The whitewater rafting is genuinely thrilling – and not as uncomfortable as you'd expect, thanks to the full wet-suit, helmet, boots and gloves, and to the exertion involved. The rivers have some exciting rapids. One route even passes through a tunnel excavated in the gold-mining days, after which comes a small but steep waterfall where your souvenir shots are snapped.

Reference section

Tour operators

Arranging your own accommodation in a resort is not difficult. But most people still prefer the convenience of a package holiday, which is what most of the companies listed below are set up to provide. Note that we've also included some operators that offer accommodation without travel arrangements.

Absolute Ski
Chalet in Méribel
Tel 01788 860800
Fax 01788 860358
holiday@absoluteski.com
www.absoluteski.com

Airtours
Mainstream operator
Tel 0870 608 1950
Fax 01706 232977
www.airtours.co.uk

All Canada Ski
Holidays in Canada
Tel 01502 585825
Fax 01502 500681
mail@all-canada.com
www.all-canada.com

Alp Active
Holidays in Les Gets
Tel 01223 568220
Fax 01223 519314
info@alpactive,com
www.alpactive.com

Alpine Action
Chalets in Les Trois Vallées
Tel 01903 761986
Fax 01903 766007
alpineaction@mistral.co.uk
www.alpine-action.co.uk

Alpine Tours
Mainly Austria, Italy and Slovenia
Tel 01227 454777
Fax 01227 451177
alpinetoursltd@btinternet.com

American Ski Classics
North American holidays
Tel 020 8392 6660
Fax 020 8392 6606
sales@holidayworld.ltd.uk
www.americanskiclassics.com

APT Holidays Ltd
Weekend breaks by coach to Austria and Switzerland
Tel 01268 783878
Fax 01268 782656
apt.holidays@virgin.net
www.apt-holidays.co.uk

Aravis Alpine Retreat
Chalet in St Jean-de-Sixt (La Clusaz)
Tel 00 33 450 023 625
Fax 00 33 450 023 982
info@aravis-retreat.com

Avant-ski
Mainly holidays in France
Tel 0191 212 1173
Fax 0191 239 9459
sales@avant-ski.com
www.avant-ski.com

Balkan Holidays
Holidays in Bulgaria and Slovenia
Tel 020 7543 5555
Fax 020 7543 5577
sales@balkanholidays.co.uk
www.balkanholidays.co.uk

Barrelli Ski
Eclectic selection of French resorts
Tel 0890 220 1500
Fax 0890 230 1501
whiplash@barrelliski.co.uk
www.barrelliski.co.uk

Bien Ski
Chalet holidays in Méribel
Tel 020 7793 4269
Fax 020 7793 4249
info@bienski-com
www.bienski.com

Big Country Ski and Activity Holidays
Holidays to North America
Tel 029 2067 5205
Fax 029 2073 9204
enquiries@big-country.co.uk
www.big-country.co.uk

Bigfoot
Variety of holidays in Chamonix
Tel 01491 579601
Fax 01491 576568
ann@bigfoot-travel.co.uk
www.bigfoot-travel.co.uk

Bladon Lines
Chalet arm of Inghams
Tel 020 8780 8800
Fax 020 8780 8805
bladonlines@inghams.co.uk
www.inghams.co.uk

Board and Lodge
Catered snowboarding holidays in Chamonix
Tel 020 8444 6381
Fax 020 7916 2275
info@boardnlodge.com
www.boardnlodge.com

Bonne Neige Ski Holidays
Catered chalets in Méribel
Tel 01270 256966
Fax 01270 251033
ukoffice@bonne-neige-ski.com
www.bonne-neige-ski.com

Borderline
Specialist in Barèges
Tel 00 33 562 92 68 95
Fax 00 33 562 92 83 43
sorbiers@sudfr.com
www.borderlinehols.com

Chalet Beaumont
Large chalet in Chamonix
Tel 020 8544 0404
Fax 020 8544 0404
stay@beau-mont.com
www.beau-mont.com

The Chalet Company
Catered chalets in Morzine and Ardent (Avoriaz)
Tel 00 33 450 79 68 40
Fax 00 33 450 74 84 81
moran@wanadoo.fr

Chalet Snowboard
Snowboard holidays in France and US
Tel 01235 767575
Fax 01235 767576
info@chalet-snowboard.co.uk
www.chalet-snowboard.co.uk

Chalet World
Chalets in big-name resorts
Tel 01952 840462
Fax 01952 840463
www.chaletworld.co.uk

Chalets de St Martin
Chalets in St-Martin
Tel 01202 473255
Fax 01202 480042
les.chalets@virgin.net
www.skifrance.fr/73992/chalets/chstma-a.htm

Chalets 'Unlimited'
Chalets worldwide
Tel 0191 212 1173
Fax 0191 239 9459
sales@avant-ski.com
www.avant-ski.com

Challenge Activ
Chalets and apartments in Morzine
Tel 0800 328 0513
Fax 0800 328 0513
challenge_activ_morzine@compuserve.com
www.challenge-activ.com

Classic Ski Limited
Holidays for 'mature' skiers/beginners
Tel 01590 623400
Fax 01590 624387
info@classicski.co.uk
www.classicski.co.uk

Club Med
All-inclusive holidays in 'ski villages'
Tel 0700 258 2633
Fax 020 7536 5414
clubmed@compuserve.com
www.clubmed.com

Collineige
Chamonix valley specialist
Tel 01276 24262
Fax 01276 27282
info@collineige.com
www.collineige.com

Connick Ski
Hotel in Châtel
Tel 00 33 450 73 22 12
Fax 00 33 450 81 30 45

Contiki
Coach-travel holidays for 18-35s
Tel 020 8290 6422
Fax 020 8225 4246
travel@contiki.co.uk
www.contiki.com

Cooltip Mountain Holidays
Chalets in Méribel
Tel 01964 563563
Fax 01964 563094
ski@cooltip.com
www.cooltip.com

The Corporate Ski Company
Corporate specialists
Tel 020 7627 5500
Fax 020 7622 6701
ski@vantagepoint.co.uk
www.vantagepoint.co.uk

Crystal
Major mainstream operator
Tel 0870 848 7000
Fax 0870 848 7032
travel@crystalholidays.co.uk
www.crystalski.co.uk

Crystal Schools
Schools arm of major mainstream operator
Tel 0870 888 0025
Fax 0870 888 0240
schools@crystalholidays.co.uk
www.crystalholidays.co.uk

Descent International
Chalets in Méribel and Verbier
Tel 020 7989 8989
Fax 020 7989 8990
ski@descent.co.uk
www.descent.co.uk

Elegant Resorts
Luxury ski holidays
Tel 0870 333 3330
Fax 0870 333 3331
enquiries@elegantresorts.co.uk
www.elegantresorts.co.uk

Equity School Ski
School group holidays
Tel 01273 299299
Fax 01273 203212
schoolski@equity.co.uk
www.equity.co.uk

Equity Total Ski
All-in holidays
Tel 01273 298298
Fax 01273 203212
travel@equity.co.uk
www.equity.co.uk

Erna Low
Hotel and self-catering holidays to France and Switzerland
Tel 020 7584 2841
Fax 020 7589 9531
info@ernalow.co.uk
www.ernalow.co.uk

Eurotunnel Motoring Holidays
Self-drive holidays to France
Tel 0870 333 2001
Fax 0870 333 2002
ethols@crestahols.co.uk

FMTA Skiing
Chalets in Maurienne Valley and Megève
Tel 01483 452500
Fax 01483 452001
faith@fmta.freeserve.co.uk
www.fmtaski.freeserve.co.uk

Fairhand Holidays
Ski-drive holidays to France
Tel 01959 540796
Fax 01959 540797
fairhand.holidays@cwcom.net
www.fairhand.holidays.cwcom.net

Fantiski
Chalet holidays in France and USA
Tel 01622 844302
Fax 01622 842458
fctravel@dircon.co.uk
www.fantiski.co.uk

Finlays
Mainly chalets in France
Tel 01835 830562
Fax 01835 830550
finlayski@aol.com
www.finlayski.com

First Choice Ski
Major mainstream operator
Tel 0870 754 3477
Fax 0870 333 0329
fcski@lineone.net
www.first-choice.com

FlexiSki
Specialists in flexible breaks
Tel 0870 909 0754
Fax 0870 909 0329
flexi@btinternet.com
www.flexiski.co.uk

Freedom Holidays
Weekends and 'flexible duration' holidays in Switzerland
Tel 01798 342034
Fax 01798 343320

Freedom 2 Travel
Coach or self-drive trips to Les Trois Valleés
Tel 01375 396688
Fax 01375 394488
sales@harris-travel.com
www.freedom2travel.net

Frontier Ski
Holidays in Canada
Tel 020 8776 8709
Fax 020 8778 0149
info@frontier-travel.co.uk
www.frontier-ski.co.uk

Frosty's
Chalet in St-Jean-de-Sixt (La Clusaz)
Tel 00 33 450 02 37 28
Fax 00 33 450 02 37 28
info@frostys.co.uk
www.frostys.co.uk

Haig Ski
Hotels with guiding and nanny service in Châtel
Tel 00 33 450 811947
Fax 00 33 450 811947
haigski@compuserve.com
www.haigski.com

Handmade Holidays
Tailor-made specialists
Tel 01453 885599
Fax 01453 883768
travel@handmade-holidays.co.uk
www.handmade-holidays.co.uk

Hannibals
Holidays in Serre-Chevalier and Val-Cenis
Tel 01233 813105
Fax 01233 813432
sales@hannibals.co.uk
www.hannibals.co.uk

Headwater Holidays
Cross-country skiing holidays
Tel 01606 813333
Fax 01606 813334
info@headwater.com

High Mountain Holidays
Catered chalet in Les Praz (Chamonix)
Tel 01993 775540
Fax 01993 772388
info@highmountain.co.uk
www.highmountain.co.uk

HuSki
Holidays in Chamonix
Tel 020 7938 4844
Fax 020 7938 2312
sales@huski.com
www.huski.com

Iglu.com
Accommodation online
Tel 020 7761 6411
Fax 020 7723 8465
hcgw@iglu.com
www.iglu.com

Independent Ski Links
Mainly private catered and self-catering in France
Tel 0870 747 9121
Fax 01964 536006
david@ski-links.com
www.ski-links.com

Inghams
Major mainstream operator
Tel 020 8780 4444
Fax 020 8780 4405
reservations @inghams.co.uk
www.inghams.co.uk

Inntravel
Cross-country skiing holidays
Tel 01653 629002
Fax 01653 628741
ski@inntravel.co.uk

Interhome
Apartments and chalets in Europe
Tel 020 8891 1294
Fax 020 8891 5331
interhome.uk@ibm.net
www.interhome.co.uk

Interski
Group holidays with tuition in Italy
Tel 01623 456333
Fax 01623 456353
email@interski.co.uk
www.interski.co.uk

Kuoni
Holidays in Switzerland and Canada
Tel 01306 742500
Fax 01306 744222

Lagrange Holidays
Self-catering holidays in France
Tel 020 7371 6111
Fax 020 7371 2990
lagrange@globalnet.co.uk
www.lagrange-holidays.com

The Last Resort
Chalet in La Tania
Tel 01457 832160
Fax 01457 839548
info@lastresorthols.co.uk
www.lastresorthols.co.uk

Le Ski
Chalets in Courchevel, Val-d'Isère and La Tania
Tel 01484 548996
Fax 01484 451909
mail@leski.com
www.leski.com

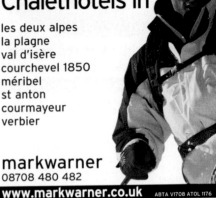

Les Deux Chalets
Chalets in Méribel
Tel 01303 246966
Fax 01303 246966
anjidelauney@tesco.net
www.chalet-de-launey.demon.co.uk

Lotus Supertravel
Holidays in North America, France and Switzerland
Tel 020 7962 9933
Fax 020 7962 9965
donald@lotusgroup.co.uk
www.supertravel.co.uk

Made to Measure
Wide variety of tailor-made holidays
Tel 01243 533333
Fax 01243 778431
madetomeasure.holidays@which.net
www.madetomeasureholidays.com

Mark Warner
Chalet hotel holidays in big name resorts
Tel 08708 480 482
Fax 020 7761 7001
www.markwarner.co.uk

MasterSki
Christian holidays
Tel 020 8942 9442
Fax 020 8949 4396
holidays@mastersun.co.uk
www.mastersun.co.uk

McNab Mountain Sports
Chalets in Argentière
Tel 01546 830243
Fax 01546 830243
inf@www.mcnab.co.uk
www.mcnab.co.uk

Meriski
Chalet specialist in Méribel
Tel 01451 843100
Fax 01451 844799
sales@meriski.co.uk
www.meriski.co.uk

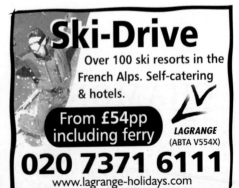

Momentum Ski
Tailor-made specialists
Tel 020 7371 9111
Fax 020 7610 6287
sales@momentum.uk.com
www.momentum.uk.com

Moswin Tours
Small German programme
Tel 0116 271 9922
Fax 0116 271 6016
germany@moswin.com
www.moswin.com

Motours
French ski-drive operation
Tel 01892 677777
Fax 01892 677711
sales@motours.co.uk
www.motours.co.uk

Mountain Highs
Chalet specialist in Morzine
Tel 01288 381457
Fax 01288 381135
mhighs@dircon.co.uk
www.mountain highs.com

Neilson
Major mainstream operator
Tel 08705 141414
Fax 01274 387740
sales@neilson.co.uk
www.neilson.co.uk

Optimum Ski
Chalet in Les Arcs
Tel 01992 561085
Fax 00 33 479 169356
info@optimumski.com
www.optimumski.com

The Oxford Ski Company
Chalets in Crans-Montana
Tel 07000 785349
Fax 07000 785340
info@oxfordski.com
www.oxfordski.com

Panorama
Budget-oriented holidays in Italy, Andorra and Spain
Tel 01273 427777
Fax 01273 427111
panorama@pavilion.co.uk
www.panoramaholidays.co.uk

Pavilion Tours
Budget holidays
Tel 0870 241 0427
Fax 0870 241 0426
sales@paviliontours.co.uk
www.paviliontours.co.uk

Peak Ski
Chalets in Verbier
Tel 01442 832629
Fax 01442 834303
peakski@which.net
www.peak-ski.co.uk

PGL Ski Europe
Specialist in school group holidays
Tel 01989 768168
Fax 01989 768376
ski@pgl.co.uk
www.pgl.co.uk

PGL Teenski
Holidays for teenagers
Tel 0500 749147
Fax 01989 766306
holidays@pgl.co.uk
www.pgl.co.uk

Piste Artiste
Holidays in Champéry and Whistler
Tel 020 7436 0100
Fax 00 41 24 479 3490
ski@pisteartiste.com
www.pisteartiste.com

Plus Travel
Specialists in Swiss resorts
Tel 020 7259 0199
Fax 020 7259 0190
sales@plustravel.freeserve.co.uk

Powder Byrne
Small programme of luxury holidays
Tel 020 8246 5300
Fax 020 8246 5322
enquiries@powderbyrne.co.uk
www.powderbyrne.com

Powder Skiing in North America Limited
Heli-skiing holidays in Canada
Tel 020 7736 8191
Fax 020 7384 2592

Ramblers
Cross-country holidays
Tel 01707 331133
Fax 01707 333276
info@ramblersholidays.co.uk

Rocky Mountain Snowboard Tours
Snowboarding holidays in the Rockies
Tel 0151 733 7593
Fax 0151 734 4300
snowboarding@rockymountain.co.uk
www.rockymountain.co.uk

Scandinavian Travel Service
Holidays in Sweden
Tel 020 7559 6666
Fax 020 7559 6677
sales@scantravel.com

Scott Dunn Latin America
Holidays to South America
Tel 020 8767 8989
Fax 020 8767 2026
latin@scottdunn.com
www.scottdunn.com

Scott Dunn Ski
Upmarket holidays
Tel 020 8767 0202
Fax 020 8767 2026
ski@scottdunn.com
www.scottdunn.com

Silver Ski
Chalet holidays in France
Tel 01622 735544
Fax 01622 738550
karen@silverski.co.uk
www.silverski.co.uk

Simply Ski
Holidays in big-name resorts
Tel 020 8541 2209
Fax 020 8541 2280
ski@simply-travel.com
www.simplyski.co.uk

Ski Activity
Holidays in big-name resorts
Tel 01738 840888
Fax 01738 840079
sales@skiactivity.com
www.skiactivity.com

Ski Addiction
Chalets and hotels in Châtel and St Anton
Tel 01580 819354
Fax 01580 819354
sales@skiaddiction.co.uk
www.skiaddiction.co.uk

Ski Amis
Chalet holidays in the La Plagne area
Tel 01233 732187
Fax 01233 732769
skiamis@compuserve.com
www.skiamis.com

Ski Arrangements
Chalets/apartments in France. Also Austria and E USA
Tel 01629 822900
Fax 01629 826345
www.go2ski.co.uk

SkiAway Holidays
Holidays in the Pyrenees and French Alps
Tel 01903 824823
Fax 01903 821858
skiaway@tourplaneurope.com
www.tourplaneurope.com

Ski Balkantours
Holidays in E Europe for schools and groups
Tel 028 9024 6795
Fax 028 9023 4581
mail@balkan.co.uk

Ski Barrett-Boyce
Chalet in Megève with tuition
Tel 020 8288 0042
Fax 020 8288 0761
skibb@atlas.co.uk
www.skibb.com

Ski Beat
Chalets in La Plagne, Tignes and Méribel
Tel 01243 780405
Fax 01243 533748
ski@skibeat.co.uk
www.skibeat.co.uk

Ski Blanc
Chalets in Méribel
Tel 020 8502 9082
Fax 01737 213617
www.merinet.com/skiblanc

Ski Bon
Chalets in Méribel
Tel 020 8649 8458
mik_g@compuserve.com
www.skibon.com

SkiBound
Schools division of First Choice
Tel 0870 900 3200
Fax 0870 333 0329

Ski Chamois
Holidays in Morzine
Tel 01302 369006
Fax 01302 326640
skichamois@morzine1550.freeserve.co.uk
www.ski-chamois.freeserve.co.uk

Ski Choice
Mainly hotels and self-catering
Tel 01491 837607
Fax 01491 833836

Ski Club Europe
Schools trips to Austria, France and Italy
Tel 020 8699 7788
Fax 020 8699 7770
ski@club-europe.co.uk
www.club-europe.co.uk

Ski Club of GB
Holidays for club members
Tel 020 8410 2022
Fax 020 8410 2001
skiers@skiclub.co.uk
www.skiclub.co.uk

The Ski Company
Holidays in France and US, with tuition
Tel 01279 653746
Fax 01279 654705
info@theskicompany.co.uk
www.theskicompany.co.uk

The Ski Company Ltd
Luxury chalets in France and Switzerland
Tel 01451 843123
Fax 01451 844799
sales@skicompany.co.uk
www.skicompany.co.uk

Ski Connections
Canada and US operator
Tel 01494 473173
Fax 01494 473588
enquiries@connectionsworldwide.net
www.canadaski.net

Ski Cuisine
Chalets in Méribel
Tel 01702 589543
Fax 01702 588671
skicuisine@dial.pipex.com
www.skicuisine.co.uk

Ski Deep
Chalets in La Tania and Le Praz
Tel 00 33 479 081905
Fax 0870 164 5870
ski@skideep.com
www.skideep.com

Ski Equipe
Upmarket chalet operator
Tel 0161 440 0010
Fax 0161 440 0080
ski@skiequipe.fsbusiness.co.uk
www.ski-equipe.com

Skiers World
School trips to North America and Europe
Tel 0870 333 3620
Fax 029 2076 4455
info@skiersworld.com
www.skiersworld.com

Ski Esprit
Chalet holidays for families
Tel 01252 618300
Fax 01252 618328
travel@esprit-holidays.co.uk
www.ski-esprit.co.uk

Ski Etoile
Chalet in Montgenèvre
Tel 01588 640442
Fax 01588 640442
skietoile@clun25.freeserve.co.uk

Ski Famille
Family holidays in Les Gets
Tel 01223 363777
Fax 01223 519314
info@skifamille.co.uk
www.skifamille.co.uk

Ski France
Chalets and catered apartments
Tel 020 8313 0690
Fax 020 8466 0653
ski@skifrance.co.uk
www.skifrance.co.uk

SkiGower
School and group trips, mainly Switzerland
Tel 01527 851411
Fax 01527 851417
linda@gowstrav.demon.co.uk

Ski Hillwood
Austrian and French family holidays
Tel 01923 290700
Fax 01923 290340
sales@hillwood-holidays.co.uk

Ski Hiver
Chalets in Peisey and Val-d'Isère
Tel 023 9242 8586
Fax 023 9242 8904
skihiver@aol.com
www.skihiver.co.uk

Ski Independence
USA and Canada and self-drive to France and Switzerland
Tel 0870 555 0555 (US/Can); 0870 600 1462 (Europe)
Fax 0870 550 2020
ski@ski-independence.co.uk
www.ski-independence.co.uk

Ski La Cote
Chalet holidays in Chapelle d'Abondance
Tel 01482 668357
Fax 01482 668357
adrian@ski-la-cote.karoo.co.uk

Ski Leisure Direction
Mainly self-catering in France
Tel 020 8324 4042
Fax 020 8324 4030
richard@ldl.u-net.com
www.leisuredirection.co.uk

Ski Line
Catered chalets in Europe and USA
Tel 020 8777 0440
info@skiline.co.uk
www.skiline.co.uk

Ski McNeill
Tailor-made to US and European weekends
Tel 028 9066 6699
Fax 028 9068 3888
mail@skimcneill.com
www.skimcneill.com

Ski Miquel
Small but eclectic programme
Tel 01457 821200
Fax 01457 821209
ski@miquelhols.co.uk
www.miquelhols.co.uk

Ski Morgins Holidays
Chalet holidays in Morgins
Tel 01568 770681
Fax 01568 770153
info@skimorgins.co.uk
www.skimorgins.co.uk

Ski 'n' Action
Chalets in Courchevel and Le Praz
Tel 01707 251696
Fax 01707 259874
info@ski-n-action.co.uk
www.ski-n-action.co.uk

Ski Olympic
Chalet holidays in France
Tel 01709 579999
Fax 01709 579898
info@ski-olympic.co.uk
www.ski-olympic.co.uk

Ski Partners
Schools programme
Tel 0117 925 3545
Fax 0117 929 3697

Ski Peak
Vaujany specialist operator
Tel 01428 741144
Fax 01428 741155
sales@ski-peak.ltd.uk
www.ski-peak.ltd.uk

SkiPlan incorporating STS
Schools holidays
Tel 01273 774666
Fax 01273 734042
sales@topstravel.co.uk

Ski Rosie
Hotels and apartments in Chatel
Tel 01442 235142 or 00 33 450 813100
Fax 01442 235142 or 00 33 450 813100
skirosie@dial.pipex.com

Ski Safari
Canadian specialist
Tel 020 7740 1221
Fax 020 7740 1223
info@skisafari.com
www.skisafari.com

Skisafe Travel
Mainly holidays in Scotland
Tel 0141 812 0925
Fax 0141 812 1544
aviemoreski@osa-travel.co.uk
www.osa-travel.co.uk

Skisar US
Hotels and B&Bs in N America
Tel 01959 540796
Fax 01959 540797
ian.porter@skiarus.com
www.skiarus.com

Ski Scott James
Chalets in Argentière
Tel 020 7381 0115
Fax 020 7681 2035
jamie@skiscottjames.co.uk
www.skiscottjames.co.uk

Ski Solutions
Tailor-made holidays
Tel 020 7471 7777
Fax 020 7471 7771
alc@skisolutions.com
www.skisolutions.com

Ski Success
Group holidays to the US and to the Italian Dolomites
Tel 01225 764205
Fax 01225 777520

Ski Supreme
Coach and self-drive to France
Tel 01355 260547
Fax 01355 229232
roddy@skisupreme.co.uk
www.skisupreme.co.uk

Ski The American Dream
Major operator to North America
Tel 020 8552 1201
Fax 020 8552 7726
holidays@skidream.com
www.skidream.com

Ski Total
European and US holidays
Tel 020 8948 3535
Fax 020 8332 1268
sales@skitotal.com
www.skitotal.com

Ski Vacation Canada
Holidays in Canada
Tel 0870 70 70 444
Fax 0141 353 0135
vacationcanada@btinternet.com

Ski-Val
Holidays in France, Austria and the US
Tel 01822 611200
Fax 01822 611400
reservations@skival.co.uk
www.skival.co.uk

Ski Valkyrie
European programme
Tel 01622 763745
Fax 01622 690964

Ski Verbier
Specialises in Verbier
Tel 020 7385 8050
Fax 020 7385 8002
info@skiverbier.com
www.skiverbier.com

Ski Weekend
Weekend and ten-day holidays
Tel 01367 241636
Fax 01367 243833
sales@skiweekend.com
www.skiweekend.com

Ski with Julia
Swiss hotels and catered apartments
Tel 01386 584478
Fax 01386 584629
julia@skijulia.co.uk
www.skijulia.co.uk

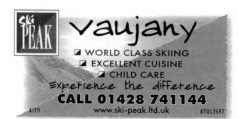

Skiworld
European and North American programme
Tel 020 7602 4826/7444
Fax 020 7371 1463
sales@skiworld.ltd.uk
www.skiworld.unet.com

Ski Yogi
Tailor-made holidays
Tel 01799 531886
Fax 01799 531887

Sloping Off
Schools and tailor-made, by coach
Tel 01725 552247
Fax 01725 552489
victory.tours@dial.pipex.com
www.victorytours.co.uk

Snowbizz Vacances
Holidays in Puy-St-Vincent
Tel 01778 341455
Fax 01778 347422
wendy@snowbizz.co.uk
www.snowbizz.co.uk

Snowcoach
Andorra, Austria and France
Tel 01727 833141
Fax 01727 843766
info@snowcoach.co.uk
www.snowcoach.co.uk

Snowfocus
Chalet in Châtel with nannies
Tel 01872 553003
Fax 01872 553050
chalet@snowfocus.com
www.snowfocus.com

Snowlife
Holidays in La Clusaz
Tel 01534 863630
Fax 01534 862222
snowlife@psilink.co.uk

Snowline
Chalet holidays in France
Tel 020 8870 4807
Fax 020 8875 9236
ski@snowline.co.uk
www.snowline.co.uk

Snowman Holidays
Own hotel near Megève
Tel 00 33 450 931183
Fax 00 33 450 931491
kieron@belleettoile.com
www.belleetoile.com

Snow Plus
Holidays with guiding based in Nendaz
Tel 0704 145 0100
Fax 0870 137 1080
scottfree@compuserve.com
www.snowplus.co.uk

Solo's
Singles' holidays, ages 30-49 or 50-69
Tel 020 8951 2800
Fax 020 8951 1051
travel@solosholidays.co.uk
www.solosholidays.co.uk

Stanford Skiing
Megève specialist
Tel 020 8789 2929
Fax 020 8516 7670
stanskiing@aol.com
www.lattimore.co.uk/stanford/

St Anton Ski Company
Hotels and chalets in St Anton
Tel 0831 822 878
jonathanverney@compuserve.com

Swiss Travel Service
Hotels in Switzerland
Tel 01992 456123
Fax 01992 448855
swiss@bridge-travel.co.uk
www.swisstravel.co.uk

Thomson Ski & Snowboarding
Major mainstream operator
Tel 0870 606 1470
Fax 020 8939 0402
reservations@thomson-ski.com
www.thomson-ski.com

Top Deck
Lively, informal holidays
Tel 020 7370 4555
Fax 020 7373 6201
res@topdecktravel.co.uk
www.topdeckski.co.uk

Tops Ski Chalets and Club Hotels
Chalets in France
Tel 01273 774666
Fax 01273 734042
marketing@topstravel.co.uk

Trail Alpine
Chalet in Morzine
Tel 01745 570106
Fax 01745 570641
rjonestrailalpine@compuserve.com
www.trailalpine.co.uk

UCPA
All-inclusive budget trips to France
Tel 0161 442 6130
Fax 0161 442 6130
av4ucpa@btinternet.com
www.ucpa.co.uk

United Vacations Ski Freedom USA
US and Canada programme
Tel 0870 606 2222
Fax 020 8313 3547
uvuk@unitedvacations.com
www.unitedvacations.co.uk

Val d'Isère A La Carte
Holidays in Val d'Isère
Tel 01481 241024
Fax 01481 243885
valnorman@skialacarte.freeserve.co.uk
www.skivaldisere.co.uk

Val d'Isère Properties (VIP)
Specialist in Val d'Isère
Tel 020 8875 1957
Fax 020 8875 9236
ski@valdisere.co.uk
www.valdisere.co.uk

Vanilla Ski
Chalet in Seez (near La Rosière and Les Arcs)
Tel 01932 860696
Fax 01932 860696
vanillaski@compuserve.com
www.vanillaski.com

Virgin Ski
Holidays to America
Tel 01293 544889
Fax 01293 536957
brochure.requests@virginholidays.co.uk
www.virginholidays.co.uk

Waymark Holidays
Cross-country skiing holidays
Tel 01753 516477
Fax 01753 517016

Weekends in Val d'Isère
Weekends – and not just in Val d'Isère
Tel 020 8944 9762
Fax 020 8944 9762
valweekends@btinternet.com
www.val-disere-ski.com

White Mountain Lodge
Chalets in Argentière
Tel 01403 265966
Fax 01403 265966

White Roc
Weekends and short breaks
Tel 020 7792 1188
Fax 020 7792 1956
ski@whiteroc.co.uk
www.whiteroc.co.uk

YSE
Variety of holidays in Val-d'Isère
Tel 020 8871 5117
Fax 020 8871 5229
sales@yseski.co.uk
www.yseski.co.uk

Black-and-white pages

A classified listing of the names, numbers and addresses you are likely to need.

Airlines

Air Canada
Tel 0870 524 7226
Air France
Tel 0845 0845 111
Air New Zealand
Tel 020 8741 2299
Alitalia
Tel 0870 544 8259
American Airlines
Tel 020 8572 5555
Austrian Airlines
Tel 0345 581333
British Airways
Tel 0845 77 333 77
Buzz
Tel 0870 240 7070
Canadian Airlines
Tel 0345 616767
Continental Airlines
Tel 0800 776464
Delta Airlines
Tel 0800 414767
Easyjet
Tel 0870 6 000 000
Go
Tel 0845 605 4321
KLM
Tel 0990 074074
Lauda Air
Tel 020 7434 7391
Freephone 0800 767737
Lufthansa German Airlines
Tel 0845 773 7747
Qantas
Tel 0345 747 767
Ryanair
Tel 0870 1 569 569
Swissair
Tel 0845 601 0956
United Airlines
Tel 0845 844 4777
Virgin Atlantic Airways
Tel 01293 747 747

Airports

Aberdeen
Tel 01224 722331
Belfast
Tel 01849 422888
Birmingham
Tel 0121 767 5511
Bournemouth
Tel 01202 364000
Bristol
Tel 01275 474444
Cardiff
Tel 01446 711111
Dublin
Tel 00 353 1 814 1111
East Midlands
Tel 01332 852852
Edinburgh
Tel 0131 333 1000
Exeter
Tel 01392 367433
Glasgow
Tel 0141 887 1111
Leeds-Bradford
Tel 0113 250 9696
London Gatwick
Tel 01293 535353
London Heathrow
Tel 020 8759 4321
London Luton
Tel 01582 405100
London Stansted
Tel 01279 680500
Manchester
Tel 0161 489 3000
Newcastle
Tel 0191 286 0966
Teesside
Tel 01325 332811

Airport Transfers

Airport Transfer Service
Tel 00 33 450 536397
The Alpine Cab Company
Tel 00 33 450 731938

Breakdown Insurance

AA Five Star Service
Tel 0800 444 500
Autohome
Tel 01604 232334
Fax 01604 231304
Britannia Continental
Tel 01484 514848
Fax 01484 518961
Only available to Britannia Rescue members
Direct Line Rescue
Tel 0845 246 8999
Europ Assistance
Tel 01444 442211
Fax 01444 455204
First Assist Group
Tel 020 8763 1550
Fax 020 8668 1262
Green Flag
Tel 0113 236 3236
Leisurecare Insurance Services
Tel 01793 750150
Fax 01793 750661
Mondial Assistance UK
Tel 020 8681 2525
Fax 020 8680 2769
RAC Travel Services
Tel 0800 550055

Car Hire

Alamo Rent-a-Car
Tel 0990 994000
Fax 01273 223315
Avis
Tel 020 8848 8765
Fax 020 8561 2604
Budget Car and Van Rental
Tel 0541 565656
Fax 01442 276000
Europcar UK
Tel 0345 222525
Fax 01923 811010
Hertz UK
Tel 0990 996699
Fax 020 8679 0181
Holiday Autos International Ltd
Tel 0990 300400
Fax 0990 300410
Suncars
Tel 0990 005566

Car Winter Equipment

Brindley Chains Ltd
1 Tatton Court, Kingsland Grange, Warrington WA1 4RR
Tel 01925 825555
Fax 01925 825338
Pewag snowchains
DAP (Cambridge) Ltd
122 Newmarket Road, Cambridge CB5 8HE
Tel 01223 323488
Fax 01223 324952
Thule roof systems, Kar Rite boxes, Skandibox, Konig snowchains

GT Towing Ltd
6 Hatfield Rd, Potters Bar, Hertfordshire EN6 1HP
Tel 01707 652118
Fax 01707 644638
Ski boxes and snowchains

Kar Rite Europe Ltd
One and Two Falconer Road, Haverhill, Suffolk CB9 7XU
Tel 01440 760000
Fax 01440 760001
Ski boxes and roof racks

Lakeland Roof Box Centre
Lake District Business Park, Mint Bridge Road, Kendal, Cumbria LA9 6NH
Tel 01539 732793
Fax 01539 732818

Latchmere Motor Spares
93-97 Latchmere Road, London SW11 2DR
Tel 020 7223 5491
Fax 020 7228 3907
Snowchains, roof bars, ski clamps, boxes

Motor Traveller
225 St Leonards Road, Windsor SL4 3DR
Tel 01753 833442
Fax 01753 832495
Thule racks and boxes, Milz snowchains

RUD Chains Ltd
Units 10-14, John Wilson Business Park, Thanet Way, Whitstable, Kent CT5 3QT
Tel 01227 276611
Fax 01227 276586
Snowchains

Snowchains Ltd
Wrotham Road, Borough Green, Kent TN15 8DG
Tel 01732 884408
Fax 01732 884564
Thule ski boxes, roof bars and ski racks, Weissenfels snowchains

Spikes Spiders
Auto Cavity Seal, 5 Bridgewater Street, Castlefield, Manchester M3 4NN
Tel 0161 834 4153
Fax 0161 839 2941

The Roof Box Company
Unit 1A, Toll Bar Estate, Fedbergh, Cumbria LA10 5HA
Tel 01539 621884
Fax 01539 621886

Thule Ltd
Units 4 & 5 Concorde Drive, 5c Business Centre, Clevedon, Bristol BS21 6UH
Tel 01275 340404
Fax 01275 340686

Cross Channel Travel

Brittany Ferries
Tel 0870 90 12 400
Fax 0870 90 20 300
Portsmouth–Caen

Eurotunnel
Tel 08705 35 35 35
Fax 01303 288784
Folkestone–Calais/Coquelles via the Channel Tunnel

Hoverspeed Fast Ferries
Tel 0870 524 0241
Fax 01304 865203
Dover–Calais, Folkestone–Boulogne

P&O North Sea Ferries
Tel 01482 377177
Fax 01482 706438
Hull–Zeebrugge, Hull–Rotterdam

P&O Portsmouth
Tel 0870 242 4999
Portsmouth–Cherbourg, Portsmouth–Le Havre

P&O Stena Line
Tel 0870 600 0600
Fax 01304 863464
Dover–Calais

SeaFrance
Tel 08705 711 711
Dover–Calais

Stena Line
Tel 0990 707070
Fax 01233 202349
Harwich–Hook

Dry Ski Slopes

South-West England

Avon Ski Centre
Lyncombe Lodge, Churchill, North Somerset BS19 5PQ
Tel 01934 852335

Christchurch Ski Centre
Matchams Lane, Hurn, Christchurch, Dorset BH23 6AW
Tel 01202 499155

Exeter and District Ski Club
Belmont Road, Exeter EX1 2DJ
Tel 01392 211422

John Nike Leisuresport - Plymouth
Plymouth Ski Centre, Alpine Park, Marsh Mills, Plymouth PL6 8LQ
Tel 01752 600220

Warmwell Ski and Snowboard Centre
Warmwell, Near Dorchester, Dorset DT2 8JE
Tel 01305 853245

Wellington Sports Centre
Corams Lane, Wellington, Somerset TA21 8LL
Tel 01823 663010

Wessex Ski Club
Barton Hall, Kinkerswell Road, Torquay, Devon TQ2 8JY
Tel 01803 313350

Yeovil Ski Centre
Addlewell Lane, Nine Springs, Yeovil, Somerset BA20 1QW
Tel 01935 421702

South-East England

Alpine Ski Centre
Gallwey Road, Aldershot, Hants GU11 2DD
Tel 01252 325889

Beckton Alpine Centre
Alpine Way, London E6 4LA
Tel 020 7511 0351

Bishop Reindorp Ski Centre
Larch Avenue, Guildford, Surrey
Tel 01483 504988

Bowles Outdoor Centre
Eridge Green, Tunbridge Wells TN3 9LW
Tel 01892 665665

Bromley Ski Centre
Sandy Lane, St Paul's Cray, Orpington, Kent BR5 3HY
Tel 01689 876812

Calshot Activities Centre
Calshot Spit, Fawley, Southampton SO45 1BR
Tel 023 8089 2077

Crystal Palace National Sports Centre
Norwood, London SE19 2BL
Tel 020 8778 9876

Folkestone Sports Centre Ski Slope
Radnor Park Avenue, Folkestone, Kent CT19 5HX
Tel 01303 850333

Hillingdon Ski and Snowboard Centre
Gatting Way, Park Road, Uxbridge, Middlesex UB8 1NR
Tel 01895 255183

John Nike Leisuresport - Bracknell
Bracknell Ski Centre, John Nike Way, Amen Corner, Bracknell, Berkshire RG12 8TN
Tel 01344 789000

John Nike Leisuresport - Chatham
Chatham Ski Centre, Alpine Park, Capstone Road, Chatham, Kent ME7 3JH
Tel 01634 827979

Sandown Ski Centre
More Lane, Esher, Surrey KT10 8AN
Tel 01372 467132

Southampton Ski Centre
The Sports Centre, Bassett, Southampton SO16 7AY
Tel 023 8079 0970

Wycombe Summit
Abbey Barn Lane, High Wycombe, Bucks HP10 9QQ
Tel 01494 474711

Wales

Cardiff Ski Centre
Fairwater Park, Fairwater, Cardiff CF5 3JR
Tel 029 2056 1793

Dan-yr-Ogof Ski Slopes
Abercrave, Upper Swansea Valley, Powys SA9 1GJ
Tel 01639 730284

John Nike Leisuresport - Llandudno
Great Orme, Llandudno LL30 2QL
Tel 01492 874707

Plas y Brenin
Capel Curig, Gwynedd LL24 0ET
Tel 01690 720214

Pontypool Ski Centre
Pontypool Leisure Park, Pontypool, Gwent NP4 8AT
Tel 01495 756955

Rhiwgoch Ski Centre
Bron Aber, Trawsfynydd, Gwynedd LL41 4UR
Tel 01766 540578

Ski Pembrey
Pembrey Country Park, Llanelli, Carmarthenshire SA16 0EJ
Tel 01554 834443

MIDDLE ENGLAND

Gloucester Ski and Snowboard Centre
Robinswood Hill, Matson Lane, Gloucester GL4 6EA
Tel 01452 414300

Healthland Snozone
Xscape, 602 Marlborough Gate, Central Milton Keynes MK9 3DD
Tel 01908 230260

John Nike Leisuresport Swadlincote
Swadlincote Ski Centre, Hill Street, Swadlincote, Derbyshire DE11 8LP
Tel 01283 217200

Kidsgrove Ski Cetre
Kidsgrove, Stoke-on-Trent ST7 4EF
Tel 01782 784908

Skew Bridge Ski Slope
Northampton Road, Rushden, Northants NN10 9AW
Tel 01933 359939

Stoke Ski Centre
Festival Park, Stoke-on-Trent ST1 5PU
Tel 01782 204159

Tallington Ski and Snowboard Centre
Barholm Road, Tallington, Nr Stamford, Lincs PE9 4RJ
Tel 01778 344990

Tamworth Snowdome
Leisure Island, River Drive, Tamworth, Staffordshire B79 7ND
Tel 08705 000011

Telford Ski Centre
Court Street, Madeley, Telford, Shropshire TF7 5DZ
Tel 01952 586862

The Ackers
Golden Hillock Road, Small Heath, Birmingham B11 2PY
Tel 0121 772 5111

EASTERN ENGLAND

Brentwood Park Ski Centre
Warley Gap, Brentwood, Essex CM13 3LG
Tel 01277 211994

Gosling Ski Centre
Stanborough Road, Welwyn Garden City, Hertfordshire AL8 6XE
Tel 01707 391039

Harlow Ski Centre
Hammarskjold Road, Harlow, Essex CM20 2JF
Tel 01279 307360

Hemel Ski Centre
St Albans Hill, Hemel Hempstead, Herts HP3 9NH
Tel 01442 241321

Norfolk Ski Club
Whitlingham Lane, Trowse, Norwich, Norfolk NR14 8TW
Tel 01603 662781

Suffolk Ski Centre
Bourne Terrace, Wherstead, Ipswich IP2 8NQ
Tel 01473 602347

NORTHERN ENGLAND

Alston Training and Adventure Centre
High Plains Lodge, Alston, Cumbria CA9 3DD
Tel 01434 381886

Halifax Ski Centre
Bradford Old Road, Swalesmoor, Halifax HX3 6UG
Tel 01422 340760

Kendal Ski Club
Canal Head North, Kendal, Cumbria LA9 7AL
Tel 01539 732948/733031

Oldham Ski Centre
Counthill Road, Moorside, Oldham OL4 2PZ
Tel 0161 911 4081

Pendle Ski Club
Clitheroe Road, Sabden, Clitheroe BB7 9HN
Tel 01200 425222

Sheffield Ski Village
Vale Road, Parkwood Springs, Sheffield S3 9SJ
Tel 0114 276 9459

Ski Rossendale
Haslingden Old Road, Rawtenstall, Rossendale, Lancashire BB4 8RR
Tel 01706 222426

Ski Runcorn
Town Park, Palace Fields, Runcorn, Cheshire WA7 2PS
Tel 01928 701965

Spectrum Ski and Snowboard School
Spectrum Leisure Complex, Hunwick Lane, Willington, Crook, Co Durham DL15 0JA
Tel 01388 747000

Sunderland Ski Centre
Silsworth Sports Complex, Silsworth Lane, Sunderland SR3 2AN
Tel 0191 553 5785

The Oval Ski Club
Old Chester Road, Bebington CH63 7LF
Tel 0151 645 0551

Whickham Thorns Outdoor Centre
Market Lane, Dunston NE11 9NX
Tel 0191 460 1193

SCOTLAND

Aberdeen Ski Centre
Gartree Road, Aberdeen AB10 7BA
Tel 01224 311781

Alford Ski Centre
Greystone Road, Alford, Aberdeenshire AB33 8TY
Tel 01975 563024

Ancrum Outdoor Education Resource Centre
10 Ancrum Road, Dundee, Tayside DD2 2HZ
Tel 01382 435911

Bearsden Ski Club
Stockiemuir Road, Bearsden, Glasgow G61 3RS
Tel 0141 943 1500

Firpark Ski Centre
Tillycoultry, Clackmannanshire FK13 6PL
Tel 01259 751772

Glasgow Ski Centre
Bellahouston Park, 16 Dumbreck Road, Glasgow G41 5BW
Tel 0141 427 4991

Glenmore Lodge
Scottish National Sports Centre, Aviemore, Inverness-shire PH22 1QU
Tel 01479 861256

Hillend Ski Centre
Biggar Road, Midlothian EH10 7DU
Tel 0131 445 4433

Loch Rannoch Outdoor Activity Centre
Kinloch Rannoch, Perthshire PH16 5PS
Tel 01882 632201

Lochanhully Woodland Club
Carrbridge, Inverness-shire PH23 3NA
Tel 01479 841234

Newmilns Ski Slope
High Street, Newmilns KA16 9EB
Tel 01560 322320

Polmonthill Ski Centre
Polmont, Falkirk FK2 0YE
Tel 01324 503835

Stakis Royal Deeside and Craigendarroch Country Club
Braemar Road, Ballater, Royal Deeside AB35 5XA
Tel 01339 755858

NORTHERN IRELAND

Craigavon Golf and Ski Centre
Turmoyra Lane, Silverwood, Lurgan BT66 6NG
Tel 01762 326606

Mount Ober Ski Centre
Ballymaconaghy Road, Knockbracken, Belfast BT8 6SB
Tel 028 9079 5666

Equipment Distributors

Ardblair Sports Ltd
Tel 01250 873863
Fax 01250 875289
Leki ski poles

Big Bear Sports
Tel 020 8998 4553
Fax 020 8998 4844
Look bindings, Dynastar skis, Lange boots, Original Sin snowboards

Blue Ridge
Tel 020 8991 9244
Fax 020 8991 9255
Tecnica

Europa Sportsystems
Tel 01539 724740
Fax 01539 730955
Nordica boots, Kästle skis and poles, Killer Loop snowboards

Euroski
Tel 01273 701004
Fax 01273 701004
Alpina

Mast Co
Tel 0118 947 1735
Fax 0118 946 1213
Fischer, Dynafit, Raichle, Scott, Marker, Volkl

Phoenix Mountaineering Ltd
Tel 01475 746000
Fax 01475 746001
Rossignol

Salomon
Tel 01256 479555
Fax 01256 479357
Salomon

Sportline Ltd
Tel 01635 555800
Fax 01635 38682
Head

Ultra Sport
Tel 0115 973 1001
Fax 0115 946 1067
Palmer boards, Flow and Northwave boots, Flow and Drake bindings, Neil Pryde accessories

Insurance Companies

ABC Holiday Extras
Tel 0800 171000
Fax 0870 844 4310

AUL
Tel 01206 577770

Aon Suretravel Ltd
Tel 01372 749191
Fax 01372 749701

BUPA Travel Services
Tel 0990 858585

British Activity Holiday Insurance Services
Tel 020 7251 6821
Fax 020 7490 0708

CGU
Tel 020 7283 7500
Fax 020 7662 8140

Columbus Travel Insurance Direct
Tel 020 7375 0011
Fax 020 7375 0022

Cork, Bays & Fisher
Tel 020 7680 4000

Direct Travel Insurance
Tel 01903 812345
Fax 01903 813555

Douglas Cox Tyrie
Tel 020 8534 9595

Europ Assistance
Tel 01444 442211
Fax 01444 459292

Hamilton Barr Insurance Brokers
Tel 01483 255666
Fax 01483 255660

JS Insurance Management Ltd
Tel 01784 430043

Jardine Lloyd Thompson
Tel 0161 957 8000

Ketteridge SkiGuard Travel Insurance
Tel 01277 630770
Fax 01277 630770

Matthew Gerard Travel Insurance Services
Tel 01483 730900
Fax 01483 730969

McLean, Kent and Coomber (MKC)
Tel 01268 590658
Fax 01268 590860

P J Hayman & Co
Tel 01730 260222
Fax 01730 266655

Perry, Gamble & Co
Tel 020 8542 1122

Preferential Travel Insurance
Tel 01702 423393

Snowcard Insurance Services Ltd
Tel 01327 262805
Fax 01327 263227

Sportscover Direct Ltd
Tel 0117 922 6222
Fax 0117 922 1666

Supreme Travel
Tel 01355 260547

Whiteley Insurance Consultants
Tel 01422 348411
Fax 01422 330345

WorldCover Direct
Tel 0800 365121
Fax 0180 557 4941

Worldwide Travel Insurance Services Ltd
Tel 01892 833338

National Tourist Offices

Andorran Delegation
Tel 020 8874 4806

Argentinian Tourist Board
Tel 020 7318 1340
Fax 020 7318 1349

Australian Tourist Commission
Tel 020 8780 2229
Fax 020 8780 1496

Austrian National Tourist Office
Tel 020 7629 0461
Fax 020 7499 6038

Canadian Tourism Commission
Tel 0891 715000
Fax 020 7839 1149

Chile – Consulate General
Tel 020 7580 1023
Fax 020 7436 5204

Czech Republic Tourist Authority
Tel 09063 640641

Finnish Tourist Board
Tel 020 7839 4048
Fax 020 7321 0696

French Government Tourist Office
Tel 0891 244123
Fax 020 7493 6594

German National Tourist Office
Tel 0891 600100
Fax 020 7495 6129

Italian State Tourist Office
Tel 020 7408 1254
Fax 020 7493 6695
Brochure line: 0891 600280

Japanese Tourist Commission
Tel 020 7734 9638

New Zealand Tourism Board
Tel 09069 10 10 10
Fax 020 7839 8929

Norwegian Tourist Board
Tel 020 7839 6255
Fax 020 7839 6014

Romanian Tourist Office
Tel 020 7224 3692
Fax 020 7935 6435

Scottish Tourist Board
Tel 0131 332 2433
Fax 0131 343 1513

Slovenian Tourist Office
Tel 020 7287 7133
Fax 020 7287 5476

Spanish Tourist Office
Tel 0900 166 9920
Fax 020 7486 8034

Swedish Travel and Tourism Council
Tel 020 7870 5605
Fax 020 7724 5872

Switzerland Tourism
Tel 020 7734 1921
Fax 020 7437 4577

Visit USA Association
Tel 09065 508972

Railways

Deutsche Bahn (German Railways)
Tel 0870 243 5363

Eurostar
Tel 0990 186186

Rail Europe
Tel 08705 848 848

Swiss Federal Railways
Tel 020 7734 1921
Fax 020 7437 4577

Retailers

These retailers of ski/board equipment also stock *Where to Ski and Snowboard.*

SOUTH-WEST ENGLAND

Snow & Rock
Units 1-3 Shield Retail Centre, Gloucester Road North, Filton, Bristol, Bristol BS34 7BQ
Tel 0117 914 3000

Team Ski & Leisure
37 High East Street, Dorchester, Dorset DT1 1HN
Tel 01305 268035

SOUTH-EAST ENGLAND

Captain's Cabin
93 High Street, Chatham, Chatham, Kent ME4 4DL
Tel 01634 819777
Fax 01634 819777

Captain's Cabin
14 St George's Walk, Croydon, Croydon CR0 1YG
Tel 020 8680 6968

Captain's Cabin
19 Wincheap, Canterbury, Kent CT1 3TB
Tel 01227 457906
Fax 01227 763292

Captain's Cabin Sevenoaks
113-115 St John's Hill, Sevenoaks, Kent TN13 3PE
Tel 01732 464463
Fax 01732 464463

Carters
99-113 Caversham Road, Reading, Berkshire RG1 8AN
Tel 0118 959 9022
Fax 0118 950 0618

John Pollock
157 High Road, Loughton, Essex IG10 4LF
Tel 020 8508 6626

John Pollock
119 High Road, East Finchley, London N2 8AG
Tel 020 8883 4364

John Pollock
67 High Street, Barnet EN5 5UR
Tel 020 8440 3994

Mountain Bike & Ski Co
18 Gillingham Street, Victoria, London SW1V 1HU
Tel 020 7834 8933
Fax 020 7834 8933

Snow & Rock
188 Kensington High Street, London W8 7RG
Tel 020 7937 0872

Snow & Rock
4 Mercer Street, Covent Garden, London WC2H 9QA
Tel 0845 100 1000

Snow & Rock
150 Holborn, Corner of Grays Inn Road, London EC1N 2LC
Tel 020 7831 6900

Snow & Rock
99 Fordwater Road, Chertsey, Surrey KT16 8HH
Tel 01932 566886

Snow Boats
8-10 The Street, Wrecclesham, Farnham, Surrey GU10 4PR
Tel 01252 715169
Fax 01428 714013

MIDDLE ENGLAND

Active
Cornhill House, Market Square, Banbury, Oxfordshire
Tel 01295 273700
Fax 01295 254108

Attwoolls Ski Shop
Bristol Road, Whitminster, Gloucestershire GL2 7LX
Tel 01452 742200
Fax 01452 742244

Lockwoods Ski Shop
125-129 Rugby Road, Leamington Spa, Warwickshire CV32 6DJ
Tel 01926 339388
Fax 01926 470408

Snow & Rock
14 Priory Queensway, Birmingham B4 6BS
Tel 0121 236 8280

Sporting Triangle
18 West Street, Hereford HR4 0BX
Tel 01432 271500

EASTERN ENGLAND

John Pollock
Harlow Ski Slope, Harlow Sports Centre, Hammarskjold Way, Harlow, Essex CM20 2JF
Tel 01279 425009

Ski Surf 2000
13 Peartree Centre, Peartree Lane, Stanway, Colchester, Essex CO3 5JN
Tel 01206 502000
Fax 01206 502002

Snow & Rock
Hemel Ski Centre, St Albans Hill, Hemel Hempstead, Hertfordshire HP3 9NH
Tel 01442 235305

Two Seasons
34 Chesterton Road, Cambridge CB4 1EN
Tel 01223 356207
Fax 01223 566432

NORTHERN ENGLAND

BAC Outdoor Leisure
Central Hall, Coronation Street, Elland, Halifax, West Yorkshire HX5 0DF
Tel 01422 371146
Fax 01422 371146

LD Mountain Centre Limited
34 Dean Street, Newcastle-upon-Tyne NE1 1PG
Tel 0191 232 3561
Fax 0191 222 0082

Severn Sports/Boardworx
80 Town Street, Armley, Leeds, West Yorkshire LS12 3AA
Tel 0113 279 1618
Fax 0113 231 0231

Snow & Rock
Sheffield Ski Centre, Vale Road, Parkwood Springs, Sheffield S3 9SJ
Tel 0114 275 1700

SCOTLAND

Summits
36 Moss Street, Paisley PA1 1BA
Tel 0141 887 5536

Summits
5 Bridge Street, Dunfermline
Tel 01383 730181
Fax 01383 730184

IRELAND

The Alpine Shop
17-18 Temple Lane, Templebar, Dublin 2, Ireland
Tel 00 353 1672 7088
Fax 00 353 1672 7089

The Great Outdoors
Chatham Street, Dublin 2, Ireland
Tel 00 353 1679 4293
Fax 00 353 1679 4554

Ski organisations

Artificial Ski Slope Instructors (ASSI)
Tel 0121 501 2314
Fax 0121 585 6448

British Association of Ski Instructors (BASI)
Tel 01479 861717
Fax 01479 861718

British Ski Club for the Disabled
Tel 01895 271104

British Ski and Snowboard Federation
Tel 0131 445 7676
Fax 0131 445 7722

British Snowboarding Association
Tel 07000 360540
Fax 07000 720540

English Ski Council
Tel 0121 501 2314
Fax 0121 585 6448

Ski Club of Great Britain
Tel 020 8410 2000
Fax 020 8410 2001

Snowsport Scotland
Tel 0131 445 4151
Fax 0131 445 4949

Snowsport Wales
Tel 029 2056 1904
Fax 029 2056 1924

The Uphill Ski Club
Tel 01479 861272
Fax 01479 861272
Ski organisation for the disabled

Ski travel agents

Alpine Answers
Tel 020 8871 4656
Fax 020 8871 9676
www.alpineanswers.co.uk

Avant-ski
Tel 0191 212 1173
Fax 0191 239 9459
www.avant-ski.com

Chalet Connections
Tel 0113 237 0371
Fax 0113 269 3305

Iglu.com
Tel 020 7761 6410
Fax 020 7535 8826
www.iglu.com

Independent Ski Links
Tel 0870 747 9121
Fax 01964 536006
www.ski-links.com

Ski Expectations
Tel 01799 531888
Fax 01799 531887

Ski McNeill
Tel 028 9066 6699
Fax 028 9068 3888
www.skimcneill.com

Ski Solutions
Tel 020 7471 7700
Fax 020 7471 7701
www.skisolutions.com

Ski Travel Centre
Tel 0141 649 9696
Fax 0141 649 2273
www.ski-travel-centre.co.uk

Ski the Rockies
Tel 020 7649 9894

Ski-holidays.com
Tel 0870 010 2100
www.ski-holidays.com

Skiers Travel
Tel 0113 292 0893
www.skiers-travel.co.uk

Snow Line
Tel 01858 828000
Fax 01858 828020
www.snow-line.co.uk

Ski Line
Tel 020 8777 0440
www.skiline.co.uk

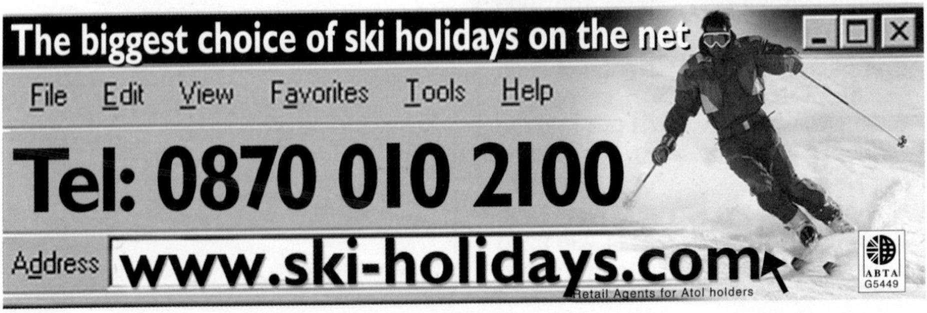

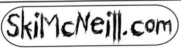

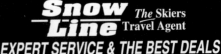

Resort index / directory / packages

This is an index to the resort chapters in the book; you'll find page references for about 400 resorts described elsewhere. But you'll also find brief descriptions here of another 700 resorts, most of them much smaller than those we've covered in full, but often still worth a short visit. We also list here the companies offering package holidays to each resort. To get in touch with one of these tour operators, look them up in the list starting on page 602. Note: all places named after saints are ordered in a single sequence, regardless of local spellings of Saint, San, Sankt or whatever.

Key

🚡 *Lifts*
⛷ *Pistes*
⊠ *UK tour operators*

49 Degrees North USA
Best snow in Washington State; 120-acre bowl reserved for powder weekends.
1195m; slopes 1195–1760m
🚡 *4* ⛷ *780 acres*

Abetone Italy
Resort in the exposed Appennines, less than two hours from Florence and Pisa.
1390m; slopes 1390–1900m
🚡 *25* ⛷ *50km*
⊠ *Alpine Tours*

Abtenau Austria
Sizeable village in Dachstein-West region near Salzburg, on large plain ideal for cross-country for which it's known.
710m; slopes 710–1260m
🚡 *6* ⛷ *10km*
⊠ *Thomson*

Achenkirch Austria
Unspoilt, low-altitude Tirolean village close to Niederau and Alpbach, overlooking a lake.
930m; slopes 930–1800m
🚡 *10* ⛷ *25km*
⊠ *Ramblers*

Adelboden 376
⊠ *Interhome, Kuoni, Made to Measure, Plus Travel, Swiss Travel Service*

Les Aillons France
Traditional village near Chambéry. Nicely sheltered.
1000m; slopes 1000–1900m
🚡 *24*

Akakura Japan
Old spa of some oriental charm, 150km from Tokyo; modern lifts and easy runs.
770m; slopes 770–1500m
🚡 *41* ⛷ *85km*

Alagna 351
Small resort on the western fringe of Monterosa Ski area.
⊠ *Ski Club of GB, Ski Weekend*

Alba Italy
Picturesque Dolomite village with a small area; access to Sella Ronda at Canazei.
1515m; slopes 1515–2440m
🚡 *5* ⛷ *10km*
⊠ *Crystal*

Alleghe Italy
Dolomite village in a pretty lakeside setting. Cheap base for visiting Cortina.
980m
🚡 *24* ⛷ *80km*
⊠ *Crystal*

Alpbach 87
⊠ *Crystal, Independent Ski Links, Inghams, Interhome, Made to Measure, Thomson*

Alpe-d'Huez 185
⊠ *Airtours, Chalet World, Chalets 'Unlimited', Club Med, Crystal, Erna Low, Fairhand Holidays, First Choice Ski, Iglu.com, Independent Ski Links, Inghams, Interhome, Lagrange Holidays, Made to Measure, Motours, Neilson, Panorama, Ski Arrangements, Ski Club of GB, Ski France, Ski Independence, Ski Leisure Direction, Ski Line, Ski Miquel, Ski Valkyrie, SkiAway Holidays, Skiworld, Thomson, Tops Ski Chalets and Club Hotels*

Alpe-du-Grand-Serre France
Tiny resort near Alpe-d'Huez and Les Deux-Alpes. Good for bad-weather days.
1400m; slopes 1400–2200m
🚡 *20*

Alpendorf Austria
Hamlet 4km from St Johann im Pongau, with access to the Salzburger Sportwelt area.
850m; slopes 850–2185m
🚡 *120* ⛷ *320km*

Alpine Meadows 455

Alps Korea
Korea's most northerly, snow-reliable resort. An hour from Seoul.

Alta 505
⊠ *Ski The American Dream*

Altenmarkt Austria
Unspoilt village well placed for snowsure Obertauern and Wagrain.
855m; slopes 855–2130m
🚡 *28* ⛷ *150km*
⊠ *Made to Measure, Sloping Off*

Alto Campoo Spain
Barren, desolate place with undistinguished slopes, but magnificent wilderness views.
1700m; slopes 1650–2175m
🚡 *10*

Alt St Johann Switzerland
Old cross-country village near Liechstenstein.
900m; slopes 900–2260m
🚡 *21* ⛷ *50km*

Alyeska USA
Alaskan area 60km from Anchorage, with luxury hotel.
75m; slopes 75–1200m
🚡 *9* ⛷ *785 acres*
⊠ *Big Country Ski*

Aminona 384
Purpose-built resort on east side of Crans-Montana area.
⊠ *Lagrange Holidays*

Andalo Italy
Atmospheric Dolomite village near Madonna, with low wooded slopes.
1050m; slopes 1035–2125m
🚡 *17* ⛷ *60km*
⊠ *Equity Total Ski*

Andermatt 377
⊠ *Iglu.com, Made to Measure, Ski Weekend*

Andorra la Vella 570
Andorra's capital, with plenty for non-skiers.

Angel Fire USA
Intermediate neighbour of Taos, New Mexico. Height usually ensures good snow.
2620m; slopes 2620–3255m
🚡 *6* ⛷ *455 acres*

Les Angles France
Attractive resort in one of the best Pyrenean ski areas. Pretty, tree-lined, easy skiing.
1600m; slopes 1650–2400m
🚡 *23*
⊠ *Lagrange Holidays*

Annaberg-Lungötz Austria
Peaceful village in a pretty setting; shares a sizeable area with Gosau.
775m; slopes 775–1615m
🚡 *33* ⛷ *65km*

Antagnod Italy
Weekend day-tripper area on way up to Champoluc, above Aosta valley. No village.
1710m; slopes 1710–2000m
🚡 *4* ⛷ *7km*

Anzère Switzerland
Sympathetically designed modern resort on a sunny balcony near Crans-Montana; intermediate slopes.
1500m; slopes 1500–2460m
🚡 *13* ⛷ *40km*
⊠ *Fairhand Holidays, Interhome, Lagrange Holidays, Made to Measure*

Apex 544
⊠ *Frontier Ski, Made to Measure, Ski Connections, Ski Safari, Skisar US*

Aprica Italy
Ugly, straggling village between Lake Como and Brenta Dolomites, with bland slopes and limited facilities.
1180m; slopes 1180–2310m
🚡 *24* ⛷ *50km*
⊠ *Interhome*

Arabba 358
Tiny village with the Sella Ronda on its doorstep.
⊠ *Crystal, Independent Ski Links, Inghams, Momentum Ski, Neilson*

Aragnouet-Piau France
Purpose-built mid-mountain satellite of St-Lary, best suited to families, beginners and early intermediates.
1850m; slopes 1420–2500m
🚡 *32* ⛷ *80km*

Arapahoe Basin 479
Small resort a few minutes from Keystone by road.

Arcalis 570
⊠ *Snowcoach*

Les Arcs 193
⊠ *Airtours, Avant-ski, Chalet Snowboard, Chalets 'Unlimited', Club Med, Crystal, Erna Low, Fairhand Holidays, First Choice Ski, Iglu.com, Independent Ski Links, Inghams, Interhome, Lagrange Holidays, Made to Measure, Motours, Neilson, Optimum Ski, Ski Activity, Ski Amis, Ski Arrangements, Ski Club of GB, Ski France, Ski Independence, Ski Leisure Direction, Ski Line, Ski Olympic, Ski Supreme, SkiAway Holidays, Skiworld, Solo's, Thomson, Vanilla Ski*

Ardent 199
Quiet hamlet with access to Avoriaz and Châtel.
⊠ *The Chalet Company*

Åre 588
⊠ *Crystal, Independent Ski Links, Neilson*

Arêches-Beaufort France
Secluded little resort accessible only from Mont Blanc region to the north.
1050m; slopes 1050–2300m
15

Argentière 203
Old village beneath Chamonix's Grands Montets.
⊠ *Bigfoot, Chalets 'Unlimited', Collineige, Crystal, Fairhand Holidays, Independent Ski Links, Interhome, Lagrange Holidays, McNab Mountain Sports, Motours, Ski Arrangements, Ski Club of GB, Ski Hillwood, Ski Scott James, Ski Valkyrie, White Mountain Lodge, White Roc*

Arinsal 570
⊠ *Airtours, Chalets 'Unlimited', Crystal, First Choice Ski, Independent Ski Links, Inghams, Neilson, Panorama, Thomson*

Arnoldstein/Dreiländereck Austria
One of several little areas overlooking town of Villach.
680m; slopes 680–1455m
8 12km

Arolla Switzerland
Tiny village in pretty riverside setting south of Sion. Main attraction is heli-skiing.
2005m; slopes 2005–2890m
5 47km

Arosa 378
⊠ *Independent Ski Links, Inghams, Interhome, Kuoni, Made to Measure, Plus Travel, Powder Byrne, Ski Choice, Swiss Travel Service*

Artesina Italy
Purpose-built resort lacking character and atmosphere. Old lifts – nearly all drags.
1350m; slopes 1320–2100m
14 60km

Asiago Italy
Sizeable resort close to Verona, but low and limited.
1000m; slopes 1000–1380m
17

Aspen 462
⊠ *American Ski Classics, Big Country Ski, Chalet World, Chalets 'Unlimited', Crystal, Elegant Resorts, Fantiski, Iglu.com, Independent Ski Links, Lotus Supertravel, Made to Measure, Momentum Ski, Rocky Mountain Snowboard Tours, Ski Activity, Ski Club of GB, Ski Connections, Ski Independence, Ski Line, Ski Safari, Ski The American Dream, Ski Total, Skisar US, Skiworld, Thomson, United Vacations*

Attitash USA
One of the best ski areas in eastern US. Close to other New Hampshire areas, too.
slopes 180–715m
11 280 acres
⊠ *Big Country Ski, Neilson, Ski Success, Skisar US, Virgin Ski*

Auffach 170
Unexceptional village in the Wildschönau area.

Auris-en-Oisans 185
Quiet hamlet linked across the valley to Alpe d'Huez.
⊠ *Fairhand Holidays, Lagrange Holidays*

Auron France
Pleasant village with varied, sheltered slopes; a stark contrast to nearby Isola 2000.
1600m; slopes 1165–2450m
27 130km

Auronzo di Cadore Italy
Sizeable village – a cheaper base for visiting Cortina.
865m; slopes 865–1585m
5 7km

Aussois France
One of many rustic working villages near Modane that share Maurienne valley pass.
1500m; slopes 1500–2750m
11 30km

Autrans France
Major cross-country centre village, close to Grenoble.
1050m; slopes 1050–1710m
15 30km
⊠ *Headwater Holidays, Lagrange Holidays*

Avila Canada
Ugly base lodge that shares most popular area in Montréal region with Mont St Sauveur.
215m; slopes 215–415m
9 175 acres

Avon USA
Small town – an inexpensive base from which to ski Beaver Creek, Vail and Breckenridge.
⊠ *Skisar US*

Avoriaz 199
⊠ *Airtours, Chalet Snowboard, Chalets 'Unlimited', Club Med, Crystal, Erna Low, Eurotunnel Motoring Holidays, Fairhand Holidays, First Choice Ski, Iglu.com, Independent Ski Links, Lagrange Holidays, Made to Measure, Motours, Neilson, Ski Arrangements, Ski Choice, Ski Club of GB, Ski Independence, Ski Leisure Direction, Thomson*

Axamer Lizum 103
⊠ *Pavilion Tours*

Axams 103
Quiet village near Innsbruck.
⊠ *Lagrange Holidays*

Ax-les-Thermes France
Sizeable spa village with own train station, near Font-Romeu and Andorra.
1400m; slopes 1400–2400m
16

Bad Gastein 88
⊠ *Crystal, First Choice Ski, Independent Ski Links, Inghams, Made to Measure, Ski Miquel*

Badger Pass USA
Centre for 350 miles of superb backcountry touring in Yosemite National Park.
2195m; slopes 2195–2435m
5 90 acres

Bad Hofgastein 88
Relaxed and spacious spa resort in the Gastein Valley.
⊠ *Crystal, Inghams, Made to Measure*

Bad Kleinkirchheim Austria
Spacious, sophisticated, quiet, spa village in south-east of Austria, with queue-free, intermediate terrain.
1100m; slopes 1100–2055m
29 80km
⊠ *Alpine Tours, Crystal, Sloping Off*

Banff 547
⊠ *Airtours, All Canada Ski, Crystal, Elegant Resorts, Equity Total Ski, First Choice Ski, Frontier Ski, Handmade Holidays, Independent Ski Links, Inghams, Kuoni, Lotus Supertravel, Made to Measure, Neilson, Pavilion Tours, Ski Activity, Ski Club of GB, Ski Connections, Ski Equipe, Ski Independence, Ski Line, Ski Safari, Ski The American Dream, Ski Vacation Canada, Skisar US, Skiworld, Thomson, United Vacations*

Bansko Bulgaria
Old traditional cobble-street town. Skiing very limited and 12km away.
935m; slopes 1760–2500m
3 5km
⊠ *Balkan Holidays*

Baqueira-Beret 578
⊠ *Ski Miquel*

Barboleuse Switzerland
Quiet base from which to ski Villars and Les Diablerets.
slopes 1130–2970m
46 125km

Bardonecchia 326
⊠ *Airtours, Crystal, Equity Total Ski, Independent Ski Links, Neilson, Thomson*

Barèges 322
⊠ *Borderline, Fairhand Holidays, Lagrange Holidays, SkiAway Holidays, Thomson*

Les Barzettes 384
Smaller base along the road from Crans-Montana.

Bear Mountain USA
Southern California's main area, in the beautiful San Bernardino National Forest region. 100% snowmaking.
slopes 2170–2685m
12 195 acres

Bear's Town Korea
Ugly modern resort with pistes cut out of thick forest; 10 slopes. Only 40 minutes from Seoul, so crowded.
11

Beaulard Italy
Little place just off the road between Sauze d'Oulx and Bardonecchia.
1215m; slopes 1215–2120m
6 20km

Beaver Creek 491
⊠ *Crystal, Handmade Holidays, Independent Ski Links, Made to Measure, Ski Club of GB, Ski Connections, Ski Equipe, Ski Independence, Ski The American Dream, Ski Total, Skisar US, United Vacations*

Beaver Mountain USA
Small Utah area north of Salt Lake City, too far from Park City for a day trip.
2195m; slopes 2195–2680m
3 525 acres

Belleayre Mountain USA
State-owned resort near Albany, NY State. Cheap prices but old lifts/short runs.
775m; slopes 775–1015m
8 135 acres

Belle-Plagne 275
Satellite of La Plagne.
⊠ *Motours*

Berchtesgaden Germany
Pleasant old town close to Salzburg, known for its Nordic skiing but with several little Alpine areas nearby.
550m; slopes 630–1800m
21 50km
⊠ *Moswin Tours*

Bergün Switzerland
Traditional, quiet little family resort on the rail route between Davos and St Moritz.
1375m; slopes 1400–2550m
5 25km

Berwang Austria
Unspoilt village in a spacious valley, close to Lermoos.
1335m; slopes 1335–1740m
14 40km

Bessans France
Old cross-country village well placed for touring Maurienne valley resorts.
1710m; slopes 1740–2200m
4
⊠ *Headwater Holidays*

Besse France
Charming old village built out of lava, 6km from purpose-built satellite Super-Besse.
1050m; slopes 1350–1800m
21 80km
⊠ *Lagrange Holidays*

Bethel USA
Pleasant, historic town in Maine, attractive alternative to staying in Sunday River.
⊠ *Skisar US*

Le Bettex 248
Small base above St-Gervais; links to the Megève network.

Bettmeralp Switzerland
Central village of the sizeable Aletsch area near Brig, perched high above the Rhône valley, amid spectacular glacial scenery.
1955m; slopes 1925–2710m
31 90km

Beuil-les-Launes France
Alpes Maritimes resort closest to Nice. Shares area with Valberg.
1400m; slopes 1400–2100m
27

Bezau Austria
Virtually no slopes, but main village in low Bregenzerwald region north-west of Lech.
650m; slopes 1210–1630m

Biberwier Austria
Limited little base from which to cover the Zugspitz area.
1000m; slopes 1000–1880m
5 9km

Bichlbach Austria
Smallest of the Zugspitz villages with very limited slopes of its own.
1070m; slopes 1070–1620m
3 7km

Bielmonte Italy
Milanese day-tripper spot. Good for bad-weather days.
1200m; slopes 1200–1620m
13 20km

Big Mountain USA
Impressive ski area close to Montana's Glacier National Park. Fog is commonplace.
1370m; slopes 1370–2135m
10 3000 acres
⊠ *Inghams, Ski Independence, Skisar US*

Big Powderhorn USA
South Lake Superior resort. Extensive regional lift pass but area suffer from winds.
370m; slopes 370–560m
9 250 acres

Big Sky 519
⊠ *Ski Independence, Ski The American Dream, Skisar US*

Big White 544
⊠ *Frontier Ski, Made to Measure, Ski Activity, Ski Connections, Ski Independence, Ski Safari, Ski The American Dream, Ski Vacation Canada, Skisar US*

Bischofshofen Austria
Working town near St Johann im Pongau with limited runs of its own.
545m; slopes 545–100m
2 22km

Bivio Switzerland
Quiet village near St Moritz with easy slopes opened up by a few drag lifts.
1775m; slopes 1780–2600m
4 40km

Bizau Austria
One of two main areas in low Bregenzerwald region north-west of Lech.
680m; slopes 680–1700m
6 24km

Björkliden 587

Björnrike 587

Blackcomb 560
⊠ *Frontier Ski*

Blatten-Naters Switzerland
Stunning glacial scenery, immediately above Brig, with larger Aletsch slopes nearby.
675m; slopes 1325–2880m
9 60km

Bled 582
⊠ *Alpine Tours, Crystal, Thomson*

Blue Cow 592

Blue Mountain Canada
Largest area in Ontario, with glorious views of Lake Huron. High-capacity lift system. 100% snowmaking.
230m; slopes 230–450m
15 275 acres
⊠ *All Canada Ski*

Blue River Canada
Base of Mike Wiegele heli-ski operation in Cariboo and Monashee mountains.
⊠ *Scott Dunn Ski*

Bluewood USA
Particularly remote area even by American NW standards.
1355m; slopes 1355–1725m
3 530 acres

Bogus Basin USA
Sizeable area overlooking Idaho's capital, Boise. Good two-centre trip with Sun Valley.
1760m; slopes 1760–2310m
8 2600 acres

Bohinj 582
⊠ *Alpine Tours, Crystal, Thomson*

Bois-d'Amont France
One of four resorts that make up Les Rousses area in Jura region. Useful stopover.
1050m; slopes 1120–1680m
40
⊠ *Lagrange Holidays*

Bolognola Italy
Tiny area in Macerata region near Adriatic Riviera.
1070m; slopes 1070–1845m
7 5km

Bolton Valley USA
Neighbour of Stowe. Mostly intermediate slopes. Ski train to nearby Waterbury and Burlington.
465m; slopes 465–960m
6 155 acres

Le Bonhomme France
One of several areas near Strasbourg. Snowmakers.
830m; slopes 830–1235m
11

Bonneval-sur-Arc France
Unspoilt, remote old village in the Haute Maurienne valley Pass to neighbouring Val-d'Isere closed in winter.
1800m; slopes 1800–3050m
18

Bons 233
Rustic, unspoilt old hamlet linked to Les Deux-Alpes.

Boreal USA
Closest area to north Lake Tahoe town, Truckee. Limited slopes, best for novices.
2195m; slopes 2195–2375m
9 380 acres

Bormio 327
⊠ *Airtours, Inghams, Interhome, Sloping Off, Thomson*

Borovets 579
⊠ *Balkan Holidays, Crystal, First Choice Ski, Independent Ski Links, Inghams, Neilson, Ski Balkantours, Thomson*

Bosco Chiesanuova Italy
Day tripper's place near Verona.
1105m; slopes 1105–1805m
18 20km

La Bourboule France
Spa village cum cross-country centre with Alpine slopes of Le Mont-Dore nearby.
850m; slopes 1050–1850m
41 80km
⊠ *Lagrange Holidays*

Bourg-d'Oisans France
Civilised valley town from which to visit Alpe-d'Huez and Les Deux-Alpes.

Bourg-St-Maurice 193
French valley town, useful as a base for visiting nearby resorts. Funicular to Les Arcs.
⊠ *Interhome*

Bovec 582

Boyne Highlands USA
Area with impressive, high-capacity lift system for weekend Detroit crowds. Fierce winds a drawback.
225m; slopes 225–390m
10 240 acres

Boyne Mountain USA
Weekend Detroit crowds. Not as windy as sister Boyne Highlands. Shared lift pass.
190m; slopes 190–340m
12 115 acres

Bramans France
Old cross-country village (50km of trails) near Modane. Well placed for touring Maurienne resorts.
1230m

Bramberg Austria
Village near Pass Thurn (Kitzbühel area). Shares area with Neukirchen.
820m; slopes 820–900m
13 11km

Brand Austria
Old family favourite, with small, low area.
1050m; slopes 1050–1920m
8 30km
⊠ *Crystal, Interhome*

Cervinia 330
✉ *Airtours, Crystal, Elegant Resorts, Equity Total Ski, First Choice Ski, Iglu.com, Independent Ski Links, Inghams, Momentum Ski, Neilson, Ski Club of GB, Ski Solutions, Thomson*

Cesana Torinese 265
Little Italian village linked to Montgenèvre in France.
✉ *First Choice Ski*

Le Châble 421
Small village below Verbier, linked by gondola.

Chacaltaya Bolivia
Highest ski area in the world; altitude headache guaranteed. 4WD from nearby La Paz. Primitive facilities.
5190m; slopes 5220–5420m
1 2km

Chaillol France
Cross-country centre at edge of beautiful Ecrins National Park, near Gap.
1600m; slopes 1450–2000m
11

Chamois Italy
Neighbour of Cervinia close to Valtournenche. Good when bad weather in higher areas.
1815m; slopes 1815–2270m
8 20km

Chamonix 203
✉ *Airtours, Avant-ski, Bigfoot, Board and Lodge, Chalet Beaumont, Chalets 'Unlimited', Club Med, Collineige, Crystal, Elegant Resorts, Erna Low, Fairhand Holidays, First Choice Ski, Handmade Holidays, HuSki, Iglu.com, Independent Ski Links, Inghams, Interhome, Lagrange Holidays, Made to Measure, Momentum Ski, Motours, Neilson, Simply Ski, Ski Arrangements, Ski Club of GB, Ski Esprit, Ski Independence, Ski Leisure Direction, Ski Line, Ski Solutions, Ski Valkyrie, Ski Weekend, Skiworld, Sloping Off, The Ski Company, Thomson, White Roc*

Champagny-en-Vanoise 275
Charming village linked to the La Plagne network.
✉ *Barrelli Ski, Fairhand Holidays, Independent Ski Links, Lagrange Holidays, Made to Measure, Motours, Ski Leisure Direction*

Champéry 379
✉ *Iglu.com, Made to Measure, Piste Artiste, Plus Travel, White Roc*

Champex Switzerland
Lakeside hamlet tucked away in the trees above Orsières. A nice quiet, unspoilt base from which to visit Verbier's area.
1470m; slopes 1470–2220m
4 8km

Champfér 415
Lakeside hamlet between St Moritz and Silvaplana.
✉ *Made to Measure*

Champoluc 351
Unspoilt village at one end of the the Monterosa Ski area.
✉ *Chalets 'Unlimited', Crystal, Handmade Holidays, Thomson*

Champoussin 379
Quiet village linked to the rest of the Champéry slopes.

Chamrousse France
Functional family resort near Grenoble, with sheltered area close to accommodation.
1650m; slopes 1400–2255m
26
✉ *Fairhand Holidays, Lagrange Holidays, Motours*

Chandolin Switzerland
Picturesque, unspoilt village near Zinal and Grimentz. Extensive intermediate slopes.
1935m; slopes 1660–2895m
15 70km

Chantemerle 291
Valley village with direct access to Serre-Chevalier.

Chapelco Argentina
Year-round resort, 15 km from St Martin de Los Andes.
slopes 1250–1980m
9

La Chapelle-d'Abondance 211
Unspoilt village 5km down the valley from Châtel.
✉ *Ski La Cote*

Charlotte Pass 592

Château d'Oex Switzerland
Pleasant village at the opposite end of the White Highlands ski area to Gstaad.
970m; slopes 950–3000m
69 250km
✉ *Alpine Tours, Crystal, Erna Low, Ski Valkyrie*

Châtel 211
✉ *Avant-ski, Chalets 'Unlimited', Fairhand Holidays, First Choice Ski, Freedom Holidays, Haig Ski, Interhome, Lagrange Holidays, Made to Measure, Motours, Ski Addiction, Ski Arrangements, Ski Club of GB, Ski Independence, Ski Leisure Direction, Ski Line, Ski Rosie, SkiAway Holidays, Snowfocus, Tops Ski Chalets and Club Hotels*

Le Chatelard France
Small resort in remote Parc des Bauges between Lake Annecy and Chambéry.

Chiesa Italy
Attractive venue with a fairly high plateau of easy runs.
1000m; slopes 1700–2335m
10 25km
✉ *First Choice Ski*

Le Chinaillon 216
Village at base of lifts above Le Grand-Bornand.
1300m; slopes 1000–2100m
38 65km

Chiomonte Italy
Tiny resort east of Sauze d'Oulx and Bardonecchia.
745m; slopes 745–2210m
6 10km

Chonmasan Korea
Dreary, purpose-built resort 50 minutes from Seoul; gets very crowded. 6 slopes.
7

Chsea Algeria
Largest of Algeria's skiable areas, 135km south-east of coastal town of Alger.
1860m; slopes 1860–2510m

Churwalden Switzerland
Hamlet on fringe of Lenzerheide-Valbella area.
1230m; slopes 1230–2865m
35 155km

Clavière 265
Small Italian village linked to Montgenèvre in France.
✉ *Crystal, Equity Total Ski, Independent Ski Links, Neilson*

La Clusaz 216
✉ *Aravis Alpine Retreat, Classic Ski Limited, Erna Low, Fairhand Holidays, First Choice Ski, Interhome, Lagrange Holidays, Made to Measure, Motours, Ski Activity, Ski Amis, Ski Arrangements, Ski Club of GB, Ski Leisure Direction, Ski Valkyrie, Ski Weekend, Snowlife*

Les Coches 275
Small, purpose-built village, linked to the La Plagne area.
✉ *Crystal, Fairhand Holidays, Lagrange Holidays, Made to Measure, Motours, Ski Esprit, Ski Leisure Direction, Ski Olympic*

Cogne Italy
One of Aosta valley's larger villages. Small area worth a short visit from nearby Pila.
1530m; slopes 1530–2245m
5 8km
✉ *Inntravel, Waymark Holidays*

Colfosco 358
Small but sprawling village, part of the Sella Ronda.

Colle di Tenda Italy
Dour, modern resort that shares a good area with nicer Limone, not far from Nice.
1400m; slopes 1120–2040m
33 80km

Colle Isarco Italy
Brenner Pass area. Well known bargain-shopping town Vipiteno nearby.
1095m; slopes 1095–2720m
5 15km

Le Collet-d'Allevard France
Ski area of sizeable summer spa in remote spot east of Chambéry-Grenoble road.
1450m; slopes 1450–2100m
13

Collio Italy
Tiny area of short runs in remote spot between lakes Garda and d'Iseo.
840m; slopes 840–1715m
14

Combelouvière France
Quiet hamlet tucked away in the trees at the foot of Valmorel's pistes.
1250m; slopes 1250–2550m
50 163km
✉ *Fairhand Holidays, Lagrange Holidays*

Combloux France
Quiet, unspoilt alternative to linked Megève.
900m; slopes 1100–1850m
80
✉ *Lagrange Holidays*

Les Contamines 222
✉ *Chalets 'Unlimited', Classic Ski Limited, Fairhand Holidays, First Choice Ski, Interhome, Lagrange Holidays, Ski Activity, Ski Arrangements, Ski Line, Ski Total, Skiworld*

Copper Mountain 474
✉ *Club Med, Made to Measure, Ski Independence, Ski The American Dream, Solo's, United Vacations, United Vacations*

Le Corbier France
Tower-block resort with an extensive but low area linked with La Toussuire, off the Maurienne valley.
1500m; slopes 1400–2400m
24
✉ *Equity Total Ski, Fairhand Holidays, Interhome, Lagrange Holidays, Motours*

Coronet Peak 597

Ehrwald Austria
Friendly, pretty village with nicely varied areas, notably the Zugspitz glacier, nearby.
1000m; slopes 1000–3000m
21 25km

Eldora Mountain USA
Varied terrain close to Denver. Crowded at weekends; low lift capacity.
2795m; slopes 2795–3220m
8 386 acres

Elk Meadows USA
Small area south of Salt Lake City.
2775m; slopes 2775–3170m
5 420 acres

Ellmau 95
✉ *Airtours, Crystal, Inghams, Interhome, Motours, Neilson, Thomson*

Encamp 570
Unattractive town linked to the Pas de la Casa slopes.
✉ *First Choice Ski, Thomson*

Enego Italy
Limited weekend day trippers' area near Vicenza and Trento.
1300m; slopes 1300–1445m
7 30km

Engelberg 395
✉ *Crystal, Iglu.com, Interhome, Kuoni, Made to Measure, SkiGower, Swiss Travel Service*

Entrèves 340
Characterless cluster of hotels at base of cable-car up to Courmayeur slopes.

Etna Italy
Scenic, uncrowded, short-season area on the volcano; easy off-piste.
1800m; slopes 1800–2350m
5km

Evolène Switzerland
Rustic village south of Sion, with Verbier's slopes accessed at nearby Les Masses.
1380m; slopes 1300–3330m
100 400km

Faak am See Austria
Limited area, one of five overlooking town of Villach.
550m; slopes 840–1045m
2 2km

Fairmont Hot Springs Canada
Major luxury spa complex ideal for relaxing holiday with some gentle skiing thrown in.
1280m; slopes 1280–1585m
2 60 acres

Faistenau Austria
Cross-country centre close to Salzburg and St Wolfgang. Limited Alpine area.
785m; slopes 785–1000m
5 3km

Falcade Italy
Little ski areas close to but not part of Sella Ronda.
1145m; slopes 1145–2170m
11 39km
✉ *Alpine Tours*

Falera 396
Small, rustic village, with access to Flims/Laax area.

Le Falgoux France
One of the most beautiful old villages in France. In very scenic Volcano National Park.
930m; slopes 930–1350m

Falkertsee Austria
Base area with bleak, open slopes in contrast to nearby Badkleinkirchheim.
1690m; slopes 1690–2385m
5 15km

Falls Creek 592

Farellones/El Colorado Chile
Chile's best ski area, an hour from Santiago. Crowded at weekends.
✉ *Scott Dunn Latin America*

La Feclaz France
One of several little resorts in remote Parc des Bauges.

Fernie 556
✉ *Airtours, All Canada Ski, Frontier Ski, Independent Ski Links, Inghams, Ski Activity, Ski Connections, Ski Independence, Ski Safari, Skisar US*

Fieberbrunn Austria
Jolly old traditional village, an inconvenient distance from its small but attractive ski area.
800m; slopes 800–2020m
14 30km

Fiesch Switzerland
Traditional Rhône valley resort close to Brig. Lift into the beautiful Aletsch area.
1060m; slopes 1050–2870m
10
✉ *SkiGower*

Filzmoos Austria
Charming, friendly village; leisurely slopes, ideal for novices. Good snow record.
1055m; slopes 1055–1645m
12 32km
✉ *Inghams, Neilson*

Finkenberg 125
Between Mayrhofen and Hintertux, with gondola link to Mayrhofen's main area.
✉ *Crystal, First Choice Ski*

Fiss Austria
Compact, quiet village with a sunny area protected by snow-guns. Linked to Serfaus.
1435m; slopes 1200–2540m
17 70km
✉ *Alpine Tours, Interhome*

Flachau Austria
Quiet village in a pretty setting at one end of three-valley lift network.
925m; slopes 925–1980m
53 220km
✉ *Interhome, Thomson*

Flachauwinkl Austria
Well placed within the Salzburger Sportwelt area, but with the Salzburg-Villach autobahn carving through it.
930m; slopes 800–2185m
120 320km

Flaine 238
✉ *Airtours, Classic Ski Limited, Club Med, Crystal, Erna Low, Fairhand Holidays, First Choice Ski, Iglu.com, Independent Ski Links, Inghams, Lagrange Holidays, Made to Measure, Motours, Neilson, Ski Arrangements, Ski Choice, Ski Club of GB, Ski Independence, Ski Leisure Direction, Skisafe Travel, Thomson*

Flims 396
✉ *Freedom Holidays, Interhome, Kuoni, Made to Measure, Momentum Ski, Plus Travel, Powder Byrne, Ski Choice, Ski Weekend, Swiss Travel Service, White Roc*

Flumet France
Large resort, well placed for whole Mont Blanc area. Cheap alternative to Megève.
1000m; slopes 1000–2070m
11

Flumserberg Switzerland
Collective name for villages sharing a varied area an hour south-east of Zurich.
1220—1400m; slopes 1220–2220m
17

Folgaria Italy
Largest of several resorts east of Trento. Old lift system.
1165m; slopes 1185–2005m
38 70km
✉ *Alpine Tours*

Folgarida 350
Pleasant Dolomite village, with links to Madonna.
✉ *Equity Total Ski, Sloping Off*

Foncine-le-Haut France
Major cross-country centre with 220km of trails, relatively close to Channel.
✉ *Headwater Holidays, Lagrange Holidays*

Fonni Gennaragentu Italy
Sardinia's only 'ski area'.
1 5km

Font-Romeu France
Family resort set in woodland, with the biggest snowmaking set-up in the Pyrenees.
1800m; slopes 1750–2250m
29
✉ *Lagrange Holidays*

Foppolo Italy
Relatively unattractive but user-friendly village, a short transfer from Bergamo.
1510m; slopes 1610–2160m
10 45km
✉ *Equity Total Ski*

Forca Canapine Italy
Limited area near Adriatic. Weekend day tripper spot.
1450m; slopes 1450–1690m
11 20km

Formazza Italy
Centre for cross-country skiing with some downhill slopes, too.
1280m; slopes 1275–1755m
8km

Formigal 577
✉ *Independent Ski Links, Thomson*

Le Fornet 303
Rustic, old hamlet 3km down the valley from Val-d'Isère.

Forstau Austria
Secluded hamlet above Radstadt-Schladming road. Very limited area with old lifts, but nice and quiet.
930m; slopes 930–1885m
7 14km

Fortress Mountain Canada
Primitive, wild little mountain between Banff and Calgary, renowned for powder snow, dramatic scenery and uncrowded slopes.
2040m; slopes 2040–2370m
6 325 acres

La Foux-d'Allos France
Purpose-built resort that shares a good intermediate area with Pra-Loup.
1800m; slopes 1800–2600m
53 230km
✉ *Fairhand Holidays, Lagrange Holidays*

Frabosa Soprana Italy
One of numerous little areas south of Turin, well placed for combining winter sports with Riviera sightseeing.
850m; slopes 860–1740m
40km

Frisco 469
Small town down the valley from Breckenridge.

Frontignano Italy
Best lift system in Macerata region near Adriatic Riviera.
1340m; slopes 1340–2000m
8 10km

Fügen Austria
Unspoilt village with limited area best suited to beginners, poorly placed for other Zillertal resorts.
560m; slopes 560–2400m
19 48km
✉ *Lagrange Holidays*

Fulpmes Austria
Sizeable village in a beautiful valley, with a small area of its own, Schlick 2000, part of the Innsbruck pass.
960m; slopes 960–2260m
9 20km
✉ *Crystal*

Funäsdalen Sweden
Cross-country Mecca. Home of world's longest ski trails, with 600m vertical of Alpine runs. Top-class facilities.
600m; slopes 600–1200m
30 85km

Furano Japan
Small Hokkaido resort. One of the few Japanese areas to get reasonable powder.
235m; slopes 235–1065m
17

Fusch Austria
Across golf course from Kaprun and Schuttdorf. Cheap(er), quiet place to stay when visiting Zell am See.
805m; slopes 805–1050m
2 5km

Fuschl Austria
Attractive lakeside village close to Salzburg, 30 min from its slopes. Best suited to skiers-cum-sightseers.
670m

Gala Norway
Centre for downhill and cross-country skiing an hour's drive north of Lillehammer.
930m
7
✉ *Inntravel, Scandinavian Travel Service*

Gallio Italy
One of several low resorts near Vicenza and Trento. Weekend day trippers' place.
1100m; slopes 1100–1550m
11 50km

Galtür 106
✉ Charming traditional village near Ischgl.
✉ *Made to Measure, Ski Choice*

Gambarie d'Aspromonte Italy
Italy's second most southerly ski area (after Mt Etna). On toe of Italian 'boot' near Reggio di Calabria.
1310m; slopes 1310–1650m
3

Gantschier Austria
No slopes of its own but well placed for visiting all the Montafon areas.
700m

Gargellen 130
✉ *Interhome, Made to Measure*

Garmisch-Partenkirchen
Germany
Superb main area of wooded runs when the unreliable snowcover allows; great glacier views when it doesn't.
700m; slopes 700–2830m
38 118km
✉ *Moswin Tours*

Gaschurn 130

Geilo 584
✉ *Crystal, Independent Ski Links, Inntravel, Neilson, Thomson, Waymark Holidays*

Gérardmer France
Nearest slopes to Channel, near Strasbourg. Sizeable resort with plenty of amenities. Night skiing too.
660m; slopes 750–1150m
20
✉ *Fairhand Holidays, Lagrange Holidays*

Gerlitzen Alpe Austria
Modern gondola ride above Villach. Great views. Worthwhile excursion from Badkleinkirchheim.
500m; slopes 1003–1911m
14 20km

Gerlos Austria
One of Austria's inexpensive but fairly snowsure resorts, now linked to Zell im Zillertal and Königsleiten to form a fair-sized intermediate area.
1250m; slopes 1250–2300m
23 70km
✉ *Interhome*

Les Gets 269
Sprawling chalet resort on low pass near Morzine.
✉ *Alp Active, Avant-ski, Chalets 'Unlimited', Fairhand Holidays, Fantiski, Iglu.com, Lagrange Holidays, Made to Measure, Motours, Ski Activity, Ski Famille, Ski Hillwood, Ski Independence, Ski Total, Tops Ski Chalets and Club Hotels*

La Giettaz France
Small resort between La Clusaz and Megève with no particular attractions.

Gitschtal/Weissbriach Austria
One of many little areas near Hermagor in eastern Austria close to Italian border.
690m; slopes 690–1400m
3 5km

Glaris Switzerland
Hamlet base station for the uncrowded Rinerhorn section of the Davos slopes.
1455m; slopes 1455–2490m
5 30km

Glencoe 589

Glenshee 589

Going 95
Small local area near Ellmau.

Goldegg Austria
Year-round resort famous for lakeside castle; with Wagrain (Salzburg Sportwelt) and Grossarl (Gastein) nearby.
825m; slopes 825–1250m
5 12km

Gore Mountain USA
In New York State, near Lake Placid, sufficiently far north to avoid worst weekend crowds. Intermediate terrain.
455m; slopes 455–1095m
9 290 acres

Göriach Austria
Hamlet connecting into one of longest, most snowsure cross-country networks in Europe.
1250m

Gortipohl Austria
Traditional village in pretty Montafontal.
920m; slopes 900–2370m
26 100km

Gosau Austria
Straggling village with plenty of pretty, if low, pistes. Snowsure Obertauern and Schladming are within reach.
765m; slopes 765–1800m
37 65km

Göstling Austria
One of Austria's easternmost resorts, between Salzburg and Vienna. A traditional village in wooded setting.
530m; slopes 530–1800m
12 20km

Götzens Austria
Valley village base for Axamer Lizum area.
870m

Gourette France
Most snowsure resort in the French Pyrenees. Very popular with local families, best avoided at weekends.
1400m; slopes 1400–2400m
26
✉ *Lagrange Holidays*

Grächen Switzerland
Uncommercialised, quiet little family village with a scenic but small intermediate area. Tricky access road.
1615m; slopes 1615–2890m
13 50km
✉ *Interhome*

Le Grand-Bornand 216
✉ *Fairhand Holidays, Lagrange Holidays, Motours*

Grand Targhee 520
Powder skiing paradise an hour from Jackson Hole.
✉ *Lotus Supertravel, Ski The American Dream, Skisar US*

Grangesises Italy
Small satellite of Sestriere, with lifts to the main slopes.

Grau Roig 570
Expanding base giving access to Pas de la Casa's runs.
✉ *Inghams, Panorama*

La Grave 244
✉ *Lagrange Holidays, Ski Arrangements, Ski Club of GB, Ski Valkyrie, Ski Weekend*

Gray Rocks Canada
Very popular family resort, 130km north of Montreal.
250m; slopes 250–440m
4 200 acres

Great Divide USA
Area near Helena, Montana, best for experts. Mostly bowls, and near-extreme Rawhide Gulch.
1765m; slopes 1765–2195m
4 720 acres

Gresse-en-Vercors France
Resort south of Grenoble. Sheltered slopes worth noting for bad-weather days.
1250m; slopes 1250–1800m
16
✉ *Interhome, Lagrange Holidays*

Gressoney-la-Trinité 351
Village in Monterosa Ski area.
✉ *Crystal, Motours*

Gressoney-St-Jean 351
Village in Monterosa Ski area.

Grimentz Switzerland
Captivating rustic village with varied pistes. Modern lifts; near Valais town of Sierre.
1570m; slopes 1570–3000m
12 50km

Grindelwald 401
✉ *Crystal, Elegant Resorts, Iglu.com, Independent Ski Links, Inghams, Interhome, Kuoni, Made to Measure, Plus Travel, Powder Byrne, Ski Club of GB, SkiGower, Swiss Travel Service, Thomson, White Roc*

Grossarl Austria
Secluded village over the mountain from the Gastein valley. Shares sizeable area with Dorfgastein.
920m; slopes 920–2035m
24 80km

Grosskirchheim Austria
Very limited neighbour of Heiligenblut.
1025m; slopes 1025–1400m
2 3km

Grouse Mountain Canada
Vancouver area with largest lift capacity. Mostly easy slopes.
880m; slopes 880–1245m
11 120 acres

Grünau Austria
Attractive, riverside village in lake-filled part of eastern Austria. Varied area, but low.
525m; slopes 600–1600m
14 40km

Gryon 430
Village below Villars, with which it shares a ski area.

Gstaad 405
✉ *Crystal, Elegant Resorts, Interhome, Made to Measure, Ski Independence, SkiGower, White Roc*

Gunstock USA
New Hampshire resort close to Boston, popular with families. Easy slopes.
275m; slopes 275–700m
7 220 acres

Guthega 592

Hallanrinteet Finland
Twin ski areas 20 minutes apart. Good lake views. Short intermediate runs.
14

Happo One Japan
Pseudo-European resort near Nagano.One of Japan's more challenging areas.
750m; slopes 750–1830m
34

Harrachov Czech Republic
Closest resort to Prague, with enough terrain to justify a day trip. No nursery area.
685m; slopes 650–1020m
4 8km

Hasliberg Switzerland
Four rustic hamlets on sunny plateau overlooking Meiringen and Lake Brienz. Varied intermediate area.
1055m; slopes 600–2435m
16 60km

Haus in Ennstal 158
Village next to Schladming.

Heavenly 450
✉ *American Ski Classics, Big Country Ski, Crystal, Independent Ski Links, Inghams, Ski Activity, Ski Independence, Ski Line, Ski Success, Ski The American Dream, Skisar US, Skiworld, Solo's, Thomson, United Vacations, Virgin Ski*

Hebalm Austria
One of many small areas in Austria's easternmost ski region near Slovenian border. No major resorts in vicinity.
1350m; slopes 1350–1400m
6 11km

Heiligenblut Austria
Picturesque village with mostly high terrain. Its remote position west of Bad Gastein ensures crowds don't invade.
1300m; slopes 1300–2900m
14 55km

Hemlock Resort Canada
Area E of Vancouver with amazing snowfall (600 inches). Mostly intermediate terrain. Lodging at base area.
1000m; slopes 1000–1375m
4 350 acres

Hemsedal 586
✉ *Crystal, Independent Ski Links, Neilson*

Heremence Switzerland
Quiet village in unspoilt attractive setting south of Sion. Verbier slopes accessed at Les Masses.
1250m; slopes 1300–3330m
100 400km

Hermagor Austria
Carinthian village below the Sonnenalpe ski area.
600m; slopes 1210–2005m
23 101km

Himos Finland
Varied Alpine skiing, half-pipes and snowboard park, cross-country.
80m; slopes 80–220m
10

Hintersee Austria
Close to Salzburg. Several long top-to-bottom pistes and lifts, so size of area greatly reduced if snowline high.
745m; slopes 750–1470m
9 40km

Hinterstoder Austria
Quiet, unspoilt traditional village, 80km east of Salzburg, with a good snow record for its height.
600m; slopes 600–1860m
15 35km

Hintertux 100
✉ *Alpine Tours, Lagrange Holidays*

Hippach Austria
Hamlet near a queue-free lift into Mayrhofen's main area.
600m; slopes 630–1830m
7 20km

Hochgurgl 133
Quiet hotel-village above Obergurgl.
✉ *Inghams, Thomson*

Hochpillberg Austria
Peaceful hamlet with fabulous views towards Innsbruck. Varied terrain.
1330m
5 10km

Hochsölden 163
Quieter satellite above lively, sprawling Sölden.

Hochybrig Switzerland
Purpose-built complex only 64km south of Zurich, with facilities for families.
1050m; slopes 1050–2200m
16 50km

Hohuanshan Taiwan
Limited ski area with short season in wild inaccessible Miitaku mountains.
3275m

Hollersbach Austria
Pass Thurn hamlet near Mittersill. Uncrowded base from which to visit Kitzbühel.
805m; slopes 805–1000m
2 5km

Homewood USA
Area with unsurpassed Lake Tahoe views, near Tahoe City. Mostly sheltered slopes so a good choice in bad weather.
1895m; slopes 1895–2400m
10 1260 acres

Hoodoo Ski Bowl USA
East of Eugene. Typical Oregon area – sizeable but short runs.
1420m; slopes 1420–1740m
4 800 acres

Hopfgarten 164
Chalet village with link into Ski Welt shared with Söll.
✉ *Contiki, First Choice Ski*

Horseshoe Resort Canada
Toronto region resort with high-capacity lift system, 100% snowmaking.
310m; slopes 310–405m
7 60 acres

Hospental 377
Village with slopes included on the Andermatt lift pass.

Les Houches 203
Spread-out village at entrance to the Chamonix valley.
✉ *Avant-ski, Barrelli Ski, Bigfoot, Chalets 'Unlimited', Motours, Ski Leisure Direction*

Hovden Norway
Luxury lakeside hotel in wilderness midway between Oslo and Bergen. Cross-country centre.
760m; slopes 760–1205m
2

Huez 185
Charming old hamlet on the road up to Alpe-d'Huez.

Hunter Mountain USA
New Yorkers' favourite area so very crowded at weekends.
485m; slopes 485–975m
11 230 acres

Hüttschlag Austria
Hamlet in dead-end valley with lifts into Gastein area at neighbouring Grossarl.
1020m; slopes 840–1215m
2 5km

Hyundai Sungwoo Korea
Massive high-rise monstrosity, 2 hours from Seoul.
8

Idre Sweden
Collective name for four areas whose lifts and buses are on one pass. Snowsure but only 305m vertical.
710m; slopes 710–890m
30 28km

Igls 103
✉ *Inghams, Lagrange Holidays, Made to Measure*

Iizuna Japan
Tiny area one hour from Nagano, 4 hours from Tokyo.
5

Incline Village 455
Large village on northern edge of Lake Tahoe.

Indianhead USA
South Lake Superior area with most snowfall in region. Intermediate cruising terrain too. Winds are a problem.
395m; slopes 395–585m
9 190 acres

Inneralpbach 87
Small satellite 3km up the valley from Alpbach.

Innerarosa 378
The prettiest part of Arosa.

Innsbruck 103
✉ *Made to Measure*

Interlaken 431
Large town at entrance to the valleys leading to Wengen, Grindelwald and Mürren.
✉ *Kuoni, Made to Measure, SkiGower, Swiss Travel Service*

Ischgl 106
✉ *Fairhand Holidays, Inghams, Made to Measure, Momentum Ski, Ski Solutions*

Ishiuchi Maruyama-Yuzawa Kogen Japan
Sizeable resorts that share lift pass offering largest area in central Honshu region.
255m; slopes 255–920m
36

Isola 2000 245
✉ *Avant-ski, Erna Low, Fairhand Holidays, Lagrange Holidays, Made to Measure, Pavilion Tours, Ski Arrangements*

Isoyöte Finland
Southernmost downhill skiing in Finland, mostly easy skiing. Main hotel at mountain-top.
430m; slopes 240–430m
11 *21km*

Itter 164
Next to Söll; skiing linked to the whole of the Ski Welt.
✉ *Neilson, Panorama*

Jackson USA
Classic New England village, and major cross-country centre.

Jackson Hole 520
✉ *American Ski Classics, Big Country Ski, Crystal, Elegant Resorts, Independent Ski Links, Inghams, Lotus Supertravel, Made to Measure, Momentum Ski, Neilson, Scott Dunn Ski, Ski Activity, Ski Connections, Ski Independence, Ski Line, Ski Safari, Ski Success, Ski The American Dream, Skisar US, Skiworld, United Vacations*

Jasper 544
✉ *All Canada Ski, Crystal, Frontier Ski, Independent Ski Links, Inghams, Made to Measure, Neilson, Ski Activity, Ski Connections, Ski Independence, Ski Safari, Ski The American Dream, Ski Vacation Canada, Skisar US, Thomson*

Jay Peak 529

Jochberg 111
Straggling village, 8km from Kitzbühel.

La Joue-du-Loup France
Purpose-built little family resort. Shares intermediate area with Superdévoluy.
1500m; slopes 1500–2510m
31 *100km*
✉ *Lagrange Holidays, Motours*

Jouvenceaux 353
Quieter base from which to ski Sauze d'Oulx's terrain.

Jukkasjärvi Sweden
Centuries-old resort with unique ice hotel – rebuilt every December out of 3,000 tons of snow and ice.

June Mountain USA
Well liked by day-visitors from nearby Mammoth. Quiet slopes and superb school.
2300m; slopes 2300–3090m
8 *500 acres*

Juns 100
Spread out village between Lanersbach and Hintertux.
✉ *Alpine Tours*

Kals am Grossglockner Austria
Village in remote valley north of Lienz.
1325m; slopes 1325–2305m
7 *15km*

Kaltenbach Austria
Village with one of the larger, quieter Zillertal areas.
560m; slopes 560–2300m
16 *60km*

Kananaskis Canada
Small, mainly intermediate area near Calgary, nicely set in woods.
slopes 1525–2465m
12 *605 acres*
✉ *All Canada Ski, Frontier Ski, Made to Measure*

Kandersteg Switzerland
Good cross-country base amid beautiful scenery near Interlaken.
1175m; slopes 1175–2000m
7 *13km*
✉ *Headwater Holidays, Inntravel, Kuoni, Made to Measure, Waymark Holidays*

Kanin 582

Kaprun 173
Classic Austrian village near Zell am See.
✉ *Crystal, Made to Measure, Neilson, Ski Club of GB*

Les Karellis France
Resort with slopes that offer more scenic, challenging and snowsure pistes than better-known Valloire, nearby.
1600m; slopes 1600–2550m
19 *40km*

Kastelruth Italy
Charming picture-book village in the south Tirolean Italian Dolomites with good cross-country trails. Near the Sella Ronda circuit.
✉ *Inntravel*

Kasurila Finland
Siilinjarvi area ski centre popular with boarders.
5

Katschberg Austria
Lovely hamlet above St Michael in southern Austria.
1140m; slopes 1650–2220m
15 *80km*
✉ *Alpine Tours, Crystal*

Keystone 479
✉ *Big Country Ski, Crystal, Handmade Holidays, Made to Measure, Ski Club of GB, Ski Connections, Ski Independence, Ski The American Dream, Ski Total, Skisar US, United Vacations*

Kicking Horse Mountain 544

Killington 533
✉ *Big Country Ski, Chalets 'Unlimited', Crystal, Equity Total Ski, First Choice Ski, Iglu.com, Independent Ski Links, Inghams, Lotus Supertravel, Made to Measure, Neilson, Ski Activity, Ski Arrangements, Ski Connections, Ski Independence, Ski Line, Ski Safari, Ski Success, Ski The American Dream, Skisar US, Thomson, United Vacations, Virgin Ski*

Kimberley 544
✉ *Frontier Ski, Inghams, Ski Safari, Skisar US*

Kirchberg 111
Lively little town close to Kitzbühel.
✉ *First Choice Ski, Interhome, Lagrange Holidays, Solo's, Top Deck*

Kirchdorf 154
Attractive village near St Johann in Tirol.
✉ *Crystal, Snowcoach*

Kirkwood 455

Kitzbühel 111
✉ *Airtours, Avant-ski, Bladon Lines, Chalets 'Unlimited', Crystal, Elegant Resorts, First Choice Ski, Iglu.com, Independent Ski Links, Inghams, Interhome, Lagrange Holidays, Made to Measure, Neilson, Panorama, Ski Arrangements, Ski Club of GB, Ski Solutions, Solo's, Thomson*

Kleinarl Austria
Secluded traditional village up a side valley from Wagrain, with lifts into the Salzburger Sportwelt area.
1015m; slopes 800–1980m
11 *60km*

Klippitztorl Austria
One of many little areas in Austria's easternmost ski region near Slovenian border. Typically, all lifts are drags.
1460m; slopes 1460–1820m
6 *20km*

Klosters 389
Affluent chalet village that shares ski area with Davos.
✉ *Elegant Resorts, Inghams, Kuoni, Made to Measure, Momentum Ski, Plus Travel, Powder Byrne, Ski Club of GB, Ski Solutions, Ski with Julia, SkiGower, The Ski Company Ltd, White Roc*

Kobla 582

Kolsass-Weer Austria
Dated resort; low, limited, inconvenient slopes; now loses out to cheaper Andorra.
555m; slopes 555–1010m
3 *14km*

Königsleiten Austria
Quiet, high resort sharing fairly snowsure area with Gerlos, now also linked to Zell im Zillertal to form a fair-sized intermediate area.
1600m; slopes 1245–2300m
25 *70km*

Kopaonik Serbia
Modern, sympathetically designed family resort in a pretty setting.
1770m; slopes 1110–2015m
21 *57km*

Koralpe Austria
Largest and steepest of many gentle little areas in Austria's easternmost ski region near Slovenian border.
1550m; slopes 1550–2050m
10 *25km*

Korea Condo Korea
Odd resort – a single condo complex built some away from the 3 slopes.
2

Kössen Austria
Near St Johann in Tirol; very low, scattered, limited slopes.
600m; slopes 600–1700m
11 *25km*

Kötschach-Mauthen Austria
One of many little areas near Hermagor in eastern Austria close to Italian border.
710m; slopes 710–1300m
5 *6km*

Kranjska Gora 582
✉ *Alpine Tours, Balkan Holidays, Crystal, Solo's, Thomson*

Krimml Austria
Sunny area high enough to usually have good snow. Shares regional pass with Wildkogel resorts.
1075m; slopes 1640–2040m
8 *33km*

Krispl-Gaissau Austria
Close to Salzburg. Several long top-to-bottom lifts, so area greatly reduced if snowline high. Easy slopes.
925m; slopes 750–1570m
11 *40km*

Kühtai Austria
Huddle of good hotels with a small, snowsure area suited to intermediates.
2020m; slopes 2010–2520m
11 *40km*
✉ *Inghams*

Kurumayama Kogen Japan
Remote resort, 6 hours from Osaka. Probably the least crowded slopes in Japan.
11

Kusatsu Onsen Japan
Spa village with attractive hot springs, 3 hours from Tokyo.
15

Laax **396**
Old farming community linked to Flims.
⊠ *Made to Measure*

Ladis Austria
Smaller alternative to Serfaus and Fiss, with lifts that connect into the same area.
1200m; slopes 1200–2540m
4 *18km*
⊠ *Alpine Tours*

Le Laisinant **303**
Tiny hamlet a bus-ride down the valley from Val-d'Isère.

Lake Tahoe **455**
⊠ *Equity Total Ski, Independent Ski Links, Ski Activity, Ski Connections, Ski Independence, Ski Safari, Skisar US, Solo's, Thomson, United Vacations, Virgin Ski*

Lake Louise **547**
⊠ *Airtours, All Canada Ski, Crystal, Elegant Resorts, First Choice Ski, Frontier Ski, Independent Ski Links, Inghams, Kuoni, Lotus Supertravel, Made to Measure, Neilson, Ski Activity, Ski Club of GB, Ski Connections, Ski Equipe, Ski Independence, Ski Line, Ski The American Dream, Ski Vacation Canada, Skisar US, Solo's, Thomson, United Vacations*

Lake Placid USA
Attractive lakeside resort 15km from Whiteface in New York. Good snowmaking.
975m; slopes 975–1340m
9 *150 acres*

Lanersbach **100**
Attractive village with Hintertux glacier nearby.

Lans-en-Vercors France
Neighbour of Villard-de-Lans, near Grenoble. Highest slopes in region; few snowmakers.
1020m; slopes 1020–1805m
16

Lauterbrunnen **406**
Valley town in the Jungfrau, with a funicular up to Mürren.
⊠ *Ski Miquel, Top Deck*

Le Lavancher **203**
Quiet village between Chamonix and Argentière.

Lavarone Italy
One of several areas east of Trento, for weekend day-trip.
1195m; slopes 1075–1555m
13 *12km*

Leadville USA
Old mining town full of historic buildings. Own easy area (Ski Cooper) plus snowcat operation.
slopes 3200–3555m
4 *385 acres*

Lech **117**
⊠ *Avant-ski, Chalets 'Unlimited', Elegant Resorts, Fairhand Holidays, FlexiSki, Iglu.com, Independent Ski Links, Inghams, Made to Measure, Momentum Ski, Simply Ski, Ski Choice, Ski Solutions, Ski Total, Ski Yogi, White Roc*

The Lecht **589**

Lélex France
Family resort with pretty wooded slopes between Dijon and Geneva.
900m; slopes 900–1680m
29 *50km*
⊠ *Lagrange Holidays*

Las Leñas Argentina
Up-market, Euro-style modern resort, 3 hours south of Mendoza, with varied, beautiful terrain.
2240m; slopes 2240–3340m
12 *65km*
⊠ *Scott Dunn Latin America*

Lenk Switzerland
Traditional village that shares a sizeable area of easy, pretty terrain with Adelboden.
1070m; slopes 1070–2100m
21
⊠ *Made to Measure, Swiss Travel Service*

Lenzerheide Switzerland
Spacious village, separated by a lake from Valbella; shares a large intermediate area.
1500m; slopes 1230–2865m
35 *155km*
⊠ *Interhome, Made to Measure, Plus Travel, Ski Choice*

Leogang **139**
Quiet, spread-out village with link to Saalbach-Hinterglemm.
⊠ *Equity Total Ski*

Lermoos Austria
Focal resort of the Zugspitz area, a delightful base for beginners and for cross-country enthusiasts.
1005m; slopes 1005–2250m
10 *29km*

Lessach Austria
Hamlet with trail connecting into one of the longest, most snowsure cross-country networks in Europe.
1210m

Leukerbad Switzerland
Major spa resort with spectacular scenery and high runs including a World Cup downhill course.
1410m; slopes 1410–2700m
17 *60km*

Leutasch Austria
Traditional cross-country village with limited slopes but a pleasant day trip from nearby Seefeld or Innsbruck.
1130m; slopes 1130–1605m
4 *9km*
⊠ *Headwater Holidays, Inntravel*

Levi Finland
Finland's most Alpine-like resort. Easy to get to – Kittila airport is 10 minutes away.
205m; slopes 205–530m
15
⊠ *Inghams*

Leysin Switzerland
Large resort near Aigle, with a good range of facilities, but low, sunny terrain.
1400m; slopes 1400–2300m
19 *60km*
⊠ *Club Med, Crystal, Plus Travel, SkiGower*

Lienz Austria
Pleasant town-cum-resort in pretty surroundings.
675m; slopes 730–2290m
12 *55km*

Lillehammer **584**
⊠ *Independent Ski Links, Neilson*

Limone Italy
Pleasant old railway town not far from Turin, with a pretty area (far from snowsure).
1010m; slopes 1030–2050m
29 *80km*

Lincoln **529**
New Hampshire town from which to visit Loon Mountain.
⊠ *Crystal, Neilson, Virgin Ski*

Lindvallen-Hogfjallet Sweden
Largest area in Scandinavia. Start of Vasalopp, world's largest cross-country race.
800m; slopes 800–1000m
72 *85km*

Livigno **345**
⊠ *Airtours, Chalets 'Unlimited', Crystal, First Choice Ski, Iglu.com, Independent Ski Links, Inghams, Neilson, Panorama, Ski Club of GB, Thomson*

Lizzola Italy
Small base development in remote spot north of Bergamo.
1250m; slopes 1250–2070m
9 *30km*

Llaima Chile
Exotic ski touring area around and below a mildly active volcano; trails through trees.
1500m

Loch Lomond Canada
On shores of Lake Superior. Challenging slopes – steep, narrow, bumpy.
215m; slopes 215–440m
3 *90 acres*

Lofer Austria
Traditional village close to Salzburg with own area, and Waidring's Steinplatte nearby.
640m; slopes 640–1745m
14 *46km*

Longchamp **312**
Purpose-built resort that shares Valmorel's ski area.

Loon Mountain **529**
⊠ *Crystal, Equity Total Ski, Skisar US, Virgin Ski*

Lost Trail USA
Remote Montana area, open only Thursday to Sunday and holidays. Mostly intermediate.
2005m; slopes 2005–2370m
4 *600 acres*

Loveland USA
High, varied slopes, a day trip from Keystone and renowned for snow. Long season.
3220m; slopes 3220–3730m
10 *836 acres*

Luchon France
Sizeable village with plenty of amenities and train station, with gondola to its ski area.
630m; slopes 1440–2260m
16 *35km*
⊠ *Lagrange Holidays*

Lurisia Italy
Sizeable spa resort. Good base for visits to surrounding little ski areas and Nice.
750m; slopes 850–1800m
30km

Luz-Ardiden France
Spa village below its ski area. Cauterets and Barèges nearby. Near Carcassone.
710m; slopes 1730–2450m
19

Macugnaga Italy
Pretty two-part village set amid stunning scenery. Novice and intermediate slopes.
1330–1390m; slopes 1330–2970m
12 *40km*
⊠ *Interhome, Neilson, Thomson*

Mad River Glen 529

Madesimo 349
⊠ *Inghams*

Madonna di Campiglio 350
⊠ *Alpine Tours, Crystal, Equity Total Ski, Inghams, Interhome, Ski Club of GB, Sloping Off, Solo's, Thomson*

La Magdelaine Italy
Neighbour of Cervinia, good on bad weather days.
1645m; slopes 1645–1870m
4 4km

Maishofen Austria
Cheap(er) place to stay when visiting equidistant Saalbach and Zell am See.
765m

Malbun Liechtenstein
Quaint, civilised, user-friendly little family resort, 16km from the capital, Vaduz. Limited slopes, with short easy runs.
1600m; slopes 1595–2100m
6 16km

Malcesine Italy
Large summer resort on Lake Garda with fair area.
1430m; slopes 1430–1830m
8 12km

Malga Ciapela Italy
Resort at the foot of the Marmolada glacier massif, with a link into the Sella Ronda, and Cortina nearby.
1445m; slopes 1445–3270m
8 18km

Mallnitz Austria
Village in a pretty valley close to Slovenia, with varied areas giving a mix of wooded and open runs and good off-piste.
1200m; slopes 1300–2650m
11 31km

Mammoth Mountain 457
⊠ *Big Country Ski, Crystal, Independent Ski Links, Ski Activity, Ski Independence, Ski Line, Ski Safari, Ski The American Dream, Skisar US, United Vacations, Virgin Ski*

Manigod France
Valley village over the Col de la Croix-Fry from La Clusaz.

Marble Mountain Canada
Area near Newfoundland town Corner Brook and Gros Morne National Park. One of highest snowfall records in the east.
85m; slopes 85–570m
5 126 acres
⊠ *Frontier Ski*

Maria Alm Austria
Charming unspoilt village east of Zell am See with a varied area over five mountains.
800m; slopes 800–2000m
36 150km

Mariapfarr Austria
Village at centre of one of longest, most snow-reliable cross-country networks in Europe. St Michael Alpine area on doorstep.
1120m
7 30km

Mariazell Austria
Traditional Styria village with an impressive basilica, that has a real antiquated feel to it. Limited slopes.
870m; slopes 870–1265m
5 11km

Maribor 582

Marilleva 350
Small resort, with links to Madonna di Campiglio.
⊠ *Sloping Off*

Masella 577
⊠ *Pavilion Tours*

La Massana 570
Lively base for several areas, notably Pal and Arinsal.
⊠ *Inghams*

Le Massif 567
⊠ *Ski Safari*

Matrei in Osttirol Austria
Large market village south of Felbertauern tunnel. Mostly high slopes.
1000m; slopes 1000–2400m
6 29km

Mauterndorf Austria
Village near Obertauern with tremendous snow record.
1120m; slopes 1075–2360m
10 25km
⊠ *Sloping Off*

Maverick Mountain USA
Plenty of terrain accessed by few lifts. Cowboy Winter Games venue – rodeo one day, ski races the next.
2155m; slopes 2155–2800m
2 500 acres

Mayens de Riddes Switzerland
Tiny hamlet next to La Tzoumaz with links up to Savoleyres and the Verbier network.
slopes 1400–3330m
100 410km
⊠ *Interhome*

Mayens-de-Sion Switzerland
Hamlet off road up to Les Collons (part of Verbier area).
1180m; slopes 1300–3330m
100 400km

Mayrhofen 125
⊠ *Airtours, Crystal, Equity Total Ski, First Choice Ski, Independent Ski Links, Inghams, Made to Measure, Neilson, Ski Arrangements, Ski Club of GB, Snowcoach, Thomson*

Méaudre France
Small resort near Grenoble with good snowmaking to make up for low altitude.
1000m; slopes 1000–1600m
10

Megève 248
⊠ *Avant-ski, Chalets 'Unlimited', Classic Ski Limited, Elegant Resorts, Erna Low, FMTA Skiing, Fairhand Holidays, Iglu.com, Interhome, Lagrange Holidays, Made to Measure, Momentum Ski, Motours, Powder Byrne, Ski Arrangements, Ski Barrett-Boyce, Ski Independence, Ski Solutions, Ski Weekend, SkiAway Holidays, Stanford Skiing, Thomson, White Roc*

Meiringen Switzerland
Conan Doyle's death place for Sherlock Holmes. Varied terrain, a good outing from the nearby Jungfrau resorts.
600m; slopes 600–2435m
16 60km
⊠ *Made to Measure*

Les Menuires 254
⊠ *Club Med, Crystal, Erna Low, Fairhand Holidays, First Choice Ski, Iglu.com, Independent Ski Links, Interhome, Lagrange Holidays, Made to Measure, Motours, Ski Arrangements, Ski Independence, Ski Leisure Direction, Ski Olympic, Ski Supreme, SkiAway Holidays, SkiAway Holidays*

Merano Italy
Purpose-built base on high plateau near Bolzano.
2000m; slopes 2000–2240m
18 28km

Méribel 257
⊠ *Absolute Ski, Airtours, Alpine Action, Avant-ski, Bien Ski, Bien Ski, Bladon Lines, Bonne Neige Ski Holidays, Chalet World, Chalets 'Unlimited', Club Med, Cooltip Mountain Holidays, Crystal, Descent International, Erna Low, Eurotunnel Motoring Holidays, Fairhand Holidays, First Choice Ski, Iglu.com, Independent Ski Links, Inghams, Interhome, Lagrange Holidays, Les Deux Chalets, Lotus Supertravel, Made to Measure, Mark Warner, MasterSki, Meriski, Momentum Ski, Motours, Neilson, Panorama, Scott Dunn Ski, Silver Ski, Simply Ski, Ski Activity, Ski Arrangements, Ski Blanc, Ski Bon, Ski Choice, Ski Club of GB, Ski Cuisine, Ski France, Ski Independence, Ski Leisure Direction, Ski Line, Ski Olympic, Ski Solutions, Ski Total, Ski Valkyrie, SkiAway Holidays, Skiworld, Snowcoach, Snowline, Solo's, The Ski Company, The Ski Company Ltd, Thomson, Tops Ski Chalets and Club Hotels, Weekends in Val d'Isère, White Roc*

Métabief-Mont-d'Or France
Twin villages in Jura region. Worthwhile stopover for self-drivers en route to major areas beyond Geneva.
900m; slopes 900–1460m
33

Methven 594

Mijoux France
Pretty wooded slopes between Dijon and Geneva. Shares lift pass with neighbour Lélex.
1000m; slopes 900–1680m
29 50km

Mission Ridge USA
Area in dry region that gets higher-quality but less snow than other Seattle resorts. Good intermediate slopes.
1390m; slopes 1390–2065m
4 300 acres

Misurina Italy
Tiny village near Cortina. Cheap alternative base.
1755m; slopes 1755–1900m
4 13km

Mittersill Austria
Valley-junction village near Pass Thurn. Quieter base from which to visit Kitzbühel.
790m; slopes 1265–1895m
15 25km

Moena Italy
Large village between Cavalese and Sella Ronda resorts, ideal for touring.
1180m; slopes 1180–2515m
24 35km
⊠ *Thomson, Waymark Holidays*

La Molina 577
⊠ *Pavilion Tours*

Molltall Glacier Austria
Little-known high slopes other side of Tauern tunnel from Bad Gastein.
slopes 2570–3122m
4 11km

Monarch USA
Uncrowded area near Crested Butte. Great powder. Good for all except expert.
3290m; slopes 3290–3645m
5 670 acres

Monesi Italy
Southernmost of resorts south of Turin, surprisingly close to Monaco and Nice.
1310m; slopes 1310–2180m
🚡 *5* ⛷ *38km*

Le Monêtier **291**
Quiet little village with access to Serre-Chevalier's slopes.

La Mongie **322**
⊠ *Erna Low, Lagrange Holidays, SkiAway Holidays*

Montafon **130**

Montalbert **275**
Traditional village with access to the La Plagne network.
⊠ *Crystal, Interhome, Ski Amis, Ski Arrangements*

Mt Blanc **567**

Montchavin **275**
Attractive village on fringe of La Plagne ski area.
⊠ *Crystal, Made to Measure, Ski Esprit*

Mont-de-Lans **233**
Low village on the way up to Les Deux-Alpes.

Le Mont-Dore France
Largest resort in stunningly beautiful volcanic Auvergne region near Clermont-Ferrand. Attractive traditional village.
1050m; slopes 1350–1850m
🚡 *20* ⛷ *80km*
⊠ *Lagrange Holidays*

Monte Bondone Italy
Essentially a Trento weekenders' area (some of the lifts are closed weekdays).
slopes 1300–2100m
🚡 *8* ⛷ *13km*
⊠ *Solo's*

Monte Campione Italy
Tiny purpose-built resort. Snowmaking helps offset low altitude. Area spread thinly over four mountainsides.
1100m; slopes 1200–2010m
🚡 *18* ⛷ *100km*
⊠ *Equity Total Ski*

Monte Livata Italy
Closest resort to Rome, with plenty of accommodation for weekenders.
1430m; slopes 1430–1750m
🚡 *8* ⛷ *8km*

Monte Piselli Italy
Tiny area with highest slopes of the many little resorts east of Rome.
2100m; slopes 2100–2690m
🚡 *3* ⛷ *5km*

Monte Pora Italy
Tiny resort near Lake d'Iseo and Bergamo. Several other little areas nearby.
1350m; slopes 1350–1880m
🚡 *8* ⛷ *20km*

Montezuma USA
One of the best cross-country ski areas in Colorado. No resort as such, but just up the road from Keystone.

Mont Gabriel Canada
Montreal area with runs on 4 sides of mountain, though 2 south-facing sides rarely open. 2 short but renowned double-black-diamond runs.
🚡 *9*
⊠ *Ski Connections*

Montgenèvre **265**
⊠ *Airtours, Crystal, Equity Total Ski, Erna Low, Fairhand Holidays, First Choice Ski, Iglu.com, Independent Ski Links, Lagrange Holidays, Made to Measure, Neilson, Ski Etoile, Thomson*

Mont Glen Canada
Least crowded of areas close to Montreal.
680m; slopes 680–1035m
🚡 *4* ⛷ *110 acres*

Mont Grand Fonds Canada
Small area sufficiently far from Québec not to get overrun at weekends.
400m; slopes 400–735m
🚡 *4*

Mont Habitant Canada
Very limited area (215m vertical) but with nicest base lodge of any resort in Montreal region.
🚡 *3*

Mont Olympia Canada
Small, 2-mountain area near Montreal, one mostly novice terrain, the other best suited to experts.
🚡 *6*

Mont Orford Canada
Cold, windswept lone peak (there's no resort), worth a trip from nearby Montreal on a fine day.
slopes 305–855m
🚡 *8* ⛷ *180 acres*

Mont Ste Anne **567**
⊠ *All Canada Ski, Frontier Ski, Inghams, Ski Connections, Ski Safari, Ski Vacation Canada, Skisar US*

Mont St Sauveur **567**

Mont Sutton Canada
Varied area with perhaps the best glade skiing in eastern Canada, including some for novices.
🚡 *9* ⛷ *175 acres*

Morgins **379**
Chalet resort indirectly linked to Champéry.
⊠ *Ski Morgins Holidays*

Morillon **238**
Valley village linked to the Flaine network.
⊠ *Fairhand Holidays, Lagrange Holidays, Motours*

Morin Heights Canada
One of the best areas in the Montreal region. 100% snowmaking. Attractive base lodge.
🚡 *6*

Morzine **269**
⊠ *Airtours, Avant-ski, Chalet Snowboard, Chalets 'Unlimited', Challenge Activ, Crystal, Fairhand Holidays, First Choice Ski, Iglu.com, Independent Ski Links, Inghams, Lagrange Holidays, Made to Measure, Momentum Ski, Motours, Mountain Highs, Ski Arrangements, Ski Chamois, Ski Choice, Ski Esprit, Ski France, Ski Valkyrie, Ski Weekend, Snowline, Solo's, The Chalet Company, Thomson, Trail Alpine, Weekends in Val d'Isère, White Roc*

Les Mosses Switzerland
Uninteresting resort and area, best for a day trip.
1500m; slopes 1500–2200m
🚡 *13* ⛷ *25km*
⊠ *APT Holidays Ltd*

Mottaret **257**
Purpose-built but attractive component of Méribel.
⊠ *First Choice Ski, Ski Club of GB, Ski Leisure Direction, Skiworld, Thomson*

Mottarone Italy
Closest slopes to Lake Maggiore. No village – just a base area.
1200m; slopes 1200–1490m
⛷ *25km*

Mt Abram USA
Small, pretty, tree-lined area renowned for its immaculately groomed easy runs.
295m; slopes 295–610m
🚡 *5* ⛷ *170 acres*

Mountain High USA
Best snowfall record and highest lift capacity in Los Angeles vicinity. Mostly intermediate cruising.
2010m; slopes 2010–2500m
🚡 *10* ⛷ *220 acres*

Mt Arrowsmith Canada
On Vancouver Island, a short drive from city ferry.
1280m; slopes 1280–1600m
🚡 *3*

Mt Ashland USA
Arty town in Oregon renowned for Shakespeare Glaciated bowl rimmed with steeps. Best for experts.
1935m; slopes 1935–2285m
🚡 *4* ⛷ *200 acres*

Mt Bachelor USA
Interesting 360 degree area (there's no resort) on an extinct volcano in central Oregon. Gets a lot of rain.
1740m; slopes 1740–2765m
🚡 *13* ⛷ *3680 acres*

Mt Baker USA
Almost on the coast near Seattle. Plenty of challenging slopes. Known for spectacular avalanches.
1115m; slopes 1115–1540m
🚡 *10* ⛷ *1000 acres*

Mt Baldy Canada
Tiny area but worthwhile excursion from Big White. Gets ultra light snow – great glades/powder chutes.
slopes 1705–2150m
🚡 *2* ⛷ *150 acres*

Mt Baldy USA
Some of the longest and steepest runs in California. Limited snowmaking and old lifts are a major drawback.
1980m; slopes 1980–2620m
🚡 *4* ⛷ *400 acres*

Mt Baw Baw Australia
Small but entertaining intermediate area in attractive woodland, with great views. 2.5 hours from Melbourne.
1480m; slopes 1340–1565m
🚡 *8* ⛷ *61 acres*

Mt Buffalo **592**

Mt Buller **592**
⊠ *Ski Connections*

Mt Dobson New Zealand
Best of smaller areas. Wide treeless basin with long runs by NZ standards. Good snow-cover; mostly intermediate.
1630m; slopes 1630–2045m
🚡 *4* ⛷ *990 acres*

Mt Hood Meadows USA
Sizeable area with magnificent Oregon scenery. Impressive snowfall record but snow and weather tends to be wet.
1375m; slopes 1375–2535m
🚡 *12* ⛷ *2150 acres*

Mt Hood Ski Bowl USA
Sizeable area set amid magnificent Oregon scenery. Weather can be damp.
1095m; slopes 1095–1540m
🚡 *9* ⛷ *960 acres*

Mt Hotham 592

Mt Hutt 594

Mt Lemmon USA
Southernmost area in North America. close to famous Old West town Tombstone, Arizona. Reasonable snowfall.
2515m; slopes 2515–2790m
3 80 acres

Mt Lyford New Zealand
Limited but developing area close to the whale- and seal-watching centre, Kaikoura, 140km north of Christchurch.
1200m; slopes 1200–1640m
6 395 acres

Mt McKay 592

Mt Olympus Greece
Ski mountaineering site with chain of huts on both faces.

Mt Rose USA
Only 22 miles from Reno. Good slopes of its own and well placed for trips to other Tahoe resorts.
2515m; slopes 2515–2955m
5 900 acres

Mt Selwyn Australia
Popular with beginners and families. Surprisingly good lift system. 6 hours from Sydney.
1520m; slopes 1490–1610m
13 111 acres

Mt Snow/Haystack 529
⊠ *Ski Success, Virgin Ski*

Mt Spokane USA
Little intermediate area outside Spokane (Washington State) with cheap lift pass.
1160m; slopes 1160–1795m
5 350 acres

Mt St Louis/Moonstone Canada
Premier area in Toronto region, spread over 3 peaks, with very high-capacity lift system. 100% snowmaking.
13 175 acres

Mt Sunapee USA
Closest area of any size to Boston; primarily intermediate terrain.
375m; slopes 375–835m
8 210 acres

Mt Washington Resort Canada
Main area in remote part of Vancouver Island; beautiful scenery. Impressive snowfall but rain is a problem.
1110m; slopes 1110–1590m
6 970 acres
⊠ *Frontier Ski, Ski Safari*

Mt Waterman USA
Small Los Angeles area where kids ski free. Little snowmaking is a drawback.
2135m; slopes 2135–2440m
3 210 acres

Mühlbach Austria
Village near Bischofshofen, a bus-ride from one end of five-mountain area that stretches for miles towards Maria Alm.
855m; slopes 790–1825m
23 80km

Mühltal 170
Small village halfway between Niederau and Auffach in the Wildschönau. No local skiing of its own.

Muhr Austria
Village by Katschberg tunnel well placed for visiting St Michael, Badkleinkirchheim, Flachau, Obertauern.
1110m

Muju Korea
Largest area in Korea and the furthest from Seoul (3.5 hours away). Not as ugly/crowded as most Korean resorts.
13

Mürren 406
⊠ *Independent Ski Links, Inghams, Kuoni, Made to Measure, Plus Travel, Ski Club of GB, Ski Solutions, SkiGower, Swiss Travel Service, Thomson*

Mutters 103

Myoko Kogen Japan
Japan's best all-round area. Extensive slopes spread over 5 distinct, interconnected sections with longer, wider runs than Japanese norm.
57

Naeba Japan
Attracts the fashion-conscious. North of Tokyo.
900m; slopes 900–1800m
34

Nakiska Canada
Small area of wooded runs between Banff and Calgary, with state-of-the-art snowmaking.
1525m; slopes 1525–2215m
5 230 acres

Nasserein 146
Quiet suburb of St Anton.

Nauders Austria
Attractive village on Italian border with a high intermediate area and lots of snowmakers.
1400m; slopes 1400–2750m
16 65km

Nax Switzerland
Quiet, sunny village overlooking Rhône valley. Own little area and short drive from Veysonnaz.
1300m; slopes 1300–3330m
100 400km

Nendaz 421
Apartment development offering alternative to Verbier.
⊠ *Interhome, Snow Plus*

Neukirchen Austria
Quiet, pretty beginners' resort with a fairly snowsure plateau at the top of its mountain. Ziller valley nearby.
855m; slopes 855–2150m
14 35km

Neustift 132
⊠ *Alpine Tours, Crystal, Interhome, Made to Measure, Ski Valkyrie*

Nevegal Italy
Weekend day-trippers' place near Belluno, south of Cortina.
1030m; slopes 1030–1650m
14 28km

Nevis Range 589

Niederau 170
Amorphous chalet-style village in the Wildschönau region.
⊠ *First Choice Ski, Inghams, Neilson, Thomson*

Niedernsill Austria
Crowd-free slopes tucked behind Kaprun. Also well placed for visiting uncrowded, snowy Gerlos and Matrei.
770m; slopes 770–1000m
3

Niseko Kogen Japan
Hokkaido's main resort. Very exposed with unpredictable weather. Small area with very short runs.
22

Nockberge Innerkrems Austria
Area just south of Katschberg tunnel. Gets weather from east (Tirol gets it from west).
1500m; slopes 1500–2300m
10 33km

Nordic Valley USA
Utah cross-country area close to Salt Lake City. Powder Mountain and Snowbasin are nearby Alpine areas.
slopes 1675–1980m
2 85 acres

Nordseter Norway
Cluster of hotels in forest 14 km north of Lillehammer. Basic Alpine facilities but better cross-country centre.
1000m

Norefjell Norway
120km north-west of Oslo. Norway's toughest run, a very steep unpisted 600m drop.
750m; slopes 185–1185m
11

La Norma France
Traffic-free purpose-built resort near Modane and Val-Cenis, with easy terrain.
1350m; slopes 1350–2750m
18 65km
⊠ *Erna Low, Fairhand Holidays, Interhome, Lagrange Holidays*

Norquay 547

North Conway USA
Attractive factory-outlet-shopping town in New Hampshire close to Attitash and Cranmore ski areas.
⊠ *Skisar US, Virgin Ski*

Northstar-at-Tahoe 455
⊠ *United Vacations*

Nosawa Onsen Japan
Shinetsu spa village with good hot springs. Pistes cut out of heavy vegetation.
500m; slopes 500–1650m
27

Nôtre-Dame-de-Bellecombe 248
Inexpensive base from which to visit Megève.
⊠ *Barrelli Ski, Motours*

Nova Levante Italy
Little area used mostly by weekend day-trippers.
1180m; slopes 1180–2200m
14 20km

Nub's Nob USA
Sheltered Great Lakes ski area (many others suffer fierce winds). Weekend crowds from Detroit. Wooded slopes.
275m; slopes 275–405m
8 245 acres

Oberau 170
Very pretty village in the Wildschönau region.
⊠ *Inghams, Neilson, Thomson*

Obereggen Italy
Tiny resort used mainly by weekend day-trippers.
1550m; slopes 1550–2200m
6 10km

Obergurgl 133
⊠ *Airtours, Crystal, Independent Ski Links, Independent Ski Links, Inghams, Made to Measure, Neilson, Ski Club of GB, Ski Solutions, Thomson*

Oberlech 117
Car- and crowd-free family resort alternative to Lech.

Oberndorf 154
Quiet hamlet connected to St Johann in Tirol.
⊠ *Lagrange Holidays*

Oberstdorf Germany
Attractive winter-sports town near the Austrian border. Famous ski-jumping hill.
815m; slopes 800–2220m
31 30km
⊠ *Moswin Tours*

Obertauern 138
⊠ *Inghams, Made to Measure, Thomson*

Ochapowace Canada
Main area in Saskatchewan, east of Regina. Doesn't get a huge amount of snow but 75% snowmaking helps.
4 100 acres

Ohau New Zealand
Some of NZ's steepest slopes. Great views of Lake Ohau. Base has accommodation.
1425m; slopes 1425–1825m
3 310 acres

Okemo 529

Oppdal 584

Orcières-Merlette France
Good family resort; convenient snowsure nursery slopes, longer runs mostly funnel safely back to town.
1850m; slopes 1850–2650m
27 100km
⊠ *Fairhand Holidays, Lagrange Holidays, Motours*

Oropa Italy
Little area just off Aosta-Turin motorway. Easy change of scene from Courmayeur.
1180m; slopes 1200–2390m
15km

Les Orres France
Friendly modern resort with great views. Intermediate terrain; unreliable snow; long transfer from Lyon.
1550m; slopes 1550–2720m
24 63km
⊠ *Fairhand Holidays, First Choice Ski, Lagrange Holidays*

Orsières Switzerland
Traditional, sizeable winter resort near Martigny. Well-positioned for visiting Verbier and Chamonix valley.
900m

Ortisei 358
Charming market town with links to the Sella Ronda.
⊠ *Inghams*

Oslo Norway
Capital city with cross-country ski trails in its parks. Alpine slopes just north of city.

Otre il Colle Italy
Smallest of many little resorts near Bergamo.
1100m; slopes 1100–2000m
7 7km

Oukaimeden Morocco
Slopes 75km from Marrakesh with a surprisingly long season. A few simple hotels and equipment available.
2600m; slopes 2600–3260m
8 15km

Ovindoli Italy
One of smallest areas in L'Aquila region east of Rome. Higher slopes than most and one of the better lift systems.
1375m; slopes 1375–2220m
9 10km
⊠ *Thomson*

Ovronnaz Switzerland
Pretty village set on a sunny shelf above the Rhône valley. Limited area but Crans-Montana and Anzère close.
1350m; slopes 1350–2080m
10 25km

Owl's Head Canada
Steep mountain with superb views, in a remote spot bordering Vermont.
7 90 acres

Oz-en-Oisans 185
Attractive old village, with higher satellite at base of lifts into Alpe-d'Huez area.
⊠ *Lagrange Holidays*

Pajarito Mountain USA
Los Alamos area with steep, ungroomed slopes. Fun day out from Taos.
2685m; slopes 2685–3170m
5 220 acres

Pal 570
⊠ *Panorama*

Pamporovo 579
⊠ *Balkan Holidays, Crystal, First Choice Ski, Independent Ski Links, Neilson, Ski Balkantours*

Panarotta Italy
Smallest of resorts east of Trento. Higher altitude than nearby Andalo.
1500m; slopes 1500–2000m
6 7km

Panorama 559
⊠ *All Canada Ski, Frontier Ski, Inghams, Ski Safari, Skisar US*

Panticosa 577

Park City 508
⊠ *American Ski Classics, Crystal, Iglu.com, Independent Ski Links, Made to Measure, Momentum Ski, Ski Activity, Ski Connections, Ski Independence, Ski Line, Ski Safari, Ski The American Dream, Skisar US, Skiworld, United Vacations*

Parnassus Greece
Biggest and best area in Greece with surprisingly good slopes and lifts, 30km from Delphi. Wonderful sea views.
slopes 1600–2250m
10

Parpan Switzerland
Pretty village linked to the large intermediate area of Lenzerheide.
1510m; slopes 1230–2865m
35 155km

Partenen Austria
Traditional village in pretty setting at end of Montafontal (dead-end in winter). Slopes start at neighbour Gaschurn.
1100m; slopes 900–2300m
27 100km

La Parva Chile
Chile's best and most well liked ski area, an hour from Santiago. Weekend crowds.
2815m; slopes 2815–3570m
14
⊠ *Scott Dunn Latin America*

Pas de la Casa 570
⊠ *Airtours, Chalets 'Unlimited', Crystal, First Choice Ski, Independent Ski Links, Lagrange Holidays, Neilson, Panorama, Thomson, Top Deck*

Passo Lanciano Italy
Closest area to Adriatic. Weekend crowds from nearby Pescara when snow good.
1305m; slopes 1305–2000m
13

Passo Tonale Italy
Ugly resort in a bleak setting with guaranteed snow at a bargain price. Pretty Madonna is nearby.
1885m; slopes 1885–3025m
30 80km
⊠ *Airtours, Alpine Tours, Crystal, Equity Total Ski, First Choice Ski, Inghams, Sloping Off, Thomson*

Pass Thurn 111
Road-side lift base for Kitzbühel's most snowsure, but unconnected, ski area.

Pebble Creek USA
Small area on Utah-Jackson Hole route. Blend of open and wooded slopes.
1920m; slopes 1920–2530m
3 600 acres

Pec Pod Snezkou
Czech Republic
Collection of hamlets leading to the main lifts. Piste skiing very limited. Strictly for ultra-tight budgets.
770m; slopes 710–1190m
5 12km

Peisey-Nancroix 193
Small village linked to the Les Arcs network.
⊠ *Ski Hiver*

Pejo Italy
Unspoilt traditional village in a pretty setting, with a limited area. A cheap base for nearby Madonna.
1340m; slopes 1340–2800m
6 15km

Perisher/Smiggins 592

Pescasseroli Italy
One of numerous areas east of Rome in L'Aquila region.
1250m; slopes 1250–1945m
6 25km

Pescocostanzo Italy
One of numerous areas east of Rome in L'Aquila region. Summer mountain retreat.
1395m; slopes 1395–1900m
4 25km

Pettneu 146
Snow-sure resort with a bus link to nearby St Anton.

Petzen Austria
One of many little areas in Austria's easternmost ski region near Slovenian border.
600m; slopes 600–1700m
6 13km

Peyragudes-Peyresourde
France
Small Pyrenean resort with better snow record than neighbouring Barèges.
1000m; slopes 1600–2400m
15 37km
⊠ *Lagrange Holidays*

Pfunds Austria
Picturesque valley village close to Ischgl and to Swiss and Italian resorts.
970m

Phoenix Park Korea
Characterless golf complex with 12 ski slopes to keep things ticking over in winter. 2 hours from Seoul.
7

Piancavallo Italy
Uninspiring yet curiously trendy purpose-built village, an easy drive from Venice.
1270m; slopes 1270–1830m
17 45km

Piani delle Betulle Italy
One of several little areas near east coast of Lake Como.
730m; slopes 730–1850m
6 10km

Piani di Artavaggio Italy
Small base complex rather than village. One of several little areas near Lake Como.
875m; slopes 875–1875m
7 15km

Piani di Bobbio Italy
Largest of several tiny resorts above Lake Como.
770m; slopes 770–1855m
🚡 10 ⛷ 20km

Piani di Erna Italy
Small base development – no village. One of several little areas above Lake Como.
600m; slopes 600–1635m
🚡 7 ⛷ 6km

Piau-Engaly France
User-friendly St-Lary satellite similar in appearance to Les Arcs 1600, in one of the best areas in the Pyrenees.
1850m; slopes 1420–2500m
🚡 21
✉ Lagrange Holidays

Piazzatorre Italy
One of many little areas in Bergamo region.
870m; slopes 870–2000m
🚡 6 ⛷ 15km

Pico **533**
Low-key little family area (no resort) close to Killington in central Vermont.

Piesendorf Austria
Cheap(er), quiet place to stay when visiting Zell am See. Tucked behind Kaprun near Niedernsill.
780m; slopes 780–1275m
🚡 3 ⛷ 3km

Pievepelago Italy
Much the smallest and most limited of Appennine ski resorts. Less than 2 hours from Florence and Pisa.
1115m; slopes 1115–1410m
🚡 7 ⛷ 8km

Pila **352**
✉ Crystal, Independent Ski Links, Interski, Sloping Off

Pilion Greece
350m vertical. Pleasant slopes cut out of dense forest, only 15km from holiday resort Portaria above town of Volos.
🚡 3

Pinzolo Italy
Atmospheric village with slopes well equipped with snowmakers. Cheap base for nearby Madonna.
800m; slopes 780–2100m
🚡 8 ⛷ 29km
✉ Alpine Tours, Equity Total Ski

Pitztal Austria
Long valley with good glacier area at its head, accessed by underground funicular.
1250m; slopes 1735–3440m
🚡 12 ⛷ 40km

Pla-d'Adet France
Purpose-built complex at foot of St-Lary ski area. Limited.
1680m; slopes 1420–2450m
🚡 32 ⛷ 80km
✉ Lagrange Holidays

La Plagne **275**
✉ Airtours, Chalet World, Chalets 'Unlimited', Club Med, Crystal, Erna Low, Fairhand Holidays, First Choice Ski, Handmade Holidays, Iglu.com, Independent Ski Links, Inghams, Interhome, Lagrange Holidays, Made to Measure, Mark Warner, Motours, Neilson, Silver Ski, Simply Ski, Ski Activity, Ski Amis, Ski Arrangements, Ski Beat, Ski Club of GB, Ski France, Ski Independence, Ski Leisure Direction, Ski Line, Ski Olympic, Ski Supreme, SkiAway Holidays, Skiworld, Thomson, Tops Ski Chalets and Club Hotels, UCPA

Poiana Brasov **581**
✉ Balkan Holidays, Independent Ski Links, Inghams, Neilson, Ski Balkantours

Pomerelle USA
Small area in Idaho on the Utah-Sun Valley route.
2430m; slopes 2430–2735m
🚡 3 ⛷ 300 acres

Pontechianale Italy
Highest, largest area in remote region south-west of Turin. Day-tripper place.
1600m; slopes 1600–2680m
🚡 8 ⛷ 30km

Ponte di Legno Italy
Attractive sheltered alternative to bleak, ugly neighbour Tonale.
1255m; slopes 1255–1920m
🚡 5 ⛷ 15km

Pontresina **415**
Small, sedate base linked to nearby St Moritz by road.
✉ Club Med, Made to Measure

Porter Heights New Zealand
Closest skiing to Christchurch (1 hour). Open, sunny bowl; mostly intermediate plus back bowls for powder hounds.
1300m; slopes 1300–1980m
🚡 5 ⛷ 200 acres

Porterillos Argentina
Limited area near Mendoza, just over the border from Chilean resort Portillo.

Portillo Chile
Luxury hotel 150km north-east of Santiago, with more snowsure, less crowded pistes than Las Leñas in Argentina.
2880m; slopes 2510–3290m
🚡 12 ⛷ 25km
✉ Scott Dunn Latin America

Powderhorn USA
Area in west Colorado perched on world's highest flat-top mountain, Grand Mesa. Sensational views.
2490m; slopes 2490–2975m
🚡 4 ⛷ 300 acres

Powder King Canada
In British Columbia, the most remote and northerly of Canadian resorts. Great powder. Plenty of lodging.
880m; slopes 880–1520m
🚡 3 ⛷ 160 acres

Powder Mountain USA
Sizeable Utah area, a feasible day out from Park City. Renowned for bowls of fluffy virgin powder.
2315m; slopes 2315–2710m
🚡 6 ⛷ 1600 acres

Pozza di Fassa Italy
Pretty Dolomite village with its own slopes and access to the Sella Ronda.
1340m; slopes 1340–2155m
🚡 6 ⛷ 20km

Pragelato Italy
Inexpensive base short drive east of Sestriere. Own area worth a try for half a day.
1535m; slopes 1535–2580m
⛷ 35km

Prägraten am Grossvenediger Austria
Traditional mountaineering/ski touring village in lovely setting south of Felbertauern tunnel.
1310m; slopes 1310–1490m
🚡 2 ⛷ 3km

Prali Italy
Tiny resort east of Sestriere. Worthwhile half-day change of scene from Milky Way.
1455m; slopes 1450–2500m
🚡 6 ⛷ 25km

Pralognan-la-Vanoise France
Unspoilt traditional village overlooked by spectacular peaks. Champagny and Courchevel are close by.
1410m; slopes 1410–2355m
🚡 12
✉ Lagrange Holidays, Motours

Pra-Loup France
Convenient, purpose-built family resort with extensive, varied intermediate area linked to La Foux-d'Allos.
1600m; slopes 1500–2600m
🚡 53 ⛷ 167km
✉ Equity Total Ski, Fairhand Holidays, Independent Ski Links, Lagrange Holidays, Thomson

Prati di Tivo Italy
Sizeable resort by southern Italy standards. East of Rome near town of Teramo.
1450m; slopes 1450–1800m
🚡 6 ⛷ 16km

Prato Nevoso Italy
Purpose-built resort with rather bland slopes. Novel mountain-top skidoo transfer to/from Artesina.
1500m; slopes 1500–1950m
🚡 13 ⛷ 30km
✉ Equity Total Ski

Prato Selva Italy
Tiny base development east of Rome near Teramo.
1370m; slopes 1370–1800m
🚡 4 ⛷ 10km

Les Praz **203**
Quiet hamlet 4km from Chamonix.
✉ High Mountain Holidays

Le Praz **223**
Lowest and most attractive of the Courchevel resorts.

Praz-de-Lys France
Little known snow-pocket area near Lake Geneva that can have good snow when nearby resorts do not.
1500m; slopes 1200–2000m
🚡 23 ⛷ 50km
✉ Lagrange Holidays

Praz-sur-Arly **248**
Traditional village just down the road from Megève.
✉ Lagrange Holidays, Motours

Le Pré **193**
Charming, rustic hamlet with lifts up to Arc 2000.

Predazzo Italy
Small quiet place between Cavalese and Sella Ronda resorts. Well positioned for touring Dolomites area.
1015m; slopes 995–2205m
🚡 8 ⛷ 17km

Premanon France
One of four resorts that make up Les Rousses area in Jura region.
1050m; slopes 1120–1680m
🚡 40
✉ Lagrange Holidays

La Presolana Italy
Large summer resort near Bergamo. Several other little areas nearby.
1250m; slopes 1250–1650m
🚡 *6* ⛷ *15km*

Punta Arenas Chile
Most southerly organised slope in the world, in Patagonia, near Cape Horn.
🚡 *1*

Puy-St-Vincent **284**
✉ *Fairhand Holidays, Interhome, Lagrange Holidays, Snowbizz Vacances*

Pyhä Finland
Finland's steep and deep resort (280m vertical), popular with good skiers and boarders.
🚡 *6*

Pyrenees 2000 France
Tiny resort built in pleasing manner. Shares pretty area of short runs with Font-Romeu. Impressive snowmaking.
2000m; slopes 1750–2250m
🚡 *32* ⛷ *52km*

Québec **567**
✉ *Inghams*

Queenstown **597**
✉ *Ski Connections*

Radium Hot Springs Canada
Commercialised resort near Panorama offering alternative to slope-side resort.
slopes 975–2135m
🚡 *8* ⛷ *300 acres*
✉ *Skisar US*

Radstadt Austria
Interesting, unspoilt medieval town near Schladming with own small area and the Salzburger Sportwelt accessed from nearby Zauchensee.
855m; slopes 855–1680m
🚡 *10* ⛷ *17km*
✉ *Thomson*

Rainbow New Zealand
Northernmost area on South Island, 90 minutes from Nelson. Wide and treeless. Novice and intermediate.
1440m; slopes 1440–1760m
🚡 *4* ⛷ *865 acres*

Ramsau am Dachstein Austria
Charming village overlooked by the Dachstein glacier. Renowned for cross-country, but it has Alpine slopes on the glacier and at Schladming.
1200m; slopes 1100–2700m
🚡 *17* ⛷ *30km*

Ramundberget **587**

Rauris Austria
Old roadside village close to Kaprun and Zell am See, with a long narrow area that has snowmakers on lower slopes.
950m; slopes 950–2200m
🚡 *10* ⛷ *30km*
✉ *APT Holidays Ltd*

Ravascletto Italy
Resort close to Austria in a pretty wooded setting, with most of its terrain high above on an open plateau.
920m; slopes 920–1735m
🚡 *12* ⛷ *40km*

Reallon France
Traditional-style village, with splendid views from above Lac de Serre-Ponçon.
1560m; slopes 1560–2115m
🚡 *6* ⛷ *20km*
✉ *Lagrange Holidays*

Red Lodge USA
Characterful Old West Montana town. Great two-centre trip with Big Sky or Jackson Hole.
1800m; slopes 2155–2860m
🚡 *8* ⛷ *1600 acres*
✉ *Skisar US*

Red Mountain **544**
✉ *Frontier Ski, Ski Safari, Skisar US*

Red River USA
New Mexico western town – complete with saloons and with intermediate slopes above. Neighbour of Taos.
2665m; slopes 2665–3155m
🚡 *7* ⛷ *290 acres*

Reichenfels Austria
One of many small areas in Austria's easternmost ski region near Slovenian border.
810m; slopes 810–1400m
🚡 *4* ⛷ *8km*

The Remarkables **597**

Rencurel-les-Coulumes France
One of seven little resorts just west of Grenoble totalling 200km of piste.

Reutte Austria
500-year old market town with many suitably traditional hotels, and rail links to nearby Lermoos.
855m; slopes 855–1900m
🚡 *9* ⛷ *18km*

Revelstoke Canada
Town from which you can heli-ski the Monashees. Local terrain on Mt McKenzie for bad-weather days.
460m
✉ *Powder Skiing in North America Limited*

Rhêmes-Notre-Dame Italy
Unspoilt village in the beautiful Rhêmes valley, south of Aosta. Courmayeur and La Thuile within reach.
🚡 *2* ⛷ *5km*

Riederalp Switzerland
Pretty, car-free village above the Rhône valley amid the glorious scenery. Access by cable-car from near Brig.
1900m; slopes 1900–2710m
🚡 *32* ⛷ *90km*

Rigi-Kaltbad Switzerland
Resort on a mountain rising out of Lake Lucerne, with superb views, accessed by the world's first mountain railway.
1440m; slopes 1195–1795m
🚡 *9* ⛷ *30km*

Riihivouri Finland
Unusual in having its 'base' area at the top of the mountain. 20km from city of Jyvaskyla.
🚡 *4*

Riksgränsen **587**

Riscone Italy
Dolomite village sharing area with San Vigilio. Good snowmaking. Short easy runs.
1200m; slopes 1200–2275m
🚡 *35* ⛷ *40km*

Risoul **285**
✉ *Crystal, Erna Low, Fairhand Holidays, First Choice Ski, Iglu.com, Interhome, Lagrange Holidays, Made to Measure, Motours, Neilson, Ski Arrangements, Ski Independence, Ski Leisure Direction, Thomson*

Rivisondoli Italy
Sizeable summer mountain retreat east of Rome. Lift system better than most in vicinity.
1350m; slopes 1350–2050m
🚡 *7* ⛷ *16km*

Rjukan Norway
Gateway to ultimate cross-country region – Hardanger Vidda. Trails to Voss take a week.
300m

Roccaraso Italy
Largest of the resorts east of Rome, at least when snowcover is complete.
1280m; slopes 1280–2200m
🚡 *12* ⛷ *56km*

Rohrmoos **158**
Situated below small mountain in Dachstein-Tauern region, next to Schladming.

La Rosière **286**
✉ *Erna Low, Iglu.com, Interhome, Lagrange Holidays, Motours, Ski Arrangements, Ski Esprit, Ski Olympic, Vanilla Ski*

Rossland Canada
Main place to stay for Red Mountain, 5km away.
slopes 1155–2005m
🚡 *4*

Rougemont **405**
Part of the Gstaad ski region.

Ruka Finland
Finland's best-known ski resort. Most slopes have snow guns. Spacious area by Finnish standards.
🚡 *18*

Russbach Austria
Secluded village tucked up side valley, linked into Gosau-Annaberg-Lungotz area.
815m; slopes 780–1620m
🚡 *33* ⛷ *65km*

Saalbach-Hinterglemm **139**
✉ *Airtours, Crystal, First Choice Ski, Iglu.com, Independent Ski Links, Inghams, Interhome, Made to Measure, Neilson, Panorama, Ski Club of GB, Sloping Off, Thomson*

Saalfelden Austria
Ideally placed for touring eastern Tirol. Maria Alm, Saalbach nearby.
745m; slopes 745–1550m
🚡 *3* ⛷ *3km*

Saanen Switzerland
Cheaper and more convenient alternative to staying in Gstaad – but much quieter.
slopes 950–3000m
🚡 *69* ⛷ *250km*
✉ *SkiGower*

Saanenmöser **405**
Small village alternative to staying in Gstaad.
✉ *SkiGower*

Saas-Almagell Switzerland
Compact village up the valley from Saas-Grund, with good cross-country trails and walks, and limited Alpine area.
1670m
🚡 *6*

Saas-Fee **410**
✉ *Avant-ski, Crystal, Erna Low, First Choice Ski, Independent Ski Links, Inghams, Interhome, Kuoni, Made to Measure, Momentum Ski, Plus Travel, Powder Byrne, Ski Choice, Ski Club of GB, Ski Independence, Ski Solutions, SkiGower, Swiss Travel Service, Thomson*

Saas-Grund Switzerland
Sprawling valley village below Saas-Fee.
1560m; slopes 1560–3100m
7 45km
✉ *SkiGower*

Saddleback USA
Small area between Maine's premier resorts. High slopes by local standards.
695m; slopes 695–1255m
5 100 acres

Sahoro Japan
Ugly, purpose-built complex on Hokkaido island. Limited area.
400m; slopes 400–1100m
9 15km
✉ *Club Med*

St Andrä im Lungau Austria
Valley-junction village ideally placed for one of the longest, most snowsure cross-country networks in Europe. Close to Tauern pass and St Michael.
1045m

St Anton **146**
✉ *Airtours, Alpine Tours, Avant-ski, Bladon Lines, Chalet World, Chalets 'Unlimited', Crystal, Elegant Resorts, First Choice Ski, FlexiSki, Iglu.com, Independent Ski Links, Inghams, Lotus Supertravel, Made to Measure, Mark Warner, Momentum Ski, Simply Ski, Ski Addiction, Ski Arrangements, Ski Club of GB, Ski Equipe, Ski Line, Ski Solutions, Ski Total, Ski Valkyrie, Ski Yogi, Ski-Val, Skiworld, St Anton Ski Company, Thomson, White Roc*

S Bernardino Switzerland
Pretty resort south of the road tunnel, close to Madesimo.
1625m; slopes 1600–2595m
8 35km

S Candido Italy
Austrian border resort on road to Lienz.
1175m; slopes 1175–1580m
4 15km

S Carlos de Bariloche
Argentina
South America's only year-round resort, with 5 areas nearby. Cerro Catedral is the best but crowded in August.
790m; slopes 1050–2300m
29 26km
✉ *Scott Dunn Latin America*

S Cassiano **358**
Pretty village linked to Sella Ronda.
✉ *First Choice Ski*

Sta Caterina Italy
Pretty, user-friendly village near Bormio, with a snowsure novice and intermediate area.
1740m; slopes 1740–2725m
8 25km
✉ *Airtours, Thomson*

St Cergue Switzerland
Limited resort less than an hour from Geneva, good for families with young children.
1045m; slopes 1045–1700m
9 20km

St Christoph **146**
Small village on Arlberg pass above St Anton.
✉ *Elegant Resorts, Made to Measure*

St-Colomban-des-Villards
France
Small resort in next side valley to La Toussuire. Good base for visiting Valloire and Val-Cenis.

Sta Cristina **358**
Quiet village on the periphery of the Sella Ronda.
✉ *Crystal, Inghams*

Sainte-Foy-Tarentaise **290**
✉ *Independent Ski Links, Ski Arrangements, Ski Weekend, Weekends in Val d'Isère*

St-François-Longchamp **312**
Sunny, gentle slopes linked to Valmorel.
✉ *Interhome, Lagrange Holidays*

St Gallenkirch **130**

St-Gervais **248**
Small town sharing its ski area with Megève.
✉ *Fairhand Holidays, Interhome, Lagrange Holidays, Snowcoach, Snowman Holidays*

S Grée di Viola Italy
Easternmost of resorts south of Turin, surprisingly close to Italian Riviera.
1100m; slopes 1100–1800m
30km

St Jakob in Defereggen Austria
Unspoilt traditional village in a pretty, sunny valley close to Lienz and Heiligenblut.
1390m; slopes 1390–2520m
9 35km

St Jakob in Haus Austria
Snowpocket village with its own slopes, and a shared lift pass with nearby Fieberbrunn, Waidring and St Johann.
855m; slopes 855–1500m
7 22km

St-Jean-de-Sixt **216**
Hamlet base for La Clusaz.
✉ *Frosty's*

St-Jean-Montclar France
Small village at foot of thickly forested slopes. Good day out from nearby Pra-Loup.
1300m; slopes 1300–2500m
18 50km

St Johann im Pongau Austria
Bustling, lively town with own area and access to the Salzburger Sportwelt area.
650m; slopes 800–1850m
26 70km

St Johann in Tirol **154**
✉ *Crystal, Panorama, Thomson*

St-Lary-Soulan **322**
✉ *Fairhand Holidays, Lagrange Holidays*

St Leonhard in Pitztal Austria
Village beneath a fine glacier in the Oetz area, accessed by underground funicular.
1250m; slopes 1735–3440m
12 40km

St Luc Switzerland
Quiet, unspoilt rustic village on the south side of the Rhône valley, with plenty of high, easy pistes.
1650m; slopes 1650–3025m
15 75km
✉ *Iglu.com, Inntravel*

St Margarethen Austria
Village near Obertauern in remarkable snow pocket.
1065m; slopes 1075–2210m
14 50km

Sta Maria Maggiore Italy
South of Simplon Pass from Rhône valley, near Lake Maggiore.
820m; slopes 820–1890m
5 10km

St Martin bei Lofer Austria
Traditional village in lovely setting. Cross-country centre with Alpine slopes at Lofer.
635m

St-Martin-de-Belleville **288**
✉ *Chalets de St Martin, Independent Ski Links, Made to Measure, Motours, Ski Miquel*

S Martin de los Andes
Argentina
Limited area on the slopes of Cerro Chapelco. Neighbour to main resort, Bariloche.
6
✉ *Scott Dunn Latin America*

S Martino di Castrozza Italy
Plain village in the southern Dolomites with varied slopes in four disjointed areas, none very extensive.
1465m; slopes 1465–2610m
20 50km
✉ *Equity Total Ski, Interhome*

St Martin/Tennengebirge
Austria
Highest village in Dachstein-West region near Salzburg. Limited slopes of its own but close to Annaberg's area.
1000m; slopes 1000–1350m
5 4km

St-Maurice-sur-Moselle France
One of several areas near Strasbourg. Unlike most resorts in this region, no snowmakers.
550m; slopes 900–1250m
8

St Michael im Lungau Austria
Quiet, unspoilt village in the Tauern pass snowpocket with disjointed intermediate area. Close to Obertauern.
1075m; slopes 1075–2360m
25 60km
✉ *Alpine Tours, Equity Total Ski*

St Moritz **415**
✉ *Club Med, Crystal, Elegant Resorts, FlexiSki, Iglu.com, Independent Ski Links, Inghams, Interhome, Kuoni, Made to Measure, Plus Travel, Ski Club of GB, Ski Solutions, Ski with Julia, SkiGower, Swiss Travel Service, Weekends in Val d'Isère*

St-Nicolas-de-Véroce **248**
Small hamlet on the fringes of the Megève network.

St-Nizier-du-Moucherotte
France
One of seven little resorts just west of Grenoble totalling 200km of piste. Unspoilt, inexpensive place to tour.

St-Pierre-de-Chartreuse France
Locals' weekend place near Grenoble. Unreliable snow.
900m; slopes 900–1800m
19

S Simone Italy
Tiny development north of Bergamo. Lift pass shared with unappealing Foppolo area, 10 minutes' drive away.
2000m; slopes 1105–2300m
9 45km

St Stephan Switzerland
Unspoilt old farming village at the foot of the largest area in the Gstaad Super Ski region.
995m; slopes 950–2155m
69 250km

St Veit im Pongau Austria
Spa resort with limited slopes at Goldegg but Wagrain (Salzburg Sportwelt) and Grossarl (Gastein) are nearby.
765m

St-Veran France
Highest 'real' village in Europe. Close to Serre-Chevalier and Milky Way. Snow-reliable cross-country skiing.
2040m; slopes 2040–2800m
15 30km

S Vigilio Italy
Charming, atmospheric Dolomite village with a delightful, sizeable area well covered by snow guns.
1200m; slopes 1200–2275m
33 40km

S Vito di Cadore Italy
Sizeable alternative place to stay to Cortina. Own slopes of negligible interest.
1010m; slopes 1010–1380m
9 12km

St Wolfgang Austria
Charming lakeside resort near Salzburg, some way from any slopes.
540m; slopes 665–1350m
9 17km
✉ *Airtours, Crystal, Inghams, Neilson, Thomson*

Les Saisies France
Traditional-style Albertville Olympics cross-country venue and varied four-mountain Alpine slopes.
1650m; slopes 1150–2000m
24
✉ *Classic Ski Limited, Inntravel, Lagrange Holidays, Motours*

Sälen 587
✉ *Scandinavian Travel Service*

Salt Lake City USA
Underrated base from which to ski Utah. Cheaper and livelier than the resorts.
✉ *Pavilion Tours, Skisar US*

Salzburg-Stadt Austria
Single long challenging run off back of Salzburg's local mountain, accessed from suburb of Grodig.
425m; slopes 450–1805m
1 8km

Samedan Switzerland
Valley town, just down the road from St Moritz.
1720m; slopes 1740–2570m
3 7km

Samnaun 106
Shares large ski area with Ischgl.

Samoëns 238
Beautiful rural valley village, a bus-ride from lifts into Flaine's skiing.
✉ *Fairhand Holidays, Inntravel, Interhome, Lagrange Holidays, Motours*

Sandia Peak USA
World's longest cable-car trip ascends from Albuquerque. Mostly gentle slopes.
slopes 2645–3165m
7 100 acres

Sansicario 353
Small, stylish, modern resort near Sauze d'Oulx.
✉ *Equity Total Ski*

Santa Fe USA
One of America's most interesting towns. Varied slopes – glades, bowls and cruiser pistes.
3145m; slopes 3145–3645m
7 600 acres

Sappada Italy
Isolated resort close to the Austrian border below Lienz.
1215m; slopes 1215–2050m
17 50km

Sappee Finland
Southern resort within easy reach of Helsinki, popular with telemarkers and boarders. Lake views.
4

Sarnano Italy
Main resort in Macerata region near Adriatic Riviera. Valley village with ski slopes accessed by cable-car.
540m
9 11km

Le Sauze France
Fine area near Barcelonnette, sadly remote from airports.
1400m; slopes 1400–2440m
24

Sauze d'Oulx 353
✉ *Airtours, Chalets 'Unlimited', Crystal, Equity Total Ski, First Choice Ski, Independent Ski Links, Inghams, Neilson, Panorama, Ski Club of GB, Thomson*

Savognin Switzerland
Pretty village with a good mid-sized area; a good base for top nearby resorts – St Moritz, Davos/Klosters, Flims.
1200m; slopes 1200–2715m
17 80km

Scheffau am Wilden Kaiser 95
Rustic beauty 4km from Ellmau.
✉ *Crystal, Thomson*

Schia Italy
Only area near Parma. No village. Very limited – short runs served by drags.
1245m; slopes 1245–1415m
7 15km

Schilpario Italy
Only one of many little areas near Bergamo.
1125m; slopes 1125–1635m
7 15km

Schladming 158
✉ *Crystal, Equity Total Ski, Independent Ski Links, Interhome, Made to Measure, Neilson*

Schönried 405
A cheaper, quieter alternative to staying in Gstaad.
✉ *Interhome*

Schoppernau Austria
Scattered farming community, one of two main areas in Bregenzerwald NW of Lech.
860m; slopes 860–2050m
7 35km

Schröcken Austria
Bregenzerwald area village close to the German border.
1260m; slopes 1260–2100m
16 56km

Schruns 130
✉ *Interhome*

Schüttdorf 173
Characterless dormitory satellite of Zell am See.

Schwarzach im Pongau Austria
Riverside village with railway station. Slopes at Goldegg. Wagrain (Salzburg Sportwelt) and Grossarl (Gastein valley).
600m

Schweitzer USA
In Idaho but near Spokane (Washington State). Good snowfall record; uncrowded, varied slopes.
1215m; slopes 1215–1945m
6 2350 acres
✉ *Skisar US*

Scopello Italy
Low area close to Aosta valley, worth considering for day trip in bad weather.
slopes 690–1740m
9 26km

Scuol Switzerland
Year-round spa resort close to Austria and Italy, with an impressive range of pistes.
1250m; slopes 1250–2785m
15 80km

Searchmont Resort Canada
Fine Lake Superior views. Modern lift system and 95% snowmaking.
275m; slopes 275–485m
4 65 acres

Sedrun Switzerland
Charming, unspoilt old village on the Glacier Express rail route close to Andermatt.
1440m; slopes 1450–2350m
12 50km

Seefeld 162
✉ *Crystal, Independent Ski Links, Inghams, Interhome, Lagrange Holidays, Made to Measure, Neilson, Thomson*

Le Seignus-d'Allos France
Neighbour of La Foux-d'Allos (shares large area with Pra-Loup). Own little area too. Lift pass share arrangement.
1400m; slopes 1400–2425m
13

Sella Nevea Italy
Limited resort in a beautiful setting on the Slovenian border. Summer glacier.
1140m; slopes 1190–1800m
11 8km

Selva 358
✉ *Airtours, Bladon Lines, Chalets 'Unlimited', Crystal, First Choice Ski, Independent Ski Links, Inghams, Momentum Ski, Thomson*

Selvino Italy
Closest resort to Bergamo.
960m; slopes 960–1400m
6 20km

Semmering Austria
Civilised winter-sports resort amid pretty scenery, 100km from Vienna, towards Graz. Mostly intermediate terrain.
1000m; slopes 1000–1340m
5 14km

Seoul Korea
Small, unattractive, barren area 25 minutes from the capital. 3 very crowded slopes; short season.
3

Les Sept-Laux France
Ugly, user-friendly family resort near Grenoble, like a small Avoriaz. Pretty slopes for all grades.
1350m; slopes 1350–2400m
31 100km
✉ *Lagrange Holidays*

Serfaus Austria
Charming traffic-free village (with underground people-mover) at foot of long, narrow ski area, mainly easy and intermediate. Linked to Fiss.
1425m; slopes 1200–2700m
19 80km
✉ *Alpine Tours, Interhome, Made to Measure*

Serrada Italy
Very limited area near Trento.
slopes 1250–1605m
5
✉ *Alpine Tours, Equity Total Ski*

Serre-Chevalier 291
✉ *Airtours, Chalets 'Unlimited', Crystal, Equity Total Ski, Erna Low, Fairhand Holidays, First Choice Ski, Handmade Holidays, Hannibals, Iglu.com, Independent Ski Links, Inghams, Lagrange Holidays, Made to Measure, Motours, Neilson, Ski Arrangements, Ski France, Ski Independence, Ski Leisure Direction, Ski Miquel, Skiworld, Sloping Off, Thomson, Tops Ski Chalets and Club Hotels*

Sesto Italy
Dolomite village on the road to Cortina, surrounded by pretty little areas.
1310m
31 *50km*

Sestola Italy
Appennine village near Florence almost completely equipped with snowmakers.
900m; slopes 1280–1975m
23 *50km*

Sestriere 366
✉ *Club Med, Crystal, Equity Total Ski, Independent Ski Links, Interhome, Momentum Ski, Motours, Motours, Neilson, Thomson*

Shames Mountain Canada
Remote spot inland from coastal town Prince Rupert. Impressive snowfall record and gets deep powder.
670m; slopes 670–1195m
3 *183 acres*

Shawnee Peak USA
Small area near Sunday River renowned for its night skiing. Spectacular views. Mostly groomed cruising.
185m; slopes 185–580m
5 *225 acres*

Shemshak Iran
Most popular of the three mountain resorts within 65km of Teheran. Packed at weekends, but few go to ski.

Shiga Heights Japan
Largest area in Japan, site of Nagano's 1998 Olympic skiing events, 150km from Tokyo. Happo One is nearby.
930m; slopes 1220–2305m
73 *130km*

Showdown USA
Intermediate area in Montana cut out of forest north of Bozeman.
2065m; slopes 2065–2490m
4 *640 acres*

Sierra-at-Tahoe 455

Sierra Nevada 577
✉ *First Choice Ski, Independent Ski Links, Neilson, Thomson*

Sierra Summit USA
Sierra Nevada area accessible only from the west. 100% snowmaking.
2160m; slopes 2160–2645m
8 *250 acres*

Silbertal Austria
Low secluded village, linked to Schruns. Good base for touring numerous areas.
890m; slopes 700–1450m
3 *6km*

Sils Maria 415
Pretty lakeside village, linked to St Moritz.
✉ *Interhome, Made to Measure*

Silvaplana 415
Pretty village near St Moritz.
✉ *Interhome, Made to Measure*

Silver Creek USA
Winter Park's little neighbour. Very child-oriented. Low snowfall record for Colorado.
2490m; slopes 2490–2795m
5 *250 acres*

Silver Mountain USA
Northern Idaho area, near delightful Couer d'Alene. Best for experts and intermediates.
1215m; slopes 1215–1915m
6 *1500 acres*

Silver Star 544
✉ *All Canada Ski, Frontier Ski, Made to Measure, Ski Independence, Ski Safari, Ski The American Dream, Ski Vacation Canada, Skisar US*

Sinaia 581

Sipapu USA
Great little New Mexico area, but with unreliable snow-cover. Mostly tree-lined runs.
slopes 2500–2765m
3

Siviez 421
Quiet base for skiing Verbier's Four Valleys circuit.
✉ *Interhome*

Sixt France
Traditional village near Samoëns, at foot of piste down from Flaine area.
770m; slopes 700–2560m
80 *260km*

Sjusjoen Norway
Cluster of hotels in deep forest close to Lillehammer. Basic Alpine facilities but better cross-country centre.
885m
✉ *Headwater Holidays, Inntravel, Waymark Holidays*

Ski Apache USA
Apache-owned area south of Albuquerque noted for groomed steeps.
2925m; slopes 2925–3505m
11 *750 acres*

Ski Cooper USA
Small area close historic town of Leadville. Good ski/sightseeing day out from nearby Vail-Beaver Creek.
slopes 3200–3565m
4

Ski Windham USA
2 hours from New York City. Decent slopes by eastern standards.
485m; slopes 485–940m
7 *220 acres*

Smokovec Slovakia
Spa town near Poprad, with 3 small areas known collectively as High Tatras.
1000m; slopes 1000–1500m
5

Smugglers' Notch 537
✉ *Ski The American Dream*

Snowbasin 513
✉ *Skisar US*

Snowbird 515
✉ *Crystal, Independent Ski Links, Made to Measure, Ski Connections, Ski Independence, Ski The American Dream, Skisar US, United Vacations*

Snowbowl (Arizona) USA
Near Flagstaff, Arizona, atop extinct volcano and with stunning desert views. Good snowfall record.
2805m; slopes 2805–3505m
5 *135 acres*

Snowbowl (Montana) USA
Montana area renowned for powder. Intermediate pistes plus 700 acres of extreme slopes.
1520m; slopes 1520–2315m
4 *1400 acres*

Snowmass 462
Purpose-built village with big mountain near Aspen.
✉ *Big Country Ski, Crystal, Fantiski, Independent Ski Links, Lotus Supertravel, Made to Measure, Ski Independence, Ski The American Dream, Ski Total, Skisar US, United Vacations*

Snow Summit USA
San Bernardino National Forest ski area near Palm Springs. 100% snowmaking and high-capacity lift system.
2135m; slopes 2135–2500m
12 *230 acres*

Snow Valley USA
Area quite near Palm Springs. Fine desert views. High-capacity lift system to cope with weekend crowds.
2040m; slopes 2040–2390m
11 *230 acres*

Solda Italy
Other side of Stelvio Pass from Bormio. Very long airport transfers.
1905m; slopes 1905–2625m
19 *25km*
✉ *Inghams*

Sölden 163
✉ *Made to Measure*

Soldeu 570
✉ *Airtours, Chalets 'Unlimited', Crystal, First Choice Ski, Independent Ski Links, Inghams, Lagrange Holidays, Neilson, Panorama, Pavilion Tours, Ski Club of GB, Solo's, Thomson, Top Deck*

Solfonn Norway
Tiny development west of Geilo with some of Norway's most challenging Alpine slopes. Extensive, interesting cross-country trails too.
550m; slopes 550–760m
2

Solitude 503
✉ *Skisar US*

Söll 164
✉ *Airtours, Crystal, First Choice Ski, Independent Ski Links, Inghams, Interhome, Motours, Neilson, Panorama, Ski Club of GB, Ski Hillwood, Thomson*

Sommand France
Purpose-built base that shares area with Praz-de-Lys.
1420m; slopes 1200–1800m
22 *50km*

Sorenberg Switzerland
Popular weekend retreat between Berne and Lucerne, with a high proportion of steep, low pistes.
1165m; slopes 1165–2350m
18 *50km*

South Lake Tahoe 455

South Tatras Slovakia
An area (there's no resort) covering both sides of Mount Chopok near Poprad.
slopes 1240–2005m
19 *20km*

Spindleruv Mlyn
Czech Republic
Largest Giant Mountains region resort but few facilities. Several scattered little low areas.
750m; slopes 750–1300m
9 *25km*

Spital am Pyhrn Austria
Limited village east of Schladming, 4km from its easy intermediate slopes.
650m; slopes 810–1885m
10 18km

Spittal/Drau Austria
Historic Carinthian town with a limited area. A good day-trip from Bad Kleinkirchheim.
555m; slopes 1650–2140m
12 22km

Sportgastein **88**
Characterless mountain village in the Badgastein valley.

Squaw Valley **455**
⊠ *Crystal, Ski Activity, Ski Independence, Ski Safari, Ski The American Dream, United Vacations, Virgin Ski*

Srinagar India
Himalayan resort in Kashmir, with a small pisted area but excellent heli-skiing.
2720m; slopes 2645–3645m
7 5km

Stafal **351**
Tiny, isolated village, with good access to the Monterosa Ski area.

Steamboat **484**
⊠ *American Ski Classics, Big Country Ski, Chalets 'Unlimited', Crystal, Independent Ski Links, Inghams, Lotus Supertravel, Made to Measure, Neilson, Ski Activity, Ski Connections, Ski Independence, Ski Line, Ski Safari, Ski The American Dream, Ski Total, Skiworld, Thomson, United Vacations*

Steinach Austria
Pleasant village in picturesque surroundings just off the autobahn near the Brenner Pass.
1050m; slopes 1050–2205m
6 16km
⊠ *Alpine Tours*

Stevens Pass USA
Mostly intermediate slopes, a day trip from Seattle. Low snowfall.
1235m; slopes 1235–1785m
14 1125 acres

Stoneham **567**
⊠ *Frontier Ski, Inghams, Ski Safari*

Stoos Switzerland
Small, unspoilt village an hour from Zurich. Weekends crowded. Amazing views of Lake Lucerne from summits.
1300m; slopes 570–1920m
7

Storlien Sweden
Small family resort amid magnificent scenery, 30 mins from top resort Åre.
600m; slopes 600–790m
7 15km
⊠ *Independent Ski Links*

Stowe **540**
⊠ *Chalets 'Unlimited', Crystal, Independent Ski Links, Inghams, Made to Measure, Neilson, Ski Arrangements, Ski Connections, Ski Independence, Ski Line, Ski The American Dream, Skisar US, Thomson, United Vacations, Virgin Ski*

Stratton **529**

Strobl Austria
Neighbour of St Wolfgang in beautiful lakeside setting.
545m; slopes 545–1510m
9 12km

Stuben **117**
Small, unspoilt village linked to St Anton.
⊠ *Ski Total*

Sugar Bowl USA
Exposed area north of Lake Tahoe with one of highest snowfall in California, best for experts.
2095m; slopes 2095–2555m
8 1500 acres

Sugarbush **529**
⊠ *Big Country Ski, Made to Measure, Ski Arrangements, Ski Success, Virgin Ski*

Sugarloaf **529**
⊠ *Big Country Ski, First Choice Ski, Independent Ski Links, Ski Success*

Summit at Snoqualmie USA
Four areas – Summit East (formerly Hyak), Summit Central (formerly Ski Acres), Summit West (formerly Snoqualmie Pass) and Alpental.
slopes 915–1645m
24 2000 acres

Sun Alpina Japan
Collective name for 3 tiny neighbouring areas that share lift pass. 4 hours from Tokyo, 3 hours from Osaka.
23

Sundance **503**
⊠ *Skisar US*

Sunday River **541**
⊠ *Big Country Ski, Crystal, First Choice Ski, Made to Measure, Neilson, Ski Independence, Ski Success, Skisar US*

Sunlight USA
Quiet little area worth the easy trip from Vail. Varied terrain.
2405m; slopes 2405–3015m
4 460 acres

Sun Peaks **544**
⊠ *All Canada Ski, Frontier Ski, Made to Measure, Ski Connections, Ski Independence, Ski Safari, Ski The American Dream, Ski Vacation Canada, Skisar US*

Sunrise Park USA
Arizona's largest area. Slopes spread over 3 mountains; best for novices and leisurely intermediates.
2805m; slopes 2805–3350m
12 800 acres

Sunshine Village **547**
⊠ *Airtours*

Sun Valley **526**
⊠ *Big Country Ski, Ski Activity, Ski The American Dream, Skisar US*

Suommu Finland
No village – just a lodge right on the Arctic Circle. A few pistes but mostly ski-touring centre. 60km from Rovaniemi.
140m; slopes 140–410m

Superbagnères France
Little more than a particularly French-dominated Club Med, best for a low-cost, low-effort family trip to the Pyrenees.
1880m; slopes 1440–2260m
16 35km
⊠ *Lagrange Holidays*

Super-Besse France
Purpose-built resort amid spectacular extinct-volcano scenery. Shares area with Mont-Dore. Limited village.
1350m; slopes 1350–1850m
21 80km
⊠ *Lagrange Holidays*

Superdévoluy France
Ugly, purpose-built, user-friendly family resort, an hour south-east of Grenoble, with a sizeable intermediate area.
1500m; slopes 1500–2510m
32 100km
⊠ *Fairhand Holidays, Lagrange Holidays, Motours*

Super-Lioran France
Purpose-built satellite of Le Lioran, Auvergne village. Spectacular volcano scenery.
1160m; slopes 1160–1850m
24
⊠ *Lagrange Holidays*

Supermolina **577**

Tahko Finland
Largest resort within 500km of Helsinki. Intermediate slopes in attractive, wooded, frozen-lake setting.
8

Tahoe City **455**

Talisman Mountain Resort
Canada
One of the best areas in Toronto region. Low lift capacity; 100% snowmaking.
235m; slopes 235–420m
8

Tamsweg Austria
Large village in snowy region close to Tauern Pass and St Michael. Cross-country centre.
1025m

La Tania **223**
Small, purpose-built resort within the Courchevel area.
⊠ *Airtours, Alpine Action, Avant-ski, Barrelli Ski, Chalet World, Chalets 'Unlimited', Crystal, Erna Low, Fairhand Holidays, First Choice Ski, Freedom 2 Travel, Independent Ski Links, Lagrange Holidays, Le Ski, Made to Measure, Motours, Neilson, Silver Ski, Simply Ski, Ski Amis, Ski Arrangements, Ski Beat, Ski Club of GB, Ski Deep, Ski France, Ski Leisure Direction, Snowline, The Last Resort, Thomson*

Taos **527**
⊠ *Made to Measure, Ski Independence, Ski The American Dream, Skisar US*

Tärnaby-Hemavan Sweden
Only Swedish area with its own airport. Snowsure.
slopes 265–830m
7 44km

El Tarter **570**
Relatively quiet, convenient alternative to Soldeu.
⊠ *Panorama, Solo's, Top Deck*

Tarvisio Italy
Interesting old town bordering Austria and Slovenia. A major cross-country centre with fairly limited Alpine slopes.
750m; slopes 750–1860m
12 15km

Täsch **436**
The final base by road on the way to car-free Zermatt.
⊠ *Interhome*

Tauplitz Austria
Traditional village at the foot of an interestingly varied area north of Schladming.
900m; slopes 900–2000m
18 25km

Tazawako Japan
Small area 4 hours from Tokyo. One of the few Japanese areas to get reasonable powder.
10

Telluride **490**
⊠ *American Ski Classics, Elegant Resorts, Iglu.com, Lotus Supertravel, Made to Measure, Ski Independence, Ski Safari, Ski The American Dream, Skisar US, Skiworld*

Temu Italy
Sheltered hamlet near Tonale. Worth a visit in bad weather.
1155m; slopes 1155–1955m
4 *5km*

Tengendai Japan
Tiny area 3 hours from Tokyo with one of Japan's best snow records, including occasional powder.
5

Termignon France
Traditional rustic village. Good slopes of its own, and good base for touring Maurienne valley resorts.
1300m; slopes 1300–2500m
6 *35km*
⊠ *Fairhand Holidays, Lagrange Holidays*

Terminillo Italy
Purpose-built resort 100km from Rome with a worthwhile area when its lower runs have snowcover.
1500m; slopes 1500–2210m
15 *40km*

Thollon-les-Mémises France
Attractive base for relaxed holiday. Close to Evian, Lake Geneva, Portes du Soleil.
1000m; slopes 1600–1900m
20
⊠ *Lagrange Holidays*

Thredbo **592**

La Thuile **368**
⊠ *Chalets 'Unlimited', Crystal, Equity Total Ski, First Choice Ski, Independent Ski Links, Inghams, Interski, Motours, Neilson, Ski Valkyrie, Thomson*

Thyon 2000 **421**
Limited resort in the Verbier ski area.

Tignes **296**
⊠ *Airtours, Avant-ski, Chalet World, Chalets 'Unlimited', Club Med, Crystal, Erna Low, Fairhand Holidays, First Choice Ski, Iglu.com, Independent Ski Links, Inghams, Interhome, Lagrange Holidays, Made to Measure, MasterSki, Motours, Neilson, Silver Ski, Ski Activity, Ski Amis, Ski Arrangements, Ski Beat, Ski Choice, Ski Club of GB, Ski France, Ski Independence, Ski Leisure Direction, Ski Line, Ski Olympic, Ski Solutions, Ski Supreme, Ski Valkyrie, Skiworld, The Ski Company, Thomson, UCPA*

Timberline (Palmer Snowfield) USA
East of Portland, Oregon. Lift-served summer skiing.
slopes 1830–2600m
6 *2500 acres*

Togari Japan
One of several areas close to 1998 Olympic site Nagano.
16

Torgnon Italy
Neighbour of Cervinia, good for bad weather.
1500m; slopes 1500–1965m
4 *6km*

Torgon Switzerland
Old village in a pretty wooded setting, with a lift connection to the Portes du Soleil.
1150m; slopes 975–2275m
219 *650km*
⊠ *Interhome*

Le Tour France
Charming, unspoilt hamlet at the head of the Chamonix valley.
1465m; slopes 1465–2185m
9 *40km*

La Toussuire France
Dreary, downmarket, modern resort off Maurienne valley.
1800m; slopes 1400–2600m
54 *200km*
⊠ *Fairhand Holidays, Lagrange Holidays*

Trafoi Italy
Quiet, traditional (Austrian-style) village near Bormio.
1570m; slopes 1570–2550m
6 *10km*

Treble Cone **594**

Tremblant **569**
⊠ *All Canada Ski, Crystal, Elegant Resorts, First Choice Ski, Frontier Ski, Iglu.com, Independent Ski Links, Inghams, Made to Measure, Neilson, Pavilion Tours, Ski Connections, Ski Independence, Ski Safari, Ski The American Dream, Ski Vacation Canada, Skisar US, Thomson*

Troodos Cyprus
A good outing from Greek-sector coastal resorts. Pretty, wooded pistes and fine views.
1920m
4 *5km*

Trysil **584**
⊠ *Scandinavian Travel Service*

Tschagguns Austria
Village with a varied little area of its own and Schruns close by.
700m; slopes 700–2300m
13 *33km*

Tsugaike Kogen Japan
Sizeable resort 4 hours from Tokyo, 3 hours from Osaka.
800m; slopes 800–1700m
28

La Tuca Spain
Purpose-built development near Viella. Worthwhile excursion from nearby Baqueira-Beret.
1050m; slopes 1270–2250m
7

Tulfes **103**

Turoa **594**

Turracherhöhe Austria
Tiny resort on a mountain shelf, with varied intermediate slopes. A good outing from Bad Kleinkirchheim.
1765m; slopes 1400–2200m
11 *30km*
⊠ *Alpine Tours*

Tyax Lodge Canada
Heli-skiing operation in Chilcotin mountains. Transfers from Whistler or Vancouver.

Uludag Turkey
Surprisingly suave, laid-back, well-equipped, purpose-built resort near Bursa, south of Istanbul. Popular with posers.
1850m; slopes 1850–2320m
14 *15km*

Unken Austria
Traditional village with closest slopes to Salzburg, hidden in side valley.
565m; slopes 1000–1500m
4 *8km*

Untergurgl **133**
Valley-floor alternative to Obergurgl or Hochgurgl.

Unternberg Austria
Riverside village with trail connecting into one of longest, most snowsure cross-country networks in Europe. Large.
1030m

Unterwasser Switzerland
Old but not especially attractive resort 90 min from Zurich. More challenging half of area shared with Wildhaus.
910m; slopes 900–2260m
21 *50km*

Uttendorf-Weiss-See Austria
Astute choice for crowd-free slopes when snowline high and Kaprun queues long. Tucked behind Kaprun.
805m; slopes 1485–2600m
9 *20km*

Vail **491**
⊠ *American Ski Classics, Big Country Ski, Chalet World, Crystal, Elegant Resorts, Handmade Holidays, Iglu.com, Independent Ski Links, Inghams, Lotus Supertravel, Made to Measure, Momentum Ski, Neilson, Rocky Mountain Snowboard Tours, Ski Activity, Ski Club of GB, Ski Equipe, Ski Independence, Ski Line, Ski Safari, Ski The American Dream, Ski Total, Skisar US, Skiworld, Thomson, United Vacations*

Valbella Switzerland
Convenient but characterless village sharing intermediate Lenzerheide area.
1540m; slopes 1470–2865m
35 *155km*
⊠ *Club Med, Kuoni, Made to Measure*

Valberg France
Surprisingly large Alpes Maritimes resort (bigger than better-known Isola 2000) close to Nice.
1650m; slopes 1400–2100m
27

Val-Cenis **246**
⊠ *Erna Low, Hannibals, Inghams, Lagrange Holidays, Motours*

Val d'Illiez Switzerland
Peaceful, unspoilt village a few minutes below Champoussin. Thermal baths. Good views of Dents du Midi.
950m; slopes 1050–2280m
228 *650km*

Val-d'Isère **303**
⊠ *Airtours, Avant-ski, Bladon Lines, Chalet World, Chalets 'Unlimited', Club Med, Crystal, Elegant Resorts, Erna Low, Fairhand Holidays, Fantiski, Finlays, First Choice Ski, Handmade Holidays, Iglu.com, Independent Ski Links, Inghams, Interhome, Lagrange Holidays, Le Ski, Lotus Supertravel, Made to Measure, Mark Warner, Momentum Ski, Motours, Neilson, Scott Dunn Ski, Silver Ski, Ski Activity, Ski Amis, Ski Arrangements, Ski Choice, Ski Club of GB, Ski*

Waiorau Nordic New Zealand
Specialist cross-country centre just over an hour from Queenstown.
1600m

Wald im Pinzgau Austria
Cross-country centre surrounded by Alpine areas – with Pass Thurn also nearby.
885m

Wanaka 594

Waterville Valley 529
⊠ *Neilson, Virgin Ski*

Weinebene Austria
One of many gentle little areas in Austria's easternmost ski region near Slovenian border.
1560m; slopes 1560–1835m
5 12km

Weissbach bei Lofer Austria
Traditional resort between Lofer and Saalfelden. No slopes of own but well placed for touring Tirol.
665m

Weissensee Naggeralm Austria
Famous for Europe's largest frozen lake. One of many little areas in eastern Austria.
930m; slopes 930–1330m
4 7km

Weisspriach Austria
Hamlet in very snowy pass near Obertauern which shares area with Mauterndorf and St Michael.
1115m; slopes 1115–2050m
7 20km

Wengen 431
⊠ *Club Med, Crystal, Iglu.com, Independent Ski Links, Independent Ski Links, Inghams, Kuoni, Made to Measure, Plus Travel, Ski Club of GB, Ski Solutions, SkiGower, Swiss Travel Service, Thomson*

Wentworth Canada
Long-established Nova Scotia area. Harsh climate ensures snow arrives and stays despite low altitude.
55m; slopes 55–300m
6 150 acres

Werfen Austria
Traditional village spoilt by Tauern autobahn passing between it and slopes. Good touring to Dachstein West.
620m

Werfenweng Austria
Hamlet with advantage over main village Werfen of being away from autobahn and by the slopes. Best for novices.
1000m; slopes 1000–1835m
11 40km

Westendorf 169
⊠ *Independent Ski Links, Inghams, Neilson, Thomson*

Whakapapa 594
⊠ *Ski Connections*

Whistler 560
⊠ *All Canada Ski, American Ski Classics, Chalet World, Chalets 'Unlimited', Crystal, Elegant Resorts, First Choice Ski, FlexiSki, Frontier Ski, Handmade Holidays, Iglu.com, Independent Ski Links, Inghams, Kuoni, Lotus Supertravel, Made to Measure, Momentum Ski, Neilson, Pavilion Tours, Piste Artiste, Simply Ski, Ski Activity, Ski Arrangements, Ski Club of GB, Ski Connections, Ski Equipe, Ski Independence, Ski Line, Ski Miquel, Ski Safari, Ski The American Dream, Ski Total, Ski Vacation Canada, Ski Yogi, Skisar US, Skiworld, Solo's, The Ski Company, Thomson, United Vacations*

Whitecap Mountains Resort USA
Largest, snowiest area in Wisconsin close to Lake Superior. Winds and weekend crowds.
435m; slopes 435–555m
8 390 acres

White Pass Village USA
Closest area to Mt St Helens. Remote and uncrowded with a good snowfall record. Mostly intermediate cruising.
1370m; slopes 1370–1825m
6 635 acres

Whitewater 544
⊠ *Skisar US*

Wildcat Mountain USA
New Hampshire area famous for bad weather, but one of the best areas on a nice day.
slopes 600–1250m
6 225 acres

Wildhaus Switzerland
Undeveloped farming community in stunning scenery, near Liechtenstein.
1100m; slopes 1100–2075m
9 50km

Wildschonau 170
⊠ *Interhome*

Wiler Switzerland
Remote, picturesque dead-end valley near Lotschberg rail tunnel north of Rhône valley. Very limited slopes.
1380m; slopes 1380–2700m
6

Willamette Pass USA
Speed skiing training centre in national forest near Crater Lake, Oregon. Small but varied piste area.
1560m; slopes 1560–2035m
5 550 acres

Williams USA
Tiny area above the main accommodation centre for Grand Canyon.
slopes 2010–2270m
2 50 acres

Windischgarsten und Umgebung Austria
Working village on same railway line as Schladming. Slopes at Hinterstoder/Spital.
600m; slopes 810–1870m
11 18km

Winter Park 498
⊠ *American Ski Classics, Chalets 'Unlimited', Crystal, Independent Ski Links, Made to Measure, Neilson, Ski Independence, Ski Safari, Ski The American Dream, Skisar US, Skiworld, Thomson, United Vacations*

Wolf Creek USA
Remote area with highest snowfall record in Colorado. Uncrowded; good for all levels; wonderful powder.
3155m; slopes 3155–3590m
6 800 acres
⊠ *Skisar US*

Xonrupt France
Cross-country centre only 3km from nearest Alpine slopes to Channel at Gérardmer.
715m; slopes 666–1150m
20 40km
⊠ *Lagrange Holidays*

Yangji Pine Korea
Modern resort with pistes cut out of forest. 40 minutes south of Seoul. Very crowded.
7

Ylläs Finland
Largest ski centre in the Arctic area, 170km from Lapland's capital Rovaniemi. Open slopes for Finland.
255m; slopes 255–715m
18
⊠ *Inghams*

Yong Pyeong Korea
Largest resort in Korea, 200km east of Seoul, with 100% snowmaking.
750m; slopes 750–1460m
16 20km

Zakopane Poland
An interesting old town near Cracow and Auschwitz. Mostly intermediate pistes.
830m; slopes 1000–1960m
20 10km

Zao Japan
3 interconnected areas. Very cold temperatures. Renowned for 'chouoh' – pines frozen into weird shapes.
780m; slopes 780–1660m
42

Zauchensee Austria
Purpose-built resort with lifts fanning out into the Salzburger Sportwelt area.
855m; slopes 800–2185m
120 320km
⊠ *Made to Measure*

Zell am See 173
⊠ *Airtours, Crystal, First Choice Ski, Inghams, Interhome, Made to Measure, Neilson, PGL Teenski, Panorama, Solo's, Thomson*

Zell im Zillertall Austria
Sprawling valley town with pistes on two mountains, now linked to higher Gerlos and Königsleiten to form a fair-sized intermediate area.
580m; slopes 930–2410m
22 47km
⊠ *First Choice Ski, Thomson*

Zermatt 436
⊠ *Bladon Lines, Chalet World, Chalets 'Unlimited', Crystal, Elegant Resorts, Erna Low, Iglu.com, Independent Ski Links, Inghams, Interhome, Kuoni, Lotus Supertravel, Made to Measure, Momentum Ski, Plus Travel, Powder Byrne, Scott Dunn Ski, Ski Choice, Ski Club of GB, Ski Independence, Ski Solutions, Ski Total, Ski with Julia, SkiGower, Swiss Travel Service, Thomson, White Roc*

Zinal Switzerland
Pretty, rustic village with high slopes.
1680m; slopes 1680–2895m
9 70km
⊠ *Interhome*

Zug 117
Tiny village with Lech's toughest skiing.

Zürs 117
High, smart but soulless village on road to Lech.
⊠ *Elegant Resorts, Iglu.com, Made to Measure*

Zweisimmen Switzerland
Limited but inexpensive base for slopes around Gstaad.
965m; slopes 965–2000m
7 25km

MONEY BACK VOUCHER – PART 1

To be sent to
SKI SOLUTIONS, 84 Pembroke Road, London W8 6NX
along with your booking form

Name ______________________________

Address ______________________________

____

E-mail address ______________________________

Daytime phone number ______________________________

Tour operator (if applicable) ______________________________

Departure date ______________ **Number in party** ______________

I have bought a copy of Where to Ski and Snowboard 2001 and claim a refund of the £15.99 cover price. I understand this amount will be deducted from the cost of the holiday I am booking through Ski Solutions. Offer valid for bookings for 2000/01 and 2001/02 seasons holidays made before 30 April 2002.

Signature ______________ **Date** ______________

MONEY BACK VOUCHER – PART 2

To be sent to
WHERE TO SKI AND SNOWBOARD,
The Old Forge, Norton St Philip, Bath BA3 6LW

Name ______________________________

Address ______________________________

____

E-mail address ______________________________

Daytime phone number ______________________________

Resort(s) to be visited ______________________________

Departure date ______________ **Number in party** ______________

I have booked a ski holiday through Ski Solutions and claimed a refund of the £15.99 cover price of Where to Ski and Snowboard 2001.

Signature ______________ **Date** ______________

Have you booked any other holiday through Ski Solutions in the last two seasons? ☐ **Yes** ☐ **No**

WHERE *to* SKI AND *Snowboard* 2001

WHERE *to* SKI AND *Snowboard* 2001

WHERE *to* SKI AND *Snowboard* 2001

WHERE *to* SKI AND *Snowboard* 2001

WHERE *to* SKI AND *Snowboard* 2001